D1533496

Shooter's Bible®

ABOUT OUR COVER

The two guns pictured are 20 gauge sidelock shotguns built by F. III. Rizzini of Magno, Italy. Each one is painstakingly hand-made by the finest Italian artisans under the direction of Guido Rizzini. With an annual production of 15-20 guns, they combine the finest wood, mechanical craftmanship and finish quality attainable. Considered the world's finest side-by-side shotguns, they are available in all gauges, styles and imaginitive engraving embellishments, each designed to the singular specifications of the individual customer. The two guns shown on our cover were commissioned by New England Arms Company of Kittery Point, Maine, which imports F. III. Rizzini guns to the U.S. Engravings are by Master Engravers Firmo Fracassi and S. Muffolini.

NEW!

NEW!

NEW!

NEW!

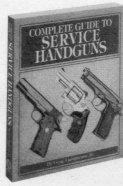

NEW!

Shooter's Bible

NO. 90
1999 EDITION

EDITOR
William S. Jarrett

PROJECT MANAGER
Dominick S. Sorrentino

PRODUCTION & DESIGN
Lesley A. Notorangelo/D.S.S.

ELECTRONIC IMAGING
Lesley A. Notorangelo/D.S.S.

FIREARMS CONSULTANTS
Kevin De Forge
Bill Meade
Frank Zito

COVER PHOTOGRAPHER
Ray and Matt Wells

PUBLISHER
David C. Perkins

PRESIDENT
Brian T. Herrick

STOEGER PUBLISHING COMPANY

Every effort has been made to record specifications and descriptions of guns, ammunition and accessories accurately, but the Publisher can take no responsibility for errors or omissions. The prices shown for guns, ammunition and accessories are manufacturers' suggested retail prices (unless otherwise noted) and are furnished for information only. These were in effect at press time and are subject to change without notice. Purchasers of this book have complete freedom of choice in pricing for resale.

Published by Stoeger Publishing Company
5 Mansard Court
Wayne, New Jersey 07470

Library of Congress Catalog Card No.: 63-6200
International Standard Book No.: 0-88317-205-4

Manufactured in the United States of America

In the United States:
Distributed to the book trade and to the sporting goods trade by
Stoeger Industries
5 Mansard Court
Wayne, New Jersey 07470
Tel: 973-872-9500 Fax: 973-872-2230

In Canada:
Distributed to the book trade and to the sporting goods trade by
Stoeger Canada Ltd.
1801 Wentworth Street, Unit 16
Whitby, Ontario, L1N 8R6, Canada

Contents

ARTICLES

A New Breed Of Custom Rifles	8
Cowboy Action Shooting: A Sport For All Shooters	18
The Secrets Of Successful Field Gunning	26
The Sharps 1859: A Modern Replica That Shoots!	33
New Bolt Action Designs Take Muzzleloading Into The New Century	41
Ad Topperwein: World's Greatest Trick Shooter	49
The 22-250 Improved: An Old Wildcat Made Better	57
The Fine Art Of Softshell Reloading	65
One Rifle For All Seasons	77

MANUFACTURER'S SHOWCASE   89

SPECIFICATIONS

Handguns	97
Rifles	203
Shotguns	323
Blackpowder	401
Sights & Scopes	459
Ammunition	499
Ballistics	505
Reloading	521

REFERENCE

Directory of Manufacturers & Suppliers	558
Caliberfinder	563
Gunfinder	572

Foreword

As we approach the millennium, this 90th edition of Shooter's Bible takes on added significance. It's a milestone that calls for comparisons with the past and expectations for the future. With that in mind, we've put together a new, updated edition that pays respect to what's gone before, while at the same time welcoming the technology of the year 2000 and beyond (in other words, we've been digitized).

This last edition of the 20th century leads off with a series of articles by well known and experienced outdoor writers, led by Wayne van Zwoll, who describes the evolution from the elegant walnut stocks of the past to the custom-made synthetic-stocked rifles of the present (and future). Next, Ron Harris entertains us with his report on the popular sport of "Cowboy Action Shooting," which has attracted lots of media attention. Veteran writer Nick Sisley reveals his secrets of shotgunning for feathered targets, and Stan Warren offers his insights on the Sharps 1859 muzzleloader, which he describes as a "modern replica that shoots!" Toby Bridges, another muzzleloading expert, reveals how new bolt action designs are taking this sport into the new century as well.

Then, for a nice change of pace, Sam Fadala kicks in with a lively biography of Ad Topperwein, "The World's Greatest Trick Shooter," who amazed audiences in the early 1900s with his uncanny accuracy. Don Lewis, who has been our reloading expert for several decades now, explains how the 22-250 Improved Wildcatter came into its own; and Ralph Quinn, another regular, demonstrates how making your own shotshells can save money while improving accuracy. And finally, our Canadian friend, Wilf Pyle, suggests how "One Rifle For All Seasons" can do the job for most hunters.

Our Manufacturers' Showcase, which follows, has several new faces, including Desert Mountain, Dillon Precision, Forrest, Grizzly Industrial, Gutman Cutlery, and Triple K. We invite readers to "shop at the Showcase" for products made by these and other firms listed, most of which are not represented in the Specifications section. Turn the page following the Showcase and you'll find the beginning of the Handgun section. Among the major companies we've added are Bond Arms and Enterprise Arms. Gone is the Star line along with Daewoo and Erma. Brno is no longer represented in the Rifle section, nor are Maverick (formerly affiliated with Mossberg) and County among the shotguns listed. Welcome, meanwhile, to Tristar, Heckler & Koch and Fabarms. The new Blackpowder entries include Browning, Fort Worth and Markesbury. Not listed are Peifer and White Systems. Among the many makers of scopes, we've added Leica and dropped Williams.

That leads us to the all-important Ammunition, Ballistics and Reloading sections, followed by a complete Directory of Manufacturers and Suppliers where all the addresses, phone and fax numbers of each and every company featured in this edition can be found (so let your fingers do the walking). Finally, we've repeated the popular Caliberfinder and Gunfinder reference guides. Looking for a particular caliber? Simply check the Caliberfinder, then find the guns that will accommodate it in the Gunfinder.

We appreciate your continuing interest in this, America's oldest and most respected gun reference annual. Browsers, critics and interested parties everywhere are always welcome!

William S. Jarrett,
Editor

A New Breed Of Custom Rifles   8
BY WAYNE VAN ZWOLL

Cowboy Action Shooting: A Sport For All Shooters   18
BY RON "El Escritor" HARRIS

The Secrets Of Successful Field Gunning   26
BY NICK SISLEY

The Sharps 1859: A Modern Replica That Shoots!   33
BY STAN WARREN

New Bolt Action Designs Take Muzzleloading Into The New Century   41
BY TOBY BRIDGES

Ad Topperwein: World's Greatest Trick Shooter   49
BY SAM FADALA

The 22-250 Improved: An Old Wildcat Made Better   57
BY DON LEWIS

The Fine Art Of Softshell Reloading   65
BY RALPH F. QUINN

One Rifle For All Seasons   77
BY WILF E. PYLE

Articles

A New Breed Of Custom Rifles

BY WAYNE VAN ZWOLL

Ever since R.F. Sedgely and Griffin & Howe carved out their first elegant stocks for the 1903 Springfields, custom bolt rifles have worn pretty wood. In fact, for decades a "custom" rifle had less to do with custom fit than with an expensive look. Colorful, neatly-checkered walnut adorned with engraved metal and gold inlay transformed rifles into art. Accouterments like trap grip caps and sculpted quarter-ribs evolved more as the craftsman's *tour de force* than as the hunter's tools. Eventually, though, top-quality English walnut became scarce and expensive, forcing artisans to raise their fees. And with custom rifles from the best shops displaying ever more beauty and refinement, many hunters decided they'd become "too purty to beat up in the brush." Meanwhile, factory-built rifles kept improving, offering better accuracy and shooting comfort. Factory chamberings now included so many useful cartridges that building a rifle for a wildcat round made little sense. After-market parts and services, such as muzzle brakes and pillar bedding, enabled shooters to "customize" a standard rifle at a cost well below the price of a custom rifle made from scratch.

A pivotal moment in the evolution of hand-built rifles arrived with the synthetic stock, though its looks at first impressed few shooters. Black plastic! But like the girl next door, synthetic stocks improved with time. Riflemen slowly came around to appreciate their stability, durability and (in some cases) lighter weight. When manufacturing tolerances shrank far enough to produce "drop-in" fit, glass bedding became unnecessary. Big gun companies began to equip their flagship bolt rifles with synthetic stocks. Small-volume entrepreneurs competed with ordinary barreled actions nested in commercial stocks of compounds with space-ship names like Kevlar. Men who dressed rifles in walnut found themselves serving mainly collectors and traditionalists.

KENNY JARRETT'S BEANFIELD RIFLES

Enter a South Carolina riflesmith named Kenny Jarrett, who worked hard to maintain a hillbilly image while selling sub-minute accuracy from pillar-bedded bolt guns chambered for long-range wildcat cartridges. A fourth-generation farmer who liked to shoot, Jarrett began building rifles full time in 1979, calling them "beanfield rifles" and marketing them well. Using techniques he'd

Synthetic stocks have become so popular that in some product lines they're featured more often than wood. These synthetic-stocked Browning A-Bolts come with chrome-moly or stainless steel metal.

Weatherby is not limiting its snythetic stocks to the big magnums. Its new lightweight and ultralight rifles wear them. Here the author fires a .30-.378 Mark V.

Kenny Jarrett's rifles still turn up wherever serious hunters gather. This fine bull elk fell to a single 200-grain Nosler Partition from a .300 Jarrett (essentially an 8mm Remington case necked down). The author guided this hunter in northeastern Utah.

learned from Texas gunmaker Harold Broughton, he fitted Remington Model 700 actions with Hart barrels and McMillan synthetic stocks. By 1990, he had 13 employees on his payroll and was grossing half a million dollars. His original shop, built of cypress lumber and cedar shakes, had grown into a 6,000-square-foot facility with five lathes. Over the years, Kenny Jarrett has chambered rifles for at least 75 cartridges, some of his own design. Customers can choose from several metal finishes and can specify any suitable rifle action. Before assembling his rifles, Jarrett trues bolt faces and barrel shanks and laps lugs. He also offers "switch-barrel" guns that permit in-the-field barrel changes.

Because they're guaranteed to deliver fine accuracy, with metal contoured and barrels chambered to each customer's specs, Jarrett's rifles are truly custom-made. Purists might argue that stocks made from a mold cannot be shaped or checkered like

wood, hence they don't qualify as custom stocks. Fair enough, but in a beanfield rifle any rifleman can discern the bloodline of a Griffin & Howe. Most apparent, though, is its bench-rifle ancestry. Kenny Jarrett's aim is to build sporting rifles that shoot as well as Broughton's bench guns. Synthetic stocks enable him to do that.

A beanfield rifle has never come cheap, and prices have climbed. In an interview with Jarrett in 1991, he commented: "You can only make accurate rifles the way we're making them, slowly and with great care. We use the best of modern machinery, and we all work hard to build 125 rifles a year. I've scrapped as many as three barrels on one rifle because I couldn't get the half-minute groups I wanted. I've even had to discard actions. That's expensive. But my goal is to build the most accurate rifles you can buy anywhere in the world, for any amount of money."

While still a commercial pilot, Don Allen, founder of Dakota Arms, began making rifle stocks in his spare time. The Model 97 is his third centerfire sporting rifle, the first with a synthetic stock.

He went on to note that while some of his clients were quite wealthy, he knew a local farm boy who'd saved hay money for three years to get a Jarrett. Kenny sent the lad home with a new Leupold scope at no extra charge.

DON ALLEN'S MODEL 97 DAKOTA

While Kenny Jarrett was plowing new ground with his high-priced synthetic-stocked rifles, Don Allen was getting ready to bring back the pre-64 Winchester Model 70 as a semi-custom rifle. Then a commercial pilot for Northwest Airlines, Don had been a part-time stockmaker for five years before incorporating in 1977. He subsequently deigned and built a stock duplicating machine before moving from Minneapolis to Sturgis, South Dakota, in 1984. There, with Oregon riflesmith Pete Grisel, he redesigned the early Model 70. The new action, called the Dakota 76, featured the M70's trigger, safety and extractor; but the coned breech was replaced by Mauser-style breeching. Other distinguishing characteristics of the Dakota were its side-swing bolt stop and a one-piece trigger-guard assembly and a blind rear guard screw hole. The initial price—$1750—was four times the cost of a new Model 70, but each Dakota rifle was enhanced by fine wood and checkering. After Pete Grisel left the firm, Don Allen kept on building rifles with "classic, elegant styling, top-drawer workmanship and first-rate materials at a sensible price." His 21,000-square-foot facility has since

turned out a .22 bolt rifle and a nice dropping-block single-shot that Dakota Arms chambers for just about any cartridge.

Don Allen's newest rifle, though, is a synthetic-stocked bolt gun. This from a man who talks about wood the way houndsmen refer to their dogs. He has bought walnut all over the world and acted as a wood broker for other gunmakers. His Dakota 76 rifles and Model 10 single-shots have been dressed in highly-figured Turkish walnut, tightly inletted and cleanly checkered. "We won't stop making elegant, traditional rifles," Don point out. "But the market has a spot for a synthetic-stocked rifle we can sell for less money."

Except for its H-S Precision stock, the Model 97 Dakota, introduced in 1997, closely resembles the Model 76 but costs half as much. The top profile and trigger bow are similar, as are the three-position M70 safety and Mauser claw

The straight-combed stock made by H-S Precision with its sweeping, open grip make the Dakota 97 a handsome rifle. It points quickly in the field and absorbs recoil well.

a camming groove *inside* the bridge. Unlike these two actions, the Model 97 has a blind magazine. It holds three standard rimless or belted magnum cartridges, or two Dakota cartridges, which are large-diameter rimless rounds based on the .404 Jeffery case. To cut coats, the feed lips are stamped into the Model 97's boxes, not machined into the rails. No wonder its action costs about half as much to produce as the Model 76 action!

Don Allen's choice for a stock made sense. Besides installing synthetic stocks on its own rifles and providing them to firms like Dakota Arms, H-S Precision sells them to Remington, Weatherby and Winchester. With their aluminum bedding blocks, conservative lines and appealing finish, sporter- and varmint-style stocks made by Dakota Arms have earned a large share of the market. The bedding block on its Dakota 97 is machined to the same radius as the receiver, so there's no need to glass bed. The block extends down to the trigger bow to serve as a "stop" or pillar between guard assembly and receiver. The recoil lug contacts only the rear of its mortise.

The 26-inch Lothar Walther barrel is button-rifled. Standard chamberings include the .257 Roberts, .25-06, .270, .30-06, 7mm Remington Magnum and .300 Winchester Magnum, not to mention the 7mm, .300, .330 and .375 Dakotas. The barrels are free-floated because, according to Don Allen, any synthetic stock will bend with

Most Dakota cartridges are available in the Model 97, with several popular rimless and belted magnum rounds. The rifle has a round action.

extractor. Up close, though, some differences are noted. For example, the Model 97 action, like the Remington 700, is machined from tube stock. The Dakota 76, patterned after Winchester's Model 70, starts off as a large block of steel, much of which is subsequently milled away. The new round action, lacking the integral recoil lug of its forebear, is fitted with a 700-style lug in the form of a collar that fits between barrel and receiver face. "This recoil lug is twice as thick as the Remington's," Don notes, explaining that such a design reduces manufacturing costs in the receiver and also makes headspacing easy. "We can buy barrels already chambered and headspace them by machining a few thousandths off the lug. It's an inexpensive, yet precise method."

The Model 97 bolt handle protrudes from a collar welded around the bolt body, so it can't come off. The camming surface for primary extraction is on the rear of the bridge, much like a Mauser. The Dakota 76 and Winchester 70 have

The author shot this Wyoming pronghorn at 200 yards with a Model 97 in .300 Dakota. The scope is a 2.5-10x Swarovski, ideal for a versatile big game rifle.

D'Arcy Echols examines one of the first of his synthetic- stocked semi-custom rifles. After 15 years of hand-building walnut-stocked guns, he was persuaded by a number of clients to add this "working rifle" to his line.

Model 1898. These extractors are costly, and they require several broaching operations in the receiver. A bolt-face extractor lets Remington cut the lug races through its Model 700 receivers in one pass. We decided to save money elsewhere."

Allen's stock features a long, open grip for fast handling; but the rifle is no wand. At 9½ pounds trailside, it has the heft of a conventional custom rifle, partly because of its 26-inch barrel. But that weight is intelligently distributed and helps counter recoil. It also keeps the rifle from bobbing around in the gale-force winds of Wyoming and other northern states.

D'ARCY ECHOLS: CRAFTSMAN IN WOOD

Another gunmaker noted for his craftsmanship in wood and who has turned to building synthetic-stocked rifles is D'Arcy Echols, of Providence,

temperature changes. "Synthetics have a reputation for stability," he explains. "But that only describes their refusal to warp when wet. Heat will move them away from pressure. Unlike wood, they have no memory, so when the temperature drops, they don't move back. That's why a synthetic stock must never contact the forward section of a barrel."

Like Kenny Jarrett, who fashioned his own stock for McMillan to duplicate, Allen wanted a stock profile to help identify the Model 97 rifle, shaping it to mirror the Model 76 stock. It has sharp, clean checkering and a high, straight comb that quickly puts the shooter's eye in line with the scope. A soft recoil pad is standard, as are sling swivel studs. Length of pull is 13⅝ inches. Designed to sell at a low price, the Model 97 Dakota comes with few options. A muzzle brake, sights, even a quarter-rib can be ordered at extra charge. So can an off-beat chambering or (within limits) a non-standard length of pull. But this rifle was not designed to compete with a Model 76 or even a Jarrett rifle. Its chief rivals are the synthetic-stocked rifles from Remington's custom shop, which, as Don Allen points out, lack the Mauser claw extractor that many hunters find essential for positive functioning.

"Not only does the Mauser claw prevent double feeding and take a big, strong bite of the rim; it is easy to replace in the field," he advises. "Quick field repair is a military concern, and it almost surely influenced Paul Mauser when he designed the

D'Arcy Echols' synthetic-stocked rifle is available in seven chamberings, with the .375 H&H and .458 Lott rated among the most powerful and popular. D'Arcy builds his rifles on Winchester M70 Classic actions.

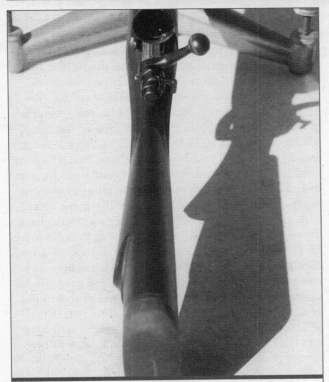

The butt angles away from bore-line on this D'Arcy Echols stock. Aiming is easier when the shooter can put his eye quickly behind the sight without losing comb support.

Utah. He has specialized in top-grade walnut-stocked bolt guns now for 15 years, faithfully shipping only four rifles a year; but their clean styling, impeccable inletting and faultless functioning keep the orders coming. "I *shoot* my rifles," he says. "They must not only be very accurate, but one hundred percent reliable. Many wind up in Africa, where ornery beasts take advantage of malfunctions."

A few years ago, one of D'Arcy's friends suggested he build a rifle that was more affordable for the average hunter. He was also impressed with a magazine box D'Arcy had designed to hold four magnum cartridges in proper stacking configuration—one more than most bolt guns offer. A few years ago, D'Arcy decided to design his own synthetic-stocked rifle, but not one that looked like others on the market. D'Arcy's new stock made of walnut featured a straight comb, point-pattern checkering, and a long, open grip.

Castoff at toe and heel (the buttstock angles to the right) enables shooters to line up their eyes directly behind the sight. There's also a one-inch Decelerator recoil pad, and a long forend that keeps the forward swivel well away from the left hand. Lengths of pull range from $13\frac{1}{2}$ to $14\frac{1}{2}$ inches.

The heart of D'Arcy's rifle is Winchester's new Model 70 Classic action, which he buys from wholesalers as complete rifles, then strips off the barrels and stocks (because he was unable to buy the actions only). He then squares lug seats, bolt and receiver faces and installs his own four-round magazine box. D'Arcy reworks the feed rails and ramp to ensure smooth, positive functioning. He also remachines trigger and sear surfaces and replaces the trigger pin with a bigger, harder one that eliminates wiggling. Then he opens the ejection port slightly to improve breech access and drills out the 6-48 scope mount screw holes to 8-40. The bigger screws offer more security under the brutish recoil of the magnum cartridges D'Arcy offers as standard chamberings; namely: 7mm Remington .300 Winchester, .300 Weatherby, .338 Winchester, .375 H&H, .416 Remington and the wildcat .458 Lott (a .375 case necked up). The 26-inch barrels are chrome-moly, cut-rifled Kriegers, cryogenically stress-relieved. The front swivel stud on the .375, .416 and .458 rifles is installed on a barrel-mounted pedestal ahead of the forend tip.

Krieger does the chambering and headspacing, in accordance with D'Arcy's specifications. He has

The author found this D'Arcy Echols rifle in .300 Weatherby pleasant to shoot, even without a muzzle brake. Intelligent stock design is the key.

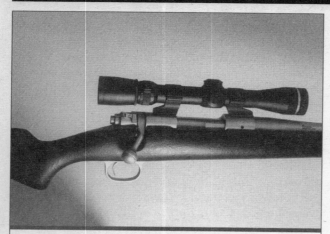

Lex Webernick's small shop in Cedar City, Utah, produces what is currently the lightest synthetic stock on the market—11 ounces out of the mold. The stock's slim lines are appealing, but the author found this grip a bit short for his big hands. Iron Sighter alloy mounts hold the Leupold variable scope.

walnut. He, Kenny Jarrett and Don Allen have proved that synthetic stocks can complement the best barrels and actions, producing rifles that look, not cheap or ugly, but businesslike. There's no doubt that the stability and durability of synthetics contribute to the accuracy and serviceability of these rifles.

Years ago, when companies like Brown Precision pioneered the synthetic rifle stock, one of the major selling points was its light weight. But Jarrett, Allen and Echols are all building rifles that weigh as much or more than wood-stocked rifles from a production line. The reason? First, demand for long-range rifles has picked up in the last few years. Big game rounds with great reach have become more popular, as have the powerful scopes and long barrels that make them effective. Short barrels can't squeeze top speeds from high-performance rounds, and compact scopes lack resolving power from a distance. Weight may still be a concern among hunters who log lots of foot miles in the mountains, but heavy rifles do a better job of absorbing the recoil of cross- canyon cartridges, and they keep bullets in the middle longer during sustained fire.

RIFLES, INCORPORATED

Another reason is that lightweight rifles haven't disappeared by any means. The big gun companies offer them and several custom shops specialize in

found that to stay under a reasonable pressure ceiling with the .300 Weatherby he must allow a quarter-inch of freebore (i.e., bullet travel between launch and rifling engagement), which is a little less than the .354 freebore in Weatherby rifles but more than some gunsmiths allow. "If you short-throat a Weatherby," D'Arcy says, "you may run into trouble with Weatherby factory loads on hot days. Norma puts plenty of pep in its ammunition, which is made specifically for rifles with substantial freebore." Short throats generally give the best accuracy, but D'Arcy's compromise has proven itself at the range. He says he won't guarantee bench-grade accuracy, "Mainly because few shooters can hold well enough to get it." But he prides himself in shipping only rifles that shoot exceptionally well.

Those who've seen D'Arcy's synthetic-stocked rifle would hardly call it ugly, but it *is* a departure from the walnut-stocked masterpieces that come, albeit slowly, from his shop. "It was a painful transition," he acknowledges, "But the market was there, and now I'm really excited about the possibilities. Five of these new rifles have already seen action in Africa, with no problems reported." At $5000 each, there *shouldn't* be a problem. D'Arcy doesn't apologize for the price, though, which not long ago would have been steep for a top-grade rifle in English

The slender, open grip of the Webernick rifle (center) contrasts with the standard grip of a Remington Model 700 (left) and a snythetic-stocked Weatherby Mark V (right). The Webernick rifle, a .260 Remington built on a Model 70 action with 24-inch barrel of medium-light contour, weighs only six pounds without scope.

Some custom gunmakers prefer stainless steel. Webernick typically uses Shilen barrels. The author's stainless Model 70 from Rifles, Inc. shoots well with a variety of handloads.

them. One of the best known is Rifles, Incorporated (Cedar City, Utah) where Lex Webernick built a business by restocking, rebarreling and remachining Remington 700 actions. In 1987 he designed his own lightweight synthetic rifle stock which may still be the lightest around—only 11 ounces out of the mold and less than a pound trail-ready. Comprised of laminates of Kevlar, graphite and boron, its stock is trim as well as light. The comb is properly proportioned for use with a low-mounted scope that keeps recoil from bruising the shooter's face. The forend is short and dubbed off at an angle to accommodate the front swivel stud. This arrangement, which may look strange at first, is eminently practical. There's no need for forend beyond the stud; and a stud that protrudes below board can bite a hand. On the bench, a front-mounted stud allows the forend free travel rearward without tearing the sandbag.

This featherweight stock allows Lex Webernick to pare dozens of ounces from his rifles. In fact, he offers a 4½-pound centerfire bolt gun (available from Rifles, Incorporated). He also offers 200 chamberings, and if there still isn't one to a customer's liking his shop will add another to that list. Lex prefers Remington actions because they're easily obtained, reasonably priced, and light in weight. They've also established a reputation for accuracy on the bench. As for barrels, he follows the recommended break-in procedure. The result

is a level of accuracy that amazes disciples of heavier tubes. The barrel and mid-section of Lex's rifles do not make contact with the stock. Bedding pads at the tang and a receiver ring cap the pillars around the guard screws. Lex Webernick's rifles differ from those of other makers in that they are truly lightweight as well as accurate. They're not normally chambered for big-fisted slammers like the .375 H&H and the .458 Lott; but a friend who carries a Webernick rifle in .300 Winchester claims that with a brake the five-pounder is pleasant to shoot.

In addition to relieving hunters of weight on the trail, synthetic stocks have given new life to take-down rifles that never worked very well wearing wood. Pre-war Winchester and Savage lever-action take-down designs served their owners well enough, given the limited effectiveness of their iron sights and mild cartridges. But they eventually became loose, and even when tight they typically gave mediocre accuracy. Efforts at building bolt-action take-downs produced nothing of note for sportsmen, until H-S Precision announced its Pro-Series Take-Down rifle in the late 1980s. Not only

The new H-S Precision Model 2000 looks like other bolt rifles–except for a couple of steel plates sandwiched together in front of the magazine. Unlike the earlier Pro-Series take-down, which was built on the Remington 700 action, this less costly version features H-S Precision's own mechanism. A heavy, fluted barrel is standard, chambered in .22-250, .270, .308 and .300 Winchester Magnum. The magazine is a detachable box.

The breech end of the Model 2000 barrel assembly has three rows of interrupted threads that turn into mating surfaces in the receiver. The forend latch locks the two halves of the rifle into a single, solid unit. There's no rattle, no play. The latch slugs into a recess in the forend.

would the rifle come apart easily just forward of the receiver, it accommodated different bolts and barrels without special fitting. Simply rotate the front (barrel and forend) assembly 90 degrees and insert it into the receiver. Twist it tight, then snap the forend lever flush into its locking recess.

THE MODEL 2000

The only troubling thing about that rifle was its high price. But recently the H-S people came up with a new take-down called the Model 2000, which hitches up like the old Pro-Series. But rather than build the rifle around a 700 Remington action, H-S Precision developed a new action in-house. Also, the Model 2000 is *not* a custom rifle. It has no option list, and its synthetic-stocked rifle evolved to meet a price ($1795, which is half of what the Pro-Series rifle sold for a few years ago). It features a 23½-inch cut-rifled H-S barrel with six grooves and six flutes. It measures .830 at the muzzle and is chambered only in .22-250, .270, .308 and .300 Winchester Magnum. Two action lengths offer

appropriate magazine fit and bolt throw. The detachable box magazine protrudes a quarter-inch from the belly of the stock. Its capacity is three magnum and four standard cartridges, but even with this modest payload, there's no snapping the box home with the bolt closed.

At any rate, this hefty rifle isn't for Midwest deer hunters who pop in and out of automobiles all day, motoring from one woodlot to the next. Quick loading seems an unnecessary convenience. A staggered blind magazine would hold as many cartridges as the in-line box and look much better. It would also be easier to charge. Inserting rounds with sharp bullet noses proved painful because they had to enter from the front against considerable resistance (the magazine is long enough for shallow bullet seating). The bolt is a hybrid, its face recessed like the Remington 700's, and its leading rim is beveled much like the Winchester 70. It has two big locking lugs, a face-mounted claw extractor and a plunger ejector. There's also a three-position Model 70 safety, with a red dot cleverly inset in the stem so the shooter can see while aiming with the tab set forward. The bolt

The H-S Precision take-down rifle has a fully enclosed bolt face with plunger ejector and an ample front-mounted extractor. The window in the takedown plate receives the forend latch.

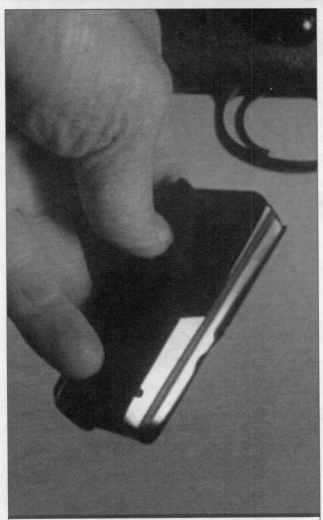

The H-S 2000 take-down rifle features a detachable box magazine. While increasingly popular with hunters, it is less appealing to some enthusiasts than a blind or hinged-cover magazine. The H-S box is narrow and of limited capacity, despite its protrusion from the rifle's belly.

is delicate enough to look like a switch, not a jack handle.

The rifle's main metal parts are made of 416 stainless steel finished nicely in black matte Teflon. The stock has a wide forend that houses the take-down locking lever flush. Stock-to-metal fit is exceptionally tight. The floating barrel centers the forend lips. Like other H-S stocks, this one has a slender grip and high, supportive comb. The battleship-gray color is accented by fine white flecks. A black recoil pad comes standard. Assembling and disassembling the Model 2000 requires a firm grip but no foul language. The breech end of the barrel mates with the receiver via three rows of interrupted threads. Once cinched into place, the two pieces become one. There's no wiggle or rattle. The locking lever snaps into place with authority. A ring on the barrel immediately in front of the take-down junction can be snugged with a spanner wrench should the rifle loosen through wear. Leupold's QRW scope mounts allow for further disassembly. Though it's not pegged as a custom rifle, the H-S Precision Model 2000 has features many shooters identify with custom rifles. Its take-down design should appeal to travelers who want a rifle that fits easily into panniers and the crowded gear compartments of Super Cubs. A furnished test target indicated a level of accuracy that should appeal to the increasing number of sportsmen glassing for big antlers far across canyons and clear cuts. The rifle's weight will not endear it to climbers, however.

As synthetic stocks evolve, enterprising gunmakers like Kenny Jarrett, Don Allen, D'Arcy Echols and Lex Webernick will find new applications for them. The warmth and color of figured walnut can't yet be duplicated in synthetic materials (though companies like Bell & Carlson have simulated wood color and grain in their stocks). Nor can molded stocks be shaped like wood. But utility has more than cosmetic appeal, and a clever designer can offer most people good stock fit from a mold, given the option of cutting the butt to proper length. Most shooters now acknowledge the benefits of synthetic stocks on factory rifles. Their popularity on custom-built rifles—and those with custom-rifle features and price tags —will no doubt increase.

comes apart like a Winchester 70, revealing a fast titanium striker. The bolt handle is short and hugs the lock tightly. H-S designed its own trigger for the Model 2000. Adjustable for sear engagement, weight and overtravel, it performed consistently on a prototype rifle. The trigger scale registered a letoff of less than two pounds (production triggers will adjust between $2\frac{1}{2}$ and $3\frac{1}{2}$ pounds). The smooth finger-piece has a pronounced hook and

Cowboy Action Shooting: A Sport For All Shooters

By Ron "El Escritor" Harris

From the driver's seat of the stagecoach, the scenery ahead looked lovely—until the bandits attacked. After that, the view was all to the rear. Swiveling around, Tutler downed three of the thugs, but the six rounds it took were the last in his Winchester. Meantime, five more gang members were gaining ground and spreading out. It took all five .45s from Tutler's Colt Peacemaker to neutralize the ne'er-do-wells. Suddenly, the remaining felons appeared at the side of the creaking Concord coach, certain of success. Tutler was still riding shotgun, with only four 12 gauge "howdys!" left to defend against the marauding horsemen. Soon Tutler ran out of ammo and adversaries simultaneously. Quite literally, the stage had been saved.

If that reads like a scene from a John Wayne film, you're close. Actually it's a description of Stage Two of Colt's End of Trail, the World Championship of Cowboy Action Shooting, held each April for the past 17 years in Norco, California. The recurring theme of these main match stages—11 in all—derives from westerns starring John Wayne, several of which were shown as part of the four-day Cowboy Action Shooting Championships and Wild West Jubilee. Proceeds from the huge event benefit the Children's Hospital of Orange County (California) and the Happy Trails Children's Foundation founded by Roy Rogers and Dale Evans.

The three-gun, 15-round course of fire described above took World Champion Tom "Tutler" Filbeck just 22.72 seconds, from the starter's beep to his final, clock-stopping shotgun blast. While not all stages utilize multiple weapons, most are designed

Single shot rifle events bring out the Sharps and Spencers. Here World Champion Tom Tutler competes in an E.O.T. World Championship with his '73 Trap Door Springfield carbine.

to afford shooters the opportunity to shoot two or more 19th Century firearms at reactive steel, and occasionally at cardboard, balloon or clay targets as well.

The "action" part in Cowboy Action Shooting is what propels the popularity and growth of these games. Shooters face the same challenges of time, space and movement as in other three-gun disciplines, but in difficult and usually humorous scenarios. These sometimes silly scenes are plagerized from western movies, novels, documented history, and the fertile imaginations of diabolical match officials.

"Cowboy Action" means media attention and Colt's End of Trail gets plenty of it. Here, "Tequila" ignores the TV cameras and concentrates instead on his front sight.

Surprised by "bad guys" at her garden party, "Mesa" drives them off with her Winchester carbine, while Australia's "Josey Wales" counts seconds and misses.

At major Cowboy Action events, such as the World Championships at "Colt's End of Trail" and "Ruger's Winter Range," or the National Championships held in Phoenix each February, the stage configurations can rival the movie sets of Hollywood westerns. Shooting bays are disguised as saloon false fronts, adobe pueblos and mining operations. In addition to stagecoaches and celerity wagons, there are freight wagons and buckboards to shoot from, over, around or under. Comical, old-time set decorations sometimes interfere with concentration, and procedural instructions often include reciting lines and performing distracting chores before, during or at the end of a course of fire.

A typical scenario involves a contestant sitting at a poker table with a couple of dummies. On the table there are playing cards, money, a pistol and saddlebags. Suddenly the man hollers, "You varmints have cheated me fer the last time!" With that, he picks up his pistol and shoots two paper targets positioned at the other side of the table.

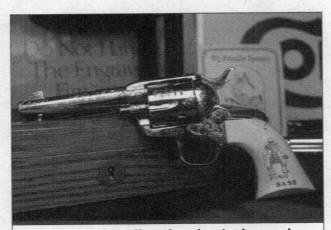

The engraved scroll work and scrimshaw make awards like this Colt a "Frontier Six Shooter" to aim for.

As "Sharpshooter" shoots his way down the streets of Colt's End of Trail, he is timed and watched carefully for misses and procedural errors.

"Cimarron Sue" shoots a stage at Ruger's Winter Range. Note the empty brass above her Winchester '73 as she levers up a round.

Cowboy Action competitors are sticklers for authenticity of clothing and gear, witness these galoots passing as Texas Rangers.

Blackpowder smoke belches from "El Escritor's" 1860 Army Colt. The dummy's friends are unable to save him.

This antique Colt is worn cross-draw in a typical Mexican two-loop holster. Many shooters invest more on research than on revolvers and rifles.

Colt's End of Trail features fine firearms vendors (left), as well as purveyors of 19th century goods of all kinds (right).

Gun carts may be large or small, but all shooters use them; and there's also a "Best Guncart" prize at many matches.

The author and his mount finish a stage at the Winter Range Cowboy Mounted Shooting event by shooting the last of ten balloons. Mounted Shooting is barrel racing, gymkhana and pistol shooting all rolled into one.

He then shoots the next three steel targets twelve feet or so downrange. Holstering his pistol, he scoops up the money, stuffs it in the saddlebags, busts through swinging doors and throws the loot up on the saddle of a plastic horse. Drawing his rifle from its scabbard, he twice sweeps the five 10-inch steel targets winking at him downrange. Replacing the long gun, he snatches up a shotgun that happens to be staged, open and empty, against the hitching post and engages the last four targets until they all fall down.

Thanks to fun like this, a proliferation of Cowboy Action matches blooms, like Brigadoon, into villages of white canvas tents, teepees, chuck wagons and stagecoaches, often larger than the original frontier towns they replicate. The streets teem with cowboys in chaps, bankers in frock coats, ladies in bonnets and, of course, the daringly draped *demimonde*. Peddlers and drummers hawk everything the 19th Century could offer, especially the Colts, Winchesters, Greeners and their reproductions, all historic embodiments of the "Spirit of the Game" philosophy of Cowboy Action Shooting. Matches are *fiestas*—celebrations of our western heritage—as much as they are competitions. With virtually everyone armed, these events might seem a bizarre and dangerous venue, but the opposite is true. An armed society is a polite society, and the re-created Wild West of Cowboy Action Shooting is only as wild as

strict firearms safety allows.

Sticklers for authenticity, Cowboy Action shooters take pains that their clothing and equipment match their persona accurately, as expressed by their choice of registered aliases. Sometimes comical, occasionally revealing and often an honest tribute, shooters choose their alter egos for personal reasons. Aliases, which were common in the Old West, are as humorous now as they were then. "Wild Bill Hiccup" is a favorite, along with "Iona Gunn," "Butch Chastity" and "Some Dense Kid." Once an alias is registered, shooters are thereafter known by this moniker and its abbreviations. It's the only name on their score card and no one else can use it.

The organization, which currently registers more than 16,000 of these notorious nicknames, is the Single Action Shooting Society, or SASS, with headquarters in Orange, CA. Administered by a board of directors called *"The Wild Bunch,"* SASS was created to administer and promote Cowboy Action Shooting worldwide. It endorses regional matches conducted by 160 affiliated clubs world-wide, produces *"Colt's End of Trail,"* and publishes *The Cowboy Chronicle*, a bi-monthly journal. The SASS also publishes a 35-page SASS "Shooters Handbook," which has become the

One of the last events at Ruger's Winter Range is the "Man-on-Man Shootout." Always exciting, it becomes historic when the shooters are "China Camp" (reloading) and "Tutler," both World Champions.

which Cowboy Action refers allows *aficionados* a variety of options. Shooters can choose smokeless, black powder cartridge, or percussion pistols. There's also a class for one-handed *pistoleros*; or one can opt for the more effective, if less romantic, two-handed "Squaw Hold."

During the early period, shooters choose from among Colt, Remington or other percussion revolvers and such long arms as the 1860 Henry and 1866 "Yellowboy" Winchester. At the other end of the period, the favorites include Smith and Wesson Schofields, 1892 Winchesters, and Model '97 Winchesters. The most commonly observed arsenal at Cowboy Action matches consists of two Colt SAA revolvers, a Winchester '73 rifle or carbine and a Rossi coach gun (the names Colt, Winchester and Remington also refer to reproduction firearms such as Uberti, Rossi and others.)

As the match begins, each shooter's outfit goes into a strange cart-like contraption that substitute for a horse and wagon. Often designed and built by the contestants themselves, these colorful carts convey arms and ammo from stage-to-stage. Since Cowboy Action Shooting is a family sport,

"The Gov" loads his nickel-plated Colt Peacemaker with .45 Colt blackpowder cartridges, while in the background "Tex" charges his 1851 Colt Navy Models at "Colt's End of Trail," the World Championships of Cowboy Action.

Cowboy Action shooters are divided into posses. All fire together to cut a log in half at Ruger's Winter Range in Arizona.

bible of Cowboy Action Shooting. Issued to every SASS member, it describes the firearms and equipage greenhorn shooters need in order to compete. While various affiliated clubs may add their own rules and colloquial customs to local matches, SASS rules are what define Cowboy Action Shooting.

The "Big Three" of Cowboy Action Shooting, which some refer to as "The Guns That Won the West," are the Colt Single Action Army, the Henry/Winchester lever action rifles and carbines, and some version of a period shotgun. At many matches, there are also stages for derringers, pocket revolvers, long range, single-shot rifles, and a cowboy version of sporting clays. On the other hand, the broad scope of competition categories and the historic period—roughly 1865 to 1900—to

A typical posse gathers at Ruger's Winter Range, the National Championships of Cowboy Action Shooting held in Phoenix, AZ, each February.

husbands and wives team up with other couples to load the gun carts with six long guns, at least four revolvers, two or more gunbelts, several hundred rounds of ammunition, a cleaning and tool kit, food, camera, a coffee thermos, canteen, rain gear, umbrellas and assorted personal gear.

Ammunition hauled in the carts, bandoleers and pistol belts is apt to be pistol ammo, from .32-20 through .45 Colt (by far the most popular round). The .44-40, .44 Special and .38 also rank high in popularity. What's really important, however, is that each caliber must match the period correctly. Reloading Single Action Army revolvers and lever action rifles under pressure is tough enough without having to sort through different calibers as well.

There's much more to Cowboy Action than just shooting, and there's a lot more to a shooter's outfit as well. You don't have to go to the line dressed to the nines, although most shooters do, but the sport also represents a lifestyle. It exists because of a community feeling referred to as the "Cowboy Way," "The Code of the West" or the "Spirit of the Game." It's in this spirit that everyone wears clothing and equipment appropriate to the era being re-created. Most folks research and develop an image based on real or imagined characters. For some, collecting the gear and accessories is a large part of the fun, whereas others manage somehow to keep it simple and save money.

Cowboy Action shooters disdain the term "costume" in favor of "outfit", but either way it's an important part of the fun. Most events include costume competitions and matches boasting bodacious bays and firing lines that look like movie scenes. Since stages require contestants to move from position to position with loaded firearms—following complex directions and even speaking lines as they go— shooting a championship match can be a lot like being in a western movie. It's this "Cowboy Way," this "Spirit of the Game" that engenders good humor, sportsmanship among cowboy competitors, and cooperation among range officials.

"Aliases and costuming keep our great game from getting too serious," says Harper "Judge Roy Bean" Creigh, and he should know. Cowboy Action Shooting was largely his idea, which explains why he wears SASS badge Numeber One. In 1978, Creigh and holster/saddle-maker Gordon "Diamond Jim Chisholm" Davis got together with 20 or so friends to shoot the old Colts and Winchesters that everybody owned but never shot anymore. So much fun was had that Creigh and Davis had no trouble organizing more matches. In 1982 they, along with founder Boyd "U.S. Grant" Davis, IPSC champion Jerry Usher and Marine Captain Bill "Moss Horn" Hahn, put together the first World Championships, which Creigh named *End of Trail.* The rest is Western History.

Truth be told, Cowboy Action Shooting is

A group of Ladies-at-Arms cover an old Studebaker roundup chuck wagon at Ruger's Winter Range in Phoenix. Cowboy Action Shooting appeals to both sexes and all ages.

"The Canyon Kid" models his well researched kit, a fine example of an 1870s cowboy.

devised a match known as "Cowboy Mounted Shooting," which added horses but removed live ammunition. In this event, cowboys and cowgirls race against the clock around an arena course lined with ten balloons, breaking them in sequence with blanks from two pistols.

Afoot or on horseback, it's the spirit of the Cowboy Action game that sets this unique lifestyle apart. That and a wise decision by Judge Roy Bean and his "Wild Bunch" that no money ever be awarded at *Colt's End of Trail.* That prohibition has remained in effect and is honored at *Ruger's Winter Range* and all other SASS-affiliated matches. Cowboy Action Shooting is strictly for fun. The competition for bragging rights and sponsor-donated prizes is merely another phase of the fun and fellowship this shooting sport affords.

In these sometimes tedious, high-tech times, there is something soothing about blazing away with six-shooters at targets you once thought were too large or too close to miss. Compared to other shooting sports, Cowboy Action Shooting may seem anachronistic and imprecise. But it's our way of remembering and re-creating America's precious western heritage. Cowboy Action Shooting is more than simply a shooting sport or a hobby. It's a delightful family pursuit and an increasingly popular reenactment of the living history left behind by the Great American West.

For further information about Cowboy Action Shooting, readers may contact the following organizations:

SINGLE ACTION SHOOTING SOCIETY (SASS)

1938 N. Batavia Street, Suite M
Orange, CA 92865
(714) 998-1899
Internet: http://SASSnet.com
E-mail: SASSEOT@aol.com

COWBOY MOUNTED SHOOTING ASSOCIATION

4101 W. Willow
Phoenix, AZ 85029
(602) 978-8328
Internet: http//www.futureone.com/~bobbie/index.html

nothing more than good-humored recreational shooting in an Old West fantasy setting. Without their fantastic history, the old guns and their reproductions would be nothing more than obsolete antique firearms. But the world's fascination with the American West of the 19th century only deepens with the passage of time. Our 19th century firearms become momentary time machines, and for that moment we experience some of what it must have felt like to defend the cabin, wagon or ranch with the ordinary firearms of the day.

This combination of enjoyable activities—shootin' match, historical re-enactment, costume party and old-time social—has swollen SASS membership, created businesses and fueled our renewed interest in all things Western. An entire industry has evolved to serve the varied interests of the practitioners of this arcane but romantically entertaining diversion. For several years, the only thing missing were the horses, so Cowboy Action shooters Phil Spangen-berger and Jim Rodgers

The Secrets Of Successful Field Gunning

By Nick Sisley

A gaudy cock pheasant erupts with a noisy explosion out of the jing weeds. After regaining your composure, you know it's still a relatively easy shot. But you miss! Twice! A roaring ruffed grouse scares you halfway into the middle of next week. It's disappearing fast as you try desperately to catch up with the shotgun muzzle. But you can't. The gun explodes before you can get to the target. The stillness is deafening, and you wonder about the state of your wing-gunning abilities. Tomorrow, or the next day, it could be a flock of mallards, their flight successfully diverted by a guide with some expert calling. Not only have the birds turned, they are headed for the decoy spread, their wings cupped. Now

they tilt back and forth, catching the wind just right for a controlled descent, a planned landing for your opening in the fakes. "Take 'em," comes the word from the guide. You want to show your mettle, but three steel shot loads find only empty air. Each of the several targets flies off unscathed. The guide makes a remark that sounds something like, "We'll get 'em next time." But you notice he's now loading his own gun.

We all miss our share of feathered targets, so a mere miss is no reason to get down in the dumps. Too many Americans assume that skill with shooting a shotgun is something we're born with—that we either have it or we don't. Not true. Like any other skill, shotgun shooting is something you learn,

Sometimes a gaudy ringneck rooster provides an easy straightaway—and still you miss.

Excellent certified instruction is available simply by calling the National Sporting Clays Association or the National Skeet Shooting Association for the names of certified shooting instructors in your area.

beginning with the basics. Just as in golf, bowling, tennis or whatever you pursue, we all need a solid foundation. Without it any attempts at improvement will be so much wasted effort. Accordingly, the best way to start is by obtaining instruction from a qualified instructor. All you have to do is call 1-800-877-5338, which is the toll-free number for both the National Sporting Clays Association (NSCA) and the National Skeet Shooting Association (NSSA). They'll supply you with a list of certified instructors in your area.

Let's assume you've already learned some solid basics in shotgun shooting. Following is a series of shots that are often encountered in the uplands or in waterfowling, along with a primer of sorts on how you can practice these shots in the proper manner.

THE EASY STRAIGHTAWAY

Often the "easy straightaway" isn't so easy. The place to practice this target is on a skeet field, specifically the Low House at Station Seven or any straightaway target found at a local sporting clays course. At the Station Seven Low House, you know the target is going to fly over the center stake. Plant both feet on the ground, shoulder-width apart, your belly button facing slightly to the right of the center stake (to the left for right-handed shooters). Take a half step forward

with your left foot, placing your belly button even further to the right of the center stake. With the gun pointed down, place the muzzle slightly below the flight path of the target. Get loose by moving and shaking your shoulders around.

Now, without ever looking at the muzzle, call for the target. Focus on it completely; in fact, stare a hole through it. How you bring the gun up at this point is very important. Shift your weight to the left foot, maybe even taking a one-inch step forward. Then, at first sight of the clay, push the gun slightly forward. Here, it's like a doctor telling you to take an aspirin. He doesn't mean you should take the whole bottle. Don't make that forward movement of your body and gun anything but *very* slight.

Next, bring the gun forward—only a half-inch or so—and then up. At the same time, you don't want the muzzle waving around, which is easy to do. With the gun mounted to your shoulder, the goal is for the muzzle to move slightly upward until it meets the escaping straightaway target. Bringing the muzzle up too high won't work, because then you won't be able to see the bird and you'll instinctively lift your head, a definite no-no. Let the muzzle dip down and the smooth, even flow of gun to target will be ruined. You must compensate and get the muzzle back on track. In doing so, odds are you're going to look at the

Lazy incoming targets, like this dove, can sometimes be exasperating. You can take care of that by learning and practicing the basics.

Practicing at a Low Seven Station on a skeet field or at a sporting clays course is an excellent idea for improving straightaway shots.

muzzle (though you probably won't realize it) and take your eye off the target. Those negatives are really mounting. The solution is to practice the mount over and over, getting the basics down pat and developing the muscle memory that will take over automatically when a pheasant, grouse or quail presents a straightaway opportunity.

THE QUICK CROSSER: RIGHT TO LEFT OR LEFT TO RIGHT

This shot is fairly common in ruffed grouse shooting, but it occurs in other upland encounters as well. What invariably happens is that the bird flies out and there's no way the shooter can get the muzzle in position for a sustained lead shot. This bird is *always* head of the muzzle; or more properly, the muzzle is *always* behind the quick crosser. What this means is, simply, the shot must come from behind, which scares shooter after shooter. They know the bird will soon disappear into heavy cover. The natural tendency is to shoot fast, which often means getting the muzzle to the bird too soon.

Take the advice of someone who has compiled thousands of experiences: You can't kill a game bird if you fire while still trying to catch up. Depending upon the angle, it's essential that you at least get the muzzle to the bird, if not in front of it.

Probably the ideal place to practice this target is on a skeet field at High Two or Low Six, or at a local sporting clays range. The true quick crosser on a skeet field is a High or Low Station Four, but for the sake of practice the High Two and Low Six will work even better. It's so easy for either one of these targets to get the jump on a shooter, and for the clay to get ahead of the muzzle. Consequently, the idea is to set up so either target gets ahead of the muzzle from the start. You want to break the targets near the center stake. Begin by placing your feet shoulder-width apart and facing the stake. Then take a half step forward with your left foot (for right-handed shooters). Gun down, insert the muzzle at about a point parallel to and just below the target's flight path. Before calling for the target, distribute your weight evenly on both feet, knees bent slightly.

When you jump up from a waterfowl blind, the ducks will flare, often providing a quartering away shot.

As the bird flies out, almost every shooter makes the same mistake by starting the gun butt toward the shoulder. This causes the muzzle to dip down and away from the bird's flight path. When that happens, you must make several compensations, one or all of which will further contribute to a miss. Instead, try this method: first, move the muzzle along the target's flight path. Only then should you start the butt toward your shoulder. Starting the butt to your shoulder any sooner will result in a herky-jerky movement that won't produce anything positive. Instead, start the muzzle on the bird's flight path first, then blend in the butt stock mount. You'll love what you see! That one-piece fluid movement will be a definite help in making the target easier. It also eliminates the problem of the butt stock hanging up on your clothes. Remember, don't take that whole bottle of aspirin. The muzzle should move only an inch or so before you blend in the mount of the butt stock toward your shoulder. Practice this move in your living room, den or office before even

One key to hitting hard, fast crossing shots more consistently is to start the muzzle moving along the target line—before starting the butt stock to your shoulder.

A hunter practices the lazy incomer shot at a sporting clays station.

Two shooters discuss the importance of follow-through, which is just as important in shotgunning as it is in golf, bowling, or throwing a ball.

attempting to experiment with it over and over on a High Two and Low Six.

You've now reached a point where the basics are solidly in force. It's time to return to the target range. Whether shooting a High Two or a Low Six, the clay is now ahead of the muzzle, exactly as you want. Practice coming from behind and *not* pulling the trigger until you've caught up with the target. Do this over and over, both High Two and Low Six. Get comfortable with the sight picture. Feel confident in coming from behind. Not only is this natural, it's the *only* way a high percentage of upland birds can be taken, because the gun's muzzle almost always starts behind these upland birds—particularly the quick, hard crossers.

THE FLOATING INCOMERS

In this shot, which occurs fairly often in dove shooting, an incomer flies off to the left or the right of the shooting position. Sometimes these incomers are anything but floaters—they're on full after burner! To practice this shot, use a Low One and Two and a High Six and Seven on a skeet

field or on most sporting clays courses. In many instances, incomers can arrive at longer distances, which makes for some good practice. Most learners are taught to take the bird on a sustained lead, which is the natural way to make this shot. Start off in the same manner as outlined for previous shots, facing the center stake, then taking a half step forward with the left foot. Insert the muzzle slightly below the bird's flight path, gun down, and call for the target. Starting the muzzle first, track the bird only briefly before hitting the trigger. If you measure this target—which is easy to do since there's time—the tendency is to look back and forth between the gun and the bird. This "measuring" of the lead isn't good basics; moreover, it's not conducive to hitting the target. Another mistake in tracking a lazy incomer too long is that it's natural to slow or stop the swing. Further, if you take that first shot—and miss—while the target is still well to the front, there's still plenty of time to shoot again without having to turn and shoot while the bird is going away.

Once you feel comfortable with shooting the

Ruffed grouse that offer hard and fast crossing shots are invariably ahead of the muzzle, which means you must come from behind and swing through the target.

closer-in targets, use a sporting clays course for those high, long incomers. You'll discover that appreciably more lead is needed as the bird flies farther and farther away. Again, practice this shot in your office, living room or den, beginning with foot and body position, starting with the muzzle first, then shooting that first shot quickly, following through, your head welded to the stock. Some may argue that all this practice is well and good, but how can it help in the field, where push often comes to shove? The answer: by practicing foot and body position over and over for specific shots, getting the muzzle moving along the target's flight path, staring holes through targets, following through, keeping the head welded to the wood, that all these solid basics will eventually pay off in the field.

THE LONG QUARTERING SHOTS

These tough shots occur when, for example, decoying ducks are suddenly panicked when they see a hunter suddenly rise up in the blind to shoot. In their attempts to escape, the ducks neither go straightaway nor are they hard crossers.

One place to practice your swing through is at Station Low Six on a skeet field, or a similar target on a sporting course. The idea is to let the clay get in front of the muzzle, then learn to swing through the target.

Shotgun basics are important, especially when you're learning to keep your head welded to the stock.

They are at something like a quarter angle, and often the distance is significant. You may find such a shot on a sporting clays course for practice. If not, seek special permission at a skeet range to shoot the High Two and the Low Six, but from several *yards* behind the regular shooting pad. You may even want to position yourself slightly toward Station Three or Five for a more realistic quartering angle. It's easy to shoot behind this kind of target, for there's a common tendency to shoot right *at* it. The most natural way to come up on a quartering duck is simply to insert the muzzle in front of the bird at the start. You won't need much lead, but some is essential. Depending upon the angle, at least some "daylight" is needed between the muzzle and the bird—more if there's an acute angle to the shot.

Practice doing this on an "extended" High Two and a Low Six skeet target, or on a sporting clays range. Experiment with that slight step forward to get your weight started forward. Extend the gun forward slightly, rather than bringing it directly to your shoulder. With this method, the muzzle moves right or left only a little. You start with the gun down, the muzzle just below the bird's flight path; then you call for the bird and make your move. It's all similar to making straightaway shots. Just get that muzzle in a straight line and slightly ahead of the bird. Another method that might

work equally well is to make a pass-through shot. Set up as before, but with the muzzle back a tad closer to the house. You *want* the bird to get ahead of the muzzle. As the clay flies out, start your swing, then your mount. Overtake the fake quarry and immediately hit the trigger. Because the muzzle moves faster than the bird, there's no need actually to get ahead of the quartering shot. Simply hit the trigger when you blot out the clay, keep your head down, and follow through.

You won't necessarily poleax a distant duck with this scenario. That's because, unless you break a wing, the shot has to penetrate all the way up through the vitals to be lethal. The farther the bird is from the gun, the less likely you'll experience full penetration. But don't be discouraged. Any bird that's flying away from you, where considerable distance is involved, is extremely hard to kill. Center the bird quartering away in the distance with a full pattern and it will come down. Your retriever can then earn its keep.

Don't be discouraged if your wing-shooting skills have been less than satisfactory in the past. And don't assume that you have to be born a good shotgunner. Natural ability is an obvious factor in any endeavor, but you can learn to be more effective with your shotgun. The basics we've discussed here can bring significant improvement. But it does take practice, and no one can do that for you. As they say, the ball's in your court.

The quartering away duck shot can be a real nemesis.

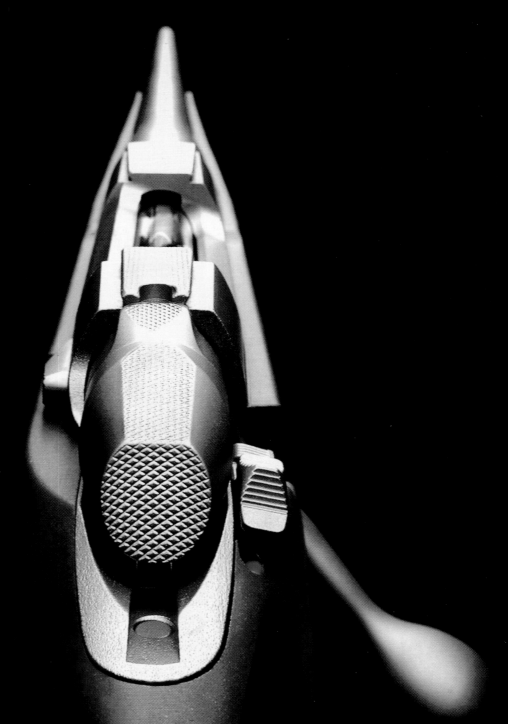

The Sharps 1859: A Modern Replica That Shoots!

By Stan Warren

In modern terms, the new brand of "muzzleloaders" personified by the Sharps Model 1859 fits the old phrase, "Neither fish nor fowl." Although a true black powder percussion arm, it does not load from the muzzle; hence, the laws in most states do not allow its use during special big game hunting seasons. To carry it afield when other nimrods are toting their long-shooting centerfires is the equivalent of getting into a game of "Five Card Stud" and insisting that you'd prefer playing with three cards.

Why, then, the urge to sally forth with such an oddball beast? The answer is simple: the Model 1859—whether a .45 or .54 caliber—*shoots*. This should not come as a great surprise; after all, the term "sharpshooter" is nothing more than a corruption of the complimentary name given Christian Sharps' shooters during the dark and troubled days of the Civil War. Bear in mind, this was well before the advent of what became known as the "Buffalo Gun" of song and fable, and well before the days when wonderful, fancy grades of sporting rifles arrived on the scene. These were taken from the ranks of the finer models of 1874, 1877 and beyond. Nor, except as a step in history, does the percussion rifle figure in the great American victory over the Irish rifle team at the famous Creedmore Match on Long Island (NY) in 1873.

The Model 1859 was indeed a weapon of war. Some 2,000 of them were carried into battle in 1862 by Col. Hiram Berdan's 1st and 2nd

While strong and massive, the breech block of the Sharps removes easily for cleaning it and virtually every other working part of the rifle.

In the closed position, the breech of this falling-block Sharps replica is strong enough to handle full-chamber black powder loads and produce shot-to-shot consistency.

Regiment of U.S. Sharpshooters. With their 30-inch round barrels, bull forends with three-barrel-band fasteners and steel patch boxes, these guns looked somewhat like traditional military muskets. Another 1,500 were built to fulfill an Army contract, followed by 2,800 more going to the Navy, with more to come. By then, the reputation of the Sharps for accuracy, strength and dependability had been secured.

Following hostilities, many of these rifles remained quite serviceable. Naturally, some wound up as part of that mighty migration of settlers heading to the open West, away from the war-ravaged lands in the east. Those that were left over in the military were mostly converted later on to .50-70 centerfire, especially the carbine version. As for the westward migrators, there was certainly game, if not wealth, beyond the Mississippi. The average Sharps with its .52 caliber bore proved effective in thumping bison, bear and anything else that came within its limited range. Tossing a chunk of lead with a diameter of .535 to .555 and weighing in the neighborhood of 425 to 450 grains, the rifle proved itself even

with a muzzle velocity slightly more than 1,200 feet per second, or a muzzle energy in excess of 1,300 foot-pounds. Big bullet fans will claim that numbers can be deceptive, but the wide-girthed, soft lead bullet was mighty efficient in its day.

I first became aware of the history of the Sharps rifle after using a Shiloh Sharps replica of a .50-70 Model 1874 cartridge Sharps to collect various bucks and boars running wild in the hills of Tennessee. Then came the urge to slip back a notch farther to the wartime rifle that had been an important stepping stone in the development of self-contained ammunition. An invitation to hunt with Pierangelo Pedersoli, whose factory in Italy produces many of the modern Sharps copies, was enough to provide the final push. Also included on that trip to Montana's pronghorn flats was Dan McKenney, a black powder shooter whose experience with these rifles made his comments especially pertinent.

In its time, the '59 Sharps was truly a marvel. Soldiers could actually prepare their ammunition before going into battle, something unknown by the U.S. military prior to the acceptance of this rifle. Once they'd run out of their "cartridges," they could load from the breech with bullets and loose powder. And when fouling really got bad—and the breech block was too gritty to lower—troopers could simply load from the muzzle. Not a perfect situation, but certainly well in advance of most military arms up to and including the Civil War era.

"This same flexibility has some drawbacks," Dan McKenney observed one day during our hunt. "With a conventional muzzleloader, it's possible to alter your bullet/powder charge combination substantially without any trouble. The design of the Sharps percussion rifle provides a finite amount of space. As bullet weight is increased, powder capacity decreases. This may work fine in our centerfire-rifle-way of doing things, but the effect really restricts what is inherently an already restricted shooting situation. For instance, with a .50 caliber percussion rifle of the Hawken type, you can realistically load down and shoot round balls with fair effect on small game. Then you can turn around and use a conical bullet

with a hefty charge on deer, elk or whatever. To try anything similar with Sharps' falling block design, you have to think things out a bit."

Since the ability to use prepared ammunition is what made the Sharps rifle unique in its day, it's only fitting that the process be followed for a modern hunting excursion of the kind I made in Montana with Mr. Pedersoli.

PREPARING FOR THE HUNT

Although molds are available for producing period-style Sharps bullets—complete with a cantilevered base for easy assembly and typing—my preparations for the hunt were concerned mainly with the selection of pure lead projectiles already on hand. Thompson/Center's Maxi-Ball and Maxi-Hunter 320-grain and 255-grain were among the first tried, as was Hornady's 285-grain Great Plains Bullet, followed quickly by the 285-grain Buffalo Bullet. During the production of paper cartridges, bullet design plays an important—even unique—role having nothing to do with accuracy or performance on game.

Musket or "top hat" caps used with the Sharps provide the spark necessary to ignite charges in the chamber. The big caps put out substantially more fire than standard #11 versions.

Excellent accuracy beyond 100 yards is possible with the replica Sharps percussion rifles. Surprisingly, the scoped version (.45 caliber at top) handled small targets at more than twice that distance.

To tie off the paper tube effectively, there must be a good amount of lubricating groove near the base. Of the four configurations mentioned above, the T/C Maxi-Hunter was easiest to use, while the Buffalo Bullet and Great Plains Bullet were noticeably more difficult because they lacked what amounted to a tying groove. When the Maxi-Hunter proved to be the least accurate of the lot, things naturally got complicated. It would have been fine for use on whitetails, but on the wind-swept plains of Montana accuracy became a comforting factor. The nod, therefore, went to a longer, more ballistically-efficient shape.

Given the different bullet shapes, weights and lengths, Dan McKinney's comments on the use of "finite space" were borne out. A wonderfully accurate Whiteworth-style bullet had to be put aside because, at 475 grains, it simply took up too much room. With powder space reduced, the long slug's easy-to-use grooves—the same ones that made cartridge preparation a cinch—could

not muster the necessary speed. On a Pro-Chrono chronograph, the Whitworth lumbered along at just over 1,200 fps, while the Maxi-Ball averaged close to 1,300 and the Great Plains Bullet consistently exceeded 1,340.

With the details established, actual production of cartridges got under way in earnest. Both nitrated paper and cigarette-rolling papers functioned quite well; but since the latter are more readily available, most shooters lean in that direction. A few tales exist concerning the failure of nitrated paper to exhibit complete combustion, especially along the glued seam. Fortunately, that problem failed to develop. Only on a rare occasion did a sliver or two remain in the breech after firing. Nor did leaving them where they lay make a noticeable difference in loading ease or performance.

Having been raised in an era when practically every farm kid tried his hand at rolling cigarettes, I found that working with this type of paper did not pose any great challenge. Two papers are simply

Paper cartridges are shown with a percussion Sharps replica. The author used numerous conventional-type muzzleloading bullets as well as the cantilever base style originally intended for these rifles.

fastened together, rolled around a dowel, then refastened using nothing more than the tip of one's tongue. With ammo meant for carrying afield, the seams are lightly glued with a natural flour paste. With either type of casing material, the silk thread is lightly secured with the same paste (you'll need the longest cigarette papers available to ensure enough load to fill a chamber).

When describing the use of components, the key word is *simple*. Merely tie the tip of a paper tube into a lubricating groove and fill the tube almost to the end with powder. Then twist it, like we used to do with penny candy wrappers, or fold it over and glue. Properly done, the cartridge should be jut long enough for the breech block to shave off a bit of the tube.

In preparing for the hunt, another question arose:0 how to carry the prepared ammo? The cartridges had an annoying habit of converting themselves, without warning, back into their component parts. Clearly, some sort of protection

was required. Since nothing that was commercially available served the purpose, a friend who runs a saddle shop created a traveling device that fit nicely into a belt, took up little room, and held five rounds securely without sacrificing accessibility.

During the test period, the one thing that became obvious with virtually every bullet/powder charge combination was that the rifle could really *shoot*. The twist rate—one turn in 21 inches—was rather fast considering the rifle. Using the T/C Maxi-Ball, all groups fired were substantially under two inches at 100 yards with no sighting aids other than the factory sights. Average groups with other bullets ran less than three inches. A .54 caliber Pedersoli Sharps, sporting a one in 48" twist, did about as well with bullets that were more squat and stubby.

Consistent velocity readings were somewhat unexpected. After all, the Sharps is not a solid breech rifle in the sense that any design with a fire-carrying channel is solid. The breech block on the Sharps slides down to expose the chamber; enough, one would think, to equate pressure changes and lost pressure from gases produced by the burning powder. Not so. The seal was quite efficient, even though modern replicas sport barrel sleeves without benefit of the platinum sealing rings found in some originals. Even today, after several hundred trigger pulls and full-pressure loads, the breech block on my Sharps displays nothing more than a polished ring on the breech block edge. The outer face of the chamber section, meanwhile, shows polish marks that suggest a tiny bit more gas was escaping toward the upper right side of the junction. The gas-polished portion measures about an eight of an inch, which isn't bad.

Also unexpected was the fast, consistent ignition of the Sharps. After all, the separate chamber and breech block/nipple assembly means that the spark from the nipple and percussion cap must travel a fair distance to get the job done.

This problem is handled partially by a musket cap that throws a much bigger spark than standard #11 percussion caps.

"Follow the tilt and thump drill and she'll go off," Dan McKenney stated flatly. "Whether you decide to use cartridges or loose bullet and powder, put the charge in place, then tilt the barrel up to a vertical position and thump the action solidly with the butt of your hand. Enough powder will get into the flash channel to transfer the fire."

That's good advice in any man's language.

THE HUNT BEGINS

Near the Montana-Wyoming border, along its eastern edge, rains are not supposed to amount to biblical proportions. Still, the Powder River crawled steadily toward the upper limits of its banks while we hunters checked zeroes on water-logged targets from a shooting bench partially sheltered by a blue tarp. The winds were strong

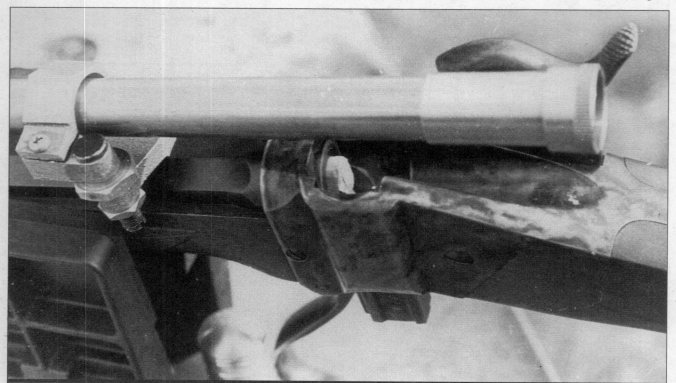

A paper cartridge should extend slightly beyond the mouth of the chamber. Lifting the breech lever effectively shaves off the rear portion, leaving a full chamber. Only a percussion cap is needed then to fire the rifle.

enough to jerk stove pipes out of sheepherder stoves and fill tents with smoke. One of the hunters left his pipe where it had fallen outside, duct-taped the pipe vent and lit the igniter on a propane heater. Recreating a touch of the past was one thing, but being miserable on the verge of asphyxiation was quite another.

The wind and rain were so nasty that ducks walked rather than flew, and migratory birds went in the direction of the prevailing gusts rather than southward as they'd have preferred. Twice on that first day, rifles of types other than the Sharps either hung fire or misfired. Despite the proven accuracy of the replica Sharps, hitting a target at an unknown distance had played a major role in our preparations for hunting pronghorn on their turf. Zeroed at 100 yards, my powder-bullet combo proved effective at that range but lost enthusiasm at a fast clip after that. At 150 yards, for example, the bullet hit nine inches below the point of aim.

Beyond that, a shooter would have to be an incredible judge of distance (or be extremely lucky). Accordingly, my plan was to make whatever careful stalks it took to restrict my shots to the 100-yard range. Most pronghorn country, after all, has its share of folds, breaks and depressions that can be used to a hunter's advantage. Working in his favor as well are the prairie goats, who tend to follow a reasonably set pattern when not being shoved around by hunting pressure.

When the sporting gods smile, lots of thing work. By the third day, the rains had been chased away by an approaching high pressure system and the mornings turned chilly but clear. With the help of a hunting partner, we planned to ambush a herd we'd spotted previously, one that moved along a predictable path to a small, bowl-shaped basin below our vantage point. Assistance came from a fellow hunter who approached the herd from the other side, moving slowly and hopefully

Range work with both .45 and .50 caliber Sharps copies moved out to the 100-yard mark with excellent results. Here the author checks the results of another bullet through the Pro-Chrono. At around 1,360 fps, the replica Sharps (made by Pedersoli) produced more than enough punch to take on game the size of deer and antelope.

This pronghorn was taken with the .45 caliber Sharps replica at very short range. Although prepared to handle long shots, smart black powder rifle hunters are more than willing to take an easy one when the opportunity arises.

pushing the animals in a direction they would normally prefer to travel.

Hiding behind some tumbleweed, I watched the animals gradually reduce the distance between us. At about 80 yards, it was rather easy to deliver a 285-grain Great Plains Bullet right on the shoulder point of a nice buck. The solid lead bullet with its conspicuous hollow point did what is best described as a "smashing job" in stopping the pronghorn. Actually, many black powder shooters agree there's no need to build hollow-point bullets, since the soft nature of the projectile pretty much ensures expansion. But it may also restrict penetration, and perhaps it does. However, the amount of tissue through which my slug penetrated another buck later on that memorable day was mighty impressive. It all came about in an unusual fashion. While stalking a herd that was feeding peacefully, my partner glanced around to see another buck moving toward him. The animal failed to notice the hunter creeping up a slight draw off to the right. At forty paces, the buck looked up, but

there was no time to react. The Sharps' sights were already lined up just to the side of his breast bone.

Few pronghorn have ever been knocked flatter, regardless of the caliber used. Upon performing an autopsy, we quickly discovered why the hit had been so deadly. Due to the angle, the bullet had ranged upward after impact. The top of the heart was, for all practical purposes, gone. Both lungs were shredded, too; but even after doing all that damage the bullet had plowed onward, finally coming to rest just short of the offside ham joint. Over two feet of tissue had been penetrated, proof that lead bullets at modest velocities are capable of handling even heavy game.

Having worked so well on pronghorn, the Model '59 Sharps will doubtless continue to see duty in the game fields. Like the hunters and soldiers who carried the original version knew only too well, this transitional black powder arm, keeping in mind its limitations imposed by velocity, is a truly impressive performer.

New Bolt Action Designs Take Muzzleloading Into The New Century

By Toby Bridges

Among the new breed of muzzleloading hunters, few could care less whether or not their rifles display historically correct lines and styling. In fact, most black powder hunters today are making new demands on the performance of their frontloading rifles, with the expectation that they'll perform more like a modern centerfire big game rifle. Fortunately, some significant changes and improvements in muzzleloader design and performance have occurred. Muzzle-loading has gone modern and some of the newer rifles on the market are already

fully capable of delivering centerfire rifle quality accuracy at 100 yards and farther. Among them, one stands out: the Knight MK-85 in-line percussion rifle, introduced in the mid-1980s and now recognized as the model that first brought modern technology into the centuries' old sport of muzzleloading.

Among the important features of this modernistic frontloader is a fast plunger-style hammer designed to fire a percussion cap on a nipple located in the rear center of the breech plug. Fire from the exploding cap must travel only a fraction of an inch

Bill's Custom Guns of Greensboro, North Carolina, utilized a Howa centerfire rifle action to customize a modern bolt action frontloader.

The Knight XK-97 D.I.S.C. Rifle is shown with some of the loading components that turn it into a tack driver.

Both the Fire-Bolt and Accu-Bolt models from Connecticut Valley Arms utilize the same short-throw bolt action.

to reach the powder charge in the barrel. Ignition is spontaneous and more sure-fire than older traditional side-hammer percussion ignition systems. The Knight MK-85 couples this improved ignition with modern lines that handle nicely and a barrel with a fast rate of rifling twist for improved performance with today's conical and saboted bullets. The overnight success of this muzzleloader has caused nearly every muzzleloading gun manufacturer to include an in-line percussion rifle of similar design in its lineup. As muzzleloading continues to mature into a hunting sport, the development of frontloaders worldwide has become strictly performance-driven. Modern black powder hunters are no longer content with the standard in-line percussion designs. They want a hunting rifle with still hotter ignition, faster lock time, better accuracy, and more user-friendly. The muzzleloading industry has responded with an entirely new breed of bolt action in-line percussion hunting rifle. Following is a review of some of the more popular, more advanced models that are destined to take muzzleloading into the 21st Century.

THE REMINGTON MODEL 700 ML/MLS

Remington Arms Company shook up the shooting world in 1996 when it introduced the company's respected Model 700 bolt action centerfire rifle in a brand new muzzleloading version. Not content merely to jump onto the bandwagon, Remington's Model 700 in frontloader form took muzzleloader development to a new level. Offered in a choice of .50 or .54 caliber with black or camouflaged composite stock, the Model 700 ML (blued) and MLS (stainless) retain the basic stock design, trigger, receiver and bolt of the centerfire version. Modifications include a removable breech plug and nipple threaded into the rear of the barrel, replacement of the standard bolt firing pin with a larger flat-faced striker (for positive ignition of a No. 11 percussion cap), and the addition of a solid aluminum ramrod mounted on the bottom side of the barrel.

THE TRADITIONS LIGHTNING RIFLE

In recent years, Traditions, Inc. has ridden the wave of in-line percussion rifle popularity with a selection of affordable hunting rifles. Retailing for about half the price of similar models from other markers, Traditions' in-line models may not have been built with the fit, finish and refined features of more costly rifles, but its guns have provided cost-conscious black powder hunters with the performance and reliability of an in-line hunting rifle. Now the company is out to change its image and reputation with the introduction of a new bolt action model called the Lightning. Among its features is a short bolt design for extremely fast lock time. It also has an adjustable trigger, breech plug and nipple, all easily removed from the barrel and receiver to make cleaning a snap. Remove the ramrod and ramrod guide from the bottom of the barrel and this rifle would have the appearance and lines of a stylish bolt action centerfire. Actually, some bolt action centerfire riflemakers could learn a thing or two about nice lines from this rifle.

As much as this frontloader may look like a bolt action cartridge rifle, though, it's a hunting muzzleloader through and through. Available in .50 or .54 caliber, it features a 24-inch barrel and comes in blued or stainless steel with a variety of stock options ranging from walnut or laminated to black or camouflaged composite. For some reason, Traditions offers the .50 caliber models with a one-turn-in-32 inches rate of rifling twist, while the .54

caliber model comes with a much slower one-turn-in-48 inches rate. The faster twist of the .50 caliber models is ideally suited for most saboted bullets, while the slow twist of the .54 caliber barrels restricts shooters to loading and firing either patched round balls or the heavy lead bore-sized conicals.

The stainless steel .50 caliber rifle tested for this article performed best with saboted .44 and .45 caliber handgun bullets of 240, 250 and 260 grains. The most accurate load consisted of two 50 grain Pyrodex Pellets and a .45 caliber Speer jacketed hollow-point bullet (260 grain) loaded with a black sabot made by Muzzleload Magnum Products. Several 100-yard groups were exactly one inch center-to-center. Weighing in at less than seven pounds, this rifle would make an excellent hunting muzzleloader for women or younger shooters. Even with loads as light as 70 grains of Pyrodex "Select," the Lightning still prints the 260 grain Speer bullet inside of 1½ inches at 100 yards, with not too much recoil.

THE CONNECTICUT VALLEY ARMS FIRE-BOLT AND ACCU-BOLT RIFLES

This long-time muzzleloading gun supplier has added two bolt action models to it's line—the low-cost Fire-Bolt and a premium version known as the

Traditions, Inc. makes a bold statement with its slim, trim Lightning. Shown is a lightweight bolt action in-line muzzleloader that shoots well with a wide range of saboted bullets.

Pure class is the best way to describe the new Model 420 LR offered by Austin & Halleck. Note the clean lines, superb wood and nicely executed cut checkering.

Accu-Bolt—which share the same short throw bolt and receiver. What really sets the higher priced Accu-Bolt apart is a custom-cut Badger barrel featuring .005" grooves that spin with a one-turn-in-26 inches rate of twist. The Fire-Bolt model, featuring a slower one-turn-in-32 inches rate of twist, is built with an extruded and hammer-forged barrel, which the company advertises as "The Most Accurate Production Barrel in The World." The Accu-Bolt is available in .50 caliber only and comes with a special Accu-System bullet sizer made from a section of the barrel installed. Connecticut Valley Arms has also developed a lubaloy-coated Accu-System bullet specifically for this rifle. Once forced through the sizer, the 300 grain copper clad bullets offer a precise fit with the Accu-Bolt's Badger barrel. With a 100 grain charge of either FFg black powder or Pyrodex "Select," the Accu-Bolt can print the bore-sized conical inside three inches at 100 yards with consistency.

The Accu-Bolt's fast twist 24" barrel prefers a wide range of saboted handgun bullets, along with several new all-copper bullets such as the Remington Premier Copper Solid or the Barnes Expander MZ. Both the 250 and 300 grain .45 caliber Hornady XTP jacketed hollow-points loaded with a black sabot out-performed everything else in our tests. With a 100-grain charge of Pyrodex "Select," either bullet would print 1½- to 2½-inch groups at 100 yards.

The Fire-Bolt is available in both .50 and .54 caliber. Its slower one-turn-in-32 inches rate of twist may not handle the much longer saboted all-copper bullets as effectively as the Accu-Bolt's faster twist barrel. But the 24" production barrel on this rifle can fire the shorter mid-200 grain weight bullets with authority.

THE AUSTIN & HALLECK MODEL 420 LR

The Austin & Halleck bolt action Model 420 brings to muzzleloading a new level of class that was heretofore missing from other production guns. Most bolt action in-line rifles, in fact, come off as "Plain Janes" when compared to the Model

Austin & Halleck Model 420 designer Ted Hatfield checks out a tight 1¼-inch 100-yard group fired with one of the company's Monte Carlo versions.

The Remington Model 700 MLS (stainless) utilizes basically the same action as the company's line of bolt action centerfire rifles. The 1½-inch group shown is a typical 100-yard performance for this ultra-modern muzzleloader.

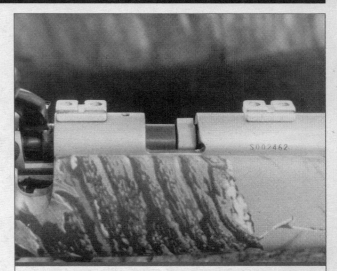

A plastic ignition disc sits in the priming port of a Knight XK-97 D.I.S.C. Rifle. The bolt will cam forward to compress the disc as the handle is pushed downward, forming a tight fit against the rear of the breech plug.

420. The line and workmanship—especially the quality of the wood—that make up this rifle rival the work found in custom modern centerfire rifles with price tags exceeding $2,500. Indeed, for about one-third the cost of a Dakota or Steyr-Mannlicher centerfire rifle, a discerning muzzleloading hunter can own a top-of-the-line Austin & Halleck muzzleloader of equal quality.

The Model 420 is offered in two versions—the 420 LR Monte Carlo and the 420 LR Classic—with the only difference being the configuration of their fancy tiger-striped curly maple stocks. As the model designation indicates, the 420 LR Monte Carlo has the European flair of a high-combed Monte Carlo butt, while the Classic version features the lines of a high-quality American sporter. Both models feature clean 20-lines-per-inch cut checkering at the wrist and along the forearm. They also shoot as well as they look. The .50 caliber frontloaders with their forged 26-inch barrels are rifled with a one-turn-in-28 inches rate of twist and perform well with a wide range of saboted bullets. One of the best shooting sabot and bullet combinations is the .45 caliber 260 grain Speer jacketed hollow-point and a black sabot made by Muzzleload Magnum Products. Loaded ahead of two 50 grain Pyrodex Pellets, this bullet

printed one-hole groups measuring only an inch cross at 100 yards. Both rifles shot nearly as well with Speer's slightly heavier 300 grain jacketed flat nose .45 bullet.

Other features of the Austin & Halleck Model 410 rifles include easy take down and a removable breech plug for cleaning, a fully adjustable Timney trigger and a removable plastic weather shroud for weather-proof hunting in wet conditions.

THE RUGER MODEL 77/50

The recognition of muzzleloading as a fast-growing and popular sport took a giant leap with the introduction of Sturm, Ruger's Model 77/50. Like Remington's bolt action muzzleloader, Ruger's new frontloader, based on an already existing action, features a modified version of the company's well-received Model 77/22 bolt action, producing a handsome, nice-handling modern bolt action .50 caliber muzzleloading hunting rifle. Built with a 22-inch barrel, this .50 caliber rifle has a one-turn-in-28 inches rate of rifling twist, which has become something of a standard for rifles designed to shoot saboted bullets. Slower rates of twist often fail to stabilize the longer all-copper bullets, such as Barnes Expander-MZ. Considering the

Only a ramrod located at the bottom of the barrel indicates this custom rifle by Henry Ball is indeed a front-loader. This particular rifle was designed to shoot modern smokeless powders.

high quality of Ruger's centerfire rifles, there's no reason to doubt the ability of this bolt action muzzleloader to handle any of the sabot and bullet combinations that have performed well in other rifles with the same rate of rifling twist.

Features that are sure to cause serious black powder big game hunters to take a close look at the new Ruger frontloader include its low profile and stylish scope bases machined right onto the top of the Model 77/50 receiver. There are also a removable one-piece nipple and breech plug for easy cleaning, plus an overall slim look and nice feel. Ruger's "Old Army" percussion revolver set new standards for black powder handguns when it was introduced during the early 1970s. Now, with the new Model 77/50 in production, it seems they're out to do the same thing with modern bolt action in-line percussion muzzleloaders.

THE KNIGHT D.I.S.C. RIFLE

Not to be outdone by the latest round of in-line percussion rifle developments, Knight Rifles has entered the field with a new bolt action design that

gives shooters a choice of the standard No. 11 percussion cap or a much hotter No. 209 shotshell primer for ignition. Knight's new XK-97 D.I.S.C. Rifle utilizes a special plastic ignition disc which can be fitted with an insert for firing a No. 11 percussion cap or primed with a No. 209 shotshell primer. The bolt operates unlike the bolt firing systems found on other bolt action in-line rifles. The shooter simply lifts upward on the bolt handle, camming the face of the bolt away from the breech plug and exposing a priming port at the front of the bolt. After inserting an ignition disc into the opening, then pushing the bolt handle downward, the bolt cams forward to compress the plastic disc between the face of the bolt and the breech plug. Fire from either the No. 11 percussion cap or the shotshell primer reaches the powder charge through a tiny flash hole in the breech plug.

The hotter flame produced by the No. 209 shotshell primers does a noticeably better job of igniting the compressed Pyrodex Pellets. Ignition with the primers is faster than with No. 11 caps, and when fired across a chronograph loads touched off with a primer indicated a velocity that was two percent faster. This usually worked out to a velocity about 30 to 40 f.p.s. higher. The improved ignition of primer discs has led Knight Rifles to promote the loading and firing of three 50 grain Pyrodex Pellets behind a saboted bullet. With some of the lighter 200 and 220 grain bullets, velocity has exceeded 2,200 f.p.s. In our test, however, the D.I.S.C. rifle consistently turned in the best accuracy when loaded with only two of the pellets, producing 1^1/$_2$-inch groups at 100 yards with several sabot and bullet combinations.

The Knight XK-97 D.I.S.C. has many of the same features found on standard in-line percussion Knight rifles, including the Knight double safety system, removable breech plug, and a top quality 22-inch Green Mountain barrel with a one-turn-in-28 inches rate of rifling twist. Owners should keep plenty of the plastic ignition discs on hand, though. The hotter fire from the shotshell primers destroys the discs after only one or two uses. Moreover, finding this radically different setting on the shelf of a local gun shop may not be all that easy.

INTO THE FUTURE

These and other products on the market, now or in the near future, indicate what a great selection of in-line percussion rifles is available. Still, as fast as in-line percussion ignition systems have evolved, there looms on the horizon still another system that is sure to change this old sport one more time. For example, Bill's Custom Guns in Greensboro, North Carolina, is now hand-crafting a unique bolt-muzzleloading rifle—one gun at a time—that may make obsolete most of the advanced bolt action designs we've reviewed here. The brainchild of custom riflemaker Henry Ball, this system takes muzzleloader performance to an entirely new level. The heart of this rifle is a modern centerfire rifle action using commercial Mauser, Sako and Howa actions. Each is fitted with a custom-cut McGowan rifle barrel with a one-turn-in-24 inches rate of twist, plus a breech plug threaded into the rear of the fully tapered steel barrel. That's about as close as this bolt action muzzleloader comes to any of the rifles we've tested.

For ignition, Henry Ball's system relies on precision-machined stainless steel ignition modules primed with No. 209 shotshell primers, chambered into the rear of the breech plug for a totally enclosed, weatherproof ignition system. All of the fire from the primer goes through a tiny flash hole at the front of the breech plug and into the barrel for the most positive muzzleloading ignition system yet made available. The stainless steel ignition modules are easily deprimed with a punch pin and

Henry Ball's innovative ignition system relies on a reusable stainless steel ignition module and a No. 209 shotshell primer for fully protected, enclosed ignition that puts 100 percent of fire into the barrel.

Cleaning a bolt action in-line muzzleloader means the bolt must be disassembled to remove fouling. Selecting a model with a bolt that breaks down quickly and easily will make the job less tedious.

The easier a bolt action in-line rifle is to break down for cleaning, the more popular the gun will be with hunters who dislike cleaning corrosive fouling from the bore and other parts. Shown here is the removable breech plug and nipple from a Traditions Lightning rifle.

measured slightly more than three-quarters of an inch. This load, moreover, is good for 2,350 f.p.s. at the muzzle and only about five inches of drop from 100 to 200 yards. Best of all, the bore doesn't have to be wiped clean of fouling between shots, and there's no rush to clean the small amount of non-corrosive fouling left in the barrel at the end of a day's shooting. (Note: Do not attempt to load and shoot smokeless powder in any other muzzleloader!)

At this point, traditionalist readers are probably shaking their heads. Has this old sport suddenly gone too far, too fast? Only the future and the demands of muzzleloading hunters will tell. One thing is for certain, muzzleloading is still one of the fastest-growing segments of the shooting and hunting sports. And as more hunters leave the ranks of modern gun and archery hunters, state governments will continue to expand opportunities for hunting with a muzzleloader. Whether shooters prefer the aesthetics of a traditional longrifle from the past or the improved performance of a modern bolt action in-line muzzleloader, these new opportunities mean more time in the field for hunters everywhere.

can be reused a hundred or more time. A Henry Ball test rifle built around a Howa action with a .50 caliber barrel performed extremely well with measured charges of Pyrodex "Select" ranging from 100 to 130 grains, and with both two and three 50 grain Pyrodex Pellet loads. Most groups fired with saboted .45 caliber handgun bullets printed in tight clusters at 100 yards, averaging only an inch or so across.

A rifle of this technology, however, was not designed to be loaded and fired with only black powder or Pyrodex. Henry Ball, a long time center-fire benchrest shooter, built this rifle to handle prescribed loads of smokeless powder safely; in other words, he has designed and built a muzzle-loader that can handle the higher pressures of smokeless powder. With a 35 grain charge of Alliant 2400 behind a saboted 260 grain Speer .45 caliber jacketed hollow-point, a .50 caliber test rifle with a Howa action produced accuracy one would consider impossible for a muzzleloader. One ten-shot 100-yard group, for example,

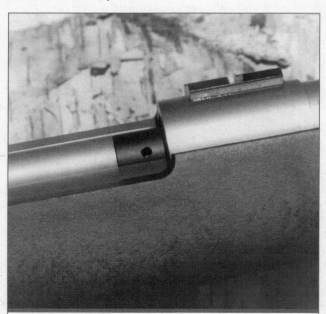

When fitted into the face of a Remington muzzle-loader bolt, this removable plastic weather shroud protects the capped nipple from rain or snow.

Ad Topperwein: World's Greatest Trick Shooter

By Sam Fadala

The early American settlers revered their firearms far beyond their primary use as work tools. Certainly guns were required for protection and "making meat," but they were never treated like hoes, picks or shovels. Gun makers in Europe had long since learned to create works of art. Dutch and German craftsmen, in particular, appreciated the rifles, fowlers and pistols they produced far beyond their practical value. For that reason, this era became known as "The Golden Age of Firearms," when one-man shops turned out graceful Kentucky/Pennsylvania longarms unsurpassed in beauty, balance and embellishment. The special feelings that transplanted Europeans expressed for their guns during the early 18th century and beyond grew into interesting and even exciting competitions along the eastern seaboard. The men who competed in those early days gained considerable local fame through their marksmanship abilities. The tradition lived on in the Far West as fur trappers, known as mountain men, competed in shooting games at what became known as rendezvous, as described in the following announcement:

HUNTERS, AND OTHERS LOOK THIS WAY

The Great Shooting Match Will Take Place on
DECEMBER 15TH AND 16TH, 1727
DANIEL YOEMANS BY THE BIG CREEK
FIRST PRIZE *is a* BIG FAT OX *for the First Day*
Second Day, a **SNAP-HAUNCE GUN** *With a Long Barl*
Distance 15 rods

A charge of two shillings for each man. Only one shot for each two shillings.

There will be more prizes, such as traps, robes, knives and skins at less charges.
Hunters coming from a long distance can be kept for one shilling a day.
Horses at one-half shilling. Plenty to eat and drink for all that come!

ANYONE GOING BACK TO SETTLEMENTS MUST
TELL EVERY MAN TO COME TO THE MATCH.

LINCOLN WAS RIGHT
by Ad Topperwein

*You may hit some of your
targets most of the time.*

*And most of your
targets some of the time*

*But you can't hit all your
targets every time all the time.*

*No matter how great your skill
and how hard you try, sooner
or later you'll let one go by.*

*But no matter whether you
hit'em or miss'em you are
always having a lot of fun.*

*Keep up your shooting. You will
never regret it, and you may
make a better score tomorrow.*

This advertisement for a shooting match was no small thing and people took it very seriously. There were, of course, no movies to attend, and certainly no television. Entertainment from Europe arrived slowly in the cities of the 18th century, and it took even longer to reach outlying villages. What drew large crowds well into the late 19th century were these shooting exhibitions, which continued right into the next century.

Enter Fred Toepperwein, who had settled in New Braunfels, Texas, in 1869. A German by descent and a farmer by trade, Fred was also a shooter, gunsmith and firearms designer by avocation, once earning a patent on one of his inventions that he later sold to Winchester. A pilot model was created by that famous firearms company, but the idea never went into production. Nonetheless, Fred's son, Adolph, whom everyone called "Ad," looked upon his father with pride for his accomplishments in the world of firearms, as he should have.

Fred had been a Scheutzenfest marksman of renown in his mother country and worked tirelessly to keep the tradition alive in his new home in Texas, where many other Bavarian settlers had established a new life. The elder Toepperwein, himself among the best riflemen in the group, organized his neighbors into a shooting club. "Ad" Topperwein (the extra "e" had been dropped along the way) was born into this environment and quickly displayed a talent for shooting passed on from father to son. Just as the famous trick-shooting artist, Annie Oakley, had begun her career gathering food for her family, so did Ad hone his skills hunting for meat. His interests soon turned, however, to aerial tricks as he grew increasingly fascinated with the art of hitting targets tossed high in the air.

Ad's first rifle, a .40 caliber muzzleloader, was soon replaced by a Model 1873 Winchester lever-action repeater chambered for the .44 W.C.F. (Winchester Center Fire) cartridge and featuring a 24-inch octagon barrel. While Ad's interest in hunting game never waned during his early years, the desire to shoot was even greater. What turned the tide was the acquisition of a Winchester Model 1890 slide-action .22 rimfire rifle, which proved an ideal choice for aerial shooting. Easy and cheap to shoot, it enabled Ad to pull off feats of marksmanship that amazed Ad's friends and admirers. His uncanny ability, born out of natural talent, was backed by a steady hand, keen eye and an innate ability to aim at moving objects in such a way that bullet and target met with amazing precision high in the air.

But Ad Topperwein had more to offer than his gifted shooting talent. Tall, slim, blue-eyed and fine-featured, he presented a crowd-pleasing appearance. For those who were qualified to judge such things, his achievements soon earned him the title of "World's Greatest Trick Shooter," surpassing even the legendary Annie Oakely. He became, in essence, an exhibition shooter, a respected profession followed by the likes of Herb Parsons, Tom Trye and others who made a living through their ability to shoot with unerring accuracy at all manner of stationary or moving targets. Interestingly, shooting at bulls'-eyes on a stationary target never captured Ad's imagination. His true love was shooting at airborne targets, especially with a .22 rimfire rifle and standard lead bullets. He wasn't opposed to shot, per se, but he had a special fondness for the single

Ad Topperwein—greatest trick shooter of them all. Blessed with supreme coordination, he could "shoot the pips out of an orange" and the orange didn't have to be stationary at the time.

Topperwein was not only a wizard with a handgun, rifle or shotgun, he was a great showman as well. He would purposely invite criticism of a trick, then show his audience what he could do.

drawing cartoons did indeed pay the rent and keep food on the table, nothing could prevent "Top," as he was also known, from shooting. He could often be found standing along the river plinking, for that was his main passion. The more interesting the target, the better, especially if it was airborne. Indeed, no tin can was safe. He loved riddling them full of .22 caliber holes with his rimfire rifle.

Then one day, something happened that completely changed Ad's life for good: the Sells-Floto Circus came to town. Little did its owners know they would find a great new act in San Antonio. They already had a trick shooter, a man who shot balloons while riding horseback in the style of Buffalo Bill. While this may appear easy, considerable skill was required, as those who tried to copy Buffalo Bill's act with shot cartridges had long since discovered. But now word reached the circus owners that a local man named Topperwein could outshoot their exhibition marksman.

Perhaps a showdown took place between the two sharpshooters, or maybe the circus simply asked Ad to show off his ability solo. Either way, Ad got the job and was soon headed for Mexico, where the Sells-Floto circus had scheduled its next engagement. Mexican audiences, well known for their enthusiasm, loved Ad, who quickly proved his talent with both handgun and rifle. Trouble was, he could hit targets with a single missile that others could only accomplish with shot cartridges. As a result, his .22 projectiles soon undermined the circus tent until—wham!—down it came. The beleaguered manager pleaded with Ad to forget about solid bullets and start using shot cartridges.

Top had lit the match and started a small brush fires with his prowess, and now the flames spread country-wide. One of his best acts involved breaking 2¼-inch clay discs tossed into the air. Still using .22 rimfire bullets, Ad routinely broke 955 out of 1,000 targets, improving that record to 989 as time went on. Later, he hit 1,500 airborne clay pigeons with 1,500 bullets—not a single miss!— the first thousand shot from 30 feet and the final 500 from a distance of 40 feet. He was still only in his late twenties, a handsome young man and a great showman with a long list of innovative shooting tricks. He involved the audience by purposely inviting criticism. When he shot at a metal washer, for example, claiming to pass a bullet through its center, he invited a challenge

bullet, especially when wed with his fast-handling Winchester slide-action 1890 rifle. A Winchester Model 1903 autoloader, fired from the unique .22 auto cartridge, was followed by the Winchester Model 63, another semi-auto model but chambered for the standard .22 Long Rifle round.

Despite the American public's continuing interest in trick shooting, young Ad realized he couldn't make a living at it, so he called upon another natural gift: drawing cartoons. In 1887, at the age of 18, he left home and established himself in San Antonio, then a town of only 10,000. At first, he worked as a sales clerk in a clothing store, but that job was short-lived, for his artistic talent soon won Ad the position of cartoonist for the San Antonio Express. While

Three weeks after their marriage, "Plinky" Topperwein, who had never fired a shot, was hitting bits of chalk Ad held between his fingers. She once hit 1,460 square 2 1/4-inch wooden blocks out of the air with a 22 rifle–without a miss.

The great Topperwein shot a Winchester Model 1903 Autoloader firing the 22 Auto cartridge at aerial targets.

shooter for 55 years. Still another important change in Top's life lay on the horizon, however. For some odd reason, he had suddenly begun to question the quality of his ammunition, something he had never done before. He became concerned over each round he took on tour, insisting on inspecting each batch personally before hitting the road. Ad's boss at Winchester, Edwin Pugsley, decided at first to let the sharpshooter have his way. But one day curiosity turned to outright suspicion when Top returned to the plant from a trip to Oregon to check on the quality of Winchester's highly regarded shooting fodder. Pugsley approved, but this time he kept a close eye on Top. Soon the riddle was solved. It wasn't the ammo he was so interested in, but the pretty lady who worked in the ballistic lab. Her name was Elizabeth "Plinky" Servaty, and they were married in 1903. Under her husband's tutorage, Plinky became an established aerial shooting expert in her own right. Her accomplishments with a shotgun were particularly remarkable. Firing a Winchester Model 1897—and later its successor, the Model 12—she set numerous records, breaking 1,952 our of 2,000 regulation clays in three hours and 25 minutes (some sources list five hours and 20 minutes). Whatever, she accomplished this amazing feat at the Montgomery (Alabama) Country Club.

During this period, Ad became a valuable advertisement for Winchester, traveling by train from one city to the next, covering vast stretches of both the U.S. and Canada. As part of his job, he visited local gun shops carrying Winchester products, chatting with store owners and local shooters alike. Sometimes Ad would head for the edge of town, and there, to the delight of his followers, he would shatter frangible aerial targets with a .22 rimfire rifle, hitting five out of five clay pigeons tossed into the air simultaneously. Making the trick even more difficult, he would turn his back as the clays were tossed. Then, on command, the athletic Adolph would do a back flip, grab his shotgun and smoke the five clays, working the Model 12 Winchester pump-action shotgun like a semi-auto. At other times, he would run forward, do a flip in the air, land on his feet, grab his scattergun off a table, and proceed to powder five clay birds out of the sky. Another favorite act was shooting ejected rounds out of the air with his Model 63 semi-auto .22 rifle. With the port side

from onlookers. How did they know he really put a bullet through the center of the washer, rather than simply missing it altogether? He would prove it by pasting a postage stamp over the hole and drilling the stamp with a bullet. He also amazed crowds by tossing a loaded .32-20 cartridge in the air, then shooting the bullet right out of its case.

In time, though, Top outgrew the circus. In the early 1900s, while still in his twenties, he went to work for Winchester Repeating Arms Company as an exhibition shooter. Ad enjoyed his job so much that he remained Winchester's top exhibition up, he'd fire a round, and as the spent cartridge case leaped out and up, Ad would shoot the brass case out of the air with one well-aimed bullet. The hand-eye coordination required for such a feat boggles the imagination even to this day. One of his favorite tricks was firing two .22 sixshooters simultaneously, one in the normal manner, the other aimed rearward with the aid of a mirror. Crack! Crack! The target in front would fold just as the one behind toppled over.

Plinky wasn't left out of the act, though. She would amaze audiences by shooting the ash from a cigarette held in Ad's lips, using a 38 Special revolver, not a rifle. Ad was always working on new tricks, too. He would, for example, toss a tin can in the air, followed immediately by another, until five cans were in the air at once. Not one can made it to the ground without a bullet hole. In another trick, he would outline a wooden Uncle Sam or an Indian Chief with 350 to 450 bullets fired at the rate of one shot per second. These outlines were extremely well-defined, possibly reflecting Ad's background as a cartoon artist. Trick shooters who followed in Top's footsteps did the same, creating outlines of figures in soft metal with bullet holes.

With exhibition shooting still popular in the U.S., many others tried to outdo the master, among them "Doctor Carver." Neither a physician nor a scholar, Doc Carver was nonetheless a fine

Ad Topperwein cradles his favorite Model M92 sometime during the 1940s.

Around 1912, Plinky Topperwein practices one of her favorite trick shots using a mirror.

marksman who proclaimed himself the world champion trick shooter after breaking a multitude of two and one-half-inch glass balls tossed in the air. Doc once went on a 10-day shooting spree, keeping 11 Model 1890 slide-action Winchester .22 rimfire rifles hot for 12 hours a day as he blazed away at 60,000 glass balls. In all, 55,000 of those glass targets were shattered. Still not satisfied, he repeated the stunt, firing at 60,000 glass balls and missing only 650 of them. Carver's glory was short-lived, however, and Topperwein never challenged him. Then along came a trick shooter named B.A. Bartlett, who could flick spent brass out of his Winchester .22 rifles at 60,000 regulation-sized glass balls, missing only 280. Instead of trying to break the glass ball record himself, Ad chose wooden blocks, which had been long-time standard aerial targets. After firing at 50,000 blocks tossed in the air one day, someone shouted, "Get him more ammo!" So Ad shot at 22,500 more blocks,

Tom Frye, the Remington shooter, broke Topperwein's record by shooting 100,010 wooden blocks in the air, while missing only six. Frye died in 1978.

twice each, missing only nine times. At one point, he recorded 14,500 hits in a row without a miss, shooting at split blocks and then at pieces of blocks, a record that stood for half a century. The man who beat it was Tom Frye, Remington's then hot-shot shooter who accomplished the feat with a Remington Nylon Model 66 semi-auto rifle, eventually missing only six shots out of 100,000 blocks. And whom do you suppose was the first trick shooter to congratulate him? None other than Adolph Topperwein.

Top went on to thrill crowds with many different types of firearms, including Winchester's self-load chambered for the unique 401 cartridge, as well as the famous Model 94 30-30. According to one story, John Browning himself fired his own BAR (Browning Automatic Rifle) for the U.S. Secretary of Defense at a time when the Winchester company was trying to sell that rifle to the military. After Browning fired his invention, Ad Topperwein proceeded to hit aerial targets using full-throttle 30-06 ammunition. He did so well, in fact, that one of his skyborne targets—a tomato can—erupted like a volcano, scattering its contents all over the Secretary of State. On another occasion, a certain professor of archeology frequented an

area where Ad like to shoot. Having picked out a granite ledge to practice on, Top produced an image of an Indian chief with bullet spatterings. Later, the professor came roaring into town with exciting news. He had discovered a remarkable caricature of a Native American chief etched in rock, a genuine pictograph heretofore unknown. The amazing likeness, he declared, had been tattooed into the granite with wonderful detail, right down to a full feathered headdress.

After his beloved Plinky died suddenly in 1945, Top gave up most of his trick-shooting appearances and concentrated instead on a shooting range and camp he owned near San Antonio. Failing eyesight finally brought to an end the remarkable career of the world's greatest trick shooter. Finally, in 1962, he passed on at the ripe old age of 93. Whereas the era of trick shooting has faded into the shadows of history, Ad Topperwein has not been forgotten. A few great marksmen keep the sport alive, but the name "Topperwein" is the one mentioned most often whenever the subject of the world's greatest trick shooter comes up. For truly, there has never been another quite like him.

Ad and Plinky strike an informal pose in 1912.

The 22-250 Improved: An Old Wildcat Made Better

By Don Lewis

One day recently, as I was necking down some 250-3000 Savage cases for the old 22-250 Wildcat, a friend of mine asked, "Why do you go to all the bother of making shells for a 22-250 Varminter when the 220 Swift is a much superior cartridge and factory shells are available?" A dedicated Swift owner, he went on, "It seems to me that, with all your interest in guns, you should know that Swift is the best woodchuck shell around."

"You're just repeating words that Swift owners have been saying for years," I responded. "The whole argument is based on the Swift's 4,000 feet per second velocity. It's true that with 40/45-grain bullets the Swift can reach velocities above that speed. But if you'll check the new Speer Reloading Manual for Wildcat cartridges, you'll note that the 22-250 Varminter has a muzzle velocity of 4,001 feet per second with 43 grains of H-380 behind a 45 grain Speer bullet. The Swift is only a few feet faster."

My friend responded: "But it's superior with lightweight bullets, and it is significantly faster with 55 grain bullets. Facts are facts."

"Hold on," I cut in. "Take a look at the 1959 Speer Reloading Manual. With a 55 grain Speer bullet, the Swift generates velocities slightly more than 3,800 fps with maximum powder charges. The Speer Manual for Wildcat cartridges shows velocity readings for the 22-250 in the 3,700 fps range with a number of powder charges for the 55 grain bullet. If my math is correct, there's less than 100 fps between the two cartridges using 55 grain bullets. I wouldn't call that 'significant'."

"Well, if the 22-250 is such a notable cartridge," he argued, "why hasn't a factory standardized it?"

"That's a question I can't answer. Your Model 54 Winchester 220 Swift may have more speed, but it can't compete in accuracy. The Swift is seldom seen in benchrest competition, but the 22-250 Varminter holds a slew of benchrest accuracy records. In my book, it's even more accurate than the Remington 222. It's hard to believe that the old 22-250 Varminter from the mid-1930s is still a wildcat in 1961. I rest my case."

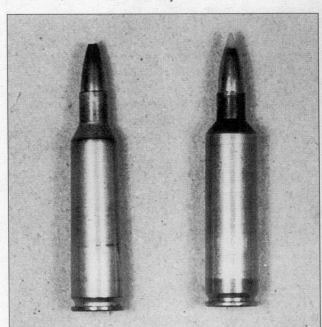

A remington 22-250 case (left) is shown with a 22-250 Ackley Improved (right). Note the sharper shoulder (40%) and less body taper on the improved case.

A strain gauge is glued to the barrel just ahead of the receiver. Two of the wires are plugged into the M-43 PBL. The strain gauge area has been sanded white for a solid bond between gauge and barrel. The third wire shown is grounded to the rifle, usually on the recoil lug screw.

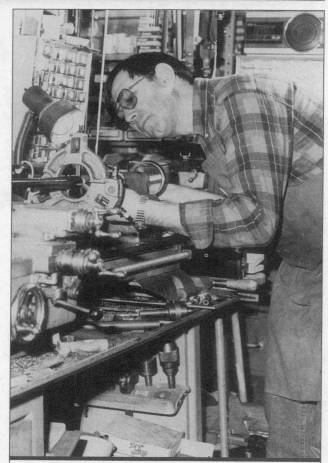

Custom rifle-builder Jim Peightal feeds a reamer into the author's Dumoulin barrel, matching the chamber to the Ackley Improved 22-250.

FILLING THE GAPS WITH WILDCATS

It's possible the day of the wildcat cartridge is waning. The gaps that existed in factory cartridges in the 20s and 30s were the prime reasons why wildcatters created cartridges that would fill them. A major change in factory cartridge design back then would be dropping an older cartridge or one that was unpopular. Since the factories didn't offer new cartridges to replace the ones that were dropped or discontinued, the wildcat crowd worked unceasingly to fill the gaps. Their efforts produced a multitude of cartridges. Some were good, but many never got past the designer's reloading bench. Unfortunately, some of the wildcat designs were claimed to be vastly superior to factory rounds.

In those days, the home chronograph was only a dream. With no credible method for measuring velocities, wildcatters used several unscientific methods for determining the muzzle velocity of their creations. Probably the oldest was shooting through inch-thick boards stacked tightly together. A factory round of known velocity, carrying the same bullet diameter and weight as a wildcatter, was fired into the boards along with one of the new creations. If the wildcat passed through more boards, its velocity was estimated to be higher than the factory round. How much higher was a matter of sheer speculation.

Another method was to fire into a steel plate. If the wildcat made a deeper indentation in the

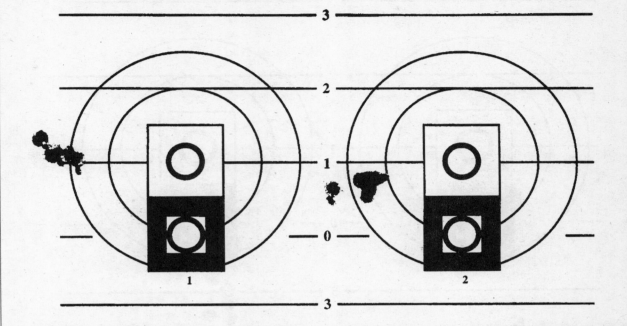

A five-shot fire form group (left) measures about 5/8". Groups are not usually this tight when fire forming cases. Another five-shot group with fire-formed cases (right) is about 5/8" in spread, with four shots making one jagged hole.

plate, its velocity was assumed to be higher. Wildcatters could send a batch of ammo to a factory for chronographing, but this was slow and expensive. Since wildcatters weren't too keen about allowing factories to see their creations, they simply estimated velocities. It's reasonable to assume many wildcatters were overly optimistic and their velocity readings greatly exaggerated.

Basically, most of the wildcats come from four styles of cartridges. First, there are the wildcats from the 30-30 family of rimmed cartridges. Rimmed and with the same rim size and thickness in common, they are well adapted to single shots and lever action rifles. As examples, they include the 22 Savage Hi-Power, 219 Zipper, 30-30, 25-35, 32 Special Winchester, 32-40 and 38-55. Any wildcat based on this family—such as the .219 Donaldson Wasp—could be made from any or all of these cartridges.

The second style is the rimless group, sometimes referred to as "standard" head size. This group ranges through a significant number of cartridges, from the 250-3000 Savage to the 30-06. Known as the magnum family, this group is easily recognizable by its belted head design. It could be described as a hybrid between the rimmed and rimless cases. Some of its more popular cartridges are the 7mm Remington Magnum, 264 Winchester Magnum, 300 H&H Magnum, 338 and 458 Winchesters. Finally, there's a group made up of large rimmed cartridges, including the 30-40 Krag and the 405 Winchester.

One of the first wildcats to gain a fair share of popularity was the 22/3000 Lovell, created by a gunsmith named Hervey Lovell, who tried necking down the dying 25-20 single shot case to the 224 caliber. With heavy loads of 4227 powder behind a 50-grain 224 caliber bullet, Lovell obtained velocities around 3,000 fps, a considerable increase over

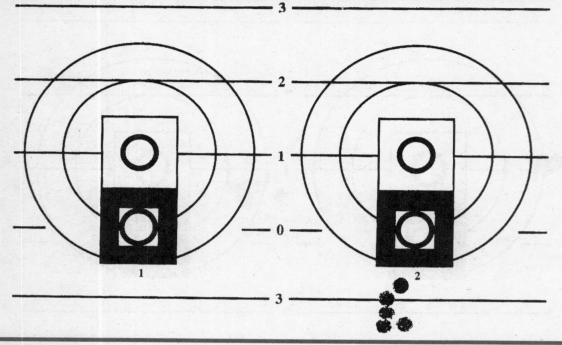

This five-shot group (target #2) was fired for accuracy in bright sunlight. The horizontal spread is about 1/4-inch.

the popular 22 Hornet. Accuracy was good, so varmint hunters now had themselves a 250-yard varmint cartridge. Later, Harvey Donaldson, who created the 219 Donaldson Wasp, decided to improve the 22/3000 Lovell with the help of a gunsmith named Risley. Their new improved case was formed simply by firing the 22/3000 Lovell in the improved chamber. Fire-forming pushed the neck out from the original 5 degree 30 minutes to a sharper 12 degrees. When fired in the improved chamber, the case expanded some, gave slightly more muzzle velocity, and presumably better combustion of powder. Donaldson named his creation the 22/3000 2-R (later shortened to 2-R Lovell), which means "2" for a second reamer and "R" for Risley, who did most of the work.

Some confusion has always existed between an "improved" round and a "wildcat" round. Actually, there's a wide chasm between the two. Improving a cartridge normally means changing the shoulder angle to a sharper degree, or perhaps removing some

of the body taper. In essence, the blown-out version allows the use of more powder, which increases velocity somewhat. A conventional factory shell is fired in the improved chamber and then blown out to the new chamber's dimensions. A wildcat cartridge, on the other hand, is made by necking down (or up) a factory round for another caliber. For example, the 22 CHeetah wildcat case is made from regular 308 Winchester brass. Converting the 308 to the Mark 1 (a 40-degree shoulder angle) 22 caliber CHeetah requires a number of swaging operations, shortening the case and fire-forming with a stiff load of powder. It's obvious that the 308 round cannot be fired in the chamber of a CHeetah.

During the 1920s and 30s, many 22 caliber wildcat or improved cartridges were hailed as super varmint rounds. The 218 Mashburn Bee, which was an improved version of the factory 218 Bee, comes to mind. The 219 Donaldson Wasp failed to achieve factory status, but it was a top benchrest cartridge for years. This flexible

Author Don Lewis is shown range-testing a Dumoulin 22-250 Ackley Improved topped with a Burris 8x32x scope.

cartridge is as much at home in a prairie dog town as it is on the competition line. Cases were formed with vise-type dies from a variety of rimmed cases, such as the 219 Zipper, 25-35, 32 Special and 30-30. When Remington's 222 made its debut, the Wasp was relegated to the ranks of the unwanted. With modern reloading press dies, however, cases become easier to make and case loss was minimal. Even though it lost out to the 222 Remington, the old Wasp is a better cartridge.

Other strange names included the 22/303 Sprinter and 22/4000 Senior Varminter, but the best of the bunch was the 22-250. In the beginning, its case was made by shoving a 250-3000 Savage case into a 22-250 full length resizing die, retaining the same 26 1/2-degree shoulder. Most firearm historians agree that Captain Grosvenor Wotkyns and J.B. Sweany are responsible for the original development of the 22-250 sometime in the 1920s as a prototype of the 220 Swift. Later on, it became known as the "Wotkyns original Swift."

In 1935, Winchester introduced the 220 Swift, and a few years later Jerry Gebby named his version of the 22-250 the "22 Varminter," copyrighting the name to prevent other gunsmiths from using it. Regardless, 22-250s were turned out by the hundreds under that name. With its inherent accuracy, the 22-250 soon caught the attention of the benchrest clan, although it faced stiff opposition from the 219 Zipper and 219 Donaldson Wasp, which eventually rode into the sunset. Remington standardized the old 22-250 wildcat in 1965, calling it the 22-250 Remington, introducing it in their Model 700 bolt action rifle and Model 40XB match rifle. The Model 700, with its adjustable trigger, was a perfect vehicle for the new varmint round. And later, when Remington offered the 22-250 chambering in its new "Varmint Special" Model 700 heavy barrel, varmint hunters finally had a 350-yard factory varmint outfit to work with. This new entry represented the most versatile long range 224 varmint round available. In fact, it still is.

Jay Postman, technical service manager at RCBS and noted consultant on handloading problems, helped the author in his 22-250 Ackley Improved project.

As the 22-250 gained in popularity, several top varmint cartridges—including the 222 Remington, 244 Remington and 243 Winchester—began losing ground. All these cartridges are still available, but the 22-250 remains number one in popularity with varmint-hunting fans. Yet, with all this wildcat has in its favor, it never got out from under the shadow of the 220 Swift, whose proponents firmly believed that the Swift's higher velocity makes it a better varmint round. In fact, the Winchester 220 Swift was a barrel burner and case consumer, and it lacked accuracy with lightweight bullets. Most of these claims were false, but Swift was fighting a losing battle, and in 1964 Winchester discontinued it in favor of the 225 Winchester. Undaunted, Swift fans claimed it was superior to the popular 22-250,

and they still do today.

After word spread about the 22-250's winning performances on the benchrest line, the wildcat began to infiltrate the ranks of the varmint hunting crowd. Its inherent accuracy and ease of case forming won hundreds of converts. Still, the cries rang out that the 22-250 was inferior to the 220 Swift, and these accusations prompted such wildcatters as P.O. Ackley to improve the case. Many experimenters worked with the 22-250, but Ackley's Improved version, with its blown-out 40-degree shoulder angle and literally no body taper, proved the best of the bunch. Ackley's Improved case can now handle 220 Swift charges with a variety of powders; in one sense, then, the improved 22-250 *is* equal in velocity to the Swift.

Acting on an article in *Precision Shooting* by Roy Towers, Jr., back in 1977, this writer visited custom gunsmith Jim Peightal to discuss rechambering a 22-250 Dumoulin to the Ackley Improved 40-degree version. I also contacted Jay Postman, a reloading specialist at RCBS (Blount), for technical help. Tower's goal was to build a varmint rifle that would exit a 50/52 grain bullet at velocities over 4,000 fps and still produce 1/3-minute of angle three-shot groups. "You need a big engine to drive a 50/52 grain bullet at 4,000 fps," Towers noted. "Loading manuals show that the 220 Swift can drive 50 grain bullets to that velocity at the upper limits of its loading capacity. The manuals, however, indicate you are living on the edge when you load the Swift to these capacities."

Improved cases normally have increased capacity over the parent cartridge, and this is true with the 22-250 Ackley Improved case. A blown-out 22-250 Ackley case offers not only a greater powder capacity, it also has less taper. It's possible that the straight sides of the Ackley Improved grip the sides of the chamber, reducing back thrust against the bolt face and preventing the case from stretching. Towers says that after firing his improved cases at least ten times, they are still in excellent shape, with little or no case stretching, thickening of the neck or expansion of the primer pocket. More importantly, no signs of incipient case separation are observed.

Meanwhile, two weeks after ordering a reamer for the 22-250 Ackley Improved Chamber, Jim Peightal finished the Dumoulin and shot several chronograph tests through an Oehler 35P Skyscreen

III system. His best results came from a Remington 9 1/2 primer igniting 43 1/2 grains of H-380 powder behind a 50 grain Nosler Ballistic Tip bullet. Instrumental velocity at 12 feet from the muzzle was a sizzling 3,783 fps (true muzzle velocity would be around 3,808 fps). High velocity, however, means nothing if accuracy is missing. It was obvious from Roy Towers' testing that other load combinations would push the velocity beyond the 4,000 fps mark in his custom rig.

But how well would the Dumoulin improved 22-250 perform in the accuracy column at velocities above 3800? Peightal's first five-shot groups were good, but not spectacular. After a brisk barrel scrubbing with Shooter's Choice, group measurements fell to the 5/8-inch mark on a consistent basis, with several 3/8-inch groups included. The Dumoulin had always performed to this degree with reloaded 22-250 ammo, and rechambering it to the Ackley Improved didn't impair its accuracy potential. A charge of 40 1/2 grains of H-380 behind a 50 grain Sierra Spitzer bullet was used for fire forming, with an Oehler Model 43 Personal Ballistic Laboratory used to obtain data during the fire forming process. The Spitzer bullet generated an average instrumental velocity (at 14 feet) of 3,486 fps. The Model 43 PBL indicated that the average true muzzle velocity of the group was 3,529 fps. Chamber pressure was on the high side with an average peak pressure of 66,800 pounds per square inch. The Nosler

Number 4 Reloading Guide explains that the maximum average pressure limit for a standard 22-250 Remington is 65,000 PSI; but Dr. Kenneth Oehler (of Oehler Research) warns that 60,000 PSI should be followed as the maximum pressure limit with all reloaded ammunition.

A five-shot accuracy test during the fire forming operation printed a 3/4-inch group. Using fire formed cases with the same load combination produced a 5/8-inch group with four shots appearing in one jagged hole. A charge of 43 1/2 grains of H-380 ignited by a Remington 9 1/2 primer shoved a 50 grain Nosler Boattail out of the muzzle with an instrumental velocity (at 14 feet from the muzzle) of 3,783 fps. This same load in Roy Towers' rifle produced an instrumental velocity (at 10 feet from the muzzle) of 3,826 fps and cut a three-shot group measuring .205 (less than 1/4-inch) at 100 yards. A five-shot group fired from the Dumoulin at 100 yards measured 5/8-inches, while another four-shot group printed 3/8-inches. It's unfair to compare the old Dumoulin's barrel against Towers' custom rig; but the Dumoulin's accuracy level is more than adequate for long range varmint shooting. No further pressure or velocity tests were conducted. The Nosler #4 Reloading Guide and Towers' Ballistic Sheet show velocities in excess of 4,000 fps with certain load combinations.

There's no question that the 22-250 Ackley Improved can match the Swift's velocities, but speed alone should not be the main criterion for evaluating a cartridge. As powder charges are increased, chamber pressure is bound to rise. The handloader should keep a sharp eye out for subjective pressure signs, and this is doubly true when working with wildcat or improved cartridges. These signs include head expansion, hard extraction, loose primers, leaking primer pockets and primers extruded into the firing pin hole (primer craters). These signs are less reliable than pressure measurements from sophisticated ballistic instruments, but they do indicate when a particular load combination is generating excessive pressures. Should any one of these signs appear, cut back on the powder charge by at least five percent.

When all is said and done, the 22-250 Remington is a terrific varmint cartridge with few peers in the .224 caliber. Re-chambering to the 22-250 Ackley Improved may not be for everyone, but nonetheless it remains truly an old wildcat made better.

John Novak fire-forms a Hornady 40-grain Varmint Express load. His Dumoulin barrel is topped with a Tasco 10x40x scope. A wire extending from his rifle is plugged into an Oehler M-43 PBL for chamber pressure reading and other ballistic data.

```
Test: Ack Imp 6        1    Gun Name: Ackley Imp      Load Name: 22-250 AckImp
Muzl to Scr1:  10.0 ft      Mfg/Model: Dumoulin Cust  Bullet Mfg: Hornady
Scr1 to Scr3:   8.0 ft         Caliber: 22-250 Ack Imp  Bullet Wgt:   40.0 Gr
Scr4 to Scr6: -N/A- ft        Serial #: 89839               Style: Var Express
Muzl to Trgt: 311.5 ft         Bore Dia:  0.224 in        G1 BC:  0.212
 Target Size:  42.5 in     Barrel Length: 24.0  in        Powder: Factory
 Temperature:  78  Deg F    Sight Height:  1.5   in    Powder Wgt:   0.0 Gr
    Humidity:   0   %         Gage Factor:  2.000      Lot Number:
    Altitude:   0  ft       Outside Dia:  1.156 in        Primer: Factory
  Baro Press: 29.92 in Hg    Inside Dia:  0.460 in         Brass: Hornady
  Wind Speed:   0  MPH      Maximum PSI: 60000           Load OAL:  2.422 in
   Wind Dir: 12:00 O'clk     Offset PSI:  7000          Note: Fire-Form 2nd test
Date 03-04-98  Time 10:23   TESTINFO.DAT               OD 1.156
```

--- SHOT DATA ---

			298 ft			--TARGET--		--EST PRESSURE--		
RND	VEL13	PRF	TOF2T	VEL-T	BC	HORZ	VERT	PEAK	AREA	RISE
1	4022	20	79310	3502	0.210	0.6	4.8	582	301	194
2	4003	31	79733	3482	0.209	-0.2	3.9	580	299	192
3	4036	29	78978	3519	0.212	0.8	4.7	591	303	185
4	4022	29	79135	3517	0.217	-0.7	4.5	591	306	188
5	4005	25	79611	3490	0.212	0.5	4.9	574	305	192

--- SUMMARY ---

			298 ft			--TARGET--		--EST PRESSURE--		
	VEL13	PRF	TOF2T	VEL-T	BC	HORZ	VERT	PEAK	AREA	RISE
AV	4018	27	79354	3502	0.212	0.2	4.6	583	303	190
SD	14	4	316	16	0.003	0.6	0.4	7	3	3
HI	4036	31	79733	3519	0.217	0.8	4.9	591	306	194
LO	4003	20	78978	3482	0.209	-0.7	3.9	574	299	185
ES	33	11	755	38	0.008	1.4	1.0	16	7	8

```
                      RAD SD:   0.7
                      GROUP:    1.4
```

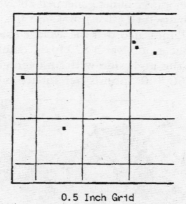

0.5 Inch Grid

--- STANDARD ATMOSPHERE BALLISTICS ---

Zero Rng: 100

				Yards				
	MUZ	INST	50	100	200	300	400	500
BULLET PATH	-1.50	-1.38	-0.44	0.0	-1.4	-6.6	-17.2	-35.4
10 MPH WIND	0.00	0.00	0.24	1.01	4.26	10.22	19.53	33.12
VELOCITY	4045	4018	3760	3493	3005	2568	2171	1811
ENERGY	1454	1434	1256	1084	802	586	419	291
POWER FACTOR	161.8	160.7	150.4	139.7	120.2	102.7	86.8	72.4

Ballistic Chart On Fire-Forming The 22-250 Ackley Improved

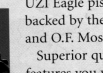

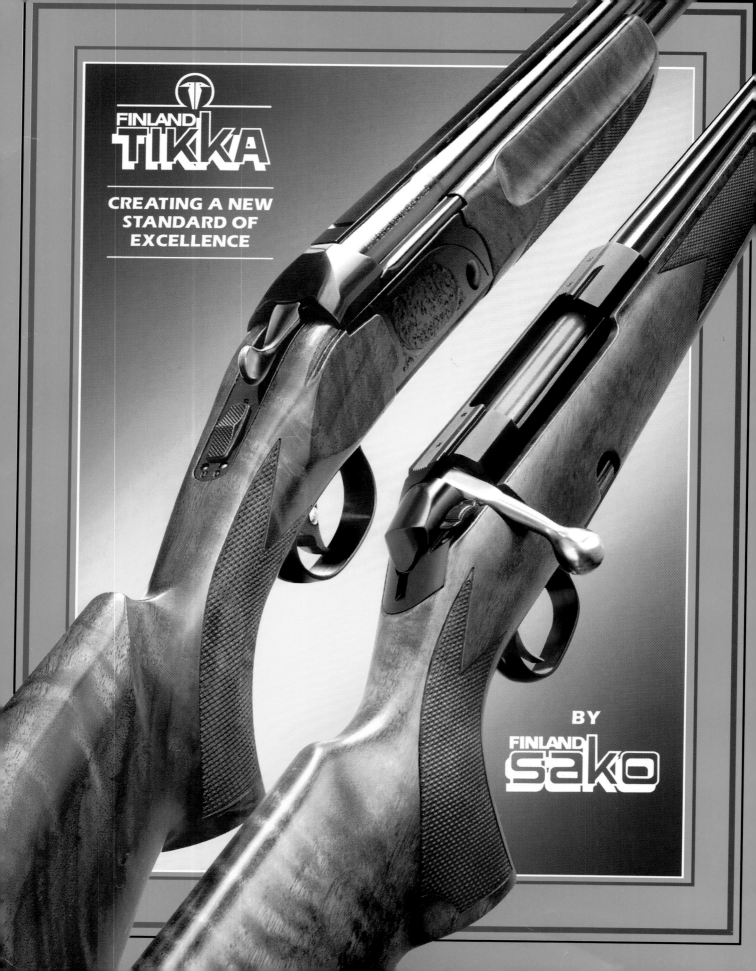

FINLAND TIKKA

CREATING A NEW STANDARD OF EXCELLENCE

BY

FINLAND sako

The Fine Art Of Softshell Reloading

BY RALPH F. QUINN

For those who've joined the growing army of scattergunners who participate regularly in sanctioned trap, skeet and sporting clays events across the U.S., chances are good the economic benefits of shotshell reloading really hit home after that first 250-round outing. On average, 50 to 75 percent of the cost of factory ammo can be saved by reloading—but cost isn't the only reason for taking up the art of shotshell reloading. Hunters and target shooters alike have the added advantage of "tuning," or tailoring, their shells toward specific needs. Birding, for example, involves close-in gunning in tight cover, which means quail, grouse or woodcock spreader loads can be fabricated using post or x-shaped wads. When combined with deformed or reclaimed shot, success with these loads is assured.

Likewise, small gauge—.410 and 28—aficionados can create super patterns at 25 yards using high antimony shot, while sporting clays fanciers can load to International specifications of 24 grams (7/8 oz.) of shot at 1,350 feet per second (fps). This makes it easier to hit at long ranges with the added advantage of reduced recoil. Exactly how many benefits and pleasures can be gained by reloading shotshell? The answer is "virtually endless," especially for those scattergunners who hunt a wide variety of upland game and migratory waterfowl, or who participate regularly in registered claybird events. Aside from the obvious benefit of shotshell reloading, there's nothing quite like the satisfaction of breaking a target, downing a fast-flying grouse or scoring a hit on high-flying geese using shells fashioned for a specific job.

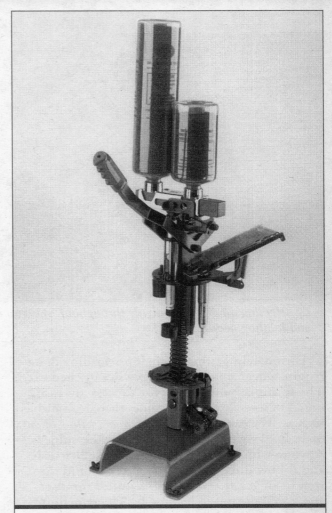

MEC's Sizemaster is a semi-auto single stage tool with auto primer feed and sizing of shell base.

By selecting quality ingredients throughout, shotgun enthusiasts can fashion reloads tailored to both target and hunting needs.

Fortunately, getting started in reloading doesn't require a degree in ballistics, physics or chemistry. The formulas and recipes for success are easily found in several reloading guides that are available, such as *Winchester's Reloaders Manual (15th edition)*, or in books written specifically on the subject. Anyone who can read a powder or bullet scale and follow directions to the letter should do well in the craft. Having a technical mindset and a well-organized loading bench are definite pluses. In fact, reloading can be great for putting the whole family to work in a highly profitable pursuit of profit and just plain fun.

SELECTING THE RIGHT EQUIPMENT AND COMPONENTS

With more than 4.5 million sportsmen reloading shotshells today, a host of equipment manufacturers stand ready to cater to their needs. Selecting the loader is governed by several factors, including convenience, speed and the availability of cash. Basically, there are three types of reloading presses to choose from: manual, semi-automatic single stage and semi-automatic progressive. Where price is a major consideration, a manual reloader is the way to go; but some trade-offs are involved,

Beginning reloaders should select a wad that accepts the proper shot charge and powder and then stick with them until reloading becomes second nature.

Winchester's Ball Powder AA plus is an ideal powder for both clay targets and hunting. Follow manufacturers' recommendations and good results will follow.

namely speed, convenience and, depending on one's measurement skills, uniformity of shell performance, shot to shot.

Semi-automatic reloaders, both single and progressive, cost more, but they are fast and relatively easy to use, resulting in shells that perform with uniformity. In a single-stage tool, the hull is processed and moved from one station to another singly and finished before a new shell starts through the cycle. These tools are ideal for hunters who don't require high volume and maximum speed. With a well-organized bench, reloading eight to ten boxes per hour is well within the range of a single-stage reloader.

Progressive reloaders—including the MEC 650, Hornady Apex I, Ponsness/Warren, Dillon SL 900 or Spolars' high-tech Gold Premier—can process five to eight shells through several reloading steps simultaneously, completing a finished shell with each pull of the handle. Sporting clays, skeet and trap fanciers who shoot eight or more boxes of shells per event and perhaps 10-20,000 rounds per year generally prefer progressive models that can reload a large number of shells fast. If manual labor is not desirable, several hydraulically-operated models are available for true high-speed operation.

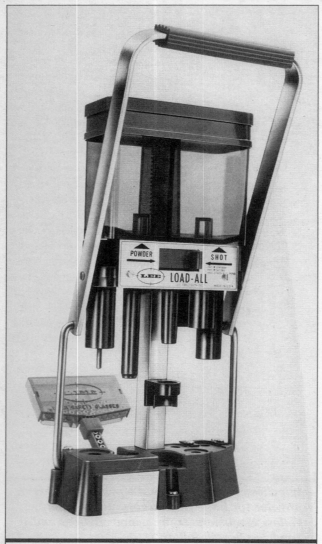

Lee Precision's "Load All" is an entry level reloader that's priced right and does the job adequately.

Spolar's Gold Premier is a progressive top-of-the-line reloader with true high-speed shell production.

Although more expensive, they quickly pay for themselves in time saved and efficiency of operation.

As with other loading specialties, what results is the sum total of its individual ingredients, and shot shell reloaders are no different. Using quality materials selected wisely for the job at hand and matched to a shell's interior dimensions or case capacity can result in superior hulls. As already mentioned, reloading can reduce ammo costs from 50 to 75 percent, but not at the expense of performance. Loads that have been customized for each shooting situation are critical to shotgunning success.

CHOOSING THE HULL

One of the most important considerations a shooter must make in keeping the reloading process simple is the proper choice of empty hulls. Too many beginners choose the wrong hulls and quickly become discouraged. Not all shells have the same capacity, nor do they have the same crimp. Each time a hull with a different capacity

Reloading shotshells is a fun activity for all family members. The author's daughter, Jennifer Quinn, is a seasoned veteran at 11 and reloads her own .410 shells for clay birds. With proper supervision, it's an ideal way to introduce youngsters to the shooting sports.

Empties should, of course, be examined closely for splint ends or bases and other visible damage.

THE SHOT

Four kinds of shot are currently available: soft, hard and extra hard lead, and steel. Shot size selection is usually dictated by the diameter of the pellet needed for the job at hand, from No. 9s (smallest) to 2s (largest). Larger shot pellets (BB and Buckshot) are available for special applications. Other shot shell data is easily found in shotshell reloading manuals, but there are other considerations, such as shot hardness, which has a great deal to do with pattern size and uniformity. Since hard shot resists deformation during initial acceleration, the pellets fly truer and faster—and they hit harder. Reloaders who seek top performance from magnum hunting loads or top trap and skeet loads should use shot with a high antimony content (five to six percent in small shot and two percent in larger pellets). Antimony lowers shot density, so each pellet weighs less; but what counts are the high percentage patterns.

Chilled, dropped or soft shot contain between .5 and 2.0 percent antimony. Soft shot deforms easily through compression and choking, so pellets quickly become unstable and fall from the main shot column. This so-called "stringing" is responsible for poor patterning in the smaller gauges, particularly .410s and 28s. And whereas lead and steel shot reload easily, it's essential to follow reloading data to the letter. For example, *never substitute steel shot for lead shot.* Chamber pressure that results could cause injury or worse. When loading steel, it's also important to use steel shot components in accordance with each manufacturer's directions.

THE RIGHT WAD

The wad is that part of the shotshell which lies between the powder and the shot. A tight seal allows expanding gases from the burning powder to propel the shot column out of the barrel with maximum velocity. Modern "wad columns," which combine the shot cup and wad in one piece, are by far the easiest to use and have become quite popular. The problem is to select a wad column that's compatible with the components selected. The first step is to pick a wad that can hold a given

is used, a new set of wad and powder components must be assembled to fill the case properly. Start by selecting one of the popular low brass trap or skeet hulls available along with a set of components to get the shell in question. Since most shooters don't reload, low-priced discards can be bought at local clubs. Winchester AAs, Federal Gold Medal or Remington Premiers are extremely strong and durable, providing 15 to 20 reloadings. It's important to remember that low brass hulls can be safely loaded to magnum and high-velocity levels.

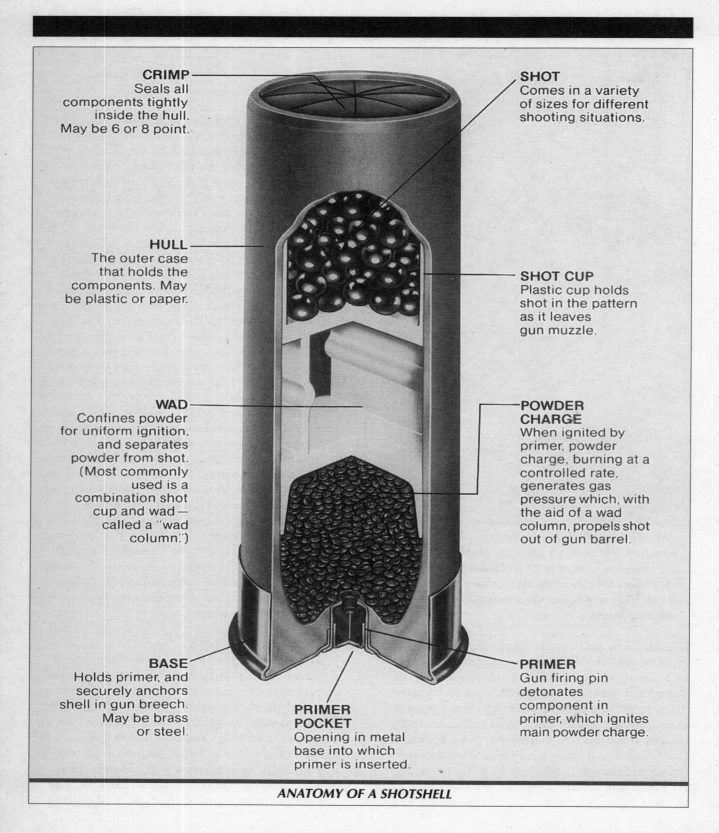

CRIMP
Seals all components tightly inside the hull. May be 6 or 8 point.

SHOT
Comes in a variety of sizes for different shooting situations.

HULL
The outer case that holds the components. May be plastic or paper.

SHOT CUP
Plastic cup holds shot in the pattern as it leaves gun muzzle.

WAD
Confines powder for uniform ignition, and separates powder from shot. (Most commonly used is a combination shot cup and wad — called a "wad column.")

POWDER CHARGE
When ignited by primer, powder charge, burning at a controlled rate, generates gas pressure which, with the aid of a wad column, propels shot out of gun barrel.

BASE
Holds primer, and securely anchors shell in gun breech. May be brass or steel.

PRIMER POCKET
Opening in metal base into which primer is inserted.

PRIMER
Gun firing pin detonates component in primer, which ignites main powder charge.

ANATOMY OF A SHOTSHELL

HOW TO LOAD SHOTSHELLS

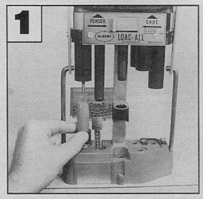

1 Remove spent primer and push full length resizer onto shell.

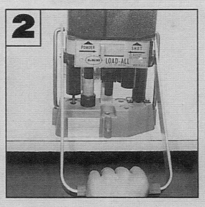

2 Install live primer and push off full length sizer.

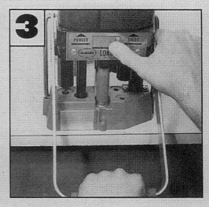

3 Add powder.

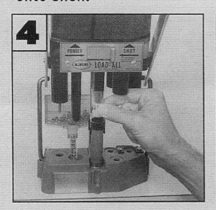

4 Install wad and shot. (To load slugs, simply substitute the shot with a Lee Drive Key slug).

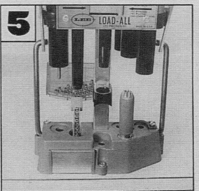

5 Start crimp with built-in crimp starter.

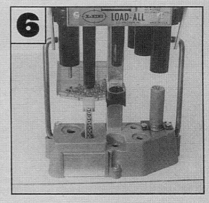

6 Finish crimp with perfect taper.

amount of shot, otherwise excess shot could cause barrel fouling and more open patterns. Since crimps are important to ensure uniform pressures and velocities, load recipes should be selected with the idea in mind of achieving a good crimp on the finished load. Remington RXP, Winchester WAA12, Federal 12SE, Active TG-30 and Hornady's Versatile are only a few of the quality choices available.

ALL POWDER IS NOT ALIKE

Powder selection can be a confusing issue for the beginning reloader. Different powders have varying burning speeds, so it's important to pick the right propellant for the job. For instance, heavy shot loads require slow-burning powders, simply because it takes longer to accelerate a heavy shot load than it does a light one. A fast-burning powder behind heavy shot can cause excessive

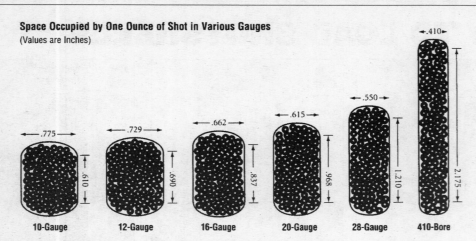

Space Occupied by One Ounce of Shot in Various Gauges
(Values are Inches)

.775	.729	.662	.615	.550	.410
1.010	.690	.837	.968	1.210	2.175
10-Gauge	**12-Gauge**	**16-Gauge**	**20-Gauge**	**28-Gauge**	**410-Bore**

Internal Diameter of the Barrel in Several Shotgun Gauges

10-Gauge—0.775-Inch	16-Gauge—0.662-Inch	28-Gauge—0.550-Inch
12-Gauge—0.729-Inch	20-Gauge—0.615-Inch	.410-Bore—0.410-Inch

Standard Shot Size

Shot Charge	Shot Size							
	#2	**#4**	**#5**	**#6**	**#7 1/2**	**#8**	**#8 1/2**	**#9**
1/2 oz.	45	67	85	112	175	205	242	292
3/4 oz.	67	101	127	168	262	308	363	439
7/8 oz.	79	118	149	197	306	359	425	512
1 oz.	90	135	170	225	350	410	485	585
1 1/8 oz.	101	152	191	253	393	461	545	658
1 1/4 oz.	112	169	213	281	437	513	605	731
1 3/8 oz.	124	186	234	309	481	564	665	804
1 1/2 oz.	135	202	255	337	525	615	730	877
1 5/8 oz.	146	220	276	366	569	666	790	951
1 7/8 oz.	169	253	319	422	656	769	850	1097
2 oz.	180	270	340	450	700	820	970	1170
2 1/4 oz.	202	304	382	506	786	922	1090	1316

This tabulation gives the approximate number of pellets per shotshell load for shot sizes 2 through 9. The exact number of pellets will vary, depending on exact alloy content. For example, chilled shot vs. soft shot. Variations in shot pellet diameter will also affect the exact number of pellets per load when shot charge is thrown by volume rather than by weight.

Component Shot Chart– Diameter In Inches

Winchester uniform, chilled lead shot provides consistent shot patterns and better penetration. Strict quality control throughout the manufacturing process assures the ultimate in performance. All Winchester shot available in 25 pound bags.

9	8	7 1/2	6	5	4	2	BB
●	●	●	●	●	●	●	●
.08	.09	.095	.11	.12	.13	.15	.18
APPROXIMATE NUMBER OF PELLETS TO THE OUNCE							
600	405	345	220	170	135	90	50

By knowing the space occupied by shot in various gauges and shot count, it's possible to fashion shotshells matched to "internal" capacity, with crimps that are uniform in shape.

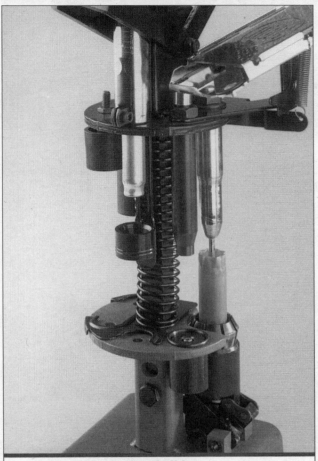

1. Deprimes and sizes shell base

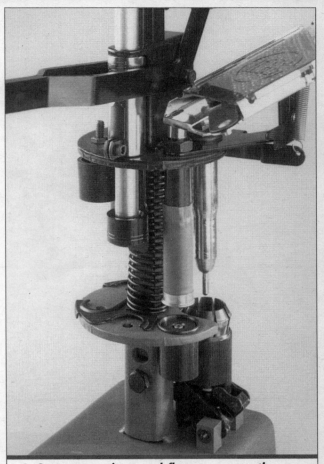

2. Seats new primer and flares case mouth

breech pressure; yet the same powder propelling a light load won't produce the right pressure buildup. The result: poor velocity.

As a rule of thumb, reloaders should use the fastest burning powder appropriate for the velocity level required in accordance with a reloader's manual. Choosing one powder over another can provide the keys to success: lower costs and more uniform velocities, pressures and superior crimps. Those who want to vary shot charges or use many different gauges and loads should select slower burning powder. Faster burning powders burn cleaner, are economical to use and provide uniform ballistics. Alliant (formerly Hercules), Hodgdon, Remington and Winchester all offer powders to fit

virtually every need. It's important to use a reloading scale periodically when checking charges thrown through a complete load cycle.

WHICH PRIMER TO USE

As shown in the accompanying illustration, the function of a primer is to ignite the main powder charge. All modern cases use the 209 primer. Remington, CCI (209/109), Federal and Winchester are interchangeable, but performance many vary. Use only the primer recommended by the manufacturer from whom the hull, powder, wad and shot were purchased. Compatibility of primer and powder are especially important. When ball or spherical powders are employed, a foil-

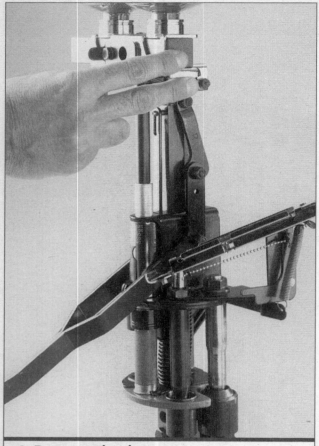

3. Drops powder charge

4. Seats wad (wad in position)

covered flash hole can prevent the intrusion of powder into the anvil area; otherwise, firing could cause primer pressure to reach a critical high.

LET'S START RELOADING

Throughout the loading procedure described below, a MEC Sizemaster single stage reloader has been used. The descriptions given are not intended as a substitute for the instructions provided with any particular tool. Always read the instructions and use the components exactly as shown in the loading data. The case, primer, powder charge, wad and shot charge listed in the tables must be followed precisely to ensure safe load assembly. The only exception is CCI 109 primer, which may be substituted for CCI's 209. Also, powder and shot charges that weigh five percent less than normal are acceptable.

STEP ONE: Place an empty hull into the deprime resize station with the right hand. Depress the handle with the left hand to the bottom of its stroke, removing the primer and resizing the brass base. With the right hand, remove the shell and place it on the reprime punch (the primer should now be in the reprime pocket). With an automatic primer feed, this phase is completed with each handle stroke; otherwise, the primer must be placed in the reprime pocket manually.

STEP TWO: With the left hand, depress the handle until the primer is firmly seated. Use enough pressure to seat the primer so that it's level with the bottom of the case head. Now raise the handle with the left hand and remove the primed shell from the reprime punch and place it on the shell holder at station #3 (center)

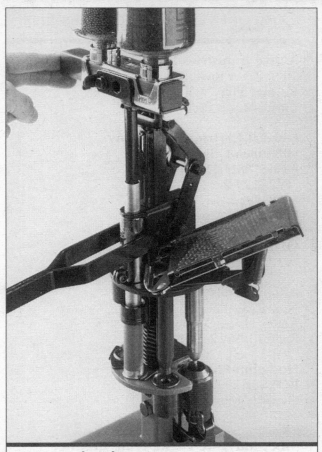

5. Drops shot charge

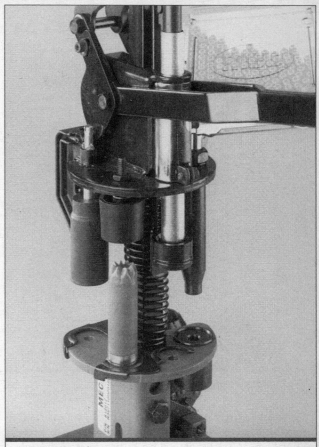

6. Starts Crimp

STEP THREE: Depress the handle until the rammer tube enters the shell. To charge the case with powder, hold the handle in this position and move the charge bar to the left.

STEP FOUR: Lift the handle to the top of its stroke and place a wad on the rammer tube. Depress the handle to the bottom, seating the wad over the powder charge.

STEP FIVE: Grasp the handle with the right hand and lift the handle, with the rammer rube remaining in the shell mouth. Move the charging bar all the way to the right position. This charges the hull with shot.

STEP SIX: Lift the handle to the top of its stroke and place the shell into the crimp start station. Depress the handle to the bottom position and start the crimp. Trap and skeet loads (except the 28 and .410 gauges) are 8-point crimps. Field

loads often use 6-point folds. It's important to crimp hulls using the same fold as the original.

STEP SEVEN: Lift the handle and move the shell to crimp station #5. With a smooth motion, close the shell by moving the handle to the bottom of its stroke. By following these instructions, the correct hand position can be developed. With enough practice, it's possible to load six to ten boxes of shells per hour with ease.

SAFETY AND RELOADING

By following the directions supplied by the various component manufacturers, and with common sense always in mind, reloading is a safe and rewarding activity, but there are some safety rules that must be followed. To begin, when purchasing powder be sure to request a copy of the SAAMI (Sporting Arms and Manufacturers

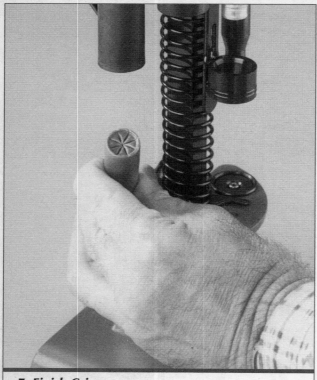

7. Finish Crimp

Institute) pamphlet on the properties and storage of smokeless powders. Modern powders are propellants, not explosives. The containers in which powders are packaged have been designed to keep powder dry, but they will burst if accidentally ignited. Therefore, store these containers away from flames, fires or sparks and keep them locked in a place where children can't reach them. Primers should also be handled with care. Never remove primers from their container until it's time to use them. Store away from excessive heat and handle gently. Do not store primers near powder or any place where children have access.

To repeat: always avoid experimenting or substituting components when reloading, and always follow the manufacturer's recommended components. Ballistic experts have tested recommended loads extensively and know how they perform. Also, safety glasses should be worn at all times, and there should be absolutely no smoking while reloading. By following these simple directives, all reloading activities should prove safe, profitable and relaxing fun for all concerned.

COMPONENT MANUFACTURERS LIST

Active Industries Inc.
1000 Zigor Road
Kearneysville, WV 25430
(304) 725-0451

Federal Cartridge Company
900 Ehlen Drive
Anoka, MN 55303
(612) 323-2300

Fiocchi of America, Inc.
5030 Fremont Road
Ozark, MO 65721
(417) 725-4118

Alliant Techsystems
New River Energetics
Route 114, P.O. Box 6
Radford, VA 24141-0096

Hodgdon Powder Co., Inc.
P.O. Box 2932
Shawnee Mission, KS 66201
(913) 362-9455

MEC, Mayville Engineering Co. Inc.
714 South Street
Mayville, WI 53050
(920) 387-4500

Polywad Shotgun Shell
P.O. Box 7916
Macon, GA 31209
(912) 477-0669

Winchester Components Div.
427 North Shamrock
East Alton, IL 62024-1197
(618) 258-2000

Remington Arms Co., Inc.
870 Remington Drive
P.O. Box 700
Madison, NC 27025-0700
(910) 548-8546

One Rifle For All Seasons

By Wilf E. Pyle

Suppose you could have only one rifle for all your hunting needs. Which one would you choose? Historically, many shooters have been restricted to carrying one rifle at any one time. There was no such thing as a Sunday afternoon trip to the range with five different rifles. The restrictions of wilderness travel limited most shooters to one specific firearm; moreover, it has always been difficult to carry two rifles. As the late, great Jack O'Connor was quick to point out, "You can only shoot one at a time." For some shooters, practical economics dictate. Why have two when one will do the job?

There are good, practical and time-tested reasons for shooting exclusively with one particular rifle. Those who do usually shoot that rifle well and are frequently skilled marksmen. Good shooting—that is, accurate and consistent shooting—is best achieved with a familiar arm. The best shooters usually have a few different firearms, but only one rifle in particular is a favorite. Most often, it's the one they shoot best and feel most comfortable with. It brings them success at the target range, in the hunting fields and when plinking.

WHICH ACTION TYPE IS FOR YOU?

If it comes down to one action type, the bolt is the hands-down choice. The reasons are many, starting with a great selection of cartridge choices. There's a bolt action available for nearly every modern cartridge covering all hunting situations, from plains to woods, from swamps to fields, and from mountains to valleys. The bolt's stronger camming action, especially when compared to other action types, grows in importance when dirty cartridges are encountered or reloads are used. Another reason for favoring a bolt action is its reliability, which refers to a rifle's ability to be

Suppose this shooter was limited to the use of one rifle. Which one should he choose—or is that a fair question?

The clip-fed rifle is critical to sport hunters. Strangely, few commercial bolt action rifles carry clips.

loaded and fired consistently without cartridge jamming, misfires or misfeeds. All these qualities are major assets in most of today's rifles, but they are most noticeable in bolt actions. Rifles in bolt action also come in many different styles, and they readily accept scopes. Trigger pulls, too, are considered by many to be best in a bolt action rifle, especially those featuring adjustable triggers. A 2 2/3- to three-pound trigger pull is considered adequate for most sport hunting. Other repeating models lack this feature or require the services of a competent gunsmith to make the necessary adjustments.

LEVER ACTION: CHOICE OF MILLIONS

Many shooters doubtless prefer a lever as their favorite action type. Even today, on ranches and farms across North America, an aging lever still hangs above many a kitchen door ready for imme-diate use. Indeed, more than seven million lever rifles are in use in the U.S. In a country that occupies 3.6 million square miles, that equals nearly two lever rifles per square mile. Little wonder that these rifles have taken on a "family gun" kind of presence, what with their prowess in putting down stock, shooting predators, protecting livestock and informal plinking. When these guns are called into service, it's likely something is going to be shot.

Lever guns are still preferred by eastern white-tailed deer hunters, including those who are fortunate enough to use horses in their hunting. The fabled Winchester Model '94 is less popular today than it once was, while the Model 81 Browning lever rifle is considered a boon to deer hunters who travel by horseback or on foot. Its design, which is much different than older levers, features a compact lever that moves a seven-lugged bolt into position. This multi-lugged bolt head enables the rifle to use modern, high-powered cartridges that have taken the place of the .30-30 and other older cartridges. A few years ago, Browning introduced a long-action version that moved the lever into magnum territory, allowing this action to compete head to head with the now firmly entrenched bolt action. The Browning rifle is now available in two action lengths covering .30-06, .270, .300 Winchester, .338 Winchester and 7mm Remington Magnum cartridges, to name a few. There is also a lightweight version.

The Browning lever differs from traditional Marlins and Winchester levers with its four-round detachable magazine, a very practical feature not available on all bolt action rifles. This rifle also ejects to the side, like a bolt, which makes scope mounting easy. The Browning is also a good-looking rifle; indeed, some of the original models from 1981 have quite generous stocks with exceptionally well-blued actions and barrels. Watch these early versions become collectors' pieces in the not too distant future.

Other action types—the pump, semi-automatic, single shot and the various combination guns—have their followers, too, and should not be dismissed. Not surprisingly, hunters who own only one rifle frequently choose one of these action types. Autoloader big game rifles are really not practical for those who seek one all-purpose rifle. The selection of models available is poor and cartridge choices are limited. For all but the .22 rimfire, the configurations are slanted toward military-style choices. Some, though, are quite comfortable with these different styles and quickly regale their fellow hunters with the advantages enjoyed by autoloaders over other action types. The autoloader actually delivers the fastest follow-up shot of any action type; many older .30 calibers are, in fact, adequate for today's hunting and shooting in North America. This writer feels quite comfortable with an aging Winchester Model 100 carbine in .284 Winchester, as do others he knows.

THE SINGLE SHOT RIFLE

The popularity of the single shot rifle has never really declined. In fact, there is currently great interest in single shot rifles because of the vast array of intermediate to high intensity cartridges that are chambered in these models. Reliability, accuracy, strength and simplicity are the traits which, when compared to levers, pumps and bolts, account for the enduring life of this action. A wide array of available stock types and barrel lengths means that those who are dedicated to the single shot as their only gun can find one to cover most hunting applications.

The single shot has a history of being a "gun crank's" gun, because many wildcat cartridges were designed from the older medium-powered cartridges, specifically the .25-35, .30-30, .30-40 Krag, .303 British, .32 Special, .33 Winchester, .35 Winchester and the .405 Winchester (also known from time to time as the old Winchester High Wall). A reasonably competent gun crank could easily rework a trigger to achieve a signifi-

In recent years barrels have undergone a transition in weight, from standard to lightweight. Many shooters claim that a short, lightweight rifle is easier to use in close bush conditions and is handier to move from one place to another.

Most consider the modern sporting stock near-perfect for the average shooter. Would-be one-rifle owners should check it out by throwing the rifle to a shoulder to see how the sights line up, where the butt lands on the shoulder, and how the forend sits in the hand.

cantly better pull than earlier bolts or modified military rifles. Sometimes the action was given additional heat treating and the firing pins were bushed; but such old techniques are not necessary with modern single shots like the Ruger Numbers One and Three centerfire single shots.

The best application for the single shot is in varmint hunting or limited forms of predator shooting. In such situations, it's entirely possible for a hunter to take only one shot at an animal before it rapidly disappears in flight or slips silently down a hole. Most modern hunting situations, however, require an easily accessible second shot. For that reason the single shot rifle is not recommended for hunters who seek one rifle for all their shooting.

THE PUMP ACTION RIFLE: AN AMERICAN ORIGINAL

Pump action rifles have a place in the one-gun lineup. There's a long-held notion that pumps survive because there are so many shotgun shooters who gravitate naturally to a pump centerfire for their big game hunting experiences. These rifles, by the way, can be fired conveniently by either left or right-handed shooters—a big plus in favor of the pump. About the only knock against the pump action is its poor selection of models and cartridges, a situation that is getting worse each year. This means that more good pump buys are found on the second-hand gun market than other actions. And, while pumps are uniquely American,

Over seven million lever rifles are in use in the U.S., which covers a land mass of 3.6 million square miles. That means nearly two lever rifles per square mile are in use in the U.S. today. Small wonder that they're used for a wide range of services, from plinking to shooting predators.

they have failed to gather the kind of interest that translates into market sales.

Perhaps the most interesting pump for modern hunters is the .35 Whelan in the Remington Model 7600. This cartridge, which is a .30-06 blown out to .35 caliber, uses a 200 or 250 grain hunting bullet. Browning recently introduced a pump rifle that looks much like the well-known Browning Automatic Rifle. Called the Model BPR, it's available in calibers .243, .308, .270, .30-06, .300 Winchester Magnum and 7mm Remington Magnum. Interestingly, the pumps have held on in the limited .22 centerfire market. Its large magazine capacity is doubtless one reason, and the slick look of these little rifles is probably another. Pumps capable of digesting .32-20s, .357 Magnums and some

of the older mid-powered ammunition—the .38-40 and even the .44 Magnum among them—would be exciting rifles for the short range varmint shooter. But where are they?

FINDING THE PERFECT BARREL

Selecting a rifle based on a particular barrel can be accomplished only by actually shooting the rifle under controlled conditions. We often hear shooters say, "This rifle or that rifle has a good barrel." What they are really doing is comparing the overall performance of one rifle to their own set of criteria involving accuracy. Most barrels made today are excellent, although there is much support among shooters for custom-made barrels, which they claim are more accurate

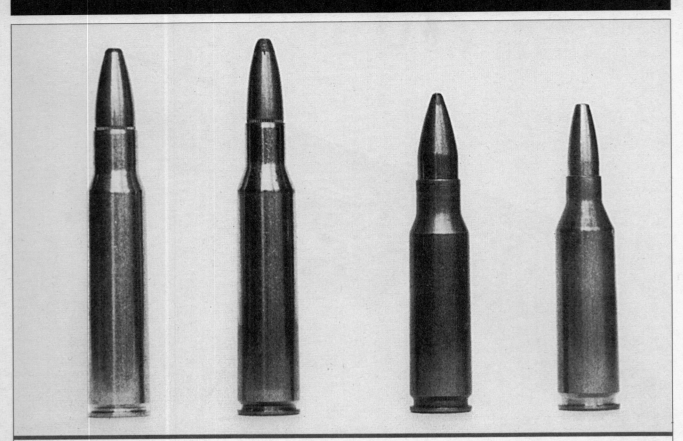

Only a few cartridges make the basic list of one-rifle must- haves: the venerable .30-06, the aging .270 Winchester, the lightweight .243 Winchester, and the .308 Winchester.

than commercially available factory kinds.

While it's generally recognized that modern commercial barrels meet a certain standard in terms of accuracy, their length, weight, configuration and style are choices the one-rifle shooter must face. Carbine barrels, which are typically 18 inches in length, are handy to have, but they create more muzzle blast and flash in all cartridges, even mild calibers like the .243 Winchester. Carbines get the nod for their light weight, their use in close bush country, and in situations where fewer shots are needed in the field.

For the one-rifle shooter who goes after varmints, heavy barrels in a standard caliber are recommended. They hold steadier, manage heat better during extended shooting sessions, and are capable of accurate bullet placement with a wider range of bullet weights as opposed to regular barrels. These factors are critical when choosing a rifle for predator or varmint shooting; but they are less critical for deer hunters who must sacrifice some accuracy in exchange for less weight and maneuverability.

Modern, lightweight barrels are generally 18 to 20 inches long and are finely tapered toward the muzzle. The newer style rifles are called Ultra-light, Mountain or Featherweight. While the saving is strictly that of weight—about three pounds lighter than standard rifles—many shooters will argue that a short, lightweight rifle is simply easier to use in close bush conditions and handier to carry around. Short barrels increase muzzle blast and lightweight barrels make a rifle that's more difficult to hold. Against these considerations one must estimate how long a lightweight rifle must be carried and how many shots will be fired in the course of a hunt. A true carbine wears a short barrel in combination with a shorter action and a slightly shorter stock.

Carbine barrels are typically 18 inches in length, making them handy but creating more muzzle blast and flash in all cartridges—even mild calibers like the .243 Winchester.

Stainless steel barrels have become an important option in picking the perfect sporting rifle. Hunters in the north, where temperatures go from hot to cold over short periods of time, need barrels that require less external care and don't show abuse as readily as more traditional blue steel barrels. You can bang a favorite blue steel rifle barrel against the door of a truck and leave a mark for the life of the rifle, but a stainless steel model will take innumerable knocks without marring. Debates over the accuracy of stainless versus blue steel are pointless. For most purposes, there's no difference. There is merit, however, in the fact that stainless barrels are more reflective; but then most hunting takes place in the dull, overcast days of fall or winter, when reflection is not an issue. Barrel weights vary greatly, with most manufacturers offering five or six choices. Most commercial sporting rifles come with number three barrels,

but some may have 2s and 4s depending on caliber. A .22 caliber barrel of the same length and taper weighs more than a .338. The heavier sporting barrel sits in the hand better, producing superior accuracy. Carbines are often used for mountain hunting on horseback, while deer hunters in the bush favor lightweight carbines. When it's time to take the stand—or point, as it's called—experienced hunters are likely to retire the carbine and pick up a sporter weight rifle.

SCOPES, LENGTH OF PULL, GRIPS AND TRIGGERS

In the past, carbines have generally been used without scopes. Students of hunting arms often note that older carbines frequently carry aperture sights, which have largely become a thing of the past. Because lever action rifles, such as the Winchester Model 94, were top ejecting, mounting

A heavy barrel in a standard caliber is one way to go. Heavy barrel rifles hold steadier, manage heat better during extended shooting sessions, and are capable of accurate bullet placement with a wide range of bullet weights.

a scope became difficult. Now, however, the carbine bolt action rifle has pretty much replaced the carbine lever. Modern, rugged compact scopes and mounts are readily available, making the carbine more useful for general hunting purposes. Levers have also benefitted from the improved scope mounts, making it relatively easy to outfit a top ejecting lever with a scope. Perhaps that's one reason why the lever continues to be so popular.

With most rifles now carrying a scope, it's important that your eye lines up with the scope. The dimensions of the comb will indicate where the eye will naturally fall. If it's necessary to twist your chin, stretch your neck or creep forward on the stock to see through the scope, then the rifle is a poor fit to the body. Snapping the rifle to the shoulder a few times should clearly reveal

the nature of the fit. A rifle that fits properly can make the difference between so-so and superior accuracy.

Length of pull—the distance from the center of the trigger to the center of the butt plate—is important, too. A hunter's physical build determines what length of pull to choose. Shooters with long necks, arms or hands typically require greater pull lengths. The current standard is 13 3/8 inches, with true carbines falling shorter by as much as an inch and many California-style stocks being as much as an inch longer. Little variation in length of pull occurs among modern rifles compared to what was available in the 1950s. This standardization was brought about largely by the writings of shooters like Jack O'Connor and Warren Page. For the average shooter who

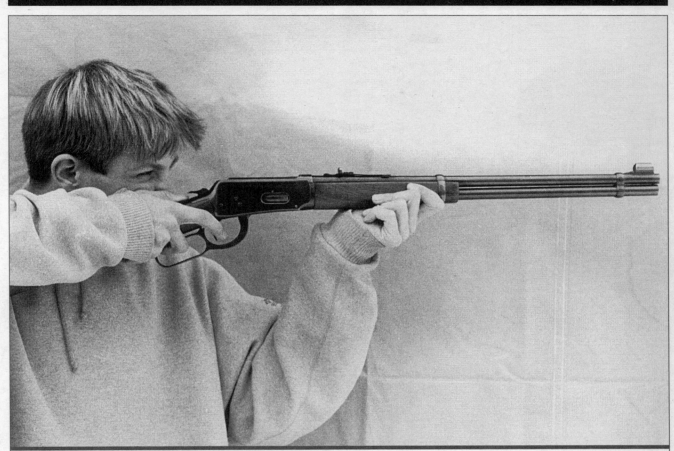

Lever guns are preferred by many hunters of eastern white- tailed deer. The fabled Winchester Model '94, while less popular than it once was, remains a boon to deer hunters traveling by horseback or on foot.

uses a modern sporting rifle, drop at the heel and drop at comb are handy indicators of how the stock fits the shooter. "Drop at the heel" represents the vertical distance between the line of sight and the top edge of the butt. "Drop at the comb" is the vertical distance between the line of sight and the forward end of the comb. *Drop* in part determines felt recoil while helping to align the eye, scope and target. A well-designed stock should have a comb high enough so that the eye can look through the scope.

Pistol grip is important, too. Recently, this factor has been largely ignored as more rifle stocks have been designed around the lightweight or short rifle concept. Rifles that are used for general hunting and shooting require a curved pistol grip, enough so that a shooter can pull a rifle

into the shoulder with a hand that is in a natural, uncramped position. A full grip allows the shooter to throw the rifle to the shoulder faster and on target sooner. It also lets the hunter line up better. A straight grip, or one that isn't quite full, can cause the hand to search for a natural position. It provides no guidance for the hand to line up with the eye during the period when the mind is busy searching for the target and sorting out lead. A few stock designs feature something called a "Wundhammer swell;" i.e., a swollen pistol grip that helps position the hand quicker and securely.

For many years, the forends of stocks varied considerably. Like other stock characteristics, they have undergone tremendous standardization. Untrained shooters feel the urge to pull the rifle into their shoulder with an arm extended on the

For those who seek one rifle for all shooting purposes, the autoloader action is limited.

forend. This creates tension in the shoulder and produces an unsteady stance. The forend need only be thick enough to provide a good support for the hand, so that it can grip the rifle firmly and help guide the rifle as it follows through on a running shot. Forends that are not so thick enable the hunter to get on target quickly for a smooth follow-through.

Discussions about stock material or composition have become fashionable among the shooting intelligentsia. Walnut stocks, for example, have endured every kind of weather condition and abuse, from wars to neglect, yet there is a common notion that composition material is superior to wood. Only time will tell. There are as yet no 200-year-old synthetic stocks out there. The best advice to riflemen deciding whether to go with composition or wood is *relax*. Pick wood with a clear conscience, but feel free to choose composition, too.

Our leanings toward lightweight rifles in recent years have been offset by a desire for heavy, multi-powered scopes. The scope has indeed undergone its own kind of technological improvements that have caused their weight to rise sharply. Well into the 1950s, hunters were never really confident about the scope, and reliability was always suspect. Today, it's commonly acknowledged that no big game rifle should be fired without a scope. One-rifle shooters are urged to buy the best they can afford. The scope, after all, allows the hunter to shoot as well as he can see, an advantage we all need.

Scopes obviously offer a great capacity for gathering light, which is why the objective lenses on most models are so large. The scope places the eye and target on the same plane, which is a great advantage over the old iron sights, which shooters had to line up, front and rear, with the target. While the choice among modern variable scopes is large, a four-power scope remains the best choice overall for most hunters. Six-power scopes are preferred by some plains hunters, but recently there has been a major move by hunters to embrace variable multi-powered models that run from three- to twelve-power. Medium levels of magnification reduce the potential for aiming error, while high powers increase shakiness while taking aim. The bottom line for a one-gun owner is to make sure the rifle is equipped with a quality scope.

GOOD CARTRIDGE SELECTION: A MUST

Some feel that cartridge selection is more important than the type and style of rifle preferred by the one-gun hunter. We're not talking about shooters who recognize these choices as particularly valuable, though, but rather those who desire one rifle to cover all kinds of shooting. Cartridges are important to know about in terms of different hunting applications, but one cartridge can usually cover a broad range of hunting applications when combined with smart bullet selection. Every gun crank has a personal favorite—along with strong arguments to support their choice. Fortunately, most one-gun owners are not gun cranks. Still, a few cartridges stand out as basic choices. These include the venerable .30-06, the aging .270 Winchester, the lightweight .243 Winchester, and the .308 Winchester. Note that the list does not include a single cartridge with a magnum designation, nor does it have any small caliber, high-intensity rounds. The list is based on several factors: ease of shooting, broadness of application, and availability in most types of rifle action. As for ammunition, the average shooter is as likely to find ammo for a .30-06 in Saskatchewan as he is in Beemerville, New Jersey. High velocity, a large selection in bullet weights, and great striking power mean nothing if the desired cartridges aren't available.

The .30-06 makes the list because it's a highly versatile cartridge available in most rifle types. An adequate long range round, it's available in 125, 150, 165, 180, 200 and 220 grain bullets in shapes ranging from pointed to hollow. The .30-06 is applicable to almost all game shooting situations in North America, from prairie dogs to moose. It's also about the easiest cartridge with

which to establish point-blank range. Sighted-in to hit three inches high at 100 yards, it offers a point-blank range of just under 300 yards on deer and most other big game without having to hold high or low in order to change the point of impact.

The standard 150 grain bullet leaves a .30-06 at 2,900 feet per second, while at 300 yards it offers 1,295 foot pounds of energy—plenty for deer, antelope, moose and even black bear. And when teamed with lightweight bullets, such as the Remington 125 grain factory load, varmints and coyotes come into the picture. At one time, lightweight bullets in the .30-06 had a bad reputation; but accuracy performance is now as good as it gets with modern factory rifles, ammo and scopes. A sabot carrying 55 grain Remington can also give casual shooters a chance at most predators. Premium high energy rifle rounds produced by Federal and others offer 180 grain factory loads that are slightly under ten percent more powerful at all ranges than standard loadings. Those that seek .30-06 magnums may have their wish in these new rounds.

Barrel weights vary greatly, with most manufacturers offering five to six choices. Commercial sporting rifles are usually outfitted with number 3 barrels, but a few may have 2s and 4s varying in caliber.

We don't hear much about the aging .270 Winchester anymore, but a lot of rifles are chambered for this round. In fact, more rifle models are now being produced for the .270 than at its high point in the early 1950s. Actually, the .270 evolved from the .30-06 case in 1925 and was first offered in Winchester's legendary Model 54. Producing 3,140 feet per second from the muzzle with a 130 grain bullet, the .270 has gained a solid reputation as a big game cartridge, one that can step down to varmint and back up to moose or bear without losing a beat. Indeed, the .270 was the first cartridge to offer that kind of versatility to the American shooter. It remains a viable choice for the one-rifle owner, offering mild recoil, an abundant selection of actions, and a multitude of hunting bullets to cover most current shooting applications.

Another favorite is the .243 Winchester, which owes its existence to Warren Page. The cartridge, which is simply the .308 Winchester necked down, first arrived on the shooting scene in 1955, and the first commercial rifle to use it was the Model 88 Lever Action Winchester. From the start, the cartridge was popular and its reputation expanded quickly from a limited varmint role to a broader selection of game animals up to the black bear. Its light recoil and low-level muzzle blast made this round a training round of sorts for young shooters and women who were just getting into the shooting and hunting sports. For many, the .243 Winchester

The .243 Winchester is a favorite for the one-rifle shooter. The cartridge first came on the shooting scene in 1955 for Winchester's Model 88 Lever Action.

remains the gateway to magnum rifles.

The .308 is also mild on recoil and quite accurate for a sporting weight firearm. It started life as a military round in one of the best military rifles ever invented: the M-14. The Winchester company immediately recognized the value of this short, stubby round in lever and semiautomatic rifles, producing the Model 100 Winchester in .308, arguably the most popular semiautomatic rifle of all time. The .308 is light in weight and offers good trajectory, making it an ideal round for hunting deer out to 300 yards. Bullet selection is large as well, making the .308 one of the most popular and versatile hunting cartridges available.

To sum up, those wanting an iron-clad recommendation on the single best rifle model, make, style and cartridge won't find it here. There is really no such thing as the "perfect" choice for the one-gun owner. The sporting rifle, as it has evolved, is probably the best choice for most hunting applications, while the bolt action offers the greatest flexibility in configuration and cartridge choices. The real key is *choice*, which allows shooters to match hunting conditions to rifle style. This freedom to choose lets hunters select any number of options they might face in the field. As hunters, as one-gun shooters, as shooters of all types, we all need the power to choose. We need choices in barrel weight, stock type, barrel length, sighting equipment and cartridges. Give shooters a choice and there will always be satisfied one-gun shooters.

A stainless steel barrel has become an important option in rifle selection. These barrels need less care than the more traditional blue steel gun barrel.

I.G.A.'s Deluxe Uplander Side-By-Side

The new Stoeger Deluxe Uplander Side-by-Side shotgun is offered for the first time with semi-fancy American Walnut stock and forend. Each stock is fitted with a thin black Pachmayr rubber recoil pad and the wood is finished in a soft matte lacquer. Internal choke tubes are standard on the 12 and 20 gauge as well as 3" chambers. The 28 gauge comes with a 26" barrel—chambered for 2.75" shells—and is choked, improved cylinder and modified. Our Deluxe .410 Uplander also features a 26" barrel and is choked, modified, and full (3" chambers are standard). Double gold triggers, positive extractors and automatic safety are all standard features. Sighting is made easy with the aid of a red bead front and mid-rib sight. For information contact:

STOEGER INDUSTRIES
5 Mansard Court
Wayne, New Jersey 07470
Tel: 800-631-0722
Fax: 973-872-2230

MANUFACTURERS' SHOWCASE

MODEL G1004, G1008 A1S-A TYPE VERTICAL MILLING MACHINES

These vertical mills feature a 1½ HP single phase motor, one-shot lubrication, fine feed spindle attachment, built-in chip tray, swiveling mast, tilting head and complete coolant system. The Model G1008 also features a variable-speed longitudinal table power feed. Shipping weight approximately 1050 lbs.. Selling price for the Model **G1004** is **$2,295.00** and the Model **G1008** is **$2,650.00**. Both are F.O.B. our warehouse.

3 LOCATIONS
Bellingham, WA / Williamsport, PA / Memphis, TN

GRIZZLY INDUSTRIAL, INC.
TEL: 1-800-523-4777   FAX: 1-800-438-5901

BEAMSHOT
PROFESSIONAL LASER SIGHTING SYSTEMS™

SIGHTS DESIGNED FOR REVOLVERS

Designed specifically for the special demands of revolver use, BEAMSHOT PROFESSIONAL LASER SIGHTING SYSTEMS will maintain their accuracy in extreme conditions. Constructed of high-grade, lightweight aluminum, they are available in black or silver. BEAMSHOT'S 1000 series and 3000 series have various ranges from 670mm/300 yards to 635mm/800 yards. A special BEAMSHOT 780mm is visible only when viewed through night vision equipment. All BEAMSHOTS are quality constructed and powered by unmatched, continuous "on" operation (20+ hours). Easily mounted to virtually all revolvers. One year warranty.

QUARTON USA
7042 Alamo Downs Pkwy, Suite 370, San Antonio, TX 78238
Tel: 800-520-8435 *Fax:* 210-520-8433

NUFACTURERS' SHOWCASE

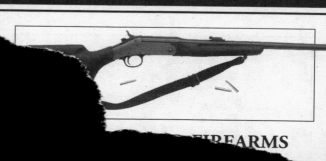

FIREARMS

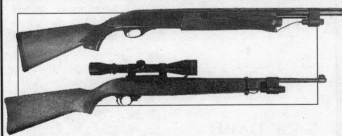

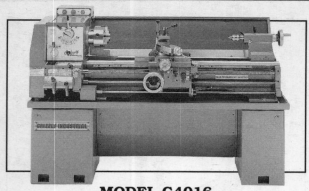

MODEL G4016
13½" x 40"
GEAR HEAD LATHE W/STAND

Our 8-speed, 13½" x 40" metal lathe combines a 2-horsepower motor with a precision gear head system. 78 to 2100 RPM. Features rock-solid cast iron construction with heavy-gauge steel chip tray and backsplash. Shipping weight approximately 1200 lbs.. The price is only **$2,695.00** and is F.O.B. our warehouse.

3 LOCATIONS
Bellingham, WA / Williamsport, PA / Memphis, TN

GRIZZLY INDUSTRIAL, INC.
TEL: 1-800-523-4777   FAX: 1-800-438-5901

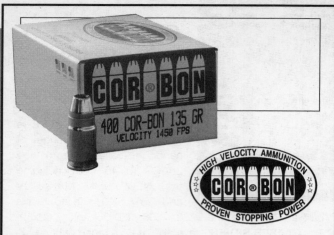

COR-BON is a manufacturer of premium self-defense ammunition for law enforcement, special operations and personal self-defense. In addition, COR-BON *Handgun Hunting* ammunition is offered in various loads, from 10mm to 454 Casull. Plus, a special *Single Shot Hunter* line is specifically designed to give optimum ballistics in the reduced barrel length of high-performance pistols.

COR-BON BULLET CO.
1311 Industry Road
Sturgis, SD 57785
Tel: 800-626-7266
Fax: 800-923-2666

MANUFACTURERS' SHOWCASE

SIGHTS DESIGNED FOR YOUR PISTOL

Designed specifically for the harsh use and extreme conditions associated with pistols, BEAMSHOT PROFESSIONAL LASER SIGHTING SYSTEMS are built to take a beating while maintaining superior accuracy. Available in black or silver, BEAMSHOT's 1000 and 3000 series have various ranges, from 670mm/300 yards to 635mm/800 yards. There's even a special BEAMSHOT 780mm visible only when viewed through night vision equipment. All BEAMSHOTS are constructed of lightweight, high-grade aluminum, powered by batteries for continuous "on" operation (20+ hours). Easily mounted to virtually all pistols. One year warranty.

BEAMSHOT
PROFESSIONAL LASER SIGHTING SYSTEMS™

QUARTON USA
7042 Alamo Downs Pkwy, Suite 370, San Antonio, TX 78238
Tel: 800-520-8435 *Fax:* 210-520-8433

CASE GARD JAMMIT TARGET STAND

The Jammit Target Stand is easy to set up and move to different yardages. Ideal for unlevel ground, like the side of a hill. Made of engineering grade plastic. Includes one 17.5" X 23" cardboard target backer. Breaks down fast for compact storage. Write us and send one dollar for our full color catalog.

MTM MOLDED PRODUCTS
P.O. Box 14117
Dayton, OH 45423
Tel: 937-890-7461 *Fax:* 937-890-1747

STAINLESS STEEL FLASKS

The name Smith and Wesson has long been associated with fine quality handguns. A reputation that takes years to build and once attained, worth more than money can buy. Smith & Wesson hip flasks proudly pay tribute to that fine name with embossed Smith & Wesson logos.

Distributed worldwide exclusively by Gutmann Cutlery.

WHOLESALE ONLY

FOR A FREE CATALOG AND A DEALER NEAR YOU, PLEASE CALL
1-800-CUTLERY

GUTMANN CUTLERY, INC.
P.O. Box 2219, Bellingham, WA 98227-2219
Tel: 1-800-288-5379   Fax: 360-715-2091

HARRINGTON & RICHARDSON®
OFFERS WHITETAILS UNLIMITED 1998
COMMEMORATIVE EDITION RIFLE

To help ensure the future success of the North American whitetail deer, Harrington & Richard joins forces with Whitetails Unlimited to create the new 1998 Commemorative Edition rifle chambered in the venerable 30-30 Win. Produced on a high-tensile, investment cast steel frame, this rifle is fitted to a classic pistol grip stock with sling swivel studs and a premium rocoil pad. The wood is American black walnut and the stocks and forends are precisely carved, hand-sanded, carefully finished and cut checkered by hand. Each rifle features a special laser engraving of the WTU logo and a pewter-finished Whitetails Unlimited medallion is inletted into the stock. H&R's patented Transfer Bar System virtually eliminates the possibility of an accidental discharge. The 22" barrel is fitted with fully adjustable rifle sights and is hand-fitted to the action for proper headspace and superior performance. For more information contact:

H&R 1871, INC.
60 Industrial Rowe, Gardner, MA 01440
Tel: 978-632-9393   *Fax:* 978-632-2300

MANUFACTURERS' SHOWCASE

GUNLINE TOOLS FOR GUN STOCKERS

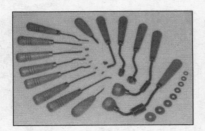

GUNLINE TOOLS is offering a complete line of checkering, bottoming and barrel bedding tools to both professional and amateur gun stockers. Made of high quality materials and careful manufacturing processes, these tools can be relied upon to give superior service and durability. All cutting units are replaceable so that there is a minimum of fuss in maintaining precise operation. Checkering sets come with full instructions, sample patterns and pitch gage to provide the new gun stocker with more than adequate assistance.

GUNLINE TOOLS
2950-O Saturn St.
Brea, CA 92821
Tel: 714-993-5100
Fax: 714-572-4128
www.gunline.com

"Quick Access When Needed, While Secure From Curious Hands"

The Versa Mount Security Box comes with mounting rails on both sides. This means you never have to mount is upside down, which changes the sequence and feel of the lock. The Box is constructed of welded steel in 8", 10" and 12" sizes. It has a rubber lining, a line pull-out tray, and a five-button Simple combination lock. Simply slide the Box onto the mounted bracket, shut the door, and the Box is locked in place. *For information call or fax (817) 594-1482.*

T&T ENTERPRISES
4003 Hogle Street
Weatherford, TX 76086

PRO EARS® "LE" (LINEAR ELITE)

Today's Most Advanced Hearing Protection/Enhancement System

PRO EARS "LE", ultra-comfortable units with "DSC"™ (Dynamic Sound Compression), instantly protect against hearing damage by compressing noise vibrations, starting at 72 db. Unlike other brands that shut off their amplifications system, "LE" models eliminate gaps in hearing, letting users hear every sound safely. **PRO EARS "LE"** models also feature "DSR"™ (Dynamic Sound Range) for clear, natural sound enhancement for close and distant sounds. Also features soft, comfortable Sealing Rings, adjustable Head band, 250 hours minimum battery life, and the industry's longest warranty (5 years). For more information on the new **PRE EARS "LE"** models, see your local Pro Ears dealer or contact:

RIDGELINE, INC.
P.O. Box 930 • Dewey, AZ 86327-0930
Tel: 520-632-5800 *Fax:* 320-632-5900
800-891-3660 *(dealers only)*
E-mail: ProEars@neta.com, or visit us on the Internet at:
http://www.neta.com/~ProEars

BENCH MASTER RIFLE REST

The Bench Master Rifle Rest is a rugged, compact and highly adjustable rifle-shooting accessory—one that offers precision line-up and recoil reduction when sighting in a rifle, testing ammunition or shooting varmints. It features three course positions totaling 5.5", with 1.5" fine adjustment in each course position, plus leveling and shoulder height adjustments for maximum control and comfort. Because of its unique design, the Bench Master can easily double as a rifle vise for scope mounting, bore sighting and cleaning. It comes with a LIFETIME Warranty and a list price of only $119.95. For a free brochure, call or write:

DESERT MOUNTAIN MFG.
P.O. Box 130184, Coram, MT 59913
Tel: 800-477-0762 (Toll Free)

MANUFACTURERS' SHOWCASE

PROTECTIVE METAL CASES

ICC, Impact Case Company and KK AIR International offer a complete line of two- and three-piece "Flat Style" and "Trunk Style" Protective Aluminum Transport/Shipping Cases. In addition to the standard sizes, KK AIR offers special cases in any quantity. NEW PRODUCTS include Cordura Nylon Concealment Duffels and Jackets. The Standard Size Cases carry a "Lifetime Material and Workmanship Warranty." Before buying any case products or firearm duffels, be sure to check out ICC/KK AIR offerings. For detailed specification sheets describing this rugged equipment, contact:

ICC/KK AIR INTERNATIONAL
P.O. Box 9912
Spokane, WA 99209
Tel: 1-800-262-3322
Fax: 1-509-326-5436

SERIES S MODEL L

HARRIS
ENGINEERING, INC.

ULTRALIGHT BIPODS
- *Versatile*
- *Sturdy*
- *Light*
- *Fast*

SERIES S BIPODS
Pivoting Bipod
with tension
adjustment

Harris Bipods clamp quickly and securely to most stud equipped bolt-action rifles. Folding legs have completely adjustable spring-return telescoping extensions. Time proven design and quality manufacture. Thirteen models available plus adapters for various guns.

HARRIS ENGINEERING INC.
Barlow, Kentucky 42024

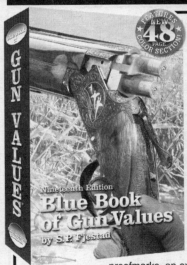
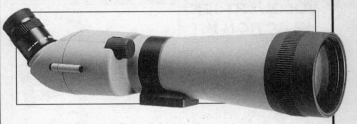

STOEGER INTRODUCES THE I.G.A. WATERFOWL 12 GAUGE MODEL

Stoeger Industries has added a new dimension to hunting by introducing the I.G.A. Waterfowl over-and-under with its low profile matte blue receiver. This affordable, rugged and reliable waterfowl gun is finished in Advantage® camouflage over the 30" barrels and durable Brazilian walnut stock and forend. Its massive monoblock, which connects the barrel assembly to the receiver, assures a tight lock up every time. The moly-chrome steel barrels are fitted with recessed interchangeable screw-in choke tubes and are capable of handling 2.75" or 3" steel shot. Upon opening the barrel assembly, automatic ejectors throw the fired shells clear of the chamber. Other standard features include a single selective trigger and automatic safety. Here's the ideal gun for fowl in the fowlest conditions. For information contact:

STOEGER INDUSTRIES
5 Mansard Court
Wayne, New Jersey 07470
Tel: 800-631-0722 • Fax: 973-872-2230

U.S.A. Magazines, the world's largest manufacturer of American-made rifle and handgun magazines, offers high-precision magazines made to meet manufacturers' specs. We carry a full line of 10-round magazines for the top-selling pistols in the world, plus any other hard to find models. Extended capacity magazines are also available for law enforcement agencies, military and export. U.S.A. Magazines also has a good supply of extended capacity magazines manufactured prior to the enactment of the U.S. Crime Bill. A full color catalog is available for $2.00 by mail and is **FREE** when ordered via U.S.A. Magazine's popular web site. Or you may phone us.

U.S.A MAGAZINES, INC.
P.O. Box 39115
Tel: 800-USA-2577 • Fax: 562-903-7857
www.usa.magazines.com

MANUFACTURERS' SHOWCASE

VOLQUARTSEN HP ACTION KIT

The **HP ACTION KIT** consists of our target hammer with a special tungsten disulfide finish, a trigger with an over-travel adjustment, sear and disconnector—all with a special coating. It also comes with a trigger plunger with improved radius, trigger plunger spring and special hammer spring. Also included in the kit is a vibration dampening bolt stop pin to reduce wear on the action and/or bolt. The new **HP ACTION KIT** will give the shooter one of the crispest, smoothest and cleanest trigger pulls they could have regardless of materials or cost. Satisfaction Guaranteed! For information contact:

VOLQUARTSEN CUSTOM LTD.
24276 240th St., P.O. Box 397
Carroll, Iowa 51401
Tel: 712-792-4238
Fax: 712-792-2542
E-mail: VCL@NETINS.NET
HTTP://WWW.VOLQUARTSEN.COM

NOBODY BEATS BEAMSHOT

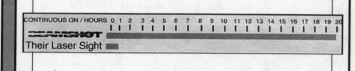

Only **BEAMSHOT LASER SIGHTS** can supply continuous "on" usage for more than 20 hours—25 times the life of other laser sights. Designed and built better than other average laser sights, these sights cost less initially and less in battery usage over the long run. And what good is a laser sight if you can't mount it securely to your firearm? Other manufacturers claim their lasers will mount "any" arm. In fact, **BEAMSHOT** produces the widest variety of mounts available—and all in stock.

Is there a gun **BEAMSHOT** can't be mounted to with ease? *Not likely.*

PROFESSIONAL LASER SIGHTING SYSTEMS™

QUARTON USA
7042 Alamo Downs Pkwy, Suite 370, San Antonio, TX 78238
Tel: 800-520-8435 Fax: 210-520-8433

You can pay more. You just can't get more.

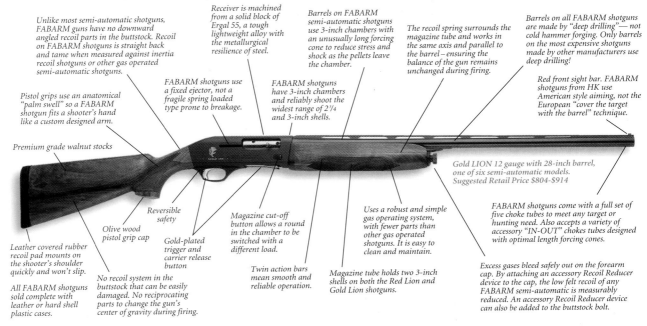

Unlike most semi-automatic shotguns, FABARM guns have no downward angled recoil parts in the buttstock. Recoil on FABARM shotguns is straight back and tame when measured against inertia recoil shotguns or other gas operated semi-automatic shotguns.

Receiver is machined from a solid block of Ergal 55, a tough lightweight alloy with the metallurgical resilience of steel.

Barrels on FABARM semi-automatic shotguns use 3-inch chambers with an unusually long forcing cone to reduce stress and shock as the pellets leave the chamber.

The recoil spring surrounds the magazine tube and works in the same axis and parallel to the barrel – ensuring the balance of the gun remains unchanged during firing.

Barrels on all FABARM shotguns are made by "deep drilling"— not cold hammer forging. Only barrels on the most expensive shotguns made by other manufacturers use deep drilling!

FABARM shotguns use a fixed ejector, not a fragile spring loaded type prone to breakage.

FABARM shotguns have 3-inch chambers and reliably shoot the widest range of 2¾ and 3-inch shells.

Red front sight bar. FABARM shotguns from HK use American style aiming, not the European "cover the target with the barrel" technique.

Pistol grips use an anatomical "palm swell" so a FABARM shotgun fits a shooter's hand like a custom designed arm.

Premium grade walnut stocks

Gold LION 12 gauge with 28-inch barrel, one of six semi-automatic models. Suggested Retail Price $804-$914

Reversible safety

Olive wood pistol grip cap

Gold-plated trigger and carrier release button

Magazine cut-off button allows a round in the chamber to be switched with a different load.

Uses a robust and simple gas operating system, with fewer parts than other gas operated shotguns. It is easy to clean and maintain.

FABARM shotguns come with a full set of five choke tubes to meet any target or hunting need. Also accepts a variety of accessory "IN-OUT" chokes tubes designed with optimal length forcing cones.

Leather covered rubber recoil pad mounts on the shooter's shoulder quickly and won't slip.

All FABARM shotguns sold complete with leather or hard shell plastic cases.

No recoil system in the buttstock that can be easily damaged. No reciprocating parts to change the gun's center of gravity during firing.

Twin action bars mean smooth and reliable operation.

Magazine tube holds two 3-inch shells on both the Red Lion and Gold Lion shotguns.

Excess gases bleed safely out on the forearm cap. By attaching an accessory Recoil Reducer device to the cap, the low felt recoil of any FABARM semi-automatic is measurably reduced. An accessory Recoil Reducer device can also be added to the buttstock bolt.

FABARM shotguns

Feature for feature, premium grade semi-automatic shotguns from Italian gun maker Fabbrica Bresciana Armi (FABARM) are unsurpassed. Deep-drilled barrels. Forged double action bars. Rugged and simple design. Straight-back low recoil. All translate into the finest autoloading shotguns made.

Plus HK/FABARM has a full line of quality shotguns, including over-&-unders, side-by-sides, and a pump action utility gun—all designed and manufactured with a synthesis of old world craftsmanship and advanced engineering.

HK/FABARM shotguns are made for any and every shooting need you have...sporting clays, trap, skeet, waterfowl, upland bird, turkey, and personal security.

Best of all, HK/FABARM shotguns are covered by a lifetime warranty—the only shotgun with such a guarantee.

MAX LION 12 gauge with 28-inch barrels, one of eight over-and-under models. Suggested Retail Price $1,053-$1,807

Classic Lion Grade II 12 gauge with 26-inch barrels, one of two side-by-side models. Suggested Retail Price $1,488-$2,110

FP6 12 gauge pump action with 20-inch barrel. Suggested Retail Price $472

Exclusively from
HECKLER & KOCH, INC.
21480 Pacific Boulevard
Sterling, Virginia 20166 U.S.A.

FABARM • Fabbrica Bresciana Armi

STOEGER

IGA

DELUXE SERIES
SHOTGUNS

American Arms	98		Kahr Arms	140
American Derringer	99		KBI	141
AMT	101		Kimber	142
Auto-Ordnance	103		L.A.R. Grizzly	144
Beretta	104		Laseraim Arms	145
Bernardelli	108		Llama	146
Bersa	109		Luger, American Eagle	148
Brolin	110		Magnum Research	149
Browning	111		MOA Maximum	151
Colt	114		Navy Arms	151
Coonan Arms	119		New England Firearms	153
Davis	120		North American Arms	154
Downsizer	121		Para-Ordnance	155
EMF/Dakota	121		Rossi	157
Entréprise	124		Ruger	160
European American Armory	126		Safari	169
FEG	128		Savage	170
Freedom Arms	128		Sig-Sauer	171
Glock	130		Smith & Wesson	173
Hämmerli	132		Springfield	188
Harrington & Richardson	133		Taurus	192
Heckler & Koch	134		Thompson/Center	197
Heritage	136		Uberti	198
Hi-Point	137		Unique	199
High Standard	137		Walther	200
Israel Arms	139		Wichita Arms	202
Jennings Firearms	140		Wildey	202

Handguns

*For addresses and phone/fax numbers of manufacturers and distributors included in this section, please turn to **DIRECTORY OF MANUFACTURERS AND SUPPLIERS** on page 558.*

AMERICAN ARMS

ESCORT .380 ACP

REGULATOR SINGLE
ACTION REVOLVER

ESCORT .380 ACP

SPECIFICATIONS
Caliber: .380 ACP *Action:* DA
Capacity: 7-shot magazine
Barrel Length: 3 ³/₈" *Overall Length:* 6 ¹/₈"
Width: ¹³/₁₆" *Weight:* 19 oz.
Sights: Fixed; low profile
Features: Stainless steel frame, slide & trigger; nickel-steel barrel; soft polymer grips; loaded chamber indicator
Price: $349.00

REGULATOR
DELUXE

REGULATOR DELUXE

SPECIFICATIONS
Caliber: 44 Special, 44-40, 45LC
Barrel Length: 4.25" or 5.5"
Features: Blued steel backstrap and trigger guard; hammer block safety;
Prices:
BIRD'S-HEAD GRIP. $425.00
TWO-CYLINDER SET $495.00
Also available:
BISLEY SINGLE ACTION 45 LC. *Barrel Length:* 4.75", 5.5", 7.5". *Features:* Walnut grips; "hump back" backstrap; low profile wide spur hammer $475.00

REGULATOR SINGLE ACTION

SPECIFICATIONS
Calibers: 45 Long Colt, 44-40, 357 Mag.
Barrel Length: 4.75", 5.5" and 7.5"
Overall Length: 8 ¹/₁₆"
Weight: 2 lb. 3 oz. (4.75" barrel)
Sights: Fixed
Safety: Hammer block
Features: Brass trigger guard and backstrap; two-cylinder combos avail. (45 L.C./45 ACP and 44-40/44 Special
Prices:
REGULATOR SINGLE ACTION REVOLVER $365.00
TWO-CYLINDER SET 435.00

MATEBA AUTO REVOLVER (not shown)

This firearm incorporates the quickness and handling of a semi-auto pistol with the reliability and accuracy of a revolver. May be fired as a single-action or double-action handgun. When fired, the cylinder and slide assembly move back and the recoil causes the cylinder to rotate. The speed of firing is comparable to a semi-auto pistol. The "auto pistol" aspect of this gun aligns the barrel with the bottom chamber of the cylinder. This reduces muzzlle recoil allowing the shooter to stay "on target" with the least amount of movement.

SPECIFICATIONS
Caliber: 357
Capacity: 6 rounds
Overall Length: 8.77"
Barrel Length: 4"
Weight: 2.75 lbs.
Features: The mateba has an all blue finish, solid steel alloy frame and walnut grips
Price: $1,295.00

UBERTI .454 SINGLE ACTION (not shown)

SPECIFICATIONS
Caliber: .454
Barrel Lengths: 6", 7.5"
Features: Top ported barrels; satin nickel finish; fully adj. sight; hammer block safety; hardwood grips; wide serrated trigger guard with off-hand finger rest for two-handed hold
Price: $869.00

AMERICAN DERRINGER PISTOLS

MODEL 1

38 DOUBLE ACTION DERRINGER

SPECIFICATIONS

Calibers: See below
Action: Single action w/automatic barrel selection
Capacity: 2 shots **Barrel Length:** 3"
Overall Length: 4.82" **Weight:** 15 oz. (in 45 Auto)
Calibers:

22 Long Rifle w/rosewood grips	$260.00
22 Magnum	265.00
10mm Auto	280.00
223	420.00
32 Magnum/S&W Long	265.00
32-20	260.00
357 Magnum w/rosewood grips	275.00
357 Maximum w/rosewood grips	285.00
9mm Luger, 38 Special w/rosewood grips	260.00
38 Super w/rosewood grips	275.00
38 Special +P+ (Police)	268.00
38 Special Shot Shells	275.00
38 Special	260.00
380 Auto	255.00
40 S&W, 45 Auto, 30 M-1 Carbine	275.00
45 Colt	325.00
45/.410	338.00
45-70 (single shot)	327.00
44-40 Win., 44 Special	338.00
45 Win. Mag., 44 Magnum, 41 Magnum	400.00
30-30 Win., Comm. Ammo dual calibers	400.00
Engraved Series	1,317.00

MODEL 7 ULTRA LIGHTWEIGHT SINGLE ACTION (7.5 oz.) (not shown)

22 LR, 22 Mag. Rimfire, 32 Mag./32 S&W Long, 38 Special, 380 Auto	$265.00
44 Special	505.00

MODEL 8 TARGET (not shown)

45/410	$425.00
Engraved	1,917.00

SPECIFICATIONS

Calibers: See below **Capacity:** 2 shots **Barrel Length:** 3"
Overall Length: 4.85" **Weight:** 14.5 oz. **Height:** 3.3" **Width:** 1.1"
Finish: Stainless steel **Safety:** Hammerblock thumb
Calibers:

22 LR, 38 Special	$325.00
9mm Luger	335.00
357 Magnum, 40 S&W	365.00

MODEL 6 STAINLESS STEEL DOUBLE DERRINGER

SPECIFICATIONS

Calibers: See below **Capacity:** 2 shots **Barrel Length:** 6"
Overall Length: 8.2" **Weight:** 21 oz.
Calibers:

22 Win. Mag.	$365.00
357 Mag.	365.00
45 Auto	365.00
45/.410, 45 Colt	375.00

MODEL 10 STAINLESS STEEL BARREL (10 oz.) (not shown)

38 Special	$245.00
45 Auto	270.00
45 Colt	325.00

MODEL 11 LIGHTWEIGHT DOUBLE DERRINGER (11 oz.) (not shown)

22 LR, 22 Mag. Rim., 32 Mag./SW, 38 Special, 380 Auto	$250.00

AMERICAN DERRINGER PISTOLS

MODEL 4

MODEL 4 STAINLESS STEEL DOUBLE DERRINGER

SPECIFICATIONS
Calibers: 45 Colt and 3" .410 *Capacity:* 2 shots
Barrel Length: 4.1" *Overall Length:* 6"
Weight: 16.5 oz.
Finish: Satin or high-polish stainless steel
Price: $357.00
Also available:
In 357 Mag.. . . . . $350.00
  357 Maximum 355.00
In 45-70, both barrels 500.00
In 44 Mag. w/oversized grips 445.00
  45/410. . . . . 365.00
  45 Automatic 355.00
MODEL M-4 ALASKAN SURVIVAL
  in 45-70/45-.410, 45-70/45 Colt 400.00
ENGRAVED SERIES. 1,717.00
SEMMERLONG LM-4 (not shown)
  45 ACP. 2,500.00

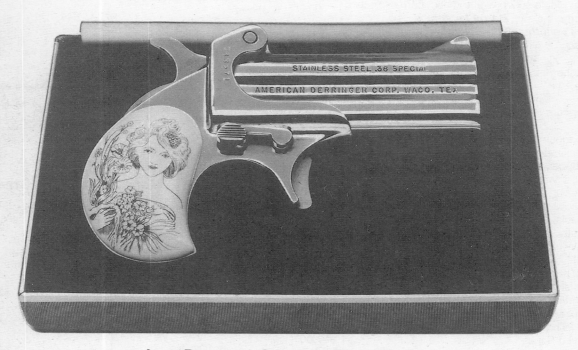

LADY DERRINGER STAINLESS STEEL DOUBLE

LADY DERRINGER (Stainless Steel Double)

Calibers:
38 Special $290.00
32 Mag. 305.00
357 Mag. 335.00
45 Colt, 45/410 . . . . 365.00

TEXAS DOUBLE DERRINGER COMMEMORATIVE (not shown)

Calibers:
38 Special (Brass) $295.00
45 Colt (Brass). 380.00
45 Colt Brass Frame Special SN. 405.00
44-40 (Brass). 350.00

AMT PISTOLS

BACKUP DAO

SPECIFICATIONS
Calibers: 357 SIG, 380 ACP (9mm Short), 38 Super, 400 Corbon, 40 S&W, 45 ACP
Capacity: 5-shot (40 S&W, 45 ACP); 6-shot (other calibers)
Barrel length: 3" *Overall length:* 5.75"
Weight: 23 oz. *Width:* 1"
Features: Locking-barrel action, checkered fiberglass grips, grooved slide sight
Prices:
In 380 ACP, 40 S&W, 45 ACP, 9mm $319.00
In 38 Super, 357 Sig. 400 Corbon 369.00

BACKUP
(380 OR 9mm SHORT)

380 BACKUP II

SPECIFICATIONS
Caliber: 380 ACP
Action: Single
Capacity: 5 shots
Barrel length: 2.5"
Overall length: 5"
Weight: 18 oz. Width: 11/16"
Sights: Open
Grips: Carbon fiber
Price:
Single Action only $369.00

380 BACKUP II

1911 GOVERNMENT
45 ACP LONGSLIDE (not shown)

SPECIFICATIONS
Caliber: 45 ACP *Capacity:* 7 shots
Barrel length: 7" Overall length: 10.5"
Weight: 46 oz. *Sights:* 3-dot, adjustable
Features: Wide adjustable trigger; Neoprene wraparound grips
Price: $459.00

1911 GOVERNMENT MODEL

SPECIFICATIONS
Caliber: 45 ACP
Capacity: 7 shots
Barrel length: 5" *Overall length:* 8.5"
Weight: 38 oz. *Width:* 1.25" *Sights:* Fixed
Features: Long grip safety; rubber wraparound Neoprene grips; beveled magazine well; wide adjustable trigger
Price: $399.00
Also available:
1911 HARDBALLER. Same specifications as Standard Model, but with adjustable sights and matte rib. $425.00
400 ACCELERATOR (7" 400 Corbon barrel) 525.00
COMMANDO (40 S&W 4" barrel) 425.00

1911 GOVERNMENT

AMT PISTOLS

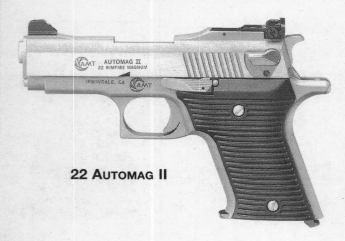

22 AUTOMAG II

22 AUTOMAG II RIMFIRE MAGNUM

The only production semiautomatic handgun in this caliber, the Automag II is ideal for the small-game hunter or shooting enthusiast who wants more power and accuracy in a light, trim handgun. The pistol features a bold open-slide design and employs a unique gas-channeling system for smooth, trouble-free action.

SPECIFICATIONS
Caliber: 22 Rimfire Magnum
Barrel lengths: 3 ³/₈", 4.5" or 6"
Magazine capacity: 9 shots (4.5" & 6"), 7 shots (3 ³/₈")
Weight: 32 oz. (6"), 30 oz. (4.5"), 24 oz. (3 ³/₈")
Sights: Adjustable 3-dot *Finish:* Stainless steel
Features: Squared trigger guard; grooved carbon fiber grips; gas channeling system
Price: $399.00

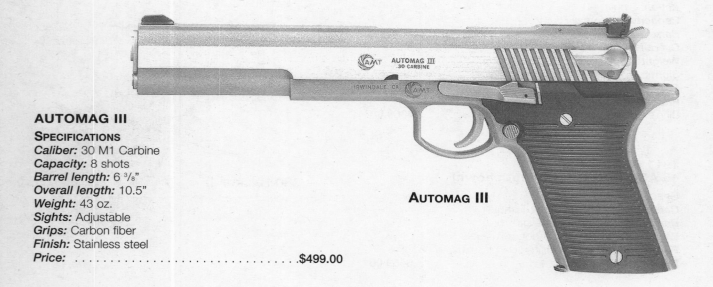

AUTOMAG III

AUTOMAG III
SPECIFICATIONS
Caliber: 30 M1 Carbine
Capacity: 8 shots
Barrel length: 6 ³/₈"
Overall length: 10.5"
Weight: 43 oz.
Sights: Adjustable
Grips: Carbon fiber
Finish: Stainless steel
Price: $499.00

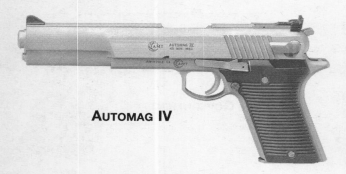

AUTOMAG IV

AUTOMAG IV
SPECIFICATIONS
Caliber: 45 Win. Mag.
Capacity: 7 shots
Barrel length: 6.5"
Overall length: 10.5"
Weight: 46 oz.
Sights: Adjustable
Grips: Carbon fiber
Finish: Stainless steel
Price: $599.00

Auto-Ordnance

MODEL 1911A1
PITBULL

MODEL 1911A1 THOMPSON

SPECIFICATIONS
Caliber: 45 ACP
Capacity: 7 rounds (45 ACP)
Barrel Length: 5"
Overall Length: 8 1/2"
Weight: 39 oz. (with fixed sights)
Sights: Blade front; rear adjustable for windage
Stock: Checkered plastic with medallion
Prices:
45 ACP, blued $425.00
PIT BULL MODEL (45 ACP w/3 1/2" barrel) 474.50
WW II PARKERIZED PISTOL (45 cal. only) 399.95
DELUXE MODEL (45 cal. only) 438.00
  CUSTOM HIGH POLISH. 585.00

MODEL 1911A1
PARKERIZED

MODEL 1911A1
CUSTOM HIGH POLISH
(5" barrel)

BERETTA PISTOLS

COMPACT FRAME COUGAR PISTOLS

MODEL 8000 (9mm) MODEL 8040 (40 CAL.) MODEL 8045 (45 ACP)

Beretta's 8000/8040/8045 Cougar Series semiautomatics use a proven locked-breech system with a rotating barrel. This design makes the pistol compact and easy to conceal and operate with today's high-powered 9mm, 40 cal. and 45 ACP cal. ammunition. When the pistol is fired, the initial thrust of recoil energy is partially absorbed as it pushes slide and barrel back, with the barrel rotating by cam action against a tooth on the rigid central block. When the barrel has turned about 30 degrees, the locking lugs on the barrel clear the locking recesses, which free the slide to continue rearward. The recoil spring absorbs the remaining recoil energy as the slide extracts and ejects the spent shell casing, rotates the hammer, and then reverses direction to chamber the next round. By channeling part of the recoil energy into barrel rotation and by partially absorbing the barrel and slide recoil shock through the central block before it is transferred to the frame, the Cougar shows an unusually low felt recoil.

MODEL 8000/8040 COUGAR

SPECIFICATIONS
Calibers: 9mm, 40 semiauto, 45 ACP
Capacity: 10 rounds (8 rounds in 45 ACP)
Action: Double/Single or Double Action only
Barrel length: 3.6"
Overall length: 7"
Weight: 32.6 oz.
Overall height: 5.5"
Sight radius: 5.2"
Sights: Front and rear sights dovetailed to slide
Finish: Bruniton/Plastic
Features: Firing-pin block; chrome-lined barrel; short recoil, rotating barrel; anodized aluminum alloy frame
Prices:
Double action only (9mm and 40 cal.) $629.00
Double or Single action (9mm and 40 cal.) 651.00
Double action only (45 ACP) 679.00
Double or Single action (45 ACP) 701.00

MODEL 8040 MINI-COUGAR

MODEL 8000/8040 MINI-COUGAR
SPECIFICATIONS
Caliber: 9mm and 40 S&W
Capacity: 10 rounds (9mm); 8 and 10 rounds (40 S&W
Action: Double/Single or Double Action only
Barrel length: 3.6"
Weight: 27.6 oz. (9mm); 27.4 oz. (40 S&W)
Features: One inch shorter in the grip than the standard Cougar
Prices:
Double action only $629.00
Double or Single actions .651.00

BERETTA PISTOLS

SMALL FRAME PISTOLS

MODEL 3032 TOMCAT

SPECIFICATIONS
Caliber: 32 Auto
Capacity: 7-shot magazine
Barrel length: 2.45"
Overall length: 4.9"
Weight: 14 1/2 oz.
Sights: Blade front, drift-adjustable rear
Features: Double or single action, thumb safety, tip-up barrel for direct loading/unloading, blued or matte finish
Prices:
Matte/Plastic $317.00
Blued/Plastic 346.00

MODEL 3032 TOMCAT

MODEL 21 BOBCAT DA SEMIAUTOMATIC
A safe, dependable, accurate small-bore pistol in 22 LR or 25 Auto. Easy to load with its unique barrel tip-up system.

SPECIFICATIONS
Caliber: 22 LR or 25 ACP
Magazine capacity: 7 rounds (22 LR); 8 rounds (25 ACP)
Overall length: 4.9"
Barrel length: 2.4"
Weight: 11.5 oz. (25 ACP); 11.8 oz. (22 LR)
Sights: Blade front: V-notch rear
Safety: Thumb operated
Grips: Plastic or Walnut
Frame: Forged aluminum
Prices:
Matte/Plastic $236.00
Blued/Plastic 266.00
Nickel/Plastic 317.00
Blued/Engraved/Wood 307.00

MODEL 21 BOBCAT

MODEL 950 JETFIRE
SINGLE-ACTION SEMIAUTOMATIC

SPECIFICATIONS
Calibers: 25 ACP
Barrel length: 2.4"
Overall length: 4.7"
Overall height: 3.4"
Safety: External, thumb-operated
Magazine capacity: 8 rounds
Sights: Blade front; V-notch rear
Weight: 9.9 oz.
Frame: Forged aluminum.
Prices:
Matte/Plastic $215.00
Blued/Plastic 236.00
Nickel/Plastic 293.00
Blued/Engraved/Wood 329.00

MODEL 950 JETFIRE

BERETTA PISTOLS

MEDIUM-FRAME CHEETAH PISTOLS

MODEL 84 CHEETAH

This pistol is pocket size with a large magazine capacity. The first shot (with hammer down, chamber loaded) can be fired by a double-action pull on the trigger without cocking the hammer manually.

The pistol also features a favorable grip angle for natural pointing, positive thumb safety (designed for both right- and left-handed operation), quick takedown (by means of special takedown button) and a conveniently located magazine release. Black plastic grips. Wood grips extra.

SPECIFICATIONS

Caliber: 380 Auto (9mm Short). *Magazine capacity:* 10 rounds. *Barrel length:* 3.8". (approx.) *Overall length:* 6.8". (approx.) *Weight:* 23.3 oz. (approx.). *Sights:* Fixed front; rear dovetailed to slide. *Height overall:* 4.85" (approx.).

Prices: Bruniton/Plastic $529.00
Bruniton/Wood 557.00
Nickel/Wood 600.00

MODEL 84 CHEETAH

MODEL 85 CHEETAH (not shown)

Some basic specifications as the model 84 Cheetah, except has a single line 8-round magazine, ambidextrous safety.

Prices: Bruniton/Plastic $500.00
Bruniton/Wood 530.00
Nickel/Wood 559.00
Also available: MODEL 87 in 22 LR. *Capacity:* 8 rounds. Straight blow-back open slide design. *Width:* 1.3". *Barrel length:* 3.8". *Overall length:* 6.8". *Overall height:* 4.7". *Weight:* 20.1 oz. *Finish:* Blued with wood $529.00
Long Barrel (6") Model .529.00

MODEL 86 CHEETAH

SPECIFICATIONS

Caliber: 380 Auto (9mm Short). *Barrel length:* 4.4". *Overall length:* 7.3". *Capacity:* 8 rounds. *Weight:* 23.3 oz. *Sight radius:* 4.9". *Overall height:* 4.8". *Overall width:* 1.4". *Grip:* Walnut. *Features:* Same as other Medium Frame, straight blow-back models, plus safety and convenience of a tip-up barrel (rounds can be loaded directly into chamber without operating the slide).

Price: Bruniton/Wood Grips $530.00
Also available: MODEL 87 CHEETAH (22 LR). Features straight blow-back, open slide design; 7 round capacity; blued finish; wood grips. *Weight:* 20.1 oz.
Price: $529.00

MODEL 86 CHEETAH

MODEL 89 GOLD STANDARD SA

This sophisticated single-action, target pistol features an eight-round magazine, adjustable target sights, and target-style contoured walnut grips with thumbrest.

SPECIFICATIONS

Caliber: 22 LR. *Capacity:* 8 rounds. *Barrel length:* 6". *Overall length:* 9.5". *Height:* 5.3" *Weight:* 41 oz. *Features:* Adjustable target sights, and target style contoured walnut grips with thumbrest
Price: $750.00

MODEL 89 GOLD STANDARD

BERETTA PISTOLS

LARGE FRAME 92/96 SERIES PISTOLS

**MODELS 92FS (9mm)
& 96 (40 Cal.)**

MODEL 92D/96D

MODELS 92FS (9MM) & 96 (40 CAL.)
SPECIFICATIONS

Calibers: 9mm and 40 cal. *Capacity:* 10 rounds
Action: Double/Single *Barrel length:* 4.9"
Overall length: 8.5" *Weight:* 34.4 oz.
Overall height: 5.4" *Overall width:* 1.5" *Sights:* Integral
front; windage adjustable rear; 3-dot or tritium night sights
Grips: Wood or plastic *Finish:* Bruniton (also available in
blued, stainless, silver or gold) *Features:* Chrome-lined
bore; visible firing-pin block; open slide design; safety drop
catch (half-cock); combat trigger guard; external hammer;
reversible magazine release
Also available: MODELS 92D (9mm) and 96D (40 cal.).
Same specifications but in DA only and with Bruniton finish
and plastic grips only. Also features chamber loaded indicator on extractor; bobbed external hammer; "slick" slide
(no external levers).
MODEL CENTURION (9mm and 40 cal.). Same as above but
more compact upper slide barrel assembly.
Barrel length: 4.3". *Overall length:* 7.8". *Weight:* 33.2 oz.
MODEL 92 COMPACT L TYPE M (9mm)
Barrel length: 4.3" *Overall length:* 7.8" *Weight:* 30.9 oz.

MODEL 96 COMBAT/MODEL 96 STOCK
SPECIFICATIONS

Calibers: 40 *Capacity:* 10 rounds *Action:* Single action
only (Combat); single/double (Stock) *Barrel length:* 4.9"
(Stock); 5.9" (Combat) *Overall length:* 8.5" (Stock); 9.5"
(Combat) *Weight:* 35 oz. (Stock); 40 oz. (Combat) *Sights:*
3 interchageable front sights (Stock) *Features:* Rubber
magazine bumpers; replaceable accurizing barrel bushings;
checkered grips; machine-checkered front and backstraps;
fitted ABS cases; Brigadier slide; extended frame-mounted
safety; competition-tuned trigger and adjustable rear target
set and tool set (Combat only)
Prices: MODEL 96 STOCK (double or single action) . . $1,371.00
MODEL 96 COMBAT (single action only) 1,593.00
   w/plastic grip 1,308.00
COMBAT COMBO (4.9" or 5.9" barrels) 1,559.00

Prices: MODEL 92 COMPACT L TYPE M (9mm)
DA OR SA $613.00
   w/Tritium 704.00
DA Only 586.00
   w/Tritium 676.00
MODEL 92FS PLASTIC w/3-Dot sights 613.00
   For wood grips, **add** 22.00
   For tritium sights, **add** 91.00
MODEL 92F Stainless w/3-dot sights 679.00
MODEL 92FS Plastic Centurion
   9mm/40 cal. w/3-dot sights (double action) 586.00
   w/tritium sights (double action) 676.00
MODEL 92D (DA only, bobbed hammer)
   w/3-dot sights 586.00
   w/tritium sights 676.00
MODEL 92F Deluxe gold or silver plated engraved . . 5,434.00
MODEL 96 w/3-dot sights 586.00
w/tritium sights 676.00
MODEL 96D (DA only) 586.00
   w/tritium sights 676.00
MODEL 96 CENTURION 613.00
   w/tritium sights 704.00

MODEL 96 COMBAT

BERNARDELLI PISTOLS

MODEL P.018 TARGET PISTOL

SPECIFICATIONS
Caliber: 9mm
Capacity: 16 rounds
Barrel length: 4.8"
Overall length: 8.25"
Weight: 34.2 oz.
Sights: Low micrometric sights adjustable for windage and elevation *Sight radius:* 5.4"
Features: Thumb safety decocks hammer; magazine press button release reversible for right- and left-hand shooters; hardened steel barrel; can be carried cocked and locked; squared and serrated trigger guard and grip; frame and barrel forged in steel and milled with CNC machines; manual thumb, half cock, magazine and auto-locking firing-pin block safeties; low-profile 3-dot interchangeable combat sights
Prices:
Black Plastic $725.00
Chrome. 780.00

MODEL P.018
TARGET PISTOL

MODEL P.018 COMPACT TARGET PISTOL

SPECIFICATIONS
Calibers: 380, 9mm, 40 S&W (chrome only)
Capacity: 14 rounds
Barrel length: 4"
Overall length: 7.44"
Weight: 31.7 oz.
Sight radius: 5.4"
Grips: Walnut or plastic
Features: Same as Model P.018
Prices:
Black Plastic $725.00
Chrome. 780.00

MODEL P.018
COMPACT TARGET

MODEL P.010 TARGET PISTOL

SPECIFICATIONS
Caliber: 22 LR
Capacity: 5 or 10 rounds
Barrel length: 5.9"
Weight: 40 oz.
Sights: Interchangeable front sight; rear sight adjustable for windage and elevation
Sight radius: 7.5"
Features: All steel construction; external hammer with safety notch; external slide catch for hold-open device; inertia safe firing pin; oil-finished walnut grips for right- and left-hand shooters; matte black or chrome finish; pivoted trigger with adjustable weight and take-ups
Price: $899.00

MODEL P.010
TARGET

BERSA AUTOMATIC PISTOLS

THUNDER 22

SPECIFICATIONS
Caliber: 22 LR
Capacity: 10 rounds
Action: Double
Barrel length: 3.5"
Overall length: 6 5/8"
Weight: 23 oz.
Sights: Notched-bar dovetailed rear; blade integral with slide front; 3-dot
Safety: Manual firing pin
Grips: Black polymer
Prices:
Matte $264.95
Satin Nickel 281.95

THUNDER 22

THUNDER 380

SPECIFICATIONS
Caliber: 380 ACP
Capacity: 7 rounds
Barrel length: 3.5"
Overall length: 6 5/8"
Weight: 23 oz.
Sights: Notched-bar dovetailed rear; blade integral with slide front
Safety: Manual firing pin
Grips: Black polymer
Finish: Blue, satin nickel.
Prices:
Matte $264.95
Satin Nickel 281.95
9-Shot Deluxe 274.95
Also Available:
THUNDER 380 DELUXE (29 oz.; 9 shots)
Price: $274.95

THUNDER 380

SERIES 95

SPECIFICATIONS
Caliber: 380 ACP
Capacity: 7 rounds
Action: Double
Barrel length: 3.5"
Overall length: 6 5/8"
Weight: 23 oz.
Sights: Notched-bar dovetailed rear; blade integral with slide front
Safety: Manual firing pin
Grips: Black polymer
Finish: Matte blue, satin nickel
Prices:
Matte $241.95
Nickel 264.95

SERIES 95

BROLIN ARMS

TAC SERIES

MODEL TAC-11 PISTOL

SPECIFICATIONS
Caliber: 45 ACP *Capacity:* 8+1
Action: Single *Barrel length:* 4" *Overall length:* 8.5"
Weight: 37 oz. *Finish:* Blue, Stainless or Two-Tone
Features: Signature wood grip; beveled magazine well; beavertail grip safety; adj. rear sight; black ramp front sight; recoil guide rod; adj. aluminum match trigger; slotted commander hammer
Prices: $919.00
Stainless or Two-Tone 929.00

TAC SERIES

GOLD SERIES

GOLD MODEL .45ACP

SPECIFICATIONS
Caliber: 45 ACP *Capacity:* 8+1
Action: Single *Barrel length:* 3.25"
Overall length: 7.5" *Weight:* 33 oz.
Features: Heavy conical lock-up match barrel; orange dovetail front sight, fully adjustable rear sight; slotted commander hammer; beavertail grip safety; checkered wood grip; adj. aluminum match trigger; full length guide rod
Prices: $689.00
Stainless or Blue 709.00
Compact 699.00

MODEL P45C COMP COMPACT

LEGEND SERIES

MODEL L45 STANDARD

SPECIFICATIONS
Caliber: 45 ACP *Capacity:* 7+1
Action: Single *Barrel length:* 5"
Overall length: 8.5"
Weight: 46 oz. *Finish:* Matte blue
Features: Throated match barrel; orange-ramp front sight; white-outlined rear sight; beveled magazine well; checkered walnut grip; aluminum match trigger
Prices: $459.00
Also available:
MODEL 45C COMPACT. Same specifications as the L45 Standard, except with integral conical lock-up.
Price $489.00

LEGEND SERIES L45 STANDARD

BROWNING AUTOMATIC PISTOLS

9MM HI-POWER
SINGLE ACTION

HI-POWER SINGLE ACTION

Both the 9mm and 40 S&W models come with either a fixed-blade front sight and a windage-adjustable rear sight or a nonglare rear sight, screw adjustable for both windage and elevation. The front sight is an 1/8-inch-wide blade mounted on a ramp. The rear surface of the blade is serrated to prevent glare. All models have an ambidextrous safety. See table below for specifications and prices.

HI-POWER SPECIFICATIONS 9mm & 40 S&W

MODEL	SIGHTS	GRIPS	BARREL LENGTH	OVERALL LENGTH	OVERALL WIDTH	OVERALL HEIGHT	WEIGHT*	MAG. CAP.	PRICE
Mark III	Fixed	Molded	4.75"	7.75"	1 $3/8$"	5"	32 oz.	10	$550.95
Standard	Fixed	Walnut	4.75"	7.75"	1 $3/8$"	5"	32 oz.	10	584.95
Standard	Adj.	Walnut	4.75"	7.75"	1 $3/8$"	5"	32 oz.	10	635.95
HP-Practical	Fixed	Molded Rubber	4.75"	7.75"	1 $3/8$"	5"	36 oz.	10	629.95
HP-Practical	Adj.	Molded Rubber	4.75"	7.75"	1 $3/8$"	5"	36 oz.	10	681.95
Silver Chrome	Adj.	Molded Rubber	4.75"	7.75"	1 $3/8$"	5"	36 oz.	10	650.95
Capitan (9mm only)	Adj.	Walnut	4.75"	7.75"	1 $3/8$"	5"	32 oz.	10	692.95

* 9mm weight listed. Overall weight of the 40 S&W Hi-Power is 3 oz. heavier than the 9mm.

MODEL BDM 9mm DOUBLE ACTION

Browning's Model BDM (for Browning Double Mode) pistol provides shooters with convenience and safety by combining the best advantages of double-action pistols with those of the revolver. In just seconds, the shooter can set the BDM to conventional double-action "pistol" mode or to the all-new double-action "revolver" mode.

SPECIFICATIONS
Caliber: 9mm Luger
Capacity: 10 rounds
Barrel Length: 4.73" *Overall Length:* 7.85"
Weight: 31 oz. (empty) *Sight Radius:* 6.26"
Height: 5.45" *Width:* 1.34"
Sights: Low-profile front (removable); rear screw adjustable for windage; includes 3-dot sight system
Finish: Matte blue
Features: Dual-purpose ambidextrous decocking lever/safety designed with a short stroke for easy operation (also functions as slide release); contoured grip is checkered on all four sides

MODEL BDM
9MM DOUBLE ACTION
(SILVER CHROME)

Prices:
Standard $550.95
Practical 570.95
Silver Chrome 570.95

BROWNING AUTOMATIC PISTOLS

MODEL BDA-380

MODEL BDA-380

A high-powered, double-action semiautomatic pistol with fixed sights in 380 caliber.

SPECIFICATIONS
Capacity: 10 shots
Barrel Length: 3 $^{13}/_{16}$"
Overall Length: 6.75"
Weight: 23 oz.
Sights: Fixed
Grips: Walnut
Prices:
Nickel Finish $606.95
Blued Finish. 563.95

BUCK MARK 22 LR SERIES

BUCK MARK STANDARD
(5.5" BARREL)

BUCK MARK PLUS NICKEL

BUCK MARK SPECIFICATIONS

BUCK MARK MODELS	MAG. CAP.	BARREL LENGTH	OVERALL LENGTH	WEIGHT	OVERALL HEIGHT	SIGHT RADIUS	GRIPS	PRICE
Standard	10	5.5"	9.5"	36 oz.	5 $^3/_8$"	8"	Molded Composite, Ambidextrous	$256.95
Micro Standard	10	4"	8"	32 oz.	5 $^3/_8$"	9 $^9/_{16}$"	Molded Composite, Ambidextrous	256.95
Nickel	10	5.5"	9.5"	36 oz.	5 $^3/_8$"	8"	Molded Composite, Ambidextrous	301.95
Micro Nickel	10	4"	8"	32 oz.	5 $^3/_8$"	9 $^9/_{16}$"	Molded Composite, Ambidextrous	301.95
Plus Nickel	10	5.5"	9.5"	36 oz.	5 $^3/_8$"	8"	Laminated Hardwood	342.95
Micro Plus Nickel	10	4"	8"	32 oz.	5 $^3/_8$"	9 $^9/_{16}$"	Laminated Hardwood	342.95
Plus	10	5.5"	9.5"	36 oz.	5 $^3/_8$"	8"	Laminated Hardwood	313.95
Micro Plus	10	4"	8"	32 oz.	5 $^3/_8$"	9 $^9/_{16}$"	Laminated Hardwood	313.95

Finishes are matte blue w/polished barrel flats or nickel plated slide and barrel. Pro Target rear sight and $^1/_8$" wide front sight standard.

BROWNING AUTOMATIC PISTOLS

BUCK MARK BULLSEYE

BUCK MARK
5.5 TARGET

BUCK MARK
SILHOUETTE

BUCK MARK SPECIFICATIONS (cont.)

BUCK MARK MODELS	MAG. CAP.	BARREL LENGTH	OVERALL LENGTH	WEIGHT	OVERALL HEIGHT	SIGHT RADIUS	GRIPS	PRICE
Bullseye, Standard	10	7.25"	11 5/16"	36 oz.	5 3/8"	9 7/8"	Molded Composite, Ambidextrous	$376.95
Bullseye, Target	10	7.25"	11 5/16"	36 oz.	5 3/8"	9 7/8"	Contoured Rosewood	484.95
	10	7.25"	11 5/16"	36 oz.	5 3/8"	9 7/8"	Wraparound fingergroove	484.95
5.5 Field	10	5.5"	9 5/8"	35.5 oz.	5 5/16"	8.25"	Contoured Walnut	411.95
	10	5.5"	9 5/8"	35.5 oz.	5 5/16"	8.25"	Wraparound fingergroove	411.95
5.5 Target	10	5.5"	9 5/8"	35.5 oz.	5 5/16"	8.25"	Contoured Walnut	411.95
	10	5.5"	9 5/8"	35.5 oz.	5 5/16"	8.25"	Wraparound fingergroove	411.95
5.5 Nickel Target	10	5.5"	9 5/8"	35.5 oz.	5 5/16"	8.25"	Contoured Walnut	462.95
	10	5.5"	9 5/8"	35.5 oz.	5 5/16"	8.25"	Wraparound fingergroove	462.95
5.5 Gold Target	10	5.5"	9 5/8"	35.5 oz.	5 5/16"	8.25"	Contoured Walnut	462.95
	10	5.5"	9 5/8"	35.5 oz.	5 5/16"	8.25"	Wraparound fingergroove	462.95
Silhouette	10	9 7/8"	14"	53 oz.	5 5/16"	13"	Contoured Walnut	434.95
	10	9 7/8"	14"	53 oz.	5 5/16"	13"	Wraparound fingergroove	434.95
Unlimited Silhouette	10	14"	14"	64 oz.	5 5/16"	15"	Contoured Walnut	535.95
	10	14"	18 11/16"	64 oz.	5 5/16"	15"	Wraparound fingergroove	535.95
Varmint	10	9 7/8"	14"	48 oz.	5 5/16"		Contoured Walnut	390.95
	10	9 7/8"	14"	48 oz.	5 5/16"		Wraparound fingergroove	390.95
Extra Magazine								24.95

COLT AUTOMATIC PISTOLS

COLT .22 SEMIAUTOMATIC DA

SPECIFICATIONS
Caliber: 22 LR *Capacity:* 10 rounds
Barrel Length: 4.5" *Overall Length:* 8 ⁵/₈"
Weight: 33.5 oz. *Sights:* Fixed
Sight Radius: 5.75"
Grips: Composite Monogrip
Finish: Stainless steel
Price: $248.00
Also Available:
COLT .22 TARGET w/6" stainless steel barrel (10 ¹/₈" overall)
Weight: 40.5 oz. *Sight Radius:* 9.25" *Sights:* Front,
adjustable Patridge; white outline rear
Price: 377.00

.22 SEMIAUTOMATIC DA

M1991A1 MKIV SERIES 80 PISTOLS

SPECIFICATIONS
Caliber: 45 ACP *Capacity:* 7 rounds
Barrel Length: 5" *Overall Length:* 8.5"
Weight: 38 oz. *Sights:* Fixed
Sight Radius: 6.5" *Grips:* Checkered rubber
Finish: Matte blue
Features: Smooth trigger; 4-way safety
Price: $556.00
Also Available:
COMPACT M1991A1 w/3.5" barrel; *Weight:* 34 oz. 556.00
COMMANDER M1991A1 w/4.25" barrel and
    7-round capacity 556.00
Stainless (5" barrel only) 610.00

**M1991A1 MKIV
SERIES 800 Pistols**

COMBAT COMMANDER MKIV SERIES 80

The single action semiautomatic Combat Commander,
available in 45 ACP and 38 Super, features an all-steel frame
that supplies the pistol with an extra measure of heft and
stability. This Colt pistol also offers 3-dot high-profile sights,
lanyard-style hammer and thumb and beavertail grip safety. Also
available in lightweight version with alloy frame (45 ACP only.)

SPECIFICATIONS
Caliber: 38 Super or 45 ACP *Capacity:* 8 rounds
Barrel Length: 4.25" *Overall Length:* 7.75"
Weight: 35 oz. *Finish:* Stainless steel
Features: Firing pin safety; upswept grip safety; extended
manual thumb safety; Hogue grips, lightweight trigger
Price: $813.00
Also Available:
With blue slide, two-tone finish, combat sights,
    stainless steel receiver. 813.00

**COMBAT COMMANDER
4.25" barrel only**

DOWNSIZER PISTOLS

MODEL WSP
"WORLD'S SMALLEST PISTOL"

SPECIFICATIONS
Action: Single-shot double-action only
Caliber: 9mm, 40 S&W, 45 ACP, 357 Mag., 380 ACP,
32 Mag., 22 Mag.
Barrel length: 2.1", tip-up barrel w/o extractor
Overall length: 3.25"
Weight: 11 oz. Height: 2.25"
Width: 0.9"
Materials: Stainless steel; CNC machines from solid bar
stock
Price: $329.00

**"WORLD'S
SMALLEST PISTOL"**

EMF/DAKOTA REVOLVERS

E.M.F. HARTFORD SINGLE-ACTION REVOLVERS

Hartford Single Action revolvers are the most authentic of all the colt reproduction single actions. All parts are interchangeable with the original Colt 1st and 2nd generation revolvers.

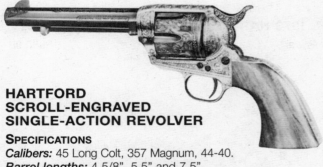

**HARTFORD
SCROLL-ENGRAVED
SINGLE-ACTION REVOLVER**

SPECIFICATIONS
Calibers: 45 Long Colt, 357 Magnum, 44-40.
Barrel lengths: 4 5/8", 5.5" and 7.5".
Features: Classic original-type scroll engraving.
Price: $800.00
Nickel 900.00

**HARTFORD MODELS
"CAVALRY COLT" AND "ARTILLERY"**
The Model 1873 Government Model Cavalry revolver is an exact reproduction of the original Colt made for the U.S. Cavalry in caliber 45 Long Colt with barrel length of 7.5". The Artillery Model has 5.5" barrel.

Price: $700.00
Also available:
SHERIFF'S MODEL (3.5" barrel) $585.00

HARTFORD PINKERTON

SPECIFICATIONS
Caliber: 45 LC *Barrel length:* 4".
Bird's-head grip with ejector tube.
Price: $570.00

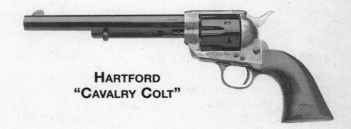

**HARTFORD
"CAVALRY COLT"**

EMF/Dakota Revolvers

E.M.F. Hartford Single-Action Revolvers

1st and 2nd generations models available. Parts are interchangeable with the original Colts. Forged steel frames, case hardened, steel backstrap & trigger guard. Original blue finish, walnut grips. Barrel lengths: 4.75", 5.5", 7.5", 12" buntline.

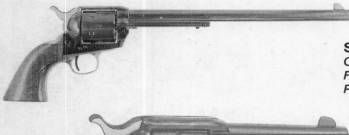

1873 HARTFORD "BUNTLINE"

SPECIFICATIONS
Caliber: 45 LC *Barrel Length:* 12"
Features: Steel backstrap & trigger
Price: $670.00

1873 HARTFORD "SIXSHOOTER"

SPECIFICATIONS
Calibers: 45, 357 Magnum, 44-40 *Barrel Lengths:* 4.75",
5.5", 7.5" *Features:* Brass backstrap & trigger guard
Price: $550.00

1873 HARTFORD COMBO "SIXSHOOTER"

Price: $680.00

1895 HARTFORD "BISLEY"

SPECIFICATIONS
Caliber: 45 LC *Barrel Lengths:* 5.5" & 7.5"
Features: Steel backstrap & trigger guard
Price: $600.00

1893 HARTFORD "EXPRESS"

SPECIFICATIONS
Calibers: 45 LC *Barrel Lengths:* 4.75" & 5.5"
Features: Steel backstrap & trigger guard
Price: $570.00

EMF/DAKOTA REVOLVERS

1873 DAKOTA SINGLE ACTION

SPECIFICATIONS
Calibers: 357 Mag., 44-40, 45 Long Colt. *Barrel lengths:*
4.75", 5.5" and 7.5". *Finish:* Blued, casehardened frame.
Grips: One-piece walnut. *Features:* Classic Colt design,
set screw for cylinder pin release; black nickel backstrap
and trigger design
Price: $400.00

1873 DAKOTA SINGLE ACTION
WITH 5.5" BARREL

MODEL 1875 "OUTLAW" SINGLE ACTION
(not shown)

SPECIFICATIONS
Calibers: 44-40, 45 Long Colt, 357. *Barrel length:* 5.5"
and 7.5". *Finish:* Blued or nickel. *Special features:*
Casehardened frame, walnut grips; brass trigger guard; an
exact replica of the Remington No. 3 revolver produced
from 1875 to 1889.
Price: $575.00

1873 DAKOTA SINGLE ACTION
WITH 7.5" BARREL

1875 REMINGTON SA REVOLVER

MODEL 1875 REMINGTON
SINGLE ACTION REVOLVER

SPECIFICATIONS
Features: Factory engraved; casehardened frame
Price:
Blued $575.00
Nickel 740.00

MODEL 1890 REMINGTON POLICE

MODEL 1890 REMINGTON POLICE

SPECIFICATIONS
Calibers: 44-40, 45 Long Colt and 357 Magnum. *Barrel
length:* 5.75". *Finish:* Blued or nickel. *Features:* Original
design (1891-1894) with lanyard ring in buttstock; casehardened frame; walnut grips
Price: $610.00

ENTRÉPRISE ARMS

ELITE P500

SPECIFICATIONS
Caliber: .45 ACP, 10 round magazine
Barrel: 5" *Weight:* 40 oz. *Length:* 8.5" overall.
Stocks: Black ultra-slim double diamond checkered grip panels
Sights: 3 Dot fixed sights (dovetail cut front sight)
Features: Reinforced dustcover, lowered & flared ejection port, squared trigger guard, adjustable match trigger, bolstered front strap, high grip cut, hardened steel magazine release, high ride beavertail grip safety, steel flat mainspring housing (checkered 20 LPI), checkered slide release, extended thumb lock, EDM skeletonized match hammer & sear, match grade disconnector with polished contact points and Wolff springs throughout.
Price: $739.90

ELITE P500

TACTICAL P500

SPECIFICATIONS
Caliber: .45 ACP, 10 round magazine
Barrel: 5" *Weight:* 40 oz. *Length:* 8.5" overall
Stocks: Black ultra slim double diamond checkered grip panels.
Sights: Tactical Ghost Ring sight or Novak lo-mount sight.
Features: Same as the Elite model plus extended ambidextrous thumb safety, front & rear cocking serrations, full length guide rod, barrel throated & frame ramp polished, tuned match extractor, fitted barrel & bushing, stainless steel firing pin, serrated & ramped front sight, slide lapped frame, de-horned and action set at a crisp 4.5 pounds.
Price: $979.00

TACTICAL P500

BOXER P500

SPECIFICATIONS
Caliber: .45 ACP, 10 round magazine.
Barrel: 5" *Weight:* 40 oz. *Length:* 8.5" overall
Stocks: Black ultra-slim double diamond checkered grip panels.
Sights: Adjustable Competizione "melded" rear sight with dovetail Patridge front sight.
Features: Same as the Elite model plus high mass chiseled slide, sweep cut on slide, machined slide parallel rails with polished breech face & barrel channel, front & rear cocking serrations, lowered & flared ejection port, full length stainless steel one-piece guide rod with plug, National match barrel 5" Government length, match bushing, stainless steel firing pin, match extractor, oversized firing pin stop, fitted barrel & bushing, slide lapped to frame, barrel throated & frame ramp polished, extractor tuned and action set at 4.5 pounds.
Price: $1,099.00
Also available: TITLEIST P500 (45 ACP and 40 cal.) Same as Elite model plus features included above.
Price: $979.00

BOXER P500

ENTRÉPRISE ARMS

MODEL I

TOURNAMENT SHOOTERS MODEL I
SPECIFICATIONS
Caliber: .45 ACP, 40 cal., 38 Super
Barrel: 5" ***Weight:*** 40 oz. ***Length:*** 8.5" overall
Stocks: Black ultra-slim double diamond checkered grip panels
Sights: Adjustable Competizione "melded" rear sight with dovetail Patridge front sight
Features: Same as the Elite model plus oversized magazine release button, ambidextrous thumb lock, flared extended magazine well, fully machined parallel slide rails, polished barrel channel, polished breech face, front & rear cocking serrations, serrated top of slide, stainless steel ramped bull barrel with fully supported chamber, full length stainless steel one piece guide rod with plug, stainless steel firing pin, match extractor, oversized firing pin stop, fitted Bull Barrel, slide lapped to frame, polished ramp, extractor tuned, hard chrome finish and action set at a 2 pounds.
Price: $2,300.00

MODEL II

TOURNAMENT SHOOTERS MODEL II
SPECIFICATIONS
Caliber: .45 ACP, 10 round magazine
Barrel: 6" ***Weight:*** 44 oz. ***Length:*** 9.5" overall
Stocks: Black ultra slim double diamond checkered grip panels
Sights: Adjustable Competizione "melded" rear sight with dovetail Patridge front sight
Features: Same as the Elite model plus oversized magazine release button, ambidextrous thumb lock, front strap checkered (20 LPI), long slide fully machined, parallel slide rails, polished barrel channel, polished breech face, front & Rear Cocking Serrations, lowered & flared ejection port, serrated top of slide, 6" stainless steel national match barrel, national match bushing, full length stainless steel two piece guide rod with plug, stainless steel firing pin, match extractor, oversized firing pin stop, fitted barrel & bushing, slide lapped to frame, barrel throated & frame pamp polished, extractor tuned, black oxide finish and action set at 4.5 pounds.
Price: $2,000.00

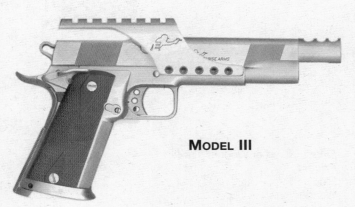

MODEL III

TOURNAMENT SHOOTERS MODEL III
SPECIFICATIONS
Caliber: .45 ACP, 40 cal., 38 Super
Barrel: 6" ***Weight:*** 44 oz. ***Length:*** 9.5" overall
Stocks: Black ultra slim double diamond checkered grip panels
Features: Same as the Elite model plus fitted barrel and compensator, oversized magazine release button, ambidextrous extended thumb lock, extended slide stop, front strap checkered (20 LPI), trigger guard checkered (20 LPI), frame mounted scope base, flared extended magazine well, slide fully machined, seven port cone-style compensator, full length stainless steel one piece guide rod with plug, stainless steel firing pin, match extractor, oversized firing pin stop, slide lapped to frame, extractor tuned, polished ramp, hard chrome finish and action Set at 2 pounds.
Price: $2,700.00

EUROPEAN AMERICAN ARMORY

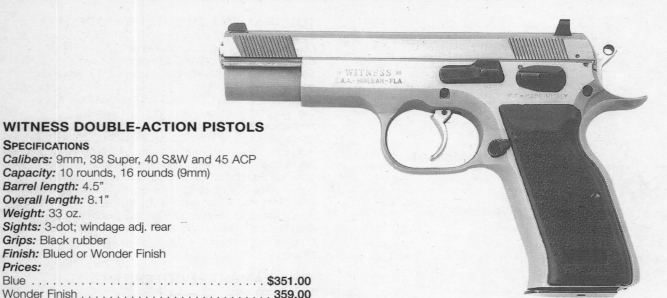

WITNESS DOUBLE-ACTION PISTOLS

SPECIFICATIONS
Calibers: 9mm, 38 Super, 40 S&W and 45 ACP
Capacity: 10 rounds, 16 rounds (9mm)
Barrel length: 4.5"
Overall length: 8.1"
Weight: 33 oz.
Sights: 3-dot; windage adj. rear
Grips: Black rubber
Finish: Blued or Wonder Finish
Prices:
Blue $351.00
Wonder Finish 359.00

WITNESS GOLD TEAM

SPECIFICATIONS
Calibers: 9mm, 40 S&W, 38 Super, 9X21mm, 45 ACP
Capacity: 10 rounds; 16 rounds (9mm); 19 rounds (38 Super)
Barrel length: 5.25" *Overall length:* 10.5"
Weight: 38 oz.
Finish: Hard chrome
Features: Triple chamber comp, S/A trigger, extended safety
competition hammer, checkered front strap and backstrap,
low-profile competition grips, square trigger guard
Price: $2,150.00
Also available:
WITNESS SILVER TEAM. Same calibers as above. Features
double chamber compensator, competition hammer,
extended safety & magazine release, blued finish. *O.A.
length:* 9.75" *Weight:* 34 oz.
Price: 967.45

WITNESS SUBCOMPACT (not shown)

SPECIFICATIONS
Calibers: 9mm, 40 S&W, 45 ACP. *Capacity:* 10 rounds
(9mm); 9 rounds (40 S&W); 8 rounds (45 ACP)
Barrel length: 3.66"
Overall length: 7.24"
Weight: 30 oz.

Finish: Blued or Wonder Finish
Prices:
Blue $351.00
Wonder Finish 365.00
Polymer. 335.00
Ported or Carry Comp 405.00

EUROPEAN AMERICAN ARMORY

EUROPEAN SINGLE ACTION COMPACT

SPECIFICATIONS
Caliber: 380 ACP *Capacity:* 7 rounds
Barrel length: 3.2" *Overall length:* 6.5"
Weight: 26 oz. *Finish:* Blued or Wonder Finish
Features: All-steel construction; automatic ejection; single-action trigger; European wood grips; rear sight adj. for windage; positive sighting system
Prices:
Blued Finish $132.50
Wonder Finish 164.00

EUROPEAN SA COMPACT

WINDICATOR REVOLVER

SPECIFICATIONS
Calibers: 38 Special, 357 Mag. *Capacity:* 6 rounds
Action: Single/Double action *Barrel length:* 2" or 4"
Sights: Fixed (No-Snag) or windage adj. *Finish:* Blued only
Features: Swing-out cylinder; black rubber grips; hammer block safety
Prices:
38 SPECIAL w/2" barrel $170.00
38 SPECIAL w/4" barrel 195.00
357 MAGNUM w/2" barrel 190.00
357 MAGNUM w/4" barrel 233.50

WINDICATOR REVOLVER

BIG BORE BOUNTY HUNTER
SINGLE ACTION

BIG BORE BOUNTY HUNTER
SINGLE ACTION

SPECIFICATIONS
Calibers: 357 Mag., 45 Long Colt and 44 Mag.
Capacity: 6 rounds *Barrel length:* 4.5" or 7.5"
Sights: Fixed *Weight:* 2.45 lbs. (4.5" bbl.); 2.7 lbs. (7.5" bbl.)
Finish: Blued, color casehardened or nickel
Features: Transfer-bar safety, 3 position hammer; hammer-forged barrel; walnut grips (polymer grips optional)
Prices:
Blued or color casehardened receiver $281.00
Also available:
In 22 LR/WMR
   (4.75" or 6.75" barrel) w/blue finish 185.50

SMALL BORE BOUNTY HUNTER
(not shown)

SPECIFICATIONS
Caliber: 22 LR/22 WMR
Capacity: 6 or 8 shots
Action: Single action
Barrel length: 4.75" or 6.75" (8 lands and grooves)
Overall length: 9.5" or 11.5"
Height: 5.25"
Weight: 38 oz. (average)
Grips: European walnut
Sights: Fixed
Finish: Blue or nickel
Features: Transfer bar safety
Prices: $187.20
Nickel 205.00

FEG/INTERARMS

MARK II APK $269.00

SPECIFICATIONS
Caliber: 380 ACP
Capacity: 7 rounds
Action: Single or double action
Barrel Length: 3.4"
Overall Length: 6.4"
Height: 4.7"
Width: 1.2"
Weight: 25 oz.
Sights: Windage-adjustable sights
Features: Grooved non-reflective integral sighting rib; safety acts as decocker; thumbrest target grip and field cleaning rod w/padded carrying case included

MARK II APK

MARK II AP $269.00

SPECIFICATIONS
Caliber: 380 ACP
Capacity: 7 rounds
Action: Single or double action
Barrel Length: 3.9"
Overall Length: 6.9"
Height: 4.7"
Width: 1.2"
Weight: 27 oz.
Sights: Windage-adjustable sights
Features: Same as Model APK

MARK II AP22 (not shown) $269.00

SPECIFICATIONS
Caliber: 22 LR
Capacity: 8 rounds
Action: Single or double action
Barrel Length: 3.4"
Overall Length: 6.3"
Height: 4.2"
Width: 1.28"
Weight: 23 oz.
Finish: Blue
Sights: Windage-adjustable sights
Features: Same as Model APK

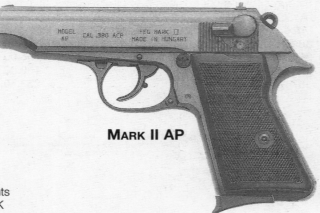

MARK II AP

FREEDOM ARMS

MODEL 1997 PREMIER GRADE
FIXED SIGHT $1361.00
ADJUSTABLE SIGHT $1462.00

SPECIFICATIONS
Caliber: 357 Magnum
Capacity: 6 shots
Action: Single Action
Barrel Lengths: 5.5" and 7.5"
Sights: Removable front blade; adjustable rear; fixed sight
Grips: Impregnated hardwood or optional black micanta

MODEL 1997
PREMIER GRADE

Beretta Sport clothing and accessories shown above.

WITHOUT OUR EXCLUSIVE, ADJUSTABLE STOCK, YOU'RE NOT SHOOTING WHERE YOU'RE LOOKING.

The **Beretta AL390** is the only *semi-automatic* designed with a *fully adjustable stock* so you can fit it to your body type and shooting style...putting your eye right where it belongs for **more instinctive shooting**.

That's just one of the ways the AL390 fits into your hunting plans. Its **proven, state-of-the-art, self-regulating, self-cleaning gas system** gives you all-load versatility, reliability and reduced recoil. Its bore and chamber are **hard chromed for corrosion resistance and long life**. The trigger group is easily removed for cleaning and maintenance.

The AL390's Stock Drop & Cast Spacer System utilizes spacers for quick adjustment of both the vertical and horizontal angles to fit each shooter's size and shape.

A full range of field grade models are available in **12, 20, or 20 gauge youth**

Our unique self-regulating gas system accommodates all loads automatically, for reduced stress and lower felt recoil.

models with *Mobilchoke® barrels* in your choice of gloss, matte, Advantage® camo or synthetic stocks.

Be sure to explore the full line of

For best results, use Beretta Gun Oil.

Beretta Sport clothing and accessories at your Beretta dealer today.

BERETTA

A tradition of excellence since 1526

Beretta U.S.A. Corp., 17601 Beretta Dr., Accokeek, MD 20607, www.beretta.com. For a Beretta Worldwide Catalog of firearms & Beretta Sport clothing and accessories, call 1-800-528-7453 ($3.00 shipping). Visit The Beretta Gallery in New York and Dallas.

AMERICAN EAGLE

YESTERDAY'S TRADITION - TODAY'S TECHNOLOGY

FREEDOM ARMS

MODEL 252 REVOLVER
SILHOUETTE CLASS 10" BARREL

454 CASULL FIELD GRADE

SPECIFICATIONS
Caliber: 22 LR (optional 22 Magnum cylinder)
Barrel Lengths: 5.13", 7.5" (Varmint Class) and
10" (Silhouette Class)
Sights: Silhouette competition sights (Silhouette Class);
adjustable rear express sight; removable front express
blade; front sight hood
Grips: Black micarta (Silhouette Class); black and green
(laminated hardwood (Varmint Class)
Finish: Stainless steel
Features: Dual firing pin; lightened hammer; pre-set
trigger stop; accepts all sights and/or scope mounts
Prices:
SILHOUETTE CLASS (10" barrel) $1564.00
VARMINT CLASS (5.13" & 7.5" barrels) 1499.00
22 MAG. CYLINDER 264.00

SILHOUETTE/COMPETITION MODELS
(not shown)

SPECIFICATIONS
Calibers: 357 Magnum, 41 Rem. Mag. and 44 Rem. Mag.
Barrel Lengths: 9" (357 Mag.) and 10" (41 Rem. Mag., 44 Rem. Mag.)
Sights: Silhouette competition *Grips:* Pachmayr
Trigger: Pre-set stop; trigger over travel screw
Finish: Field Grade
Price: $1417.85

MODEL 353 REVOLVER
FIELD GRADE 7 1/2" BARREL

SPECIFICATIONS
Caliber: 357 Magnum *Action:* Single action
Capacity: 5 shots *Barrel Lengths:* 4.75", 6", 7.5", 9"
Sights: Removable front blade; adjustable rear
Grips: Pachmayr Presentation grips (Premier Grade
has impregnated hardwood grips
Finish: Nonglare Field Grade (standard model); Premier
Grade brushed finish (all stainless steel)
Prices:
FIELD GRADE. $1310.00
PREMIER GRADE 1730.00

MODEL 555
PREMIER GRADE (50 AE)

454 CASULL & MODEL 555
PREMIER & FIELD GRADES

SPECIFICATIONS
Calibers: 454 Casull, 41 Rem. Mag., 44 Rem. Mag. 50 AE
Action: Single action *Capacity:* 5 rounds
Barrel Lengths: 4.75", 6", 7.5", 10"
Overall Length: 14" (w/7.5" barrel)
Weight: 3 lbs. 2 oz. (w/7.5" barrel)
Safety: Patented sliding bar
Sights: Notched rear; blade front (optional adjustable rear
and replaceable front blade)
Grips: Impregnated hardwood (Premier Grade) or rubber
Pachmayr (Field Grade)
Finish: Brushed stainless (Premier Grade); Matte Finish (Field)
Features: Patented interchangeable forcing cone bushing
(optional); ISGW silhouette, Millett competition and express
sights are optional; SSK T'SOB 3-ring or 2-ring Leupold
scope mount optional; optional cylinder in 454 Casull, 45
ACP, 45 Win. Mag. ($264.00)
Prices:
MODEL FA-454AS AND 50AE PREMIER GRADE
W/adjustable sights $1790.00
W/fixed sights 1620.00
44 Remington w/adjustable sights. 1730.00
W/fixed sights 1571.00
MODEL FA-454FGAS FIELD GRADE
With stainless-steel matte finish, adj. sight,
Pachmayr presentation grips $1370.00
W/fixed sights 1218.00
44 Remington w/adjustable sights. 1310.00
MODEL 555 PREMIER 50 Action Express 1790.00
MODEL 555 FIELD 1370.00
MODEL 654 PREMIER (41 Rem. Mag.) 1730.00
MODEL 654 FIELD (41 Rem. Mag.) 1310.00

GLOCK

MODEL 17L COMPETITION

MODEL 19 COMPACT
(Fixed Sight)

SPECIFICATIONS
Caliber: 9mm Parabellum *Magazine capacity:* 10 rounds
(15 and 17 rounds optional)* *Barrel length:* 4"
Overall length: 6.85" *Weight:* 21 oz.
Price: Fixed Sight $646.00
Also available: MODEL 21. *Caliber:* 45 ACP. *Capacity:* 10
rounds (13 rounds optional)*
Price: Fixed Sight $688.00

MODEL 20
SPECIFICATIONS
Caliber: 10mm *Magazine capacity:* 10 rounds (15
rounds optional)* *Action:* Double action *Barrel length:*
4.6" *Overall length:* 7.59" *Height:* 5.47" (w/sights)
Weight: 27.68 oz. (empty) *Sights:* Fixed (adjustable
$29.00 add'l) *Features:* 3 safeties, "safe-action" system,
polymer frame
Price: Fixed Sight $668.00

MODEL 24 COMPETITION
SPECIFICATIONS
Caliber: 40 S&W *Capacity:* 10 rounds (15 rounds optional)*
Barrel length: 6.02" *Overall length:* 8.85" *Weight:* 26.7
oz. (empty) *Safety:* Manual trigger safety; passive firing
block and drop safety *Finish:* Matte (Tenifer process); nonglare
Price: $800.00
w/Compensated Barrel, Fixed Sights 830.00

For law enforcement and military use only

MODEL 17L COMPETITION
SPECIFICATIONS
Caliber: 9mm Parabellum
Magazine capacity: 10 rounds (17 and 19 rounds
optional)*
Barrel length: 6.02"
Overall length: 8.85"
Weight: 23.35 oz. (without magazine)
Sights: Fixed (adjustable rear sights **$28.00** add'l)
Price: Fixed Sight $800.00

MODEL 17 (Not Shown)
SPECIFICATIONS
Caliber: 9mm Parabellum
Magazine capacity: 10 rounds (17 and 19 rounds
optional)*
Barrel length: 4.5" (hexagonal profile with right-hand twist)
Overall length: 7.32"
Weight: 22 oz. (without magazine)
Sights: Fixed (adjustable rear sights **$28.00** add'l)
Price: Fixed Sight $616.00

MODEL 20

MODEL 24 COMPETITION

GLOCK

MODEL 23 COMPACT SPORT/SERVICE MODEL

SPECIFICATIONS
Caliber: 40 S&W *Capacity:* 10 rounds
Barrel length: 4.02"
Overall length: 6.85"
Weight: 21.16 oz.
Price: $616.00
Also available:
MODEL 22 (Sport and Service models)
Caliber: 40 S&W
Capacity: 10 rounds (15 rounds optional)*
Barrel length: 4.5" *Overall length:* 7.32"
Price: Fixed Sight $616.00

MODEL 23

MODEL 29 SUBCOMPACT

SPECIFICATIONS
Caliber: 10 mm auto *Capacity:* 10 rounds
Barrel length: 3.78" *Overall length:* 6.77"
Weight: 24.7 oz. (approx.) *Height:* 4.5"
Finish: Matte (Tenifer process); nonglare
Features: Safe Action trigger system; two magazines
provided
Price: $668.00

MODEL 29

MODEL 26

SPECIFICATIONS
Caliber: 9mm *Action:* DA
Capacity: 10 rounds
Barrel length: 3.47" *Overall length:* 6.3"
Weight: 19.77 oz.
Finish: Matte (Tenifer process); nonglare
Features: 3 safeties; Safe Action trigger system;
polymer frame
Price: $616.00
Also available:
MODEL 27. Same specifications as Model 26 but in
.40 S&W
Capacity: 9 rounds
Price: Fixed Sight $616.00

MODEL 26

MODEL 30 SUBCOMPACT

SPECIFICATIONS
Caliber: 45 ACP
Capacity: 10 rounds (9 round optional)
Barrel length: 3.78"
Overall length: 6.8"
Weight: 24 oz. (approx.)
Height: 4.5"
Finish: Matte (Tenifer process); nonglare
Features: Safe Action trigger system; two magazines
provided; magazine has an extended floorplate that serves
as a finger rest; 6.7-inch slide
Price: $668.00

MODEL 30

HÄMMERLI U.S.A. PISTOLS

MODEL 160 FREE PISTOL
$2085.00

SPECIFICATIONS
Caliber: 22 LR *Barrel Length:* 11.3"
Overall Length: 17.5" *Height:* 5.7" *Weight:* 45 oz.
Trigger Action: Infinitely variable set trigger weight;
cocking lever located on left of receiver; trigger length
variable along weapon axis
Locking Action: Martini-type locking action w/side-
mounted locking lever
Barrel: Free floating, cold swaged precision barrel w/low
axis relative to the hand
Ignition: Horizontal firing pin (hammerless) in line w/barrel
axis; firing pin travel 0.15"
Grips: Selected walnut w/adj. hand rest for direct arm to
barrel extension

MODEL 160
FREE PISTOL

MODEL 162 ELECTRONIC PISTOL
$2295.00

SPECIFICATIONS
Same as **Model 160** except trigger action is electronic.
Features: Short lock time (1.7 milliseconds between
trigger actuation and firing pin impact), light trigger pull,
and extended battery life.

MODEL 162
ELECTRONIC PISTOL

MODEL 208S STANDARD PISTOL
$1925.00

SPECIFICATIONS
Caliber: 22 LR *Capacity:* 8 rounds *Action:* Single
Barrel Length: 5.9" *Overall Length:* 10" *Height:* 5.9"
Weight: 36.7 oz. *Sight Radius:* 8.2"
Sights: Micrometer rear sight w/notch width; adj. for
windage & elevation; standard front blade
Trigger: Adj. for pull weight, travel, slackweight & creep
Safety: Rotating knob on rear of frame

MODEL 208S
STANDARD PISTOL

MODEL 280 TARGET PISTOL
$1565.00 ($1765.00 in 32 S&W)

SPECIFICATIONS
Calibers: 22 LR and 32 S&W
Capacity: 6 rounds (22 LR); 5 rounds (32 S&W)
Action: Single *Barrel Length:* 4.58"
Overall Length: 11.8" *Height:* 5.9"
Weight: (excluding counterweights) 34.6 oz. (22 LR);
   41.8 oz. (32 S&W)
Sight Radius: 8.7" *Sights:* Micrometer adjustable
Grips: Orthopedic type; stippled walnut w/adj. palm shelf
Features: 3 steel & 3 carbon fiber barrel weight; combina-
tion tool; 4 Allen wrenches; dry fire plug; magazine loading
tool; extra magazine
Also available:
MODEL 280 TARGET PISTOL COMBO
With carrying case $2595.00
Conversion Unit (22 LR) 765.00
In 32 S&W. 965.00

MODEL 280
TARGET PISTOL

HARRINGTON & RICHARDSON

MODEL 929 SIDEKICK REVOLVER

SPECIFICATIONS
Calibers: 22 Short, Long, Long Rifle
Action: Single and double action
Capacity: 9 rounds
Barrel Length: 6" (w/sighting rib)
Weight: 36 oz.
Sights: Fixed front; fully adjustable rear
Grips: Walnut finished hardwood; nickel medallion
Finish: High-polish blue
Price: $159.95

**MODEL 929
SIDEKICK**

MODEL 939 PREMIER TARGET REVOLVER

SPECIFICATIONS
Calibers: 22 Short, Long, Long Rifle
Capacity: 9 rounds
Barrel Length: 6"
Weight: 36 oz.
Grips: Walnut hardwood; nickel medallion
Sights: Fully adjustable rear; fixed front
Features: Two-piece walnut-stained hardwood western-styled grip frame profile, transfer bar system; made of high-quality ferrous metals
Price: $184.95

**MODEL 939 PREMIER
TARGET REVOLVER**

**FORTY-NINER CLASSIC
WESTERN REVOLVER**

FORTY-NINER CLASSIC WESTERN REVOLVER

SPECIFICATIONS
Calibers: 22 Short, Long and Long Rifle
Capacity: 9 rounds
Barrel Length: 5.5" or 7.5" (case colored)
Weight: 36 oz. (5.5" barrel); 38 oz. (7.5" barrel)
Sights: Fixed front; drift-adjustable rear
Grips: Two-piece walnut-stained hardwood; nickel medallion
Price: $184.95

SPORTSMAN 999 REVOLVER

SPECIFICATIONS
Calibers: 22 Short, Long, Long Rifle
Action: Single and double
Capacity: 9 rounds
Barrel Lengths: 4" and 6" (both fluted)
Weight: 30 oz. (4" barrel); 34 oz. (6" barrel)
Sights: Windage adjustable rear; elevation adjustable front
Grips: Walnut-finished hardwood
Finish: Blued
Price: $279.95

**SPORTSMAN 999
REVOLVER**

HECKLER & KOCH

MODEL HK USP 9 &40 UNIVERSAL SELF-LOADING PISTOL

SPECIFICATIONS

Calibers: 9mm and 40 S&W *Capacity:* 10 + 1
Operating System: Short recoil, modified Browning action
Barrel Length: 4.25" *Overall Length:* 7.64"
Weight: 1.74 lbs. (40 S&W); 1.66 lbs. (9mm)
Height: 5.35" *Sights:* Adjustable 3-dot
Grips: Polymer receiver and integral grips
Prices:

9mm & 40 S&W	$655.00
W/control lever on right	676.00
Stainless steel	701.00
W/control lever on right	722.00

Also available:
HK USP45 TACTICAL PISTOL
w/cleaning kit & case 965.00

MODEL HK USP45 TACTICAL PISTOL

MODEL USP45 UNIVERSAL SELF-LOADING PISTOL

SPECIFICATIONS

Caliber: 45 ACP *Capacity:* 10 rounds
Action: DA/SA or DAO *Barrel Length:* 4.41"
Overall Length: 7.87" *Height:* 5.55" *Weight:* 1.90 lbs.
Grips: Polymer frame & integral grips
Prices:

Variants* 1, 3, 5, 7, 9	$717.00
Variants* 2, 4, 6, 10	737.00
Stainless steel, **add**	46.00

*Variants refers to availability of control lever options for right- or left-hand shooters
Also available:
in 9mm and 40 S&W. *Barrel Length:* 4.25". *Overall Length:* 7.64". *Weight:* 1.75 lbs. . . . . 685.00 ($706.00 w/control lever on right). Add **$46.00** for stainless steel

MODEL HK USP45 UNIVERSAL SELF-LOADING PISTOL

HK USP COMPACT UNIVERSAL SELF-LOADING PISTOL

SPECIFICATIONS

Calibers: 9mm and 40 S&W *Capacity:* 10 rounds
Operating System: Short recoil, modified Browning action
Barrel Length: 3.58" *Overall Length:* 6.81"
Weight: 1.70 lbs. (40 S&W); 1.60 lbs. (9mm)
Height: 5" *Sights:* Adjustable 3-dot
Grips: Polymer frame and integral grips
Prices:

9mm and 40 S&W	$685.00
W/control lever on right	706.00

Also available:
Same specifications as above but with stainless

steel slide:	731.00
W/control lever on right	752.00

HK USP45 COMPACT UNIVERSAL SELF-LOADING PISTOL

HECKLER & KOCH

HK USP45 MATCH PISTOL

HK USP45 MATCH PISTOL

SPECIFICATIONS
Caliber: 45 ACP
Capacity: 10 rounds
Operating System: Short recoil, modified Browning action
Barrel Length: 6.02"
Overall Length: 9.45"
Weight: 2.38 lbs.
Height: 5.90"
Sights: Adjustable 3-dot
Grips & Stock: Polymer frame and integral grips
Prices:
Blued $1,369.00
Stainless Steel 1,441.00

MARK 23 SPECIAL OPERATIONS PISTOL (SOCOM)

SPECIFICATIONS
Caliber: 45 ACP
Capacity: 10 rounds
Operating System: Short recoil, modified Browning action
Barrel Length: 5.87"
Overall Length: 9.65"
Height: 5.9"
Weight: 2.66 lbs.
Sights: 3-dot
Grips: Polymer frame & integral grips
Price: $2,055.00

MARK 23 SPECIAL OPERATIONS PISTOL (SOCOM)

MODEL P7M8

MODEL P7M8

SPECIFICATIONS
Caliber: 9mmX19 (Luger)
Capacity: 8 rounds
Barrel Length: 4.13"
Overall Length: 6.73"
Weight: 1.75 lbs. (empty)
Sight Radius: 5.83"
Sights: Adjustable rear
Grips: Plastic   *Finish:* Blue or nickel
Operating System: Recoil-operated; retarded inertia slide
Price: $1,187.00

HERITAGE MANUFACTURING

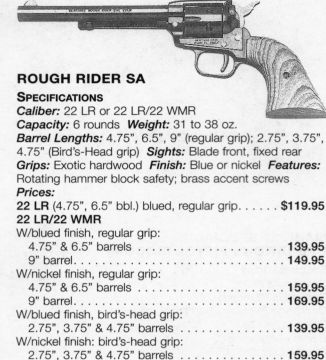

ROUGH RIDER SA

SPECIFICATIONS
Caliber: 22 LR or 22 LR/22 WMR
Capacity: 6 rounds *Weight:* 31 to 38 oz.
Barrel Lengths: 4.75", 6.5", 9" (regular grip); 2.75", 3.75", 4.75" (Bird's-Head grip) *Sights:* Blade front, fixed rear
Grips: Exotic hardwood *Finish:* Blue or nickel *Features:* Rotating hammer block safety; brass accent screws
Prices:
22 LR (4.75", 6.5" bbl.) blued, regular grip. $119.95
22 LR/22 WMR
W/blued finish, regular grip:
   4.75" & 6.5" barrels 139.95
   9" barrel. 149.95
W/nickel finish, regular grip:
   4.75" & 6.5" barrels 159.95
   9" barrel. 169.95
W/blued finish, bird's-head grip:
   2.75", 3.75" & 4.75" barrels 139.95
W/nickel finish: bird's-head grip:
   2.75", 3.75" & 4.75" barrels 159.95

SENTRY DOUBLE ACTION

SPECIFICATIONS
Caliber: 38 Special *Capacity:* 6 rounds *Barrel Length:* 2"
Overall Length: 6.5" *Weight:* 23.1 oz. (with fixed sights)
Sights: Ramped front, fixed rear *Grips:* Black polymer
Finish: Blue or nickel *Features:* Internal hammer block; additional safety plug in cylinder, transfer bar safety.
Prices:
  Blued. **$139.95**
  Nickel 149.95

STEALTH COMPACT PISTOL

SPECIFICATIONS
Caliber: 9mm and 40 S&W
Capacity: 10 rounds
Barrel Length: 3.9"
Overall Length: 6.3"
Weight: 20 oz. *Height:* 4.2"
Triggerpull: 4 lbs. *Frame:* Black polymer
Styles: Model C-1000 17-4 Stainess steel slide; Model C-2000 17-4 Black chrome slide; Model C-1010 17-4 Two-tone stainless steel/black chrome slide
Features: Striker-fire trigger; gas-delayed blow back action; frame-mounted ambidextrous trigger safety; drop safety; closed breech safety; magazine disconnect safety
Prices:
  9mm **$289.95**
  40 S&W. 329.95

MODEL H25S

SPECIFICATIONS
Caliber: 25 ACP
Capacity: 6 rounds
Action: Single
Barrel Length: 2.25"
Overall Length: 4.58"
Weight: 13.5 oz.
Safety: Frame-mounted trigger safety; magazine disconnect safety
Triggerpull: 5 lbs. *Frame:* Black polymer
Features: All-steel frame and slide; exposed hammer
Prices:
  Blued. **$149.95**
  Nickel 159.95

HI-POINT FIREARMS

MODEL 9mm

380 POLYMER

MODEL 9MM

SPECIFICATIONS
Caliber: 9mm Parabellum
Capacity: 9 shots
Barrel length: 4.5"
Overall length: 7.72"
Weight: 39 oz.
Sights: 3-dot type
Features: Quick on-off thumb safety; nonglare military black finish
Price: $139.95

MODEL 380 POLYMER

SPECIFICATIONS
Caliber: 380 ACP *Capacity:* 8 shots *Barrel length:* 3.5"
Price: $79.95
Also available in 45 ACP. Same specifications as the 9mm except w/7-shot capacity and military black finish.
Price: $148.95
MODEL 40 in 40 S&W. Same specifications as the 45 ACP w/8-shot capacity 148.95
MODEL 9mm COMPACT w/3.5" barrel 124.95
Also available w/polymer frame (same price)

HIGH STANDARD

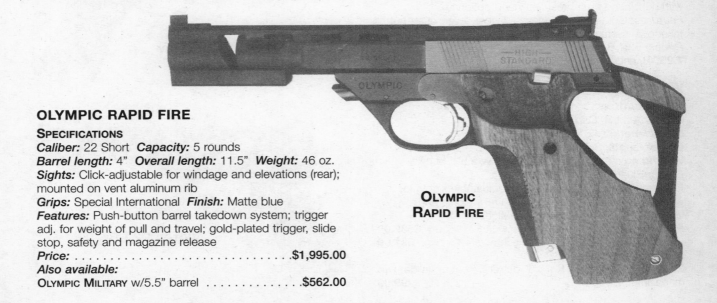

OLYMPIC RAPID FIRE

OLYMPIC RAPID FIRE

SPECIFICATIONS
Caliber: 22 Short *Capacity:* 5 rounds
Barrel length: 4" *Overall length:* 11.5" *Weight:* 46 oz.
Sights: Click-adjustable for windage and elevations (rear); mounted on vent aluminum rib
Grips: Special International *Finish:* Matte blue
Features: Push-button barrel takedown system; trigger adj. for weight of pull and travel; gold-plated trigger, slide stop, safety and magazine release
Price: $1,995.00
Also available:
OLYMPIC MILITARY w/5.5" barrel $562.00

HIGH STANDARD

CITATION

SPECIFICATIONS
Caliber: 22 LR *Capacity:* 10 rounds
Barrel length: 5.5" *Overall length:* 9.5"
Weight: 44 oz. *Finish:* Blued or Parkerized
Features: Optional Universal Mount to replace open-sight rib (deduct $30.00)
Price: $468.00
Also available:
SUPERMATIC CITATION MS. Similar to Citation above, except 10" barrel (14" overall), 54 oz. weight, RPM sights click-adjustable for windage and elevation, checkered right-hand thumbrest and matte blue finish $657.00
TROPHY/CITATION 22 SHORT CONVERSION KIT
(incl. barrel w/sight, slide, 2 magazines) $299.00

CITATION

OLYMPIC

SPECIFICATIONS
Caliber: 22 LR *Capacity:* 10 rounds
Barrel length: 5.5" *Overall length:* 9.5"
Weight: 44 oz. *Finish:* Matte frame
Features: Fully adjustable rear sight; non-adjustable trigger
Price: $590.00

TROPHY

SPECIFICATIONS
Caliber: 22 LR *Capacity:* 10 rounds
Actions: Recoil-operated semiautomatic
Barrel length: 5.5" bull or 7.25" fluted
Overall length: 9.5 (w/5.5" bbl.) and 11.25" (w/7.25" bbl.)
Weight: 44 oz. (w/5.5" bbl.) and 46 oz. (w/7.25" bbl.)
Sights: Click-adjustable rear for windage/elevation; undercut ramp front *Grips:* Checkered American walnut with right-hand thumbrest (left-hand optional)
Features: Gold-plated trigger; slide lock lever; push-button takedown system; magazine release
Prices: 5.5" BARREL $569.00
7.25" BARREL 650.00

OLYMPIC

VICTOR 22 LR

SPECIFICATIONS
Caliber: 22 LR *Capacity:* 10 rounds
Barrel lengths: 4.5" and 5.5"
Overall length: 8.5" and 9.5"
Weight: 45 oz. (w/4.5" bbl.); 46 oz. (w/5.5" bbl.)
Finish: Blued or Parkerized frame
Features: Optional steel rib; click-adjustable sights for windage and elevation; optional barrel weights and Universal Mount (to replace open-sight rib)
Prices: $532.00
  w/5.5" barrel 591.00
Also available:
22 SHORT CONVERSION KIT 5.5" barrel w/vent rib, slide, two magazines $299.00

TROPHY

VICTOR 22 LR

ISRAEL ARMS & FIREARMS INT'L

M-1500

SPECIFICATIONS
Caliber: 9mm, 40 S&W
Capacity: 10 rounds
Barrel Length: 3.9"
Overall Length: 6"
Height: 5.1"
Weight: 32.2 oz.
Features: Ambidextrous safety; rubberized grips;
41/40 steel; extended hammer protection; improved
trigger guard
Price: $450.00

M-1500

M-5000

SPECIFICATIONS
Caliber: 45 ACP
Capacity: 8 rounds
Barrel Length: 4.25"
Overall Length: 6"
Height: 5.25"
Weight: 42 oz.
Finish: Blued and satin
Sights: Low-profile fixed three-dot configuration
Features: Slide grooved across top; competition
trigger, hammer and slide stop; wraparound combat-
style grips
Price: $480.00

M-5000

M-2500

SPECIFICATIONS
Calibers: 9mm, 40 S&W
Capacity: 10 rounds
Barrel Length: 3.9"
Overall Length: 7"
Height: 5.4"
Weight: 34 oz.
Features: Double action; forged steel slide; ambidextrous
controls; drop proof safety; chromed barrel; internal
automatic safety
Price: $649.50
Also available:
In 45 ACP, 8 shots, 4.25" barrel (7.75" overall), weight 36
oz. rubberized wraparound grip, forged-steel frame and
slide, competition trigger, hammer, slide stop, standard
two-tone.
Price: $525.00

M-2500

JENNINGS FIREARMS

T-22 Target Pistol

SPECIFICATIONS
Caliber: 22 *Capacity:* 10 rounds *Barrel length:* 5"
Weight: 28 oz. *Sights:* Screw adjustable sights; red front
Features: Steel thumb safety on left grip blocks sear, locks
side and becomes slide hold open after last round; red
loaded chamber indicator; serrated trigger; quick magazine
release
Price: $90.00

LAZER NINE (not shown)
SPECIFICATIONS
Caliber: 9mm *Capacity:* 7 shots
Overall length: 6"
Height: 4" *Weight:* 14 oz.
Sights: Laser sights
Features: Polymer frame; slide hold open; locked breech;
extra 7-shot magazine
Price: $170.00

JENNINGS NINE (not shown)
SPECIFICATIONS
Caliber: 9mm
Capacity: 12 rounds (law enforcement only)
Barrel length: 6.7"
Height: 4.8" *Weight:* 30 oz.
Sights: Red front sight
Features: Serrated target trigger; slide hold open (last
round); internal drop safety; improved grip contour; loaded
chamber indicator; screw adjustment sight; internal drop
safety; quick magazine release
Price: $90.00

KAHR ARMS

MODEL K9 PISTOL

All key components of the Kahr K9-
frame, slide, barrel, etc. are made
from 4140 steel, allowing the pistol to
chamber reliably and fire virtually any
commercial 9mm ammo, including +P
rounds. The frame and sighting surfaces
are matt blued, and the sides of the slide
carry a polished blue finish.

SPECIFICATIONS
Caliber: 9mm (9x19), 40 S&W *Capacity:* 7 rounds (6
rounds 40 S&W) *Barrel length:* 3.5" *Overall length:* 6"
(6.1" 40 S&W) *Height:* 4.5" (4.55" 40 S&W) *Weight
(empty):* 25 oz.; 26 oz. (40 S&W) *Grips:* Wraparound soft

polymer *Sights:* Drift-adjustable, low-profile white bar-dot
combat sights *Finish:* Nonglare matte black finish on
slide, frame sighting surfaces, electroless nickel, black titanium, satin hard chrome (matte black, electroless nickel
only in 40 S&W) *Features:* Trigger cocking safety; passive
firing-pin block; no magazine disconnect; locked breech
Also available: MODEL MK9 MICRO-COMPACT 9mm.
Overall length: 5.5" *Barrel length:* 3" *Weight:* 22 oz.
Price: $605.00
w/night sights 692.00
In duo-tone 749.00
w/night sights 836.00

Prices: **K9 PISTOL**
Matte black $538.00
Matte black w/night sights 624.00
Matte electroless nickel 612.00
Electroless nickel w/night sights 699.00
Black titanium 664.00
Black titanium w/night sights 750.00
Matte stainless 588.00
w/night sights 675.00

Prices: **LADY K9**
Lightened recoil spring, matte black 545.00
W/night sights 631.00
Satin electroless nickel 619.00
Electroless nickel w/night sights 706.00

KBI HANDGUNS

FEG SMC AUTO PISTOL

SPECIFICATIONS
Calibers: 380 ACP *Capacity:* 6 rounds
Barrel Length: 3.5" *Overall Length:* 6 ⅛"
Weight: 18.5 oz.
Stock: Checkered composition w/thumbrest
Sights: Blade front; rear adjustable for windage
Features: Alloy frame; steel slide; double action; blue finish; two magazines and cleaning rod standard
Price: $255.00

FEG SMC-22

FEG MODEL PJK-9HP (HI-POWER)

SPECIFICATIONS
Caliber: 9mm Luger Parabellum
Magazine capacity: 10 rounds
Action: Single *Barrel Length:* 4.75"
Overall Length: 8" *Weight:* 21 oz.
Grips: Hand-checkered walnut *Safety:* Thumb safety
Sights: 3-dot system *Finish:* Blue
Features: One 10-round magazine, cleaning rod
Price: $269.00

**FEG MODEL
PJK-9HP**

FEG MODEL SMC-380

SPECIFICATIONS
Calibers: 380 ACP *Capacity:* 6 rounds
Action: Double *Barrel Length:* 3.5"
Overall Length: 6 ⅛" *Weight:* 18.5 oz.
Safety: Thumb safety w/decocking
Grips: Black composite
Features: High-luster blued steel slide; blue anodized aluminum alloy frame
Price: $255.00

**FEG MODEL
SMC-380**

ARMSCOR MODEL M-200DC REVOLVERS

SPECIFICATIONS
Calibers: 38 Special *Capacity:* 6 rounds
Action: Double *Barrel Lengths:* 2.5", 4", 6"
Overall Lengths: 7 ⅜", 9", 11 ⅜"
Weight: 22 oz. (2.5"), 28 oz. (4"), 34 oz. (6")
Finish: Blued
Features: Serrated target hammer spur; floating-type firing pin (mounted in frame); transfer bar safety; full shroud; combat style rubber grips (Model M-200 DC) or checkered wood grips (Model M-200TC)
Price: 2.5" barrel $199.00
4" barrel 205.00
6" barrel 215.00

**ARMSCOR MODEL
M-200DC/TC**

KIMBER PISTOLS

CUSTOM
$657.00

CUSTOM STAINLESS
$774.00

SPECIFICATIONS .45 CUSTOM SERIES

	BARREL LENGTH	FINISH	SIGHTS	SIGHT RADIUS	APPROX. WEIGHT	OVERALL LENGTH	MAGAZINE CAPACITY	GRIPS
CUSTOM	5"	Matte Black Oxide	McCormick Low Profile Combat	6.7"	38 oz.	8.7"	7	Black Synthetic
CUSTOM STAINLESS	5"	Satin Stainless Steel	McCormick Low Profile Combat	6.7"	38 oz.	8.7"	7	Black Synthetic
CUSTOM ROYAL	5"	Highly Polished Blue	McCormick Low Profile Combat	6.7"	38 oz.	8.7"	7	Hand Checkered Rosewood
CUSTOM WALNUT	5"	Matte Black Oxide	McCormick Low Profile Combat	6.7"	38 oz.	8.7"	7	Hand Checkered Walnut

CUSTOM WALNUT (NOT SHOWN) – **$670.00**

CUSTOM ROYAL
$787.00

COMPACT STAINLESS
$794.00

SPECIFICATIONS .45 COMPACT

	BARREL LENGTH	FINISH	SIGHTS	SIGHT RADIUS	APPROX. WEIGHT	OVERALL LENGTH	MAGAZINE CAPACITY	GRIPS
COMPACT	4"	Matte Black Oxide	McCormick Low Profile Combat	5.7"	34 oz.	7.7"	7	Black Synthetic
COMPACT STAINLESS	4"	Satin Stainless Steel	McCormick Low Profile Combat	5.7"	34 oz.	7.7"	7	Black Synthetic
CUSTOM ALUMINUM	4"	Matte Black	McCormick Low Profile Combat	5.7"	28 oz.	7.7"	7	Black Synthetic

COMPACT (NOT SHOWN) – **$677.00** **COMPACT ALUMINUM** (NOT SHOWN) – **$677.00**

KIMBER PISTOLS

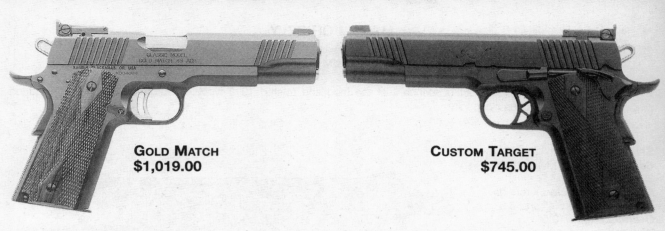

GOLD MATCH
$1,019.00

CUSTOM TARGET
$745.00

SPECIFICATIONS

	BARREL LENGTH	FINISH	SIGHTS	SIGHT RADIUS	APPROX. WEIGHT	OVERALL LENGTH	MAGAZINE CAPACITY	GRIPS
CUSTOM TARGET	5"	Matte Black Oxide	Kimber Adjustable	6.7"	38 oz.	8.7"	7	Black Synthetic
STAINLESS TARGET	5"	Satin Stainless Steel	Kimber Adjustable	6.7"	38 oz.	8.7"	7	Black Synthetic
GOLD MATCH	5"	Highly Polished Blue	Kimber Adjustable	6.7"	38 oz.	8.7"	8	Hand Checkered Rosewood
STAINLESS GOLD MATCH	5"	Highly Polished Stainless Steel	Kimber Adjustable	6.7"	38 oz.	8.7"	8	Hand Checkered Rosewood

STAINLESS TARGET (NOT SHOWN) – **$863.00** **STAINLESS GOLD MATCH** (NOT SHOWN) – **$1,168.00**

POLYMER
$869.00

POLYMER TARGET
$957.00

SPECIFICATIONS .45 POLYMERS

	BARREL LENGTH	FINISH	SIGHTS	SIGHT RADIUS	APPROX. WEIGHT	OVERALL LENGTH	MAGAZINE CAPACITY	GRIPS
POLYMER	5"	Matte Black Oxide	McCormick Low Profile Combat	6.7"	34 oz.	8.75"	14	N/A
POLYMER STAINLESS	5"	Satin Stainless Steel Slide	McCormick Low Profile Combat	6.7"	34 oz.	8.75"	14	N/A
POLYMER TARGET	5"	Matte Black Oxide Slide	McCormick Low Profile Combat	6.7"	34 oz.	8.75"	14	N/A
POLYMER STAINLESS TARGET	5"	Satin Stainless Steel Slide	McCormick Low Profile Combat	6.7"	34 oz.	8.75"	14	N/A

POLYMER STAINLESS (NOT SHOWN) – **$948.00** **POLYMER STAINLESS TARGET** (NOT SHOWN) – **$1,036.00**

L.A.R. GRIZZLY

MARK I GRIZZLY
45 WIN MAG $1000.00
357 MAGNUM $1014.00

This semiautomatic pistol is a direct descendant of the tried and trusted 1911-type .45 automatic, but with the added advantage of increased caliber capacity.

SPECIFICATIONS
Calibers: 45 Win. Mag., 45 ACP, 357 Mag., 10mm
Magazine Capacity: 7 rounds
Barrel Lengths: 5.4" and 6.5"
Overall Length: 10.5"
Weight (empty): 48 oz.
Height: 5.75"
Sights: Fixed, ramped blade (front); fully adjustable for elevation and windage (rear)
Grips: Checkered rubber, nonslip, combat-type
Safeties: Grip depressor, manual thumb, slide-out -of-battery disconnect
Materials: Mil spec 4140 steel slide and receiver with non-corrosive, heat-treated, special alloy steels for other parts. All models available in blue, Parkerized, chrome, two-tone or nickel.
Also available:
GRIZZLY WIN MAG CONVERSION UNITS
  In 45 Win. Mag., 45 ACP, 10mm $233.00
  In 357 Magnum 248.00
WIN MAG COMPENSATOR 119.00
  In 50 caliber 130.00

L.A.R. GRIZZLY
MARK I

GRIZZLY MARK V

SPECIFICATIONS
Caliber: 50 AE
Capacity: 6 rounds
Barrel Lengths: 5.4" and 6.5"
Overall Length: 10 5/8"
Weight: 56 oz.
Height: 5.75"
Sights: Fixed front; fully adjustable rear
Features: Browning–type short recoil; locked breech
Conversion Units available in: 44 Mag., 45 Win. Mag., 45 ACP, 357/45 Win. Mag.
Price: $1,152.00

L.A.R. GRIZZLY
MARK V

LASERAIM ARMS

**LASERAIM
SERIES I PISTOLS**

The Series I pistol features a dual port compensated barrel and vented slide to reduce recoil and improve control. Other features include stainless-steel construction, ramped barrel, accurized barrel bushing and fixed sights (Laseraim's "HOT-DOT" sight or Auto Illusion electronic red dot sight available as options).

SPECIFICATIONS
Calibers: 45 ACP, 10mm, 40 S&W, 400 Cor-Bon
Capacity: 7+1 (45 ACP) and 8+1 (10mm)
Barrel Lengths: 3 7/8" and 5.5"
Overall Length: 8.75" (3 7/8") and 10.5"
Weight: 46 oz. (3 7/8") and 52 oz.
Features: Adjustable Millet sights, ambidextrous safety, beavertail tang, non-glare slide serration, beveled magazine well, extended slide release
Price: **$399.00**
Also available:
DREAM TEAM w/Laseraim Laser, fixed sights,
   HOTDOT **$549.00**

**LASERAIM
SERIES III PISTOLS**

LASERAIM VELOCITY 400 HIGH SPEED SERIES
This all-stainless steel line of handguns features an extended slide release, skeletonized hammer and safety, and a ser rated slide. These improvements lower overall weight and reduce action time. Available in ported full-size and non-ported compact versions in the popular 357 SIG and 400 COR-BON calibers.

The **VELOCITY 400** model features the new 400 COR-BON (a 45 ACP necked down to 40 S&W), adding to its speed and stopping power by 60 percent. Available in 3 5/8" and 5" barrels.

Prices:
3 5/8" barrel **$349.00**
5" barrel 349.00

LLAMA AUTOMATIC PISTOLS

MICRO-MAX 380 AUTOMATIC

LLAMA CLASSIC AUTOMATIC PISTOL SPECIFICATIONS (prices on following page)

SPECIFICATIONS:	MICRO-MAX	COMPACT-FRAME	GOVERNMENT MODEL
CALIBERS:	380 Auto	45 Auto	45 Auto
FRAME:	Precision machined from high-strength steel	Precision machined from high-strength steel	Precision machined from high-strength steel
TRIGGER:	Serrated	Serrated	Serrated
HAMMER:	External; wide spur, serrated	External; military style	External; military style
OPERATION:	Straight blow-back	Locked breech	Locked breech
LOADED CHAMBER INDICATOR:	Yes	Yes	Yes
SAFETIES:	Extended manual & grip safeties	Extended manual & beavertail grip safeties	Extended manual & beavertail grip safeties
GRIPS:	Matte black polymer	Anatomically designed rubber grips	Anatomically designed rubber grips
SIGHTS:	Patridge-type front; square-notch rear	3-dot combat sight	3-dot combat sights
SIGHT RADIUS:	4 1/4"	6 1/4"	6 1/4"
MAGAZINE CAPACITY:	7 shots	10 shots	10 shots
WEIGHT:	23 oz.	39 oz.	41 oz.
BARREL LENGTH:	3 11/16"	4 1/4"	5 1/8"
OVERALL LENGTH:	6 1/2"	7 7/8"	8 1/2"
HEIGHT:	4 3/8"	5 7/16"	5 5/16"
FINISH:	Standard; Non-glare combat matte. Deluxe: Satin chrome, Duo-tone	Non-glare combat matte, Satin chrome	Non-glare combat matte Satin chrome, Duo-tone

LLAMA PISTOLS

MICRO-MAX/MINI-MAX/MAX-I AUTO PISTOLS

MATTE FINISH
380 Auto 7-Shot $264.95
380 Auto 7-Shot Ultra Lite 249.95
9mm Auto 8-Shot Mini Compact 281.95
40 S&W Auto 7-Shot Mini Compact 281.95
45 Auto 6-Shot Mini Compact 281.95
45 Auto 7-Shot Gov't Model. 291.95

SATIN CHROME FINISH
380 Auto 7-Shot $281.95
9mm Auto 8-Shot Mini Compact 304.95
40 S&W Auto 7-Shot Mini Compact 304.95
45 Auto 6-Shot Mini Compact 304.95
45 Auto 7-Shot Gov't Model. 314.95

DUO-TONE FINISH
45 Auto 7-Shot Gov't Model. $296.95
45 Auto 6-Shot Mini Compact Model 298.95

MINIMAX-II 45

	MAX-I 9-SHOT 9MM		MAXI-I 7-SHOT 45 AUTO	
	COMPACT FRAME	**GOVERNMENT MODEL**	**COMPACT FRAME**	**GOVERNMENT MODEL**
CALIBERS:	9 mm	9 mm	45 Auto	45 Auto
MAG. CAPACITY:	9	9	7	7
ACTION:	Single	Single	Single	Single
OPERATION:	Locked breech	Locked breech	Locked breech	Locked breech
BARREL LENGTH:	4 1/4"	5 1/8"	4 1/4"	5 1/8"
OVERALL LENGTH:	7 7/8"	8 1/2"	7 7/8"	8 1/2"
WEIGHT:	34 oz.	36 oz.	34 oz.	36 oz.
HEIGHT:	5 7/16"	5 7/16"	5 7/16"	5 5/16"
FRAME:	Precision machined from high-strength steel		Precision machined from high-strength steel	
TRIGGER:	Serrated	Serrated	Serrated	Serrated
HAMMER:	Skeletonized combat-style		Skeletonized combat-style	
LOADED CHAMBER INDICATOR:	Yes	Yes	Yes	Yes
SAFETIES:	Extended manual & beavertail grip safeties		Extended manual & beavertail grip safeties	
SIGHTS:	3-dot combat sights		3-dot combat sights	
SIGHT RADIUS:	6 1/4"	6 1/4"	6 1/4"	6 1/4"
GRIPS:	Anatomically designed rubber grips		Anatomically designed rubber grips	
FINISH:	Non-glare combat matte.		Non-glare combat matte	

AMERICAN EAGLE LUGER

AMERICAN EAGLE LUGER®

9mm AMERICAN EAGLE LUGER®
STAINLESS STEEL

It is doubtful that there ever was a pistol created that evokes the nostalgia or mystique of the Luger pistol. Since its beginnings at the turn of the 20th century, the name Luger® conjures memories of the past. Stoeger Industries is indeed proud to have owned the name Luger® since the late 1920s and is equally proud of the stainless-steel version that graces this page.

The "American Eagle" name was introduced around 1900 to capture the American marketplace. It served its purpose well, the name having become legendary along with the Luger® name. The "American Eagle" inscribed on a Luger® also distinguishes a firearm of exceptional quality over some inexpensive models that have been manufactured in the past. Constructed entirely of stainless steel, the gun is available in 9mm Parabellum only, with either a 4" or 6" barrel, each with deeply checkered American walnut grips.

The name Luger®, combined with Stoeger's reputation of selling only quality merchandise since 1918, assures the owner of complete satisfaction.

SPECIFICATIONS
Caliber: 9mm Parabellum
Capacity: 7 + 1
Barrel Length: 4" (P-08 Model); 6" (Navy Model)
Overall Length: 8.25" (w/4" bbl.), 10.25" (w/6" bbl.)
Weight: 30 oz. w/4" barrel, 32 oz. w/6" barrel
Grips: Deeply checkered American walnut
Features: All stainless-steell construction
Price:. $699.00
In matte black 789.00

MAGNUM RESEARCH

MARK XIX COMPONENT SYSTEM

The Mark XIX Component system allows for three caliber changes in two different barrel lengths.

The Desert Eagle Pistol Mark XIX Component System is based on a single platform that transforms into six different pistols–three Magnum calibers, each with a 6-inch or 10-inch barrel. Changin calibers is a simple matter of switching barrels and magazines. (Converting to or from .357 Magnum also involves changing the bolt.)

The barrel design alone sports several improvements. Each barrel is now made of a single piece of steel instead of three. All six barrels, including the optional 10-inch barrels, have a $^7/_8$" dovetailed design with cross slots to accommodate scope rings; no other scope mounts are required. The .50 A.E.'s new 10-inch barrel will fit existing .50s, as well as the new Mark XIX platform.

Hogue soft rubber grips are standard equipment on the new gun. The pistol's well-know gas operation, polygonal rifling, low recoil and safety features remain the same, as do the Mark VII adjustable trigger, slide release and safety levers.

SPECIFICATIONS
Calibers: 357 Magnum, 44 Magnum and 50 A.E.
Capacity: 9 rounds (357 Mag.); 8 rounds (44 Mag.); 7 rounds (50 A.E.)
Barrel Lengths: 6" and 10"
Overall Length: 10.74" (w/6" bbl.); 14.75" (w/10" bbl.)
Weight: 4 lbs. 6.5 oz. (w/6" bbl.); 4 lbs. 15 oz. (w/10" bbl.) (empty)
Height: 6.25" **Width:** 1.25"
Finish: Standard black
Prices:

357 MAG. w/6" barrel	$1099.00
357 MAG. w/10" barrel	1160.00
44 MAG. w/6" barrel	1099.00
44 MAG. w/10" barrel	1160.00
50 A.E. MAG. w/6" barrel	1099.00
50 A.E. w/10" barrel	1160.00

LONE EAGLE

LONE EAGLE SINGLE SHOT BARRELED ACTION
$319.00

This specialty pistol is designed for hunters, silhouette enthusiasts, long-range target shooters and other marksmen. The pistol can fire 15 different calibers of ammo. Available w/interchangeable 14-inch barreled actions. Calibers: 22 Hornet, 22-250, 223 Rem., 243 Win., 30-06, 30-30, 308 Win., 35 Rem., 358 Win., 44 Mag., 444 Marlin, 7mm-08, 7mm Bench Rest., 7.62x39, 260 Rem., 440 Cor-Bon. Features ambidextrous grip, new cocking indicator and lever.

Also available:

Barreled action w/muzzle brake	$418.00
Barreled action w/chrome finish	$359.00
Barreled action w/chrome finish, muzzle brake	$469.00
Ambidextrous grip assembly	$119.00

Magnum Research/ASAI

ONE PRO 45 PISTOL

ONE PRO 45 PISTOL
$649.00

ASIA (Advanced Small Arms Industries) is a Swiss company founded in 1994 and based in Solothurn, an old Swiss City with long tradition in weapon and watch history. All key components of the new **One PRO .45** Series are made from chromium-nickel-molybdenium steel, allowing the pistol to fire any commercially manufactured ammunition, including +P rounds. The **One PRO .45** and **One PRO 400 Cor-Bon** are available with a patented safety system. A decocking lever allows the hammer to be lowered into the safety intercept notch without risk, and a new patented automatic firing pin lock allows the loaded, decocked gun to be carried safely.

SPECIFICATIONS
Caliber: .45 or 400 COR-BON
Capacity: 1
Barrel Length: 3.75" (4.52" in IPSC model)
Overall Length: 7.04"
Height: 5.31"
Weight (empty): 31.1 oz. (23.5 oz. in light alloy frame)
Width: 1.25"

Operation: Short recoil
Trigger Pull DA: 8.6 lbs.
Locking System: Dropping barrel
Features: Conversion kits available (includes recoil spring guide and hard plastic case).
Price: **$249.00**
 in 400 Cor-Bon Non-Compensated **$209.00**

MOA MAXIMUM PISTOLS

MAXIMUM SINGLE SHOT

MAXIMUM

This single-shot pistol with its unique falling-block action performs like a finely tuned rifle. The single-piece receiver of stainless steel is mated to a Douglas barrel for optimum accuracy and strength.

SPECIFICATIONS
Calibers: 22 Hornet to 358 Win.
Barrel Lengths: 8.5", 10.5" and 14"
Weight: 3 lbs. 8 oz. (8.5" bbl.); 3 lbs. 13 oz. (10.5" bbl.); 4 lbs. 3 oz. (14" bbl.)
Prices:
Stainless receiver, blued barrel $740.00
Stainless receiver and barrel 818.00
Extra barrels (blue) 235.00
   Stainless 293.00
Muzzle brake 125.00

NAVY ARMS REPLICAS

1873 SINGLE ACTION

1873 "PINCHED FRAME" SA REVOLVER

1873 COLT-STYLE SA REVOLVER

The classic 1873 Single Action is the most famous of all the "six shooters." From its adoption by the U.S. Army in 1873 to the present, it still retains its place as America's most popular revolver.

Calibers: 44-40 or 45 Long Colt
Barrel Lengths: 3", 4.75", 5.5" or 7.5"
Overall Length: 10.75" (5.5" barrel) **Weight:** 2.25 lbs.
Sights: Blade front; notch rear **Grips:** Walnut
Price: $390.00

1873 U.S. CAVALRY MODEL (not shown)

An exact replica of the original U.S. Government issue Colt Single-Action Army, complete with Arsenal stampings and inspector's cartouche.

Caliber: 45 Long Colt **Barrel Length:** 7.5"
Overall Length: 13.25" **Weight:** 2 lbs. 7 oz.
Sights: Blade front; notch rear **Grips:** Walnut
Price: $450.00

1873 "PINCHED FRAME" SA REVOLVER

A replica of the early "pinched frame" Colt Peacemaker, the first run commercial Single Action manufactured in 1873.

Caliber: 45 Long Colt **Barrel Length:** 7.5"
Overall Length: 13.75" **Weight:** 2 lbs. 13 oz. **Sights:** German siver blade front, U-shaped "pinched-frame" rear notch
Price: $415.00

"FLAT TOP" TARGET MODEL SA REVOLVER (not shown)

A fine replica of Colt's rare "Flat top" Single Action Army revolver that was used for target shooting.

Caliber: 45 Long Colt **Barrel Length:** 7.5"
Overall Length: 12.75" **Weight:** 2 lbs. 7 oz.
Sights: Spring-loaded German silver Patridge front, adjustable notch ear.
Grips: Walnut. **Finish:** Satin stainless
Price: $450.00

NAVY ARMS REPLICAS

1875 SCHOFIELD REVOLVER

BISLEY MODEL SA REVOLVER

1875 SCHOFIELD REVOLVER
A favorite side arm of Jesse James and General George Armstrong, the 1875 Schofield revolver was one of the legendary handguns of the Old West.

Caliber: 44-40, 45 LC
Barrel Lengths: 5" (Wells Fargo Model) or 7" (U.S. Cavalry Model)
Overall Length: 10.75" or 12.75"
Weight: 2 lbs. 7 oz.
Sights: Blade front; notch rear
Features: Top-break, automatic ejector single action
Price: **$795.00**

BISLEY MODEL SINGLE ACTION REVOLVER
Introduced in 1894, Colt's "Bisley Model" was named after the Bisley shooting range in England. Most of these revolvers were sold in the United States and were popular sidearms in the American West at the turn of the century. This replica features the unique Bisley grip style, low-profile spur hammer, blued barrel and color casehardened frame.

Calibers: 44-40 or 45 Long Colt
Barrel Lengths: 4.75", 5.5" and 7.5"
Sights: Blade front, notch rear
Grips: Walnut
Price: **$445.00**

1895 U.S. ARTILLERY MODEL (not shown)
Same specifications as the U.S. Cavalry Model, but with a 5.5" barrel as issued to Artillery units.

Caliber: 45 Long Colt
Price: **$480.00**

New England Firearms

STANDARD REVOLVER
with Swing Out Cylinders

SPECIFICATIONS
Calibers: 22 S, L or LR
Capacity: 9 shots
Barrel Lengths: 3" and 4"
Overall Length: 7" (3" barrel) and 8.5" (4" barrel)
Weight: 25 oz. (3" bbl.) and 28 (4" bbl.)
Sights: Blade front; fixed rear
Grips: American hardwood, walnut finish, NEF medallion
Finish: Blue or nickel
Also available:
In 5-shot, calibers 32 H&R Mag., 32 S&W, 32 S&W Long.
Weight: 23 oz. (3" barrel); 26 oz. (4" barrel). Other
specifications same as above.
Prices:
  Blued finish **$134.95**
  Nickel finish (3" bbl. only) **144.95**
STARTER REVOLVER (pull pin cylinder & lanyard ring) in 22 cal.
Capacity: 5 and 9 shot. *Finish:* Blued
Price: **$104.95**

STANDARD MODEL
(22 LR, 3" BARREL)

ULTRA MAG.

ULTRA MODEL
(6" BARREL)

ULTRA AND ULTRA
MAG. REVOLVERS

SPECIFICATIONS
Calibers: 22 Short, Long, Long Rifle
(Ultra); 22 Win. Mag. (Ultra Mag.)
Capacity: 9 shots (22 LR); 6 shots
(22 Win. Mag.)
Barrel Length: 6"
Overall Length: 11" *Weight:* 36 oz.
Sights: Blade on rib front; fully adjustable rear
Grips: American hardwood, walnut finish, NEF medallion
Finish: Blue
Price: **$169.95**
Also available:
LADY ULTRA in 5-shot 32 H&R Magnum. *Barrel Length:* 3"
Overall Length: 7" *Weight:* 31 oz.
Price: **$169.95**

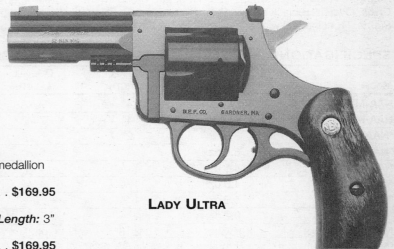

LADY ULTRA

NORTH AMERICAN ARMS

22 LR MINI-REVOLVER
w/NAA HOLSTER GRIP

MINI-REVOLVERS

SPECIFICATIONS (See also table below)
Calibers: 22 Short (1 ⅛" bbl. only), 22 LR and 22 Magnum
Capacity: 5-shot cylinder
Grips: Laminated rosewood
Safety: Half-cock safety
Sights: Blade front (integral w/barrel); fixed, notched rear
Material: Stainless steel
Finish: Matte with brushed sides

NAA .32 GUARDIAN (not shown)

North American Arms' new double-action only autoloading
pocket pistol, weighting only 14 oz., designed for concealed
carry and personal protection. See table below for specifications.

MINI-MASTER NAA-MMT-M
(22 MAG. 4" BARREL)

**MINI-MASTER NAA
BLACK WIDOW**

MINI-MASTER SERIES

SPECIFICATIONS (Standard on all models)
Calibers: 22 LR (NAA-MMT-L, NAA-BW-L) and 22 Magnum
(NAA-MMT-M, NAA-BW-M)
Barrel: Heavy vent
Rifling: 8 land and grooves, 1:12 R.H. button broach twist
Grips: Oversized black rubber *Cylinder:* Bull
Sights: Front integral with barrel; rear Millett adjustable

white outlined (elelvation only) or low-profile fixed
Prices:
MINI-MASTER NAA-MMT-M $292.00
  w/Fixed sight 276.00
MINI-MASTER NAA BLACK WIDOW
  Adjustable sight $259.00
  Fixed sight 243.00

SPECIFICATIONS: MINI-REVOLVERS & MINI-MASTER SERIES

MODEL	WEIGHT	BARREL LENGTH	OVERALL LENGTH	OVERALL HEIGHT	OVERALL WIDTH	PRICE
NAA-MMT-M	10.7 oz.	4"	7 ¾"	3 ⅞"	⅞"	$292.00
NAA-MMT-L	10.7 oz.	4"	7 ¾"	3 ⅞"	⅞"	292.00
*NAA-BW-M	8.8 oz.	2"	5 ⅞"	3 ⅞"	⅞"	243.00
*NAA-BW-L	8.8 oz.	2"	5 ⅞"	3 ⅞"	⅞"	243.00
NAA-22LR**	4.5 oz.	1 ⅛"	4 ¼"	2 ⅜"	¹³⁄₁₆"	162.00
NAA-22LLR**	4.6 oz.	1 ⅝"	4 ¾"	2 ⅜"	¹³⁄₁₆"	162.00
*NAA-22MS	5.9 oz.	1 ⅛"	5"	2 ⅞"	⅞"	184.00
*NAA-22M	6.2 oz.	1 ⅝"	5 ⅜"	2 ⅞"	⅞"	184.00
NAA 32 GUARDIAN	13.5 oz.	2.18"	4.3"	3.23"	.85"	425.00

*Available with Conversion Cylinder chambered for 22 Long Rifle **($281.00)** **Available with holster gip **($195.00)**

PARA-ORDNANCE

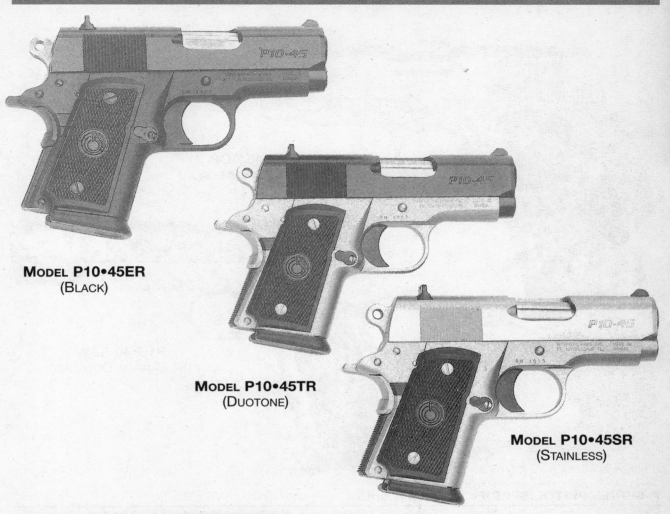

MODEL P10•45ER
(BLACK)

MODEL P10•45TR
(DUOTONE)

MODEL P10•45SR
(STAINLESS)

P-SERIES PISTOL SPECIFICATIONS *(continued on following page)*

MODEL	CALIBER	BARREL LENGTH	WEIGHT (OZ.)	OVERALL LENGTH)	HEIGHT (W/MAG.)	RECEIVER TYPE	MATTE FINISH	PRICES
P10•40ER	40 S&W	3"	31	6 5/8"	4.5"	Steel	Black	$750.00
P10•40RR	40 S&W	3"	23	6 5/8"	4.5"	Alloy	Black	745.00
P10•40TR	40 S&W	3"	31	6 5/8"	4.5"	Stainless	Duotone	785.00
P10•40SR	40 S&W	3"	31	6 5/8"	4.5"	Stainless	Stainless	799.00
P10•45ER	45 ACP	3"	31	6 5/8"	4.5"	Steel	Black	750.00
P10•45RR	45 ACP	3"	23	6 5/8"	4.5"	Alloy	Black	740.00
P10•45TR	45 ACP	3"	31	6 5/8"	4.5"	Stainless	Duotone	785.00
P10•45SR	45 ACP	3"	31	6 5/8"	4.5"	Stainless	Stainless	799.00
P12•45ER	45 ACP	3.5"	34	7 5/8"	5"	Steel	Black	750.00
P12•45RR	45 ACP	3.5"	26	7 5/8"	5"	Alloy	Black	740.00
P12•45TR	45 ACP	3.5"	34	7 5/8"	5"	Stainless	Duotone	785.00
P12•45SR	45 ACP	3.5"	34	7 5/8"	5"	Stainless	Stainless	799.00
P13•45ER	45 ACP	4.25"	36	7.75"	5.25"	Steel	Black	750.00
P13•45RR	45 ACP	4.25"	28	7.75"	5.25"	Alloy	Black	740.00
P13•45TR	45 ACP	4.25"	36	7.75"	5.25"	Stainless	Duotone	785.00
P13•45SR	45 ACP	4.25"	36	7.75"	5.25"	Stainless	Stainless	799.00

For recreational purposes, magazine capacities are restricted to 10 rounds.

PARA-ORDNANCE

MODEL P12•45 ACP
(3.5" BARREL, STAINLESS)

P16•40 S&W
(5" BARREL, DUOTONE)

P-SERIES PISTOL SPECIFICATIONS *(Cont.)*

MODEL	CALIBER	BARREL LENGTH	WEIGHT (OZ.)	OVERALL LENGTH)	HEIGHT (W/MAG.)	RECEIVER TYPE	MATTE FINISH	PRICES
P14•45ER	45 ACP	5"	40	8.5"	5.75"	Steel	Black	$750.00
P14•45RR	45 ACP	5"	31	8.5"	5.75"	Alloy	Black	740.00
P14•45TR	45 ACP	5"	40	8.5"	5.75"	Stainless	Duotone	785.00
P14•45SR	45 ACP	5"	40	8.5"	5.75"	Stainless	Stainless	799.00
P14•40ER	40 S&W	3.5"	34	71/8"	5"	Steel	Black	750.00
P14•40RR	40 S&W	3.5"	26	71/8"	5"	Alloy	Black	740.00
P14•40TR	40 S&W	3.5"	34	71/8"	5"	Stainless	Duotone	785.00
P14•40SR	40 S&W	3.5"	34	71/8"	5"	Stainless	Stainless	799.00
P15•40ER	40 S&W	4.25"	36	7.75"	5.25"	Steel	Black	750.00
P15•40RR	40 S&W	4.25"	28	7.75"	5.25"	Alloy	Black	740.00
P15•40TR	40 S&W	4.25"	36	7.75"	5.25"	Stainless	Duotone	785.00
P15•40SR	40 S&W	4.25	36	7.75"	5.25"	Stainless	Stainless	799.50
P16•40ER	40 S&W	5"	40	8.5"	5.75"	Steel	Black	750.00
P16•40TR	40 S&W	5"	40	8.5"	5.75	Stainless	Duotone	785.00
P16•40SR	40 S&W	5"	40	8.5"	5.75"	Stainless	Stainless	799.00

For recreational purposes, magazine capacities are restricted to 10 rounds.

Also available: P109RR 3" or 5" barrel in 9mm: **$740.00**
P1010SR 10mm w/3" stainless barrel: **$799.00** (**$850.00** w/5" stainless barrel)

ROSSI REVOLVERS

MODEL 720

SPECIFICATIONS
Caliber: 44 S&W Special
Capacity: 5 shots
Barrel Length: 3"
Overall Length: 8"
Weight: 30 oz.
Height: 5.37" (5.15" Model 720C)
Sights: Adjustable rear; red insert front
Finish: Stainless steel
Features: Rubber combat grips; fulll ejector rod shroud;
available in hammerless mode
Price: $290.00

MODEL 720

MODEL 68

SPECIFICATIONS
Caliber: 38 Special
Capacity: 5 rounds
Barrel Lengths: 2" and 3"
Overall Length: 6.87" (2" barrel); 7.87" (3" barrel)
Weight: 22 oz. (2" barrel); 23 oz. (3" barrel)
Grips: Wood or rubber
Finish: Blued or nickel (3" barrel only)
Features: Frames machined from chrome-molybdenum
SAE 4140
Price: $225.00

MODEL 68

MODEL 88

SPECIFICATIONS
Caliber: 38 Special
Capacity: 5 rounds, swing-out cylinder
Barrel Lengths: 2" and 3"
Overall Length: 6.87" (2" barrel); 7.87" (3" barrel)
Weight: 22 oz. (2"); 23 oz. (3")
Sights: Ramp front, square-notched rear adjustable
for windage
Grips: Wood or rubber (2" barrel only)
Finish: Stainless steel
Price: $255.00

MODEL 88

ROSSI REVOLVERS

MODEL 88 "THE LADY ROSSI"

SPECIFICATIONS
Caliber: 38 Special
Capacity: 5 rounds
Barrel Length: 2"
Overall Length: 6.5"
Weight: 21 oz.
Grips: Rosewood
Finish: Stainless steel
Features: Fixed sights, velvet bag
Price: $285.00

MODEL 88
"THE LADY ROSSI"

MODELS 515/518

SPECIFICATIONS
Calibers: 22 LR (Model 518) and 22 Mag. (Model 515)
Capacity: 6 rounds
Barrel Length: 4"
Overall Length: 8.8"
Weight: 30 oz.
Grips: Checkered wood and rubber wraparound supplied
Prices:
22 LR, 518 . . . . $255.00
22 Mag., 515. . . . . 270.00

MODEL 515
22 MAG.

MODEL 851

SPECIFICATIONS
Caliber: 38 Special
Capacity: 6 rounds
Barrel Length: 4"
Overall Length: 9"
Weight: 31 oz.
Grips: Full-size checkered Brazilian hardwood
Finish: Stainless
Features: Ventilated rib; full-length ejector shroud; fully
adjustable rear sight; red insert front sight; wide target-style
hammer and trigger
Price: $255.00

MODEL 851

ROSSI REVOLVERS

MODEL 877
$290.00

SPECIFICATIONS
Caliber: 357 Magnum
Capacity: 6 rounds
Barrel Length: 2" heavy
Overall Length: 6.87"
Weight: 26 oz.
Height: 5"
Grips: Rubber
Finish: Stainless
Features: Fully enclosed ejector rod; serrated ramp
front sight
Also available:
MODEL 677 w/matte blued finish $260.00

MODEL 677 357 MAGNUM

CYCLOPS
$429.00

SPECIFICATIONS
Caliber: 357 Magnum
Capacity: 6 rounds
Barrel Length: 6" and 8"
Overall Length: 11.75" and 13.75"
Height: 5.75"
Width: 1.47"
Weight: 44 oz., 51 oz. (8" barrel)
Finish: Stainless steel
Grips: Rubber
Features: Four recessed compensator ports on each
side of muzzle, plus extra heavy barrel; mounts and
rings included

MODEL 877

MODEL 971 (not shown)
$299.00 ($255.00 Blued)

SPECIFICATIONS
Caliber: 357 Magnum
Capacity: 6 rounds
Barrel Lengths: 2.5:, 3.25", 4" and 6"
Overall Length: 7 1/2", 8 1/4", 9", 11"
Weight: 30.4 oz. (2.5"), 32 oz. (3.25"), 31.5 oz. (4"), 35.4 oz.
(4" w/rubber grips), 40.5 oz. (6")
Finish: Blued (4" barrel only) or stainless steel
Also available:
MODEL 971 VRC. In 357 Magnum, stainless, rubber grips.
Weight: 30.4 oz. (2.5"); 34.7 oz. (4"); 38.9 oz. (6").
Price: $340.00

MODEL 971 VRC
37 MAG. STAINLESS

RUGER REVOLVERS

REDHAWK REVOLVER

STAINLESS REDHAWK
MODEL KRH-44

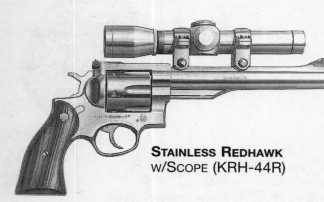

STAINLESS REDHAWK
w/SCOPE (KRH-44R)

SUPER REDHAWK STAINLESS
MODEL KSRH-9

BLUED STEEL REDHAWK REVOLVER

The popular Ruger Redhawk® double-action revolver is available in an alloy steel model with blued finish or high-gloss standard steel in 44 Magnum caliber. Constructed of hardened chrome-moly and other alloy steels, this Redhawk is satin polished to a high luster and finished in a rich blue.

SPECIFICATIONS
Capacity: 6 rounds

CATALOG NUMBER	CALIBER	BARREL LENGTH	OVERALL LENGTH	APPROX. WEIGHT (OUNCES)	PRICE
RUGER BLUED REDHAWK REVOLVER					
RH-445	44 Mag.	5.5"	11"	49	$490.00
RH-44	44 Mag.	7.5"	13"	54	490.00
RH-44R*	44 Mag.	7.5"	13"	54	527.00

Scope model, with Integral Scope Mounts, 1" Ruger Scope rings.

STAINLESS REDHAWK DOUBLE-ACTION REVOLVER

CATALOG NUMBER	CALIBER	BARREL LENGTH	OVERALL LENGTH	APPROX. WEIGHT (OUNCES)	PRICE
RUGER STAINLESS REDHAWK REVOLVER					
KRH-445	44 Mag.	5.5"	11"	49	$547.00
KRH-44	44 Mag.	7.5"	13"	54	547.00
KRH-44R*	44 Mag.	7.5"	13"	54	589.00
KRH-455	45 LC	5.5"	11"	49	547.00
KRH-45	45 LC	7.5"	13"	54	547.00
KRH-45R*	45 LC	7.5"	13"	54	589.00

Scope model, with Integral Scope Mounts, 1" Stainless Steel Ruger Scope rings.

SUPER REDHAWK STAINLESS DOUBLE-ACTION REVOLVER

The Super Redhawk double-action revolver in stainless steel features a heavy extended frame with 7.5" and 9.5" barrels. Cushioned grip panels contain Goncalo Alves w/wood grip panel inserts to provide comfortable, non-slip hold. Comes with case and lock, integral scope mounts and 1" stainless steel Ruger scope rings.

SPECIFICATIONS
Caliber: 44 Magnum
Barrel Lengths: 7.5" and 9.5"
Overall Length: 13" w/7.5" bbl.; 15" w/9.5" bbl.
Weight (empty): 53 oz. (7.5" bbl.); 11.25" (9.5" bbl.)
Sight radius: 9.5" (7.5" bbl.); 11.25" (9.5" bbl.)
Finish: Stainless steell; satin polished

KSRH-7 (7.5" barrel) $589.00
KSRH-9 (9.5" barrel)) 594.00

RUGER SINGLE-ACTION REVOLVERS

**VAQUERO SINGLE ACTION
$434.00 (ALL MODELS)**

BISLEY-VAQUERO

The original Bisley single-action design developed in the 1890s was created for England's famous target shooting matches held at Bisley Common. Modification and repositioning of the grip to a nearly vertical position greatly reduced a tendency of some standard frame single-action grips to "ride-up" in the shooter's hand during recoil. Maintaining the same hand positioning on a revolver's grip from shot to shot is an important part of target shooting. The Bisley hammer is lower and has a wide hammer spur. This enables a shooter to cock the hammer with a minimum amount of disturbance

to the hand and revolver position. The Ruger Vaquero has been extremely popular since its introduction a few years ago. Its "color case finish" fixed sight frames combined the latest Ruger new model single-action revolver mechanism with the classic appearance of the revolver of a century ago. The design of the Bisley-Vaquero has captured renewed interest among serious single-action Target Shooters and Cowboy Action Shooters alike. As with the Vaquero, the new Ruger Bisley-Vaquero is based on the Ruger New Model Blackhawk, single-action revolver, in production since 1973.

BISLEY-VAQUERO SINGLE-ACTION REVOLVER

SPECIFICATIONS
Calibers: .44 Magnum and .45 Long Colt
Capacity: 6 rounds
Barrel Length: 5.5" *Overall Length:* 11.375"
Safety: Transfer bar and loading gate interlock
Sights: Blade front; notch rear; fixed
Sights Radius: 6.5"
Weight (Approx.): 40 oz.
Grips: Smooth rosewood with inletted Ruger medallion

Finish: Blued: "color case finish" on frame; polished and blued barrel and cylinder
Features: Instruction manual, lockable plastic case with lock; heat treated Chrome-moly steel frame, barrel and grip (blued version); 400 stainless steel
Prices:
MODELS RBNV-475 AND RBNV-455 . . . . $450.00
MODELS KRBNV-475 AND KRBNV-455 . . . . 487.00
 (Simulated ivory grips **$36.00** additional)

SPECIFICATIONS: VAQUERO SA

CATALOG NUMBER	CALIBER	FINISH*	BARREL LENGTH	OVERALL LENGTH	APPROX. WT (OZ.)	CATALOG NUMBER	CALIBER	FINISH*	BARREL LENGTH	OVERALL LENGTH	APPROX. WT (OZ.)
BNV34	357 Mag.+	CB	4 5/8"	10.25"	39	BNV475	44 Mag.	CB	5.5"	11.5"	40
KBNV34	357 Mag.+	SSG	4 5/8"	10.25"	39	KBNV475	44 Mag.	SSG	5.5"	11.5"	40
BNV35	357 Mag.+	CB	5.5"	11.5"	40	BNV477	44 Mag.	CB	7.5"	13 1/8"	41
KBNV35	357 Mag.+	SSG	5.5"	11.5"	40	KBNV477	44 Mag.	SSG	7.5"	13 1/8"	41
BNV40	44-40	CB	4 5/8"	10.25"	39	BNV44	45 Long Colt	CB	4 5/8"	10.25"	39
KBNV40	44-40	SSG	4 5/8"	10.25"	39	KBNV44	45 Long Colt	SSG	4 5/8"	10.25"	39
BNV405	44-40	CB	5.5"	11.5"	40	BNV455	45 Long Colt	CB	5.5"	11.5"	40
KBNV405	44-40	SSG	5.5"	11.5"	40	KBNV455	45 Long Colt	SSG	5.5"	11.5"	40
BNV407	44-40	CB	7.5"	13 1/8"	41	BNV45	45 Long Colt	CB	7.5"	13 1/8"	41
KBNV407	44-40	SSG	7.5"	13 1/8"	41	KBNV45	45 Long Colt	SSG	7.5"	13 1/8"	41

*Finish: high-gloss stainless steel (SSG); "color-cased finish" on steel cylinder frame w/blued steel grip, barrel and cylinder (CB).
**With simulated ivory grips: *$475.00* (add *$53.00* for engraved cylinder).

RUGER SINGLE-ACTION REVOLVERS

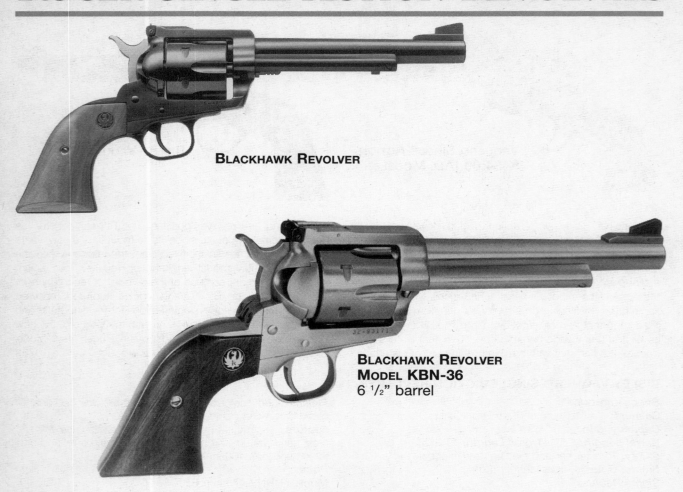

BLACKHAWK REVOLVER

**BLACKHAWK REVOLVER
MODEL KBN-36**
6 ¹/₂" barrel

SPECIFICATIONS: NEW MODEL BLACKHAWK AND BLACKHAWK CONVERTIBLE

CAT. NUMBER	CALIBER	FINISH**	BBL. LENGTH	O.A. LENGTH	WEIGHT (OZ.)	PRICE
BN34	357 Mag.++	B	4 ⁵/₈"	10 ³/₈"	40	**$360.00**
KBN34	357 Mag.++	SS	4 ⁵/₈"	10 ³/₈"	40	**443.00**
BN36	357 Mag.++	B	6.5"	12.25"	42	**360.00**
KBN36	357 Mag.++	SS	6.5"	12.5"	42	**443.00**
BN34X*	357 Mag.++	B	4 ⁵/₈"	10 ³/₈"	40	**380.00**
BN36X*	357 Mag.++	B	6.5"	12.25"	42	**380.00**
BN44	45 Long Colt	B	4 ⁵/₈"	10.25"	39	**360.00**
KBN44	45 Long Colt	SS	4 ⁵/₈"	10.25"	39	**443.00**
BN455	45 Long Colt	B	5.5"	11 ¹/₈"	39	**360.00**
BN45	45 Long Colt	B	7.5"	13 ¹/₈"	41	**360.00**
KBN45	45 Long Colt	SS	7.5"	13 ¹/₈"	41	**443.00**

*Convertible: Designated by an X in the Catalog Number, this model comes with an extra interchangeable .38 Special cylinder; price includes extra cylinder. **Finish: blued (B); stainless steel (SS); high-gloss stainless steel (HGSS); color-cased finish on the steel cylinder frame with blued steel grip, barrel, and cylinder (CB). Also available: Models BN44X and BN455X in .45 Convertible (6-shot). Price: **$380.00**

RUGER REVOLVERS

NEW SUPER MODEL BLACKHAWK
SINGLE-ACTION REVOLVER

NEW MODEL SUPER BLACKHAWK SINGLE-ACTION REVOLVER

SPECIFICATIONS
Caliber: 44 Magnum; interchangeable with 44 Special
Barrel Lengths: 4 ⁵/₈", 5.5", 7.5", 10.5"
Overall Length: 13 ³/₈" (7.5" barrel)
Weight: 45 oz. (4 ⁵/₈" bbl.), 46 oz. (5.5" bbl.), 48 oz. (7.5" bbl.) and 51 oz. (10.5" bbl.)
Frame: Chrome molybdenum steel or stainless steel
Springs: Music wire springs throughout
Sights: Patridge style, ramp front matted blade 18" wide; rear sight click-adjustable for windage and elevation
Grip Frame: Chrome molybdenum or stainless steel, enlarged and contoured to minimize recoil effect
Trigger: Wide spur, low contour, sharply serrated for convenient cocking with minimum disturbance of grip

Finish: Polished and blued or brushed satin stainless steel
Features: Case and lock included
Prices:
KS45N
    5.5" bbl., brushed or high-gloss stainless **$450.00**
KS458N
    4 ⁵/₈" bbl., brushed or high-gloss stainless **450.00**
KS47N
    7.5" bbl., brushed or high-gloss stainless **450.00**
KS411N 10.5" bull bbl., stainless steel **455.00**
S45N 5.5" bbl., blued **413.00**
S458N 4 ⁵/₈" bbl., blued **413.00**
S47N 7.5" bbl., blued **413.00**
S411N 10.5" bull bbl., blued. **418.00**

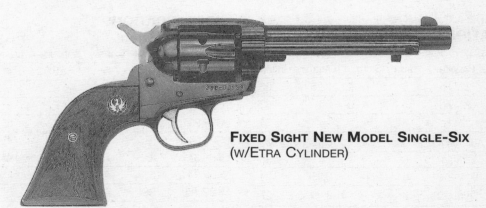

FIXED SIGHT NEW MODEL SINGLE-SIX
(w/Etra Cylinder)

FIXED SIGHT NEW MODEL SINGLE-SIX

SPECIFICATIONS
Caliber: 22 LR (fitted with 22 WMR cylinder)
Barrel Lengths: 4 ⁵/₈", 5.5", 6.5", 9.5"; stainless steel model in 5.5" and 6.5" lengths only
Weight (approx.): 33 oz. (with 5.5" barrel); 38 oz. (with 9.5" barrel)
Sights: Patridge-type ramp front sight; rear sight click adjustable for elevation and windage; protected by integral

frame ribs. Fixed sight model available with 5.5" or 6.5" barrel (same prices as adj. sight models).
Finish: Blue or stainless steel *Features:* Case and lock incl.
Prices:
In blue. **$313.00**
    9 ¹/₂" barrel. **318.00**
In brushed steel
    (convertible 5.5" and 6.5" barrels only) **393.00**

RUGER REVOLVERS

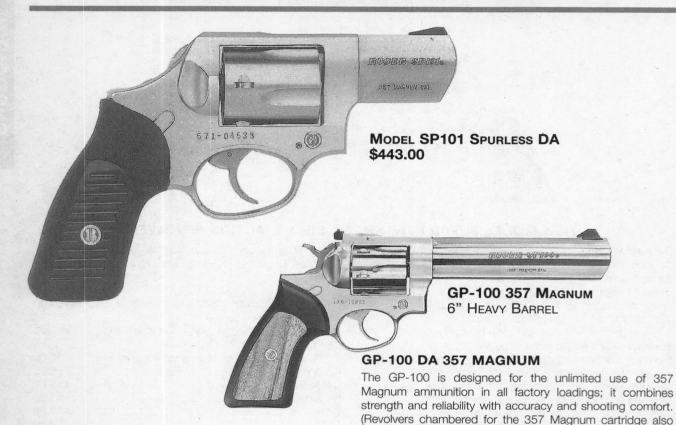

MODEL SP101 SPURLESS DA
$443.00

GP-100 357 MAGNUM
6" HEAVY BARREL

GP-100 DA 357 MAGNUM

The GP-100 is designed for the unlimited use of 357 Magnum ammunition in all factory loadings; it combines strength and reliability with accuracy and shooting comfort. (Revolvers chambered for the 357 Magnum cartridge also accept the 38 Special cartridge.)

SPECIFICATIONS SP101 REVOLVERS

CATALOG NUMBER	CALIBER	CAP.*	SIGHTS	BARREL LENGTH	APPROX WT. (Oz.)
KSP-221	22 LR	6	A	2.25"	32
KSP-240	22 LR	6	A	4"	33
KSP-241	22 LR	6	A	4"	34
KSP-3231	32 Mag.	6	A	3 1/16"	30
KSP-3241	32 Mag.	6	A	4"	33
KSP-921	9mmx19	5	F	2.25"	25
KSP-931	9mmx19	5	F	3 1/16"	27
KSP-821	38+P	5	F	2.25"	25
KSP-831	38+P	5	F	3 1/16"	27
KSP-321X**	357 Mag.	5	F	2.25"	25
KSP-321XL**	357 Mag.	5	F	2.25"	25
KSP-331X**	357 Mag.	5	F	3 1/16"	27

*Indicates cylinder capacity
**Revolvers chambered for 357 Magnum also accept 38 Special cartridges.
Model KSP-240 has short shroud; all others have full.

SPECIFICATIONS

CATALOG NUMBER	FINISH	SIGHTS+	SHROUD++	BARREL LENGTH	WT. (Oz.)	PRICE
GP-141	B	A	F	4"	41	$440.00
GP-160	B	A	S	6"	43	440.00
GP-161	B	A	F	6"	46	474.00
GPF-331	B	F	F	3"	36	423.00
GPF-340	B	F	S	4"	37	423.00
GPF-341	B	F	F	4"	38	457.00
KGP-141	SS	A	F	4"	41	474.00
KGP-160	SS	A	S	6"	43	474.00
KGP-161	SS	A	F	6"	46	474.00
KGPF-330	SS	F	S	3"	35	457.00
KGPF-331	SS	F	F	3"	36	457.00
KGPF-340	SS	F	S	4"	37	457.00
KGPF-341	SS	F	F	4"	38	457.00
KGPF-840*	SS	F	S	4"	37	457.00
GPF-841*	SS	F	F	4"	38	457.00

*38 Special only. B = blued; SS = stainless; A = adjustable;
F = fixed. ++ F = full; S = short.

RUGER REVOLVERS

BISLEY SINGLE-ACTION TARGET GUN

BISLEY SINGLE-ACTION TARGET GUN

The Bisley single-action was originally used at the British National Rifle Association matches held in Bisley, England, in the 1890s. Today's Ruger Bisleys are offered in two frame sizes, chambered from 22 LR to 45 Long Colt. These revolvers are the target-model versions of the Ruger single-action line.

Special Features: Unfluted cylinder roll-marked with classic foliate engraving pattern; hammer is low with smoothly curved, deeply checkered wide spur positioned for easy cocking.

Prices:
22 LR $380.00
357 Mag., 44 Mag., 45 Long Colt. 450.00

BISLEY SPECIFICATIONS

Catalog Number	Caliber	Barrel Length	Overall Length	Sights	Approx. Wt. (Oz.)
RB22AW	22 LR	6.5"	11.5"	Adj.	41
RB35W	357 Mag.	7.5"	13"	Adj.	48
RB44W	44 Mag.	7.5"	13"	Adj.	48
RB45W	45 LC	7.5"	13"	Adj.	48

Dovetail rear sight adjustable for windage only.

THE NEW BEARCAT

THE NEW BEARCAT

Originally manufactured between 1958 and 1973, the 22-rimfire single-action Bearcat features an all-steel precision investment-cast frame and patented transfer-bar mechanism. The New Bearcat also has walnut grips with the Ruger medallion.

SPECIFICATIONS
Caliber: 22 LR
Capacity: 6 shots
Barrel Length: 4"
Grips: Walnut
Finish: Blued chrome-moly steel
Price:
   Blued $320.00

RUGER P-SERIES PISTOLS

MODEL P93 (not shown)

SPECIFICATIONS (See also table below)
Barrel Length: 3.9" **Overall Length:** 7.3"
Height: 5.75" **Width:** 1.5"
Weight: 31 oz.
Sights: 3-dot system; square-notch rear, drift adjustable for windage; square post front (both sights have white dots)
Mechanism: Recoil-operated, double action, autoloading
Features: Oversized trigger guard with curved trigger guard bow; slide stop activated automatically on last shot (w/magazine in pistol); all stainless steel models made with "Terhune Anticorro" steel for maximum corrosion resistance

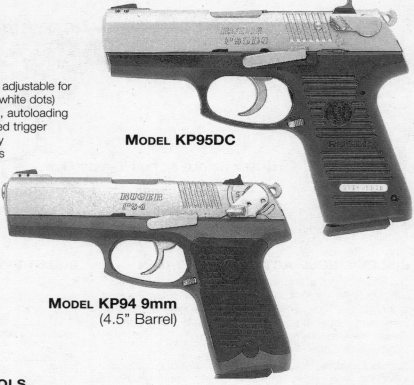

MODEL KP95DC

MODEL KP94 9mm
(4.5" Barrel)

MODEL P94

SPECIFICATIONS (See also table below)
Barrel Length: 4.5"
Capacity: 10 rounds
Overall Length: 7.5"
Weight: 33 oz. (empty magazine)
Height: 5.5"
Width: 1.5"
Sight Radius: 5"
Sights: 3-dot system
Features: See Model P93

SPECIFICATIONS P SERIES PISTOLS

CAT. NUMBER	MODEL	FINISH	CALIBER	MAG. CAP.	PRICE
P89	Manual Safety	Blued	9mm	10	$410.00
KP89	Manual Safety	Stainless	9mm	10	452.00
P89D	Decock Only	Blued	9mm	10	410.00
KP89D	Decock Only	Stainless	9mm	10	452.00
KP89DAO	Double-Action Only	Stainless	9mm	10	452.00
KP90*	Manual Safety	Stainless	45 ACP	7	488.65
KP90D	Decock Only	Stainless	45 ACP	7	488.65
KP93D**	Decock Only	Stainless	9mm	10	520.00
KP93DAO	Double-Action Only	Stainless	9mm	10	520.00
KP94***	Manual Safety	Stainless	9mm	10	520.00
KP94D	Decock Only	Stainless	9mm	10	520.00
KP94DAO	Double-Action Only	Stainless	9mm	10	520.00
KP944	Manual Safety	Stainless	40 Auto	10	520.00
KP944D	Decock Only	Stainless	40 Auto	10	520.00
KP944DAO	Double-Action Only	Stainless	40 Auto	10	520.00
KP95D	Decock Only	Stainless	9mm	10	369.00
KP95DAO	Double-Action Only	Stainless	9mm	10	369.00
P95D	Decock Only	Blued, Stainless Frame	9mm	10	351.00
P95DAO	Double-Action Only	Blued, Stainless Frame	9mm	10	351.00

*Available w/ambidextrous safety, blued (**$454.00**) Model P90. **Available w/ambidextrous decocker, blued (**$421.50**) Model P93D.
***Available w/ambidextrous safety, blued (**$421.50**) Model P94.

RUGER 22 AUTOMATIC PISTOLS

**MARK II
STANDARD MODEL**

MARK II STANDARD MODEL

The Ruger Mark II models represent continuing refinements of the original Ruger Standard and Mark I Target Model pistols. More than two million of this series of autoloading rimfire pistol have been produced since 1949.

The bolts on all Ruger Mark II pistols lock open automatically when the last cartridge is fired, if the magazine is in the pistol. The bolt can be operated manually with the safety in the "on" position for added security while loading and unloading. A boltstop can be activated manually to lock the bolt open.

The Ruger Mark II pistol uses 22 Long Rifle ammunition in a detachable, 10-shot magazine (standard on all Mark II models except Model 22/45, whose 10-shot magazine is not interchangeable with other Mark II magazines). Designed for easy insertion and removal, the Mark II magazine is equipped with a magazine follower button for convenience in reloading.

For additional specifications, please see chart on the next page.

MARK II GOVERNMENT MODEL

MARK II STANDARD MODEL

RUGER PISTOLS

MODEL P-4 22/45

MARK II 22/45
w/Zytel Frame

22/45 TARGET MODEL P-512
(w/11-degree angle)

SPECIFICATIONS: RUGER 22 MARK II PISTOLS

CATALOG NUMBER	MODEL*	FINISH**	BARREL LENGTH	OVERALL LENGTH	APPROX. WT. (OZ.)	PRICE
MK-4	Std.	B	4 3/4"	8 5/16"	35	$252.00
MK-4B	Bull	B	4"	8.25"	38	336.50
KMK-4	Std.	SS	4 3/4"	8 5/16"	35	330.25
KP-4***22/45	Std.	SS	4 3/4"	8 13/16"	28	280.00
P-4	Bull	B	4"	8"	31	237.50
MK-6	Std.	B	6"	10 5/16"	37	252.00
KMK-6	Std.	SS	6"	10 5/16"	37	330.25
MK-678	Target	B	6 7/8"	11 1/8"	42	310.50
KMK-678	Target	SS	6 7/8"	11 1/8"	42	389.00
P-512***22/45	Bull	B	5.5"	9 3/4"	35	237.50
MK-512	Bull	B	5.5"	9 3/4"	42	310.50
KMK-512	Bull	SS	5.5"	9 3/4"	42	389.00
KP-512***22/45	Bull	SS	5.5"	9 3/4"	35	330.00
MK-10	Bull	B	10"	14 5/16"	51	314.50
KMK-10	Bull	SS	10"	14 5/16"	51	393.00
MK-678G	Bull	B	6 7/8"	11 1/8"	46	356.50
KMK-678G	Bull	SS	6 7/8"	11 1/8"	46	427.25
KMK-678GC	Bull	SS	6 7/8"	11 1/8"	45	441.00

*Model: Std.=standard **Finish: B=blued; SS=stainless steel ***22 cartridge, 45 grip angle and magazine latch

SAFARI ARMS PISTOLS

MATCHMASTER

SPECIFICATIONS
Caliber: 45 ACP
Capacity: 7 rounds
Barrel length: 5" or 6"
Overall length: 8.25"
Weight: 40.3 oz.
Finish: Stainless steel or black Parkerized carbon steel
Features: Extended safety & slide stop; wide beavertail grip safety; LPA fully adjustable rear sight; full-length recoil spring guide; squared trigger guide & finger-groove front strap frame; laser-etched walnut grips
Prices:
5" Barrel $750.00
6" Barrel 825.00

ENFORCER

SPECIFICATIONS
Caliber: 45 ACP
Capacity: 6 rounds
Barrel length: 4" conical
Overall length: 7.3"
Height: 4 $^7/_8$"
Weight: 36 oz.
Sight radius: 5.75"
Finish: Stainless steel or matte black Parkerized carbon steel
Features: Beavertail grip safety; extended thumb safety and slide release; smooth walnut stock w/laser-etched Black Widow logo
Price: $780.00

COHORT

SPECIFICATIONS
Caliber: 45 ACP
Capacity: 7 rounds
Barrel length: 4" conical
Overall length: 7.3"
Height: 5.5"
Weight: 37 oz.
Sights: Ramped blade front, LPA adjustable rear
Finish: Stainless steel or black Parkerized carbon steel
Features: Beavertail grip safety; extended thumb safety and slide release; commander-style hammer; smooth walnut stock
Price: $800.00

SAVAGE ARMS

BOLT-ACTION HUNTING HANDGUN

SPECIFICATIONS
Calibers: 22-250 Rem., 243 Win. and 308 Win.
Capacity: 3 + 1 *Barrel Length:* 14"
Overall Length: 22.5" *Weight:* Approx. 5 lbs.
Sights: None. Drilled and tapped for scope mounts
Stock: Mid-grip, ambidextrous composite, with grooved
forend and dual pillar bedding
Finish: Blued alloy steel
Features: Bolt-action hunting handgun with left hand bolt
and right hand ejection.

MODEL 510F
"STRIKER"

Price: $400.00

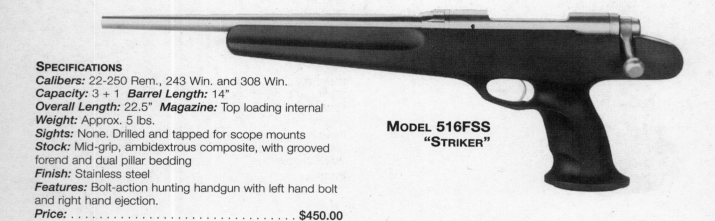

SPECIFICATIONS
Calibers: 22-250 Rem., 243 Win. and 308 Win.
Capacity: 3 + 1 *Barrel Length:* 14"
Overall Length: 22.5" *Magazine:* Top loading internal
Weight: Approx. 5 lbs.
Sights: None. Drilled and tapped for scope mounts
Stock: Mid-grip, ambidextrous composite, with grooved
forend and dual pillar bedding
Finish: Stainless steel
Features: Bolt-action hunting handgun with left hand bolt
and right hand ejection.

MODEL 516FSS
"STRIKER"

Price: $450.00

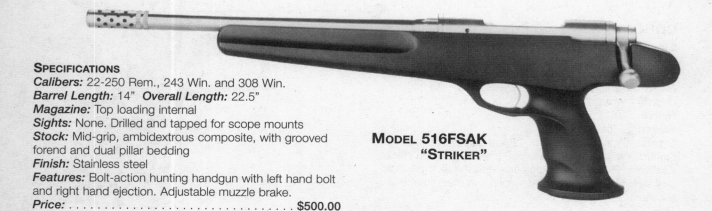

SPECIFICATIONS
Calibers: 22-250 Rem., 243 Win. and 308 Win.
Barrel Length: 14" *Overall Length:* 22.5"
Magazine: Top loading internal
Sights: None. Drilled and tapped for scope mounts
Stock: Mid-grip, ambidextrous composite, with grooved
forend and dual pillar bedding
Finish: Stainless steel
Features: Bolt-action hunting handgun with left hand bolt
and right hand ejection. Adjustable muzzle brake.

MODEL 516FSAK
"STRIKER"

Price: $500.00

SIG-SAUER PISTOLS

MODEL P220 "AMERICAN"

SPECIFICATIONS

Calibers: 38 Super, 45 ACP
Capacity: 9 rounds; 7 rounds in 45 ACP
Barrel Length: 4.4"
Overall Length: 7.79"
Height: 5.6"
Width: 1.4"
Weight (empty): 26.5 oz.; 25.7 oz. in 45 ACP
Finish: Blue, K-Kote or Two-tone
Prices:
Blued $750.00
  w/"Siglite" night sights 845.00
w/K-Kote finish 795.00
  w/K-Kote and "Siglite" night sights 885.00

**MODEL P220
"AMERICAN"**

MODEL P225

SPECIFICATIONS

Caliber: 9mm Parabellum *Capacity:* 8 rounds
Action: DA/SA or DA only *Barrel Length:* 3.9"
Overall Length: 7.1" *Weight (empty):* 26.1 oz.
Height: 5.2" *Width:* 1.3" *Finish:* Blue, K-Kote or Two-tone
Prices:
Blued finish $725.00
Blued w/"Siglite" night sights 830.00
w/K-Kote. 770.00
w/K-Kote and "Siglite" night sights 860.00

MODEL P225

MODEL P210 (not shown)

SPECIFICATIONS

Single-action 8-round pistol in 9mm Luger. *Barrel Length:* 4.75" *Overall Length:* 8.5" *Weight:* 32 oz. *Height:* 5.4" *Width:* 1.3" *Sights:* Blade front; notch rear (drift adjustable for windage) *Safety:* Thumb-operated manual safety lever; magazine safety *Finish:* Blue only. Long Rifle conversion kit available (**add $300.00**)
Price: $2,100.00

MODEL P226

SPECIFICATIONS

Calibers: 357 SIG and 40 S&W *Capacity:* 10 rounds
Action: DA/SA or DA only *Barrel Length:* 4.4"
Overall Length: 7.7"
Weight (empty): 26.5 oz.; 30.1 oz. in 357 SIG
Height: 5.5" *Finish:* Blue, K-Kote or Two-tone
Prices:
Blackened stainless steel slide $795.00
  w/"Siglite" night sight 885.00
  w/Double Action only 885.00
Nickel finish stainless steel slide, DA only
  w/"Siglite" night sights 925.00

MODEL P226

SIG-SAUER PISTOLS

MODEL P232

MODEL P229

SPECIFICATIONS
Calibers: 9mm, 357 and 40 S&W
Capacity: 10 rounds
Action: DA/SA or DA only
Barrel Length: 3.8"
Overall Length: 7.1"
Weight (empty): 27.5 oz.
Height: 5.4"
Width: 1.5"
Finish: Blackened stainless steel
Features: Stainless steel slide; automatic firing-pin lock; wood grips (optional); aluminum alloy frame
Prices:
Model P229. . . . . $795.00
w/"Siglite" night sight 885.00
w/Nickel slide 830.00
w/Nickel slide/"Siglite" night sight 925.00

MODEL P239

SPECIFICATIONS
Calibers: 9mm Luger, 357 SIG and 40 S&W
Action: DA/SA or DA only
Capacity: 7 rounds (357 SIG); 8 rounds (9mm)
Barrel Length: 3.6"
Overall Length: 6.6"
Weight: 25.2 oz.
Height: 5.1"
Width: 1.2"
Finish: Blackened stainless steel
Features: Mechanically locked, recoil-operated semiauto; automatic firing-pin lock
Prices:
Blackened stainless steel slide $595.00
w/"Siglite" night sight 685.00

MODEL P232

SPECIFICATIONS
Calibers: 9mm Short (380 ACP) and 32 ACP
Action: DA/SA or DAO
Capacity: 7 rounds (380 ACP); 8 rounds (32 ACP)
Barrel Length: 3.6" *Overall Length:* 6.6"
Weight (empty): 16.2 oz.; (16.4 oz. in 32 ACP)
Height: 4.7" *Width:* 1.2"
Safety: Automatic firing-pin lock *Finish:* Blued or stainless steel
Prices:
Blued finish $485.00
Stainless steel 525.00
w/Stainless slide, alloy frame 505.00
w/"Siglite" night sight, Hogue grips, DA only 560.00

MODEL P229

MODEL P239

SMITH & WESSON PISTOLS

COMPACT SERIES

MODEL 3900 COMPACT SERIES

SPECIFICATIONS
Caliber: 9mm Parabellum DA Autoloading Luger
Capacity: 8 rounds
Barrel Length: 3.5"
Overall Length: 6 $\frac{7}{8}$"
Weight (empty): 25 oz.
Sights: Post w/white dot front; fixed rear adj. for windage only w/2 white dots. Adjustable sight models include micrometer click, adj. for windage and elevation w/2 white dots. Deduct $25 for fixed sights.
Finish: Satin stainless
Prices:
MODEL 3913 . . . . $633.00
MODEL 3913 LADYSMITH (single side) 651.00
MODEL 3953 (double action only) 633.00

MODEL 3913 DA
STAINLESS

MODEL 3913
LADYSMITH

MODEL 6906

MODEL 6900 COMPACT SERIES

SPECIFICATIONS
Caliber: 9mm Parabellum; traditional DA autoloading Luger
Capacity: 12 rounds
Barrel Length: 3.5"
Overall Length: 6 $\frac{7}{8}$"
Weight (empty): 26.5 oz.
Sights: Post w/white dot front; fixed rear adj. for windage only w/2 white dots
Grips: Curved backstrap
Finish: Blue (Model 6904); satin stainless (Model 6906)
Prices:
MODEL 6904 . . . . $625.00
MODEL 6906 . . . . 688.00
MODEL 6906 Fixed Novak night sight. 801.00
MODEL 6946 DA only, fixed sights 688.00

MODEL 6906 DA
STAINLESS

SMITH & WESSON PISTOLS

FULL-SIZE CENTERFIRE DOUBLE-ACTION PISTOLS

Smith & Wesson's double-action semiautomatic Third Generation line includes the following features: fixed barrel bushing for greater accuracy • smoother trigger pull plus a slimmer, contoured grip and lateral relief cut where trigger guard meets frame • beveled magazine well • ambidextrous safety lever • low-glare bead-blasted finish.

MODEL 4006
WITH FIXED SIGHT

MODEL 4506
ADJUSTABLE SIGHT

MODEL 4046

MODEL 4586
FIXED SIGHT

MODEL 4000 SERIES

SPECIFICATIONS
Caliber: 40 S&W
Capacity: 11 rounds
Barrel Length: 4"
Overall Length: 7.5"
Weight: 38.5 oz. (with fixed sights)
Sights: Post w/white dot front; fixed w/white 2-dot rear
Grips: Straight backstrap
Finish: Stainless steel
Prices:

MODEL 4006 w/fixed sights $798.00
  Same as above w/adj. sights 788.00
  w/fixed night sight 880.00
MODEL 4043 DA only (28 oz.) 750.00
MODEL 4046 Fixed sights, DA only (39.5 oz.) 768.00
  Double action only, fixed Tritium night sight 880.00

MODEL 4500 SERIES

SPECIFICATIONS
Caliber: 45 ACP Autoloading DA
Capacity: 8 rounds
Barrel Lengths: 5" (Model 4506); 4.25" (Models 4566 & 4586)
Overall Length: 8.5" (Model 4506)
Weight (empty): 40.5 oz. (Model 4506); 38.5 oz. (Model 4566)
Sights: Post w/white-dot front; fixed rear, adj. for windage only. Adj. sight incl. micrometer click, adj. for windage and elevation w/2 white dots. Add **$29.00** for adj. sights.
Grips: Delrin one-piece wraparound, arched backstrap, textured surface
Finish: Satin stainless
Prices:

MODEL 4506 w/adj. sights, 5" bbl. $830.00
  With fixed sights 798.00
MODEL 4566 w/4.25" bbl., fixed sights 798.00
MODEL 4586 DA only, 4.25" bbl., 39.5 oz.,
  fixed 2-dot rear sight, white dot front 798.00

SMITH & WESSON PISTOLS

FULL-SIZE DOUBLE-ACTION PISTOLS

MODEL 5900 SERIES

SPECIFICATIONS
Caliber: 9mm Parabellum DA Autoloading Luger
Capacity: 15 rounds
Barrel Length: 4"
Overall Length: 7.5"
Weight (empty): 28 oz. (Models 5903, 5904); 37.5 oz. (Model 5906); 38 oz. (Model 5906 w/adj. sight)
Sights: Front, post w/white dot; fixed rear, adj. for windage only w/2 white dots. Adjustable sight models include micrometer click, adj. for windage and elevation w/2 white dots.
Finish: Blue (Model 5904); satin stainless (Models 5903 and 5906)
Prices:
MODEL 5904 Blue $663.00
MODEL 5906 Satin stainless 765.00
   With fixed sights 729.00
   With Tritium night sight 841.00
MODEL 5946 Double action only 729.00

MODEL 5906 DA
STAINLESS

MODEL 410

SPECIFICATIONS
Caliber: 40 S&W
Capacity: 10 rounds
Barrel Length: 4"
Overall Length: 7.5"
Weight: 28.5 oz.
Sights: 3-dot sights
Grips: Straight backstrap
Features: Right-hand slide-mounted manual safety; decocking lever; aluminum alloy frame; blue carbon steel slide; nonreflective matte blued finish; beveled edge slide
Price: $500.00

MODEL 410

MODEL 900 SERIES (MODEL 908)

SPECIFICATIONS
Caliber: 9mm
Capacity: 8 rounds
Barrel Lengths: 3.5"
Overall Length: 6 13/16"
Weight: 28.8 oz.
Sights: White dot front; fixed 2-dot rear
Grips: Straight backstrap
Safety: External, single side
Finish: Matte blue
Features: Carbon steel slide; alloy frame
Price: $453.00

MODEL 910

SMITH & WESSON PISTOLS

SIGMA SERIES

Smith & Wesson's Sigma Series pistols are a combination of traditional craftmanship and the latest technological advances that allow the guns to be assembled without the usual "fitting" process required for other handguns. The polymer frame provides unprecedented comfort and pointability. The low barrel centerline combined with the ergonomic design allows low muzzle flip and fast reaction for the next shot.

SIGMA SERIES MODEL SW40F
FULL SIZE DA

SIGMA SERIES SW380
COMPACT DA

SIGMA SERIES SW40C/SW40F FULL SIZE DA

SPECIFICATIONS
Calibers: 40 S&W
Capacity: 10 rounds
Barrel Length: 4" (SW40C); 4.5" (SW40F)
Overall Length: 6.9" (SW40C); 7.75" (SW40F)
Weight (empty): 24.4 oz. (SW40C); 26 oz. (SW40F)
Sights: 3-dot system (Tritium night sights available)
Finish: Satin black/Melonite
Price: $541.00

SIGMA SERIES SW380 COMPACT DA (380 ACP)

SPECIFICATIONS
Calibers: 38 ACP *Capacity:* 6 rounds
Barrel Length: 3" *Overall Length:* 5.8" *Weight:* 14 oz.
Sights: Post w/channel front; fixed channel rear
Finish: Blue
Features: Lightweight polymer frame with integral thumbrest; two-piece trigger; corrosion-resistant steel slide
Price: $319.00
Also available:
MODEL SW9M in 9mm w/3..25" barrel (6.25" overall).
Weight: 17.9 oz. Sights: Post .060" front; fixed channel rear
Price: $366.00

SIGMA SERIES SW9V/SW40V

SPECIFICATIONS
Caliber: 9mm and 40 S&W
Capacity: 10 rounds
Action: Traditional double action
Barrel Length: 4"
Overall Length: 7.25"
Weight: 24.7 oz.
Finish: Satin stainless
Sights: White dot front; fixed 2-dot rear
Features: Strike firing system; grips integral with frame; stainless steel slide
Price: $382.00

SIGMA SERIES SW40V

SMITH & WESSON PISTOLS

TARGET PISTOLS

MODEL 457

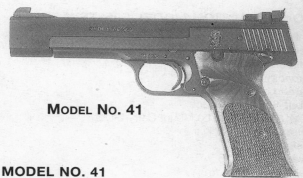

MODEL No. 41

MODEL 457

SPECIFICATIONS
Caliber: 45 ACP
Capacity: 7 rounds
Barrel Length: 3.75"
Overall Length: 7.25"
Weight: 29 oz. *Grips:* Straight backstrap
Sights: White dot front; fixed 2-dot rear *Finish:* Blued
Features: Carbon steel slide and alloy frame; .260"
bobbed hammer; single side external safety
Price: $500.00

MODEL NO. 41

SPECIFICATIONS
Caliber: 22 LR *Magazine Capacity:* 12 rounds
Barrel Lengths: 5.5" and 7" *Weight:* 41 oz. (5.5" barrel)
Overall Length: 10.5" (7" bbl.)
Sights: Front, 1/8" Patridge undercut; rear, S&W micrometer
click sight adjustable for windage and elevation
Grips: Hardwood target *Finish:* S&W Bright blue
Trigger: .365" width; S&W grooving, adj. trigger stop
Features: Carbon steel slide and frame
Price: $778.00

MODEL 2213
"SPORTSMAN"

MODEL 22A SPORT (not shown)

SPECIFICATIONS
Caliber: 22 LR *Capacity:* 10 rounds *Action:* Single
Barrel Lengths: 4", 5.5" (standard or bull barrel and 7"
Overall Length: 8" (4"), 9.5" (5.5"), 11" (7")
Grips: Two-piece polymer (4"); 2-piece Soft Touch (5.5" and 7"
Weight: 28 oz. (4"), 32 oz. (5.5"), 33 oz. (7")
Sights: Patridge front, adjustable rear *Finish:* Blue
Features: Single slide external safety
Prices:
   4" $224.00
   5.5" 247.00
   5.5" Bull Barrel 311.00
   5.5" Stainless 287.00
   7" 281.00
Also available: in stainless steel (5.5" and 7" only)
Prices:
   5.5" Standard $303.00
   5.5" Bull Barrel 368.00
   7" Standard 334.00

MODEL 2213/2214 RIMFIRE "SPORTSMAN"

SPECIFICATIONS
Caliber: 22 LR *Capacity:* 8 rounds *Barrel Length:* 3"
Overall Length: 6 1/8"" *Weight:* 18 oz.
Sights: Patridge front, adjustable rear
Finish: Stainless steel slide w/alloy frame (Model 2214 has
blued carbon steel slide w/alloy frame and blued finish)
Prices:
   Blue $284.00
   Stainless 330.00

SMITH & WESSON PISTOLS

TSW TACTICAL SERIES

DOUBLE ACTION MODEL 3953TSW

SPECIFICATIONS
Action: Double Action Only
Caliber: 9mm
Capacity: 7 Rounds
Barrel Length: 3.5"
Front Sight: White Dot
Rear Sight: Novak Lo Mount Carry 2-Dot
Grips: Straight Backstrap
Weight: 24.7 oz.
Overall Length: 6 5/8"
Height: 4 7/8" *Width:* 1.00"
Material: Aluminum Alloy/Stainless Steel
Finish: Satin Stainless
Price: $674.00
Also available: MODEL 3913TSW
   Same as above but width is 1.30"

MODEL 3953TSW
DOUBLE ACTION

TRADITIONAL DA MODEL 4013TSW

SPECIFICATIONS
Action: Traditional Double Action
Caliber: .40 S&W
Frame: Compact
Capacity: 9 rounds
Barrel Length: 3.5"
Front Sight: White Dot
Rear Sight: Novak Lo Mount Carry 2-Dot
External Safety: Ambidextrous
Grips: Curbed Backstrap
Weight: 26.4 oz. *Overall Length:* 6 7/8"
Height: 5" *Width:* 1.30"
Material: Aluminum Alloy/Stainless Steel
Finish: Satin Stainless
Price: $799.00
Also available: MODEL 4053STW
   Same as above but width is 1.24" and weight is 27.2 oz.

MODEL 4013TSW
TRADITIONAL DA

TRADTIONAL DA MODEL 4513TSW

SPECIFICATIONS
Action: Traditional Double Action
Caliber: .45 ACP *Frame:* Compact
Capacity: 6 Rounds *Barrel Length:* 3.75"
Front Sight: White Dot
Rear Sight: Novak Lo Mount Carry 2-Dot
Grips: Straight Backstrap *Weight:* 28 oz.
Overall Length: 6 7/8"
Height: 5" *Width:* 1.30"
Material: Aluminum Alloy/Stainless Steel
Finish: Satin Stainless
Price: $758.00
Also available: MODEL 4553TSW
   Same as above but weight is 29 oz. and height is 4 7/8"

MODEL 4513TSW
TRADITIONAL DA

SMITH & WESSON PISTOLS

SMALL FRAME

MODEL 60LS LADYSMITH
38 S&W Special

MODEL 37
CHIEFS SPECIAL AIRWEIGHT
38 S&W Special

MODEL 60
38 CHIEFS SPECIAL
Stainless

LADYSMITH HANDGUNS
MODEL 36-LS AND MODEL 60-LS

SPECIFICATIONS
Calibers: 38 S&W Special and 357 Magnum
Capacity: 5 shots *Barrel Lengths:* 2" (2 ¹/₈" 357 Magnum)
Overall Length: 6 ⁵/₁₆" *Weight:* 20 oz. (23 oz. 357 Magnum)
Sights: Serrated ramp front (black pinned ramp in 357 Mag.); fixed notch rear
Grips: Contoured laminated rosewood, round butt
Finish: Glossy deep blue or stainless
Features: Both models come with soft-side LadySmith carry case
Prices:
MODEL 36-LS Blue $425.00
MODEL 60-LS Stainless 479.00

MODEL 36
38 CHIEFS SPECIAL

SPECIFICATIONS
Caliber: 38 S&W Special *Capacity:* 5 shots
Barrel Length: 2" *Overall Length:* 6 ⁵/₁₆"
Weight: 20 oz.
Sights: Serrated ramp front; fixed, square-notch rear
Grips: Uncle Mike's Boot
Finish: S&W blued carbon steel; satin stainless Model 637
Features: .312" smooth combat-style trigger; .240" service hammer
Prices:
MODEL 36 38 CHIEFS SPECIAL $394.00
MODEL 37 CHIEFS SPECIAL AIRWEIGHT:
    Same as Model 36, except finish is blue or
    nickel aluminum alloy. 429.00
MODEL 637 CHIEFS SPECIAL AIRWEIGHT:
    With 2" barrel, synthetic round butt, stainless finish.
    Weight: 13.5 oz.. . . . . 446.00

MODEL 60
38 CHIEFS SPECIAL, STAINLESS

SPECIFICATIONS
Calibers: 38 S&W Special *Capacity:* 5 shots
Barrel Lengths: 2 1/8" (357 Mag.); 3" full lug (38 S&W Spec.)
Overall Length: 6 ⁵/₁₆" (2 ¹/₈" bbl.)); 7.5" (3" bbl.)
Weight: 23 oz. (2 1/8" barrel); 24.5 oz. (3" full lug barrel)
Sights: Micrometer click rear, adj. for windage and elevation; pinned black front (3" full lug model only); standard sights as on Model 36
Grips: Uncle Mike's Combat *Finish:* Satin stainless
Features: .312" smooth combat-style trigger
Prices:
2 ¹/₈" Barrel. $449.00
3" Barrel. 476.00

SMITH & WESSON PISTOLS

SMALL FRAME

MODEL 442
38 SPECIAL

MODEL 649
BODYGUARD

38 CENTENNIAL "AIRWEIGHT" MODEL 442

SPECIFICATIONS
Caliber: 38 S&W Special
Capacity: 5 rounds
Barrel Length: 2" *Overall Length:* 6 5/16"
Weight: 15.8 oz.
Sights: Serrated ramp front; fixed, square-notch rear
Finish: Matte blue
Price: $445.00
Also available:
MODEL 642 CENTENNIAL AIRWEIGHT
   Stainless steel w/2" barrel, synthetic round butt grip,
   double-action only. $460.00
LADYSMITH MODEL (satin stainless). 490.00

MODEL 649 BODYGUARD

SPECIFICATIONS
Caliber: 38 S&W Special/357 S&W Mag.
Capacity: 5 rounds
Barrel Length: 1 7/8" and 2 1/8"
Overall Length: 6 5/16"
Weight: 20 oz.
Sights: Black pinned ramp front; fixed, square-notch rear
Grips: Uncle Mike's Combat
Finish: Satin stainless
Price: $488.00

38 BODYGUARD "AIRWEIGHT" MODEL 38 (not shown)

SPECIFICATIONS
Caliber: 38 S&W Special
Capacity: 5 rounds
Barrel Length: 2" *Overall Length:* 6 3/8"
Weight: 14 oz.
Sights: Front serrated ramp; square-notch rear
Grips: Checkered walnut Service with S&W monograms
Finish: S&W blue
Price: $462.00
Also available:
MODEL 638 in nickel aluminum alloy

MODEL 696 (not shown)

SPECIFICATIONS
Caliber: 44 S&W Special
Capacity: 5 rounds
Action: Single or double action
Barrel Length: 3"
Overall Length: 8 3/16"
Weight: 48 oz.
Sights: Red ramp front; adjustable white outline rear
Grips: Hogue rubber
Finish: Satin stainless
Features: .500" target hammer; .400" smooth combat trigger
Price: $509.00

SMITH & WESSON REVOLVERS

SMALL FRAME

MODEL 317 AIRLITE

MODEL 317 AIRLITE

SPECIFICATIONS
Caliber: 22 LR **Action:** Single or double action
Capacity: 8 rounds **Barrel Length:** 1 $\frac{7}{8}$" and 3"
Overall Length: 6 $\frac{3}{16}$"
Weight: 9.9 oz. (10.5 oz. w/rubber grip) **Finish:** Clear Cote
Sights: Serrated ramp front; fixed notch rear
Prices:
1 $\frac{7}{8}$" barrel w/synthetic grips $451.00
1 $\frac{7}{8}$" barrel w/Dymondwood. 484.00
3" barrel w/Dymondwood grip 518.00
3" barrel w/rubber grips 477.00

MODEL 317 LADYSMITH

MODEL 317 LADYSMITH

SPECIFICATIONS
Same as **MODEL 317 AIRLITE** with round butt grip, fixed
sights and Dymondwood grip.
Price: $505.00

MODEL 940 CENTENNIAL

SPECIFICATIONS
Caliber: 9mm Parabellum
Capacity: 5 rounds
Action: Double action only
Barrel Length: 2"
Overall Length: 6 $\frac{5}{16}$"
Weight: 23 oz.
Sights: Serrated ramp front; fixed, square-notch rear
Grips: Synthetic round-butt grips
Finish: Satin stainless
Price: $493.00

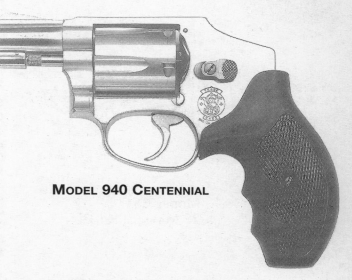

MODEL 940 CENTENNIAL

SMALL FRAME

MODEL 63

MODEL 63 – 22/32 KIT GUN

SPECIFICATIONS
Caliber: 22 Long Rifle *Capacity:* 6 shots
Barrel Lengths: 2" and 4"
Overall Length: 6.25" (w/2" bbl.) 8 11/16 (w/4" bbl.)
Weight: 22 oz. (2" barrel); 24.5 oz. (4" barrel)
Sights: 1/8" red ramp front sight; rear sight is black stainless steel S&W micrometer click, square-notch, adjustable for windage and elevation
Grips: Synthetic round butt *Finish:* Satin stainless
Prices:
2" Barrel $476.00
4" Barrel 481.00

MODEL 640

MODEL 640 CENTENNIAL

SPECIFICATIONS
Calibers: 357 Magnum and 38 S&W Special
Action: Double action only
Capacity: 5 rounds
Barrel Length: 1 7/8" and 2 1/8"
Overall Length: 6 3/4"
Weight: 23 oz. (1 7/8" barrel)
Sights: Pinned black ramp front; fixed, square-notch rear
Features: Fully concealed hammer; smooth hardwood service stock; satin stainless steel finish; round-butt synthetic grips
Price: $488.00

MODEL 651
22 MAGNUM KIT GUN

MODEL 651
22 MAGNUM KIT GUN

SPECIFICATIONS
Calibers: 22 Magnum
Capacity: 6 shots
Barrel Length: 4"
Overall Length: 8 11/16"
Weight: 24.5 oz.
Sights: Red ramp front; micrometer click rear, adjustable for windage and elevation
Grips: Synthetic round-butt grips
Finish: Satin stainless
Features: .375" hammer; .312" smooth combat trigger
Price: $478.00

SMITH & WESSON REVOLVERS

MEDIUM FRAME

MODEL 10
HEAVY BARREL

MODEL 10
38 MILITARY & POLICE

SPECIFICATIONS
Caliber: 38 S&W Special *Capacity:* 6 shots
Barrel Length: 4" heavy barrel *Overall Length:* 9.25"
Weight: 33.5 oz.
Sights: Front, fixed 1/8" serrated ramp; square-notch rear
Grips: Uncle Mike's Combat *Finish:* S&W blue
Price: $408.00

MODEL 64
38 MILITARY & POLICE STAINLESS

SPECIFICATIONS
Caliber: 38 S&W Special *Capacity:* 6 shots
Barrel Length: 4" heavy barrel, square butt; 3" heavy
barrel, round butt; 2" regular barrel, round butt
Overall Length: 9.25" w/4" bbl.; 7 7/8" w/3" bbl.;
6 7/8" w/2" barrel
Weight: 28 oz. w/2" barrel; 30.5 oz. w/3" bbl.;
33.5 oz. w/4" barrel
Sights: Fixed, 1/8" serrated ramp front; square-notch rear
Grips: Uncle Mike's Combat *Finish:* Satin stainless
Prices:
   2" Bbl. $433.00
   3" & 4" Bbl. 441.00

MODEL 64

MODEL 13 (HEAVY BARREL)
357 MILITARY & POLICE

SPECIFICATIONS
Caliber: 357 Magnum and 38 S&W Special
Capacity: 6 shots *Barrel Lengths:* 3" and 4"
Overall Length: 9.25" (w/4" bbl.) *Weight:* 36 oz. (w/4" bbl.)
Sights: Front, 1/8" serrated ramp; square-notch rear
Grips: Uncle Mike's Combat *Finish:* S&W blue
Price: $411.00

MODEL 13

MODEL 65

MODEL 65 (HEAVY BARREL)
357 MILITARY & POLICE

SPECIFICATIONS
Same specifications as **MODEL 13**, except **MODEL 65** is
satin stainless steel.
Price: $445.00
Also available:
MODEL 65 LADYSMITH
Same specifications as **MODEL 65** but with 3" barrel only
(weights 32 oz.) and rosewood laminate stock; satin stain-
less finish, smooth combat wood grips.
Price: $479.00

SMITH & WESSON REVOLVERS

MEDIUM FRAME

MODEL 14
K-38 MASTERPIECE

MODEL 15
38 COMBAT MASTERPIECE

SPECIFICATIONS
Caliber: 38 S&W Special *Barrel Length:* 6" full lug barrel
Overall Length: 11 1/8" *Weight:* 41.5 oz.
Sights: Micrometer click rear, adjustable for windage and
elevation; pinned blackk Patridge-style front
Grips: Synthetic square butt (on round-butt frame)
Finish: Blue carbon steel
Features: .500 target hammer; .312" smooth combat trigger
Price: $484.00

SPECIFICATIONS
Caliber: 38 S&W Special *Capacity:* 6 shots
Barrel Length: 4" *Overall Length:* 9 5/16"
Weight (loaded): 36 oz.
Sights: Serrated ramp front; S&W micrometer click sight
adjustable for windage and elevation
Grips: Uncle Mike's Combat *Finish:* S&W blue
Features: .375" semi-target hammer; .312" smooth combat-
style trigger
Price: $437.00
Also available:
MODEL 67. Same specifications as MODEL 15 but with satin
stainless finish, red ramp front sight and .375" semi-target
hammer.
Price: $485.00

MODEL 617

MODEL 17

SPECIFICATIONS
Caliber: 22 Long Rifle *Capacity:* 6 shots
Barrel Length: 4", 6" or 8 3/8"
Overall Length: 9 1/8" (4" barrel); 11 1/8" (6" barrel);
13.5" (8 3/8" barrel)
Weight (loaded): 42 oz. with 4" barrel; 48 oz. with
6" barrel; 54 oz. with 8 3/8" barrel
Sights: Front pinned Patridge; rear, S&W micrometer
click sight adjustable for windage and elevation
Grips: Hogue rubber, square butt *Finish:* Satin stainless
Features: Target hammer and trigger; drilled and tapped
for scope
Prices:

4" Barrel.	$478.00
6" Barrel	508.00
8.75" Barrel	520.00
6" Bbl. 10-Shot	524.00

SPECIFICATIONS
Caliber: 22 LR *Capacity:* 10 rounds
Action: Single/Double *Barrel Length:* 6"
Overall Length: 11 1/8" *Weight:* 42 oz.
Sights: Pinned Patridge front; adjustable black blade rear
Grips: Hogue rubber *Finish:* Blue dcarbon steel
Features: .312" smooth combat trigger; .375" semi-target
hammer
Price: $508.00

SMITH & WESSON REVOLVERS

MEDIUM FRAME

MODEL 19

MODEL 19
357 COMBAT MAGNUM

SPECIFICATIONS
Caliber: 357 S&W Magnum (actual bullet dia. 38 S&W Spec.)
Capacity: 6 shots
Barrel Lengths: 2.5" and 4"
Overall Length: 9.5" w/4" bbl.; 7.5" w/2.5" bbl.
Weight: 30.5 oz. (2.5" bbl.); 36 oz. (4" bbl.)
Sights: Serrated ramp front; adjustable black rear
Grips: Uncle Mike's Combat
Finish: S&W bright blue
Prices:
  2.5" Bbl. $434.00
  4" Bbl. 443.00

MODEL 66

MODEL 66
357 COMBAT MAGNUM

SPECIFICATIONS
Caliber: 357 Magnum (actual bullet dia. 38 S&W Spec.)
Capacity: 6 shots
Barrel Lengths: 4" or 6" with square butt; 2.5" with round butt
Overall Length: 7.5" w/2.5" bbl.; 9.5" w/4" bbl.; 11 3/8" w/6" bbl.
Weight: 30.5 oz. w/2.5" bbl.; 36 oz. w/4" bbl.; 39 oz. w/6" bbl.
Sights: Front, 1/8"; rear, S&W Red Ramp on ramp base, S&W Micrometer Click, adjustable for windage and elevation
Grips: Uncle Mike's Combat
Trigger: .312" Smooth Combat
Finish: Satin stainless
Prices:
  2.5" Bbl. $484.00
  4" Bbl. 490.00

MODEL 586

MODEL 586
DISTINGUISHED COMBAT MAGNUM

SPECIFICATIONS
Calibers: 357 Magnum and 38 S&W Special
Capacity: 6 shots
Barrel Lengths: 4" or 6"
Overall Length: 9 9/16" w/4" bbl.; 11 15/16" w/6" bbl.
Weight: 41 oz. w/4" bbl.; 46 oz. w/6" bbl.
Sights: Front, S&W Red Ramp; rear, S&W Micrometer Click, adjustable for windage and elevation; white outline notch
Grips: Hogue rubber square butt
Finish: S&W Blue
Prices:
  4" Bbl. $480.00
  6" Bbl. 484.00

SMITH & WESSON REVOLVERS

MEDIUM FRAME

MODEL 686

MODEL 686
POWERPORT

SPECIFICATIONS
Same specifications as MODEL 586 (see preceding page), except also available with 2.5" barrel (35.5 oz.) and 8 ³/₈" barrel (53 oz.). All models have stainless steel finish, combat or target stock and/or trigger; adjustable sights optional.

Prices:
2.5" Barrel $499.00
8 ³/₈" Barrel 550.00

SPECIFICATIONS
Same general specifications as the MODEL 686 except this revolver features 6" full lug barrel with intergral compensator, Hogue rubber grips and black-pinned Patridge front sight.
Price: $548.00
Also available:
MODEL 686 PLUS DISTINGUISHED COMBAT MAGNUM
Capacity: 7 rounds **Barrel Lengths:** 2.5", 4" or 6" full lug.
Overall Length: 7.5" – 11 ¹⁵/₁₆" **Weight:** 34.5 oz. – 45 oz.
Prices:
2.5" bbl. $518.00
4" Barrel 526.00
6" Barrel 534.00

LARGE FRAME

MODEL 29
44 MAGNUM

MODEL 625

SPECIFICATIONS
Calibers: 44 Magnum and 44 S&W Spec.
Capacity: 6 shots **Barrel Lengths:** 6" and 8 ³/₈"
Overall Length: 11 ³/₈" with 6" bbl.; 13 ⁷/₈" with 8 ³/₈" bbl.
Weight: 47 oz. w/6" bbl.; 54 oz. w/8 ³/₈" bbl.
Sights: Front, red ramp on ramp base; rear, S&W micrometer click, adjustable for windage and elevation; white outline notch
Grips: Hogue rubber **Hammer:** .500" Target
Trigger: .400" serrated **Finish:** Blued carbon steel
Prices:
6" Bbl. $574.00
8 ³/₈" Bbl. 586.00

SPECIFICATIONS
Caliber: 45 ACP
Capacity: 6 shots
Barrel Length: 5" full lug barrel
Overall Length: 10 ³/₈"
Weight (empty): 45 oz.
Sights: Front, Patridge on ramp base; S&W Micrometer Click rear, adjustable for windage and elevation
Grips: Hogue rubber, round butt
Finish: Satin stainless
Price: $618.00

SMITH & WESSON PISTOLS

LARGE FRAME

MODEL 629

MODEL 629
CLASSIC DX

MODEL 629
SPECIFICATIONS
Calibers: 44 Magnum, 44 S&W Special *Capacity:* 6 shots
Barrel Lengths: 4", 6", 8 ³/₈" *Overall Length:* 9 ⁵/₈", 11 ³/₈", 13 ⁷/₈"
Weight (empty): 44 oz. (4" bbl.); 47 oz. (6" bbl.); 54 oz. (8 ³/₈" bbl.)
Sights: S&W Red Ramp front; white outline rear w/S&W
Micro-[ljmeter Click, adjustable for windage and elevation;
drilled and tapped
Grips: Hogue rubber *Finish:* Satin stainless steel
Features: Combat trigger, target hammer
Prices: 4" Bbl. $607.00
    6" Bbl. 613.00
    8 ³/₈" Bbl. 627.00

MODEL 629 CLASSIC
SPECIFICATIONS
Calibers: 44 Magnum, 44 S&W Special *Capacity:* 6 rounds
Barrel Lengths: 5", 6.5", 8 ³/₈" *Overall Length:* 10.5", 12", 13 ⁷/₈"
Weight: 51 oz. (5" bbl.); 52 oz. (6.5" bbl.); 54 oz. (8 ³/₈" bbl.)
Grips: Hogue rubber
Prices: 5" & 6.5" Bbl. $650.00
    8 ³/₈" Bbl. 671.00
Also available:
MODEL 629 CLASSIC DX. Same features as the **MODEL
629 CLASSIC** above, plus interchangeable front sights.
    With 6.5" barrel. $835.00
    With 8 ³/₈" barrel. 862.00
MODEL 629 POWERPORT w/6.5" barrel (12" overall
length), weighs 52 oz. Patridge front sight, adjustable black
blade rear sight.
Price: $650.00

MODEL 657

MODEL 610
CLASSIC HUNTER

MODEL 657 STAINLESS
SPECIFICATIONS
Calibers: 41 Magnum *Capacity:* 6 shots
Barrel Length: 6" *Overall Length:* 11 ³/₈"
Weight (empty): 48 oz.
Sights: Front, pinned ramp on ramp base; black blade
rear, adjustable for windage and elevation; drilled and
tapped
Grips: Hogue rubber *Finish:* Satin stainless steel
Price: $548.00

MODEL 610 CLASSIC HUNTER
SPECIFICATIONS
Calibers: 10mm *Frame:* N-Large *Capacity:* 6 rounds
Barrel Length: 6.5" *Overall Length:* 12"
Weight: 52 oz.
Sights: Interchangeable front; micrometer click adj.
black blade
Grips: Hogue rubber *Finish:* Stainless steel
Feature: Unfluted cylinder
Price: $664.00

SPRINGFIELD PISTOLS

MODEL 1911-A1 PISTOLS

**MODEL 1911-A1
STANDARD MIL-SPEC**

**MODEL 1911-A1
STANDARD & LIGHTWEIGHT**

SPECIFICATIONS
Calibers: 45 ACP and 38 Super
Capacity: 7 rounds (45 ACP); 9 rounds (38 Super)
Barrel Length: 5" *Overall Length:* 8 ⁵⁄₈"
Trigger Pull: 5-6.5 lbs. *Sight Radius:* 6.25"
Weight: 38.5 oz. *Finish:* Parkerized
Features: Black plastic grips; military hammer; 3-dot fixed combat sights
Price: $519.00

**MODEL 1911-A1
TROPHY MATCH BI-TONE**

SPECIFICATIONS
Calibers: 45 ACP and 9mm *Capacity:* 7 rounds
Barrel Length: 5" *Overall Length:* 8 ⁵⁄₈" *Weight:* 40 oz.
Trigger Pull: 4-5.5 lbs. *Sights:* Fully adjustable target sights
Sight Radius: 6.75" *Finish:* Blued, Bi-tone or stainless
Features: Match grade barrel; Videcki speed trigger; serrated front strap & top of slide
Prices:
Blued $989.00
Bi-Tone (w/fitted beavertail safety) 999.00
Stainless (w/fitted beavertail safety) 1,029.00

SPECIFICATIONS
Calibers: 45 ACP, 9mm and 38 Super
Capacity: 8 rounds (45 ACP), 9 rounds (9mm & 38 Super)
Barrel Length: 5" *Overall Length:* 8 ⁵⁄₈"
Weight: 38.5 oz. (31.5 oz. Lightweight)
Features: Walnut grips; Bo-Mar-type sights optional
Prices:
45 ACP Blued or Lightweight Matte $549.00
45 ACP Stainless 589.00
45 ACP Stainless Steel V-12 (ported) 719.00
9mm Blued 549.00
9mm Stainless 599.00
38 Super Stainless Steel 599.00

MODEL 1911-A1 HIGH-CAPACITY STANDARD
(not shown)

SPECIFICATIONS
Caliber: 45 ACP
Capacity: 10 rounds (13-round & 17-round capacity available for law enforcement and military use only)
Barrel Length: 5"
Trigger Pull: 5-6.5 lbs.
Sight Radius: 6.14"
Finish: Blued, stainless or Parkerized
Prices:
45 ACP Parkerized $659.00
45 ACP & 9mm Blued 679.00
45 ACP & 9mm Stainless 709.00

In addition to the models listed above and in the following pages, Springfield Armory also produces a broad line of customized pistols including the Super Tuned series (described later). These include the following: Bullseye Wadcutter, National Match Hardball, PPC Auto, High Capacity Full House Racegun, and more. New for 1998-1999 is the **BUREAU MODEL 1911-A1 .45 ACP** with extensive features.
Price: $1,895.00

SPRINGFIELD PISTOLS

MODEL 1911-A1 CHAMPION SERIES

MODEL 1911-A1 CHAMPION

MODEL 1911-A1 MIL-SPEC CHAMPION

SPECIFICATIONS
Calibers: 45 ACP *Capacity:* 7 rounds *Barrel Length:* 4"
Overall Length: 7.75" *Weight:* 36.3 oz. *Trigger Pull:* 5-6.5 lbs.
Sight Radius: 5.25" *Sights:* 3-dot fixed combat sights
Finish: Blued, stainless
Prices:
Blued $569.00
Stainless 579.00
V-10 (Ported) stainless w/ultra compact slide 749.00
Champion .45 (Ported) stainless 719.00
Champion .45 w/ultra compact slide stainless 698.00

SPECIFICATIONS
Caliber: 45 ACP
Capacity: 7 rounds
Barrel Length: 4"
Overall Length: 7.75"
Weight: 36.3 oz.
Sights: 3-dot Combat
Finish: Parkerized
Price: $519.00
    V-10 MIL-SPEC .45 w/ultra compact slide 598.00

MODEL 1911-A1 MIL-SPEC CHAMPION ULTRA COMPACT

MODEL 1911-A1 LIGHTWEIGHT COMPACT

SPECIFICATIONS
Calibers: 45 ACP *Capacity:* 7 rounds *Barrel Length:* 4"
Overall Length: 7.75" *Weight:* 36.3 oz.
Trigger Pull: 5-6.5 lbs. *Sight Radius:* 5.25"
Sights: 3-dot fixed Combat sights *Finish:* Parkerized
Price: $549.00

SPECIFICATIONS
Caliber: 45 ACP *Capacity:* 7 rounds
Barrel Length: 4" *Overall Length:* 7.75"
Weight: 32 oz. (27 oz. alloy) *Trigger Pull:* 5-6.5" *Sights:*
3-dot fixed combat sights *Sight Radius:* 5.25"
Finish: Matte
Price: $669.00

SPRINGFIELD PISTOLS

SUPER TUNED SERIES

CHAMPION 1911-A1

CHAMPION 1911-A1
SPECIFICATIONS
Caliber: 45 ACP *Capacity:* 7 + 1 *Barrel Length:* 4"
Overall Length: 7.75" *Weight:* 36.3 oz. *Sight Radius:* 5.25"
Trigger Pull: 4.4-5.5 lbs. crisp *Grips:* Lightweight combat
Finish: Blue or Parkerized *Sights:* Novak fixed low-mount;
dovetailed serrated ramp front *Features:* Tuned and
polished extractor and ejector; beavertail grip safety;
polished feed ramp and throat barrel
Prices:
Parkerized $959.00
Blued 989.00
Also available: SUPER TUNED V10 1911-A1.
  In stainless $1,119.00
    Bi-tone w/3.5" barrel. 1,049.00
SUPER TUNED STANDARD 1911-A1.
  In stainless w/5" barrel $995.00

ULTRA COMPACT SERIES

HIGH-CAPACITY ULTRA COMPACT MODELS
(not shown)

SPECIFICATIONS
Caliber: 45 ACP and 9mm *Capacity:* 10 rounds (11-
round capacity available for law enforcement and military
use only) *Barrel Length:* 3.5" *Weight:* 33.6 oz.
Sight Radius: 5.25" *Trigger Pull:* 5-6.5 lbs.

Finish: Blue or stainless *Features:* 3-dot fixed combat
sights; flared ejection port; beveled magazine well
Prices:
Stainless $759.00
Mil-Spec Parkerized 689.00
V-10 (PORTED) ULTRA COMPACT
MIL-SPEC .45 PARKERIZED $729.00
  In stainless. 799.00

**1911-A1 V-10
ULTRA COMPACT
BI-TONE**

SPECIFICATIONS
Caliber: 45 ACP *Capacity:* 7 rounds *Barrel Length:* 3.5"
Overall Length: 7.75" *Weight:* 34.8 oz. *Sights:* 3-dot
fixed combat sights *Sight Radius:* 5.25"
Trigger Pull: 5-6.5 lbs. *Finish:* Bi-Tone or Parkerized
Prices:
Bi-Tone $675.00
Parkerized 579.00

**1911-A1 ULTRA
COMPACT BI-TONE**

SPECIFICATIONS
Caliber: 45 ACP
Capacity: 7 rounds
Barrel Length: 3.5" *Overall Length:* 7 1/8"
Weight: 31 oz. *Finish:* Bi-Tone or Parkerized
Prices:
Bi-Tone $629.00
Parkerized 519.00

SPRINGFIELD PISTOLS

MODEL 1911-A1 PDP SERIES

DEFENDER

DEFENDER

SPECIFICATIONS
Caliber: 45 ACP
Capacity: 8 rounds
Barrel Length: 5"
Overall Length: 9"
Weight: 42.2 oz.
Sight Radius: 6 ³/₈"
Sights: 3-dot adjustable
Finish: Bi-Tone
Features: Videcki speed trigger, extended safety
Price: **$993.00**

FACTORY COMP

FACTORY COMP

SPECIFICATIONS
Calibers: 45 ACP and 38 Super
Capacity: 8 rounds (9 rounds 38 Super)
Barrel Length: 5 ⁵/₈"
Overall Length: 10"
Weight: 42.8 oz.
Finish: Blued
Sights: Adjustable 3-dot rear; ramp front
Features: Videcki speed trigger; checkered walnut grips; extended thumb safety; skeletonized hammer
Price:
   45 ACP blued. **$947.00**

HIGH-CAPACITY FACTORY COMP

HIGH-CAPACITY FACTORY COMP

SPECIFICATIONS
Calibers: 45 ACP and 38 Super
Capacity: 10 rounds (13 rounds and 17 rounds available for law-enforcement and military use only)
Barrel Length: 5.5"
Overall Length: 10"
Weight: 40 oz.
Finish: Blued
Features: Triple port comp, skeletonized hammer and grip safety; match barrel & bushing; extended thumb safety; lowered & flared ejection port
Price:
   45 ACP. **$1,075.00**

TAURUS PISTOLS

SMALL & MEDIUM FRAME

MODEL PT 22

SPECIFICATIONS
Caliber: 22 LR *Action:* Semiautomatic (DA only)
Capacity: 8 shots *Barrel Length:* 2.75"
Overall Length: 5.25" *Weight:* 12.3 oz. *Sights:* Fixed
Safety: Manual *Grips:* Rosewood grip panels
Finish: Blue, nickel, duotone or gold trimmed
Prices:
Blue, Nickel or DuoTone $203.00
Gold Trim 220.00

MODEL PT-25

SPECIFICATIONS
Caliber: 25 ACP *Capacity:* 9 rounds
Action: Double action semiauto
Barrel Length: 2.75" *Overall Length:* 5.25"
Weight: 12.3 oz.
Finish: Blue, stainless steel, duotone or gold trimmed
Sights: Fixed *Features:* Rosewood grip panels; tip-up
barrel; push button magazine release
Prices:
Blue, Nickel or DuoTone $162.00
Blue w/Gold Trim 220.00

MODEL PT-938 COMPACT (not shown)

SPECIFICATIONS
Caliber: 380 ACP *Capacity:* 10 rounds
Action: Double action semiauto
Barrel Length: 3" *Overall Length:* 6.75"
Weight: 27 oz. *Finish:* Blue or stainless steel
Sights: Fixed *Grips:* Checkered rubber grips
Prices:
Blue $438.00
Stainless 450.00

PT 911 COMPACT (not shown)

SPECIFICATIONS
Caliber: 9mm *Capacity:* 10 rounds
Action: Double action semiauto *Barrel Length:* 4"
Overall Length: 7" *Weight:* 28.2 oz.
Safeties: Manual, ambidextrous hammer drop; intercept
notch; firing pin block; chamber load indicator
Grips: Santoprene II *Sights:* Fixed 3-dot combat
Finish: Blue or stainless *Features:* Floating firing pin
Prices:
Blue $438.00
Stainless 450.00
Also available:
PT-111 9MM MILLENNIUM. *Barrel Length:* 3 1/8" *Sights:* Fixed
3-dot *Capacity:* 10 rounds, polymer frame $344.00
Stainless 360.00

MODEL PT 22

MODEL PT-25

**MODEL PT 111
MILLENNIUM**

TAURUS PISTOLS

LARGE FRAME

MODEL PT-92

SPECIFICATIONS
Caliber: 9mm Parabellum *Action:* Semiautomatic double action *Capacity:* 10 + 1 *Hammer:* Exposed
Barrel Length: 5" *Overall Length:* 8.5"
Height: 5.39" *Width:* 1.45" *Weight:* 34 oz. (empty)
Rifling: R.H., 6 grooves *Sights:* Front, fixed; rear, drift adjustable, 3-dot combat *Safeties:* (a) Ambidextrous manual safety locking trigger mechanism and slide in locked position; (b) half-cock position; (c) inertia-operated firing pin; (d) chamber-loaded indicator *Slide:* Hold open upon firing last cartridge *Grips:* Checkered rubber
Finish: Blue or stainless steel
Prices:
Blue $490.00
Stainless 510.00
Also available:
MODEL PT-99 Same specifications as Model PT 92, but has micrometer click-adjustable rear sight.
Blue $530.00
Stainless 550.00

MODEL PT-92

MODEL PT-945

SPECIFICATIONS
Caliber: 45 ACP *Capacity:* 8 shots
Action: Semiautomatic double *Barrel Length:* 4.25"
Overall Length: 7.48" *Weight:* 29.5 oz.
Sights: Drift-adjustable front and rear; 3-dot combat
Grips: Checkered rubber
Safety Features: Manual safety; ambidextrous; chamber load indicator; intercept notch; firing-pin block; floating firing pin
Finish: Blue or stainless
Prices:
Blue $470.00
Stainless 485.00
Also available:
MODEL 945C w/factory porting (blue) $510.00
    w/factory porting (stainless) 525.00

MODEL PT-945

MODEL PT-940 (not shown)

SPECIFICATIONS
Caliber: 40 S&W *Action:* Semiautomatic double
Capacity: 10 rounds *Barrel Length:* 3.75"
Overall Length: 7" *Weight:* 28.2 oz.
Grips: Santoprene II *Sights:* Low-profile 3-dot combat
Finish: Blue or stainless
Features: Factory porting standard
Prices:
Blue $450.00
Stainless 470.00

**MODEL PT 99
STAINLESS**

TAURUS REVOLVERS

MODEL 44

SPECIFICATIONS
Caliber: 44 Mag. *Capacity:* 6 rounds
Barrel Lengths: 4" (solid rib ported); 6.5" and 8 ³/₈" (vent. rib)
Weight: 44 oz. (4"); 52.5 oz. (6.5"); 57.25 oz. (8 ³/₈")
Sights: Serrated ramp front; rear micrometer click, adjustable for windage and elevation
Grips: Santoprene I
Finish: Blue or stainless steel
Features: Transfer bar safety
Prices:
4" barrel blue, ported solid rib. $447.00
   stainless steel, ported solid rib. 508.00
6.5" and 8 ³/₈" blue, ported vent. rib 465.00
   stainless steel, ported vent. rib 529.00

MODEL 454 CASULL

MODEL 454 CASULL "RAGING BULL" DA
SPECIFICATIONS
Caliber: 454 Casull *Capacity:* 5 rounds
Barrel Length: 6.5" or 8.375" w/integral vent rib
Overall Length: 12" (6.5" barrel); 14" (8.375" barrel)
Weight: 53 oz. (6.5" barrel); 62.75 oz. (8.375" barrel)
Safety: Transfer bar ignition system
Sights: Black Patridge front blade; micrometer click adj. black rear
Finish: Polished stainless steel or bright blue steel
Grips: Soft black rubber w/recoil-absorbing insert
Features: Ported barrel w/internal gas expansion chamber; front and rear cylinder lock
Prices:
Blue ported $750.00
Stainless 850.00

MODEL 82

SPECIFICATIONS
Caliber: 38 Special *Capacity:* 6 shot
Action: Double *Barrel Length:* 4" heavy barrel
Weight: 34 oz. (4" barrel) *Sights:* Notched rear; serrated ramp front *Grips:* Brazilian hardwood
Finish: Blue or stainless
Prices:
Blue $296.00
Stainless 344.00

MODEL 85

SPECIFICATIONS
Caliber: 38 Special *Capacity:* 5 shot
Action: Double *Barrel Length:* 2" and 3"
Weight: 21 oz. (2" barrel) *Sights:* Fixed sights
Grips: Brazilian hardwood *Finish:* Blue or stainless steel
Prices:
Blue $258.00
Stainless Steel 306.00
Also available:
MODEL 85CH. Same specifications and prices as Model 85, except has concealed hammer and 2" barrel only.
MODEL 85UL w/2" barrel only and optional porting; weights 17 oz. Features Ultra-Lite Integral Key Lock
Blue $299.00
Stainless 330.00
MODELS 85CHB2C/85B2C w/2" barrel, blue finish, ported barrels $276.00
Stainless 325.00
MODELS 85B2KL/85SS2KL w/Integral Key Lock . . . $277.00
Stainless 326.00

TAURUS REVOLVERS

MODEL 941

MODEL 94

SPECIFICATIONS
Caliber: 22 LR **Number Of Shots:** 9
Action: Double **Barrel Lengths:** 2", 3", 4",
and 5" heavy, solid rib **Weight:** 25 oz. (w/4"
barrel) **Sights:** Serrated ramp front; rear
micrometer click adjustable for windage and elevation
Grips: Brazilian hardwood (3", 4", 5")
Finish: Blue or stainless steel
Prices:
Blue $308.00
Stainless Steel 356.00
Also available:
MODEL 941 in 22 Magnum, 8-shot capacity; 2", 3", 4",
5" barrel lengths available; ejector shroud.
In blue $331.00
In stainless steel 384.00

MODEL 96

SPECIFICATIONS
Caliber: 22 LR
Capacity: 6 shot
Action: Double
Barrel Length: 6" **Weight:** 34 oz.
Sights: Patridge-type front; rear, micrometer click
adjustable for windage and elevation
Safety: Transfer bar
Grips: Brazilian hardwood
Finish: Blue only
Features: Target hammer; adjustable target trigger
Price: $376.00

MODEL 445 DOUBLE ACTION

SPECIFICATIONS
Caliber: 44 Special **Capacity:** 5 shots
Barrel Length: 2" **Weight:** 28.25 oz.
Grips: Santoprene I
Sights: Serrated ramp front; notched rear
Finish: Blue or stainless
Features: Optional porting; heavy solid rib barrel
Prices:
Blue $304.00
Stainless 351.00
Also available:
MODEL 445CH. Same specifications as Model 445 but features
concealed hammer

MODEL 605

SPECIFICATIONS
Caliber: 357 Magnum
Capacity: 5 shot
Barrel Length: 2.25"
Weight: 24.5 oz.
Sights: Notched rear; serrated ramp front
Grips: Santoprene I
Safety: Transfer bar
Finish: Blue or stainless
Features: Optional porting ($19.00 add'l.)
Prices:
Blue $296.00
Stainless 344.00
Also available:
MODEL 605CH w/concealed hammer and ported barrel
MODELS 605021KL/605029KL w/Integral Key Lock
($20.00 add'l.)

TAURUS REVOLVERS

MODEL 606 COMPACT

SPECIFICATIONS
Caliber: 357 Magnum/38 Special
Capacity: 6 shots *Action:* Double action
Barrel Length: 2" *Weight:* 29 oz.
Sights: Notched rear; serrated ramp front
Grips: Santoprene I
Finish: Blue or stainless *Features:* Transfer bar safety; heavy solid rib barrel; ejector shroud; floating firing pin; optional porting
Prices:
Blue $296.00
Stainless Steel 344.00
Also available:
MODEL 606C. Same specifications as Model 606, but with concealed hammer
MODEL 606C/KL Same as Model 606, but with Integral Key Lock ($20.00 add'l); w/Ported stainless barrel $382.00

MODEL 608 DOUBLE ACTION

SPECIFICATIONS
Caliber: 357 Magnum
Capacity: 8 shots
Barrel Lengths: 3" and 4" (heavy solid rib); 6.5" and 8 $^3/_8$" (ejector shroud)
Weight: 51.5 oz. (6.5" barrel)
Grips: Santoprene I
Sights: Serrated ramp front w/red insert; micrometer click adjustable
Finish: Blue or stainless
Features: Compensated barrel; transfer bar safety; concealed hammer (3" barrel and stainless steel only $46.00 additional)
Prices:
3", 4" Blue $447.00
3", 4" Stainless 508.00
6.5", 8 $^3/_8$" Blue 465.00
6.5", 8 $^3/_8$" Stainless 529.00

MODEL 669

MODEL 669

SPECIFICATIONS
Caliber: 357 Magnum *Capacity:* 6 shot
Action: Double *Barrel Lengths:* 4" and 6"
Weight: 37 oz. (4" barrel)
Sights: Serrated ramp front; rear, micrometer click adjustable for windage and elevation
Grips: Brazilian hardwood
Finish: Royal blue or stainless
Optional feature: Recoil compensator $363.00 (Blue); $442.00 (Stainless)
Prices:
4" and 6" Blue $344.00
4" and 6" Stainless 421.00

MODEL 689

MODEL 689 STAINLESS

SPECIFICATIONS
The Model 689 has the same specifications as the Model 669, except vent rib is featured. Recoil compensator not available.

Prices:
Blue $358.00
Stainless 435.00

THOMPSON/CENTER

ENCORE HUNTER PACKAGE

ENCORE PISTOL
SPECIFICATIONS
Calibers: 22-250 Rem., 223 Rem., 243 Win., 260 Rem., 45-70 Gov't., 45 Colt/.410 ga., 270 Win., 7mm BR Rem., 7mm-08 Rem., 7.62X39mm, 308 Win., 30-06 Spfd. 44 Rem. Mag., 444 Marlin *Action:* Single break-open *Barrel lengths:* 10" and 15" *Overall length:* 14.5" (10" bbl.); 19.5" (15" bbl.) *Weight:* 4 lbs. (10" bbl.); 4.5 lbs. (15" bbl.) *Trigger:* Adjustable *Safety:* Automatic hammerblock w/bolt interlock *Grips:* Ambidextrous walnut pistol grip w/finger grooves and butt cap; composite grips as accessory. *Sights:* Adjustable rear; ramp front sight blade *Features:* Interchangeable barrels (**$215.00** 10" bbl., **$445.00** 15" bbl.); drilled and tapped for T/C scope mounts; barrel lug welded by electronic beam process
Price: 10" barrel **$485.00**
    15" barrel 495.00
Also available: ENCORE HUNTER PACKAGE in 22-250 Win., 270 Win., 308 Win. *Barrel length:* 15" *Features:* Weaver-style base and rings, 2.5-7X Recoil Proof pistol scope; blued frame and barrel; black composite grip and forend; soft carry case; no iron sights.
Price: **$759.00**

THOMPSON/CENTER CONTENDER SHOOTER'S PACKAGE
SPECIFICATIONS
Calibers: 7-30 Waters, 223 Rem., 30-30 Win., 22 LR Match *Barrel length:* 14" (10" 22 LR Match) *Overall length:* 16" (12" 22 LR Match) *Weight:* 4 lbs.
Features: Mounted T/C Recoil Proof 2.5 X 7 scope plus carrying case
Price: Blued steel **$730.00**

CONTENDER SUPER "16" (Not Shown)
SPECIFICATIONS
Calibers: 22 LR, 223 Rem., 45-70 (bull barrel); 45 Colt/.410 ga.
Prices:
Blued (22 LR, 223 Rem.) **$491.00**
    45-70 Gov't. w/Muzzle Tamer 506.00
    45 Colt/.410 ga. 522.00
Stainless steel (223 Rem. only) 546.00
    45 Colt/.410 ga. 579.00
    45-70 Gov't. w/Muzzle Tamer 568.00

CONTENDER SUPER "14" BULL BARREL MODELS
SPECIFICATIONS
Calibers: 22 LR, 22 LR Match Grade Chamber, 22 Hornet, 223 Rem., 7-30 Waters, 30-30 Win., and 44 Mag. (Blued version also available in 22 Hornet, 222 Rem., 300 Whisper, 357 Rem. Max.). *Barrel length:* 14" bull barrel.
Features: Fully adjustable target rear sight and Patridge-style ramped front sight with 13.5-inch sight radius.
Overall length: 18.25" *Weight:* 3.5 lbs.
Prices:
Blued **$473.80**
    Match Grade Chamber 484.00
    17 Rem. 504.00
Stainless 504.70
Vent Rib Model (14") in 45 Colt/.410, blue 504.70
Stainless 535.60

CONTENDER BULL BARREL MODELS
These pistols with 10-inch barrel feature fully adjustable Patridge-style iron sights. All stainless steel models (including the Super "14" and Super "16") are equipped with Rynite finger-groove grip with rubber recoil cushion and matching Rynite forend, plus Cougar etching on the steel frame.
Standard calibers available: 22 WMR, 22 LR, 22 Hornet, 22 LR Match, 223 Rem., 300 Whisper, 30-30 Win., 7mm T.C.U., 357 Mag., 44 Mag. and 45 Colt/.410. Custom calibers also available.

Prices:
Bull Barrel Blue **$475.00**
Bull Barrel Stainless 529.00
    In 45/.410 . . . . 535.00
Vent Rib Model Stainless 551.00
Match Grade Barrel (22 LR only, stainless) 540.00

UBERTI REPLICAS

1871 ROLLING BLOCK TARGET PISTOL

SPECIFICATIONS
Calibers: 22 LR, 22 Magnum, 22 Hornet and 357 Mag.
Capacity: Single shot
Barrel Length: 9.5" (half-octagon/half-round or full round
Navy Style)
Overall Length: 14" *Weight:* 2.75 lbs.
Sights: Fully adjustable rear; ramp front or open sight on
Navy Style barrel
Grip and forend: Walnut *Trigger guard:* Brass
Frame: Color casehardened steel
Price: $410.00

**1871 ROLLING BLOCK
TARGET PISTOL**

1873 CATTLEMAN S.A.

SPECIFICATIONS
Calibers: 357 Magnum, 44-40, 45 L.C., 45 ACP
Capacity: 6 shots
Barrel Lengths: 4.75", 5.5", 7.5" round, tapered; 18" (Buntline)
Overall Length: 10.75" w/5.5" barrel
Weight: 2.42 lbs. *Grip:* One-piece walnut
Frame: Color casehardened steel; also available in
charcoal blue or nickel
Price: $410.00-475.00
Also available:
45 L.C./45 ACP Convertible $485.00

1873 CATTLEMAN

1875 "OUTLAW"/1890 POLICE

SPECIFICATIONS
Calibers: 357 Magnum, 44-40, 45 ACP, 45 Long Colt
Capacity: 6 shots *Barrel Lengths:* 5.5", 7.5" round, tapered
Overall Length: 13.75" *Weight:* 2.75 lbs.
Grips: Two-piece walnut *Finish:* Color casehardened steel
Price: $435.00
Also available:
In nickel plate $435.00
45 L.C./45 ACP Convertible 475.00

**1875 "OUTLAW"/
1890 POLICE**

American Arms/Uberti	204		L.A.R. Grizzly	238
AMT	205		Lazzeroni	239
Arnold	206		Magnum Research	240
A-Square	208		Magtech	240
Auto-Ordnance	209		Marlin	241
Beretta	210		Mauser	250
Blaser	211		Navy Arms	251
Brown Precision	212		New England Firearms	257
Browning	214		Pedersoli	258
Christensen Arms	219		Prairie Gun Works	258
Colt	221		Remington	259
Cooper Arms	222		Rifles	269
Dakota Arms	224		Rossi	270
EMF	226		Ruger	271
European American Armory	226		Sako	279
Francotte	227		Sauer	286
Harrington & Richardson	228		Savage	287
Harris Gunworks	229		Springfield	298
Heckler & Koch	232		Steyr-Mannlicker	300
Henry Repeating Arms	232		Thompson/Center	301
Howa	233		Tikka	302
Jarrett	233		Uberti	304
KBI/Charles Daly	234		Ultra Light Arms	306
Kimber	235		Unique	307
Kongsberg	237		Weatherby	308
Krieghoff	238		Winchester	314

Rifles

*For addresses and phone/fax numbers of manufacturers and distributors included in this section, please turn to **DIRECTORY OF MANUFACTURERS AND SUPPLIERS** on page 558.*

AMERICAN ARMS/UBERTI LEVER ACTION RIFLES

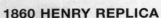

1860 HENRY REPLICA

SPECIFICATIONS
Caliber: 44-40 or 45 LC
Barrel Length: 24.25" half-octagonal barrel w/forged steel tubular magazine
Overall Length: 43.75"
Weight: 9.25 lbs.
Features: Brass frame, elevator, magazine follower and buttstock; straight-grip walnut buttstock
Price: $996.00

1866 WINCHESTER REPLICA

SPECIFICATIONS
Caliber: 44-40 or 45 LC
Barrel Length: 24.25" tapered octagonal or 19" round tapered carbine barrel
Overall Length: 43.25" (w/24.25" barrel)
Weight: 8.15 lbs.
Features: Tubular magazine; brass frame, elevator and buttplate; walnut buttstock and forend
Prices: $829.00
19" barrel 797.00

1873 WINCHESTER

SPECIFICATIONS
Caliber: 44-40 or 45 LC
Barrel Length: 24.25" tapered octagonal barrel (tubular magazine)
Features: Color casehardened steel frame with ejection port cover; brass elevator; walnut buttstock with steel buttplate
Price: $984.00
Also available:
DELUXE 1873 WINCHESTER REPLICA w/pistol grip and deluxed hand-checkered stock; vertically adjustable rear sight and horizontally adjustable front sight; special checkered pistol grip walnut stock and forearm w/upgraded wood.. . . . . $1,299.00

AMT RIFLES

22 RIMFIRE MAGNUM

22 MAGNUM HUNTER

AMT's rimfire magnum rifle delivers big-bore velocity with minimum cost ammunition. Jacketed bullets combine with magnum velocity to yield high impact. Greater power flattens trajectory and improves accuracy.

SPECIFICATIONS
Caliber: 22 Rimfire Magnum
Capacity: 10 rounds
Barrel length: 20" *Weight:* 6 lbs.
Sights: No sights; drilled and tapped for 87-A Weaver scope mount base
Features: Stainless steel construction
Price: (scope not included)................. $459.00

TARGET MODEL SEMIAUTOMATIC

SPECIFICATIONS
Caliber: 22 LR
Capacity: 10 rounds
Barrel length: 20" target barrel .920 O.D.
Weight: 7.5 lbs.
Features: Button rifled barrel w/target crown; one-piece receiver w/built-in integral Weaver-style mount; left or right hand Fajen laminated Aristocrat-style stock or Hogue composite stock; cryogenic-treated barrel
Prices:
FAJEN STOCK. $599.99
w/HOGUE STOCK 549.00

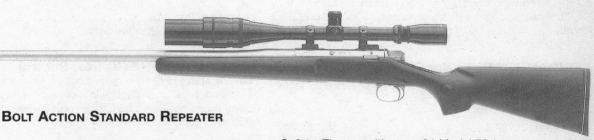

BOLT ACTION STANDARD REPEATER

STANDARD RIFLES
(Single Shot & Repeater)

SPECIFICATIONS
Caliber: Single Shot—22 Hornet, 222, 223, 22-250, 243 Win., 243A, 22 PPC, 6 PPC, 6.5X08, 708, 308
Repeaters—223, 22-250, 243, 243A, 6 PPC, 25-06, 6.5X08, 270, 30-06, 308, 7mm Mag., 300 Win. Mag., 338 Win. Mag., 375 H&H, 416 Rem., 458 Win. Mag., 416 Rigby, 7.62X39, 7X57, 7.62mm
Action: Push feed post-64 Win. Type
Magazine: Mauser type
Barrels: Match grade up to 28" long #3
Weight: Approximately 8.5 lbs.
Trigger: Custom-type adjustable

Safety: Three position pre-64 Model 70-type
Stock: Classic Composite
Pull: 13.5" stock length
Features: Pillar bedding; sliding ejector 2/30° cone bolt; stainless and chrome moly steel; sights drilled and tapped for scope mount
Prices:
STANDARD SINGLE SHOT $1,109.99
STANDARD REPEATER. 1,109.99
DELUXE SINGLE SHOT 2,399.99
DELUXE REPEATER 1,595.00
ACTIONS (Left-Hand models available)
   SINGLE SHOT. 550.00
   REPEATER 650.00
    Magnum actions 690.00

ARNOLD ARMS RIFLES

AFRICAN SERIES

Arnold Arms Company introduces a full line of rifles built on its "Apollo" action with the strongest and hardest chrome-moly and stainless steels available. Alignment of bolt face, receiver and barrel centerline axis results in optimum accuracy. Lapping the bolt lugs, squaring the bolt and truing the receiver are unnecessary—the Apollo action assures perpendicular alignment and equal pressure lock-up. A perfect mating of the receiver, recoil lug and stock, achieved only through the process of glass bedding, assures uniformity of recoil bearing points shot after shot. The revolutionary positive feed and extraction features designed and machined into the "Apollo" bolt face assure full extraction and ejection as well as next cartridge feeding with every complete bolt cycling. The 3-position positive-lock safety locks up the bolt and firing pin to prevent accidental discharge until the rifle is ready to fire.

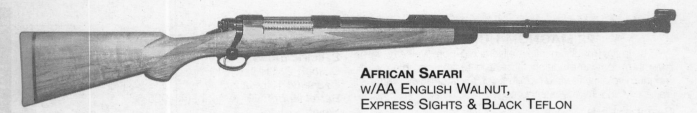

AFRICAN SAFARI
w/AA English Walnut,
Express Sights & Black Teflon

AFRICAN SAFARI

SPECIFICATIONS
Calibers: 243 to 458 Win. Magnum
Barrel Length: 22" to 26" (Contours #2 to #7 C-M; #4 to #7 S.S.)
Sights: Scope mount standard or with optional M70 Express sights
Finish: Chrome-moly in matte blue, polished or stainless steel matte finish
Stock: A and AA Fancy Grade English walnut stock with #5 standard wraparound checkering pattern (patterns 1-4 & 6-10 available at extra charge); includes ebony forend tip
Price:. **$6,472.00**

AFRICAN TROPHY (Not Shown)
Same as African Safari but with AAA Extra Fancy English walnut stock with #9 checkering.

Prices:
C-M Matte **$6,921.00**
Std. Polish 7,021.00
Hi-Luster 7,121.00
Stainless Steel Matte. 6,971.00
Add **$499.00** for Express sights

GRAND AFRICAN (Not Shown)
Same as above but in calibers .338 Magnum to .458 Win. Mag. Other standard features include: Exhibition Grade stock with #10 checkering pattern; choice of ebony or Cape Buffalo forend tip; barrel band; scope mount w/Express sights w/front ring & hood. **Barrel Length:** 24"-26".

Prices:
C-M Hi-Luster Polish only **$8,172.00**
Stainless Steel Matte. 8,022.00

WITH "A" GRADE ENGLISH WALNUT
Matte Blue. **$5,528.00**
Std. Polish 5,628.00
Hi-Luster 5,728.00
Stainless Steel Matte 5,578.00
WITH "AA" GRADE ENGLISH WALNUT
C-M Matte Blue. **$5,588.00**
Std. Polish 5,688.00
Hi-Luster 5,788.00
Stainless Steel Matte 5,638.00
Add **$499.00** for Express sights

AFRICAN SYNTHETIC (Not Shown)
Same as above but in fibergrain stock with or without cheekpiece and traditional checkering pattern or stipple finish (Camo colors also available); Whitworth Express folding leaf optional w/front hood sight.

Prices:
C-M Matte **$4,463.00**
Std. Polish 4,563.00
Stainless Steel Matte. 4,513.00

SERENGETI SYNTHETIC (Not Shown)
Same as above but in calibers 243 to 300 Magnum; choice of classic or Monte Carlo cheekpiece; scope mount only. **Barrel Length:** 22"-26" (Contours Featherweight to #5 C-M, #4 to #6 S.S.

Prices:
C-M Matte **$3,769.00**
Std. Polish 3,869.00
Stainless Steel Matte. 3,819.00
Add **$195.00** for fibergrain stock

ARNOLD ARMS RIFLES

ALASKAN SERIES

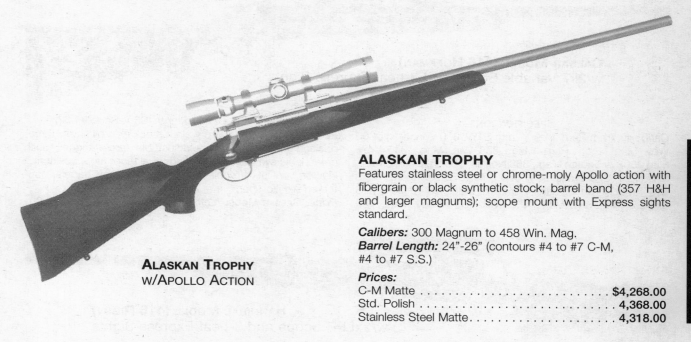

ALASKAN TROPHY
w/APOLLO ACTION

ALASKAN TROPHY
Features stainless steel or chrome-moly Apollo action with fibergrain or black synthetic stock; barrel band (357 H&H and larger magnums); scope mount with Express sights standard.

Calibers: 300 Magnum to 458 Win. Mag.
Barrel Length: 24"-26" (contours #4 to #7 C-M, #4 to #7 S.S.)

Prices:
C-M Matte $4,268.00
Std. Polish 4,368.00
Stainless Steel Matte 4,318.00

GRAND ALASKAN (Not Shown)
Same as above but with AAA fancy select or Exhibition grade English walnut, barrel band and ebony forend; Express sights & scope mount standard. *Calibers:* 300 Magnum to 458 Win. Mag.

Prices:
"AAA" GRADE SELECT ENGLISH WALNUT
C-M Matte. $7,570.00
Std. Polish 7,670.00
Stainless Steel Matte 7,620.00
"EXHIBITION" GRADE, EXTRA FANCY SELECT ENGLISH WALNUT
C-M Matte. $8,621.00
Std. Polish 8,721.00
Hi-Luster. 8,821.00
Stainless Steel Matte 8,671.00

ALASKAN SYNTHETIC RIFLE (Not Shown)
Same as Alaskan Trophy but with fibergrain stock; scope mounts or Express sights optional.

Calibers: 257 to 338 Magnum.

Prices:
C-M Matte $4,463.00
Std. Polish 4,563.00
Stainless Steel Matte. 4,513.00

ALASKAN RIFLE (Not Shown)
Features stainless steel or chrome-moly Apollo action with black, woodland, or Arctic camo stock; scope mount only.

Calibers: 300 Magnum to 458 Win. Mag.
Barrel Length: 24"-26" (Contours #4 to #7 C-M, #4 to #7 S.S.)

Prices:
C-M Matte $3,769.00
Std. Polish 3,869.00
Stainless Steel 3,819.00

ALASKAN GUIDE (Not Shown)
Same as above but with choice of either "A" English walnut or synthetic stock; scope mount only.

Calibers: 257 to 338 Magnum.
Barrel Length: 22"-26" depending on caliber (Contours #4 to #6 C-M, #4 to #6 S.S.)

Prices:
C-M Matte $5,528.00
Std. Polish 5,628.00
Stainless Steel Matte. 5,578.00

A-Square Rifles

CAESAR MODEL (416 HOFFMAN)
w/2x7 Variable Scope and 3-Leaf Express Sights

SPECIFICATIONS

Calibers: 7mm Rem. Mag., 7mm STW, 300 Win. Mag., 300 Wby. Mag., 8mm Rem. Mag., 338 Win. Mag., 340 Wby. Mag., 338 A-Square Mag., 358 Norma, 358 STA, 9.3x64mm, 375 H&H, 375 Weatherby, 375 JRS, 375 A-Square Mag., 416 Taylor, 416 Hoffman, 416 Rem. Mag., 404 Jeffery, 425 Express, 458 Win. Mag., 458 Lott, 450 Ackley Mag., 460 Short A-Square, 470 Capstick and 495 A-Square Mag.
Features: Selected Claro walnut stock with oil finish; three-position safety; three-way adjustable target trigger; flush detachable swivels; leather sling; dual recoil lugs; coil spring ejector; ventilated recoil pad; premium honed barrels; contoured ejection port
Price: CAESAR MODEL (Left Hand). $3,295.00

HANNIBAL MODEL (416 RIGBY)
w/2xLER Scope and 3-Leaf Express Sights

SPECIFICATIONS

Calibers: 300 Pegasus, 8mm Rem. Mag., 338 Win., 340 Wby., 338 A-Square Mag., 338 Excalibur, 358 Norma Mag., 358 STA, 9.3x64, 375 A-Square, 375 JRS, 375 H&H, 375 Wby., 378 Wby., 404 Jeffery, 416 Hoffman, 416 Rem., 416 Rigby, 416 Taylor, 416 Wby., 425 Express, 450 Ackley, 458 Lott, 458 Win., 460 Short A-Square, 460 Weatherby, 470 Capstick, 495 A-Square, 500 A-Square, 577 Tyrannosaur
Barrel Length: 20" to 26"
Length of Pull: 12" to 15.25" **Weight:** 9.5 lbs.-13.25 lbs.
Finish: Deluxe walnut stock; oil finish; matte blue
Features: Flush detachable swivels, leather sling, dual recoil lugs, coil spring ejector, ventilated recoil pad, premium honed barrels, contoured ejection port, three-way adjustable target-style trigger, Mauser-style claw extractor and controlled feed, positive safety
Price: $3,295.00

HAMILCAR

SPECIFICATIONS

Calibers: 25-06, 257 Wby., 6.5x55 Swedish, 264 Win., 270 Win., 270 Wby., 7x57 Mauser, 280 Rem., 7mm Rem., 7mm Wby., 7mm STW, 30-06, 300 Win., 300 Wby., 338-06, 9.3x62 **Barrel Length:** 20" to 26" **Length of Pull:** 12" to 15.25" **Weight:** 8.5 lbs. **Finish:** Deluxe walnut stock; oil finish; matte blue **Features:** Flush detachable swivels, leather sling, coil spring ejector, vent. recoil pad; honed barrels; contoured ejection port; target-style adjustable trigger, Mauser-style claw extractor; controlled feed; positive safety
Price: $3,295.00
Also available: GENGHIS KHAN MODEL in 22-250, 243 Win., 6mm Rem., 25-06, 257 Wby., 264 Win. Features benchrest-quality heavy taper barrel and coilchek stock. **Weight:** 11 lbs. (w/scope & iron sights)
Price: $3,295.00

AUTO-ORDNANCE

SEMIAUTOMATIC RIFLES

THOMPSON MODEL M1 CARBINE

SPECIFICATIONS
Caliber: 45 ACP *Barrel Length:* 16.5"
Overall Length: 38" *Weight:* 11.5 lbs.
Sights: Blade front; fixed rear

Stock: Walnut stock and horizontal foregrip
Features: Side cocking lever; frame and receiver milled from solid steel
Price: $815.00

THOMPSON DELUXE MODEL 1927 A1

SPECIFICATIONS
Caliber: 45 ACP
Barrel Length: 16.5"
Overall Length: 41" *Weight:* 13 lbs.
Sights: Blade front; open rear adjustable

Stock: Walnut stock; vertical foregrip
Also available:
THOMPSON **1927A1C** LIGHTWEIGHT (45 Cal.). Same as the 1927 A1 model, but weighs only 9.5 lbs.
Price: $825.00

MODEL 1927 A1 COMMANDO

SPECIFICATIONS
Caliber: 45 ACP
Barrel Length: 16.5"
Overall Length: 41"

Weight: 13 lbs.
Sights: Blade front; open rear (adjustable)
Finish: Black (stock and forend)
Price: $820.00

BERETTA RIFLES

455 EXPRESS

EXPRESS RIFLES

Express Rifles must withstand the extreme pressures generated by high caliber express cartridges. This requires action and locking systems designed and manufactured with extra strength, all joined with absolute precision for optimum convergence. The SS06 and SS06EELL Over- and Under Express Rifles offer rifled barrels of special steel cold-hammered in three calibers: 9.3x74R, .375 H&H Mag. and .458 Win. Mag. For those wishing to hunt with a traditional shotgun, an extra set of matching 12 gauge barrels is available. Hand-finished, hand-checkered stocks and forends are made from select walnut or walnut briar with a cheek-piece. A special trap door compartment for extra cartridges is fitted inside the stock, and an area under the pistol-grip cap holds a set of spare front sights. The SS-06 is finished with light engraving on the color case-hardened receiver. The SS06 EELL sports a receiver hand-engraved with game scenes, or a color case-hardened version with gold inlaid animals. For additional specifications see the table below.

The 455 Side-by-Side Express Rifle action is made of special high-strength steel and forged with an elongated 60mm plate. This increases the distance between the hinge pin and the three-lug locking system to compensate for stress when shooting. To withstand the pressure of high-powered cartridges, the sealed receiver has reinforced sides, and the top tang extends fully up to the stock comb to strengthen attachment of the stock. An articulated front trigger and automatic blocking device eliminate the possibility of simultaneous discharge. The safety (automatic on request) provides for quick, reliable and positive on/off operation. The Boehler steel barrels are joined with Demibloc chamber system.

SS06 EXPRESS RIFLE
SPECIFICATIONS
Calibers: 375 H&H, 458 Win. Mag., 9.3x94R
Barrel length: 24" (12 ga. matching interchangeable barrels available)
Weight: 11 lbs.
Sights: Blade front sight; V-notch rear sight w/folding leaf (claw mounts for Zeiss scope factory fitted and sighted-in at 100 meters)
Price: **$50,000.00**
Note: MODEL SS06 EELL is also available in same calibers and features hand-engraved game scenes on the receiver or color case-hardened w/gold inlaid animals. **$50,000.00**

455 EXPRESS RIFLE
SPECIFICATIONS
Calibers: 375 H&H, 410 Rigby, 458 Win. Mag., 470 N.E., 500 N.E.
Barrel length: 23" - 25"
Weight: 11 lbs.
Sights: Fixed front sight w/folding blade; V-notch rear sight
Price: **$50,000.00**
Note: MODEL 455 EELL is also available (same price and calibers) featuring Bulino-style game scene engraving or intricate scroll work and walnut briar stock and forend.

PREMIUM GRADE EXPRESS RIFLE SPECIFICATIONS

MODEL	9.3x 74R	.375 H&H MAG.	CALIBER* .416 RIGBY	.458 H&H MAG.	.470 N.E.	.500 N.E.	BARREL LENGTH (CM/IN)	AVERAGE WEIGHT (KG/LBS)**
SS06	√	√		√			62/24	5.00/11.0
SS06 EELL	√	√		√			62/24	5.00/11.0
455		√	√	√	√	√	60/23 to 65/25	5.00/11.0
455 EELL		√	√	√	√	√	60/23 to 65/25	5.00/11.0

*SS06 EELL Models are available with interchangeable 12 gauge shotgun barrels upon request.
**Weights are approximate, dependent on wood density and barrel length.

BERETTA RIFLES

MATO RIFLES

Beretta's new Mato (the Dakota Indian word for "bear") is designed for hunters. Based on the Mauser 98 action, it has a drop-out box magazine that releases quickly. The barrels are machined from high-grade chrome-moly steel. Other features include ergonomic bolt handle, adjustable trigger, wraparound hand checkering and three-position safety.

SPECIFICATIONS
Calibers: 270 Win., 280 Rem., 30-06 Springfield, 7mm Rem. Mag., 300 Win. Mag., 338 Win. Mag., 375 H&H Mag. **Barrel length:** 23.6" **Overall length:** 44.5" **Weight:** 7.97 lbs. (Deluxe); 8 lbs. (Standard) **Stock:** Matte grey composite synthetic (Standard); Triple-X Grade Claro walnut w/hand-rubbed satin oil finish and black forend tip (Deluxe) **Length of pull:** 13.5" **Drop at comb:** .56" **Drop at heel:** .81" **Twist:** 1:10" (1:12" 375 H&H Mag.)

Prices: Standard Synthetic $1,660.00
in H&H mag.. . . . . 2,015.00
Deluxe Synthetic 2,478.00
in H&H Mag.. . . . . 2,795.00

BLASER RIFLES

MODEL R93 CLASSIC

MODEL R 93 BOLT ACTION SERIES

SPECIFICATIONS (CLASSIC)
Calibers: (interchangeable)
Standard: (22-250, 243 Win., 270 Win., 30-06, 308 Win.
Magnum: 257 Weatherby Mag., 7mm Rem. Mag., 300 Win. Mag., 300 Wby. Mag., 338 Win. Mag., 375 H&H, 416 Rem. Mag..
Barrel lengths: 22" (Standard) and 26" (Magnum)
Overall length: 40" (Standard) and 42" (Magnum)
Weight: (w/scope mounts) 7 lbs. (Standard) and 7.25 lbs. (Magnum) **Safety:** Cocking slide
Stock: Two-piece Custom and Deluxe Walnut recoil pad, hand-cut checkering (18 lines/inch, borderless)
Length of pull: 13.75"

Prices:
CLASSIC $3,495.00
LX 1,795.00
SYNTHETIC. 1,495.00
ATTACHÉ 5,125.00
SAFARI SYNTHETIC 2,120.00
SAFARI LX 2,545.00
SAFARI CLASSIC 4,245.00
SAFARI ATTACHÉ 5,875.00
Also available:
SAFARI MODEL. 416 Rem. Mag. only. 24" heavy barrel (42" overall); open sights. **Weight:** 9.5 lbs
Prices: Standard. $3,300.00
Deluxe 3,600.00
Super Deluxe 4,000.00

BROWN PRECISION RIFLES

PRO-HUNTER RIFLE

Designed for the serious game hunter or guide, this custom version of Brown Precision's Pro-Hunter rifle begins as a Winchester Model 700 Super Grade action with controlled feed claw extractor. The trigger is tuned to crisp let-off at each customer's specified weight. A Shilen Match Grade stainless-steel barrel is custom crowned and hand fitted to the action.

The Pro-Hunter Elite features choice of epress rear sight or custom Dave Talley removable peep sight and banded front ramp sight with European dovetail and replaceable brass bead. An optional flip-up white night sight is also available, as is a set of Dave Talley detachable T.N.T. scope mount rings and bases installed with Brown's Magnum Duty 8X40 screws. QD sling swivels are standard.

All metal parts are finished in either matte electroless nickel or black Teflon. The barreled action is glass bedded to a custom Brown Precision Alaskan-configuration fiberglass stock, painted according to customer choice and fitted w/premium 1" buttpad and Dave Talley trapdoor grip cap. Weight ranges from 7 to 15 lbs., depending on barrel length, coutour and options.

Optional equipment includes custom steel drop box magazine, KDF or Answer System muzzle brake, Mag-Na-Port, Zeiss, Swarovski or Leupold scope and Americase aluminum hard case.

Prices: **$3565.00**

PRO-VARMINTER RIFLE

The standard Pro-Varminter is builllt on the Remington 700 or Rremington 40X action (right or left hand) and features a hand-fitted Shilen Match Grade Heavy Benchrest stainless-steel barrel in bright or bead-blasted finish. The barreled action is custom-bedded in Brown Precision's Varmint Special Hunter Bench or 40X Benchrest-style custom fiberglass, Kevlar or graphite stock.

Other standard features include custom barrel length and contour, trigger tuned for crisp pull to customer's specified weight, custom length of pull, and choice of recoil pad. Additional options include metal finishes, muzzle brakes, Leupold target or varmint scopes and others.

Prices:

Right-hand Model 700 Action	**$1965.00**
For Left-hand Model, **add**.	**$120.00**
40X Action.	**$2450.00**

BROWN PRECISION RIFLES

HIGH COUNTRY YOUTH RIFLE

This custom rifle has all the same features as the standard High Country rifle, but scaled-down to fit the younger or smaller shooter. Based on the Remington Model 7 barreled action, it is available in calibers 223, 243, 7mm-08, 6mm and 308. The rifle features a shortened fiberglass, Kevlar or graphite stock, which can be lengthened as the shooter grows, a new recoil pad installed and the stock refinished. Custom features/options include choice of actions, custom barrels, chamberings, muzzle brakes, metal finishes, scopes and accessories.

All Youth Rifles include a deluxe package of shooting, reloading and hunting accessories and information to increase a young shooter's interest.

Price: starts at **$1355.00**

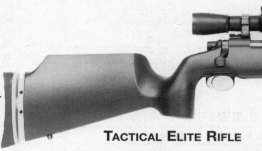

TACTICAL ELITE RIFLE

Brown Precision's Tactical Elite is built on a Remington 700 action and features a bead-blasted Shilen Select Match Grade Heavy Benchrest Stainless Steel barrel custom-chambered for 223 Rem., 308 Win., 300 Win. Mag. (or any standard or wildcat caliber). A nonreflective custom black Teflon metal finish on all metal surfaces ensures smooth bolt operation and 100 percent weatherproofing. The barreled action is bedded in a target-style stock with high rollover comb/cheekpiece, vertical pistol grip and palmswell. The stock is an advanced, custom fiberglass/Kevlar/graphite composite for maximum durability and rigidity, painted in flat black (camouflage patterns are also available). QD sling swivel studs and swivels are standard.

Other standard features include: three-way adjustable buttplate/recoil pad assembly with length of pull, vertical and cant angle adjustments, custom barrel length and contour, and trigger tuned for a crisp pull to customer's specifications. Options include muzzle brakes, Leupold or Kahles police scopes, and others, and are priced accordingly.

Price: **$2750.00**

CUSTOM TEAM CHALLENGER

This custom rifle was designed for use in the Chevy Trucks Sportsman's Team Challenge shooting event. It's also used in metallic silhouette competition as well as in the field for small game and varmints. Custom built on the Ruger 10/22 semi-automatic rimfire action, which features an extended magazine release, a simplified bolt release and finely tuned trigger, this rifle is fitted with either a Brown Precision fiberglass or Kevlar stock with custom length of pull up to 15". The stock can be shortened at the butt and later relengthened and repainted to accommodate growing youth shooters. Stock color is also optional. To facilitate shooting with scopes, the lightweight stock has high-comb classic styling. The absence of a cheekpiece accommodates either right- or left-handed shooters, while the stock's flat-bottom, 1 3/4" forearm ensures maximum comfort in both offhand and rest shooting. Barrels are custom-length Shilen Match Grade .920" diameter straight or lightweight tapered.

Prices:

With blued action/barrel **$975.00**
With blued action/stainless barrel **1050.00**
With stainless action/stainless barrel **1095.00**

BROWNING RIFLES

MODEL BL-22 LEVER-ACTION RIFLE

RIMFIRE RIFLE SPECIFICATIONS

Model	Caliber	Barrel Length	Sight Radius	Overall Length	Average Weight	Price
Semi-Auto 22 Grade I	22 LR	19.25"	16.25"	37"	4 lbs. 12 oz.	$398.95
Semi-Auto 22 Grade VI*	22 LR	19.25"	16.25"	37"	4 lbs. 12 oz.	819.00
BL-22 Grade I	22 LR, Long, Short	20"	15.875"	36.75"	5 lbs.	345.95
BL-Grade II	22 LR, Long, Short	20"	15.875"	36.75"	5 lbs.	359.95

Blued or Grayed

22 SEMIAUTOMATIC RIMFIRE RIFLES GRADES I AND VI (See table above for prices)

SPECIFICATIONS (See also table above)
Capacity: 11 cartridges in magazine, 1 chamber
Safety: Cross-bolt type **Trigger:** Grade I is blued; Grade VI is gold colored **Sights:** Gold bead front, adjustable folding leaf ear; drilled and tapped for Browning scope mounts
Stock & Forearm: Grade I, select walnut with checkering (18 lines/inch); Grade VI, high-grade walnut with checkering (22 lines/inch).

STOCK DIMENSIONS

	Semi-Auto	BL-22
Length of Pull	13.75"	13.5"
Drop at Comb	1 3/8"	.625"
Drop at Heel	2.375"	2.25"

GRADE VI ENGRAVED
(24-KARAT GOLD PLATED)

BROWNING RIFLES

MODEL 1885 LOW WALL RIFLE
(HIGH & LOW WALL MODELS)
$939.95

SPECIFICATIONS MODEL 1885 LOW WALL OR HIGH WALL

CALIBERS*	BARREL LENGTH	SIGHT RADIUS	OVERALL LENGTH	APPROXIMATE WEIGHT	RATE OF TWIST (R. HAND)
HIGH WALL					
22-250 Rem.	28"	—	43.5"	8 lbs. 13 oz.	1 in 14"
270 Win.	28"	—	43.5"	8 lbs. 12 oz.	1 in 10"
30-06 Sprg.	28"	—	43.5"	8 lbs. 12 oz.	1 in 10"
7mm Rem. Mag.	28"	—	43.5"	8 lbs. 11 oz.	1 in 9.5"
45-70 Govt.	28"	21.5"	43.5"	8 lbs. 14 oz.	1 in 20"
LOW WALL					
22 Hornet	24"	—	39.5"	6 lbs. 4 oz.	1 in 16"
223 Rem.	24"	—	39.5"	6 lbs. 4 oz.	1 in 12"
243 Win.	24"	—	39.5"	6 lbs. 4 oz.	1 in 10"

Also available in 454 Casull

LOW WALL TRADITIONAL HUNTER
SPECIFICATIONS
Calibers: 357 Mag., 44 Mag., 45 Colt
Barrel Length: 24" *Overall Length:* 40.25" *Sight Radius:*
31" *Weight:* 6 lbs. 8 oz. *Length of Pull:* 13.5"
Price:. **$1,215.00**

MODEL 1885 HIGH WALL TRADITIONAL HUNTER
SPECIFICATIONS
Calibers: 30-30 Win., 38-55 Win., 45-70 Govt.
Barrel Length: 28" *Overall Length:* 44.25" *Weight:* 9 lbs.
Rate of Twist: 1 in 12" (30-30 Win.); 1 in 15" (38-55 Win.);
1 in 20" (45-70 Gov't.)
Price:. **$1,149.95**

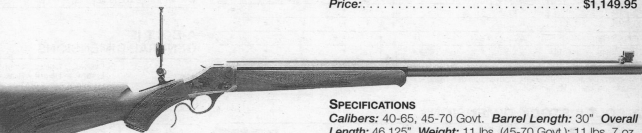

MODEL 1885 BPCR
(BLACK POWDER CARTRIDGE RIFLE)

SPECIFICATIONS
Calibers: 40-65, 45-70 Govt. *Barrel Length:* 30" *Overall*
Length: 46.125" *Weight:* 11 lbs. (45-70 Govt.); 11 lbs. 7 oz.
(40-65) *Sight Radius:* 34" *Rate of Twist:* 1 in 16" (R.H.)
Price:. **$1,664.95**
Also available:
BPCR "CREEDMORE TYPE" LONG RANGE with *Barrel Length:* 34"

BROWNING RIFLES

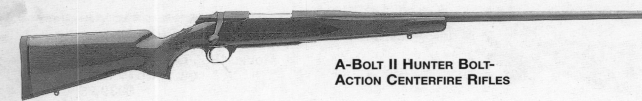

A-BOLT II HUNTER BOLT-ACTION CENTERFIRE RIFLES

BOSS (Ballistic Optimizing Shooting System) is now optional on all A-Bolt II models (except standard on Varmint). BOSS adjusts barrel vibrations to allow a bullet to leave the rifle muzzle at the most advantageous point in the barrel oscillation, thereby fine-tuning accuracy with any brand of ammunition regardless of caliber.

This hard-working rifle features a practical grade of walnut and low-luster bluing ideal for rugged conditions. Includes the standard A-Bolt II fast-cycling bolt, crisp trigger, calibrated rear sights and ramp-style front sights. Optional BOSS.

Scopes: Closed. Clean tapered barrel. Receiver is drilled and tapped for a scope mount; or select HUNTER model has open sights.
Prices: w/BOSS, No Sights $606.85
No Sights 545.35
Open Sights 613.75

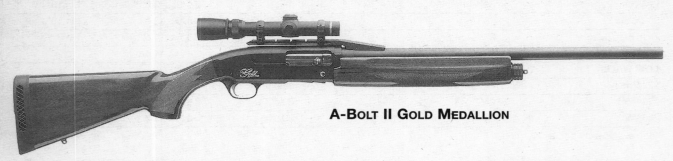

A-BOLT II GOLD MEDALLION

A-BOLT II SPECIFICATIONS (See following page for additional A-Bolt II prices)

CALIBER	TWIST (R.H.)	MAGAZINE CAPACITY	HUNTER	GOLD MEDAL.	MEDAL.	MICRO MEDAL.	STAINLESS STALKER	COMP STALKER	VARMINT	ECLIPSE
LONG ACTION MAGNUM CALIBERS										
375 H&H	1:12"	3	—	—	•	—	•	—	—	—
338 Win. Mag.	1:10"	3	•	—	•	—	•	•	—	—
300 Win. Mag.	1:10"	3	•	•	•	—	•	•	—	•
7mm Rem. Mag.	1:9.5"	3	•	•	•	—	•	•	—	•
LONG ACTION STANDARD CALIBERS										
25-06 Rem.	1:10"	4	•	—	•	—	•	•	—	—
270 Win.	1:10"	4	•	•	•	—	•	•	—	•
280 Rem.	1:10"	4	•	—	•	—	•	•	—	•
30-06 Sprg.	1:10"	4	•	•	•	—	•	•	—	•
SHORT ACTION CALIBERS										
243 Win.	1:10"	4	•	—	•	•	•	•	—	•
308 Win.	1:12"	4	•	—	•	•	•	•	•	•+
7mm-08 Rem.	1:9.5"	4	•	—	•	•	•	•	—	—
22-250 Rem.	1:14"	4	•	—	•	•	•	•	•	•+
223 Rem.	1:12"	6*	•	—	•	•	•	•	—	+

• Magazine capacity of 223 Rem. models is up to 5 rounds on Micro-Medallion (up to 6 on other models).
+ = also available in Varmint version of Eclipse

A-BOLT II AVERAGE WEIGHTS

MODEL	LONG ACTION MAGNUM CALIBERS	LONG ACTION STANDARD CALIBERS	SHORT ACTION CALIBERS
Composite/ Stainless Steel	7 lbs. 3 oz.	6 lbs. 11 oz.	6 lbs. 4 oz.
Micro-Medal.			6 lbs. 1 oz.
Gold Medal.	7 lbs. 11 oz.	7 lbs. 3 oz.	
Medallion & Hunter	7 lbs. 3 oz.	6 lbs. 11 oz.	6 lbs. 7 oz.
Varmint			9 lbs.
Eclipse	8 lbs.	7 lbs. 8 oz.	7 lbs. 10 oz.
Eclipse Varmint			9 lbs. 1 oz.
M-1000	9 lbs. 13 oz.		

A-BOLT II GENERAL DIMENSIONS

LENGTH	OVERALL LENGTH	BARREL LENGTH	SIGHT RADIUS*
Long Action Mag. Cal.	46.75"	26"	18"
Long Action Std. Cal.	42.75"	22"	18"
Short Action Cal.	41.75"	22"	16"
Micro-Medallion	39 9/16"	20"**	—
Varmint Models	44.5"	24"	26"

*Open sights available on A-Bolt Hunter and all models in 375 H&H.
**22 Hornet Micro-Medallion has a 22" barrel. BOSS equipped rifles have the same dimensions.

A-BOLT II STOCK DIMENSIONS

	MICRO-MED.	GOLD MEDAL.	HUNTER	VARMINT	STALKER	ECLIPSE	ECLIPSE VARMINT M-1000
Length Of Pull	13 5/16"	13 5/8"	13 5/8"	13 3/4"	13 5/8"	14"	14"
Drop At Comb	3/4"	3/4"-1"	3/4"	9/16"	5/8"	7/16"	1/2"
Drop At Heel	1 1/8"	1 3/4"	1 1/8"	7/16"	1/2"	1 1/16"	1"

BROWNING RIFLES

A-BOLT II M-1000 ECLIPSE
300 WIN. MAG.

A-BOLT II ECLIPSE MODELS WITH THUMBHOLE STOCK

Some of the most advanced, specialized developments of the A-Bolt II have evolved into the A-Bolt II Eclipse Series. Each rifle is fitted with a newly designed thumbhole stock configuration. To hold accuracy under changing humidity and precipitation conditions the stock itself is crafted from rugged gray/black, multi-laminated hardwood. This gives the Eclipse a camouflaged look. The custom thumbhole-style stock provides a solid grip and secure feel that adds up to accuracy. The Eclipse is available in two versions: long and short action hunting model with standard A-Bolt II barrel, and a short action varmint version with a heavy barrel. All are BOSS equipped.

A-BOLT II STAINLESS STALKER

The barrel, receiver and bolt are machined from solid stainless steel for a high level of corrosion and rust resistance and also to prolong the life of the rifle bore. The advanced graphite-fiberglass composite stock shrugs off wet weather and rough handling and isn't affected by humidity. A palm swell on both right- and left-hand models offers a better grip. A lower comb directs recoil away from the face. Barrel, receiver and stock have a durable matte finish. The BOSS is optional in all calibers.

A-BOLT II SERIES	Prices
GOLD MEDALLION no sights	$854.95
MEDALLION no sights, BOSS	697.95
MEDALLION no sights	636.25
MEDALLION L.H., no sights, BOSS	722.95
MEDALLION L.H., no sights	661.45
MEDALLION 375 H&H no sights, BOSS	798.95
MEDALLION 375 H&H L.H., no sights, BOSS	823.75
MEDALLION 375 H&H L.H., sights	762.25
MICRO MEDALLION no sights	636.25
VARMINT, hvy. bbl., BOSS, gloss or satin/matte	819.25

A-BOLT II SERIES	Prices
STAINLESS STALKER no sights, BOSS	$769.75
STAINLESS STALKER no sights	708.25
STAINLESS STALKER L.H., no sights, BOSS	792.25
STAINLESS STALKER L.H., no sights	792.25
STAINLESS STALKER 375 H&H, BOSS	867.85
STAINLESS STALKER 375 H&H, open sights	806.35
STAINLESS STALKER 375 H&H, L.H., BOSS	893.00
COMPOSITE STALKER, no sights, BOSS	623.95
COMPOSITE STALKER, no sights	562.45
ECLIPSE, no sights, BOSS	895.75
ECLIPSE VARMINT no sights, BOSS	922.75
ECLIPSE M-1000, w/BOSS	922.75

CUSTOM TROPHY (Not Shown)

SPECIFICATIONS
Caliber: 270 Win., 30-06 Sprfd., 7mm Rem. Mag., 300 Win. Mag. **Capacity:** 4 rounds (3 rounds in Magnum calibers) **Barrel Length:** 22" (26" in Magnum)
Overall Length: 42.75" (44.75" in Magnum)
Weight: 7 lbs. 11 oz. (7 lbs. 3 oz. in Magnum)

Stock: American walnut
Features: Octagon barrel; skeleton pistol grip; tang safety; gold highlights; removable magazine w/hinged floorplate; 60° bolt throw; canted bolt knob; adjustable trigger system; cocking indicator; streamlined shroud.
Price: $1,295.00

RIFLES

BROWNING RIFLES

LIGHTNING BLR

SPECIFICATIONS

Calibers: *Long Action*–223 Rem., 270 Win., 30-06 Springfield (7mm Rem. Mag.) 300 Win. Mag. *Short Action*–22-250 Rem., 243 Win., 7mm-08 Rem., 308 Win. **Capacity:** 4 rounds; 3 in magnum calibers **Barrel Length:** *Long Action*–22" (24" magnum calibers) *Short Action*–20" **Overall Length:** *Long*

Action–42 ⁷⁄₈" (44 ⁷⁄₈" magnum calibers) *Short Action*–39.5" **Approximate Weight:** *Long Action*–7 lbs. 4 oz. (7 lbs. 12 oz. magnum calibers) *Short Action*–6 lbs. 8 oz. **Sight Radius:** 17.75" (19.75" magnum calibers)
Prices: Short Action........................ $576.95
    Long Action............................ 608.95

MODEL BPR PUMP RIFLE

SPECIFICATIONS

Calibers: 243 Win., 308 Win., 270 Win., 30-06 Springfield; 7mm Rem. Mag., 300 Win. Mag. **Capacity:** 4 rounds; 3 in magnum calibers **Action:** Pump action **Barrel Length:** 22" (24" magnum calibers) **Overall Length:** 43"; 45" magnum calibers **Weight:** 7 lbs. 3 oz. (7 lbs. 9 oz. magnum calibers) **Safety:** Crossbolt w/enlarged head **Sight Radius:** 17.5" (19.5" magnum calibers) **Sights:** Adjustable rear sight;

hooded front sight w/gold bead **Stock Dimensions:** Length of pull; 13.75"; Drop at comb: 1 ⁵⁄₈" (1.75" magnum calibers) Drop at heel: 2" **Features:** Drilled and tapped for scope mounts; multiple lug rotating bolt locks directly into barrel; detachable box magazine w/hinged floorplate; single-stage trigger; recoil pad standard; full pistol grip
Price:............................... $689.95
    Magnum............................... 741.95

BAR MARK II SAFARI

BAR MARK II SAFARI & LIGHTWEIGHT SEMIAUTOMATIC RIFLES

The BAR Mark II features an engraved receiver, a redesigned bolt release, new gas and buffeting systems, and a removable trigger assembly. Additional features include: crossbolt safety with enlarged head; hinged floorplate, gold trigger; select walnut stock and forearm with cut-checkering and swivel studs; 13.75" length of pull; 2" drop at heel; 1 ⁵⁄₈" drop at comb; and a recoil pad (magnum calibers only). The New Lightweight model features alloy receiver and shortened barrel. Open sights are standard.

BAR MARK II SPECIFICATONS

Calibers: *Standard*–243 Win., 25-06, 270 Win., 308 Win.; *Magnum*–7mm Rem. Mag., 300 Win. Mag., 338 Win. Mag.; *Lightweight*–243 Win., 270 Win., 30-06 Springfield; 308 Win.
Capacity: 4 rounds; 3 in magnum
Barrel Length: *Standard*–22"; *Magnum*–24"; *Lightweight*–20"
Overall Length: *Standard*–43"; *Magnum*–45"; *Lightweight*–41"
Average Weight: *Standard*–7 lbs. 6 oz.; *Magnum*–8 lbs. 6 oz.; *Lightweight*–7 lbs. 2 oz.
Sight Radius: *Standard*–17.5"; *Magnum*–19.5"; *Lightweight*–15.5"

Prices:
STANDARD CALIBERS
  No sights, BOSS........................ $785.25
  Open sights, no BOSS 729.95
  No sights, no BOSS 713.95
MAGNUM CALIBERS
  No sights, BOSS........................ $837.25
  Open sights 765.95
  No sights, no BOSS 781.95
BAR MARK II LIGHTWEIGHT
  Open sights, no BOSS $729.95

CHRISTENSEN ARMS

CARBONCANNON SERIES

Custom lightweight graphite barreled precision magnum big-game class rifle. All popular Magnum calibers available. Up to 28" long match-grade stainless steel barrel liner, head spaced minimum, accurized action, custom trigger, synthetic or wood stock and fitted for scope mounts. Bedded with graphite barrel free floating. **Weight:** 6.5 pounds (or less). **Accuracy:** 3 shots .5" or less at 100 yards (shoots straight when barrel is hot).
Price:. **$2,950.00**

CARBONTACTICAL SERIES

Custom lightweight graphite, barreled precision tactical-class rifle. All popular calibers available. Up to 28" long match-grade stainless steel barrel liner, head spaced minimum, muzzle break optional, accurized action, custom trigger, synthetic or wood stock and fitted for scope mounts. Bedded with free-floating graphite barrel. **Weight:** 6.5 pounds **Accuracy:** 3 shots .5" or less at 100 yards (shoots straight when barrel is hot).
Price:. **$2,950.00**

CARBONONE SERIES

Custom lightweight graphite barreled precision varmint-class rifle. .17 thru .243 calibers available. Up to 28" long match-grade stainless steel barrel liner, head spaced minimum, accurized action, custom trigger, synthetic or wood stock; fitted for scope mounts. Bedded with free-floating graphite barrel. **Weight:** 6 pounds (or less) **Accuracy:** 3 shots .5" or less at 100 yards (shoots straight when barrel is hot).
Price:. **$2,950.00**

CARBONRANGER SERIES

Custom lightweight long range precision sniper rifle. Available in 50 caliber. Up to 36" long stainless steel barrel liner, chambered to minimum tolerances. E.D.M. precision machined Omni Wind Runner accurized action (or an action of choice), custom trigger, retractable stock. 5 shots 8" at 1000 yards. Shoots straight with a hot barrel.
Prices:. . . . . **$6,550.00-$10,625.00**

CHRISTENSEN ARMS

CARBONLITE SERIES

Custom ultra-lightweight graphite, barreled precision mountain-class rifle. .17 and .243 calibers available. Up to 28" long match-grade stainless steel barrel liner, head spaced minimum, accurized action, custom trigger, synthetic or wood stock and fitted for scope mounts. Bedded with free-floating graphite barrel. **Weight:** 6 pounds (or less) **Accuracy:** 3 shots .5" or less at 100 yards (shoots straight when barrel is hot).
Price:................................$2,950.00

CARBONKING SERIES

Custom lightweight graphite, barreled precision hunting-class rifle. .25 thru .308 calibers available. Up to 28" long match-grade stainless steel barrel liner, head spaced minimum, accurized action, custom trigger, synthetic or wood stock and fitted for scope mounts. Bedded with free-floating graphite barrel. **Weight:** 6.5 pounds or less. **Accuracy:** 3 shots .5" or less at 100 yards (shoots straight when barrel is hot).
Price:................................$2,950.00

CARBONCHALLENGE SERIES

Custom ultra-lightweight graphite barreled precision target and small-game rimfire-class rifle. Up to 20" long match-grade stainless steel barrel liner, semi-auto action, custom trigger, synthetic or wood stock and fitted for scope mounts. Bedded with action free floating. **Weight:** 3-4.5 pounds **Accuracy:** 3 shots .5" or less at 50 yards.
Price:.......................$990.00-$1,299.00

CARBONCHALLENGER THUMBHOLE

COLT RIFLES

LIGHTWEIGHTS

The Colt Match Target Lightweight semiautomatic rifle fires from a closed bolt, is easy to load and unload, and has a buttstock and pistol grip made of tough nylon. A round, ribbed handguard is fiberglass-reinforced to ensure better grip control.
Calibers: 223 Rem.

Barrel Length: 16"
Overall Length: 34.5" (35.5" in 7.62 X 39mm)
Weight: 6.7 lbs
Capacity: 5 rounds (7.62 X 39mm); 8 rounds (223 Rem. and 9mm)
Price:. $1,010.00

COMPETITION H-BAR

MATCH TARGET RIFLES
The Colt Target and H-Bar rifles are range-selected for top accuracy. They have a 3-9x rubber armored variable-power scope mount, carry handle with iron sight, Cordura nylon case and other accessories.
Caliber: 223 Rem.
Barrel Length: 20: (16" H-BAR II)
Overall Length: 39" (34.5" H-BAR II)

Weight: 8.5 lbs (Competition/Match H-Bar); 8 lbs. (Target H-BAR); 7.5 lbs. (Target); 7.1 lbs. (H-Bar II)
Capacity: 8 rounds
Prices:
MATCH TARGET. $1,040.00
MATCH TARGET H-BAR. 1,085.00
COMPETITION H-BAR 1,090.00
COMPETITION H-BAR II. 1,065.00

COLT ACCURIZED RIFLE (not shown)
SPECIFICATIONS
Caliber: 223 Rem.
Capacity: 8 rounds
Action: Semiauto; gas operated; locking bolt
Barrel Length: 24" heavy
Overall Length: 43"

Weight: 9.25 oz.
Rifling Twist: 1 turn in 9", 6 grooves
Trigger: Smooth
Finish: Matte black w/matte stainless steel barrel
Features: Flattop upper receiver for low scope mount (1" rings)
Price:. $1,295.00

COOPER ARMS RIFLES

VARMINT EXTREME SERIES

MODEL 21 VARMINT EXTREME

MODEL 21 VARMINT EXTREME

SPECIFICATIONS
Calibers: 17 Rem., 17 Mach IV, 221 Fireball, 222 Rem., 222 Rem. Mag., 22 PPC, 223 **Barrel Length:** 24"
Stock: AAA Claro walnut; flared oval forearm
Other specifications same as Model 36 RF.

Price:	$1,695.00
Also available:	
MODEL 21 CUSTOM CLASSIC	$1,895.00
MODEL 21 WESTERN CLASSIC	1,995.00

MODEL 22 VARMINT EXTREME

MODEL 22 REPEATER CUSTOM CLASSIC

MODEL 22 BR-50 SINGLE SHOT

MODEL 22 SINGLE SHOT VARMINT EXTREME

SPECIFICATIONS
Calibers: 22-250, 220 Swift, 243, 25-06, 308, 6mm PPC
Capacity: Single shot **Barrel Length:** 24"
Action: 3 front locking lug; glass-bedded
Trigger: Single-stage Match, fully adjustable; Jewell 2-stage (optional)
Stock: McMillan black-textured synthetic, beaded, w/Monte Carlo cheekpiece; 4-panel checkering print;

Pachmayr recoil pad
Price:

MODEL 22 VARMINT EXTREME	$1,795.00
Also available:	
MODEL 22 BR-50 BENCH REST (w/Jewell Trigger)	$2,195.00
MODEL 22 REPEATER CUSTOM CLASSIC	2,675.00

COOPER ARMS RIFLES

COMPETITION SERIES

MODEL 36 BR-50

MODEL 36 CUSTOM CLASSIC

MODEL 36 FEATHERWEIGHT

MODEL 36 CLASSIC

SPECIFICATIONS
Caliber: 22 LR *Capacity:* 5-shot magazine
Action: bolt-action repeater
Barrel Length: 23.75" (chrome moly); free-floated barrel
w/competition step crown
Stock: AAA Claro, side panel checkering, Pachmayr recoil
pad, steel grip cap (Classic Model); AAA Claro, wraparound custom checkering, beaded cheekpiece, ebony tip,
steel grip cap (Custom Classic)
Features: Glass-bedded adjustable trigger; bases and
rings optional; 3 mid-locking lugs

Prices:
CUSTOM CLASSIC $1,795.00
WESTERN CLASSIC 1,995.00
VARMINT CLASSIC 1,695.00
Also available:
MODEL 36 RF/CF FEATHERWEIGHT: Same specifications
   as Model 36 RF, but weights 6.5 lbs. $1,695.00
MODEL 36 RF BR-50: Same specifications as Model 36 RF,
but w/22" stainless steel bbl. 6.8 lbs. 1,895.00
MODEL IR 50/50 . . . . 1,895.00

DAKOTA ARMS

DAKOTA 76 AFRICAN GRADE

DAKOTA 76 RIFLES
SPECIFICATIONS

Calibers:
SAFARI GRADE: 338 Win. Mag., 300 Mag., 375 H&H Mag., 458 Win. Mag.
CLASSIC GRADE: 22-250, 257 Roberts, 270 Win., 280 Rem., 30-06, 7mm Rem. Mag., 338 Win. Mag., 300 Win. Mag., 375 H&H Mag., 458 Win. Mag.
AFRICAN GRADE: 404 Jeffery, 416 Dakota, 416 Rigby, 450 Dakota
Barrel Lengths: 21" or 23" (Classic); 23" only (Safari); 24" (African)
Weight: 7.5 lbs. (Classic); 9.5 lbs. (African); 8.5 lbs. (Safari)
Safety: Three-position striker-blocking safety allows bolt operation with safety on

Sights: Ramp front sight; standing-leaf rear
Stock: Choice of X grade oil-finished English, Bastogne or Claro walnut (Classic); choice of XXX grade oil-finished English or Bastogne walnut w/ebony forent tip (Safari)
Prices:

CLASSIC GRADE	$2,995.00
SAFARI GRADE	3,995.00
AFRICAN GRADE	4,495.00
Barreled Actions:	
Classic Grade	2,000.00
Safari Grade	2,350.00
African Grade	2,950.00
Actions:	
Classic Grade	1,750.00
Safari Grade	1,900.00
African Grade	2,500.00

DAKOTA 10 SINGLE SHOT

SPECIFICATIONS
Calibers: Most rimmed/rimless commercially loaded types
Barrel Length: 23" **Overall Length:** 39.5" **Weight:** 6 lbs.
Features: Receiver and rear of breech block are solid steel without cuts or holes for maximum lug area (approx. 8 times more bearing area than most bolt rifles); crisp, clean trigger pull; removable trigger plate allows action to adapt to single-set triggers; straight-line coil-spring action and short hammer fall combine for fast lock time; smooth, quiet top

tang safety blocks the striker forward of the main spring; strong, positive extractor and manual ejector adapted to rimmed/rimless cases. XX grade oil-finished English, Bastogne or Claro walnut stock.

Price:	$3,295.00
BARRELED ACTIONS	2,050.00
ACTIONS ONLY	1,775.00
Also Available:	
DAKOTA 10 MAGNUM SINGLE SHOT	$3,295.00
Barreled actions	2,050.00
Actions only	1,775.00

DAKOTA 22 LR SPORTER

SPECIFICATIONS
Calibers: 22 LR **Capacity:** 5-round clip
Barrel Length: 22" (chrome-moly, 1 turn in 16")

Weight: 6.5 lbs.
Stock: X Claro or English walnut with hand-cut checkering
Features: Plain bolt handle; swivels and single screw studs; .5" black pad; 13 5/8" length of pull
Price: $1,795.00

DAKOTA ARMS

VARMINT HUNTER

LIGHTWEIGHT HUNTER

DAKOTA 97 VARMINT & LIGHTWEIGHT HUNTER RIFLES

SPECIFICATIONS

Caliber: 22-250 to 330 Dakota Magnum (Lightweight models); also available in 375 H&H Mag. and 375 Dakota Mag. (Varmint) *Action:* Single shot
Barrel Length: 22" (Lightweight); 26" (375 H&H and 375 Dakota Mag.) *Overall Length:* 43"-45" (Lightweight); 45"-47" (375 H&H Mag. and 375 Dakota Mag.)
Length Of Pull: 13 ⅝" *Weight:* 6.16 lbs.-6.5 lbs. (Lightweight); 7.7 lbs. (375 H&H Mag. and 375 Dakota Mag.) *Stock:* Composite black fiberglass stock (X walnut in 375 H&H Mag. and 375 Dakota Mag.) *Features:* Sling swivel studs; 1" recoil pad; fully adjustable match trigger; free-floating barrel; cylindrical machined receiver; Model 76 ejection system; 3-position striker-block safety; cloverleaf tang
Price:................................$1,695.00
Action...................................1,000.00
Barreled Action............................1,200.00

LONG BOW TACTICAL E.R. (ENGAGEMENT RIFLE)

SPECIFICATIONS

Caliber: 338 Capua Mag., 300 Dakota Mag., 330 Dakota Mag.
Action: Blind magazine
Barrel Length: 28" stainless steel
Overall Length: 50"-51"
Length Of Pull: 12 ⅞"-14 ⅜"
Weight: 13.7 lbs. (w/o scope)
Stock: McMillan fiberglass (black or olive drab green); matte finish
Features: Adjustable cheekpiece; 3 sling swivel studs; bipod spike in forend; controlled round feeding; claw extraction system; one-piece optical rail; 3-position firing pin block safety; deployment kit; muzzlebrake
Price:................................$4,250.00
Action only..............................2,500.00

LONG BOW TACTICAL

EMF REPLICA RIFLES

1860 HENRY RIFLE

SPECIFICATIONS
Calibers: 44-40 and 45 LC *Barrel length:* 24.25";
upper half-octagonal w/magazine tube in one-piece steel
Overall length: 43.75" *Weight::* 9.25 lbs.

Stock: Varnished American walnut wood
Features: Polished brass frame; brass buttplate
Price:. $1,230.00

MODEL 1866
YELLOW BOY RIFLE & CARBINE

These exact reproductions of guns used over 100 years
ago are available in 45 Long Colt, 38 Special and 44-40.
Both carbine and rifle are offered with blued finish, walnut
stock and brass frame.
Prices:
Rifle $920.00
Carbine. 900.00

MODEL 1873 SPORTING RIFLE

SPECIFICATIONS
Calibers: 357, 44-40, 45 Long Colt *Barrel length:* 24.25"
octagonal *Overall length:* 43.25" *Weight::* 8.16 lbs.
Features: Magazine tube in blued steel; frame is casehard-
ened steel; stock and forend are walnut wood
Price $1,150.00

Also available:
MODEL 1873 CARBINE. Same features as
the 1873 Sporting Rifle, except in 45 Long Colt only
with 19" barrel, overall length 38.25" and weight 7.38 lbs.
Price:. $1,150.00

EUROPEAN AMERICAN ARMORY

HW 660 WEIHRAUCH RIMFIRE
TARGET RIFLE (SINGLE SHOT)

SPECIFICATIONS
Caliber: 22 LR *Barrel length:* 26" *Overall length:* 45.33"
Weight: 10.8 lbs. *Finish:* Blue *Stock:* European walnut

w/adjustable black rubber buttplate and comb
Features: Adjustable match trigger; left-handed stock
available; aluminum adjustable sling swivel; adj. vertical
and lateral cheekpiece; rear sight click-adjustable for
windage and elevation; aluminum forend rail; polished
feed ramp; external thumb safety
Price: $951.60
Laminated 998.40

FRANCOTTE RIFLES

August Francotte rifles are available in all calibers for which barrels and chambers are made. All guns are custom made to the customer's specifications; there are no standard models. Most bolt-action rifles use commercial Mauser actions; however, the magnum action is produced by Francotte exclusively for its own production. Side-by-side and mountain rifles use either boxlock or sidelock action. Francotte system sidelocks are back-action type. Options include gold and silver inlay, special engraving and exhibition and museum grade wood. Francotte rifles are distributed in the U.S. by Armes de Chasse (see Directory of Manufacturers and Distributors for details).

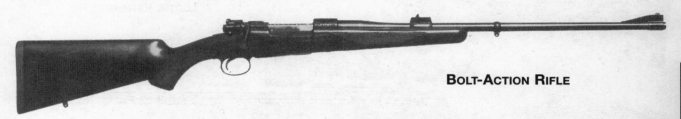

BOLT-ACTION RIFLE

SPECIFICATIONS
Calibers: 300 WM, 375 H&H, 9.3X62, 416 Rigby
Barrel length: To customer's specifications
Weight: 8 to 12 lbs., or to customer's specifications
Stock: A wide selection of wood in all possible styles according to customer preferences; prices listed below do not include engraving or select wood.
Engraving: Per customer specifications
Sights: All types of sights and scope

BOLT-ACTION RIFLES	Prices
Standard Bolt Action (416 Rigby)	$7,000.00
Magnum Action 300 WM, 375 H&H	8,900.00

BOXLOCK SIDE-BY-SIDE DOUBLE RIFLES	Prices
Std. boxlock double rifle (9.3X74R, 8X57JRS, 7X65R, etc.)	$12,700.00
Std. boxlock double (Magnum calibers)	27,500.00

SIDELOCK S/S DOUBLE RIFLES	
Std. sidelock double rifle (9.3X74R, 8X57JRS, 7X65R, etc.)	$17,500.00
Std. sidelock double (Magnum calibers)	27,250.00

MOUNTAIN RIFLES	
Standard boxlock	$12,000.00
Std. boxlock (Mag. & rimless calibers)	**Price on request**
Standard sidelock (7RM and .243 WM)	36,334.00

**MOUNTAIN RIFLE
w/ELABORATE ENGRAVING**

HARRINGTON & RICHARDSON

ULTRA VARMINT

ULTRA COMP

ULTRA SINGLE-SHOT RIFLES
SPECIFICATIONS
Calibers: 223 Rem. & 243 (Varmint), 25-06, 308 Win. and 357 Rem. Max.
Action: Break-open; side lever release; positive ejection
Barrel Length: 22" (308 Win., 357 Rem. Max.); 24" bull barrel (223 Rem. Varmint; 26" (25-06)
Weight: 7 to 8 lbs.
Sights: None (scope mount included)
Length Of Pull: 14.25"
Drop At Comb: 1.25" **Drop At Heel:** 1 ¹/₈"

Forend: Semibeavertail
Stock: Monte Carlo; hand-checkered curly maple; Varmint model has light laminate stock
Features: Sling swivels on stock and forend; patented transfer bar safety; automatic ejection; hammer extension; rebated muzzle
Price:
    Ultra Varmint **$254.95**
Also available:
ULTRA COMP in 30-06 and 270 Win. **Barrel Length:** 24".
Weight: 7-8 lbs. Camo laminate stock. **289.95**

WHITETAILS UNLIMITED 1998 COMMEMORATIVE RIFLE

WHITETAILS UNLIMITED 1998 COMMEMORATIVE EDITION RIFLE
in cooperation with Whitetails Unlimited
The 1998 Harrington & Richardson® commemorative edition is chambered in 30-30 Win. caliber, America's most popular whitetail cartridge. This limited edition is produced on a high tensile, investment cast steel frame, and is fitted to a classic pistol grip stock with sling swivel studs and a premium recoil pad. The wood is pure American black walnut. The stocks and forends are precisely carved, hand-sanded and cut checkered by hand. Also featured are a laser engraving of the WTU logo and a pewter finished Whitetails Unlimited medallion inletted into the stock. A patented Transfer Bar System virtually eliminates the possibility of accidental discharge.

SPECIFICATIONS
Caliber: 30-30 Win. **Barrel Length:** 22"
Weight: 7 lbs. **Sights:** Ramp front; fully adjustable rear
Length Of Pull: 14" **Features:** Side lever release; positive ejection; swivel stud; break open action
Price: **$289.95**

Harris Gunworks Rifles

Signature Series

Classic Sporter

SPECIFICATIONS
Calibers:
Model SA: 22-250, 243, 257 Roberts, 6mm Rem., 6mm BR, 7mm BR, 7mm-08, 284, 308, 350 Rem. Mag.
Model LA: 25-06, 270, 280 Rem., 30-06, 35 Whelen
Model MA: 7mm STW, 7mm Rem. Mag., 300 Win. Mag.,

300 Weatherby, 300 H&H, 338 Win. Mag., 340 Weatherby, 375 H&H, 416 Rem., 416 Hoffman, 416 Taylor, 458 Win., 458 Lott, 257 Wby. Mag., 358 Norma, 358 STA
Capacity: 4 rounds; 3 rounds in magnum calibers
Weight: 7 lbs.; 7 lbs. 9 oz. in long action
Barrel lengths: 22", 24", 26"
Options: Wooden stock, optics, 30mm rings, muzzle brakes, steel floor plates, iron sights
Price: $2,700.00

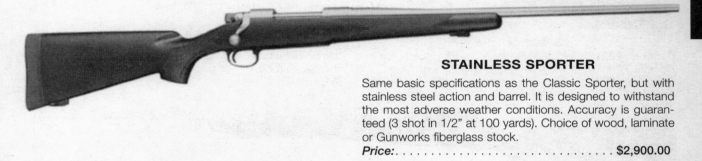

STAINLESS SPORTER

Same basic specifications as the Classic Sporter, but with stainless steel action and barrel. It is designed to withstand the most adverse weather conditions. Accuracy is guaranteed (3 shot in 1/2" at 100 yards). Choice of wood, laminate or Gunworks fiberglass stock.
Price: $2,900.00

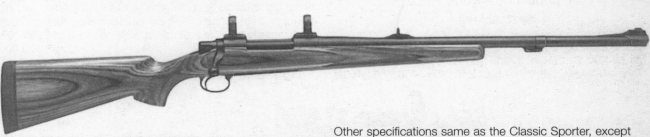

ALASKAN

SPECIFICATIONS
Calibers:
Model LA: 270, 280, 30-06, 35 Whelen
Model MA: 7mm Rem. Mag., 300 Win. Mag., 300 H&H, 300 Weatherby, 358 Win., 340 Weatherby, 375 H&H, 416 Rem., 416 Taylor, 458 Win., 458 Lott

Other specifications same as the Classic Sporter, except Harris action is fitted to a match-grade barrel, complete with single-leaf rear sight, barrel band front sight, 1" detachable rings and mounts, steel floorplate, electroless nickel finish. Monte Carlo stock features cheekpiece, palm swell and special recoil pad.
Price: $3,800.00
Also available:
Stainless Steel Receiver, **add** $150.00

HARRIS GUNWORKS RIFLES

TALON SPORTER

The all-new action of this model is designed and engineered specifically for the hunting of dangerous (African-type) game animals. Patterned after the renowned pre-64 Model 70, the Talon features a cone breech, controlled feed, claw extractor, positive ejection and three-position safety. Action is available in chromolybdenum and stainless steel. Drilled and tapped for scope mounting in long, short or magnum, left or right hand.

Same basic specifications as Harris Signature series, but offered in the following **calibers:**
Standard Action: 22-250, 243, 257 Roberts, 6mm Rem., 6mm BR, 7mm BR, 7mm-08, 284, 308, 350 Rem. Mag.
Long Action: 25-06, 270, 280 Rem., 30-06, 35 Whelen, 257 Wby. Mag., 300 Win. Mag., 300 Wby., 358 STA, 7mm STA
Magnum Action: 300 H&H, 338 Win. Mag., 340 Weatherby, 375 H&H, 416 Hoffman, 416 Taylor, 416 Rem.
Price:. **$2,900.00**

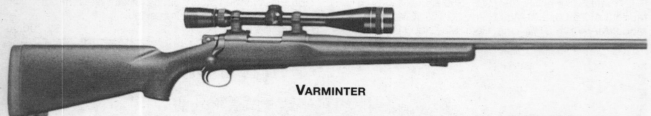

VARMINTER

SPECIFICATIONS
Calibers: 223, 22-250, 220 Swift, 243, 257 Roberts, 6mm Rem., 25-06, 7mm BR, 7mm-08, 308, 350 Rem. Mag. Other specifications same as the Classic Sporter, except

the Super Varminter comes with heavy contoured barrel, adjustable trigger, field bipod and hand-bedded fiberglass stock.
Price:. **$2,700.00**

TITANIUM MOUNTAIN RIFLE
SPECIFICATIONS
Calibers:
Model LA: 270, 280 Rem., 30-06, 35 Whelen, 458 Lott
Model MA: 7mm Rem. Mag., 300 Win. Mag., 300 Win. Mag., 300 Wby, 338 Win. Mag., 340 Wby., 458 Win., 458

Lott, 300 H&H, 375 H&H, 357 Wby., 358 STA, 358 Norma, 416 Rem., 416 Hoffman, 416 Taylor
Weight: 5 1/2 lbs.
Other specifications same as the Classic Sporter, except barrel is made of chrome-moly (titanium alloy light contour match-grade barrel is available at additional cost of **$500.00**.)
Prices:. **$3,300.00**
w/GRAPHITE-STEEL COMPOSITE
   LIGHTWEIGHT BARREL. **3,700.00**

.300 PHOENIX

SPECIFICATIONS
Caliber: 300 Phoenix. **Barrel length:** 27 1/2". **Weight:** 12 1/2 lbs. **Stock:** Fiberglass with adjustable cheekpiece.
Feature: Available in left-hand action.
Price:. **$3,380.00**

HARRIS GUNWORKS RIFLES

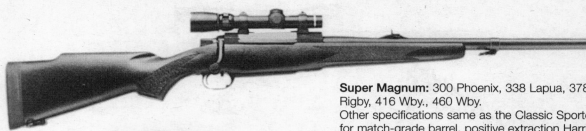

TALON SAFARI

SPECIFICATIONS
Calibers:
Magnum: 300 Win. Mag., 300 Weatherby, 300 H&H, 338 Win. Mag., 340 Weatherby, 375 H&H, 404 Jeffrey, 416 Rem., 416 Hoffman, 416 Taylor, 458 Win., 458 Lott

Super Magnum: 300 Phoenix, 338 Lapua, 378 Wby., 416 Rigby, 416 Wby., 460 Wby.
Other specifications same as the Classic Sporter, except for match-grade barrel, positive extraction Harris Safari action, quick detachable 1" scope mounts, positive locking steel floorplate, multi-leaf express sight, barrel band ramp front sight, barrel band swivels, and Harris Safari stock.
Prices:
MAGNUM **$3,900.00**
SUPER MAGNUM **4,200.00**

NATIONAL MATCH RIFLE

SPECIFICATIONS
Calibers: 308, 7mm-08
Mag. Capacity: 5 rounds
Weight: Approx. 11 lbs. (12 1/2 lbs. w/heavy contour

barrel). Available for right-hand shooters only. Features Harris fiberglass stock with adjustable buttplate, stainless steel match barrel with barrel band and Tompkins front sight; Harris repeating bolt action with clip shot and Canjar trigger. Barrel twist is 1:12".
Price: **$3,500.00**

LONG RANGE RIFLE

SPECIFICATIONS
Calibers: 300 Win. Mag., 300 Phoenix, 7mm Mag., 338 Lapua
Barrel length: 26"

Weight: 14 lbs.
Available in right-hand only. Features a fiberglass stock with adjustable butt plate and cheekpiece. Stainless steel match barrel comes with barrel band and Tompkins front sight. Harris solid bottom single-shot action and Canjar trigger. Barrel twist is 1:12".
Price: **$3,620.00**

HARRIS BENCHREST RIFLE (not shown)

SPECIFICATIONS
Caliber: 6mm PPC, 243, 6mm BR, 6mm Rem., 308. Built to individual specifications to be competitive in hunter, light varmint and heavy varmint classes. Features solid bottom

or repeating bolt action, Canjar trigger, fiberglass stock with recoil pad, stainless steel match-grade barrel and reloading dies. Right- or left-hand models.
Price: **$3,050.00**

HECKLER & KOCH RIFLES

MODEL KH PSG-1 HIGH PRECISION MARKSMAN'S RIFLE

SPECIFICATIONS

Caliber: 308 (7.62mm) **Capacity:** 5 rounds
Barrel Length: 25.6" **Overall Length:** 47.5"

Rifling: 4 groove, polygonal **Twist:** 12", right hand
Weight: 17.8 lbs. **Height:** 8.26 lbs. **Sights:** Hensoldt
6X42 telescopic **Stock:** Matte black, high-impact plastic
Finish: Matte black, phosphated **Features:** Aluminum
case; tripod; sling; adj. buttstock and contoured grip
Price: $10,811.00

HENRY REPEATING ARMS

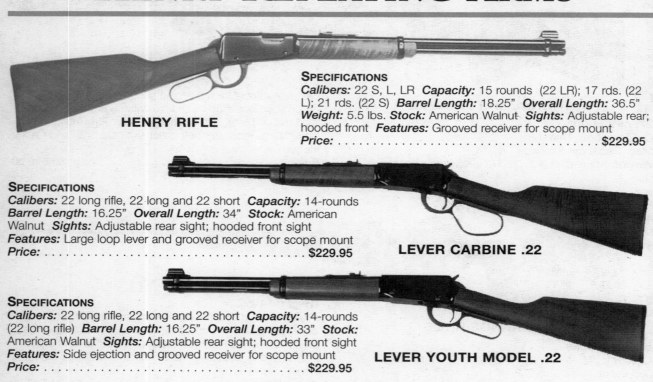

HENRY RIFLE

SPECIFICATIONS

Calibers: 22 S, L, LR **Capacity:** 15 rounds (22 LR); 17 rds. (22
L); 21 rds. (22 S) **Barrel Length:** 18.25" **Overall Length:** 36.5"
Weight: 5.5 lbs. **Stock:** American Walnut **Sights:** Adjustable rear;
hooded front **Features:** Grooved receiver for scope mount
Price: $229.95

SPECIFICATIONS

Calibers: 22 long rifle, 22 long and 22 short **Capacity:** 14-rounds
Barrel Length: 16.25" **Overall Length:** 34" **Stock:** American
Walnut **Sights:** Adjustable rear sight; hooded front sight
Features: Large loop lever and grooved receiver for scope mount
Price: $229.95

LEVER CARBINE .22

SPECIFICATIONS

Calibers: 22 long rifle, 22 long and 22 short **Capacity:** 14-rounds
(22 long rifle) **Barrel Length:** 16.25" **Overall Length:** 33" **Stock:**
American Walnut **Sights:** Adjustable rear sight; hooded front sight
Features: Side ejection and grooved receiver for scope mount
Price: $229.95

LEVER YOUTH MODEL .22

U.S. SURVIVAL RIFLE .22

SPECIFICATIONS

Calibers: 22 long rifle **Capacity:** 9-shot **Barrel Length:** 16.25"
Overall Length: 35.25" **Sights:** Adjustable rear sight **Features:**
Barrel and action fit in floating waterproof stock; comes with two
8-round magazines
Price: $165.00

HOWA LIGHTNING RIFLES

LIGHTNING BOLT-ACTION RIFLE

The rugged mono-bloc receivers on all Howa rifles are machined from a single billet of high carbon steel. The machined steel bolt boasts dual-opposed locking lugs and triple relief gas ports. Actions are fitted with a button-release hinged floorplate for fast reloading. Premium steel sporter-weight barrels are hammer-forged. A silent sliding thumb safety locks the trigger for safe loading or clearing the chamber. The stock is ultra-tough polymer.

SPECIFICATIONS
Calibers: 22-250, 223, 243, 270, 308, 30-06, 300 Win. Mag., 338 Win. Mag., 7mm Rem. Mag.
Capacity: 5 rounds (3 in Magnum)
Barrel length: 22" (24" in Magnum)
Overall length: 42.5"
Weight: 7.5 lbs. (7.7 lbs. in Magnum) *Finish:* Blue
Price:
STANDARD MODEL **$425.00**
   In Magnum calibers **445.00**
BARRELED ACTIONS **325.00**
   In Magnum calibers **345.00**

JARRETT CUSTOM RIFLES

MODEL NO. 1

Jarrett's Standard Hunting Rifle uses McMillan's fiberglass stock and is made primarily for hunters of big game and varmints.
Price: $3,050.00
Also available:
MODEL NO. 3 COUP DE GRACE. Same specifications as the Standard model, but can use a Remington or Winchester receiver. Includes a muzzlebreak kit (Serial No. 1-100) and weatherproofing metal finish. Model 70-style bolt release installed on a Rem. 700.
Price: $3,695.00

This lightweight rifle—called the "Walkabout"—is based on Remington's Model 7 (or Short 700) receiver. It is available in any short-action caliber and is pillar-bedded into a McMillan Model 7-style or Mountain stock.
Price: $3,050.00

MODEL NO. 2

MODEL NO. 4 (not shown)

This model—the "Professional Hunter"—is based on a Winchester controlled round-feed Model 70. It features a quarter rib and iron sights and comes with two Leupold scopes with quick-detachable scope rings. A handload is developed for solids and soft points (40 rounds each). It is then pillar-bedded into a McMillan fiberglass stock. Available in any Magnum caliber. Comes with takedown rifle case.
Price: $6,200.00

KBI/CHARLES DALY RIFLES

MODEL CDGA 6345 EMPIRE GRADE SEMIAUTOMATIC

MODEL CDGA 4103 FIELD GRADE BOLT ACTION

STANDARD M-20P SEMIAUTOMATIC

MODEL M-12Y YOUTH BOLT ACTION

KBI/CHARLES DALY RIFLE SPECIFICATIONS

Item No.	Capacity	Caliber	Barrel Length	Length	Overall Price
FIELD GRADE					
CDGA 4103	6	22LR	22 5/8"	41"	$119.00
CDGA 4164	10	22LR	20 1/4"	40 1/2"	119.00
CDGA 4238	Single Shot	22LR	16 1/4"	32"	144.00
CDGA 4279	6	22LR	17 1/2"	34 3/8"	119.00
SUPERIOR GRADE					
CDGA 5047	6	22LR	22 5/8"	41 1/4"	169.00
CDGA 5159	5	22 MRF	22 5/8"	41 1/4"	189.00
CDGA 5261	5	22 Hornet	22 5/8"	41 1/4"	339.00
CDGA 5302	10	22LR	20 1/4"	40 1/2"	169.00
EMPIRE GRADE					
CDGA 6116	6	22LR	22 5/8"	41 1/4"	334.00
CDGA 6208	5	22 MRF	22 5/8"	41 1/4"	359.00
CDGA 6270	5	22 Hornet	22 5/8"	41 1/4"	439.00
CDGA 6345	10	22LR	20 1/4"	40 1/4"	334.00

KIMBER RIFLES

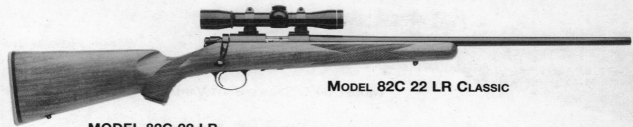

MODEL 82C 22 LR CLASSIC

MODEL 82C 22 LR

Prices:
CLASSIC $920.00
STAINLESS CLASSIC 970.00
SVT (SHORT/VARMINT/TARGET) 730.00

HS (HUNTER SILHOUETTE) $730.00
VARMINT STAINLESS (LTD. ED.) 1,030.00
SUPERAMERICA 1,490.00
CUSTOM MATCH 2,168.00

MODEL 82C 22 LR SPECIFICATIONS

MODEL:	MODEL 82C CLASSIC	MODEL 82C STAINLESS CLASSIC	MODEL 82C SVT	MODEL 82C SUPERAMERICA	MODEL 82C CUSTOM MATCH
WEIGHT:	6.5 lbs.	6.5 lbs.	7.5 lbs.	6.5 lbs.	6.75 lbs.
OVERALL LENGTH:	40.5"	40.5"	36.5"	40.5"	40.5"
ACTION TYPE:	Rear Locking Repeater	Rear Locking Repeater	Rear Locking Single Shot	Rear Locking Repeater	Rear Locking Repeater
CAPACITY:	4-Shot Clip 5 & 10 Shot (opt.)	4-Shot Clip 5 & 10 Shot (opt.)		4-Shot Clip 5 & 10 Shot (opt.)	4-Shot Clip 5 & 10 Shot (opt.)
TRIGGER: PRESSURE	Fully Adjustable Set at 2.5 lbs.	Fully Adjustable Set at 2.5 lbs.	Fully Adjustable Set at 2.5 lbs.	Fully Adjustable Set at 2.5 lbs.	Fully Adjustable Set at 2.5 lbs.
BARREL LENGTH: GROOVES TWIST	22" 6 16"	22" 6 16"	18" Fluted 6 16"	22" 6 16"	22" 6 16"
STOCK: GRADE WALNUT CHECKERING (LPI) COVERAGE	A Claro 18 Side Panel	A Claro 18 Side Panel	A Claro None NA	AAA Claro 22 Full Coverage Wrap Around	AA French 22 Full Coverage Wrap Around
LENGTH OF PULL	13 5/8"	13 5/8"	13 5/8"	13 5/8"	13 5/8"
METAL FINISH:	Polished & Blued	Stainless steel bbl. Matte blued action	Stainless steel bbl. Matte blued action	Polished & Blued	Matte "rust" type blue

MAUSER 98 SPORTER

MAUSER 98 SPORTER

The Mauser 98 Sporter features a new match-grade plain matte or fluted stainless steel barrel. The action is finished in a deep matte blue. Each rifle incorporates a high quality synthetic stock with a 1" recoil pad and comes with scope mount bases. For proper scope mounting, Kimber installs a new steel Buehler-style safety and repositions the bolt handle.

SPECIFICATIONS

Calibers: .270 Win., .30-06 Sprg., 7mm Rem. Mag., .300 Win. Mag., .338 Win Mag *Barrel Length:* 24" (25" in magnum calibers) *Overall Length:* 46" (47" in magnum calibers) *Weight:* 7.5 lbs. *Sights:* None. Comes with scope mount bases *Stock:* High quality synthetic stock with a 1" recoil pad *Finish:* Deep matte blue
Prices:
Standard $535.00
Matte Magnum 339.00
Stainless Magnum 560.00

KIMBER RIFLES

MODEL 84 C SINGLE SHOT VARMINT

MODEL 84C

The Kimber Model 84C is a scaled-down mini-Mauser with controlled round feeding. Like other Kimber rifles, the 84C action is machined from solid steel. Designed for the .223 Rem. family of cartridges, it is available in both single shot and repeater versions. Every Model 84C is test-fired for accuracy at the factory. Each rifle must shoot a 5-shot group measuring .400" or less center-to-center at 50 yards.

Prices:

SINGLE SHOT VARMINT .223 CALIBER	$1,032.00
in .17 Caliber	1,117.00
CLASSIC	1,275.00
SUPERAMERICA	1,770.00
VARMINT STAINLESS	1,390.00

MODEL 84C SPECIFICATIONS

MODEL:	MODEL 84C SINGLE SHOT VARMINT	MODEL 84C CLASSIC	MODEL 84C SUPERAMERICA	MODEL 84C VARMINT STAINLESS
CALIBERS:	17 Rem., 223 Rem.	222 Rem., 223 Rem.	17 Rem., 222 Rem. 223 Rem.	223 Rem.
WEIGHT:	7.5 lbs.	6.75 lbs.	6.75 lbs.	7.5 lbs.
OVERALL LENGTH:	43.5"	40.5"	40.5"	42.5"
ACTION TYPE:	Front Locking Single Shot	Front Locking Controlled Feed Repeater Hinged floorplate 5-shot box magazine	Front Locking Controlled Feed Repeater Hinged floorplate 5-shot box magazine	Front Locking Controlled Feed Repeater Hinged floorplate 5-shot box magazine
TRIGGER: PRESSURE	Fully Adjustable Set at 2.5 lbs.	Fully Adjustable Set at 2.5 lbs.	Fully Adjustable Set at 2.5 lbs.	Fully Adjustable Set at 2.5 lbs.
BARREL LENGTH: GROOVES TWIST	25" (Fluted) 6 17 Rem.-10"/223 Rem.-12"	22" 6 222 Rem.-12"/223 Rem.-12"	22" 6 17 Rem.-10"/222 Rem.-12" 223 Rem.-12"	24" (Fluted) 6 12"
STOCK: GRADE WALNUT CHECKERING (LPI) COVERAGE	A Claro 18 Side Panel	A Claro 18 Side Panel	AAA Claro 22 Full Coverage Wrap Around	A Claro 18 Side Panel
LENGTH OF PULL	13 ⅝"	13 ⅝"	13 ⅝"	13 ⅝"
METAL FINISH:	Stainless steel barrel, Matte blue action	Polished & Blued	Polished & Blued	Stainless steel barrel, Matte blue action

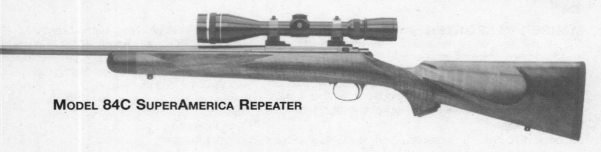

MODEL 84C SUPERAMERICA REPEATER

KONGSBERG RIFLES

MODEL 393 CLASSIC

HUNTER 393 MODELS

SPECIFICATIONS
Calibers: 243 Win., 6.5mmx55 Swedish, 270 Win., 30-06, 308 Win., 7mm Rem. Mag., 300 Win. Mag., 338 Win. Mag.
Capacity: 4 rounds (3 rounds in Magnum calibers)
Barrel Length: 22.8" (26" in Magnum calibers)
Muzzle Diameter: 0.63" (0.69" in Magnum calibers)
Weight: 7.5 lbs.
Stock: Turkish walnut; Select and Deluxe Models have Monte Carlo stock

Prices:

SELECT (STANDARD) MODEL	$980.00
Left Hand	1118.00
In Magnum calibers	1093.00
CLASSIC MODEL	995.00
In Magnum calibers	1109.00
DELUXE MODEL	1124.00
Left Hand	1261.00
In Magnum calibers	1236.00

SPORTER 393 THUMBHOLE

SPORTER 393 THUMBHOLE MODEL

SPECIFICATIONS
Calibers: 308 Win.
Capacity: 4 rounds
Barrel Length: 22.4"
Muzzle Diameter: 0.75"

Weight: 9 lbs.
Stock: American walnut thumbhole stock
Features: Adjustable comb, release in front of bolt handle for easy bolt removal
Price: (scope not included) $1579.00

KRIEGHOFF DOUBLE RIFLES

CLASSIC SIDE-BY-SIDE DOUBLE RIFLE

Krieghoff's new Classic Side-by-Side offers many standard features, including: Schnable forearm...classic English-style stock with rounded cheekpiece...UAS anti-doubling device...extractors...1" quick-detachable sling swivels... decelerator recoil pad...short opening angle for fast loading ...compact action with reinforced sidewalls...sliding, self-adjusting wedge for secure bolt...large underlugs...automatic hammer safety...horizontal firing-pin placement...Purdey-style extension between barrels.

SPECIFICATIONS
Calibers: *Standard*—7x65R, 308 Win., 30-06, 8x57 JRS, 8X75JRS, 9.X74R; *Magnum*—375 Flanged Mag. N.E., 470 N.E., 500 N.E., 500/.416 N.E.

Action: Cocking device for optimum safety
Barrel length: 23.5"
Trigger: Double triggers with steel trigger guard
Weight: 7.5 to 11 lbs. (depending on caliber and wood density) **Options:** 21.5" barrel; engraved sideplates

Prices:
STANDARD $7,850.00
Interchangeable barrels
   (installed, w/extra forearm) 4,500.00
MAGNUM 9,450.00
Interchangeable barrels 5,500.00

L.A.R. GRIZZLY RIFLE

BIG BOAR COMPETITOR

BIG BOAR COMPETITOR
SPECIFICATIONS
Caliber: 50 BMG
Capacity: Single shot
Action: Bolt action, bull pup, breechloading
Barrel length: 36"
Overall length: 45 1/2" **Weight:** 30.4 lbs.
Safety: Thumb safety

Features: All-steel construction; receiver made of 4140 alloy steel, heat-treated to 42 R/C; bolt made of 4340 alloy steel; low recoil (like 12 ga. shotgun)
Prices: $2,570.00
PARKERIZED 2,670.00
NICKEL FRAME 2,820.00
FULL NICKEL 2,920.00

LAZZERONI RIFLES

These new, state-of-the-art rifles feature 4340 chrome-moly steel receivers with two massive locking lugs, a match-grade 416R stainless steel barrel, fully adjustable benchrest-style trigger and a Lazzeroni-designed synthetic stock that is hand-bedded using aluminum pillar blocks. Included is a precision-machined floorplate/triggerguard assembly.

MODEL L2000ST

SPECIFICATIONS
Calibers: 6.17 (243) Flash™; 6.53 (257) Scramjet™; 6.71 (264) Blackbird™; 9.53 (375) Saturn™; 10.57 (416) Meteor™
Capacity: 3 rounds (1 in chamber)

Barrel Length: 27" (24" in Saturn & Meteor)
Overall Length: 47.5" (44.5" Saturn & Meteor)
Weight: 8.1 lbs. (10 lbs. in Saturn & Meteor)
Stock: Lazzeroni fiberglass sporter; right or left hand available; "fibergrain" finish on Saturn & Meteor stock
Prices:
MODEL L2000ST $3,995.00
SATURN & METEOR 4,395.00

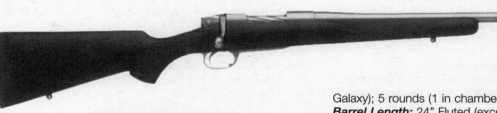

MODEL L2000SA

SPECIFICATIONS
Calibers: 6.17 (243) Spitfire™; 6.71 (264) Phantom™; 7.21 (284) Tomahawk™; 7.82 (308) Patriot™; 8.59 (338) Galaxy™
Capacity: 4 rounds (1 in chamber Tomahawk, Patriot,

Galaxy); 5 rounds (1 in chamber Spitfire, Phantom)
Barrel Length: 24" Fluted (except Galaxy)
Overall Length: 42.5"
Weight: 6.8 lbs.
Stock: Lazzeroni Slimline Stock
Price:
MODEL L2000SA $3,995.00

MODEL L2000SP

SPECIFICATIONS
Calibers: 6.17 (243) Flash™; 6.53 (257) Scramjet™; 6.71 (264) Blackbird™; 7.82 (308) Warbird™; 8.59 (338) Titan™; 9.53 (375) Saturn™; 10.57 (416) Meteor™

Capacity: 3 rounds (1 in chamber)
Barrel Length: 23" (21" Ladies and Youth)
Overall Length: 43.5" (40.5" Ladies and Youth)
Weight: 7.8 lbs.
Stock: Lazzeroni fiberglass thumbhole (right hand only)
Price:
MODEL L2000SP $3,995.00

MAGNUM RESEARCH

MOUNTAIN EAGLE

VARMINT MODEL
w/STAINLESS STEEL KRIEGER BARREL

MOUNTAIN EAGLE BOLT-ACTION RIFLE

SPECIFICATIONS
Calibers: 270 Win., 280 Rem., 30-06 Springfield, 7mm Mag., 300 Wby. Mag., 300 Win. Mag., 338 Win. Mag., 340 Wby. Mag., 357 H&H Mag., 416 Rem. Mag.
Capacity: 5-shot magazine (long action); 4-shot (Magnum action) *Action:* SAKO-built to MRI specifications
Barrel length: 24" with .004" headspace tolerance
Overall length: 44" *Weight:* 7 lb. 13 oz.
Sights: None *Stock:* Fiberglass composite
Length of pull: 13 ⅝" *Features:* Adjustable trigger; high comb stock (for mounting and scoping); one-piece forged bolt; free-floating, match-grade, cut-rifles, benchrest barrel; recoil pad and sling swivel studs; Platform Bedding System front lug; pillar-bedded rear guard screw; lengthened receiver ring; solid steel hinged floorplate

Price: **$1,499.00**
    Left Hand **1,549.00**
    357 H&H Mag. and 416 Rem. Mag. **1,799.00**
Also available:
VARMINT EDITION. In 222 Rem. and 223 Rem. with stainless steel Krieger barrel (26") **$1629.00**
STANDARD (add **$300.00** for 357 H&H or 416 Rem) **1,499.00**
    Left Hand. **1,549.00**

MAGTECH RIFLES

MODEL MT 122.2R

MODEL MT 122.2S/R/T BOLT-ACTION RIFLE

SPECIFICATIONS
Calibers: 22 Short, Long, Long Rifle
Capacity: 6- or 10-shot clip *Action:* Bolt action
Barrel length: 25" (8-groove rifling), free-floating
Overall length: 43" *Weight:* 6.5 lbs.
Safety: Double locking bolt, red cocking indicator, safety lever (disconnects trigger from firing mechanism in "safe" position) *Finish:* Brazilian hardwood

Features: Double extractors; beavertail forearm; sling swivels. No mechanical sight (for mounting scope or sight later) on Model 122.2S.
Price: **$100.00**
Also available:
MODEL MT 122.2R. With adjustable rear sight and post front sight.
Price: **$115.00**
MODEL MT 122.2T. With adjustable micrometer-type rear sight and ramp front sight; positive click stops for precise adjustment.
Price: **$120.00**

MARLIN 22 RIFLES

MODEL 60

SPECIFICATIONS

Caliber: 22 Long Rifle *Capacity:* 14-shot tubular magazine with patented closure system *Barrel Length:* 22" *Overall Length:* 40.5" *Weight:* 5.5 lbs. *Sights:* Ramp front sight with brass bead and Wide-Scan hood; adjustable open rear, receiver grooved for scope mount *Action:* Self-loading; side ejection; manual and automatic "last-shot" hold-open devices; receiver top has serrated, nonglare finish; crossbolt safety *Stock:* One-piece Maine birch Monte Carlo stock, press-checkered, with full pistol grip; Mar-Shield® finish
Price: $161.00

MODEL 60SB

SPECIFICATIONS

Caliber: 22 LR only *Action:* Same as Model 60SS *Capacity:* 14-shot tubular magazine w/patented closure system *Barrel Length:* 22" w/Micro-Groove rifling (16 grooves) *Overall Length:* 40.5" *Weight:* 5.5 lbs. *Sights:* Same as Model 60SS *Stock:* Monte Carlo walnut finished Maine birch; full pistol grip; Mar-Shield® finish
Price: $204.00

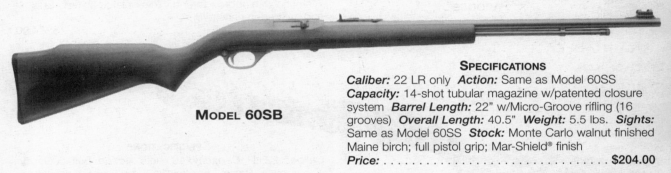

MODEL 60SS

SPECIFICATIONS

Caliber: 22 Long Rifle *Capacity:* 14 rounds *Barrel Length:* 22" *Overall Length:* 40.5" *Weight:* 5.5 lbs.

Sights: Adjustable folding semibuckhorn rear; ramp front sight with high-visibility post and removable Wide Scan™ hood *Stock:* Laminated two-tone Maine birch with nickel-plated swivel studs and rubber rifle buttpad *Features:* Micro-Groove® rifling; side ejection; manual bolt hold-open; automatic last-shot bolt hold-open; crossbolt safety
Price: $257.00

MODEL 60SSK

SPECIFICATIONS

Caliber: 22 LR only *Capacity:* 14-shot tubular magazine w/patented closure system *Barrel Length:* 22" w/Micro-Groove rifling (16 grooves) *Overall Length:* 40.5" *Weight:* 5 lbs. *Sights:* Same as Model 60SS *Stock:* Monte Carlo black fiberglass-filled synthetic w/nickel plated swivel studs and molded in checkering
Price: $223.00

MARLIN 22 RIFLES

MODEL 70PSS "PAPOOSE"

SPECIFICATIONS
Caliber: 22 Long Rifle **Capacity:** 7-shot clip **Barrel Length:** 16.25" **Overall Length:** 35.25" **Weight:** 3.25 lbs. **Action:** Self-loading; side ejection; manual bolt hold-open; crossbolt safety; stainless-steel breech bolt and barrel **Sights:** Screw adjustable open rear; ramp front; receiver grooved for scope mount **Stock:** Black fiberglass-filled synthetic with abbrev. forend, nickel-plated swivel studs and molded-in checkering
Price: $264.00

MODEL 7000

SPECIFICATIONS
Caliber: 22 LR **Capacity:** 10 shots **Action:** Self-loading; side ejection **Barrel Length:** 18" heavy target; recessed muzzle (12 grooves) **Overall Length:** 37" **Weight:** 5.5 lbs. **Stock:** Monte Carlo black fiberglass-filled synthetic **Sights:** No sights; receiver grooved for scope mount (1" scope ring mounts standard) **Features:** Manual bolt hold-open; cross-bolt safety; steel charging handle
Price: $219.00
Also available:
MODEL 795. Same specifications as Model 7000 but w/screw-adjustable open rear sight w/brass bead; barrel has 16 grooves; **Weight:** 4.5 lbs. $152.00
w/scope 159.00

MODEL 995SS

SPECIFICATIONS
Caliber: 22 LR only **Capacity:** 7-shot nickel-plated clip magazine **Action:** Same as Model 70PSS **Barrel Length:** 18" stainless steel w/Micro-Groove Rifling (16 grooves) **Overall Length:** 37" **Weight:** 4.5 lbs. **Sights:** Same as Model 70PSS **Stock:** Monte Carlo black fiberglass synthetic w/nickel-plated swivel studs and molded-in checkering
Price: $249.00

MARLIN RIFLES

MODEL 922 MAGNUM

SPECIFICATIONS

Caliber: 22 Win. Mag. Rimfire **Capacity:** 7-shot clip magazine **Barrel Length:** 20.5" **Overall Length:** 39.75" **Weight:** 6.5 lbs. **Sights:** Adjustable semibuckhorn rear; ramp front sight with brass bead and removable Wide-Scan hood™ **Stock:** Monte Carlo checkered American black walnut with rubber rifle buttpad and swivel studs **Features:** Side ejection; manual bolt hold-open; automatic last-shot bolt hold-open; magazine safety; Garand-type safety; Micro-Groove® rifling

Price: $423.00

MODEL 883

SPECIFICATIONS

Caliber: 22 WMR (not interchangeable with other 22 cartridges) **Capacity:** 12-shot tubular magazine with patented closure system **Action:** Bolt action; positive thumb safety; red cocking indicator **Barrel Length:** 22" with Micro-Groove® rifling (20 grooves) **Overall Length:** 41" **Weight:** 6 lbs. **Sights:** Adjustable folding semibuckhorn rear; ramp front with Wide-Scan hood™; receiver grooved for scope mount **Stock:** Checkered Monte Carlo American black walnut with full pistol grip; rubber buttpad; swivel studs; tough Mar-Shield® finish

Price: $290.00

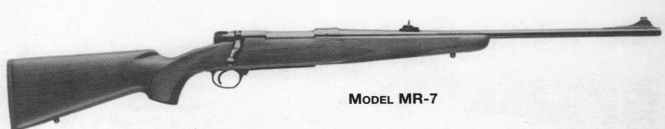

MODEL 883SS
(STAINLESS STEEL)

SPECIFICATIONS

Same as Model 883, except with stainless barrel and receiver, laminated two-tone brown Maine birch stock with nickel-plated swivel studs and rubber rifle buttpad

Price: $309.00

MODEL MR-7

SPECIFICATIONS

Calibers: 25-06 Rem., 270 Win., 30-06 Sprfd, 308 Win., 243 Win., 22-250 Rem. **Action:** Bolt action **Capacity:** 4-shot detachable box magazine **Barrel Length:** 22" (6-groove rifling), recessed muzzle **Overall Length:** 43" **Weight:** 7.5 lbs. **Sights:** Rear, optional Williams streamlined ramp w/brass bead; front, Williams blade **Stock:** American black walnut w/cut checkering; Mar-Shield™ finish **Features:** 3-position safety; shrouded striker; red cocking indicator; drilled and tapped receiver, rubber recoil pad

Price: $638.00

MARLIN BOLT-ACTION RIFLES

MARLIN 15YN "LITTLE BUCKAROO™"
SINGLE SHOT 22 BEGINNER'S RIFLE

SPECIFICATIONS
Caliber: 22 Short, Long or Long Rifle *Capacity:* Single shot *Action:* Bolt action; easy-load feed throat; thumb safety; red cocking indicator *Barrel Length:* 16.25" (16 grooves) *Overall Length:* 33.25" *Weight:* 4.25 lbs. *Sights:* Adjustable open rear; ramp front sight *Stock:* One-piece walnut-finished press-checkered Maine birch Monte Carlo w/full pistol grip; tough Mar-Shield® finish
Price: $181.00

MODEL 25MN

SPECIFICATIONS
Caliber: 22 WMR (not interchangeable w/other 22 cartridges) *Capacity:* 7-shot clip magazine *Barrel Length:* 22" with Micro-Groove® rifling *Overall Length:* 41" *Weight:* 6 lbs. *Sights:* Adjustable open rear; ramp front sight; receiver grooved for scope mount *Stock:* One-piece walnut finished press-checkered Maine birch Monte Carlo w/full pistol grip; Mar-Shield® finish; swivel studs
Price: $209.00

MODEL 25N

SPECIFICATIONS
Same specifications as Model 25MN, except *caliber* 22 LR and *weight* 5.5 pounds.
Price: $183.00

MARLIN 15N

SPECIFICATIONS
Caliber: 22 Short, Long, Long Rifle *Capacity:* Single shot *Action:* Bolt action; easy load feed ramp; thumb safety; red cocking indicator *Barrel Length:* 14.25" w/Micro-Groove® rifling (16 grooves) *Overall Length:* 35.25" *Weight:* 4.25 lbs. *Sights:* Screw-adjustable open rear; ramp front; grooved for scope mount *Stock:* Same as Model 25N but w/full pistol grip
Price:. $181.00

MARLIN BOLT-ACTION RIFLES

MODEL 882 SSV

MODEL 882

SPECIFICATIONS
Caliber: 22 WMR *Action:* Bolt action; thumb safety; red cocking indicator *Capacity:* 7-shot clip *Barrel Length:* 22" *Overall Length:* 41" *Weight:* 6 lbs. *Sights:* Adj. semibuckhorn folding rear; ramp front w/brass bead and Wide-Scan™ front sight hood *Stock:* Monte Carlo

American black walnut with swivel studs; full pistol grip; classic cut-checkering; rubber rifle buttpad
Price: $293.00
Also available: MODEL 882SS W/FIRE SIGHTS. Same as Model 882, except stainless-steel barrel; receiver front breechbolt striker knob and trigger stud; orange front sight post; black fiberglass-filled synthetic stock w/nickel-plated swivel studs and molded-in checkering. $297.00
MODEL 882SSV w/thumb safety with red cocking indicator; stainless barrel; black synthetic stock

MODEL 882L

SPECIFICATIONS
Caliber: 22 WMR (not interchangeable with other 22 cartridges) *Capacity:* 7-shot clip magazine *Barrel Length:* 22" Micro-Groove® *Overall Length:* 41" *Weight:* 6.25 lbs. *Sights:* Ramp front w/brass bead and removable

Wide-Scan™ hood; adj. folding semibuckhorn rear *Stock:* Laminated hardwood Monte Carlo w/Mar-Shield® finish
Features: Swivel studs; rubber rifle butt pad; receiver grooved for scope mount; positive thumb safety; red cocking indicator
Price: $296.00

MODEL MR-7B

SPECIFICATIONS
Caliber: 270 Win. and 30-06 Springfield *Capacity:* 4-shot blind magazine *Barrel Length:* 22" w/6-groove precision

rifling and recessed muzzle *Overall Length:* 43" *Weight:* 7.25 lbs. *Sights:* With or without sights (front sight: Williams streamlined ramp w/brass bead; rear sight: Williams blade) *Stock:* Maine birch pistol grip stock w/cut checkering; swivel studs; rubber rifle butt pad; Mar-Shield® finish
Price: w/sights $518.00

MODEL 81TS

SPECIFICATIONS
Caliber: 22 Short, Long or Long Rifle *Capacity:* Tubular magazine holds 25 Short, 19 Long, 17 Long Rifle cartridges

Barrel Length: 22" w/Micro-Groove® rifling (16 grooves) *Overall Length:* 41" *Weight:* 6 lbs. *Sights:* Screw-adjustable open rear; ramp front *Stock:* Monte Carlo black fiberglass-filled synthetic w/swivel studs and molded-in checkering
Price: $180.00
w/scope 187.00

MARLIN SELF-LOADING RIFLES

MODEL 922M SELF-LOADER

SPECIFICATIONS
Caliber: 22 WMRF *Capacity:* 7-shot clip magazine
Barrel Length: 20.5" Micro-Groove *Overall Length:*
39.75" *Weight:* 6.5 lbs. *Sights:* Adjustable folding semi-
buckhorn rear sight; ramp front sight w/brass bead and
removable Wide-Scan™ hood *Stock:* Monte Carlo
American black walnut checkered stock w/rubber rifle
butt pad and swivel studs *Features:* Garand type safety;
magazine safety; receiver sandblasted to prevent glare;
manual bolt hold-open; automatic last-shot bolt hold-open
Price: $423.00

MODEL 9 CAMP CARBINE

SPECIFICATIONS
Caliber: 9mm *Capacity:* 10-shot clip (12-shot avail.)
Action: Self-loading. Manual bolt hold-open. Garand-type
safety, magazine safety, loaded chamber indicator. Solid-top,
machined steel receiver is sandblasted to prevent glare, and
is drilled/tapped for scope mounting. *Barrel Length:* 16.5"
with Micro-Groove® rifling *Overall Length:* 35.5" *Weight:*
6.75 lbs. *Sights:* Adjustable folding rear, ramp front sight
with high-visibility, orange front sight post; Wide-Scan™
hood. *Stock:* Press-checkered walnut-finished hardwood
w/pistol grip; tough Mar-Shield™ finish; rubber rifle buttpad;
swivel studs
Price: $438.00

MODEL 45

SPECIFICATIONS
Caliber: 45 Auto *Capacity:* 7-shot clip *Barrel Length:*
16.5" *Overall Length:* 35.5" *Weight:* 6.75 lbs. *Sights:*
Adjustable folding rear; ramp front sight with high-visibility,
orange front sight post; Wide-Scan™ hood *Stock:* Press-
checkered walnut-finished Maine birch with pistol grip;
rubber rifle buttpad; swivel studs
Price: $438.00

MARLIN LEVER-ACTION CARBINES

MODEL 30AS

SPECIFICATIONS

Caliber: 30-30 **Capacity:** 6-shot tubular magazine
Action: Lever w/hammer block safety; solid top receiver
w/side ejection **Barrel Length:** 20" w/Micro-Groove®

Overall Length: 38.25" **Weight:** 7 lbs. **Sights:** Tapped for
scope mount and receiver sight; also available in combination w/4x, 32mm, 1" scope **Stock:** Walnut-finished Maine birch stock w/pistol grip; cut checkering; Mar-Shield® finish; swivel studs
Price: **$399.00**
Also available: MODEL30AW. Same specifications as Model 30AS but with blued steel barrel band w/integral swivel; padded nylon sling. **$402.00**

MARLIN GOLDEN 39AS

Introduced in 1891, the Marlin lever-action 22 is the oldest shoulder gun still being manufactured.

SOLID RECEIVER TOP. You can easily mount a scope on your Marlin 39 by screwing on the machined scope adapter base provided. The screw-on base is a neater, more versatile method of mounting a scope on a 22 sporting rifle. The solid top receiver and scope adapter base provide a maximum in eye relief adjustment. If you prefer iron sights, you'll find the 39 receiver clean, flat and sandblasted to prevent glare. Exclusive brass magazine tube

MICRO-GROOVE® BARREL. Marlin's famous rifling system of multi-grooving has consistently produced fine accuracy because the system grips the bullet more securely, minimizes distortion, and provides a better gas seal.

And the Model 39 maximizes accuracy with the heaviest barrels available on any lever-action 22.

SPECIFICATIONS

Caliber: 22 Short, Long and Long Rifle **Capacity:** Tubular magazine holds 26 Short, 21 Long and 19 LR cartridges
Action: Lever; solid top receiver; side ejection; one-step takedown; deeply blued metal surfaces; receiver top sandblasted to prevent glare; hammer block safety; rebounding hammer **Barrel:** 24" with Micro-Groove® rifling (16 grooves) **Overall Length:** 40" **Weight:** 6.5 lbs. **Sights:** Adjustable folding semibuckhorn rear, ramp front sight with Wide-Scan™ hood; solid top receiver tapped for scope mount or receiver sight; scope adapter base; offset hammer spur for scope use—works right or left **Stock:** Two-piece cut-checkered American black walnut w/fluted comb; full pistol grip and forend; blued-steel forend cap; swivel studs; grip cap; white butt and pistol-grip spacers; Mar-Shield® finish; rubber buttpad
Price: **$470.00**

MODEL 336CS

SPECIFICATIONS

Caliber: 30/30 Win. and 35 Rem. **Capacity:** 6-shot tubular magazine **Barrel Length:** 20" w/Micro-Groove® rifling (12 grooves) **Overall Length:** 38.25" **Weight:** 7 lbs. **Sights:**

Adjustable semi-buckhorn folding rear; ramp front sight w/brass bead and Wide-Scan hood. Solid top receiver tapped for scope mount or receiver sights; offset hammer spur for scope use. **Stocks:** American black walnut pistol grip stock w/fluted comb; cut checkering; rubber rifle butt pad; white butt and pistol grip spacers; blued steel barrel band w/integral swivel stud
Price: **$459.00**

MARLIN LEVER-ACTION CARBINES

MODEL 1894 COWBOY II

SPECIFICATIONS
Calibers: 357 Mag./38 Special, 44-40, 44 Mag./44 Special, 45 LC
Action: Lever action w/squared finger lever

Capacity: 10-shot tubular magazine
Barrel Length: 24" tapered octagon (6 grooves)
Overall Length: 41.5" **Weight:** 7.5 lbs.
Sights: Adjustable semi-buckhorn rear; carbine front
Stock: Straight-grip American black walnut w/cut-checkering and hard rubber buttplate
Features: Mar-Shield™ finish; blued steel forend cap; side ejection; blued metal surfaces; hammer block safety
Price: $704.00

MARLIN 1894S

SPECIFICATIONS
Calibers: 44 Rem. Mag./44 Special, 45 Colt
Capacity: 10-shot tubular magazine
Action: Lever action w/square finger lever; hammer block safety

Barrel Length: 20" w/deep-cut Ballard-type rifling
Sights: Ramp front sight w/brass bead; adjustable semi-buckhorn folding rear and Wide-Scan™ hood; solid-top receiver tapped for scope mount or receiver sight
Overall Length: 37.5" **Weight:** 6 lbs.
Stock: Checkered American black walnut stock w/Mar-Shield® finish; blued steel forend cap; swivel studs
Price: $477.00

MARLIN 1894CS 357 MAGNUM

SPECIFICATIONS
Calibers: 357 Magnum, 38 Special
Capacity: 9-shot tubular magazine
Action: Lever action w/square finger lever; hammer block safety; side ejection; solid top receiver; deeply blued metal

surfaces; receiver top sandblasted to prevent glare
Barrel Length: 18.5" w/deep-cut Ballard-type rifling (12 grooves)
Sights: Adjustable semibuckhorn folding rear, ramp front w/brass bead and Wide-Scan™ hood; solid top receiver tapped for scope mount or receiver sight; offset hammer spur for scope use-adjustable for right or left hand
Overall Length: 36" **Weight:** 6 lbs.
Stock: Cut-checkered straight-grip two-piece American black walnut Mar-Shield® finish; swivel studs; rubber rifle buttpad
Price: $477.00

MARLIN LEVER-ACTION CARBINES

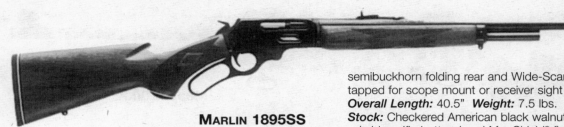

MARLIN 1895SS

SPECIFICATIONS
Caliber: 45-70 Government
Capacity: 4-shot tubular magazine
Action: Lever action; hammer block safety; receiver top sandblasted to prevent glare
Barrel: 22" w/deep-cut Ballard-type rifling
Sights: Ramp front sight w/brass bead; adjustable semibuckhorn folding rear and Wide-Scan™ hood; receiver tapped for scope mount or receiver sight
Overall Length: 40.5" *Weight:* 7.5 lbs.
Stock: Checkered American black walnut pistol-grip stock w/rubber rifle buttpad and Mar-Shield® finish; white pistol grip, butt spacers; swivel studs
Price: $555.00
Also available:
MODEL 1895G "GUIDE GUN" WITH PORTED BARREL. Same caliber, capacity, action, sights. Stock has straight grip, ventilated recoil pad. *Barrel Length:* 18.5" *Overall Length:* 37" *Weight:* 6.75 lbs.
Price: $562.00

MARLIN 336CS

SPECIFICATIONS
Calibers: 30-30 Win., and 35 Rem.
Capacity: 6-shot tubular magazine
Action: Lever action w/hammer block safety; deeply blued metal surfaces; receiver top sandblasted to prevent glare
Barrel: 20" Micro-Groove® barrel
Sights: Adjustable folding semibuckhorn rear; ramp front sight w/brass bead and Wide-Scan™ hood; tapped for receiver sight and scope mount; offset hammer spur for scope use (works right or left)
Overall Length: 38.5" *Weight:* 7 lbs.
Stock: Checkered American black walnut pistol-grip stock w/fluted comb and Mar-Shield® finish; rubber rifle buttpad; swivel studs
Price: $459.00

MODEL 444SS

SPECIFICATIONS
Caliber: 444 Marlin
Capacity: 5-shot tubular magazine
Barrel: 22" Micro-Groove®
Overall Length: 40.5" *Weight:* 7.5 lbs.
Stock: Checkered American black walnut pistol grip stock with rubber rifle buttpad; swivel studs
Sights: Ramp front sight with brass bead and Wide-Scan™ hood; adjustable semibuckhorn folding rear; receiver tapped for scope mount or receiver sight
Price: $555.00

MARLIN 22 TARGET RIFLE

MODEL 2000L

SPECIFICATIONS

Caliber: 22 LR only
Capacity: Single shot
Action: Bolt action; thumb safety; patented two-stage target trigger; red cocking indicator
Barrel Length: 22" heavy, selected Micro-Groove w/match chamber and recessed muzzle

Overall Length: 41" *Weight:* 8 lbs.
Sights: Fully adjustable target rear peep sight; hooded front sight w/10 aperture inserts
Stock: Laminated black/grey w/ambidextrous pistol grip; butt plate adjustable for length of pull, height, angle; aluminum forearm
Price: $639.00

MAUSER RIFLES

MODEL 96 BOLT ACTION

MODEL 96

SPECIFICATIONS

Calibers: 243 Win., 25-06, 270 Win., 30-06 S'fld, 308 Win., 7mm Rem. Mag., 300 Win. Mag.
Capacity: 5 rounds
Action: Sliding bolt action
Barrel length: 22" (24" magnum)
Overall length: 42" (44" magnum)
Weight: 6.25 lbs.
Safety: Rear tang, 3-position
Trigger: Single *Stock:* Checkered walnut
Sights: None; drilled and tapped for Rem. 700 scope mounts and bases

Features: Quick-detachable 1" sling swivels; 16 locking lugs
Price: $699.00
Also available:
MODEL SR 86 W/28.75" barrel in 308 Win. w/muzzle brake; adjustable black laminated thumbhold stock w/bipod rail. *Weight:* 13.6 lbs. $11,795.00
MODEL M94 w/22" barrel (24" magnum) in 25-06 Rem., 243 Win., 308 Win., 270 Win., 30-06 S'fld, 7mm Rem. Mag., 300 Win. Mag. Features aluminum bedding block, interchangeable barrels ($799.00), combo or single-set trigger, detachable mag., walnut stock.
Weight: 7.25 lbs. $2,295.00

NAVY ARMS REPLICA RIFLES

HENRY MILITARY RIFLE

This Civil War replica features a highly polished brass frame and blued barrel; sling swivels to the original specifications are located on the left side.

SPECIFICATIONS
Caliber: 44-40 or 45 Colt *Capacity:* 13 rounds

Barrel Length: 24"
Overall Length: 43"
Weight: 9.25 lbs. *Stock:* Walnut
Price: $895.00

IRON FRAME HENRY

SPECIFICATIONS
Caliber: 44-40 *Capacity:* 13 rounds
Barrel Length: 24" *Overall Length:* 43"
Weight: 9 lbs.
Stock: Walnut
Finish: Blued or casehardened
Feature: Iron frame
Price: $945.00

HENRY CARBINE

The arm first utilized by the Kentucky Cavalry, with blued finish and brass frame.

SPECIFICATIONS
Caliber: 44-40
Capacity: 11 rounds
Barrel Length: 22"
Overall Length: 41"
Weight: 8 ³/₄ lbs.
Price: $875.00

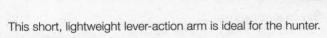

This short, lightweight lever-action arm is ideal for the hunter.

SPECIFICATIONS
Caliber: 44-40
Capacity: 8 rounds
Barrel Length: 16 ¹/₂"
Overall Length: 34 ¹/₂"
Weight: 7 lbs. 7 oz.
Price: $875.00

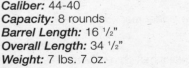

HENRY TRAPPER MODEL

RIFLES

NAVY ARMS REPLICA RIFLES

1866 "YELLOWBOY" RIFLE

The 1866 model was Oliver Winchester's improved version of the Henry rifle. Called the "Yellowboy" because of its polished brass receiver, it was popular with Indians, settlers and cattlemen alike.

SPECIFICATIONS
Caliber: 38 Special, 44-40, 45 Colt
Barrel Length: 24" full octagon *Overall Length:* 42.5"
Weight: 8.25 lbs. *Sights:* Blade front; open ladder rear
Stock: Walnut
Price: $685.00

1866 "YELLOWBOY" CARBINE

This is the "saddle gun" varient of the rifle described above.

SPECIFICATIONS
Caliber: 38 Special, 44-40 or 45 Colt
Barrel Length: 19" round *Overall Length:* 38.25"
Weight: 7.25 lbs. *Sights:* Blade front; open ladder rear
Stock: Walnut
Price: $675.00

1873 WINCHESTER SPORTING RIFLE

This replica of the state-of-the-art Winchester 1873 Sporting Rifle features a checkered pistol grip, buttstock, casehardened receiver and blued octagonal barrel.

SPECIFICATIONS
Caliber: 44-40 or 45 Colt
Barrel Length: 24" or 30"
Overall Length: 48 ³/₄" (w/30" barrel)
Weight: 8 lbs. 14 oz.
Sights: Blade front; buckhorn rear
Prices:
30" Barrel. $960.00
24" Barrel. 930.00

1873 WINCHESTER STYLE RIFLE

Known as "The Gun That Won the West," the 1873 was the most popular lever-action rifle of its time. This fine replica features a casehardened receiver.

SPECIFICATIONS
Caliber: 357 Mag., 44-40 or 45 Colt
Barrel Length: 24" *Overall Length:* 43"
Weight: 8.25 lbs.
Sights: Blade front; open ladder rear
Stock: Walnut
Price: $820.00
Also available: 1873 WINCHESTER-STYLE CARBINE
(19" barrel) $800.00

NAVY ARMS REPLICA RIFLES

1873 SPRINGFIELD CAVALRY CARBINE

A reproduction of the classic U.S. "Trapdoor" Springfield carbine used by the 7th Cavalry at The Battle of Little Big Horn.

SPECIFICATIONS
Caliber: 45-70 Government
Barrel Length: 22"
Overall Length: 40.5"
Weight: 7 lbs.
Sights: Blade front, military ladder rear
Stock: Walnut   *Features:* Saddle bar with ring
Price: $870.00
Also available:
1873 SPRINGFIELD INFANTRY RIFLE (32.5" bbl.) . . **$1,060.00**

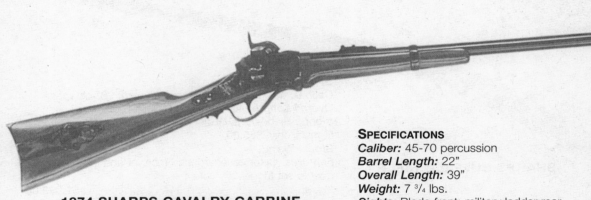

1874 SHARPS CAVALRY CARBINE

This cavalry carbine version of the Sharps rifle features a side bar and saddle ring.

SPECIFICATIONS
Caliber: 45-70 percussion
Barrel Length: 22"
Overall Length: 39"
Weight: 7 ³/₄ lbs.
Sights: Blade front; military ladder rear
Stock: Walnut
Price: $935.00

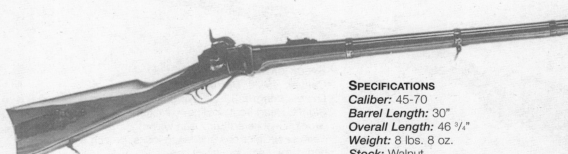

1874 SHARPS SNIPER RIFLE

This replica of the 1874 three-band sharpshooter's rifle was a popular target rifle at the Creedmoor military matches and was the issue longarm of the New York State Militia.

SPECIFICATIONS
Caliber: 45-70
Barrel Length: 30"
Overall Length: 46 ³/₄"
Weight: 8 lbs. 8 oz.
Stock: Walnut
Features: Double-set triggers; casehardened receiver; patchbox and furniture
Price: $1,115.00
Also available:
SINGLE TRIGGER INFANTRY MODEL $1,060.00

RIFLES

NAVY ARMS REPLICA RIFLES

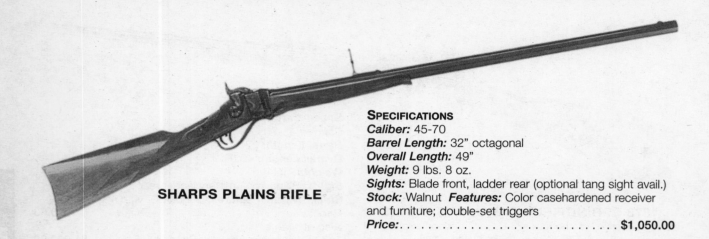

SHARPS PLAINS RIFLE

SPECIFICATIONS
Caliber: 45-70
Barrel Length: 32" octagonal
Overall Length: 49"
Weight: 9 lbs. 8 oz.
Sights: Blade front, ladder rear (optional tang sight avail.)
Stock: Walnut *Features:* Color casehardened receiver and furniture; double-set triggers
Price: $1,050.00

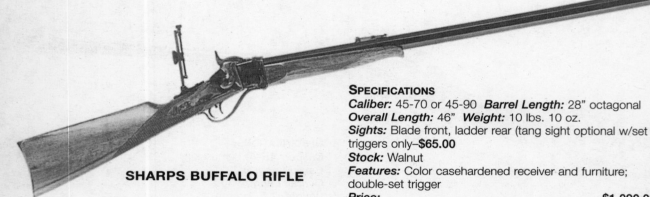

SHARPS BUFFALO RIFLE

SPECIFICATIONS
Caliber: 45-70 or 45-90 *Barrel Length:* 28" octagonal
Overall Length: 46" *Weight:* 10 lbs. 10 oz.
Sights: Blade front, ladder rear (tang sight optional w/set triggers only–**$65.00**
Stock: Walnut
Features: Color casehardened receiver and furniture; double-set trigger
Price: $1,090.00

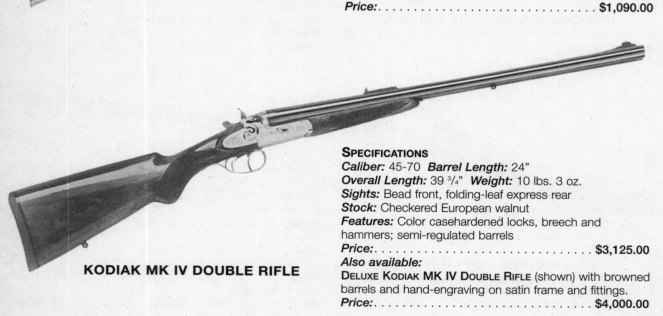

KODIAK MK IV DOUBLE RIFLE

SPECIFICATIONS
Caliber: 45-70 *Barrel Length:* 24"
Overall Length: 39 ³/₄" *Weight:* 10 lbs. 3 oz.
Sights: Bead front, folding-leaf express rear
Stock: Checkered European walnut
Features: Color casehardened locks, breech and hammers; semi-regulated barrels
Price: $3,125.00
Also available:
DELUXE KODIAK MK IV DOUBLE RIFLE (shown) with browned barrels and hand-engraving on satin frame and fittings.
Price: $4,000.00

NAVY ARMS REPLICA RIFLES

NO. 2 CREEDMOOR TARGET RIFLE

This reproduction of the Remington No. 2 Creedmoor Rifle features a color casehardened receiver and steel trigger guard, tapered octagon barrel, and walnut forend and butt-stock with checkered pistol grip.

SPECIFICATIONS
Caliber: 45-70
Barrel Length: 30", tapered
Overall Length: 46"
Weight: 9 lbs.
Sights: Globe front, adjustable Creedmoor rear
Stock: Checkered walnut stock and forend
Price: **$900.00**

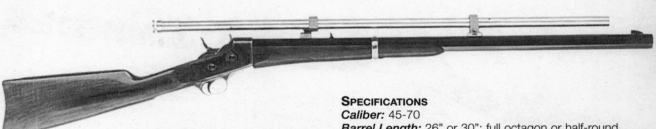

REMINGTON-STYLE ROLLING BLOCK BUFFALO RIFLE

This replica of the rifle used by buffalo hunters and plainsmen of the 1800s features a casehardened receiver, solid brass trigger guard and walnut stock and forend. The tang is drilled and tapped to accept the optional Creedmoor sight.

SPECIFICATIONS
Caliber: 45-70
Barrel Length: 26" or 30"; full octagon or half-round
Sights: Blade front, open notch rear
Stock: Walnut stock and forend
Feature: Shown with optional 32.5" Model 1860 brass telescopic sight **$210.00**; Compact Model (18"): **$200.00**
Price: **650.00**
Also available:
With casehardened steel (no brass furniture) **745.00**

GREENER LIGHT MODEL HARPOON GUN

Designed for large game fish, the Greener Harpoon gun utilizes the time-proven Martini action. The complete outfit consists of gun, harpoons, harpoon lines, line release frames, blank cartridges and cleaning kit, all housed in a carrying case.

SPECIFICATIONS
Caliber: 38 Special (blank)
Barrel Length: 20"   *Overall Length:* 36"
Weight: 6 lbs. 5 oz.
Stock: Walnut
Price: **$995.00**

NAVY ARMS REPLICA RIFLES

1892 RIFLE

SPECIFICATIONS
Caliber: 357 Mag., 44-40 or 45 Colt
Barrel Length: 24.25" octagon
Weight: 7 lbs.
Sights: Blade front; semi-buckhorn rear
Stock: American walnut
Price: $525.00

1892 BRASS FRAME RIFLE

SPECIFICATIONS
Calibers: 44-40 or 45 Colt
Barrel Length: 24.25" octagonal
Weight: 7.25 lbs.
Sights: Blade front; semi-buckhorn rear
Stock: American walnut
Price: $525.00

1892 SHORT RIFLE

Replica of the "Texas Special" 92 Winchester that featured a 20" full octagonal barrel. Available with color casehardened or blue receiver and furniture.

SPECIFICATIONS
Calibers: 357 Mag., 44-40 or 45 Colt
Barrel Length: 20" octagon *Weight:* 6.25 lbs.
Sights: Blade front; semibuckhorn rear
Stock: American walnut
Price: $525.00

NEW ENGLAND FIREARMS RIFLES

SYNTHETIC HANDI-RIFLE

New England Firearms® Handi-Rifle now features a black Monte Carlo synthetic stock and forend. This version includes a factory-mounted scope base and an offset hammer extension to ease cocking when a scope is mounted. The rifles all include the patented NEF Transfer Bar System, which virtually eliminates the possibility of accidental discharge. A wide range of additional rifle barrels are available for factory retrofitting through NEF's Accessory Barrel Program.

SPECIFICATIONS
Calibers: 22 Hornet, 223 Rem., 243 Win., 270 Win., 280 Rem., 30-30 Win., 30-06 Springfield; 44 Rem. Mag., 45-70 Gov't **Action:** Break-open; side lever release; automatic ejection **Barrel Length:** 22" (26" in 270 Win.) **Overall Length:** 38" (40" in 270 Win.) **Length Of Pull:** 14.25" **Drop At Heel:** 2.25" **Drop At Comb:** 1.5" **Weight:** 7 lbs. **Sights:** Ramp front; fully adjustable rear; tapped for scope mount **Stock:** High density polymer; black matte finish; sling swivels; recoil pad
Price: **$219.95**
   In 270 Win. **224.95**

SUPER LIGHT YOUTH HANDI-RIFLE™

For 1998 New England Firearms introduces a youth version of its Superlight Handi-Rifle in 22 Hornet. Proper gun fit is provided by a special youth-sized, lightweight synthetic stock and forend. Weight is further reduced with a new Super Light taper on the quick handling barrel. The matte black synthetic stock and forend feature a non-slip finish plus a sling, swivels and recoil pad. Other features include the patented New England Firearms Transfer Bar System, which virtually

eliminates the possibility of accidental discharge. As a young shooter grows, New England Firearms offers a variety of adult-sized rifle and shotgun barrels for factory retrofitting.

SPECIFICATIONS
Caliber: 22 Hornet **Action:** Single shot; break-open; side lever release; automatic ejection **Barrel Length:** 20" **Overall Length:** 33" **Drop At Heel:** 1 1/8" **Drop At Comb:** 1 1/8" **Length Of Pull:** 11.75" **Weight:** 5 1/3 lbs. **Sights:** Ramp front; fully adjustable rear; tapped for scope mount **Stock:** High density polymer; black matte finish; sling swivels; recoil pad
Price: **$219.95**

PEDERSOLI REPLICA RIFLES

ROLLING BLOCK TARGET RIFLE

SPECIFICATIONS
Calibers: 45-70 and 357 *Barrel length:* 30" octagonal (blued)
Weight: 91/2 lbs. (45-70); 10 lbs. (357) *Sights:* Adjustable
rear sight; tunnel modified front (all models designed for fit-
ting of Creedmoor sight)
Prices: $740.00
w/Creedmoor sight 810.00
Also available: Cavalry, Infantry, Long Range Creedmoor
Prices: . . . . $675.00–$900.00

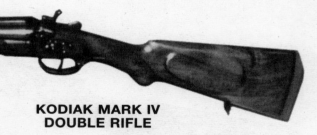

SPECIFICATIONS
Caliber: 54 *Barrel length:* 22" round (6 grooves)
Overall length: 39" *Weight:* 7.5 lbs.
Sights: Fully adjustable rear; fixed front
Price: w/Patchbox $885.00
Also available:
Sharps 1859 Military Rifle (set trigger, 30" barrel, 8.4 lbs.).
Price: $1,080.00

SHARPS CARBINE MODEL 766

SPECIFICATIONS
Calibers: 45-70, 9.3x74R, 8x57JSR *Barrel length:*
22" (24" 45-70) *Overall length:* 39" (40.5" 45-70)
Weight: 8.24 lbs. (9.7 lbs. 45/70)
Price: $3,125.00
Also available:
Kodiak Mark IV w/interchangeable 20-gauge barrel
Price: $4,125.00

KODIAK MARK IV DOUBLE RIFLE

PRAIRIE GUN WORKS

MODEL M-15 ULTRA LITE (not shown)

SPECIFICATIONS
Caliber: Most Short Action calibers
Action: Remington 700 Short Action
Barrel length: 22" Douglas Match Grade
Length of pull: 13.5" *Weight:* 4.5-5.25 lbs.
Stock: Fiberglass-Kevlar composite w/integral recoil lug;
recoil pad installed *Finish:* Black or grey textured finish
Sights: Custom aircraft-grade aluminum scope mounts

Features: Trigger set and polished for 3 lb. pull; bolt fluted,
hollowed and tapped w/Ultra Lite custom firing pin and
bolt shroud
Price: $1,750.00
Also available:
Model M-18. Same specifications and price as Model M-
15, except chambered for long-action calibers (up to 340
Weatherby)

REMINGTON BOLT-ACTION RIFLES

MODEL 700 BDL DM

MODEL 700 BDL SS DM
(Stainless/Synthetic)

MODEL 700 BDL DM

The **MODEL 700 DM** (Detachable Magazine) models feature detachable 4-shot magazines (except the 3-shot magnum-caliber models), stainless-steel latches, latch springs and magazine boxes. **MODEL 700 BDL DM** rifles feature the standard Remington BDL barrel contour with 22" barrels on standard-caliber models and 24" barrels on magnum-caliber rifles. All barrels have a hooded front sight and adjustable rear sight. Additional features include polished blued-metal finish, high-gloss, Monte Carlo-style cap, white line spacers, 20 lines-per-inch skipline checkering, recoil pad and swivel studs. All models feature fine-line engraving on receiver front rings, rear bridges, non-ejection receiver sides and floorplates. For calibers, see Model 700 table.

Prices:
MODEL 700 BDL DM. $702.00
    Magnum 729.00

RIFLES

MODEL 700 BDL SS

MODEL 700 BDL

This Model 700 features the Monte Carlo American walnut stock finished to a high gloss with fine-cut skipline checkering. Also includes a hinged floorplate, sling swivels studs, hooded ramp front sight and adjustable rear sight. Also available in stainless synthetic version (Model 700 BDL SS) with stainless-steel barrel, receiver and bolt plus synthetic stock for maximum weather resistance. For additional specifications, see Model 700 table.

MODEL 700 BDL
Prices:
In 17 Rem., 7mm Rem. Mag., 300 Win. Mag. . . . **$612.00**
In 222 Rem., 22-250 Rem., 223 Rem., 243 Win.,
   25-06 Rem., 270 Win., 30-06. . . . . **585.00**
In 338 Win. Mag.. . . . . **612.00**
Left Hand in 2700 Win., 30-06.. . . . . **612.00**
Left Hand in 7mm Rem. Mag.. . . . . **639.00**
MODEL BDL SS (Stainless Synthetic)
In 270 Win. 30-06.. **641.00**
In 7mm Rem. Mag., 300 Win. Mag.. . . . . **668.00**
In 338 Win. Mag. and 375 H&H Mag. **668.00**

MODEL 700 BDL SS DM-B

Available in *calibers:* 7mm Rem. Mag., 7mm STW, 30 Win. Mag., 3000 Wby. Mag. and 338 Win. Mag. *Barrel length:* 25.5" (magnum contour barrel). Stainless synthetic detachable magazine with muzzle brake.
Price: $789.00

REMINGTON BOLT-ACTION RIFLES

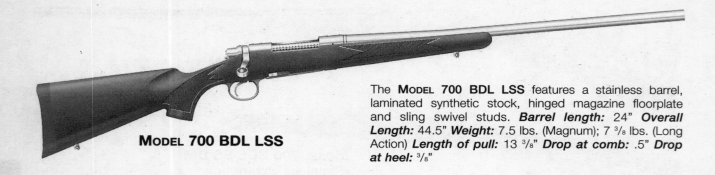

MODEL 700 BDL LSS

The **MODEL 700 BDL LSS** features a stainless barrel, laminated synthetic stock, hinged magazine floorplate and sling swivel studs. **Barrel length:** 24" **Overall Length:** 44.5" **Weight:** 7.5 lbs. (Magnum); 7 3/8 lbs. (Long Action) **Length of pull:** 13 3/8" **Drop at comb:** .5" **Drop at heel:** 3/8"

MODEL 700 "SENDERO SPECIAL"

Remington's Sendero rifle combines the accuracy features of the Model 700 Varmint Special with long action and magnum calibers for long-range hunting. The 26-inch barrel has a heavy varmint profile and features a spherical concave crown. For additional specifications, see table on the following page.

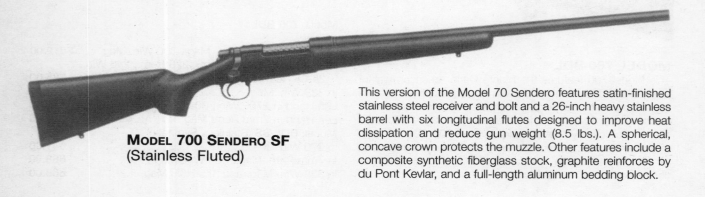

MODEL 700 SENDERO SF
(Stainless Fluted)

This version of the Model 70 Sendero features satin-finished stainless steel receiver and bolt and a 26-inch heavy stainless barrel with six longitudinal flutes designed to improve heat dissipation and reduce gun weight (8.5 lbs.). A spherical, concave crown protects the muzzle. Other features include a composite synthetic fiberglass stock, graphite reinforces by du Pont Kevlar, and a full-length aluminum bedding block.

MODEL 700 ADL (not shown)

Synthetic model has a fiberglass-reinforced synthetic stock, positive checkering, straight comb, raised cheekpiece and black rubber recoil pad. Stock and blued metalwork have a non-reflective black matte finish.

(See also table on the following page for prices, calibers and additional specifications)

MODEL 700 VLS
(VARMINT LAMINATED STOCK)

MODEL 700/CALIBERS
Prices:
MOUNTAIN 25-06, 260 Rem., 27 Win., 280 Rem.,
7mm-08, 30-06 . . . . $639.00
SENDERO 25-6, 270 Win. 705.00
7mm Rem. Mag., 30 Win. Mag. 732.00

SENDERO SF 25-06, 7mm Rem. Mag., 7mm STW,
300 Win. Mag., 300 Wby. Mag. 879.00
BDL SS DM 25-06 Rem., 260 Rem., 270 Win.,
280 Rem., 7mm-08, 30-06, 308 Win. 702.00
7mm Rem. Mag., 300 Win. Mag. and
300 Wby. Mag. 729.00

MODEL 700™ CENTERFIRE RIFLE SPECIFICATIONS

CALIBERS	MAGAZINE CAPACITY	BARREL LENGTH	TWIST (R-H) 1 TURN IN	MOUNTAIN RIFLE (DM)	SENDERO	SENDERO SF	BDL Stainless Synthetic DM	BDL SS	DM-B	BDL LSS
17 Rem.	5	24"	9"							
220 Swift	4	26"	14"							
222 Rem.	5	24"	14"							
22-250 Rem.	4	24"	14"							
223 Rem.	5	24"	12"							
243 Win.	4	22"	9 1/8"	●						
	4	24"	9 1/8"							
25-06 Rem.	4	24"	10"		●	●	●			
	4	22"	10"	●						
260 Rem.	4	24"	9"	●			●			
270 Win.	4	22"	10"	●						
	4	22"	10"							
	4	24"	10"		●		●	●		●
280 Rem.	4	22"	9 1/4"	●						
	4	24"	9 1/4"				●			
7mm-08 Rem.	4	22"	9 1/4"	●						
	4	24"	9 1/4"							
7mm Rem. Mag.	3	24"	9 1/4"		●	●		●	●	●
	3	24"	9 1/4"							●
7mm STW	3	24"	9 1/2"			●			●	
30-06	4	22"	10"	●						
	4	24"	10"				●	●		
308 Win.	4	22"	10"							
	4	24"	12"				●			
300 Win. Mag.	3	24"	10"		●	●	●	●		●
	3	24"	12"						●	●
300 Wby. Mag.	3	24"	12"			●	●			
338 Win. Mag.	3	24"	10"					●		
375 H&H Mag.	3	24"	12"					●		

All Model 700™ rifles come with sling swivel studs. The BDL, ADL, and Seven™ are furnished with sights. The BDL Stainless Synthetic, LSS, Mountain Rifle, Classic, Sendero and Varmint guns have clean barrels. All Remington CF rifles drilled and tapped for scope mounts.

RIFLES

REMINGTON BOLT-ACTION RIFLES

MODEL 700/CALIBERS (cont.)
Prices:

BDL SS DM-B 7mm Rem., 7mm STW,
300 Win. Mag. **$789.00**
BDL Stainless Synthetic 270 Win., 30-06 . . . . . . **641.00**
7mm Rem. Mag., 3000 Win. Mag.,
338 Win. Mag., 375 H&H Mag. **668.00**
LLS 270 Win, 7mm Rem. Mag., 300 Win. Mag. . . **715.00**
BDL 222 Rem., 270 Win. LH, 7mm Rem. Mag.,
30-06 LH, 300 Win. Mag., 338 Win. Mag. **612.00**
222 Rem., 22-250, 223 Rem., 243 Win.,
25-06, 270 Win., 30-06. . . . . **585.00**
7mm Rem. Mag. LH **639.00**
BDL DM 243 Win., 25-06 Rem., 270 Win.,
280 Rem., 7mm-08 Rem., 30-06. . . . . **639.00**

270 Win. LH **$665.00**
7mm Rem. Mag. LH, 300 Win. Mag. LH **692.00**
ADL 270 Win., 30-06, 308 Win. **492.00**
7mm Rem. Mag. **519.00**
ADL Synthetic 223 Rem., 243 Win., 270 Win.,
30-06, 308 Win. **425.00**
7mm Rem. Mag., 300 Win. Mag. **452.00**
VLS 22-25 Rem., 223 Rem., 243 Win.,
6mm Rem., 7mm-08 Rem., 308 Win. **625.00**
VS w/26" Heavy Barrel in 22-250 Rem.,
223 Rem., 243 Win., 308 Win. **705.00**
w/26" Fluted Barrel in 220 Swift, 22-250 Rem.,
223 Rem., 308 Win. **852.00**
Ported barrels. **872.00**

MODEL 700™ CENTERFIRE RIFLE SPECIFICATIONS (cont.)

Calibers	Magazine Capacity	Barrel Length	Twist (R-H) 1 Turn In	BDL	BDL (DM)	ADL	ADL Synthetic	VLS* 26" Heavy BBL	VS (Varmint Synthetic) 26" Heavy BBL	VS (Varmint Synthetic) 26" Stainless Fluted BBL
17 Rem.	5	24"	9"	●						
220 Swift	4	26"	14"							●
222 Rem.	5	24"	14"	●						
22-250 Rem.	4	24"	14"	●				●	●	●
223 Rem.	5	24"	12"	●			NEW	●	●	●
243 Win.	4	20"	9 1/8"	●	●		NEW			
	4	22"	9 1/8"					●	●	
25-06 Rem.	4	24"	10"	●						
	4	22"	10"							
260 Rem.	4	24"	9"					NEW		
270 Win.	4	22"	10"	●	●	●	●			
	4	22"	10"	●	●					
	4	24"	10"							
280 Rem.	4	22"	9 1/4"		●					
	4	24"	9 1/4"							
7mm-08 Rem.	4	22"	9 1/4"		●					
	4	24"	9 1/4"					●		
7mm Rem. Mag.	3	24"	9 1/4"	●	●	●	●			
	3	24"	9 1/4"	●	●					
7mm STW	3	24"	9 1/2"							
30-06	4	22"	10"	●	●	●	●			
	4	22"	10"	●	●					
308 Win.	4	20"	10"			●	●			
	4	22"	12"				●	●	●**	NEW**
300 Win. Mag.	3	24"	10"	●	●		NEW			
	3	24"	12"		●					
300 Wby. Mag.	3	24"	12"							
338 Win. Mag.	3	24"	10"	●						
375 H&H Mag.	3	24"	12"							

*Varmint Laminated Stock (also available in 6mm Rem.) **Available w/24" barrel

REMINGTON BOLT-ACTION RIFLES

MODEL 700 CLASSIC (8mm. Rem.)

Since Remington's series of Model 700 Classics began in 1981, the company has offered this model in a special chambering each year. The 300 Win. Mag. was introduced in 1963 for the Model 70 bolt-action rifle following the development of the 338 Win. Mag., 30-338 Wildcat and 308 Norma Mag. The 300 Win. Mag. has slightly longer body and a shorter neck than its predecessors and is recommended for all North American big-game hunting. The 8mm Rem. shown above was introduced in 1998.

The Model 700 Classic features an American walnut, straight-combed stock without a cheekpiece for rapid mounting, better sight alignment and reduced felt recoil. A hinged magazine flloorplate, sling swivel studs and satin wood finish with cut-checkering are standard, along with 24" barrel (44.5" overall) and 1:10" twist (no sight). Receiver drilled/tapped for scope mounts.
Price: **$612.00**

MODEL 700 MOUNTAIN DM (DETACHABLE MAGAZINE) RIFLE

The Remington Model 700 MTN DM rifle features the traditional mountain rifle-styled stock with a pistol grip pitched lower to position the wrist for a better grip. The cheekpiece is designed to align the eye for quick, accurate sighting. The American walnut stock has a handrubbed oil finish and comes with a brown recoil pad and deep-cut checkering. The Model 700 MTN DM also features a lean contoured 22" barrel that helps reduce total weight to 6.75 pounds (no sights). All metalwork features a glass bead-blasted, blued-metal finish. *Calibers:* 25-06 Rem., 260 Rem., 270 WWin., 280 Rem., 7mm-08 Rem., and 30-06 Springfield.
Price: **$639.00**

MODEL 700 ALASKAN WILDERNESS RIFLE (AWR)

This custom-built rifle has the same rate of twist and custom magnum barrel contour as the African Plains Rifle below, but features a Kevlar-reinforced composite stock. *Calibers:* 7mm Rem. Mag., 300 Win. Mag., 300 Wby. Mag., 338 Win. Mag., 375 H&H Mag. *Capacity:* 3 shots *Barrel length:* 24" *Overall Length:* 44.5" *Weight:* 6 lbs. 12 oz.
Price: **$1,376.00**

MODEL 700 AFRICAN PLAINS RIFLE (APR)

The custom-built Model 70 APR rifle has a laminated classic wood stock and the following specifications. *Calibers:* 7mm Rem. Mag., 300 Win. Mag., 300 Wby. Mag., 338 Win. Mag., 375 H&H Mag. *Capacity:* 3 shots *Barrel length:* 26" *Overall Length:* 46.5" *Weight:* 7.75 lbs. *Rate Of Twist:* R.H. 1 turn in 9.25" (7mm Rem. Mag.); 10" (300 Win. Mag. and 338 Win. Mag.); 12" (30 Wby. Mag. and 375 H&H Mag.)
Price: **$1,466.00**

REMINGTON BOLT-ACTION RIFLES

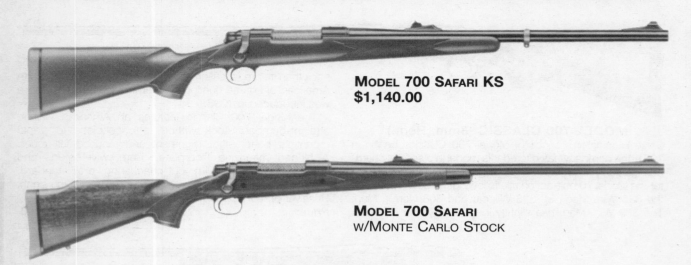

MODEL 700 SAFARI KS
$1,140.00

MODEL 700 SAFARI
w/MONTE CARLO STOCK

MODEL 700™ SAFARI GRADE bolt-action rifles provide big-game hunters with a choice of either wood or synthetic stocks. Model 700 Safari Monte Carlo (with Monte Carlo comb and cheekpiece) and Model 700 Safari Classic (with straight-line classic comb and no cheekpiece) are the satin-finished wood-stock models. Both are decorated with hand-cut checkering 18 lines to the inch and fitted with two reinforcing crossbolts covered with rosewood plugs. The Monte Carlo model also has rosewood pistol-grip and forend caps. All models are fitted with sling swivel studs and 22" or 24" barrels. Synthetic stock has simulated wood-grain finish, reinforced with Kevlar® (KS).
Calibers: 8mm Rem. Mag., 375 H&H Magnum, 416 Rem. Mag. and 458 Win. Mag. **Capacity:** 3 rounds. **Avg. Weight:** 9 lbs. **Overall Length:** 44.5" **Rate of Twist:** 10" (8mm Rem. Mag.); 12" (375 H&H Mag.); 14" (416 Rem. Mag., 458 Win. Mag.)
Price: **$1,136.00**

MODEL 40-XR KS TARGET RIMFIRE POSITION RIFLE w/KEVLAR STOCK

Action: Bolt action, single shot
Caliber: 22 Long Rifle rimfire Capacity: Single loading
Barrel: 24" medium weight target barrel countersunk at muzzle. Drilled and tapped for target scope blocks. Fitted with front sight base
Bolt: Artillery style with lockup at rear; 6 locking lugs, double extractors
Overall Length: 43.5"
Average Weight: 100.5 lbs.
Sights: Optional at extra cost; Williams Receiver No. FPTK and Redfield Globe front match sight
Safety: Positive serrated thumb safety
Receiver: Drilled and tapped for receiver sight

Trigger: Adjustable from 2 to 4 bls.
Stock: Position style with Monte Carlo, cheekpiece and thumb groove; five-way adj. buttplate and full-length guide rail
Price: **$1,441.00**
Also Available:
MODEL 40-XR BR with 22" stainless-steel barrel (heavy contour), 22 LR match chamber and bore dimensions. Receiver and barrel drilled and tapped for scope mounts (mounted on green, duPont Kevlar reinforced fiberglass benchrest stock. Fully adjustable trigger (2 oz. trigger optional).
Price: **$1,548.00**
(Additional target rifles are available through Remington's Custom Shop.)

REMINGTON BOLT-ACTION RIFLES

MODEL SEVEN CARBINE

Every **MODEL SEVEN** is built to the accuracy standards of the famous Model 700 and is individually test fired to prove it. its tapered 18.5" Remington special steel barrel is f ree floating out to a single pressure point at the forend tip. And there is ordnance-quality steel in everything from its fully enclosed bolt and extractor system to its steel trigger guard and floorplate. Ramp front and fully adjustable rear sights, sling swivel studs are standard. The Youth Model features a hardwood stock that is 1 inch shorter for easy control. Chambered in 243 Win. and 7mm-08 for less recoil. See table at right for additional specifications.

Prices:

18.5" Barrel	$585.00
20" Barrel	641.00
Youth	479.00

SPECIFICATIONS MODEL SEVEN™

CALIBERS	CLIP MAG. CAPACITY	BARREL LENGTH	OVERALL LENGTH	TWIST R-H 1 TURN IN	AVG. WT. (LBS.)
223 Rem.*	5	18.5"	37 3/4"	12"	6 1/4"
243 Win.	4	18.5"	37 3/4"	9 1/8"	6 1/4"
	4	18.5"	36 3/4" (Youth)	9 1/8"	6
	4	20"	39 1/4"	9 1/8"	6 1/4"
260 Rem.*	4	18.5"	37 3/4"	9"	6 1/4"
7mm-08 Rem.	4	18.5"	37 3/4"	9 1/4"	6 1/4"
	4	18.5"	36 3/4" (Youth)	9 1/4"	6
	4	20"	39 1/4"	9 1/4"	6 1/4"
308 Win.	4	18.5"	37 3/4"	10"	6 1/4"
	4	20"	39 1/4"	10"	6 1/4"

Stock Dimensions: 13 3/16" length of pull, 9/16" drop at comb, 5/16" drop at heel. youth gun has 12.5" length of pull. 17. Rem. provided without sights.
Note: *New Model Seven Mannlicher and Model Seven KS versions are availlable from the Remington Custom Shop through your local dealer.*
*Also available in 20" barrel (stainless only).

MODEL SEVEN YOUTH
(243 Win., 260 Rem., 7mm-08 Rem.)
$479.00

MODEL SEVEN SS
(STAIINLESS SYNTHETIC 20" BBL.)
(243 Win., 260 Rem.,7mm-08 Rem., 308 Win.)
$641.00

RIFLES

REMINGTON REPEATING RIFLES

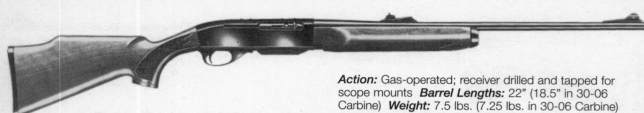

MODEL 7400 (High Gloss Stock)

Calibers: 243 Win., 270 Win., 280 Rem., 30-06, 30-06 Carbine, 308 Win.
Capacity: 5 centerfire cartridges (4 in the magazine, 1 in the chamber); extra 4-shot magazine available

Action: Gas-operated; receiver drilled and tapped for scope mounts **Barrel Lengths:** 22" (18.5" in 30-06 Carbine) **Weight:** 7.5 lbs. (7.25 lbs. in 30-06 Carbine) **Overall Length:** 42" **Sights:** Standard blade ramp front; sliding ramp rear **Stock:** Satin or high-gloss (270 Win. and 300-06 only walnut stock and forend; curved pistol grip; also available with Special Purpose nonreflective finish (270 Win. and 30-06 only) **Length Of Pull:** 13 3/8"
Drop At Heel: 2.25" **Drop At Comb:** 1 13/16"
Price: $573.00

MODEL 7600 (High Gloss Stock)

The Model 7600 shares nearly the same specifications as the Model 7400 featured above, except the 7600 is pump action.
Drop At Heel: 15/16"
Drop At Comb: 9/16"
Price: $540.00

MODEL 7400
CUSTOM ENGRAVED

MODEL 7600 CUSTOM
Closeup of Engraved Receiver

REMINGTON RIMFIRE RIFLES

RIFLES

MODEL 541-T BOLT ACTION
Price: **$465.00**
HEAVY BARREL 492.00
MODEL 581-S 239.00

MODEL 552 BDL SPEEDMASTER

The rimfire semiautomatic 552 BDL Deluxe sports Remington custom-impresses checkering on both stock and forend. Tough Du Pont RK-W lifetime finish brings out the lustrous beauty of the walnut while protecting it. Sights are ramp-style in front and rugged big-game type fully adjustable in rear.
Price: **$340.00**

MODEL 572 BDL FIELDMASTER

Features of this rifle with big-game feel and appearance are: Du Pont's tough RK-W finish; centerfire-rifle-type rear sight fully adjustable for both vertical and horizontal sight alignment; big-game style ramp front sight; Remington impressed checkering on both stock and forend.
Price: **$353.00**

(See following page for additional specifications.)

REMINGTON RIMFIRE RIFLES

MODEL 597 SERIES

Remington's new autoloading rimfire rifles–the Model 597™ Series–are made for those outdoorsmen who view rimfire shooting as a serious activity. They are available in three versions, offering a choice of carbon or stainless steel barreled actions, synthetic or laminated wood stocks, and chambering for either standard 22 Long Rifle or 22 Magnum ammo. All three M597™ rifles feature beavertail-style forends rounded with finger grooves for hand-filling control. The top of the receiver blends into the pistol grip, creating a rimfire autoloader that points like a shotgun but aims like a rifle. Features include a bolt guidance system of twin steel rails for smooth bolt travel and functional reliability. The 20-inch barrels are free-floated for consistent accuracy with all types of rimfire ammunition. A new trigger design creates crisp let-off for autoloading rifles. Bolts on the two 22 LR versions are nickel-plated. The magnum-version bolt is constructed of a special alloy steel to provide controlled, uniform function with magnum cartridges. All receivers are grooved for standard tip-off mounts and are also drilled and tapped for Weaver-type bases. Adjustable open sights and one-piece scope mount rails are standard, as are spare magazine clips.

RIMFIRE RIFLE SPECIFICATIONS

MODEL	ACTION	BARREL LENGTH	OVERALL LENGTH	AVERAGE WT. (LBS.)	MAGAZINE CAPACITY
597™	Auto	20"	40"	5.5	10-Shot Clip
597™ LSS	Auto	20"	40"	5.5	10-Shot Clip
597™ Mag.	Auto	20"	40"	5.5	8-Shot Clip
522 Viper	Auto	20"	40"	4 $5/8$	10-Shot Clip
541-T	Bolt	24"	42.5"	5 $7/8$*	5-Shot Clip
541-T HB Heavy Barrel	Bolt	24"	42.5"	6.5*	5-Shot Clip
552 BDL Deluxe Speedmaster	Auto	21"	40"	5 $3/4$	15 Long Rifle
572 BDL Deluxe Fieldmaster	Pump	21"	40"	5.5	15 Long Rifle
581-S	Bolt	24"	42.5"	5 $7/8$	5-Shot Clip

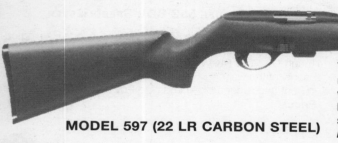

MODEL 597 (22 LR CARBON STEEL)

The M597™ is chambered for 22 Long Rifle ammunition and matches Remington's carbon steel barrel with a strong, light-weight, alloy receiver. All metal has a non-reflective, matte black finish. The rifle is housed in a one-piece, dark gray synthetic stock.
Price: **$159.00**

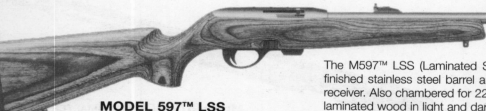

MODEL 597™ LSS

The M597™ LSS (Laminated Stock Stainless) has a satin-finished stainless steel barrel and matching, gray-tone alloy receiver. Also chambered for 22 LR cartridges, its stock is of laminated wood in light and dark brown tones.
Price: **$212.00**
W/Laminated Stock **265.00**

MODEL 597™ MAGNUM

Chambered for 22 Win. Mag. rimfire cartridges, the M597™ MAGNUM features a carbon steel barrel, alloy receiver and black synthetic stock.
Price: **$305.00**
W/Laminated Stock **359.00**

RIFLES, INC.

CUSTOM RIFLES

CLASSIC MODEL

SPECIFICATIONS
Calibers: Customized for varmint, target or hunter specifications, up to 375 H&H
Action: Remington or Winchester stainless steel Control-round with lapped bolt

Barrel Length: 26"-28" depending on caliber; stainless-steel match grade, lapped
Weight: 6.5 lbs. (approx.)
Stock: Pillar glass bedded; laminated fiberglass, finished with textured epoxy
Features: Fine-tuned and adjustable trigger; hinged floor-plate trigger guard
Price: $1,800.00

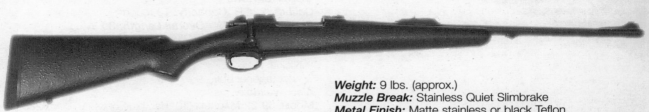

SAFARI MODEL

SPECIFICATIONS
Action: Winchester Model 70 Control-round feed; hand lapped and honed bolt; drilled and tapped for 8X40 base screws
Barrel Length: 23"-25" depending on caliber; stainless-steel match grade, lapped

Weight: 9 lbs. (approx.)
Muzzle Break: Stainless Quiet Slimbrake
Metal Finish: Matte stainless or black Teflon
Stock: Pillar glass bedded; double reinforced laminated fiberglass/graphite; finished with textured epoxy
Features: Fine-tuned and adjustable trigger; hinged floor-plate
Options: Drop box for additional round; express sights; barrel band; quarter ribs
Price: $2,400.00
   w/Options $3,385.00

LIGHTWEIGHT STRATA STAINLESS MODEL

SPECIFICATIONS
Calibers: Up to 375 H&H
Action: Stainless Remington; fluted, tapped and handle-hollowed bolt; aluminum bolt shroud
Barrel Length: 22"-24" depending on caliber; stainless-steel match grade
Weight: 4.75 lbs. (approx.)

Stock: Pillar glass bedded; laminated Kevlar/Boron/Graphite, finished with textured epoxy
Features: Matte stainless metal finish; aluminum blind or hinged floorplate trigger guard; custom Protektor pad
Price: $2,400.00
Also Available:
LIGHTWEIGHT 70 in calibers up to 375 H&H. *Barrel Length:* 22" to 24" (depending on caliber)) stainless steel match grade. *Weight:* 5.75 lbs. *Stock:* Pillar glass bedded; laminated Kevlar/Graphite/Boron finished with textured epoxy. Trigger is fine-tuned and adjusted.
Price: $2,300.00

ROSSI RIFLES

PUMP-ACTION GALLERY GUNS

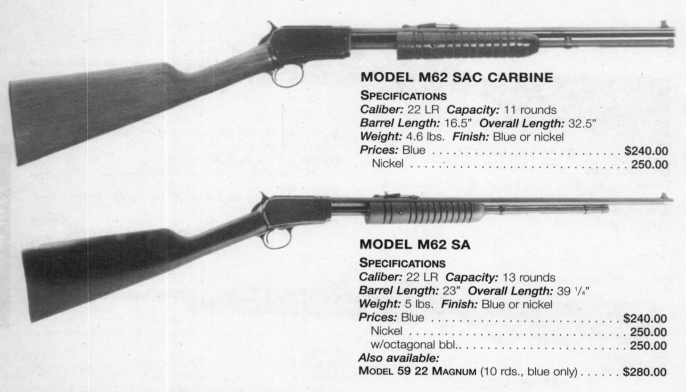

MODEL M62 SAC CARBINE

SPECIFICATIONS
Caliber: 22 LR *Capacity:* 11 rounds
Barrel Length: 16.5" *Overall Length:* 32.5"
Weight: 4.6 lbs. *Finish:* Blue or nickel
Prices: Blue $240.00
      Nickel 250.00

MODEL M62 SA

SPECIFICATIONS
Caliber: 22 LR *Capacity:* 13 rounds
Barrel Length: 23" *Overall Length:* 39 1/4"
Weight: 5 lbs. *Finish:* Blue or nickel
Prices: Blue $240.00
      Nickel 250.00
      w/octagonal bbl.. . . . . 250.00
Also available:
MODEL 59 22 MAGNUM (10 rds., blue only) $280.00

MODEL M92SRC LEVER-ACTION OLD WEST CARBINES

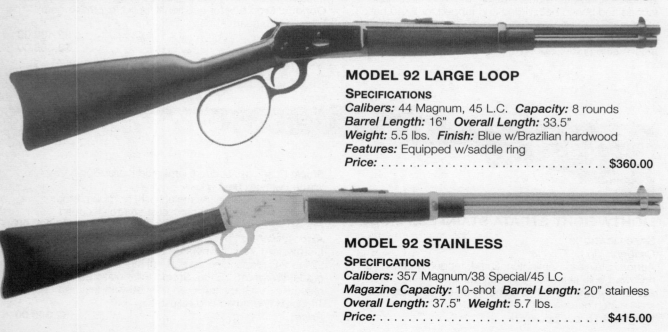

MODEL 92 LARGE LOOP

SPECIFICATIONS
Calibers: 44 Magnum, 45 L.C. *Capacity:* 8 rounds
Barrel Length: 16" *Overall Length:* 33.5"
Weight: 5.5 lbs. *Finish:* Blue w/Brazilian hardwood
Features: Equipped w/saddle ring
Price: $360.00

MODEL 92 STAINLESS

SPECIFICATIONS
Calibers: 357 Magnum/38 Special/45 LC
Magazine Capacity: 10-shot *Barrel Length:* 20" stainless
Overall Length: 37.5" *Weight:* 5.7 lbs.
Price: $415.00

ROSSI RIFLES

MODEL 92SRC LEVER-ACTION OLD WEST CARBINES *(cont.)*

MODEL M92 SRC

SPECIFICATIONS
Caliber: 38 Special or 357 Magnum, **Capacity:** 10 rounds
Barrel Length: 20" **Overall Length:** 37.5"
Weight: 5.7 lbs. **Finish:** Blue
Price: $360.00
Also available:
MODEL M92 SRC in 45 LC w/24" half-
ocatgonal barrel 429.00
MODEL M92 SRS in 38 Spec., 357 Mag. & 44 Mag.
w/16" barrel, 8-shot magazine. **Overall Length:** 33".
Weight: 5.5 lbs. 360.00
MODEL M92 CARBINE w/16" barrel, 8-shot magazine.
Weight: 5.5 lbs. 360.00

RUGER CARBINES

MODEL PC9 AUTOLOADING CARBINE
SPECIFICATIONS

After four years of research, Ruger engineers have combined 10/22 and P-series technology to create an autoloading rifle that uses popular pistol cartridges and Ruger pistol magazines. This handy carbine meets the needs of personal defense, sporting use, law enforcement and security agencies. Advanced synthetics and prescision investment-casting technologies allow for improved performance and substantially reduced costs. The Ruger Carbine has a chrome-moly steel barrel, receiver, slide and recoil springs, and features a checkered Zytell stock with rubber buttplate. Adjustable open sights and patented integral scope mounts are standard. The Ruger Carbine also features a combination firing-pin block and slide lock. Trigger engagement is required for the firing pin to strike the primer. The slide locks to prevent chambering or ejection of a round if the riffle is struck on the buttpad. This safety system is backed up by a manual crossbolt safety located at the rear of the trigger guard. A slide stop locks the slide open for inspection and cleaning.

Caliber: 9 x 19mm/40 auto **Capacity:** 10 rounds
Action: Mass impulse delayed blowback
Barrel Length: 15.25" **Overall Length:** 34.75"
Weight: 6 lbs. 4 oz. **Trigger Pull:** Approx. 6 lb.
Rifling: 6 grooves, 1 turn in 10" RH
Stock: du Pont "Zytel" matte black
Finish: Matte black oxide
Sights: Blade front, open rear plus provision for scope mounts (ghost ring version also available)
Sight Radius: 12.65"
Safety: Manual push-button crossbolt safety (locks trigger mechanism) and internal firing-pin block safety
Features: Bolt lock to prevent accidental unloading or chambering of a cartridge; steel barrel, receiver, slide and recoil spring unit w/black composite stock
Price: $550.00
w/Receiver Sight 580.00

RUGER CARBINES

RUGER MINI-14/5

Mechanism: Gas-operated, semiautomatic. **Materials:** Heat-treated chrome molybdenum and other alloy steels as well as music wire coil springs are used throughout the mechanism to ensure reliability under field-operating conditions. **Safety:** The safety blocks both the hammer and sear. The slide can be cycled when the safety is on. The safety is mounted in the front of the trigger guard so that it may be set to Fire position without removing finger from trigger guard. **Firing pin:** The firing pin is retracted mechanically during the first part of the unlocking of the bolt. The rifle can only be fired when the bolt is safely locked. **Stock:** One-piece American hardwood reinforced with steel liner at stressed areas. Sling swivels standard. Handguard and forearm separated by air space from barrel to promote cooling under rapid-fire conditions. **Field stripping:** The Carbine can be field-stripped to its eight (8) basic sub-assemblies in a matter of seconds and without use of special tools.

RUGER MINI-14
SPECIFICATIONS
Caliber: 223 (5.56mm) **Barrel Length:** 18.5"
Overall Length: 37 ¼" **Weight:** 6 lbs. 8 oz.
Magazine: 5-round, detachable box magazine
Sights: Rear adj. for windage/elevation.
Prices: MINI-14/5 Blued $516.00
K-MINI-14/5 Stainless Steel 569.00
(Scopes rings not included)

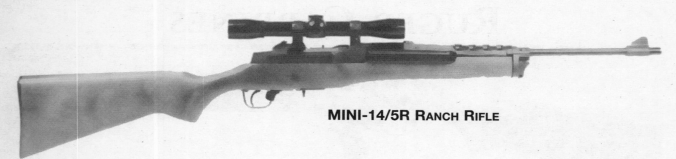

MINI-14/5R RANCH RIFLE

SPECIFICATIONS
Caliber: 223 (5.56mm) **Barrel Length:** 18.5"
Overall Length: 37 ¼" **Weight:** 6 lbs. 8 oz.
Magazine: 5-round detachable box magazine.

Sights: Fold-down rear sight; 1" scope rings (factory machined scope mount system available on all Ranch models)
Prices: MINI-14/5R Blued $556.00
K-MINI-14/5R Stainless Steel 609.00

MINI-THIRTY

This modified version of the Ruger Ranch rifle is chambered for the 7.62 x 39mm Soviet service cartridge. Designed for use with telescopic sights, it features low, compact scope-mounting for greater accuracy and carrying case, and a buffer in the receiver. Sling swivels are standard.

SPECIFICATIONS
Caliber: 7.62 x 39mm **Barrel Length:** 18.5"
Overall Length: 37 ⅛" **Weight:** 6 lbs. 14 oz. (empty)
Magazine Capacity: 5 shots **Rifling:** 6 grooves, R.H. twist, 1:10"
Finish: Blued or stainless
Stock: One-piece American hardwood w/stee liners in stressed areas
Sights: Blade front; peep rear (factory machined scope mount system available on all Ranch models).
Prices: Blued $556.00
Stainless Steel 609.00

RUGER CARBINES

STANDARD 10/22 CARBINE

MODEL K10/22RP "ALL WEATHER"

MODEL K10/22RBI INTERNATIONAL CARBINE STAINLESS

MODEL 10/22T TARGET

Construction of the 10/22 Carbine is rugged and follows the Ruger design practice of building a firearm from integrated sub-assemblies. For example, the trigger housing assembly contains the entire ignition system, which employs a high-speed, swinging hammer to ensure the shortest possible lock time. The barrel is assembled to the receiver by a unique dual-screw dovetail system that provides unusual rigidity and strength—and accounts, in part, for the exceptional accuracy of the 10/22.

SPECIFICATIONS
Mechanism: Blow-back, semiautomatic. **Caliber:** 22 LR, high-speed or standard-velocity loads. **Magazine:** 10-shot capacity, exclusive Ruger rotary design; fits flush into stock. **Barrel:** 18.5", assembled to the receiver by dual-screw dovetail mounting for added strength and rigidity. **Overall Length:** 37 1/4". **Weight:** 5 lbs. **Sights:** 1/16" brass bead front; single folding-leaf rear, adjustable for elevation; receiver drilled and tapped for scope blocks or tip-off mount adapter (included). **Trigger:** Curved finger surface, 3/8" wide. **Safety:** Sliding cross-button type; safety locks both sear and

hammer and cannot be put in safe position unless gun is cocked. **Stocks:** 10/22 RB is birch; 10/22 SP Deluxe Sporter is American walnut. **Finish:** Polished all over and blued or anodized or brushed satin bright metal.

Prices:

MODEL 10/22 RB STANDARD
(Birch carbine stock) $213.00
MODEL 10/22 DSP DELUXE
(Hand-checkered American walnut) 274.00
MODEL K10/22 RB STANLESS 255.00
MODEL K10/22 RBI INTERNATIONAL CARBINE w/full-length
hardwood stock, stainless-steel bbl. 282.00
MODEL 10/22 RBI INTERNATIONAL CARBINE
w/blued barrel 262.00
MODEL 10/22T TARGET (no sights) Hammer-
forged barrel, laminated target-style stock 392.50
w/stainless steel 440.00
MODEL K10/22RP stainless `All Weather"
w/synthetic stock 255.00

RUGER SINGLE-SHOT RIFLES

The following illustrations show the variations currently offered in the Ruger No. 1 Single-Shot Rifle Series. Ruger No. 1 rifles have a Farquharson-type falling-block action and select American walnut stocks. Pistol grip and forearm are hand-checkered to a borderless design. Price for any listed model is **$685.00** (except the No. 1 RSI International Model: **$699.00**). Barreled Actions (blued only): **$465.00**

NO. 1A LIGHT SPORTER
Calibers: 243 Win., 270 Win., 30-06, 7x57mm. *Barrel Length:* 22". *Sights:* Adjustable folding-leaf rear sight mounted on quarter rib with ramp front sight base and dovetail-type gold bead front sight; open. *Weight:* 7 1/4 lbs.

NO. 1S MEDIUM SPORTER
Calibers: 218 Bee, 7mm Rem. Mag., 300 Win. Mag., 338 Win. Mag., 45-70. *Barrel Length:* 26" (22" in 45-70). *Sights:* (same as above). *Weight:* 8 lbs. (7 1/4 lbs. in 45-70).

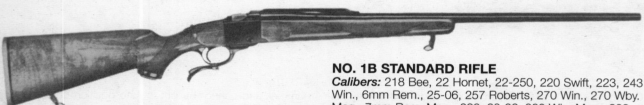

NO. 1B STANDARD RIFLE
Calibers: 218 Bee, 22 Hornet, 22-250, 220 Swift, 223, 243 Win., 6mm Rem., 25-06, 257 Roberts, 270 Win., 270 Wby. Mag., 7mm Rem. Mag., 280, 30-06, 300 Win. Mag., 300 Wby. Mag., 338 Win. Mag. *Barrel Length:* 26". *Sights:* Ruger 1" steel tip-off scope rings. *Weight:* 8 lbs.

NO. 1V SPECIAL VARMINTER
Calibers: 22-250, 220 Swift, 223, 25-06, 6mm. *Barrel Length:* 24" (26" in 220 Swift). *Sights:* Ruger target scope blocks, heavy barrel and 1" tip-off scope rings. *Weight:* 9 lbs.
Also available:
NO. 1H TROPICAL RIFLE (24" heavy barrel) in 375 H&H Mag., 458 Win. Mag., 416 Rigby and 416 Rem. Mag.
NO 1. RSI INTERNATIONAL (20" lightweight barrel) in 243 Win., 270 Win., 30-06 and 7x57mm

RUGER BOLT-ACTION RIFLES

MARK II SERIES

MODEL M-77R MKII

Integral Base Receiver, 1" scope rings. No sights.
Calibers: (Long action) 6mm Rem., 6.5x55mm, 7x57mm, 257 Roberts, 270, 280 Rem., 30-06 (all with 22" barrels); 7mm Rem. Mag., 300 Win. Mag., 338 Win. Mag. (all with 24" barrels); and (Short Stroke action) 223, 243, 308 (22" barrels).
Weight: Approx. 7 lbs.
Price: $574.00
Also available: **M-77LR MKII** (Left Hand).
Calibers: 270, 30-06, 7mm Rem. Mag., 300 Win. Mag
Price: 574.00

MODEL M-77RS MKII

Integral Base Receiver, Ruger steel 1" rings, open sights.
Calibers: 243, 25-06, 270, 7mm Rem. Mag., 30-06, 300 Win. Mag., 308, 338 Win. Mag., 458 Win. Mag.
Weight: Approx. 7 lbs.
Price: $635.00

MODEL M-77RL MKII ULTRA LIGHT

This big-game, bolt-action rifle encompasses the traditional features that have made the Ruger M-77 one of the most popular centerfire rifles in the world. It includes a sliding top tang safety, a one-piece bolt with Mauser-type extractor and diagonal front mounting system. American walnut stock is hand-checkered in a sharp diamond pattern. A rubber recoil pad, pistol-grip cap and studs for mounting quick detachable sling swivels are standard. Available in both long- and short-action versions, with Integral Base Receiver and 1" Ruger scope rings.
Calibers: 223, 243, 257, 270, 30-06, 308.
Barrel length: 20". *Weight:* Approx. 6 lbs.
Price: $610.00

RUGER BOLT-ACTION RIFLES

MODEL 77/22RH HORNET
$489.00 ($499.00 w/Sights)

The Model 77/22RH is Ruger's first truly compact centerfire bolt-action rifle. It features a 77/22 action crafted from heat-treated alloy steel. Exterior surfaces are blued to match the hammer-forged barrel. The action features a right-hand turning bolt with a 90-degree bolt throw, cocking on opening. Fast lock time (2.7 milliseconds) adds to accuracy. A three-position swing-back safety locks the bolt; in its center position firing is blocked, but bolt operation and safe loading and unloading are permitted. When fully forward, the rifle is ready to fire. The American walnut stock has recoil pad, grip cap and sling swivels installed. One-inch diameter scope rings fit integral bases.

SPECIFICATIONS
Caliber: 22 Hornet
Capacity: 6 rounds (detachable rotary magazine)
Barrel length: 20" *Overall length:* 40"
Weight: 6 lbs. (unloaded)
Sights: Single folding-leaf rear; gold bead front
Length of pull: 13 3/4"
Drop at heel: 2 3/4" Drop at comb: 2"
Finish: Polished and blued, matte, nonglare receiver top
Also available: **MODEL K77/22VHZ** Varmint w/stainless-steel heavy barrel, laminated American hardwood stock.
Price: (w/o sights) $535.00

MODEL 77/22RS

MODEL K77/22BVZ VARMINT

MODEL 77/22 RIMFIRE RIFLE

The Ruger 22-caliber rimfire 77/22 bolt-action rifle has been built especially to function with the patented Ruger 10-Shot Rotary Magazine concept. The magazine throat, retaining lips and ramps that guide the cartridge into the chamber are solid alloy steel that resists bending or deforming.

The 77/22 weighs just under six pounds. Its heavy-duty receiver incorporates the integral scope bases of the patented Ruger Scope Mounting System with 1-inch Ruger scope rings. With the 3-position safety in its "lock" position, a dead bolt is cammed forward, locking the bolt handle down. In this position the action is locked closed and the handle cannot be raised.

All metal surfaces are finished in nonglare deep blue or satin stainless. Stock is select straight-grain American walnut, hand checkered and finished with durable polyurethane.

An All-Weather, all-stainless steel **MODEL K77/22RS** features a stock made of glass-fiber reinforced Zytel. *Weight:* Approx. 6 lbs.

SPECIFICATIONS
Calibers: 22 LR and 22 Magnum. *Barrel length:* 20".
Overall length: 39 1/4". *Weight:* 6 lbs. (w/o scope, magazine empty). *Feed:* Detachable 10-Shot Ruger Rotary Magazine.
Prices: **77/22R** Blue, w/o sights, 1" Ruger rings . **$473.00**
77/22RM Blue, walnut stock, plain barrel,
no sights, 1" Ruger rings, 22 Mag. **473.00**
77/22RS Blue, sights included, 1" Ruger rings . . . **481.00**
77/22RSM Blue, American walnut, iron sights **481.00**
K77/22-RP Synthetic stock, stainless steel, plain
barrel with 1" Ruger rings **473.00**
K77/22-RMP Synthetic stock, stainless steel,
plain barrel, 1" Ruger rings **473.00**
K77/22-RSP Synthetic stock, stainless steel, gold
bead front sight, folding-leaf rear, Ruger 1"rings . **481.00**
K77/22RSMP Synthetic stock, metal sights,
stainless. **481.00**
K77/22VBZ Varmint Laminated stock, scope
rings, heavy barrel, stainless **499.00**

RUGER BOLT-ACTION RIFLES

MODEL 77/44
Chambered in .44 Magnum, the new 77/44 is a short (18.5" barrel), lightweight (6 lbs.) deluxed grade carbine based on the same action used in the 77/22 (see preceeding page). Action features right-hand turning bolt with 90-degree bolt throw.
Capacity: 4 rounds
Price: $575.00

MARK II SERIES (w/THREE POSITION SAFETY/FIXED EJECTORS)

MODEL K77RBZ MKII

MODEL K77RBZ MKII
Stainless steel, laminated stock, scope rings, no sights.
SPECIFICATIONS
Calibers: 223, 22-250, 243, 270 Win., 7mm Rem. Mag., 308, 30-06, 300 Win. Mag., 338 Win. Mag.
Price: $606.00

MODEL K77RSBZ MKII

MODEL K77RSBZ MKII
Stainless steel, laminated stock, scope rings, open sights.
Calibers: 243, 270 Win., 7mm Rem. Mag., 30-06, 308 Win. Mag., 338 Win. Mag.
Price: $667.00
Also available:
MODEL K77RSP MKII
Stainless steel, laminated stock, scope rings, open sights.
Calibers: 243, 270 Win., 7mm Rem. Mag., 30-06, 300 Win. Mag., 338 Win. Mag.
Price: $635.00

MODEL M-77RSI MKII

MODEL M-77RSI MKII INTERNATIONAL MANNLICHER
Mannlicher-type stock, Integral Base Receiver, open sights, Ruger 1" steel rings. *Calibers:* 243, 270, 30-06, 308 *Barrel Length:* 18.5" *Weight:* Approx. 6 lbs.
Price: $642.00

RUGER BOLT-ACTION RIFLES

MARK II SERIES (w/THREE POSITION SAFETY/FIXED EJECTORS)

**MODEL M-77VT MK II
HEAVY BARREL TARGET**

MODEL M-77VT MK II HEAVY-BARREL TARGET

Features Mark II stainless-steel bolt action, gray matte finish, two-stage adjustable trigger. No sights.

SPECIFICATIONS
Calibers: 22-250, 220 Swift, 223, 243, 25-06 and 308.
Barrel Length: 26", hammer-forged, free-floating stainless steel. *Weight:* 9 ¾ lbs. Stock: Laminated American hardwood with flat forend.
Price: KM-77VT MKII $684.00

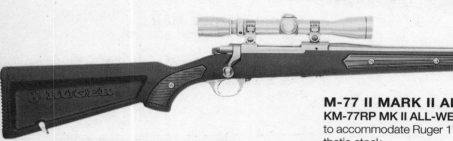

M-77 MARK II ALL-WEATHER

M-77 II MARK II ALL-WEATHER

KM-77RP MK II ALL-WEATHER Receiver w/integral dovetails to accommodate Ruger 1" rings, no sights, stainless steel, synthetic stock.
Calibers: 223, 22-50, 243, 25-06, 270, 280, 30-06, 7mm Rem. Mag., 300 Win. Mag., 308, 338 Win. Mag. $574.00
MODEL K77RSP MKII Receiver w/integral dovetails to accommodate Ruger 1" rings, metal sights, stainless steel, synthetic stock.
Calibers: 243, 270, 7mm Rem. Mag., 30-06, 300 Win. Mag., 338 Win. Mag. 635.00

RUGER 77 RSM MK II MAGNUM RIFLE

This "Bond Street" quality African safari hunting rifle features a sighting rib machined from a single bar of steel; Circassian walnut stock with black forend tip; steel floorplate and latch; a new Ruger Magnum trigger guard with floorplate latch designed flush wwith the contours of the trigger gurad (to eliminate accidental dumping of cartridges); a three-position safety mechanism; Express rear sight; and front sight ramp with gold bead sight. Also available in Express Model (long action, no heavy barrel).

Calibers: 375 H&H, 416 Rigby. *Capacity:* 4 rounds (375 H&H) and 3 rounds (416 Rigby). *Barrel Length:* 22"
Overall Length: 42 ⅛" *Barrel Thread Diameter:* 1⅛"
Weight: 9 ¼ lbs. (375 H&H); 10 ¼ lbs. (416 Rigby).
Price: $1550.00
Also available:
EXPRESS RIFLE. *Calibers:* 270, 7mm, 30-06, 338 Win. Mag.
Features: Deluxe wood, solid rib, long action, scope rings.
Price: $1550.00

SAKO RIFLES

SAKO 75

SAKO 75 HUNTER

The SAKO 75 Hunter is the first rifle to offer an action furnished with both a bolt with three locking lugs and a mechanical ejector. This combination results in unprecedented smoothness and reliability. The sturdy receiver helps to zero the rifle with different bullets and loads. The new bolt provides a solid, well-balanced platform for the cartridge. The traditional safety catch is either on or off. Cartridge removal or loading is done by pressing a separate bolt release button in front of the safety. No need to touch the safety to remove a cartridge and then disengage it by mistake under difficult or stressful conditions. The new cold hammer-forged barrel is manufactured in an advanced custom-built robotic cell. The New SAKO features a totally free-floating barrel. Instead of checkering, this all-stainless, all-weather model has soft rubbery grips molded in the stock to provide a firmer, more comfortable hold than with conventional synthetic stocks. The selected moisture stabilized high-grade walnut ensures quality and craftsmanship. Other features include:

- Five bolt siding guides
- 70° Bolt Lift
- Totally free-floating cold hammer-forged barrel
- Positive safety system with separate bolt release button for safe unloading

- Detachable staggered 5-round magazine
- Five (5) action sizes for perfect cartridge match
- All-Stainless metal parts and All-Weather synthetic stock with special grips
- Selected moisture stabilized walnut stock with hand-crafted checkering
- Integral scope rails

Prices:
SAKO 75 HUNTER
22"barrel (17 Rem., 222 Rem., 223 Rem., 22-250 Rem., 243 Win., 7mm-08, 308 Win., 25-06 Rem., 270 Win., 280 Win., 30-06) **$1,099.00**
24" barrel (7mm Rem. Mag., 300 Win. Mag., 338 Win. Mag., 375 H&H Mag., 416 Rem. Mag. **1,129.00**
26" barrel (270 Wby. Mag., 7mm STW, 7mm Wby. Mag., 300 Wby. Mag., 340 Wby.) **1,129.00**

SAKO 75 STAINLESS SYNTHETIC
22" barrel (22-250 Rem., 243 Win., 308 Win., 7mm-08 25-06 Rem., 270 Win., 30-06) **$1,195.00**
24" barrel (7mm Rem. Mag., 300 Win. Mag., 338 Win. Mag., 375 H&H Mag. **1,225.00**
26" barrel (7mm STW)

SAKO 75 STAINLESS SYNTHETIC

SAKO RIFLES

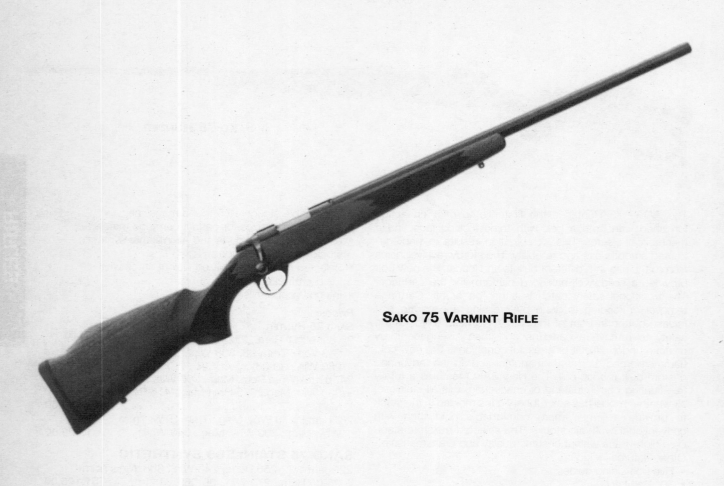

SAKO 75 VARMINT RIFLE

SAKO 75 VARMINT RIFLE

The new SAKO 75 Varmint Rifle uses only the highest grade steel in the construction of the action, bolt, barrel and all internal parts. SAKO cold hammer-forges heavyweight bar stock into one of the truest, most accurate barrels available. The 24" barrel is matched to the appropriate action size to eliminate excessive weight. The barreled action assembly is then cradled into a specially designed stock and is free floating for greater accuracy. The matte lacquered walnut stock features a beavertail forearm for additional stability and support when shooting from sandbags or whenever top accuracy is necessary. The SAKO 75 is the first and only rifle with three locking lugs and a mechanical ejector. Other SAKO features include a one-piece forged bolt with five gliding surfaces, a detachable magazine, and a smooth 70 degree bolt lift.

Calibers:
Short Action—17 Rem., 222 Rem., 223 Rem.
Medium Action—22-250 Rem.
Price:. **$1,275.00**

SAKO RIFLES

**FINNFIRE
22 LONG RIFLE**

**FINNFIRE
HEAVY BARREL**

FINNFIRE 22 LR BOLT-ACTION RIFLE

SAKO of Finland, acclaimed as the premier manufacturer of bolt-action centerfire rifles, presents its 22 Long Rifle Finnfire. Designed by engineers who use only state-of-the-art technology to achieve both form and function and produced by craftsmen to exacting specifications, this premium grade bolt-action rifle exceeds the requirements of even the most demanding firearm enthusiast.

The basic concept in the design of the Finnfire was to make it as similar to its "big brothers" as possible—just scaled down. For example, the single-stage adjustable trigger is a carbon copy of the trigger found on any other big-bore hunting model. The 22-inch barrel is cold-hammered to ensure superior accuracy.

SPECIFICATIONS
Overall length: 37 1/2" *Weight:* 5 1/4 lbs.; 7 1/2 lbs. (w/heavy barrel) *Rate of twist:* 16 1/2"
Other outstanding features include:
- European walnut stock
- Luxurious matte lacquer finish
- 50° bolt lift
- Free-floating barrel
- Integral 11mm dovetail for scope mounting
- Two-position safety that locks the bolt
- Cocking indicator
- Five-shot detachable magazine
- Ten-shot magazine available
- Available with open sights
Price: $764.00
HEAVY BARREL 849.00

COMMITMENT TO EXCELLENCE — A SAKO TRADITION

SAKO RIFLES

DELUXE BOLT-ACTION RIFLE

SAKO 75 DELUXE BOLT-ACTION RIFLE

All the fine-touch features you expect of the deluxe grade SAKO are here: **1**-Reliable safety sysem with a separate bolt release button. **2**-First ever bolt with three locking lugs and a mechanical ejector. Five guiding surfaces prevent bolt binding and provide smooth operation. Four action sizes for perfect cartridge fit. **3**-Totally free-floating cold hammer forged barrel for ultimate accuracy. Test with a slip of paper. **4**-Sako Deluxe 75 Hunting Rifle has stainless steel lined staggered magazine with hinged floorplate and aluminum follower for faultless operation. Positive feeding angle is only 3-5 degrees. **5**-Fancy grade, high-grained walnut. Olld-world craftmanship Rosewood pistol grip cap with silver inlay. **6**-Classic detail–Rosewood fore-end tip. And of course the accuracy, reliability and superior field performance for which SAKO is so

justly famous are still here too. It's all here—it just weighs less than it used to. Think of it as more for less.

In addition, the scope mounting system on these SAKOS are among the strongest in the world. Instead of using separate bases, a tapered dovetail is milled into the receiver, to which the scope rings are mounted. A beautiful system that's been proven by over 20 years of use. SAKO Original Scope Mounts and SAKO scope rings are available in low, medium and high in one-inch and 30mm.

Prices:

ACTION I
in 17 Rem., 222 Rem. & 223 Rem. **$1,565.00**

ACTION III
In 22-250 Rem., 243 Win., 7mm-08 and
308 Win. **1,565.00**

ACTION IV
In 25-06 Rem., 270 Win., 280 Rem., 30-06 . . . . **1,565.00**

ACTION V
In 270 Wby. Mag., 7mm Rem. Mag., 300 Win.
Mag. and 338 Win. Mag. **1,598.00**
In 7mm STW, 300 Wby. Mag., .340 Wby. Mag.,
375 H&H Mag., 416 Rem. Mag. **1,598.00**

SUPER DELUXE

SUPER DELUXE

SAKO offers the Super Deluxe for the most discriminating gun buyer. This one-of-a-kind beauty is available on special order.

Price:
SUPER DELUXE **$3,400.00**

SAKO RIFLES

MODEL TRG-21

SAKO, known for manufacturing the finest and most accurate production sporting rifles available today, presents the ultimate in sharpshooting systems: the sleek **TRG-21 TARGET RIFLE**. Designed for use when nothing less than total precision is demanded, this SAKO rifle features a cold-hammer forged receiver, "resistance-free" bolt, stainless-steel barrel and a fully adjustable polyurethane stock. Chambered in .308 Win. A wide selection of optional accessories is also available. Designed, crafted and manufactured in Finland.

- Cold-hammer forged receiver
- "Resistance-free" bolt
- Cold-hammer forged, stainless steel barrel
- Three massive locking lugs
- 60° bolt lift
- Free-floating barrel
- Detachable 10-round magazine

- Fully adjustable cheekpiece
- Infinitely adjustable buttplate
- Adjustable two-stage trigger pull
- Trigger adjustable for both length and pull
- Trigger also adjustable for horizontal or vertical pitch
- Safety lever inside and trigger guard
- Reinforced polyurethane stock

Optional features:
- Muzzle brake
- Quick-detachable one-piece scope mount base
- Available with 1" or 30mm rings
- Collapsible and removable bipod rest
- Quick-detachable sling swivels
- Wide military-type nylon sling

Price: **$3,575.00**
Also available:
TRG-41 in 338 Lapua Mag. **$4,200.00**

MODEL TRG-S

The TRG-S has been crafted and designed around SAKO's highly sophisticated and extremely accurate TRG-21 Target Rifle (above). The "resistance-free" bolt and precise balance of the TRG-S, plus its three massive locking lugs and short 60-degree bolt lift, are among the features that attract the shooter's attention. Also of critical importance is the cold-hammer forged receiver—unparalleled for strength and durability. The detachable 5-round magazine fits securely into the polyurethane stock. The stock, in turn, is molded around a synthetic skelton that provides additional support and maximum rigidity. *Calibers: Standard*—25-06 Rem., 270 Win., 6.5X55, 30-06; *Magnum*—7mm Rem. Mag., 7mm Wby. Mag., 7mm STW, 270 Wby. Mag., 300 Win Mag., 300 Wby., 30-378 Wby. Mag., 338 Win. Mag., 338 Lapua Mag., 340 Wby. Mag., 375 H&H Mag., 416 Rem. Mag.

Price:
STANDARD CALIBERS **$825.00**
MAGNUM CALIBERS **865.00**

SAKO RIFLES

SAKO 75 RIFLE MODELS

Model	Available (est.)	Action	Total length inch.	Barrel length inch.	Weight lbs	17 Rem 10"	222 Rem 14"	223 Rem 12"	22 PPC USA 14"	6 PPC USA 11"	7.62x39 14"	22-250 Rem 10"	243 Win 9,5"	7mm-08 Rem 11"	308 Win 10"	25-06 Rem 9"	6.5x55 SE 10"	270 Win 10"	7x64 10"	280 Rem 10"	30-06 11"	9.3x62 14"	270 Wby Mag 10"	7mm Rem Mag 9,5"	7mm Wby Mag 9,5"	7mm STW 9,5"	300 Win Mag 11"	300 Wby Mag 11"	338 Win Mag 10"	340 Wby Mag 10"	375 H&H Mag 12"	416 Rem Mag 14"	Matte lacquered	Lacquered	Oiled	Injection moulded	Open sights	Without sights	Single-stage trigger	Double-stage trigger	Single-set trigger	Detachable	Single-shot	Fixed	Magazine capacity	Left-handed	Stainless steel barrel	Stainless steel action
HUNTER	1998	I	41¾	22	6⅛	•	•	•																									•	+	+		+		•		•		+		•	6	+		
	1998	II	42 3/16	22 7/16	7				•	•	•																						•	+	+		+		•		•		+		•	5	+		
	10/97	III	42⅞	22 7/16	7¼							•	•	•	•																		•	+	+		+		•		•		+		•	5	+		
	2/97	IV	43¾	22 7/8	7 15/16											•	•	•	•	•	•	•											•	+	+		+		•		•		+		•	5	+		
	10/97	V	45⅝	24⅛	8⅝																		•	•	•	•	•	•	•	•			•	+	+		+		•		•		+		•	4	+		
	10/97	V	45⅜	24⅛	9																										•	•	•	+	+		+		•		•		+		•	4	+		
DELUXE	1998	I	41¾	22	6⅛	•	•	•																									•	+	+		+		•		+		•			6	+		
	1998	II	42 3/16	22 7/16	7				•	•	•																						•	+	+		+		•		+		•			5	+		
	10/97	III	42⅞	22 7/16	7¼							•	•	•	•																		•	+	+		+		•		+		•			5	+		
	2/97	IV	43¾	22 7/8	7 15/16											•	•	•	•	•	•	•											•	+	+		+		•		+		•			5	+		
	10/97	V	45⅝	24⅛	8⅝																		•	•	•	•	•	•	•	•			•	+	+		+		•		+		•			4	+		
	10/97	V	45⅜	24⅛	9																										•	•		+	+		+		•		+		•			4	+		
SUPER DELUXE	1998	I	41¾	22	6⅛	•	•	•																									•	+	+		+		•		+		•			6	+		
	1998	II	42 3/16	22 7/16	7				•	•	•																						•	+	+		+		•		+		•			5	+		
	1998	III	42⅞	22 7/16	7¼							•	•	•	•																		•	+	+		+		•		+		•			5	+		
	1998	IV	43¾	22 7/8	7 15/16											•	•	•	•	•	•	•											•	+	+		+		•		+		•			5	+		
	1998	V	45⅝	24⅛	8⅝																		•	•	•	•	•	•	•	•			•	+	+		+		•		+		•			4	+		
	1998	V	45⅜	24⅛	9																										•	•			+		+		•		+		•			4	+		
SAFARI	1998	V	45⅜	24⅛	9																								•	•	•	•			+		•				•		•			5			
EURO *	1998	I	41¾	22	6⅛	•	•	•																									•		+		+	+		•		•		+			6	+		
	1998	II	42 3/16	22 7/16	7				•	•	•																						•		+		+	+		•		•		+			5	+		
	1998	III	42⅞	22 7/16	7¼							•	•	•	•																		•		+		+	+		•		•		+			5	+		
	1998	IV	43¾	22 7/8	7 15/16											•	•	•	•	•	•	•											•		+		+	+		•		•		+			5	+		
	1998	V	45⅝	24⅛	8⅝																		•	•	•	•	•	•	•	•			•		+		+	+		•		•		+			4	+		
CARBINE *	1998	III	39¼	19¼	7¼							•	•	•	•																				•		•		+	+		•		•		+		5	+		
	1998	IV	40⅛	19¼	7 15/16											•	•	•	•	•	•	•													•		•		+	+		•		•		+		5	+		
	1998	V	40½	19¼	8⅛																		•	•	•	•	•	•	•	•					•		•		+	+		•		•		+		4	+		
BATTUE *	1998	III	39¼	19¼	7							•	•	•	•																		•	+	+		•	+		•		•		+		5	+		
	1998	IV	40⅛	19¼	7 15/16											•	•	•	•	•	•	•											•	+	+		•	+		•		•		+		5	+		
	1998	V	40½	19¼	7 15/16																		•	•	•	•	•	•	•	•			•	+	+		•	+		•		•		+		4	+		
VARMINT	1998	I	45⅝	26	8⅛	•	•	•																										+		•		+	•	+		•	+		6	+		
	1998	II	45⅞	26	8⅝				•	•	•																							+		•		+	•	+		•	+		5	+		
	1998	III	46½	26	8 15/16							•	•	•	•																			+		•		+	•	+		•	+		5	+		
	1998	IV	46⅞	26	9											•		•		•														+		•		+	•	+		•	+		5	+	+	
	1998	V	47¼	26	9¼																		•	•	•	•	•	•	•	•				+		•		+	•	+		•	+		4	+	+	
STAINLESS *	1998	III	42⅞	22 7/16	7							•	•	•	•																		•	+	+		•	+		•		•		+		5	+	•	•
	1998	IV	43¾	22 7/8	7¼											•		•		•													•	+	+		•	+		•		•		+		5	+	•	•
	1998	V	45⅜	24⅛	8⅛																		•		•			•					•	+	+		•	+		•		•		+		4	+	•	•
SYNTHETIC *	1998	III	42⅞	22 7/16	7¼							•	•	•	•																				•	+	•		+	•		+	•			+		5			
	1998	IV	42¼	22 7/8	7 15/16											•	•	•	•	•	•	•													•	+	•		+	•		+	•			+		5			
	1998	V	45⅜	24⅛	8⅝																		•	•	•	•	•	•	•	•					•	+	•		+	•		+	•			+		4			
SYNTHETIC STAINLESS	6/97	III	42⅞	22 7/16	7							•	•	•	•																				•	+	•		+	•		+	•			+		5		•	•
	2/97	IV	43¾	22 7/8	7¼											•		•		•															•	+	•		+	•		+	•			+		5		•	•
	8/97	V	45⅜	24⅛	8⅛																		•		•			•							•	+	•		+	•		+	•			+		4		•	•

• = as standard   + = as option   26" Barrel Standard on 7mm STW & Weatherby calibers.
*For updated availability of these products, contact Stoeger Industries at 800-631-0722

SAKO ACTIONS

Only by building a rifle around a SAKO action do shooters enjoy the choice of three different lengths, each scaled to a specific family of cartridges. The S 491-1 (Short) action is miniaturized in every respect to match the 222 family, which includes everything from 17 Remington to 223 Remington. The M 591 (Medium) action is scaled down to the medium-length cartridges of standard bolt face—22—250, 243, 408, 7mm-08 or similar length cartridges. The L 691 (Long) action is offered in either standard or Magnum bolt face and accommodates cartridges of up to 3.65 inches in overall length, including rounds like the 300 Weatherby and 375 H&H Magnums. **For left-handers, the Medium and Long actions are offered in either standard or Magnum bolt face.** All actions are furnished in-the-white only.

S 491 SHORT ACTION (formerly Al-1)

SPECIFICATIONS
Calibers:
17 Rem., 222 Rem.
222 Rem. Mag.
223 Rem.
Price: $565.00

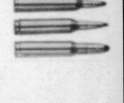

S 491-PPC SHORT ACTION SINGLE SHOT

SPECIFICATIONS
Calibers:
22 PPC
6 PPC
Price: $643.00

M 591 MEDIUM ACTION (formerly All-1)

SPECIFICATIONS
Calibers:
22-250 Rem. (M 591-3)
243 Win.
308 Win.
7mm-08
Price: $565.00

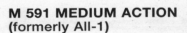

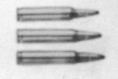

L 691 LONG ACTION (formerly AV-4)

SPECIFICATIONS
Calibers:
25-06 Rem. (L 691-1)
270 Win. (L 691-1
280 Rem. (L 691-1)
30-06 (L 691-1)
7mm Rem. Mag. (L 691-4)
300 Win. Mag. (L 691-4)
300 Wby. Mag. (L 691-4)
338 Win. Mag. (L 691-4)
375 H&H Mag. (L 691-4)
416 Rem. Mag. (L 691-4)
Price: $599.00

SAUER RIFLES

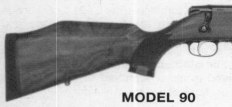

MODEL 90

SPECIFICATIONS
Calibers: 22-250, 243 Win., 25-06, 270, 30-06, 308 Win.; *Supreme Magnum calibers:* 7mm Rem. Mag., 300 Win. Mag., 300 Wby. Mag., 338 Win. Mag., and 375 H&H
Barrel Length: 23.6"; 26" (Supreme Magnum)
Overall Length: 42.5"; 46.5" (Supreme Magnum)
Weight: 7.5 lbs.; 7.7 lbs. (Supreme Magnum)
Sights: None furnished; drilled and tapped for scope mount
Stock: Monte Carlo cut with sculptured cheekpiece, hand-

MODEL 90 SUPREME

checkered pistol grip and forend, rosewood pistol grip cap and forend tip, black rubber recoil pad, and fully inletted sling swivel studs.
Features: Rear bolt cam-activated locking lug action; jeweled bolt with an operating angle of 65°; fully adjustable gold-plated trigger; chamber loaded signal pin; cocking indicator; tang-mounted slide safety with button release; bolt release button (to operate bolt while slide safety is engaged); detachable 3 or 4-round box magazine; sling slide scope mounts; leather sling (extra)
Prices:
Standard $1,350.00
Magnum 1,382.00

MODEL SHR 970 SYNTHETIC

SPECIFICATIONS
Calibers: 270 Win., 30-06 S'field **Capacity:** 4 rounds
Barrel Length: 22" **Overall Length:** 41.9" **Weight:** 7.2 lbs.
Sights: Drilled and tapped for scope base
Stock: Reinforced synthetic stock, rubber butt pad, QD swivel studs
Price: $499.00

SAUER .458 SAFARI

The Sauer .458 Safari features a rear bolt cam-activated locking-lug action with a low operating angle of 65°. It has a gold plated trigger, jeweled bolt, oil finished bubinga stock and deep luster bluing. Safety features include a press

bottom slide safety that engages the trigger sear, toggle joint and bolt. The bolt release feature allows the sportsman to unload the rifle while the safety remains engaged to the trigger sear and toggle joint. The Sauer Safari is equipped with a chamber loaded signal pin for positive identification. Specifications include: **Barrel Length:** 24" (heavy barrel contour). **Overall Length:** 44". **Weight:** 10 lb. 6 oz. **Sights:** Williams open sights (sling swivels included).
Price: $1,995.00

MODEL 202 SUPREME BOLT ACTION
(not shown)

SPECIFICATIONS
Calibers: 25-06 Rem., 243 Win., 270 Win., 308, 30-06 S'field; *Supreme Magnum calibers:* 7mm Rem. Mag., 300 Win. Mag., 300 Wby. Mag., 375 Win. Mag.
Action: Bolt takedown **Capacity:** 3 rounds
Barrel Length: 23.6"; 26" (Supreme Magnum)
Overall Length: 44.3"; 46" (Supreme Magnum)
Weight: 7.7 lbs.; 8.4 lbs. (Supreme Magnum)
Stock: Select American claro walnut with high-gloss epoxy finish and rosewood forend and grip caps; Monte Carlo comb with cheekpiece; 22 line-per-inch diamond pattern,

hand-cut checking **Sights:** Drilled and tapped for sights and scope bases **Features:** Adjustable two-stage trigger; polished and jeweled bolt; quick-change barrel; tapered bore; QD sling swivel studs; black rubber recoil pad; Wundhammer palm swell; dual release safety; six locking lugs on bolt head; removable box magazine; fully enclosed bolt face; three gas relief holes; firing-pin cocking indicator on bolt rear
Prices: Standard $985.00
Magnum 1,056.00
Also available: In Left Hand model (270 Win., 30-06 S'field, 7mm Rem. Mag. only). $1,056.00
Magnum 1,115.00

SAVAGE ARMS

CENTERFIRE RIFLES

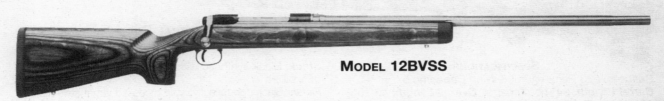

MODEL 12BVSS

MODEL 12BVSS SHORT ACTION VARMINT

SPECIFICATIONS

Calibers: 223 Rem., 22-250 Rem., and 308 Win. Single-shot Model 12FVSS available in 223 Rem. and 22-250 Rem.
Capacity: 5 + 1
Barrel Length: 26" fluted heavy barrel
Overall Length: 46.75"
Magazine: Top loading internal
Weight: 9.5 lbs.

Sights: None. Drilled and tapped for scope mounts
Stock: Laminated hardwood with high comb, ambidextrous grip and ebony tip
Finish: Fluted stainless steel with recessed target style muzzle
Features: Short Action precision long range rifle with dual pillar bedding
Price: **$560.00**

MODEL 12FVSS

MODEL 12FVSS SHORT ACTION VARMINT

SPECIFICATIONS

Calibers: 223 Rem., 22-250 Rem., and 308 Win. (Single-shot Model 12FVSSs available in 223 Rem. and 22-250 Rem.)
Capacity: 5 *Barrel Length:* 26" heavy barrel
Overall Length: 46.75"
Magazine: Top loading internal *Weight:* 9 lbs.

Sights: None. Drilled and tapped for scope mounts
Stock: Laminated hardwood with high comb, ambidextrous grip and ebony tip
Finish: Fluted stainless steel with recessed target style muzzle
Features: Short Action Long Range rifle with dual pillar bedding and 26" fluted heavy barrel
Price: **$534.00**

MODEL 12FV

MODEL 12FV SHORT ACTION VARMINT

SPECIFICATIONS

Calibers: 223 Rem. and 22-250 Rem
Capacity: 5
Barrel Length: 26"
Overall Length: 46.75"
Magazine: Top loading internal
Weight: 9 lbs.

Sights: None. Drilled and tapped for scope mounts
Stock: Durable black synthetic with scrolled checkering and dual pillars
Finish: Blued with recesses target style muzzle
Features: Short action varmint rifle with 26" button rifled heavy barrel
Price: **$429.00**

SAVAGE ARMS

MODEL 10FP SHORT ACTION TACTICAL RIFLE

SPECIFICATIONS
Calibers: 223 Rem. and 308 Win. **Capacity:** 5
Barrel Length: 24" heavy barrel **Overall Length:** 43.75"
Magazine: Top loading internal **Weight:** 8 lbs.
Sights: None. Drilled and tapped for scope mounts

Stock: Black synthetic with scrolled checkering and dual pillars
Finish: Black non-reflective with recessed target style muzzle
Features: Short action heavy barrel rifle with twin pillar bedding
Price: $446.00

MODEL 16FSS SHORT ACTION WEATHER WARRIOR

SPECIFICATIONS
Calibers: 243 Win. and 308 Win. **Capacity:** 5
Barrel Length: 22" **Overall Length:** 40.75"
Magazine: Top loading internal **Weight:** 6 lbs.
Sights: None. Drilled and tapped for scope mounts

Stock: Durable black synthetic with scrolled checkering and dual pillars **Finish:** Stainless steel
Features: Short action satin finished 400 series stainless steel barreled action
Price: $515.00

MODEL 10FM SIERRA LIGHTWEIGHT

SPECIFICATIONS
Calibers: 243 Win., 270 Win., 30-06 Splfd., 308 Win.
Capacity: 5 + 1 **Barrel Length:** 20"
Overall Length: 41.5" **Magazine:** Top loading internal
Weight: 6.25 lbs. **Sights:** None. Drilled and tapped for

scope mount; bases included
Stock: Lightweight graphite/fiberglass filled composite stock with positive checkering **Finish:** Blued
Features: Blue alloy steel barreled action
Price: $440.00

MODEL 110FP TACTICAL

SPECIFICATIONS
Calibers: 223 Rem., 25-06 Rem., 30-06 Spfd., 308 Win., 7mm Rem. Mag., 300 Win. Mag. **Capacity:** 5 rounds (1 in chamber)
Barrel Length: 24" (w/recessed target-style muzzle) **Overall Length:** 45.5" **Weight:** 8.5 lbs. **Sights:** None; drilled and tapped for scope mount; bases included **Features:** Black matte nonreflective finish on metal parts; bolt coated with titanium nitride; stock made of black graphite/fiberglass-filled composite with positive checkering; left-hand model available

Price: $429.00
Also Available: MODEL 110CY **Calibers:** 223 Rem., 243 Win., 270 Win., 308 Win. **Capacity:** 5 rounds (1 in chamber); top-loading internal magazine. **Barrel Length:** 22" blued. **Overall Length:** 42.5" **Weight:** 6 3/8 lbs. **Sights:** Adjustable; drilled and tapped for scope mounts **Stock:** High comb, walnut-stained hardwood w/cut checkering and short pull.
Price: $360.00

SAVAGE ARMS RIFLES

MODEL 11F SHORT ACTION HUNTER

SPECIFICATIONS
Calibers: 223 Rem., 22-250 Rem., 243 Win. and 308 Win.
Capacity: 5 **Barrel Length:** 22" standard weight
Overall Length: 42.75" **Magazine:** Top loading internal
Weight: 6.75 lbs. **Sights:** Available in right/left hand.
Drilled and tapped for scope mounts
Stock: Durable black synthetic with scrolled checkering
and dual pillars **Finish:** Blued
Features: Short Action with dual pillar bedded stock
Price: $395.00

MODEL 11G SHORT ACTION CLASSIC AMERICAN STYLE HUNTER

SPECIFICATIONS
Calibers: 223 Rem., 22-250 Rem., 243 Win. and 308 Win.
Capacity: 5 **Barrel Length:** 22" **Overall Length:** 42.75"
Magazine: Top loading internal **Weight:** 6.75 lbs.
Sights: Available with or without (11GNS) Available in
right/left hand. Drilled and tapped for scope mounts
Stock: American style walnut finished hardwood with fancy
scrolled, diamond point checkering and black recoil pad
Finish: Blued
Price: $374.00

MODEL 10GY SHORT ACTION LADIES/YOUTH RIFLE

SPECIFICATIONS
Calibers: 223 Rem., 243 Win. and 308 Win.
Capacity: 5
Barrel Length: 22" standard weight
Overall Length: 39.25"
Magazine: Top loading internal
Weight: 6.25 lbs.
Sights: None. Drilled and tapped for scope mounts
Stock: American style walnut finished hardwood with
cut checkering
Finish: Blued
Price: $374.00

SAVAGE CENTERFIRE RIFLES

LONG RANGE/PILLAR BEDDED STOCKS

MODEL 112FVSS STAINLESS

SPECIFICATIONS

Calibers: 22-250 Rem., 223 Rem., 25-06 Rem., 30-06, 308 Win., 7mm Rem. Mag., 300 Win. Mag. (single-shot model available in 220 Swift, 22-250, 223 Rem., 300 Win. Mag.)

Capacity: 4 + 1 **Barrel Length:** 26" fluted, stainless steel **Overall Length:** 47.5" **Weight:** 8 7/8 lbs. **Sights:** Graphite/fiberglass-filled composite w/positive checkering
Price: $515.00

MODEL 112BVSS VARMINT

SPECIFICATIONS

Calibers: 22-250 Rem., 223 Rem., 25-06, 7mm Rem. Mag., 300 Win Mag., 30-06 Sprgfld., 308 Win. (single-shot model also available in 220 Swift, 22-250, 223 Rem., 300 Win. Mag.) **Capacity:** 4 + 1 **Barrel Length:** 26" fluted

heavy barrel, stainless steel **Overall Length:** 47.5" **Weight:** 10 lbs. (approx.) **Sights:** None; drilled and tapped **Stock:** Laminated hardwood w/high comb; ambidextrous grip
Price: $535.00

MODEL 112FV VARMINT
w/Graphite Fiberglass Polymer Stock
Price: $410.00

MODEL 112 BT COMPETITION GRADE

SPECIFICATIONS

Calibers: 223 Rem. and 308 Win. Mag. (single-shot available in 300 Win. Mag.)
Capacity: 5 + 1
Barrel Length: 26"; blackened stainless steel w/recessed

target/style muzzle
Overall Length: 47.5"
Weight: 10 7/8 lbs.
Stock: Laminated brown w/straight comb
Price: $1,000.00

SAVAGE CENTERFIRE RIFLES

ALL-WEATHER 116 SERIES

MODEL 116FSS "WEATHER WARRIOR"

Savage Arms combines the strength of a black graphite fiber-glass polymer stock and the durability of a stainless-steel barrel and receiver in this bolt-action rifle. Major components are made from stainless steel, honed to a low refllective satin finish. Drilled and tapped for scope mounts. Left-hand model available (116FLSS).

SPECIFICATIONS
Calibers: 223, 243, 270 30-06, 308 Win., 7mm Rem. Mag., 300 Win. Mag., 338 Win. Mag. **Capacity:** 4 (7mm Rem. Mag., 300 Win. Mag., 338 Win. Mag.); 5 (223, 243, 270, 30-06) **Barrel Length:** 22" (223, 243, 270, 30-06); 24" (7mm Rem. Mag., 300 Win. Mag., 338 Win. Mag.) **Overall Length:** 43.5"-45.5" **Weight:** 6.5 lbs.
Price: **$495.00**

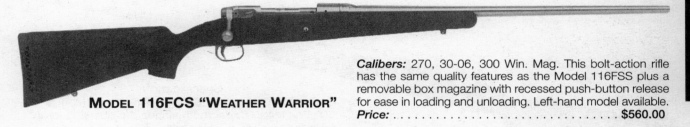

MODEL 116FCS "WEATHER WARRIOR"

Calibers: 270, 30-06, 300 Win. Mag. This bolt-action rifle has the same quality features as the Model 116FSS plus a removable box magazine with recessed push-button release for ease in loading and unloading. Left-hand model available.
Price: **$560.00**

MODEL 116FCSAK WEATHER WARRIOR RIFLE

SPECIFICATIONS
Calibers: 270 Win. 30-06 Spfld., 7mm Rem. Mag., 300 Win. Mag. **Capacity:** 5 (standard) 4 (magnum) plus one in chamber **Barrel Length:** 22" **Overall Length:** 43.5" **Magazine:** Detachable staggered box type **Weight:** 7.25 lbs.

Sights: None. Drilled and tapped for scope mount
Stock: Lightweight black synthetic with positive checkering
Finish: Fluted, satin finished stainless steel
Features: Fluted 400 series stainless steel barreled action with Adjustable Muzzle Brake (AMB)
Price: **$650.00**

MODEL 116FSK "KODIAK"

Features a compact barrel with "shock suppressor" that reduces average linear recoil by more than 30" without loss of Magnum stopping power. Left-hand model available.

SPECIFICATIONS
Calibers: 270 Win., 30-06 Sprg., 7mm Rem. Mag., 300 Win. Mag., 338 Win. Mag. **Capacity:** 5 rounds (4 in Magnum) **Barrel Length:** 22" **Overall Length:** 43.5" **Weight:** 7 lbs.
Price: **$554.00**
Also available: MODEL 116FSAK. Same specifications as above except includes adj. muzzle brake.
Price: **$585.00**

SAVAGE ARMS

MODEL 116SE
SAFARI EXPRESS

SPECIFICATIONS
Calibers: 300 Win. Mag., 338, 458 Win. Mag.
Capacity: 4 rounds (1 in chamber)
Barrel Length: 24" stainless steel w/AMB
Overall Length: 45.5" **Weight:** 8.5 lbs. **Sights:** 3-leaf express **Stock:** Classic-style select-grade walnut w/cut checkering; ebony tip; stainless-steel crossbolts; internally vented recoil pad
Price: $900.00

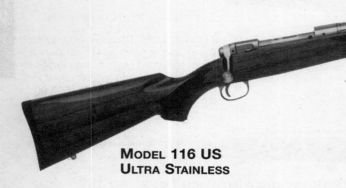

MODEL 116 US
ULTRA STAINLESS

SPECIFICATIONS
Caliber: 270 Win., 30-06 Spfld., 7mm Rem. Mag. and 300 Win Mag. **Capacity:** 5 standard calibers **Overall Length:** 43.5"-45.5" **Magazine:** Top loading internal **Weight:** Approx. 7 1/8 lbs. **Sights:** None. Drilled and tapped for scope mount **Stock:** American walnut with cut checkering and ebony tip **Finish:** Stainless steel **Features:** High gloss finished stock with stainless steel barreled action
Price: $700.00

MODEL 114CE
"CLASSIC EUROPEAN"

Weight: 7 1/8 lbs. (approx.)
Finish: Oil-finished walnut stock w/schnabel tip, cheekpiece and French skip-line checkering on grip and forend
Features: Rubber recoil pad; pistol-grip cap with gold medallion; high-luster blued finish on receiver barrel and bolt handle; side button release; adjustable metal sights; precision rifled barrel; drilled and tapped
Price: $600.00
Also available:
MODEL 114C "CLASSIC." Same specifications as above except barrel twist is 1 in 10". Plus select grade oil-finished American walnut stock; laser-etched Savage logo on bolt body; custom high lustre blued finish on receiver and bolt handle

SPECIFICATIONS
Calibers: 270 Win., 30-06 Sprgfld., 7mm Rem. Mag., 300 Win. Mag. **Capacity:** 3 rounds (magnum); 4 rounds (standard); plus 1 in each chamber
Barrel Length: 22" (standard); 24" (magnum)
Overall Length: 43.5" (standard); 45.5" (magnum)

SAVAGE RIFLES

HUNTER SERIES 111

MODEL 111GC CLASSIC HUNTER

SPECIFICATIONS

Calibers: 270 Win., 30-06 Springfield, 7mm Rem. Mag., 300 Win. Mag. *Capacity:* 5 rounds (4 rounds in Magnum calibers) *Overall Length:* 43.5" (45.5" Magnum calibers) *Weight:* 6 3/8-7 lbs. *Sights:* Adjustable

Stock: American-style walnut-finished hardwood; cut checkering
Features: Detachable staggered box-type magazine; left-hand model available
Price: $410.00

MODEL 111FAK EXPRESS

SPECIFICATIONS

Calibers: 270 Win., 30-06 Splfd., 7mm Rem. Mag., 300 Win. Mag., 338 Win. Mag. *Capacity:* 5 standard calibers (4 magnums + 1) *Barrel Length:* 22" *Overall Length:* 43.5 *Magazine:* Top loading *Weight:* 6.75 lbs. *Sights:* None.

Drilled and tapped for scope mount. *Stock:* Durable lightweight graphite/fiberglass filled composite with positive checkering *Finish:* Blued *Features:* Blue alloy steel barreled action with Adjustable Muzzle Brake (AMB)
Price: $450.00

MODEL 111FC CLASSIC HUNTER

SPECIFICATIONS

Same specifications as CLASSIC HUNTER above, except stock is lightweight graphite/fiberglass-filled composite w/positive checkering. Left-hand model available. *Calibers:* 270 Win., 30-06 Splfd., 7mm Rem. Mag. and 300 Win. Mag.
Price: $420.00

MODEL 111G CLASSIC HUNTER

SPECIFICATIONS

Same specifications as MODEL 111GC CLASSIC HUNTER, except available also in *calibers* 22-250 Rem., 223 Rem., 243 Win., 25-06, 270 Win., 7mm-08, 7mm Rem. Mag., 30-06 Sprgfld., 300 Win. Mag., 308. Stock is American-style walnut-finished hardwood with cut-checkering. Left-hand model available. YOUTH MODEL available in 223 Rem., 243 Win., 270 Win., 308 Win.
Price: $360.00

MODEL 111F CLASSIC HUNTER

SPECIFICATIONS

Same specifications as MODEL 111G CLASSIC HUNTER, except stock is black nonglare graphite/fiberglass-filled polymer with positive checkering. Left-hand model available.
Price: $380.00

RIFLES

SAVAGE RIFLES

MODEL 93 FSS STAINLESS

SPECIFICATIONS
Caliber: 22 WMR *Capacity:* 5 shots *Barrel Length:* 20.75" (1 in 16 twist) *Overall Length:* 39.5" *Weight:* 5.5 lbs. *Sights:* Front bead sight; sporting rear sight w/step elevator. *Features:* Precision button-rifled, free-floated barrel; black graphite/polymer filled stock w/positive checkering on grip and forend; corrosion and rust-resistant stainless steel barreled action.
Price: $175.00

MODEL 93G MAGNUM

SPECIFICATIONS
Caliber: 22 WMR *Capacity:* 5-shot clip *Barrel Length:* 20.75" *Overall Length:* 39.5" *Weight:* 5.75 lbs. *Stock:* Cut-checkered walnut-stained hardwood. *Sights:* Bead front; sporting rear with step elevator *Feature:* Free-floated precision button rifling.
Price: $145.00

MODEL 93F MAGNUM

SPECIFICATIONS
Calibers: 22 WMR *Capacity:* 5 *Barrel Length:* 20.75" free floated *Overall Length:* 39.5" *Magazine:* 5 shot detachable clip *Weight:* 5 lbs. *Sights:* Bead front sight, adjustable rear. Receiver dovetailed for scope mount *Stock:* Black synthetic with positive checkering *Finish:* Blued, button rifled *Features:* Blue alloy steel barreled action
Price: $139.00

MODEL 93FVSS

SPECIFICATIONS
Caliber: 22 WMR *Capacity:* 5 rounds *Barrel Length:* 21" heavy weight *Overall Length:* 40" *Weight:* 6 lbs. *Sights:* None. Drilled and tapped for scope mount. Weaver style bases included *Stock:* Black synthetic with positive checkering *Finish:* Stainless steel, recessed target style muzzle *Features:* Stainless steel heavy barrel in 22 WMR
Price: $201.00

SAVAGE SPORTING RIFLES

MODEL 64FV
SEMI-AUTOMATIC HEAVY BARREL

SPECIFICATIONS
Caliber: 22 LR *Capacity:* 10 shots
Barrel Length: 21" heavy weight *Overall Length:* 40.75"
Magazine: 10 shot detachable clip *Weight:* 6 lbs.
Sights: None. Weaver style bases included
Stock: Black synthetic with positive checkering
Finish: Blued, button rifled with recessed target style muzzle
Features: Semiauto blue alloy steel barreled action
Price: $149.00

MODEL 64F SEMIAUTO

SPECIFICATIONS
Caliber: 22 LR *Capacity:* 10 shots
Action: Semiautomatic side-ejecting
Barrel Length: 20.25" (1 in 16" twist)
Overall Length: 40" *Weight:* 5.5 lbs.
Sights: Front bead; adjustable open rear
Finish: Matte blue *Stock:* Black graphite/polymer synthetic
Features: Detachable clip magazine; free-floated precision
button-rifled barrel
Price: $145.00

MODEL 64G SEMIAUTO

SPECIFICATIONS
Caliber: 22 LR *Capacity:* 10-shot clip
Action: Semiautomatic side-ejecting
Barrel Length: 20.25" *Overall Length:* 40"
Weight: 5.5 lbs. *Sights:* Open bead front; adjustable rear
Stock: One-piece, walnut-finish hardwood, Monte Carlo
buttstock w/full pistol grip; checkered pistol grip and forend
Features: Bolt hold-open device; thumb-operated
rotary safety
Price: $123.00

SAVAGE SPORTING RIFLES

MARK I-G SINGLE SHOT

SPECIFICATIONS

Caliber: 22 Short, Long or LR **Capacity:** Single shot **Action:** Self-cocking bolt action, thumb-operated rotary safety **Barrel Length:** 20.75" **Overall Length:** 39.5"

Weight: 5.5 lbs.
Sights: Open bead front; adjustable rear
Stock: One-piece, walnut-finish hardwood, Monte Carlo buttstock w/full pistol grip; checkered pistol grip and forend
Features: Receiver grooved for scope mounting
Price: $119.00
Also available:
MARK I-G "SMOOTHBORE" (20.75" barrel) **119.00**
MARK I-G YOUTH (19" barrel) **119.00**

MARK II-FV HEAVY BARREL REPEATER

SPECIFICATIONS

Caliber: 22 LR **Capacity:** 5 shots **Barrel Length:** 21" heavy weight **Overall Length:** 39.75" **Magazine:** 5 shot detachablle clip **Weight:** 6 lbs. **Sights:** None. Weaver style bases included **Stock:** Black synthetic with positive checkering **Finish:** Blued free floated, button rifled with recessed target style muzzle **Features:** Heavy barrel with synthetic stock in 22 LR
Price: $174.00

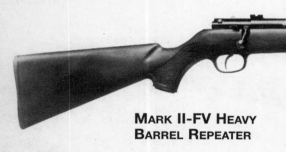

MARK II-FSS

SPECIFICATIONS

Caliber: 22 LR **Capacity:** 10-shot clip **Barrel Length:** 20.75" (1 in 16" twist) **Overall Length:** 39.5" **Weight:** 5 lbs. **Stock:** Synthetic **Sights:** Bead front sight; adjustable open rear **Features:** Stainless steel barrelled action

Price: $150.00
Also available: **MARK II-G** w/one-piece walnut-finished Monte Carlo-style hardwood stock, blued steel bolt-action receiver, bead front sight **$126.00**
MARK II-GY LADIES/YOUTH w/19" barrel (37" overall)
        Weight: 5 lbs. **126.00**
MARK II-GXP w/4x15mm scope (LH model avail.) . **131.00**
MARK II-F synthetic stock. **119.00**

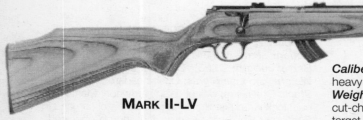

MARK II-LV

SPECIFICATIONS

Caliber: 22 LR **Capacity:** 10-shot **Barrel Length:** 21" heavy barrel (1 in 16" twist) **Overall Length:** 39.75" **Weight:** 6.5 lbs. **Stock:** Grey laminated hardwood stock; cut-checkered **Features:** Precision button rifled with recessed target-style muzzle; machined blued steel barreled action; dovetailed for scope mounting
Price: $200.00

SAVAGE SPORTING RIFLES

MODEL 900TR
TARGET REPEATER

SPECIFICATIONS
Caliber: 22 Long Rifle
Capacity: 5-shot clip magazine
Action: Self-cocking bolt action, thumb-operated rotary safety
Overall Length: 43 5/8"
Approx. Weight: 8 lbs.
Stock: One-piece, target-type with walnut finish hardwood; comes with shooting rail and hand stop
Sights: Receiver peep sights with 1/4 min. click micrometer adjustments, target front sight with inserts
Price: $415.00

MODEL 24F COMBINATION
RIFLE/SHOTGUN
$400.00

SPECIFICATIONS MODEL 24F COMBINATION RIFLE/SHOTGUN

O/U COMB. MODEL	GAUGE/ CALIBER	CHOKE	CHAMBER	BARREL LENGTH	O.A. LENGTH	TWIST R.H.	STOCK
24F-20 24F-12	20/22 LR	20 gauge: Modified Barrel 12 gauge: 3 Chokes	3"	24"	40.5"	1 in 14"	Black Graphite Fiberglass Polymer
	12 or 20/22 Hornet					1 in 14"	
	12 or 20/223					1 in 14"	
	12 or 20/30-30					1 in 12"	

SPRINGFIELD RIFLES

MODEL SAR-8 SPORTER RIFLE

SPECIFICATIONS
Caliber: 7.62mm **Barrel Length:** 18" (1:12" twist, 4-groove)
Overall Length: 40.38" **Weight:** 10.6 lbs.
Sights: Protected front post; rotary-style adjustable rear aperture

Features: Recoil-operated w/delayed roller-lock locking system; synthetic thumbhole stock
Price:. $1,249.00
Also available:
SAR-8 HEAVY BARREL TACTICAL RIFLE $1,989.00

MODEL SAR-4800 SPORTER RIFLE

SPECIFICATIONS
Caliber: 7.62mm, 5.56mm
Barrel Length: 21" (7.62mm); 18" (5.56mm)
Overall Length: 43.3" (7.62mm); 38.25" (5.56mm)
Weight: 11.1 lbs. (7.62mm); 10.45 lbs. (5.56mm)

Sights: Protected front post; adjustable rear
Features: Forged receiver and bolt; hammer-forged chrome-lined barrel; adjustable gas system; synthetic thumbhole stock
Price:. $1,249.00

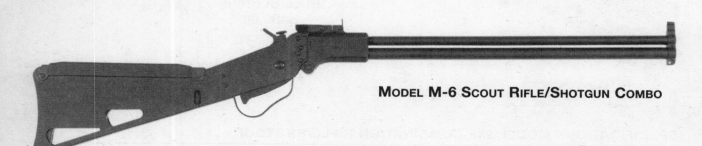

MODEL M-6 SCOUT RIFLE/SHOTGUN COMBO

SPECIFICATIONS
Calibers: 22 LR/.410 and 22 Hornet/.410
Barrel Length: 18.25" (1:15" R.H. twist in 22 LR; 1:13" R.H. twist in 22 Hornet)
Overall Length: 32"
Weight: 4 lbs.

Sight Radius: 16 1/8" **Finish:** Parkerized or stainless steel
Features: .410 shotgun barrel (2.5" or 3" chamber) choked Full; drilled and tapped for scope mount with Weaver base; lockable plastic carry case
Price:. $169.00
Stainless Steel. 199.00

SPRINGFIELD RIFLES

M1A STANDARD

SPECIFICATIONS
Calibers: 308 Win./7.62mm NATO (243 or 7mm-08 optional)
Capacity: 5- or 10-round box magazine
Barrel Length: 22"
Rifling: 6 groove, RH twist, 1 turn in 11"
Overall Length: 44 ¹/₃"
Weight: 9.2 lbs.
Sights: Military square post front; military aperture rear, adjustable for windage and elevation

Sight Radius: 26.75"
Prices:
 Standard w/walnut stock **$1,381.00**
Also available:
BASIC M1A RIFLE w/painted black fiberglass stock,
 caliber 308/7.62mm only **$1,249.00**
 w/bipod and stabilizer **1,460.00**
M1A SCOUT RIFLE w/scope mount and handguard, black
fiberglass stock. **$1,459.00**
w/walnut stock **1,479.00**

M1A NATIONAL MATCH

SPECIFICATIONS
Caliber: 308 Win.
Barrel Length: 22"
Overall Length: 44.375"
Trigger Pull: 4.5 lbs. *Weight:* 10.8 lbs.
Features: Comes with National Match barrel, flash suppressor, gas cylinder, special glass-bedded walnut stock

and match-tuned trigger assembly.
Price: **$1,729.00**
Also available:
M1A SUPER MATCH. Heavy match barrel and permanently attached figure-8-style operating rod guide, plus heavy walnut match stock, longer pistol grip and contoured area behind rear sight for better grip; 11.2 lbs. **$2,050.00**

M1A-A1 BUSH RIFLE

SPECIFICATIONS
Calibers: 308 Win./7.62mm
Barrel Length: 18" (w/o flash suppressor)
Overall Length: 40.5"
Weight: 8.9 lbs. (9 lbs. w/walnut stock)

Sight Radius: 22.75"
Prices:
w/walnut stock. **$1,410.00**
w/black fiberglass stock. **1,396.00**
w/black laminated stock. **1,466.00**

STEYR-MANNLICHER RIFLES

STEYR SSG-PI

The Steyr SSG features a black synthetic Cycolac stock (walnut optional), heavy Parkerized barrel, five-round standard (and optional 10-round) staggered magazine, heavy-duty milled receiver.

SPECIFICATIONS
Calibers: 243 Win. and 308 Win. *Barrel Length:* 26"
Overall Length: 44.5" *Weight:* 8.5 lbs.

Sights: Iron sights; hooded ramp front with blade adjustable for elevation; rear standard V-notch adjustable for windage. **Features:** Sliding safety; 1" swivels.
Prices:
MODEL SSG-PI Cycolac half-stock (26" bbl. with sights in 308 Win.) **$2,195.00**
MODEL SSG-PII (20" or 26" heavy bbl. in 308 Win.) 2,195.00
MODEL SSG-P-IV URBAN in 308 Win. w/16.75" heavy barrel. 2,660.00
MODEL SSG Scope Mount (1"). 244.00
MODEL SSG-PIIK (20" heavy barrel). 2,195.00

STEYR SCOUT (not shown)

The Steyr "Jeff Cooper" Scout system is equally effective as a sporter, tactical or survival rifle. Among its features are a spare magazine storage compartment, safe bolt system, roller tang safety and non-skid neutral grey Zytel stock; also an integral bipod, flush sling sockets and forward-mounted Leupold 2.5X Scout Scope.

SPECIFICATIONS
Caliber: 308 Win. (7.62 X 5mm)

Capacity: 5 rounds **Barrel Length:** 19" fluted cold-hammer-forged barrel **Overall Length:** 39.57" w/2 buttstock spacers
Weight: 7 lbs. (w/scope and mounts)
Sights: Factory-installed Leupold 2.5 X 28mm IER
Stock: Synthetic grey Zytel w/13.58" length of pull (adjustable)
Price: **$2,595.00**

SBS (SAFE BOLT SYSTEM) MANNLICHER EUROPEAN MODEL

SPECIFICATIONS
Calibers: 243 Win., 25-06, 308 Win., 270 Win., 7mm-08, 30-06 S'fld, 7mm Rem. Mag., 300 Win. Mag. *Capacity:* 4 rounds (3 rounds in Magnum, Prohunter and Forester); detachable staggered box magazine *Barrel Lengths:* 23.6"; 26" (magnum calibers) *Overall Length:* 44.5"
Weight: 7.5 lbs. *Safety:* 3-position roller safety
Trigger: Single adjustable trigger *Sights:* Ramp front w/balck adjustment for elevations; rear standard V-notch adjustable for windage; drilled and tapped for mounts

Finish: Blued; hand-checkered fancy European oiled walnut stock **Features:** Rotary cold hammer-forged barrel; front locking lug bolt
Prices:
Standard Calibers **$2,795.00**
Magnum Calibers 2,995.00
Full Stock 2,995.00
Half Stock 2,895.00
Also available:
STEYR SBS PROHUNTER in 243 Win., 25-06, 270 Win., 7mm-08 Rem., 308 Win., 30-06, w/synthetic half stock; no sights **$799.00**
STEYR MAGNUM MODEL in 7mm Rem. Mag. or 300 Win. Mag. w/25.6" barrel 899.00
STEYR SBS FORESTER in 243 Win, 25-06, 270 Win., 7mm-08 Rem., 308 Win., 30-06 w/23.6" bbl.. . . 929.00
STEYR SBS FORESTER MAGNUM in 7mm Rem. Mag. or 300 Win. Mag.. . . . . 1,045.00

THOMPSON/CENTER RIFLES

CONTENDER CARBINE

SPECIFICATIONS

Available in 5 *calibers:* 22 LR Match, 22 Hornet, 223 Rem., 7x30 Waters, 30-30 Win. *Barrels:* 21 inches, interchangeable. Adjustable iron sights; tapped and drilled for scope mounts. *Weight:* 5 lbs. 3 oz.
Price: $460.00

Also available:
CONTENDER CARBINE w/standard walnut stock in 22 Hornet, 223 Rem. 7x30 Waters 30-30 Win. **$530.00**
CONTENDER CARBINE with Match Grade 22 LR barrel 541.00

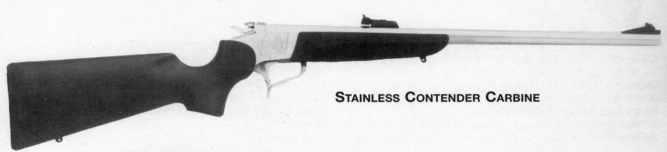

STAINLESS CONTENDER CARBINE

SPECIFICATIONS

Available in 22 LR Match, 22 Hornet, 223 Rem., 7x30 Waters, 30-30 Win. Same specifications as standard model, with walnut or composite stock. All stainless-steel components interchange readily with blued components

(barrels and frames can be mixed or matched).
Prices:
Stainless Carbine, Standard **$546.00**
In 22 LR Match 556.00

ENCORE RIFLE

SPECIFICATIONS

Calibers: 22-250 Rem., .223 Rem., .243 Win., .260 Rem., .270 Win., .280 Rem., 7mm-08 Rem., 7mm Rem. Mag., .308 Win., .30-06 Spfd., .300 Win. Mag., 45-70 Govt.
Action: Single-shot, break-open
Barrel lengths: 24" and 26" heavy barrel (.22-250 Rem., 7mm Rem. Mag., and 300 Win. Mag. only)
Overall length: 38 1/2" (24" barrel); 40 1/2" (26" barrel)

Weight: 6 3/4 lbs. (24"); 7 1/2 lbs. (26")
Trigger: Adjustable for overtravel
Safety: Automatic hammerblock w/bolt interlock
Stock: American walnut with Schnabel forend and Monte Carlo buttstock
Features: Interchangeable barrels, sling swivel studs
Price: $562.00
In 45-70 Govt. only 577.00

TIKKA RIFLES

WHITETAIL HUNTER

SPECIFICATIONS
Calibers: 22-250, 223, 243, 308 (Medium); 25-06, 270, 30-06 (Long); 7mm Mag., 300 Win. Mag., 338 Win. Mag.
Capacity: 3 rounds (5 rounds optional); detachable magazine
Barrel Lengths: 22.5" (24.5" Magnum)
Overall Length: 42" (Medium); 42.5" (Long); 44.5" (Magnum)
Weight: 7 lbs. (Medium); 7 ¼ lbs. (Long); 7.5 lbs. (Magnum)

Sights: No sights; integral scope mount rails; drilled and tapped
Safety: Locks trigger and bolt handle
Features: Oversized trigger guard; short bolt throw; customized spacer system; walnut stock with palm swell and matte lacquer finish; cold hammer-forged barrel
Price: **$598.00**
   Magnum 624.00

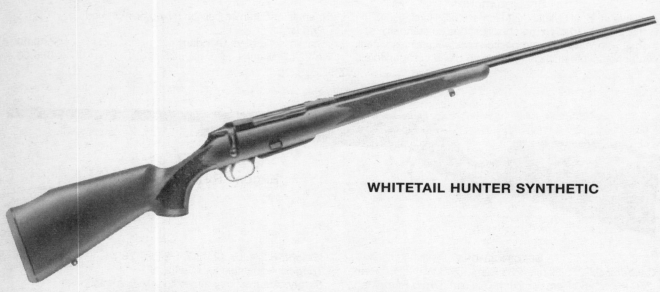

WHITETAIL HUNTER SYNTHETIC

SPECIFICATIONS
Same specifications as the standard Whitetail Hunter, except with All-Weather synthetic stock.
Price: **$598.00**
   Magnum 624.00

Also available:
WHITETAIL HUNTER STAINLESS SYNTHETIC.
Same specifications as above, except with stainless steel receiver, barrel and bolt. **$655.00**
In Magnum calibers 685.00

TIKKA RIFLES

CONTINENTAL VARMINT

SPECIFICATIONS
Calibers: 22-250, 223, 308
Capacity: 3 rounds (5 rounds optional)
Barrel Length: 26 *Overall Length:* 46"
Weight: 8 lbs. 10 oz.

Finish: Matte lacquer walnut stock w/palm swell
Features: Recoil pad spacer system; quick-release detachable magazine; beavertail forend; cold hammer-forged barrel; integral scope mount rails; adjustable trigger
Price: $694.00

CONTINENTAL LONG-RANGE HUNTING RIFLE

SPECIFICATIONS
Calibers: 25-06 Rem., 270 Win., 7mm Rem. Mag., 300 Win. Mag.
Capacity: 3 rounds (5 rounds in standard calibers, 4 rounds in magnum calibers)
Barrel Length: 26" heavy barrel

Overall Length: 46.5"
Weight: 8 lbs. 12 oz.
Finish: Matte lacquer walnut stock w/palm swell
Features: Same as Continental Varmint model
Price: $694.00
   Magnum Calibers. 724.00

RIFLES

UBERTI REPLICAS

ALL UBERTI FIREARMS AVAILABLE IN
SUPER GRADE, PRESTIGE AND ENGRAVED FINISHES

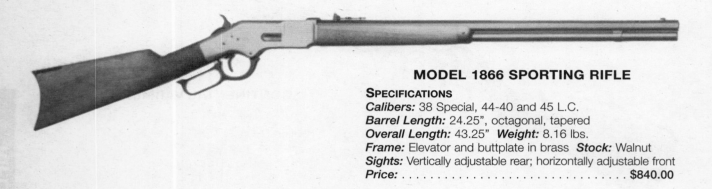

MODEL 1866 SPORTING RIFLE

SPECIFICATIONS
Calibers: 38 Special, 44-40 and 45 L.C.
Barrel Length: 24.25", octagonal, tapered
Overall Length: 43.25" *Weight:* 8.16 lbs.
Frame: Elevator and buttplate in brass *Stock:* Walnut
Sights: Vertically adjustable rear; horizontally adjustable front
Price: $840.00

MODEL 1866 YELLOWBOY CARBINE
The frist gun to carry the Winchester name, this model was born as the 44-caliber rimfire cartridge Henry and is now chambered for 22 LR and 44-40.

SPECIFICATIONS
Calibers: 22 LR, 22 Magnum, 38 Special, 44-40, 45 L.C.
Barrel Length: 19", round, tapered *Overall Length:* 38.25"
Weight: 7.380 lbs. *Frame:* Brass *Stock and forend:* Walnut
Sights: Vertically adjustable rear; horizontally adjustable front
Price: $760.00
In 22 LR or 22 Mag.. .... 820.00

MODEL 1871
ROLLING BLOCK BABY CARBINE

SPECIFICATIONS
Calibers: 22 LR, 22 Hornet, 22 Magnum, 357 Magnum
Barrel Length: 22" *Overall Length:* 35.5"
Weight: 4.85 lbs. *Stock and forend:* Walnut
Trigger guard: Brass
Sights: Fully adjustable rear; ramp front
Frame: Color-casehardened steel
Price: $490.00

UBERTI REPLICAS

MODEL 1873 SPORTING RIFLE

SPECIFICATIONS
Calibers: 357 Magnum, 44-40 and 45 LC. Hand-checkered. Other specifications same as Model 1866 Sporting Rifle. Also available with 24.25" or 30" octagonal barrel and pistol-grip stock (extra).
Price: In 357 Mag........................ $970.00
In 44-40 or 45 LC........................ 940.00
Also available: With pistol grip............ $1,020.00
With pistol grip and 30" barrel............. 1,050.00

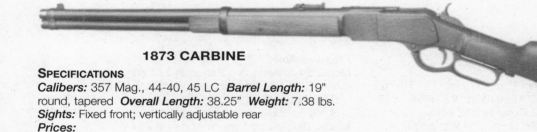

1873 CARBINE

SPECIFICATIONS
Calibers: 357 Mag., 44-40, 45 LC *Barrel Length:* 19" round, tapered *Overall Length:* 38.25" *Weight:* 7.38 lbs.
Sights: Fixed front; vertically adjustable rear
Prices:
In 357 Mag............................... $920.00
In 44-40 or 45 LC......................... 900.00

HENRY RIFLE

SPECIFICATIONS
Calibers: 44-40, 45 LC *Barrel Length:* 24.25" (half-octagon, with tubular magazine) *Overall Length:* 43.75"
Weight: 9.26 lbs.
Frame: Brass *Stock:* Varnished American walnut
Price: $940.00

HENRY CARBINE (not shown)

SPECIFICATIONS
Caliber: 44-40
Capacity: 12 shots
Barrel length: 22.25"
Weight: 9.04 lbs.
Price: $950.00

Also available:
HENRY TRAPPER. *Barrel length:* 16.25" or 18". *Overall length:* 35.75" or 37.75". *Weight:* 7.383 lbs. or 7.9034 lbs. *Capacity:* 8 or 9 shots.
Price: $950.00
HENRY RIFLE w/STEEL FRAME. (24.25" barrel; 44/40 cal.)
Price: $995.00

RIFLES

ULTRA LIGHT ARMS

MODEL 20
MOUNTAIN RIFLE

MODEL 28

MODEL 20 SERIES

SPECIFICATIONS

Calibers (Short Action): 6mm Rem., 17 Rem., 22 Hornet, 222 Rem., 222 Rem. Mag., 22-250 Rem., 223 Rem., 243 Win., 250-3000 Savage, 257 Roberts, 257 Ackley, 7x57 Mauser, 7X57 Ackley, 7mm-08 Rem., 284 Win., 300 Savage, 308 Win., 358 Win.
Barrel Length: 22" **Weight:** 4.75 lbs.
Safety: Two-position safety allows bolt to open or lock with sear blocked
Stock: Kevlar/Graphite composite; choice of 7 or more colors
Price:. **$2,500.00**
   Left Hand **2,600.00**

Also Available:
MODEL 24 SERIES (Long Action) in 270 Win., 30-06, 25-06, 7mm Express **Weight:** 5.25 lbs.
   Barrel Length: 22". **$2,600.00**
   Same as above in Left-Hand Model **2,700.00**
MODEL 28 SERIES (Magnum Action) in 264 Win., 7mm Rem., 300 Win., 338 **Weight:** 5.75 lbs.
   Barrel Length: 24". **2,900.00**
   Same as above in Left-Hand Model **3,000.00**
MODEL 40 SERIES (Magnum Action) in 300 Wby. and 416 Rigby **Weight:** 7.5 lbs.
   Barrel Length: 26". **2,900.00**
   Same as above in Left-Hand Model **3,000.00**

MODEL 20 RF

SPECIFICATIONS

Caliber: 22 LR
Barrel Length: 22" (Douglas Premium #1 Contour)
Weight: 5.25 lbs.
Sights: None (drilled and tapped for scope)
Stock: Composite
Features: Recoil pad; sling swivels; fully adjustable Timney trigger; 3-function safety; color options
Price:
   Single Shot **$800.00**
   Repeater **850.00**

UNIQUE RIFLES

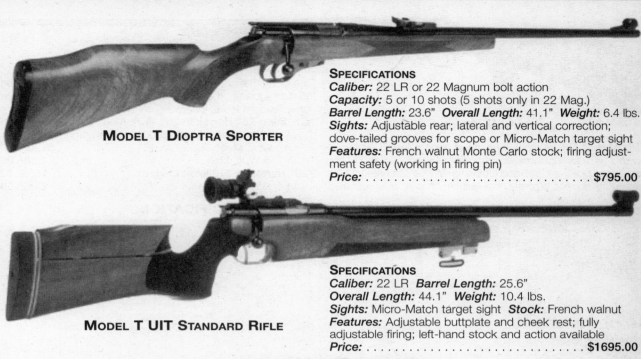

MODEL T DIOPTRA SPORTER

SPECIFICATIONS
Caliber: 22 LR or 22 Magnum bolt action
Capacity: 5 or 10 shots (5 shots only in 22 Mag.)
Barrel Length: 23.6" *Overall Length:* 41.1" *Weight:* 6.4 lbs.
Sights: Adjustable rear; lateral and vertical correction;
dove-tailed grooves for scope or Micro-Match target sight
Features: French walnut Monte Carlo stock; firing adjust-
ment safety (working in firing pin)
Price: $795.00

MODEL T UIT STANDARD RIFLE

SPECIFICATIONS
Caliber: 22 LR *Barrel Length:* 25.6"
Overall Length: 44.1" *Weight:* 10.4 lbs.
Sights: Micro-Match target sight *Stock:* French walnut
Features: Adjustable buttplate and cheek rest; fully
adjustable firing; left-hand stock and action available
Price: $1695.00

MODEL T/SM SILHOUETTE

SPECIFICATIONS
Caliber: 22 LR or 22 Magnum
Capacity: 5- or 10-shot magazine (5-shot only in 22 Mag.)
Barrel Length: 20.5" *Overall Length:* 38.4" *Weight:* 6.6 lbs.
Sights: Dove-tailed grooves on receiver for scope or
Micro-Match target sight
Stock: French walnut Monte Carlo stock (left-hand stock
available)
Price: $950.00

MODEL TGC CENTERFIRE

SPECIFICATIONS
Caliber: 243 Win., 270 Win., 7mm-08, 7mm Rem. Mag.,
308 Win., 30-06, 300 Win. Mag.
Capacity: 3- or 5-shot magazine
Barrel Length: 24" bolt action (interchangeable barrel)
Overall Length: 44.8" *Weight:* 8.4 lbs.
Sights: Dovetailed grooves on receiver for scope
Stock: French walnut Monte Carlo stock (left-hand stock
available)
Price: $1295.00

WEATHERBY MARK V RIFLES

MARK V DELUXE

The Mark V Deluxe stock is made of hand-selected American walnut with skipline checkering, traditional diamond-shaped inlay, rosewood pistol-grip cap and forend tip. Monte Carlo design with raised cheekpiece properly positions the shooter while reducing felt recoil. The action and hammer-forged barrel and hand-bedded for accuracy, then deep blued to a high-luster finish. See also specifications tables below and on the following page.

Calibers: **26" Barrel:** In 257 Wby. Mag., 270 Wby. Mag., 7mm Wby. Mag., 300 Wby. Mag. and 340 Wby. Mag. **$1,499.00**
In 378 Wby. Mag. 1,586.00
28" Barrel: In 416 Wby. Mag. 1,758.00
In 460 Wby. Mag. 2,056.00

MARK V® MAGNUM RIFLE SPECIFICATIONS

Caliber	Model	Barrelled Action	Weight*	Overall Length	Magazine Capacity	Barrel Length/Contour	Rifling	Length Of Pull	Drop At Comb	Monte Carlo	Drop At Heel
.257 Wby. Mag.	Mark V Sporter	RH 26"	8 1/2 lbs.	46 5/8"	3+1 in chamber	26" #2	1-10" twist	13 5/8"	1"	1/2"	1 5/8"
	Eurosport	RH 26"	8 1/2 lbs.	46 5/8"	3+1 in chamber	26" #2	1-10" twist	13 5/8"	1"	1/2"	1 5/8"
	Mark V Deluxe	RH 26"	8 1/2 lbs.	46 5/8"	3+1 in chamber	26" #2	1-10" twist	13 5/8"	7/8"	3/8"	1 3/8"
	Euromark	RH 26"	8 1/2 lbs.	46 5/8"	3+1 in chamber	26" #2	1-10" twist	13 5/8"	7/8"	3/8"	1 3/8"
	Lazermark	RH 26"	8 1/2 lbs.	46 5/8"	3+1 in chamber	26" #2	1-10" twist	13 5/8"	7/8"	3/8"	1 3/8"
	Synthetic	RH 26"	8 lbs.	46 5/8"	3+1 in chamber	26" #2	1-10" twist	13 5/8"	7/8"	1/2"	1 1/8"
	Fluted Synthetic	RH 26"	7 1/2 lbs.	46 5/8"	3+1 in chamber	26" #2	1-10" twist	13 5/8"	7/8"	1/2"	1 1/8"
	Stainless	RH 26"	8 lbs.	46 5/8"	3+1 in chamber	26" #2	1-10" twist	13 5/8"	7/8"	1/2"	1 1/8"
	Fluted Stainless	RH 26"	7 1/2 lbs.	46 5/8"	3+1 in chamber	26" #2	1-10" twist	13 5/8"	7/8"	1/2"	1 1/8"
	Accumark	RH 26"	8 1/2 lbs.	46 5/8"	3+1 in chamber	26" #3	1-10" twist	13 5/8"	1"	9/16"	1 1/2"
	SLS	RH 26"	8 1/2 lbs.	46 5/8"	3+1 in chamber	26" #2	1-10" twist	13 5/8"	1"	1/2"	1 5/8"
.270 Wby. Mag.	Mark V Sporter	RH 26"	8 1/2 lbs.	46 5/8"	3+1 in chamber	26" #2	1-10" twist	13 5/8"	1"	1/2"	1 5/8"
	Eurosport	RH 26"	8 1/2 lbs.	46 5/8"	3+1 in chamber	26" #2	1-10" twist	13 5/8"	1"	1/2"	1 5/8"
	Mark V Deluxe	RH 26"	8 1/2 lbs.	46 5/8"	3+1 in chamber	26" #2	1-10" twist	13 5/8"	7/8"	3/8"	1 3/8"
	Euromark	RH 26"	8 1/2 lbs.	46 5/8"	3+1 in chamber	26" #2	1-10" twist	13 5/8"	7/8"	3/8"	1 3/8"
	Lazermark	RH 26"	8 1/2 lbs.	46 5/8"	3+1 in chamber	26" #2	1-10" twist	13 5/8"	7/8"	3/8"	1 3/8"
	Synthetic	RH 26"	8 lbs	46 5/8"	3+1 in chamber	26" #2	1-10" twist	13 5/8"	7/8"	1/2"	1 1/8"
	Fluted Synthetic	RH 26"	7 1/2 lbs.	46 5/8"	3+1 in chamber	26" #2	1-10" twist	13 5/8"	7/8"	1/2"	1 1/8"
	Stainless	RH 26"	8 lbs.	46 5/8"	3+1 in chamber	26" #2	1-10" twist	13 5/8"	7/8"	1/2"	1 1/8"
	Fluted Stainless	RH 26"	7 1/2 lbs.	46 5/8"	3+1 in chamber	26" #2	1-10" twist	13 5/8"	7/8"	1/2"	1 1/8"
	Accumark	RH 26"	8 1/2 lbs.	46 5/8"	3+1 in chamber	26" #3	1-10" twist	13 5/8"	1"	9/16"	1 1/2"
	SLS	RH 26"	8 1/2 lbs.	46 5/8"	3+1 in chamber	26" #2	1-10" twist	13 5/8"	1"	1/2"	1 5/8"
7mm Rem. Mag.	Mark V Sporter	RH 24"	8 lbs.	44 5/8"	3+1 in chamber	24" #2	1-9 1/2" twist	13 5/8"	1"	1/2"	1 5/8"
	Eurosport	RH 24"	8 lbs.	44 5/8"	3+1 in chamber	24" #2	1-9 1/2" twist	13 5/8"	1"	1/2"	1 5/8"
	Synthetic	RH 24"	8 lbs.	44 5/8"	3+1 in chamber	24" #2	1-9 1/2" twist	13 5/8"	7/8"	1/2"	1 1/8"
	Fluted Synthetic	RH 24"	7 1/2 lbs.	44 5/8"	3+1 in chamber	24" #2	1-9 1/2" twist	13 5/8"	7/8"	1/2"	1 1/8"
	Stainless	RH 24"	8 lbs.	44 5/8"	3+1 in chamber	24" #2	1-9 1/2" twist	13 5/8"	7/8"	1/2"	1 1/8"
	Fluted Stainless	RH 24"	7 1/2 lbs.	44 5/8"	3+1 in chamber	24" #2	1-9 1/2" twist	13 5/8"	7/8"	1/2"	1 1/8"
	Accumark	RH 26"	8 1/2 lbs.	46 5/8"	3+1 in chamber	26" #3	1-9 1/2" twist	13 5/8"	1"	9/16"	1 1/2"
	SLS	RH 24"	8 1/2 lbs.	44 5/8"	3+1 in chamber	24" #2	1-9 1/2" twist	13 5/8"	1"	1/2"	1 5/8"
7mm Wby. Mag.	Mark V Sporter	RH 26"	8 1/2 lbs.	46 5/8"	3+1 in chamber	26" #2	1-10" twist	13 5/8"	1"	1/2"	1 5/8"
	Eurosport	RH 26"	8 1/2 lbs.	46 5/8"	3+1 in chamber	26" #2	1-10" twist	13 5/8"	1"	1/2"	1 5/8"
	Mark V Deluxe	RH 26"	8 1/2 lbs.	46 5/8"	3+1 in chamber	26" #2	1-10" twist	13 5/8"	7/8"	3/8"	1 3/8"
	Euromark	RH 26"	8 1/2 lbs.	46 5/8"	3+1 in chamber	26" #2	1-10" twist	13 5/8"	7/8"	3/8"	1 3/8"
	Lazermark	RH 26"	8 1/2 lbs.	46 5/8"	3+1 in chamber	26" #2	1-10" twist	13 5/8"	7/8"	3/8"	1 3/8"
	Synthetic	RH 26"	8 lbs.	46 5/8"	3+1 in chamber	26" #2	1-10" twist	13 5/8"	7/8"	1/2"	1 1/8"
	Fluted Synthetic	RH 26"	7 1/2 lbs.	46 5/8"	3+1 in chamber	26" #2	1-10" twist	13 5/8"	7/8"	1/2"	1 1/8"
	Stainless	RH 26"	8 lbs.	46 5/8"	3+1 in chamber	26" #2	1-10" twist	13 5/8"	7/8"	1/2"	1 1/8"
	Fluted Stainless	RH 26"	7 1/2 lbs.	46 5/8"	3+1 in chamber	26" #2	1-10" twist	13 5/8"	7/8"	1/2"	1 1/8"
	Accumark	RH 26"	8 1/2 lbs.	46 5/8"	3+1 in chamber	26" #3	1-10" twist	13 5/8"	1"	9/16"	1 1/2"
	SLS	RH 26"	8 1/2 lbs.	46 5/8"	3+1 in chamber	26" #2	1-10" twist	13 5/8"	1"	1/2"	1 5/8"
7mm STW	Accumark	RH 26"	8 1/2 lbs.	46 5/8"	3+1 in chamber	26" #3	1-10" twist	13 5/8"	1"	9/16"	1 1/2"
.300 Win Mag.	Mark V Sporter	RH 24"	8 lbs.	44 5/8"	3+1 in chamber	24" #2	1-10" twist	13 5/8"	1"	1/2"	1 5/8"
	Eurosport	RH 24"	8 lbs.	44 5/8"	3+1 in chamber	24" #2	1-10" twist	13 5/8"	1"	1/2"	1 5/8"
	Synthetic	RH 24"	8 lbs.	44 5/8"	3+1 in chamber	24" #2	1-10" twist	13 5/8"	7/8"	1/2"	1 1/8"
	Fluted Synthetic	RH 24"	7 1/2 lbs.	44 5/8"	3+1 in chamber	24" #2	1-10" twist	13 5/8"	7/8"	1/2"	1 1/8"
	Stainless	RH 24"	8 lbs.	44 5/8"	3+1 in chamber	24" #2	1-10" twist	13 5/8"	7/8"	1/2"	1 1/8"
	Fluted Stainless	RH 24"	7 1/2 lbs.	44 5/8"	3+1 in chamber	24" #2	1-10" twist	13 5/8"	7/8"	1/2"	1 1/8"
	Accumark	RH 26"	8 1/2 lbs.	46 5/8"	3+1 in chamber	26" #3	1-10" twist	13 5/8"	1"	9/16"	1 1/2"
	SLS	RH 24"	8 1/2 lbs.	44 5/8"	3+1 in chamber	24" #2	1-10" twist	13 5/8"	1"	1/2"	1 5/8"

WEATHERBY MARK V RIFLES

MARK V EUROMARK

The Euromark features a hand-rubbed oil finish and Monte Carlo stock of American walnut, plus custom grade, hand-cut checkering with an ebony pistol-grip cap and forend tip.

Prices: **26" Barrel**
In Weatherby Magnum calibers 257, 270, 7mm,
300 and 340 . . . . **$1,499.00**
In 378 Wby. Mag. **1,586.00**
28" Barrel
In 416 Wby. Mag. **1,758.00**
24" Barrel
In 7mm Rem. Mag., 300 Win. Mag., 338 Win. Mag. and
375 H&H Mag. **1,499.00**

ACCUMARK

Built on the proven performance of the Mark V action, the Accumark is a composite of several field-tested features that help make it the utmost in accuracy, including a hand-laminated raised-comb Monte Carlo synthetic stock by H-S Precison (a combiniation of Kevlar, unidirectional fibers and fiberglass). There's also a molded-in, CNC-machined aluminum bedding plate that stiffens the receiver area of the rifle when the barreled action is secured to the block, providing a solid platform for the action. The Accumark is available in Weatherby Magnum calibers from 257 through 340, 7mm Rem. Mag. and .300 Win. Mag. Please see the specifications on the previous pages for additional information.

Prices: **26" Barrel**
In 257, 270, 7mm, 7mm STW, 300-340
Magnum calibers **$1,299.00**
28" Barrel
In 30-378 Wby. and 338-378 Magnum
calibers **1,499.00**

WEATHERBY MARK V RIFLES

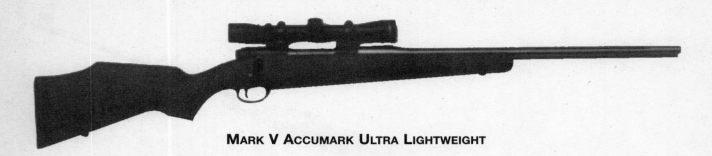

MARK V ACCUMARK ULTRA LIGHTWEIGHT

Weatherby's new **MARK VR ACCUMARK ULTRA LIGHTWEIGHT** rifle is based on Weatherby's Mark V lightweight action for standard cartridges. It features a chrome moly receiver, bolt and sleeve. To reduce weight, the bolt handle is skeletonized and the flutes on the boot are deeper and wider than those on other Weatherby Mark V rifles. To reduce weight further without sacrificing strength and structural integrity, the follower, floor plate, trigger housing and other non-critical components are made of lighter alloys. A stainless steel 24-inch barrel with weight-reducing flutes increases portability while maintaining velocity. A recessed target crown on the barrel enhances accuracy. The Ultra Lightweight also features a specially designed Monte Carlo stock with a pillar bedding system. Hand-laminated of Kevlar and fiberglass materials to provide a sure grip, the stock is teamed with a Pachmayr decelerator pad to dampen recoil. Stock colors are dark gray with black spiderwebbing. Additional specifications include **Calibers:** .243 Winchester, 7mm-08 Remington, .308 Winchester, .25-06 Remington, .270 Winchester, .280 Remington, .30-06 Springfield, and .240 Weatherby Mag. **Overall length:** 44". **Weight:** 5.75 lbs.
Price: **$1,199.00**

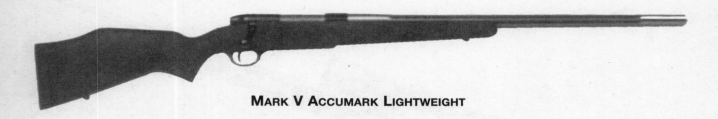

MARK V ACCUMARK LIGHTWEIGHT

Weatherby's new **MARK VR ACCUMARK LIGHTWEIGHT** is a standard- cartridge rifle designed for hunting varmints, deer and other big-game animals with extended-range accuracy. A lightweight version of Weatherby's legendary Mark V Magnum action, its lightweight action is scaled and designed specifically for standard cartridges, with six locking lugs compared to the Magnum action's nine. Both feature a short 54-degree bolt lift. Action metalwork is black oxide coated with a bead blast matte finish to eliminate glare. Six deep flutes help lighten the overall barrel weight without reducing stiffness while increasing the surface area of the barrel by 40 percent. This helps extend barrel life by reducing heat buildup in the barrel. Muzzle diameter is .722. The barrel, which has a low-lustre brushed finish, is free floated and includes a recessed target crown. Trigger presettings are four pounds of pull with .012-.015 of an inch of sear engagement for extremely crisp and consistent let-off. The trigger is fully adjustable for sear engagement and let-off weight. The Accumark Lightweight also features a composite stock made of Kevlar and fiberglass. The bedding block is computer-designed and CNC-machined from aircraft quality aluminum. This system stiffens the receiver area of the rifle when the barreled action is secured into the block. The combination of CNC machining and precision molding of the bedding block into the stock helps ensure perfect fit and alignment of the barreled action. The hand-laminated, raised-comb Monte Carlo stock is black with gray spiderwebbing.
Additional specifications include:
Calibers: .22-250 Remington, .243 Winchester, 7mm-08 Remington, .308 Winchester, .25-06 Remington, .270 Winchester, .280 Remington, .30-06 Springfield, and .240 Weatherby Mag. **Barrel length:** 24". **Overall length:** 44". **Weight:** 7.5 lbs.
Price: **$1,199.00**

WEATHERBY MARK V RIFLES

MARK V SPORTER

SPECIFICATIONS

Calibers: **26" Barrel:** In 257 Wby. Mag., 270 Wby.
Mag., 7mm Wby. Mag., 300 Wby. Mag. and
340 Wby. Mag. $949.00
24" Barrel: In 7mm Rem. Mag., 300 Win. Mag.,
338 Win. Mag. and 375 H&H Mag. $949.00
Also available: EUROSPORT. Same specifications and prices
but with hand-rubbed satin oil finish.

MARK V® MAGNUM RIFLE SPECIFICATIONS (cont.)

CALIBER	Model	Barrelled Action	Weight*	Overall Length	Magazine Capacity	Barrel Length/ Contour	Rifling	Length Of Pull	Drop At Comb	Monte Carlo	Drop At Heel
.300 WBY. MAG.	Mark V Sporter	RH 26"	8 1/2 lbs.	46 5/8"	3+1 in chamber	26" #2	1-10" twist	13 5/8"	1"	1/2"	1 5/8"
	Eurosport	RH 26"	8 1/2 lbs.	46 5/8"	3+1 in chamber	26" #2	1-10" twist	13 5/8"	1"	1/2"	1 5/8"
	Mark V Deluxe	RH 26"	8 1/2 lbs.	46 5/8"	3+1 in chamber	26" #2	1-10" twist	13 5/8"	7/8"	3/8"	1 3/8"
	Euromark	RH 26"	8 1/2 lbs.	46 5/8"	3+1 in chamber	26" #2	1-10" twist	13 5/8"	7/8"	3/8"	1 3/8"
	Lazermark	RH 26"	8 1/2 lbs.	46 5/8"	3+1 in chamber	26" #2	1-10" twist	13 5/8"	7/8"	3/8"	1 3/8"
	Synthetic	RH 26"	8 lbs.	46 5/8"	3+1 in chamber	26" #2	1-10" twist	13 5/8"	7/8"	1/2"	1 1/8"
	Fluted Synthetic	RH 26"	7 1/2 lbs.	46 5/8"	3+1 in chamber	26" #2	1-10" twist	13 5/8"	7/8"	1/2"	1 1/8"
	Stainless	RH 26"	8 lbs.	46 5/8"	3+1 in chamber	26" #2	1-10" twist	13 5/8"	7/8"	1/2"	1 1/8"
	Fluted Stainless	RH 26"	7 1/2 lbs.	46 5/8"	3+1 in chamber	26" #2	1-10" twist	13 5/8"	7/8"	1/2"	1 1/8"
	Accumark	RH 26"	8 1/2 lbs.	46 5/8"	3+1 in chamber	26" #3	1-10" twist	13 5/8"	1"	9/16"	1 1/2"
	SLS	RH 26"	8 1/2 lbs.	46 5/8"	3+1 in chamber	26" #2	1-10" twist	13 5/8"	1"	1/2"	1 5/8"
.338 WIN. MAG.	Mark V Sporter	RH 24"	8 lbs.	44 5/8"	3+1 in chamber	24" #2	1-10" twist	13 5/8"	1"	1/2"	1 5/8"
	Eurosport	RH 24"	8 lbs.	44 5/8"	3+1 in chamber	24" #2	1-10" twist	13 5/8"	1"	1/2"	1 5/8"
	Synthetic	RH 24"	8 lbs.	44 5/8"	3+1 in chamber	24" #2	1-10" twist	13 5/8"	7/8"	1/2"	1 1/8"
	Stainless	RH 24"	8 lbs.	44 5/8"	3+1 in chamber	24" #2	1-10" twist	13 5/8"	7/8"	1/2"	1 1/8"
	SLS	RH 24"	8 1/2 lbs.	44 5/8"	3+1 in chamber	24" #2	1-10" twist	13 5/8"	1"	1/2"	1 5/8"
.340 WBY. MAG.	Mark V Sporter	RH 26"	8 1/2 lbs.	46 5/8"	3+1 in chamber	26" #2	1-10" twist	13 5/8"	1"	1/2"	1 5/8"
	Eurosport	RH 26"	8 1/2 lbs.	46 5/8"	3+1 in chamber	26" #2	1-10" twist	13 5/8"	1"	1/2"	1 5/8"
	Mark V Deluxe	RH 26"	8 1/2 lbs.	46 5/8"	3+1 in chamber	26" #2	1-10" twist	13 5/8"	7/8"	3/8"	1 3/8"
	Euromark	RH 26"	8 1/2 lbs.	46 5/8"	3+1 in chamber	26" #2	1-10" twist	13 5/8"	7/8"	3/8"	1 3/8"
	Lazermark	RH 26"	8 1/2 lbs.	46 5/8"	3+1 in chamber	26" #2	1-10" twist	13 5/8"	7/8"	3/8"	1 3/8"
	Synthetic	RH 26"	8 lbs.	46 5/8"	3+1 in chamber	26" #2	1-10" twist	13 5/8"	7/8"	1/2"	1 1/8"
	Stainless	RH 26"	8 lbs.	46 5/8"	3+1 in chamber	26" #2	1-10" twist	13 5/8"	7/8"	1/2"	1 1/8"
	Accumark	RH 26"	8 1/2 lbs.	46 5/8"	3+1 in chamber	26" #2	1-10" twist	13 5/8"	1"	9/16"	1 1/2"
	SLS	RH 26"	8 1/2 lbs.	46 5/8"	3+1 in chamber	26" #2	1-10" twist	13 5/8"	1"	1/2"	1 5/8"
.375 H&H MAG.	Mark V Sporter	RH 24"	8 1/2 lbs.	44 5/8"	3+1 in chamber	24" #3	1-12" twist	13 5/8"	1"	1/2"	1 5/8"
	Eurosport	RH 24"	8 1/2 lbs.	44 5/8"	3+1 in chamber	24" #3	1-12" twist	13 5/8"	1"	1/2"	1 5/8"
	Euromark	RH 24"	8 lbs.	44 5/8"	3+1 in chamber	24" #3	1-12" twist	13 5/8"	1"	1/2"	1 5/8"
	Synthetic	RH 24"	8 lbs.	44 5/8"	3+1 in chamber	24" #3	1-12" twist	13 5/8"	7/8"	1/2"	1 1/8"
	Stainless	RH 24"	8 lbs.	44 5/8"	3+1 in chamber	24" #3	1-12" twist	13 5/8"	7/8"	1/2"	1 1/8"
**.30-378 WBY. MAG.	Accumark	RH 26"	8 1/2 lbs.	46 5/8"	2+1 in chamber	26" #3	1-10" twist	13 5/8"	1"	9/16"	1 1/2"
	Synthetic	RH 26"	8 lbs.	46 5/8"	2+1 in chamber	26" #2	1-10" twist	13 5/8"	7/8"	1/2"	1 1/8"
	Stainless	RH 26"	8 lbs.	46 5/8"	2+1 in chamber	26" #2	1-10" twist	13 5/8"	7/8"	1/2"	1 1/8"
**.338-378 WBY. MAG.	Accumark	RH 26"	8 1/2 lbs.	46 5/8"	2+1 in chamber	26" #3	1-10" twist	13 5/8"	1"	9/16"	1 1/2"
.378 WBY. MAG.	Mark V Deluxe	RH 26"	9 1/2 lbs.	46 5/8"	2+1 in chamber	26" #3	1-12" twist	13 7/8"	7/8"	3/8"	1 3/8"
	Euromark	RH 26"	9 1/2 lbs.	46 5/8"	2+1 in chamber	26" #3	1-12" twist	13 7/8"	7/8"	3/8"	1 3/8"
	Lazermark	RH 26"	9 1/2 lbs.	46 5/8"	2+1 in chamber	26" #3	1-12" twist	13 7/8"	7/8"	3/8"	1 3/8"
**.416 WBY. MAG.	Mark V Deluxe	RH 26"	9 1/2 lbs.	46 3/4"	2+1 in chamber	26" #3	1-14" twist	13 7/8"	7/8"	3/8"	1 3/8"
	Euromark	RH 26"	9 1/2 lbs.	46 3/4"	2+1 in chamber	26" #3	1-14" twist	13 7/8"	7/8"	3/8"	1 3/8"
	Lazermark	RH 26"	9 1/2 lbs.	46 3/4"	2+1 in chamber	26" #3	1-14" twist	13 7/8"	7/8"	3/8"	1 3/8"
**.460 WBY. MAG.	Mark V Deluxe	RH 26"	10 1/2 lbs.	46 3/4"	2+1 in chamber	26" #4	1-16" twist	14"	7/8"	3/8"	1 3/8"
	Lazermark	RH 26"	10 1/2 lbs.	46 3/4"	2+1 in chamber	26" #4	1-16" twist	14"	7/8"	3/8"	1 3/8"

WEATHERBY MARK V RIFLES

LAZERMARK

26" Barrel
Prices:
In Weatherby Magnum calibers 257, 270, 7mm,
   300 and 340 . . . . **$1,599.00**

LAZERMARK

In 378 Wby. Mag. **1,701.00**
28" Barrel
In 416 Wby. Mag. **1,869.00**
In 460 Wby. Mag. **2,196.00**

MARK V MAGNUM STAINLESS

Features 400 Series stainless steel. The action is hand-bedded to a lightweight, injection-molded synthetic stock. A custom floorplate on stainless-steel trigger guard with engraved flying "W" monogram is standard.

Prices: MARK V STAINLESS
26" Barrel
In Weatherby Magnum calibers 257, 270, 7mm
   Rem. Mag., 300 and 340 . . . . **$999.00**

MARK V MAGNUM STAINLESS

24" Barrel
In 7mm Rem. Mag., 300 Win. Mag., 338 Win.
   Mag. and 375 H&H Mag. **999.00**
28" Barrel
In 30-378 Wby. Mag.. . . . . **1,149.00**
Also available:
MODEL SLS (Stainless Laminated Sporter) **1,249.00**
FLUTED STAINLESS **1,149.00**
FLUTED SYNTHETIC **949.00**

MARK V SYNTHETIC

MARK V SYNTHETIC

Features an injection-molded synthetic stock with dual-tapered checkered forearm. Comes with custom floorplate release/trigger guard assembly and engraved flying "W" monogram.

Prices: MARK V SYNTHETIC
26" Barrel
In Weatherby Magnum calibers 257, 270, 7mm,
   300 and 340 . . . . **$799.00**
24" Barrel
In 7mm Rem. Mag., 300 Win. Mag., 338 Win.
   Mag. and 375 H&H Mag. **799.00**
28" Barrel
In 30-378 Wby. Mag. **949.00**

For complete specifications on the above rifles, please see the tables on the preceding pages.

WEATHERBY MARK V RIFLES

MARK V LIGHTWEIGHT SPORTER

MARK V LIGHTWEIGHT CARBINE

NEW MARK V LIGHTWEIGHT RIFLES

Virtually identical in design to the Mark V magnum action, Weatherby's new lightweight version is shorter, narrower and lighter than the original. It accommodates up to 30-06 length cartridges, including the 240 Weatherby Magnum. For complete specifications, see table below.

Prices: LIGHTWEIGHT SYNTHETIC (24" barrel)
22-250 to 308 Win. Mag. $699.00
CARBINE MODEL (20" in 243 Win., 7mm-08
Rem., 308 Win.) 699.00
LIGHTWEIGHT STAINLESS 899.00
LIGHTWEIGHT SPORTER 849.00

MARK V® LIGHTWEIGHT RIFLE SPECIFICATIONS

Caliber	Model	Barrelled Action	Weight*	Overall Length	Magazine Capacity	Barrel Length/ Contour	Rifling	Length Of Pull	Drop At Comb	Monte Carlo	Drop At Heel
.240 WBY. MAG.	Mark V Sporter	RH 24"	6 3/4 lbs.	44"	5+1 in chamber	24" #1	1-10" twist	13 5/8"	3/4"	3/8"	1 1/8"
	Mark V Stainless	RH 24"	6 1/2 lbs.	44"	5+1 in chamber	24" #1	1-10" twist	13 5/8"	3/4"	3/8"	1 1/8"
	Mark V Synthetic	RH 24"	6 1/2 lbs.	44"	5+1 in chamber	24" #1	1-10" twist	13 5/8"	3/4"	3/8"	1 1/8"
	Accumark	RH 24"	7 lbs.	44"	5+1 in chamber	24" #3	1-10" twist	13 5/8"	3/4"	3/8"	1 1/8"
	Accumark Ultra Lightweight	RH 24"	5 3/4 lbs.	44"	5+1 in chamber	24" #2	1-10" twist	13 5/8"	3/4"	3/8"	1 1/8"
.22-250 REM.	Mark V Sporter	RH 24"	6 3/4 lbs.	44"	5+1 in chamber	24" #1	1-14" twist	13 5/8"	3/4"	3/8"	1 1/8"
	Mark V Stainless	RH 24"	6 1/2 lbs.	44"	5+1 in chamber	24" #1	1-14" twist	13 5/8"	3/4"	3/8"	1 1/8"
	Mark V Synthetic	RH 24"	6 1/2 lbs.	44"	5+1 in chamber	24" #1	1-14" twist	13 5/8"	3/4"	3/8"	1 1/8"
	Accumark	RH 24"	7 lbs.	44"	5+1 in chamber	24" #3	1-14" twist	13 5/8"	3/4"	3/8"	1 1/8"
	Mark V Stainless Carbine	RH 20"	6 lbs.	40"	5+1 in chamber	20" #1	1-14" twist	13 5/8"	3/4"	3/8"	1 1/8"
	Mark V Synthetic Carbine	RH 20"	6 lbs.	40"	5+1 in chamber	20" #1	1-14" twist	13 5/8"	3/4"	3/8"	1 1/8"
.243 WINCHESTER	Mark V Sporter	RH 24"	6 3/4 lbs.	44"	5+1 in chamber	24" #1	1-10" twist	13 5/8"	3/4"	3/8"	1 1/8"
	Mark V Stainless	RH 24"	6 1/2 lbs.	44"	5+1 in chamber	24" #1	1-10" twist	13 5/8"	3/4"	3/8"	1 1/8"
	Mark V Synthetic	RH 24"	6 1/2 lbs.	44"	5+1 in chamber	24" #1	1-10" twist	13 5/8"	3/4"	3/8"	1 1/8"
	Accumark	RH 24"	7 lbs.	44"	5+1 in chamber	24" #3	1-10" twist	13 5/8"	3/4"	3/8"	1 1/8"
	Accumark Ultra Lightweight	RH 24"	5 3/4 lbs.	44"	5+1 in chamber	24" #2	1-10" twist	13 5/8"	3/4"	3/8"	1 1/8"
	Mark V Stainless Carbine	RH 20"	6 lbs.	40"	5+1 in chamber	20" #1	1-10" twist	13 5/8"	3/4"	3/8"	1 1/8"
	Mark V Synthetic Carbine	RH 20"	6 lbs.	40"	5+1 in chamber	20" #1	1-10" twist	13 5/8"	3/4"	3/8"	1 1/8"
7MM-08 REM.	Mark V Sporter	RH 24"	6 3/4 lbs.	44"	5+1 in chamber	24" #1	1-9 1/2" twist	13 5/8"	3/4"	3/8"	1 1/8"
	Mark V Stainless	RH 24"	6 1/2 lbs.	44"	5+1 in chamber	24" #1	1-9 1/2" twist	13 5/8"	3/4"	3/8"	1 1/8"
	Mark V Synthetic	RH 24"	6 1/2 lbs.	44"	5+1 in chamber	24" #1	1-9 1/2" twist	13 5/8"	3/4"	3/8"	1 1/8"
	Accumark	RH 24"	7 lbs.	44"	5+1 in chamber	24" #3	1-9 1/2" twist	13 5/8"	3/4"	3/8"	1 1/8"
	Accumark Ultra Lightweight	RH 24"	5 3/4 lbs.	44"	5+1 in chamber	24" #2	1-9 1/2" twist	13 5/8"	3/4"	3/8"	1 1/8"
	Mark V Stainless Carbine	RH 20"	6 lbs.	40"	5+1 in chamber	20" #1	1-9 1/2" twist	13 5/8"	3/4"	3/8"	1 1/8"
	Mark V Synthetic Carbine	RH 20"	6 lbs.	40"	5+1 in chamber	20" #1	1-9 1/2" twist	13 5/8"	3/4"	3/8"	1 1/8"
.308 WINCHESTER	Mark V Sporter	RH 24"	6 3/4 lbs.	44"	5+1 in chamber	24" #1	1-12" twist	13 5/8"	3/4"	3/8"	1 1/8"
	Mark V Stainless	RH 24"	6 1/2 lbs.	44"	5+1 in chamber	24" #1	1-12" twist	13 5/8"	3/4"	3/8"	1 1/8"
	Mark V Synthetic	RH 24"	6 1/2 lbs.	44"	5+1 in chamber	24" #1	1-12" twist	13 5/8"	3/4"	3/8"	1 1/8"
	Accumark	RH 24"	7 lbs.	44"	5+1 in chamber	24" #3	1-12" twist	13 5/8"	3/4"	3/8"	1 1/8"
	Accumark Ultra Lightweight	RH 24"	5 3/4 lbs.	44"	5+1 in chamber	24" #2	1-12" twist	13 5/8"	3/4"	3/8"	1 1/8"
	Mark V Stainless Carbine	RH 20"	6 lbs.	40"	5+1 in chamber	20" #1	1-12" twist	13 5/8"	3/4"	3/8"	1 1/8"
	Mark V Synthetic Carbine	RH 20"	6 lbs.	40"	5+1 in chamber	20" #1	1-12" twist	13 5/8"	3/4"	3/8"	1 1/8"
.25-06 REM.	Mark V Sporter	RH 24"	6 3/4 lbs.	44"	5+1 in chamber	24" #1	1-10" twist	13 5/8"	3/4"	3/8"	1 1/8"
	Mark V Stainless	RH 24"	6 1/2 lbs.	44"	5+1 in chamber	24" #1	1-10" twist	13 5/8"	3/4"	3/8"	1 1/8"
	Mark V Synthetic	RH 24"	6 1/2 lbs.	44"	5+1 in chamber	24" #1	1-10" twist	13 5/8"	3/4"	3/8"	1 1/8"
	Accumark	RH 24"	7 lbs.	44"	5+1 in chamber	24" #3	1-10" twist	13 5/8"	3/4"	3/8"	1 1/8"
	Accumark Ultra Lightweight	RH 24"	5 3/4 lbs.	44"	5+1 in chamber	24" #2	1-10" twist	13 5/8"	3/4"	3/8"	1 1/8"
.270 WINCHESTER	Mark V Sporter	RH 24"	6 3/4 lbs.	44"	5+1 in chamber	24" #1	1-10" twist	13 5/8"	3/4"	3/8"	1 1/8"
	Mark V Stainless	RH 24"	6 1/2 lbs.	44"	5+1 in chamber	24" #1	1-10" twist	13 5/8"	3/4"	3/8"	1 1/8"
	Mark V Synthetic	RH 24"	6 1/2 lbs.	44"	5+1 in chamber	24" #1	1-10" twist	13 5/8"	3/4"	3/8"	1 1/8"
	Accumark	RH 24"	7 lbs.	44"	5+1 in chamber	24" #3	1-10" twist	13 5/8"	3/4"	3/8"	1 1/8"
	Accumark Ultra Lightweight	RH 24"	5 3/4 lbs.	44"	5+1 in chamber	24" #2	1-10" twist	13 5/8"	3/4"	3/8"	1 1/8"
.280 REM.	Mark V Sporter	RH 24"	6 3/4 lbs.	44"	5+1 in chamber	24" #1	1-10" twist	13 5/8"	3/4"	3/8"	1 1/8"
	Mark V Stainless	RH 24"	6 1/2 lbs.	44"	5+1 in chamber	24" #1	1-10" twist	13 5/8"	3/4"	3/8"	1 1/8"
	Mark V Synthetic	RH 24"	6 1/2 lbs.	44"	5+1 in chamber	24" #1	1-10" twist	13 5/8"	3/4"	3/8"	1 1/8"
	Accumark	RH 24"	7 lbs.	44"	5+1 in chamber	24" #3	1-10" twist	13 5/8"	3/4"	3/8"	1 1/8"
	Accumark Ultra Lightweight	RH 24"	5 3/4 lbs.	44"	5+1 in chamber	24" #2	1-10" twist	13 5/8"	3/4"	3/8"	1 1/8"
.30-06 SPRINGFIELD	Mark V Sporter	RH 24"	6 3/4 lbs.	44"	5+1 in chamber	24" #1	1-10" twist	13 5/8"	3/4"	3/8"	1 1/8"
	Mark V Stainless	RH 24"	6 1/2 lbs.	44"	5+1 in chamber	24" #1	1-10" twist	13 5/8"	3/4"	3/8"	1 1/8"
	Mark V Synthetic	RH 24"	6 1/2 lbs.	44"	5+1 in chamber	24" #1	1-10" twist	13 5/8"	3/4"	3/8"	1 1/8"
	Accumark	RH 24"	7 lbs.	44"	5+1 in chamber	24" #3	1-10" twist	13 5/8"	3/4"	3/8"	1 1/8"
	Accumark Ultra Lightweight	RH 24"	5 3/4 lbs.	44"	5+1 in chamber	24" #2	1-10" twist	13 5/8"	3/4"	3/8"	1 1/8"

MODEL 70 CUSTOM SHARPSHOOTER

- Pre-'64 type action
- Choice of round, round fluted, half-octagon, half-round or full-tapered octagon barrels
- Fancy Grade American walnut stock
- Hand-crowned, match-grade barrel
- Special Custom Shop serial numbers and proof stamp
- Inletted swivel bases
- Red 1/2" or 1" recoil pad, depending on caliber
- 70-point cut-checkering
- Hard case

For additional specifications, see table below.

MODEL 70 CUSTOM CLASSICS

The Model 70 Ultimate Classic features a stock configuration with slimmer, classic styling and special rounded forend. The design offers ideal eye-to-scope alignment without using a Monte Carlo or cheekpiece configuration. The fluted barrel option gives the barrel the stiffness of that of a larger diameter barrel with greatly reduced weight. Both blued steel or all-stainless-steel versions are offered. Other options include:

MODEL 70 CUSTOM MODELS

Suggested Retail Right Handed	Left Handed	Caliber	Magazine Capacity*	Barrel Length	Overall Length	Nominal Length of Pull	Nominal Drop at Comb	Nominal Drop at Heel	Nominal Weight (Lbs.)	Rate of Twist 1 Turn In	BOSS Options**	Features
CUSTOM TAKE-DOWN												
$2,495	—	375 H&H	3	24"	44-3/4"	13-1/2"	5/8"	5/8"	9	12"	N/A	H-S Pro-Series Stock
2,495	—	416 Rem. Mag.	3	24"	44-3/4"	13-1/2"	5/8"	5/8"	9	14"	N/A	H-S Pro-Series Stock
CUSTOM FLUTED TAKE-DOWN												
$2,495	—	300 Win. Mag.	3	26"	46-3/4"	13-1/2"	5/8"	5/8"	8-1/2	10"	N/A	H-S Pro Series Stock
2,495	—	7mm STW	3	26"	46-3/4"	13-1/2"	5/8"	5/8"	8-1/2	10"	N/A	H-S Pro Series Stock
ULTIMATE CLASSIC												
$2,386	$2,386	25-06 Rem.	5	24"	44-2/4"	13-3/4"	5/8"	9/16"	7-1/2	10"	YES	B&R
2,386	2,386	264 Win. Mag.	3	26	46-3/4	13-3/4	5/8	9/16	7-3/4	9	YES	B&R
2,386	2,386	270 Win.	5	24	44-3/4	13-3/4	5/8	9/16	7-1/2	10	YES	B&R
2,386	2,386	30-06 Spfld.	5	24	44-3/4	13-3/4	5/8	9/16	7-1/2	10	YES	B&R
2,386	2,386	35 Whelen	5	24	44-3/4	13-3/4	5/8	9/16	7-1/2	16	YES	B&R
2,386	2,386	7mm Rem. Mag.	3	26	46-3/4	13-3/4	5/8	9/16	7-3/4	9-1/2	YES	B&R
2,386	2,386	7mm STW	3	26	46-3/4	13-3/4	5/8	9/16	7-3/4	10	YES	
2,386	2,386	300 Win. Mag.	3	26	46-3/4	13-3/4	5/8	9/16	7-3/4	10	YES	B&R
2,386	2,386	300 H&H	3	26	46-3/4	13-3/4	5/8	9/16	7-3/4	10	N/A	
2,386	2,386	300 Weath. Mag.	3	26	46-3/4	13-3/4	5/8	9/16	7-3/4	10	YES	
2,386	2,386	338 Win. Mag.	3	26	46-3/4	13-3/4	5/8	9/16	7-3/4	10	YES	B&R
2,386	2,386	340 Weath. Mag.	3	26	46-3/4	13-3/4	5/8	9/16	7-3/4	10	N/A	
CLASSIC CUSTOM EXPRESS												
$2,512	2,512	375 H&H	3	24"	44-3/4"	13-3/4"	9/16"	13/16"	10	12"	N/A	Express Sights
2,512	2,512	416 Rem. Mag.	3	24	44-3/4	13-3/4	9/16	13/16	10	14	N/A	Express Sights
2,512	—	458 Win. Mag.	3	22	42-3/4	13-3/4	9/16	13/16	10	14	N/A	Express Sights
CLASSIC CUSTOM SPORTING SHARPSHOOTER II												
$1,875	1,875	7mm STW	3	26"	46-3/4"	13-1/2"	5/8"	3/4"	8-1/2	10"	N/A	F.S. Accu Block
1,875	1,875	300 Win. Mag.	3	26	46-3/4	13-1/2	5/8	3/4	8-1/2	10	N/A	B&R, F.S. Accu Block
CLASSIC CUSTOM SHARPSHOOTER II (STAINLESS STEEL)												
$1,994	—	22-250 Rem.	5	26"	46-3/4"	13-1/2"	7/16"	9/16"	11-1/4	14"	N/A	F.S. Accu Block
1,994	—	308 Win.	5	24	46-3/4	13-1/2	7/16	9/16	11	12	N/A	F.S. Accu Block
1,994	1,994	30-06 Spfld.	5	26	46-3/4	13-1/2	7/16	9/16	11-1/4	10	N/A	F.S. Accu Block
1,994	1,994	22-250 REM.	5	26	46-3/4	13-1/2	7/16	9/16	11-1/4	10	N/A	F.S. Accu Block

*For additional capacity, add one round in chamber. **BOSS available on round barrel models only. Drops are measured from center line of bore. Twist is right hand. Certain combinations of barrel type, stainless steel option, and stock grade vary with models. Details are available on request. B&R = Bases and rings included. N/A = BOSS accuracy system not available. Code numbers and specifications in red indicate a new product or new specifications for 1997.*

WINCHESTER BOLT-ACTION RIFLES

CLASSIC FEATHERWEIGHT ALL-TERRAIN

MODEL 70 CLASSIC MODELS WITH PRE-'64 TYPE ACTION

SUGGESTED RETAIL RIGHT HANDED	LEFT HANDED	CALIBER	MAGAZINE CAPACITY*	BARREL LENGTH	NOMINAL OVERALL LENGTH	NOMINAL LENGTH OF PULL	NOMINAL DROP AT COMB	NOMINAL DROP AT HEEL	NOMINAL WEIGHT (LBS.)	RATE OF TWIST I TURN IN	FEATURES
CLASSIC FEATHERWEIGHT (BLUED)											
$620	—	22-250 Rem.	5	22"	42"	13-1/2"	9/16"	7/8"	7	14"	Walnut Stock
620	—	243 Win.	5	22	42	13-1/2	9/16	7/8	7	10	Walnut Stock
620	—	6.5 x 55mm Swed.	5	22	42	13-1/2	9/16	7/8	7	8	Walnut Stock
620	—	308 Win.	5	22	42	13-1/2	9/16	7/8	7	12	Walnut Stock
620	—	7mm-08 Rem.	5	22	42	13-1/2	9/16	7/8	7	10	Walnut Stock
620	—	270 Win.	5	22	42-1/2	13-1/2	9/16	7/8	7-1/4	10	Walnut Stock
620	—	280 Rem.	5	22	42-1/2	13-1/2	9/16	7/8	7-1/4	10	Walnut Stock
620	—	30-06 Spfld.	5	22	42-1/2	13-1/2	9/16	7/8	7-1/4	10	Walnut Stock
CLASSIC FEATHERWEIGHT (STAINLESS)											
$716	—	22-250 Rem.	5	22"	42"	13-1/2	9/16	7/8"	7	14"	Walnut Stock
716	—	243 Win.	5	22	42	13-1/2	9/16	7/8	7	10	Walnut Stock
716	—	308 Win.	5	22	42	13-1/2	9/16	7/8	7	12	Walnut Stock
716	—	270 Win.	5	22	42-1/2	13-1/2	9/16	7/8	7-1/4	10	Walnut Stock
716	—	30-06 Spfld.	5	22	42-1/2	13-1/2	9/16	7/8	7-1/4	10	Walnut Stock
716	—	7mm Rem. Mag.	3	24	44-1/2	13-1/2	9/16	7/8	7-1/2	9-1/2	Walnut Stock
716	—	300 Win. Mag.	3	24	44-1/2	13-1/2	9/16	7/8	7-1/2	10	Walnut Stock
CLASSIC FEATHERWEIGHT ALL-TERRAIN™											
$672	—	270 Win.	5	22"	42-3/4"	13-3/4"	9/16"	13/16"	7	10"	Composite Stock
672	—	30-06 Spfld.	5	22	42-3/4	13-3/4	9/16	13/16	7	10	Composite Stock
672	—	7mm Rem. Mag.	3	24	44-3/4	13-3/4	9/16	13/16	7-1/4	9-1/2	Composite Stock
672	—	300 Win. Mag.	3	24	42-3/4	13-3/4	9/16	13/16	7-1/4	10	Composite Stock

For additional capacity, add one round in chamber when ready to fire. Drops are measured from center line of bore. Rate of twist: RH.

CLASSIC TRADITIONS

SUGGESTED RETAIL	CALIBER	MAGAZINE CAPACITY	BARREL LENGTH	OVERALL LENGTH	NOMINAL LENGTH OF PULL	NOMINAL DROP AT COMB	NOMINAL DROP AT HEEL	NOMINAL WEIGHT (LBS.)	RATE OF TWIST I TURN IN	FEATURES
MODEL 1886 LEVER ACTION HIGH GRADE										
$1,588	45-70	8	26"	45"	12-3/4"	2"	2-7/8"	9-1/4	20"	SG, FM, CBP, Rifle Sights, THS, TM
MODEL 1886 LEVER ACTION GRADE 1										
$996	45-70	8	26"	45"	12-3/4"	2"	2-7/8"	9-1/4	20"	SG, FM, CBP, Rifle Sights, THS, TM
MODEL 1892 LEVER ACTION GRADE 1										
$722	45 Colt	11	24"	45-1/4"	13"	1-1/2"	2-3/8"	6-1/4	38"	SG, FM, CBP, Rifle Sights, THS, TM
$722	.357 Mag.	11	24"	41-1/4"	13"	1-1/2"	2-2/3"	6-1/4	16"	SG, FM, CBP, Rifle Sights, THS, TM
$722	44-40 Win.	11	24"	41-1/4"	13"	1-1/2"	2-3/8"	6-1/4	36"	SG, FM, CBP, Rifle Sights, THS, TM
MODEL 63 SEMI-AUTO HIGH GRADE										
$1,083	22 Long Rifle	10	23"	39"	13-1/4"	1-3/8"	2-1/2"	6-1/4	16"	TM, Rifle Sights, Grooved Receiver
MODEL 63 SEMI-AUTO GRADE 1										
$678	22 Long Rifle	10	23"	39"	13-1/4"	1-3/8"	2-1/2"	6-1/4	16"	TM, Rifle Sights, Grooved Receiver
MODEL 52B BOLT ACTION GRADE 1										
$635	22 Long Rifle	5	24"	41-3/4"	13-1/2"	1-3/8"	2-5/16"	7	16"	DM, D&T
MODEL 1895 LEVER ACTION HIGH GRADE										
$1,360	30-06 Spfld.	4	24"	42	13-1/4"	2-7/8	3-5/8"	8	10	Rifle Sights, THS, TM
MODEL 1895 LEVER ACTION GRADE 1										
$909	270 Win.	4	24"	42"	13-1/4"	2-7/8"	3-5/8"	8	10"	Rifle Sights, THS, TM
909	30-06 Spfld.	4	24	42	13-1/4	2-7/8	3-5/8	8	10	Rifle Sights, THS, TM

WINCHESTER BOLT-ACTION RIFLES

MODEL 70 CLASSIC SUPER GRADE

SPECIFICATIONS & PRICES: MODEL 70 CLASSIC MODELS *(Continued on following page)*

Suggested Retail Right Handed	Left Handed	Caliber	Magazine Capacity*	Barrel Length	Nominal Overall Length	Nominal Length of Pull	Nominal Drop at Comb	Nominal Drop at Heel	Nominal Weight (Lbs.)	Rate of Twist 1 Turn In	Features
CLASSIC SUPER EXPRESS											
$865	$894	375 H&H Mag.	3	24"	44-3/4"	13-3/4"	9/16"	1 5/16"	8-1/2	12"	Sights, Walnut Stock
865	—	416 Rem. Mag.	3	24	44-3/4	13-3/4	9/16	1 5/16	8-1/2	14	Sights, Walnut Stock
865	—	458 Win. Mag.	3	22	42-3/4	13-3/4	9/16	1 5/16	8-1/4	14	Sights, Walnut Stock
CLASSIC SUPER GRADE											
$840	—	270 Win.	5	24"	44-3/4"	13-3/4"	9/16"	13/16"	7-3/4	10"	B&R, Walnut Stock
840	—	30-06 Spfld.	5	24	44-3/4	13-3/4	9/16	13/16	7-3/4	10	B&R, Walnut Stock
840	—	7mm Rem. Mag.	3	26	46-3/4	13-3/4	9/16	13/16	8	9-1/2	B&R, Walnut Stock
840	—	300 Win. Mag.	3	26	46-3/4	13-3/4	9/16	13/16	8	10	B&R, Walnut Stock
840	—	338 Win. Mag.	3	26	46-3/4	13-3/4	9/16	13/16	8	10	B&R, Walnut Stock
CLASSIC SPORTER (BLUED)											
$613	—	25-06 Rem.	5	24"	44-3/4"	13-3/4"	9/16"	13/16"	7-3/4	10"	Walnut Stock
613	—	264 Win. Mag.	3	26	46-3/4	13-3/4	9/16	13/16	8	9	Walnut Stock
613	$641	270 Win.	5	24	44-3/4	13-3/4	9/16	13/16	7-3/4	10	Walnut Stock
613	641	30-06 Spfld.	5	24	44-3/4	13-3/4	9/16	13/16	7-3/4	10	Walnut Stock
613	—	270 Weath. Mag.	3	26	46-3/4	13-3/4	9/16	13/16	8	10	Walnut Stock
613	641	7mm STW	3	26	46-3/4	13-3/4	9/16	13/16	8	9-1/2	Walnut Stock
613	641	7mm Rem. Mag.	3	26	46-3/4	13-3/4	9/16	13/16	8	9-1/2	Walnut Stock
613	641	300 Win. Mag.	3	26	46-3/4	13-3/4	9/16	13/16	8	10	Walnut Stock
613	—	300 Weath. Mag.	3	26	46-3/4	13-3/4	9/16	13/16	8	10	Walnut Stock
613	641	338 Win. Mag.	3	26	46-3/4	13-3/4	9/16	13/16	8	10	Walnut Stock

WINCHESTER BOLT-ACTION RIFLES

MODEL 70 BLACK SHADOW

SPECIFICATIONS & PRICES: MODEL 70 CLASSIC MODELS *(Cont.)*

Suggested Retail Right Handed	Left Handed	Caliber	Magazine Capacity*	Barrel Length	Nominal Overall Length	Nominal Length of Pull	Nominal Drop at Comb	Nominal Drop at Heel	Nominal Weight (Lbs.)	Rate of Twist I Turn In	Features
BOSS® CLASSIC STAINLESS (COMPOSITE)											
$788	—	270 Win.	5	24"	44-3/4"	13-3/4"	9/16"	13/16"	7-1/4	10"	Composite Stock
788	—	30-06 Spfld.	5	24	44-3/4	13-3/4	9/16	13/16	7-1/4	10	Composite Stock
788	—	7mm Rem. Mag.	3	26	46-3/4	13-3/4	9/16	13/16	7-1/2	9-1/2	Composite Stock
788	—	300 Win. Mag.	3	26	46-3/4	13-3/4	9/16	13/16	7-1/2	10	Composite Stock
788	—	338 Win. Mag.	3	26	46-3/4	13-3/4	9/16	13/16	7-1/2	10	Composite Stock
CLASSIC COMPACT											
$620	—	243 Win.	4	20"	39-1/2"	13"	9/16"	3/4"	6-1/2	10"	Walnut Stock
620	—	308 Win.	4	20	39-1/2	13	9/16	3/4	6-1/2	12	Walnut Stock
620	—	7mm-08 Rem.	4	20	39-1/2	13	9/16	3/4	6-1/2	9-1/2	Walnut Stock
CLASSIC LAREDO											
$764	—	7mm STW	3	26"	46-3/4"	13-3/4"	5/8"	1/2"	9-1/2	9-1/2"	Composite Stock
764	—	7mm Rem. Mag.	3	26	46-3/4	13-3/4	5/8	1/2	9-1/2	9-1/2	Composite Stock
764	—	300 Win. Mag.	3	26	46-3/4	13-3/4	5/8	1/2	9-1/2	10	Composite Stock
CLASSIC LAREDO FLUTED											
$894	—	7mm STW	3	26"	46-3/4"	13-3/4"	5/8"	1/2"	9-1/2	9-1/2"	Fluted Barrel/Composite Stock
894	—	7mm Rem. Mag.	3	26	46-3/4	13-3/4	5/8	1/2	9-1/2	9-1/2	Fluted Barrel/Composite Stock
894	—	300 Win. Mag.	3	26	46-3/4	13-3/4	5/8	1/2	9-1/2	10	Fluted Barrel/Composite Stock
BOSS® • CLASSIC LAREDO											
$879	—	7mm STW	3	25"	46-3/4"	13-3/4"	5/8"	1/2"	9-1/2	9-1/2"	Composite Stock
CLASSIC LAMINATED (STAINLESS)											
$735	—	270 Win.	5	24"	44-3/4"	13-3/4"	9/16"	13/16"	8	10"	Gray/Black Laminated Stock
735	—	30-06 Spfld.	5	24	44-3/4	13-3/4	9/16	13/16	8	10	Gray/Black Laminated Stock
735	—	7mm Rem. Mag.	3	26	46-3/4	13-3/4	9/16	13/16	8-1/4	9-1/2	Gray/Black Laminated Stock
735	—	300 Win. Mag.	3	26	46-3/4	13-3/4	9/16	13/16	8-1/4	10	Gray/Black Laminated Stock
735	—	338 Win. Mag.	3	26	46-3/4	13-3/4	9/16	13/16	8-1/4	10	Gray/Black Laminated Stock
CLASSIC CAMO (STAINLESS)											
$745	—	270 Win.	5	24"	44-3/4"	13-1/2"	9/16"	13/16"	7-1/4	10"	Mossy Oak® Composite Stock
745	—	30-06 Spfld.	5	24	44-3/4	13-1/2	9/16	13/16	7-1/4	10	Mossy Oak® Composite Stock
745	—	7mm Rem. Mag.	3	26	46-3/4	13-1/2	9/16	13/16	7-1/2	9-1/2	Mossy Oak® Composite Stock
745	—	300 Win. Mag.	3	26	46-3/4	13-1/2	9/16	13/16	7-1/2	10	Mossy Oak® Composite Stock

WINCHESTER BOLT-ACTION RIFLES

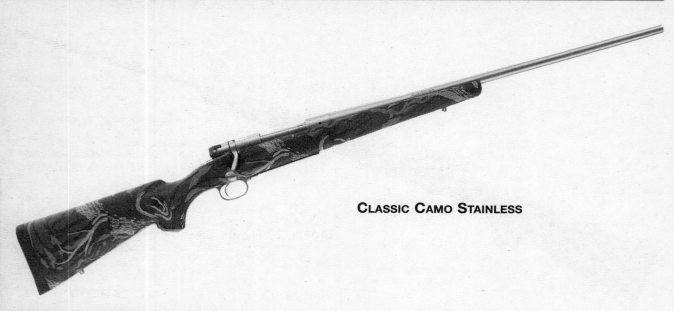

CLASSIC CAMO STAINLESS

MODEL 70 PUSH FEED MODELS

SUGGESTED RETAIL RIGHT HANDED	LEFT HANDED	CALIBER	MAGAZINE CAPACITY*	BARREL LENGTH	NOMINAL OVERALL LENGTH	NOMINAL LENGTH OF PULL	NOMINAL DROP AT COMB	NOMINAL DROP AT HEEL	NOMINAL WEIGHT (LBS.)	RATE OF TWIST I TURN IN	FEATURES
HEAVY VARMINT											
$764	—	220 Swift	5	26"	46"	13-1/2"	3/4"	1/2"	10-3/4	14"	Accu Block
764	—	222 Rem.	6	26	46	13-1/2	3/4	1/2	10-3/4	14	Accu Block
764	—	223 Rem.	6	26	46	13-1/2	3/4	1/2	10-3/4	9	Accu Block
764	—	22-250 Rem.	5	26	46	13-1/2	3/4	1/2	10-3/4	14	Accu Block
764	—	243 Win.	5	26	46	13-1/2	3/4	1/2	10-3/4	10	Accu Block
764	—	308 Win.	5	26	46	13-1/2	3/4	1/2	10-3/4	12	Accu Block
HEAVY VARMINT (FLUTED BARREL)											
$894	—	220 Swift	5	26"	46"	13-1/2"	3/4"	1/2"	10-1/4	14"	Accu Block
894	—	222 Rem.	6	26	46	13-1/2	3/4	1/2	10-1/4	14	Accu Block
894	—	223 Rem.	6	26	46	13-1/2	3/4	1/2	10-1/4	9	Accu Block
894	—	22-250 Rem.	5	26	46	13-1/2	3/4	1/2	10-1/4	14	Accu Block
894	—	243 Win.	5	26	46	13-1/2	3/4	1/2	10-1/4	10	Accu Block
894	—	308 Win.	5	26	46	13-1/2	3/4	1/2	10-1/4	12	Accu Block
BLACK SHADOW®											
$475	—	270 Win.	5	22"	42-3/4"	13-3/4"	9/16"	13/16"	7-1/4	10"	Composite Stock
475	—	30-06 Spfld.	5	22	42-3/4	13-3/4	9/16	13/16	7-1/4	10	Composite Stock
475	—	7mm Rem. Mag.	3	24	42-3/4	13-3/4	9/16	13/16	7-1/4	9-1/2	Composite Stock
475	—	300 Win. Mag.	3	22	42-3/4	13-3/4	9/16	13/16	7-1/4	10	Composite Stock
RANGER™											
$482	—	223 Rem.	6	22"	42"	13-1/2"	9/16"	7/8"	6-3/4	12"	Sights, Hardwood Stock
482	—	243 Win.	5	22	42	13-1/2	9/16	7/8	6-3/4	10	Sights, Hardwood Stock
482	—	270 Win.	5	22	42-1/2	13-1/2	9/16	7/8	7	10	Sights, Hardwood Stock
482	—	30-06 Spfld.	5	22	42-1/2	13-1/2	9/16	7/8	7	10	Sights, Hardwood Stock
482	—	7mm Rem. Mag.	3	24	44-1/2	13-1/2	9/16	7/8	7-1/2	9-1/2	Sights, Hardwood Stock
RANGER™ LADIES/YOUTH											
$482	—	223 Rem.	6	22"	41"	12-1/2"	3/4"	1"	6-1/2	12"	Sights, Hardwood Stock
482	—	243 Win.	5	22	41	12'1/2	3/4	1	6-1/2	10	Sights, Hardwood Stock
482	—	7mm 08 Rem.	5	22	41	12'1/2	3/4	1	6-1/2	9-1/2	Sights, Hardwood Stock
482	—	308 Win.	5	22	41	12'1/2	3/4	1	6-1/2	12	Sights, Hardwood Stock

WINCHESTER BOLT-ACTION RIFLES

For prices, see tables on preceeding pages

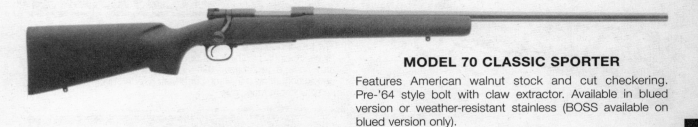

MODEL 70 CLASSIC SPORTER

Features American walnut stock and cut checkering. Pre-'64 style bolt with claw extractor. Available in blued version or weather-resistant stainless (BOSS available on blued version only).

MODEL 70 CLASSIC LAREDO

Features heavy 26" barrel H-S Precision gray synthetic stock with full-length "Pillar Plus Accu-Block."
Calibers: 7mm Rem. Mag., 7mm STW, 300 Win. Mag.
Overall length: 46.75". 3-shot capacity

WINCHESTER RANGER® BOLT-ACTION CENTERFIRE RIFLE

The Ranger Bolt-Action Rifle comes with an American hardwood stock, a wear-resistant satin walnut finish, ramp beadpost front sight, steel barrel, hinged steel magazine floorplate, three-position safety and engine-turned, anti-bind bolt. The receiver is drilled and tapped for scope mounting; accuracy is enhanced by thermoplastic bedding of the receiver. Barrel and receiver are brushed and blued.

WINCHESTER RANGER® LADIES'/YOUTH BOLT-ACTION CARBINE

Scaled-down design to fit the younger, smaller shooter, this carbine features anti-bind bolt design, jeweled bolt, three-position safety, contoured recoil pad, ramped bead front sight, semibuckhorn folding-leaf rear sight, hinged steel magazine floorplate, and sling swivels. Receiver is drilled and tapped for scope mounting.

WINCHESTER LEVER-ACTION CARBINES/RIFLES

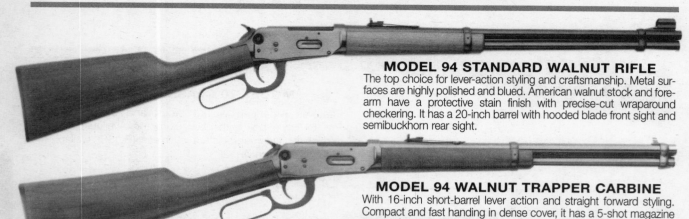

MODEL 94 STANDARD WALNUT RIFLE

The top choice for lever-action styling and craftsmanship. Metal surfaces are highly polished and blued. American walnut stock and forearm have a protective stain finish with precise-cut wraparound checkering. It has a 20-inch barrel with hooded blade front sight and semibuckhorn rear sight.

MODEL 94 WALNUT TRAPPER CARBINE

With 16-inch short-barrel lever action and straight forward styling. Compact and fast handing in dense cover, it has a 5-shot magazine capacity (9 in 45 Colt or 44 Rem. Mag./44 S&W Special). *Calibers:* 30-30 Win., 357 Mag., 45 Colt, and 44 Rem. Mag./44 S&W Special.

MODEL 94

Suggested Retail	Caliber	Magazine Capacity*	Barrel Length	Overall Length	Nominal Length of Pull	Nominal Drop at Comb	Nominal Drop at Heel	Nominal Weight (Lbs.)	Rate of Twist I Turn In	Features
BLACK SHADOW										
$348	30-30 Win.	4	24"	42-1/8"	13-3/4"	3/4"	3/4"	6-1/2	12"	Comp. Hunting Stock, Rifle Sights, SL
348	30-30 Win.	4	20	38-1/8	13-3/4	3/4	3/4	6-1/4	12	Comp. Hunting Stock, Rifle Sights, SL
348	44 Rem. Mag. & 44 S&W Spec.	5	20	38-1/8	13-3/4	3/4	3/4	6-1/4	38	Comp. Hunting Stock, Rifle Sights, SL
BLACK SHADOW®BIG BORE										
$360	444 Marlin	4	20"	38-1/8"	13-3/4"	3/4"	3/4"	6-1/2	38"	Comp. Hunting Stock, Rifle Sights, SL
RANGER COMPACT										
$320	30-30 Win.	5	16"	33-1/4"	12-1/2"	1-1/8"	1-3/4"	5-7/8	12"	Rifle Sights, SL
320	357 Mag.	9	16	33-1/4	12-1/2	1-1/8	1-3/4	5-7/8	16	Rifle Sights, SL
LEGACY										
$393	30-30 Win.	6	20"	38-1/8"	13-1/2"	1-1/8"	1-7/8"	6-1/2	12"	PG, Rifle Sights, SL
393	357 Mag.	11	20	38-1/8	13-1/2	1-1/8	1-7/8	6-1/2	16	PG, Rifle Sights, SL
393	45 Colt	11	20	38-1/8	13-1/2	1-1/8	1-7/8	6-1/2	38	PG, Rifle Sights, SL
393	44 Rem. Mag. & 44 S&W Spec.	11	20	38-1/8	13-1/2	1-1/8	1-7/8	6-1/2	38	PG, Rifle Sights, SL
407	30-30 Win.	7	24	42-1/8	13-1/2	1-1/8	1-7/8	6-3/4	12	PG, Rifle Sights, SL
407	357 Mag.	12	24	42-1/8	13-1/2	1-1/8	1-7/8	6-3/4	16	PG, Rifle Sights, SL
407	45 Colt	12	24	42-1/8	13-1/2	1-1/8	1-7/8	6-3/4	38	PG, Rifle Sights, SL
407	44 Rem. Mag. & 44 S&W Spec.	12	24	42-1/8	13-1/2	1-1/8	1-7/8	6-3/4	38	PG, Rifle Sights, SL
WALNUT										
$393	30-30 Win. Checkered	6	20"	38-1/8"	13-1/2"	1-1/8"	1-7/8"	6-1/4	12"	Rifle Sights, SL
363	30-30 Win. (Non-Checkered)	6	20"	38-1/8"	13-1/2	1-1/8	1-7/8	6-1/4	12	Rifle Sights, SL
RANGER										
$320	30-30 Win.	6	20"	38-1/8"	13-1/2"	1-1/8"	1-7/8"	6-1/4	12"	Rifle Sights, SL
376	30-30 Win. (with scope)	6	20"	38-1/8"	13-1/2	1-1/8	1-7/8	6-1/4	12	Rifle Sights/Scope, SL
TRAILS END										
$398	44-40 Win.	11	20"	38-1/8"	13-1/2"	1-1/8"	1-7/8"	6-1/2	36"	Rifle Sights, SL
398	357 Mag.	11	20	38-1/8	13-1/2	1-1/8	1-7/8	6-1/2	16	Rifle Sights, SL
398	44 Rem. Mag. & 44 S&W Spec.	11	20	38-1/8	13-1/2	1-1/8	1-7/8	6-1/2	38	Rifle Sights, SL
398	45 Colt	11	20	38-1/8	13-1/2	1-1/8	1-7/8	6-1/2	38	Rifle Sights, SL
420	357 Mag.	11	20	38-1/8	13-1/2	1-1/8	1-7/8	6-1/2	16	Rifle Sights, SL
420	44 Rem. Mag. & 44 S&W Spec.	11	20	38-1/8	13-1/2	1-1/8	1-7/8	6-1/2	38	Rifle Sights, SL
420	45 Colt	11	20	38-1/8	13-1/2	1-1/8	1-7/8	6-1/2	38	Rifle Sights, SL
BIG BORE										
$404	444 Marlin	6	20"	38-1/8"	13-1/2"	1-1/8"	1-7/8"	6-1/2	38	Rifle Sights, LL
404	307 Win.	6	20	38-1/8	13-1/2	1-1/8	1-7/8	6-1/2	12	Rifle Sights, SL
404	356 Win.	6	20	38-1/8	13-1/2	1-1/8	1-7/8	6-1/2	12	Rifle Sights, SL
TRAPPER										
$363	30-30 Win.	5	16"	34-1/4"	13-1/2"	1-1/8"	1-7/8"	6	12	Rifle Sights, SL
363	44 Rem. Mag. & 44 S&W Spec.	9	16	34-1/4	13-1/2	1-1/8	1-7/8	6	38	Rifle Sights, SL
363	357 Mag.	9	16	34-1/4	13-1/2	1-1/8	1-7/8	6	16	Rifle Sights, SL
363	45 Colt	9	16	34-1/4	13-1/2	1-1/8	1-7/8	6	38	Rifle Sights, SL
WRANGLER										
$384	30-30 Win.	5	16"	34-1/4"	13-1/2"	1-1/8"	1-7/8"	6	12"	Rifle Sights, LL
404	44 Rem. Mag. & 44 S&W Spec.	9	16	34-1/4	13-1/2	1-1/8	1-7/8	6	38	Rifle Sights, LL

*Bushnell 4X32 scope and see-thru mounts available.

WINCHESTER RIFLES

LEVER ACTION

MODEL 94 RANGER

MODEL 94 RANGER is an economical version of the Model 94. Lever action is smooth and reliable. In 30-30 Winchester, the rapid-firing six-shot magazine capacity provides two more shots than most other centerfire hunting rifles. *Also available:* RANGER COMPACT in 30-30 Win. and 357 Mag. See also Specifications table.

Price: $320.00
   With Scope 376.00

MODEL 94 BIG-BORE WALNUT

Winchester's powerful 307 and 356 hunting calibers combined with maximum lever-action power and angled ejection provide hunters with improved performance and economy. Now available in 444 Marlin. See also Specification table.

Price: $404.00

MODEL 94 TRAILS END

SPECIFICATIONS
Calibers: 357 Mag., 44 Rem. Mag., 45 Colt. *Capacity:* 11 shot magazine. *Barrel length:* 20". *Overall length:* 38 $1/8$". *Weight:* 6.5 lbs. Features include rifle sights and standard loop or large loop. Now available in 44-40 Win.

Prices:
   Standard Loop Lever $398.00
   Large Loop Lever 420.00

MODEL 94 LEGACY
Standard Loop Lever

SPECIFICATIONS
Calibers: 30-30 Win., 357 Mag., 44 Rem. Mag., 45 Colt. *Capacity:* 6 shots (30-30 Win.); 11 shots (other calibers); add 1 shot for 24" barrel. *Barrel length:* 20" or 24". *Overall length:* 38 1/8" w/20" barrel. *Weight:* 6.5 lbs. w/20" bbl.; 6.75 w/24" bbl. Features include pistol-grip stock, rifle sights and standard loop lever.

Price: $393.00
   w/24" barrel 407.00

WINCHESTER RIFLES

MODEL 9422 LEVER-ACTION RIMFIRE RIFLES

Positive lever action and bolt design ensure feeding and chambering from any shooting position. The bolt face is T-slotted to guide the cartridge with complete control from magazine to chamber. Receivers are grooved for scope mounting. Stock and forearm are checkered American walnut with high-luster finish and straight-grip design. Internal parts are carefully finished for smoothness of action.

MODEL 9422 WALNUT

MODEL 9422 WALNUT MAGNUM gives exceptional accuracy at longer ranges than conventional 22 rifles. It is designed specifically for the 22 WMR and holds 11 cartridges.

Otherwise same basic specifications as the 9422 Walnut. Considered one of the world's finest production sporting arms, this lever-action holds 21 Short, 17 Long or 15 Long Rifle rimfire cartridges. *Barrel length:* 20.5". *Overall length:* 37 1/8". *Weight:* 6.25 lb. Features rifle sights.

MODEL 9422 WINCAM™ MAGNUM features laminated non-glare, green-shaded stock and forearm. American hardwood stock is bonded to withstand all climates. Holds 11 22 WMR cartridges and has same basic specifications as the 9422 Walnut Magnum.

MODEL 9422 WINTUFF™ RIFLE

Includes all features and specifications of standard Model 94 plus tough laminated hardwood styled for the brush-gunning hunter who wants good concealment and a carbine that can stand up to all kinds of weather. In standard and magnum rimfire.

MODEL 9422

Suggested Retail	Caliber	Magazine Capacity*	Barrel Length	Overall Length	Length Of Pull	Nominal Drop At Comb	Nominal Drop At Heel	Nominal Weight (Lbs.)	Rate Of Twist I Turn In	Features
WINTUFF™										
$407	22 Rimfire	21 Short, 17 Long, 15 Long Rifle	20-1/2"	37-1/8"	13-1/2"	1-1/8"	1-7/8"	6-1/4	16"	R. Sights
424	22 WMR	11	20-1/2	37-1/8	13-1/2	1-1/8	1-7/8	6-1/4	16	R. Sights
LEGACY										
$436	22 Rimfire	21 Short, 17 Long, 15 Long Rifle	22-1/2"	39-1/8"	13-1/2"	1-1/8"	1-7/8"	6	16"	Pistol Grip Stock, R.S.
WALNUT										
$407	22 Rimfire	21 Short, 17 Long, 15 Long Rifle	20-1/2"	37-1/8"	13-1/2"	1-1/8"	1-7/8"	6	16"	R. Sights
424	22 WMR	11	20-1/2	37-1/8	13-1/2	1-1/8	1-7/8	6	16	R. Sights
429	22 Rimfire	21 Short, 17 Long, 15 Long Rifle	20-1/2	37-1/8	13-1/2	1-1/8	1-7/8	6	16	R. Sights, Large Loop
HIGH GRADE SERIES II										
$504	22 Rimfire	21 Short, 17 Long, 15 Long Rifle	20-1/2"	37/1/8"	13-1/2"	1-1/8"	1-7/8"	6	16"	R. Sights
25TH ANNIVERSARY EDITION GRADE I										
$606	22 Rimfire	21 Short, 17 Long, 15 Long Rifle	20-1/2"	37-1/8"	13-1/2"	1-1/8"	1-7/8"	6-1/4	16"	R. Sights
TRAPPER										
$407	22 Rimfire	15 Short, 12 Long, 11 Long Rifle	16-1/2"	33-1/8"	13-1/2"	1-1/8"	1-7/8"	5-3/4	16"	R. Sights
424	22 WMR	8	16-1/2	33-1/8	13-1/2	1-1/8	1-7/8	5-3/4	16	R. Sights

Shotguns

American Arms	324		Magtech	360
American Arms/Franchi	327		Marlin	360
AYA	328		Marocchi	362
Benelli	330		Merkel	363
Beretta	333		Mossberg	365
Bernardelli	339		New England Firearms	372
Brolin	340		Parker Reproductions	374
Browning	341		Perazzi	375
Charles Daly	347		Piotti	377
Dakota Arms	350		Remington	378
A.H. Fox	350		Rizzini	387
Francotte	351		Ruger	388
Garbi	351		Savage	389
Harrington & Richardson	352		Sigarms	389
Heckler & Koch/Fabarms	354		SKB	390
Ithaca	356		Stoeger IGA	393
KBI/Armscor	357		Weatherby	397
Krieghoff	358		Winchester	399

*For addresses and phone/fax numbers of manufacturers and distributors included in this section, please turn to **DIRECTORY OF MANUFACTURERS AND SUPPLIERS** on page 558.*

AMERICAN ARMS SHOTGUNS

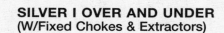

SILVER I OVER AND UNDER
(W/Fixed Chokes & Extractors)

Features polished white frame w/outline engraving; blued trigger guard, top lever and forward latch; radiused rubber recoil pad.

SILVER II
(W/Choke Tubes & Automatic Selective Ejectors)

Same features as Silver I, but with more refined engraving. Models in 16, 20 and .410 gauge have fixed chokes.

SILVER SPORTING
(Ported, w/Choke Tubes)

SPECIFICATIONS

MODEL	GAUGE	BBL. LENGTH	CHAMBER	CHOKES	AVG. WEIGHT	PRICES
Silver I	12	26" – 28"	3"	IC/M-M/F	6 lbs. 15 oz.	$625.00
	20	26" – 28"	3"	IC/M-M/F	6 lbs. 12 oz.	625.00
	28	26"	2.75"	IC/M	5 lbs. 14 oz.	650.00
	.410	26"	3"	IC/M	6 lbs. 6 oz.	650.00
Silver II*	12	26" – 28"	3"	CT-3	6 lbs. 15 oz.	750.00
	16	26"	2.75"	IC/M	6 lbs. 13 oz.	750.00
	20	26"	3"	CT-3	6 lbs. 12 oz.	750.00
	28	26"	2.75"	IC/M	5 lbs. 14 oz.	775.00
	.410	26"	3"	IC/M	6 lbs. 6 oz.	775.00
Sporting**	12	28" – 30"	2.75"	CTS	7 lbs. 6 oz.	925.00
	20	28"	3"	CTS	7 lbs. 3 oz.	925.00

CT-3 Choke Tubes IC/M/F Cast Off = $^3/_8$" CTS = SK/SK/IC/M   Silver I and II: Pull = 14 $^1/_8$"; Drop at Comb = 1 $^3/_8$"; Drop at Heel = 2 $^3/_8$"
Silver I and II: Pull = 14 $^1/_4$"; Drop at Comb = 1 $^1/_2$"; Drop at Heel = 2 $^1/_2$"   * 2 Barrel Set: **$115.00** **Silver Upland Lite (12 and 20 ga.) = $925.00**

AMERICAN ARMS SHOTGUNS

BRITTANY SIDE-BY-SIDE

SPECIFICATIONS
Gauges: 12, 20
Chamber: 3"
Chokes: CT-3

Barrel Length: 26"
Weight: 6 lbs. 7 oz. (20 ga.); 6 lbs. 15 oz. (12 ga.)
Features: Engraved case-colored frame; single selective trigger with top tang selector; automatic selective ejectors; manual safety; hard chrome-lined barrels; walnut English-style straight stock and semi-beavertail forearm w/cut checkering and oil-rubbed finish; ventilated rubber recoil pal; and choke tubes with key
Price: $860.00

GENTRY SIDE-BY-SIDE

Features boxlocks with engraved English-style scrollwork on side plates; one-piece, steel-forged receiver; chrome barrels; manual thumb safety; independent floating firing pin.

SPECIFICATIONS
Gauges: 12, 20, 28, .410
Chamber: 3" (except 28 gauge, 2.75")

Barrel Lengths: 26", choked IC/M (all gauges; 28", choked M/F (12 and 20 gauges)
Weight: 6 lbs. 15 oz. (12 ga.); 6 lbs. 7 oz. (20 and .410 ga.); 6 lbs. 5 oz. (28 ga.)
Drop At Comb: 1 $^3/_8$"
Drop At Heel: 2 $^3/_8$"
Other Features: Fitted recoil pad; flat matted rib; walnut pistol-grip stock and beavertail forend with hand-checkering; gold front sight bead
Prices:
   12 or 20 ga. $735.00
   28 or .410 ga. 775.00

FRANCHI MODEL 610 VARIOPRESS SYSTEM

SPECIFICATIONS
Gauge: 12 ga. semiauto gas-operated
Barrel Lengths: 26" and 28"
Overall Length: 47.5" (26" barrel)

Weight: 7 lbs. 2 oz.
Length Of Pull: 14.25"
Drop At Comb: 1.5"
Drop At Heel: 2.5"
Finish: Alloy frame w/non-glare finish
Features: Patented Variopress System; shoots all shot-shells up to 3"; chrome-lined barrel w/Franchoke system (IC-M-F); pistol-grip stock
Price: $750.00
   w/Engraved Receiver 795.00

SHOTGUNS

AMERICAN ARMS SHOTGUNS

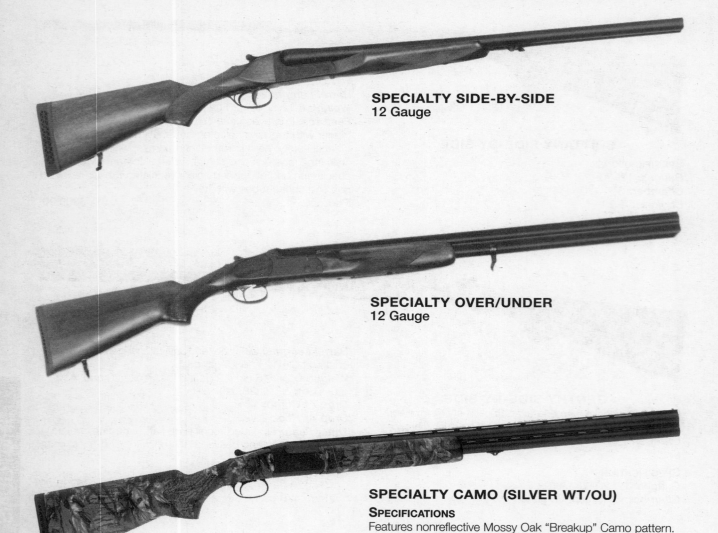

SPECIALTY SIDE-BY-SIDE
12 Gauge

SPECIALTY OVER/UNDER
12 Gauge

SPECIALTY CAMO (SILVER WT/OU)

SPECIFICATIONS

Features nonreflective Mossy Oak "Breakup" Camo pattern. Specifications same as WS/OU 12 ga., including auto selective ejectors and AA1 choke tubes (IC-M-F). *Price* on request.

SPECIFICATIONS

MODEL	GAUGE	BBL. LENGTH	CHAMBER	CHOKES	AVG. WGT.	PRICES
WT/OU	10	26"	3.5"	CT-2	9 lbs. 10 oz.	$995.00
WS/OU	12	28"	3.5"	CT-3	7 lbs. 2 oz.	775.00
WT/OU Camo	12	26"	3.5"	CT-3	7 lbs.	850.00
TS/SS	12	26"	3.5"	CT-3	7 lbs. 6 oz.	785.00

CT-3 Choke Tubes IC/M/F. CT-2 = Choke tubes F/F. Drop at Comb = 1 1/8"; Drop at Heel = 2 3/8"

AMERICAN ARMS/FRANCHI

FALCONET 2000 OVER/UNDER

SPECIFICATIONS
Gauge: 12 ga. (2.75" chamber)
Barrel Length: 26"
Overall Length: 43 1/8"
Weight: 6 lbs. 2 oz.
Length Of Pull: 14.25"
Drop At Comb: 1.5" *Drop At Heel:* 2.5"

Finish: Select European walnut stock and forend w/fine-line checkering
Features: Gold-plated gamebird scene engraved on frame; chrome- lined barrels w/Franchoke system; safety and barrel selector on top tang; ventilated top rib and separated barrels; hard case standard
Price:. $1,375.00

SPORTING 2000

SPECIFICATIONS
Gauge: 12 ga. *Choke:* Franchoke (F-1M-M-1C-SK)
Barrel Length: 28"
Overall Length: 45 3/8"
Length Of Pull: 14.25"
Drop At Comb: 1 3/8" *Drop At Heel:* 2.25"
Weight: 7 lbs. 12 oz. *Stock:* Select European walnut

stock and forend w/fine-line checkering
Features: Gold-plated gamebird scene engraved on frame; chrome- lined barrels w/Franchoke system; safety and barrel selector on top tang; ventilated top rib and separated barrels; hard case standard; ventilated 10mm rib w/white bead front sight
Price:. $1,495.00

MODEL 48/AL
RECOIL OPERATED SEMIAUTOMATIC

SPECIFICATIONS
Gauges: 12 ga. *Action:* Franchoke (F-1M-M-1C-SK)
Chamber: 12 ga. *Barrel Lengths:* 28"
Choke: 45 3/8" *Weight:* 7 lbs. 12 oz.

Length Of Pull: 14.25"
Drop At Comb: 1 3/8" *Drop At Heel:* 2.25"
Price:. $649.00
    In 28 gauge 725.00

ALCIONE 2000 SX O/U (not shown)
SPECIFICATIONS
Gauges: 12 ga. (2.75" chamber)
Choke: Franchoke (F-M-1C)
Barrel Length: 28"
Overall Length: 45 1/8" *Weight:* 7 lbs. 4 oz.
Length Of Pull: 14.25" *Drop At Comb:* 1.5"

Drop At Heel: 2.5"
Stock: Select European walnut stock and forend w/fine-line checkering
Features: Engraved chrome steel frame; chrome-lined barrels; safety and barrel selector on top tang; ventilated 10mm top rib and separated barrels
Price:. $1,895.00

AYA SHOTGUNS

SIDELOCK SHOTGUNS

AYA sidelock shotguns are fitted with London Holland & Holland system sidelocks, double triggers with articulated front trigger, automatic safety and ejectors, cocking indicators, bushed firing pins, replaceable hinge pins and chopper lump barrels. Stocks are of figured walnut with hand-cut checkering and oil finish, complete with a metal oval on the buttstock for engraving of initials. Exhibition grade wood is available as are many special options, including a true left-hand version and self-opener. Available from Armes de Chasse (see Directory of Manufacturers and Suppliers). **Barrell lengths:** 26", 27", 28", 29" and 32". **Weight:** 5 to 7 pounds, depending on gauge.

MODEL	Prices
MODEL 1: Sidelock in 12 and 20 ga. w/special engraving and exhibition quality wood	**$6,895.00**
DELUXE	.7,495.00
MODEL 2: Sidelock in 12, 16, 20, 28 ga. and .410 bore	.3,295.00
MODEL 53: Sidelock in 12, 16 and 20 ga. with 3 locking lugs and side clips	.4,602.00
MODEL 56: Sidelock in 12 ga. only with 3 locking lugs and side clips	.7,595.00
MODEL XXV/SL: Sidelock in 12 and 20 ga. only w/Churchill-type rib	.3,892.00

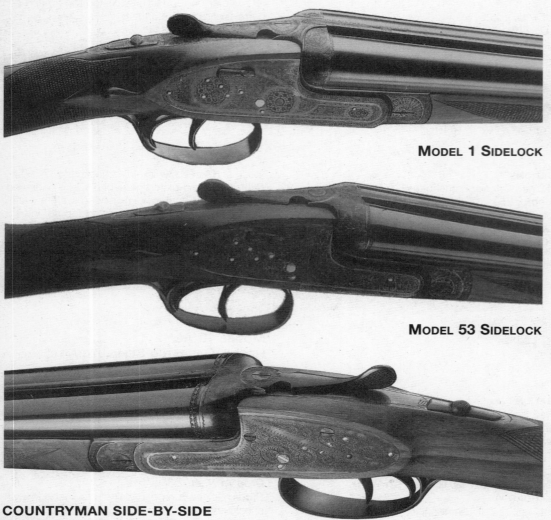

MODEL 1 SIDELOCK

MODEL 53 SIDELOCK

COUNTRYMAN SIDE-BY-SIDE

SPECIFICATIONS
Gauges: 12 and 10 **Barrel lengths:** 26", 27" or 28" **Length of pull:** up to 15" **Features:** Selective ejectors; automatic safety; Cordura covered case; hand-detachable side locks; disc set starters; chopper lump barrels; hand-rubbed select Spanish walnut stock with hand-cut checkering.
Price: .$2,295.00

AYA SHOTGUNS

BOXLOCK SHOTGUNS

AYA boxlocks use the Anson & Deeley system with double locking lugs, incorporating detachable cross pin and separate plate to allow easy access to the firing mechanism. Barrels are chopper lump, firing pins are bushed, plus automatic safety and ejectors and metal oval for engraving of initials. Other features include disc set strikers, replaceable hinge pin, split bottom plate.
Barrel lengths: 26", 27" and 28"

Weight: 5 to 7 pounds, depending on gauge.

MODEL	Price
MODEL XXV BOXLOCK: 12 and 20 gauge only	$2,635.00
MODEL 4 BOXLOCK: 12, 16, 20, 28, .410 ga.	1,695.00
MODEL 4 DELUXE BOXLOCK: Same gauges as above	2,995.00

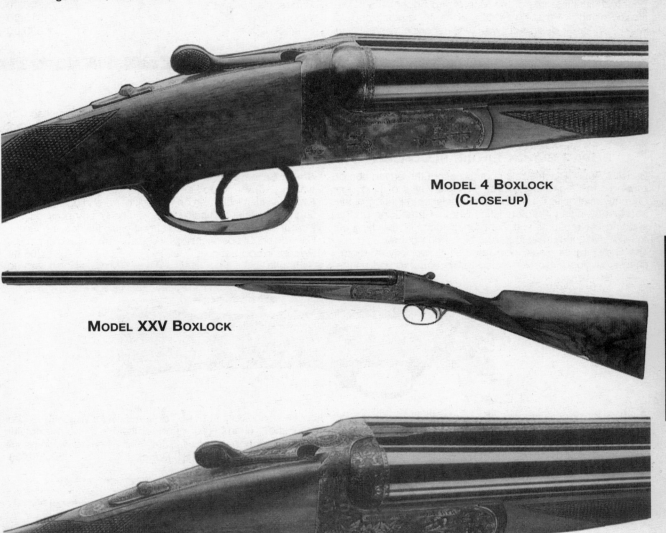

MODEL 4 BOXLOCK (CLOSE-UP)

MODEL XXV BOXLOCK

MODEL XXV BOXLOCK

SHOTGUNS

BENELLI SHOTGUNS

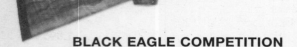

BLACK EAGLE COMPETITION

Benelli's Black Eagle Competition shotgun combines the best technical features of the Montefeltro Super 90 and the classic design of the old SL 80 Series. It comes standard with a specially designed two-piece receiver of steel and aluminum, adding to its reliability and resistance to wear. A premium high-gloss walnut stock and gold-plated trigger are included, along with a Montefeltro rotating bolt. The Black Eagle Competition has no complex cylinders and pistons to maintain. Features include etched receiver, competition stock and mid-rib bead.

Prices: Camo Synthetic $1,300.00
Wood Satin 1,215.00
Synthetic 1,200.00

SUPER BLACK EAGLE SLUG GUN

Benelli's Super Black Eagle shotgun offers the advantage of owning one 12-gauge auto that fires every type of 12 gauge currently available. It has the same balance, sighting plane and fast-swinging characteristics whether practicing on the sporting clays c0urse with light target loads or touching off a 3 1/2" Magnum steel load at a high-flying goose.
The Super Black Eagle also features a specially strengthened steel upper receiver mated to the barrel to endure the toughest shotgunning. The alloy lower receiver keeps the overall weight low, making this model as well balanced and point-able as possible. Distinctive high-gloss or satin walnut stocks and a choice of full finish or blued metal add up to a universal gun for all shotgun hunting and sports.

Stock: Satin walnut (28") with drop adjustment kit; high-gloss walnut (26") with drop adjustment kit; or synthetic stock
Finish: Matte black finish on receiver, barrel and bolt (28"); blued finish on receiver and barrel (26") with bolt mirror polished
Features: Montefeltro rotating bolt with dual locking lugs
For additional specifications, see table on folllowing page.
Prices: Wood Satin $1,255.00
Synthetic 1,245.00

LEGACY

Features lower alloy receiver and upper steel receiver cover and interchangeable barrel with mid-point bead and red light-gathering bar front sight. Also Benelli's inertia recoil operating system; cartridge drop lever (to indicate "hammer-cocked condition; set of 5 choke tubes for use with lead or steel shot); chambered round removable without emptying the magazine; handles all 2 3/4" and 3" shells within gauge with over 1 1/2 oz. of shot. *Price:* $1,320.00

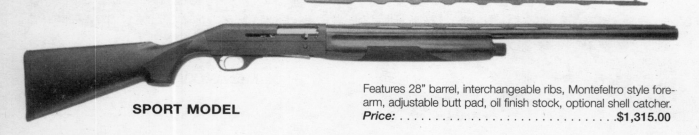

SPORT MODEL

Features 28" barrel, interchangeable ribs, Montefeltro style fore-arm, adjustable butt pad, oil finish stock, optional shell catcher.
Price: $1,315.00

BENELLI SHOTGUNS

EXECUTIVE TYPE II

EXECUTIVE SERIES

ENGRAVED I	. . . .$4,950.00
ENGRAVED II	. . . . 5,600.00
ENGRAVED III	. . . . .6,550.00

BENELLI SHOTGUN SPECIFICATIONS

DESCRIPTION	GAUGE	BARREL LENGTH CHAMBER	STOCK	RECEIVER	CHOKE FINISH	SIGHTS	MAGAZINE CAPACITY*	OVERALL LENGTH	WEIGHT (POUNDS)
Super Black Eagle-Ltd. Ed.	12/3.5"	26"Vent. Rib	Satin Walnut	Engraved	S,IC,M,IM,F**	Mid & Front Red Bar	3	47.63"	7.4
Super Black Eagle	12/3.5"	28"Vent. Rib	Satin Walnut	Matte	S,IC,M,IM,F**	Mid & Front Red Bar	3	49.63"	7.5
Super Black Eagle	12/3.5"	26"Vent. Rib	Satin Walnut	Blued	S,IC,M,IM,F**	Mid & Front Red Bar	3	47.63"	7.4
Super Black Eagle	12/3.5"	26"Vent. Rib	Satin Walnut	Matte	S,IC,M,IM,F**	Mid & Front Red Bar	3	47.63"	7.4
Super Black Eagle	12/3.5"	28" Vent. Rib	Synthetic	Matte	S,IC,M,IM,F**	Mid & Front Red Bar	3	49.63"	7.5
Super Black Eagle	12/3.5"	26"Vent. Rib	Synthetic	Matte	S,IC,M,IM,F**	Mid & Front Red Bar	3	47.63"	7.4
Super Black Eagle	12/3.5"	24" Vent. Rib	Synthetic	Matte	S,IC,M,IM,F**	Mid & Front Red Bar	3	45.63"	7.3
Super Black Eagle	12/3.5"	28"Vent. Rib	Camo	Camo	S,IC,M,IM,F**	Mid & Front Red Bar	3	49.63"	7.5
Super Black Eagle	12/3.5"	26"Vent. Rib	Camo	Camo	S,IC,M,IM,F**	Mid & Front Red Bar	3	47.63"	7.4
Super Black Eagle	12/3.5"	24"Vent. Rib	Camo	Camo	S,IC,M,IM,F**	Mid & Front Red Bar	3	45.63"	7.3
Super Black Eagle SLUG	12/3"	24"	Matte	Matte	Rifled Barrel	Drilled/Tapper	3	45.63"	7.6
Super Black Eagle SLUG	12/3"	24"	Matte	Matte	Rifled Barrel	Drilled Tapped	3	45.63"	7.6
Montefeltro	12/3"	28"Vent. Rib	Satin Walnut	Blued	S,IC<M,IM,F**	Front Red Bar	4	49.5"	7.1
Montefeltro	12/2"	26"Vent. Rib	Satin Walnut	Blued	S,IC<M,IM,F**	Front Red Bar	4	47.5"	6.9
Montegeltro	12/3"	24"Vent. Rib	Satin Walnut	Blued	S,IC<M,IM,F**	Front Red Bar	4	45.5"	6.8
Montefeltro	12/3"	28"Vent. Rib	Satin Walnut	Blued	S,IC<M,IM,F**	Front Red Bar	4	49.5"	7.1
Montefeltro	12/3"	26"Vent. Rib	Satin Walnut	Blued	S,IC<M,IM,F**	Front Red Bar	4	47.5"	6.9
Montefeltro	20/3"	26"Vent. Rib	Satin Walnut	Blued	S,IC<M,IM,F**	Mid & Front Red Bar	4	47.5"	6.0
Montefeltro- Left Hand	20/3"	24"Vent. Rib	Satin Walnut	Blued	S,IC<M,IM,F**	Mid & Front Red Bar	4	45.5"	6.0
Montefeltro - Left Hand	20/3"	26"Vent. Rib	Camo/Wood	Blued	S,IC<M,IM,F**	Mid & Front Red Bar	4	45.5"	6.0
Legacy	12/3"	28"Vent. Rib	Satin Walnut	Nickel	S,IC,M,IM,F**	Mid & Front Red Bar	4	49.63"	7.5
Legacy	12/3"	26"Vent. Rib	Satin Walnut	Nickel	S,IC,M,IM,F**	Mid & Front Red Bar	4	47.63"	7.4
Executive Type I	12/3"	All Vent. Rib	All are Select	Engraved	S,IC,M,IM,F**	Mid & Front Red Bar	4		
Type II		in 28", 26"	Grade	to Level	S,IC,M,IM,F**	Mid & Front Red Bar	4		
Type III		26" or 21"	Satin Walnut	I, II, III	S,IC,M,IM,F**	Mid & Front Red Bar			
Sport - Supplied with 2 Vent Ribs	12/3"	28"Vent. Rib	Satin Walnut	Matte	S,IC,M,IM,F**	Mid & Front Red Bar	4	49.63"	7.1
Sport - Supplied with 2 Vent Ribs	12/3"	26"Vent. Rib	Satin Walnut	Matte	S,IC,M,IM,F**	Mid & Front Red Bar	4		
M1 Filed	12/3"	28"Vent. Rib	Satin Walnut	Matte	S,IC,M,IM,F**	Front Red Bar	3	49.5"	7.4
M1 Field	12/3"	28"Vent. Rib	Synthetic	Matte	S,IC,M,IM,F**	Front Red Bar	3	49.5"	7.4
M1 Field	12/3"	26" Vent. Rib	Satin Walnut	Matte	S,IC,M,IM,F**	Front Red Bar	3	47.5"	7.3
M1 Field	12/3"	26"Vent. Rib	Synthetic	Matte	S,IC,M,IM,F**	Front Red Bar	3	45.5"	7.3
M1 Field	12/3"	24"Vent. Rib	Synthetic	Mate	S,IC,M,IM,F**	Front Red Bar	3	42.5"	7.2
M1 Field	12/3"	21"Vent. Rib	Synthetic	Matte	S,IC,M,IM,F**	Front Red Bar	3	45.5"	7.0
M1 Field	12/3"	28"Vent Rib	Camo	Camo	S,IC,M,IM,F**	Front Red Bar	3	49.5	7.4
M1 Field	12/3"	26"Vent. Rib	Camo	Camo	S,IC,M,IM,F**	Front Red Bar	3	47.5"	7.3
M1 Field	12/3"	24"Vent. Rib	Camo	Camo	S,IC,M,IM,F**	Front Red Bar	3	45.5"	7.2
M1 Field	12/3"	21" Vent. Rib	Camo	Camo	S,IC,M,IM,F**	Front Red Bar	3	42.5"	7.0
M1 Field - SLUG	12/3"	24"	Synthetic	Matte	Rifled Barrel	Drilled/Tapped	3	45.63"	7.6
M1 Practical	12/2"	26"	Synthetic	Matte	IC, M, F**	Military Ghost Ring	9	47.63"	7.6
M1 Tactical M	12/3"	18.5"	Synthetic	Matte	IC ,M, F**	Military Ghost Ring	s5	39.75"	7.1
M1 Tactical	12/3"	18.5"	Synthetic - PG	Matte	IC, M, F**	Ghost Ring	5	39.75"	7.0
M1 Tactical	12/2"	18.5"	Synthetic	Matte	IC, M, F**	Rifle Sights	s5	39.75"	6.7
M1 Entry	12/3"	14"	Synthetic	Matte	Cylinder Bore	Rifle Sights	5	35.5"	6.6
M1 Entry	12/3"	14"	Synthetic - PG	Matte	Cylinder Bore	Ghost Ring	5	35.5"	6.7
M3 Auto/Pump	12/3"	19.75"	Synthetic	Matte	Cylinder Bore	Rifle Sights	5	41"	7.2
M3 Auto/Pump	12/3"	19.75"	Synthetic	Matte	Cylinder Bore	Ghost Ring	5	41"	7.4

BENELLI SHOTGUNS

MODEL M1 SUPER 90 SERIES

M1 SUPER 90 FIELD W/REALTREE

The M1 Field 12-gauge shotgun combines the M1 Super 90 receiver with a choice of polymer or walnut stocks, including a camouflaged model with an Xtra Brown pattern sealed on the matte finish metal and polymer stock. Available in 21", 24", 26" or 28" barrels with vent rib.

M1 SUPER 90 FIELD W/REALTREE
Camo finish, camo polymer buttstock
and forearm $990.00

MODEL M1 SUPER 90 FIELD

Also available:
MODEL M1 SUPER 90 TACTICAL w/18 1/2" bbl. . . .$875.00
    With pistol-grip stock, ghost ring sights 950.00
PRACTICAL SUPER 90, 26" barrel, ghost ring sight,
    synthetic stock 1,175.00
MODEL M1 SUPER 90 FIELD (polymer stock)
    w/21", 24", 26", 28" bbl. 900.00
MODEL M3 SUPER 90 PUMP/AUTO SERIES
    Standard stock, 19 3/4" barrel 1,040.00
    w/Ghost Ring Sight and standard stock 1,080.00

MONTEFELTRO SUPER 90 VENT RIB

Prices:
12 Ga.—24", 26", or 28" Barrel
    (20 ga.—24" or 26" barrel only) $925.00
Left Hand w/26" or 28" Barrel. 945.00
20 ga. w/Camo Wood, 26" VR 1,010.00

See table on the preceding page for all Benelli specifications.

BERETTA SHOTGUNS

SERIES 682 GOLD COMPETITION TRAP OVER/UNDER

MODEL 682 GOLD TRAP w/ADJUSTABLE STOCK

These 12 gauge Model 682 Trap guns feature adjustable gold-plated, single-selective sliding trigger; low-profile improved boxlock action; manual safety w/barrel selector; 2.75" chambers; auto ejector; competition recoil pad buttplate; hand-checkered walnut stock.
Weight: Approx. 8 lbs. **Barrel Lengths/Chokes:** 30 Imp. Mod./Full (Black); 30" or 32" Mobilchoke® (Black); Top Single 32" or 34" Mobilchoke®; "Live Bird" (Flat rib, Silver);

Combo: 30" or 32" Mobilchoke® (Top), 30" IM/F (Top), 32" Mobilchoke® (Mono), 30" or 32" Mobilchoke® ported
Prices:

MODEL 682 GOLD TRAP	$2,910.00
MODEL 682 GOLD TRAP COMBO	3,845.00
MODEL 682 GOLD "LIVE BIRD"	2,910.00
MODEL 682 GOLD TRAP w/Adjustable Stock	3,725.00
TOP COMBO	4,555.00

MODEL 682 GOLD COMPETITION SKEET O/U

This 12-gauge skeet gun sports a hand-checkerd premium walnut stock w/silver oval for initials, forged and hardened receiver w/Greyston finish, manual safety with trigger selector, auto ejector, silver inlaid on trigger guard.
Action: Low-profile hard chrome-plated boxlock **Trigger:**

Single adjustable sliding trigger **Barrels:** 28" bllued barrels with 2.75" chambers **Stock dimensions:** Length of pull 14.75"; drop at comb 1 ³/₈"; drop at heel 2.25" **Sights:** fluorescent front and metal middle bead **Weight:** Approx. 7.5 lbs.
Price: (incl. fitted case) $2,850.00

MODEL 682 GOLD SPORTING

These competition-stye sporting clays features 28" or 30" barrels with four flush-mounted screw-in choke tubes (Full, Modified, Improved Cylinder and Skeet), pllus hand-checkered stock and forend of fine walnut, 2.75" or 3" chambers and adjustable trigger. MODEL 682 GOLD features Greystone finish–an ultra-durable finish in gunmetal grey w/gold accents. MODEL 686 ONYX SPORTING has black matte receiver and MODEL 686 SILVER

PIGEON SPORTING has coin silver receiver with scroll engraving.
Prices:

682 GOLD SPORTING	$2,910.00
PORTED	3,035.00
686 ONYX SPORTING	1,500.00
686 SILVER PIGEON SPORTING	1,795.00
COMBO	2,210.00

BERETTA SHOTGUNS

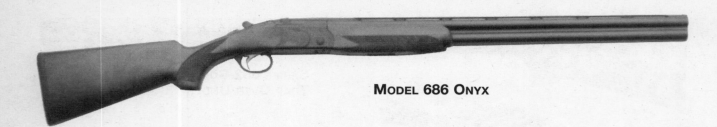

MODEL 686 ONYX

SPECIFICATIONS
Gauges: 12, 20
Chambers: 3" and 3.5"
Barrel Lengths: 26"" and 28"
Chokes: Mobilchoke® screw-in system

Weight: 6 lbs. 12 oz. (12 ga.); 6.2 lbs. (20 ga.)
Stock: American walnut with recoil pad (English stock available)
Features: Automatic ejectors; matte black finish on barrels and receiver to reduce glare
Price: $1,470.00

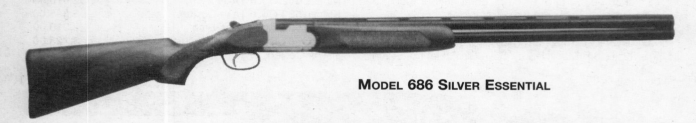

MODEL 686 SILVER ESSENTIAL

SPECIFICATIONS
Gauge: 12 (2.75" and 3" chambers)
Choke: MC3 Mobilchoke® (F, M, IC)
Barrel Length: 26"" or 28"
Overall Length: 45.7"
Weight: 6.7 lbs.

Stock: American walnut
Drop At Comb: 1.4"
Drop At Heel: 2.2"
Length Of Pull: 14.5"
Features: Satin chrome receiver
Price: $1,070.00

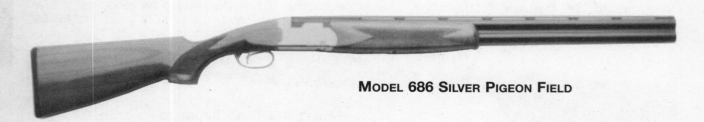

MODEL 686 SILVER PIGEON FIELD

SPECIFICATIONS
Gauges: 12, 20 and 28
Barrels/Chokes: 26" and 28" with Mobilchoke® screw-in choke tubes
Action: Low-profile, improved boxlock
Weight: 6.8 lbs.
Trigger: Selective single trigger, auto safety
Extractors: Auto ejectors
Stock: Choice walnut, hand-checkered and hand-finished with

a tough gloss finish
Prices: $1,070.00
STANDARD $1,740.00
   TRAP TOP MONO 1,740.00
COMBO 20 OR 28 GAUGE 2,410.00
Also available:
MODEL 686 SILVER PIGEON TRAP & SKEET O/U. In 12 gauge, w/30" barrels, 7.7 lbs. weight, matte finish
Price: $1,795.00

BERETTA SHOTGUNS

MODEL 687 SILVER PIGEON SPORTING

This sporting over/under features enhanced engraving pattern, schnabel forend and an electroless nickel finished receiver. *Chamber:* 3". Mobilchoke® screw-in tube system. *Gauges:* 12, 20 and 28 (Field Models)
Prices:
MODEL 687 SILVER PIGEON SPORTING $2,575.00
MODEL 687 SILVER PIGEON SPORTING COMBO 3,395.00

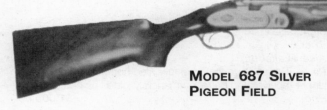

MODEL 687 SILVER PIGEON FIELD

The **687** features Mobilchoke® in 12 and 20 gauge; strong boxlock action handsomely tooled with engraved gamescene receiver, fines quality walnut stock accented with silver monogram plate, selective auto ejectors and fitted case.
Price: $2,115.00

MODEL 687EELL DIAMOND PIGEON (not shown)
MODEL 687EELL COMBO (20 and 28 ga.)
In 12, 20 or 28 ga., this model features the Mobilchoke® engraved choke system, a special premium walnut stock and silver receiver with engraved sideplate.
Prices:
MODEL 687 EELL DIAMOND PIGEON $5,215.00
MODEL 687EELL COMBO (20 and 28 ga.) 5,815.00
Also available:
MODEL 687 EEL DIAMOND PIGEON TRAP O/U $4,815.00
MODEL 687EELL DIAMOND PIGEON SKEET 4,785.00
TRAP TOP MONO (Fuil) 5,055.00
TRAP TOP MONO FMCT 5,105.00
DIAMOND PIGEON SPORTING (12 ga.) 5,310.00
4-BARREL SET 8,405.00

MODEL 687EL GOLD PIGEON FIELD (not shown)
Features game-scene engraving on receiver with gold highlights. Available in 12, 20 gauge (28 ga. and .410 in small frame).

SPECIFICATIONS
Barrels/Chokes: 26" and 28" with Mobilchoke®
Action: Low-profile improved boxlock
Weight: 6.8 lbs. (12 ga.)
Trigger: Single selective with manual safety
Extractors: Auto ejectors
Prices:
MODEL 687EL (12, 20, 28 ga.; 26" or 28" bbl.) . . . $3,670.00
MODEL 687EL SMALL FRAME (28 ga./.410) 3,835.00
MODEL 687EL SPORTING (12 ga. only) 4,470.00

MODEL ULTRALIGHT OVER/UNDER

SPECIFICATIONS
Stock: Select walnut *Features:* Nickel finish receiver w/game scene engraving; black rubber recoil pad; single selective trigger
Price: $1,740.00
Also available:
ULTRALIGHT DELUXE w/matte electroless nickel finish receiver w/gold game scene engraving; walnut stock and forend; light aluminum alloy receiver reinforced w/titanium breech plate
Price: $1,925.00

BERETTA SHOTGUNS

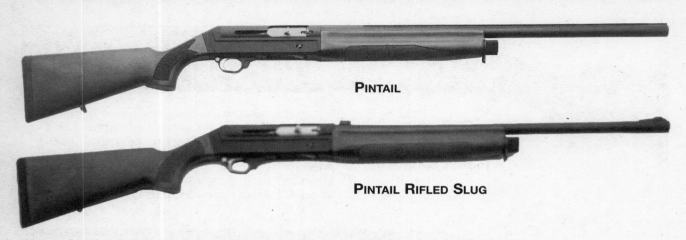

PINTAIL

PINTAIL RIFLED SLUG

This 12-gauge semiautomatic shotgun with short-recoil operation is available with 24" or 26" barrels and Mobilchoke®. Finish is nonreflective matte on alll exposed wood and metal surfaces; receiver is aluminum alloy.

SPECIFICATIONS
Barrel Lengths: 24", 26"; 24" Slug
Weight: 7.3 lbs.

Stock: Checkered selected hardwood
Sights: Bead front
Price: $780.00
Also Available:
PINTAIL RIFLED SLUG featuring fully rifed barrel w/1 in 28" twist. Upper receiver and barrel permanently joined as one unit.
Price: $1,000.00

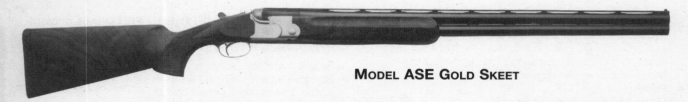

MODEL ASE GOLD SKEET

SPECIFICATIONS
Barrel Lengths: 28" (Gold Sporting, Gold Skeet), 30" (Gold Sporting, Gold Trap), 31" (Gold Sporting), 30"/32" (Gold Trap), 30"/34" (Gold Trap) *Chokes:* MC4 (Gold Sporting); SK/SK (Gold Skeet); MCT (Gold Trap)

Prices:
MODEL ASE GOLD SKEET $12,060.00
MODEL ASE GOLD SPORTING CLAYS 12,145.00
MODEL ASE GOLD TRAP 12,145.00
MODEL ASE GOLD TRAP COMBO 16,055.00

MODEL 1201 FP RIOT

This all-weather semiautomatic shotgun features an adjustable space-age technopolymer stock and forend with recoil pad. Lightweight, it sports a unique weather-resistant matte black finish to reduce glare, resist corrosion and aid in heat dispersion; short recoil action for light and heavy load.

SPECIFICATIONS
Gauge: 12 *Chamber:* 3" *Capacity:* 6 rounds *Choke:* Cylinder (fixed) *Barrel Length:* 18" *Weight:* 6.3 lbs. *Sights:* Blade Front; adjustable rear
Price: $760.00
w/Tritium Sights 840.00

BERETTA SHOTGUNS

FIELD GRADE SEMIAUTOMATICS

MODEL AL390 SILVER MALLARD

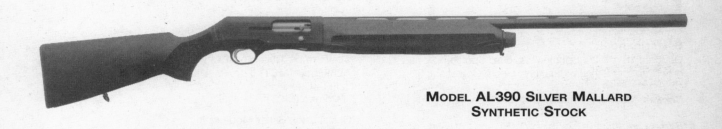

**MODEL AL390 SILVER MALLARD
SYNTHETIC STOCK**

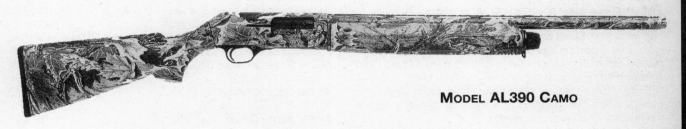

MODEL AL390 CAMO

SPECIFICATIONS
Gauges: 12; Silver Mallard 12 and 20; Youth 20 ga. only; 3" chamber
Chokes: Mobilchoke® tubes; CL (Cylinder choke on Silver Mallard Slug only); fixed chokes available on request
Barrel Lengths: 24", 26", 28", 30" (22" and 24" Silver Mallard Slug only)
Overall Length: 41.7" (22" Slug model only); 44.1" w/24" Youth bbl.; 47.6" w/28" bbl.
Weight: 6.4 lbs. (Youth); 6.8 lbs. (Slug); 7.2-7.5 lbs. (other 12 ga. models)
Features: All models equipped with vent, field-type rib, except Slug model, which has no rib. Silver Mallard is available w/matte, satin finish & cut checkering on stock & forend. Silver Mallard Slug comes w/special rifle sights and shorter barrels. Camo (new) has Advantage camouflage w/eight different earth tones, natural shapes and open areas to produce four patterns in one (limb, leaf, bark, sky)

Prices:
FIELD GRADE MODELS
AL390 SILVER MALLARD (12 or 20 ga.) $860.00
AL390 SILVER MALLARD–MATTE, BLACK SYNTHETIC
   OR SLUG (12 ga. only) 860.00
AL390 GOLD MALLARD (12 and 20 ga.) 1,025.00
AL390 CAMO (12 ga. only) 994.00
AL390 YOUTH (20 ga. only) 860.00

BERETTA SHOTGUNS

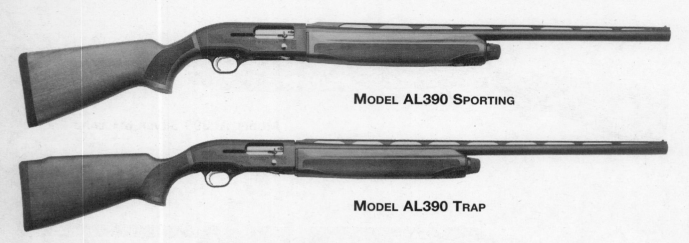

MODEL AL390 SPORTING

MODEL AL390 TRAP

SPECIFICATIONS

Gauges: 12 and 20 (Sporting and Gold Sporting; 12 ga. only (Trap and Skeet); 20 ga. only (Youth/Collection); 3" chamber

Chokes: Mobilchoke® tubes; MC/Fixed on Trap; Fixed on Skeet

Barrel Lengths: 26" (Youth only)); 26" and 28" (Skeet); 28" and 30" (Sporting, Gold Sporting & Trap); 32" avail. on Trap only

Overall Length: 47.8" w/28" bbl.

Weight: 7.6 lbs. (approx.)

Features: All models equipped with wide vent rib. **Trap** has white front and mid-rib bead sights, Monte Carlo stock, special trap recoil pad. **Skeet** has Skeet stock, interchangeable rubber skeet pad. **Sporting** has slim competition stock, rounded receiver, interchangeable rubber sporting-type recoil pad. **Gold Sporting** has engraved receiver w/gold-filled game scenes, "PB" logo, satin black or silver side panels. **Sport Sporting** collection has multi-colored stock and forend, plus anti-glare matte black finish w/scroll engraving.

Prices:

COMPETITION TRAP MODELS	
AL39 TRAP (MCT)	$900.00
FULL CHOKE	890.00
PORTED (MCT)	1,005.00

COMPETITION SKEET MODELS	
AL390 SKEET	$890.00
PORTED	995.00
AL390 SUPER SKEET Semiauto	1,160.00

COMPETITION SPORTING	
AL390 SPORT SPORTING Semiauto 12 & 20 ga.	$900.00
PORTED	995.00
AL390 SPORT DIAMOND SPORTING Semiauto (12 ga.)	3,865.00
AL390 SPORT SPORTING COLLECTION Semiauto (12 ga.)	Price On Request
AL390 GOLD SPORTING	1,115.00
AL390 YOUTH	900.00
AL390 YOUTH COLLECTION	TBA

MODEL 470 SILVER HAWK SIDE-BY-SIDE

SPECIFICATIONS

Gauge: 12 and 2 **Chamber:** 3"

Action: Low profile, improved box lock

Choke: IC/IM, M/F **Barrel Length:** 26" and 28" **Weight:** 6.5 lbs. (12 ga.); 5.9 lbs. (20 ga.)

Sights: Metal front bead **Stock:** Select walnut, checkered

Features: Silver satin chrome finish on receive, trigger guard, forend iron, top lever, trigger, trigger plate and safety/select lever; hand-chased scroll, engraving on receiver, top lever, forend iron and triggerguard; gold inlaid hawk's head on top lever.

Price: $3,210.00

BERNARDELLI SHOTGUNS

Bernardelli shotguns are the creation of the Italian firm of Vincenzo Bernardelli, known for its fine quality firearms and commitment to excellence for more than a century. Most of the long arms featured below can be built with a variety of options, customized for the discriminating sportsman. With the exceptions indicated for each gun respectively, options include choice of barrel lengths and chokes; pistol or straight English grip stock; single selective or non-selective trigger; long tang trigger guard; checkered butt; beavertail forend; hand-cut rib; automatic safety; custom stock dimensions; standard or English recoil pad; extra set of barrels; choice of luggage gun case. Engravings are available in three grades.

MODEL 112 12 GAUGE

Features extractors or automatic ejectors, English or half pistol-grip stock and splinter forend. **Barrel length:** 26.75"

(3" chamber). **Choke:** Improved Cylinder and Improved Modified. **Safety:** Manual. **Weight:** 6.5 lbs.
Prices:

Single Trigger	$1,770.00
Double Trigger	1,625.00
Ejector & Multichoke	2,135.00

ROMA S/S BOXLOCK SERIES

Features include Anson & Deeley action, Purdey triple lock, concave rib, engraved sideplates, double trigger, ejectors.
Prices:

Roma 3	$1,950.00
Roma 9	5,000.00

S.UBERTO 2
$1,850.00 – $2,295.00

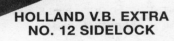

HOLLAND V.B. EXTRA NO. 12 SIDELOCK

This 12-gauge Holland & Holland-style side-by-side feature sidelocks with double safety levers, reinforced breech, three-round Purdey locks, automatic ejectors, single or double triggers, right trigger folding, striker retaining plates, best-quality walnut stock and finely chiseled English scroll engraving
Price: $1,200.00

HEMINGWAY S/S LIGHTWEIGHT BOXLOCK

This lightweight boxlock side-by-side shotgun features automatic ejectors, single selective or double triggers and concave rib. **Gauges:** 12, 20 and 28. **Weight:** 6.25 lbs.

Price:	$2,295.00
Deluxe	2,625.00

SHOTGUNS

BROLIN SHOTGUNS

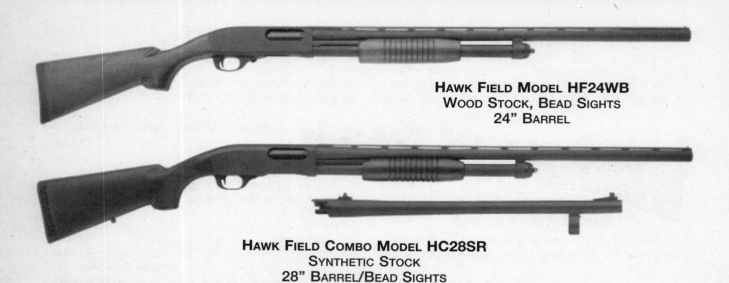

HAWK FIELD MODEL HF24WB
WOOD STOCK, BEAD SIGHTS
24" BARREL

HAWK FIELD COMBO MODEL HC28SR
SYNTHETIC STOCK
28" BARREL/BEAD SIGHTS
18.5" BARREL/RIFLE SIGHTS

HAWK FIELD SERIES

SPECIFICATIONS
Gauge: 12
Choke: Screw-in Modified Hawk choke
Barrel lengths: 24" and 28"
Overall length: 44" and 48"
Weight: 7.3 lbs. (24" barrel); 7.4 lbs. (28" barrel)
Stock: Synthetic or oil-finished wood
Length of pull: 14"
Drop at comb: 1.5" *Drop at heel:* 2.5"
Finish: Non-reflective metal

Features: Bead sights, vent rib, positive cross-bolt
safety, swivel studs
Price: $269.95
Also available:
HAWK FIELD COMBO. Combines 18.5" short barrel with 28"
field barrel; choice of oil-finished wood or black synthetic
stock; bead or rifle sights on shorter barrel only
Prices:
Synthetic or wood stock, bead sights $299.95
Synthetic or wood stock, rifle and bead sights 319.95

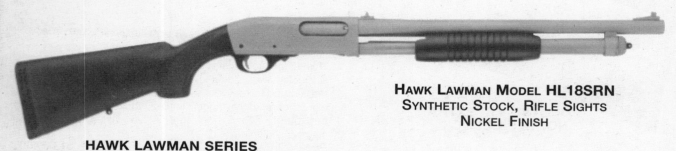

HAWK LAWMAN MODEL HL18SRN
SYNTHETIC STOCK, RIFLE SIGHTS
NICKEL FINISH

HAWK LAWMAN SERIES

SPECIFICATIONS
Gauge: 12 (3" chamber)
Choke: Cylinder
Barrel length: 18.5"
Overall length: 38.5"
Weight: 7 lbs.
Stock: Black synthetic or wood
Length of pull: 14"
Drop at comb: 1.5"

Drop at heel: 2.5"
Sights: Bead, rifle or ghost ring sights
Finish: Matte or nickel
Features: Dual operating bars
Prices:
Wood stock, bead sights $249.95
Synthetic stock, rifle sights 259.95
Same as above w/nickel finish 269.95

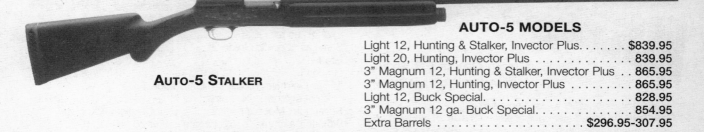

AUTO-5 STALKER

AUTO-5 MODELS

Light 12, Hunting & Stalker, Invector Plus	$839.95
Light 20, Hunting, Invector Plus	839.95
3" Magnum 12, Hunting & Stalker, Invector Plus	865.95
3" Magnum 12, Hunting, Invector Plus	865.95
Light 12, Buck Special	828.95
3" Magnum 12 ga. Buck Special	854.95
Extra Barrels	$296.95-307.95

**GOLD SPORTING CLAYS
12 GAUGE**

GOLD DEER HUNTER (12 Gauge) (not shown)

Features 5" rifled choke tube, special cantilever scope mount, sling posts, magazine cap, select walnut forearm and stock w/vented recoil pad, non-gllare black finish on receiver, satin-finish 22" barrel, 42.5" overall length; weighs 7 lbs. 12 oz.
Price: **$798.95**

SPECIFICATIONS AUTO-5 SHOTGUNS

MODEL	CHAMBER	BARREL LENGTH	OVERALL LENGTH	AVERAGE WEIGHT	CHOKES AVAILABLE
12 Gauge					
Light	2.75"	30"	49.5"	8 lbs. 7 oz.	Invector-Plus
Light	2.75"	28"	47.5"	8 lbs. 4 oz.	Invector-Plus
Light	2.75"	26"	45.5"	8 lbs. 1 oz.	Invector-Plus
Lt. Buck Special	2.75"	24"	43.5"	8 lbs.	Slug/buckshot
Light	2.75"	22"	41.5"	7 lbs. 13 oz.	Invector-Plus
Magnum	3"	32"	51.25"	9 lbs. 2 oz.	Invector-Plus
Magnum	3"	30"	49.25"	8 lbs. 13 oz.	Invector-Plus
Magnum	3"	28"	47.25"	8 lbs. 11 oz.	Invector-Plus
Magnum	3"	26"	45.25"	8 lbs. 9 oz.	Invector-Plus
Mag. Buck Special	3"	24"	43.25"	8 lbs. 8 oz.	Slug/buckshot
Light Stalker	2.75"	28"	47.5"	8 lbs. 4 oz.	Invector-Plus
Light Stalker	2.75"	26"	45.5"	8 lbs. 1 oz.	Invector-Plus
Magnum Stalker	3"	32"	51.25"	8 lbs. 15 oz.	Invector-Plus
Magnum Stalker	3"	30"	49.25"	8 lbs. 13 oz.	Invector-Plus
Magnum Stalker	3"	28"	47.25"	8 lbs. 11 oz.	Invector-Plus
20 Gauge					
Light	2.75"	28"	47.125"	6 lbs. 10 oz.	Invector-Plus
Light	2.75"	28"	45.25"	6 lbs. 8 oz.	Invector-Plus

GOLD HUNTER & STALKER SEMIAUTOMATIC SHOTGUNS: $734.95   SPORTING CLAYS: $759.95
SPECIFICATIONS GOLD 12 AND 20

GAUGE	MODEL	BARREL LENGTH	OVERALL LENGTH	AVERAGE WEIGHT	CHOKES AVAILABLE
12	Hunting	30"	50.5"	7 lbs. 9 oz.	Invector-Plus
12	Hunting	28"	48.5"	7 lbs. 6 oz.	Invector-Plus
12	Hunting	26"	46.5"	7 lbs. 3 oz.	Invector-Plus
20	Hunting	28"	48.25"	6 lbs. 14 oz.	Invector
20	Hunting	26"	46.25"	6 lbs. 12 oz.	Invector

SPECIFICATIONS GOLD 10 HUNTING & STALKER: $1,007.95

CHAMBER	BARREL LENGTH	OVERALL LENGTH	AVERAGE WEIGHT	CHOKES
3.5	30"	52"	10 lbs. 13 oz.	Standard Invector
3.5	28"	50"	10 lbs. 100 oz.	Standard Invector
3.5	26"	48"	10 lbs. 7 oz.	Standard Invector

Extra barrels are available for **$261.95**

SHOTGUNS

BROWNING CITORI SHOTGUNS

CITORI GRADE I HUNTING
12 GAUGE 3.5" MAGNUM

Grade I = Blued steel w/scroll engraving
Grade III = Grayed steel w/light relief **Grade VI** = Blued or grayed w/engraved ringneck pheasants and mallard ducks;
GL (Gran Lightning) = High-grade wood w/satin finish

CITORI PRICES (all Invector-Plus chokes unless noted otherwise)
HUNTING MODELS (w/pistol-grip stock, beavertail forearm, high-gloss finish) 12 ga., 3.5" Mag.,28" & 30" barrels .. **$1,418.00**
Same as above in 12 & 2 ga. w/3" chamber 26", 28", 30" barrels 1,334.00
SPORTING HUNTER 12 ga., 3.5" Mag., 28 & 36" barrels . 1,519.00
Same as above in 12 & 20 ga. 3" chamber, 26", 28", 36" barrels 1,435.00
SATIN HUNTER in 12 ga., 3.5" chamber, 28" barrel 1,352.00
Same as above w/3" chamber (26" barrel available) . . . 950.00
WHITE LIGHTNING 12 & 20 ga., Grade I, 3" chamber . . . 1,421.00
LIGHTNING MODELS (w/classic rounded pistol grip, Lightning-style forearm) Grade I, 12 & 2 ga., 3" chamber 26"

& 28" barrels 1,376.00
Same as above in Grade GL 1,869.00
Grade III. 2,006.00
Grade VI 2,919.00
MICRO LIGHTNING MODEL (20 Ga.) Grade I,
2.75" chamber, 24" barrel 1,428.00
SUPERLIGHT MODELS (w/straight-grip stock, slimmed-down Schnabel forearm; 2.75" chamber, 12 or 20 ga.)
Grade I 1,376.00
Grade III. 2,006.00
Grade VI 2,919.00
LIGHTNING MODELS w/Standard Invector chokes (Lightning models only, 28 and .410 ga., 2.75" chamber, 26" & 28" barrels
Grade I 1,418.00
Grade GL 1,969.00
Grade III. 2,242.00
Grade VI 3,145.00
STANDARD INVECTOR (28 & .410 ga.)
Grade I 1,418.00
Grade III. 2,242.00
Grade VI 3,145.00
UPLAND SPECIAL (12 & 20 ga.)
Grade I only, 24" barrel 1,386.00

CITORI FIELD MODEL SPECIFICATIONS

GAUGE	MODEL	CHAMBER	BARREL LENGTH	OVERALL LENGTH	AVERAGE WEIGHT	CHOKES AVAILABLE 1	GRADES AVAILABLE
12	Hunter	3.5" Mag.	30"	47"	8 lbs. 10 oz.	Invector-Plus	I
12	Hunter	3.5" Mag.	28"	45"	8 lbs. 9 oz.	Invector-Plus	I
12	Sporting Hunter	3.5" Mag.	30"	47"	8 lbs. 9 oz.	Invector-Plus	I
12	Sporting Hunter	3"	28"	45"	8 lbs. 5 oz.	Invector-Plus	I
12	Hunter	3"	30"	47"	8 lbs. 4 oz.	Invector-Plus	I
12	Hunter	3"	28"	45"	8 lbs. 1 oz.	Invector-Plus	I
12	Hunter	3"	26"	43"	7 lbs. 15 oz.	Invector-Plus	I
12	Sporting Hunter	3"	30"	47"	8 lbs. 5 oz.	Invector-Plus	I
12	Sporting Hunter	3"	28"	45"	8 lbs. 1 oz.	Invector-Plus	I
12	Sporting Hunter	3"	26"	43"	7 lbs. 13 oz.	Invector-Plus	I
12	Lightning	3"	28"	45"	8 lbs. 1 oz.	Invector-Plus	I, GL, III, VI
12	Lightning	3"	26"	43"	7 lbs. 15 oz.	Invector-Plus	I, GL, III, VI
12	White Lightning	3"	28"	45"	8 lbs. 1 oz.	Invector-Plus	I
12	White Lightning	3"	26"	43"	7 lbs. 13 oz.	Invector-Plus	I
12	Superlight	2.75"	28"	45"	6 lbs. 12 oz.	Invector-Plus	I, III, VI
12	Superlight	2.75"	26"	43"	6 lbs. 11 oz.	Invector-Plus	I, III, VI
12	Upland Special	2.75"	24"	41"	6 lbs. 9 oz.	Invector-Plus	I
20	Hunter	3"	28"	45"	6 lbs. 12 oz.	Invector-Plus	I
20	Hunter	3"	26"	43"	6 lbs. 10 oz.	Invector-Plus	I
20	Lightning	3"	28"	45"	6 lbs. 14 oz.	Invector-Plus	I, GL, III, VI
20	Lightning	3"	26"	43"	6 lbs. 9 oz.	Invector-Plus	I, GL, III, VI
20	Lightning	3"	24"	41"	6 lbs. 6 oz.	Invector-Plus	I
20	Micro Lightning	2.75"	24"	41"	6 lbs. 3 oz.	Invector-Plus	I
20	Superlight	2.75"	26"	43"	6 lbs. 3 oz.	Invector-Plus	I, III, VI
20	Upland Special	2.75"	24"	41"	6 lbs.	Invector-Plus	I
28	Lightning	2.75"	28"	45"	6 lbs. 11 oz.	Invector	I
28	Lightning	2.75"	26"	43"	6 lbs. 10 oz.	Invector	I, GL, III, VI
28	Superlight	2.75"	26"	43	6 lbs. 10 oz.	Invector	I, III, VI
.410	Lightning	3"	28"	45"	7 lbs.	Invector	I
.410	Lightning	3"	26"	43"	6 lbs. 14 oz.	Invector	I, GL, III, VI
.410	Superlight	3"	28"	45"	6 lbs. 14 oz.	Invector	I
.410	Superlight	3"	26"	43"	6 lbs. 13 oz.	Invector	I, III, VI

1. *Full & Modified Choke installed; Improved Cylinder and wrench included. GL=Gran Lightning grade.*

BROWNING CITORI SHOTGUNS

LIGHT SPORTING MODEL 802ES

Sporting 12 ga. O/U. **Barrel Length:** 28"
Overall Length: 45.5". Invector-Plus stainlless steel choke tubes. **Weight:** 7 lbs. 5 oz.
Price:. $1,880.00

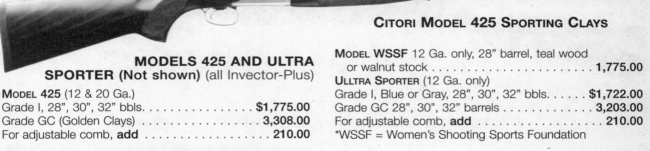

CITORI MODEL 425 SPORTING CLAYS

MODELS 425 AND ULTRA SPORTER (Not shown) (all Invector-Plus)

MODEL 425 (12 & 20 Ga.)
Grade I, 28", 30", 32" bbls. $1,775.00
Grade GC (Golden Clays) 3,308.00
For adjustable comb, **add** 210.00

MODEL WSSF 12 Ga. only, 28" barrel, teal wood
   or walnut stock **1,775.00**
ULTRA SPORTER (12 Ga. only)
Grade I, Blue or Gray, 28", 30", 32" bbls. $1,722.00
Grade GC 28", 30", 32" barrels 3,203.00
For adjustable comb, **add** 210.00
*WSSF = Women's Shooting Sports Foundation

425 & ULTRA SPORTER SPECIFICATIONS

MODEL	CHAMBER	BARREL LENGTH	OVERALL LENGTH	AVERAGE WEIGHT	CHOKES AVAILABLE	GRADES AVAILABLE
425						
12 ga.	2.75"	32"	49.5"	7 lbs. 15 oz.	Invector-Plus	Gr. I, Golden Clays
12 ga.	2.75"	30"	47.5"	7 lbs. 14 oz.	Invector-Plus	Gr. I, Golden Clays
12 ga.	2.75"	28"	45.5"	7 lbs. 13 oz.	Invector-Plus	Gr. I, Golden Clays
20 ga.	2.75"	30"	47.5"	6 lbs. 13 oz.	Invector-Plus	Gr. I, Golden Clays
20 ga.	2.75"	28"	45.5"	6 lbs. 12 oz.	Invector-Plus	Gr. I, Golden Clays
WSSF 12 ga. Paint	2.75"	28"	45.5"	7 lbs. 4 oz.	Invector-Plus	Custom WSSF Exclusive
WSSF 12 ga. Walnut	2.75"	28"	45.5"	7 lbs. 4 oz.	Invector-Plus	Gr. I
Ultra Sporter						
12 ga. Sporter	2.75"	32"	49"	8 lbs. 4 oz.	Invector-Plus	Gr. I, Golden Clays
12 ga. Sporter	2.75"	30"	47"	8 lbs. 2 oz.	Invector-Plus	Gr. I, Golden Clays
12 ga. Sporter	2.75"	28"	45"	8 lbs.	Invector-Plus	Gr. I, Golden Clays
Light Sporting 802 ES						
12 ga. Sporter	2.75"	28"	45"	7 lbs. 5 oz.	Invector-Plus 802 ES Tubes*	Gr. I

*Sporting Clays models: One modified, one Improved Cylinder and one Skeet tube supplied. Other chokes available as accessories. *Choke tubes included with 802 ES (Six tubes total)*

SPECIFICATIONS SPECIAL SPORTING CLAYS, TRAP & SKEET & LIGHTNING SPORTING (prices on following page)

GAUGE	MODEL	CHAMBER	BARREL LENGTH	OVERALL LENGTH	AVERAGE WEIGHT	CHOKES	GRADES AVAILABLE
Special							
12	Sporting Clays	2.75"	32"	49"	8 lbs. 5 oz.	Inv.-Plus	I, Golden Clays
12	Sporting Clays	2.75"	30"	47"	8 lbs. 3 oz.	Inv.-Plus	I, Golden Clays
12	Sporting Clays	2.75"	28"	45"	8 lbs. 1 oz.	Inv.-Plus	I, Golden Clays
12	Conventional Trap	2.75"	32"	49"	8 lbs. 11 oz.	Inv.-Plus	I, III, Golden Clays
12	Monte Carlo Trap	2.75"	32"	49"	8 lbs. 10 oz.	Inv.-Plus	I, III, Golden Clays
12	Skeet	2.75"	30"	47"	8 lbs. 7 oz.	Inv.-Plus	I, III, Golden Clays
12	Skeet	2.75"	30"	47"	8 lbs. 6 oz.	Inv.-Plus	I, III, Golden Clays
12	Skeet	2.75"	28"	45"	8 lbs.	Inv.-Plus	I, III, Golden Clays
12	Skeet	2.75"	26"	43"	7 lbs. 15 oz.	Inv.-Plus	I
20	Skeet	2.75"	28"	45"	7 lbs. 4 oz.	Inv.-Plus	I, III, Golden Clays
20	Skeet	2.75"	26"	43"	7 lbs. 1 oz.	Inv.-Plus	I
28	Skeet	2.75"	28"	45"	6 lbs. 15 oz.	Invector	I, III, Golden Clays
28	Skeet	2.75"	26"	43"	6 lbs. 10 oz.	Invector	I
.410	Skeet	2.5"	28"	45"	7 lbs. 6 oz.	Invector	I, III, Golden Clays
.410	Skeet	2.5"	26"	43	7 lbs. 3 oz.	Invector	I
Lightning Sporting*							
12	Sporting Clays	3"	30"	47"	8 lbs. 8 oz.	Inv.-Pus	I, Golden Clays
12	Sporting Clays	3"	28"	45"	8 lbs. 6 oz.	Inv.-Plus	I, Golden Clays

SHOTGUNS

BROWNING CITORI SHOTGUNS

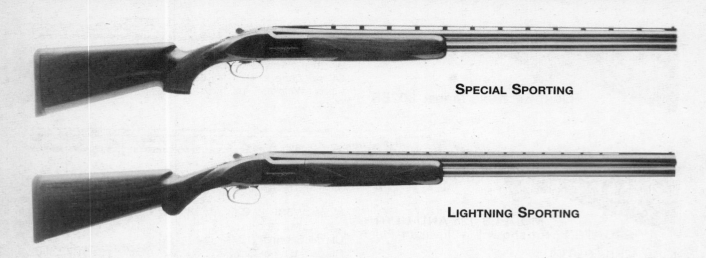

SPECIAL SPORTING

LIGHTNING SPORTING

CITORI SPECIAL SPORTING AND LIGHTNING SPORTING

Prices:

SPECIAL SPORTING
Grade I, ported barrels $1,565.00
Grade I, ported bbls., adj. comb 1,775.00
Golden Clays, ported barrels 3,203.00
Golden Clays, adj. comb 3,413.00

LIGHTNING SPORTING
Grade I, high rib, ported bbl., 3" $1,565.00
Grade I, high rib, adj. comb 1,775.00

Grade I, low rib, ported bbls., 3" 1,496.00
Grade I, low rib, adj. comb 1,706.00
Golden Clays, low rib, ported bbls., 3" 3,092.00
Golden Clays, low rib, adj. comb 3,302.00
Golden Clays, high rib, ported bbls., 3" 3,203.00
Golden Clays, high rib, adj. comb 3,413.00

SPORTING HUNTER
Grade I, 3.5" chamber, tapered rib, 12 ga. $1,519.00
Grade I, 3" chamber, 12 & 20 ga., tapered rib. . . 1,435.00

(See previous page for specifications)

CITORI SPECIAL TRAP

SPECIAL TRAP MODELS

Prices:

12 GAUGE, INVECTOR-PLUS, PORTED BARRELS
Grade I, Monte Carlo stock $1,586.00
Grade I, adj. comb 1,796.00
Grade III, Monte Carlo stock 2,179.00
Grade III, adj. comb 2,389.00
Golden Clays, Monte Carlo stock 3,239.00
Golden Clays, adj. comb 3,449.00

SPECIAL SKEET MODELS

Prices:

12 & 20 GAUGE, INVECTOR-PLUS, PORTED BARRELS
Grade I, high post rib $1,586.00
Grade I, high post rib, adj. comb 1,796.00
Grade III, high post rib 2,179.00
Grade III, high post rib, adj. comb 2,389.00
Golden Clays, high post rib 3,239.00
Golden Clays, high post rib, adj. comb 3,449.00

28 GA. AND .410 BORE STD. INVECTOR
Grade I, high post rib $1,549.00
Grade III, high post rib 2,184.00
Golden Clays, high post rib 3,166.00

BROWNING SHOTGUNS

BT-100 SINGLE BARREL TRAP

GRADE I, INVECTOR-PLUS

Monte Carlo stock	$1,995.95
Adjustable comb	2,205.00
Full choke barrel	1,948.00
Full choke barrel, adj. comb	2,158.00
Thumbhole stock	2,270.00
Full choke barrel	2,225.00

BT-100 TRAP

LOW LUSTER
Grade I, 12 ga., 32" and 34", adj. trigger pull, conventional satin stock 1,587.00

STAINLESS, INVECTOR-PLUS

Monte Carlo stock	2,415.00
Adjustable comb	2,625.00
Full choke barrel	2,368.00
Full choke barrel, adj. comb	2,625.00
Thumbhole stock	2,690.00
Full choke barrel	2,645.00
TRIGGER ASSEMBLY REPLACEMENT	525.00

A-BOLT HUNTER WITH RIFLED BARREL

A-BOLT STALKER WITH RIFLED CHOKE TUBE

A-BOLT SHOTGUNS

HUNTER. With choke tube	$828.95
Without sights	804.95
With rifled barrel	881.95
Without sights	856.95
STALKER. With choke tube	744.95
Without sights	719.95
With rifled barrel	797.95
Without sights	772.95

STOCK DIMENSIONS BT-100

	ADJUSTABLE CONVENTIONAL	THUMBHOLE	MONTE CARLO
Length of Pull	14 3/8"	14 3/8"	14 3/8"
Drop at Comb	Adj.*	1.75"	1 9/16"
Drop at Monte Carlo	—	1.25"	1 7/16"
Drop at Heel	Adj.*	2 1/8"	2"

Adjustable Drop at Comb and Heel.

SPECIFICATIONS BT-100

GAUGE	MODEL	CHAMBER	BARREL LENGTH	OVERALL LENGTH	AVERAGE WEIGHT	CHOKES	GRADES AVAILABLE
12	BT-100	2.75"	34"	50.5"	8 lbs. 10 oz.	Invector Plus[1]	I, Stainless
12	BT-100	2.75"	32"	48.5"	8 lbs. 9 oz.	Invector Plus[1]	I, Stainless
12	BT-100 Monte Carlo	2.75"	34"	50.5"	8 lbs. 10 oz.	Invector Plus	I, Stainless
12	BT-100 Monte Carlo	2.75"	32"	48.5"	8 lbs. 9 oz.	Invector Plus	I, Stainless
12	BT-100 Thumbhole	2.75"	34"	50.75"	8 lbs. 8 oz.	Invector Plus	I, Stainless
12	BT-100 Thumbhole	2.75"	32"	48.75"	8 lbs. 6 oz.	Invector Plus	I, Stainless

F=Full, M=Modified, IM=Improved Modified, S=Skeet, Invector=Invector Choke System – Invector-Plus Trap models: Full, Improved Modified, Modified, and wrench included.
[1]Also available with conventional full choke barrel.

SPECIFICATIONS A-BOLT SHOTGUNS

MODEL	CHAMBER	MAGAZINE CAPACITY	BARREL LENGTH	OVERALL LENGTH	AVERAGE WEIGHT	CHOKE/BARREL AVAILABLE
Hunter/Choke Tube	3"	2[1]	23"	44.75"	7 lbs. 2 oz.	Standard Invector*
Hunter/Rifle Barrel	3"	2[1]	22"	43.75"	7 lbs.	Fully rifled barrel
Stalker/Choke tube	3"	2[1]	23"	44.75"	7 lbs. 2 oz.	Standard Invector*
Stalker/Rifled Barrel	3"	2[1]	22"	43.75"	7 lbs.	Fully rifled barrel

*Standard Invector interchangeable choke tube system: One rifled choke tube and one X-Full Turkey choke tube included. [1]Total capacity is 2 shells in magazine, one in chamber.

SHOTGUNS

BROWNING SHOTGUNS

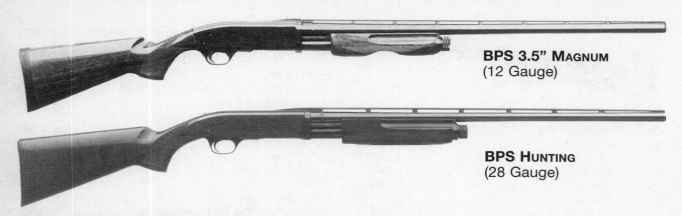

BPS 3.5" MAGNUM
(12 Gauge)

BPS HUNTING
(28 Gauge)

BPS MAGNUMS SPECIFICATIONS

Gauge	Model	Chamber	Capacity[2]	Barrel Length	Overall Length	Average Weight	Chokes Available[1]
10 Mag	Hunter & Stalker	3.5"	4	30"	52"	9 lbs. 8 oz.	Invector
10 Mag	Hunter & Stalker	3.5"	4	28"	50"	9 lbs. 6 oz.	Invector
10 Mag	Hunter & Stalker	3.5"	4	26"	48"	9 lbs. 4 oz.	Invector
10 Mag	Hunter & Stalker	3.5"	4	24"	46"	9 lbs. 4 oz.	Invector
12, 3.5" Mag	Hunter	3.5"	4	30"	51"	8 lbs. 6 oz.	Invector-Plus
12, 3.5" Mag	Stalker	3.5"	4	30"	51"	8 lbs. 4 oz.	Invector-Plus
12, 3.5" Mag	Hunter	3.5"	4	28"	49"	8 lbs. 3 oz.	Invector-Plus
12, 3.5" Mag	Stalker	3.5"	4	28"	49"	8 lbs. 1 oz.	Invector-Plus
12, 3.5" Mag	Hunter	3.5"	4	26"	47"	8 lbs.	Invector-Plus
12, 3.5" Mag	Stalker	3.5"	4	26"	47"	7 lbs. 14 oz.	Invector-Plus
12, 3.5" Mag	Hunter	3.5"	4	24"	45"	7 lbs. 13 oz.	Invector-Plus
12, 3.5" Mag	Stalker	3.5"	4	24"	45"	7 lbs. 11 oz.	Invector-Plus

SPECIFICATIONS BPS 12, 20 & 28 Ga. (3")

Gauge	Model	Chamber	Capacity[3]	Barrel Length	Overall Length	Average Weight	Chokes Available[1,2]
12	Hunter & Stalker	3"	4	30"	50.75"	7 lbs. 12 oz.	Invector-Plus
12	Hunter & Stalker	3"	4	28"	48.75"	7 lbs. 11 oz.	Invector-Plus
12	Hunter & Stalker	3"	4	26"	46.75"	7 lbs. 10 oz.	Invector-Plus
12	Standard Buck Special	3"	4	24"	44.75"	7 lbs. 10 oz.	Slug/Buckshot
12	Upland Special	3"	4	22"	42.5"	7 lbs. 8 oz.	Invector-Plus
12	Hunter & Stalker	3"	4	22"	42.5"	7 lbs. 7 oz.	Invector-Plus
12	Game Gun Turkey Special	3"	4	20.5"	40 7/8"	7 lbs. 7 oz.	Invector
12	Game Gun Deer Special/Rifled	3"	4	20.5"	40 7/8"	7 lbs. 7 oz.	Fully Rifled Barrel
12	Game Gun Deer Special/Smooth	3"	4	20.5"	40 7/8"	7 lbs. 7 oz.	Special Inv./Rifled
12	Game Gun Cantilever Mount	3"	4	20.5"	40 7/8"	7 lbs. 9 oz.	Fully Rifled
20	Hunter	3"	4	28"	48.75"	7 lbs. 1 oz.	Invector-Plus
20	Hunter	3"	4	26"	46.75"	7 lbs.	Invector-Plus
20	Micro	3"	4	22"	41.75"	6 lbs. 11 oz.	Invector-Plus
20	Upland Special	3"	4	22"	42.75"	6 lbs. 12 oz.	Invector-Plus
28	Hunter	2.75"	4	28"	48.75"	7 lbs. 1 oz.	Invector
28	Hunter	2.75"	4	26"	46.75"	7 lbs.	Invector

BPS FIELD MODEL PRICES
SPECIFICATIONS
Prices:

GRADE II 3" chamber 26", 28", 30" barrels $423.95

STALKER Same as above w/synthetic stock
& forearm 423.95

GAME GUN Deer Special (20.5" barrel) w/5"
rifled slug choke tube 492.95

TURKEY SPECIAL w/X-Full Turkey choke tube 460.95

SMALL GAUGE FIELD (28" barrel) w/bottom loading
and ejection 423.95

MAGNUM MODELS Hunting & Stalker Grades
(10 ga. and 12 ga.) w/3.5" Mag. chamber
(26" and 28" barrels) 508.95

CHARLES DALY SHOTGUNS

IMPORTED BY K.B.I., INC.

FIELD OVER/UNDER

FIELD HUNTER OVER/UNDER

SPECIFICATIONS
Gauges: 12, 20, 28 and .410 (3" chambers); 28 ga. (2.75")
Barrel Lengths/Chokes: 28" Mod./Full; 26" IC/Mod.; .410 ga. Full/Full *Weight:* Approx. 7 lb. *Stock:* Checkered walnut pistol-grip and forend *Features:* Blued engraved receiver; chrome-moly steel barrels, gold single-selective trigger, automatic safety, extractors, gold bead front sight
Prices: FIELD HUNTER
12 or 20 ga. $699.00

28 ga. **779.00**
.410 ga. **819.00**
FIELD HUNTER AE w/auto-ejectors (not available in 12 or 20 ga.)
28 ga. **859.00**
.410 ga. **899.00**
FIELD HUNTER AE-MC. Same as Field Hunter but w/5
   choke tubes (12 and 20 ga. only) **899.00**
SUPERIOR HUNTER AE. Gold single-sellective trigger,
gold bead front sight, silver engraved receiver
28 ga. **999.00**
.410 ga. **1,059.00**
SUPERIOR HUNTER AE-MC. Same as above in 12
   and 20 ga. w/5 choke tubes **1,129.00**

SUPERIOR SPORTING

SPECIFICATIONS
Gauges: 12 and 20 ga. (3" chambers)
Barrel Lengths/Chokes: 28" & 30" with multi-choke (5 tubes)
Weight: Approx. 7 lb.
Stock: Checkered walnut pistol-grip buttstock w/semi-beavertail forend

Features: Silver engraved receiver, ported chrome-moly steel barrels, gold single-selective trigger, automatic safety, auto-ejectors, red bead front sight
Prices:
SUPERIOR SPORTING $1,099.00
SUPERIOR TRAP-MC. Same as above in 12 ga.
   only (2.75" chamber) 30" bbl. only **1,219.00**
SUPERIOR TRAP. Same as above w/Full/Full
   choke **1,099.00**

SUPERIOR SKEET

SUPERIOR SKEET-MC

SPECIFICATIONS
Gauges: 12 and 20 ga.; 3" chambers
Barrel Length/Choke: 26" with multi-choke (5 choke tubes)
Weight: Approx. 7 lb.

Sights: Red bead front; metal bead center
Stock: Checkered walnut pistol-grip w/semibeavertail forend
Features: Silver engraved receiver, chrome-moly steel barrels, gold single-selective trigger, automatic safety, auto-ejectors, recoil pad
Prices:
SUPERIOR SKEET-MC $1,159.00
SUPERIOR SKEET w/SK1 & SK2 chokes **1,039.00**

SHOTGUNS

CHARLES DALY SHOTGUNS

IMPORTED BY K.B.I., INC.

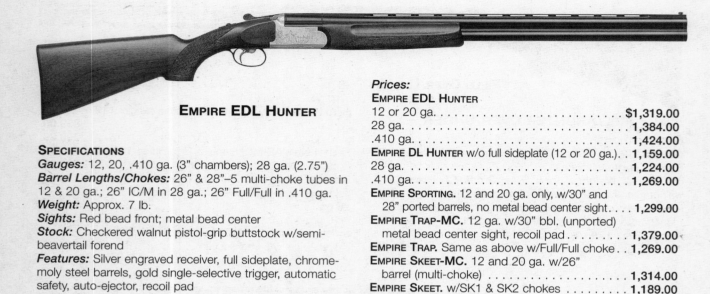

EMPIRE EDL HUNTER

SPECIFICATIONS
Gauges: 12, 20, .410 ga. (3" chambers); 28 ga. (2.75")
Barrel Lengths/Chokes: 26" & 28"–5 multi-choke tubes in 12 & 20 ga.; 26" IC/M in 28 ga.; 26" Full/Full in .410 ga.
Weight: Approx. 7 lb.
Sights: Red bead front; metal bead center
Stock: Checkered walnut pistol-grip buttstock w/semi-beavertail forend
Features: Silver engraved receiver, full sideplate, chrome-moly steel barrels, gold single-selective trigger, automatic safety, auto-ejector, recoil pad

Prices:
EMPIRE EDL HUNTER
12 or 20 ga. $1,319.00
28 ga. 1,384.00
.410 ga. 1,424.00
EMPIRE DL HUNTER w/o full sideplate (12 or 20 ga.). . 1,159.00
28 ga. 1,224.00
.410 ga. 1,269.00
EMPIRE SPORTING. 12 and 20 ga. only, w/30" and
    28" ported barrels, no metal bead center sight. . . . 1,299.00
EMPIRE TRAP-MC. 12 ga. w/30" bbl. (unported)
    metal bead center sight, recoil pad 1,379.00
EMPIRE TRAP. Same as above w/Full/Full choke . . 1,269.00
EMPIRE SKEET-MC. 12 and 20 ga. w/26"
    barrel (multi-choke) 1,314.00
EMPIRE SKEET. w/SK1 & SK2 chokes 1,189.00

DIAMOND GTX COMPETITION

Prices:
DIAMOND GTX TRAP & SPORTING MC-5
12 or 20 ga. $5,455.00
DIAMOND GTX TRAP AE 5,289.00
DIAMOND GTX SKEET MC-5 . . . . 5,289.00
DIAMOND GTX SKEET AE 5,149.00

DIAMOND GRADE OVER & UNDER COMPETITION SHOTGUNS

MODEL	GAUGE	BARREL LENGTH	CHAMBER	CHOKES	WEIGHT LBS. (approx.)
Diamond GTX Sporting AE-MC	12	30"	3"	MC-5	8
Diamond GTX Sporting AE-MC	12	28"	3"	MC-5	8
Diamond GTX Sporting AE-MC	20	28"	3"	MC-5	8
Diamond GTX Trap AE-MC	12	30"	2.75"	MC-5	8
Diamond GTX Trap AE	12	30"	2.75"	F&F	8
Diamond GTX Skeet AE-MC	12	26"	3"	MC-5	7.5
Diamond GTX Skeet AE-MC	20	26"	3"	MC-5	7.5
Diamond GTX Skeet AE	12	26"	3"	SK1&2	7.5
Diamond GTX Skeet AE	20	26"	3"	SK1&2	7.5

CHARLES DALY SHOTGUNS

IMPORTED BY K.B.I., INC.

FIELD HUNTER SIDE BY SIDE

SPECIFICATIONS
Gauges: 10, 12, 20 and .410 (3" chambers); 28 ga. (2.75")
Barrel Lengths/Chokes: 32" Mod./Mod.; 30" Mod./Full;
28" Mod./Full; 26" IC/Mod.; .410 ga. Full/Full
Weight: Approx. 6 lbs.-11.4 lbs.
Stock: Checkered walnut pistol-grip and forend

SUPERIOR GRADE (not shown)

SPECIFICATIONS
Gauges: 12 and 20; 3" chambers
Barrel Lengths/Chokes: 28" Mod./Full; 26" IC/Mod.
Weight: Approx. 7 lb.
Stock: Checkered walnut pistol-grip buttstock and
splinter forend
Features: Silver engraved receiver, chrome-lined steel
barrels, gold single trigger, automatic safety, extractors,
gold bead front sight
Prices:
SUPERIOR HUNTER. $929.00
EMPIRE HUNTER
Same as above w/hand-checkered stock auto ejectors,
    game scene engraved receiver **1,259.00**

Features: Silver engraved receiver; gold single-selective
trigger in 10, 12 and 20 ga.; double trigger in 28 and 410
ga.; automatic safety, extractors, gold bead front sight.
Imported from Spain
Prices:
10 ga. **$919.00**
12 or 20 ga. 749.00
28 or .410 ga. 799.00
FIELD HUNTER-MC (5 multi-choke tubes)
10 ga. 1,019.00
12 or 20 ga. 879.00

DIAMOND DL HUNTER (not shown)

SPECIFICATIONS
Gauges: 12, 20, .410 ga. (3" chambers; 28 ga. (2.75")
Barrel Lengths/Chokes: 28" Mod./Full; 26" IC/Mod.; 26"
Full/Full in .410 ga. *Weight:* Approx. 5-7 lbs.
Stock: Select fancy European walnut, English-styled,
beavertail forend, hand-checkered, hand-rubbed oil finish
Features: Fine steel drop-forged action with gas escape
valves; fine steel demiblock barrels w/concave rib; selective
auto ejectors, hand-detachable double safety sidelocks
w/hand-engraved rose and scrollwork; front-hinged trigger,
casehardened receive. Imported from Spain.
Prices:
DIAMOND DL 12 or 20 ga. **$5,599.00**
28 or .410 ga.. . . . . 6,079.00

RIFLE/SHOTGUN COMBINATION GUNS

SUPERIOR COMBINATION

SPECIFICATIONS
Gauge/Calibers: 12/22 Hornet, 22-250, 223 Rem., 243
Win., 270 Win., 308 Win., 30-006 Sprgfld.
Barrel Length/Choke: 23.5", shotgun choke IC
Weight: Approx. 7.5 lbs.
Stock: Checkered walnut pistol-grip buttstock and semi-
beavertail forend

Features: Silver engraved receiver forged and milled from
a solid block of high-strength steel; chrome-moly steel bar-
rels, double trigger, extractors, sling swivels, gold bead
front sight
Prices:
SUPERIOR COMBINATION. $1,159.00
EMPIRE COMBINATION. Same as above w/deluxe walnut
European-style comb/cheekpiece, slim forend . . **1,625.00**

SHOTGUNS

DAKOTA ARMS INC.

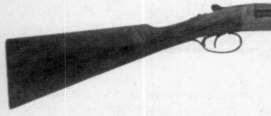

DAKOTA ARMS AMERICAN LEGEND
(LIMITED EDITION)

The Dakota American Legend 20-gauge side-by-side double shotgun is built in the United States and reflects the best fit and finish found on game guns the world over. Cased in a Marvis Huey oak and leather trunk case, these limited-edition shotguns are made from bar stock steel and special selection English walnut. This shotgun features precision-machined receiver and intricate hand checkering. Standard features include custom-fitted stock, full-coverage hand engraving, gold inlays, straight-hand grip, double triggers, selective ejectors, 24-lines-per-inch hand checkering, French gray receiver, concave rib, splinter forend, checkered butt and ivory beads. Options include a single trigger, leather-covered pad, skeleton butt, semi-beavertail forend and screw-in chokes.

SPECIFICATIONS
Barrel length: 27" ***Weight:*** 6 lbs.
Price: **$18,000.00**
Also available:
CLASSIC GRADE features hard rubber buttplate w/logo, game rib with gold bead, double triggers, and hand-rubbed oil finish
Price: **$7,950.00**
PREMIER GRADE w/50% engraving coverage, Exhibition English walnut, 14.25" length of pull
Price: **$9,950.00**

A.H. FOX SHOTGUNS

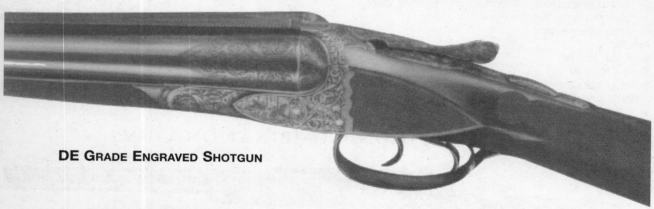

DE GRADE ENGRAVED SHOTGUN

CUSTOM BOXLOCKS

SPECIFICATIONS
Gauges: 16, 20, 28 and .410 ***Barrel:*** Any barrel lengths and chokes; rust blued Chromox or Krupp steel barrels ***Weight:*** 5 /to 6/lbs. ***Stock:*** Custom stock dimensions including cast; hand-checkered Turkish Circassian walnut stock and forend with hand-rubbed oil finish; straight grip, full pistol grip (with cap), or semi-pistol grip; splinter, schnabel or beavertail forend; traditional pad, hard rubber plate, checkered, or skeleton butt ***Features:*** Boxlock action with automatic ejectors; scalloped, rebated and color casehardened receiver; double or Fox single selective trigger; hand-finished and hand-engraved. This is the same gun that was manufactured between 1905 and 1930 by the A.H. Fox Gun Company of Philadelphia, PA, now manufactured in the U.S. by the Connecticut Shotgun Mfg. Co. (New Britain, CT).

Prices:*
CE GRADE **$9,500.00**
XE GRADE **11,000.00**
DE GRADE **13,500.00**
FE GRADE **18,500.00**
EXHIBITION GRADE **26,000.00**

*Grades differ in engraving and inlay, grade of wood and amount of hand finishing needed.

FRANCOTTE SHOTGUNS

CLOSE-UP OF BOXLOCK S6

"CUSTOM" BOXLOCKS/SIDELOCKS

There are no standard Francotte models, since every shotgun is custom made in Belgium to the purchaser's individual specifications. Features and options include Anson & Deeley boxlocks or Auguste Francotte system sidelocks. All guns have custom-fitted stocks. Available are exhibition-grade stocks as well as extensive engraving and gold inlays. U.S. agent for Auguste Francotte of Belgium is Armes de Chasse (see Directory of Manufacturers and Distributors).

SPECIFICATIONS
Gauges: 12, 16, 20, 28, .410; also 24 and 32
Chambers: 2 1/2", 2 3/4" and 3" *Barrel length:* To customer's specifications *Forend:* To customer's specifications *Stock:* Deluxe to exhibition grade; pistol, English or half-pistol grip
Prices: BASIC BOXLOCK $11,090.00
BASIC BOXLOCK (28 & .410 ga.) 15,250.00
BASIC SIDELOCK .27,935.00
BASIC SIDELOCK (28 & .410 ga.) 31,552.00

GARBI SIDELOCK SHOTGUNS

MODEL 100 SIDELOCK

MODEL 101

MODEL M100 SIDELOCK

Like this Model 100 shotgun, all Spanish-made Garbi models are Holland & Holland pattern sidelock ejector guns with chopper lump (demibloc) barrels. They are built to English gun standards with regard to design, weight, balance and proportions, and all have the characteristic "feel" associated with the best London

guns. Models offer fine 24-line hand-checkering, with outstanding quality wood-to-metal and metal-to-metal fit. The Model 100 is available in 12, 16, 20 and 28 gauge and sports Purdey-style fine scroll and rosette engraving, partly done by machine.
Price: MODEL 100 SIDELOCK $4,300.00
Also available: MODEL 101 . . . .$5,550.00
MODEL 103A 6,850.00
MODEL 103B 9,750.00
MODEL 103A ROYAL 10,850.00
MODEL 103B ROYAL 13,750.00

MODEL 200

The Model 200 double is available in 12, 16, 20 or 28 gauge; features Holland-pattern stock ejector design, heavy-duty locks, heavy proof, Continental-style floral and scroll engraving, walnut stock.
Price: $9,350.00

HARRINGTON & RICHARDSON

SINGLE-BARREL SHOTGUNS

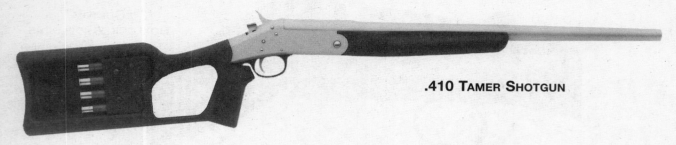

.410 TAMER SHOTGUN

This barreled .410 snake gun features single-shot action, transfer-bar safety and high-impact synthetic stock and forend. Stock has a thumbhole design that sports a full pistol grip and a recessed open side, containing a holder for storing ammo. Forend is modified beavertail configuration.

Other features include a matte, electroless nickel finish.
Weight: 5-6 lbs.
Barrel Length: 20" (3" chamber)
Choke: Full
Price: $124.95

ULTRA SLUG HUNTER

Features: 12-gauge 24" barrel, 3" chamber, fully rifled heavy slug barrel (1:35" twist); Monte Carlo stock and forend of American hardwood w/dark walnut stain; matte black receiver; transfer-bar safety system; scope rail, swivels and sling; ventilated recoil pad.
Price: $209.95

ULTRA SLUG HUNTER DELUXE

SPECIFICATIONS
Gauge: 20 rifled slug (3" chamber)
Action: 12 gauge action
Barrel Length: 24" heavy target-stylle
Rate Of Twist: 1:35" **Finish:** Low-luster blue
Stock: Select hand-checkered camo laminate wood
Features: Transfer-bar safety system, scope rail, vent recoil pad, matte black receiver, swivels and black nylon sling

Price: $239.95
Also available:
ULTRA YOUTH SLUG HUNTER. Features 12-gauge barrel blank underbored to 20 gauge and shortened to 22"; factory-mounted Weaver-style scope base; reduced Monte Carlo stock of American hardwood with dark walnut stain; vent recoil pad, sling swivels and black nylon sling.
Price: $209.95

HARRINGTON & RICHARDSON

SINGLE-BARREL SHOTGUNS

TOPPER MODEL 098

SPECIFICATIONS
Gauges: 12, 20 and .410 (3" chamber); 16 and 28 ga. (2.75" chamber) *Barrel Lengths:* 26" and 28" *Weight:* 5 to 6 lbs. *Action:* Break-open; side lever release; automatic ejection *Stock:* Full pistol grip; American hardwood; black finish with white buttplate spacer *Length Of Pull:* 14.5"
Price: $114.95

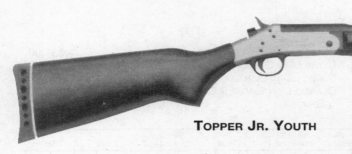

TOPPER JR. YOUTH

SPECIFICATIONS
Gauges: 20 and .410 (3" chamber) *Chokes:* Modified (20 ga.); Full (.410 ga.) *Barrel Length:* 22" and 28" *Weight:* 5 to 6 lbs. *Stock:* Full pistol grip; American hardwood; black finish; white line spacer; recoil pad *Finish:* Satin nickel frame; blued barrel
Price: $119.95

TOPPER JUNIOR CLASSIC

SPECIFICATIONS
Same specifications as the Standard Topper, but with 22" barrel, American black walnut stock and 12.5" pull.
Price: $144.95

TOPPER DELUXE MODEL 098

SPECIFICATIONS
Gauge: 12 (3.5" chamber) *Chokes:* Screw-in Modified (Full, Extra-Full Turkey and Steel Shot also available) *Action:* Break-open; side lever release; positive ejection *Barrel Length:* 28" *Weight:* 5 to 6 lbs. *Stock:* American hardwood, black finish, full pistol-grip stock with semi-beavertail forend; white line spacer; ventilated recoil pad *Finish:* Satin nickel frame; blued barrel

Price: $134.95
Also available:
TOPPER DELUXE RIFLED SLUG GUN. In gauges 12, 20 and 20 Youth; 24" compensated choke barrel, 3" chamber (1:35" twist); nickel frame; black finished American hardwood stock w/recoil pad and swivel studs; fully adjustable rifle sights; transfer-bar safety system.
Price: $169.95

SHOTGUNS

HECKLER & KOCH SHOTGUNS

FABARM SERIES

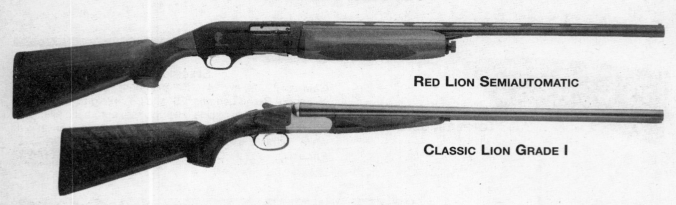

RED LION SEMIAUTOMATIC

CLASSIC LION GRADE I

Prices:

RED LION Semiautomatics 12 ga.	$804.00
GOLD LION Semiautomatic 12 ga.	914.00
FP6 Pump Action 12 ga.	472.00
MAX LION O/U.	1,807.00
BLACK LION COMPETITION 12 & 20 ga.	1,529.00
SILVER LION O/U 12 & 20 ga.	1,331.00
ULTRA MAG LION O/U 12 ga.	1,120.00
SUPER LIGHT LION O/U 12 ga.	1,053.00
CLASSIC LION GRADE II S/S.	2,110.00
GRADE I.	1,488.00

SPECIFICATIONS

Description & Article Number	Gauge (Chamber)	Operation	Magazine Capacity*	Barrel Length	Overall Length	Weight (in pounds)	Choke	Receiver Finish	Stock	Sights
Red Lion #14120	12 (3in)	semi-automatic gas operated	3	24 in.	45.5 in.	7	C,IC,M,IM,F**	matte	gloss walnut	red front bar
Red Lion #16130	12 (3 in.)	semi-automatic gas operated	3	26 in.	47.5 in.	7.1	C,IC,M,IM,F**	matte	gloss walnut	red front bar
Red Lion #18120	12 (3 in.)	semi-automatic gas operated	3	28 in.	49.5 in.	7.2	C,IC,M,IM,F**	matte	gloss walnut	red front bar
Gold Lion #14220	12 (3 in.)	semi-automatic gas operated	3	24 in.	45.5 in.	6.9	C,IC,M,IM,F**	matte	oil finished walnut with olive grip cap	red front bar
Gold Lion #16220	23 (3 in.)	semi-automatic gas operated	3	26 in.	47.5 in.	6	C,IC,M,IM,F**	matte	oil finished walnut with olive grip cap	red front bar
Gold Lion #18220	12 (3 in.)	semi-automatic gas operated	3	28 in.	49.5 in.	7.2	C,IC,M,IM,F**	matte	oil finished walnut with olive grip cap	red front bar
FP6 #40621	12 (3 in.)	pump action	5	20 in.	41.25 in.	6.6	cylinder, barrel threaded for chokes	matte	polymer	blade front
Max Lion #26320	12 (3 in.)	over-and-under	n/a	26 in.	47.5 in.	7.4	C,IC,M,IM,F**	silver	walnut	red front bar
Max Lion #28320	12 (3 in.)	over-and-under	n/a	28 in.	49.5 in.	7.6	C,IC,M,IM,F**	silver	walnut	red front bar
Max Lion #23320	12 (3 in.)	over-and-under	n/a	30 in.	51.5 in.	7.8	C,IC,M,IM,F**	silver	walnut	red front bar
Max Lion 20 Gauge #26300	20 (3 in.)	over-and-under	n/a	26 in.	47.6 in.	6.8	C,IC,M,IM,F**	silver	walnut	red front bar
Max Lion 20 Gauge #28300	20 (3 in.)	over-and-under	n/a	28 in.	49.6 in.	7	C,IC,M,IM,F**	silver	walnut	red front bar
Black Lion Competition #26420	12 (3 in.)	over-and-under	n/a	26 in.	47.5 in.	7	C,IC,M,IM,F**	black	deluxe walnut	red front bar
Black Lion Competition #28420	12 (3 in.)	over-and-under	n/a	28 in.	49.5	7.4	C,IC,M,IM,F**	black	deluxe walnut	red front bar
Black Lion Competition #23420	12 (3 in.)	over-and-under	n/a	30 in.	51.5 in.	7.8	C,IC,M,IM,F**	black	deluxe walnut	red front bar
Black Lion Competition 20 Ga. #26400	20 (3 in.)	over-and-under	n/a	26 in.	47.6 in.	6.8	C,IC,M,IM,F**	black	deluxe walnut	red front bar
Black Lion Competition 20 Ga. #28400	20 (3 in.)	over-and-under	n/a	28 in.	49.6 in.	7	C,IC,M,IM,F**	black	deluxe walnut	red front bar
Silver Lion #26520	12 (3 in.)	over-and-under	n/a	26 in.	47.5 in.	7.2	C,IC,M,IM,F**	silver	walnut	red front bar
Silver Lion #28520	12 (3 in.)	over-and-under	n/a	28 in.	49.5 in.	7.5	C,IC,M,IM,F**	silver	walnut	red front bar
Silver Lion #23520	12 (3 in.)	over-and-under	n/a	30 in.	51.5 in.	7.7	C,IC,M,IM,F**	silver	walnut	red front bar
Silver Lion 20 Gauge #26500	20 (3in.)	over-and-under	n/a	26 in.	47.6 in.	6.8	C,IC,M,IM,F**	silver	walnut	red front bar
Silver Lion 20 Gauge #28500	20 (3 in.)	over-and-under	n/a	28 in.	49.6 in.	7.1	C,IC,M,IM,F**	silver	walnut	red front bar
Ultra Mag Lion #58520	20 (3 in.)	over-and-under	n/a	28 in.	50 in.	7.9	SS-F,SS-M,C,IC,M,IM,F**	silver	black colored walnut	red front bar
Super Light Lion #64520	12 (3 in.)	over-and-under	n/a	24 in.	45.5 in.	6.5	C,IC,M,IM,F**	silver	walnut	red front bar
Classic Lion Grade I #38320	12 (3 in.)	side-by-side	n/a	26 in.	47.6 in.	7	C,IC,M,IM,F**	silver	walnut	red front bar
Classic Lion Grade II #36520	12 (3 in.)	side-by-side	n/a	26 in.	47.6 in.	7.2	C,IC,M,IM,F**	silver	walnut	red front bar

*Magazine capacity given for 2.75 inch shells, size variations among some brands may result in less capacity.
**Cylinder, Improved Cylinder, Modified, Improved Modified, Full, SS-F (Steel Shot-Full) SS-M (Steel Shot-Modified)Specifications & models subject to change without notice.

HECKLER & KOCH SHOTGUNS

FABARM SERIES

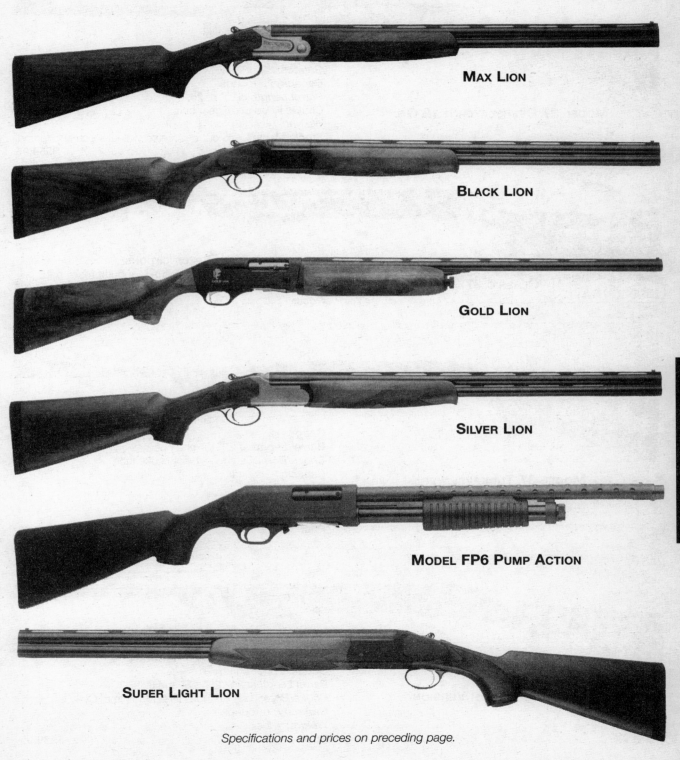

MAX LION

BLACK LION

GOLD LION

SILVER LION

MODEL FP6 PUMP ACTION

SUPER LIGHT LION

Specifications and prices on preceding page.

SHOTGUNS

ITHACA SHOTGUNS

MODEL 37 DEERSLAYER II 12 GA.

SPECIFICATIONS
Gauges: 12 or 20 (3" chamber)
Capacity: 5 rounds
Barrel Lengths: 20" or 25"
Choke: Rifled bore; deer bore
Weight: 7 lbs.
Stock: Monte Carlo cut-checkered walnut stock and forend
Price: $559.95

CLASSIC 37

SPECIFICATIONS
Features corncob ringtail forearm, sunburst recoil pad, American walnut stock, screw-in choke tubes.
Price: . . . . **Available on request**

MODEL 37 TURKEYSLAYER

SPECIFICATIONS
Gauge: 12
Barrel Lengths: 22" (3" chamber)
Choke/Bore: Caton Tightshot choke tube
Capacity: 5 rounds
Weight: 7 lbs.
Stock: Monte Carlo
Features: Four camouflage options
Price: $559.95

MODEL 37 ENGLISH VERSION

SPECIFICATIONS
Gauge: 20 (3" chamber)
Barrel Lengths: 24", 26", 28" and 30"
Choke/Bore: 3 choke tubes (Full, Mod., Imp. Cyl.)
Capacity: 5 rounds
Weight: 7 lbs.
Price: $539.95

KBI/ARMSCOR SHOTGUNS

ARMSCOR MODEL M-30F FIELD

ARMSCOR FIELD PUMP SHOTGUN

SPECIFICATIONS
Gauge: 12 (3" chamber)
Capacity: 6 shot
Choke: Modified (Model M-30F); 2 ICT (Model M-30F/MC)
Barrel Length: 28" *Overall Length:* 47.5"

Weight: 7.6 lbs.
Stock: Walnut-finished hardwood buttstock and forend
Features: Double slide-action bars; damascened bolt
Prices:
MODEL M-30F $239.00
MODEL M-30F/MC. 269.00

ARMSCOR MODEL M-30R8

ARMSCOR MODELS M-30R8/M-306 RIOT PUMP SHOTGUNS

SPECIFICATIONS
Gauge: 12 (3" chamber) *Choke:* Cylinder
Capacity: 6-shot (M-30R6); 8-shot (M-30R8)
Barrel Lengths: 18.5" (M-30R6); 20" (M-30R8)
Overall Length: 37.75" and 39.75"
Weight: 7 lbs. and 7.2 lbs.

Stock: Walnut-finished hardwood buttstock and forend
Features: Double-action slide bar; damascened bolt; blued finish
Prices:
M-30R6 . . . . $209.00
M-30R8 . . . . 224.00

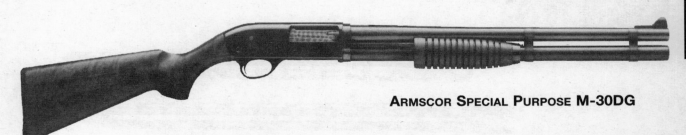

ARMSCOR SPECIAL PURPOSE M-30DG

ARMSCOR SPECIAL PURPOSE SHOTGUN

SPECIFICATIONS
Gauge: 12 (3" chamber)
Choke: Cylinder *Barrel Length:* 20"
Overall Length: 39.25" *Weight:* 7.5 lbs.
Stock: Walnut-finished hardwood (Model 30SAS has speedfeed 4-shot capacity buttstock and synthetic forend)

Features: Double-action slide bar; damascened bolt; Model M-30DG has 7-shot magazine in traditional stocked/blued pump shotgun with iron sights; Model M-30SAS has ventilated shroud and parkerized finish
Prices:
MODEL M-30DG. $249.00
MODEL M-30SAS. 289.00

KRIEGHOFF SHOTGUNS

(See following page for additional Specifications and Prices)

MODEL K-80 SPORTING CLAY

MODEL K-80 TRAP, SKEET, SPORTING CLAY AND LIVE BIRD

Barrels: Made of Boehler steel; free-floating bottom barrel with adjustable point of impact; standard Trap and Live Pigeon ribs are tapered step; standard Skeet, Sporting Clay and International ribs are tapered or parallel flat.

Receivers: Hard satin-nickel finish; casehardened; blue finish available as special order

Triggers: Wide profile, single selective, position adjustable.

Weight: 8 1/2" lbs. (Trap); 8 lbs. (Skeet)

Ejectors: Selective automatic

Sights: White pearl front bead and metal center bead

Stocks: Hand-checkered and epoxy-finished Select European walnut stock and forearm; stocks available in seven different styles and dimensions

Safety: Push button safety located on top tang.

Also available:

SKEET SPECIAL 28" and 30" barrel; tapered flat or 8mm rib; 5 choke tubes.

Price: Standard $7,575.00

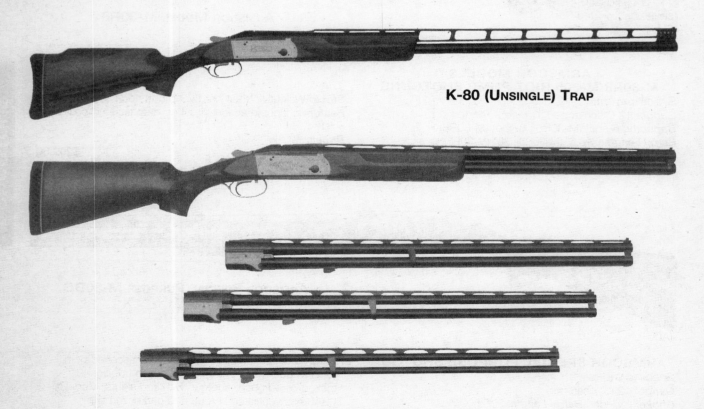

K-80 (UNSINGLE) TRAP

**K-80 AMERICAN SKEET
(4-BARREL SET)**

KRIEGHOFF SHOTGUNS

SPECIFICATIONS AND PRICES MODEL K-80 *(see also preceding page)*

MODEL	DESCRIPTION	BBL. LENGTH	CHOKE	STANDARD	BAVARIA	DANUBE	GOLD TARGET	EXTRA BARRELS
TRAP	Over & Under	30"/32"	IMI/F	$7,375.00	$12,525.00	$23,625.00	$27,170.00	$2,900.00
		30"/32"	CT/CT	8,025.00	13,175.00	24,275.00	27,820.00	3,550.00
	Unsingle	32"/34"	Full	7,950.00	13,100.00	24,200.00	27,745.00	3,575.00
	Combo	30" + 34"	IM/F&F	20,475.00	15,625.00	26,725.00	30,270.00	
	(Top Single)	32" + 34"	CT/CT&CT	11,550.00	16,700.00	27,800.00	31,345.00	
		30" + 32"						
	Combo	30" + 34"	IM/F&F	9,975.00	15,125.00	26,225.00	29,770.00	2,950.00
	(Unsingle)							
		32" + 34"	CT/CT&CT	11,050.00	16,200.00	27,300.00	30,845.00	3,375.00
Optional Features:								
Screw-in chokes (Top or Unsingle)		$425.00						
Single factory release		425.00						
Double factory release		750.00						
SKEET	4-Barrel Set	28"/12 ga.	Tula					$2,990.00
		28"/20 ga.	Skeet					2,880.00
		28"/28 ga.	Skeet	$16,950.00	$22,100.00	$33,200.00	$36,845.00	2,990.00
		28"/.410 ga.	Skeet					2,880.00
	2-Barrel Set	28"/12 ga.	Tula	11,840.00	18,990.00	28,090.00	31,685.00	4,150.00
	Lightweight	28" + 30"/12 ga.	Skeet	6,900.00	N/A	N/A	N/A	2,650.00
	1-Barrel Set	28"	Skeet	8,825.00	13,975.00	25,075.00	28,620.00	4,150.00
	International	28"/12 ga.	Tula	7,825.00	12,975.00	24,075.00	27,620.00	2,990.00
	Skeet Special			7,575.00	12,725.00	23,825.00	27,370.00	3,300.00
SPORTING CLAYS	Over/Under w/screw-in tubes (5)	28" + 30" + 32"/ 12 ga. 30" Semi-Light	Tubes IC/ICTF	$8,150.00	$13,300.00	$24,400.00	$27,945.00	$2,900.00

Optional engravings: Super Scroll – $1,995.00; Gold Super Scroll – $4,450.00; Parcours – $2,100.00; Parcours Special – $3,950.00

MODEL KS-5

The KS-5 is a single barrel trap gun made by KRIEGHOFF, Ulm/Germany—the K-80 people— and marketed by Krieghoff International. Standard specifications include: 12 gauge, 2 3/4" chamber, ventilated tapered step rip, and a casehardened receiver (satin gray finished in electroless nickel). The KS-5 features an adjustable point of impact from 50/50 to 70/30 by means of different optional fronthangers. Screw-in chokes and factory adjustable comb stocks are available options. An adjustable rib (AR) and comb stock (ADJ) are standard features.

The KS-5 is available with pull trigger or optional factory release trigger, adjustable externally for poundage. The KS-5 can be converted to release by the installation of the release parts. To assure consistency and proper functioning, release triggers are installed ONLY by Krieghoff International. Release parts are NOT available separately. These shotguns are available in Standard grade only. Engraved models can be special ordered.

Prices:
KS-5 32" or 34" barrel, Full choke, case $3,695.00
KS-5 SPECIAL 32" or 34" barrel, Full choke, AR ADJ, cased .4,695.00
Options available:
KS-5 SCREW-IN CHOKES (M, IM, F), add to base price $425.00
KS-5 FACTORY ADJ (adjustable comb stock), **add** to base price $395.00
Other Features and Accessories:
KS-5 REGULAR BARREL $2,100.00
KS-5 SPECIAL BARREL (F) 2,750.00
KS-5 SCREW-IN CHOKE BARREL 2,525.00
KS-5 SPECIAL SCREW-IN CHOKE BARREL 3,175.00
KS-5 FACTORY ADJUSTABLE STOCK 1,145.00
KS-5 STOCK 750.00
KS-5 FOREARM 290.00
KS-5 RELEASE TRIGGER (INSTALLED) 295.00
KS-5 FRONTHANGER 70.00
KL-5 ALUMINUM CASE 425.00
KS-5 INDIVIDUAL CHOKE TUBES 75.00

MAGTECH SHOTGUNS

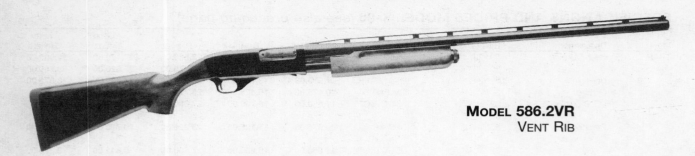

MODEL 586.2VR
VENT RIB

MODEL 586.2VR SERIES

The Magtech 586.2VR Series 12-gauge pump shotguns handle 2.75" and 3" magnum shells interchangeably and give the shooter custom features, including: • ordnance-grade, deep-blued steel receiver • double-action sllide bars • hand-finished Brazilian Embuia wood stock and forearm • hammer-forged chrome-moly barrel • high-profile steel rib • brass mid-bead and ivory-colored front sight • chrome-plated bolt • screw-in Magchokes in IC, Mod. and Full • crossbolt safety • special magazine release for unloading without cycling round through the chamber.

SPECIFICATIONS
Guage: 12 (2.75" or 3" shells)
Capacity: 5 rounds (8 in Model 586.2P)
Chokes: Magchokes in IC, Mod. & Full (IC only in Model 586.2P)
Barrel: 26" and 28", vent rib (19" plain in Model 586.2P)
Overall Length: 46.25" and 48.25" (39.25" in Model 586.2P)
Sights: Two beads (one bead in Model 586.2P)
Prices:
MODEL 586.2VR26 AND 586.2VR28 . . . . $255.00
MODEL 586.2P 235.00

MARLIN SHOTGUNS

MODEL 512DL w/FIRE SIGHTS

MODEL 512DL SLUGMASTER

SPECIFICATIONS
Guage: 12 (up to 3" shells)
Capacity: 2-shot box magazine (+1 in chamber)
Action: Bolt action; thumb safety; red cocking indicator
Barrel Length: 21" rifled (1:28" right-hand twist)
Overall Length: 44.75"
Weight: 8 lbs. (w/o scope and mount)

Sights: Adjustable folding semi-buckhorn rear; ramp front with brass bead and removable cutaway Wide-Scan® hood; receiver drilled and tapped for scope mount
Stock: Black fiberglass-filled synthetic w/molded-in checkering and padded black nylon sling
Prices: $372.00

MARLIN SHOTGUNS

MODEL 512 SLUGMASTER

SPECIFICATIONS
Gauge: 12 (up to 3" shells)
Capacity: 2-shot box magazine (+1 in chamber)
Action: Bolt action; thumb safety; red cocking indicator
Barrel Length: 21" rifled (1:28" right-hand twist)
Overall Length: 44.75" *Weight:* 8 lbs. (w/o scope and mount)

Sights: Adjustable folding semi-buckhorn rear; ramp front with brass bead and removable cutaway Wide-Sacn® hood; receiver drilled and tapped for scope mount
Stock: Walnut finished, press-checkered Maine birch w/pistol grip and Mar-Shield® finish, swivel studs, vent, recoil pad
Price: $356.00

MODEL 50DL

SPECIFICATIONS
Gauge: 12 ga. (2.75" or 3" chamber)
Capacity: 2-shot clip
Action: Bolt action
Barrel Length: 28" (Modified choke)

Overall Length: 48.75" *Weight:* 7.5 lbs.
Sights: Brass bead front; U-groove rear
Stock: Black synthetic w/ventilated rubber recoil pad
Features: Thumb safety; red cocking indicator; swivel studs
Price: $326.00

MARLIN MODEL 55GDL GOOSE GUN

High-flying ducks and geese are the Goose Gun's specialty. The Marlin Goose Gun has an extra-long 36-inch full-choked barrel and Magnum capability, making it the perfect choice for tough spots at wary waterfowl. It also features a quick-loading 2-shot clip magazine, a convenient leather carrying strap and a quality ventilated recoil pad.

SPECIFICATIONS
Gauge: 12; 2.75" Magnum, 3" Magnum or 2.75" regular shells (also handles rifled slugs and buckshot)

Choke: Full
Capacity: 2-shot detachable box magazine
Action: Bolt action; positive thumb safety; red cocking indicator
Barrel Length: 36"
Overall Length: 56.75"
Weight: 8 lbs.
Sights: Bead front sight and U-Groove rear sight
Stock: Black fiberglass-filled synthetic stock w/molded-in checkering
Price: $380.00

MAROCCHI SHOTGUNS

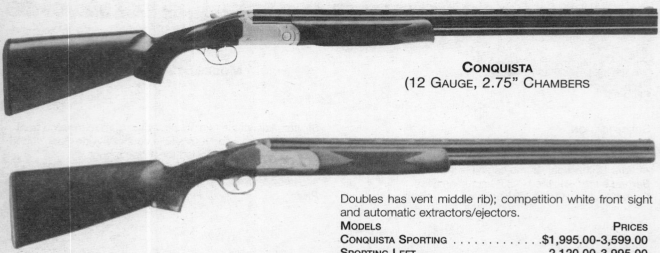

CONQUISTA
(12 GAUGE, 2.75" CHAMBERS)

CONQUISTA SPORTING CLAYS GRADE III

The Marocchi shotguns listed below all feature 10mm concave ventilated upper rib; Classic middle rib (Classic Doubles has vent middle rib); competition white front sight and automatic extractors/ejectors.

MODELS	PRICES
CONQUISTA SPORTING	$1,995.00-3,599.00
SPORTING LEFT	2,120.00-3,995.00
LADY SPORT	2,120.00-2,300.00
CONQUISTA TRAP	1,995.00-3,599.00
CONQUISTA SKEET	1,995.00-3,599.00
CLASSIC DOUBLES	1,598.00

SPECIFICATIONS CONQUISTA SHOTGUNS (all 12 Gauge)

	CONQUISTA SPORTING	SPORTING LEFT	LADY SPORT	CONQUISTA TRAP	CONQUISTA SKEET	CLASSIC DOUBLES
BARRELS						
Gauge	12	12	12	12	12	12
Chamber	2 3/4"	2 3/4"	2 3/4"	2 3/4"	2 3/4"	2 3/4"
Barrel Length	28",30",32"	28",30",32"	28",30"	29",30"	28	30"
Chokes	Contrechokes	Contrechokes	Contrechokes	Full/Full	Skeet/Skeet	Contre Plus
TRIGGER						
Trigger type	Instajust Selective	Instajust Selective	Instajust Selective	Instajust	Instajust Selective	Instajust Selective
Trigger Pull (Weight)	3.5 - 4.0 lb.s	3.5 - 4.0 lb.s	3.5 - 4.0 lb.s	3.5 - 4.0 lb.s	3.5 - 4.0 lb.s	3.5 - 4.0 lb.s
Trigger Pull (Length)	14 1/2" - 14 7/8"	14 1/2" - 14 7/8"	13 7/8" - 14 1/4"	14 1/2" - 14 7/8"	14 1/2" - 14 7/8"	14 1/4" - 14 5/8"
STOCK						
Drop at comb	1 7/16"	1 7/16"	1 11/32"	1 9/32"	1 1/2"	1 3/8"
Drop at heel	2 3/16"	2 3/16"	2 9/32"	1 11/16"	2 3/16"	2 1/8"
Cast at heel	3/16" Off	3/16" Off	3/16" Off	3/16" Off	3/16" Off	N/A
Cast at toe	3/8" Off	3/8" On	3/8" Off	5/16" Off	3/16" Off	N/A
Stock			Select Walnut			
Checkering	20 lines/inch	20 lines/inch	20 lines/inch	20 lines/inch	20 lines/inch	18 lines/inch
OVERALL						
Length Overall	45" - 45"	45" - 49"	44 3/8"-46 3/8"	47" - 49"	45"	47"
Weight Approx.*	7 7/8 lbs.	7 7/8 lbs.	71/2 lbs.	8 1/4 lbs.	7 3/4 lbs.	8 1/8 lbs.

MERKEL SHOTGUNS

OVER/UNDER SHOTGUNS

Merkel over-and-unders are the first hunting guns with barrels arranged one above the other, and they have since proved to be able competitors of the side-by-side gun. Merkel superiority lies in the following details:

- Available in 12, 16 and 20 gauge (28 ga. in Model 201E with 26 ³/₄" barrel)
- Lightweight from 6.4 to 7.28 lbs.
- The high, narrow forend protects the shooter's hand from the barrel in hot or cold climates
- The forend is narrow and therefore lies snugly in the hand to permit easy and positive swinging
- The slim barrel line provides an unobstructed field of view and thus permits rapid aiming and shooting
- The over-and-under barrel arrangement reduces recoil error; the recoil merely pushes the muzzle up vertically

**MODEL 203E
SIDELOCK**

MODEL 2001EL

MERKEL OVER/UNDER SHOTGUN

SPECIFICATIONS
Gauges: 12, 16, 20, 28
Barrel Lengths: 26.75" and 28"
Weight: 6.4 to 7.28 lbs.
Stock: English or pistol grip in European walnut
Features: All models include three-piece forearm, automatic ejectors, Kersten double crossbolt lock, Blitz action and single selective or double triggers.
Prices:
MODEL 2001EL
12 ga. 28" IC/Mod, Mod/Full $5,895.00
20 ga. 26.75" IC/Mod, Mod/Full 5,895.00
28 ga. 26.75" IC/Mod 6,495.00

MODEL 2000EL Kersten double cross-bolt lock; scroll engraved silver-grey receiver; modified Anson & Deeley box action; ejectors; single or double triggers, luxury grade wood; pistol grip or English-style stock.
12 ga. 28" IC/Mod, Mod/Full 4,995.00
20 ga. 26.75" IC/Mod, Mod/Full 4,995.00
MODEL 2002EL Same features as Model 2000EL but with hunting scenes w/arabesque engraving
12 ga. 28"; 20 ga. and 28 ga., 26.75" 9,995.00
SIDELOCKS
MODEL 203E 12 or 16 ga., 28" IC/Mod, Mod/Full (w/English-style engraving) 11,995.00
MODEL 210E Kersten double cross-bolt lock; scroll engraved, case hardened receiver; Blitz action, double-triggers; pistol grip stock w/cheekpiece; ejectors 6,195.00
MODEL 211E Same as Model 210E but with engraved hunting scenes on silver-grey receiver 7,495.00

MODEL 203E

MERKEL SHOTGUNS

SIDE-BY-SIDE SHOTGUNS

MODEL 47E BOXLOCK

MODEL 147E BOXLOCK

SPECIFICATIONS
Gauges: 12 and 200 (28 ga. in Models 147E and 147S)
Barrel Lengths: 26" and 28" (25.5" in Models 47S and 147S)
Weight: 6-7 lbs.
Stock: English or pistol grip in European walnut
Features: Models 47E and 147E are boxlocks; Models 47S and 147S are sidelocks. All guns have cold hammer-forged barrels, double triggers, double lugs and Greener crossbolt locking systems and automatic ejectors.
Prices:
MODEL 47E (Holland & Holland ejectors) $2,695.00

MODEL 122 (H&H ejectors, engraved
   hunting scenes **4,995.00**
MODEL 147 (H&H ejectors). **2,995.00**
MODEL 147E (engraved hunting scenes)
   12, 16 & 20 ga. **3,195.00**
   28 ga. **3,895.00**
MODEL 47SL SIDELOCK (H&H ejectors) **5,295.00**
MODEL 147SL SIDELOCK 12, 16 & 20 ga. **6,695.00**
   28 ga. **6,995.00**
MODEL 247S (English-style engraving). **6,995.00**
MODEL 447SL **8,995.00**

MODEL 47S SIDE-BY-SIDE

MODEL 247S SIDELOCK

MOSSBERG PUMP SHOTGUNS

MODEL 500 SPORTING

All Mossberg Model 500 pump-action shotguns feature 3" chambers, Milspec tough, lightweight alloy receivers with "top thumb safety." Standard models includes 6-shot capacity with 2 3/4" shells, cut-checkered stock, Quiet Carry forearms, gold trigger, engraved receiver, blued Woodland Camo or Marinecote metal finish and the largest selection of accessory barrels. Ten-year limited warranty.

MODEL 500 SPORTING

SPECIFICATIONS & PRICES MODEL 500 CROWN GRADE (FIELD & SLUGSTER)

Ga.	Stock #	Bb;/ Length	Barrel Type	Sights	Chokes	Stock	Length O/A	Wt.	Q.D. Studs	Notes	Prices
12	54220	28"	Vent rib, ported	2 Beads	Accu-Choke	Walnut Finish	48"	7.2		IC, Mod. & Full Tubes	$312.00
12	54116	26"	Vent rib, ported	2 Beads	Accu-Choke	Walnut Finish	46"	7.1		IC, Mod. Tubes	312.00
	Bantam									Mod. Tube Only, Bantam	
20	54132	22"	Vent Rib	2 Beads	Accu-Choke	Walnut Finish	42"	6.9		Stock	312.00
20	54136	26"	Vent Rib	2 Beads	Accu-Choke	Walnut Finish	46"	7.0		IC, Mod. & Full Tubes	312.00
	Bantam										
.410	50149	24"	Plain	2 Beads	Full	Synthetic	43"	6.8		Fixed Choke, Bantam Stock	300.00
.410	58104	24"	Vent Rib	2 Beads	Full	Walnut Finish	44"	6.8		Fixed Choke	307.00
12	54232	24"	Trophy Slugster™ Ported	Scop Mount	Rifled Bore	Walnut Finish	44"	7.3	Y	Dual-Comb™ Stock	369.00
12	54244	24"	Slugster, ported	Rifle	Rifled Bore	Walnut Finish	44"	7.0	Y		341.00
12	54844	24"	Slugster, ported	Rifle	Rifled Bore	Walnut Finish	44"	7.0	Y		371.00
20	54233	24"	Trophy Slugster™ Ported	Scope[e Mount	Rifled Bore	Walnut Finish	44"	s6.9	Y	Dual-Comb™ Stock	369.00
	Bantam										
20	58252	24"	Slugster	Rifle	Rifled Bore	Walnut Finish	44"	s6.9	Y	Bantam Stock	341.00

SPECIFICATIONS MODEL 500 COMBOS

Ga.	Stock #	Bb;/ Length	Barrel Type	Sights	Chokes	Stock	Length O/A	Wt.	Q.D. Studs	Notes	Prices
12	54243	28" / 24"	Vent rib, ported / Trophy Slugster™ ported	2 Beads / Scope Mount	Accu-Choke / Rifled Bore	Walnut Finish	48"	7.2	Y	IC, Mod. & Full Tubes / Dual-Comb™ Stock	425.00
12	54264	24"	Vent rib, ported / Slugster, ported	2 Beads / Rifle	Accu-Choke / Rifled Bore	Walnut Finish	48"	7.2	Y	IC, Mod. & Full Tubes	409.00
12	58483	28" / 18.5"	Plain / Plain	Bead / Bead	Modified / Cyl. Bore	Walnut Finish	48"	7.2		Fixed Choke, Pistol Grip Kit	340.00
20	54282	26" / 24"	Vent Rib / Slugster, ported	2 Beads / Rifle	Accu-Choke / Rifled Bore	Walnut Finish	46"	7.0	Y	IC, Mod. & Full Tubes	393.00
12	54169	28" / 18.5"	Vent rib, ported / Plain	2 Beads / Bead	Accu-Choke / Cyl. Bore	Walnut Finish	48"	7.2		IC, Mod. & Full Tube Pistol Grip Kit	359.00
.410	58456	24" / 18.5"	Vent Rib / Plain	2 Beads / Bead	Full / Cyl. Bore	Walnut Finish	44"	6.8		Fixed Choke, Pistol Grip Kit	362.00
20	54283	26" / 24"	Vent Rib / Trophy Slugster™ Ported	2 Beads / Scope Mount	Accu-Choke / Rifled Bore	Walnut Finish	46"	7.0		IC, Mod. & Full Tubes / Dual-Comb Stock	425.00
20	54188	22" / 24"	Vent Rib / Slugster, ported	2 Beads / Rifle	Accu-Choke / Rifled Bore	Walnut Finish	42"	7.0		IC, Mod. & Full Tubes / Bantam Stock & Forearm	386.00

Also available: **#54158**, same as **#54264** but w/o Q.D. studs. **$374.00**

MOSSBERG PUMP SHOTGUNS

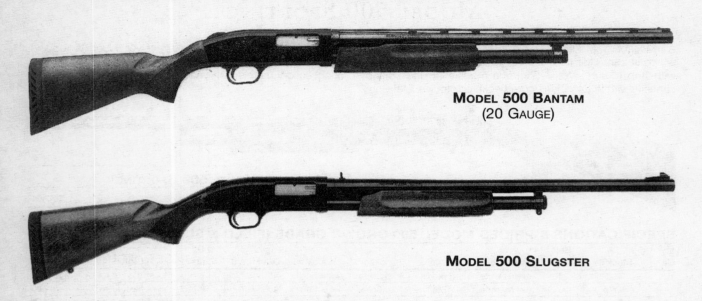

MODEL 500 BANTAM
(20 GAUGE)

MODEL 500 SLUGSTER

SPECIFICATIONS MODEL 500 WOODLAND CAMO (6-SHOT)

12	52193	28"	Vent rib, ported	2 Beads	Accu-Choke	Synthetic	48"	7.2	Y	IC, Mod. & Full Tubes	$336.00
12	50195	24"	Vent Rib	2 Beads	Accu-Choke	Synthetic	44"	7.1	Y	IC, Mod., Full & X-Full Tubes	339.00
	Bantam										
20	58135	22"	Vent Rib	2 Beads	Accu-Choke	Synthetic	42"	6.8	Y	X-Full Tubes only	322.00
	Combo	28"	Vent Rib, Ported	2 Beads	Accu-Choke						
12	52213	24"	Slugster, Ported	Rifle	Rifled Bore	Synthetic	48"	7.2	Y	IC, Mod. & Full Tubes	434.00
	Combo	24"	Vent Rib, Ported	2 Beads	Accu-Choke					X-Full Tube	
12	58143	24"	Slugster, Ported	Scope Base	Rifled Bore	Synthetic	46"	6.9	Y	Dual-Combo Stock	445.00

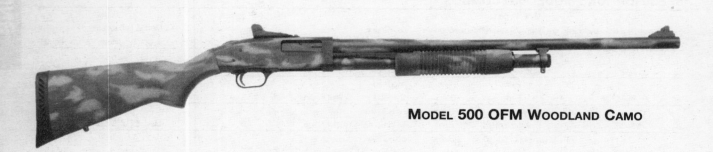

MODEL 500 OFM WOODLAND CAMO

MODEL 500 AMERICAN FIELD (Pressed Checkered, Blued Barrel)

12	50120	28"	Vent Rib	2 Beads	Accu-Choke	Walnut Finish	48"	7.2		IC, Mod. & Full Tubes	$309.00
20	50136	26"	Vent Rib	2 Beads	Accu-Choke	Walnut Finish	46"	7.1		Mod. Tube Only	309.00
.410	50104	24"	Vent Rib	2 Beads	Full	Walnut Finish	44"	7.0		Fixed Choke	301.00
12	50044	24"	Slugster, Ported	Rifle	Rifled Bore	Walnut Finish	44"	7.0	Y		336.00

MOSSBERG PUMP SHOTGUNS

MODEL 500/590 SPECIAL PURPOSE

Mossberg's Special Purpose Models 500 and 590 pump shotguns feature lightweight alloy receivers with ambidextrous "top thumb safety" button, walnut-finished wood or durable synthetic stocks with Quiet Carry™ forearms, rubber recoil pads, dual extractors, two slide bars and twin cartridge stops, Ten-year limited warranty.

SPECIFICATIONS

Gauge	Barrel Length	Sight	Stock #	Finish	Stock	Capacity	Overall Length	Weight	Notes	Price
MODEL 500/590 MARINER™ (CYLINDER BORE BARRELS)										
12	18.5"	Bead	50273	Marinecote™	Synthetic	6	38.5"	6.8	Includes Pistol Grip	$412.00
12	20"	Bead	50299	Marinecote™	Synthetic	9	40"	7.0	Includes Pistol Grip	425.00
12	20"	Ghost Ring™	50296	Marinecote™	Synthetic	9	40"	7.0		480.00
MODEL 500 SPECIAL PURPOSE (CYLINDER BORE BARRELS) PERSUADER/CRUISER										
12	18.5"	Bead	50404	Blue	Walnut Finish	6	38.5"	6.8	Includes Pistol Grip	$282.00
12	18.5"	Bead	50411	Blue	Synthetic	6	38.5"	6.8	Includes Pistol Grip	282.00
12	18.5"	Bead	50440	Blue	Pistol Grip	6	28"	5.6	Includes Heat Shield	282.00
20	18.5"	Bead	50452	Blue	Synthetic	6	38.5"	6.8	Includes Pistol Grip	281.00
20	18.5"	Bead	50450	Blue	Pistol Grip	6	28"	5.6		274.00
.410	18.5"	Bead	50455	Blue	Pistol Grip	6	28"	5.3		281.00
12	20"	Bead	50564	Blue	Walnut Finish	8	40"	7.0	Includes Pistol Grip	282.00
12	20"	Bead	50579	Blue	Synthetic	8	40"	7.0	Includes Pistol Grip	282.00
12	20"	Bead	50580	Blue	Pistol Grip	8	40"	7.0		282.00
20	21"	Bead	50581	Blue	Synthetic	8	38.5"	6.9	Includes Pistol Grip	281.00
20	21"	Bead	50582	Blue	Pistol Grip	8	28.5"	5.6		274.00
MODEL 590 SPECIAL PURPOSE (CYLINDER BORE BARRELS)										
12	20"	Bead	50645	Blue	Synthetic	9	40"	7.2	w/Acc. Lug & Heat Shield	341.00
12	20"	Bead	50650	Blue	Speed Feed	9	40"	7.2	w/Acc. Lug & Heat Shield	374.00
12	20"	Bead	50660	Parkerized	Synthetic	9	40"	7.2	w/Acc. Lug & Heat Shield	393.00
12	20"	Bead	50665	Parkerized	Speed Feed	9	40"	7.2	w/Acc. Lug & Heat Shield	425.00
MODEL 500/590 GHOST RING™ (CYLINDER BORE BARRELS)										
12	18.5"	Ghost Ring™	50402	Blue	Synthetic	6	38.5"	6.8		$332.00
12	18.5"	Ghost Ring™	50517	Parkerized	Synthetic	6	38.5"	6.8		385.00
12	20"	Ghost Ring™	50652	Blue	Synthetic	9	40"	7.2	w/Acc. Lug	391.00
12	20"	Ghost Ring™	50663	Parkerized	Synthetic	9	40"	7.2	w/Acc. Lug	447.00
12	20"	Ghost Ring™	50668	Parkerized	Speed Feed	9	40"	7.2	w/Acc. Lug	481.00
HS 410 HOME SECURITY (SPREADER CHOKE)										
.410	18.5"	Bead	50359	Blue	Synthetic	6	39.5"	6.6	Includes Vertical Foregrip	$294.00

MOSSBERG PUMP SHOTGUNS

MODEL 835 ULTI-MAG

Mossberg's Model 835 Ulti-Mag pump action shotgun has a 3 1/2" 12-gauge chamber but can also handle standard 2 3/4" and 3" shells. Field barrels are overbored and ported for optimum patterns and felt recoil reduction. Cut-checkered walnut and walnut-finished stocks and Quiet Carry™ forearms are standard, as are gold triggers and engraved receivers. Camo models are drilled and tapped for scope and feature detachable swivels and sling. All models include a Cablelock™ and 10-year limited warranty.

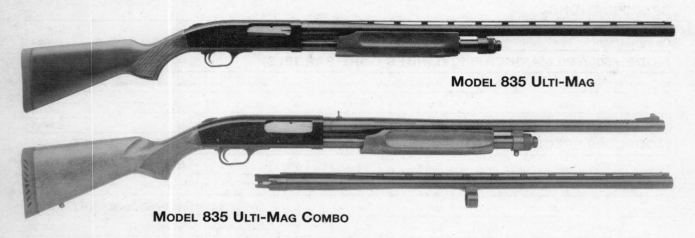

MODEL 835 ULTI-MAG

MODEL 835 ULTI-MAG COMBO

SPECIFICATIONS AND PRICES MODEL 835 ULTI-MAG (12 GAUGE, 6 SHOT)

Ga	Stock No.	Barrel Length	Type	Sights	Choke	Finish	Stock	O.A. Length	W.	Studs	Notes	Price
ULTI-MAG™ 835 CROWN GRADE												
12	68232	24"	Trophy Slugster™, Ported	Scope Mount	Rifled Bore	Blue	Walnut	44.5"	7.3	Y	Dual-Comb™ Stock	$388.00
12	68220	28"	Vent Rib, Ported	2 Beads	Accu-Mag	Blue	Walnut Finish	48.5"	7.7		Mod. Tube Only	334.00
12	68225	24"	Vent Rib, Ported	2 Beads	Accu-Mag	Matte	Walnut Finish	44.5"	7.3		X-Full Tube	341.00
12	68244	28" 24"	Vent Rib, Ported Trophy Slugster™ Ported	2 Beads Scope Mount	Accu-Mag Rifled Bore	Blue	Walnut	48.5"	7.7		Mod. Tube only Dual-Comb™ Stock	448.00
12	68223	28" 24"	Vent Rib, Ported Slugster, Ported	2 Beads Rifle	Accu-Mag Rifled Bore	Blue	Walnut	48.5"	7.7		Mod. Tube only	448.00
12	68260	28" 24"	Vent Rib, Ported Slugster	2 Beads Rifle	Accu-Mag Cyl. Bore	Blue	Walnut Finish	48.5"	7.7		Mod. Tube Only	400.00
ULTI-MAG™ CAMO												
12	61134	24"	Vent Rib, Ported	2 Beads	Accu-Mag	Realtree® A.P.	Synthetic	44.5"	7.3	Y	4 Tube w/Turkey	531.00
12	61434	24"	Vent Rib, Ported	2 Beads	Accu-Mag	Mossy Oak™	Synthetic	44.5"	7.3	Y	4 Tube w/Turkey	531.00
12	62035	28"	Vent Rib, Ported	2 Beads	Accu-Mag	Realtree® A.P.	Synthetic	48.5"	7.7		4 Tubes	531.00
12	68235	28"	Vent Rib, Ported	2 Beads	Accu-Mag	OFM Woodland	Synthetic	48.5"			Mod. Tube	369.00
12	68230	24"	Vent Rib, Ported	2 Beads	Accu-Mag	OFM Woodland	Synthetic	44.5"	7.3	Y	X-Full Tube Only	369.00
12	61247	24"	Vent Rib, Ported Slugster, Ported	2 Beads Rifle	Accu-Mag Rifled Bore	Realtree® A.P.	Synthetic	44.5"	7.3	Y	4 Tube w/Turkey Includes Hard Case	659.00
12	62148	28" 24"	Vent Rib, Ported Slugster, Ported	2 Beads Rifle	Accu-Mag Rifled Bore	OFM Woodland	Wood/ Synthetic	48.5"	7.7	Y	4 Tubes Dual-Comb™ Stock	556.00

MOSSBERG SHOTGUNS

MODEL 9200 W/VENT RIB

SPECIFICATIONS AND PRICES MODEL 9200 (12 Gauge, 5 Shot)

GA	STOCK NO.	BBL. LENGTH	BARREL TYPE	SIGHTS	CHOKE	FINISH	STOCK	LENGTH O.A.	WT.	Q.D. STUDS	NOTES	PRICES
MODEL 9200 CROWN GRADE												
12	49420	28"	Vent Rib, Ported	2 Beads	Accu-Choke	Blue	Walnut	48"	7.7		IC, Mod. & Full Tubes	$534.00
12	49432	24"	Trophy Slugster™	Scope	Rifled Bore	Blue	Walnut	44"	7.3	Y	Dual-Comb™ Stock	554.00
12	49444	24"	Slugster	Rifle	Rifled Bore	Blue	Walnut	44"	7.3			531.00
12	49403	26"	Vent Rib	2 Beads	Accu-Choke	Blue	Walnut	46"	7.5		USST,IC,Mod., Full & Skeet	564.00
12	49435	22"	Vent Rib	2 Beads	Accu-Choke	Blue	Walnut	42"	7.2		IC/Mod., Full Bantam	531.00

MODEL 9200 COMBO

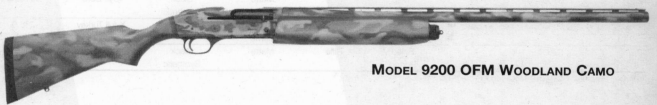

MODEL 9200 OFM WOODLAND CAMO

MODEL 9200 CAM

GA	STOCK NO.	BBL. LENGTH	BARREL TYPE	SIGHTS	CHOKE	FINISH	STOCK	LENGTH O.A.	WT.	Q.D. STUDS	NOTES	PRICES
12	49434	24"	Vent Rib	2 Beads	Accu-Choke	Mossy Oak	Synthetic	44"	7.3	Y	IC, Mod., Full & X-Full Tubes	$595.00
12	49134	24"	Vent Rib	2 Beads	Accu-Choke	Realtree® A.P.	Synthetic	44"	7.3	Y	IC, Mod., Full & X-Full Tubes	595.00
12	49491	28"	Vent Rib	2 Beads	Accu-Choke	OFM Woodland	Synthetic	48"	7.7	Y	IC, Mod. & Full Tubes	516.00
12	49430	24"	Vent Rib	2 Beads	Accu-Choke	OFM Woodland	Synthetic	44"	7.3	Y	X-Full Tubes Only	476.00
12		28"	Vent Rib	2 Beads	Accu-Choke	OFM Woodland	Synthetic	48"	7.7	Y	IC, Mod. & Full Tubes	595.00
	49466	24"	Slugster	Rifle	Rifle Bore	OFM Woodland						
				2 Beads								
12	49443	28"	Vent Rib	Scope	Accu-Choke	Blued	Walnut	48"	7.7		IC, Mod. & Full Tubes	625.00
		24"	Trophy Slugster™	Mount	Rifled Bore						Dual-Comb™ Stock	
12	49464	28"	Vent Rib	2 Beads	Accu-Choke	Blued	Walnut	48"	7.7		IC, Mod., & Full Tubes	605.00
		24"	Slugster	Rifle	Rifled Bore							

SHOTGUNS

MOSSBERG SHOTGUNS

MODEL 695 BOLT ACTION

The 3-inch chambered 12-gauge Model 695 bolt-action shotgun features a 22-inch barrel and rugged synthetic stock. This combination delivers the fast handling and fine balance of a classic sporting rifle. Every Model 695 comes with a two-round detachable magazine and Weaver-style scope bases to give hunters the advantage of today's specialized slug and turkey optics. Mossberg's fully rifled slug barrels are specially "ported" to help soften the recoil and reduce muzzle jump. Mossberg's pioneering involvement with turkey hunting has generated the development of the special Extra-full Accu-Choke Tube. The Model 695 Turkey Gun provides the precise pattern placement to make the most of this remarkably tight patterning choke tube. Non-rotating dual claw extractors ensure reliable ejection and feeding. Ten-year limited warranty.

MOSSBERG MODEL 695 BOLT ACTION

695 OEM CAMO

SPECIFICATIONS

GAUGE	MODEL NO.	BARREL LENGTH	BARREL TYPE	SIGHT	PRICE
12	59001	22"	Rifled Ported	Rifle	$319.00
12	59005	22"	Plain	Bea	286.00
12	59001	22"	Rifled Ported	R	447.00

Includes Bushnell 1.5X-4.5X scope and Protecto case

MOSSBERG LINE LAUNCHER

The line Launcher (20" barrel) is the first shotgun devoted to rescue and personal safety. It provides an early self-contained rescue opportunity for boaters, police and fire departments, salvage operations or whenever an extra-long throw of line is the safest alternative. This shotgun used a 12-gauge blank cartridge to propel a convertible projectile with a line attached. With a floating head attached, the projectile will travel 250 to 275 feet. Removing the floating head increases the projectile range to approx. 700 feet.
Prices: $899.00
LAUNCHER KIT 599.00

MOSSBERG SHOTGUNS

VIKING SERIES

VIKING SERIES
12 GAUGE PUMP ACTION

Mossberg's Viking Series shotguns are available in Models 500 and 835 pump actions or as a Model 9200 Autoloader.

Viking Models are identified by their "Moss-Green" synthetic stocks and matte-metal finish.

SPECIFICATIONS

MODEL	MODEL No.	GAUGE	BARREL LENGTH	BARREL TYPE	CHOKE/FEATURES	OVERALL LENGTH	WEIGHT	PRICE
9200 Autoloader	47420	12	28"	Vent Rib	Accu-choke w/3 tubes	48"	7.7 lbs.	$429.00
835 Ulti-Mag	67220	12	28"	Vent Rib, Ported	Mod. Tube	48"	7.7 lbs.	316.00
	57418	12	28"	Vent Rib, Ported	3 Tubes	48"	7.2 lbs.	287.00
	57125	12	24"	Vent Rib, Ported	Turkey Tube	44"	7.1 lbs.	286.00
	57437	20	26"	Vent Rib	Accu-choke w/3 Tubes	46"	7.1 lbs.	287.00
500 Pump	57244	12	24"	Rifled, Ported	Rifle sights	44"	7.1 lbs.	326.00
Scope Combo	57432	12	24"	Rifled, Ported	Scope base w/bore-sighted scope and Protecto case	44"	7.2 lbs.	394.00

MAVERICK BY MOSSBERG

MAVERICK MODEL 31002

Maverick 12-gauge-only shotguns features durable synthetic stocks and forearms and a crossbolt safety located in front of the trigger. All models have a 3" chamber and a 6-shot capacity with 2 3/4" shells. Barrels are interchangeable with Mossberg brand barrels.

Prices:
MODEL 31002 features 28" barrel, Mod. choke, 48" overall length, bead sight, weights 7.2 lbs. $221.00
MODEL 31017 features 24" barrel with rifle sights, Cyl. Bore, 44" overall length and weight of 7.1 lbs. 235.00
MODEL 31023 features the shorter 18 1/2" barrel with bead sight and Cyl. Bore, overall length of 39" and weight of 6.9 pounds 213.00

NEW ENGLAND FIREARMS

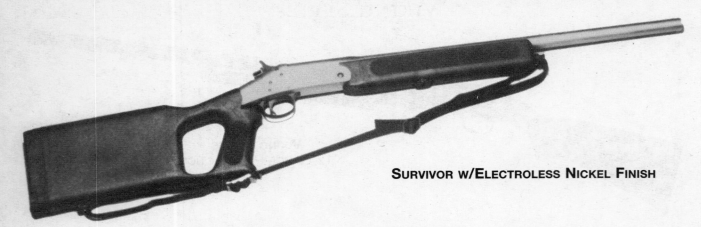

SURVIVOR W/ELECTROLESS NICKEL FINISH

SURVIVOR SERIES

This series of survival arms is available in 12 and 20 ga. with either a blued or electroless nickel finish. All shotguns feature the New England Firearms action with a patented transfer bar safety and high-impact, synthetic stock and forend. The stock is a modified thumbhole design with a full and secure pistol grip. The buttplate is attached at one end with a large thumbscrew for access to a large storage compartment holding a wide variety of survival gear or extra ammunition. The forend, which has a hollow cavity for storing three rounds of ammunition, is accessible by removing a thumbscrew (also used for takedown.)

SPECIFICATIONS
Action: Break open, side-lever release, automatic ejection
Guage: 12, 20, .41/45 Colt (Combo)   **Barrel Length:** 22"
Choke: Modified
Chamber: 3" (Combo also available w/2.5" chamber)
Overall Length: 36"   **Weight:** 6 lbs.   **Sights:** Bead
Stock: High-density polymer, black matte finish, sling swivels
Prices:
Blued finish **$129.95**
Nickel finish **145.95**
.41/45 Colt Combo, blued **145.95**
    Nickel **164.95**

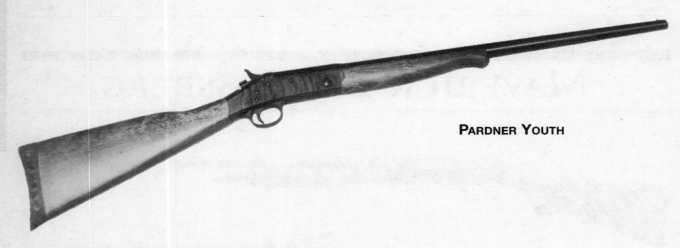

PARDNER YOUTH

PARDNER SINGLE-BARREL SHOTGUNS

SPECIFICATIONS
Guages: 12, 16, 20, 28 and .410
Barrel Lengths: 22" (Youth); 26" (20, 28, .410); 28" (12 and 16 ga.), 32" (12 ga.)
Chokes: Full (alll gauges, except 28); Modified (12, 20 and 28 ga.)

Chamber: 2.75" (16 and 28 ga.); 3" (all others)
Price: **$99.95**
    w/32" barrel **104.95**
Also available:
PARDNER YOUTH. With 22" barrel in gauges 20, 28 and .410 . . . . **$109.95**

NEW ENGLAND FIREARMS

PARDNER TURKEY & GOOSE GUN

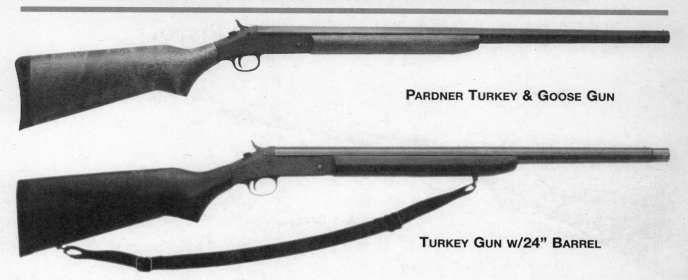

TURKEY GUN w/24" BARREL

TURKEY & GOOSE GUN

SPECIFICATIONS
Guage: 10 (3.5" chamber) *Choke:* Full
Barrel Length: 28" *Overall Length:* 44"
Weight: 9.5 lbs. *Sights:* Bead sights
Stock: American hardwood; walnut or camo finish; full
pistol grip; ventilated recoil pad. *Length Of Pull:* 14.5"

Price: **$149.95**
w/Camo Paint, Swivels & Sling **159.95**
w/32" Barrel, Camo Paint, Swivels & Sling. **179.95**
Also Available:
TURKEY GUN. With 24" screw-in barrel, turkey Full choke,
black matte finish, swivels and sling **$184.95**

SPECIAL PURPOSE
WATERFOWL SINGLE SHOT (10 ga.)

This sporting shotgun features a 32" barrel, (48" overall),
Modified choke, camo paint finish, swivels and sling.
Weight: 9.5 lbs.
Price: **$179.95**

TRACKER II RIFLED SLUG GUN

SPECIFICATIONS
Guages: 12 and 20 (3" chamber)
Choke: Rifled bore
Barrel Length: 24" *Overall Length:* 40"
Weight: 6 lbs. *Sights:* Adjustable rifle sights

Length Of Pull: 14.5" *Stock:* American hardwood; walnut
or camo finish; full pistol grip; recoil pad; sling swivel studs
Price: **$139.95**
Also available:
TRACKER SLUG GUN w/Cylinder Bore: **129.95**

SHOTGUNS

PARKER PRODUCTIONS

FULL-SIZE DOUBLE-ACTION PISTOLS

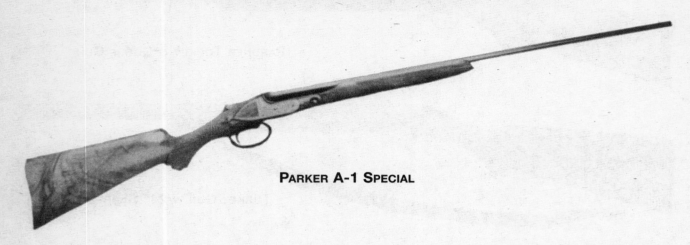

PARKER A-1 SPECIAL

Recognized by the shooting fraternity as the finest American shotgun ever produced, the Parker A-1 Special is again available. Exquisite engraving and rare presentation-grade French walnut distinguish the A-1 Special from any other shotguns in the world. Currently offered in 12 and 20 gauge, each gun is custom-fitted in its own oak and leather trunk case. Two models are offered: Hand Engraved and Custom Engraved. Also available in D Grade.

Standard features: Automatic safety, selective ejectors, skeleton steel butt plate, splinter forend, engraved snap caps, fitted leather trunk case, canvas and leather case cover, chrome barrel interiors, hand-checkering. The A-1 Special also features a 24k gold initial plate or pistol cap, 32 lines-per-inch checkering, selected wood and fine hand-

engraving. Choose from single or double trigger, English or pistol grip stock (all models). Options include beavertail forend, additional barrels.

In addition to the A-1 Special, the D-Grade is available in 12, 20, 16/20 and 28 gauge. A 16-gauge, 28" barrel can be ordered with a 20-gauge one or two-barrel set. The two-barrel sets come in a custom leather cased with a fitted over cover.

Prices: **D-GRADE**
One Barrel—12, 20, 28 gauge $3370.00
Two-barrel set 4200.00
16/20 Combo 4870.00
20/20/16 Combo 5630.00

SPECIFICATIONS

GAUGE	BARREL LENGTH	CHOKES	CHAMBERS	DROP AT COMB	DROP AT HEEL	LENGTH OF PULL	NOMINAL WEIGHT (LBS.)	OVERALL LENGTH
12	26"	Skeet I and II or IC/M	2.75"	1 3/8"	2 3/16"	14 1/8"	6.75	42 5/8"
12	28"	IC/M or M/F	2.75" & 3"	1 3/8"	2 3/16"	14 1/8"	6.75	44 5/8"
20	26"	Skeet I and II or IC/M	2.75"	1 3/8"	2 3/16"	14 3/8"	6.5	42 3/8"
20	28"	M/F	3"	1 3/8"	2 3/16"	14 3/8"	6.5	44 5/8"
16 on 20 frame	28"	Skeet I and II, IC/M or M/F	2.75"	1 3/8"	2 3/16"	14 3/8"	6.25	44 5/8"
28	26"	Skeet I and II or IC/M	2.75"	1 3/8"	2 3/16"	14 3/8"	5 1/3	42 5/8"
28	28"	M/F	2.75" & 3"	1 3/8"	2 3/16"	14 3/8"	5 1/3	44 5/8"

Note: The 16-gauge barrels are lighter than the 20-gauge barrels.

PERAZZI SHOTGUNS

The heart of the Perazzi line is the classic over/under, whose barrels are soldered into a monobloc that holds the shell extractors. At the sides are the two locking lugs that link the barrels to the action, which is machined from a solid block of forged steel. Barrels come with flat, step or raised ventilated rib. The finely checkered walnut forend is available with schnabel, beavertail or English styling, and the walnut stock can be of standard, Monte Carlo, Skeet or English design. Double or single nonselective or selective triggers. Sideplates and receiver are masterfully engraved.

OVER/UNDER GAME MODELS

GAME MODEL MX20C

GAME MODELS MX8, MX12, MX16, MX20, MX8/20, MX28 & MX410

SPECIFICATIONS
Gauges: 12, 20, 28 & .410
Chambers: 2.75"; also available in 3"
Barrel Lengths: 26" and 27.5"
Weight: 6 lbs. 6 oz. to 7 lbs. 4 oz.
Trigger Group: Nondetachable with coil springs and selective trigger
Stock: Interchangeable and custom; schnabel forend
Prices:

STANDARD GRADE	$7,210.00 - $16,990.00
SC3 GRADE	14,400.00 - 22,880.00
SCO GRADE	24,520.00 - 33,060.00
SCO GOLD GRADES	27,668.00 - 36,140.00

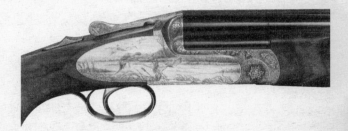

SCO SIDEPLATE ENGRAVING
(applicable to MX8 and MX12 models of any version)

AMERICAN TRAP SINGLE BARREL MODELS

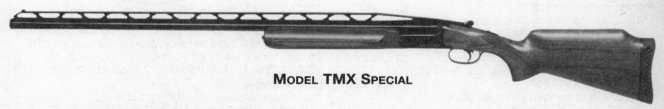

MODEL TMX SPECIAL

AMERICAN TRAP SINGLE-BARREL MODELS MX15, MX15L & TMX SPECIAL

SPECIFICATIONS
Gauge: 12
Chamber: 2.75"
Barrel Lengths: 32" and 34"
Weight: 8 lbs. 6 oz.
Choke: Full

Trigger Group: Detachable and interchangeable with coil springs
Stock: Interchangeable and custom made
Forend: Beavertail
Prices:

TMX SPECIAL	$6,930.00
MX15	7,220.00
MX15L	8,760.00

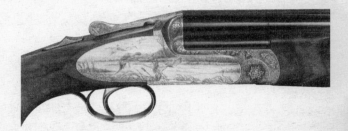

SHOTGUNS

PERAZZI SHOTGUNS

COMPETITION OVER/UNDER SHOTGUNS
Olympic, Double Trap, Skeet, Pigeon & Electrocibles

MODEL MX10

MODEL DB81 TRAP

MX8 SPORTING

MX8 SKEET

SPECIFICATIONS STANDARD GRADE
Gauges: 12 and 20
Barrel Lengths: 27.5", 28 ³/₈", 29.5", 30.75", 31.5"
Prices:
MX8 12 ga., removable trigger group 29.5",
   30.75" and 31.5" barrels **$8,500.00**
MX10 12 & 20 ga., w/adj. stock and rib 29.5",
   30.75" and 31.5" bbl.. . . . . **10,830.00**
MX11 12 ga., removable trigger group 29.5",
   30.75" and 31.5" bbl. **8,010.00**
MX8/20 20 ga. removable trigger group
   26.75", 27.5", 28 ³/₈", 29.5", 30.75"
   and 31.5" barrels **8,500.00**
MX8 12 ga. w/adj. trigger, 28 ³/₈", 29.5",
   31.5" barrels **9,010.00**
MX8 SPORTING 12 ga. w/external selector
   and 5 chokes; 27.5", 28 ³/₈", 29.5",
   and 31.5" barrels **9,430.00**
MX8 CLASSIC 12 ga. **10,730.00**
MX8 SPECIAL 12 ga. w/adjustable trigger, 29.5",
   and 31.5" barrels. **9,010.00**

DB81 SPECIAL w/adjustable trigger 29.5",
   30.75"and 31.5" barrels **9,260.00**
Note: PIGEON & ELECTROCIBLE MODELS available in MX1B,
Mirage, Mirage Special, MX10 & MX11 only w/27.5",
28.75", 29.5" & 31.5" barrels. **$7,210.00-10,838.00**
Also Available:
SC3 GRADE (Models MX8, MX10, MX10/20,
   MX8/20, MX8 Special, Mirage Spec.
   DB81 Spec.) **$14,400.00-16,400.00**
SCO GRADE (same models as
   SC3 Grade) **24,520.00-25,900.00**
SCO GOLD GRADE
   (same models as above) **27,660.00-28,840.00**
SCO GRADE SIDEPLATES
   (same models as above) **37,600.00-38,110.00**
SCO GOLD GRADE SIDEPLATES
   (same models above) **43,660.00-44,170.00**

PIOTTI SHOTGUNS

One of Italy's top gunmakers, Piotti limits its production to a small number of hand-crafted, best-quality double-barreled shotguns whose shaping, checkering, stock, action and barrel work meets or exceeds the standards achieved in London before WWII. All of the sidelock models exhibit the same overall design, materials and standards of workmanship; they differ only in the quality of the wood, shaping and sculpturing of the action, type of engraving and gold inlay work and other details. The Model Piuma differs from the other shotguns only in its Anson & Deeley boxlock design. Piotti's new over/under model appears below.

SPECIFICATIONS
Gauges: 10, 12, 16, 20, 28, .410 **Chokes:** As ordered **Barrels:** 12 ga., 25" to 32"; other gauges, 25" to 30"; chopper lump (demi-bloc) barrels with soft-luster blued finish; level, file-cut rib or optional concave **Action:** Boxlock, Anson & Deeley; Sidelock, Holland & Holland pattern; both have automatic ejectors, double triggers with yielding front trigger (non-selective single trigger optional), coin finish or optional color casehardening **Stock:** Hand-rubbed oil finish on straight grip stock with checkered butt (pistol grip optional) **Forend:** Classic (splinter); optional beavertail **Weight:** 5 lbs. 4 oz. (.410 ga.) to 8 lbs. 4 oz. (12 ga.)

SIDELOCK OVER/UNDER
Available in 12 or 20 ga. w/2.75" or 3" chambers and 26" to 32" barrels. Weight varies from 6 lbs. to 6 lbs. 12 oz. (20 ga.) and 7-8 lbs. (12 ga.). Single or double triggers. Circassion (Turkish) wood
Price: And up depending on engraving $39,200.00

MODEL PIUMA BOXLOCK
Anson & Deeley boxlock ejector double with chopper lump (demi-bloc) barrels, and scalloped frame. Very attractive scroll and rosette engraving is standard.
Price: $12,900.00

MODEL KING NO. 1 SIDELOCK
Best-quality Holland & Holland pattern sidelock ejector double with chopper lump barrels, choice of rib, very fine, full coverage scroll engraving with small floral bouquets, finely figured wood.
Price: $22,500.00

MODEL LUNIK SIDELOCK
Best quality Holland & Holland pattern sidelock ejector double with chopper lump (demi-bloc) barrels, choice of rib, Renaissance-style, large scroll engraving in relief, finely figured wood.
Price: $24,400.00

MODEL KING EXTRA
(not shown)
Best-quality Holland & Holland pattern sidelock ejector double with chopper lump barrels, choice of rib and bulino game-scene engraving or game-scene engraving with gold inlays; engraved and signed by a master engraver.
Price: And up depending on engraving $28,200.00

SHOTGUNS

REMINGTON SHOTGUNS

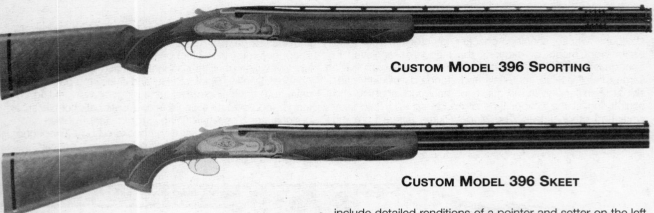

CUSTOM MODEL 396 SPORTING

CUSTOM MODEL 396 SKEET

CUSTOM MODEL 396 OVER/UNDER SHOTGUN (SKEET AND SPORTING CLAYS)

The Model 396 is produced in 12-gauge Skeet and Sporting Clays versions. Chrome-moly barrels in both versions have lengthened forcing cones, are fitted with side ribs, and have a flat 10-millimeter-wide parallel vent rib. Barrel lengths are 28" or 30". All barrels are fitted for the interchangeable Rem Choke system. Skeet and Improved Skeet choke tubes are supplied for the Model 396 Skeet, and four choke tubes— Skeet, Improved Skeet, Improved Cylinder and Modified configurations—for the Model 396 Sporting. The Sporting Clays version also features factory porting on both barrels.

The Barrels and side ribs are finished with high-polished deep bluing. The receiver and sideplates, trigger guard, top lever and forend metal are finished with gray nitride coloring.

Extensive scroll work appears on the receiver, trigger guard, tang, hinge pins and forend metal. The sideplates include detailed renditions of a pointer and setter on the left and right sides, respectively. Identifying individual versions of the Model 396 on both sideplates are the words "Sporting" or "Skeet" in script lettering. Additional scroll work, the Remington logo and the model designation appear on the floorplate.

Stocks on both models are selected from fancy American walnut and given a soft satin finish. Several stock design features are specifically adapted to clay target shooting, including a wider, target-style forend, a comb with larger radius and a universal palm swell on the pistol grip.

SPECIFICATIONS
Gauge: 12 *Chamber:* 2.75" *Choke:* Rem Choke
Length of pull: 14 3/16" *Drop at comb:* 1½"
Drop at heel: 2.25" *Barrel lengths:* 28" and 30"
Overall lengths: 45" and 47" *Weight:* 7.5 lbs. and 7⅜ lbs.
Prices:
MODEL 396 SPORTING $2,126.00
MODEL 396 SKEET 1,993.00

PEERLESS OVER/UNDER SHOTGUN w/Vent Rib and Engraved Sideplates

Practical, lightweight, well-balanced and affordable are the attributes of this Remington shotgun. Features include an all-steel receiver, boxlock action and removable sideplates (engraved with a pointer on one side and a setter on the other). The bottom of the receiver has the Remington logo, plus the words "Peerless, Field" and the serial number. Cut-checkering appears on both pistol grip and forend (shaped with finger grooves and tapered toward the front). The American walnut stock is fitted w/black, vented recoil pad.

SPECIFICATIONS
Gauge: 12 (3" chamber) *Chokes:* REM Choke System (1 Full, 1 Mod., 1 Imp. Cyl.) *Barrel lengths:* 26", 28", 30" with vent rib *Overall length:* 42" (26" barrel); 45" (28" barrel); 47" (30" barrel) *Weight:* 7.25 lbs. (26"); 7 ⅜ lbs. (28"); 7.5 lbs. (30") *Trigger:* Single, selective, gold-plated *Safety:* Automatic safety *Sights:* Target gun style with mid-bead and Bradley-type front bead
Length of pull: 14 3/16" *Drop at comb:* 1.5"
Drop at heel: 2.25" *Features:* Solid, horseshoe-shaped locking bar with two rectangular lug extensions on either side of the barrel's midbore; fast lock time (3.28 milliseconds)
Price: $1,172.00

REMINGTON SHOTGUNS

MODEL 870 EXPRESS "YOUTH" GUN

The MODEL 870 EXPRESS "YOUTH" GUN has been specially designed for youths and smaller-sized adults. It's a 20-gauge lightweight with a 1-inch shorter stock and 21-inch barrel. Yet it is still all 870, complete with REM Choke and ventilated rib barrel. Also available with a 20" fully rifled, rifle-sighted deer barrel.

SPECIFICATIONS
Barrel length: 21" *Stock Dimensions:* Length of pull 12.5" (including recoil pad); drop at heel; 2.5" drop at comb 1 ⅝"
Overall length: 39" (40.5" w/deer barrel) *Average weight:* 6 lbs.
Choke: REM Choke-Mod. (vent-rib version).
Price:
20-Gauge Lightweight **$305.00**
w/Deer Barrel **339.00**
Price:
w/Real Tree Advantage camo stock and forend . . . **372.00**

MODEL 870 EXPRESS SYNTHETIC HOME DEFENSE

This shotgun is designed specifically for home defense use. The 12-gauge pump-action shotgun features an 18" plain barrel with Cylinder choke and front bead sight. Barrel and action have the traditional Express-style metal finish. The synthetic stock and forend have a textured black, nonreflective finish and feature positive checkering.

SPECIFICATIONS
Capacity: 4 rounds.
Price: **$292.00**

MODEL 870 EXPRESS COMBO

The MODEL 870 EXPRESS in 12 and 20 gauge offers all the features of the standard Model 870, including twin-action bars, quick changing 28" barrels, REM Choke and vent rib plus low-luster, checkered hardwood stock and no-shine finish on barrel and receiver. The Model 870 Combo is packaged with an extra 20" deer barrel, fitted with rifle sights and fixed, Improved Cylinder choke (additional REM chokes can be added for special applications). The 3-inch chamber handles all 2.75" and 3" shells without adjustment. *Weight:* 7.5 lbs.
Price: **$399.00**
Also available: w/26" REM choke barrel w/vent rib and 20" fully rifled deer barrel w/rifle sights (12 and 20 ga.).
Weight: 7.5 lbs.
Price: **439.00**

SHOTGUNS

REMINGTON PUMP SHOTGUNS

MODEL 870 EXPRESS

MODEL 870 EXPRESS features the same action as the Wingmaster and is available with 3" chamber and 26" or 28" vent-rib barrel. It has a hardwood stock with low-luster finish and solid buttpad. Choke is Modified REM Choke tube and wrench. *Overall length:* 48.5" (28" barrel). *Weight:* 7.25" lbs (26" barrel).
Prices: 12 & 20 ga. $305.00
Left Hand 12 ga. 332.00
w/Black Synthetic Stock & Forend
 (Right Hand only) 312.00

MODEL 870 EXPRESS TURKEY GUN

The **MODEL 870 EXPRESS TURKEY GUN** boasts all the same features as the Model 870 Express, except has 21" vent-rib barrel and Turkey Extra-Full REM Choke.
Price: $319.00
Now available:
 w/stock and forend in Advantage Camo 372.00

MODEL 870 EXPRESS DEER GUN

This 12-gauge, pump action deer gun is for hunters who prefer open sights. Features a 20" barrel, quick-reading iron sights, fixed Imp. Cyl. choke and Monte Carlo stock. Also available with fully rifled barrel.
Price: With Rifle Sights $300.00
 Fully Rifled 339.00

MODEL 870 EXPRESS SUPER MAGNUM
(not shown)

For those who seek the power and range of 12 gauge 3.5" magnum shotshells, the new MODEL 870 EXPRESS SUPER MAGNUM represents a good value. In addition to having the strength and reliability of the Model 870 Wingmaster, this model has the added versatility of handling 12 ga. 2.75" to 3.5" loads. The existing breech bolt and receiver have been designed to accommodate the big shells (capacity: 3 (3.5") and 4 (2.75" or 3") shells. Also available is a Turkey Camo shotgun with a 23" vent rib and 3.5" chamber with a synthetic stock and forend, plus checkering and vented recoil pad. Fully camouflaged with Real Tree Advantage. Remington also offers Synthetic and Combo models

Prices:
MODEL 870 EXPRESS SUPER MAGNUM $332.00
 TURKEY CAMO 439.00
 Synthetic Model (26" vent rib) 339.00
 Turkey Camo 439.00
Combo (20" fully rifled deer barrel and 26" vent rib
 w/wood stock and forend, vented recoil pad . . . 465.00

REMINGTON PUMP SHOTGUNS

SPECIAL PURPOSE

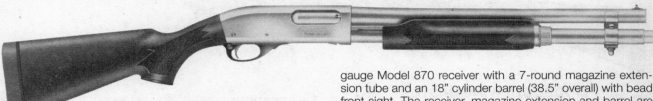

MODEL 870 SPECIAL PURPOSE MARINE MAGNUM

Remington's **MODEL 870 SPECIAL PURPOSE MARINE MAGNUM** is a versatile, multipurpose security gun featuring a rugged synthetic stock and extensive, electroless nickel plating on all metal parts. This new shotgun utilizes a standard 12-gauge Model 870 receiver with a 7-round magazine extension tube and an 18" cylinder barrel (38.5" overall) with bead front sight. The receiver, magazine extension and barrel are protected (inside and out) with heavy-duty, corrosion-resistant nickel plating. The synthetic stock and forend reduce the effects of moisture. The gun is supplied with a black rubber recoil pad, sling swivel studs, and positive checkering on both pistol grip and forend. *Weight:* 7.5 lbs.
Price: **$500.00**

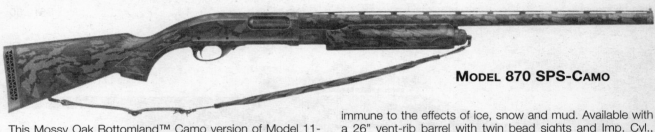

MODEL 870 SPS-CAMO

This Mossy Oak Bottomland™ Camo version of Model 11-87 and Model 870 Special Purpose Synthetic shotguns features a durable camo finish and synthetic stocks that are immune to the effects of ice, snow and mud. Available with a 26" vent-rib barrel with twin bead sights and Imp. Cyl., Modified, and Full REM Choke tubes.
Price: **$496.00**

MODEL 870 SPST ALL BLACK TURKEY GUN

Same as the Model 870 SPS above, except with a 21" vent-rib turkey barrel and Extra-Full REM Choke tube.
Price: **$425.00**

Also Available:
Mossy Oak Greenleaf Camo finish. **$511.00**
20" fully rifled cantilever deer barrel (All Black) 496.00

MODEL 870 SP (SPECIAL PURPOSE) ALL BLACK DEER GUN

SPECIFICATIONS
Gauge: 12. *Choke:* Fully rifled with rifle sights, recoil pad. *Barrel length:* 20". *Overall length:* 40.5". *Average weight:* 7 lbs.
Price: **$435.00**

REMINGTON SHOTGUNS

MODEL 870 WINGMASTER
12 Gauge, Light Contour Barrel

This restyled **870 "WINGMASTER"** pump has cut-checkering on its satin-finished American walnut stock and forend for confident handling, even in wet weather. Also available in Hi-Gloss finish. An ivory bead "Bradley"-type front sight is included. Rifle is available with 26", 28" and 30" barrel with REM Choke and handles 3" and 2.75" shells interchangeably.

SPECIFICATIONS
Overall length: 46.5" (26" barrel), 48.5" (28" barrel), 50.5" (30" barrel).
Weight: 7.25 lbs. (w/26" barrel).
Price: $519.00
Also available:
MODEL 870 WINGMASTER. 20 Ga. Lightweight (6.5 lbs.), American walnut stock and forend.
Price: $519.00

MODEL 870 WINGMASTER
CANTILEVER DEER BARREL
(12 & 20 Ga.)

Price: Fully Rifled, Satin Wood $599.00

MODEL 11-87 PREMIER SPORTING CLAYS

Remington's **MODEL 11-87 PREMIER SPORTING CLAYS** features a target-grade, American walnut competition stock with a length of pull that is 3/16" longer and 1/4" higher at the heel. The tops of the receiver, barrel and rib have a nonreflective matte finish. The rib is medium high with a stainless mid-bead and ivory front bead. The barrel (26" or 28") has a lengthened forcing cone to generate greater pattern uniformity; and there are 5 REM choke tubes—

Skeet, Improved Skeet, Improved Cylinder, Modified and Full. All sporting clays choke tubes have a knurled end extending .45" beyond the muzzle for fast field changes. Both the toe and heel of the buttpad are rounded.

SPECIFICATIONS
Weight: 7.5 lbs. (26"); 7 5/8 lbs. (28")
Price: $779.00
   Nickel Plated 827.00

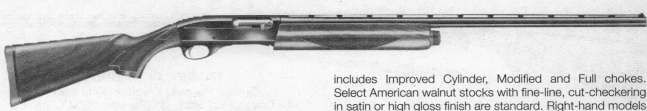

MODEL 11-87 PREMIER AUTOLOADER

Remington's redesigned 12-gauge **MODEL 11-87 PREMIER AUTOLOADER** features new, light-contour barrels that reduce both barrel weight and overall weight (more than 8 ounces). The shotgun has a standard 3-inch chamber and handles all 12-gauge shells interchangeably— from 2.75" field loads to 3" Magnums. The gun's interchangeable REM choke system includes Improved Cylinder, Modified and Full chokes. Select American walnut stocks with fine-line, cut-checkering in satin or high gloss finish are standard. Right-hand models are available in 26", 28" and 30" barrels (left-hand models are 28" only). A two-barrel gun case is supplied.

Prices:

Light Contour Barrel	$692.00
Left Hand, 28" Barrel	743.00

Also available:

MODEL 11-87 PREMIER SC (Sporting Clays)	779.00
MODEL 11-87 SC NP (Nickel Plated)	827.00

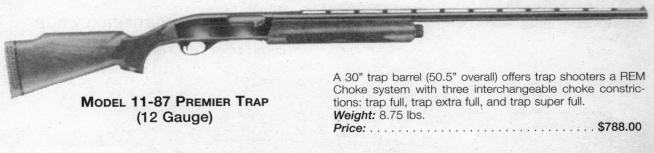

MODEL 11-87 PREMIER TRAP
(12 Gauge)

A 30" trap barrel (50.5" overall) offers trap shooters a REM Choke system with three interchangeable choke constrictions: trap full, trap extra full, and trap super full.
Weight: 8.75 lbs.
Price: $788.00

MODEL 11-87 PREMIER SKEET
(12 Gauge)

This model features American walnut wood and distinctive cut checkering with satin finish, plus new two-piece buttplate. REM Choke system includes option of two skeet chokes—skeet and improved skeet. Trap and skeet guns are designed for 12-gauge target loads and are set to handle 2.75" shells only. *Barrel length:* 26" *Overall length:* 46" *Weight:* 8 1/8 lbs.
Price: $765.00

MODEL 11-87 PREMIER DEER GUN

Price:
With Cantilever Scope Mount and Fully Rifled
21" Barrel (Satin Finish) $759.00

SHOTGUNS

REMINGTON AUTO SHOTGUNS

MODEL 11-87 SPS
(Special Purpose Wood or Synthetic)
12 Gauge Autoloader, 3" Chamber/REM/Chokes
26" or 28" Vent-Rib Barrels
Price: $679.00

MODEL 11-87 SPST TURKEY GUN
12 Gauge Autoloader, 3" Chamber All-Black
Synthetic Stock Extra-Full REM Choke Turkey Tube
Price: $692.00
w/Mossy Oak Break-Up Camo Finish 767.00

MODEL 11-87 SPS-T TURKEY GUN
12 Gauge Autoloader, 3" Chamber, 21" barrel/REM/Chokes
Synthetic Stock in Realtree™ X-tra Camo
Price: $770.00

MODEL 11-87 SPS SPECIAL PURPOSE
SYNTHETIC ALL-BLACK DEER GUN

Features the same finish as other SP models plus a padded, camo-style carrying sling of Cordura nylon with QD sling swivels. Barrel is 21" (41" overall) with rifle sights and rifled and IC choke (handles all 2.75" and 3" rifled slug and buckshot loads as well as high-velocity field and magnum loads; does not function with light 2.75" field loads). *Weight:* 8.5 lbs.
Price: 3" Magnum $703.00
Fully Rifled Cantilever 765.00

REMINGTON AUTO SHOTGUNS

MODEL 1100 AUTOLOADING SHOTGUNS

The Remington **MODEL 1100** is a 5-shot gas-operated autoloader with a gas-metering system designed to reduce recoil. This design enables the shooter to use 2 ³/₄-inch standard velocity "Express" and 2.75-inch Magnum loads without gun adjustments. Barrels, within gauge and versions, are interchangeable. All 12- and 20-gauge versions include REM™ Choke; interchangeable choke tubes in 26" and 28" (12 gauge only) barrels. American walnut stocks come with fleur-de-lis design fine-line checkering and a scratch-resistant finish.

MODEL 1100 SPECIAL FIELD (12 & 20 Ga.)
Price: $659.00

MODEL 1100 LT-20
Price: $651.00
Also Available:
MODEL 1100 LT-20 MAGNUM 659.00
MODEL 1100 LT-20 YOUTH 659.00

MODEL 1100 SYNTHETIC (20 Gauge)
Price: $492.00
Also Available:
MODEL 1100 SYNTHETIC FR RS
   (fully rifled, rifle sights) 475.00
MODEL 1100 SYNTHETIC FR CL
   (fully rifled, cantilever) 585.00

MODEL 1100 SYNTHETIC 12 Gauge
Price: $492.00

SHOTGUNS

REMINGTON AUTO SHOTGUNS

MODEL 11-96 EURO LIGHTWEIGHT

Based on the Model 11-87™ action, the Model 11-96™ features modifications to the 11-87 action to reduce the overall weight of the 26" barrel version (from 7 5/8 lbs. to just 6 7/8 lbs.). These modifications include changing the profile of the receiver and shortening the magazine assembly (capacity of 3 shells).

This shotgun is now available with 26" or 28" barrels and features Remington's pressure-compensated, low-recoil gas system, which handles both 2.75" field and 3" magnum shells interchangeably; three flush-fitting REM™ chokes (for steel or lead shot) are supplied. Each gun has fine-line embellishments on the receivers and cut-checkered, Claro walnut stocks and forends. Barrels are chrome-moly steel with chrome-plated bores and 6mm vent ribs.
Price: **$852.00**

SP-10 MAGNUM SHOTGUN

Remington's **SP-10 MAGNUM** is the only gas-operated semi-automatic 10-gauge shotgun made today. Engineered to shoot steel shot, the SP-10 delivers up to 34 percent more pellets to the target than standard 12-gauge shotgun and steel shot combinations. This autoloader features a vented, noncorrosive, stainless-steel gas system, in which the cylinder moves—not the piston. This reduces felt recoil energy by spreading the recoil over a longer time. The receiver is machined from a solid billet of ordnance steel for total integral strength. The SP-10 has a 3/8" vent rib with mid and front sights for a better sight plane. The American walnut stock and forend have a protective, low-gloss satin finish for

reduced glare, and positive deep-cut checkering. The receiver and barrel have a matte finish, and the stainless-steel breech bolt features a non-reflective finish. The SP-10 also has a brown-vented recoil pad and a padded camo sling of Cordura nylon. *Barrel lengths/choke:* 26" or 30"/REM Choke. *Overall length:* 51.5" (30" barrel) and 47.5" (26" barrel). *Weight:* 11 lbs. (30" barrel) and 10.75 lbs. (26" barrel).
Price: **$1,085.00**
Also available: SP-10 Magnum in Turkey Camo NWTF 25th Anniversary.
Price: **1,225.00**

MODEL SP-10 MAGNUM CAMO
10 Gauge Autoloader with 23" Vent-Rib Barrel and Mossy Oak Break-Up Camo Pattern
Price: **$1,179.00**

RIZZINI SHOTGUNS

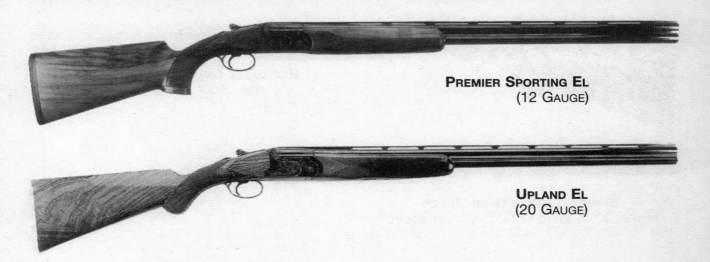

PREMIER SPORTING EL
(12 GAUGE)

UPLAND EL
(20 GAUGE)

Rizzini builds a well-finished boxlock ejector over/under that is available in all gauges and in many different configurations. Rizzini guns are manufactured in Marcheno, Italy, in the fa~mous Val Trompia gunmaking region. All Rizzini guns have special steel barrels that are proof-tested at 1200 Bars, as well as pattern-tested at the factory. The guns are built in field, sporting clays and express rifle configurations.

The **ARTEMIS** and **PREMIER** are production guns built to standard specifications. The EL models, which include the Upland EL, the Sporting EL and the High Grades feature higher grade wood, checkering and hand finishing.

FIELD guns are available with case-colored or coin-finish actions with straight grips or round knob semi-pistol grips. Also available are multi-gauge field sets with .410, 28 or 20 gauge barrels in any combination. These sets are available in EL or High Grade level guns. On custom orders, stock dimensions, chokes and barrel length may be specified. Screw-in chokes are available on 12 and 20 gauge guns.

SPORTING guns, in 12 and 20 gauge only, feature heavier weight and a target-style rib, stock and forearm. The Sporting models are available in three versions: Premier Sporting, Sporting EL and S790EL.

High Grade models, built with or without sideplates, are available in four engraving styles, including game scenes and gold inlays.

Prices:
SPORTING EL (12 gauge)................$3,250.00
UPLAND EL (20 gauge) 2,850.00
S790 EMEL HIGH GRADE................ 8,750.00
ARTEMIS EL HIGH GRADE................ 12,650.00

SHOTGUNS

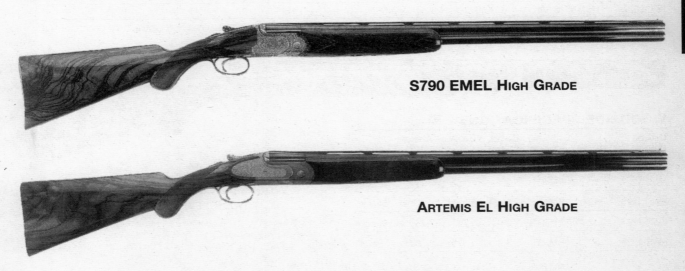

S790 EMEL HIGH GRADE

ARTEMIS EL HIGH GRADE

RUGER OVER/UNDER SHOTGUNS

RED LABEL OVER/UNDER SHOTGUN
(INC. SCREW-IN CHOKES)
Price:............................... $1,215.00

SPORTING CLAYS OVER/UNDER
MODEL KRL-2036 (20 Ga. shown above)
Price: w/Screw-in Chokes & 30" Barrels $1,349.00

SPECIFICATIONS RED LABEL AND SPORTING CLAYS OVER/UNDERS

CATALOG NUMBER	GAUGE	CHAMBER	CHOKE*	BARREL LENGTH	OVERALL LENGTH	LENGTH PULL	DROP COMB	DROP HEEL	SIGHTS**	APPROX. WT. (LBS.)	TYPE STOCK
KRL-1226	12	3"	F,M,IC,S+	26"	43"	14 1/8"	1 1/2"	2 1/2"	GBF	7 3/4	Pistol Grip
KRL-1227	12	3"	F,M.IC,S+	28"	45"	14 1/8"	1 1/2"	2 1/2"	GBF	8	Pistol Grip
KRLS-1226	12	3"	F,M.IC,S+	26"	43"	14 1/8"	1 1/2"	2 1/2"	GBF	7 1/2	Straight
KRLS-1227	12	3"	F,M.IC,S+	28"	45"	14 1/8"	1 1/2"	2 1/2"	GBF	7 3/4	Straight
KRL-1236	12	3"	M,IC,S+	30"	47"	14 1/8"	1 1/2"	2 1/2"	GBF/GBM	7 3/4	Pistol Grip
KRL-2029	20	3"	F,M,IC,S+	26"	43"	14 1/8"	1 1/2"	2 1/2"	GBF	7	Pistol Grip
KRL-2030	20	3"	F,M,IC,S+	28"	45"	14 1/8"	1 1/2"	2 1/2"	GBF	7 1/4	Pistol Grip
KRLS-2029	20	3"	F,M,IC,S+	26"	43"	14 1/8"	1 1/2"	2 1/2"	GBF	6 3/4	Straight
KRLS-2030	20	3"	F,M,IC,S+	28"	45"	14 1/8"	1 1/2"	2 1/2"	GBF	7	Straight
KRL-2036	20	3"	M,IC,S+	30"	47"	14 1/8"	1 1/2"	2 1/2"	GBF/GBM	7	Pistol Grip
KRLS-2826	28	2 3/4"	F,M,IC,S+	26"	43"	14 1/8"	1 1/2"	2 1/2"	GBF	5 7/8	Straight
KRLS-2827	28	2 3/4"	F,M,IC,S+	28"	45"	14 1/8"	1 1/2"	2 1/2"	GBF	6	Straight
KRL-2826	28	2 3/4"	F,M,IC,S+	26"	43"	14 1/8"	1 1/2"	2 1/2"	GBF	6	Pistol Grip
KRL-2827	28	2 3/4"	F,M,IC,S+	28"	45"	14 1/8"	1 1/2"	2 1/2"	GBF	6 1/8	Pistol Grip

*F-Full, M-Modified, IC-Improved Cylinder, S-Skeet. +Two skeet chokes standard with each shotgun. **GBF-Gold-Bead Front Sight, GBM-Gold-Bead Middle

WOODSIDE SPECIFICATIONS

CATALOG NUMBER	GAUGE	CHOKE*	BARREL LENGTH	OVERALL LENGTH	APPROX. WT.	STOCK
KWK-1226	12	F,M,IC,S	26"	43"	7.75 lbs.	Pistol
KWS-1227	12	F,M,IC,S	28"	45"	8 lbs.	Pistol
KWS-1226	12	F,M,IC,S	26"	43"	7.5 lbs.	Straight
KWS-1227	12	F,M,IC,S	28"	45"	7.75 lbs.	Straight
KWS-1236	12	F,M,IC,S	30"	47"	7.75 lbs.	Pistol

WOODSIDE OVER/UNDER SHOTGUN
(W/SCREW-IN CHOKES)
Price:............................... $1,675.00

SAVAGE SHOTGUNS

MODEL 210FT "MASTER SHOT" SHOTGUN

SPECIFICATIONS
Gauge: 12 *Choke:* Full choke tube *Barrel length:* 24"
Overall length: 43.5" *Weight:* 7.5 lbs.

Finish: Advantage™ camo pattern
Features: Barrel threaded for interchangeable Winchester-style choke tubes; drilled and tapped for scope mounting; positive checkering; ventilated rubber recoil pad and swivel studs; bead front sight with U-notch blade rear; short lift 60° bolt rotation, controlled round feed; triple front locking lugs
Price: $440.00

MODEL 210F SLUG GUN

Also available:
210F "MASTER SHOT" SLUG GUN (12 gauge). Features full-length baffle; 24" barrel chambered for 2.75" or 3" shells; three-position, top tang rifle-style safety; no sights; 1 in 35" twist (8-groove precision button rifled).
Price: $380.00

SIGARMS SHOTGUNS

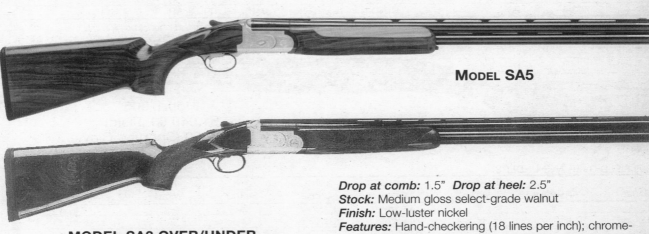

MODEL SA5

MODEL SA3 OVER/UNDER

SPECIFICATIONS
Gauge: 12 (3" chamber)
Choke: Full, Modified & Improved Cylinder
Action: Automatic ejectors w/single selective trigger
Barrel lengths: 26" and 28" w/vented rib
Weight: 6.8 lbs. *Length of pull:* 14.5"

Drop at comb: 1.5" *Drop at heel:* 2.5"
Stock: Medium gloss select-grade walnut
Finish: Low-luster nickel
Features: Hand-checkering (18 lines per inch); chrome-lined bores; screw-in multi-choke system; hardened monobloc; rolled game scenes on receiver
Prices:
MODEL SA3 FIELD $1,335.00
  SPORTING MODEL 1,675.00
MODEL SA5 FIELD 2,670.00
  SPORTING MODEL 3,185.00

SHOTGUNS

SKB SHOTGUNS

MODEL 385 SIDE-BY-SIDE

Model 385 features silver nitride receiver with engraved scroll and game scene design; solid boxlock action w/double locking lugs; single selective trigger; selective automatic ejectors; automatic safety; sculpted American walnut stock; pistol or English straight grip; semi-beavertail forend; stock and forend finished w/18-line fine checkering; standard series choke tube system; solid rib w/flat matte finish and metal front bead. For additional specifications, see table below.

Price:. **$1,799.00**
Field Set 2,579.00
Also available:
MODEL 485 SERIES. Features engraved upland game scene; semi-fancy American walnut stock and beavertail forend; raised vent rib with flat matte finish.
Price:. **$2,439.00**
Field Set 3,479.00

SPECIFICATIONS MODEL 385 & 485

FIELD MODELS

GAUGE	CHAMBER	BARREL LENGTH	OVERALL LENGTH	INTER CHOKE	SIGHTS✔	RIB WIDTH	STOCK	AVERAGE WEIGHT* 385	AVERAGE WEIGHT* 485
12	3"	28"	44 1/2"	STND-A	MFB	5/16"	PISTOL	7 lb. 3 oz.	7 lb. 1 oz.
12	3"	28"	44 1/2"	STND-A	MFB	5/16"	ENGLISH	7 lb. 1 oz.	7 lb. 5 oz.
12	3"	26"	42 1/2"	STND-A	MFB	5/16"	PISTOL	7 lb. 1 oz.	7 lb. 5 oz.
12	3"	26"	42 1/2"	STND-A	MFB	5/16"	ENGLISH	7 lb. 0 oz.	7 lb. 4 oz.
20	3"	26"	42 1/2"	STND-B	MFB	5/16"	PISTOL	6 lb. 10 oz.	6 lb. 14 oz.
20	3"	26"	42 1/2"	STND-B	MFB	5/16"	ENGLISH	6 lb. 10 oz.	6 lb. 14 oz.
28	2 3/4"	26"	42 1/2"	STND-B	MFB	5/16"	PISTOL	6 lb. 13 oz.	7 lb. 2 oz.
28	2 3/4"	26"	42 1/2"	STND-B	MFB	5/16"	ENGLISH	6 lb. 13 oz.	7 lb. 2 oz.

2 BARREL FIELD SETS

GAUGE	CHAMBER	BARREL LENGTH	OVERALL LENGTH	INTER CHOKE	SIGHTS✔	RIB WIDTH	STOCK	AVERAGE WEIGHT* 385	AVERAGE WEIGHT* 485
20	3"	26"	42 1/2"	STND-B	MFB	5/16"	PISTOL	6 lb. 10 oz.	
28	2 3/4"	26"	42 1/2"	STND-B	MFB	5/16"	PISTOL	6 lb. 13 oz.	
20	3"	26"	42 1/2"	STND-B	MFB	5/16"	ENGLISH	6 lb. 10 oz.	
28	2 3/4"	26"	42 1/2"	STND-B	MFB	5/16"	ENGLISH	6 lb. 13 oz.	

*Weights may vary due to wood density. Specifications may vary. *INTER-CHOKE SYSTEMS: COMP - Competition series includes Mod., Full, Imp. Cyl. STND-A - Standard series includes Mod., Full, Imp. Cyl. STND-B- Standard series includes Imp. Cyl., Mod. Skeet STOCK DIMENSIONS: Length of Pull - 14 1/8" Drop at Comb - 1 1/2" Drop at Heel - 2 3/4" ✔MFB-Metal Front Bead

MODEL 505
$1,049.00 (Field)
$1,149.00 (Sporting Clays)

505 FIELD OVER AND UNDERS

GAUGE	CHAMBER	BARREL LENGTH	OVERALL LENGTH	INTER CHOKE	SIGHTS✔	RIB WIDTH	AVERAGE WEIGHT*
12	3"	28"	45 3/8"	STND-A	MFB	3/8"	7 lb. 12 oz.
12	3"	26"	45 3/8"	STND-B	MFB	3/8"	7 lb. 11 oz.
20	3"	26"	45 3/8"	STND-B	MFB	3/8"	6 lb. 10 oz.

505 SPORTING CLAYS

GAUGE	CHAMBER	BARREL LENGTH	OVERALL LENGTH	INTER CHOKE	SIGHTS	RIB WIDTH	AVERAGE WEIGHT* 505
12	3"	30"	47 3/8"	STND-B	CP/WFB	15/32" CH/STP	8 lb. 5 oz.
12	3"	28"	45 3/8"	STND-B	CP/WFB	15/32" CH/STP	8 lb. 1 oz.

*Weights may vary due to wood density. Specifications may vary. *INTER-CHOKE SYSTEMS: STND-A-Standard series includes Full, Mod, Imp. Cyl. STND-B- Standard series includes Imp. Cyl., Mod, Skeet STOCK DIMENSIONS: Length of Pull-14 1/8" Drop at Comb-1 1/2" Drop at heel-2 3/16" **MFB-Metal Front Bead**

SKB SHOTGUNS

MODEL 585 AND 785 SERIES

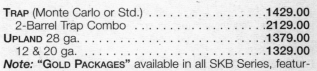

MODEL 585 SPORTING CLAYS

MODEL 585   *Prices*
FIELD/YOUTH/LADIES (12 & 20 ga.) $1329.00
Field (28 or .410 ga.) .1379.00
Two-BARREL FIELD SET (12 & 20 ga.) 2129.00
  20/28 ga. or 28/.410 ga 2179.00
Skeet (12 or 20 ga.) 1429.00
  28 or .410 ga.) 1479.00
  3-Bbl. Set (20, 28 & .410 ga.) 3329.00
SPORTING CLAYS (12 or 20 ga.) 1479.00
  28 gauge 1529.00

TRAP (Monte Carlo or Std.) 1429.00
  2-Barrel Trap Combo 2129.00
UPLAND 28 ga. 1379.00
  12 & 20 ga. 1329.00
Note: "GOLD PACKAGES" available in all SKB Series, featuring gold plated triggers, two gold-plated game scenes, and hand-finished schnabel forends.

FIELD MODELS

GAUGE	CHAMBER	BARREL LENGTH	OVERALL LENGTH	INTER CHOKE	SIGHTS✔	RIB WIDTH	AVERAGE WEIGHT* 785	585
12	3"	28"	45 3/8"	COMP.	MFB	3/8"	8 lb. 0 oz.	7 lb. 12 oz.
12	3"	26"	43 3/8"	COMP.	MFB	3/8"	8 lb. 0 oz.	7 lb. 11 oz.
20	3"	28"	45 3/8"	STND-A	MFB	5/16"	7 lb. 4 oz.	6 lb. 12 oz.
20	3"	26"	43 3/8"	STND-B	MFB	5/16"	7 lb. 3 oz.	6 lb. 10 oz.
28	2 3/4"	28"	45 3/8"	STND-A	MFB	5/16"	7 lb. 4 oz.	6 lb. 14 oz.
28	2 3/4"	26"	43 3/8"	STND-B	MFB	5/16"	7 lb. 3 oz.	6 lb. 13 oz.
410	3"	28"	45 3/8"	M/F	MFB	5/16"	7 lb. 4 oz.	7 lb. 0 oz.
410	3"	26"	43 3/8"	IC/M	MFB	5/16"	7 lb. 3 oz.	6 lb. 14 oz.

2 BARREL FIELD SETS

GAUGE	CHAMBER	BARREL LENGTH	OVERALL LENGTH	INTER CHOKE	SIGHTS✔	RIB WIDTH	AVERAGE WEIGHT* 785	585
12	3"	28"	45 3/8"	COMP	MFB	3/8"	8 lb. 1 oz.	7 lb. 11 oz.
20	3"	26"	43 3/8"	STND-B	MFB	3/8"	8 lb. 4 oz.	7 lb. 12 oz.
20	3"	28"	45 3/8"	STND-A	MFB	5/16"	7 lb. 5 oz.	7 lb. 2 oz.
28	2 3/4"	28"	45 3/8"	STND-A	MFB	5/16"	7 lb. 5 oz.	7 lb. 1 oz.
20	3"	26"	43 3/8"	STND-B	MFB	5/16"	7 lb. 3 oz.	7 lb. 1 oz.
28	2 3/4"	26"	43 3/8"	STND-B	MFB	5/16"	7 lb. 3 oz.	7 lb. 0 oz.
28	2 3/4"	28"	45 3/8"	STND-A	MFB	5/16"	7 lb. 6 oz.	7 lb. 1 oz.
410	3"	26"	43 3/8"	IC/M	MFB	5/16"	7 lb. 5 oz.	7 lb. 0 oz.

*Weights may vary due to wood density. Specifications may vary. *INTER-CHOKE SYSTEMS: COMP - Competition series include Mod. Full. Imp. Cyl. STND A - Standard series includes Mod. Full. Imp. Cyl. STND B - Standard series includes Imp. Cyl.. Mod. Skeet STOCK DIMENSIONS: Length of Pull - 14 1/8" Drop at Comb. - 1 1/2" Drop at Heel - 2 3/16" ✔MFB - Metal Front Bead*

SPORTING CLAY MODELS

GAUGE	CHAMBER	BARREL LENGTH	OVERALL LENGTH	INTER CHOKE	SIGHTS✔	RIB WIDTH	AVERAGE WEIGHT* 785	585
12	3"	32"	49 3/8"	COMP.	CP/WFB	15/32" CH/STP	8 lb. 14 oz.	8 lb. 7 oz.
12	3"	30"	47 3/8"	COMP.	CP/WFB	15/32" CH/STP	8 lb. 12 oz.	8 lb. 5 oz.
12	3"	30"	47 3/8"	COMP.	CP/WFB	3/8" SW	8 lb. 9 oz.	8 lb. 1 oz.
12	3"	28"	45 3/8"	COMP.	CP/WFB	15/32" CH/STP	8 lb. 8 oz.	8 lb. 1 oz.
12	3"	28"	45 3/8"	COMP.	CP/WFB	3/8" SW	8 lb. 5 oz.	7 lb. 14 oz.
20	3"	28"	45 3/8"	STND-B	CP/WFB	15/32" CH/STP	7 lb. 6 oz.	6 lb. 14 oz.
28	2 3/4"	28"	45 3/8"	STND-B	CP/WFB	5/16" SW	7 lb. 4 oz.	6 lb. 14oz.

2 BARREL SPORTING CLAY SET

GAUGE	CHAMBER	BARREL LENGTH	OVERALL LENGTH	INTER CHOKE	SIGHTS✔	RIB WIDTH	AVERAGE WEIGHT* 785	585
12	3"	30"	47 3/8"	COMP.	CP/WFB	15/32" CH/STP	8 lb. 14 oz.	
20	3"	28"	45 3/8"	STND-B	SP/WFB	15/32" CH/STP	8 lb. 10 oz.	

*Weights may vary due to wood density. Specifications may vary *INTER-CHOKE SYSTEMS: COMP - Competition series includes SKII/SCIII, SK I/SCI and MOD/SC IV STND B - Standard series includes Mod. Imp. Cyl. Skeet STOCK DIMENSIONS: Length of Pull - 14 1/4" Drop at Comb - 1 7/16" Drop at Heel - 1 7/8" ✔CP/WFB - Center Post White Front Bead ✔CH/STP - Center Channeled, Semi Wide Step Up Rib ✔SW - Semi Wide Step Up Rib*

SKB Shotguns

Model 585 and 785 Series

Model 785 Over/Under

The SKB 785 Series features chrome-lined oversized chambers and boreds, lengthened forcing cones, chrome-plated ejectors and competition choke tube system.

MODEL 785   *Prices*
Field (12 & 20 ga.) $1,949.00
  28 or .410 ga. 2,029.00

Two-Barrel Field Set (12 & 20 ga.) 2,829.00
  20/28 ga. or 28/.410 ga 2,929.00
Skeet (12 or 20 ga.) 2,029.00
  28 or .410 ga. 2,069.00
  2-Bbl. Set 2,929.00
Sporting Clays (12 or 20 ga.) 2,099.00
  28 gauge 2,169.00
  2-Barrel Set (12 or 20 ga.) 2,999.00
Trap (Monte Carlo or Std.) 2,029.00
  2-Barrel Trap Combo 2,829.00

TRAP MODELS

Gauge	Stock	Barrel√ Length	Overall Length	Inter Choke	Sights√	785 Rib Width	585 Rib Width	Average Weight* 785	Average Weight* 585	Manufacturers ID# 785	Manufacturers ID# 585
12	STND	30"	47 3/8"	COMP-A	CP/WFB	15/32" CH/STP	3/8" STP	8 lb. 15 oz.	8 lb. 7 oz.	A7820CVTN	A5820CVTN
12	MONTE	30"	47 3/8:	COMP-A	CP/WFB	15/32" CH/STP	3/8" STP	9 lb. 0 oz.	8 lb. 7 oz.	A7820CVTM	A5420CVTM
12	STND	32"	49 3/8"	COMP-A	CP/WFB	15/32" CH/STP	3/8" STP	9 lb. 1 oz.	8 lb. 10 oz.	A7822CVTN	A5822CVTN
12	MONTE	32"	49 3/8:	COMP-A	CP/WFB	15/32" CH/STP	3/8" STP	9 lb. 1 oz.	8 lb. 9 oz.	A7822CVTM	A5822CVTM
TRAP COMBO'S – STANDARD											
12	STND	O/U-30"	47 3/8"	COMP.	CP/WFB	15/32" CH/STP	3/8" STP	8 lb. 15 oz.	8 lb. 6 oz.	A7820TN/7822	A5820TN/5822
12	STND	S/O-32"	49 3/8"	COMP.	CP/WFB	15/32" CH/STP	3/8" STP	9 lb. 0 oz.	8 lb. 6 oz.		
12	STND	O/U-30"	47 3/8"	COMP.	CP/WFB	15/32" CH/STP	3/8"STP	9 lb. 0 oz.	8 lb. 4 oz.	A7820TN/7824	A5820TN/5824
12	STND	S/O-34"	51 3/8"	COMP.	CP/WFB	15/32" CH/STP	3/8"STP	9 lb. 1 oz.	8 lb. 6 oz.		
12	STND	O/U-32"	49 3/8"	COMP.	CP/WFB	15/32" CH/STP	3/8" STP	9 lb. 0 oz.	8 lb. 7 oz.	A7822TN/7824	A5822TN/5824
12	STND	S/O-34"	51 3/8"	COMP.	CP/WFB	15/32" CH/STP	3/8" STP	9 lb. 1 oz.	8 lb. 8 oz.		
TRAP COMBO'S – MONTE CARLO											
12	MONTE	O/U-30"	47 3/8"	COMP.	CP/WFB	15/32" CH/STP	3/8" STP	8 lb. 15 oz.	8 lb. 6 oz.	A7820TM/7822	A5820TM/5822
12	MONTE	S/O-32"	49 3/8"	COMP.	CP/WFB	15/32" CH/STP	3/8" STP	9 lb. 0 oz.	8 lb. 6 oz.		
12	MONTE	O/U-30"	47 3/8"	COMP.	CP/WFB	15/32" CH/STP	3/8"STP	8 lb. 15 oz.	8 lb. 4 oz.	A7820TM/7824	A5820TM/5824
12	MONTE	S/O-34"	51 3/8"	COMP.	CP/WFB	15/32" CH/STP	3/8"STP	9 lb. 1 oz.	8 lb. 6 oz.		
12	MONTE	O/U-32"	49 3/8"	COMP.	CP/WFB	15/32" CH/STP	3/8" STP	9 lb. 0 oz.	8 lb. 7 oz.	A7822TM/7824	A5822TM/5824
12	MONTE	S/O-34"	51 3/8"	COMP.	CP/WFB	51/32" CH/STP	3/8" STP	9 lb. 1 oz.	8 lb. 9 oz.		

*Weights may vary due to wood density. Specifications may vary. *INTER-CHOKE SYSTEMS COMP. - Competition series includes Full, Mod., Imp. Cyl. STND. B - Standard series includes Imp. Cyl. Mod. and Skeet STOCK DIMENSIONS Length of Pull - 13 1/2" Drop at Comb - 1/1/2" Drop at Heel - 2 1/4" √MFB - Metal Front Bead

YOUTH & LADIES

Gauge	Chamber	Barrel Length	Overall Length	Inter Choke	Sights√	Rib Width	Average Weight* 785	Average Weight* 585	Manufacturers ID# 785	Manufacturers ID# 585
12	3"	28"	44 1/2"	COMP.	MFB	3/8"		7 lb. 11 oz.		A5828CFY
12	3"	26"	42 1/2"	COMP.	MFB	3/8"		7 lb. 9 oz.		A5826CFY
20	3"	26"	42 1/2"	STND-B	MFB	3/8"		6 lb. 7 oz.		A5806CFY
SKEET MODELS										
12	3"	30"	47 1/4"	COMP.	CP/WFB	3/8"	8 lb. 9 oz.	8 lb. 1 oz.	A7820CV	A5820CV
12	3"	28"	45 1/4"	COMP.	CP/WFB	3/8"	8 lb. 6 oz.	7 lb. 12 oz.	A7828CV	A5828CV
20	3"	28"	45 1/4"	STND.	CP/WFB	5/16"	7 lb. 2 oz.	6 lb. 15 oz.	A7808CV	A5808CV
28	2.75"	28"	45 1/4"	STND.	CP/WFB	5/16"	7 lb. 5 oz.	6 lb. 15 oz.	A7888CV	A5888CV
410	3"	28"	45 1/4"	SK/SK	CP/WFB	5/16"	7 lb. 5 oz.	7 lb. 0 oz.	A7848CV	A5848V
3 BARREL SKEET SETS										
20	3"	28"	45 1/4"	STND.	CP/WFB	5/16"	7 lb. 2 oz.	6 lb. 15 oz.		
28	2.75"	28"	45 1/4"	STND.	CP/WFB	5/16"	7 lb. 5 oz.	7 lb. 0 oz.	A78088	A58088
410	3"	28"	45 1/4"	SK/SK	CP/WFB	5/16"	7 lb. 5 oz.	7 lb. 0 oz.		

*Weights may vary due to wood density. Specifications may vary. *INTER-CHOKE SYSTEMS: COMP. - Competition series includes 2 -SKI/SCI, 1-Mod/SCIV STND - Standard series includes Skeet, Skeet and Imp. Cyl. NOTE: 785's Are Equipped with Step-Up Style Ribs STOCK DIMENSIONS: Length of Pull - 14 1/8" Drop at Comb - 1 1/2" Drop at Heel - 2 3/16" √CP/WFB - Center Post/White Front Bead

STOEGER IGA SHOTGUNS

COACH GUN

ENGRAVED COACH GUN

The **IGA CLASSIC SIDE-BY-SIDE COACH GUN** sports a 20-inch barrel. Lightning fast, it is the perfect shotgun for hunting upland game in dense brush or close quarters. This endurance-tested workhorse of a gun is designed from the ground up to give you years of trouble-free service. Two massive underlugs provide a super-safe, vise-tight locking system for lasting strength and durability. The mechanical extraction of spent shells and double-trigger mechanism

assures reliability. The automatic safety is actuated whenever the action is opened, whether or not the gun has been fired. The polish and blue is deep and rich, and the solid sighting rib is matte-finished for glare-free sighting. Chrome-moly steel barrels with micro-polished bores give dense, consistent patterns. Nickel finish is now available. The classic stock and forend are of durable hardwood...oil finished, hand-rubbed and hand-checkered.
Improved Cylinder/Modified choking and its short barrel make the IGA coach gun the ideal choice for hunting in close quarters, security and police work. Three-inch chambers.
Prices: In 12 and 20 Gauge or .410 Bore.. . . . . . **$409.00**
Nickel, shown **464.00**
Also available with Engraved Stagecoach scene
on the stock:. **479.00**

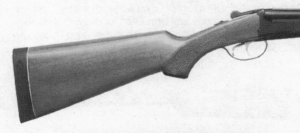

UPLANDER LADIES SIDE-BY-SIDE

UPLANDER LADIES SIDE-BY-SIDE
Crafted specifically with women in mind, IGA's new model features a lightweight 20 gauge with 24" barrel and is equipped with IC/M choke tubes. The durable 13" Brazilian hardwood stock is fitted with a ventilated pad to reduce recoil. Standard features include extractors, double triggers and automatic safety.
Price: **$478.00**

UPLANDER YOUTH SIDE-BY-SIDE (not shown)
IGA's new Youth gun is a lightweight .410 gauge with 24" barrels bored modified and full. Both barrels will handle 2 1/2'' or 3" shells. The 13" Brazilian hardwood stock includes a recoil pad. Standard features include double triggers, extractors and an automatic safety (activated when the gun is open). This shotgun is easy to load, light to carry and safe to handle with a second shot available when needed.
Price: **$438.00**

UPLANDER IGA SIDE-BY-SIDE (not shown)
The **IGA SIDE-BY-SIDE** is a rugged shotgun, endurance-tested and designed to give years of trouble-free service. A vise-tight, super-safe locking system is provided by two massive underlugs for lasting strength and durability. Two design features that make the IGA a standout for reliability are its positive mechanical extraction of spent shells and its traditional double-trigger mechanism. The safety is automatic in that every time the action is opened, whether or not the gun has been fired, the safety is actuated. The polish and bluing are deep and rich. The solid sighting rib carries a machined-in matte finish for glare-free sighting. Barrels are of chrome-moly steel with micro-polished bores to give dense, consistent patterns. The stock and forend are available with either traditional stock or the legendary English-style stock. Both are of durable Brazilian hardwood, oil-finished, hand-rubbed and hand-checkered.
Prices:
In 12, 20, 28 Gauge or .410 Bore. **$424.00**
In 12 and 20 Gauge w/Choke Tubes. **464.00**
Also available with English stock w/choke tubes (IC/M)
and fixed (M/M).

See table on page 396 for additional specifications

STOEGER IGA SHOTGUNS

CONDOR I OVER/UNDER SINGLE TRIGGER

The **IGA CONDOR I O/U SINGLE TRIGGER** is a workhorse of a shotgun, designed for maximum dependability in heavy field use. The super-safe lock-up system makes use of a sliding underlug, the best system for over/under shotguns. A massive monobloc joins the barrel in a solid one-piece assembly at the breech end. Reliability is assured, thanks to the mechanical extraction system. Upon opening the breech, the spent shells are partially lifted from the chamber, allowing easy removal by hand. IGA barrels are of chrome-moly steel with micro-polished bores to give tight, consistent patterns. They are specifically formulated for use with steel shot where Federal migratory bird regulations require. Atop the barrel is a sighting rib with an anti-glare surface. The buttstock and forend are of durable hardwood, hand-checkered and finished with an oil-based formula that takes dents and scratches in stride.

The **IGA CONDOR I** over/under shotgun is available in 12 and 20 gauge with 26- and 28-inch barrels with choke tubes and 3-inch chambers.

Price: w/Choke Tubes $559.00

CONDOR SUPREME SINGLE SELECTIVE TRIGGER

The **IGA CONDOR SUPREME** truly compliments its name. The stock is selected from upgraded Brazilian walnut, and the hand-finished checkering is sharp and crisp. A matte-laquered finish provides a soft warm glow, while maintaining a high resistance to dents and scratches. A massive monoblock joins the barrel in a solid one-piece assembly at the breech end. Upon opening the breech, the automatic ejectors cause the spent shells to be thrown clear of the gun. The barrels are of moly-chrome steel with micro-polished bores to give tight, consistent patterns; they are specifically formulated for use with steel shot. Choke tubes are provided. Atop the barrel is a sighting rib with an anti-glare surface with both mid- and front bead.

Price: $629.00

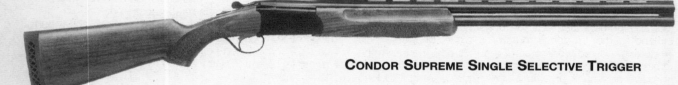

SIDE-BY-SIDE TURKEY MODEL
Price: $559.00

OVER/UNDER WATERFOWL MODEL

The 12-gauge **SIDE-BY-SIDE TURKEY MODEL** features IGA's new Advantage™ camouflage finish, plus double triggers, 3" chamber with 24" barrel and wide beavertail forend. The 30" barrel over/under **WATERFOWL MODEL** also features the new Advantage™ camouflage pattern on the barrel, stock and forend, plus single trigger, automatic ejector and Full/Full flush-mounted choke tubes and ventilated recoil pad. *Also available:* **TURKEY MODEL O/U** w/26" barrel in camouflage.

Price: $729.00

See table on page 396 for additional specifications

Stoeger IGA Shotguns

Deluxe Uplander Side-By-Side

Offered in 12 and 20 gauge with internal choke tubes along with 28 and .410 gauge with 26" fixed chokes; semi-fancy American walnut stock and forend; wood is finished in matte lacquer and stocks are fitted with a soft black recoil pad; front and mid-rib bead sight, gold double trigger and positive extractor are standard.

Price: 12 & 20 gauge $559.00
28 & .410 gauge 519.00

Deluxe Hunter Clay

Features include a matte lacquer finish, select grade semi-fancy American walnut stock and forend with a black target-style recoil pad. Also red bead front and mid-rib beads ensure accuracy. Over/under barrels are 28 inches long with 3" chambers.

Price: $699.00

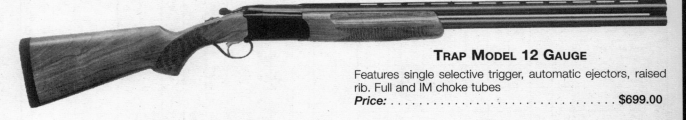

Trap Model 12 Gauge

Features single selective trigger, automatic ejectors, raised rib. Full and IM choke tubes

Price: $699.00

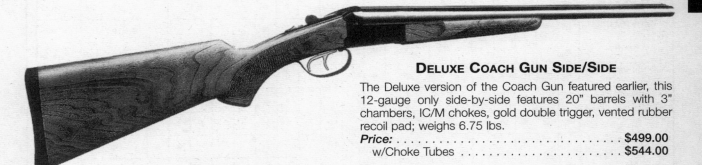

Deluxe Coach Gun Side/Side

The Deluxe version of the Coach Gun featured earlier, this 12-gauge only side-by-side features 20" barrels with 3" chambers, IC/M chokes, gold double trigger, vented rubber recoil pad; weighs 6.75 lbs.

Price: $499.00
w/Choke Tubes $544.00

See table on following page for additional specifications

SHOTGUNS

STOEGER IGA SHOTGUNS

	GAUGE					BARREL LENGTH					CHOKES		SPECIFICATIONS					SAFETY		BUTT-PLATES		DIMENSIONS			
	12	16	20	28	.410	20"	22"	24"	26"	28"	Fixed	Choke Tubes	Chamber	Weight (lbs.)	Extractors	Ejectors	Triggers	Manual	Automatic	Molded	Rubber-Ventilated	Length of pull	Drop of comb	Drop of heel	Overall length
COACH GUN Side by Side	■		■		■	■					IC/M		3"	6 3/4	■		D.T.		■	■		14 1/2"	1 1/2"	2 1/2"	36 1/2"
COACH GUN Nickel	■		■		■	■					IC/M		3"	6 3/4	■		D.T.		■	■		14 1/2"	1 1/2"	2 1/2"	36 1/2"
COACH GUN Engraved	■		■		■	■					IC/M		3"	6 3/4	■		D.T.		■	■		14 1/2"	1 1/2"	2 1/2"	36 1/2"
COACH GUN Deluxe	■					■					IC/M		3"	6 3/4	■		D.T.		■		■	14 1/2"	1 1/2"	2 1/2"	36 1/2"
UPLANDER Side by Side	■		■						■		IC/M		3"	6 3/4	■		D.T.		■	■		14 1/2"	1 1/2"	2 1/2"	42"
UPLANDER Side by Side	■		■							■	M/F		3"	6 3/4	■		D.T.		■	■		14 1/2"	1 1/2"	2 1/2"	42"
UPLANDER Side by Side		■		■					■		IC/M		2 3/4"	6 3/4	■		D.T.		■			14 1/2"	1 1/2"	2 1/2"	42"
UPLANDER Side by Side	■									■	M/F		3"	6 3/4	■		D.T.		■	■		14 1/2"	1 1/2"	2 1/2"	45 1/2"
UPLANDER Side by Side	■								■		IC/M		3"	6 3/4	■		D.T.		■	■		14 1/2"	1 1/2"	2 1/2"	42"
UPLANDER Side by Side				■					■		F/F		3"	6 3/4	■		D.T.		■	■		14 1/2"	1 1/2"	2 1/2"	42"
UPLANDER English			■					■			-	IC/M	3"	6 3/4	■		D.T.		■	■		14 1/2"	1 1/2"	2 1/2"	40"
UPLANDER English				■				■			M/M		3"	6 3/4	■		D.T.		■	■		14 1/2"	1 1/2"	2 1/2"	40"
UPLANDER Ladies			■					■			IC/M		3"	6 3/4	■		D.T.		■		■	13"	1 1/2"	2 1/2"	40"
UPLANDER Youth				■				■			M/F		3"	6 3/4	■		D.T.		■		■	13"	1 1/2"	2 1/2"	40"
UPLANDER Deluxe	■									■	M/F		3"	6 3/4	■		D.T.		■		■	14 1/2"	1 1/2"	2 1/2"	44"
UPLANDER Deluxe			■						■		IC/M		3"	6 3/4	■		D.T.		■		■	14 1/2"	1 1/2"	2 1/2"	42"
UPLANDER Deluxe				■					■		IC/M		2 3/4"	6 3/4	■		D.T.		■		■	14 1/2"	1 1/2"	2 1/2"	42"
UPLANDER Deluxe				■					■		M/F		3"	6 3/4	■		D.T.		■		■	14 1/2"	1 1/2"	2 1/2"	42"
CONDOR I Over / Under	■		■						■		IC/M		3"	8	■		S.T.	■			■	14 1/2"	1 1/2"	2 1/2"	43 1/2"
CONDOR I Over / Under	■									■	M/F		3"	8	■		S.T.	■			■	14 1/2"	1 1/2"	2 1/2"	45 1/2"
CONDOR II Over / Under	■								■		IC/M		3"	8	■		D.T.	■		■		14 1/2"	1 1/2"	2 1/2"	43 1/2"
CONDOR II Over / Under	■									■	M/F		3"	8	■		D.T.	■		■		14 1/2"	1 1/2"	2 1/2"	45 1/2"
CONDOR Supreme	■		■						■		IC/M		3"	8		■	S.T.	■			■	14 1/2"	1 1/2"	2 1/2"	43 1/2"
CONDOR Supreme	■		■							■	M/F		3"	8		■	S.T.	■			■	14 1/2"	1 1/2"	2 1/2"	45 1/2"
UPLANDER Camo	■							■			F/F		3"	6 3/4	■		D.T.		■	■		14 1/2"	1 1/2"	2 1/2"	40"
CONDOR Supreme Camo	■								■		F/F		3"	8		■	S.T.	■			■	14 1/2"	1 1/2"	2 1/2"	45 1/2"
HUNTERS-CLAYS	■									■	IC M/F		3"	8		■	S.T.	■			■	14 1/2"	1 1/2"	2 1/2"	45 1/2"

WEATHERBY SHOTGUNS

ATHENA GRADE V CLASSIC FIELD

The Athena receiver houses a boxlock action, sidelock-type plates with fine floral engraving. The hinge pivots are made of high-strength steel alloy. The locking system employs the Greener crossbolt design. The single selective trigger is mechanically operated for a fully automatic switchover, allowing the second barrel to be fired on a subsequent trigger pull, even during a misfire. The selector lever, located in front of the trigger, enables the shooter to fire the lower barrel or upper barrel first.

The breech block is hand-fitted to the receiver. Every Athena is equipped with a matted, ventilated rib and bead front sight. Ejectors are fully automatic. The safety is a slide type located on the upper tang atop pistol grip. Each stock is carved from Claro walnut, with fine line hand-checkering and high-luster finish. Trap model has Monte Carlo stock only. *See* the Athena and Orion table on the following page for additional information and specifications.

GRADE IV CHOKES
Fixed Choke
Field, .410 Gauge
Skeet, 12 or 20 Gauge
IMC Multi-Choke
Field, 12, 20 or 28 Gauge
Trap, 12 Gauge
Trap, single barrel, 12 Gauge
Trap Combo, 12 Gauge
Prices:
ATHENA GRADE IV $2,259.00
ATHENA GRADE V 2,599.00

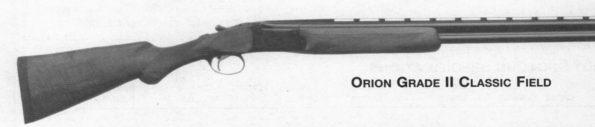

ORION GRADE II CLASSIC FIELD

ORION GRADES I, II & III OVER/UNDERS

For greater versatility, the Orion incorporates the integral multichoke (IMC) system. Available in Extra-full, Full, Modified, Improved Modified, Improved Cylinder and Skeet, the choke tubes fit flush with the muzzle without detracting from the beauty of the gun. Three tubes are furnished with each gun. The precision hand-fitted monobloc and receiver are machined from high-strength steel with a highly polished finish. The boxlock design uses the Greener cross-bolt locking system and special sears maintain hammer engagement. Pistol grip stock and forearm are carved of Claro walnut with hand-checkered diamond inlay pattern and high-gloss finish. Chrome-moly steel barrels, and the receiver, are deeply blued. The Orion also features selective automatic ejectors, single selective trigger, front bead sight and ventilated rib. The trap model boasts a curved trap-style recoil pad and is available with Monte Carlo stock only.
Weight: 12 ga. Field, 7 1/2 lbs.; 20 ga. Field, 7 1/2 lbs.; Trap, 8 lbs.
See following page for prices and additional specifications.

ORION CHOKES
Grade I
IMC Multi-Choke, Field, 12 or 20 Gauge
Grade II
Fixed Choke, Field, .410 Gauge
Fixed Choke, Skeet, 12 or 20 Gauge
IMC Multi-Choke, Field, 12, 20 or 28 Gauge
IMC Multi-Choke, Trap, 12 Gauge
Grade II Sporting Clays
12 Gauge only
Grade III
IMC Multi-Choke, Field, 12 or 20 Gauge

SHOTGUNS

WEATHERBY SHOTGUNS

ORION GRADE II CLASSIC FIELD
12 GAUGE OVER/UNDER

ORION SUPER SPORTING CLAYS O/U

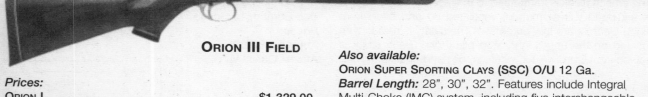

ORION III FIELD

Prices:
ORION I $1,329.00
ORION II CLASSIC FIELD 1,399.00
ORION II SPORTING CLAYS 1,499.00
ORION III FIELD & CLASSIC FIELD 1,699.00

Also available:
ORION SUPER SPORTING CLAYS (SSC) O/U 12 Ga.
Barrel Length: 28", 30", 32". Features include Integral Multi-Choke (IMC) system, including five interchangeable screw-in stainless steel Briley choke tubes; Calro walnut stock w/Sporter style pistol grip. *Weight:* 8 lbs.
Price: $1,749.00

WEATHERBY SHOTGUN SPECIFICATIONS

MODEL	GAUGE	CHAMBER	BARREL LENGTH	OVERALL LENGTH	LENGTH OF PULL	DROP AT HEEL	DROP AT COMB	BEAD SIGHT	APPROX. WEIGHT (LBS.)
Athena Grade V Classic Field	12	3"	28" or 26"	45" or 43"	14.25"	2.25"	1.5"	Brilliant front	6.5-8
	20	3"	28" or 26"	45" or 43"	14.25"	2.25"	1.5"	Brilliant front	6.5-8
Athena Grade IV Field	12	3"	28" or 26"	45" or 43"	14.25"	2.5"	1.5"	Brilliant front	6.5-8
	20	3"	28" or 26"	45" or 43"	14.25"	2.5"	1.5"	Brilliant front	6.5-8
Orion Grade III Classic Field	12	3"	28" or 26"	45" or 43"	14.25"	2.25"	1.5"	Brilliant front	6.5-8
	20	3"	28" or 26"	45" or 43"	14.25"	2.25"	1.5"	Brilliant front	6.5-8
Orion Grade III English Field	12	3"	28"	45"	14.25"	2.5"	1.5"	Brilliant front	7-7.5
	20	3"	28" or 26"	45" or 43"	14.25"	2.5"	1.5"	Brilliant front	6.5-7
Orion Grade III Field	12	3"	28" or 26"	45" or 43"	14.25"	2.25"	1.5"	Brilliant front	6.5-8
	20	3"	28" or 26"	45" or 43"	14.25"	2.25"	1.5"	Brilliant front	6.5-8
Orion Grade II Classic Field	12	3"	30", 28" or 26"	47", 45" or 43"	14.25"	2.25"	1.5"	Brilliant front	6.5-8
	20	3"	28" or 26"	45" or 43"	14.25"	2.25"	1.5"	Brilliant front	6.5-8
	28	2.75"	26"	43"	14.25"	2.25"	1.5"	Brilliant front	6.5-8
Orion Grade I Field	12	3"	30", 28" or 26"	47", 45" or 43"	14.25"	2.5"	1.5"	Brilliant front	6.5-8
	20	3"	28" or 26"	45" or 43"	14.25"	2.5"	1.5"	Brilliant front	6.5-8
Orion Grade II Classic Sporting	12	3"	30" or 28"	47" or 45"	14.25" 14.25"	2.25"	1.5" 1.5"	Midpoint w/white front	7.5-8
Orion Grade II Sporting	12	3"	30" or 28"	47" or 45"	14.25"	2.25"	1.5"	Midpoint w/white front	7.5-8

WINCHESTER SHOTGUNS

MODEL 1300 RANGER LADIES/YOUTH PUMP-ACTION SHOTGUN

MODEL 1300 RANGER 12 GAUGE DEER COMBO
22" Rifled w/Sights & 28" Vent-Rib Barrels

MODEL 1300

Suggested Retail	Gauge	Barrel Length & Type	Chamber	Shotshell Capacity*	Choke	Overall Length	Nominal Length of Pull	Nominal Drop at Comb	Nominal Drop at Heel	Nominal Weight (Lbs.)	Features
FIELD MODELS											
WALNUT											
$340	12	28"VR	3" Mag.	5	W3	49"	14"	1-1/2"	2-1/2"	7-3/8	Walnut Stock, MBF
340	12	26VR	3" Mag.	5	W3	47	14	1-1/2	2-1/2	7-1/8	Walnut Stock, MBF
BLACK SHADOW (SYNTHETIC STOCK)											
296	12	28VR	3" Mag.	5	WIM	49	14	1-1/2	2-1/2	7-1/4	MBF
296	12	26VR	3" Mag.	5	WIM	47	14	1-1/2	2-1/2	7	MBF
296	20	26VR	3" Mag.	5	WIM	47	14	1-1/2	2-1/2	6-7/8	MBF
RANGER MODELS											
RANGER											
$309	12	28"VR	3" Mag.	5	W3	49"	14"	1-1/2"	2-1/2"	7-3/8	MBF
309	20	28VR	3" Mag.	5	W3	49	14	1-1/2	2-1/2	7-1/8	MBF
RANGER LADIES/YOUTH											
309	20	22VR	3" Mag.	5	W3	42	13"	1-1/2	2-3/8	6-5/8	UP, MBF
RANGER DEER COMBO (CYLINDER DEER BARREL AND EXTRA VENT RIB BARREL)											
$379	12	22 Smooth	3" Mag.	5	Cyl	42-3/4	14	1-1/2	2-1/2	6-7/8	SB, D&T, Rifle Sights
	12	38VR	3" Mag.	5	W3	49	14	1-1/2	2-1/2	7-3/8	MBF
RANGER DEER COMBO (RIFLED DEER BARREL AND EXTRA VENT RIB BARREL)											
401	12	22 Rifled	3" Mag.	5	Rifled Barrel	42-3/4	14	1-1/2	2-1/2	6-7/8	SB,D&T,Rifle Sights
	12	28VR	3" Mag.	5	W3	49	14	1-1/2	2-1/2	7-3/8	MBF
TURKEY MODELS											
TURKEY ADVANTAGE® FULL CAMO											
$432	12	22"VR	3" Mag.	5	W3W	43	14"	1-1/2"	2-1/2"	6-3/4"	Studs, Sling, D&T, MBF
410	12	22Smooth	3" Mag.	5	WIC&WXF	43	14	1-1/2	2-1/2	6-3/4	Studs,Sling, D&T, Rifle Sights
TURKEY REALTREE® ALL-PURPOSE FULL CAMO											
432	12	22VR	3" Mag.	5	W3W	43	14	1-1/2	2-1/2	6-3/4	Studs,Sling,D&T,MBF
TURKEY REALTREE® GRAY ALL-PURPOSE FULL CAMO											
432	12	22VR	3" Mag.	5	W3W	43	14"	1-1/2	2-1/2	6-3/4	Studs,Sling,D&T,MBF
TURKEY REALTREE® GRAY ALL-PURPOSE PATTERN (MATTE METAL)											
370	12	22VR	3" Mag.	5	W3W	43	14"	1-1/2	2-1/2	6-3/4	Studs,Sling,D&T,MBF
TURKEY BLACK SHADOW (SYNTHETIC STOCK)											
296	12	22VR	3" Mag.	5	WXF	43	14	1-1/2	2-1/2	6-5/8	D&T,MBF
296	12	22 VR	3" Mag.	5	WIF	43	14	1-1/2	2-1/2	6-5/8	D&T,MBF
DEER MODELS											
DEER (WALNUT STOCK)											
$404	12	22"Rifled	3" Mag.	5	Rifled Barrel	42-3/4"	14"	1-1/2"	2-1/2"	6-7/8	Studs,B&R,D&T,Rifle Sights
DEER BLACK SHADOW (SYNTHETIC STOCK)											
296	12	22" Smooth	3" Mag.	5	WIC	43	14	1-1/2	2-1/2	6-7/8	Studs,D&T,Rifle Sights
317	12	22 Rifled	3" Mag.	5	Rifled Barrel	42-3/4	14	1-1/2	2-1/2	6-3/4	D&T,Rifle Sights
DEER ADVANTAGE® FULL CAMO PATTERN											
432	12	22" Rifled	3" Mag.	5	Rifled Barrel	42-3/4	14	1-1/2	2-1/2	6-3/4	Studs,Sling,D&T,Rifle Sights
410	12	22 Smooth	3" Mag.	5	WIC & WXF	43	14	1-1/2	2-1/2	7-1/4	Studs,Sling,D&T,Rifle Sights
BLACK SHADOW DEER COMBO (CYLINDER DEER BARREL AND 12 GA. EXTRA VENT RIB BARREL)											
366	12	22" Smooth	3" Mag.	5	Cyl.	42-3/4	14	1-1/2	2-1/2	6-3/4	Studs,D&T,Rifle Sights
	12	28VR	3" Mag.	5	WIM	49	14	1-1/2	2-1/2	6-3/4	Studs,MBF

Includes one shotshell in chamber. For Model 1300 Feature & Choke and Barrel Abbreviations see following page.

SHOTGUNS

WINCHESTER SECURITY SHOTGUNS

These tough 12-gauge shotguns provide backup strength for security and police work as well as all-around utility. The action is one of the fastest second-shot pumps made. It features a front-locking rotating bolt for strength and secure, single-unit lockup into the barrel. Twin-action slide bars prevent binding.

The shotguns are chambered for 3-inch shotshells. They handle 3-inch Magnum, 2.75-inch Magnum and standard 2.75-inch shotshells interchangeably. They have a crossbolt

safety, walnut-finished hardwood stock and forearm, black rubber buttpad and plain 18-inch barrel with Cylinder Bore choke. All are ultra-reliable and easy to handle.

Special chrome finish on Police and Marine guns are actually triple-plated: first with copper for adherence, then with nickel for rust protection, and finally with chrome for a hard finish. This triple-plating assures durability and quality. Both guns have a forend cap with swivel to accommodate sling.

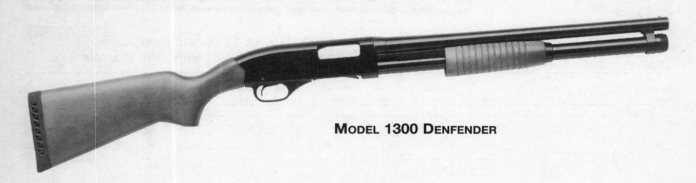

MODEL 1300 DENFENDER

SPECIFICATIONS MODEL 1300 DEFENDER

Suggested Retail	Gauge	Barrel Length & Type	Chamber	Shotshell Capacity*	Choke	Overall Length	Nominal Length of Pull	Nominal Drop at Comb	Nominal Drop at Heel	Nominal Weight (Lbs.)	Features
DEFENDER MODELS											
COMBO, HARDWOOD STOCK AND SYNTHETIC PISTOL GRIP, 5 SHOT											
$393	12	18"	3 Mag.	5	Cyl.	29-1/8"	—	—	—	5-5/8	Studs, MBF
	12	28VR	3" Mag.	5	WIM	49	14	1-1/2	2-1/2	7-3/8	Studs, MBF
HARDWOOD STOCK, 8 SHOT											
290	12	18	3" Mag.	8**	Cyl.	39-1/2	14	1-1/2	2-1/2	6-3/4	Studs, MBF
290	12	24	3" Mag.	8**	Cyl.	44-3/4	14	1-1/2	2-1/2	6-3/4	Studs, MBF
SYNTHETIC PISTOL GRIP, 8 SHOT											
290	12	18	3" Mag.	8**	Cyl.	29-1/8	—	—	—	5-1/2	Studs, MBF
SYNTHETIC STOCK, 8 SHOT											
290	12	18	3" MAG.	8**	Cyl..	39-1/2	14	1-1/2	2-1/2	6-3/8	Studs, MBF
LADY DEFENDER SYNTHETIC STOCK, 8 SHOT											
290	20	18	3" Mag.	8**	Cyl.	39-1/2	14	1-1/2	2-1/2	6-1/4	Studs, MBF
LADY DEFENDER SYNTHETIC PISTOL GRIP, 8 SHOT											
290	20	18	3" Mag.	8**	Cyl.	29-1/8	—	—	—	5-3/8	Studs, MBF
STAINLESS MARINE SYNTHETIC STOCK											
490	12	18	3" Mag.	7**	Cyl.	39-1/2	14	1-1/2	2-1/2	6-3/8	Studs, MBF

Model 1300 Feature Abbreviations: MBF=Metal bead front, Rifle=Rifle type front and rear sights. Rifle sights=Adjustable rear sight and ramp style front sight.
SB=Scope Bases Included. B&R=Scope, Bases and Rings included. D&T=Drilled and tapped to accept scope bases. Studs=Buttstock and magazine cap sling studs provided (sling loop on pistol grip models).
UP=Ladies/Youth models are supplied with universal plug for limiting magazine capacity to one, two, or three shells. Sling=Adjustable Cordura sling included.

Model 1300 Choke and Barrel Abbreviations: VR=Ventilated rib. W3W=WinChoke, Extra Full, Full and Modified Tubes. W3=WinChoke, Full, Modified and Improved Cylinder Tubes.
Cyl.=Non-WinChoke, choked Cylinder Bore. WIM=Modified Tube. WIC=Cylinder Choke Tube. WF=Full Choke Tube. WXF=Extra Full Choke Tube. Smooth=Non-Rifled Bore.

American Arms   402
American Frontier Firearms   403
Austin & Halleck   405
Cabela's   406
Colt Blackpowder Arms   407
CVA   410
Dixie   413
EMF Hartford   419
Euroarms of America   421
Fort Worth Firearms   425
Gonic Arms   426
Lyman   427
Markesbery   429
Marlin   430
Modern Muzzleloading   430
Navy Arms   433
Prairie River Arms   441
Remington   442
Ruger   443
Shiloh Sharps   444
Thompson/Center   445
Traditions   449
Uberti   457

Blackpowder

*For addresses and phone/fax numbers of manufacturers and distributors included in this section, please turn to **DIRECTORY OF MANUFACTURERS AND SUPPLIERS** on page 558.*

AMERICAN ARMS

1851 COLT NAVY

This replica of the most famous revolver of the percussion era was used extensively during the Civil War and on the Western frontier.

SPECIFICATIONS
Caliber: 36
Capacity: 6 shots
Barrel length: 7.5" octagonal w/hinged loading lever
Overall length: 13"
Weight: 44 oz.
Features: Solid brass frame, trigger guard and backstrap; one-piece walnut grip; engraved blued steel cylinder
Price:
Brass Frame $165.00
Steel Frame 195.00

1851 COLT NAVY

1858 REMINGTON ARMY

This replica of the last of Remington's percussion revolvers saw extensive use in the Civil War.

SPECIFICATIONS
Caliber: 44
Capacity: 6 shots
Barrel length: 8" octagonal w/creeping loading lever
Overall length: 13"
Weight: 38 oz.
Features: Two-piece walnut grips
Also Available:
Prices:
Brass Frame $179.00
Steel Frame 225.00
1858 ARMY STAINLESS STEEL TARGET. Same specifications as 1858 Remington, but with adjustable rear trigger sight and blade front sight; stainless steel frame, barrel and cylinder.
Price: $375.00

1858 REMINGTON ARMY

**1858 ARMY
STAINLESS STEEL TARGET**

1860 COLT ARMY

Union troops issued this sidearm during the Civil War and subsequent Indian Wars.

SPECIFICATIONS
Caliber: 44
Capacity: 6 shots
Barrel length: 8" round w/creeping loading lever
Overall length: 13.5"
Weight: 44 oz.
Features: Solid brass or steel frame, trigger guard and backstrap; one-piece walnut grip; engraved blued steel cylinder
Prices:
Brass Frame $179.00
Steel Frame 225.00

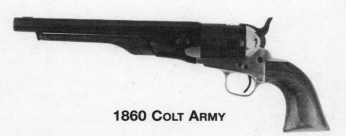

1860 COLT ARMY

AMERICAN FRONTIER FIREARMS

1871-2 OPEN-TOP FRONTIER MODEL

Available in 38 or 44 caliber with non-rebated cylinder, 7.5" and 8" round barrels; standard-finish high-polish blued steel parts, colorcase hardened hammer and walnut varnished navy-sized grips.
Price: $795.00

1871-2 OPEN-TOP FRONTIER MODEL

1871-2 OPEN-TOP TIFFANY MODEL

Available in 38 and 44 calibers, non-rebated cylinder, 4.75", 5.5", 7.5" and 8" round barrels; Tiffany grips; silver and gold finish with engraving.
Price: $995.00

1871-2 OPEN-TOP TIFFANY MODEL

REMINGTON NEW ARMY CAVALRY MODEL

Available in 38, 44, and 45 calibers with 5.5", 7.5" and 8" barrels; high-polish blued finish, colorcase hardened hammer. Comes with an ejector assembly, loading gate and government inspector's cartouche on left grip and sub-inspector's initials on various other parts.
Price: $795.00

REMINGTON NEW ARMY CAVALRY MODEL

POCKET REMINGTON

Available in 22, 32, and 38 calibers with 3.5" barrel, with or without ejector rod or gate, high-polish blued steel parts, colorcase hardened hammer, varnished walnut grips.
Price: and up $495.00

POCKET REMINGTON

BLACK POWDER

AMERICAN FRONTIER FIREARMS

RICHARDS 1851 MODEL
NAVY CONVERSION

Available in 38 and 44 calibers with non-rebated cylinder, 4.75", 5.5" & 7.5" octagon barrels, colorcase hardened hammer and trigger, ramrod and plunger, blued steel backstrap and trigger guard; walnut varnished navy-sized grips (Note: No ejector rod assembly on this model)
Price: $695.00

**RICHARDS 1851
MODEL NAVY CONVERSION**

RICHARDS 1860 ARMY
MODEL CONVERSION

Available in 38 or 44 caliber with rebated cylinder with or without ejector assembly; 4.75", 5.5" and 7.5" round barrels, standard finishes are high-polish blued steel parts (including backstrap); trigger guard is silver-plated brass; colorcase hardened hammer and trigger, walnut varnished army-sized grips.
Price: $695.00

**RICHARDS AND MASON
CONVERSION 1851 NAVY MODEL**

RICHARDS AND MASON
CONVERSION 1851 NAVY MODEL

Available in 38 and 44 calibers with Mason ejector assembly and non-rebated cylinder, 4.75", 5.5" and 7.5" octagon barrels, high-polish blued steel parts, colorcase hammer and trigger, blued steel backstrap and trigger guard with ejector rod; varnished walnut grips.
Price: $695.00

**POCKET RICHARDS AND
MASON NAVY CONVERSION**

POCKET RICHARDS AND
MASON NAVY CONVERSION

Available in 32 caliber, non-rebated cylinder, five shot, high-polish blued steel parts, silver-plated brass backstrap and trigger guard with ejector assembly, colorcase hardened hammer and trigger, varnished walnut grips.
Price: and up $495.00

**RICHARDS 1860
ARMY MODEL CONVERSION**

RICHARDS 1861 MODEL
NAVY CONVERSION (not shown)

Same as 1860 Model, except with non-rebated cylinder and navy-sized grips. All blue with silver trigger guard and backstrap.
Price: $695.00

AUSTIN & HALLECK RIFLES

MODEL 320 LR/SS

MODEL 420 LR CLASSIC

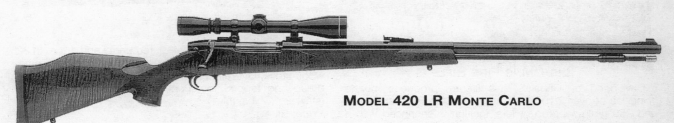

MODEL 420 LR MONTE CARLO

SPECIFICATIONS

Caliber: 50 *Action:* In-line percussion (removable weather shroud) *Barrel Length:* 26" (1:28"); 8 lands & grooves; .75" tapered round *Overall length:* 47.5" *Weight:* 7 7/8 lbs. *Length of pull:* 13.5" *Stock:* Select grade tiger-striped curly maple (Classic model has filled-grain luster finish w/steel pistol grip; Monte Carlo has filled-grain high-gloss finish) *Features:* Timney-adjustable target triggers w/sear block safety; 1" recoil pad; shadow line (optional); scope not included

Prices:

MODEL 420 LR MONTE CARLO & CLASSIC STANDARD	$518.00
Fancy	619.00
Stainless Steel Standard	613.00
Fancy Stainless Steel	689.00
Hand Select	729.00
Hand Select Stainless Steel	825.00
Exhibition Grade	1300.00
MODEL 320 LR BLU w/Synthetic Stock	455.00
MODEL 320 LR S/S	506.00

MOUNTAIN RIFLE

MOUNTAIN RIFLE
SPECIFICATIONS
Caliber: 50 percussion or flintlock
Barrel length: 32" (1:66"); 1" octagonal; slow rust brown finish
Overall length: 49" *Weight:* 7.5 lbs.

Stock: Select grade tiger-striped curly maple; filled-grain luster finish
Sights: Fixed buckhorn rear; silver blade brass bead front
Features: Double throw adjustable set triggers
Price: $499.00
   Hand Select w/wo Bullet Barrel 592.00

CABELA'S RIFLES

HAWKEN RIFLE

Traditional "plains rifle" styling with American walnut stock, brass furniture including patch box, and color-casehardened lockplate. Adjustable double-set trigger, hardened coil-spring three-stage lock with hardened steel sear. Screw adjustable rear sight with bead and ramp front. *Calibers:* 45, 50 and 54 percussion (R.H./L.H.); flintlock (R.H. only). *Barrel Length:* 28"

(1:48" twist and 12 grooves in 45 cal.; 1:48" twist, 6 grooves in 50 cal.; 1:48" twist with 5 grooves in 54 caliber).
Price: **$174.99**
   Left Hand. **184.99**
Also available: SPORTERIZED HAWKEN. Same as standard percussion model except blued steel furniture and fittings, rubber recoil pad, checkered walnut stock and leather sling. Also in carbine and synthetic stock carbine versions (right- and left-hand except in synthetic)
Price: **$184.99**
   Left Hand. **194.99**

LIGHTNING FIRE RIFLE

Developed by Cabela's, this firearm produces muzzle velocities of over 2,100 fps using Hodgdon Pyrodex Pellets and 250 grain saboted bullets. Ignition is enhanced with a musket nipple and percussion caps that deliver five times the

spark of standard #11 caps.
   SPECIFICATIONS INCLUDE: 24" fluted barrel and 1 turn in 32" twist rate. Stainless steel and blued barrel have laminated wood stock. *Overall Length:* 43". Fully adjustable rear sight, drilled and tapped for scope mounts. *Weight:* 7.25 lbs. (stainless); 7 lbs. (blue)
Price: Blue **$299.99**
   Stainless **379.99**

ROLLING BLOCK MUZZLELOADER

The breechblock/firing-pin mechanism on this model completely shrouds the nipple area, keeping caps dry and secure. Features include black engraved receiver, tapered 26.5"

barrel with 1:24" twist. Block, hammer and buttplate are color-casehardened steel; breech plug is easily removable. American walnut stock w/sling swivel studs. *Calibers:* 50 and 54 *Overall Length:* 43.5" *Weight:* 8.5 lbs.
Price: **$339.99**
Also available:
ROLLING BLOCK CARBINE. Same as above, but with 22.25" round barrel, screw-adj. rear sight and front blade/bead sight, rubber butt pad. *Overall Length:* 38.75" *Weight:* 7.75 lbs.
Price: **$319.99**

KODIAK EXPRESS DOUBLE RIFLE

Early explorers of Africa and Asia often had to rely on large-bore express rifles like this handsome sidelock replica featuring oil-finished, hand-checkered European walnut stock with

casehardened steel buttplate. Ramp-mounted, adjustable folding double rear sights, ramp front sight, drilled and tapped for folding tang sight. Color-casehardened lock, blued top tang and trigger guard are all polished and engraved. *Calibers:* 50 and 58 *Barrels:* 28" with 1:48" twist (regulated at 75 yards); blued. *Overall Length:* 45.25" *Weight:* 9.3 lbs.
Price: **$549.99**

COLT BLACKPOWDER ARMS

SIGNATURE SERIES

COLT 1847 WALKER

SPECIFICATIONS
Caliber: 44
Barrel length: 9" *Overall length:* 15.5"
Weight: 73 oz. (empty)
Sights: Fixed blade front sight *Sight radius:* 12.25"
Stock: One-piece walnut
Finish: Colt blue with color casehardened frame; hammer, lever and plunger
Price: **$419.95**

COLT WALKER
150TH ANNIVERSARY MODEL

SPECIFICATIONS
Caliber: 44 *Weight:* 4 lbs. 9 oz.
Barrel length: 9"
Cylinder length: 2 7/16"
Finish: Color casehardened frame and hammer; smooth wooden grips
Features: Colt's Signature Series 150th anniversary re-issue carries the identical markings as the original 1847 Walker. "U.S. 1847" appears above the barrel wedge, exactly as on the Walkers produced for service in the Mexican War. The cylinder has a battle scene depicting 15 Texas Rangers defeating a Comanche war party using the first revolver invented by Sam Colt. This Limited Edition features original A Company No. 1 markings embellished in gold. Serial numbers begin with #221, a continuation of A Company numbers.
Price: **$599.95**

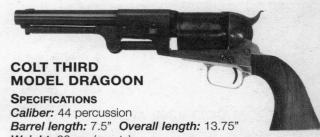

COLT THIRD
MODEL DRAGOON

SPECIFICATIONS
Caliber: 44 percussion
Barrel length: 7.5" *Overall length:* 13.75"
Weight: 66 oz. (empty)
Sight: Fixed blade front *Sight radius:* 10.75"
Stock: One-piece walnut *Finish:* Colt blue with color casehardened frame; hammer, lever and plunger
Price: **$419.95**
Also available with steel backstrap and fluted cylinder: **$540.00**

**COLT WALKER
150TH ANNIVERSARY**

COLT 1849
POCKET REVOLVER

SPECIFICATIONS
Caliber: 31
Barrel length: 4" Overall length: 9.5"
Weight: 24 oz. (empty)
Stock: One-piece walnut
Finish: Colt blue and color casehardened frame
Price: **$389.95**

COLT 1851 NAVY

SPECIFICATIONS
Caliber: 36
Barrel length: 7.5" *Overall length:* 13 1/8"
Weight: 40.5 oz. (empty)
Sights: Fixed blade front *Sight radius:* 10"
Stock: Oiled American walnut
Finish: Colt blue and color casehardened frame
Price: **$399.95**

BLACK POWDER

COLT BLACKPOWDER ARMS

SIGNATURE SERIES

COLT 1860 ARMY

A continuation in production of the famous cap-and-ball revolver used by the U.S. Cavalry with color casehardened frame, hammer and loading lever. Blued backstrap and brass trigger guard, roll-engraved cylinder and one-piece walnut grips

SPECIFICATIONS

Caliber: 44 *Barrel length:* 8" *Overall length:* 13.75"
Weight: 42 oz. (empty) *Sights:* Fixed blade front
Sight radius: 10.5" *Stock:* One-piece walnut
Finish: Colt blue with color casehardened frame; hammer, lever and plunger
Price: $399.95

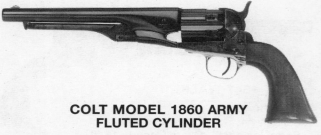

COLT MODEL 1860 ARMY FLUTED CYLINDER

The first Army revolvers shipped from Hartford were known as the "Cavalry Model"—with fluted cylinder, hardened frame, hammer, loading lever and plunger. Features blued barrel, backstrap and cylinder; brass trigger guard, fluted cylinder, one-piece walnut grip and a 4-screw frame (cut for optional shoulder stock)

SPECIFICATIONS

Caliber: 44 percussion *Barrel length:* 8"
Overall length: 13.75" *Weight:* 42 oz. (empty)
Sight: Fixed blade front *Sight radius:* 10.5"
Stock: One piece walnut *Finish:* Colt blue with color casehardened frame; hammer, lever and plunger
Price: $399.95

COLT 1861 NAVY

A personal favorite of George Armstrong Custer, who carried a pair of them during the Civil War. Loading lever and plunger; blued barrel, cylinder backstrap and trigger guard; roll-engraved cylinder; one-piece walnut grip.

SPECIFICATIONS

Caliber: 36 percussion *Barrel length:* 7.5"
Overall length: 13 1/8" *Weight:* 42 oz. (empty)
Sight: Fixed blade front *Sight radius:* 10"
Stock: One-piece walnut *Finish:* Colt blue with color casehardened frame; hammer, lever and plunger
Price: $399.95

COLT 1861 NAVY

**TRAPPER MODEL
1862 POCKET POLICE**

TRAPPER MODEL 1862 POCKET POLICE

The first re-issue of the rare and highly desirable Pocket Police "Trapper Model." The Trapper's 3.5" barrel without attached loading lever makes it an ideal backup gun, as well as a welcome addition to any gun collection. Color case-hardened frame and hammer; silver-plated backstrap and trigger guard; blued semifluted cylinder and barrel; one-piece walnut grip. Separate 4 5/8" brass ramrod.

SPECIFICATIONS

Caliber: 36 *Barrel length:* 3.5" *Overall length:* 8.5"
Weight: 20 oz. (empty) *Sight:* Fixed blade front
Sight radius: 6" *Stock:* One-piece walnut
Finish: Colt blue with color casehardened frame and hammer
Price: $389.95

COLT BLACKPOWDER ARMS

COLT MODEL 1861 MUSKET

Manufactured to original specifications using modern steels, this re-issue has the authentic Colt markings of its Civil War predecessor. Plus triangular bayonet.

SPECIFICATIONS
Caliber: .58
Barrel length: 40"
Overall length: 56"

Weight: 9 lbs. 3 oz. (empty)
Sights: Folding leaf rear; steel blade front
Sight Radius: 36"
Stock: One piece
Finish: Bright steel lockplate, hammer, buttplate, bands, ramrod and nipple; blued rear sight
Price: $569.95

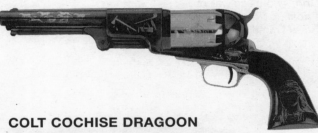

COLT COCHISE DRAGOON

SPECIFICATIONS
Caliber: .44
Weight: 4 lbs. 4 oz.   *Barrel length:* 7.5"
Features: Colt Black Diamond finish with 24 karat gold Indian-theme embellishments (peace pipe, tomahawk, wild horses, buffalo and Cochise portrait carved into blackhorn grips)
Price: $995.00

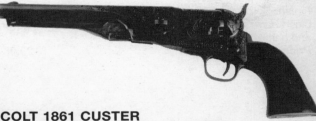

COLT 1861 CUSTER

SPECIFICATIONS
Caliber: .36
Weight: 42 oz. (empty)
Barrel length: 7.5"
Features: 70% Nimschke-style engraving, carved rosewood grip and antique silver finish
Price: $995.00

COLT 1860 GOLD U.S. CAVALRY

SPECIFICATIONS
Caliber: .44
Weight: 42 oz. (empty)
Barrel length: 8"
Features: 24 karat gold-plated cylinder with U.S. Cavalry crossed sabres emblem and gold barrel bands
Price: $667.50

CVA REVOLVERS/PISTOLS

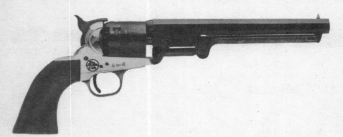

1851 NAVY REVOLVER BRASS FRAME

SPECIFICATIONS
Caliber: 44
Barrel length: 7.5" octagonal; hinged-style loading lever
Overall length: 13"
Weight: 44 oz.
Cylinder: 6-shot, engraved
Sights: Post front; hammer notch rear
Grip: One-piece walnut
Finish: Solid brass frame, trigger guard and backstrap; blued barrel and cylinder; color casehardened loading lever and hammer
Price: $129.95

1858 ARMY REVOLVER

SPECIFICATIONS
Caliber: 44
Cylinder: 6-shot, engraved
Barrel length: 8" octagonal
Overall length: 13"
Weight: 38 oz.
Sights: Blade front; adjustable target
Grip: Two-piece walnut
Price:
Brass Frame $144.95

KENTUCKY PISTOL

SPECIFICATIONS
Caliber: 50 percussion
Barrel: 9.75", rifled, octagonal
Overall length: 15.5"
Weight: 40 oz.
Finish: Blued barrel, brass hardware
Sights: Brass blade front; fixed open rear
Stock: Select hardwood
Ignition: Engraved, color casehardened percussion lock, screw adjustable sear engagement
Accessories: Brass-tipped, hardwood ramrod; stainless-steel nipple or flash hole liner
Prices:
Finished. $149.95
Percussion Kit 109.95

HAWKEN PISTOL

SPECIFICATIONS
Caliber: 50 percussion
Barrel length: 9.75", octagonal
Overall length: 16.5"
Weight: 50 oz.
Trigger: Early-style brass
Sights: Beaded steel blade front; fully adjustable rear (click adj. screw settings lock into position)
Stock: Select hardwood
Finish: Solid brass wedge plate, nose cap, ramrod thimbles, trigger guard and grip cap
Prices:
Finished. $149.95
Kit. 109.95
Laminated stock 159.95

CVA Rifles/Shotguns

ST. LOUIS HAWKEN RIFLE

SPECIFICATIONS
Calibers: 50 and 54 percussion or flintlock (50 cal. only)
Barrel: 28" octagonal 15/16" across flats; hooked breech; rifling one turn in 66", 8 lands and deep grooves
Overall length: 44" **Weight:** 8 lbs.
Sights: Dovetail, beaded blade front: adjustable open hunting-style dovetail rear
Stock: Select hardwood with beavertail cheekpiece
Triggers: Double set; fully adjustable trigger pull

Finish: Solid brass wedge plates, nose cap, ramrod thimbles, trigger guard and patchbox
Prices:
50 Caliber Flintlock. $234.95
50 Caliber Flintlock Left Hand (finished) 249.95
Also available:
PLAINSMAN (FLINTLOCK RIFLE) w/26" barrel.
Caliber: 50. **Weight:** 6.5 lbs.
Price: $159.95

TRAPPER SINGLE-BARREL SHOTGUN

SPECIFICATIONS
Gauge: 12 percussion
Barrel length: 28" round, chrome-lines bore; hooked breech
Choke: European Modified
Overall length: 46" Weight: 6 lbs.
Trigger: Early-style steel

Lock: Color Casehardened; engraves with V-type mainspring, bridle and fly
Sights: Brass bead front (no rear sight)
Stock: Select hardwood
Features: Color casehardened engraved lockplate; ventilated recoil pad, fiberglass ramrod and rear swivel
Price: $239.95

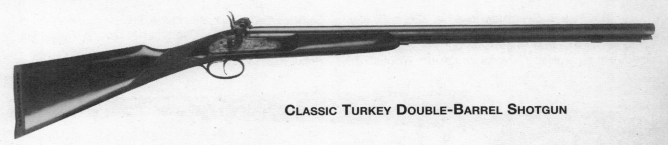

CLASSIC TURKEY DOUBLE-BARREL SHOTGUN

SPECIFICATIONS
Gauge: 12 percussion
Barrel length: 28" round, chrome-lined bore; double button-style breech
Choke: European Modified **Overall length:** 45"
Weight: 9 lbs. **Triggers:** Hinged, gold-tone double triggers
Lock: Color casehardened; engraves with V-type main-

spring, bridle and fly
Sights: Brass bead front (no rear sight)
Stock: Select hardwood; wraparound forearm with bottom screw attachment
Features: Ventilated recoil pad; rear sling swivel; fiberglass ramrod
Price: $459.95

BLACK POWDER

CVA RIFLES

IN-LINE MUZZLELOADING RIFLES

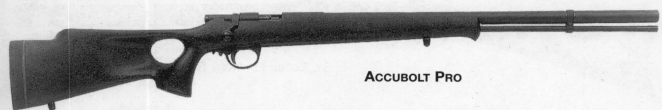

ACCUBOLT PRO

SPECIFICATIONS
Caliber: 50 *Barrel Length:* 24"
Rifling: 1:28" *Weight:* 7.5 lbs.
Price: $559.95

Also Available:
Same model as above w/hammer
forged barrel 339.95

FIREBOLT® W/ADVANTAGE CAMO

FIREBOLT™ SERIES

SPECIFICATIONS
Calibers: 50 (1:28" rifling) and (54 (1:38")
Barrel length: 24" *Weight:* 7 lbs. *Finish:* Matte blue
or stainless *Stock:* Synthetic, Synthetic w/Advantage
Camo, Thumbhole

Prices:
SYNTHETIC STOCK W/STAINLESS BARREL $299.95
SYNTHETIC STOCK W/MATTE BLUE BBL. 249.95
SYNTHETIC STOCK SNIPER CAMO 279.95
SYNTHETIC STOCK ADVANTAGE CAMO/MATTE BLUE . . . 279.95
THUMBHOLE STOCK W/MATTE BLUE. 279.95

ECLIPSE ADVANTAGE STAG HORN RIFLE

SPECIFICATIONS
Calibers: 50 and 54 *Lock:* In-line chrome-plated
percussion bolt *Barrel length:* 24" round (1.32"); blued
steel w/one-piece receiver *Overall length:* 42" *Weight:* 7 lbs.

Sights: Blued steel beaded blade front; Williams "Hunter"
sight rear *Stock:* Dura-Grip synthetic stock w/Advantage
camo
Price: $179.95

STAG HORN RIFLE
SPECIFICATIONS
Calibers: 50 and 54
Lock: In-line chrome-plated steel percussion bolt
Barrel length: 24" round (1:32") *Overall length:* 42"

Weight: 7 lbs. *Sights:* Blued steel beaded blade front;
Williams "Hunter" sight rear
Stock: Synthetic Dura-Grip stock w/pistol grip
Features: Removable breech plug; moulded oversized
black trigger guard; bottom screw barrel attachment;
black synthetic ramrod w/black tips
Price: $134.95

DIXIE

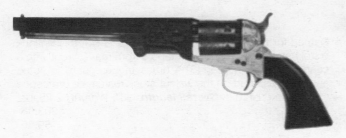

1851 NAVY BRASS-FRAME REVOLVER

This 36-caliber revolver was a favorite of the officers of the Civil War. Although called a Navy type, it is somewhat misnamed since many more of the Army personnel used it. Made in Italy; uses .376 mold or ball to fit and number 11 caps. Blued steel barrel and cylinder with brass frame.
Price:
Plain Model **$165.95**

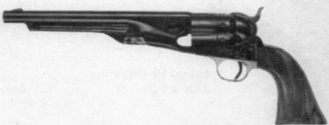

SPILLER & BURR 36 CALIBER BRASS-FRAME REVOLVER

The 36-caliber octagonal barrel on this revolver is 7 inches long. The six-shot cylinder chambers mike .378, and the hammer engages a slot between the nipples on the cylinder as an added safety device. It has a solid brass trigger guard and frame with backstrap cast integral with the frame, two-piece walnut grips and Whitney-type casehardened loading lever.
Price: **$149.95**
KIT 129.95

REMINGTON 44 ARMY REVOLVER

All steel external surfaces finished bright blue, including 8" octagonal barrel (hammer is casehardened). Polished brass guard and two-piece walnut grips are standard.
Price: **$230.00**

1860 ARMY REVOLVER

The Dixie 1860 Army has a half-fluted cylinder and its chamber diameter is .447. Use .451 round ball mold to fit this 8-inch barrel revolver. Cut for shoulder stock.
Price: **$186.75**

"WYATT EARP" REVOLVER

This 44-caliber revolver has a 12-inch octagon rifled barrel and rebated cylinder. Highly polished brass frame, backstrap and trigger guard. The barrel and cylinder have a deep blue luster finish. Hammer, trigger, and loading lever are casehardened. Walnut grips. Recommended ball size is .451.
Price: **$136.50**

WALKER REVOLVER

This 4 1/2-pound, 44-caliber pistol is the largest ever made. Steel backstrap; guard is brass with Walker-type rounded-to-frame walnut grips; all other parts are blued. Chambers measure .445 and take a .450 ball slightly smaller than the original.
Price: **$299.95**

DIXIE

QUEEN ANNE PISTOL

**CHARLES MOORE
ENGLISH DUELING PISTOL**

**MANG IN GRAZ
TARGET PISTOL**

**LePAGE
PERCUSSION DUELING PISTOL**

SCREW BARREL PISTOL

QUEEN ANNE PISTOL

Named for the Queen of England (1702-1714), this flintlock pistol has a 7 1/2" barrel that tapers from rear to front with a cannon-shaped muzzle. The brass trigger guard is fluted and the brass butt on the walnut stock features a grotesque mask worked into it. *Overall length:* 13". *Weight:* 2.25 lbs.
Price: $203.95
KIT 169.95

CHARLES MOORE ENGLISH DUELING PISTOL

This reproduction of an English percussion dueling pistol, created by Charles Moore of London, features a European walnut halfstock with oil finish and checkered grip. The 45-caliber octagonal barrel is 11" with 12 groovers and a twist of 1 in 15". Nose cap and thimble are silver. Barrel is blued; lock and trigger guard are color casehardened.
Price: FLINT $366.45
PERCUSSION 309.95

MANG TARGET PISTOL

Designed specifically for the precision target shooter, this 38-caliber pistol has a 10 7/16" octagonal barrel with 7 lands and grooves. Twist is 1 in 15". Sights: Blade front dovetailed into barrel; rear mounted on breechplug tang, adjustable for windage. *Overall length:* 17 1/4". *Weight:* 2 .5 lbs.
Price: $786.00

LePAGE PERCUSSION DUELING PISTOL

This 45-caliber percussion pistol features a blued 10" octagonal barrel with 12 lands and grooves; a brass-bladed front sight with open rear sight dovetailed into the barrel; polished silver-plated trigger guard and butt cap. Right side of barrel is stamped "LePage á Paris." Double-set riggers are single screw adjustable. *Overall length:* 16". *Weight:* 2.5 lbs.
Price: $259.95

SCREW BARREL (FOLDING TRIGGER) PISTOL

This little gun, only 6 1/2" overall, has a unique loading system that eliminates the need for a ramrod. The barrel is loosened with a barrel key, then unscrewed from the frame by hand. The recess is then filled with 10 grains of FFFg black powder, the .445 round ball is seated in the dished area, and the barrel is then screwed back into place. The .245X32 nipple uses #11 percussion caps. The pistol also features a sheath trigger that folds into the frame, then drops down for firing when the hammer is cocked. Comes with color casehardened frame, trigger and center-mounted hammer.
Price: $120.75
KIT 89.25

DIXIE

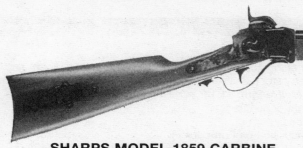

SHARPS MODEL 1859 CARBINE

About 115,000 Sharps New Model 1859 carbines and its variants were made during the Civil War. Characterized by durability and accuracy, they became a favorite of cavalry-men on both sides. Made in Italy by David Pedersoli & Co.

SPECIFICATIONS
Caliber: 54 **Barrel length:** 22" (1 in 48" twist); blued, round barrel has 7-groover rifling
Overall length: 37 1/2" **Weight:** 7 3/4 lbs.
Sights: Blade front; adjustable rear
Stock: Oil-finished walnut **Features:** Barrel band, hammer, receiver, saddle bar and ring all color casehardened
Price: $775.00

SHARPS NEW MODEL 1859 MILITARY RIFLE

Initially used by the First Connecticut Volunteers, this rifle is associated mostly with the 1st U.S. (Berdan's) Sharpshooters. There were 6,689 made with most going to the Sharpshooters (2,000) and the U.S. Navy (2,780). Made in Italy by David Pedersoli & Co.

SPECIFICATIONS
Caliber: 54 **Barrel length:** 30" (1 in 48" twist)
Overall length: 45 1/2" **Weight:** 9 lbs.
Sights: Blade front; rear sight adjustable for elevations and windage
Features: Buttstock and forend straight-grained and oil finished walnut; three barrel bands, receiver, hammer, nose cap, lever, patchbox cover and butt are all color casehardened; sling swivels attached to middle band and butt
Price: $895.00

1874 SHARPS LIGHTWEIGHT HUNTER RIFLE

This Sharps rifle in 45-70 Government caliber has a 30" octagon barrel with blued matte finish (1:18" twist). It also features an adjustable hunting rear sight and blade front, making it ideal for blackpowder hunters. The tang is drilled and threaded for tang sights. The oil-finished military-style buttstock has a blued metal buttplate. Double-set triggers. Color casehardened receiver and hammer. **Overall length:** 49 1/2". **Weight:** 10 lbs.
Price: $995.00

1874 SHARPS SILHOUETTE MODEL

This rifle in .40-65 and .45-70 caliber has a shotgun-style buttstock with a pistol grip and a metal buttplate. The 30-inch tapered octagon barrel is blued and has a 1 in 18" twist.

The receiver, hammer, lever and buttplate are color case-hardened. Ladder-type hunting rear and blade front sights are standard. Four screw holes are in the tang: two with 10 x 28 threads, two with metric threads, for attaching tang sights. Double set triggers are standard. **Weight** is 10 lbs. 3 oz. without target sights. **Overall length:** 47 1/2". Also available in .45-70
Price: $995.00

DIXIE RIFLES

DIXIE TENNESSEE MOUNTAIN RIFLE

This 50-caliber rifle features double-set triggers with adjustable set screw, bore rifled with 6 lands and grooves, barrel of 15/16 inch across the flats, brown finish and cherry stock.
Overall length: 41 1/2 inches. Right- and left-hand versions in flint or percussion.
Prices:
PERCUSSION OR FLINTLOCK $575.00
KIT 495.00

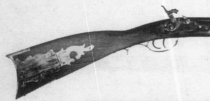

PENNSYLVANIA RIFLE

A lightweight at just 8 pounds, the 41 1/2" blued rifle barrel is fitted with an open buckhorn rear sight and front blade. The walnut one-piece stock is stained a medium darkness that contrasts with the polished brass buttplate, toe plate, patch-box, sideplate, trigger guard, thimbles and nose cap. Featuring double-set triggers, the rifle can be fired by pulling only the front trigger, which has a normal trigger pull of 4 to 5 pounds; or the rear trigger can first be pulled to set a spring-loaded mechanism that greatly reduces the amount of pull needed for the front trigger to kick off the sear in the lock. The land-to-land measurement of the bore is an exact .450: the recommended ball size is .445.
Overall length: 51 1/2".
Prices: PERCUSSION OR FLINTLOCK $450.00
KIT (Flint or Perc.) 395.00

HAWKEN RIFLE (Not Shown)

Blued barrel is 15/16" across the flats and 30" in length with a twist of 1 in 64". Stock is of walnut with a steel crescent buttplate, halfstock with brass nosecap. Double-set triggers, front-action lock and adjustable rear sight. Ramrod is equipped with jag. *Overall length:* 46 1/2". Average actual weight: about 8 lbs., depending on the caliber; shipping weight is 10 lbs. Available in either finished gun or kit.
Calibers: 45, 50 and 54.
Price: $250.00
KIT 220.00

WAADTLANDER RIFLE (Not Shown)

This authentic re-creation of a Swiss muzzloading target rifle features a heavy octagonal barrel (31") that has 7 lands and grooves. *Caliber:* 45. Rate of twist is 1 turn in 48". Double-set triggers are multilever type and are easily removable for adjustment. Sights are fitted post front and tang-mounted Swiss-type diopter rear. Walnut stock, color casehardened hardware, classic buttplate and curved trigger guard complete this reproduction. The original was made between 1839 and 1860 by Marc Bristlen, Morges, Switzerland.
Price: $1,412.00

DOUBLE-BARREL MAGNUM MUZZLELOADING SHOTGUN (Not Shown)

A full 10, 12 or 20 gauge, high-quality, double-barreled percussion shotgun with 30-inch browned barrels. Will take the plastic shot cups for better patterns. Bores are Choked, Modified and Full. Lock, barrel tang and trigger are case-hardened in a light gray color and are nicely engraved.

Prices:
12 GAUGE $449.00
12 GAUGE KIT 375.00
10 GAUGE MAGNUM (double barrel—right-hand =
   cyl. bore, left-hand = Mod.) 495.00
10 GAUGE MAGNUM KIT 395.00
20 GAUGE 495.00

DIXIE

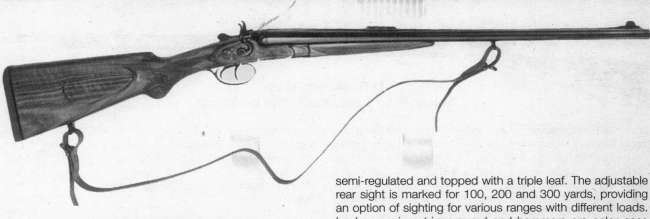

KODIAK MARK IV .45-70 DOUBLE BARREL RIFLE

Patterned after a classic, limited edition 19th century Colt double rifle, the Kodiak Mark IV has been designed for hunters and collectors. The 24-inch, browned barrels are semi-regulated and topped with a triple leaf. The adjustable rear sight is marked for 100, 200 and 300 yards, providing an option of sighting for various ranges with different loads. Locks, receiver, triggerguard and hammers are color case hardened. The two-piece stock is made from European walnut; forearm and pistol grip are checkered. The buttstock has a cheekpiece and a solid, red rubber pad. Sling swivels are standard. *Weight:* 10 lbs. *Overall length:* 40"
Price: $2,495.00

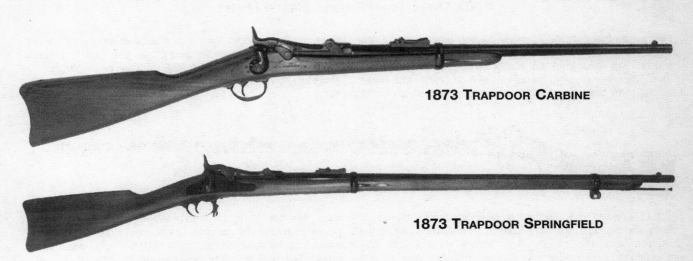

1873 Trapdoor Carbine

1873 Trapdoor Springfield

1873 SPRINGFIELD RIFLE AND CARBINE

Developed from the Allin Conversion of Springfield muskets from the Civil War, 1873 Springfield "Trapdoors" became the firearms that finished the winning of the west. Adopted in 1873 and immediately issued to troops on the frontier, the Trapdoor was the final single shot, blackpowder rifle of the U.S. military, later supplanted by the adoption of the .30-.40 Krag-Jorgensen.

RIFLE
Caliber: 45-70. *Barrel length:* 32.5" round. 1-22 twist; 3 groove rifling; all furniture blued; sling swivels; open sights; ladder style elevation rear adjustable to 500 yards. *Overall length:* 52" *Weight:* 8.5 lbs. Walnut stock
Price: $995.00

CARBINE
Caliber: 45-70. *Barrel length:* 22" round. 1-22 twist; 3 groove rifling; all furniture blued; saddle bar and ring; open sights; ladder style elevation rear adjustable to 400 yards. *Overall length:* 41" *Weight:* 8.5 lbs. Walnut stock.
Price: $895.00

OFFICER'S MODEL
Caliber: 45-70. *Barrel length:* 26" round. 1-18 twist; 6 groove rifling; pewter ramrod tip and nosecap; color case hardened hammer and lock; walnut stock; checkered wrist and forearm; single set trigger; fully adjustable tang sight. *Overall length:* 45" *Weight:* 8 lbs.
Price: $825.00

BLACK POWDER

DIXIE

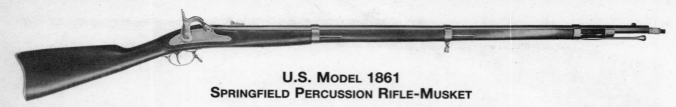

U.S. MODEL 1861
SPRINGFIELD PERCUSSION RIFLE-MUSKET

An exact re-creation of an original rifle produced by Springfield National Armory, Dixie's Model 1861 Springfield. 58-caliber rifle features a 40" round, tapered barrel with three barrel bands. Sling swivels are attached to the trigger guard bow and middle barrel band. The ramrod has a trumpet-shaped head with swell; sights are standard military rear and bayonet-attachment lug front. The percussion lock is marked "1861" on the rear of the lockplate with an eagle motif and "U.S. Springfield" in front of the hammer. "U.S." is stamped on top of buttplate. All furniture is "National Armory Bright."

Overall length: 55 13/16". *Weight:* 8 lbs.
Prices: $595.00
KIT 525.00

1862 THREE-BAND ENFIELD RIFLED MUSKET

One of the finest reproduction percussion guns available, the 1861 Enfield was widely used during the Civil War in its original version. This rifle follows the lines of the original almost exactly. The .58-caliber musket features a 39-inch barrel and walnut stock. Three steel barrel bands and the barrel itself are blued; the lockplate and hammer are case colored and the remainder of the furniture is highly polished brass. The lock is marked, "London Armory Co." *Weight:* 10.5 lbs. *Overall length:* 55".

Prices: $495.00
KIT 425.00

U.S. MODEL 1816 FLINTLOCK MUSKET

The U.S. Model 1816 Flintlock Musket was made by Harpers Ferry and Springfield Arsenal from 1816 until 1864. It had the highest production of any U.S. flintlock musket and after conversion to percussion saw service in the Civil War. It has a .69-caliber, 42" smoothbore barrel held by three barrel bands with springs. All metal parts are finished in "National Armory Bright." The lockplate has a brass pan and is marked "Harpers Ferry" vertically behind the hammer, with an American eagle placed in front of the hammer. The bayonet lug is on top of the barrel and the steel ramrod has a button-shaped head. Sling swivels are mounted on trigger guard and middle barrel band.

Overall length: 56.5"
Weight: 9.75 lbs.
Price: $725.00

1858 TWO-BAND ENFIELD RIFLE

This 33-inch barrel version of the British Enfield is an exact copy of similar rifles used during the Civil War. The .58-caliber rifle sports a European walnut stock, deep blue-black finish on the barrel, bands, breech-plug tang and bayonet mount. The percussion lock is color casehardened and the rest of the furniture is brightly polished brass.

Price: $475.00

EMF HARTFORD REVOLVERS

SHERIFF'S MODEL 1851

MODEL 1860 ARMY REVOLVER

SPECIFICATIONS
Caliber: 44 Percussion *Barrel length:* 8"
Overall length: 13 ⁵/₈" *Weight:* 41 oz.
Frame: Casehardened
Finish: High-luster blue with walnut grips
Price: Brass Frame $160.00
Also available:
CASED SET with steel frame, wood case, flask
   and mould $375.00
   Engraved cased set (brass frame only) 315.00
FLUTED CYLINDER MODEL (steel frame only) 380.00

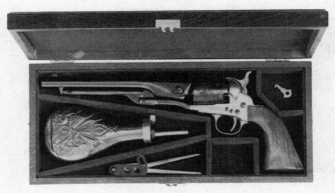

1860 ARMY BRASS FRAME CASED SET
Price: $300.00

HARTFORD 1863 TEXAS DRAGOON

SPECIFICATIONS
Caliber: 44
Barrel length: 7" (round)
Overall length: 14"
Weight: 4 lbs.
Finish: Steel casehardened frame
Price: $330.00

SHERIFF'S MODEL 1851 REVOLVER

SPECIFICATIONS
Caliber: 44 Percussion
Ball diameter: .376 round or conical, pure lead
Barrel length: 5" *Overall length:* 10.5" *Weight:* 39 oz.
Sights: V-notch groove in hammer (rear); truncated
cone in front
Percussion cap size: #11
Prices:
Brass $150.00
Steel 200.00

MODEL 1860 ARMY

HARTFORD MODEL
1862 POLICE REVOLVER

SPECIFICATIONS
Caliber: 36 Percussion
Capacity: 5-shot
Barrel length: 6.5"
Prices:
Steel $250.00
Brass 170.00

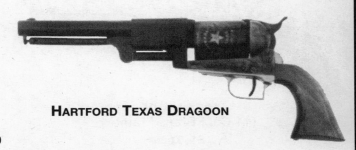

HARTFORD TEXAS DRAGOON

BLACK POWDER

EMF HARTFORD REVOLVERS

1847 WALKER
(44 Cal.)
$330.00

1851 NAVY
(36 or 44 Cal.)
$305.00

1848 DRAGOON
(44 Cal.)
$315.00

1858 REMINGTON ARMY
(44 Cal., Steel Frame)
Six-shot, 8" octagonal barrel, one-piece walnut grip.
$225.00

1849 BABY DRAGOON
(31 Cal., Brass Frame)
$150.00

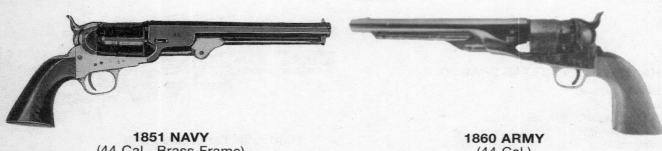

1851 NAVY
(44 Cal., Brass Frame)
$150.00

1860 ARMY
(44 Cal.)
$225.00

EUROARMS OF AMERICA

COOK & BROTHER
CONFEDERATE CARBINE MODEL 2300

Classic re-creation of the rare 1861, New Orleans-made Artillery Carbine. The lockplate is marked "Cook & Brother N.O. 1861" and is stamped with a Confederate flag at the rear of the hammer.

SPECIFICATIONS
Caliber: 58 percussion *Barrel Length:* 24"
Overall Length: 40 ⅓" *Weight:* 7.5 lbs.
Sights: Fixed blade front and adjustable dovetailed rear
Ramrod: Steel
Finish: Barrel is antique brown; buttplate, trigger guard, barrel bands, sling swivels and nose cap are polished brass; stock is walnut
Recommended ball sizes: .575 r.b., .577 Minie and .580 maxi; uses musket caps
Price: $447.00
Also available:
MODEL 2301 COOK & BROTHER FIELD
with 33" barrel 480.00

J.P. MURRAY
CARBINE MODEL 2315

Replica of an extremely rare CSA Cavalry Carbine based on an 1841 design of parts and lock.

SPECIFICATIONS
Caliber: 58
Barrel Length: 23"
Features: Brass barrel bands and buttplate; oversized trigger guard; sling swivels
Price: $453.00

C.S. RICHMOND
MUSKET MODEL 2370

SPECIFICATIONS
Caliber: 58
Barrel Length: 40" with three bands
Price: $530.00

BLACK POWDER

EUROARMS OF AMERICA

LONDON ARMORY COMPANY ENFIELD P-1858 2-BAND RIFLE MUSKET MODEL 2270

SPECIFICATIONS
Caliber: 58 percussion
Barrel Length: 33", blued and rifled
Overall Length: 49"
Weight: 8.5 to 8.75 lbs., depending on wood density
Stock: One-piece walnut; polished "bright" brass buttplate, trigger guard and nose cap; blued barrel bands
Sights: Inverted 'V' front sight; Enfield folding ladder rear
Ramrod: Steel
Price: $470.00

LONDON ARMORY COMPANY ENFIELD P-1861 MUSKETOON MODEL 2280

SPECIFICATIONS
Caliber: 58; Minie ball
Barrel Length: 24"; round high-luster blued barrel
Overall Length: 40.5"
Weight: 7 to 7.5 lbs., depending on density of wood
Stock: Seasoned walnut stock with sling swivels
Ramrod: Steel
Ignition: Heavy-duty percussion lock
Sights: Graduated military-leaf sight
Furniture: Brass trigger guard, nose cap and buttplate; blued barrel bands, lock plate, and swivels
Price: $415.00

LONDON ARMORY COMPANY 3-BAND ENFIELD P-1853 RIFLED MUSKET MODEL 2260

SPECIFICATIONS
Caliber: 58 percussion
Barrel Length: 38", blued and rifled
Overall Length: 54"
Weight: 9.5 to 9.75 lbs., depending on wood density
Stock: One-piece walnut; polished "bright" brass buttplate, trigger guard and nose cap; blued barrel bands
Ramrod: Steel; threaded end for accessories
Sights: Traditional Enfield folding ladder rear sight; inverted 'V' front sight
Price: $480.00
Also available:
MODEL 2261 w/white barrel, satin finish 520.00

EUROARMS OF AMERICA

U.S. 1803 HARPERS FERRY FLINTLOCK RIFLE MODEL 2305

SPECIFICATIONS
Caliber: 54 Flintlock
Barrel Length: 35", octagonal
Features: Walnut half stock with cheekpiece; browned barrel
Price: $640.00

U.S. 1841 MISSISSIPPI RIFLE MODEL 2310

SPECIFICATIONS
Calibers: 54 and 58 percussion
Barrel Length: 33", octagonal
Features: Walnut stock; brass barrel bands and buttplate; sling swivels
Price: $500.00

U.S. MODEL 1863 REMINGTON ZOUAVE RIFLE (2-BARREL BANDS)

SPECIFICATIONS
Caliber: 58 percussion
Barrel Length: 33", octagonal
Overall Length: 48.5"
Weight: 9.5 to 9.75 lbs.
Sights: U.S. Military 3-leaf rear; blade front
Features: Two brass barrel bands; brass buttplate and nose cap; sling swivels
Price: $430.00

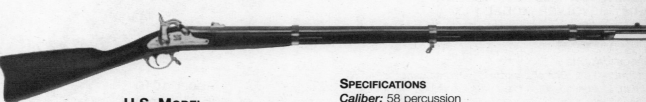

U.S. MODEL 1861 SPRINGFIELD RIFLE

SPECIFICATIONS
Caliber: 58 percussion
Barrel Length: 40"
Features: 3 barrel bands
Price: $530.00

EUROARMS OF AMERICA

MODEL 1005

ROGERS & SPENCER ARMY REVOLVER MODEL 1006 (Target)

SPECIFICATIONS

Caliber: 44; takes .451 round or conical balls; #11 percussion cap *Weight:* 47 oz. *Barrel Length:* 7.5"
Overall Length: 13.75" *Finish:* High gloss blue; flared walnut grip; solid frame design; precision-rifled barrel
Sights: Rear fully adjustable for windage and elevation; ramp front sight
Price: $239.00

ROGERS & SPENCER REVOLVER LONDON GRAY MODEL 1007 (Not Shown)

Revolver is the same as Model 1005, except for London Gray finish, which is heat treated and buffed for rust resistance; same recommended ball size and percussion caps.

Price: $245.00
Also available: MODEL 1120 COLT 1851 NAVY Steel or brass frame. 36 cal. *Barrel Length:* 7.5" octagonal.
Overall Length: 13" *Weight:* 42 oz.
Price: . . . . **To be determined**
MODEL 1210 COLT 1860 ARMY Steel frame. 44 percussion
Overall Length: 10 ⁵/₈" or 13 ⁵/₈" *Weight:* 41 oz.
Price: . . . . **To be determined**

ROGERS & SPENCER REVOLVER MODEL 1005

SPECIFICATIONS

Caliber: 44 Percussion; #11 percussion cap
Barrel Length: 7.5" *Overall Length:* 13.75" *Weight:* 47 oz.
Sights: Integral rear sight notch groove in frame; brass truncated cone front sight
Finish: High gloss blue; flared walnut grip; solid frame design; precision-rifled barrel *Recommended ball diameter:* .451 round or conical, pure lead
Price: $227.00

MODEL 1006

REMINGTON 1858 NEW MODEL ARMY ENGRAVED MODEL 1040 (Not Shown)

Classical 19th-century style scroll engraving on this 1858 Remington New Model revolver.

SPECIFICATIONS

Caliber: 44 Percussion; #11 cap *Barrel Length:* 8"
Overall Length: 14.75" *Weight:* 41 oz. *Sights:* Integral rear sight notch groove in frame; blade front sight
Recommended ball diameter: .451 round or conical, pure lead
Price: $275.00

REMINGTON 1858 NEW MODEL ARMY REVOLVER MODEL 1020

This model is equipped with blued steel frame, brass trigger guard in 44 caliber.

SPECIFICATIONS

Weight: 40 oz. *Barrel Length:* 8" *Overall Length:* 14.75"
Finish: Deep luster blue rifled barrel; polished walnut stock; brass trigger guard.
Price: $200.00
Also available: MODEL 1010 Same as Model 1020, except w/6.5" barrel and in 36 caliber: $200.00

MODEL 1010
(36 Cal. W/6.5" barrel)

FORT WORTH FIREARMS RIFLES

RIO GRANDE IN-LINE PERCUSSION

SPECIFICATIONS
Caliber: 50 *Barrel Length:* 22" or 24" (stainless steel)
Rate of twist: 1:24 *Features:* Adjustable trigger; drilled and tapped for scope; composite stock; one-piece nipple/breech plug; bolt camming action
Prices: 22" $499.95
24" 529.95

PECOS IN-LINE PERCUSSION

SPECIFICATIONS
Caliber: 50 *Barrel Length:* 22" or 24" (stainless steel)
Rate of twist: 1:24 *Features:* Slide cocking levr acts acts as secondary safety w/primary trigger safety; drilled and tapped for scope; adj. trigger
Prices: 22" $499.95
24" 529.95

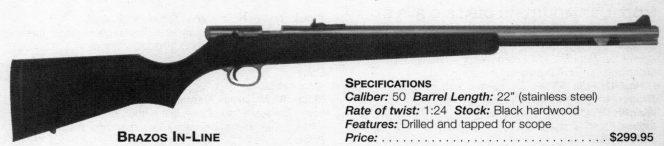

BRAZOS IN-LINE

SPECIFICATIONS
Caliber: 50 *Barrel Length:* 22" (stainless steel)
Rate of twist: 1:24 *Stock:* Black hardwood
Features: Drilled and tapped for scope
Price: $299.95

SABINE IN-LINE YOUTH

SPECIFICATIONS
Caliber: 22
Weight: 3.5 lbs. *Sights:* Positive click; hooded front sight; adjustable leaf rear sight *Stock:* Black hardwood
Features: One-piece nipple/breech plug; dovetailed for scope mount; brass ramrod w/built-in jag; 12" trigger pull
Price: $189.95

NECHES IN-LINE (not shown)

SPECIFICATIONS
Caliber: 22
Barrel Length: 18" (blue)
Weight: 4.4 lbs.

Sights: Hooded front sight; adjustable leaf rear sight
Stock: Black hardwood (full size)
Features: Same as Sabine Youth model
Price: $229.95

BLACK POWDER

GONIC ARMS

MODEL 93 RIFLE SERIES

MOUNTAIN CLASSIC

MOUNTAIN THUMBHOLE

DELUXE

MODEL 93 MOUNTAIN CLASSIC RIFLE

SPECIFICATIONS
Caliber: 50 Magnum
Barrel Length: 26" 4140 chrome-moly blued satin or 416 stainless steel w/matte finish; 1-in-24" twist
Length Of Pull: 14"
Trigger: Single, adjustable w/side safety
Weight: 6.5 to 7 lbs.
Sights: Open or peep sights, fully adjustable for windage and elevation; ramp front w/gold bead and protector hood

Stock: Walnut or laminated (left or right hand)
Features: Unbreakable ram rod; classic cheekpiece; three-point pillar bedding system; 1" decelerator recoil pad; sling swivel studs; E-Z-Load Muzzle System w/muzzle break
Price: $2,132.00
Also Available:
MODEL 93 MOUNTAIN THUMBHOLE RIFLE w/same specification and features as above, but w/thumbhole Monte Carlo rollover cheekpiece, beavertail forend and palm swell grip.
Price: 2,132.00

MODEL 93 MAGNUM RIFLE

Gonic Arm's blackpowder rifle has a unique loading system that produces better consistency and utilizes the full powder charge of the specially designed penetrator bullet (ballistics = 2,650 foot-pounds at 1,600 fps w/465-grain .500 bullet).

SPECIFICATIONS
Caliber: 50 Magnum
Barrel Lengths: 26"
Overall Length: 43"
Weight: 6 to 6.5 lbs.
Sights: Open hunting sights (adjustable)
Features: Walnut-stained hardwood stock; adjustable trigger;

nipple wrench; drilled and tapped for scope bases; ballistics and instruction manual

Prices:
Open Sights $500.00
Stainless w/Open Sights. 603.00
Also Available:
MODEL 93 SAFARI CLASSIC RIFLE w/classic walnut
   stock, open sights 1,612.00
MODEL 93 DELUXE w/grey laminated stock;
   Weaver scope base; open sights; E-Z-Load
   Muzzle System 660.25

LYMAN RIFLES

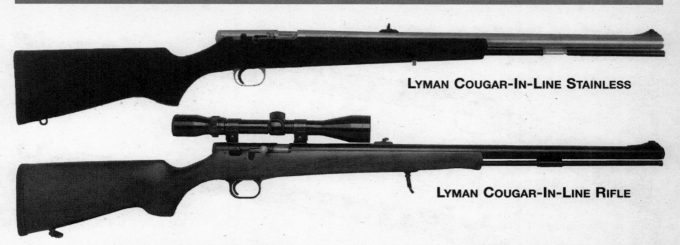

LYMAN COUGAR-IN-LINE STAINLESS

LYMAN COUGAR-IN-LINE RIFLE

The **LYMAN COUGAR IN-LINE** rifle is designed for the serious blackpowder hunter who wants a rugged and accurate muzzleloader with the feel of a centerfire bolt-action rifle. The Cougar In-Line is traditionally styled with a walnut stock and blued barrel and action. Available in 50 and 54 caliber. Features include a 22" barrel with 1:24" twist and shallow rifling grooves; dual safety system (equipped with a bolt safety notch in receiver and a sliding thumb safety that disables the trigger mechanism); drilled and tapped for Lyman 57 WTR receiver sight; fully adjustable trigger; sling swivel studs installed; unbreakable Derlin ramrod; modern folding-leaf rear and bead front sights; rubber recoil pad.
Price: $299.95
Also available in **stainless steel** on all major parts. Features same as standard version. Stock is semi-Schnabel forend with black Hard Kote finish.
Price: $382.95

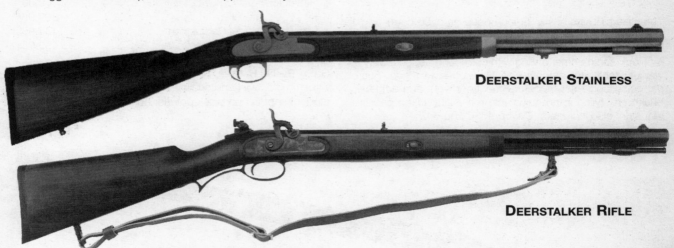

DEERSTALKER STAINLESS

DEERSTALKER RIFLE

LYMAN'S DEERSTALKER rifle incorporates • higher comb for better sighting plane • nonglare hardware • 24" octagonal barrel • casehardened sideplate • Q.D. sling swivels • Lyman sight package (37MA beaded front' fully adjustable fold-down 16A rear) • walnut stock with .5" black recoil pad • single trigger. Left-hand models available (same price). *Calibers:* 50 and 54, flintlock or percussion. *Weight:* 7.5 lbs.
Price:

Percussion	$304.95
Left-Hand	$314.95
Flintlock	$329.95
Left Hand	$339.95

Also available:
DEERSTALKER CARBINE. In .50-caliber percussion w/precision-rifled "stepped octagon" barrel (1:24" twist); fully adjustable Lyman 16A fold-down rear sight; front sight is Lyman's 37MA white bead on an 18 ramp; nylon ramrod, modern sling and swivels set. L.H. avail. *Weight:* 6.75 lbs.
Price: $324.95
    Left-Hand $329.95
DEERSTALKER STAINLESS. Features all stainless steel parts, plus walnut stock, recoil pad, Delrin ramrod, Lyman front and rear hunting sights.
Price: $382.95

BLACK POWDER

LYMAN RIFLES

GREAT PLAINS RIFLE

GREAT PLAINS HUNTER

The **GREAT PLAINS** has a 32-inch deep-grooved barrel and 1 in 66" twist to shoot patched round balls. Blued steel furniture including the thick steel wedge plates and toe plate; correct lock and hammer styling with coil spring dependability; a walnut stock w/o patchbox. A Hawken-style trigger guard protects double-set triggers. Steel front sight and authentic buckhorn styling in an adjustable rear sight. Fixed primitive rear sight also included. *Calibers:* 50 and 54.

Price:
Percussion $424.95
Kit 344.95
Flintlock 449.00
Kit 369.95
Left-Hand Model Percussion 434.95
Left-Hand Model Flintlock 459.95
Also available:
GREAT PLAINS HUNTER. Same features as standard rifle but with 1 in 32" twist and shallow rifling groove for shooting modern sabots and black powder hunting bullets.
Price: $424.95

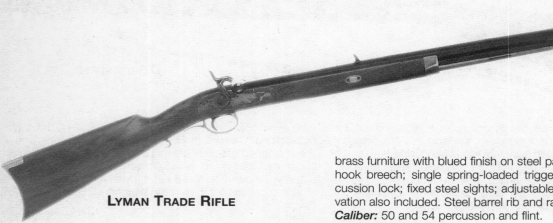

LYMAN TRADE RIFLE

The **LYMAN TRADE RIFLE** features a 28-inch octagonal barrel, rifled 1 turn at 48 inches, designed to fire both patched round balls and the popular maxi-style conical bullets. Polished

brass furniture with blued finish on steel parts; walnut stock; hook breech; single spring-loaded trigger; coil-spring percussion lock; fixed steel sights; adjustable rear sight for elevation also included. Steel barrel rib and ramrod ferrule.
Caliber: 50 and 54 percussion and flint.
Overall Length: 45"
Price:
Percussion $299.95
Flintlock $324.95

MARKESBERY MUZZLE LOADERS

Markesbery's Black Bear, Grizzly Bear and Brown Bear rifles are made of eight casted, polished molded parts, coupled with an all-casted receiver and trigger guard. Pillow mount system with interchangeable barrels in 36, 45, .50 and 54 calibers. All rifles are constructed with Markesbery's **MAGNUM HAMMER IN-LINE IGNITION SYSTEM**, the 400 SRP (small rifle primer) system or optional No. 11 cap and nipple. This system, along with a 1-26" twist button precision 24" rifle barrel, is available in either 4140 or stainless steel models. All models have a double safety system with half cock and cross bolt hammer safeties. Marble adjustable sights with double adjustment features, hammer thumb rest and rubber recoil pad are standard.

The Black Bear is made of a two-piece, handcrafted hard-wood walnut, black laminate and green laminate pistol grip. **Weight:** 6.5 lbs. **Overall Length:** 38.5". The Brown and Grizzly Bear models offer custom-checkered Monte Carlo (Grizzly Bear two-piece or Brown Bear one-piece) thumbhole stocks. **Overall Length:** 38.5" **Weight:** 6.5 lbs. (Brown Bear is 6.75 lbs.). Both models are available in black composite, crotch walnut, Mossy Oak Treestand™, Xtra-B™ and Xtra-G™. Finishes are available in glossy black blued, matte and stainless steel. All models support a solid aluminum ram rod with brass jag and bullet starter.
Price: **BLACK BEAR** (two-piece pistol grip stock)
   (depending on stock). **$536.63-573.73**

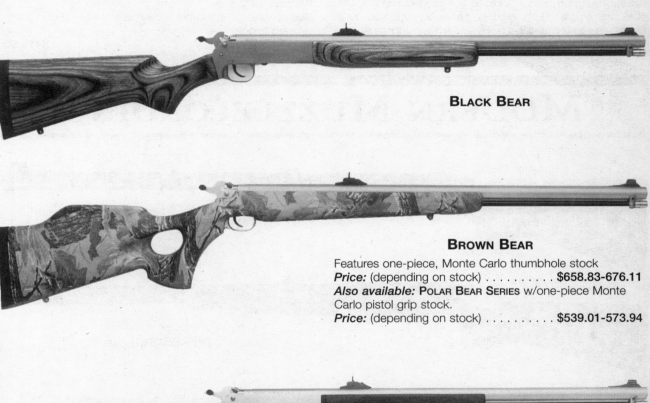

BLACK BEAR

BROWN BEAR

Features one-piece, Monte Carlo thumbhole stock
Price: (depending on stock) **$658.83-676.11**
Also available: POLAR BEAR SERIES w/one-piece Monte Carlo pistol grip stock.
Price: (depending on stock) **$539.01-573.94**

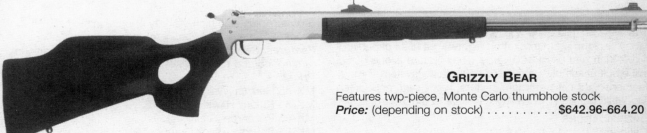

GRIZZLY BEAR

Features twp-piece, Monte Carlo thumbhole stock
Price: (depending on stock) **$642.96-664.20**

MARLIN MUZZLELOADERS

MLS-50/MLS-54
STAINLESS BARREL/BLACK RYNITE STOCK

MODELS MLS-50 & MLS-54

Marlin's new in-line muzzleloaders—the MLS-50 and MLS-54—feature stainless steel one-piece barrel/receiver construction, automatic tang safety and an ambidextrous cocking handle that disengages from the hammer for added safety. The open breech features a shrouded hammer and standard nipple. Both models come equipped with an aluminum ramrod and black Rynite stocks with molded-in checkering and swivel studs.

SPECIFICATIONS
Calibers: 50 (MLS-50) and 54 (MLS-54)
Barrel length: 22"; 1:28" rifling twist (Right hand)
Overall length: 41"
Weight: 6 1/2 lbs.
Sights: Adjustable Marble semi-buckhorn rear; ramp front w/brass beads
Price: $419.50

MODERN MUZZLELOADING

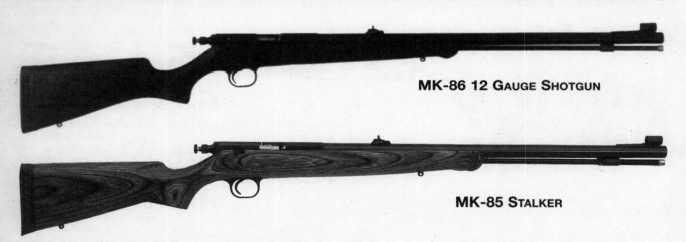

MK-86 12 GAUGE SHOTGUN

MK-85 STALKER

MK-85 AND MK-86 KNIGHT RIFLES

The MK-85 muzzleloading rifles (designed by William A. "Tony" Knight) are handcrafted, lightweight rifles capable of 1 1/2-inch groups at 100 yards. They feature a one-piece, inline bolt assembly, patented double-safety system, Timney featherweight deluxe trigger system, recoil pad, and Green Mountain barrels (1 in 28" twist in 50 and 54 caliber).

SPECIFICATIONS
Calibers: 50 and 54
Barrel length: 24"
Overall length: 43"
Weight: 7 lbs.

Sights: Adjustable high-visibility open sights
Stock: Classic walnut, laminated or composite
Features: Swivel studs installed; hard anodized aluminum ramrod; combo tool; hex keys, and more.
Prices:
MK-85 HUNTER (Walnut) $549.95
MK-85 KNIGHT HAWK 769.95
MK-85 PREDATOR (Stainless) 649.95
MK-85 STALKER (Black Composite) 619.95
Also available:
MK-86 12 GAUGE SHOTGUN (22" barrel),
   black composite 599.95

MODERN MUZZLELOADING

KNIGHT T-BOLT

SPECIFICATIONS

Caliber: 50 *Barrel Length:* 22" (blued or matte stainless) or 26" (matte stainless only) *Overall Length:* 41" *Length of pull:* 14.5" *Rate of twist:* 1 in 28" *Weight:* 6 lbs. *Sights:* Fully adjustable mettalic rear sight; front ramp and bead; drilled and tapped for scope mounting *Stock:* Composite (Black Mossy Oak Break Up or Bill Jordan's Advantage) *Features:* Sling swivel studs installed; patented double safety system; stainless steel breech plug; patented Red Hot nipple; adjustable Knight trigger; In-Line ignition system
Prices:
Blue Break-Up **$444.95**
Stainless Break-Up **519.95**
Stainless **469.95**
Blue only **399.95**

AMERICAN KNIGHT

SPECIFICATIONS

Caliber: 50
Action: Patented double safety system; one-piece removable hammer assembly; removable stainless steel breech plug w/patented Red Hot nipple
Barrel Length: 22" Green Mountain rifle barrel; blued or matte stainless steel
Rate of twist: 1 in 28" *Overall Length:* 41" *Weight:* 6 lbs. *Stock:* Full dimension hollow black composite stock; sling swivel studs installed
Features: Non-adjustable Knight trigger; In-Line ignition system
Price:
Blued only **$199.95**

BLACK POWDER

MODERN MUZZLELOADING

MODEL LK-93 WOLVERINE

SPECIFICATIONS
Calibers: 50 and 54
Barrel length: 22"; blued rifle-grade steel (1:28" twist)
Overall length: 41" *Weight:* 6 lbs.
Sights: Adjustable high-visibility rear sight; drilled and tapped for scope mount

Stock: Lightweight Fiber-Lite molded stock
Features: Patented double-safety system; adjustable Accu-Lite trigger; removable breechplug; stainless-steel hammer
Prices:

Blued	$269.95
Stainless	339.95
Advantage or Break-Up	389.95
Value Pack	299.95
Stainless Advantage or Break-up	419.95

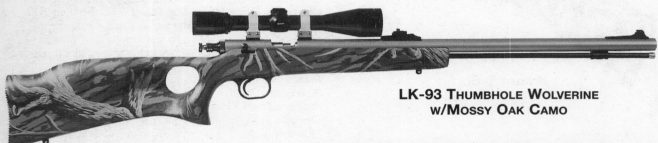

LK-93 THUMBHOLE WOLVERINE

SPECIFICATIONS
Calibers: 50 and 54
Barrel length: 22" rifle-grade steel (1:28" twist)
Overall length: 41" *Weight:* 6 lbs. 4 oz.

LK-93 THUMBHOLE WOLVERINE w/MOSSY OAK CAMO

Features: Patented double safety system: adjustable Accu-Lite trigger; removable breech plug; stainless steel hammer
Prices:

Blued w/Black Stock	$309.95
Blued w/Camo Stock	359.95
Stainless Steel w/Black Stock	379.95
Stainless Steel w/Camo Stock	429.95

DISC RIFLE

SPECIFICATIONS
Caliber: 50
Action: Patented double safety syste; one-piece
Barrel length: 24" (Green Mountain barrel; blued or matte stainless rifle grade steel)
Overall length: 43" *Rate of twist:* 1 in 28"
Length of pull: 14.5" *Weight:* 14 oz.
Sights: Metallic rear sight; front ramp and bead

Stock: Compositte (Black Mossy Oak Break-Up); Bill Jordan's Advantage w/rubber recoil pad; checkered forearm and palm swell pistol grip; patented double safety system
Features: Fully adjustable Knight trigger; In-Line ignition system; one-piece removable bolt assembly; removable stainless steel breech plug
Prices:

Blue	$449.95
Stainless	519.95
Mossy Oak Break-Up	569.95

NAVY ARMS REVOLVERS

LE MAT CAVALRY MODEL

LE MAT NAVY MODEL

LE MAT REVOLVERS

Once the official sidearm of many Confederate cavalry officers, this 9-shot .44-caliber revolver with a central single-shot barrel of approx. 65 caliber gave the cavalry man 10 shots to use against the enemy. **Barrel Length:** 7 ⁵⁄₈"
Overall Length: 14" **Weight:** 3 lbs. 7 oz.

CAVALRY MODEL	$595.00
NAVY MODEL	595.00
ARMY MODEL	595.00
18TH GEORGIA (engraving on cylinder, display case)	795.00
BEAUREGARD (hand-engraved cylinder and frame; display case and mold)	**1,000.00**

LE MAT ARMY MODEL

1862 NEW MODEL POLICE

1862 NEW MODEL POLICE

This is the last gun manufactured b y the Colt plant in the percussion era. It encompassed all the modifications of each gun, starting from the early Paterson to the 1861 Navy. It was favored by the New York Police Dept. for many years. One-half fluted and rebated cylinder, 36 cal., 5 shot. This replica features brass trigger guard and backstrap. Casehardened frame, loading lever and hammer. **Barrel Length:** 5.5"

1862 POLICE	$290.00
LAW AND ORDER SET	365.00

ROGERS & SPENCER REVOLVER

This revolver features a six-shot cylinder, octagonal barrel, hinged-type loading lever assembly, two-piece walnut grips, blued finish and casehardened hammer and lever.
Caliber: 44 **Barrel Length:** 7.5" **Overall Length:** 13.75"
Weight: 3 lbs.

ROGERS & SPENCER	$245.00

COLT 1847 WALKER

COLT 1847 WALKER

The 1847 Walker replica comes in 44 caliber with a 9-inch barrel. Weight: 4 lbs. 8 oz. Well suited for the collector as well as the blackpowder shooter. Features include: rolled cylinder scene; blued and casehardened finish; and brass guard. Proof tested.

COLT 1847 WALKER	$275.00
SINGLE CASED SET	405.00
DELUXE CASED SET	540.00

ROGERS & SPENCER REVOLVER

BLACK POWDER

NAVY ARMS REVOLVERS

FIRST MODEL DRAGOON REVOLVER

An improved version of the 1847 Walker, the First Model has a shorter barrel and cylinder as well as a loading lever latch. Used extensively during the Civil War. *Caliber:* 44 *Barrel Length:* 7.5" *Overall Length:* 13.75" *Weight:* 4 lbs. *Sights:* Blade front, notch rear. *Grip:* Walnut

FIRST MODEL DRAGOON $275.00
Also available:
THIRD MODEL DRAGOON w/oval trigger guard
   and cylinder stop 275.00

FIRST MODEL DRAGOON REVOLVER

1851 NAVY "YANK"

A favorite of "Wild Bill" Hickok, the 1851 Navy was originally manufactured by Colt from 1850 through 1876. This model was the most popular of the Union revolvers, mostly because it was lighter and easier to handle than the Dragoon. *Barrel Length:* 7.5" *Overall Length:* 14" *Weight:* 2 lbs. *Rec. Ball Diam.:* .375 R.B. (.451 in 44 cal) *Calibers:* 36 and 44 *Capacity:* 6 shot *Features:* Steel frame, octagonal barrel, cylinder roll-engraved with Naval battle scene, backstrap and trigger guard are polished brass.

1851 NAVY "YANK" $155.00
KIT 125.00
SINGLE CASED SET 280.00
DOUBLE CASED SET 455.00

REB MODEL 1860

1860 ARMY

A modern replica of the confederate Griswold & Gunnison percussion Army revolver. Rendered with a polished brass frame and a rifled steel barrel finished in a high-luster blue with genuine walnut grips. All Army Model 60s are completely proof-tested by the Italian government to the most exacting standards. *Calibers:* 36 and 44. *Barrel Length:* 7.25" *Overall Length:* 13" *Weight:* 2 lbs. 10 oz.-11 oz. *Features:* Brass frame, backstrap and trigger guard, round barrel.

REB MODEL 1860 . . . . $115.00
SINGLE CASED SET 235.00
DOUBLE CASED SET 365.00
KIT 90.00

The 1860 Army satisfied the Union Army's need for a more powerful .44-caliber revolver. The cylinder on this replica is roll engraved with a polished brass trigger guard and steel strap cut for shoulder stock. The frame, loading level and hammer are finished in high-luster color case-hardening. Walnut grips. *Weight:* 2 lbs. 9 oz. *Barrel Length:* 8" *Overall Length:* 13 ⅝" *Caliber:* 44. *Finish:* Brass trigger guard, steel backstrap, round barrel, creeping lever, rebated cylinder, engraved Navy scene.

1860 ARMY $175.00
SINGLE CASED SET 300.00
DOUBLE CASED SET 490.00
KIT 155.00

NAVY ARMS REVOLVERS

1858 NEW MODEL ARMY REMINGTON-STYLE, STAINLESS STEEL

Exactly like the standard 1858 Remington (below) except that every part except for the grips and trigger guard is manufactured from corrosion-resistant stainless steel. This gun has all the style and feel of its ancestor with all of the conveniences of stainless steel. *Caliber:* 44

1858 REMINGTON STAINLESS	$270.00
SINGLE CASED SET	395.00
DOUBLE CASED SET	680.00

REB 60 SHERRIFF'S MODEL

REB 60 SHERRIFF'S MODEL

A shortened version of the Reb Model 60 Revolver. The Sheriff's model version became popular because the shortened barrel was fast out of the leather. This is actually the original snub nose, the predecessor of the detective specials or belly guns designed for quick-draw use. *Calibers:* 36 and 44

REB 60 SHERRIFF'S MODEL	$115.00
KIT	90.00
SINGLE CASED SET	235.00
DOUBLE CASED SET	365.00

DELUXE NEW MODEL 1858 REMINGTON-STYLE 44 CALIBER (not shown)

Built to the exact dimensions and weight of the original Remington 44, this model features an 8" barrel with progressive rifling, adjustable front sight for windage, all-steel construction with walnut stocks and silver-plated trigger guard. Steel is highly polished and finished in rich blue. Barrel Length: 8" Overall Length: 14.25" Weight: 2 lbs. 14 oz.

DELUXE NEW MODEL 1858	$415.00

1858 NEW MODEL ARMY REMINGTON-STYLE REVOLVER

This rugged, dependable, battle-proven Civil War veteran with its top strap and rugged frame was considered the Magnum of C.W. revolvers, ideally suited for the heavy 44 charges. Blued finish.
Caliber: 44. *Barrel Length:* 8"
Overall Length: 14.25" *Weight:* 2 lbs. 8 oz.

NEW MODEL ARMY REVOLVER	$170.00
SINGLE CASED SET	290.00
DOUBLE CASED SET	480.00
KIT	150.00

Also available:

BRASS FRAME	$125.00
BRASS FRAME KIT	115.00
SINGLE CASED SET	250.00
DOUBLE CASED SET	395.00

NAVY ARMS

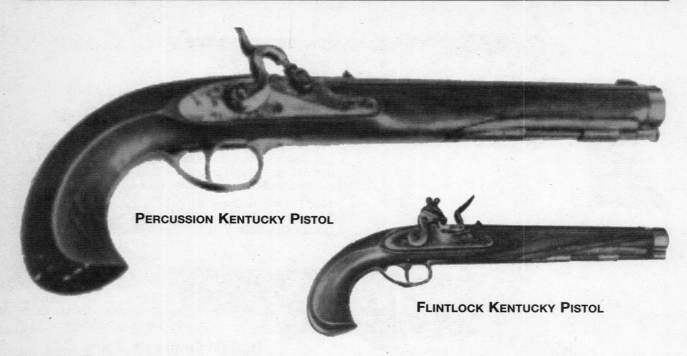

PERCUSSION KENTUCKY PISTOL

FLINTLOCK KENTUCKY PISTOL

The Kentucky Pistol is truly a historical American gun. It was carried during the Revolution by the Minutemen and was the sidearm of "Andy" Jackson in the Battle of New Orleans. Navy Arms Company has conducted extensive research to manufacture a pistol representative of its kind, with the balance and handle of the original for which it became famous. *Caliber:* 45

FLINTLOCK $225.00
SINGLE CASED FLINTLOCK SET. 350.00
DOUBLE CASED FLINTLOCK SET 580.00
PERCUSSION 215.00
SINGLE CASED PERCUSSION SET 335.00
DOUBLE CASED PERCUSSION SET 550.00

1806 HARPERS FERRY FLINTLOCK PISTOL

Of all the early American martial pistols, Harpers Ferry is one of the best known and was carried by both the Army and the Navy. Navy Arms Company has authentically reproduced the Harper's Ferry to the finest detail, providing a well-balanced and well-made pistol.

Weight: 2 lbs. 9 oz. *Barrel Length:* 10" *Overall Length:* 16"
Caliber: 58 *Finish:* Walnut stock; case-hardened lock; brass-mounted browned barrel.

HARPERS FERRY. $310.00
SINGLE CASED SET 355.00

NAVY ARMS

1853 ENFIELD RIFLE MUSKET

The Enfield Rifle Musket marked the zenith in design and manufacture of the military percussion rifle, and this perfection has been reproduced by Navy Arms Company. This and other Enfield muzzleloaders were the most coveted rifles of the Civil War, treasured by Union and Confederate troops alike for their fine quality and deadlly accuracy. *Caliber:* 58 *Barrel Length:* 39" *Weight:* 10 lbs. 6 oz. *Overall Length:* 55" *Sights:* Fixed front; graduated rear. *Stock:* Seasoned walnut with solid brass furniture.

1853 ENFIELD RIFLE MUSKET $480.00

1858 ENFIELD RIFLE

In the late 1850s the British Admiralty, after extensive experiments, settled on a pattern rifle with a 5-groove barrel of heavy construction, sighted to 1,100 yards, designated the Naval rifle, Pattern 1858. *Caliber:* 58 *Barrel Length:* 33" *Weight:* 9 lbs. 10 oz. *Overall Length:* 48.5" *Sights:* Fixed front; graduated rear. *Stock:* Seasoned walnut w/solid brass furniture.

1858 ENFIELD RIFLE $450.00

1861 MUSKETOON

The 1861 Enfield Musketoon was the favorite long arm of the Confederate Cavalry. *Caliber:* 58 *Barrel Length:* 24" *Weight:* 7 lbs. 8 oz. *Overall Length:* 40.25" *Sights:* Fixed front; graduated rear. *Stock:* Seasoned walnut with solid brass furniture.

1861 MUSKETOON $405.00
KIT 365.00

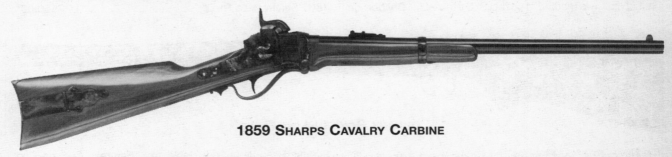

1859 SHARPS CAVALRY CARBINE

This percussion version of the Sharps is a copy of the popular breechloading Cavalry Carbine of the Civil War. It features a patchbox and bar and saddle ring on left side of the stock. *Caliber:* 54 *Barrel Length:* 22" *Overall Length:* 39" *Weight:* 7.75 lbs. *Sights:* Blade front; military ladder rear. *Stock:* Walnut

SHARPS CAVALRY CARBINE $885.00
Also available:
1859 SHARPS INFANTRY RIFLE (54 cal.) 1,030.00

NAVY ARMS RIFLES

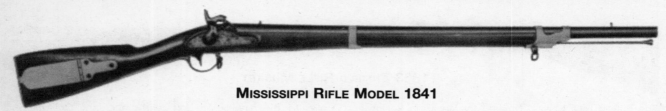

MISSISSIPPI RIFLE MODEL 1841

This historic percussion weapon gained its name because of its performance in the hands of Jefferson Davis' Mississippi Regiment during the heroic stand at the Battle of Buena Vista. Also known as the "Yager" (a misspelling of the German Jaeger), this was one of the first percussion rifles adopted by Army Ordnance. The Mississippi is handsomely furnished in brass, including patchbox ofr tools and spare parts. **Weight:** 9.5 lbs. **Barrel Length:** 32.5" **Overall Length:** 48.5" **Calibers:** 54 and 58 **Finish:** Walnut finish stock, brass mounted. **MISSISSIPPI RIFLE MODEL 1841** $465.00

SMITH CARBINE

The Smith Carbine was considered one of the finest breechloading carbines of the Civil War period. The hinged breech action allowed fast reloading for cavalry units. Available in either the Cavalry Model (with saddle ring and bar) or Artillery Model (with sling swivels). **Caliber:** 50 **Barrel Length:** 21.5" **Overall Length:** 39" **Weight:** 7.75 lbs. **Sights:** Blass blade front; folding ladder rear **Stock:** American walnut **SMITH CARBINE**. $600.00

1861 SPRINGFIELD RIFLE

One of the most popular Union rifles of the Civil War, the 1861 model featured the 1855-style hammer. The lockplate on this replica is marked "1861, U.S. Springfield." **Caliber:** 58 **Barrel Length:** 40" **Overall Length:** 56" **Weight:** 10 lbs. **Finish:** Walnut stock with polished metal lock and stock fitting. **1861 SPRINGFIELD RIFLE** $550.00

"COUNTRY BOY" IN-LINE RIFLE

The Navy Arms "Country Boy" incorporates a trap in the butt-stock for storage of a take-down tool for removing the breech plug or nipple in the field. It is also capable of replacing the #11 nipple with the hotter musket type. **Caliber:** 50 **Barrel Length:** 24" (rate of twist 1:32) **Overall Length:** 41" **Weight:** 8 lbs. **Sights:** Bead front, adjustable rear **Fetures:** Chrome-lined barrel; weather-resistant synthetic stock; drilled and tapped for scope mount. **Price** . . . . $165.00 w/Satin Chrome Finish 175.00

NAVY ARMS

PENNSYLVANIA LONG RIFLE

This new version of the Pennsylvania Rifle is an authentic reproduction of the original model. Its classic lines are accented by the long, browned octagon barrel and polished lockplate. **Caliber:** 32 or 45 (flint or percussion.) **Barrel Length:** 40.5"

Overall Length: 56.5" **Weight:** 7.5 lbs. **Sights:** Blade front; adjustable Buckhorn rear **Stock:** Walnut
PENNSYLVANIA LONG RIFLE Flintlock $485.00
   Percussion. 475.00

BROWN BESS MUSKET

Used extensively in the French and Indian War, the Brown Bess Musket proved itself in the American Revolution as well. This fine replica of the "Second Model" is marked "Grice" on the lockplate. **Caliber:** 75 **Barrel Length:** 42" **Overall Length:** 59" **Weight:** 9.5 lbs. **Sights:** Lug front **Stock:** Walnut

BROWN BESS MUSKET $815.00
KIT $690.00
Also available:
BROWN BESS CARBINE **Caliber:** 75 **Barrel Length:** 30"
Overall Length: 47" **Weight:** 7.75 lbs. $815.00

1803 HARPERS FERRY RIFLE

This 1803 Harpers Ferry rifle was carried by Lewis and Clark on their expedition to explore the Northwest territory. This replica of the first rifled U.S. Martial flintlock features a browned barrel, casehardened lock and a brass patchbox. **Caliber:** 54 **Barrel Length:** 35" **Overall Length:** 50.5" **Weight:** 8.5 lbs.
1803 HARPERS FERRY RIFLE $630.00

"BERDAN" 1859 SHARPS RIFLE

A replica of the Union sniper rifle used by Col. Hiram Berdan's First and Second U.S. Sharpshooters Regiments during the Civil War. **Caliber:** 54 **Barrel Length:** 30" **Overall Length:** 46.75" **Weight:** 8 lbs. 8 oz. **Sights:** Military-style ladder rear; blade front **Stock:** Walnut **Features:** Double-set trigger, casehardened receiver; patchbox and furniture.
"BERDAN" 1859 SHARPS RIFLE $1,095.00
Also available:
SINGLE TRIGGER INFANTRY MODEL 1,030.00

BLACK POWDER

1862 C.S. RICHMOND RIFLE

This model was manufactured by the Confederacy at the Richmond Armory utilizing 1855 Rifle Musket parts captured from the Harpers Ferry Arsenal. This replica features the unusual 1855 lockplate, stamped "1862 C.S. Richmond, V.A."

Caliber: 58 *Barrel Length:* 40" *Overall Length:* 56" *Weight:* 10 lbs. *Finish:* Walnut stock with polished metal lock and stock fittings.
1862 C.S. RICHMOND RIFLE $550.00

NAVY ARMS SHOTGUNS

STEEL SHOT MAGNUM SHOTGUN

This shotgun, designed for the hunter who must use steel shot, features engraved polished lockplates, English-style

checkered walnut stock (with cheekpiece) and chrome-lined barrels.
Gauge: 10 *Barrel Length:* 28"
Overall Length: 45.5" *Weight:* 7 lbs. 9 oz.
Choke: Cylinder/Cylinder

STEEL-SHOT MAGNUM SHOTGUN $585.00

FOWLER SHOTGUN

A traditional side-by-side percussion field gun, this fowler model features blued barrels and English-style straight stock

design. It also sports a hooked breech, engraved and color casehardened locks, double triggers and checkered walnut stock.
Gauge: 12 *Chokes:* Cylinder/Cylinder *Barrel Length:* 28"
Overall Length: 44.5" *Weight:* 7.5 lbs.

FOWLER SHOTGUN $345.00
KIT 310.00

T&T SHOTGUN

This Turkey and Trap side-by-side percussion shotgun, choked Full/Full, features a genuine walnut stock with

checkered wrist and oil finish, color casehardened locks and blued barrels.
Gauge: 12 *Barrel Length:* 28"
Overall Length: 44" *Weight:* 7.5 lbs.

T&T SHOTGUN $560.00

PRAIRIE RIVER ARMS

PRA Bullpup Rifle

SPECIFICATIONS
Calibers: 50 and 54
Barrel Length: 28" (1:28" twist)
Overall length: 31.5"
Weight: 7.5 lbs.
Stock: Hardwood or Black All Weather
Sights: Blade front, open adjustable rear
Features: Bullpup design, thumbhole stock; patented internal percussion ignition system; left-hand model available. Dovetailed for scope mount; two built-in safety positions; introduced 1995. Made in the U.S.A.
Prices:
4140 Alloy barrel, hardwood stock $375.00
4140 Alloy barrel, black stock. 390.00
Stainless barrel, hardwood stock 425.00
Stainless barrel, black stock 440.00

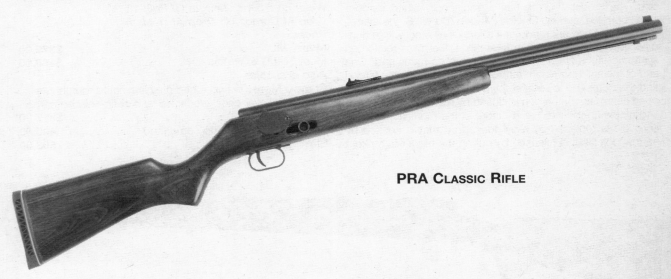

PRA Classic Rifle

SPECIFICATIONS
Calibers: 50 and 54
Barrel Length: 26" (1:28" twist)
Overall length: 40.5"
Stock: Hardwood or Black All Weather
Sights: Blade front, open adjustable rear
Features: Patented internal percussion ignition system; drilled and tapped for scope mount. Only two moving parts; flexible ramrod from hard anodixzed aluminum; sling swivel studs installed; one screw takedown; introduced 1995. Made in the U.S.A.
Prices:
4140 Alloy barrel, hardwood stock $375.00
4140 Alloy barrel, black stock. 390.00
Stainless barrel, hardwood stock 425.00
Stainless barrel, black stock 440.00

REMINGTON RIFLES

MODEL 700 ML

MODEL 700 MLS STAINLESS

MODEL 700 ML AND MLS IN-LINE MUZZLELOADING RIFLES

Remington began building flintlock muzzleloaders in 1816. These two in-line muzzleloading rifles have the same cocking action and trigger mechanism as the original versions. The difference comes from a modified bolt and ignition system. The Model 700 ML has a traditionally blued carbon-steel barreled action. On the Model 700 MLS the barrel, receiver and bolt are made of 416 stainless steel with a non-reflective, satin finish. Each is set in a fiberglass-reinforced synthetic stock fitted with a Magnum-style recoil pad. One end of the solid aluminum ramrod is recessed into the forend and the outer end is secured by a barrel band. Instead of an open chamber, the breech is closed by a stainless-steel plug and nipple. In the internal structure of the modified bolt, the firing pin is replaced by a cylindrical rod that is cocked by normal bolt lift. It is released by pulling the trigger to strike a

#11 percussion cap seated on the nipple. Lock time is 3.0 mili-seconds. Barrels are rifled with a 1 in 28" twist. The barrels are fitted with standard adjustable iron sights; receivers are drilled and tapped for short-action scope mount.

SPECIFICATIONS:
Barrel length: 24" **Overall Length:** 44.5"
Weight: 7.75 lbs. **Length Of Pull:** 13 $^3/_8$"
Drop At Comb: .5" **Drop At Heel:** $^3/_8$"
Prices:
MODEL ML $372.00
MODEL MLS STAINLESS $469.00
Also available:
CUSTOM MODEL in two-toned grey laminated thumbhole stock w/rollover cheekpiece; barrel is satin-finished carbon steel $817.00
w/Mossy Oak Break-up camo stock 405.00
Stainless Steel 503.00

MODEL 700 ML YOUTH

The **MODEL 700 ML YOUTH** rifle offers the same design as the 70 ML, but with a shorter (12 $^3/_8$") length of pull. Includes a blued, satin-finished carbon steel 21" barrel (38.5" overall), action and bolt, plus fiberglass-reinforced Model 700 stock

w/rubber recoil pad; drilled and tapped for short-action scope mounts; ram rod stored in forend.

Price: $372.00

RUGER

OLD ARMY CAP AND BALL
FIXED SIGHT

OLD ARMY CAP AND BALL

This Old Army cap-and-ball revolver with fixed sights is reminiscent of the Civil War era martial revolvers and those used by the early frontiersmen in the 1800s. This Ruger model comes in both blued and stainless-steel finishes and features modern materials, technology and design through-out, including steel music-wire coil springs. Fixed or adjustable sights. Also available with simulated ivory grips.

SPECIFICATIONS
Caliber: 45 (.443" bore; .45" groove)
Barrel Length: 7.5"
Weight: 2 $^7/_8$ lbs.
Rifling: 6 grooves, R.H. twist (1:16")
Sights: Fixed, ramp front; topstrap channel rear
Percussion cap nipples: Stainless steel (#11)
Price: $413.00
Stainless Steel 495.00

MODEL 77/50 ALL WEATHER

MODEL 77/50 RSO

MODEL 77/50 STAINLESS STEEL ALL-WEATHER BLACK POWDER RIFLE

SPECIFICATIONS
Caliber: .50 *Action:* Bolt action In-line muzzle loader
Finish: Non-glare matte stainless steel finish
Barrel Length: 22" 400 series stainless steel
Overall Length: 41.5"
Rifling: 8 grooves, right hand twist (1-turn-in-28")
Safety: Three-position wing safety
Sights: Single folding leaf rear; gold bead front; rear receiver drilled and tapped for peep sights
Stock: Black/gray laminated American hardwood w/rubber buttpad; studs for sling swivels
Length Of Pull: 13.75" *Drop At Comb:* 1.78"

Drop At heel: 1.94" *Weight (approx.):* 6.5 lbs. (unloaded)
Features: Operator's manual, set of 1" stainless steel scope range; standard breech plug wrench; bolt disassemble tool; cleaning tube; right hand 90° turn bolt
Price: $596.00
Also available:
MODEL 77/50 RS. Same specifications as above, except finish is matte blue and stock is birch w/rubber buttpad 399.00
MODEL 77/50 RSO. Same specifications as above, except for following: *Drop at Comb:* 1 $^{22}/_{32}$" *Drop At Heel:* 1 $^6/_{32}$"
Stock: Straight gripped, checkered American black walnut w/curved buttplate 550.00

SHILOH SHARPS

MODEL 1874 BUSINESS RIFLE

Calibers: 45-70, 45-90, 45-120, 50-70 and 50-90
Barrel: 28-inch heavy-tapered round; dark blue
Features: Double-set triggers adjustable set. Blade-front sight with sporting-leaf rear. Buttstock is straight grip rifle buttplate, forend sporting schnabel style. Receiver group and buttplate case-colored; wood is American walnut oil-finished

Weight: 9 lbs. 8 oz.
Price: $1,210.00
Other MODEL 1874 BLACK POWDER METALLIC CARTRIDGE RIFLES *available:*
THE HARTFORD. $1,474.00
THE SADDLE RIFLE. $1,362.00

MODEL 1874 SPORTING RIFLE NO. 1

Calibers: 45-70, 45-90, 45-120, 50-70 and 50-90
Features: 30-inch tapered octagon barrel. Double-set triggers with adjustable set, blade front sight, sporting rear with elevation leaf and sporting tang sight adjustable for elevation and

windage. Buttstock is pistol grip, shotgun butt, sporting forend style. Receiver group and buttplate case colored. Barrel is high-finish blue-black; wood is American walnut oil finish.
Price: $1,408.00

MODEL 1874 SPORTING RIFLE NO. 3

Calibers: 45-70, 45-90, 45-120, 50-70 and 50-90
Barrel: 30-inch tapered octagonal; with high finish blue-black
Features: Double-set triggers with adjustable set, blade-front sight, sporting rear with elevation leaf and sporting tang sight adjustable for elevation and wwindage. Buttstock is straight grip with rifle buttplate; trigger plate is curved and checkered to match pistol grip. Forend is sporting schnabel style. Receiver group and buttplate are case colored. Wood is oil-finished American walnut, and may be upgraded in all rifles

Weight: 9 lbs. 8 oz.
Price: $1,304.00
Also available:
MODEL 1874 LONG-RANGE EXPRESS. 1,434.00
MODEL 1874 MONTANA ROUGHRIDER. 1,304.00
Custom Rifles:
CREEDMOOR TARGET RIFLE (32" Barrel). 2,128.00
MIDRANGE RIFLE (30" Barrel). 2,284.00
SCHUETZEN RIFLE (28" Half-octagon). 2,122.00
QUIGLEY RIFLE (34" Heavy Barrel). 2,660.00

THOMPSON/CENTER

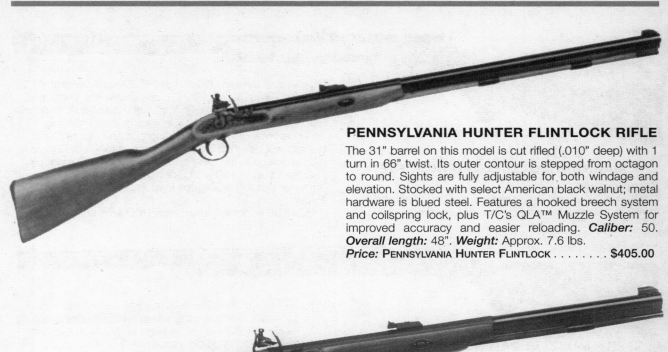

PENNSYLVANIA HUNTER FLINTLOCK RIFLE

The 31" barrel on this model is cut rifled (.010" deep) with 1 turn in 66" twist. Its outer contour is stepped from octagon to round. Sights are fully adjustable for both windage and elevation. Stocked with select American black walnut; metal hardware is blued steel. Features a hooked breech system and coilspring lock, plus T/C's QLA™ Muzzle System for improved accuracy and easier reloading. *Caliber:* 50. *Overall length:* 48". *Weight:* Approx. 7.6 lbs. *Price:* PENNSYLVANIA HUNTER FLINTLOCK $405.00

PENNSYLVANIA HUNTER FLINTLOCK CARBINE

Thompson/Center's Pennsylvania Hunter Flintlock Carbine is 50-caliber with 1:66" twist and cut-rifling. It was designed specifically for the hunter who uses patched round balls only and hunts in thick cover or brush. The 21" barrel is stepped from octagonal to round. Features T/C's QLA™ Muzzle System. *Overall length:* 38". *Weight:* 6.5 lbs. *Sights:* Fully adjustable open hunting-style rear with bead front. *Stock:* Select American walnut. *Trigger:* Single hunting-style trigger. *Lock:* Color cased, coil spring, with floral design. *Price:* PENNSYLVANIA HUNTER FLINTLOCK CARBINE . $394.00

THE NEW ENGLANDER RIFLE

This percussion rifle features a 26" round, 50- or 54-caliber rifled barrel (1 in 48" twist). Contains T/C's QLA™ Muzzle System. *Weight:* 7 lbs. 15 oz. *Prices:*
NEW ENGLANDER RIFLE $335.00
12 GAUGE ACCESSORY SHOTGUN BARREL
  (27") w/IC Choke Tube 184.00

THOMPSON/CENTER

ENCORE 209 X 50
MAGNUM MUZZLELOADING RIFLE

SPECIFICATIONS
Caliber: .50 *Action:* Break-open action muzzleloader
Ignition: 209 shotgun primer *Barrel Length:* 26" with

QLA Muzzle System *Twist:* 1 in 28" *Overall Length:* 40.5"
Weight: 7 lbs. *Sights:* Tru-Glo adjustable rear fiber optic
sight; ramp-style fiber optic front sight *Safety:* Automatic
hammerblock w/ bolt interlock *Finish:* Blued *Stock:*
American walnut with schnabel forend and Monte Carlo
buttstock *Features:* Barrel interchangeable with Encore
rifles; equipped with sling swivel studs; accepts magnum
charges of up to 150 grains of black powder or Pyrodex
equivalent (or three 50-grain Pyrodex Pellets).
Price: $562.00
($249.99 accessory muzzleloading barrel only)

BLACK DIAMOND
MUZZLELOADING RIFLE

SPECIFICATIONS
Caliber: .50 *Ignition:* In-line ignition using Flame Thrower
musket cap nipple or No. 11 nipple *Barrel:* Free-floated,
22.5" barrel with QLA *Twist:* 1 in 18" *Overall Length:*
41.5" *Weight:* 6 lbs. 9 oz. *Safety:* Patented sliding thumb
safety *Sights:* Tru-Glo Fiber Optic adjustable rear sight;
Fiber Optic ramp-style front sight *Stock:* Black Rynite
stock with molded-in checkering and pistol grip cap
Loading: Accepts magnum charges of up to 150 grains of
black powder or Pyrodex equivalent, or three 50-grain

Pyrodex Pellets *Features:* Removable universal breech
plug; synthetic ram rod; sling swivel studs; rubber recoil
pad; musket nipple wrench, 5-pack or T/C Mag Express
Sabots, and No. 11 nipple standard
Prices:
Blued $304.00
Stainless 358.00
Also Available: BLACK DIAMOND PREMIUM PACK (includes T-
Handle Short Starter, 10 Mag Express Sabots, rifle powder
measure, In-line U-View Capper, Super Jag, ball and bullet
puller, 2 Quick Shots, breech plug wrench, Hunter's Field
Pouch, Lube-N-Clean Kit, Gorilla Grease).
Prices:
Blued $339.00
Stainless 394.00

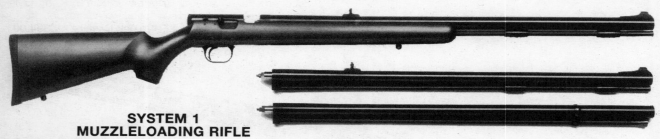

SYSTEM 1
MUZZLELOADING RIFLE

SPECIFICATIONS
Calibers: .50 and .54 (accessory barrels available in .32,
.58, and 12-gauge shotgun) *Ignition:* In-line ignition using
No. 11 nipple or accessory Flame Thrower Musket Cap
nipple *Barrel:* Free-floated, interchangeable 26" barrels
with QLA *Twist:* 1 in 38" (1 in 48" in .32 cal. only) *Overall
Length:* 44" *Weight:* 7.5 lbs. (.50 cal.) *Safety:* Patented
sliding thumb safety *Sights:* Adjustable leaf style rear;
ramp style white bead front *Stock:* American Walnut,
black composite, or Advantage camo composite *Loading:*
Accepts magnum charges of up to 150 grains of black

powder or Pyrodex equivalent, or three 50-grain Pyrodex
Pellets *Features:* Removable universal breech plug; syn-
thetic ram rod; sling swivel studs; rubber recoil pad;
Weaver-style scope bases, takedown tool, Allen wrench,
and 5 all-lead sabots standard
Prices:
Blued/Walnut. $389.00
Stainless Steel/Composite 428.00
Stainless Steel/Advantage 465.00
Accessory Barrels Blued. 270.00
Stainless Steel. 220.00

THOMPSON/CENTER

FIRE HAWK BLUED

This in-line ignition muzzleloader features a striker that is cocked and held rearward, locked in place when the thumb safety is in the rearward position. By sliding the thumb safety forward, the striker is free to fire the percussion cap when the trigger is pulled. The Fire Hawk's free-floated 24" barrel is rifled with a 1:38" twist and is designed for use with modern conical or sabot projectiles. Features T/C's QLA™ Muzzle System.

SPECIFICATIONS
Calibers: 50, 54 *Overall length:* 41.75"
Weight: 7 lbs. *Sights:* Adj. leaf-style rear; ramp-style white bead front. *Stock:* American black walnut in composite or Advantage camo composite.
Also available:
BLUED w/walnut stock in all calibers $383.00
BLUED w/thumbhole composite stock 404.00
BLUED w/Advantage camo composite stock 415.00
STAINLESS STEEL w/composite stock 425.00
STAINLESS STEEL w/walnut stock 433.00
STAINLESS STEEL w/thumbhole composite stock . . . 455.00
DELUXE SST w/walnut stock in 50 and 54 cal. 572.00
DELUXE BLUED w/walnut in 50 and 54 cal. 520.00
BANTAM (21" barrel) 50 cal. (13.25" pull), blued
   w/walnut stock 383.00

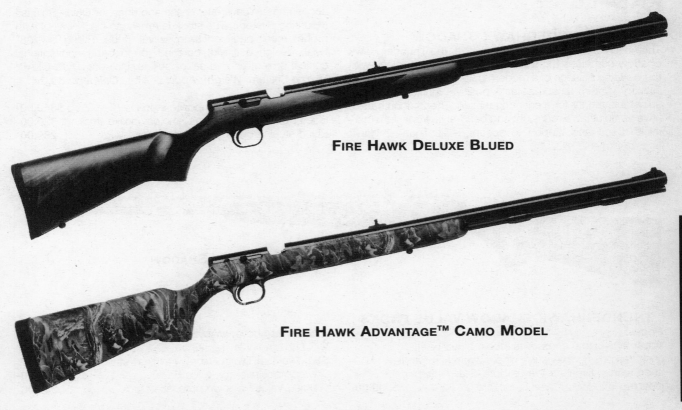

FIRE HAWK DELUXE BLUED

FIRE HAWK ADVANTAGE™ CAMO MODEL

THOMPSON/CENTER

THE HAWKEN 45, 50 AND 54 CALIBER

Similar to the famous Rocky Mountain rifles made during the early 1800s, the Hawken is intended for serious shooting. Button-rifled for ultimate precision, the Hawken is available in 45-, 50- or 54-caliber percussion or 50- caliber flintlock. It features a hooked breech, double-set triggers, first-grade American walnut stock, adjustable hunting sights, solid brass trim and color casehardened lock. Beautifully decorated; comes equipped with T/C's QLA™ Muzzle System. **Weight:** Approx. 8.5 lbs.

Prices:

HAWKEN CAPLOCK 45, 50 or 54 caliber $448.00
HAWKEN FLINTLOCK 50 caliber 459.00
KIT: Caplock (50 and 54 caliber) 315.00

Also available:

HAWKEN SILVER ELITE 50 cal. Caplock w/stainless steel barrel and lock; semi-fancy wood; right hand only 535.00

THUNDERHAWK SHADOW

Thompson/Center's in-line caplock rifle, the Thunder Hawk Shadow combines the features of an old-time caplock with the look and balance of a modern bolt-action rifle. The in-line ignition system ensures fast, positive ignition, plus an adjustable trigger for a crisp trigger pull. The 24-inch barrels have an adjustable rear sight and bead-style front sight (barrel is drilled and tapped to accept T/C's Thunder Hawk scope rings. Weaver-style base and rings, or Quick-Release Mounting System). The stock is American black walnut with rubber recoil pad and sling swivel studs. Rifling is 1:38" twist, designed to fire patched round balls, conventional conical projectiles and sabot bullets. Includes T/C's QLA™ Muzzle System. **Weight:** Approx. 7 lbs. **Calibers:** 50, 54.

Prices:

Stainless steel with composite stock $340.00
Blued steel with Advantage Camo composite stock. . . 320.00
Blued steel w/black composite stock 289.00

SST THUNDERHAWK SHADOW

THUNDERHAWK SHADOW VALUE PACKS

Prices:

Advantage Camo composite stock, blued barrel (includes powder measure, nipple wrench, T-handle short starter, Break-O-Way sabots, Star-7 capper, cleaning kit) $399.00

Same as above w/Advantage
Camo stock (21" barrel) 379.00
SST THUNDERHAWK SHADOW stainless steel barrel
w/composite stock Value Pack 428.00
Blued Value Pack w/composite stock 366.00

TRADITIONS PISTOLS

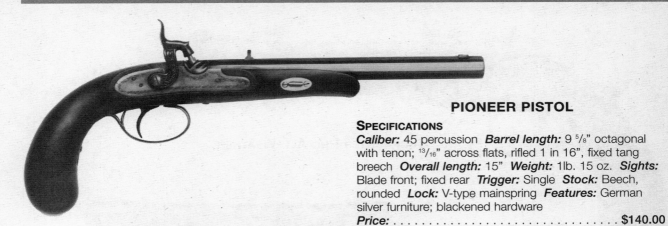

PIONEER PISTOL

SPECIFICATIONS
Caliber: 45 percussion *Barrel length:* 9 ⁵/₈" octagonal with tenon; ¹³/₁₆" across flats, rifled 1 in 16", fixed tang breech *Overall length:* 15" *Weight:* 1lb. 15 oz. *Sights:* Blade front; fixed rear *Trigger:* Single *Stock:* Beech, rounded *Lock:* V-type mainspring *Features:* German silver furniture; blackened hardware
Price: $140.00
Kit. 116.25

WILLIAM PARKER PISTOL

SPECIFICATIONS
Caliber: 50 percussion (1:20") *Barrel length:* 10 ³/₈" octagonal (15/16" across flats) *Overall length:* 17.5" *Weight:* 2 lbs. 5 oz. *Sights:* Brass blade front; fixed rear *Stock:* Walnut, checkered at wrist *Triggers:* Double set; will fire set and unset *Lock:* Adjustable sear engagement with fly and bridle; V-type mainspring *Features:* Brass percussion cap guard; polished hardware, brass inlays and separate ramrod
Price: $250.00

TRAPPER PISTOL

SPECIFICATIONS
Caliber: 50 percussion or flintlock (1:20") *Barrel length:* 9 ³/₄"; octagonal (7/8" across flats) with tenon *Overall length:* 15.5" *Weight:* 2 lbs. 14 oz. *Stock:* Beech *Lock:* Adjustable sear engagement with fly and bridle *Triggers:* Double set, will fire set and unset *Sights:* Primitive-style adjustable rear; brass blade front *Furniture:* Solid brass; blued steel on assembled pistol
Price:
Percussion. $175.00
Percussion Kit 131.00
Flintlock. 189.50

TRADITIONS PISTOLS

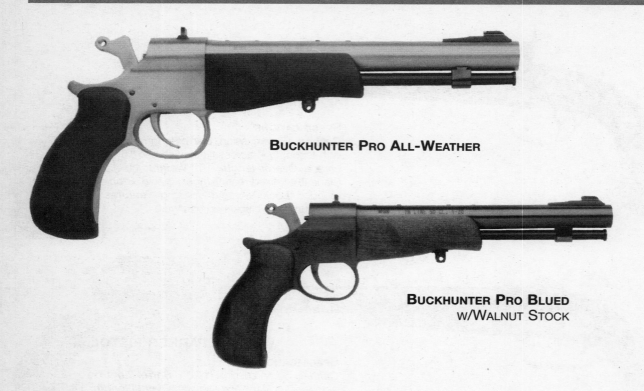

BUCKHUNTER PRO ALL-WEATHER

BUCKHUNTER PRO BLUED
w/WALNUT STOCK

BUCKHUNTER PRO-IN-LINE PISTOLS
SPECIFICATIONS
Calibers: 50 and 54 Percussion
Barrel length: 9.5" round (removable breech plug);
1:20" twist
Overall length: 14.25" (also available w/12.5" barrel in
wood) *Weight:* 3.2 oz. (.50); 3.1 oz. (54); 3.4 oz. (wood)

Trigger: Single
Sights: Fold-down adjustable rear; beaded blade front
Stock: Walnut or All-Weather
Features: Blued or C-Nickel furniture; PVC ramrod; drilled
and tapped for scop mounting; coil mainspring; thumb safety
Price: **$219.00**
   w/All-Weather Stock **233.75**

KENTUCKY PISTOL
SPECIFICATIONS
Caliber: 50 Percussion (1:20") *Barrel length:* 10"
octagon (7/8" flats); fixed tang breech; 1:20" twist
Overall length: 15" *Weight:* 2 lbs. 8 oz. *Trigger:* Single
Sights: Fixed rear; blade front *Stock:* Beechwood
Features: Brass furniture; wood ramrod; kit available
Price: **$131.00**
   Kit **101.25**

TRADITIONS

SINGLE ACTION REVOLVERS

1875 SCHOFIELD

SPECIFICATIONS
Caliber: 44/40, 45 Schofield, 45 LC
Action: Single
Barrel Length: 5.5" blued
Features: Steel frame and trigger guard; walnut grip
Price: $735.00

THUNDERER

SPECIFICATIONS
Caliber: 45 LC
Action: Single
Barrel Length: 4.75" blued
Features: Steel frame and trigger guard
Price: $397.00
w/checkered walnut grips. 459.00

1894 BISELY

SPECIFICATIONS
Caliber: 45 LC
Action: Single
Barrel Length: 4.75" blued
Features: Steel frame and trigger guard; walnut grips
Price: $425.00

1873 COLT SINGLE ACTION REVOLVERS

SPECIFICATIONS
Calibers: 22, 45 LC, 357 Mag., 44/40 *Action:* Single
Barrel Lengths: 4.75", 5.5", 7.5" blued
Features: Walnut grips; steel frame and trigger guard
Price: $395.00
w/brass trigger guard in 4.75" and 5.75"
   (45 LC and 357 Mag.). 345.00
w/brass trigger guard in 4.75" and 5.75" (44/40) . . 350.00
w/brass trigger guard and nickel frame in 4.75" and 5.75"
   (45 LC and 357 Mag.) 455.00

TRADITIONS

DEERHUNTER RIFLES

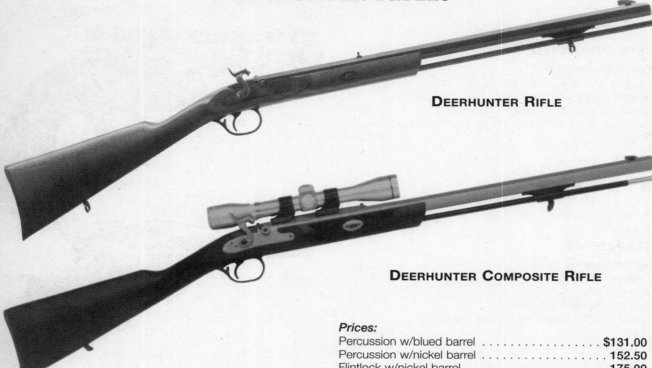

DEERHUNTER RIFLE

DEERHUNTER COMPOSITE RIFLE

Prices:
Percussion w/blued barrel **$131.00**
Percussion w/nickel barrel **152.50**
Flintlock w/nickel barrel **175.00**
Flintlock w/select hardwood stock **175.00**
Percussion w/select hardwood stock, white barrel . **135.00**
Percussion w/All-Weather/Advantage
   composite stock **$175.00**
PANTHER (50 cal.) w/All-Weather composite stock,
   fixed blade sights **116.00**
CARBINE FLINTLOCK & PERCUSSION (50 cal.)
   w/21" barrel blued and black laminated stock . . **256.00**
CARBINE (Flintlock only) w/hardwood stock **204.00**

SPECIFICATIONS
Calibers: 32, 50 and 54 percussion ***Barrel length:*** 24"
octagonal ***Rifling twist:*** 1:48" (percussion only); 1:66"
(flint or percussion) ***Overall length:*** 40" ***Weight:*** 6 lbs.
(6 lbs. 3 oz. in Small Game rifle) ***Trigger:*** Single ***Sights:***
Fixed rear; blade front ***Features:*** PVC ramrod; blackened
furniture; inletted wedge plates

PANTHER RIFLE
All-Weather Composite Stock

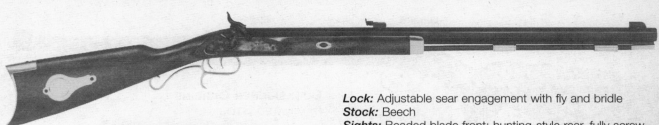

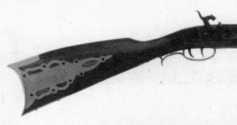

HAWKEN WOODSMAN

SPECIFICATIONS
Calibers: 50 and 54 percussion or flint (50 caliber only)
Barrel length: 28" (octagonal); hooked breech; rifled 1 turn in 48" (1 turn in 66" in 50 caliber also available)
Overall length: 44.5"
Weight: 7 lbs. 11 oz.
Triggers: Double set; will fire set or unset

Lock: Adjustable sear engagement with fly and bridle
Stock: Beech
Sights: Beaded blade front; hunting-style rear, fully screw adjustable for windage and elevation
Furniture: Solid brass, blued steel or blackened (50 cal. only); unbreakable ramrod
Prices:
Percussion. $219.00
Flint 248.00
Also available:
Left-Hand model w/1:48" twist $233.75

PENNSYLVANIA RIFLE

SPECIFICATIONS
Caliber: 50
Barrel length: 401/4"; octagonal (7/8" across flats) with 3 pins; rifled 1 turn in 66"
Overall length: 57" *Weight:* 8 lbs. 8 oz.
Lock: Adjustable sear engagement with fly and bridle

Stock: Walnut, beavertail style
Triggers: Double set; will fire set and unset
Sights: Primitive-style adjustable rear; brass blade front
Furniture: Solid brass, blued steel
Prices:
Percussion. $454.00
Flintlock 463.00

SHENANDOAH RIFLE

The Shenandoah Rifle captures the frontier styling and steady performance of Tradition's Pennsylvania Rifle in slightly shorter length and more affordable price. Choice of engraved and color casehardened flintlock or percussion V-type mainspring lock with double-set triggers. The full-length stock in walnut finish is accented by a solid brass curved buttplate, inletted patch box, nose cap, thimbles, trigger guard and decorative furniture.

SPECIFICATIONS
Caliber: 50 (1:66") flint or percussion
Barrel length: 33.5" octagon
Overall length: 49.5"
Weight: 7 lbs. 3 oz.
Sights: Buckhorn rear, blade front
Stock: Beech
Prices:
Percussion. $322.00
Flintlock 336.25

BLACK POWDER

TRADITIONS

BUCKSKINNER CARBINE

SPECIFICATIONS
Caliber: 50 percussion or flintlock
Barrel length: 21": octagonal-to-round with tenon; 15/16"
across flats; 1:66" twist (flintlock) and 1:20" (percussion)
Overall length: 36.25" Weight: 5 lbs. 15 oz.
Sights: Hunting-style, click adjustable rear; beaded blade
front with white dot

BUCKSKINNER CARBINE
LAMINATED STOCK

Trigger: Single
Features: Blackened furniture: German silver ornamenta-
tion; sling swivels; unbreakable ramrod
Prices:
Percussion. $189.50
Flintlock 204.00
Laminated Stock, Percussion. 256.00
Laminated Stock, Flintlock. 277.50
Also available:
BUCKSKINNER CARBINE DELUXE
Percussion w/nickel barrel $277.50

KENTUCKY RIFLE

SPECIFICATIONS
Caliber: 50 percussion
Barrel length: 33.5" octagon (7/8" flats); fixed tang;
1:66" twist

Overall length: 49" *Weight:* 7 lbs.
Trigger: Single *Tenons:* 2 pins
Stock: Beechwood
Sights: Fixed rear; blade front
Features: Brass furniture; ramrod; inletted wedge plates;
toe plate; V-mainspring
Price: $219.00
Kit. 175.00

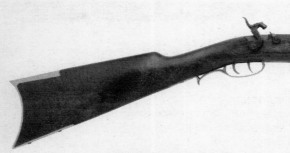

TENNESSEE RIFLE

SPECIFICATIONS
Caliber: 50 flintlock or percussion
Barrel length: 24" octagon (7/8" across flats); hooked
breech; 1:32" twist (percussion) and 1:66" (flintlock)

Overall length: 401/2"
Weight: 6 lbs.
Sights: Fixed rear; blade front
Stock: Beechwood
Features: Brass furniture; ramrod; inletted wedge plate;
stock inlays; toe plate; V-mainspring
Prices:
Percussion. $270.00
Flintlock 285.00

TRADITIONS

LIGHTNING BOLT-ACTION RIFLES

Traditions' series of Lightning Bolt rifles includes 21 different models of blued, chemical-nickel, stainless or Ultra-Coat with Teflon barrels. Stock choices are beech, brown laminated, All-Weather Composite, Advantage™Camo, X-Tra brown Camo or Break-up Camo. All models come with rugged synthetic ramrods, adjustable triggers, adjustable hunting sights, drilled and tapped barrels and field-removable stainless breech plugs.

LIGHTNING W/CHECKERED COMPOSITE STOCK
Fluted Stainless Steel Barrel w/Muzzle Break
Price: **$219.00**

LIGHTNING W/ALL-WEATHER COMPOSITE STOCK
Price: . . . . **$199.00-$336.00**

LIGHTNING W/ADVANTAGE™ CAMO COMPOSITE STOCK
Price: **$248.00**

LIGHTNING™ BOLT-ACTION RIFLES WITH LIGHTNING FIRE SYSTEM™ AND FIBER OPTIC SIGHTS

Model Number	Stock	Caliber	Barrel	Rate of Twist	Sights	Ramrod	Overall Length	Weight
R60002	Select Hardwood	.50p	24" Blued	1:32	Fiber Optic	Aluminum	43"	7 lb. 4 oz.
R60048	Select Hardwood	.54p	24" Blued	1:48	Fiber Optic	Aluminum	43"	7 lb.
R61002	AW Composite	.50p	24" Blued	1:32	Fiber Optic	Aluminum	43"	7 lb.
R61048	AW Composite	.54p	24" Blued	1:48	Fiber Optic	Aluminum	43"	6 lb. 12 oz.
R61202	AW Composite	.50p	24" Blued/Ultra Coat with Teflon	1:32	Fiber Optic	Aluminum	43"	7 lb. 6 oz.
R61802	AW Composite	.50p	24" Stiainless	1:32	Fiber Optic	Aluminum	43"	7 lb. 4 oz.
R61848	AW Composite	.54p	24" Stainless	1:48	Fiber Optic	Aluminum	43"	7 lb. 4 oz.
R62802	Brown Laminate	.50p	24" Stainless	1:32	Fiber Optic	Aluminum	43"	7 lb. 12 oz.
R610022	AW Comp/Advantage	.50p	24" Blued	1:32	Fiber Optic	Aluminum	43"	7 lb.
R610025	AW Comp/Break-Up	.50p	24" Blued	1:32	Fiber Optic	Aluminum	43"	7 lb.
R612025	AW Comp/Break-Up	.50p	24" Blued/Ultra Coat with Teflon	1:32	Fiber Optic	Aluminum	43"	7 lb.
R61702	AW Composite	.50p	24" Fluted Stainless/Muzzle Brake	1:32	Fiber Optic	Aluminum	43"	7 lb.
R610020	AW Composite	.50p	24" Blued/Muzzle Brake	1:32	Fiber Optic	Aluminum	43"	7 lb.
R618075	AW Comp/Break-Up	.50p	24" Stainless	1:32	Fiber Optic	Aluminum	43"	7 lb.

All composite stocks are checkered

BLACK POWDER

TRADITIONS

BUCKHUNTER PRO™ IN-LINE RIFLES

BUCKHUNTER PRO™ IN-LINE RIFLE

BUCKHUNTER PRO™ IN-LINE RIFLE
w/Black Composite Stock, Stainless Barrel, Optional Scope

Traditions has upgraded its Buckhunter In-line ignition rifles and shotguns with the Buckhunter Pro series. The guns feature an adjustable trigger, thumb safety and a choice of

Ultracoat Teflon, C-Nickel, blued or stainless steel barrels. New slimmed-down matte black composite stocks are available as are two camouflage patterns, laminated, thumbhole or walnut-stained stocks. All Buckhunter Pros have field-removable stainless steel breech plugs and improved adjustable hunting sights. The Buckhunter Pro rifles are available in 50 caliber (1:32") or 54 caliber (1:48") for use with conical and saboted bullets.
Prices: . . . . **$149.00 - $242.00**

BUCKHUNTER IN-LINE COMPOSITE RIFLE
SPECIFICATIONS
Calibers: 50 (1:32") and 54 (2:48") percussion **Barrel**

length: Blued 24" round **Overall length:** 42" **Weight:** 7 lbs. 6 oz. **Stock:** All-Weather Composite (matte black) **Sights:** Beaded blade front; fully adjustable rear **Features:** Blackened furniture; PVC ramrod; stainless steel removable breech plug; optional Redi-Pak (includes composite powder flask with valve dispenser, powder measure, two universal fast loaders, 5-in-1 loader, cleaning jab and patches, ball puller, 20 conical bullets, in-line nipple wrench **Price:** **$149.00**

BUCKHUNTER PRO™ IN-LINE RIFLES WITH FIBER OPTIC SIGHTS

Model Number	Stock	Caliber	Barrel	Rate of Twist	Sights	Overall Length	Weight
R50002	Select Hardwood	.50p	24" Blued	1:32	Fiber Optic	43"	7 lb. 5
R50302	Brown Laminated	.50p	24" Blued	1:32	Fiber Optic	43"	7 lb. 10 oz.
R50102	AW Composite	.50p	24" C-Nickel	1:32	Fiber Optic	43"	7 lb. 4 oz.
R50148	AW Composite	.54p	24" C-Nickel	1:48	Fiber Optic	43"	7 bl. 1 oz.
R50802	AW Composite	.50p	24" Stainless	1:32	Fiber Optic	43"	7 lb. 4 oz.
R51102	AW Composite	.50p	24" Blued	1:32	Fiber Optic	43"	7 lb. 4 oz.
R51148	AW Composite	.54p	24" Blued	1:48	Fiber Optic	43"	7 lb. 1 oz.
R51162	AW Composite	.50p	24" Blued/Ultra Coat w/Teflon®	1:32	Fiber Optic	43"	7 lb. 4 oz.
R51168	AW Composite	.54p	24" Blued/Ultra Coat w/Teflon®	1:48	Fiber Optic	43"	7 lb. 1 oz.
R511625	AW Comp/Break-Up	.50p	24" Blued/Ultra Coat w/Teflon®	1:32	Fiber Optic	43"	7 lb. 4 oz.
R511685	AW Comp/Break-Up	.54p	24" Blued/Ultra Coat w/Teflon®	1:48	Fiber Optic	43"	7 lb. 1 oz.

Replacement drop-in black and composite stocks available   FCS50101   All composite stocks are checkered

BUCKHUNTER™ IN - LINE RIFLES

Model Number	Stock	Caliber	Barrel	Rate of Twist	Sights	Overall Length	Weight
R42102	AW Composite	.50p	24" Blued	1:32	Adj/BB	43"	7 lb.
R42148	AW Composite	.54p	24" Blued	1:48	Adj/BB	43"	6 lb. 14 oz.

UBERTI REVOLVERS

PATERSON REVOLVER

Manufactured at Paterson, New Jersey, by the Patent Arms Manufacturing Company from 1836 to 1842, these were the first revolving pistols created by Samuel Colt. All early Patersons featured a five-shot cylinder, roll-engraved with one or two scenes, octagon barrel and folding trigger that extends when the hammer is cocked.

SPECIFICATIONS
Caliber: 36
Capacity: 5 shots (engraved cylinder)
Barrel Length: 7.5" octagonal
Overall Length: 11.5"
Weight: 2.552 lbs.
Frame: Color casehardened steel
Grip: One-piece walnut
Price: $399.00
w/Lever 435.00

PATERSON REVOLVER

1st MODEL DRAGOON REVOLVER

SPECIFICATIONS
Caliber: 44
Capacity: 6 shots
Barrel Length: 7.5" round forward of lug
Overall Length: 13.5"
Weight: 4 lbs.
Frame: Color casehardened steel
Grip: One-piece walnut
Price: $325.00
Also available:
2ND MODEL DRAGOON w/square cylinder bolt shot. . 325.00
3RD MODEL DRAGOON w/loading lever latch, steel
    backstrap, cut for shoulder stock 325.00
WHITNEY DRAGOON w/7.5" barrel 360.00

1st MODEL DRAGOON

WALKER REVOLVER

SPECIFICATIONS
Caliber: 44
Barrel Length: 9" (round in front of lug)
Overall Length: 15.75"
Weight: 4.41 lbs.
Frame: Color casehardened steel
Backstrap: Steel
Cylinder: 6 shots (engraved with "Fighting Dragoons" scene)
Grip: One-piece walnut
Price: $370.00

WALKER REVOLVER

BLACK POWDER

UBERTI REVOLVERS

1851 NAVY REVOLVER

SPECIFICATIONS
Caliber: 36
Barrel length: 7 1/2" (octagonal, tapered)
Cylinder: 6 shots (engraved)
Overall length: 13"
Weight: 2 3/4 lbs.
Frame: Color casehardened steel
Backstrap and trigger guard: Brass
Grip: One-piece walnut
Price: $295.00
Also available:
1851 SQUAREBACK OR OVAL. 270.00

1851 NAVY REVOLVER

1858 REMINGTON NEW ARMY 44 REVOLVER

Prices:
8" barrel, open sights $295.00
With stainless steel and open sights 420.00
TARGET MODEL w/black finish 330.00
TARGET MODEL w/stainless steel 420.00
Also available:
1858 NEW NAVY (36 cal.). 270.00
1858 NEW ARMY REVOLVING CARBINE (18" bbl.) 499.00

**1858 REMINGTON
NEW ARMY TARGET MODEL**

1860 ARMY REVOLVER

SPECIFICATIONS
Caliber: 44
Barrel length: 8" (round, tapered)
Overall length: 13 3/4"
Weight: 2.65 lbs.
Frame: One-piece, color casehardened steel
Trigger guard: Brass
Cylinder: 6 shots (engraved)
Grip: One-piece walnut
Price: $270.00
Also available:
1860 ARMY FLUTED. 295.00

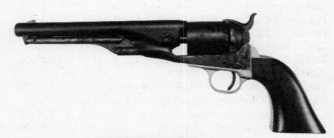

1860 ARMY REVOLVER

1861 NAVY REVOLVER

SPECIFICATIONS
Caliber: 36
Capacity: 6 shots
Barrel length: 7 1/2"
Overall length: 13"
Weight: 2.75 lbs.
Grip: One-piece walnut
Frame: Color casehardened steel
Prices: $270.00
1861 NAVY FLUTED 295.00

1861 NAVY REVOLVER

Aimpoint	460
Bausch & Lomb	461
Burris	465
Docter Optic	468
Laseraim	469
Leica	470
Leupold	471
Nikon	475
Pentax	477
Quarton	479
Redfield	480
Sako	483
Schmidt & Bender	484
Simmons	485
Swarovski	490
Tasco	492
Weaver	496
Zeiss	498

Scopes

*For addresses and phone/fax numbers of manufacturers and distributors included in this section, please turn to **DIRECTORY OF MANUFACTURERS AND SUPPLIERS** on page 558.*

AIMPOINT SIGHTS

AIMPOINT 5000 SIGHT

SPECIFICATIONS
System: Parallax free
Optical: Anti-reflex coated lenses
Adjustment: 1 click = 1/4 inch at 100 yards
Length: 5 1/2"
Weight: 5.8 oz.
Objective diameter: 36mm
Mounting system: 30mm rings
Magnification: 1X
Material: Anodized aluminum; black or stainless finish
Diameter of dot: 3" at 100 yds. or Mag Dot reticle, 10" at 100 yards.
Price: **$277.00**

SERIES 3000 UNIVERSAL

SPECIFICATIONS
System: 100% parallax free
Weight: 5.8 oz.
Length: 6.15"
Magnification: 1X
Scope attachment: 3X
Eye relief: Unlimited
Battery choices: 2X Mercury SP 675 1X Lithium or DL 1/3N
Material: Anodized aluminum, black or stainless finish
Mounting: 1" Rings (Medium or High)
Price: Black or Stainless **$232.00**

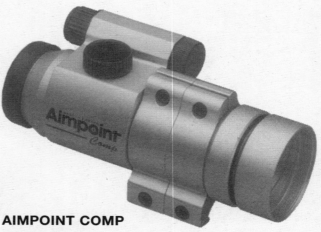

AIMPOINT 5000 2-POWER

SPECIFICATIONS
System: Parallax free
Optical: Anti-reflex coated lens
Adjustment: clock = 1/4" at 100 yards
Length: 7"
Weight: 9 oz.
Objective diameter: 46mm
Diameter of dot: 1.5" at 100 yards
Mounting system: 30mm rings
Magnification: 2X
Material: Anodized aluminum; blue finish
Price: **$367.00**

AIMPOINT COMP

SPECIFICATIONS
System: 100% Parallax free
Optics: Anti-reflex coated lenses
Eye relief: Unlimited
Batteries: 3 x Mercury SP 675
Adjustment: 1 click = 1/4-inch at 100 yards
Length: 4 3/8"
Weight: 4.75 oz.
Objective diameter: 36mm
Dot diameter: 2" at 30 yds. (7 MOA); 3" at 30 yds. (10 MOA)
Mounting system: 30mm rings
Magnification: 1X
Material: Black, blue or stainless finish
Also available with 3-minute Dot with Flip Up lens covers and captive metal adjustment covers.
Price: **$308.00**

BAUSCH & LOMB RIFLESCOPES

ELITE 3000 — 5X-15X

ELITE™ 3000 RIFLESCOPES

Model	Special Feature	Actual Magnification	Obj. Lens Aperature (MM)	Field of View @ 100yds (ft.)	Weight (oz)	Length	Eye Relief (in.)	Exit Pupil (MM)	Click Value @ 100yds (in.)	Adjust Range @ 100yds (in.)	Selection	Suggested Retail
30-2632G	Handgun (30-2632S Silver Finish) (30-2632M Matte Finish)	2x-6x	32	10-4	10	9	20	16-5.3	.25	50	Constant 20" eye relief At all powers w/max. recoil resistance	$417.95
30-2732G	(30-2732M Matte Finish)	2x-7x	32	44.6-12.7	12	11.6	3	12.2-4.6	.25	50	Compact variable for close-in brush ormed. range shooting. Excellent for shotguns	$303.95
30-3940G	(30-3940M Matte Finish, 30-3940S Silver Finish)	3x-9x	40	33.8-11.5	13	12.6	3	13.3-4.4	.25	50	For the full range of hunting. From varmint to big game. Tops in versatility.	$319.95
30-3950G	(30-3950M Matte Finish)	3x-9x	50	31.5-10-5	19	15.7	3	16-5.6	.25	50	All purpose variable with extra brightness.	$382.95
30-3955E	European Reticle Matte Finish	3x-9x	50	31.5-10.5	22	15.6	3	16-5.6	.36	70	Large exit pupil and 30mm tube for max. brightness.	$592.95
30-4124A	Adjustable Objective	4x-12x	40	26.9-9	15	13.2	3	10-3.33	.25	50	Medium to long-range variable makes a superb choice for varmint or big game	$417.95
30-5155M	Adjustable Objective	5x-15x	50	21-7	24	15.9	3	10-3.3	.25	40	Large objective for brightness	$471.95

ELITE 4000 — 2.5-10X40

ELITE™ 4000 RIFLESCOPES

Model	Special Feature	Actual Magnification	Obj. Lens Aperature (MM)	Field of View @ 100yds (ft.)	Weight (oz)	Length	Eye Relief (in.)	Exit Pupil (MM)	Click Value @ 100yds (in.)	Adjust Range @ 100yds (in.)	Selection	Suggested Retail
40-1040	Ranging reticle 30mm body tube	10X	40	10.5	22.1	13.8	3.6	4@10x	.25	120	The ultimate for precise pinpoint accuracy w/parallax focus & target adj. knobs-	$1557.00
40-1636G	(40-1636M Matte Finish)	1.5x-6x	36	61.8-16.1	15.4	12.8	3	14.6-6	.25	60	Compact wide angle for close-in & brush hunting. Max. brightness. Execel. for shotguns	$528.95
40-2104G	(40-2104M Matte Finish, 40-2104S Silver Finish)	2.5x-10x	40	41.5-10.8	16	13.5	3	15.6-4	.25	50	All purpose hunting scope w/4x zoom range for close-in brush & long range shooting	$560.95
40-3640A	Adjustable Objective	36x	40	3	17.6	15	3.2	1.1	.125	30	Ideal benchrest scope.	$850.95
40-4165M	Matte Finish	4x-16x	50	26-7.2	22	15.6	3	12.5-3.1	.25	50	The ultimate varmint, airgun and precision shooting scope. Parallax focus from 10 meter to infinity.	$738.59
40-6244A	Adjustable Objective, Sunshade (40-6244M Matte Finish)	6x-24x	40	18-4.5	20.2	16.9	3	6.7-1.7	.125	26	Varmint, target & silhouette long range shooting and airgun. Parallax focus adjust. for pinpoint accuracy. Parallax focus from 10 meter to infinity.	$640.95
40-6243A	Adjustable Objective and 1/4" MOA dot reticle	6-24x	40	18-4.5	20.2	16.9	3	6.7-1.7	.125	26	Varmint, target and silhouette long range shooting and airgun. Parallax focus adjust for pinpoint accuracy. Parallax focus from 10 meter to infinity.	$648.95

BAUSCH & LOMB/BUSHNELL

**3X-9X (40MM) TROPHY®
WIDE ANGLE RIFLESCOPE**

BUSHNELL TROPHY® RIFLESCOPES

Model	Special Feature	Actual Magnification	Obj. Lens Aperature (MM)	Field of View @ 100YDS (FT.)	Weight (OZ)	Length	Eye Relief (IN.)	Exit Pupil (MM)	Click Value @ 100YDS (IN.)	Adjust Range @ 100YDS (IN.)	Selection	Suggested Retail
73-1500	Wide Angle	1.75x-5x	32	68-23	12.3	10.8	3.5	18.3-1.75x	.25	120	Shotgun, black powder or centerfire. Close-in brush hunting.	$243.95
73-3940	Wide angle (73-3940S Silver, 73-3948 Matte)	3x-9x	40	42/14-14/5	13.2	11.7	3	13.3-4.44	.25	60	All purpose variable, excellent for use from close to long range. Circular view provides a definite advantage over "TV screen" type scopes for running game-uphill or down.	$159.95
73-3941	Illuminated reticle with back-up crosshairs	3x-9x	40	37-12.5	16	13	3	13.3-4.4	.25	70	Variable intensity light control Battery Sony CR 2032 or equivalent	$410.95
73-3942	Long mounting length designed for long-action rifles	3x-9x	42	42-14	13.8	12	3	14-4.7	.25	40	7" mounting length.	$164.95
73-3949	Wide angle with Circle-x™ Reticle	3x-9x	40	42-14	13.2	11.7	3	13.3-4.4	.25	60	Matte finish, Ideal low light reticle.	$170.95
73-4124	Wide angle, adjustable objective (73-4124M Matte)	4x-12x	40	32-11	16.1	12.6	3	10-3.3	.25	60	Medium to long range variable for varmint and big game. Range focus adjustment. Excellent air riflescope.	$285.95
73-6184	Semi-turret target adjustments, adjustable objective	6x-18x	40	17.3-6	17.9	14.8	3	6.6-2.2	.125	40	Long-range varmint centerfire or short range air rifle target precision accuracy.	$360.95
TROPHY® CA SCOPES												
73-3947	CA design (Matte)	3x-9x	40	44-14	13	12	4	13.3-4.4	.25	60	Superb optics.	$225.95
TROPHY® HANDGUN SCOPES												
73-0232	(73-0232S Silver)	2x	32	20	7.7	8.7	9	16	.25	90	Designed for target and short to med. range hunting. Magnum recoil resistant.	$202.95
73-2632	(73-2632S Silver)	2x-6x	32	11-4	10.9	9.1	18	16-5.3	.25	50	18 inches of eye relief at all powers	$268.95
TROPHY® SHOTGUN/HANDGUN SCOPES												
79-1420	Turkey Scope with Circle-x™ Reticle	1.75x-4x	32	73-30	10.9	10.8	3.5	18.8	.25	120	Ideal for turkey hunting, slug guns or blackpowder guns. Matte finish.	$237.95
73-1421	Brush Scope with Circle-x™ Reticle	1.75x-4x	32	73-30	10.9	10.8	3.5	18-8	.25	120	Ideal for turkey hunting, slug guns or blackpowder guns. Matte finish.	$237.95
TROPHY® AIR RIFLESCOPES												
73-4124	Wide angle, adjustable objective (73-4124M Matte)	4x-12x	40	32-11	16.1	12.6	3	10-3.3	.25	60	Medium to long range variable for varmint and big game. Range focus adjustment. Excellent air riflescope.	$285.95
73-6184	Semi-turret target adjustments, adjustable objective	6x-18x	40	17-6	17.9	14.8	3	6.6-2.2	.125	40	Long-range varmint centerfire or short range air rifle target precision accuracy.	$360.95

BAUSCH & LOMB/BUSHNELL

SPORTVIEW PLUS 3X-9X

BUSHNELL SPORTVIEW PLUS RIFLESCOPES

Model	Special Feature	Actual Magni-fication	Obj. Lens Aperature (mm)	Field of View @ 100yds (ft.)	Weight (oz)	Length	Eye Relief (in.)	Exit Pupil (mm)	Click Value @ 100yds (in.)	Adjust Range @ 100yds (in.)	Selection	Suggested Retail
79-0412	Adjustable objective (79-1398 Matte)	4x-12x	40	27-9	14.6	13.1	3.2	10-3.3	.25	60	Long range.	$141.95
79-1393	(79-1393S Matte Silver)	3x-9x	32	38-14	10	11.75	3.5	10.7-3.6	.25	50	All purpose variable	$68.95
79-1403	(79-1403S Silver)	4x	32	29	9.2	11.75	4	8	.25	60	General purpose.	$56.95
79-1404	Black powder	4x	32	29	9.2	11.75	4	8	.25	60	For black powder guns.	$56.95
79-1545		1.5x-4.5x	21	69-24	8.6	10.7	3	14-4.7	.25	60	Low power variable ideal for close-in brush or medium range shooting	$86.95
79-3145	Larger Objective	3.5x-10x	45	36-13	13.9	12.75	3	12.9-4.5	.25	60	Large objective for low light use.	$154.95
79-3940	Wide angle (79-3940M Matte)	3x-9x	40	42-15	12.5	12	3	4.4	.25	50	Excellent for use at any range.	$91.95
79-3142	Built-in bullet drop compensator	3x-9x	40	40-13	12	12.25	3	13.3-4.4	.25	45	All purpose. BDC adjusts for target range.	$102.95
79-6184*	Adjustable objective	6x-18x	40	19.1-6.8	15.9	14.5	3	6.7-2.2	.25	50	Excellent varmint scope.	$170.95
SPORTVIEW® AIR RIFLE SERIES												
79-0004	Adjustable objective w/rings	4x	32	31	11.2	11.7	4	8	.25	50	General purpose for air rifle and rimfire.With range focus & target adjustments	$97.95
79-0039	Adjustable objective, with rings	3x-9x	32	38-13	11.2	10.75	3.5	10.6-3.5	.25	60	Air rifle, rimfire with range focus adjustments and target adjustments	$116.95
SPORTVIEW® RIMFIRE SERIES												
79-1416	3/4" tube	4x	15	17	3.6	10.7	3.5	3.8	Friction	60	General purpose.	$11.95
79-3720	3/4" tube	3x-7x	20	23-11	5.7	11.3	2.6	6.7-2.9	Friction	50	All purpose variable.	$36.95
.22 VARMINT™ WITH RINGS												
79-0428	With rings (79-0428M Matte)	4x	28	25	8.5	7.6	3	7	.5	52	Compact for .22's	$75.95
79-3950	Wide angle	3x-9x	50	41-15	12.9	12.5	3	17-5.5	.25	50	Excellent all purpose low light scope	$164.95

BUSHNELL BANNER RIFLESCOPES

Model	Special Feature	Actual Magni-fication	Obj. Lens Aperature (mm)	Field of View @ 100yds (ft.)	Weight (oz)	Length	Eye Relief (in.)	Exit Pupil (mm)	Click Value @ 100yds (in.)	Adjust Range @ 100yds (in.)	Selection	Suggested Retail
71-1545	Wide Angle	1.5x-4.5x	32	67-23	10.5	10.5	3.5	17-7	.25	60	Ideal Shotgun and median to short range scope.	$116.95
71-3944	Black powder scope w/extended eye relief and Circle-x@ reticle	3x-9x	40	36-13	12.5	11.5	4	13-4.4	.25	60	Specifically designed for black powder and shotguns	$120.95
71-3948	Ideal scope for multi purpose guns	3x-9x	40	40-74	13	12	3	13.3-4.4	.25	60	General purpose.	$113.95
71-3950	Large objective for extra brightness in low light	3x-9x	50	31-10	19	16	3	16-5.6	.25	50	Low light conditions	$186.95
71-4124	Adjustable objective	4x-12x	40	29-11	15	12	3	10-3.3	.25	60	Ideal scope for long-range shooting.	$157.95
71-6185	Adjustable objective	6x-18x	50	17-6	18	16	3	8.3-2.8	.25	40	Long range varmint and target scope.	$209.95

BAUSCH & LOMB/BUSHNELL

BUSHNELL® HOLOSIGHT®

The BUSHNELL® HOLOsight® delivers instant target acquisition, improved accuracy, and can be tailored to virtually any shooting discipline. How does it work? A hologram of a reticle pattern is recorded on a heads-up display window. When illuminated by laser (coherent) light, a holographic image becomes visible at the target plane - where it remains in focus with the target. Critical eye alignment is not required and multi-plane focusing error is eliminated. With the BUSHNELL® HOLOsight®, simply look through the window, place the reticle image on the target and shoot. The use of holographic technology allows the creation of virtually any image as a reticle pattern, in either two or three dimensions. Shooters have the flexibly to design reticles in any geometric shape, size and in any dimension to enhance a specific shooting discipline. Since no light is cast on the target, use of the BUSHNELL® HOLOsight® is completely legal in most hunting, target and competition areas.

**BUSHNELL®
HOLOSIGHT®**

BUSHNELL HOLOSIGHT® SPECIFICATIONS

Optics	Magni-fication @ 100 yds	Field of View ft @ 100 yds	Weight (oz/g)	Length (in/mm)	Eye Relief (in/mm)	Batteries	Windage Click Value in @100 yds mm @ 100m	Elevation Click Value in @100 yds mm @ 100m	Brightness Adjustment Settings
Holographic	1x	Unlimited	8.7/247	6/152	1/2" to 10 ft. 13 to 3048 mm	2 Type N 1.5 Volt	.25 M.O.A./ 7mm @100m	.5 M.O.A./ 14mm@100m	20 levels

Model	Description		Suggested Retail
50-0021	HOLOsight Model 400	HOLOsight with mounts for Weaver rail and standard reticle.	$567.95
50-0020	HOLOsight Model 400 (without reticle)	HOLOsight with mounts for Weaver rail and no reticle. Reticle must be purchased separately.	$478.95
50-0310	HOLOsight Comp Model 430	HOLOsight with diamond reticle and integrated 1911 No-hole pattern mount.	$681.95
50-0315	HOLOsight Comp Model 430	HOLOsight with diamond reticle and integrated 1911 5 hole pattern mount.	$681.95
50-0360	HOLOsight Comp Model 430	HOLOsight with diamond reticle and integrated STI No-hole pattern mount.	$681.95
50-0364	HOLOsight Comp Model 430	HOLOsight with diamond reticle and integrated STI 5-hole pattern mount.	$681.95
50-00021	HOLOsight 2X adapter	Increases effective range of HOLOsight	$248.95

Model	Reticle	Description	Uses	
HOLOsight® RETICLES				
Included w/50-0021	Standard	2-Dimensional 65 M.O.A. ring with one M.O.A. dot and tick marks.	General all-purpose handguns, rifles, slug guns, and wing shooting	$111.95
50-0122	Dual Rings	2-Dimensional design with two rings (20 M.O.A. & 90 M.O.A.)	Wing shooting, 20" IPSC targets, slug and turkey guns	$111.95
50-0123	Open Crosshairs	2-Dimensional all-purpose design which does not cover up the target area. Inner circle covers 30" at 100 yards.	General all purpose handguns, short range rifles, slug guns and wing shooting	$111.95
50-0124	Diamond	20 M.O.A. Diamond	IPSC Shooting, and hand gun steel.	$111.95
50-0125	Dot	1 M.O.A. Dot	Precision rifle, handgun, and slug gun shooting.	$111.95
50-0126	10 MOA Ring	10 M.O.A. See-Thru Ring	All purpose handguns, slug guns, wing shooting, and rifles.	$111.95
50-0127	20 MOA Ring	20 M.O.A. See-Thru Ring	All purpose handguns, slug guns, wing shooting, and rifles.	$111.95

BURRIS SCOPES

BLACK DIAMOND RIFLESCOPES

MODEL 3X-12X-50mm

Burris's new Black Diamond line includes six models of a 30mm main tube 3X-12X-50mm with various finishes, reticles, and adjustment knobs. These riflescopes have easy-to-grip rubber-armored parallax-adjust rings, an adjustable and resettable adjustment dial, and an internal focusing eyepiece. Other features include fully multi-coated lens surfaces, 110 inches of internal adjustment, four times magnification range, and 3.5" to 4" of eye relief. Alll models come in a non-reflective matte black finish.

SPECIFICATIONS
Model: 3X-12X-50mm
Actual magnification: 3.2X-11.9X
Field of View (feet @ 100yds.): 34'-12'
Optimum eye relief: 3.5"-4.0"
Exit Pupil: 13.7mm-4.2mm

Click adjust value (@ 100 yds.): .25"
Max. internal adj. (@ 100 yds.): 110"
Objective end diameter: 60mm
Clear objective diameter: 50mm
Ocular end diameter: 42mm
Weight: 25 oz.
Length: 13.8"
Reticles available: Plex, German 3P#1, German 3P#4, Mil-Dot
Prices:
Plex w/matte finish.	$854.00
Plex w/matte finish, Posi-Lock	917.00
German 3P#1 reticle w/matte finish.	881.00
German 3P#4 reticle w/matte finish.	881.00
Plex w/matte finish, Tactical Knobs	890.00
Mil-Dot reticle w/matte finish, Tactical Knobs	890.00

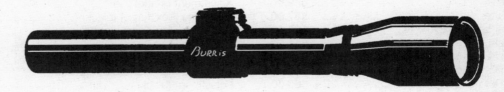

2.7X SCOUT SCOPE
W/Precision Clock Adjustments

SCOUT SCOPES
Made for hunters who need a 7- to 14 inch eye relief to mount just in front of the ejection port opening, allowing hunters to shoot with both eyes open. The 15-foot field of view and 2.75X magnification are ideal for brush guns and handgunners. Also ideal for the handgunner that uses a "two-handed hold." Rugged, reliable and 100% fog proof.

MODELS	Prices
1X XER Plex (matte)	$290.00
1X XER Plex (camo)	316.00
1.5X Heavy Plex (matte)	295.00
2.75X Plex (black)	295.00
2.75X Heavy Plex (matte)	304.00

BURRIS SCOPES

SIGNATURE SERIES

All models in the Signature Series have **HI-LUME** (multi-coated) lenses for maximum light transmission. Many models also feature **POSI-LOCK** to prevent recoil and protect against rough hunting use and temperature change. Allows the shooter to lock the internal optics of the scope in position after the rifle has been sighted in.

8X-32X SIGNATURE

6X-24X

8X-32X

4X-16X

MODELS	Prices
4X Plex (black)	$359.00
6X Plex (black)	397.00
6X Plex (matte)	415.00
1.5X-6X Plex (black)	465.00
1.5X-6X Plex (matte)	483.00
1.5X-6X Plex Posi-Lock (matte)	527.00
2X-8X Plex (black)	536.00
2X-8X Plex (matte)	554.00
2X-8X Plex Posi-Lock (black)	581.00
2X-8X Plex Posi-Lock (matte)	599.00
2.5X-10X Plex Posi-Lock Parallax Adjustment (black)	669.00
2.5X-10X Plex Posi-Lock Parallax Adjustment (matte)	686.00
2.5X-10X Plex Posi-Lock Parallax Adjustment (nickel)	695.00
3X-9X Plex (black)	549.00
3X-9X Plex (matte)	567.00
3X-9X Plex Posi-Lock (black)	593.00
3X-9X Plex Posi-Lock (matte)	611.00
3X-9X Plex Posi-Lock (nickel)	620.00
3X-9X Electro-Dot (black)	647.00
3X-9X Electro-Dot (matte)	665.00
3X-9X Electro-Dot Posi-Lock (black)	692.00
3X-9X Electro-Dot Posi-Lock (matte)	710.00
3X-9X-50mm Plex Posi-Lock (matte)	676.00
3X-9X-50mm Mil-Dot Posi-Lock (matte)	819.00
3X-12X Plex Parallax Adjustment (matte)	695.00
3X-12X Plex Posi-Lock Parallax Adjustment (black)	726.00
3X-12X Plex Posi-Lock Parallax Adjustment (matte)	744.00
4X-16X Plex Parallax Adjustment (matte)	713.00
4X-16X Plex Parallax Adjustment (black)	695.00
4X-16X Fine Plex Parallax Adjustment (black)	749.00
4X-16X Fine Plex Parallax Adjustment (matte)	749.00
4X-16X Plex Posi-Lock Parallax Adjustment (matte)	763.00
6X-24X Plex Parallax Adjustment (black)	713.00
6X-24X Plex Parallax Adjustment (matte)	731.00
6X-24X Fine Flex Target/PA (black)	749.00
6X-24X Fine Plex Target/PA (matte)	749.00
6X-24X Fine Plex Target/PA (nickel)	776.00
6X-24X Mil Dot Target (matte)	910.00
6X-24X Plex Posi-Lock Parallax Adjustment (black)	765.00
6X-24XP Plex Posi-Lock Parallax Adjustment (matte)	829.00
6X-24X Electro-Dot Parallax Adjustment (black)	812.00
6X-24X Electro-Dot Parallax Adjustment (matte)	829.00
6X-32X Fine Plex Target (black)	767.00
8X-32X Fine Plex Target (matte)	785.00
8X-32X Fine Plex Target (nickel)	794.00
8X-32X Peep Plex Target (black)	785.00
8X-32X Fine Plex Posi-Lock Parallax Adjustment (black)	820.00
8X-32X Fine Plex Posi-Lock Parallax Adjustment (matte)	838.00
NEW:	
3X-9X-50mm Plex (black)	638.00
3X-9X-50mm Mil-Dot (matte)	799.00
4X-16X Fine Plex Target/PA	734.00
4X-16X Fine Plex (matte) Target /PA	749.00
4X-16X Mil-Dot Target/PA (matte)	892.00
6X-24X 1"-.25 Dot Target/PA (matte)	803.00
8X-32X 1"-25" Dot Target/PA (matte)	820.00
8X-32X Mil-Dot Target/PA (matte)	928.00

BURRIS SCOPES

FULLFIELD SCOPES
FIXED POWER WITH HI-LUME LENSES

3X-9X GLOSS ELECTRO-DOT

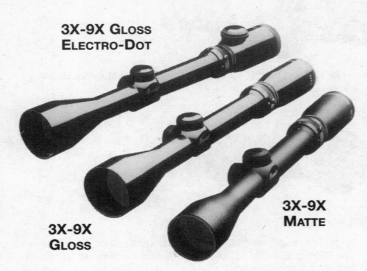

3X-9X GLOSS

3X-9X MATTE

MODELS	Prices
1.5X Shotgun Plex (matte)	$293.00
1.5X Shotgun Plex (camo)	327.00
21/2 Plex (matte)	302.00
21/2X Plex (camo)	336.00
4X Plex (black)	307.00
4X Plex (matte)	325.00
6X Plex (black)	336.00
6X Plex (matte)	354.00
1.75X-5X Plex (black)	366.00
1.75X-5X Plex (matte)	384.00
2X-7X Plex (black)	391.00
2X-7X Plex (matte)	409.00
3X-9X Plex (black) 38mm	356.00
3X-9X Plex (matte) 38mm	356.00
3X-9X Plex (nickel) 38mm	406.00
3X-9X Electro-Dot Plex (black) 40mm	477.00
3X-9X Electro-Dot Plex (matte) 40mm	495.00
3X-9X-40mm Plex (black)	379.00
3X-9X-40mm Plex (matte)	397.00
3X-9X-40mm Electro-Dot Plex (black)	477.00
3X-9X-40mm Electro-Dot Plex (matte)	495.00
3.5X-10X Plex (black)	486.00
3.5X-10X Plex (matte)	504.00
3.5X-10X Plex (nickel)	513.00
4X-12X Fine Plex Parallax Adjustment (matte)	511.00
4X-12X Fine Plex Parallax Adjustment (black)	493.00
6X-18X Plex Parallax Adjustment (matte)	534.00
6X-18X Fine Plex Parallax Adjustment (black)	517.00
6X-18X Fine Plex Target (black)	552.00
6X-18X Peep Plex PA (matte)	552.00

COMPACT SCOPES

MODELS	Prices
1X XER Plex (matte)	$290.00
1X XER Plex (camo)	324.00
1X-4X XER Plex (matte)	370.00
4X Plex (black)	257.00
4X Plex (nickel)	284.00
6X Plex (black)	273.00
6X Plex Parallax Adjustment (black)	315.00
6X HBR Fine Plex Target (black)	429.00
6X HBR .375 Dot Target (black)	465.00
6X HBR 2.7 Peep Plex Target (matte)	465.00
2X-7X Plex (black)	352.00
2Z-7X Plex (matte)	370.00
3X-9X Plex (black)	361.00
3X-9X Plex (matte)	379.00
3X-9X Plex (nickel)	388.00
4X-12X Fine Plex Parallax Adjustment (black)	475.00
4X-12X Fine Plex Target/(black)	511.00
4X-12X Fine Plex Target/PA	529.00

HANDGUN LONG EYE RELIEF SCOPE
WITH PLEX RETICLE:

3X-9X HANDGUN SCOPE

MODELS	Prices
1X XER Plex (matte)	$290.00
1X XER Plex (camo	325.00
2X Plex Posi-Lock (nickel)	311.00
2X Plex Posi-Lock (black)	293.00
2X Plex Posi-Lock (matte)	302.00
4X Plex Posi-Lock (black)	324.00
10X Plex Target (black)	447.00
1.5X-4X Plex Posi-Lock (black)	388.00
1.5X-4X Plex Posi-Lock (nickel)	406.00
2X-7X Plex Posi-Lock (black)	425.00
2X-7X Plex Posi-Lock (nickel)	443.00
3X-9X Plex Posi-Lock (black)	475.00
3X-9X Plex Posi-Lock (nickel)	493.00
NEW:	
2X Plex (black)	257.00
2X Plex (nickel)	275.00
4X Plex (Black)	288.00
4X Plex (nickel)	306.00
1.5X-4X Plex (black)	352.00
1.5X-4X Plex (nickel)	370.00
2X-7X Plex (black)	390.00
2X-7X Plex (matte)	399.00
2X-7X Plex (black) PA	431.00
2X-7X Plex (nickel)	488.00

DOCTER OPTIC RIFLESCOPES

VARIABLE POWER

MODEL 1-4X24

This is a compact, low-power riflescope ideal for close-range shooting.
Price: **$1,129.00**

3-10X40 RIFLESCOPE

Made with high-quality multi-coated optics, the 3-10X40 is ideal for late afternoon and early morning hunting. Its rugged design handles recoil from large-caliber rifles and, with a full three inches of eye relief, it protects the shooter's eye. The extended eye relief also allows those who wear eyeglasses or sunglasses to take full advantage of the scope's capabilities. Its one-inch tube and large area for mounting rings are easily mounted on all popular sporting rifles. The European-style diopter adjustment system simplifies focusing with or without glasses. It also features 1/4-inch audible click adjustments and generous elevation and windage adjustments. Field-tested in the Alaskan wilderness. *Weight:* 18 oz.
Price: **$798.00**

3-12X56 RIFLESCOPE

With its 56mm objective lens and 30mm tube, the 3-12X56M Rifle Scope has excellent light transmission properties. Its adjustable magnification factor allows shooters to zoom out for wide-field viewing or zoom in for precise bullet placement. A floating diopter makes focusing quick and easy.
Price: **$1.338.00**

VZF 2.5-1048

Docter Optic's VZF 2.5-10X48M variable riflescope delivers high-power performance yet weighs less than 19 ounces. Designed for long-range hunting and target shooting, its rugged, die-cast aluminum body and shock-proof optical system alignment have been tested and are guaranteed recoil-resistant with most rifle calibers. The VHF 2.5-10X48M also features special multi-level coating of all glass-to-air surfaces. Its large field of view extends to approx. 33 feet at 2.5X power. The focusing mechanism provides smooth, silent adjustment of the zoom range. A special sealing element ensures that the optical system is protected against all weather conditions, dust and dirt.
Price: **$1,299.00**

LASERAIM ARMS INC.

MODEL LA16
HOTDOT MIGHTY SIGHT

Ten times brighter than other laser sights, Laseraim's Hotdot Lasersights include a rechargeable NICad battery and in-field charger. Produce a 2" dot at 100 yards with a 500-yard range. **Length:** 2". **Diameter:** .75". Can be used with handguns, rifles, shotguns and bows. Fit all Laseraim mounts. Available in black or satin.
Price: **$149.00**

GI HOT CUSTOM LASERS

The GI HOT (Hotdot® laser) has been custom-designed for Glock models 17 to 30. It allows a two-handed shooting grip by locating the laser close to the bottom of the frame. This patented system internalizes the wires, leaving a clean, easy-to-use laser that conforms to the pistol and makes sighting a breeze. A pressure-sensitive pad turns the laser on and off. Four button-cell batteries power it up to one hour continuously. The Easy-lock™ windage & elevation system makes sighting quick and reliable. GI HOT range = 500 yds. **Length:** 1.5". **Weight:** 2 oz.
Price: **$229.00**

LA70 SHOTLESS LASER BORE SIGHTER™
(Not shown)

The **LA70 Shotless Laser Bore Sighter™** facilitates sighting to near perfect accuracy without wasting a shot. To check the center of the bore, simply rotate the laser on axis of the gun bore. The LA70 is equipped with a rotational **Laseraim™** with constant ON switch and six arbors fitting calibers 22 thru 45, 12-gauge shotguns and muzzleloaders (50 and 544 cal.). **Length:** 8" (w/laser and arbor).
Price: **$169.00**

LA3XHD™ HOTDOT®

This electronic red dot/laser combo can be used in all light conditions–the electronic red dot sight in bright light and the laser in low light conditions. The three-piece sighting system offers the newest technology in red dot scopes and a versatile laser. The 30mm objective lens gives an increased field of view over traditional 1" scopes and zero eye relief makes sighting a breeze. The 4 m.o.a. (about 4" at 100 yrads) dot size is ideal for hunting and target. The laser projects a 2" dot at 100 yards, has up to a 500 yd. range, and gives pin-point accuracy with Laseraim's new Easy Lock™ windage & elevation system. The LA3XHD™ HOT-DOT® Dualdot™ laser is 10 times brighter. Fits all rifles, bows, shotguns and handguns with a standard weaver base. **Weight:** 12 oz. **Overall length:** 6 inches.
Price: **$199.00**

LA93 ILLUSION III™
RED DOT SCOPE

This two-piece design offers more flexibility in mounting with less added overall weight. The 30mm objective lens gives an increased field of veiw over traditional 1" scopes and zero eye relief. The 4 m.o.a. (about 4" at 100 yards) dot size is ideal for hunting and target. Fits all rifles, bows, shotguns and handguns with a standard weaver base (sold separately). **Weight:** 5 oz. **Overall length:** 6 inches. Black or satin finish.
Price: **$99.00**

LEICA ULTRAVID RIFLESCOPES

LEICA, the world-renowned maker of high-quality cameras, binoculars and spotting scopes has earned the reputation of producing German-engineered optics with unsurpassed optical performance and mechanical precision. The LEICA ULTRAVID Riflescopes have created a complete hunting product line for the serious outdoor enthusiast. These riflescopes are designed to withstand the most extreme conditions–from frigid Alaskan bays to scorching Kalahari sands. All models provide exceptionally brilliant, high-contrast images, thanks to LEICA's Multi-Coated glass with "ballistic tough" ion-assisted coatings. The lenses are precisely positioned in a durable, one-piece 30mm housing machined from a single block of aircraft-grade aluminum to withstand accidents of all kinds. Waterproofed up to 33 feet and nitrogen-purged to provide a lifetime of fog-proof use, LEICA's ULTRAVID riflescopes are finished in a hard, anodized black matte with titanium accents. In addition, the power selector and diopter adjustment covers feature "soft touch" rubber tactile surfaces for a positive grip even with gloved hands or wet fingers.

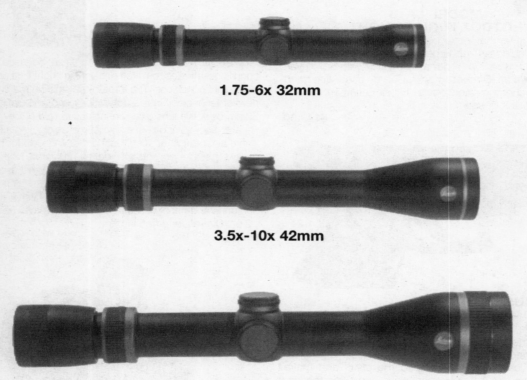

1.75-6x 32mm

3.5x-10x 42mm

4.5x-14x 42mm "F"

SPECIFICATIONS

MODEL	WEIGHT	LENGTH	FIELD OF VIEW FT. @ 100 YD.		OPTIMUM EYE RELIEF		ADJUSTMENT RANGE @ 100 YARDS	PRICES
			LOW	HIGH	LOW	HIGH		
1.75x-6x by 32 mm	14 ounces	11.25 inches	47	18 inches	4.8	3.7 inches	55 inches	$749.00
3.5x-10x by 42 mm	16 ounces	12.62 inches	29.5	10.7 inches	4.6	3.6 inches	51 inches	$849.00
4.5x-14x by 42 mm F	18 ounces	12.28 inches	20.8	7.4 inches	5.0	3.7 inches	67 inches	$949.00

LEUPOLD RIFLESCOPES

VARI-X III LINE

The Vari-X III scopes feature a power-changing system that is similar to the sophisticated lens systems in today's finest cameras. Improvements include an extremely accurate internal control system and a sharp sight picture. All lenses are coated with Multicoat 4. Reticles are the same apparent size throughout the power range and stay centered during elevation/windage adjustments. Eyepieces are adjustable and fog-free. Reticles are also available in German #1, German #1 European, German #4, Post and Duplex, and Leupold Dot.

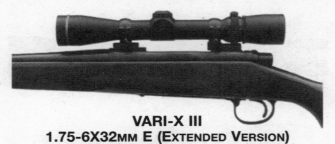

VARI-X III
1.75-6X32MM E (EXTENDED VERSION)

VARI-X III 1.5-5X20mm
This selection of hunting powers is for ranges varying from very short to those at which big game is normally taken. The field at 1.5X lets you get on a fast-moving animal quickly. With magnification at 5X, medium and big game can be hunted around the world at all but the longest ranges.
Duplex or Heavy Duplex. $592.90
In black matte finish. 614.30
Extended Version. 641.10
Also available:
VARI-X III 1.75-6X32mm. Matte finish 641.10

VARI-X III 2.5-8X36mm
This is an excellent range of powers for almost any kind of game, including varmints. The top magnification provides resolution for practically any situation.
Duplex $639.30
In matte or silver finish 660.70

VARI-X III 3.5-10X40mm
The extra power range makes these scopes the optimum choice for year-around big game and varmint hunting. The adjustable objective model, with its precise focusing at any range beyond 50 yards, also is an excellent choice for some forms of target shooting.
Duplex $664.30
With matte or silver finish 685.70

VARI-X III 3.5-10X50mm
The hunting scope is designed specifically for low-light situations. The 3.5X10-50mm scope, featuring lenses coated with Multicoat 4, is ideal for twilight hunting (especially whitetail deer) because of its efficient light transmission. The new scope delivers maximum available light through its large 50mm objective lens, which translates into an exit pupil that transmits all the light the human eye can handle in typical low-light circumstances, even at the highest magnification
Duplex or Heavy Duplex. $762.50
With matte or silver finish 783.90
With Leupold Dot. 816.10

VARI-X III 4.5-14X40mm (Adj. Objective)
This model has enough range to double as a hunting scope and as a varmint scope.
Duplex or Heavy Duplex $764.50
With matte finish 817.00
Same as above with 50mm adj. obj., Duplex or Heavy
    Duplex; matte finish only 862.50

VARI-X III 6.5-20X50mm
TARGET LONG RANGE
w/SIDE-FOCUS ADJUSTMENT

VARI-X III 6.5-20X40mm (Adj. Objective)
This scope has a wide range of power setting, with magnifications useful to hunters of all types of varmints. Can be used for any kind of big-game hunting where higher magnifications are an aid. Side-focus adjustment allows shooters to eliminate parallax while in shooting position without taking eye off target.
Gloss finish $775.00
With matte or silver finish 796.40
Also available:
6.5-20X50MM ADJ. OBJ. w/duplex matte finish. . . $894.60
6.5-20X50MM ADJ. OBJ. w/European duplex
    matte finish 948.20
6.5-20X50MM ADJ. OBJ. Long Range Duplex
    finish. 1,107.10
w/Target Dot. 1,160.75

VARI-X III 8.5-25X40mm

VARI-X III 8.5-25X40mm (Adj. Objective)
Features one-piece main tube of T-6061 aluminum, 1/4-minute click adjustments, Multicoat 4™ lens coating.
With matte finish $830.40
Target Model 937.50

LEUPOLD

VARI-X II 1-4X20mm DUPLEX

This scope, the smallest of Leupold's VARI-X II line, is noted for its large field of view: 70 feet at 100 yards.
Gloss finish only $375.00

4X20mm DUPLEX

VARI-X II 2-7X33mm DUPLEX

A compact scope, no larger than the Leupold M8-4X, offering a wide range of power. It can be set at 2X for close ranges in heavy cover or zoomed to maximum power for shooting or identifying game at longer ranges: . . . $407.10

7X33mm DUPLEX

VARI-X II 3-9X50mm

This LOV scope delivers a 5.5mm exit pupil for low-light visibility: $489.30
Matte finish (Tactical) 510.70

9X50mm

VARI-X II 3-9X40mm DUPLEX

A wide selection of powers offers the right combination of field of view and magnification to fit most hunting conditions. Many hunters use the 3X or 4X setting most of the time, cranking up to 9X for positive identification of game or for extremely long shots. The adjustable objective eliminates parallax and permits precise focusing on any object from less than 50 yards to infinity for extra-sharp definition.
Gloss finish $410.70
In matte or silver 432.10

9X40mm DUPLEX

VARI-X II 4-12X40mm (Adj. Objective)

The ideal answer for big game and varmint hunters alike. At 12.25 inches, the 4X12 is virtually the same length as Vari-X II 3X9. New fixed objective has same long eye relief and is factory-set to be free of parallax for 150 yds.
Gloss finish $564.30
Matte or silver finish 585.70
CPC 601.80
Leupold Dot 601.80
3/4 Mil. Dot 698.20

12X40mm

VARI-X II 6-18X40mm Adj. Obj. Target

Features target-style click adjustments, fully coated lenses, adj. objective for parallax-free shooting from 50 yards to infinity.
In matte. $621.40
Target Dot Model 675.00

18X40mm

LEUPOLD SCOPES

LEUPOLD PREMIER SCOPES (LPS)

This premier line of "Golden Ring" riflescopes was developed to exceed the optical and mechanical performance characteristics desired by hunters and shooters. Two products are currently available, a 1.5-6X42mm and 3.5-14X52mm. Both products have a black satin hard anodized finish and feature a new advanced scratch-resistant, multi-layer and anti-reflective coating, called "DiamondCoat™," which provides 99.65% light transmission per lens surface.

The LPS also features a 30mm one-piece main tube, which allows for a full 60 8 inches of windage and elevation adjustment at 100 yards. The main tube also provides more field-of-view than most scopes with a similar range. The power selector and adjustable objective have easy-to-grip rubber surfaces that allow for smooth adjustments. Additionally, the markings on these adjustments are angled for easy reading even in shooting positions. Low-profile windage and elevation dials are finger-adjustable. Once sighted in, pull-up/push-down dials can be reset to zero.

LPS 1.5-6X42mm (satin finish) $1,476.80
LPS 3.5-14X52mm (adjustable objective) 1,623.20
w/Leupold Dot 1,623.20

LPSTM 3.5-14X52mm ADJ. OBJ.

SHOTGUN & MUZZLELOADER SCOPES (not shown)

Leupold shotgun scopes are parallax-adjusted to deliver precise focusing at 75 yards. Each scope features a special Heavy Duplex reticle that is more effective against heavy, brushy backgrounds. All scopes have matte finish.

Prices:
VARI-X II 1-4X20mm MODEL HEAVY DUPLEX $396.40
M8-4X33mm HEAVY DUPLEX 383.90
VARI-X III 2-7X33MM HEAVY DUPLEX 428.60

COMPACT SCOPES

M8-4X28mm COMPACT & 4X RF SPECIAL

The 4X RF Special is focused to 75 yards and has a Duplex reticle with finer crosshairs $362.50

4X COMPACT & 4 RF SPECIAL

2-7X28mm COMPACT RF SPECIAL

Two ounces lighter and an inch shorter than its full-size counterpart, this 2-X7 is one of the most compact variable power scopes available for today's trend toward smaller and lighter rifles $453.60

2-7 COMPACT

3-9X33mm COMPACT

The 3X9 Compact is 3 1/2 ounces lighter and 1.3 inches shorter than a standard 3-9 . . . . $469.60
In black matte finish 491.10
EFR COMPACT (gloss) 491.10

3-9 COMPACT SILVER

LEUPOLD SCOPES

642mm TACTICAL SCOPE

The new Leupold 6X42mm features 1/4-minute click target-style adjustments for precise corrections in the field. Adjustment travel for windage or elevation is 76 inches. The combination of an exact 6X magnification, adjustable objective and target-style adjustments make it an excellent choice for Hunter Benchrest Competitions as well. Leupold's exclusive Multicoat 4 lens coating is applied to all air-to-glass surfaces to provide the 6X42mm maximum light transmission.

Length: 12". *Weight:* 11.5 ounces *Two reticles styles:* classic Duplex or a 3/4-minute Military Dot. Black matte finish.

Matte finish	$616.10
With 3/4-minute Military Dot	750.00

Also available: VARI-X III 4.5-14X50mm
LONG RANGE TACTICAL	$1,026.80
w/3/4-Mil. Dot	1,160.75
w/Target Dot	1,080.40

FIXED POWER SCOPES

M8-4X

The 4X delivers a widely used magnification and a generous
field of view	$362.50
In black matte finish	383.90

M8-4X

M8-6X

The 6X extends the range for big-game hunting and doubles in some cases as a varmint scope **$385.70**

M8-6X

M8-6X42mm

Large 42mm objective lens features increased light-gathering capability and a 7mm exit pupil. Recommended for varmint shooting at night.
Duplex or Heavy Duplex	$478.60
In matte finish	500.00

M8-6X42mm

VARMINT SCOPES

M8-12X40MM STANDARD (Adj. Obj.)

Outstanding optical qualities, resolution and magnification make the 12X a natural for the varmint shooter. Adjustable objective is standard for parallax-free focusing.
Duplex	$535.70
With CPC reticle or Dot	589.30

Also available:
VARI-X III 6.5-20X40mm VARMINT (Adj. Obj.) Target
Dot w/Multicoat 4 (matte only) **$876.80**

M8-12X40mm STANDARD

NIKON MONARCH SCOPES

6.5-20X44 AO

2-7X32

RIFLESCOPES

MODEL 6500 4x40 Lustre $284.00
MODEL 6505 4x40 Matte 304.00
MODEL 6510 2-7x32 Lustre 367.00
MODEL 6515 2-7x32 Matte 387.00
MODEL 6520 3-9x40 Lustre 371.00
MODEL 6525 3-9x40 Matte 391.00
MODEL 6530 3.5-10x50 Lustre 554.00
MODEL 6535 3.5-10x50 Matte 572.00

MODEL 6540 4-12x40 AO Lustre 476.00
MODEL 6545 4-12x40 AO Matte 496.00
MODEL 6550 6.5-20x44 AO Lustre 591.00
MODEL 6555 6.5-20x44 AO Matte 612.00
MODEL 6570 6.5-20x44 HV 591.00
MODEL 6575 6.5-20x44 HV 612.00

HANDGUN SCOPES

MODEL 6560 2x20 EER Black Lustre $213.00
MODEL 6565 2x20 EER Silver 233.00

MONARCH™ UCC RIFLESCOPE SPECIFICATIONS

Model	4x40	2-7x32	3-9x40	3.5-10x50	4-12x40 AO	6.5-20x44 AO	6.5-20x44 AO Hunting	2x20 EER
Lustre	#6500	#6510	#6520	#6530	#6540	#6550	#6570	#6560
Matte	#6505	#6515	#6525	#6535	#6545	#6555	#6575	-
Silver	-	-	-	-	-	-	-	#6565
Actual Magnification	4x	2x-7x	3x-9x	3.5-10x	4x-12x	6.5x-19.46x	6.5x-19.46x	1.75x
Objective Diameter	40mm	32mm	40mm	50mm	40mm	44mm	44mm	20mm
Exit Pupil	10mm	16-4.6mm	13.3-4.4mm	14.3-5mm	10-3.3mm	6.7-2.2mm	6.7-2.2mm	10mm
Eye Relief	89mm 3.5 in.	101-93mm 3.9-3.6 in.	93-90mm 3.6-3.5 in.	100-98mm 3.9-3.8 in.	92-87mm 3.6-3.4 in.	89-81mm 3.5-3.1 in.	89-81mm 3.5-3.1 in.	670-267mm 26.4-10.5 in.
Field of View at 100 yards	26.9 ft.	44.5-12.7 ft.	33.8-11.3 ft.	25.5-8.9 ft.	25.6-8.5 ft.	16.1-5.4 ft.	16.1-5.4 ft.	22.0 ft.
Tube Diameter	25.4mm 1 in.	25.4mm 1 in.	25.4mm 1 in.	25.4mm 1 in.	25.4mm 1 in.	25.4mm 1 in.	25.4mm 1 in.	25.4mm 1 in.
Objective Tube Diameter	47.3mm 1.86 in.	39.3mm 1.5 in	47.3mm 1.86 in.	57.3mm 2.2 in.	53.1mm 2.09 in.	54mm 2.13 in.	54mm 2.13 in.	25.4mm 1 in.
Eyepiece O.D. Diameter	38mm 1.5 in.	38mm 1.5 in.	38mm 1.5 in.	38mm 1.5 in.	38mm 1.5 in.	38mm 1.5 in.	38mm 1.5 in.	35.5mm 1.4 in.
Length	297mm 11.7 in.	283mm 11.1 in.	312mm 12.3 in.	350mm 13.7 in.	348.5mm 13.7 in.	373mm 14.6 in.	373mm 14.6 in.	207mm 8.1 in.
Weight	315 g. 11.2 oz.	315 g. 11.2 oz.	355 g. 12.6 oz.	435 g. 15.5 oz.	475 g. 16.9 oz.	565 g. 20.1 oz.	565 g. 20.1 oz.	185 g. 6.6 oz.
Adjustment Graduation	¼:1 Click ½:1 Div.	¼:1 Click ¼:1 Div.	¼:1 Click ¼:1 Div.	¼:1 Click ¼:1 Div.	¼:1 Click ¼:1 Div.	⅛:1 Click ⅛:1 Div.	⅛:1 Click ⅛:1 Div.	¼:1 Click ½:1 Div.
Max. Internal Adjustment (moa)	120	70	55	45	45	38	38	120
Parallax Setting (yards)	100	100	100	100	50 to infinity	50 to infinity	50 to infinity	100

NIKON BUCKMASTER RIFLESCOPES

SPECIAL LIMITED EDITION
3-9x40

NIKON BUCKMASTER RIFLESCOPES

Nikon has teamed with Buckmasters to produce a limited edition riflescope line. The first products in this new line are a 3-9x40 variable, a large objective 3-9x50 variable and a 4x40 fixed power scope. Built to withstand the toughest hunting conditions, the new scopes integrate shockproof, fogproof and waterproof construction, plus numerous other features seldom found on riflescopes in this price range. Nikon's Brightvue™ anti-reflective system of quality, multicoated lenses provides over 93% anti-reflection capability for high levels of light transmission and optical clarity required for dawn-to-dusk big game hunting. These riflescopes are parallax-adjusted at 100 yards and have durable matte finishes that reduce glare while afield. They also feature positive steel-to-brass, quarter-minute-click windage and elevation adjustments for instant, repeatable accuracy and a Nikoplex® reticle for quick target acquisition.

Prices:

MODEL 6405 4x40 BUCKMASTER	$237.00
MODEL 6425 3-9x40 BUCKMASTER	299.00
MODEL 6435 3-9x50 BUCKMASTER	439.00

SPECIFICATIONS

	4x40	3-9x40	3-9x50
MODEL	#6405	#6425	#6435
Actual Magnification	4x	3x-9x	3x-9x
Objective Diameter	40mm	40mm	50mm
Exit Pupil	10mm	13.3-4.4mm	16.7-5.5mm
Eye Relief	3.5 in.	3.6-3.5 in.	3.6-3.5 in.
Field of View at 100 yards	26.9 ft.	33.8-11.3 ft.	33.8-11.3 ft.
Tube Diameter	1 in.	1 in.	1 in.
Objective Tube Diameter	1.86 in.	1.86 in.	2.2 in.
Eyepiece O.D. Diameter	1.5 in.	1.5 in.	1.5 in.
Length	11.7 in.	12.3 in.	12 in.
Weight	11.2 oz.	12.6 oz.	12.7 oz.
Adjustment Graduation	1/4: 1 Click / 1/2: 1 Div.	1/4: 1 Click / 1/4: 1 Div.	1/4: 1 Click / 1/4: 1 Div.
Max. Internal Adjustment (moa)	120	55	55
Parallax Setting (yards)	100	100	100

PENTAX RIFLESCOPES

LIGHTSEEKER RIFLESCOPES

2.5 LIGHTSEEKER SG PLUS
MOSSY OAK® BREAK-UP SCOPE

ZERO-X/V SG PLUS
TURKEY STILL-TARGET COMPETITION

LIGHTSEEKER RIFLESCOPE SPECIFICATIONS

Model	Objective Diameter (MM)	Eyepiece Diameter (MM)	Exit Pupil (MM)	Eye Relief (IN.)	Field of View (FT 100 YD)	Adjustment Graduation (IN 100YD)	Maximum Adjustment (IN 100 YD)	Length (IN.)	Weight (OZ.)	Reticle*	Recommended Use**	Prices
LIGHTSEEKER 1.75X-6X	35	36	15.3-5	3.5-4.0	71-20	1/2	110	10.75	13.0	HP	BG,DB,SG/P	$546.00
LIGHTSEEKER 2X-8X	39	36	11.0-4.0	3.5-4.0	53-17	1/3	80	11.7	14.0	P	BG,DB,SG/P	594.00
LIGHTSEEKER 3X-9X	43	36	12.0-5.0	3.5-4.0	36-14	1/4	50	12.7	15.0	P or HP	BG	628.00
COLORADO CLASSIC 3X-9X	40	36	8.5-4.2	3-32.5	38-14.7	1/2	50	13.0	15.0	P	BG,SG/P	440.00
LIGHTSEEKER 3X-11X AO	43	36	11.0-3.5	3.5-4.0	38.5-13	1/4	50	13.3	19.0	P	BG,V	720.00
LIGHTSEEKER 3.5X-10X	50	36	11.0-5.0	3.5-4.0	29.5-11	1/4	50	14.0	19.5	HP	BG,V	652.00
LIGHTSEEKER 4X-16X AO	44	36	10.4-2.8	3.5-4.0	33-9	1/4	35	15.4	22.7	FP or HP	T,V,BG	816.00
LIGHTSEEKER 6X-24X AO	44	36	6.9-2.3	3.5-4.0	18-5.5	1/8	26	16.0	23.7	FP or D	T,V	856.00
LIGHTSEEKER 8.5X-32X AO	44	36	5.0-1.4	3.5-4.0	13-3.8	1/8	26	17.2	24.0	FP or MD	T,V	944.00
LIGHTSEEKER 2.5X SG PLUS	25	36	7.0	3.5-4.0	55	1/2	60	10.0	9.0	DW	BG,DG,TK	350.00
LIGHTSEEKER ZERO-X SG PLUS	27	35	19.5	4.5-15	51	1/2	196	8.9	7.9	DW	BG,DG,TK	372.00
LIGHTSEEKER ZERO-X/V SG PLUS	27	35	19.5-5.5	3.5-7	53.8-15	1/2	129	8.9	10.3	CP or HP	BG,DG,TK	454.00
LIGHTSEEKER ZERO-X/V SG PLUS TURKEY STILL-TARGET COMPETITION	27	35	19.5-5.5	3.5-7	53.8-1.5	1/2	129	8.9	10.3	CP or HP	BG,DG,TK	476.00

*All scope tubes measure 1 inch in diameter. Scopes are available in high-gloss black, matte black, satin chrome or camouflage, depending on model. *P = Penta-Plex FP = Fine-Plex DW = Deepwoods Plex D = Dot HP = Heavy Plex MD = Mil Dot **BG = Big Game SG/P = Small Game/Pinking V= Varmint DG = Dangerous Game T = Target TK = Turkey Add **$20** for matte finish*

PENTAX SCOPES

LIGHTSEEKER II RIFLESCOPES

4X-16XAO LIGHTSEEKER II
$844.00

3X-9X LIGHTSEEKER II
$636.00 (Glossy) $660.00 (Matte)

6X-24XAO LIGHTSEEKER II
$878.00

Features:

- **Scratch-resistant outer tube.** Under ordinary wear and tear, the outer tube is almost impossible to scratch.
- **High Quality cam zoom tube.** No plastics are used. The tube is made of a bearing-type brass with precision machined cam slots. The zoom control screws are precision-ground to 1/2 of one thousandth tolerance.
- **Leak Prevention.** The power rings are sealed on a separate precision-machined seal tube. The scopes are then filled with nitrogen and double-sealed with heavy-duty "O" rings, making them leak-proof and fog-proof.
- **Excellent eyepieces.** The eyepiece lenses have a greater depth of field than most others. Thus, a more focused target at 100, 200 or 500 yards is attainable. Most Pentax Riflescopes are available in High Gloss, Matte or Satin Chrome finish.

Also available:
LIGHTSEEKER PISTOLSCOPE SPECIFICATIONS

MODEL	OBJECTIVE DIAMETER (MM)	EYEPIECE DIAMETER (MM)	EXIT PUPIL (MM)	EYE RELIEF (IN.)	FIELD OF VIEW (FT 100 YD)	ADJUSTMENT GRADUATION (IN 100 YD)	MAXIMUM ADJUSTMENT (IN 100 YD)	LENGTH (IN.)	WEIGHT (OZ.)	RETICLE*
2X	22	30	29.0	10-24	21	1/2	70	8.8	6.8	P
1/5X-4X	22	30	29.0	11-25/11-18	16-11	1/4	55	10.0	11.0	P
2.5X-7X	36	30	15.1-5.7	11-28/9-14	12-7.5	1/6	40	12.0	12.5	P

QUARTON BEAMSHOT SIGHTS

BEAMSHOT 1000 ULTRA/SUPER

SPECIFICATIONS

Size: .75" X 2 $^3/_5$" (overall length)
Weight: 3.8 oz. (incl. battery & mount)
Construction: Aluminum 6061 T6
Finish: Black anodized **Cable length:** 5"
Range: 500 yards **Power:** <5mW Class IIIA Laser
Wave length: 650nm (Beamshot 1000U-635nm)
Power supply: 3V Lithium battery
Battery life: Approx. 20 hrs. (continuous)
Dot size: 5" at 10 yds.; 4" at 100 yds.
Prices:
STANDARD $50.00
SUPER 60.00
ULTRA 80.00
BORE SIGHT ARBOR 1 (.22-.264 DIAM.) 99.00
BORE SIGHT ARBOR 2 (.264-.308 DIAM.) 99.00
BORE SIGHT ARBOR 3 (.308-.35 DIAM.) 99.00

1000 (PLUS RV2 MOUNT)

1000 (PLUS P1A MOUNT)

BEAMSHOT 3000

SPECIFICATIONS

Size: $^3/_5$" X 2 (overall length)
Weight: 2 oz. (incl. battery)
Construction: Aluminum 6061 T6
Finish: Black **Cable length:** 5"
Range: 300 yards **Power:** <5mW Class IIIA Laser
Wave length: 670nm
Power supply: 3 SR44 silver oxide watch battery
Battery life: Approx. 4 hrs. (continuous)
Dot size: 0.5" at 10 yds.; 4" at 100 yds.
Prices:
SUPER $60.00
ULTRA 80.00

3000 (PLUS P4 MOUNT)

REDFIELD SCOPES

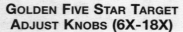

GOLDEN FIVE STAR TARGET ADJUST KNOBS (6X-18X)

LOW PROFILE WIDEFIELD 3X-9X VARIABLE

BENCHREST TARGET
40X40mm w/Abj. Obj. FCH Black Matte

LOW PROFILE WIDEFIELD

The Widefield®, with 25% more field of view than conventional scopes, lets you spot game quicker, stay with it and see other animals that might be missed.

The patented Low Profile design means a low mounting on the receiver, allowing you to keep your cheek tight on the stock for a more natural and accurate shooting stance, especially when swinging on running game.

The one-piece, fog-proof tube is machined with high tensile strength aluminum alloy and is anodized to a lustrous finish that's rust-free and virtually scratch-proof. Available in seven models.

Prices:

1 3/4X-5X LOW PROFILE VARIABLE POWER
113806 1 3/4X-5X 4 Plex $345.95

2X-7X LOW PROFILE VARIABLE POWER
111806 2X-7X 4 Plex 408.95

3X-9X LOW PROFILE VARIABLE POWER
112806 3X-9X 4 Plex 455.95

3X-9X LOW PROFILE ACCU-TRAC VARIABLE POWER
112810 3X-9X 4 Plex AT 511.95

2 3/4X LOW PROFILE FIXED POWER
141807 2 3/4X 4 Plex 292.95

4X LOW PROFILE FIXED POWER
143806 4X 4 Plex 319.95

6X LOW PROFILE FIXED POWER
146806 6X 4 Plex 345.95

3X-9X LOW PROFILE NICKEL MATTE VARIABLE POWER
112814 4 Plex 463.95

3X-9X LOW PROFILE BLACK MATTE VARIABLE POWER
112812 4 Plex 463.95

GOLDEN FIVE STAR SCOPES

This series of seven scopes incorporates the latest variable and fixed power scope features, including multi-coated and magnum recoil-resistant optical system, plus maximum light-gathering ability. Positive quarter-minute click adjustments for ease of sighting and optimum accuracy. Anodized finish provides scratch-resistant surface.

BENCHREST TARGET SCOPE

Redfield's new 40x40mm Benchrest Target Scope features Quick Zero™ windage and elevation target knobs with 1/4 minute click adjustments. It also has a fine reticle crosshair, an adjustable objective lens, and fully mult-coated lenses, in addition to standard Redfield features (one-piece aluminum alloy tube and Redfield's lifetime guarantee). Available in black matte, with an optional glare-reducing sunshade.

Price: **$695.00**

TARGET SCOPES

MODEL/DESCRIPTION	PRICE
180000/8x-32x 40mm Obj, 1/4 Dot, Blk	$712.95
180008/8x-32x 40mm Obj, 1/4 Dot, Blk/MT	729.95
185000/8x-32x 50mm Obj, 1/2 Dot, Blk	712.95
185008/8x-32x 40mm Obj, 1/2 Dot, Blk/Mt	729.95
187000/8x-32x 40mm Obj, 4 Plex Blk	712.95
187008/8x-32x 40mm Obj, 4 Plex Blk/Mt	729.95

GOLDEN FIVE STAR™ SCOPES

MODEL/DESCRIPTION	PRICE
116008/3x-9x 40mm Obj, Blk.	$363.95
116700/3x-9x 40mm Obj, Blk/Mt	371.95
116710/3x-9x 40mm Obj, Accu-Trac, Blk	414.95
116750/3x-9x 40mm Obj, Nkl/Mt	379.95
117006/4x-12x 40mm Adj. Obj, Blk	456.95
117008/4x-12x 40mm Adj. Obj, Blk/Mt	466.95
117700/4x-12x 40mm Adj. Obj, Accu-Trac, Blk/Mt	508.95
117709/4x-12x 40mm Adj. Obj, Trgt Knv, 117710/4x-12x 40mm Adj. Obj., Accu-Trac, Blk Blk/Mt	481.95
118006/6x-18x 40mm Adj. Obj. Blk	490.95
118007/6x-18x 40mm Adj. Obj, Blk/Mt	500.95
118008/6x-18x 40mm Adj. Obj, Trgt Knb, Blk	508.95
118010/6x-18x 40mm Adj. Obj, Trgt Knb	516.95
118700/6x-18x 40mm Adj. Obj, Accu-Trac, Blk/Mt	551.95

REDFIELD SCOPES

3X-9X WIDEFIELD® ILLUMINATOR
w/Nickel Matte Finish

TRACKER SE

30mm ULTIMATE ILLUMINATOR™ SCOPES

These scopes actually compensate for low light, letting you "see" contrasts between field and game. Optimum resolution, contrast, color correction, flatness of field, edge-to-edge sharpness and fidelity are improved by the air-spaced, triplet objective and advanced 5-element erector lens system. The Illuminators also feature a zero tolerance nylon cam follower and thrust washers to provide absolute point of impact hold through all power ranges. The one-piece tube construction is virtually indestructible, tested at 1200g acceleration forces, and fog-free through the elimination of potential leak paths. Offered in both the Traditional and Widefield® variable power configurations, the Illuminator is also available with the Accu-Trac® feature. Also offered in 30mm 3X-12X with a 56mm adj. obj.

Prices:

112904/3x-12x 56mm Adj. Obj, Blk **$826.95**
112908/3x-12x 56mm Adj. Obj,
   Duradize Blk/Satin **836.95**

WIDEFIELD® ILLUMINATOR SCOPES

112910/2X-7X 32mm Obj, Blk **$549.95**
112886/3X-9X 42mm Obj, Blk **623.95**
112880/3X-9X 42mm Obj, Accu-Trac, Blk **674.95**
112888/3X-9X 42mm Obj, Blk/Satin **632.95**
112890/3X-9X 42mm Obj, Accu-Trac, Blk/Satin . . **632.95**
112892/3X-9X 42mm Obj, Nkl/Mt. **632.95**
112708/3X-10X 50mm Obj, Blk/Satin **703.95**

GOLDEN FIVE STAR EXTENDED EYE RELIEF HANDGUN SCOPES

2X FIXED
140202 SCOUT SCOPE (Black matte) **$241.95**
140002 4 Plex. **234.95**
2X NICKEL PLATED FIXED
140003 4 Plex. **251.95**
4X FIXED
140005 4 Plex. **234.95**
4X NICKEL PLATED FIXED
140006 4 Plex. **251.95**
2-1/2X7-X VARIABLE
140008 4 Plex. **316.95**
2-1/2X-7X NICKEL PLATED VARIABLE
140009 4 Plex. **326.95**
2-1/2X-7X BLACK MATTE VARIABLE
140010 4 Plex. **326.95**

THE TRACKER

Redfield's Tracker SE features a rugged, one-piece tube design, fully-coated lenses, 1/4 minute click adjustments, and a hard-coat anodized finish. The Tracker SE is available in 15 models and is manufactured in the U.S. It is water-proof, shockproof, and backed by Redfield's lifetime warranty plus 90-day total satisfaction guarantee.

TRACKER SE™ SCOPES

MODEL/DESCRIPTION	PRICE
155400/Tracker SE 4x40 Black.	$200.95
125415/Tracker SE 4-40 Black Matte	207.95
125600/Tracker SE 6x40 Black.	200.95
125615/Tracker SE 6-40 Matte.	207.95
125232/Tracker SE 2-7x32 Black	241.95
125235/Tracker SE 2-7x32 Black Matte	249.95
125300/Tracker SE 3-9x40 Black/.	270.95
125315/Tracker SE 3-9x40 Matte.	278.95
125325/Tracker SE 3-9x40 Nickel.	268.95
125300/Tracker SE 3-9x50 Black	289.95
125385/Tracker SE 3-9x50 Matte	297.95
125450/Tracker SE 4-12x40 Black	292.95
125455/Tracker SE 4-12x40 Matte	301.95
125650/Tracker SE 6-18x40 Black	344.95
125655/Tracker SE 6-18x40 Matte	352.95

SCOUT SCOPE

REDFIELD SCOPES

TX-27 Scopes

REDFIELD ESD™ SCOPE

Redfield's ESD (electronic sighting device) makes sight alignment quick and easy. It features a multi-reticle selector that lets the shooter select instantly between four reticle sight patterns. By clicking the dial, the shooter can quickly change the sight pattern to match the current shooting condition. For total sight control under various lighting conditions, there is a ten-position brightness control. The ESD is constructed from aircraft-grade aluminum alloy that is shockproof, fogproof and strong, yet it weighs a mere 6 oz. Its hard-coat anodizing ensures a scratch-resistant silver matte finish. The 30mm diameter tube and fully coated double reflex lens system provides a bright, clear image free of parallax. Elevation and windage are finger adjustable in 1/4 minute clicks. Each Redfield ESD comes with rings and lens covers. It is powered by a large capacity lithium battery that last four times as long as conventional batteries.

Model/Description	Price
310000/Multi-Reticle Sight	$399.95
315000/Variable Dot Sight	366.95
315250/Silver Multi Reticle Unit	418.95
310001/ESD Replacement Battery	7.95

TX-27 SCOPE

Redfield's new TX-27 scope series features an optically optimized 27 mm diameter one-piece scope tube; exceptional quality lenses, fully multi-coated with Infinicoat IV; Quick-Zero finger adjustable low profile windage and elevation knobs; extra long eye relief; parallax and eyepiece focus adjustments; plus Duradize hard-coat anodized finish and Redfield's lifetime warranty. The TX-27 eliminates the need for a mount. The lens is sealed into the objective, then secured by the locking ring.

Model/Description	Price
160400/TX-274x40mm	$473.95
160200/TX-272.5-10x 44mm	565.95
160300/TX-27 3.5-14x40mm w/Adj., Obj.	600.95
160350/TX-27 3.5-14x50mm w/Turret Parallax Adj.	644.95
160600/TX-27 5-20x44mm w/Turret Parallax Adj.	686.95

VARMINT SCOPES (Not Shown)

Redfield's Varmint scope has 50mm objective lens that allows a better view of the target and makes parallax adjustments quick and easy. For precision adjustments for windage and elevation, Redfield offers Quick-Zero™ target knobs that are easy and convenient to adjust in changing conditions and ranges. A solid one-piece tube, machined from aircraft-grade aluminum alloy, is guaranteed not to fog, even under the most adverse conditions. Quick-Zero target knobs allow fast adjustment of the rifle for changes in elevation and wind in guaranteed 1/4-minute clicks, then reset to original "0" mark. Sight in at 100 yards, dial up for pinpoint accuracy at 300 yards, then quickly re-dial back.

The Varmint scope is available in black or black matte with a protective hard-coat anodized finish.

Model/Description	Price
119000/6x-24x50mm Obj, Fine Crosshair, Blk	$659.95
119008/6x-24x50mm Obj. Fine Crosshair, Blk/Mt	675.95
119006/6x-24x50mm Obj, 4 Plex, Blk	659.95
119116/6x-24x50mm Obj, 4 Plex, Blk/Mt	675.95
119002/6x-24x50mm Obj, 1/4 Dot, Blk	675.95
119112/6x-24x50mm Obj, 1/4 Dot, Blk/Mt	695.95

SAKO SCOPE MOUNTS

"ORIGINAL" SCOPE MOUNTS

"ORIGINAL" SCOPE MOUNTS

SAKO's "Original" scope mounts are designed and engineered to exacting specifications, which is traditional to all SAKO products. The dovetail mounting system provides for a secure and stable system that is virtually immovable. Unique to this Sako mount is a synthetic insert that provides maximum protection against possible scope damage. It also affords additional rigidity by compressing itself around the scope. Manufactured in Finland.

Prices:

1" LOW, MEDIUM & HIGH
(Short, Medium & Long Action) $98.00
30mm LOW, MEDIUM & HIGH
(Short, Medium & Long Action) 116.00
1" MEDIUM & HIGH EXTENDED BASE
SCOPE MOUNTS 154.00

"NEW" SCOPE MOUNTS

SCOPE MOUNTS

These SAKO scope mounts are lighter, yet stronger than ever. Tempered steel allows the paring of every last gram of unnecessary weight without sacrificing strength. Like the original mount, these rings clamp directly to the tapered dovetails on Sako rifles, thus eliminating the need for separate bases. Grooves inside the rings preclude scope slippage even under the recoil of the heaviest calibers. Nicely streamlined and finished in a rich blue-black to complement any Sako rifle.

Prices:

Low, medium, or high (1") $116.00
Medium or high (30mm) 135.00

SCHMIDT & BENDER RIFLE SCOPES

2.5-10X56 VARIABLE POWER SCOPE
$1298.00

Also available:
1.25-4X20 VARIABLE POWER SCOPE $945.00
1.5-6X42 VARIABLE POWER SCOPE 1073.00
3-12X42 VARIABLE POWER SCOPE. 1222.00
3-12X50 VARIABLE POWER SCOPE. 1262.00
Note: All variable power scopes have glass reticles and
are available in steel and aluminum

Also available:
4X36 FIXED POWER SCOPE
1" Steel Tube w/o Mounting Rail $725.00
6X42 FIXED POWER SCOPE
Steel Tube w/o Mounting Rail 795.00
8X56 FIXED POWER SCOPE
Steel Tube w/o Mounting Rail 915.00
10X42 FIXED POWER SCOPE
Steel Tube w/o Mounting Rail 910.00

L.E.R. 1.25-4X20

The Safari is designed for use on magnum rifles and for
hunting large game. A newly designed ocular results in a
longer eye relief, providing a wide field of view (31.5 yards at
200 yards).

Magnification: 1.25-4X
Objective lens diameter: 12.7-20mm
Field of view at 100m: 32m-10m; at 100 yards: 96'-16'
Objective housing diameter: 30mm
Scope tube diameter: 30mm
Twilight factor: 3,7-8,9
Lenses: hard multi-coating
Click value 1 click @100 meters: 15mm; @100 yards: .540"
Also available: 3-12X42 and 4-16X50
Price: $990.00

VARMINT

Designed for long-range target shooters and varmint
hunters, Schmidt & Bender 4-16X50 "Varmint" riflescope
features a precise parallax adjustment located in a third
turret on the left side of the scope, making setting adjustments quick and convenient. The fine crosshairs of Reticle
No. 6 and 8-dot cover only 1.5mm at 100 meters (.053" at
100 yards) throughout the entire magnification range.

Magnification: 4-16X *Objective lens diameter:* 50mm
Field of view at 100m: 7.5-2.5m; at 100 yards: 22.5'-7.5'
Objective housing diameter: 57mm
Scope tube diameter: 30mm *Twilight factor:* 14-28
Lenses: Hard multi-coating
Click value 1 click @100 meters: 10mm; @100 yards: .360"
Price: $1,450.00

POLICE/MARKSMAN RIFLESCOPES

This line of riflescopes was designed specifically to meet the
needs of the precision sharpshooter. It includes fixed-power
scopes in 6X42 and 10X42 magnifications and variable-
power scopes in 1.5-6X42, 3-12X42 and 3-12X50 configurations. The 3-12X50 is available in two models: Standard
(for shooting to 500 yards) and a military version (MIL)
designed for ranges up to 1000 yards. Each scope is
equipped with two elevation adjustment rings: a neutral ring
with 1/4" 100-yard clicks, which can be matched to any
caliber and bullet weight, and a second ring calibrated for

POLICE/MARKSMAN
3.12X50mm w/DETACHABLE
RUBBER SUNSHADE AND
BRYANT P-RANGEFINDING RETICLE

the .308 caliber bullet. The 1.5-6X42 is calibrated for
the 150-grain bullet, while all other rings are calibrated
for the 168-grain bullet. The military elevation adjustment
ring has 1" @100-yard clicks, except for the MIL scope
which has 1/2" @100-yard clicks.

6X42. . . . . $900.00
10X42. . . . . 950.00
1.5-6X42 . . . . 1,200.00
3-12X42. . . . . 1,360.00
3-12X50. . . . . 1,400.00
3-12X50 MI 1,425.00

SIMMONS SCOPES

SCOPES

AETEC

MODEL 2101

MODELS 2100/2101/2102
2.8-10X44 WA
Field of view: 44'-14'
Eye relief: 5"
Length: 11.9"
Weight: 15.5 oz.
Reticle: Truplex
Price: $356.95

AETEC SCOPE MODEL 2101
2.8-10x44 WA ASPHERICAL LENS SYSTEM
W/SUNSHADE, BLACK MATTE (not shown)

Also available:
MODEL 2104
3.8-12X44 WA/AO
Aspherical Lens System w/sunshade, black matte
Price: $389.95
MODEL 2107
6-20X44mm AO
Price: $412.95
MODEL 2113
6-20X50mm AO
Price: $435.95

44 MAG RIFLESCOPES

MODEL M1044 (Black Matte)
3-10X44mm
Field of view: 34'-10.5' *Eye relief:* 3"
Length: 12.8" *Weight:* 15.5 oz.
Price: $253.95

MODEL M1050DM
44 DIAMOND MAG (Black Matte)
RANGE-CALCULATING SMART RETICLE
(Black Matte)
3.8-12X44mm
Field of view: 30'-9.5' *Eye relief:* 3"
Length: 13.2" *Weight:* 18.25 oz.
Price: $356.95

MODEL M1045 (Black Matte)
4-12X44mm
Field of view: 29.5'-9.5' *Eye relief:* 3"
Length: 13.2" *Weight:* 18.25 oz.
Price: $310.95

MODEL M1050DM

MODEL M1047 (Black Matte)
6.5-20X44mm
Field of view: 16'-6' *Eye relief:* 2.6"-3.4"
Length: 12.8" *Weight:* 19.5 oz.
Price: $322.95
Also available:
MODEL M1048
6.5-20X44 Target Turrets Black Matte (1/8" MOA) . $368.95
  with Sunshade: $382.90
MODEL M3044 (Silver Matte)
3-10X44mm
Field of view: 34'-10.5' *Eye relief:* 3"
Length: 12.75" *Weight:* 15.5 oz.
Price: $278.95

PROHUNTER RIFLESCOPES

MODEL 7710

MODEL 7710
3-9X40mm Wide Angle Riflescope
Field of view: 36'-13' *Eye relief:* 3" *Length:* 12.6"
Weight: 13.5 oz. *Features:* Truplex reticle; silver matte finish
Price: $148.95
(Same in black matte or black polish, Models 7711 and 7712)

Also available:
MODEL 7700 2-7X32 Black Matte $137.95
MODEL 7716 4-12X40 Black Matte AO 176.95
MODEL 7720 6-18X40 (adj. obj. Black)......... 195.95
MODEL 7721 6-18X40 AO Black Matte 195.95
MODEL 7740 6X40 Black Matte............... 130.95

SIMMONS SCOPES
(featuring Extra Large 50mm Obj. Lenses)

PRO 50 RIFLESCOPES

MODEL 8800

MODEL #8800
SPECIFICATIONS
Magnification: 4-1X
Field Of View: 27'-9'
Eye Relief: 3.5"
Length: 13.2"
Weight: 18.25 oz.
Reticle: Truplex
Finish: Black matte
Price: $238.95

MODEL #8810 (not shown)
SPECIFICATIONS
Magnification: 6-18X
Field Of View: 17'-5.8'
Eye Relief: 3.6"
Length: 13.2"
Weight: 18.25 oz.
Reticle: Truplex
Finish: Black matte
Price: $259.95

PROHUNTER PISTOL SCOPES

MODEL 7738 (4X)

MODEL 7732 (2X)

MODEL #7732/7733 (Silver Matte)
SPECIFICATIONS
Magnification: 2X
Field Of View: 22'
Eye Relief: 9-17"
Length: 8.75"
Weight: 7 oz.
Reticle: Truplex
Finish: Black matte
Price: $148.95

MODEL #7738/7739 (Silver Matte)
SPECIFICATIONS
Magnification: 4X
Field Of View: 15'
Eye Relief: 11.8-17.6"
Length: 9"
Weight: 8 oz.
Reticle: Truplex
Finish: Black matte
Price: $160.95

SIMMONS SCOPES

*Simmons' **Whitetail Classic Series** features fully coated lenses and glare-proof BlackGranite finish.*

MODEL WTC11

MODEL WTC12

MODEL WTC13

MODEL WTC11 (Black Granite)
1.5-5X20mm
Field of view: 75'-23'
Eye relief: 3.4"
Length: 9.3"
Weight: 9.7 oz.
Price: $199.95

MODEL WTC12
2.5-8X36mm
Field of view: 45'-14'
Eye relief: 3.2"
Length: 11.3
Weight: 13 oz.
Price: $218.95

MODEL WTC13 (Black Granite)
3.5-10X40mm
Field of view: 30'-10.5'
Eye relief: 3.2"
Length: 12.4" *Weight:* 13.5 oz.
Price: $229.95

MODEL WTC15/35
3.5-10X50 Black Granite
Field of view: 29.5-11.5' *Eye relief:* 3.2"
Length: 12.75" *Weight:* 13.5 oz.
Price: $310.95

MODEL WTC16
4X40 Black Granite
Field of view: 36.8'
Eye relief: 4"
Length: 9.9"
Weight: 12 oz.
Price: $158.95

MODEL WTC23 (Black Polished)
3.5-10X40
Field of view: 30'-10.5'
Eye relief: 3.2"
Length: 12.4"
Weight: 13.5 oz.
Price: $229.95

MODEL WTC33
3.5-10X40 Silver Granite
Same specifications as
Model WTC23
Price: $229.95

MODEL WTC 45 (Black Granite)
4.5-14X40 AO
Field of view: 22.5'-8.6'
Eye relief: 3.2"
Weight: 14 oz.
Price: $287.95

SIMMONS SCOPES

GOLD MEDAL SILHOUETTE/VARMINT SERIES

Simmons Gold Medal Silhouette/Varmint Riflescopes are made of state-of-the-art drive train and erector tube design, a new windage and elevation indexing mechanism, camera-quality 100% multicoated lenses, and a super smooth objective focusing device. High silhouette-type windage and elevation turrets house 1/8 minute click adjustments. The scopes have a black matte finish and choice of dot or crosshair reticle and are fogproof, waterproof and shockproof.

MODEL 23002

MODEL 3007 V-TAC
RIFLESCOPE

MODEL #23002
6-20X44mm AO
Field of view: 17.4'-5.4' *Eye relief:* 2.6-3.4"
Length: 14.75" *Weight:* 19.75 oz.
Feature: 100% Multi-Coat Lens System, black matte finish, obj. focus
Price: Crosshair............................$646.95
Also available:
MODEL 23012 (dot reticle)...................$646.95

MODEL 3006V-TAC
3-9x40 Black Matte Range-calculating V-Tac Reticle
Field of view: 33'-14.5'
Eye relief: 4.1"-3.0"
Length: 12.5"
Weight: 17 oz.
Price: $807.95
Also available:
4.5-14X44 AO w/range-calculating reticle......$877.95

GOLD MEDAL HANDGUN SERIES

Simmons Gold Medal handgun scopes offer long eye relief, no tunnel vision, light weight, high resolution, non-critical head alignment, compact size and durability to withstand the heavy recoil of today's powerful handguns. In black and silver finishes, all have fully multicoated lenses and a Truplex reticle.

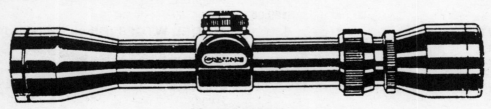

MODEL 22001

MODEL #22001
2.5-7X28mm
Field of view: 11'-4'
Eye relief: 15.7"-19.7"
Length: 9.3"
Weight: 9 oz.
Feature: Truplex reticle, 100% Multi-Coat Lens System, black polished finish.
Price: $299.95

MODEL #22002
2.5-7X28mm
Field of view: 11'-4' *Eye relief:* 15.7"-19.7"
Length: 9.3" *Weight:* 9 oz. *Feature:* Truplex reticle, 100% Multi-Coat Lens System, black polished finish.
Price: $299.95
Also Available:
MODEL #22003 2X20 ....$229.95
MODEL #22004 2X20 ....229.95
1.5-4X28 (black matte) 22008.............287.95

SIMMONS SCOPES

1022T RIMFIRE TARGET SCOPE

Magnification: 3-9X32mm AO
Finish: Black matte
Features: Adjustable for windage and elevation; adjustable objective lens, target knobs
Price: $183.95
Also available:
1022 4X32 black matte w/22 rings $77.95
1031 4X28 22 Mag Mini black matte w/22 rings ... 83.95
1032 4X28 22 Mag Mini silver matte w/22 rings ... 86.00
1033 4X32 silver matte w/22 rings 79.95
1037 3-9X32 silver matte w/22 rings........... 90.95
1039 3-9X32 black matte w/22 rings 88.95

1022T RIMFIRE TARGET SCOPE

BLACKPOWDER SCOPES

MODEL BP2732M

MODEL BP2732M
Magnification: 2-7X32 *Finish:* Black matte
Field of view: 57.7'-16.6' 100 yards *Eye relief:* 3"
Reticle: Truplex *Length:* 11.6" *Weight:* 12.4 oz.
Price: $144.95
Also available:
MODELS BP400M/400S
4X20 Black Matte or Silver Matte, Long Body

Field of view: 28' *Eye relief:* 5.0"
Length: 10.25" *Weight:* 8.7 oz. *Reticle:* Truplex
Price: $51.95

MODELS BPO420M/420S
4X20 Octagon Body
Field of view: 19.5' *Eye relief:* 4"
Length: 7.5" *Weight:* 8.3 oz. *Reticle:* Truplex
Price: $125.95

SHOTGUN SCOPES

MODEL 7790D

MODELS 21004/7790D
Magnification: 4X32
Finish: Black matte
Field of view: 16' (Model 21004); 17' (Model 7790D)
Eye relief: 5.5"
Reticle: Truplex (Model 21004); ProDiamond (Model 7790D)
Length: 8.5" (8.8" Model 21004)
Weight: 8.75 oz. (9.1 oz. Model 7790D)

Prices:
MODEL 21004 .... $90.95
MODEL 7790D 125.95
Also available:
MODEL 21005 2.5X20 Black matte (Truplex reticle). $67.95
MODEL 7789D 2X32 Black matte
  (ProDiamond reticle) 114.95
MODEL 7791D 1.5-5X20 WA Black matte
  (ProDiamond reticle) 148.95

SWAROVSKI RIFLESCOPES

HUNTER PH SERIES

(Prices on following page)

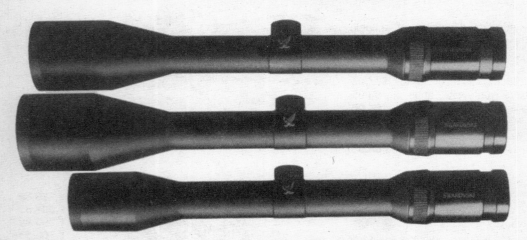

3-12X50

2.5-10X56

2.5-10X42

SPECIFICATIONS HUNTER PH SERIES (*see* following page for additional PH Models)

Type	Magnification	Effective objective lens diameter	Exit pupil diameter	Eye relief	Field of view	Field of view	Subjective field of view	Dioptric correction	Twilight performance acc. to DIN 58388	Impact point correction per click	Max. elevation/ windage adjustment range	Length	Weight (approx.)		
													S	L	LS
		in/mm	in/mm	in/mm	ft/100 yds m/100 m	degrees	degrees	dpt		in/100 yds mm/100 m	in/100 yds m/100 m	in/mm	oz/g	oz/g	oz/g
PF															
6x42	6x	1.65 42	0.28 7	3.15 80	21 7	4	23.2	+2-3	15.9	0.36 10	47 1.3	12.83 326	17.3 490	12.0 340	13.4 380
8x50	8x	1.97 50	0.25 6.25	3.15 80	15.6 5.2	3	23.2	+2-3	20	0.36 10	40 1.1	13.94 354	21.5 610	14.8 420	15.9 450
8x56	8x	2.20 56	0.28 7	3.15 80	15.6 5.2	3	23.2	+2-3	21.2	0.36 10	47 1.3	14.29 363	24.0 680	16.6 470	17.6 500
PV															
1.25-4x24	1.25-4x	0.94 24	0.49-0.24 12.5-6	3.15 80	98.4-31.2 32.8-10.4	18.6-6	23.2	+2-3	3.5-9.8	0.54 15	119 3.3	10.63 270	16.2 460	12.7 360	13.8 390
1.5-6x42	1.5-6x	1.65 42	0.52-0.28 13.1-7	3.15 80	65.4-21 21.8-7	12.4-4	23.2	+2-3	4.2-15.9	0.36 10	79 2.2	12.99 330	20.8 590	16.2 460	17.5 495
2.5-10x42	2.5-10x	1.65 42	0.52-0.17 13.1-4.2	3.15 80	39.6-12.6 13.2-4.2	7.5-2.4	23.2	+2-3	7.1-20.5	0.36 10	47 1.3	13.23 336	19.8 560	15.2 430	16.4 465
2.5-10x56	2.5-10x	2.20 56	0.52-0.22 13.1-5.6	3.15 80	39.6-12.3 13.2-4.1	7.5-2.4	23.2	+2-3	7.1-23.7	0.36 10	47 1.3	14.72 374	24.5 695	18.7 530	20.1 570
3-12x50	3-12x	1.97 50	0.52-0.17 13.1-4.2	3.15 80	33-10.5 11-3.5	6.3-2	23.2	+2-3	8.5-24.5	0.36 10	40 1.1	14.33 364	22.4 635	16.9 480	18.3 520
PF-N															
8x50	8x	1.97 50	0.25 6.25	3.15 80	15.6 5.2	3	23.2	+2-3	20	0.36 10	40 1.1	13.94 354	21.5 610	14.8 420	15.9 450
8x56	8x	2.20 56	0.28 7	3.15 80	15.6 5.2	3	23.2	+2-3	21.2	0.36 10	47 1.3	14.29 363	24.0 680	16.6 470	17.6 500

SWAROVSKI RIFLESCOPES

6-24X50mm PROFESSIONAL HUNTER "PH" RIFLESCOPE

Swarovski's 6-24X500mm "PH" riflescope was developed for long-range target, big-game and varmint shooting. Its waterproof parallax adjustment system should be popular with White Tail "Bean Field Shooters" and long-range varmint hunters looking for a choice of higher powers in a premium rifle scope and still deliver accuracy. The new scope will also appeal to many bench rest shooters who compete in certains classes where power and adjustment are limited. A non-magnifying, fine plex reticle and an all-new fine crosshair reticle with 1/8" MOA dot are available in the 6-24X50mm scope. Reticle adjustment clicks are 1/6" (minute) by external, waterproof "target turrets." The internal optical system features a patented coil spring suspension system for dependablle accuracy and positive reticle adjustment. The objective bell, 30mm middle tube, turret housing and ocular bell connection are machined from one solid bar of aluminum.

Price: **$1,665.50**

PRICES PH SERIES RIFLESCOPES

PF 6x42 (4A, 7A)	**$921.11**
PF 8x50 (4A, 7A)	**954.44**
w/illum reticle (4N, PLEXN)	**1,343.33**
PF 8x56 (4A, 7A)	**998.89**
w/illum reticle (4N, PLEXN)	**1,388.88**
PH 1.25-4x24 (4A)	**998.89**
PH 1.5-6x42 (4A, 7A)	**1,132.22**
aluminum only (#24)	**1,165.56**
PH 2.5-10x42 (4A, 7A)	**1,298.89**
aluminum only (PLEX)	**1,298.89**
PH 2.5-10x56 (4A, 7A)	**1,398.89**
aluminum only (PLEX)	**1,398.89**
w/illum reticle (4N, PLEXN)	**1,765.55**
PH 3-12x50 (4A, 7A)	**1,376.67**
aluminum only (PLEX)	**1,376.67**
w/illum reticle (4N, PLEXN)	**1,698.88**
PH 6-24x50 (aluminum only) (PLEX, DOT, FINE) .	**1,665.56**
Same as above w/4, PLEX	**1,532.22**

SPECIFICATIONS HUNTER PH SERIES (cont.)

Type	Magnification	Effective objective lens diameter	Exit pupil diameter	Eye relief	Field of view	Field of view	Subjective field of view	Dioptric correction	Twilight performance acc. to DIN 58388	Impact point correction per click	Max. elevation/windage adjustment range	Length	Weight (approx.) S	L	LS
PV-N															
2.5-10x56	2.5-10x	2.20 56	0.52-0.22 13,1-5,6	3.15 80	39.6-12.3 13.2-4.1	7.5-2.4	23.2	+2-3	7.1-23.7	0.36 10	47 1.3	14.72 374	24.5 695	18.7 530	20.1 570
3-12x50	3-12x	1.97 50	0.52-0.17 13.1-4.2	3.15 80	33-10.5 11-3.5	6.3-2	23.2	+2-3	8.5-24.5	0.36 10	40 1.1	14.33 364	22.4 635	16.9 480	18.3 520
PV-S															
6-24x50 P	6-24x	1.97 50	0.33-0.08 8.3-2.1	3.15 80	18.6-5.4 6.2-1.8	3.5-1	23.2	+2-3	7.1-34.6	0.17 4.8	E. 43/1.2 W: 25/0.7	15.43 392	–	24.5 695	–
Nova-A															
4x32 A	4x	1.26 32	0.31 8	3.15 80	30 10	5.7	22.8	±2.5	11.3	0.25 7	100 2.8	11.42 290	–	10.8 305	–
6x36 A	6x	1.42 36	0.24 6	3.15 80	21 7	4	22.8	±2.5	14.7	0.25 7	90 2.5	11.93 303	–	11.5 325	–
1.5-4.5x20 A	1.5-4.5x	0.79 20	0.50-0.17 12.7-4.4	3.35 85	75-25.8 25-8.6	14.2-4.9	22.7	±2.5	4.2-9.4	0.50 14	110 3	9.53 242	–	10.6 300	–
3-9x36 A	3-9x	1.42 36	0.47-0.16 12-4	3.35 85	39-13.5 13-4.5	7.4-2.6	22.7	±2.5	8.5-18	0.25 7	60 1.6	11.93 303	–	13.0 370	–
3-10x42 A	3.3-10x	1.65 42	0.50-0.17 12.6-4.2	3.35 85	33-11.7 11-3.9	6.3-2.2	22.7	±2.5	9.3-20.5	0.25 7	50 1.4	12.52 318	–	13.7 390	–

S: Steel • L: Alloy • LS: Alloy with rail

TASCO SCOPES

MODEL 1.75X-5X

WORLD CLASS™ WIDE-ANGLE® RIFLESCOPES

Features:
- 25% larger field of view
- Exceptional optics
- Fully coated for maximum light transmission

- Waterproof, shockproof, fogproof
- Non-removable eye bell
- Free haze filter lens caps
- TASCO's unique World Class Lifetime Warranty

The Model 1.75X-5X member of Tasco's World Class Wide Angle line offers a wide field of view — 72 feet at 1.75X and 24 feet at 5X — and quick sighting without depending on a critical view. The scope is ideal for hunting deer and dangerous game, especially in close quarters or in heavily wooded and poorly lit areas. Other features include 1/4-minute positive click stops, fully coated lenses (including Supercon process), nonremovable eyebell and windage/elevation screws. *Length:* 10", with 1" diameter tube. *Weight:* 10 ounces.

WORLD CLASS, WIDE-ANGLE VARIABLE ZOOM RIFLESCOPES

Model No.	Power	Objective Diameter	Finish	Reticle	F.O.V. @100 Yds.	Eye Relief	Tube Diameter	Length	Weight
RIFLESCOPES									
WA13.5X20	1X-3.5X	20mm	Black Gloss	30/30	103'-13'	3"	1"	9.75"	11.1 oz.
WA1.755X20	1.75X-5X	20mm	Black Gloss	30/30	72'-24'	3"	1"	10.5"	10 oz.
WA27X32	2X-7X	32mm	Black Gloss	30/30	56'-17'	3.25"	1"	11.5"	12 oz.
R-DWC39X40*	3X-9X	40mm	Black Matte	30/30	41'-15'	3"	1"	12.75"	13 oz.
R-WA39X40*	3X-9X	40mm	Black Gloss	30/30	41'-15'	3"	1"	12.75"	13 oz.
R-WA39X40TV*	3X-9X	40mm	Black Gloss	30/30 TV	41'-15'	3"	1"	12.75"	13 oz.
WA39X40ST	3X-9X	40mm	Stainless	30/30	41'-15'	3"	1"	12.75"	13 oz.
RIFLESCOPE & BINOCULAR COMBO: R-DWC39X50									
DWC39X50**	3X-9X	50mm	Black Matte	30/30	41'-13'	3"	1"	12.5"	15.8 oz.*
WC1025RB**	10X	25mm	Black Rubber	N/A	355' @ 100 yds.	12mm	N/A	4.5"	8.8 oz.

WORLD CLASS™ 1" PISTOL SCOPES

Built to withstand the most punishing recoil, these scopes feature a 1" tube that provides long eye relief to accommodate all shooting styles safely, along with fully coated optics for a bright, clear image and shot-after-shot durability. The 2X22 model is recommended for target shooting, while the 4X28 model and 1.25X-4X28 are used for hunting as well. All are fully waterproof, fogproof, shockproof and include haze filter caps. Covered by Tasco's No Fault Limited Lifetime Warranty. Should the product be damaged and fail to operate during the lifetime of the original purchaser, it will be repaired or replaced free except for a nominal handling charge.

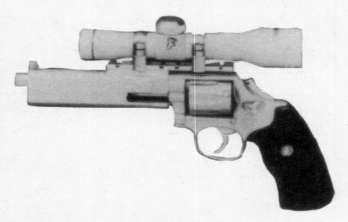

SPECIFICATIONS

Model	Power	Objective Diameter	Finish	Reticle	Field of View @ 100 Yds	Eye Relief	Tube Diam.	Scope Length	Scope Weight	Prices
PWC2X22	2X	22mm	Blk Gloss	30/30	25'	11"-20"	1"	8.75"	7.3 oz.	$288.60
PWC2X22MA	2X	22mm	Matte Alum.	30/30	25'	11"-20"	1"	8.75"	7.3 oz.	288.60
PWC4X28	4X	28mm	Blk Gloss	30/30	8'	12"-19"	1"	9.45"	7.9 oz.	339.55
PWC4X28MA	4X	28mm	Matte Alum.	30/30	8'	12"-19"	1"	9.45"	7.9 oz.	339.55
PI.254X28	1.25X-4X	28mm	Blk Gloss	30/30	23'-9'	15"-23"	1"	9.25"	8.2 oz.	339.55
P1.254X28MA	1.25X-4X	28mm	Matte Alum.	30/30	23'-9'	15"-23"	1'	9.25"	8.2 oz.	339.55

TASCO SCOPES

PROPOINT PLUS PDP6CMP

**TASCO LUMINA
MODEL 11-6x40wa-1**

PROPOINT® MULTI-PURPOSE SCOPES

Tasco's ProPoint is a true 1X-30mm scope with electronic red dot reticle that features unlimited eye relief, enabling shooters to shoot with both eyes open. It is available with a 3X booster and also has application for rifle, shotgun, bow and black powder. The compact version (PDP2) houses a lithium battery pack, making it 1.25 inches narrower than previous models and lighter as well (5.5 oz.). A mercury battery converter is provided for those who prefer standard batteries. Tasco's 3X booster with crosshair reticle weights 6.1 oz. and is 5.5 inches long. Specifications and prices are listed below.

LUMINA® RIFLESCOPES

Tasco's line of Lumina riflescopes with Rubicon™ ruby coated objective lenses filter out red light for crisp daylight viewing and are especially suited for use over snow and in other bright conditions. The line offers fixed power and variable scopes: 4X21mm, 6X40mm, 3X-12X40mm (all with 30/30 reticles) and a 3X-9X40mm model with a standard round reticle or TV reticle.
Price: **$84.95-152.95**

SPECIFICATIONS PROPOINT SCOPES

MODEL	POWER	OBJECTIVE DIAMETER	FINISH	RETICLE	FIELD OF VIEW @ 100 YDS.	EYE RELIEF	TUBE DIAM.	SCOPE LENGTH	SCOPE WEIGHT	PRICES
PDP2	1X	25mm	Black Matte	5 M.O.A. Dot	40'	Unlimited	30mm	5"	5.5 oz.	$254.65
PDP2ST	1X	25mm	Stainless	5 M.O.A. Dot	40'	Unlimited	30mm	5"	5.5 oz.	254.65
PDP2BD	1x	25mm	Black Matte	10 M.O.A. Dot	40'	Unlimited	30mm	5"	5.5 oz.	254.65
PDP2BDST	1X	25mm	Stainless	10 M.O.A. Dot	40'	Unlimited	30mm	5"	5.5 oz.	254.65
PDP3	1X	25mm	Black Matte	5 M.O.A. Dot	52'	Unlimited	30mm	5"	5.5 oz.	305.60
PDP3ST	1X	25mm	Stainless	10 M.O.A. Dot	52'	Unlimited	30mm	5"	5.5 oz.	305.60
PDP3BD	1X	25mm	Black Matte	10 M.O.A. Dot	52'	Unlimited	30mm	5"	5.5 oz.	305.60
PDPBDST	1X	25mm	Stainless	10 M.O.A. Dot	52'	Unlimited	30mm	5"	5.5 oz.	305.60
PDP3CMP	1X	30mm	Black Matte	10 M.O.A. Dot	68'	Unlimited	33mm	4.75"	5.4 oz.	390.45
PDP5CMP	1X	45mm	Black Matte	4,8,12,16 M.O.A. Dot	82'	Unlimited	47mm	4"	8 oz.	
PDP6CMP	1X	30mm	Black Matte	10 M.O.A. Dot	72'	Unlimited	38mm	3"	5.8 oz.	390.45

TASCO SCOPES

WORLD CLASS PLUS RIFLESCOPES

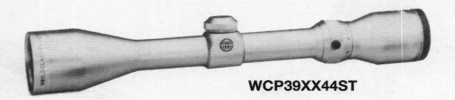

WCP39XX44ST

SPECIFICATIONS WORLD CLASS PLUS RIFLESCOPES

MODEL	POWER	OBJECTIVE DIAMETER	FINISH	RETICLE	F.O.V. @ 100 YD.S	EYE RELIEF	TUBE DIAMETER	LENGTH	WEIGHT	PRICES
WCP4X44	4X	44mm	Black Gloss	30/30	32'	3.25"	1"	12.75"	13.5 oz.	$237.70
DWCP4X44	4X	44mm	Black Matte	30/30	32'	3.25"	1"	12.75"	13.5 oz.	237.70
WCP39X44	3X-9X	44mm	Black Gloss	30/30	39'-14'	3.5"	1"	12.75"	15.8 oz.	407.45
DWCP39X44	3X-9X	44mm	Black Matte	30/30	39'-14'	3.5"	1"	12.75"	15.8 oz.	407.45
WCP39X44ST	3X-9X	44mm	Stainless Steel	30/30	39'-14'	3.5"	1"	12.75"	15.8 oz.	407.45
WCP3.510X50	3.5X-10X	50mm	Black Gloss	30/30	30'-10.5'	3.75"	1"	13"	17.1 oz.	492.35
DWCP3.510X50	3.5X-10X	50mm	Black Matte	30/30	30'-10.5'	3.75"	1"	13"	17.1 oz.	492.35
DWCP832X50	8X-32X	50mm	Black Matte	Crosshair* (1/8 M.O.A.)	13'-4'	3"	1"	14.5"	25.1 oz.	560.00
DWCP1040X50	10X-40X	50mm	Black Matte	Crosshair* (1/8 M.O.A.)	11'-2.5'	3"	1"	14.5"	25.3 oz.	611.00

*With 1/8 M.O.A.

RUBBER ARMORED SCOPES

MODEL	POWER	OBJECTIVE DIAMETER	FINISH	RETICLE	F.O.V. @ 100 YD.S	EYE RELIEF	TUBE DIAMETER	SCOPE LENGTH	SCOPE WEIGHT	PRICE
RC39X40	3-9X	400mm	Black Rubber	30/30	35'-12'	3.25"	1"	12.5"	14.3 oz.	$254.65

*Fits standard dove tail base.

OPTIMA 2000

What makes this newest ProPoint so revolutionary is that, unlike previous ProPoints, it does not have a tube design. It's smaller (only 1 1/2") and lighter (only 1/2 oz.) than any other sighting device. It's also extremely durable and rugged. After thousands of test rounds it held its point of aim and its one-piece, dovetailed-style slide mount remained immovable. Its red dot was always on, with no time lost turning it on. While used primarily on pistols, the Optima 2000 can be mounted on shotguns for skeet or trap shooting or for duck hunting. It also works well on rifles for sport or hunting. Optima 2000 is available with a bright, in-focus 3.5 or 7 M.O.A. dot on the same plane as iron sights for fast target acquisition.

OPTIMA 2000

TASCO RIFLESCOPES

BIG HORN® RIFLESCOPES

Tasco's line of Big Horn® riflescopes features two high-quality models—the 2.5-10X50mm and a 4.5X-18X50mm—with the latter offering a big 18 power and wide-angle optics for fast sighting of running game. Designed with a one-piece body tube for strength and durability, the Big Horn scopes are equipped with 50mm objective lenses that offer greater light transmission for hunting at dawn and dusk when game is most active. Multi-coating on the objective lens and ocular lenses, plus fully coated optics throughout, provide the hunter with sharp detailed images. Big Horn scopes also feature parallax adjustment rings on the objective tube.

Prices: 2.5-10X50mm $611.00
4.5-18X50mm 679.00

MAG-IV
4X-16X50mm

MAG-IV-50™ RIFLESCOPES

Tasco's MAG-IV™ riflescopes now feature large 50mm objective lenses that transmit even more light than the MAG-IV with 40mm objectives and are especially designed for dawn and dusk use. The additions to the MAG-IV line include three high-quality variable scopes: the 4X-16X50mm, the 5X20X50mm and the 5X-20X50mm with bullet drop compensation. All three models have Super-Con® multi-layered lens coating, fully coated optics, and black matte finish.

Tasco's MAG-IV scopes feature windage and elevation adjustments with 1/4-minute clickstops and an Opti-Centered® 30/30 range-finding reticle. This adjustment system allows the reticle to remain centered in the feld of view (an "image moving" system as opposed to a "reticle moving" system). Finished in black gloss.

Prices:
MODEL W416X50 . . . . $127.80
MODEL W520X50 . . . . 144.50
MODEL W520X50 BDC 155.60
Also available:
MAG-IV RIFLESCOPES 3X-12X40mm,
    4X-16X40mm, 6X-24X40mm $254.65

TITAN™ RIFLESCOPES

Tasco's Titan™ riflescopes are equipped with unusually large 42mm and 52mm objective lenses that can transmit more light than standard 40mm lenses for dim early morning and dusk conditions. Three variable scopes—the 1.5X-6X42mm, the 3X-9X42mm and the 3X-12X52mm—are available with 30/30 reticles and feature lenses with five-layer multi-coating for greater image contrast and clarity. Titan scopes also have finger-adjustable windage and elevation controls along with fast focusing eyebells. Waterproof, shockproof and fogproof, these scopes feature all-weather lubrication of each moving part for smooth functioning in any climate condition. Finished in matte black.

Now available in 1.25-4.5X26mm for close range hunting; features a German reticle and 5-layer multi-coating, long eye relief and wide field of view.

Prices:
1.25-4.5X26mm $594.00
3-9X42mm 645.00
1.5X-6X42mm 679.00
3X-12X52mm 763.95

WEAVER SCOPES

T-SERIES TARGET/VARMINT T-36

T-SERIES TARGET/VARMINT SCOPES - Fixed-power scopes featuring Weaver's patented Micro-Trac adjustment system utilizing a dual-spring, four-bearing contact design that allows independent movement of windage and elevation. Optics are fully multi-coated, delivering premium image clarity in virtually all light conditions. Adjustable objective lens allows for zero parallax from 50' to infinity. Choice of fine cross hair or dot reticles. Scopes come with sunshade, extra pair of oversize benchrest adjustment knobs, and screw-in metal lens caps.

Model: T-36
Magnification/Objective: 36X40mm
Field Of View: 3.0' **Eye Relief:** 3.0"
Length: 15.1" **Weight:** 16.7 oz.
Reticle: 1/8 or 3/8 MOA Dot, Fine Crosshair
Finish: Matte black or silver
Price: $770.95

Model: T16 (not shown)
Magnification/Objective: 16X40mm
Field Of View: 6.5' **Eye Relief:** 3.0"
Length: 15.1" **Weight:** 16.7 oz.
Reticle: 3/4 MOA Dot, Varminter Crosshair
Finish: Matte black
Price: $758.95

Model: T-24 (not shown)
Magnification/Objective: 24X40mm
Field Of View: 4.4' **Eye Relief:** 3.0"
Length: 15.1" **Weight:** 16.7 oz.
Reticle: 1/2 or 1/8 MOA Dot, Fine Crosshair
Finish: Matte black
Price: $764.95

Model: T-10 (not shown)
Magnification/Objective: 10X40mm
Field Of View: 9.3' **Eye Relief:** 3.0"
Length: 15.1" **Weight:** 16.7 oz.
Reticle: 1 1/4 MOA Dot, Varminter Crosshair
Finish: Matte black
Price: $752.95

T-SERIES MODEL T-6 RIFLESCOPE

Weaver's T-6 competition rifle scope is only 12.7 inches long and weighs less than 15 ounces. Magnification is six-power. All optical surfaces are fully multi-coated for maximum clarity and light transmission. The T-6 features Weaver's Micro-Trac precision adjustments in 1/8-minute clicks to ensure parallel tracking. The protected target-style turrets are a low-profile configuration combining ease of adjustment with weight reduction. A 40mm adjustable objective permits parallax correction from 50 feet to infinity without shifting the point of impact. A special AO lock ring eliminates bell vibration or shift. The T-6 comes with screw-in metal lens caps and features a competition matte black finish.
Reticles: .210 MOA
Price: $412.95

WEAVER SCOPES

MODEL #49837

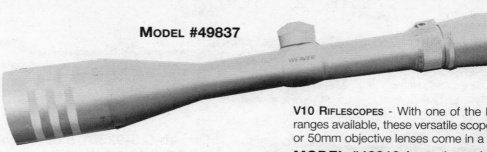

V16 RIFLESCOPES - The V16 is popular for a variety of shooting applications, from close shots that require a wide field of view to long-range varmint or benchrest shooting. Adjustable objective allows a parallax-free view from 30 feet to infinity. Features one-piece tube for strength and moisture resistance and multicoated lenses for clear, crisp images. Two finishes and three reticle options.

MODEL #49837
Magnification/Objective: 4-16X42mm
Field Of View: 26.8'-6.8' *Eye Relief:* 3.1"
Length: 13.9" *Weight:* 16.5 oz.
Reticle: Choice of Dual-X, 1/4 MOA Dot, or Fine Crosshair
Finish: Matte black or silver
Price: Black **$412.95**
Silver. 419.95

V10 RIFLESCOPES - With one of the broadest magnification ranges available, these versatile scopes in 2-10X with 38mm or 50mm objective lenses come in a choice of finishes.

MODEL #49810 (not shown)
Magnification/Objective: 2-10X38mm
Field Of View: 38.5-9.5" *Eye Relief:* 3.4-3.3" *Length:* 12.2"
Weight: 11.2 oz. *Reticle:* Dual-X *Finish:* Matte black
Price: **$251.95**
Also Available:
In gloss black, MODEL #49910 . . . . 245.95
Silver, MODEL #49710. . . . . 251.95

MODEL #49938 (not shown)
Magnification/Objective: 2-10X50mm
Field Of View: 40.2-9.2" *Eye Relief:* 2.9-2.8" *Length:* 13.75"
Weight: 15.2 oz. *Reticle:* Dual-X *Finish:* Matte black
Price: **$347.95**
Also Available:
In gloss black, MODEL #49937 . . . . 337.95
Silver, MODEL #49939 . . . . 347.95

V24 6X24 VARMINT SCOPE

RIMFIRE 4X MATTE SCOPE

V24 6X24 VARMINT SCOPE - Weaver's V24 Varmint scope is the big brother of the V16, one of Weaver's most popular scopes. The V24 zooms from 6 to 24 power, has a 42mm adjustable objective and a special varmint reticle. Reticle adjustments are in precise, 1/8-minute clicks for precision positioning. One-piece tube design and intelligent engineering make the V24 lighter than comparable high-quality scopes. Like the V16, the new scope has generous eye relief, multi-coated optics for maximum light transmission, and comes with a matte black finish. An optional 4-inch sun shade is available for shooting in critical light conditions.
Price: **$480.95**

RIMFIRE SCOPE 2.5-7X
Lenses are multi-coated for bright, clear low-light performance and the one-piece tube design is shockproof and waterproof.
Prices:
49622 2.5-7x Rimfire Matte **$166.95**
49623 2.5-7x Rimfire Silver. 168.95

RIMFIRE SCOPE 4X
Fixed 4x scope is ideal for a variety of shooting applications. It's durable, light-weight and waterproof.
Prices:
49620 4x Rimfire Matte **$144.95**
49621 4x Rimfire Silver. 147.95

ZEISS RIFLESCOPES

THE "Z" SERIES

DIAVARI-C 3-9X36
$615.00
NEW LIGHTER VERSION OF THE
GERMAN-MADE SCOPE NOW
BUILT IN THE U.S.A.

DIAVARI-C 3-9X36T (not shown)
$815.00 ($845.00 Silver)

DIATAL-Z 6X42 T
$955.00

DIAVARI-Z 1.5-6X42 T
$1,240.00

DIATAL-Z 3-12X56 T
$1,575.00 ($1,810.00 w/
Illuminated #8 Reticle)

DIAVARI-Z 2.5-10X48 T
(not shown)
$1,465.00

DIATAL-Z 8X56 T
$1,135.00

DIAVARI-Z 1.25-4x24
(not shown)
$1,085.00

ZM/Z SERIES RIFLESCOPE SPECIFICATIONS

MODEL	DIATAL-ZM/Z 6X42T	DIAVARI-ZM/Z 1.5-6x42 T	DIAVARI-ZM/Z 3-12x56 T	DIATAL-ZM/Z 8x56 T	DIAVARI-ZM/Z 2.5-10x48 T	DIAVERA-ZM/Z 1.25-4x24	DIAVARI-C 3-9x36
Magnification	6X	1.5 X 6X	3X 12X	8X	2.5X-10X	1.25-4X	3X 9X
Effective obj. diam.	42mm/1.7"	19.5/0.8" 42/1.7"	38/1.5" 56/2.2"	56mm/2.2"	33/1.30" 48/1.89"	NA	30.0/1.2" 36.0/1.4"
Diameter of exit pupil	7mm	13mm 7mm	12.7mm 4.7mm	7mm	13.2mm 4.8mm	12.6mm 6.3mm	10.0 4.0mm
Twilight factor	15.9	4.2 15.9	8.5 25.9	21.2	7.1 21.9	3.54 9.6	8.5 18.0
Field of view at 100 m/ ft. at 100 yds.	6.7m/20.1'	18/54.0' 6.5/19.5'	9.2/27.6' 3.3/9.9'	5m/15.0'	11.0/33.0 3.9/11.7	32 10	12.0/36.0 4.3/12.9
Approx. eye relief	8cm/3.2"	8cm/3.2"	8cm/3.2"	8cm/3.2"	8cm/3.2"	8cm/3.2"	3.5"
Click-stop adjustment 1 click - (cm at 200 m)/ (inch at 100 yds)	1cm/0.36"	1cm/0.36"	1cm/0.36"	1cm/0.36"	1cm/0.36"	1cm/0.36"	107/0.25"
Max adj. (elv./wind.) at 100m (cm) at 100 yds.	187	190	95	138	110/39.6	300	135/49
Center tube dia.	25.4mm/1"	30mm/1.18"	30mm/1.18"	25.4mm/1"	30mm/1.18"	30mm/1.18"	25.4mm/1.0"
Objective bell dia.	48mm/1.9"	48mm/1.9"	62mm/2.44"	62mm/2.44"	54mm/2.13"	NA	44.0/1.7
Ocular bell dia.	40mm/1.57"	40mm/1.57"	40mm/1.57"	40mm/1.57"	40mm/1.57"	NA	42.5/1.8
Length	324mm/12.8"	320mm/12.6"	388mm/15.3"	369mm/14.5"	370mm/14.57"	290mm/11.46"	
Approx. weight: ZM	350g/15.3 oz.	586g/20.7 oz.	765g/27.0 oz.	550g/19.4 oz.	715g/25.2 oz.	490g/17.3 oz.	NA
Z	400g/14.1 oz.	562g/19.8	731g/25.8 oz.	520g/18.3 oz.	680g/24 oz.	NA	430g/15.2 oz.

CENTERFIRE PISTOL & REVOLVER AMMUNITION
Federal 500
Sako 503

CENTER RIFLE AMMUNITION
Federal 500
Hornady 501
Remington 502
Sako 503
Winchester 504

RIMFIRE AMMUNITION
Remington 502

SHOTSHELL AMMUNITION
Federal 500
Remington 502
Winchester 504

Ammunition

*For addresses and phone/fax numbers of manufacturers and distributors included in this section, please turn to **DIRECTORY OF MANUFACTURERS AND SUPPLIERS** on page 558.*

FEDERAL AMMUNITION

Federal's new pistol and rifle cartridges for 1997-98 are featured below. For a complete listing of Federal ammunition, call or write the Federal Cartridge Company (see Directory of Manufacturers and Suppliers in the Reference section for address and phone number). *See* also Federal ballistics tables.

PREMIUM PERSONAL DEFENSE PISTOL

This award-winning load has a new look featuring a special clear plastic packaging that offers protection against moisture and rough treatment. Also new is a .357 Magnum handgun load.

PREMIUM TUNGSTEN-POLYMER SHOTSHELL

Federal introduces a non-toxic shot with the power and density of lead and speed of steel. Tungsten-Polymer delivers 80-85% patterns at 40 yards with excellent down-range energy.

PREMIUM WOODLEIGH WELDCORE CENTERFIRE RIFLE

Federal has expanded this load, which has been popular throughout Europe and Africa for big game and safari hunting since 1988, to include eight new Premium Centerfire and High Energy loads featuring an Australian legend called Woodleigh Weldcore. This load features a bonded-core bullet with a special heavy jacket for extra penetration power. Weight retention of 80-85% provides the energy needed to drop big game in its tracks.

PREMIUM TUNGSTEN-IRON TURKEY SHOTSHELL

This turkey load has the pellet energy of lead, a velocity of 1300 feet per second, and good penetration. Tight patterns and excellent penetration assure success of this load among turkey hunters.

HORNADY AMMUNITION

Hornady's new **SST (SUPER SHOCK TIPPED)** bullets feature a premium polymer tip which, along with its profile, combine to improve the SST's ballistic coefficient. The result: greater velocity and better accuracy. Upon impact, the tip is pushed backward into the lead core to initiate immediate expansion. The specially designed jacket grips and controls the expanding core, allowing the bullet to reach its optimum mass and momentum.

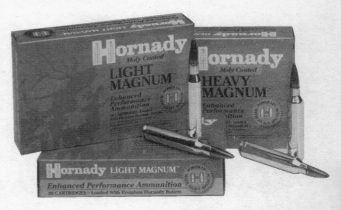

Hornady's moly-coated **LIGHT MAGNUM** ammo achieves more energy, flatter trajectory and velocities up to 200 feet per second faster than standard ammo. That same performance is now available in .280 Remington and 7mm Remington Magnum. With Light Magnum and Heavy Magnum, greater velocity is achieved from standard cartridges with no additional heat and pressure. The addition of molybdenum disulfide to these bullets cuts friction and eliminates copper fouling in the bore—more rounds can be fired without stopping to clean the rifle.

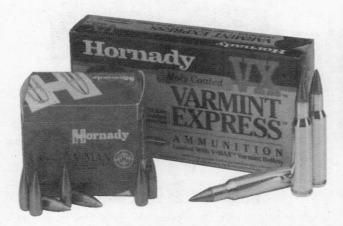

Hornady's **VARMINT EXPRESS** ammunition now features moly-coated V-MAX bullets, which offer faster speeds in most calibers. Other features include high quality brass cases, hand-inspection, individually selected primers and powders.

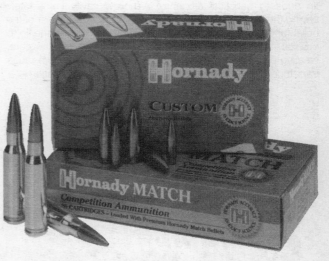

The effectiveness of Hornady's factory-loaded rifle match ammunition is assured by hand-selection and matching for premium uniformity. Cases, powder and primer are all loaded so as to guarantee superb ignition and pinpoint accuracy. These match cartridges are loaded with either Hornady **A-MAX** or **BTHP** match bullets, all available with high-performance moly-coating that reduces barrel wear and increases speed.

REMINGTON AMMUNITION

PREMIER VARMINT AMMUNITION

Initially offered in four .22-caliber selections, Remington's Premier® Varmint line has been expanded to include two larger-caliber loadings with heavier bullets for both longer range shooting and greater wind-bucking characteristics. These are the 6mm Remington and .243 Win., both loaded with sleek, high ballistic-coefficient, 75-grain Hornady V-MaxTM Green Tip bullets. The key to their performance is a unique internal design; a slim, aerodynamically efficient external shape with a boat tail base; and a uniform concentricity. All rounds are loaded with selected powders for uniformly consistent velocities. Resulting groups are often a single, ragged hole. A lightweight, sharp-nosed polymer tip adds to ballistic efficiency. A hollow cavity immediately behind the tip moves the center of gravity towards the rear of the bullet for improved stability and accuracy. It also allows the tip to develop its own kinetic energy before smashing into the core, creating explosive fragmentation on impact. Flatter down-range trajectories help minimize shooter errors in range estimation.

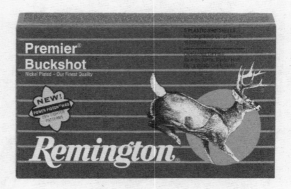

PREMIER BUCKSHOT

Power Piston wads in Remington's 12 gauge Premier Buckshot offer protection against pellet deformation on firing. All Premier Buckshot is hardened with 3 percent antimony, nickel plated for added hardness, and buffered to cushion pellets. Patterns are 25 percent tighter than normal buckshot loads. Remington produces its buckshot shells in both 2 3/4" and 3" lengths. Pellet counts range from 9 to 20.

HIGH VELOCITY GOLDEN BULLET

Remington's hollow point .22 LR ammo has a muzzle velocity of 1280 ft/sec and up to 1010 ft/sec at 100 yards. Long range trajectory at 100 yards is 3.5." Lead bullets are also available in 22LR and 22 short.

PREMIER .22 WIN. MAG.

Whether tin can plinking to one-hole perfection, or getting young shooters started, or practicing plinking or small-game hunting, Remington's rimfire lineup produces maximum performance. The .22 Win. Mag. is available in three styles: V-Max Boat Tail, Jacketed Hollow Point, and Pointed Soft Point.

SAKO AMMUNITION

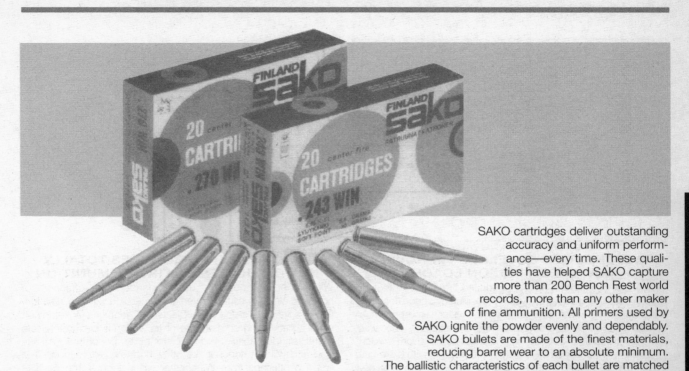

SAKO cartridges deliver outstanding accuracy and uniform performance—every time. These qualities have helped SAKO capture more than 200 Bench Rest world records, more than any other maker of fine ammunition. All primers used by SAKO ignite the powder evenly and dependably. SAKO bullets are made of the finest materials, reducing barrel wear to an absolute minimum. The ballistic characteristics of each bullet are matched perfectly to the cartridge caliber for every shooting purpose.

SAKO PREMIUM PISTOL & REVOLVER CARTRIDGES

CALIBERS	BULLET WEIGHT GR.	BULLET TYPE	SUGGESTED RETAIL PRICE
380 ACP	95	FMJ	$34.70
30 Luger	92	FMJ	31.65
9mm Luger	115	FMJ	34.70
9mm Luger	114	FMJ	60.35
32 W&W Long	98	WC	27.75
38 Special	148	WC	30.65
38 Special	158	SWC	30.65

SAKO PREMIUM CENTERFIRE RIFLE CARTRIDGES

CALIBERS	BULLET WEIGHT GR.	BULLET TYPE	SUGGESTED RETAIL PRICE
22 Hornet	45	SP	$15.95
22 Hornet	40	HP	19.25
222 Remington	50	SP	17.25
222 Remington	55	SP	17.65
222 Remington SM	52	HP	20.50
222 Rem. Mag.	50	SP	18.00
222 Rem. Mag.	55	SP	18.50
223 Remington	55	SP	18.00
22 PPC USA	52	HP	37.90
22-250 Remington	50	SP	25.85
22-250 Remington	55	SP	27.00
6 PPC USA	70	HP	37.90
243 Winchester	90	SP	23.75
6.5 X 55	139	SP	24.95
6.5 X 55	155	SP	26.90
270 Winchester	156	SP	25.35

SAKO PREMIUM CENTERFIRE RIFLE CARTRIDGES

CALIBERS	BULLET WEIGHT GR.	BULLET TYPE	SUGGESTED RETAIL PRICE
7 X 33 SAKO	78	SP	$38.75
7mm Rem. Mag.	170	SP	34.00
7.62 x 39	123	SP	25.85
308 Winchester	123	SP	22.50
308 Winchester	156	SP	24.60
308 Winchester	180	SP	23.75
308 Winchester	200	SP	24.95
308 Winchester	180	SHH	24.95
308 Win. SM	168	HP	25.40
308 Win. SM	190	HP	25.80
7.62 X 53R	156	SP	25.00
7.62 X 53R	180	SP	24.15
7.62 X 53R	200	SP	24.40
7.62 X 53R	180	SHH	25.55
30-06	123	SP	25.80
30-06	180	SHH	25.95
300 Win. Mag.	156	SHH	41.65
300 Win. Mag.	180	HH	41.00
300 Win. Mag.	168	HP	42.80
8.2 X 53R	200	SP	24.20
8 X 57 J.S.	200	SP	25.80
338 Win. Mag.	250	SP	35.65
9.3 X 53R Finish	257	SP	13.50
9.3 X 62	250	SPC	48.15
9.3 X 74R	250	SPC	59.65
375 H & H	270	SPC	64.00

WINCHESTER AMMUNITION

WINCHESTER® DEVELOPS IMPROVED AA® SUPER PIGEON LOADS

Winchester Ammunition has re-introduced three new AA® Super Pigeon loads to replace previously obsoleted pigeon loads by Winchester. The new rounds feature Winchester's time-proven AA components, including a one-piece hull, a plastic one-piece wad, Winchester's famous 209 primer, and clean-burning Ball Powder®. In addition, Winchester has improved the payload with extra-hard copper-plated pellets for hard-hitting performance. The three new loads contain 3 1/4 dram of powder and 1 1/4 oz. of shot in shot sizes 6, 7 1/2, or 8, with a muzzle velocity of 1250 fps.

WINCHESTER INTRODUCES TOTALLY NON-TOXIC CENTERFIRE AMMUNITION

Winchester Ammunition has expanded its offerings of non-lead alternatives for centerfire ammunition with the introduction of a new line called SuperClean™ NT, featuring jacketed soft point bullets using cores made of tin, which is completely safe and totally non-toxic. Tin, in a pistol bullet, performs much like lead and will not ricochet like other non-toxic alternatives. The first five offerings from Winchester will include a 105 gr. JSP bullet in the 9mm Luger with a muzzle velocity of 1200 fps. The SuperClean NT uses Winchester's lead-free, nickel-plated cup primer, which is very sensitive and ignites well even with light or off-center firing pin hits.

TWO NEW HEAVY LOADS ADDED TO WINCHESTER® UPLAND® GAME SHOTSHELL LINE

Winchester Ammunition has added two heavy 12 gauge loads to the Upland Game Shotshell line. Both 2 3/4" loads use the time-proven 3 1/4 dram of powder with 1 1/4 oz. of shot. Hunters can choose from either 7 1/2 or 8 size shot. This line offers hunters a great value in shotshells without sacrificing performance. All loads in the Upland line use proven-quality Winchester components custom tailored for optimum results. Winchester Upland Game Loads are available in a variety of shot sizes in both light and heavy loads in 20, 16, and 12 gauge rounds.

WINCHESTER® ADDS 9X23 WINCHESTER TO USA BRAND LINE

Winchester Ammunition introduced the 9x23 Winchester caliber with an initial offering of a 125-grain Silvertip™ hollow point bullet in the Super XR line. With a muzzle velocity of 1450 fps, this round has the same velocity and energy as a 357 magnum with the same bullet weight. Winchester now produces the 9x23 Win in its USA Brand ammunition. The new load uses a 124 gr. jacketed soft point bullet with a muzzle velocity of 1450 fps. The symbol number is Q4304, with 50 rounds packed in each box.

CENTERFIRE PISTOL & REVOLVER BALLISTICS

Federal	510
Hornady	511
Remington	516
Winchester	519

CENTER RIFLE BALLISTICS

Federal	506
Hornady	511
Remington	512
Sako	517
Weatherby	518
Winchester	520

RIMFIRE BALLISTICS

Federal	509

Ballistics

FEDERAL RIFLE BALLISTICS

PREMIUM® CENTERFIRE RIFLE

USAGE	NEW	FEDERAL LOAD NO.	CALIBER	BULLET WGT. GRAINS	BULLET WGT. GRAMS	BULLET STYLE*	FACTORY PRIMER NO.	VELOCITY IN FEET PER SECOND (TO NEAREST 10 FPS) MUZZLE	100 YDS.	200 YDS.	300 YDS.	400 YDS.	500 YDS.	ENERGY IN FOOT-POUNDS (TO NEAREST 5 FOOT-POUNDS) MUZZLE	100 YDS.	200 YDS.	300 YDS.	400 YDS.	500 YDS.
1		P223E	223 Rem. (5.56x45mm)	55	3.56	Sierra GameKing BTHP	215	3240	2770	2340	1950	1610	1330	1280	935	670	465	315	215
1		P22250E	22-250 Rem.	55	3.56	Sierra GameKing BTHP	210	3680	3280	2920	2590	2280	1990	1655	1315	1040	815	630	480
2	NEW	P22250T1	22-250 Rem.	55	3.56	Trophy Bonded Bear Claw	210	3600	3080	2610	2190	1810	1490	1585	1155	835	590	400	270
2	NEW	P22DT1	220 Swift	55	3.56	Trophy Bonded Bear Claw	210	3700	3170	2690	2270	1880	1540	1670	1225	885	625	430	290
2		P243C	243 Win. (6.16x51mm)	100	6.48	Sierra GameKing BTSP	210	2960	2760	2570	2380	2210	2040	1950	1690	1460	1260	1080	925
1		P243D	243 Win. (6.16x51mm)	85	5.50	Sierra GameKing BTHP	210	3320	3070	2830	2600	2380	2180	2080	1778	1510	1070	890	855
2		P243F	243 Win. (6.16x51mm)	70	4.54	Nosler Ballistic Tip	210	3400	3070	2760	2470	2200	1950	1795	1465	1185	950	755	590
2		P6C	6mm Rem.	100	6.48	Nosler Partition	210	3100	2860	2640	2420	2220	2020	2135	1820	1545	1300	1080	910
2		P257B	257 Roberts (High-Velocity + P)	120	7.77	Nosler Partition	210	2780	2560	2360	2160	1970	1790	2060	1750	1480	1240	1030	855
2		P2506C	25-06 Rem.	117	7.58	Sierra GameKing BTSP	210	2990	2770	2570	2370	2180	2000	2320	2000	1715	1465	1240	1045
2		P2506D	25-06 Rem.	100	6.48	Nosler Ballistic Tip	210	3210	2960	2720	2490	2280	2070	2290	1948	1640	1380	1150	955
2		P2506E	25-06 Rem.	115	7.45	Nosler Partition	210	2990	2750	2520	2300	2100	1900	2285	1930	1620	1350	1120	915
2		P2506T1	25-06 Rem.	115	7.45	Trophy Bonded Bear Claw	210	2990	2740	2500	2270	2050	1850	2285	1910	1590	1310	1075	870
2		P257WBA	257 Weatherby Magnum	115	7.45	Nosler Partition	210	3150	2900	2660	2440	2220	2020	2535	2145	1810	1515	1260	1040
2		P257WBT1	257 Weatherby Magnum	115	7.45	Trophy Bonded Bear Claw	210	3150	2890	2640	2400	2180	1970	2535	2125	1775	1470	1210	990
2	NEW	P655ST2	6.5X55 Swedish	140	9.07	Trophy Bonded Bear Claw	210	2550	2350	2160	1980	1810	1650	2020	1720	1450	1220	1015	845
2		P270C	270 Win.	150	9.72	Sierra GameKing BTSP	210	2850	2660	2480	2300	2130	1970	2705	2355	2040	1760	1510	1290
2		P270D	270 Win.	130	8.42	Sierra GameKing BTSP	210	3060	2830	2620	2410	2220	2030	2700	2320	1980	1680	1420	1190
2		P270E	270 Win.	150	9.72	Nosler Partition	210	2850	2590	2340	2100	1880	1670	2705	2225	1815	1470	1175	930
2		P270F	270 Win.	130	8.42	Nosler Ballistic Tip	210	3060	2840	2630	2430	2230	2050	2700	2325	1990	1700	1440	1210
2		P270T1	270 Win.	140	9.07	Trophy Bonded Bear Claw	210	2940	2700	2480	2260	2060	1860	2685	2270	1905	1580	1315	1080
2		P270T2	270 Win.	130	8.42	Trophy Bonded Bear Claw	210	3060	2810	2570	2340	2130	1930	2705	2275	1905	1585	1310	1070
2	NEW	P270WBA	270 Weatherby Magnum	130	8.42	Nosler Partition	210	3200	2960	2740	2520	2320	2120	2955	2530	2160	1835	1550	1300
2	NEW	P270WBB	270 Weatherby Magnum	130	8.42	Sierra GameKing BTSP	210	3200	2980	2780	2580	2400	2210	2955	2570	2230	1925	1655	1415
2	NEW	P270WBT1	270 Weatherby Magnum	140	9.07	Trophy Bonded Bear Claw	210	3100	2840	2600	2370	2150	1950	2990	2510	2100	1745	1440	1175
2		P730A	7-30 Waters	120	7.77	Sierra GameKing BTSP	210	2700	2300	1930	1600	1330	1140	1940	1405	990	685	470	345
2		P7C	7mm Mauser (7x57mm Mauser)	140	9.07	Nosler Partition	210	2660	2450	2260	2070	1890	1730	2200	1865	1585	1330	1110	930
2		P708A	7mm-08 Rem.	140	9.07	Nosler Partition	210	2800	2580	2370	2200	2020	1840	2435	2065	1775	1500	1265	1060
2		P708B	7mm-08 Rem.	140	9.07	Nosler Ballistic Tip	210	2800	2610	2430	2260	2100	1940	2440	2125	1840	1590	1360	1165
2		P764A	7x64 Brenneke	160	10.37	Nosler Partition	210	2650	2480	2310	2150	2000	1850	2495	2180	1895	1640	1415	1215
2		P280A	280 Rem.	150	9.72	Nosler Partition	210	2890	2620	2370	2140	1910	1710	2780	2285	1875	1520	1215	970
2		P280T1	280 Rem.	140	9.07	Trophy Bonded Bear Claw	210	2990	2740	2510	2290	2080	1880	2770	2335	1955	1625	1345	1100
2		P7RD	7mm Rem. Magnum	150	9.72	Sierra GameKing BTSP	215	3110	2920	2750	2580	2410	2250	3220	2850	2510	2210	1930	1690
3		P7RE	7mm Rem. Magnum	165	10.68	Sierra GameKing BTSP	215	2950	2800	2650	2510	2370	2230	3190	2865	2570	2300	2050	1825
2		P7RF	7mm Rem. Magnum	160	10.37	Nosler Partition	215	2950	2770	2590	2420	2250	2090	3090	2715	2375	2075	1800	1555
2		P7RG	7mm Rem. Magnum	140	9.07	Nosler Partition	215	3150	2930	2710	2510	2320	2130	3085	2660	2290	1960	1670	1415
2		P7RH	7mm Rem. Magnum	150	9.72	Nosler Ballistic Tip	215	3110	2910	2720	2540	2370	2200	3220	2825	2470	2150	1865	1610
3		P7RT1	7mm Rem. Magnum	175	11.34	Trophy Bonded Bear Claw	215	2860	2560	2350	2120	1900	1700	3180	2625	2150	1745	1400	1120
3		P7RT2	7mm Rem. Magnum	160	10.37	Trophy Bonded Bear Claw	215	2940	2660	2390	2140	1900	1680	3070	2505	2025	1620	1280	1005
3	NEW	P7RT3	7mm Rem. Magnum	140	9.07	Trophy Bonded Bear Claw	215	3150	2910	2680	2460	2250	2000	3085	2630	2230	1880	1575	1310
3		P7WBA	7mm Weatherby Magnum	160	10.37	Nosler Partition	215	3050	2850	2650	2470	2290	2120	3305	2880	2505	2165	1865	1600
3	NEW	P7WBB	7mm Weatherby Magnum	160	10.37	Sierra GameKing BTSP	215	3050	2850	2710	2540	2400	2250	3305	2945	2615	2320	2050	1805
3		P7WBT1	7mm Weatherby Magnum	160	10.37	Trophy Bonded Bear Claw	215	3050	2730	2420	2140	1830	1640	3305	2640	2085	1630	1255	955
2	NEW	P7STWA	7mm STW	160	10.37	Sierra GameKing BTSP	215	3200	3020	2850	2670	2530	2380	3640	3245	2890	2570	2275	2010
3	NEW	P7STWT1	7mm STW	150	9.72	Trophy Bonded Bear Claw	215	3250	3010	2770	2540	2350	2150	3520	3010	2565	2175	1830	1535
2		P3030D	30-30 Win.	170	11.01	Nosler Partition	210	2200	1900	1620	1380	1190	1060	1830	1355	990	720	535	425
2		P308C	308 Win. (7.62x51mm)	165	10.69	Sierra GameKing BTSP	210	2700	2520	2330	2160	1990	1830	2670	2310	1990	1700	1450	1230
2		P308E	308 Win. (7.62x51mm)	180	11.66	Nosler Partition	210	2620	2430	2240	2060	1890	1730	2745	2355	2005	1700	1430	1200
2		P308F	308 Win. (7.62x51mm)	150	9.72	Nosler Ballistic Tip	210	2820	2610	2410	2220	2040	1880	2650	2270	1935	1640	1380	1155
3	NEW	P308J	308 Win. (7.62x51mm)	180	11.66	Woodleigh Weldcore SP	210	2620	2390	2170	1960	1770	1580	2745	2280	1880	1540	1250	1010
2		P308T1	308 Win. (7.62x51mm)	165	10.69	Trophy Bonded Bear Claw	210	2700	2440	2200	1970	1760	1570	2670	2185	1775	1425	1135	900
2		P3006B	30-06 Spring (7.62x63mm)	165	10.69	Sierra GameKing BTSP	210	2800	2610	2420	2240	2070	1910	2870	2490	2150	1840	1580	1340
2		P3006F	30-06 Spring (7.62x63mm)	180	11.66	Nosler Partition	210	2700	2500	2320	2140	1970	1810	2915	2510	2150	1830	1550	1310
2		P3006G	30-06 Spring (7.62x63mm)	150	9.72	Sierra GameKing BTSP	210	2910	2690	2480	2270	2070	1880	2820	2420	2040	1710	1430	1180
3		P3006L	30-06 Spring (7.62x63mm)	180	11.66	Sierra GameKing BTSP	210	2700	2540	2380	2220	2080	1930	2915	2570	2260	1975	1720	1485
2		P3006P	30-06 Spring (7.62x63mm)	150	9.72	Nosler Partition	210	2910	2700	2490	2300	2110	1940	2820	2420	2070	1760	1485	1245
2		P3006Q	30-06 Spring (7.62x63mm)	165	10.69	Nosler Ballistic Tip	210	2800	2610	2430	2250	2080	1920	2870	2495	2155	1855	1585	1350
3	NEW	P3006W	30-06 Spring (7.62x63mm)	180	11.66	Woodleigh Weldcore SP	210	2700	2470	2240	2030	1830	1650	2915	2430	2010	1645	1340	1085
3		P3006T1	30-06 Spring (7.62x63mm)	165	10.69	Trophy Bonded Bear Claw	210	2800	2540	2290	2060	1830	1630	2870	2360	1915	1545	1230	975
3		P3006T2	30-06 Spring (7.62x63mm)	180	11.66	Trophy Bonded Bear Claw	210	2700	2460	2220	2000	1800	1610	2915	2410	1975	1605	1290	1035
3		P300WC	300 Win. Magnum	200	12.96	Sierra GameKing BTSP	215	2830	2680	2530	2380	2240	2110	3560	3180	2830	2520	2230	1970
3		P300W14	300 Win. Magnum	150	9.72	Trophy Bonded Bear Claw	215	3280	2980	2700	2430	2190	1950	3570	2450	2420	1970	1590	1270
3	NEW	P300WBC	300 Weatherby Magnum	180	11.66	Sierra GameKing BTSP	215	3190	3010	2830	2660	2490	2330	4065	3610	3195	2820	2480	2175
3		P35WT1	35 Whelen	225	14.58	Trophy Bonded Bear Claw	210	2600	2400	2200	2020	1840	1670	3375	2865	2420	2030	1690	1400

+P ammunition is loaded to a higher pressure. Use only in firearms recommended by the gun manufacturer.
*BTHP = Boat-Tail Hollow Point BTSP = Boat-Tail Soft Point SP = Soft Point
Usage Key: 1 = Varmints, predators, small game 2 = Medium game 3 = Large, heavy game 4 = Dangerous game 5 = Target shooting, training, practice 6=Self defense

FEDERAL RIFLE BALLISTICS

WIND DRIFT IN INCHES 10 MPH CROSSWIND					HEIGHT OF BULLET TRAJECTORY IN INCHES ABOVE OR BELOW LINE OF SIGHT IF ZEROED AT ⊕ YARDS, SIGHTS 1.5 INCHES ABOVE BORE LINE										TEST BARREL LENGTH INCHES	FEDERAL LOAD NO.
					AVERAGE RANGE				LONG RANGE							
100 YDS.	200 YDS.	300 YDS.	400 YDS.	500 YDS.	50 YDS.	100 YDS.	200 YDS.	300 YDS.	50 YDS.	100 YDS.	200 YDS.	300 YDS.	400 YDS.	500 YDS.		
1.3	5.8	14.2	27.7	47.6	-0.3	⊕	-2.7	-10.8	+0.4	+1.5	⊕	-6.8	-25.3	-56.6	24	P223E
0.8	3.6	8.4	15.8	26.3	-0.4	⊕	-1.7	-7.6	0.0	+0.9	⊕	-5.0	-15.1	-32.9	24	P2225OR
1.2	5.2	12.5	24.3	41.9	-0.4	⊕	-2.2	-8.5	+0.2	+1.1	⊕	-6.2	-19.8	-44.5	24	P2225OT1
1.2	5.0	12.1	23.4	40.3	-0.4	⊕	-2.0	-8.1	+0.1	+1.0	⊕	-5.9	-18.5	-41.6	24	P225OT1
0.6	2.6	6.1	11.3	18.4	-0.2	⊕	-2.1	-11.4	0.0	+1.5	⊕	-6.0	-19.0	-39.9	24	P243C
0.7	2.7	6.3	11.6	18.9	-0.3	⊕	-2.7	-9.0	+0.2	+1.1	⊕	-5.5	-16.1	-32.8	24	P243D
0.8	3.4	8.1	15.2	25.1	-0.3	⊕	-2.2	-8.8	+0.2	+1.1	⊕	-5.7	-17.1	-35.7	24	P243F
0.7	2.9	6.7	12.5	20.4	-0.3	⊕	-2.8	-10.5	+0.4	+1.4	⊕	-6.3	-18.7	-38.1	24	P8C
0.8	3.3	7.7	14.3	23.5	-0.1	⊕	-3.9	-14.0	+0.8	+1.9	⊕	-8.2	-24.0	-48.8	24	P257B
0.7	2.8	6.5	12.0	19.6	-0.2	⊕	-2.8	-11.4	+0.5	+1.5	⊕	-6.8	-19.8	-40.4	24	P2506C
0.7	2.9	6.7	12.4	20.2	-0.3	⊕	-2.5	-9.7	+0.3	+1.2	⊕	-6.0	-17.5	-35.8	24	P2506D
0.8	3.2	7.4	13.8	22.6	-0.2	⊕	-3.1	-11.7	+0.6	+1.6	⊕	-7.0	-20.8	-42.2	24	P2506E
0.8	3.4	7.9	14.8	21.4	-0.2	⊕	-3.2	-11.9	+0.6	+1.6	⊕	-7.2	-21.1	-43.2	24	P2506T1
0.7	3.0	6.9	12.9	21.1	-0.3	⊕	-2.7	-10.2	+0.4	+1.3	⊕	-6.2	-18.4	-37.5	24	P257WBA
0.7	3.1	7.3	13.7	22.4	-0.3	⊕	-2.7	-10.4	+0.4	+1.4	⊕	-6.3	-18.8	-38.5	24	P257WBT1
0.8	3.6	8.4	15.5	25.6	0.0	⊕	-4.6	-17.1	+1.2	+2.4	⊕	-9.8	-28.4	-58.2	24	MS55T2
0.7	2.7	6.3	11.6	18.9	-0.2	⊕	-3.4	-12.5	+0.7	+1.7	⊕	-7.4	-21.4	-43.0	24	P270C
0.7	2.8	6.6	12.1	19.7	-0.2	⊕	-2.8	-10.7	+0.5	+1.4	⊕	-6.5	-19.0	-38.5	24	P270D
0.9	3.9	9.2	17.3	28.5	-0.2	⊕	-3.7	-13.6	+0.8	+1.9	⊕	-8.2	-24.4	-50.5	24	P270E
0.7	2.7	6.4	11.8	19.3	-0.2	⊕	-2.8	-10.7	+0.5	+1.4	⊕	-6.5	-19.0	-38.2	24	P270F
0.8	3.2	7.6	14.2	23.6	-0.2	⊕	-3.3	-12.2	+0.8	+1.8	⊕	-7.3	-21.5	-43.7	24	P270T1
0.7	3.2	7.4	13.8	22.5	-0.2	⊕	-2.9	-11.1	+0.5	+1.5	⊕	-6.7	-19.8	-40.5	24	P270T2
0.7	2.7	6.3	11.7	19.0	-0.3	⊕	-2.5	-9.6	+0.3	+1.2	⊕	-5.8	-17.3	-35.1	24	P270WBA
0.6	2.4	5.7	10.3	16.9	-0.3	⊕	-2.4	-8.3	+0.2	+1.1	⊕	-5.7	-16.6	-33.7	24	P270WBB
0.8	3.1	7.4	13.7	22.5	-0.3	⊕	-2.8	-10.3	+0.4	+1.4	⊕	-6.0	-18.3	-39.0	24	P270WBT1
1.6	7.2	17.7	34.5	58.1	0.0	⊕	-5.2	-18.8	+1.2	+2.6	⊕	-12.0	-37.6	-81.7	24	P730A
1.3	3.2	8.2	15.4	23.4	-0.1	⊕	-4.0	-15.4	+1.0	+2.1	⊕	-8.0	-26.1	-52.9	24	P7C
0.8	3.1	7.3	13.5	21.8	-0.2	⊕	-3.7	-13.5	+0.8	+1.9	⊕	-8.0	-23.1	-46.0	24	P70BA
0.7	2.7	6.4	11.9	19.1	-0.2	⊕	-3.6	-13.1	+0.7	+1.8	⊕	-7.7	-14.1	-44.5	24	P70BB
0.7	2.9	6.8	12.3	19.5	-0.1	⊕	-4.2	-14.0	+0.8	+2.1	⊕	-8.7	-24.0	-48.4	24	P764A
0.8	3.6	8.8	16.8	27.8	-0.2	⊕	-3.8	-13.4	+0.7	+1.8	⊕	-8.0	-23.0	-48.2	24	P280A
1.2	4.9	11.6	22.5	27.3	-0.2	⊕	-3.5	-12.7	+0.7	+1.6	⊕	-8.4	-25.4	-54.3	24	P280T1
0.5	2.2	5.1	9.3	15.6	-0.3	⊕	-2.8	-9.0	+0.4	+1.3	⊕	-5.9	-17.0	-34.2	24	P780
0.5	2.0	4.6	8.4	13.5	-0.2	⊕	-3.0	-10.9	+0.5	+1.5	⊕	-6.4	-18.4	-36.6	24	P78E
0.6	2.5	5.6	10.4	16.9	-0.2	⊕	-3.1	-11.2	+0.6	+1.6	⊕	-6.7	-19.0	-38.8	24	P78F
0.6	2.6	6.0	11.1	18.2	-0.3	⊕	-2.8	-9.8	+0.4	+1.3	⊕	-6.0	-17.5	-35.6	24	P78G
0.5	2.3	5.4	9.8	16.2	-0.3	⊕	-2.8	-9.8	+0.4	+1.3	⊕	-6.0	-17.4	-35.0	24	P78H
1.0	3.8	9.1	16.7	27.8	-0.2	⊕	-3.6	-13.5	+0.7	+1.8	⊕	-8.2	-24.0	-48.0	24	P7T1
1.0	3.9	9.4	17.5	29.3	-0.2	⊕	-3.4	-12.0	+0.7	+1.7	⊕	-7.9	-23.3	-48.7	24	P7T2
0.7	2.9	6.8	12.3	20.1	-0.3	⊕	-2.8	-10.1	+0.4	+1.3	⊕	-6.1	-18.1	-38.8	24	P7T3
0.6	2.5	5.8	10.7	17.3	-0.2	⊕	-2.8	-10.5	+0.4	+1.4	⊕	-6.3	-18.4	-37.1	24	P7WBA
0.5	2.1	4.8	8.8	14.2	-0.3	⊕	-2.7	-10.2	+0.4	+1.4	⊕	-6.0	-17.4	-34.9	24	P7WBB
1.0	4.2	10.1	19.1	31.9	-0.2	⊕	-3.2	-12.4	+0.6	+1.6	⊕	-7.6	-22.7	-47.8	24	P7WBT1
0.5	1.9	4.5	8.3	13.2	-0.3	⊕	-2.3	-8.9	+0.3	+1.1	⊕	-5.5	-15.7	-31.3	24	P73TWA
0.6	2.7	6.3	11.6	18.8	-0.3	⊕	-2.4	-8.2	+0.3	+1.2	⊕	-5.7	-16.7	-34.2	24	P73TWT1
0.8	6.0	18.4	36.7	58.8	-0.3	⊕	-8.8	-29.8	+2.4	+4.1	⊕	-17.4	-52.4	-109.4	24	P3030B
0.7	3.0	7.0	13.8	21.1	-0.1	⊕	-4.0	-14.4	+0.9	+2.0	⊕	-8.4	-24.3	-49.0	24	P30C
0.8	3.3	7.7	14.3	23.3	-0.1	⊕	-4.4	-15.6	+1.0	+2.2	⊕	-9.2	-26.5	-53.6	24	P30E
0.7	3.1	7.2	13.3	21.7	-0.2	⊕	-3.5	-13.2	+0.7	+1.8	⊕	-7.8	-22.7	-46.0	24	P30F
0.9	4.0	9.4	17.8	29.1	-0.1	⊕	-4.7	-16.6	+1.1	+2.3	⊕	-9.7	-28.4	-58.6	24	P30FJ
1.0	4.2	10.0	18.7	31.1	-0.1	⊕	-4.4	-15.0	+1.0	+2.2	⊕	-9.4	-27.7	-57.5	24	P30T1
0.7	2.8	6.6	12.3	19.8	-0.2	⊕	-3.6	-13.2	+0.8	+1.8	⊕	-7.6	-22.4	-45.2	24	P3006D
0.7	3.0	7.3	13.4	27.7	-0.1	⊕	-4.0	-14.6	+0.9	+2.0	⊕	-8.6	-24.6	-49.6	24	P3006F
0.7	3.0	7.1	13.4	22.0	-0.2	⊕	-3.3	-12.4	+0.6	+1.7	⊕	-7.4	-21.5	-43.7	24	P3006G
0.6	2.6	6.0	11.0	17.8	-0.1	⊕	-3.8	-13.0	+0.8	+1.8	⊕	-8.1	-23.1	-46.1	24	P3006L
0.7	2.9	6.8	12.7	20.7	-0.2	⊕	-3.3	-12.2	+0.6	+1.6	⊕	-7.3	-21.1	-42.8	24	P3006P
0.7	2.8	6.6	12.1	19.7	-0.2	⊕	-3.6	-13.2	+0.7	+1.8	⊕	-7.7	-22.3	-45.0	24	P3006Q
0.9	3.8	9.0	16.7	27.8	-0.1	⊕	-4.2	-15.4	+1.0	+2.1	⊕	-8.1	-26.4	-54.7	24	P3006W
1.0	4.0	9.8	17.8	29.7	-0.1	⊕	-3.9	-14.5	+0.8	+2.0	⊕	-8.7	-25.4	-53.1	24	P3006T1
0.9	4.0	9.4	17.7	29.4	-0.1	⊕	-4.3	-15.0	+1.0	+2.2	⊕	-9.2	-27.0	-58.1	24	P3006T2
0.5	2.2	5.0	9.2	14.9	-0.2	⊕	-3.4	-12.2	+0.7	+1.7	⊕	-7.1	-20.4	-40.5	24	P300WC
0.8	3.3	7.8	14.8	24.0	-0.3	⊕	-2.4	-9.8	+0.3	+1.2	⊕	-6.8	-17.9	-37.1	24	P300WT4
0.5	2.0	4.8	8.8	14.6	-0.3	⊕	-2.3	-8.1	+0.3	+1.2	⊕	-5.6	-16.6	-32.0	24	P300WBC
0.8	3.5	8.3	15.3	25.3	-0.1	⊕	-4.6	-16.4	+1.1	+2.3	⊕	-9.4	-27.3	-56.0	24	P35WT1

This trajectory table was calculated using the best available data for each lead. Trajectories are representative of the nominal behavior of each lead at standard conditions (50°F temperature; barometric pressure of 29.53 inches; altitude at sea level).
Shooters are cautioned that actual trajectories may differ due to variations in altitude, atmospheric conditions, guns, sights, and ammunition.

FEDERAL RIFLE BALLISTICS

PREMIUM® HIGH ENERGY RIFLE

USAGE	FEDERAL LOAD NO.	CALIBER	BULLET WGT. IN GRAINS	GRAMS	BULLET STYLE*	FACTORY PRIMER NO.	MUZZLE	100 YDS.	VELOCITY IN FEET PER SECOND (TO NEAREST 10 FPS) 200 YDS.	300 YDS.	400 YDS.	500 YDS.	MUZZLE	100 YDS.	ENERGY IN FOOT-POUNDS (TO NEAREST 5 FOOT-POUNDS) 200 YDS.	300 YDS.	400 YDS.	500 YDS.
2	P270T3	270 Win.	140	9.07	Trophy Bonded Bear Claw	210	3100	2860	2620	2400	2200	2000	2990	2535	2140	1795	1500	1240
3	P308T2	308 Win. (7.62x51mm)	165	10.69	Trophy Bonded Bear Claw	210	2870	2600	2350	2120	1890	1690	3020	2485	2030	1640	1310	1040
3	P308G	308 Win. (7.62x51mm)	180	11.66	Nosler Partition	210	2740	2550	2370	2200	2030	1870	3080	2600	2245	1925	1645	1395
NEW 3	P308L	308 Win. (7.62x51mm)	180	11.66	Woodleigh Weldcore SP	210	2740	2500	2280	2060	1860	1680	3000	2500	2075	1705	1385	1128
3	P3006T3	30-06 Spring (7.62x63mm)	180	11.66	Trophy Bonded Bear Claw	210	2880	2630	2380	2160	1940	1740	3315	2755	2270	1855	1505	1210
3	P3006R	30-06 Spring (7.62x63mm)	180	11.66	Nosler Partition	210	2880	2690	2500	2320	2150	1980	3315	2880	2495	2150	1845	1570
NEW 3	P3006X	30-06 Spring (7.62x63mm)	180	11.66	Woodleigh Weldcore SP	210	2880	2640	2400	2180	1970	1780	3315	2775	2310	1905	1560	1265
3	P300WT3	300 Win. Mag.	180	11.66	Trophy Bonded Bear Claw	215	3100	2830	2580	2340	2110	1900	3840	3205	2660	2190	1780	1445
3	P300WE	300 Win. Mag.	200	12.96	Nosler Partition	215	2930	2740	2550	2370	2200	2030	3810	3325	2885	2495	2145	1840
NEW 3	P300WS	300 Win. Mag.	180	11.66	Woodleigh Weldcore SP	215	3100	2830	2580	2340	2120	1910	3840	3210	2665	2195	1795	1450
3	P300WST3	300 Weatherby Magnum	180	11.66	Trophy Bonded Bear Claw	215	3330	3060	2850	2750	2410	2210	4430	3795	3235	2750	2320	1950
3	P300WS8	300 Weatherby Magnum	180	11.66	Nosler Partition	215	3330	3110	2910	2710	2520	2340	4430	3875	3375	2935	2540	2190
NEW 2	P303T1	303 British	180	11.66	Trophy Bonded Bear Claw	215	2590	2350	2120	1900	1700	1520	2680	2205	1795	1445	1160	920
3	P338T2	338 Win. Mag.	225	14.58	Trophy Bonded Bear Claw	215	2940	2690	2450	2230	2010	1810	4320	3610	3000	2475	2025	1640
3	P338D	338 Win. Mag.	250	16.20	Nosler Partition	215	2800	2610	2420	2250	2080	1920	4350	3775	3260	2805	2395	2025
NEW 3	P338G	338 Win. Mag.	250	16.20	Woodleigh Weldcore SP	215	2800	2610	2420	2240	2070	1910	4350	3770	3255	2795	2385	2025
NEW 4	P375T3	375 H & H Magnum	300	19.44	Trophy Bonded Bear Claw	215	2700	2440	2190	1960	1740	1540	4855	3960	3195	2560	2020	1585

*SP = Soft Point

PREMIUM® SAFARI® RIFLE

USAGE	FEDERAL LOAD NO.	CALIBER	BULLET WGT. IN GRAINS	GRAMS	BULLET STYLE*	FACTORY PRIMER NO.	MUZZLE	100 YDS.	VELOCITY IN FEET PER SECOND (TO NEAREST 10 FPS) 200 YDS.	300 YDS.	400 YDS.	500 YDS.	MUZZLE	100 YDS.	ENERGY IN FOOT-POUNDS (TO NEAREST 5 FOOT-POUNDS) 200 YDS.	300 YDS.	400 YDS.	500 YDS.
3	P300HA	300 H&H Magnum	180	11.66	Nosler Partition	215	2880	2620	2380	2150	1930	1730	3315	2750	2270	1840	1480	1190
3	P300W92	300 Win. Magnum	180	11.66	Nosler Partition	215	2960	2700	2450	2210	1990	1780	3500	2905	2395	1955	1585	1270
3	P300WT1	300 Win. Magnum	200	12.96	Trophy Bonded Bear Claw	215	2930	2570	2350	2150	1950	1770	3480	2935	2460	2050	1690	1385
3	P300WT2	300 Win. Magnum	180	11.66	Trophy Bonded Bear Claw	215	2960	2700	2460	2220	2000	1800	3500	2915	2415	1975	1605	1290
NEW 3	P300WF	300 Win. Magnum	180	11.66	Woodleigh Weldcore SP	215	2960	2700	2460	2230	2010	1800	3500	2915	2415	1980	1610	1300
3	P300WBA	300 Weatherby Magnum	180	11.66	Nosler Partition	215	3190	2980	2780	2590	2400	2230	4055	3540	3080	2670	2305	1985
3	P300WBT1	300 Weatherby Magnum	180	11.66	Trophy Bonded Bear Claw	215	3190	2950	2720	2500	2290	2100	4065	3475	2955	2505	2105	1760
3	P300WBT2	300 Weatherby Magnum	200	12.96	Trophy Bonded Bear Claw	215	2900	2670	2440	2230	2030	1830	3735	3150	2645	2200	1820	1490
3	P338A2	338 Win. Magnum	210	13.60	Nosler Partition	215	2830	2600	2390	2180	1980	1800	3735	3160	2655	2215	1835	1505
3	P338B2	338 Win. Magnum	250	16.20	Nosler Partition	215	2660	2470	2300	2120	1960	1800	3925	3395	2925	2505	2130	1805
3	P338T1	338 Win. Magnum	225	14.58	Trophy Bonded Bear Claw	215	2800	2580	2330	2110	1900	1710	3915	3285	2700	2220	1800	1455
NEW 3	P338F	338 Win. Magnum	250	16.20	Woodleigh Weldcore SP	215	2660	2470	2290	2120	1960	1800	3925	3395	2920	2495	2120	1795
NEW 3	P340WBT1	340 Weatherby Magnum	225	14.58	Trophy Bonded Bear Claw	215	3100	2840	2600	2370	2150	1940	4800	4035	3375	2800	2310	1885
4	P375F	375 H&H Magnum	300	19.44	Nosler Partition	215	2530	2320	2120	1930	1750	1580	4265	3585	2995	2475	2040	1675
4	P375T1	375 H&H Magnum	300	19.44	Trophy Bonded Bear Claw	215	2530	2280	2040	1810	1610	1425	4265	3450	2765	2190	1725	1350
4	P375T2	375 H&H Magnum	300	19.44	Trophy Bonded Sledgehammer	215	2530	2160	1820	1520	1280	1100	4265	3105	2210	1550	1090	810
2	P458A	458 Win. Magnum	350	22.68	Soft Point	215	2470	1990	1570	1250	1060	950	4740	3065	1915	1295	870	705
4	P458B	458 Win. Magnum	510	33.04	Soft Point	215	2090	1820	1570	1360	1180	1090	4945	3730	2790	2080	1605	1320
4	P458C	458 Win. Magnum	500	32.40	Solid	215	2090	1870	1670	1480	1320	1190	4850	3880	3065	2440	1945	1585
4	P458T1	458 Win. Magnum	400	25.92	Trophy Bonded Bear Claw	215	2380	2170	1960	1770	1600	1430	5030	4165	3415	2785	2255	1825
4	P458T2	458 Win. Magnum	500	32.40	Trophy Bonded Bear Claw	215	2090	1870	1660	1480	1310	1170	4850	3870	3065	2420	1915	1550
4	P458T3	458 Win. Magnum	500	32.40	Trophy Bonded Sledgehammer	215	2090	1960	1650	1460	1300	1170	4850	3845	3075	2365	1865	1505
4	P416A	416 Rigby	410	26.57	Woodleigh Weldcore SP	215	2370	2110	1870	1640	1440	1280	5115	4050	3185	2455	1895	1485
4	P416B	416 Rigby	410	26.57	Solid	215	2370	2110	1870	1640	1440	1280	5115	4050	3185	2455	1895	1485
4	P416T1	416 Rigby	400	25.92	Trophy Bonded Bear Claw	215	2370	2150	1940	1750	1570	1410	4990	4110	3350	2715	2180	1760
4	P416T2	416 Rigby	400	25.92	Trophy Bonded Bear Claw	215	2370	2120	1890	1660	1460	1290	4990	3970	3130	2440	1895	1480
4	P416T11	416 Rem. Magnum	400	25.92	Trophy Bonded Bear Claw	215	2400	2180	1970	1770	1590	1420	5115	4215	3440	2785	2245	1800
4	P470A	470 Nitro Express	500	32.40	Woodleigh Weldcore SP	215	2150	1890	1650	1440	1270	1140	5130	3965	3040	2310	1790	1435
4	P470B	470 Nitro Express	500	32.40	Woodleigh Weldcore Solid	215	2150	1890	1650	1440	1270	1140	5130	3965	3040	2310	1790	1435
4	P470T1	470 Nitro Express	500	32.40	Trophy Bonded Bear Claw	215	2150	1940	1740	1560	1400	1260	5130	4170	3360	2685	2160	1750
4	P470T2	470 Nitro Express	500	32.40	Trophy Bonded Sledgehammer	215	2150	1940	1740	1560	1400	1290	5130	4170	3360	2695	2180	1750

*SP = Soft Point Sledgehammer = Sledgehammer Solid

GOLD MEDAL® SKEET

FEDERAL LOAD NO.	GAUGE	SHELL LENGTH INCHES	MM	DRAM EQUIV.	MUZZLE VELOCITY	SHOT CHARGE WEIGHT OUNCES	GRAMS	SHOT SIZES
GOLD MEDAL® PLASTIC								
S113	12	2¾	70	2¾	1180	1	28.35	9
S115	12	2¾	70	2¾	1145	1⅛	31.88	9
S116	12	2¾	70	3	1200	1⅛	31.88	9
GOLD MEDAL® PAPER								
S175	12	2¾	70	2¾	1180	1	28.35	9
S117	12	2¾	70	2¾	1145	1⅛	31.88	9
S118	12	2¾	70	3	1200	1⅛	31.88	9
GOLD MEDAL® EXTRA-LITE® PLASTIC (SOFT RECOIL)								
S114	12	2¾	70	Extra-Lite		1⅛	31.89	9
GOLD MEDAL® PLASTIC (SMALL GAUGE)								
S206	20	2¾	70	2½	1200	⅞	24.80	9
S280	28	2¾	70	2	1230	¾	21.25	9
S412	410	2½	63.5	Max.	1230	½	14.17	9

GOLD MEDAL® SPORTING CLAYS

FEDERAL LOAD NO.	GAUGE	SHELL LENGTH INCHES	MM	DRAM EQUIV.	MUZZLE VELOCITY	SHOT CHARGE WEIGHT OUNCES	GRAMS	SHOT SIZES
GOLD MEDAL® PLASTIC								
SC116	12	2¾	70	3	1200	1⅛	31.89	7½, 8
GOLD MEDAL® EXTRA-LITE® PLASTIC (SOFT RECOIL)								
SC114	12	2¾	70	Extra-Lite		1⅛	31.89	7½, 8
GOLD MEDAL® SPECIAL PLASTIC (HIGH VELOCITY)								
SC170	12	2¾	70	SPEC.		1⅛	31.89	7½, 8
GOLD MEDAL® PLASTIC (SMALL GAUGE)								
SC206	20	2¾	70	2½	1200	⅞	24.80	8, 8½
SC280	28	2¾	70	2	1230	¾	21.25	8½
SC412	410	2½	63.5	Max.	1230	½	14.17	8½

FEDERAL RIFLE BALLISTICS

WIND DRIFT IN INCHES 10 MPH CROSSWIND					HEIGHT OF BULLET TRAJECTORY IN INCHES ABOVE OR BELOW LINE OF SIGHT IF ZEROED AT ⊕ YARDS. SIGHTS 1.5 INCHES ABOVE BORE LINE											TEST BARREL LENGTH INCHES	FEDERAL LOAD NO.
							AVERAGE RANGE				LONG RANGE						
100 YDS.	200 YDS.	300 YDS.	400 YDS.	500 YDS.	50 YDS.	100 YDS.	200 YDS.	300 YDS.	50 YDS.	100 YDS.	200 YDS.	300 YDS.	400 YDS.	500 YDS.			
0.7	3.0	6.9	12.9	21.2	-0.2	⊕	-2.9	-10.6	+0.4	+1.4	⊕	-6.4	-19.9	-39.7		24	P27013
1.0	3.9	9.2	17.9	29.4	-0.2	⊕	-3.6	-13.6	+0.7	+1.9	⊕	-8.2	-24.6	-49.0		24	P208T2
0.7	2.9	6.8	12.6	20.2	-0.1	⊕	-3.6	-13.6	+0.6	+1.9	⊕	-8.2	-23.5	-47.1		24	P208G
0.9	3.7	8.9	16.3	27.2	-0.1	⊕	-4.1	-14.9	+0.9	+2.0	⊕	-8.8	-25.8	-52.9		24	P208L

GOLD MEDAL ULTRAMATCH RIMFIRE

USAGE	TYPE	FEDERAL LOAD NO.	CARTRIDGE PER BOX	CALIBER	BULLET WT. IN GRAINS	BULLET STYLE	VELOCITY IN FEET PER SECOND (TO NEAREST 10 FPS)					ENERGY IN FOOT-POUNDS (TO NEAREST 5 FOOT-POUNDS)					WIND DRIFT IN INCHES 10 MPH CROSSWIND				HEIGHT OF BULLET TRAJECTORY IN INCHES ABOVE OR BELOW LINE OF SIGHT IF ZEROED AT ⊕ YARDS. SIGHTS 1.5 INCHES ABOVE BORE LINE			
							MUZZLE	25 YD.	50 YD.	75 YD.	100 YD.	MUZZLE	25 YD.	50 YD.	75 YD.	100 YD.	25 YD.	50 YD.	75 YD.	100 YD.	25 YD.	50 YD.	75 YD.	100 YD.
5	UltraMatch	1000A	50	22 Long Rifle	40	Solid	1140	1050	1040	1000	970	115	105	95	90	80	0.3	1.2	2.5	4.3	0.2	⊕	-2.2	-6.6
5	UltraMatch	1000B	50	22 Long Rifle	40	Solid	1080	1030	1000	960	930	105	100	95	90	75	0.3	1.0	2.2	3.9	0.3	⊕	-2.4	-7.2
5	Match	900A	50	22 Long Rifle	40	Solid	1140	1050	1040	1000	970	115	105	95	90	80	0.3	1.2	2.5	4.3	0.2	⊕	-2.2	-6.6
5	Match	900B	50	22 Long Rifle	40	Solid	1080	1030	1000	960	930	105	95	90	90	75	0.3	1.0	2.2	3.9	0.3	⊕	-2.4	-7.2
5	Target	711	50	22 Long Rifle	40	Solid	1150	1090	1050	1010	970	115	105	95	90	80	0.3	1.2	2.8	4.5	0.2	⊕	-2.2	-6.4

These ballistic specifications were derived from test barrels 24 inches in length.

BALLISTICS

FEDERAL BALLISTICS

CLASSIC AUTOMATIC PISTOL

USAGE	FEDERAL LOAD NO.	CALIBER	BULLET WGT. IN GRAINS	GRAMS	BULLET STYLE*	FACTORY PRIMER NO.	VELOCITY IN FEET PER SECOND (TO NEAREST 10 FPS) MUZZLE	25 YDS.	50 YDS.	75 YDS.	100 YDS.	ENERGY IN FOOT-POUNDS (TO NEAREST 5 FOOT-POUNDS) MUZZLE	25 YDS.	50 YDS.	75 YDS.	100 YDS.	MID-RANGE TRAJECTORY 25 YDS.	50 YDS.	75 YDS.	100 YDS.	TEST BARREL LENGTH INCHES
5,6	25AP	25 Auto (6.35mm Browning)	50	3.24	Full Metal Jacket	200	760	750	730	720	700	65	60	60	55	55	0.5	1.9	4.5	8.1	2
5,6	32AP	32 Auto (7.65mm Browning)	71	4.60	Full Metal Jacket	100	910	880	860	830	810	130	120	115	110	105	0.3	1.4	3.2	5.9	4
5,6	380AP	380 Auto (9x17mm Short)	95	6.15	Full Metal Jacket	100	960	910	870	830	790	190	175	160	145	130	0.3	1.3	3.1	5.8	3¾
6	380BP	380 Auto (9x17mm Short)	90	5.83	Hi-Shok JHP	100	1000	940	890	840	800	200	175	160	140	130	0.3	1.2	2.8	5.5	3¾
6	9MKB	9mm Makarov (9x18 Makarov)	90	5.83	Hi-Shok JHP	100	990	950	910	880	850	195	180	165	155	145	0.3	1.2	2.8	5.3	3½
5,6	9AP	9mm Luger (9x19mm Parabellum)	124	8.03	Full Metal Jacket	100	1120	1070	1030	990	960	345	315	290	270	255	0.2	0.9	2.2	4.1	4
6	9BP	9mm Luger (9x19mm Parabellum)	115	7.45	Hi-Shok JHP	100	1160	1100	1060	1020	990	345	310	285	270	250	0.2	0.9	2.1	3.9	4
6	9MS	9mm Luger (9x19mm Parabellum)	147	9.52	Hi-Shok JHP	100	990	950	930	900	880	320	295	285	265	255	0.3	1.2	2.8	5.1	4
6	357S2	357 Sig	125	8.10	Full Metal Jacket	100	1350	1270	1190	1130	1080	510	445	395	355	325	0.2	0.7	1.8	3.1	4
6	40SWA	40 S&W	180	11.66	Hi-Shok JHP	100	990	960	910	880	860	390	365	345	320	315	0.3	1.2	2.8	5.0	4
6	40SWB	40 S&W	155	10.04	Hi-Shok JHP	100	1140	1080	1030	990	950	445	400	365	335	315	0.2	1.0	2.2	4.1	4
6	10C	10mm Auto	180	11.66	Hi-Shok JHP	150	1030	1000	970	950	920	425	400	375	355	340	0.3	1.1	2.5	4.7	5
6	10E	10mm Auto	155	10.04	Hi-Shok JHP	150	1330	1220	1140	1080	1030	605	515	450	400	360	0.2	0.7	1.8	3.3	5
6	45A	45 Auto	230	14.96	Full Metal Jacket	150	850	830	810	790	770	370	350	335	320	305	0.4	1.8	3.8	6.8	5
6	45C	45 Auto	185	11.99	Hi-Shok JHP	150	950	920	900	880	860	370	350	335	315	300	0.3	1.3	2.8	5.3	5
6	45B	45 Auto	230	14.90	Hi-Shok JHP	150	850	830	810	790	770	370	350	335	320	305	0.4	1.8	3.7	6.7	5

*JHP = Jacketed Hollow Point

CLASSIC REVOLVER

USAGE	FEDERAL LOAD NO.	CALIBER	BULLET WGT. IN GRAINS	GRAMS	BULLET STYLE**	FACTORY PRIMER NO.	VELOCITY IN FEET PER SECOND (TO NEAREST 10 FPS) MUZZLE	25 YDS.	50 YDS.	75 YDS.	100 YDS.	ENERGY IN FOOT-POUNDS (TO NEAREST 5 FOOT-POUNDS) MUZZLE	25 YDS.	50 YDS.	75 YDS.	100 YDS.	MID-RANGE TRAJECTORY 25 YDS.	50 YDS.	75 YDS.	100 YDS.	TEST BARREL LENGTH INCHES
5	32LA	32 S&W Long	98	6.35	Lead Wadcutter	100	780	700	630	560	500	130	105	85	70	55	0.5	2.2	5.8	11.1	4
5	32LB	32 S&W Long	98	6.35	Lead Round Nose	100	710	690	670	650	640	115	105	100	95	90	0.6	2.3	5.3	9.6	4
6	32HRA	32 H&R Magnum	95	6.15	Lead Semi-Wadcutter	100	1030	1000	940	930	870	225	210	195	185	170	0.3	1.1	2.5	4.7	4½
6	32HRB	32 H&R Magnum	85	5.50	Hi-Shok JHP	100	1100	1050	1020	870	930	230	210	195	175	165	0.2	1.0	2.3	4.3	4½
5	38B	38 Special	158	10.23	Lead Round Nose	100	760	740	720	710	690	200	190	185	175	170	0.5	2.0	4.6	8.3	4-V
5,6	38C	38 Special	158	10.23	Lead Semi-Wadcutter	100	760	740	720	710	690	200	190	185	175	170	0.5	2.0	4.6	8.3	4-V
1,6	38E	38 Special (High-Velocity +P)	125	8.10	Hi-Shok JHP	100	950	920	900	880	860	250	235	225	215	205	0.3	1.3	2.9	5.4	4-V
1,6	38F	38 Special (High-Velocity +P)	110	7.13	Hi-Shok JHP	100	1000	960	930	900	870	240	225	210	195	185	0.3	1.2	2.7	5.0	4-V
1,6	38G	38 Special (High-Velocity +P)	158	10.23	Semi-Wadcutter HP	100	890	870	840	840	820	280	265	250	245	235	0.3	1.4	3.3	5.8	4-V
5,6	38H	38 Special (High-Velocity +P)	158	10.23	Lead Semi-Wadcutter	100	890	870	850	840	820	270	265	250	245	235	0.3	1.4	3.3	5.9	4-V
1,6	38J	38 Special (High-Velocity +P)	125	8.10	Hi-Shok JSP	100	950	920	900	880	860	250	235	225	215	205	0.3	1.3	2.9	5.4	4-V
2,6	357A	357 Magnum	158	10.23	Hi-Shok JSP	100	1240	1160	1100	1060	1020	535	475	430	395	365	0.2	0.8	1.9	3.5	4-V
1,6	357B	357 Magnum	125	8.10	Hi-Shok JHP	100	1450	1350	1240	1160	1100	580	405	430	370	335	0.1	0.8	1.5	2.8	4-V
5	357C	357 Magnum	158	10.23	Lead Semi-Wadcutter	100	1240	1160	1100	1060	1020	535	475	430	395	365	0.2	0.8	1.9	3.5	4-V
1,6	357D	357 Magnum	110	7.13	Hi-Shok JHP	100	1300	1180	1100	1040	970	410	340	290	260	235	0.2	0.8	1.9	3.5	4-V
2,6	357E	357 Magnum	158	10.23	Hi-Shok JHP	100	1240	1160	1100	1060	1020	535	475	430	395	365	0.2	0.8	1.9	3.5	4-V
2	357G	357 Magnum	180	11.66	Hi-Shok JHP	100	1090	1030	980	930	900	475	425	385	350	320	0.2	1.0	2.4	4.5	4-V
2,6	357H	357 Magnum	140	9.07	Hi-Shok JHP	100	1360	1270	1190	1130	1080	575	500	445	315	360	0.2	0.7	1.8	3.8	4-V
1,6	41A	41 Rem. Magnum	210	13.60	Hi-Shok JHP	150	1300	1210	1130	1070	1030	790	680	595	540	495	0.2	0.7	1.9	3.3	4-V
1,6	44SA	44 S&W Special	200	12.96	Semi-Wadcutter HP	150	900	860	830	800	770	360	330	305	285	260	0.3	1.4	3.4	6.3	6½-V
2,6	44A	44 Rem. Magnum	240	15.55	Hi-Shok JHP	150	1180	1130	1080	1050	1010	740	675	625	580	550	0.2	0.9	2.0	3.7	6½-V
1,2	44B	44 Rem. Magnum	180	11.66	Hi-Shok JHP	150	1610	1480	1370	1270	1180	1035	875	750	640	550	0.1	0.5	1.2	2.3	6½-V
1,6	45LCA	45 Colt	225	14.58	Semi-Wadcutter HP	150	900	880	860	830	820	405	385	370	355	340	0.3	1.4	3.2	5.8	5½

+P ammunition is loaded to a higher pressure. Use only in firearms recommended by the gun manufacturer. "V" indicates vented barrel to simulate service conditions. *Also available in 20-pound box (A44B20). **JHP = Jacketed Hollow Point HP = Hollow Point JSP = Jacketed Soft Point Usage Key: 1=Varmints, predators, small game 2= Medium game 3 =Large, heavy game 4=Dangerous game 5=Target shooting, training, practice 6=Self defense

CLASSIC RIMFIRE

USAGE	FEDERAL LOAD NO.	CARTRIDGES PER BOX	CALIBER*	BULLET WGT. IN GRAINS	BULLET STYLE**	VELOCITY IN FEET PER SECOND (TO NEAREST 10 FPS) MUZZLE	50	100	ENERGY IN FOOT-POUNDS (TO NEAREST 5 FOOT-POUNDS) MUZZLE	50	100	WIND DRIFT IN INCHES 10 MPH CROSSWIND	50	100	HEIGHT OF BULLET TRAJECTORY IN INCHES ABOVE OR BELOW LINE OF SIGHT IF ZEROED AT 100 YARDS. SIGHTS 1.5 INCHES ABOVE BORE LINE. 50	75	100	150
1,5	710	50	22 Long Rifle HV	40	Solid, Copper Plated	1280	1100	1020	940	140	110	90	80	1.5	5.5	11.4	⊕	-6.5	-21.0	+2.7	-10.0
1,5	810	100	22 Long Rifle HV	40	Solid, Copper Plated	1280	1100	1020	940	140	110	90	80	1.5	5.5	11.4	⊕	-6.5	-21.0	+2.7	-10.0
1,5	712	50	22 Long Rifle HV	38	HP Copper Plated	1280	1120	1020	950	140	105	90	75	1.6	5.8	12.1	⊕	-6.3	-20.8	+2.7	-10.0
1,5	724	50	22 Long Rifle HV†	31	HP Copper Plated	1550	1280	1100	990	165	115	85	65	1.7	7.0	15.5	⊕	-3.8	-14.7	+1.9	-8.0
1,5	716	50	22 Long Rifle Bird Shot	25	No. 10 Lead Shot	—	—	—	—	—	—	—	—	—	—	—	—	—	—	—	—

*HV = High Velocity HV† = Hyper-Velocity **HP = Hollow Point These ballistic specifications were derived from test barrels 24 inches in length.

CLASSIC .22 MAGNUM

USAGE	FEDERAL LOAD NO.	CARTRIDGES PER BOX	CALIBER	BULLET WGT. IN GRAINS	BULLET STYLE*	VELOCITY IN FEET PER SECOND (TO NEAREST 10 FPS) MUZZLE	50	100	ENERGY IN FOOT-POUNDS (TO NEAREST 5 FOOT-POUNDS) MUZZLE	50	100	WIND DRIFT IN INCHES 10 MPH CROSSWIND	50	100	HEIGHT OF BULLET TRAJECTORY IN INCHES ABOVE OR BELOW LINE OF SIGHT IF ZEROED AT 100 YDS. SIGHTS 1.5 INCHES ABOVE BORE LINE. 50	75	100	150
1,5	757	50	22 Win. Magnum	50	Jacketed HP	1650	1450	1280	1150	300	235	180	145	1.1	4.6	10.3	⊕	-3.0	-12.5	+1.2	-8.5
1,5	737	50	22 Win. Magnum	40	Full Metal Jacket	1910	1600	1330	1140	325	225	155	115	1.3	5.7	13.4	⊕	-2.8	-10.7	+1.9	-5.8
1,5	767	50	22 Win. Magnum	30	Jacketed HP	2200	1760	1400	1130	325	205	130	85	1.4	6.3	15.4	⊕	-1.3	-7.3	+0.7	-5.2

*HP = Hollow Point These trajectory tables were calculated by computer using the best available data for each lead. Trajectories are representative of the nominal behavior of each lead at standard conditions (58°F temperature; barometric pressure of 29.53 inches; altitude at sea level). Shooters are cautioned that actual trajectories may differ due to variations in altitude, atmospheric conditions, guns, sights, and ammunition.

HORNADY BALLISTICS

BALLISTICS INFORMATION

CUSTOM AMMO	VELOCITY (FEET PER SECOND)						ENERGY (FOOT - POUNDS)						TRAJECTORY TABLES				
Barrel is 24" except for 30-30 Win., which is 20"	MUZZLE	100 yds.	200 yds.	300 yds.	400 yds.	500 yds.	Muzzle	100 yds.	200 yds.	300 yds.	400 yds.	500 yds.	100 yds.	200 yds.	300 yds.	400 yds.	500 yds.
223 Rem., 53 gr. HP	3330	2882	2477	2106	1710	1475	1305	978	722	522	369	356	+1.7	-0-	-7.4	-22.7	-49.1
223 Rem., 60 gr. SP	3150	2782	2442	2127	1837	1575	1322	1031	795	603	450	331	+1.6	-0-	-7.5	-22.5	-48.1
223 Rem., 75 gr. BTHP MATCH	2790	2554	2330	2119	1926	1744	1296	1086	904	747	617	506	2.37	-0-	-8.75	-25.06	-50.80
22-250 Rem., 53 gr. HP	3680	3185	2743	2341	1974	1646	1594	1194	886	645	459	319	+1.0	-0-	-5.7	-17.8	-38.8
22-250 Rem., 60 gr. SP	3600	3195	2826	2485	2169	1878	1727	1360	1064	823	627	470	+1.0	-0-	-5.4	-16.3	-34.8
220 Swift, 50 gr. SP	3850	3327	2862	2442	2060	1716	1645	1228	909	662	471	327	+0.8	-0-	-5.1	-16.1	-35.3
220 Swift, 60 gr. HP	3600	3199	2824	2475	2156	1868	1727	1364	1063	816	619	465	+1.0	-0-	-5.4	-16.3	-34.8
243 Win., 75 gr. HP	3400	2970	2578	2219	1890	1595	1926	1469	1107	820	595	425	+1.2	-0-	-6.5	-20.3	-43.8
243 Win., 100 gr. BTSP	2960	2728	2508	2299	2099	1910	1945	1653	1397	1174	979	810	+1.6	-0-	-7.2	-21.0	-42.8
6MM Rem., 100 gr. BTSP	3100	2861	2634	2419	2231	2018	2134	1818	1541	1300	1088	904	+1.3	-0-	-6.5	-18.9	-38.5
257 Roberts, 117 gr. BTSP	2780	2550	2331	2122	1925	1740	2007	1689	1411	1170	963	787	+1.9	-0-	-8.3	-24.4	-49.9
25-06 117 gr. BTSP	2990	2749	2520	2302	2096	1900	2322	1962	1649	1377	1141	938	+1.6	-0-	-7.0	-20.7	-42.2
270 Win., 130 gr. SP	3060	2800	2560	2330	2110	1900	2700	2265	1890	1565	1285	1045	+1.8	-0-	-7.1	-20.6	-42.0
270 Win., 140 gr. BTSP	2940	2747	2562	2385	2214	2050	2688	2346	2041	1769	1524	1307	+1.6	-0-	-7.0	-20.2	-40.3
270 Win., 150 gr. SP	2840	2641	2450	2267	2092	1926	2686	2322	1999	1712	1458	1235	+2.05	-0-	-7.83	-22.47	-45.04
7 x 57 Mau, 139 gr. BTSP	2700	2504	2316	2137	1965	1802	2251	1936	1656	1410	1192	1002	+2.0	-0-	-8.5	-24.9	-50.3
7MM Rem. Mag., 139 gr. BTSP	3150	2933	2727	2530	2341	2160	3063	2656	2296	1976	1692	1440	+1.2	-0-	-6.1	-17.7	-35.5
7MM Rem. Mag., 154 gr. SP	3035	2814	2604	2404	2212	2029	3151	2708	2319	1977	1674	1408	+1.3	-0-	-6.7	-19.3	-39.3
7MM Rem. Mag., 162 gr. BTSP	2940	2757	2582	2413	2251	2094	3110	2735	2399	2095	1823	1578	+1.6	-0-	-6.7	-19.7	-39.3
7MM Rem. Mag., 175 gr. SP	2860	2650	2440	2240	2060	1880	3180	2720	2310	1960	1640	1370	+2.0	-0-	-7.9	-22.7	-45.8
7MM Wby. Mag., 154 gr. SP	3200	2971	2753	2546	2348	2159	3501	3017	2592	2216	1885	1593	+1.2	-0-	-5.8	-17.0	-34.5
7MM Wby. Mag., 175 gr. SP	2910	2709	2516	2331	2154	1985	3290	2850	2459	2111	1803	1531	+1.6	-0-	-7.1	-20.6	-41.7
30-30 Win., 150 gr. RN	2390	1973	1605	1303	1095	974	1902	1296	858	565	399	316	-0-	-8.2	-30.0		
30-30 Win., 170 gr. FP	2200	1895	1619	1381	1191	1064	1827	1355	989	720	535	425	-0-	-8.9	-31.1		
308 Win., 150 gr. BTSP	2820	2560	2315	2084	1866	1644	2648	2183	1785	1447	1160	922	+2.0	-0-	-8.5	-25.2	-51.8
308 Win., 165 gr. BTSP	2700	2496	2301	2115	1937	1770	2670	2283	1940	1639	1375	1148	+2.0	-0-	-8.7	-25.2	-51.0
308 Win., 168 gr. BTHP MATCH	2700	2491	2292	2102	1921	1751	2719	2315	1959	1648	1377	1143	+2.36	-0-	-8.96	-25.87	-52.20
308 Win., 168 gr. A-MAX MATCH	2620	2446	2280	2120	1972	1831	2560	2232	1939	1677	1450	1251	2.60	-0-	-9.23	-25.65	-51.92
308 Win., 178 gr. BTHP MATCH	2610	2439	2274	2116	1964	1819	2692	2351	2044	1769	1524	1308	+2.49	-0-	-9.21	-26.20	-50.14
30-06 150 gr. SP	2910	2617	2342	2083	1843	1622	2820	2281	1827	1445	1131	876	+2.1	-0-	-8.5	-25.0	-51.8
30-06 150 gr. BTSP	2910	2683	2467	2262	2066	1880	2820	2397	2027	1706	1421	1177	+2.0	-0-	-7.7	-22.2	-44.9
30-06 165 gr. BTSP	2800	2591	2392	2202	2020	1848	2873	2460	2097	1777	1495	1252	+1.8	-0-	-8.0	-23.3	-47.0
30-06 168 gr. BTHP MATCH	2800	2587	2383	2189	2004	1828	2924	2496	2118	1787	1497	1247	+2.16	-0-	-8.27	-23.85	-48.57
30-06 180 gr. BTSP	2900	2695	2498	2310	2131	1959	3361	2902	2494	2133	1814	1533	+1.95	-0-	-7.54	-21.61	-43.31
300 Wby. Mag., 180 gr. SP	3120	2891	2673	2466	2268	2079	3890	3340	2856	2430	2055	1727	+1.3	-0-	-6.2	-18.1	-36.8
300 Win. Mag., 150 gr. BTSP	3275	2988	2718	2464	2224	1998	3573	2974	2461	2023	1648	1330	+1.2	-0-	-6.0	-17.8	-36.5
300 Win. Mag., 165 gr. BTSP	3100	2877	2665	2462	2269	2084	3522	3033	2603	2221	1887	1592	+1.3	-0-	-6.5	-18.5	-37.3
300 Win. Mag., 180 gr. SP	2960	2745	2540	2344	2157	1979	3501	3011	2578	2196	1859	1565	+1.9	-0-	-7.3	-20.9	-41.9
300 Win. Mag., 190 gr. BTSP	2900	2711	2529	2355	2187	2026	3549	3101	2699	2340	2018	1732	+1.6	-0-	-7.1	-20.4	-41.0
303 British, 150 gr. SP	2685	2441	2210	1992	1787	1598	2401	1984	1627	1321	1064	500	+2.2	-0-	-9.3	-27.4	-56.5

LIGHT MAGNUM	VELOCITY (FEET PER SECOND)						ENERGY FOOT - POUNDS						TRAJECTORY TABLES				
Barrel is 24".	MUZZLE	100 yds.	200 yds.	300 yds.	400 yds.	500 yds.	Muzzle	100 yds.	200 yds.	300 yds.	400 yds.	500 yds.	100 yds.	200 yds.	300 yds.	400 yds.	500 yds.
6MM Rem., 100 gr. BTSP LM	3250	2997	2756	2528	2311	2105	2345	1995	1687	1418	1186	984	1.59	-0-	-6.33	-18.25	-36.51
243 Win., 100 gr. BTSP LM	3100	2839	2592	2358	2138	1936	2133	1790	1491	1235	1014	832	+1.5	-0-	-6.81	-19.8	-40.2
257 Roberts, 117 gr. BTSP LM	2940	2694	2460	2240	2031	1844	2245	1885	1572	1303	1071	883	+1.7	-0-	-7.8	-21.8	-44.7
25-06, 117 gr. BTSP LM	3110	2855	2613	2384	2168	1966	2512	2117	1774	1476	1220	1006	1.81	-0-	-7.08	-20.28	-40.35
7 x 57 Mau, 139 gr. BTSP LM	2830	2620	2450	2250	2070	1910	2475	2135	1835	1565	1330	1115	+1.8	-0-	-7.6	-22.1	-45.0
7 x 57MM, 139 gr. SP LM-E	2950	2736	2532	2337	2152	1979	2686	2310	1978	1686	1429	1209	2.02	-0-	-7.80	-21.51	-42.25
7MM Rem. Mag., 139 gr. BTSP HM Moly	3250	3041	2822	2613	2413	2223	3300	2854	2456	2106	1797	1525	1.14	-0-	-5.66	-16.59	-33.51
7MM-08, 139 gr. BTSP LM	3000	2790	2590	2399	2216	2041	2777	2403	2071	1776	1515	1285	+1.5	-0-	-6.7	-19.4	-39.2
308 Win., 150 gr. SP LM	3000	2721	2459	2212	1979	1762	2997	2466	2014	1629	1305	1034	+1.9	-0-	-7.69	-22.49	-46.23
308 Win., 165 gr. BTSP LM	2880	2655	2441	2237	2043	1859	3038	2582	2182	1833	1529	1266	+2.03	-0-	-7.86	-22.70	-45.87
308 Win., 168 gr. BTHP LM MATCH	2840	2630	2429	2238	2056	1892	3008	2579	2201	1868	1577	1335	1.84	-0-	-7.83	-22.70	-45.23
30-06 150 gr. SP LM	3100	2815	2548	2295	2058	1835	3200	2639	2161	1755	1410	1121	+1.4	-0-	-6.8	-20.3	-42.0
30-06 165 gr. BTSP LM	3015	2790	2575	2370	2176	1994	3330	2850	2428	2058	1734	1496	+1.55	-0-	-6.96	-20.11	-39.77
30-06 180 gr. BTSP LM	2900	2695	2498	2310	2131	1959	3361	2902	2494	2133	1814	1534	+1.95	-0-	-7.54	-21.61	-43.31
303 British, 150 gr. SP LM	2830	2570	2325	2094	1884	1690	2667	2199	1800	1461	1185	952	+2.0	-0-	-8.4	-24.6	-50.3
6.5 x 55MM, 129 gr. SP LM	2750	2548	2355	2171	1995	1827	2166	1860	1589	1350	1139	956	+2.24	-0-	-8.52	-24.42	-49.57
6.5 x 55, 140 gr. SP LM-E	2740	2541	2351	2169	1999	1842	2333	2006	1717	1463	1242	1054	2.40	-0-	-8.71	-24.02	-49.33
270 Win., 140 gr. BTSP LM	3100	2894	2697	2508	2327	2155	2987	2604	2261	1956	1684	1443	1.37	-0-	-6.32	-18.30	-36.81
280 Rem., 139 gr. BTSP LM Moly	3110	2888	2675	2473	2280	2096	2985	2573	2209	1887	1604	1355	1.38	-0-	-5.66	-18.62	-37.32
300 Win. Mag., 180 gr. BTSP HM	3100	2879	2668	2467	2275	2092	3840	3313	2845	2431	2068	1749	1.39	-0-	-6.45	-18.72	-37.51
338 Win. Mag., 225 gr. SP HM	2950	2714	2491	2278	2075	1884	4347	3680	3098	2591	2151	1772	1.92	-0-	-7.52	-21.78	-44.14
375 H&H, 270 gr. SP HM	2870	2620	2385	2162	1957	1767	4937	4116	3408	2802	2296	1871	2.24	-0-	-8.39	-23.87	-48.79
375 H&H, 300 gr. FMJ-RN HM	2705	2376	2072	1804	1560	1355	4873	3760	2861	2167	1621	1222	2.73	-0-	-10.81	-32.13	-68.38

TAP	VELOCITY (FEET PER SECOND)						ENERGY (FOOT - POUNDS)						TRAJECTORY TABLES				
Tactical Application Police	MUZZLE	100 yds.	200 yds.	300 yds.	400 yds.	500 yds.	Muzzle	100 yds.	200 yds.	300 yds.	400 yds.	500 yds.	100 yds.	200 yds.	300 yds.	400 yds.	500 yds.
223 Rem., 55 gr. URBAN*	2970	2626	2307	2011	1739	1496	1077	842	650	494	369	273	1.54	-0-	-8.12	-24.87	-53.23
223 Rem., 60 gr. URBAN*	2950	2619	2312	2025	1762	1524	1160	914	712	546	413	309	1.55	-0-	-8.09	-24.72	-52.82
223 Rem., 75 gr. BTHP PRECISION	2630	2409	2199	2000	1814	1637	1152	966	805	666	548	446	-2.0	-0-	-9.21	-25.91	-55.71
308 Win., 168 gr. BTHP PRECISION	2700	2491	2292	2102	1921	1751	2719	2315	1959	1646	1377	1143	2.36	-0-	-8.99	-25.87	-52.20

*16" AR-15 Carbine

VARMINT EXPRESS™	VELOCITY (FEET PER SECOND						ENERGY (FOOT - POUNDS)						TRAJECTORY TABLES				
Barrel is 24"	MUZZLE	100 yds.	200 yds.	300 yds.	400 yds.	500 yds.	Muzzle	100 yds.	200 yds.	300 yds.	400 yds.	500 yds.	100 yds.	200 yds.	300 yds.	400 yds.	500 yds.
22 Hornet, 35 gr. V-MAX	3100	2278	1601	1135	929	811	747	403	199	100	67	51	2.75	-0-	-16.89	-60.39	-144.72
222 Rem., 40 gr. V-MAX	3600	3117	2673	2269	1911	1596	1151	863	634	457	324	226	1.07	-0-	-6.13	-18.92	-41.15
222 Rem., 50 gr. V-MAX	3140	2729	2352	2008	1710	1450	1094	827	614	448	325	233	1.67	-0-	-7.88	-24.39	52.94
223 Rem., 40 gr. V-MAX	3800	3305	2845	2424	2044	1715	1282	970	719	522	371	261	0.84	-0-	-5.34	-16.57	-36.06
223 Rem., 55 gr. V-MAX	3240	2859	2507	2181	1891	1628	1282	998	767	581	437	324	1.44	-0-	-7.10	-21.38	-45.22
22-250 Rem., 40 gr. V-MAX	4150	3631	3147	2699	2293	1932	1529	1171	879	647	467	331	0.54	-0-	-4.15	-13.30	-28.90
22-250 Rem., 50 gr. V-MAX	3800	3349	2925	2535	2178	1862	1603	1245	950	713	527	385	0.79	-0-	-5.02	-15.58	-33.34
22-250 Rem., 55 gr. V-MAX	3680	3265	2876	2517	2183	1887	1654	1302	1010	772	582	435	0.88	-0-	-5.26	-16.12	-34.13
220 Swift, 40 gr. V-MAX	4200	3678	3190	2739	2329	1962	1566	1201	904	666	482	342	0.51	-0-	-4.00	-12.88	-27.94
220 Swift, 50 gr. V-MAX	3850	3396	2970	2576	2215	1894	1645	1280	979	736	545	398	0.74	-0-	-4.84	-15.08	-32.25
220 Swift, 55 gr. V-MAX	3680	3265	2876	2517	2183	1887	1654	1302	1010	772	582	435	0.88	-0-	-5.26	-16.12	-34.13
243, 58 gr. V-MAX	3750	3319	2913	2539	2195	1889	1811	1418	1093	830	620	459	1.19	-0-	-5.46	-16.44	-34.49

BARREL LENGTH	PISTOL AMMO	VELOCITY (FEET PER SECOND)			ENERGY (FOOT - POUNDS)		
		MUZZLE	50 yds.	100 yds.	Muzzle	50 yds.	100 yds.
2"	25 Auto, 35 gr. JHP/XTP	900	813	742	63	51	43
4"	32 ACP, 60 gr. HP/XTP	1000	917	849	133	112	96
4"	32 Auto, 71 gr. FMJ	900	845	797	128	112	100
3 3/4"	380 Auto, 90 gr. JHP/XTP	1000	902	823	200	163	135
4"	9MM Luger, 115 gr. JHP/XTP	1155	1047	971	341	280	241
4"	9MM Luger, 124 gr. JHP/XTP	1110	1030	971	339	292	259
4"	9MM Luger, 124 gr. FMJ V	1110	1038	981	339	297	265
4"	9MM Luger, 147 gr. JHP/XTP	975	935	899	310	285	264
4"	9 x 18 Makarov, 95 gr. JHP/XTP	1000	930	874	211	182	161
4"V	38 Special, 125 gr. JHP/XTP	900	856	817	225	203	185
4"V	38 Special, 140 gr. JHP/XTP	900	850	806	252	225	202
4"V	38 Special, 148 gr. HBWC	800	697	610	210	160	122
4"V	38 Special, 158 gr. JHP/XTP	800	765	731	225	205	188
4"	357 SIG, 124 gr. JHP/XTP	1350	1208	1108	502	405	338
4"	357 SIG, 147 gr. JHP/XTP	1225	1138	1072	490	422	375
8"V	357 Mag., 125 gr. JHP/XTP	1500	1314	1166	624	479	377
8"V	357 Mag., 125 gr. JFP/XTP	1500	1311	1161	624	477	374
8"V	357 Mag., 140 gr. JHP/XTP	1400	1249	1130	609	485	397
8"V	357 Mag., 158 gr. JHP/XTP	1250	1150	1073	548	464	404
8"V	357 Mag., 158 gr. JFP	1250	1147	1068	548	461	400

BARREL LENGTH	PISTOL AMMO	VELOCITY (FEET PER SECOND)			ENERGY (FOOT - POUNDS)		
		MUZZLE	50 yds.	100 yds.	Muzzle	50 yds.	100 yds.
5"	10MM Auto, 155 gr. JHP/XTP	1265	1119	1020	551	431	358
5"	10MM Auto, 180 gr. JHP/XTP Full	1180	1077	1004	556	464	403
5"	10MM Auto, 200 gr. JHP/XTP	1050	994	948	490	439	399
4"	40 S&W, 155 gr. JHP/XTP	1180	1061	980	479	388	331
4"	40 S&W, 180 gr. JHP/XTP	950	903	862	361	326	297
4"	40 S&W, 180 gr. FMJ V	950	906	865	361	328	299
4 3/4" V	44-40, 205 gr. Cowboy	725	697	670	239	221	204
7 1/2"V	44 Special, 180 gr. JHP/XTP	1000	935	882	400	350	311
7 1/2"V	44 Rem. Mag., 180 gr. JHP/XTP	1550	1340	1173	960	717	550
7 1/2"V	44 Rem. Mag., 200 gr. JHP/XTP	1500	1284	1128	999	732	565
7 1/2"V	44 Rem. Mag., 240 gr. JHP/XTP	1350	1188	1078	971	753	619
7 1/2"V	44 Rem. Mag., 300 gr. JHP/XTP	1150	1084	1031	881	782	708
4 3/4" V	45 Long Colt, 255 gr. Cowboy	725	692	660	298	271	247
5"	45 ACP, 185 gr. JHP/XTP	950	880	819	371	318	276
5"	45 ACP, 200 gr. JHP/XTP	900	855	815	358	325	295
5"	45 ACP+P, 200 gr. HP/XTP	1055	982	925	494	428	380
5"	45 ACP+P, 230 gr. HP/XTP	950	904	865	462	418	382
5"	45 ACP, 230 gr. FMJ/RN	850	809	771	369	334	304
5"	45 ACP, 230 gr. FMJ/FP	850	809	771	369	334	304
5"	45 ACP, 230 gr. FMJ-FP V	850	814	779	369	338	310

REMINGTON BALLISTICS

These tables were calculated by computer. A standard scientific technique was used to predict trajectories from the best available data for each round. Trajectories shown typify the ammunition's performance at sea level, but note that they may vary due to atmospheric conditions and the equipment.

All velocity and energy figures in these charts have been derived by using test barrels of indicated lengths.

Ballistics shown are for 24" barrels, except those for .30 carbine and .44 Remington Magnum, which are for 20" barrels. These barrel lengths were chosen as representative, as it's impractical to show performance figures for all barrel lengths.

The muzzle velocities, muzzle energies and trajectory data in these tables represent the approximate performance expected of each specified loading. Differences in barrel lengths, internal firearm dimensions, temperature, and test procedure can produce actual velocities that vary from those given here.

Centerfire Rifle Velocity vs. Barrel Length

Muzzle Velocity Range (ft./sec.)	Approx. Change in Muzzle Velocity per 1" Change in Barrel Length (ft./sec.)
2000-2500	10
2500-3000	20
3000-3500	30
3500-4000	40

1. Determine how much shorter, or longer, your barrel is than the test barrel.
2. In the left column of the above table, select the muzzle-velocity class of your cartridge.
3. To the right of that class, read the approximate change in velocity per inch of barrel length.
4. Multiply this number by the difference in the length of your barrel from that of the test barrel.
5. If your barrel is shorter than the test barrel, subtract this figure from the muzzle velocity shown for your cartridge.
6. If your barrel is longer, add this figure to the muzzle velocity shown.

The trajectory figures shown in these ballistic tables are the rise or drop, in inches, of the bullet from a direct line of sight at selected yardage. Sighting-in distances have been set at 100 to 250 yards.

The line of sight used is 1½" above the axis of the bore. Since the rise or drop figures shown at the stated yardage are points of impact, you must hold low for positive figures, high for negative figures.

Many shooters who use the same cartridge often find it helpful to commit the rise and drop figures for that cartridge to memory, or tape them to their rifle stock. That way, they know instantly the right "hold" as soon as they estimate the target's range.

Specifications are nominal. Ballistics figures established in test barrels. Individual rifles may vary from test-barrel specifications.

* Inches above or below line of sight. Hold low for positive numbers, high for negative numbers.

† 280 Rem. and 7mm Express® Rem. are interchangeable.

‡ Interchangeable in 244 Rem.

¹ Bullet does not rise more than 1" above line of sight from muzzle to sighting-in range.

² Bullet does not rise more than 3" above line of sight from muzzle to sighting-in range.

NOTE: "zero" indicates yardage at which rifle was sighted in.

Centerfire Rifle Ballistics Tables

Caliber	Index/EDI Number	Wt. (grs.)	Bullet Style	Primer No.	Muzzle	100 yds.	200 yds.	300 yds.	400 yds.	500 yds.
.17 Remington	R17REM	25	Hollow Point Power-Lokt®	7½	4040	3284	2644	2086	1606	1235
.22 Hornet	R22HN1	45	Pointed Soft Point	6½	2690	2042	1502	1128	948	840
	R22HN2	45	Hollow Point	6½	2690	2042	1502	1128	948	840
.220 Swift	R220S1	50	Pointed Soft Point	9½	3780	3158	2617	2135	1710	1357
	PRV220SA	50	V-Max™, Boat Tail	9½	3780	3321	2908	2532	2185	1866
.222 Remington	R222R1	50	Pointed Soft Point	7½	3140	2602	2123	1700	1350	1107
	R222R3	50	Hollow Point Power-Lokt®	7½	3140	2635	2182	1777	1432	1172
	PRV222RA	50	V-Max™, Boat Tail	7½	3140	2744	2380	2045	1740	1471
.223 Remington	PRV223RA	50	V-Max™, Boat Tail	7½	3300	2889	2514	2168	1851	1568
	R223R1	55	Pointed Soft Point	7½	3240	2747	2304	1905	1554	1270
	R223R2	55	Hollow Point Power-Lokt®	7½	3240	2773	2352	1969	1627	1341
	R223R3	55	Metal Case	7½	3240	2759	2326	1933	1587	1301
	R223R6	62	Hollow Point Match	7½	3025	2572	2162	1792	1471	1217
.22-250 Remington	R22501	55	Pointed Soft Point	9½	3680	3137	2656	2222	1832	1493
	R22502	55	Hollow Point Power-Lokt®	9½	3680	3209	2785	2400	2046	1725
	PRV2250A	50	V-Max™, Boat Tail	9½	3725	3272	2864	2491	2147	1832
.243 Win.	R243W1	80	Pointed Soft Point	9½	3350	2955	2593	2259	1951	1670
	R243W2	80	Pointed Soft Point Power-Lokt®	9½	3350	2955	2593	2259	1951	1670
	R243W3	100	Pointed Soft Point Core-Lokt®	9½	2960	2697	2449	2215	1993	1786
	PRV243WC ★	75	V-Max™, Boat Tail	9½	3375	3065	2775	2504	2248	2008
	PRB243WA ★	100	Pointed Soft Point, Boat Tail	9½	2960	2720	2492	2275	2069	1875
	PRT243WC ★	90	Pointed Soft Point, Ballistic Tip™	9½	3120	2871	2635	2411	2199	1997
6mm Remington	R6MM4	100	Pointed Soft Point Core-Lokt®	9½	3100	2829	2573	2332	2104	1889
	PRV6MMRC ★	75	V-Max™, Boat Tail	9½	3400	3088	2797	2524	2267	2026
	PRB6MMRA ★	100	Pointed Soft Point, Boat Tail	9½	3100	2852	2617	2394	2183	1982
.25-20 Win.	R25202	86	Soft Point	6½	1460	1194	1030	931	858	797
.250 Savage	R250SV	100	Pointed Soft Point	9½	2820	2504	2210	1936	1684	1461
.257 Roberts	R257	117	Soft Point Core-Lokt®	9½	2650	2291	1961	1663	1404	1199
.25-06 Remington	R25062	100	Pointed Soft Point Core-Lokt®	9½	3230	2893	2580	2287	2014	1762
	R25063	120	Pointed Soft Point Core-Lokt®	9½	2990	2730	2484	2252	2032	1825
6.5x55 Swedish	R65SWE1	140	Pointed Soft Point Core-Lokt®	9½	2550	2353	2164	1984	1814	1654
.260 Remington	R260R1	140	Pointed Soft Point Core-Lokt®	9½	2750	2544	2347	2158	1979	1812
	PRT260RC ★	140	Pointed Soft Point, Ballistic Tip	9½	2890	2688	2494	2309	2131	1962
.264 Win. Mag.	R264W2	140	Pointed Soft Point Core-Lokt®	9½ M	3030	2782	2548	2326	2114	1914
.270 Win.	R270W1	100	Pointed Soft Point	9½	3320	2924	2561	2225	1916	1636
	R270W2	130	Pointed Soft Point Core-Lokt®	9½	3060	2776	2510	2259	2022	1801
	R270W3	130	Bronze Point™	9½	3060	2802	2559	2329	2110	1904
	R270W4	150	Soft Point Core-Lokt®	9½	2850	2504	2183	1886	1618	1385
	RS270WA	140	Swift A-Frame™ PSP	9½	2925	2652	2394	2152	1923	1711
	PRB270WA ★	140	Pointed Soft Point, Boat Tail	9½	2960	2749	2548	2355	2171	1995
	PRT270WB ★	140	Pointed Soft Point, Ballistic Tip	9½	2960	2754	2557	2366	2187	2014
7mm Mauser (7 x 57)	R7MSR1	140	Pointed Soft Point Core-Lokt®	9½	2660	2435	2221	2018	1827	1648
7mm-08 Remington	R7M081	140	Pointed Soft Point Core-Lokt®	9½	2860	2625	2402	2189	1988	1798
	R7M083	120	Hollow Point	9½	3000	2725	2467	2223	1992	1778
	PRB7M08RA★	140	Pointed Soft Point, Boat Tail	9½	2860	2656	2460	2273	2094	1923
	PRT7M08RA ★	140	Pointed Soft Point, Ballistic Tip	9½	2860	2670	2488	2313	2145	1984
.280 Remington	R280R3 †	140	Pointed Soft Point Core-Lokt®	9½	3000	2758	2528	2309	2102	1905
	R280R1 †	150	Pointed Soft Point Core-Lokt®	9½	2890	2624	2373	2135	1912	1705
	R280R2 †	165	Soft Point Core-Lokt®	9½	2820	2510	2220	1950	1701	1479
	PRB280RA ★	140	Pointed Soft Point, Boat Tail	9½	3000	2789	2588	2395	2211	2035
	PRT280RA ★	140	Pointed Soft Point, Ballistic Tip	9½	3000	2804	2616	2436	2263	2097
7mm Remington Mag.	R7MM2	150	Pointed Soft Point Core-Lokt®	9½ M	3110	2830	2568	2320	2085	1866
	R7MM3	175	Pointed Soft Point Core-Lokt®	9½ M	2860	2645	2440	2244	2057	1879
	R7MM4	140	Pointed Soft Point Core-Lokt®	9½ M	3175	2923	2684	2458	2243	2039
	RS7MMA	160	Swift A-Frame™ PSP	9½ M	2900	2659	2430	2212	2006	1812
	PRB7MMRA ★	140	Pointed Soft Point, Boat Tail	9½ M	3175	2956	2747	2547	2356	2174
	PRT7MMC ★	150	Pointed Soft Point, Ballistic Tip	9½ M	3110	2912	2723	2542	2367	2200
7mm STW	R7MSTW1	140	Pointed Soft Point Core-Lokt®	9½ M	3325	3064	2818	2585	2364	2153
	RS7MSTWA ★	140	Swift A-Frame™ PSP	9½ M	3325	3020	2735	2467	2215	1978
.30 Carbine	R30CAR	110	Soft Point	6½	1990	1567	1236	1035	923	842
.30-30 Win. Accelerator®	R3030A	55	Soft Point	9½	3400	2693	2085	1570	1187	986
.30-30 Win.	R30301	150	Soft Point Core-Lokt®	9½	2390	1973	1605	1303	1095	974
	R30302	170	Soft Point Core-Lokt®	9½	2200	1895	1619	1381	1191	1061
	R30303	170	Hollow Point Core-Lokt®	9½	2200	1895	1619	1381	1191	1061
.300 Savage	R30SV3	180	Soft Point Core-Lokt®	9½	2350	2025	1728	1467	1252	1098
	R30SV2	150	Pointed Soft Point Core-Lokt®	9½	2630	2354	2095	1853	1631	1432

★ NEW FOR 1998

REMINGTON BALLISTICS

■ = Premier® Safari Grade   ■ = Premier® Varmint   ▢ = Premier® Ballistic Tip®   ▢ = Premier® Boat Tail

Energy (ft.-lbs.)						Short-range[1] Trajectory*						Long-range[2] Trajectory*							
Muzzle	100 yds.	200 yds.	300 yds.	400 yds.	500 yds.	50 yds.	100 yds.	150 yds.	200 yds.	250 yds.	300 yds.	100 yds.	150 yds.	200 yds.	250 yds.	300 yds.	400 yds.	500 yds.	Barrel Length
906	599	388	242	143	85	-0.3	0.3	zero	-1.3	-3.8	-7.8	1.8	2.3	1.8	zero	-3.3	-16.6	-43.6	24"
723	417	225	127	90	70	-0.1	zero	-2.1	-7.1	-16.0	-30.0	1.4	zero	-4.3	-12.4	-25.8	-74.2	-162.0	24"
723	417	225	127	90	70	-0.1	zero	-2.1	-7.1	-16.0	-30.0	1.4	zero	-4.3	-12.4	-25.8	-74.2	-162.0	
1586	1107	760	506	325	204	-0.2	0.3	zero	-1.4	-4.0	-8.2	0.4	1.0	zero	-2.3	-6.2	-20.1	-46.1	24"
1586	1224	939	711	530	387	-0.3	0.3	zero	-1.2	-3.3	-6.7	0.8	0.9	zero	-1.9	-5.0	-15.4	-33.2	24"
1094	752	500	321	202	136	0.1	0.7	zero	-2.3	-6.5	-13.1	1.9	1.7	zero	-3.6	-9.7	-31.7	-72.8	24"
1094	771	529	351	228	152	0.1	0.7	zero	-2.2	-6.2	-12.5	1.8	1.6	zero	-3.5	-9.2	-29.6	-67.1	
1094	836	629	464	336	240	-0.1	0.6	zero	-1.9	-5.4	-10.7	1.6	1.5	zero	-3.0	-7.8	-23.9	-51.7	24"
1209	927	701	522	380	273	-0.1	0.5	zero	-1.7	-4.3	-9.4	-0.1	1.3	zero	-2.6	-6.9	-21.2	-45.8	24"
1282	921	648	443	295	197	-0.1	0.6	zero	-2.0	-5.6	-11.2	1.6	1.5	zero	-3.1	-8.2	-26.2	-58.6	
1282	939	675	473	323	220	-0.1	0.6	zero	-1.9	-5.4	-10.7	1.5	1.4	zero	-3.0	-7.9	-24.8	-55.1	24"
1282	929	660	456	307	207	-0.1	0.6	zero	-1.9	-5.5	-11.0	1.6	1.5	zero	-3.1	-8.1	-25.5	-57.0	
1260	911	643	442	298	204	0.2	0.7	zero	-2.3	-6.5	-12.9	1.9	1.7	zero	-3.6	-9.4	-29.9	-66.4	24"
1654	1201	861	603	410	272	-0.2	0.3	zero	-1.4	-4.0	-8.1	1.9	2.4	1.8	zero	-3.3	-15.5	-38.3	
1654	1257	947	703	511	363	-0.2	0.3	zero	-1.3	-3.7	-7.4	1.8	2.2	1.7	zero	-3.0	-13.7	-32.8	24"
1540	1188	910	689	512	372	-0.3	0.3	zero	-1.2	-3.5	-7.0	1.7	2.1	1.6	zero	-2.8	-12.8	-30.4	
1993	1551	1194	906	676	495	-0.1	0.5	zero	-1.6	-4.5	-8.8	2.2	2.7	2.0	zero	-3.5	-15.8	-37.3	
1993	1551	1194	906	676	495	-0.1	0.5	zero	-1.6	-4.5	-8.8	2.2	2.7	2.0	zero	-3.5	-15.8	-37.3	
1945	1615	1332	1089	882	708	0.1	0.7	zero	-2.0	-5.4	-10.4	1.6	1.5	zero	-2.9	-7.5	-22.1	-45.4	24"
1897	1564	1282	1044	842	671	-0.1	0.4	zero	-1.4	-4.0	-7.8	2.0	2.4	1.8	zero	-3.0	-13.3	-30.6	
1945	1642	1378	1149	950	780	0.1	0.7	zero	-1.9	-5.3	-10.1	2.8	3.2	2.3	zero	-3.8	-16.6	-37.6	
1946	1647	1388	1162	966	797	-0.1	0.5	zero	-1.7	-4.5	-8.9	1.4	1.3	zero	-2.5	-6.4	-18.8	-38.3	
2133	1777	1470	1207	983	792	-0.1	0.6	zero	-1.8	-4.8	-9.3	1.4	1.3	zero	-2.6	-6.7	-19.8	-40.8	
1925	1587	1303	1061	858	683	-0.1	0.4	zero	-1.4	-3.9	-7.6	1.9	2.3	1.7	zero	-3.0	-13.1	-30.1	24"
2134	1806	1521	1273	1058	872	-0.1	0.5	zero	-1.7	-4.7	-9.0	1.4	1.3	zero	-2.6	-6.5	-19.1	-38.9	
407	272	203	165	141	121	zero	-3.5	-13.2	-30.0	-54.7	-89.1	zero	-7.9	-22.9	-45.8	-78.5	-173.0	-315.5	24"
1765	1392	1084	832	630	474	-0.1	zero	-1.3	-4.1	-8.7	-15.3	2.0	1.8	zero	-3.6	-9.2	-27.7	-58.6	24"
1824	1363	999	718	512	373	-0.1	zero	-1.6	-5.2	-10.5	-19.5	2.6	2.3	zero	-4.1	-11.7	-36.1	-78.2	24"
2316	1858	1478	1161	901	689	-0.1	0.5	zero	-1.7	-4.6	-9.1	1.3	1.3	zero	-2.6	-6.6	-19.8	-41.7	
2382	1985	1644	1351	1100	887	0.1	0.6	zero	-1.9	-5.2	-10.1	1.4	1.4	zero	-2.8	-7.2	-21.4	-44.1	24"
2021	1720	1456	1224	1023	850	-0.1	zero	-1.5	-4.8	-9.9	-17.0	2.4	2.1	zero	-3.9	-9.8	-27.0	-57.8	24"
2351	2011	1712	1448	1217	1021	0.3	0.8	zero	-2.3	-6.1	-11.7	1.9	1.7	zero	-3.3	-8.3	-24.0	-47.2	24"
2226	1924	1657	1420	1210	1025	0.2	0.7	zero	-2.0	-5.4	-10.2	1.7	1.5	zero	-2.9	-7.3	-21.1	-42.5	
2854	2406	2018	1682	1389	1139	0.1	0.6	zero	-1.8	-5.0	-9.6	1.5	1.4	zero	-2.7	-6.9	-20.2	-41.3	24"
2448	1898	1456	1099	815	594	-0.1	0.5	zero	-1.6	-4.6	-9.1	2.3	2.8	2.0	zero	-3.6	-16.2	-38.5	
2702	2225	1818	1472	1180	936	0.1	0.6	zero	-1.8	-5.1	-9.8	1.5	1.4	zero	-2.8	-7.0	-20.9	-43.3	
2702	2267	1890	1565	1285	1046	-0.1	0.6	zero	-1.8	-4.9	-9.5	1.5	1.3	zero	-2.7	-6.8	-20.0	-41.1	
2705	2087	1587	1185	872	639	0.3	0.8	zero	-2.4	-6.7	-13.0	2.0	1.8	zero	-3.6	-9.4	-28.6	-61.2	24"
2659	2166	1782	1439	1150	910	0.2	0.7	zero	-2.1	-5.6	-10.9	1.7	1.5	zero	-3.1	-7.8	-23.2	-43.0	
2723	2349	2018	1724	1465	1237	0.1	0.6	zero	1.9	-5.1	-9.7	1.6	1.4	zero	-2.7	-6.9	-20.1	-40.7	
2724	2358	2032	1743	1487	1262	-0.1	0.5	zero	-1.9	-5.0	-9.7	1.6	1.4	zero	-2.7	-6.9	-20.0	-40.3	
2199	1843	1533	1266	1037	844	-0.1	zero	-1.4	-4.4	-9.1	-15.8	2.2	1.9	zero	-3.6	-9.2	-27.4	-55.3	24"
2542	2142	1793	1490	1228	1005	0.2	0.7	zero	-2.1	-5.7	-11.0	1.8	1.6	zero	-3.1	-7.8	-22.9	-46.8	
2398	1979	1621	1316	1058	842	0.1	0.6	zero	-1.9	-5.3	-10.2	1.6	1.4	zero	-2.9	-7.3	-21.7	-44.9	24"
2542	2192	1881	1606	1363	1150	0.2	0.7	zero	-2.0	-5.5	-10.5	1.7	1.5	zero	-3.0	-7.5	-21.7	-43.9	
2543	2217	1925	1663	1431	1224	0.2	0.7	zero	-2.0	-5.4	-10.3	1.7	1.6	zero	-2.9	-7.3	-21.2	-42.6	
2797	2363	1986	1657	1373	1128	0.1	0.6	zero	-1.9	-5.1	-9.8	1.5	1.4	zero	-2.8	-7.0	-20.5	-42.0	
2781	2293	1875	1518	1217	968	0.2	0.7	zero	-2.1	-5.8	-11.2	1.8	1.6	zero	-3.1	-8.0	-23.6	-48.8	
2913	2308	1805	1393	1060	801	-0.1	zero	-1.3	-4.1	-8.6	-15.2	2.0	1.8	zero	-3.6	-9.1	-27.4	-57.8	24"
2797	2418	2081	1783	1519	1287	0.1	0.6	zero	-1.8	-4.9	-9.3	1.5	1.4	zero	-2.7	-6.7	-19.5	-39.4	
2799	2445	2128	1848	1593	1368	0.1	0.6	zero	-1.8	-4.8	-9.2	1.5	1.3	zero	-2.6	-6.8	-19.0	-38.2	
3221	2667	2196	1792	1448	1160	-0.1	0.5	zero	-1.6	-4.6	-9.0	1.3	1.2	zero	-2.5	-6.6	-20.2	-44.8	
3178	2718	2313	1956	1644	1372	0.2	0.7	zero	-2.1	-5.6	-10.7	1.7	1.5	zero	-3.0	-7.6	-22.1	-44.8	
3133	2655	2240	1878	1564	1292	-0.1	0.5	zero	-1.6	-4.4	-8.5	2.2	2.6	1.9	zero	-3.2	-14.2	-32.0	24"
2987	2511	2097	1739	1430	1166	0.2	0.7	zero	-2.0	-5.5	-10.7	1.7	1.5	zero	-3.0	-7.6	-22.4	-44.7	
3133	2715	2345	2017	1726	1469	-0.1	0.5	zero	-1.6	-4.2	-8.2	2.2	2.6	1.6	zero	-3.1	-13.4	-30.8	
3222	2825	2470	2152	1867	1612	-0.1	0.5	zero	-1.6	-4.3	-8.3	1.2	1.2	zero	-2.3	-5.9	-17.3	-34.8	
3436	2918	2468	2077	1737	1441	-0.1	0.4	zero	-1.4	-3.9	-7.6	2.0	2.4	1.7	zero	-2.9	-12.8	-28.8	24"
3436	2834	2324	1892	1525	1215	-0.1	0.4	zero	-1.5	-4.1	-8.0	2.1	2.5	1.8	zero	-3.1	-13.8	-31.5	
967	600	373	262	208	173	0.6	zero	-4.2	-12.9	-27.2	-48.6	zero	-4.2	-12.9	-27.2	-48.6	-116.6	-225.5	20"
1412	886	521	301	172	119	-0.1	0.6	zero	-2.2	-6.2	-13.2	1.7	1.6	zero	-3.5	-9.9	-34.3	-83.3	24"
1902	1296	858	565	399	316	0.2	zero	-2.4	-7.6	-16.1	-28.8	1.6	zero	-4.3	-12.1	-24.0	-64.2	-133.2	
1827	1355	989	720	535	425	0.3	zero	-2.7	-8.3	-17.1	-29.9	1.8	zero	-4.6	-12.6	-24.5	-62.6	-125.3	24"
1827	1355	989	720	535	425	0.3	zero	-2.7	-8.3	-17.1	-29.9	1.8	zero	-4.6	-12.6	-24.5	-62.6	-125.3	
2207	1639	1193	860	626	482	0.2	zero	-2.3	-7.1	-14.7	-25.9	1.5	zero	-4.0	-10.9	-21.3	-54.8	-110.3	24"
2303	1845	1462	1143	806	685	-0.1	zero	-1.5	-4.8	-10.1	-17.6	2.4	2.1	zero	-4.1	-10.4	-30.9	-64.6	

BALLISTICS

REMINGTON BALLISTICS

VENTED TEST-BARREL BALLISTICS

This Remington® patented, industry-accepted method provides data that more precisely reflect actual use of revolver ammunition. It considers cylinder gap, barrel length, powder position, and production tolerances. Although our final values differ from conventional figures, the ammunition is unchanged. Key elements of our patented procedure include: (a) horizontal powder orientation; (b) cylinder gap: .008"; (c) barrel length: 4".

INTERCHANGEABILITY CHART

Cartridges within groups shown are interchangeable. Other substitutions should not be made without specific recommendation of the firearms manufacturer since improper combinations could result in firearm damage or personal injury.

RIMFIRE

.22 W.R.F.
.22 Remington Special
.22 Win. Model 1890 in a .22 Win. Mag. Rimfire but not conversely

CENTERFIRE

.25-20 Remington
.25-20 W.C.F.
.25-20 Win.
.25-20 Win. High Speed
.25-20 Marlin
.25 W.C.F.
6mm Rem. (80 & 90 grain)
.244 Remington
.25 Automatic
.25 Auto. Colt Pistol (ACP)
.25 (6.35mm) Automatic Pistol
6.35mm Browning
7mm Express® Remington
.280 Remington
.30-30 Sav.
.30-30 Win.
.30-30 Win. Accelerator* (SEE NOTE A)
.30-30 Marlin
.30-30 Win. High Speed
.30 W.C.F.
.32 Colt Automatic
.32 Auto. Colt Pistol (ACP)
.32 (7.65mm) Automatic Pistol
7.65mm Automatic Pistol
7.65mm Browning (not interchangeable with 7.65mm Luger)
.32 Short Colt in .32 Long Colt but not conversely
      (SEE NOTE C)
.32 S&W in .32 S. & W. Long but not conversely
.32 S&W Long
.32 Colt New Police
.32 Colt Police Positive
.32 W.C.F.* (SEE NOTE A)
.32 Win.* (SEE NOTE A)
.32-20 Win. High Speed* (SEE NOTE A)
.32-20 Colt L.M.R
.32-20 W.C.F (SEE NOTE G)
.32-20 Win. and Marlin
.38 S.&W.
.38 Colt New Police
.380 Webley
.38 Colt Special
.38 S&W Special
.38 Special Targetmaster®
.38 S&W Special Mid-Range (SEE NOTE D)
.38 Special (+P) (SEE NOTE B)
.38-44 Special (+P) (SEE NOTE B)
.38 Special
.38 Special Flat Point
.38 Short Colt in .38 Long Colt but not conversely. Both can be used in .38 Special
.38 Marlin
.38 Win.* (SEE NOTE A)
.38 Remington* (SEE NOTE A)
.38-40 Win.
.38 W.C.F.* (SEE NOTE A)
.38 Automatic in .38 Super (+P) but not conversely
.380 Automatic
9mm Browning Short (Corto Kurz)
9mm Luger (SEE NOTE E)
9mm Parabellum
.44 S&W Special (SEE NOTE F)
.44 Marlin
.44 Win.
.44 Remington
.44-40 Win.
.44 W.C.F.
.45-70 Government
.45-70 Marlin, Win.
.45-70-405

Centerfire Rifle Ballistics Tables

Caliber	Index/EDI Number	Wt. (grs.)	Bullet Style	Primer No.	Muzzle	100 yds.	200 yds.	300 yds.	400 yds.	500 yds.
.308 Win.	R308W1	150	Pointed Soft Point Core-Lokt®	9½	2820	2533	2263	2009	1774	1560
	R308W2	180	Soft Point Core-Lokt®	9½	2620	2274	1955	1666	1414	1212
	R308W3	180	Pointed Soft Point Core-Lokt®	9½	2620	2393	2178	1974	1782	1604
	R308W7	168	Boat Tail HP Match	9½	2680	2493	2314	2143	1979	1823
	PRB308WA ★	165	Pointed Soft Point, Boat Tail	9½	2700	2497	2303	2117	1941	1773
	PRT308WT ★	165	Pointed Soft Point, Ballistic Tip	9½	2700	2613	2333	2161	1996	1838
.30-06 Springfield	R30061	125	Pointed Soft Point	9½	3140	2780	2447	2138	1853	1595
	R30062	150	Pointed Soft Point Core-Lokt®	9½	2910	2617	2342	2083	1843	1622
	R30063	150	Bronze Point™	9½	2910	2656	2416	2189	1974	1773
	R3006B	165	Pointed Soft Point Core-Lokt®	9½	2800	2534	2283	2047	1825	1621
	R30064	180	Soft Point Core-Lokt®	9½	2700	2348	2023	1727	1466	1251
	R30065	180	Pointed Soft Point Core-Lokt®	9½	2700	2469	2250	2042	1846	1663
	R30067	220	Soft Point Core-Lokt®	9½	2410	2130	1870	1632	1422	1246
	RS3006A	180	Swift A-Frame™ PSP	9½	2700	2465	2243	2032	1833	1648
	PRB3006SA ★	165	Pointed Soft Point, Boat Tail	9½	2800	2592	2394	2204	2023	1852
	PRT3006A ★	150	Pointed Soft Point, Ballistic Tip*	9½	2910	2696	2492	2298	2112	1934
	PRT3006B ★	165	Pointed Soft Point, Ballistic Tip*	9½	2800	2609	2426	2249	2080	1919
.300 Win. Mag.	R300W1	150	Pointed Soft Point Core-Lokt®	9½M	3290	2951	2636	2342	2068	1813
	R300W2	180	Pointed Soft Point Core-Lokt®	9½M	2960	2745	2540	2344	2157	1979
	RS300WA	200	Swift A-Frame™ PSP	9½M	2825	2595	2376	2167	1970	1783
	PRB300WA ★	190	Pointed Soft Point, Boat Tail	9½M	2885	2691	2506	2327	2156	1993
.300 Wby. Mag.	R300WB1	180	Pointed Soft Point Core-Lokt®	9½M	3120	2866	2627	2400	2184	1979
	RS300WBB	200	Swift A-Frame™ PSP	9½M	2925	2690	2467	2254	2052	1861
	PRB300WBA ★	190	Pointed Soft Point, Boat Tail	9½M	3030	2830	2638	2455	2279	2110
.303 British	R303B1	180	Soft Point Core-Lokt®	9½	2460	2124	1817	1542	1311	1137
7.62 x 39mm	R762391	125	Pointed Soft Point	7½	2365	2062	1783	1533	1320	1154
.32-20 Win.	R32201	100	Lead	6½	1210	1021	913	834	769	712
.32 Win. Special	R32WS2	170	Soft Point Core-Lokt®	9½	2250	1921	1626	1372	1175	1044
8mm Remington Mag.	RS8MMRA ★	200	Swift A-Frame™ PSP	9½M	2900	2623	2361	2115	1885	1672
8mm Mauser	R8MSR	170	Soft Point Core-Lokt®	9½	2360	1969	1622	1333	1123	997
.338 Win. Mag.	R338W1	225	Pointed Soft Point Core-Lokt®	9½M	2780	2572	2374	2184	2003	1832
	R338W2	250	Pointed Soft Point Core-Lokt®	9½M	2660	2456	2261	2075	1898	1731
	RS338WA	225	Swift A-Frame™ PSP	9½M	2785	2517	2266	2029	1808	1605
	PRT338WB ★	200	Pointed Soft Point, Ballistic Tip	9½M	2950	2724	2509	2303	2108	1922
.35 Remington	R35R1	150	Pointed Soft Point Core-Lokt®	9½	2300	1874	1506	1218	1039	934
	R35R2	200	Soft Point Core-Lokt®	9½	2080	1698	1376	1140	1001	911
.35 Whelen	R35WH1	200	Pointed Soft Point	9½M	2675	2378	2100	1842	1606	1399
	R35WH3	250	Pointed Soft Point	9½M	2400	2197	2005	1823	1652	1496
.375 H&H Mag.	R375M1	270	Soft Point	9½M	2690	2420	2166	1928	1707	1507
	RS375MA	300	Swift A-Frame™ PSP	9½M	2530	2245	1979	1733	1512	1321
.416 Remington Mag.	R416R2	400	Swift A-Frame™ PSP	9½M	2400	2175	1962	1763	1579	1414
.44-40 Win.	R4440W	200	Soft Point	2½	1190	1006	900	822	756	699
.44 Remington Mag.	R44MG2	240	Soft Point	2½	1760	1380	1114	970	878	806
	R44MG3	240	Semi-Jacketed Hollow Point	2½	1760	1380	1114	970	878	806
	R44MG6	210	Semi-Jacketed Hollow Point	2½	1920	1477	1155	982	880	802
	RH44MGA	275	JHP Core-Lokt®	2½	1580	1293	1093	976	896	832
.444 Mar.	R444M	240	Soft Point	9½	2350	1815	1377	1087	941	846
.45-70 Government	R4570G	405	Soft Point	9½	1330	1168	1055	977	918	869
	R4570L	300	Jacketed Hollow Point	9½	1810	1497	1244	1073	969	895
.458 Win. Mag.	RS458WA	450	Swift A-Frame™ PSP	9½M	2150	1901	1671	1465	1289	1150

★ NEW FOR 1998

NOTE A: *High-speed cartridges must not be used in revolvers. They should be used only in rifles made especially for them.
NOTE B: Ammunition with (+P) on the case headstamp is loaded to higher pressure. Use only in firearms designated for this cartridge and so recommended by the gun manufacturer.
NOTE C: Not for use in revolvers chambered for .32 S&W or .32 S&W Long.
NOTE D: All .38 Special cartridges can be used in .357 Magnum revolvers but not conversely.
NOTE E: 9mm sub-machine gun cartridges should not be used in handguns.
NOTE F: .44 Russian and .44 S&W Special can be used in .44 Remington Magnum revolvers but not conversely.
NOTE G: Not to be used in Win. M-66 and M-73.

REMINGTON BALLISTICS

(continued)

= Premier® Safari Grade = Premier® Ballistic Tip® = Premier® Boat Tail

Energy (ft.-lbs.) Muzzle	100 yds.	200 yds.	300 yds.	400 yds.	500 yds.	Short-range[1] Trajectory* 50 yds.	100 yds.	150 yds.	200 yds.	250 yds.	300 yds.	Long-range[2] Trajectory* 100 yds.	150 yds.	200 yds.	250 yds.	300 yds.	400 yds.	500 yds.	Barrel Length
2648	2137	1705	1344	1048	810	-0.1	zero	-1.2	-3.9	-8.4	-14.7	2.0	1.7	zero	-3.4	-8.8	-26.2	-54.8	
2743	2066	1527	1109	799	587	-0.1	zero	-1.7	-5.3	-10.7	-19.7	2.6	2.3	zero	-4.1	-11.8	-36.3	-78.2	
2743	2288	1896	1557	1269	1028	-0.1	zero	-1.5	-4.6	-9.5	-16.5	2.3	2.0	zero	-3.8	-9.7	-28.3	-57.8	24"
2678	2318	1998	1713	1460	1239	-0.1	zero	-1.3	-4.1	-8.5	-14.7	2.1	1.8	zero	-3.4	-8.6	-24.7	-49.9	
2670	2284	1942	1642	1379	1152	-0.1	zero	-1.3	-4.1	-8.5	-14.8	2.0	1.8	zero	-3.4	-8.6	-25.0	-50.6	
2672	2314	1995	1711	1460	1239	0.1	zero	-1.3	-4.0	-6.4	-14.4	2.0	1.7	zero	-3.3	-8.4	-24.3	-48.9	
2736	2145	1662	1269	953	706	-0.1	0.6	zero	-1.9	-5.2	-10.1	1.5	1.4	zero	-2.8	-7.4	-22.4	-47.6	
2820	2281	1827	1445	1131	876	0.2	0.7	zero	-2.2	-5.9	-11.4	1.8	1.6	zero	-3.2	-8.2	-24.4	-50.9	
2820	2349	1944	1596	1298	1047	0.2	0.7	zero	-2.0	-5.6	-10.8	1.7	1.5	zero	-3.0	-7.7	-22.7	-46.6	
2872	2352	1909	1534	1220	963	0.3	0.8	zero	-2.3	-6.3	-12.1	2.0	1.7	zero	-3.4	-8.7	-25.9	-53.2	
2913	2203	1635	1192	859	625	-0.1	zero	-1.5	-4.9	-10.3	-18.3	2.4	2.1	zero	-4.3	-11.0	-33.8	-72.8	
2913	2436	2023	1666	1362	1105	-0.1	zero	-1.3	-4.2	-8.8	-15.4	2.1	1.8	zero	-3.5	-9.0	-26.3	-54.0	
2837	2216	1708	1301	988	758	0.1	zero	-2.0	-6.2	-12.9	-22.4	1.3	zero	-3.5	-9.5	-18.4	-46.4	-91.6	
2913	2429	2010	1650	1343	1085	-0.1	zero	-1.3	-4.2	-8.9	-15.4	2.1	1.8	zero	-3.6	-9.1	-26.6	-54.4	
2872	2462	2100	1780	1500	1256	0.2	0.8	zero	-2.2	-5.8	-11.2	1.8	1.6	zero	-3.1	-7.9	-23.0	-46.6	
2821	2422	2070	1769	1485	1247	0.1	0.7	zero	-2.0	-5.3	-10.2	1.6	1.5	zero	-2.9	-7.3	-21.1	-42.8	
2873	2494	2155	1854	1588	1350	0.2	0.8	zero	-2.1	-5.7	-10.9	1.8	1.6	zero	-3.1	-7.7	-22.3	-45.0	24"
3605	2900	2314	1827	1424	1095	-0.1	0.5	zero	-1.6	-4.4	-8.7	2.2	2.6	1.9	zero	-3.4	-15.0	-34.4	
3501	3011	2578	2196	1859	1565	0.1	0.6	zero	-1.9	-5.1	-9.8	1.6	1.4	zero	-2.8	-7.0	-20.2	-41.0	24"
3544	2969	2506	2086	1722	1412	0.2	0.8	zero	-2.2	-5.9	-11.3	1.6	1.6	zero	-3.2	-8.0	-23.5	-47.9	
3511	3055	2648	2285	1961	1675	0.1	0.7	zero	-2.0	-5.3	-10.1	1.6	1.5	zero	-2.9	-7.2	-20.8	-41.9	
3890	3284	2758	2301	1905	1565	-0.1	0.5	zero	-1.7	-4.6	-8.9	2.4	2.8	2.0	zero	-3.4	-14.9	-33.6	
3799	3213	2701	2256	1870	1533	0.1	0.7	zero	-2.0	-5.4	-10.4	2.8	3.2	2.3	zero	-3.9	-17.0	-38.3	24"
3873	3378	2936	2542	2190	1878	-0.1	0.6	zero	-1.7	-4.7	-9.0	1.4	1.3	zero	-2.6	-6.4	-18.6	-37.6	
2418	1803	1319	950	687	517	0.1	zero	-2.0	-5.8	-13.2	-23.3	1.3	zero	-3.1	-9.9	-19.3	-49.9	-100.8	24"
1552	1180	882	652	483	370	0.1	zero	-2.2	-6.7	-14.0	-24.5	1.5	zero	-3.8	-10.4	-20.1	-51.3	-102.5	24"
325	231	185	154	131	113	zero	-5.9	-20.0	-43.3	-77.4	-122.4	zero	-11.1	-31.6	-62.6	-104.7	-226.7	-410.6	24"
1911	1393	998	710	521	411	0.3	zero	-2.6	-8.0	-16.7	-29.3	1.7	zero	-4.5	-12.4	-24.1	-62.1	-125.3	24"
3734	3054	2476	1987	1577	1241	0.2	0.7	zero	-2.1	-5.8	-11.2	1.8	1.6	zero	-3.1	-8.0	-23.9	-49.6	24"
2102	1463	993	671	476	375	0.2	zero	-2.4	-7.6	-16.1	-28.6	1.6	zero	-4.4	-12.0	-23.7	-62.8	-128.9	24"
3860	3305	2815	2383	2004	1676	-0.3	0.8	zero	-2.2	-5.9	-11.4	1.9	1.7	zero	-3.2	-8.1	-23.4	-47.5	
3927	3348	2837	2389	1999	1663	-0.1	zero	-1.4	-4.3	-8.9	-15.4	2.1	1.9	zero	-3.5	-8.9	-26.0	-52.7	24"
3871	3165	2565	2057	1633	1286	-0.1	zero	-1.2	-4.0	-8.5	-14.8	2.0	1.8	zero	-3.5	-8.8	-25.2	-54.1	
3866	3295	2795	2357	1973	1641	0.1	0.6	zero	-1.9	-5.2	-10.0	1.6	1.4	zero	-2.8	-7.1	-20.8	-42.4	
1762	1169	755	494	359	291	0.3	zero	-2.7	-8.6	-18.2	-32.6	1.8	zero	-4.9	-13.7	-27.1	-72.5	-150.4	24"
1921	1280	841	577	445	369	0.5	zero	-3.5	-10.7	-22.6	-40.1	2.3	zero	-6.1	-16.7	-33.0	-86.6	-174.8	
3177	2510	1958	1506	1145	869	-0.1	zero	-1.5	-4.7	-9.9	-17.3	2.3	2.0	zero	-4.0	-10.3	-30.8	-64.9	24"
3197	2680	2230	1844	1515	1242	0.1	zero	-1.9	-5.7	-11.8	-20.4	1.3	zero	-3.2	-8.6	-16.6	-40.0	-76.3	
4337	3510	2812	2228	1747	1361	-0.1	zero	-1.4	-4.5	-9.4	-16.4	2.2	1.9	zero	-3.8	-9.7	-28.7	-59.8	24"
4262	3357	2608	2001	1523	1163	-0.1	zero	-1.7	-5.4	-11.4	-19.8	2.7	2.3	zero	-4.6	-11.7	-35.0	-73.6	
5115	4201	3419	2760	2214	1775	0.1	zero	-1.9	-5.9	-12.1	-20.8	1.3	zero	-3.3	-8.9	-17.0	-41.9	-80.8	24"
629	449	360	300	254	217	zero	-5.8	-20.0	-44.6	-78.6	-126.1	zero	-11.3	-33.1	-64.1	-108.7	-235.2	-422.3	24"
1650	1015	661	501	411	346	zero	-2.1	-8.7	-21.2	-40.6	-67.7	zero	-5.6	-17.0	-35.4	-61.4	-143.0	-269.9	
1650	1015	661	501	411	346	zero	-2.1	-8.7	-21.2	-40.6	-67.7	zero	-5.6	-17.0	-35.4	-61.4	-143.0	-269.9	20"
1719	1017	622	450	361	300	zero	-1.6	-7.1	-17.9	-35.1	-60.2	zero	-4.8	-14.7	-31.2	-55.5	-131.3	-253.7	
1524	1020	730	582	490	422	1.4	zero	-6.6	-19.4	-39.2	-67.5	zero	-6.6	-19.4	-39.2	-67.5	-210.8	-280.8	
2942	1755	1010	630	472	381	0.2	zero	-3.2	-9.7	-20.8	-37.8	2.2	zero	-5.4	-15.4	-31.4	-86.7	-180.0	24"
1590	1227	1001	858	758	679	zero	-4.0	-14.5	-32.0	-57.5	-90.6	zero	-8.5	-24.0	-47.4	-78.6	-169.4	-301.3	24"
2182	1492	1031	767	625	533	zero	-1.3	-6.6	-16.5	-32.0	-54.1	zero	-4.6	-13.8	-28.6	-50.1	-115.7	-219.1	
4618	3609	2789	2144	1659	1321	0.3	zero	-2.7	-8.2	-16.7	-28.9	1.8	zero	-4.6	-12.2	-23.4	-58.5	-114.7	24"

Specifications are nominal. Ballistics figures established in test barrels.
Individual rifles may vary from test-barrel specifications.
*Inches above or below line of sight. Hold low for positive numbers, high for negative numbers.
[1] Bullet does not rise more than 1" above line of sight from muzzle to sighting-in range.
[2] Bullet does not rise more than 3" above line of sight from muzzle to sighting-in range.
NOTE: "zero" indicates yardage at which rifle was sighted in.

BALLISTICS

REMINGTON BALLISTICS

Pistol and Revolver Ammunition Ballistics ☐ Golden Saber™ ☐ Core-Lokt® Hunting ☐ Disintegrator™ Frangible

Caliber	Order No.	Primer No.	Weight (grs.)	Bullet Style	Velocity (ft./sec.) Muzzle	50 yds.	100 yds.	Energy (ft.-lbs.) Muzzle	50 yds.	100 yds.	Mid-range Trajectory 50 yds.	100 yds.	B.L
.25 (6.35mm) Auto. Pistol	R25AP	1¹/₂	50	Metal Case	760	707	659	64	56	48	2.0"	8.7"	2"
6mm BR Rem.	R6MMBR	7¹/₂	100	Pointed Soft Point	Refer to Remington CF Ballistics Charts								
7mm BR Rem.	R7MMBR	7¹/₂	140	Pointed Soft Point	Refer to Remington CF Ballistics Charts								
.32 S&W	R32SW	1¹/₂	88	Lead	680	645	610	90	81	73	2.5"	0.5"	3"
.32 S&W Long	R32SWL	1¹/₂	98	Lead	705	670	635	115	98	88	2.3"	10.5"	4"
.32 (7.65mm) Auto. Pistol	R32AP	1¹/₂	71	Metal Case	905	855	810	129	115	97	1.4"	5.8"	4"
.357 Mag. (Vented Barrel Ballistics)	R357M7	5¹/₂	110	Semi-Jacketed Hollow Point	1295	1094	975	410	292	232	0.8"	3.5"	4"
	R357M1	5¹/₂	125	Semi-Jacketed Hollow Point	1450	1240	1090	583	427	330	0.6"	2.8"	4"
	GS357MA	5¹/₂	125	Brass-Jacketed Hollow Point	1220	1095	1009	413	333	283	0.8"	3.5"	4"
	RH357MA	5¹/₂	165	JHP Core-Lokt®	1290	1189	1108	610	518	450	0.7"	3.1"	8³/₈"
	R357M2	5¹/₂	158	Semi-Jacketed Hollow Point	1235	1104	1015	535	428	361	0.8"	3.5"	4"
	R357M3	5¹/₂	158	Soft Point	1235	1104	1015	535	428	361	0.8"	3.5"	4"
	R357M5	5¹/₂	158	Semi-Wadcutter	1235	1104	1015	535	428	361	0.8"	3.5"	4"
	R357M10	5¹/₂	180	Semi-Jacketed Hollow Point	1145	1053	985	524	443	388	0.9"	3.9"	8³/₈"
9mm Luger Auto. Pistol	R9MM1	1¹/₂	115	Jacketed Hollow Point	1155	1047	971	341	280	241	0.9"	3.9"	4"
	R9MM10	1¹/₂	124	Jacketed Hollow Point	1120	1028	960	346	291	254	1.0"	4.1"	4"
	R9MM2	1¹/₂	124	Metal Case	1110	1030	971	339	292	259	1.0"	4.1"	4"
	R9MM3	1¹/₂	115	Metal Case	1135	1041	973	329	277	242	0.9"	4.0"	4"
	R9MM6	1¹/₂	115	Jacketed Hollow Point (+P)‡	1250	1113	1019	399	316	265	0.8"	3.5"	4"
	R9MM8	1¹/₂	147	Jacketed Hollow Point (Subsonic)	990	941	900	320	289	264	1.1"	4.9"	4"
	R9MM9	1¹/₂	147	Metal Case (Match)	990	941	900	320	289	264	1.1"	4.9"	4"
	LF9MMA ★	1¹/₂	105	Disintegrator™ Plated Frangible	1100	1016	954	282	241	212	1.0"	4.3"	4"
	GS9MMB	1¹/₂	124	Brass-Jacketed Hollow Point	1125	1031	963	349	293	255	1.0"	4.0"	4"
	GS9MMC	1¹/₂	147	Brass-Jacketed Hollow Point	990	941	900	320	289	264	1.1"	4.9"	4"
	GS9MMD	1¹/₂	124	Brass-Jacketed Hollow Point (+P)‡	1180	1089	1021	384	327	287	0.8"	3.8"	4"
.380 Auto. Pistol	R380AP	1¹/₂	95	Metal Case	955	865	785	190	160	130	1.4"	5.9"	4"
	R380A1	1¹/₂	88	Jacketed Hollow Point	990	920	868	191	165	146	1.2"	5.1"	4"
	GS380B	1¹/₂	102	Brass-Jacketed Hollow Point	940	901	866	200	184	170	1.2"	5.1"	4"
.38 S&W	R38SW	1¹/₂	146	Lead	685	650	620	150	135	125	2.4"	10.0"	4"
.38 Special (Vented Barrel Ballistics)	R38S10	1¹/₂	110	Semi-Jacketed Hollow Point (+P)‡	995	926	871	242	210	185	1.2"	5.1"	4"
	R38S16	1¹/₂	110	Semi-Jacketed Hollow Point	950	890	840	220	194	172	1.4"	5.4"	4"
	R38S2	1¹/₂	125	Semi-Jacketed Hollow Point (+P)‡	945	898	858	248	224	204	1.3"	5.4"	4"
	GS38SB	1¹/₂	125	Brass-Jacketed Hollow Point (+P)‡	975	929	885	264	238	218	1.0"	5.2"	4"
	R38S3	1¹/₂	148	Targetmaster® Lead WC Match	710	634	566	166	132	105	2.4"	10.8"	4"
	R38S5	1¹/₂	158	Lead (Round Nose)	755	723	692	200	183	168	2.0"	8.3"	4"
	R38S14	1¹/₂	158	Semi-Wadcutter (+P)‡	890	855	823	278	257	238	1.4"	6.0"	4"
	R38S6	1¹/₂	158	Semi-Wadcutter	755	723	692	200	183	168	2.0"	8.3"	4"
	R38S12	1¹/₂	158	Lead Hollow Point (+P)‡	890	855	823	278	257	238	1.4"	6.0"	4"
.38 Short Colt	R38SC	1¹/₂	125	Lead	730	685	645	150	130	115	2.2"	9.4"	6"
.357 Sig.	R357S1	5¹/₂	125	Jacketed Hollow Point	1350	1157	1032	506	372	296	0.7"	3.2"	4"
.40 S&W	R40SW1	5¹/₂	155	Jacketed Hollow Point	1205	1095	1017	499	413	356	0.8"	3.6"	4"
	R40SW2	5¹/₂	180	Jacketed Hollow Point	1015	960	914	412	368	334	1.3"	4.5"	4"
	LF40SWA ★	5¹/₂	145	Disintegrator™ Plated Frangible	1095	1023	973	379	337	305	1.0"	4.1"	4"
	GS40SWA	5¹/₂	165	Brass-Jacketed Hollow Point	1150	1040	964	485	396	340	1.0"	4.0"	4"
	GS40SWB	5¹/₂	180	Brass-Jacketed Hollow Point	1015	960	914	412	368	334	1.3"	4.5"	4"
.41 Rem. Mag. (Vented Barrel Ballistics)	R41MG1	2¹/₂	210	Soft Point	1300	1162	1062	788	630	526	0.7"	3.2"	4"
.44 Rem. Mag. (Vented Barrel Ballistics)	R44MG5	2¹/₂	180	Semi-Jacketed Hollow Point	1610	1365	1175	1036	745	551	0.5"	2.3"	4"
	R44MG2	2¹/₂	240	Soft Point	1180	1081	1010	741	623	543	0.9"	3.7"	4"
	R44MG3	2¹/₂	240	Semi-Jacketed Hollow Point	1180	1081	1010	741	623	543	0.9"	3.7"	4"
	RH44MGA	2¹/₂	275	JHP Core-Lokt®	1235	1142	1070	931	797	699	0.8"	3.3"	6¹/₂"
.44 S&W Special	R44SW	2¹/₂	246	Lead	755	725	695	310	285	265	2.0"	8.3"	6"
	R44SW1	2¹/₂	200	Semi-Wadcutter	1035	938	866	476	391	333	1.1"	4.9"	6"
.45 Colt	R45C	2¹/₂	250	Lead	860	820	780	410	375	340	1.6"	6.6"	5"
	R45C1	2¹/₂	225	Semi-Wadcutter (Keith)	960	890	832	460	395	346	1.3"	5.5"	5"
.45 Auto.	R45AP2	2¹/₂	185	Jacketed Hollow Point	1000	939	889	411	362	324	1.1"	4.9"	5"
	R45AP4	2¹/₂	230	Metal Case	835	800	767	356	326	300	1.6"	6.8"	5"
	R45AP7	2¹/₂	230	Jacketed Hollow Point (Subsonic)	835	800	767	356	326	300	1.6"	6.8"	5"
	LF45APA ★	2¹/₂	175	Disintegrator™ Plated Frangible	1020	928	859	404	335	286	1.2"	5.1"	5"
	GS45APA	2¹/₂	185	Brass-Jacketed Hollow Point	1015	951	899	423	372	332	1.1"	4.5"	5"
	GS45APB	2¹/₂	230	Brass-Jacketed Hollow Point	875	833	795	391	355	323	1.5"	6.1"	5"
	GS45APC	2¹/₂	185	Brass-Jacketed Hollow Point (+P)‡	1140	1042	971	534	446	388	1.0"	4.0"	5"

‡Ammunition with (+P) on the case headstamp is loaded to higher pressure. Use only in firearms designated for this cartridge and so recommended by the gun manufacturer.

★ NEW FOR 1998

Caliber	Grs	Type	Muzzle	100y	200y	300y	400y	500y	Muzzle	100y	200y	300y	400y	500y	Muzzle	100y	200y	300y	400y	500y	Box Pcs
			Velocity in feet per second						**Energy in foot-pounds**						**Trajectory Inches/Yards**						
22 Hornet	45	SPEEDHEAD FMJ	2300	1724	1291	1069	944	861	524	295	165	114	89	74	-1.5	0	-14.3	-47.1	-108.9	-203.5	20
	45	SOFT POINT RN	2300	1724	1291	1069	944	861	524	295	165	114	89	74	-1.5	0	-14.3	-47.1	-108.9	-203.5	20
	42	HOLLOW PIONT	2700	2193	1764	1419	1161	1011	652	428	277	179	120	91	-1.5	0	-6.6	-24.5	-60.1	-120.9	20
22 PPC USA	52	HPBT MATCH	3400	2990	2613	2255	1920	1616	1342	1040	795	592	429	304	-1.5	1.2		-6.0	-19.1	-41.8	20
222 Remington	50	SPEEDHEAD FMJ	3200	2663	2182	1776	1447	1192	1135	786	528	350	232	158	-1.5	1.2	0	-10.3	-31.1	-67.3	20
222	50	SOFT POINT P	3200	2663	2182	1776	1447	1192	1135	786	528	350	232	158	-1.5	1.7	0	-10.3	-31.1	-67.3	20
	55	SOFT POINT P	3280	2800	2372	1978	1637	1350	1312	958	686	477	326	222	-1.5	1.4	0	-8.0	-24.8	-54.5	20
	52	HPBT MATCH	3035	2613	2235	1894	1589	1333	1072	795	581	417	294	207	-1.5	1.8	0	-9.0	-27.9	-60.7	20
222 Remington	50	SPEEDHEAD FJM	3230	2690	2207	1798	1466	1207	1159	803	540	359	238	161	-1.5	1.6	0	-10.0	-30.3	-67.0	20
	50	SOFT POINT P	3230	2690	2207	1798	1466	1207	1159	803	540	359	238	161	-1.5	1.6	0	-10.0	-30.3	-67.0	20
	55	SOFT POINT P	3330	2848	2414	2016	1671	1378	1352	989	710	495	340	231	-1.5	1.4	0	-7.7	-23.8	-51.9	20
223 Remington	50	SPEEDHEAD FJM	3230	2690	2207	1798	1466	1207	1159	803	540	359	238	161	-1.5	1.6	0	-10.0	-30.3	-67.0	20
	50	SOFT POINT P	3230	2690	2207	1798	1466	1207	1159	803	540	359	238	161	-1.5	1.6	0	-10.0	-30.3	-67.0	20
	55	SOFT POINT P	3330	2848	2414	2016	1671	1378	1352	989	710	495	340	231	-1.5	1.4	0	-7.7	-23.8	-51.9	20
22-250 Remington	50	SPEEDHEAD FMJ	3770	3168	2639	2168	1751	1396	1579	1113	773	522	340	216	-1.5	1.0	0	-6.0	-19.5	-44.0	20
	50	SOFT POINT P	3770	3168	2639	2168	1751	1396	1579	1113	7773	522	340	216	-1.5	1.0	0	-6.0	-19.5	-44.0	20
	55	SOFT POINT P	3660	3146	2681	2255	1871	1533	1631	1206	876	620	426	286	-1.5	1.0	0	-5.9	-18.7	-41.3	20
6PPC USA	70	HPBT MATCH	3200	2740	2407	2090	1793	1527	1481	1156	892	673	495	359	-1.5	1.5	0	-7.2	-22.8	-49.2	20
243 Winchester	90	SPEEDHEAD FJM	2855	2587	2340	2110	1895	1693	1618	1329	1087	884	713	569	-1.5	1.9	0	-8.2	-24.3	-49.9	20
	90	SOFT POINT P	3130	2850	2587	2343	2114	1898	1949	1612	1329	1090	887	715	-1.5	1.5	0	-6.5	-19.5	-40.2	20
6.5X55 Swedish	100	SPEEDHEAD FJM	2625	2270	1946	1651	1397	1196	1533	1147	842	606	434	319	-1.5	2.6	0	-11.9	-36.0	-76.8	20
	139	HPBT MATCH	2790	2648	2512	2381	2252	2129	2396	2161	1945	1746	1563	1396	-1.5	1.7	0	-7.2	-20.5	-40.7	20
	156	SOFT POINT RN	2625	23843	2156	1941	1740	1554	2382	1966	1607	1303	1047	835	-1.5	2.3	0	-9.8	-28.9	-59.7	20
270 Wlinchester	130	SPEEDHEAD FMJ	2820	2506	2212	1938	1687	1463	2290	1805	1407	1080	818	616	-1.5	2.0	0	-9.2	-27.5	-58.3	20
	156	HAMMERHEAD	2755	2470	2208	1967	1743	1538	2625	2111	1685	1338	1051	818	-1.5	2.2	0	-9.3	-27.6	-57.5	20
7x33 Sako	78	SPEEDHEAD FJM	2430	1920	1500	1190	1013	906	1029	643	392	247	179	143	-1.5	0	-8.5	-31.0	-78.8	-158.0	50
	78	SOFT POINT SP	2430	1920	1500	1190	1013	906	1029	643	392	247	179	243	-1.5	0	-8.5	-31.0	-78.8	-158.0	50
7mm Mauser(7x57)	78	SPEEDHEAD FJM	2950	2324	783	1362	1090	950	1522	943	555	324	208	158	-1.5	2.6	0	-14.9	-50.4	-112.2	20
	170	SOFT POINT SP	2495	2283	2086	1901	1728	1567	2324	1962	1638	1361	1125	925	-1.5	2.6	0	-10.8	-31.1	-63.3	20
7x64	120	SOFT POINT P	3100	2816	2545	2296	2069	1856	2567	2117	1730	1408	1143	920	-1.5	1.4	0	-7.3	-20.9	-42.6	20
	170	HAMMERHEAD	2790	2563	2351	2154	1967	1791	2929	2473	2081	1747	1458	1208	-1.5	1.9	0	-8.2	-23.9	-48.6	20
7x65R	170	HAMMERHEAD	2625	2409	2208	2019	1839	1670	2594	2186	1836	1535	1274	1050	-1.5	2.3	0	-9.4	-27.4	-55.6	20
7mm Remington Mag	170	HAMMERHEAD	2970	2734	2512	2303	2108	1924	3320	2814	2376	1996	1674	1394	-1.5	1.6	0	-7.2	-21.0	-42.5	20
7.62x39 Russian	123	SPEEDHEAD FMJ	2345	2096	1863	1651	1466	1305	1507	1203	951	747	589	466	-1.5	0	-6.5	-23.6	-53.2	-98.5	30
	123	SPEEDHEAD FMJ	2345	2096	1863	1651	1466	1305	1507	1203	951	747	589	466	-1.5	0	-6.5	-23.6	-53.2	-98.5	250
	123	SOFT POINT P	2345	2096	1863	1651	1466	1305	1507	1203	951	747	589	466	-1.5	0	-6.5	-23.6	-53.2	-98.5	30
30-30 Winchester	93	SPEEDHEAD FMJ	2970	2354	1818	1400	1126	976	1811	1138	679	403	260	196	-1.5	0	-4.9	-21.8	-57.7	-117.3	20
	150	SOFT POINT FP	2310	1982	1681	1439	1240	1096	1777	1304	938	688	510	400	-1.5	0	-8.1	-28.3	-65.6	-125.6	20
308 Winchester	93	SPEEDHEAD FMJ	2970	2354	1818	1400	1126	976	1811	1138	679	403	260	196	-1.5	0	-4.9	-21.8	-56.7	-117.3	20
	123	SPEEDHEAD FMJ	2920	2622	2347	2097	1868	1654	2335	1883	1509	1205	955	749	-1.5	1.8	0	-8.4	-24.5	-50.7	20
	123	SOFT POINT P	3035	2734	2455	2194	1958	1738	2523	2047	1650	1318	1050	827	-1.5	1.6	0	-7.6	-22.4	-46.2	20
	156	S-HAMMERHEAD	2790	2563	2353	2158	1973	1800	2689	2271	1914	1610	1346	1120	-1.5	2.0	0	-8.2	-23.9	-48.9	20
	180	HAMEMRHEAD	2610	2382	2169	1971	1786	1612	2273	1885	1556	1277	1041	1.3	-1.5	2.4	0	-9.9	-28.6	-58.1	20
	180	S-HAMMERHEAD	2610	2400	2204	2017	1839	1672	2725	2310	1946	1629	1355	1119	-1.5	2.3	0	-9.5	-27.5	-55.8	20
	200	HAMMERHEAD	2445	2210	1990	1782	1588	1415	2660	2172	1762	1414	1122	891	-1.5	2.8	0	-11.3	-33.7	-70.1	20
	123	RANGE	2950	2652	2378	2126	1895	1679	2388	1927	1549	1238	983	772	-1.5	1.8	0	-8.0	-23.7	-49.0	50
	102	SUPER RANGE	3120	2712	2342	2003	1695	1428	2195	1662	1240	907	649	461	-1.5	1.6	0	-8.0	-24.7	-53.7	50
	168	HPBT MATCH	2690	2500	2321	2159	2004	1857	2701	2328	2010	1739	1499	1286	-1.5	2.3	0	-8.5	-24.5	-49.1	20
	190	HPBT MATCH	2525	2372	2224	2080	1940	1679	2688	2369	2082	1822	1585	1373	-1.5	2.4	0	-9.0	-26.3	-52.9	20
7.62x53R	93	SPEEDHEAD FMJ	2970	2354	1818	1400	1126	976	1811	1138	679	403	260	196	-1.5	0	-4.9	-21.8	-56.7	-117.3	20
	123	SPEEDHEAD FMJ	2920	2622	2347	2097	1868	1654	2335	1883	1509	1205	955	749	-1.5	1.8	0	-8.4	-24.5	-50.7	20
	156	S-HAMMERHEAD	2790	2563	2353	2158	1973	1800	2689	2271	1914	1610	1346	1120	-1.5	2.0	0	-8.2	-23.9	-48.9	20
	180	S-HAMMERHEAD	2610	2400	2204	2017	1839	1672	2725	2310	1946	1629	1355	1119	-1.5	2.3	0	-9.5	-27.5	-55.8	20
	200	HAMMERHEAD	2445	2210	1990	1782	1588	1415	2660	2172	1762	1414	1122	891	-1.5	2.8	0	-11.3	-33.7	-70.1	20
	123	RANGE	2950	2652	2378	2126	1895	1679	2388	1927	1549	1238	983	772	-1.5	1.8	0	-8.0	-23.7	-49.0	50
30-06 Springfield	123	SPEEDHEAD FMJ	2920	2622	2347	2097	1868	1654	2335	1883	1509	1205	955	749	-1.5	1.8	0	-8.4	-24.5	-50.7	20
	123	SOFT POINT P	3120	2800	2510	2250	2010	1786	2661	2148	1726	1385	1106	873	-1.5	1.6	0	-7.3	-21.3	-43.9	20
	156	S-HAMMERHEAD	2900	2670	2454	2255	2070	1893	2915	2466	2083	1759	1481	1240	-1.5	1.8	0	-7.8	-22.2	-44.7	20
	180	HAMMERHEAD	2700	2465	2242	2042	1857	1682	2935	2433	2013	1670	1381	1133	-1.5	2.3	0	-9.4	-27.0	-54.5	20
	180	S-HAMMERHEAD	2700	2500	2295	2100	1920	1750	2935	2495	2105	1768	1475	1223	-1.5	2.1	0	-8.7	-25.3	-51.3	20
	220	HAMMERHEAD	2410	2200	2000	1826	1664	1517	2847	2369	1963	1632	1356	1126	-1.5	3.3	0	-12.4	-34.7	-69.6	20
	123	RANGE	2950	2652	2378	2126	1895	1679	2388	1927	1549	1238	983	772	-1.5	1.8	0	-8.0	-23.7	-49.0	50
300 Winchester Mag	156	S-HAMMERHEAD	3150	2905	2673	2453	2243	2044	3430	2918	2470	2080	1740	1445	-1.5	1.3	0	-6.1	-18.1	-37.0	20
	180	HAMMERHEAD	2950	2700	2467	2243	2031	1833	3493	2926	2438	2015	1653	1345	-1.5	1.6	0	-7.4	-21.7	-44.4	20
	180	HAMMERHEAD	2950	2730	2517	2314	2121	1938	3493	2983	2537	2144	1801	1504	-1.5	1.6	0	-7.1	-20.7	-42.0	20
	168	HPBT MATCH	3020	2816	2622	2438	2260	2090	3400	2959	2566	2217	1905	1630	-1.5	1.5	0	-6.5	-18.8	-38.0	20
8.2x57JRS	200	HAMMERHEAD	2395	2093	1815	1563	1347	1176	2553	1949	1465	1087	807	616	-1.5	3.3	0	-13.9	-42.0	-89.7	20
338 Winchester Mag	250	HAMMERHEAD	2676	2413	2169	1946	1742	1554	3966	3229	2608	21012	1683	1339	-1.5	2.3	0	-10.0	-29.1	-59.7	20
9.3x53R Finnish	256	SOFT POINT RN	2330	2000	1695	1439	1236	1091	3010	2211	1593	1148	847	660	-1.5	3.6	0	-16.9	-50.3	-107.0	20
9.3x62	250	POWERHEAD BARNES	2360	2170	1988	1815	1652	1503	3095	2612	2192	1828	1514	1253	-1.5	3.0	0	-11.8	-34.2	-69.4	10
375 H&H Mag	270	POWERHEAD BARNES	2720	2535	2354	2181	2015	1857	4440	3848	3319	2848	2432	2066	-1.5	1.9	0	-8.3	-23.8	-48.0	10

SPEEDHEAD=FMJ-Full Metal Jacket
HP = Hollow Point, Varmint, Precision
SP FP = Soft Point Flat Point

HAMMERHEAD=Soft Point Bonded Core
S-HAMMERHEAD=SUPER HAMMERHEAD=Hollow Point Bonded Core
POWERHEAD BARNES = Hollow Piont Solid Copper

HPBT=Hollow Point Boat Tail, Precision
RANGE=Full Metal Jacket
SUPER RANGE = HPBT, Varmint, Precision

SP P=Soft Point Pointed
SP SP = Soft Point Semi Pointed
SP RN = Soft Point Round Nose

WEATHERBY BALLISTICS

SUGGESTED USAGE	CARTRIDGE	Weight Grains	Bullet Type	B/C	VELOCITY in Feet per Second Muzzle	100 Yards	200 Yards	300 Yards	400 Yards	500 Yards	ENERGY in Foot-Pounds Muzzle	100 Yards	200 Yards	300 Yards	400 Yards	500 Yards	PATH OF BULLET 100 Yards	200 Yards	300 Yards	400 Yards	500 Yards
V	.224 Wby.	55	Pt-Ex	.235	3650	3192	2780	2403	2056	1741	1627	1244	944	705	516	370	2.8	3.7	0.0	-9.8	-27.9
V	.240 Wby.	87	Pt-Ex	.327	3523	3199	2898	2617	2352	2103	2397	1977	1622	1323	1069	855	2.7	3.4	0.0	-8.4	-23.3
		90	Barnes-X	.382	3500	3222	2962	2717	2484	2264	2448	2075	1753	1475	1233	1024	2.6	3.3	0.0	-8.0	-21.6
		95	Bst	.379	3420	3146	2888	2645	2414	2195	2467	2087	1759	1475	1229	1017	2.7	3.5	0.0	-8.4	-22.9
M		100	Pt-Ex	.381	3406	3134	2878	2637	2408	2190	2576	2180	1839	1544	1287	1065	2.8	3.5	0.0	-8.4	-23.0
		100	Partition	.384	3406	3136	2882	2642	2415	2199	2576	2183	1844	1550	1294	1073	2.8	3.5	0.0	-8.4	-22.9
V	.257 Wby.	87	Pt-Ex	.322	3825	3472	3147	2845	2563	2297	2826	2328	1913	1563	1269	1019	2.1	2.8	0.0	-7.1	-19.5
M		100	Pt-Ex	.357	3602	3298	3016	2750	2500	2264	2881	2416	2019	1680	1388	1138	2.4	3.1	0.0	-7.7	-21.0
		100	Bst	.393	3602	3325	3066	2822	2590	2370	2881	2455	2087	1768	1490	1247	2.3	3.0	0.0	-7.4	-19.9
		115	Barnes-X	.429	3400	3158	2929	2711	2504	2306	2952	2546	2190	1877	1601	1358	2.7	3.4	0.0	-8.1	-21.7
		117	Rn-Ex	.243	3402	2984	2595	2240	1921	1639	3007	2320	1742	1302	956	690	3.4	4.3	0.0	-11.1	-31.9
		120	Partition	.391	3305	3046	2801	2570	2350	2141	2910	2472	2091	1760	1471	1221	3.0	3.7	0.0	-8.9	-24.3
V	.270 Wby.	100	Pt-Ex	.307	3760	3396	3061	2751	2462	2190	3139	2560	2081	1681	1346	1065	2.3	3.0	0.0	-7.6	-21.0
M		130	Pt-Ex	.409	3375	3123	2885	2659	2444	2240	3288	2815	2402	2041	1724	1448	2.8	3.5	0.0	-8.4	-22.6
		130	Partition	.416	3375	3127	2892	2670	2458	2256	3288	2822	2415	2058	1744	1470	2.8	3.5	0.0	-8.3	-22.4
		140	Bst	.456	3300	3077	2865	2663	2470	2285	3385	2943	2551	2204	1896	1622	2.9	3.6	0.0	-8.4	-22.6
		140	Barnes-X	.462	3250	3032	2825	2628	2438	2257	3283	2858	2481	2146	1848	1583	3.0	3.7	0.0	-8.7	-23.2
		150	Pt-Ex	.462	3245	3028	2821	2623	2434	2253	3507	3053	2650	2292	1973	1690	3.0	3.7	0.0	-8.7	-23.3
		150	Partition	.465	3245	3029	2823	2627	2439	2259	3507	3055	2655	2298	1981	1699	3.0	3.7	0.0	-8.7	-23.3
M	7MM Wby.	139	Pt-Ex	.392	3340	3079	2834	2601	2380	2170	3443	2926	2478	2088	1748	1453	2.9	3.6	0.0	-8.7	-23.7
		140	Partition	.434	3303	3069	2847	2636	2434	2241	3391	2927	2519	2159	1841	1562	2.9	3.6	0.0	-8.5	-23.1
		140	Bst	.485	3302	3092	2892	2700	2517	2341	3389	2972	2599	2267	1969	1703	2.8	3.5	0.0	-8.2	-21.9
		150	Barnes-X	.488	3100	2901	2710	2527	2352	2183	3200	2802	2446	2127	1842	1588	3.3	4.0	0.0	-9.4	-25.3
		154	Pt-Ex	.433	3260	3028	2807	2597	2397	2206	3634	3134	2694	2307	1964	1663	3.0	3.7	0.0	-8.8	-23.8
		160	Partition	.475	3200	2991	2791	2600	2417	2241	3638	3177	2767	2401	2075	1784	3.1	3.8	0.0	-8.9	-23.8
B		175	Pt-Ex	.462	3070	2861	2662	2471	2288	2113	3662	3181	2753	2373	2034	1735	3.5	4.2	0.0	-9.9	-26.5
M	.300 Wby.	150	Pt-Ex	.338	3540	3225	2932	2657	2399	2155	4173	3462	2862	2351	1916	1547	2.6	3.3	0.0	-8.2	-22.6
		150	Partition	.387	3540	3263	3004	2759	2528	2307	4173	3547	3005	2536	2128	1773	2.5	3.2	0.0	-7.7	-20.9
		165	Pt-Ex	.387	3390	3123	2872	2634	2409	2195	4210	3573	3021	2542	2126	1765	2.8	3.5	0.0	-8.5	-23.1
		165	Bst	.475	3350	3133	2927	2730	2542	2361	4111	3596	3138	2730	2367	2042	2.7	3.4	0.0	-8.1	-21.4
B		180	Pt-Ex	.425	3240	3004	2781	2569	2366	2173	4195	3607	3091	2637	2237	1886	3.1	3.8	0.0	-9.0	-24.4
		180	Barnes-X	.511	3190	2995	2809	2631	2459	2294	4067	3586	3154	2766	2417	2103	3.1	3.8	0.0	-8.7	-23.2
		180	Partition	.474	3240	3028	2826	2634	2449	2271	4195	3665	3193	2772	2396	2062	3.0	3.7	0.0	-8.6	-23.1
		200	Partition	.481	3060	2860	2668	2485	2308	2139	4158	3631	3161	2741	2366	2032	3.5	4.2	0.0	-9.8	-26.2
		220	Rn-Ex	.300	2845	2543	2260	1996	1751	1530	3954	3158	2495	1946	1497	1143	4.9	5.9	0.0	-14.6	-40.8
B	.340 Wby.	200	Pt-Ex	.361	3221	2946	2688	2444	2213	1995	4607	3854	3208	2652	2174	1767	3.3	4.0	0.0	-9.9	-27.0
		200	Bst	.502	3221	3022	2831	2649	2473	2305	4607	4054	3559	3115	2716	2358	3.0	3.7	0.0	-8.6	-22.9
		210	Partition	400	3211	2963	2728	2505	2293	2092	4807	4093	3470	2927	2452	2040	3.2	3.9	0.0	-9.5	-25.7
		225	Pt-Ex	.397	3066	2824	2595	2377	2170	1973	4696	3984	3364	2822	2352	1944	3.6	4.4	0.0	-10.7	-28.6
		225	Barnes-X	.482	3001	2804	2615	2434	2260	2093	4499	3927	3416	2959	2551	2189	3.6	4.3	0.0	-10.3	-27.4
		250	Pt-Ex	.431	2963	2745	2537	2338	2149	1968	4873	4182	3572	3035	2563	2150	3.9	4.6	0.0	-11.1	-29.6
		250	Partition	.473	2941	2743	2553	2371	2197	2029	4801	4176	3618	3120	2678	2286	3.9	4.6	0.0	-10.9	-28.9
MB	.30-378 Wby.	165	Bst	.475	3500	3275	3062	2859	2665	2480	4488	3930	3435	2995	2603	2253	2.4	3.0	0.0	-7.4	-19.5
		180	Barnes-X	.511	3450	3243	3046	2858	2678	2504	4757	4204	3709	3264	2865	2506	2.4	3.1	0.0	-7.4	-19.6
		200	Partition	.481	3160	2955	2759	2572	2392	2220	4434	3877	3381	2938	2541	2188	3.2	3.9	0.0	-9.1	-24.3
MB	.338-378 Wby.	200	Bst	.502	3350	3145	2949	2761	2582	2409	4983	4391	3861	3386	2959	2576	2.7	3.3	0.0	-7.9	-21.0
		225	Barnes-X	.482	3180	2974	2778	2591	2410	2238	5052	4420	3856	3353	2902	2501	3.1	3.8	0.0	-8.9	-24.0
		250	Partition	.473	3060	2856	2662	2475	2297	2125	5197	4528	3933	3401	2927	2507	3.5	4.2	0.0	-9.8	-26.4
B	.378 Wby.	270	Pt-Ex	.380	3180	2921	2677	2445	2225	2017	6062	5115	4295	3583	2968	2438	1.3	0.0	-6.1	-18.1	-37.1
		270	Barnes-X	.503	3150	2954	2767	2587	2415	2249	5948	5232	4589	4013	3495	3031	1.2	0.0	-5.8	-16.7	-33.7
		300	Rn-Ex	.250	2925	2558	2220	1908	1627	1383	5699	4360	3283	2424	1764	1274	1.9	0.0	-9.0	-27.8	-60.0
		300	FMJ	.275	2925	2591	2280	1991	1725	1489	5699	4470	3461	2640	1983	1476	1.8	0.0	-8.6	-26.1	-55.4
A	.416 Wby.	350	Pt-Ex	.521	2850	2673	2503	2340	2182	2031	6312	5553	4870	4253	3700	3204	1.7	0.0	-7.2	-20.9	-41.8
		400	Swift A	.391	2650	2426	2213	2011	1820	1644	6237	5227	4350	3592	2941	2399	2.2	0.0	-9.3	-27.1	-56.0
		400	Rn-Ex	.311	2700	2417	2152	1903	1676	1470	6474	5189	4113	3216	2493	1918	2.3	0.0	-9.7	-29.3	-61.2
		400	**Mono	.304	2700	2411	2140	1887	1656	1448	6474	5162	4068	3161	2435	1861	2.3	0.0	-9.8	-29.7	-62.1
A	.460 Wby.	450	Barnes-X	.488	2700	2518	2343	2175	2013	1859	7284	6333	5482	4725	4050	3452	2.0	0.0	-8.4	-24.1	-48.2
		500	Rn-Ex	.287	2600	2301	2022	1764	1533	1333	7504	5877	4539	3456	2608	1972	2.6	0.0	-11.1	-33.5	-71.1
		500	FMJ	.295	2600	2309	2037	1784	1557	1357	7504	5917	4605	3534	2690	2046	2.5	0.0	-10.9	-33.0	-69.6

LEGEND: Pt-Ex = Pointed Expanding · Rn-Ex = Round Nose-Expanding · FMJ = Full Metal Jacket · Swift A = Divided Lead Cavity or "H" Type · Barnes-X = Barnes "X" Flat Base · Bst = Nosler Ballistic Tip*

NOTE: These tables were calculated by computer using a standard modern scientific technique to predict trajectories and recoil energies from the best available data for each cartridge. The figures shown are expected to be reasonably accurate of ammunition behavior under standard conditions. However, the shooter is cautioned that performance will vary because of variations in rifles, ammunition, atmospheric conditions and altitude. · B.C.: Ballistic Coefficients used for these tables were supplied by the bullet's manufacturers. Listed velocities were determined using 26-inch barrels. Velocities from shorter barrels will be reduced by 30 to 65 feet per second per inch of barrel removed. · Trajectories were computed with the line-of-sight 1.5 inches above the bore centerline.

*Partition is a registered trademark of Nosler, Inc. · **Monolithic Solid is a registered trademark of A-Square, Inc. · Barnes X-Bullet" is a registered trademark of Barnes Bullets.

USAGE: V-Varmint   M-Medium Game (Deer, Sheep, Pronghorn, Black Bear)   B-Big Game (Elk, Moose, Grizzly)   A-African Big Game (Elephant, Cape Buffalo, Rhino, Lion)

WINCHESTER BALLISTICS

CENTERFIRE HANDGUN BALLISTICS

SUPREME®

Cartridge	Symbol	Bullet Wt. Grs.	Type	User Guide	Velocity (fps)			Energy (ft-lbs.)			Mid Range Traj. (In.)		Barrel Length In.
					Muzzle	50 Yds.	100 Yds.	Muzzle	50 Yds.	100 Yds.	50 Yds.	100 Yds.	
380 Automatic SXT®	S380	95	SXT	PP	955	889	835	192	167	147	1.3	5.5	3-3/4
38 Special + P # SXT	S38SP	130	SXT	PP	925	887	852	247	227	210	1.3	5.5	4V
9mm Luger SXT	S9	147	SXT	PP	990	947	909	320	293	270	1.2	4.8	4
40 Smith & Wesson SXT	S401	165	SXT	PP	1110	1020	960	443	381	338	1.0	4.2	4
40 Smith & Wesson SXT	S40	180	SXT	PP	1015	959	912	412	367	333	1.1	4.7	4
45 Automatic SXT	S45	230	SXT	PP	880	846	816	396	366	340	1.5	6.1	5
357 Magnum # Partition Gold™	S357P	180	Partition Gold™	H	1180	1088	1020	557	473	416	0.8	3.6	8V
44 Magnum # Partition Gold™	S44MP	250	Partition Gold™	H	1230	1132	1057	840	711	620	0.8	2.9	6.5V
NEW 45 Winchester Magnum	SPG45WM	260	Partition Gold™	H	1200	1105	1033	832	705	617	0.8	3.5	5
NEW 454 Casull	SPG454	260	Partition Gold™	H	1800	1605	1427	1871	1485	1176	0.4	1.7	7.5V

SUPER-X®

Cartridge	Symbol	Bullet Wt. Grs.	Type	User Guide	Velocity (fps)			Energy (ft-lbs.)			Mid Range Traj. (In.)		Barrel Length In.
					Muzzle	50 Yds.	100 Yds.	Muzzle	50 Yds.	100 Yds.	50 Yds.	100 Yds.	
25 Automatic	X25AXP	45	Expanding Point**	PP	815	729	655	66	53	42	1.8	7.7	2
30 Carbine #	X30M1	110	Hollow Soft Point	H	1790	1601	1430	783	626	500	0.4	1.7	10
32 Smith & Wesson Long	X32SWLP	98	Lead-Round Nose	T	705	670	635	115	98	88	2.3	10.5	4
32 Automatic	X32ASHP	60	Silvertip® Hollow Point	PP	970	895	835	125	107	93	1.3	5.4	4
38 Smith & Wesson	X38SWP	145	Lead-Round Nose	T	685	650	620	150	135	125	2.4	10.0	4
380 Automatic	X380ASHP	85	Silvertip Hollow Point	PP	1000	921	860	189	160	140	1.2	5.1	3-3/4
38 Special	X38S9HP	110	Silvertip Hollow Point	PP	945	894	850	218	195	176	1.3	5.4	4V
38 Special Super Unleaded™	X38SSU	130	Full Metal Jacket Encapsulated	T	775	743	712	173	159	146	1.9	7.9	4V
38 Special Super Match®	X38SMRP	148	Lead-Wad Cutter	T	710	634	566	166	132	105	2.4	10.8	4V
38 Special	X38S1P	158	Lead-Round Nose	T	755	723	693	200	183	168	2.0	8.3	4V
38 Special	X38WCPSV	158	Lead-Semi Wad Cutter	T	755	721	689	200	182	167	2.0	8.4	4V
38 Special + P #	X38S7PH	125	Jacketed Hollow Point	PP	945	898	858	248	224	204	1.3	5.4	4V
38 Special + P #	X38S8HP	125	Silvertip Hollow Point	PP	945	898	858	248	224	204	1.3	5.4	4V
38 Special +P Super Unleaded	X38SSU1	158	Full Metal Jacket-Encapsulated	T	890	864	839	278	262	249	1.4	5.8	4V
38 Special + P	X38SPD	158	Lead-Semi Wad Cutter Hollow Point	PP	890	855	823	278	257	238	1.4	6.0	4V
9mm Luger Super Unleaded	X9MMSU	115	Full Metal Jacket Encapsulated	T	1155	1047	971	341	280	241	0.9	3.9	4
9mm Luger	X9MMSHP	115	Silvertip Hollow Point	PP	1225	1095	1007	383	306	259	0.8	3.6	4
9mm Luger Super Unleaded	X9MMSU2	147	Full Metal Jacket-Encapsulated	T	990	945	907	320	292	268	1.2	4.8	4
9mm Luger Subsonic	XSUB9MM	147	Jacketed Hollow Point	PP	990	945	907	320	292	268	1.2	4.8	4
9mm Luger	X9MMST147	147	Silvertip Hollow Point	PP	1010	962	921	333	302	277	1.1	4.7	4
38 Super Automatic + P*	X38ASHP	125	Silvertip Hollow Point	T/PP	1240	1130	1050	427	354	306	0.8	3.4	5
9 X 23 Winchester	X923W	125	Silvertip Hollow Point	T/PP	1450	1249	1103	583	433	338	0.6	2.8	5
357 Magnum #	X357SHP	145	Silvertip Hollow Point	PP	1290	1155	1060	535	428	361	0.8	3.5	4V
357 Magnum #	X3574P	158	Jacketed Hollow Point	H/PP	1235	1104	1015	535	428	361	0.8	3.5	4V
357 Magnum #	X3575P	158	Jacketed Soft Point	H/PP	1235	1104	1015	535	428	361	0.8	3.5	4V
40 Smith & Wesson	X40SWSTHP	155	Silvertip Hollow Point	PP	1205	1096	1018	500	414	357	0.8	3.6	4
40 Smith & Wesson Super Unleaded	X40SWSU1	165	Full Metal Jacket-Encapsulated	T	1110	1020	960	443	381	338	1.0	4.2	4
40 Smith & Wesson Super Unleaded	X40SWSU	180	Full Metal Jacket-Encapsulated	T	990	933	886	392	348	314	1.2	5.0	4
40 Smith & Wesson Subsonic	XSUB40SW	180	Jacketed Hollow Point	PP	1010	954	909	408	364	330	1.1	4.8	4
10mm Automatic	X10MMSTHP	175	Silvertip Hollow Point	PP	1290	1141	1037	649	506	418	0.7	3.3	5-1/2
41 Remington Magnum #	X41MSTHP2	175	Silvertip Hollow Point	H/PP	1250	1120	1029	607	488	412	0.8	3.4	4V
44 Smith & Wesson Special #	X44STHPS2	200	Silvertip Hollow Point	PP	900	860	822	360	328	300	1.4	5.9	6-1/2
44 Smith & Wesson Special	X44SP	246	Lead-Round Nose	T	755	725	695	310	285	265	2.0	8.3	6-1/2
44 Remington Magnum #	X44MS	210	Silvertip Hollow Point	H/PP	1250	1106	1010	729	570	475	0.8	3.5	4V
44 Remington Magnum #	X44MHSP2	240	Hollow Soft Point	H	1180	1081	1010	741	623	543	0.9	3.7	4V
45 Automatic	X45ASHP2	185	Silvertip Hollow Point	PP	1000	938	888	411	362	324	1.2	4.9	5
45 Automatic Super Unleaded	X45ASU	230	Full Metal Jacket - Encapsulated	T	835	800	767	356	326	300	1.6	6.8	5
45 Automatic Subsonic	XSUB45A	230	Jacketed Hollow Point	PP	880	842	808	396	363	334	1.5	6.1	5
45 Colt #	X45CSHP2	225	Silvertip Hollow Point	PP	920	877	839	423	384	352	1.4	5.6	5-1/2
45 Colt	X45CP2	255	Lead-Round Nose	T	860	820	780	420	380	345	1.5	6.1	5-1/2
45 Winchester Magnum #	X45WMA	260	Jacketed Hollow Point	H	1200	1099	1026	831	698	607	0.8	3.6	5
454 Casull #	X454C1	260	Jacketed Flat Point	H	1800	1577	1381	1871	1436	1101	0.4	1.8	7.5V
454 Casull #	X454C2	300	Jacketed Flat Point	H	1625	1451	1308	1759	1413	1141	0.5	2.0	7.5V

Winchester Rifle Ballistics

SUPER-X® CENTERFIRE RIFLE BALLISTICS

Cartridge	Symbol	Bullet Wt. Grs.	Bullet Type	Game Selector Guide	CXP Guide Number	Barrel Length (In.)	Velocity in Feet Per Second (fps) Muzzle	100	200	300	400	500	Energy in Foot Pounds (ft-lbs.) Muzzle	100	200	300	400	500	Trajectory, Short Range Yards 50	100	150	200	250	300	Trajectory, Long Range Yards 100	150	200	250	300	400	500
218 Bee	X218B	46	Hollow Point	V	1	24	2760	2102	1550	1155	961	850	778	451	245	136	94	74	0.3	0	-2.3	-7.2	-15.8	-29.4	1.5	0	-4.2	-12.0	-24.8	-71.4	-155.6
22 Hornet	X22H1	45	Soft Point	V	1	24	2690	2042	1502	1128	948	840	723	417	225	127	90	70	0.3	0	-2.4	-7.7	-16.9	-31.3	1.6	0	-4.5	-12.8	-26.4	-75.6	-163.4
22 Hornet	X22H2	46	Hollow Point	V	1	24	2690	2042	1502	1128	948	841	739	426	230	130	92	72	0.3	0	-2.4	-7.7	-16.9	-31.3	1.6	0	-4.5	-12.8	-26.4	-75.5	-163.3
22-250 Remington	X222501	55	Pointed Soft Point	V	1	24	3680	3137	2656	2222	1832	1493	1654	1201	861	603	410	272	0.2	0.5	0	-1.6	-4.4	-8.7	2.3	2.6	1.9	0	-3.4	-15.9	-38.9
220 Swift	X220S	50	Pointed Soft Point	V	1	24	3870	3310	2816	2373	1972	2516	1663	1226	881	625	432	290	-0.4	0	-0.4	-1.7	-4.1	-7.8	0.8	0.9	0	-2.0	-5.2	-16.7	-37.1
222 Remington	X222R	50	Pointed Soft Point	V	1	24	3140	2602	2123	1700	1350	1107	1094	752	500	321	202	136	0.5	0.9	0	-2.5	-6.9	-13.7	2.2	1.9	0	-3.8	-10.0	-32.3	-73.8
223 Remington	X223RH	53	Hollow Point	V	1	24	3330	2882	2477	2106	1770	1475	1305	978	722	522	369	256	0.3	0.7	0	-1.9	-5.3	-10.3	1.7	1.4	0	-2.9	-7.4	-22.7	-49.1
223 Remington	X223R	55	Pointed Soft Point	V	1	24	3240	2747	2304	1905	1554	1270	1282	921	648	443	295	197	0.4	0.8	0	-2.2	-6.0	-11.8	1.9	1.6	0	-3.3	-8.5	-26.7	-59.6
223 Remington	X223R2	64	Power-Point®	D	2	24	3020	2656	2320	2009	1724	1473	1296	1003	765	574	423	308	0.1	0.7	0	-2.1	-5.8	-11.4	1.7	1.6	0	-3.2	-8.2	-25.1	-53.6
225 Winchester	X2251	55	Pointed Soft Point	V	1	24	3570	3066	2616	2208	1838	1514	1556	1148	836	595	412	280	0.2	0.6	0	-1.7	-4.6	-9.0	2.4	2.8	2.0	0	-3.5	-16.3	-39.5
243 Winchester	X2431	80	Pointed Soft Point	V	1	24	3350	2955	2593	2259	1951	1670	1993	1551	1194	906	676	495	0.3	0.7	0	-1.8	-4.9	-9.4	2.6	2.9	2.1	0	-3.6	-16.2	-37.9
243 Winchester	X2432	100	Power-Point	D,O/P	2	24	2960	2697	2449	2215	1993	1786	1945	1615	1332	1089	882	708	0.5	0.9	0	-2.2	-5.8	-11.0	1.9	1.6	0	-3.1	-7.8	-22.6	-46.3
25-06 Remington	X25061	90	Positive Expanding Point	V	1	24	3440	3043	2680	2344	2034	1749	2364	1850	1435	1098	827	611	0.3	0.6	0	-1.7	-4.5	-8.8	2.4	2.7	2.0	0	-3.4	-15.0	-35.2
25-06 Remington	X25062	120	Positive Expanding Point	D,O/P	2	24	2990	2730	2484	2252	2032	1825	2382	1985	1644	1351	1100	887	0.5	0.8	0	-2.1	-5.6	-10.7	1.9	1.6	0	-3.0	-7.5	-22.0	-44.8
25-35 Winchester	X2535	117	Soft Point	D	2	24	2230	1866	1545	1282	1097	984	1292	904	620	427	313	252	0.6	0	-3.1	-9.2	-19.0	-33.1	2.1	0	-5.1	-13.8	-27.0	-70.1	-142.0
6.5 x 55 Swedish	X6555	140	Soft Point	D,O/P	2	24	2550	2359	2176	2002	1836	1680	2022	1731	1473	1246	1048	878	0	0	-1.5	-4.8	-9.8	-16.9	2.4	2	0	-3.9	-9.7	-28.1	-56.8
270 Winchester	X2705	130	Power-Point	D,O/P	2	24	3060	2802	2559	2329	2110	1904	2702	2267	1890	1565	1285	1046	0.4	0.8	0	-2.0	-5.3	-10.1	1.8	1.5	0	-2.8	-7.1	-20.6	-42.0
270 Winchester	X2703	130	Silvertip	D,O/P	2	24	3060	2776	2510	2259	2022	1801	2702	2225	1818	1472	1180	936	0.5	0.8	0	-2.0	-5.5	-10.4	1.8	1.5	0	-2.9	-7.4	-21.6	-44.3
270 Winchester	X2704	150	Power-Point	D,O/P,M	3	24	2850	2585	2336	2100	1879	1673	2705	2226	1817	1468	1175	932	0.6	1.0	0	-2.4	-6.4	-12.2	2.2	1.8	0	-3.4	-8.6	-25.0	-51.4
284 Winchester	X2842	150	Power-Point	D,O/P,M	3	24	2860	2595	2344	2108	1886	1680	2724	2243	1830	1480	1185	940	0.6	1.0	0	-2.4	-6.3	-12.1	2.1	1.8	0	-3.4	-8.5	-24.8	-51.0
NEW 7mm-08 Remington	X708	140	Power-Point	D,O/P	2	24	2800	2523	2268	2027	1802	1596	2429	1980	1599	1277	1010	792	-0.1	0	-1.2	-4.0	-8.4	-14.7	2.0	1.8	0	-3.4	-8.8	-26.0	-54.0
7mm Remington Mag.	X7MMR1	150	Power-Point	D,O/P,M	2	24	3110	2830	2568	2320	2085	1866	3221	2667	2196	1792	1448	1160	0.4	0.8	0	-1.9	-5.2	-9.9	1.7	1.5	0	-2.8	-7.0	-20.5	-42.1
7mm Remington Mag.	X7MMR2	175	Power-Point	D,O/P,M	3	24	2860	2645	2440	2244	2057	1879	3178	2718	2313	1956	1644	1372	0.6	0.9	0	-2.3	-6.0	-11.3	2.0	1.7	0	-3.2	-7.9	-22.7	-45.8
7.62 x 39mm Russian	X76239	123	Soft Point	D,V	2	20	2365	2033	1731	1465	1248	1093	1527	1129	818	586	425	327	0.5	0	-2.6	-7.6	-15.4	-26.7	3.8	3.1	0	-6.0	-15.4	-46.3	-98.4
30 Carbine #	X30M1	110	Hollow Soft Point	V	1	20	1990	1567	1236	1035	923	842	967	600	373	262	208	173	0.9	0	-4.5	-13.5	-28.3	-49.9	0	-4.5	-13.5	-28.3	-49.9	-118.6	-228.2
30-30 Winchester	X30301	150	Hollow Point	D	2	24	2390	2018	1684	1398	1177	1036	1902	1356	944	651	461	357	0.5	0	-2.6	-7.7	-16.0	-27.9	1.7	0	-4.3	-11.6	-22.7	-59.1	-120.5
30-30 Winchester	X30306	150	Power-Point	D	2	24	2390	2018	1684	1398	1177	1036	1902	1356	944	651	461	357	0.5	0	-2.6	-7.7	-16.0	-27.9	1.7	0	-4.3	-11.6	-22.7	-59.1	-120.5
30-30 Winchester	X30302	150	Silvertip	D	2	24	2390	2018	1684	1398	1177	1036	1902	1356	944	651	461	357	0.5	0	-2.6	-7.7	-16.0	-27.9	1.7	0	-4.3	-11.6	-22.7	-59.1	-120.5
30-30 Winchester	X30303	170	Power-Point	D	2	24	2200	1895	1619	1381	1191	1061	1827	1355	989	720	535	425	0.6	0	-3.0	-8.9	-18.0	-31.1	2.0	0	-4.8	-13.0	-25.1	-63.6	-126.7
30-30 Winchester	X30304	170	Silvertip	D	2	24	2200	1895	1619	1381	1191	1061	1827	1355	989	720	535	425	0.6	0	-3.0	-8.9	-18.0	-31.1	2.0	0	-4.8	-13.0	-25.1	-63.6	-126.7
30-06 Springfield	X30062	125	Pointed Soft Point	V	1	24	3140	2780	2447	2138	1853	1595	2736	2145	1662	1269	953	706	0.4	0.8	0	-2.1	-5.6	-10.7	1.8	1.5	0	-3.0	-7.7	-23.0	-48.5
30-06 Springfield	X30061	150	Power-Point	D,O/P	2	24	2920	2580	2265	1972	1704	1466	2839	2217	1708	1295	967	716	0.6	1.0	0	-2.4	-6.6	-12.7	2.2	1.8	0	-3.5	-9.0	-27.0	-57.1
30-06 Springfield	X30063	150	Silvertip	D,O/P	2	24	2910	2617	2342	2083	1843	1622	2820	2281	1827	1445	1131	876	0.6	0.9	0	-2.3	-6.3	-12.0	2.1	1.8	0	-3.3	-8.5	-25.0	-51.8
30-06 Springfield	X30065	165	Pointed Soft Point	D,O/P,M	2	24	2800	2573	2357	2151	1956	1772	2873	2426	2036	1696	1402	1151	0.7	1.0	0	-2.5	-6.5	-12.2	2.2	1.9	0	-3.6	-8.4	-24.4	-49.6
30-06 Springfield	X30064	180	Power-Point	D,O/P,M	2	24	2700	2348	2023	1727	1466	1251	2913	2203	1635	1192	859	625	0.2	0	-1.8	-5.5	-11.2	-19.5	2.7	2.3	0	-4.4	-11.3	-34.4	-73.7
30-06 Springfield	X30066	180	Silvertip	D,O/P,M,L	3	24	2700	2469	2250	2042	1846	1663	2913	2436	2023	1666	1362	1105	0.2	0	-1.6	-4.8	-9.7	-16.5	2.4	2.0	0	-3.7	-9.3	-27.0	-54.9
300 Winchester Mag.	X30WM1	150	Power-Point	D,O/P	2	24	3290	2951	2636	2342	2068	1813	3605	2900	2314	1827	1424	1095	0.3	0.7	0	-1.8	-4.8	-9.3	2.6	2.9	2.1	0	-3.5	-15.4	-35.5
300 Winchester Mag.	X30WM2	180	Power-Point	O/P,M,L	3	24	2960	2745	2540	2344	2157	1979	3501	3011	2578	2196	1859	1565	0.5	0.8	0	-2.1	-5.5	-10.4	1.9	1.6	0	-2.9	-7.3	-20.9	-41.9
300 Savage	X3001	150	Power-Point	D,O/P	2	24	2630	2311	2015	1743	1500	1295	2303	1779	1352	1012	749	558	0.3	0	-1.9	-5.7	-11.6	-19.9	2.8	2.3	0	-4.5	-11.5	-34.4	-73.0
303 British	X303B1	180	Power-Point	D	2	24	2460	2233	2018	1816	1629	1459	2418	1993	1627	1318	1060	851	0.3	0	-2.1	-6.1	-12.2	-20.8	1.4	0	-3.3	-8.8	-16.6	-40.4	-77.4
307 Winchester	X3076	180	Power-Point	D,M	2	24	2510	2179	1874	1599	1362	1177	2519	1898	1404	1022	742	554	0.3	0	-2.2	-6.5	-13.3	-22.9	1.5	0	-3.6	-9.6	-18.6	-47.1	-93.7
308 Winchester	X3085	150	Power-Point	D,O/P	2	24	2820	2488	2179	1893	1633	1405	2648	2061	1581	1193	888	657	0.2	0	-1.6	-4.8	-9.8	-16.9	2.4	2.0	0	-3.8	-9.8	-29.3	-62.0
308 Winchester	X3086	180	Power-Point	D,O/P,M	2	24	2620	2274	1955	1666	1414	1212	2743	2066	1527	1109	799	587	0.3	0	-2.0	-5.9	-12.1	-20.9	2.9	2.4	0	-4.7	-12.1	-36.9	-79.1
308 Winchester	X3083	180	Silvertip	M,L	3	24	2620	2393	2178	1974	1782	1604	2743	2288	1896	1557	1269	1028	0.2	0	-1.8	-5.2	-10.4	-17.7	2.6	2.1	0	-4.0	-9.9	-28.9	-58.8
32 Win Special	X32WS2	170	Power-Point	D	2	24	2250	1870	1537	1267	1082	971	1911	1320	892	606	442	356	0.6	0	-3.1	-9.2	-19.0	-33.2	2.0	0	-5.1	-13.8	-27.1	-70.9	-144.3
32-20 Winchester #	X32201	100	Lead	V	1	24	1210	1021	913	834	769	712	325	231	185	154	131	113	0	-6.3	-20.9	-44.9	-79.3	-125.1	0	-11.5	-32.3	-63.6	-106.3	-230.3	-413.3
8mm Mauser (8 x 57)	X8MM	170	Power-Point	D	2	24	2360	1969	1622	1333	1123	997	2102	1463	993	671	476	375	0.5	0	-2.7	-8.2	-17.0	-29.8	1.8	0	-4.5	-12.4	-24.3	-63.8	-130.7
338 Winchester Mag.	X3381	200	Power-Point	D,O/P,M, L	3	24	2960	2658	2375	2110	1862	1635	3890	3137	2505	1977	1539	1187	0.5	0.9	0	-2.3	-6.1	-11.6	2.0	1.7	0	-3.2	-8.2	-24.3	-50.4
35 Remington	X35R1	200	Power-Point	D	2	24	2020	1646	1335	1114	985	901	1812	1203	791	551	431	360	0.9	0	-4.1	-12.1	-25.1	-43.9	2.7	0	-6.7	-18.3	-35.8	-92.8	-185.5
356 Winchester	X3561	200	Power-Point	D,M	2	24	2460	2114	1797	1517	1284	1113	2688	1985	1434	1022	732	550	0.4	0	-2.3	-7.0	-14.3	-24.7	1.6	0	-3.8	-10.4	-20.1	-51.2	-102.3
357 Magnum #	X3575P	158	Jacketed Soft Point	V,D	2	20	1830	1427	1138	980	883	809	1175	715	454	337	274	229	0	-2.4	-9.1	-21.0	-39.2	-64.3	0	-5.5	-16.2	-33.1	-57.0	-128.3	-235.8
375 Winchester	X375W	200	Power-Point	D,M	2	24	2200	1841	1526	1268	1089	980	2150	1506	1034	714	527	427	0.6	0	-3.2	-9.5	-19.5	-33.8	2.1	0	-5.2	-14.1	-27.4	-70.1	-138.1
38-40 Winchester #	X3840	180	Soft Point	D	2	24	1160	999	901	827	764	710	538	399	324	273	233	201	0	-6.7	-22.2	-47.3	-83.2	-130.8	0	-12.1	-33.9	-66.4	-110.6	-238.3	-425.6
38-55 Winchester	X3855	255	Soft Point	D	2	24	1320	1190	1091	1018	963	917	987	802	674	587	525	476	0	-4.7	-15.4	-32.7	-57.2	-89.3	0	-8.4	-23.4	-45.6	-75.2	-158.8	-277.4
44 Remington Magnum #	X44MS	210	Silvertip Hollow Point	V,D	2	20	1580	1198	993	879	795	725	1164	670	460	361	295	245	0	-3.7	-13.3	-29.8	-54.2	-87.3	0	-7.7	-22.4	-44.9	-76.1	-168.0	-305.8
44 Remington Magnum #	X44MHSP2	240	Hollow Soft Point	D	2	20	1760	1362	1094	953	861	789	1650	988	638	484	395	332	0	-2.7	-10.2	-23.6	-44.2	-73.3	0	-6.1	-18.1	-37.4	-65.1	-150.3	-282.5
44-40 Winchester #	X4440	200	Soft Point	D	2	24	1190	1006	900	822	756	699	629	449	360	300	254	217	0	-6.5	-21.6	-46.3	-81.8	-129.1	0	-11.8	-33.3	-65.5	-109.5	-237.4	-426.2
45-70 Government	X4570H	300	Jacketed Hollow Point	D,M	2	24	1880	1650	1425	1235	1105	1010	2355	1815	1355	1015	810	680	0	-2.4	-8.2	-17.6	-31.4	-51.5	0	-4.6	-12.8	-25.4	-44.3	-95.5	-

Reloading

BULLETS

Hornady	522
Nosler	525
Sako	528
Sierra	529
Speer	532

GUNPOWDER

Alliant	536
Hodgdon	537

TOOLS

Dillon	538
Forster	540
Hornady	542
Lyman	544
MEC	549
MTM	551
RCBS	552
Redding	555

*For addresses and phone/fax numbers of manufacturers and distributors included in this section, please turn to **DIRECTORY OF MANUFACTURERS AND SUPPLIERS** on page 558.*

HORNADY RIFLE BULLETS

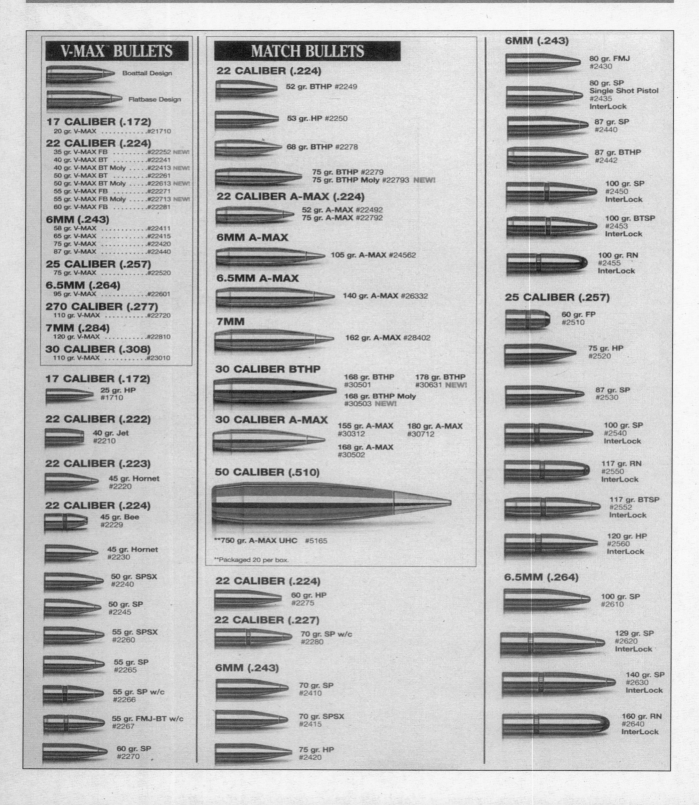

V-MAX BULLETS

Boattail Design

Flatbase Design

17 CALIBER (.172)
20 gr. V-MAX ....#21710

22 CALIBER (.224)
35 gr. V-MAX FB ....#22252 NEW!
40 gr. V-MAX BT ....#22241
40 gr. V-MAX BT Moly .....#22413 NEW!
50 gr. V-MAX BT ....#22261
50 gr. V-MAX BT Moly .....#22613 NEW!
55 gr. V-MAX FB ....#22271
55 gr. V-MAX FB Moly .....#22713 NEW!
60 gr. V-MAX FB ....#22281

6MM (.243)
58 gr. V-MAX ....#22411
65 gr. V-MAX ....#22415
75 gr. V-MAX ....#22420
87 gr. V-MAX ....#22440

25 CALIBER (.257)
75 gr. V-MAX ....#22520

6.5MM (.264)
95 gr. V-MAX ....#22601

270 CALIBER (.277)
110 gr. V-MAX ....#22720

7MM (.284)
120 gr. V-MAX ....#22810

30 CALIBER (.308)
110 gr. V-MAX ....#23010

17 CALIBER (.172)
25 gr. HP #1710

22 CALIBER (.222)
40 gr. Jet #2210

22 CALIBER (.223)
45 gr. Hornet #2220

22 CALIBER (.224)
45 gr. Bee #2229

45 gr. Hornet #2230

50 gr. SPSX #2240

50 gr. SP #2245

55 gr. SPSX #2260

55 gr. SP #2265

55 gr. SP w/c #2266

55 gr. FMJ-BT w/c #2267

60 gr. SP #2270

MATCH BULLETS

22 CALIBER (.224)
52 gr. BTHP #2249

53 gr. HP #2250

68 gr. BTHP #2278

75 gr. BTHP #2279
75 gr. BTHP Moly #22793 NEW!

22 CALIBER A-MAX (.224)
52 gr. A-MAX #22492
75 gr. A-MAX #22792

6MM A-MAX
105 gr. A-MAX #24562

6.5MM A-MAX
140 gr. A-MAX #26332

7MM
162 gr. A-MAX #28402

30 CALIBER BTHP
168 gr. BTHP #30501
178 gr. BTHP #30631 NEW!
168 gr. BTHP Moly #30503 NEW!

30 CALIBER A-MAX
155 gr. A-MAX #30312
180 gr. A-MAX #30712
168 gr. A-MAX #30502

50 CALIBER (.510)

**750 gr. A-MAX UHC #5165

*Packaged 20 per box.

22 CALIBER (.224)
60 gr. HP #2275

22 CALIBER (.227)
70 gr. SP w/c #2280

6MM (.243)
70 gr. SP #2410

70 gr. SPSX #2415

75 gr. HP #2420

6MM (.243)
80 gr. FMJ #2430

80 gr. SP
Single Shot Pistol #2435
InterLock

87 gr. SP #2440

87 gr. BTHP #2442

100 gr. SP #2450
InterLock

100 gr. BTSP #2453
InterLock

100 gr. RN #2455
InterLock

25 CALIBER (.257)
60 gr. FP #2510

75 gr. HP #2520

87 gr. SP #2530

100 gr. SP #2540
InterLock

117 gr. RN #2550
InterLock

117 gr. BTSP #2552
InterLock

120 gr. HP #2560
InterLock

6.5MM (.264)
100 gr. SP #2610

129 gr. SP #2620
InterLock

140 gr. SP #2630
InterLock

160 gr. RN #2640
InterLock

HORNADY RIFLE BULLETS

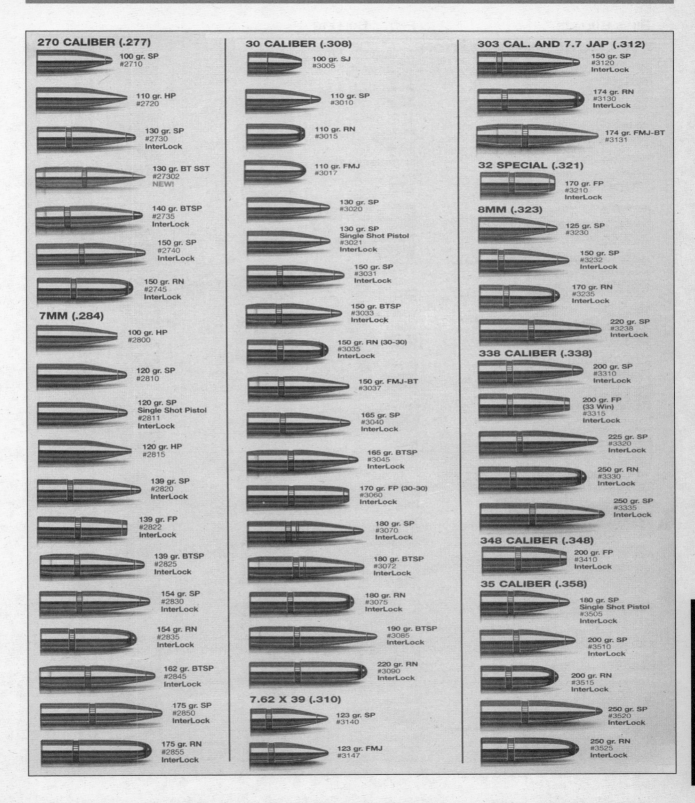

270 CALIBER (.277)

100 gr. SP #2710

110 gr. HP #2720

130 gr. SP #2730 InterLock

130 gr. BT SST #27302 NEW!

140 gr. BTSP #2735 InterLock

150 gr. SP #2740 InterLock

150 gr. RN #2745 InterLock

7MM (.284)

100 gr. HP #2800

120 gr. SP #2810

120 gr. SP Single Shot Pistol #2811 InterLock

120 gr. HP #2815

139 gr. SP #2820 InterLock

139 gr. FP #2822 InterLock

139 gr. BTSP #2825 InterLock

154 gr. SP #2830 InterLock

154 gr. RN #2835 InterLock

162 gr. BTSP #2845 InterLock

175 gr. SP #2850 InterLock

175 gr. RN #2855 InterLock

30 CALIBER (.308)

100 gr. SJ #3005

110 gr. SP #3010

110 gr. RN #3015

110 gr. FMJ #3017

130 gr. SP #3020

130 gr. SP Single Shot Pistol #3021 InterLock

150 gr. SP #3031 InterLock

150 gr. BTSP #3033 InterLock

150 gr. RN (30-30) #3035 InterLock

150 gr. FMJ-BT #3037

165 gr. SP #3040 InterLock

165 gr. BTSP #3045 InterLock

170 gr. FP (30-30) #3060 InterLock

180 gr. SP #3070 InterLock

180 gr. BTSP #3072 InterLock

180 gr. RN #3075 InterLock

190 gr. BTSP #3085 InterLock

220 gr. RN #3090 InterLock

7.62 X 39 (.310)

123 gr. SP #3140

123 gr. FMJ #3147

303 CAL. AND 7.7 JAP (.312)

150 gr. SP #3120 InterLock

174 gr. RN #3130 InterLock

174 gr. FMJ-BT #3131

32 SPECIAL (.321)

170 gr. FP #3210 InterLock

8MM (.323)

125 gr. SP #3230

150 gr. SP #3232 InterLock

170 gr. RN #3235 InterLock

220 gr. SP #3238 InterLock

338 CALIBER (.338)

200 gr. SP #3310 InterLock

200 gr. FP (33 Win) #3315 InterLock

225 gr. SP #3320 InterLock

250 gr. RN #3330 InterLock

250 gr. SP #3335 InterLock

348 CALIBER (.348)

200 gr. FP #3410 InterLock

35 CALIBER (.358)

180 gr. SP Single Shot Pistol #3505 InterLock

200 gr. SP #3510 InterLock

200 gr. RN #3515 InterLock

250 gr. SP #3520 InterLock

250 gr. RN #3525 InterLock

RELOADING

HORNADY BULLETS

RIFLE BULLETS

375 CALIBER (.375)

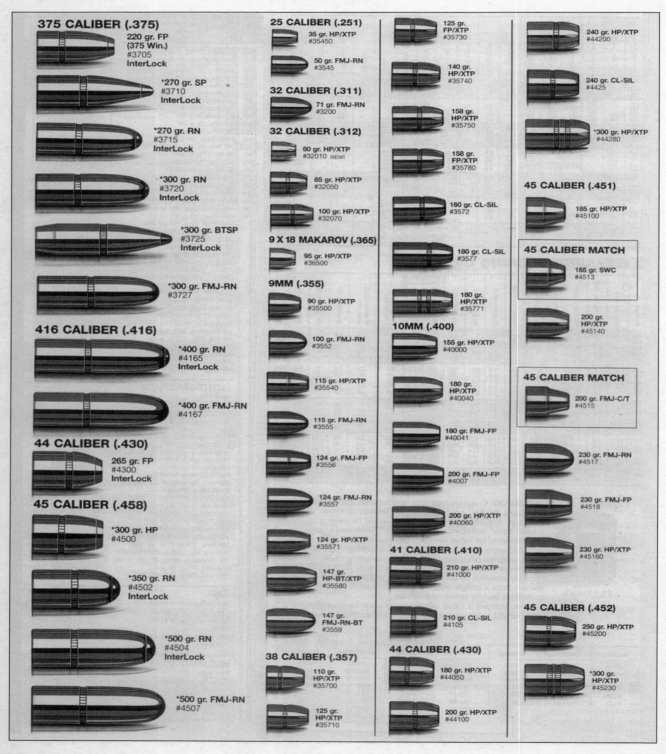

220 gr. FP
(375 Win.)
#3705
InterLock

*270 gr. SP
#3710
InterLock

*270 gr. RN
#3715
InterLock

*300 gr. RN
#3720
InterLock

*300 gr. BTSP
#3725
InterLock

*300 gr. FMJ-RN
#3727

416 CALIBER (.416)

*400 gr. RN
#4165
InterLock

*400 gr. FMJ-RN
#4167

44 CALIBER (.430)

265 gr. FP
#4300
InterLock

45 CALIBER (.458)

*300 gr. HP
#4500

*350 gr. RN
#4502
InterLock

*500 gr. RN
#4504
InterLock

*500 gr. FMJ-RN
#4507

PISTOL BULLETS

25 CALIBER (.251)

35 gr. HP/XTP
#35450

50 gr. FMJ-RN
#3545

32 CALIBER (.311)

71 gr. FMJ-RN
#3200

32 CALIBER (.312)

60 gr. HP/XTP
#32010 NEW!

85 gr. HP/XTP
#32050

100 gr. HP/XTP
#32070

9 X 18 MAKAROV (.365)

95 gr. HP/XTP
#36500

9MM (.355)

90 gr. HP/XTP
#35500

100 gr. FMJ-RN
#3552

115 gr. HP/XTP
#35540

115 gr. FMJ-RN
#3555

124 gr. FMJ-FP
#3556

124 gr. FMJ-RN
#3557

124 gr. HP/XTP
#35571

147 gr. HP-BT/XTP
#35580

147 gr. FMJ-RN-BT
#3559

38 CALIBER (.357)

110 gr. HP/XTP
#35700

125 gr. HP/XTP
#35710

125 gr. FP/XTP
#35730

140 gr. HP/XTP
#35740

158 gr. HP/XTP
#35750

158 gr. FP/XTP
#35780

160 gr. CL-SIL
#3572

180 gr. CL-SIL
#3577

180 gr. HP/XTP
#35771

10MM (.400)

155 gr. HP/XTP
#40000

180 gr. HP/XTP
#40040

180 gr. FMJ-FP
#40041

200 gr. FMJ-FP
#4007

200 gr. HP/XTP
#40060

41 CALIBER (.410)

210 gr. HP/XTP
#41000

210 gr. CL-SIL
#4105

44 CALIBER (.430)

180 gr. HP/XTP
#44050

200 gr. HP/XTP
#44100

240 gr. HP/XTP
#44200

240 gr. CL-SIL
#4425

*300 gr. HP/XTP
#44280

45 CALIBER (.451)

185 gr. HP/XTP
#45100

45 CALIBER MATCH

185 gr. SWC
#4513

200 gr. HP/XTP
#45140

45 CALIBER MATCH

200 gr. FMJ-C/T
#4515

230 gr. FMJ-RN
#4517

230 gr. FMJ-FP
#4518

230 gr. HP/XTP
#45160

45 CALIBER (.452)

250 gr. HP/XTP
#45200

*300 gr. HP/XTP
#45230

NOSLER BULLETS

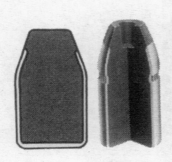 

PISTOL AND REVOLVER BULLETS

Cal. Dia.	HANDGUN *Revolver*	BULLET WEIGHT AND STYLE	SECT. DENS.	BAL. COEF.	PART#
38 .357"		125 GR. HOLLOW POINT 250 QUANTITY BULK PACK	.140	.143	42055 44840
		150 GR. SOFT POINT	.168	.153	42056
		158 GR. HOLLOW POINT 250 QUANTITY BULK PACK	.177	.182	42057 44841
		180 GR. SILHOUETTE 250 QUANTITY BULK PACK	.202	.210	42058 44851
41 .410"		210 GR. HOLLOW POINT	.178	.170	43012
44 .429"		200 GR. HOLLOW POINT 250 QUANTITY BULK PACK	.155	.151	42060 44846
		240 GR. HOLLOW POINT 250 QUANTITY BULK PACK	.186	.173	42061 44842
		240 GR. SOFT POINT	.186	.177	42068
		300 GR. HOLLOW POINT	.233	.206	42069
45 Colt .451"		250 GR. HOLLOW POINT	.176	.177	43013

Cal. Dia.	HANDGUN *Auto*	BULLET WEIGHT AND STYLE	SECT. DENS.	BAL. COEF.	PART#
9mm .355"		90 GR. HOLLOW POINT	.102	.086	42050
		115 GR. FULL METAL JACKET	.130	.103	42059
		115 GR. HOLLOW POINT 250 QUANTITY BULK PACK	.130	.110	43009 44848
38 .357"		115 GR. HOLLOW POINT PRACTICAL PISTOL™	.129	.110	44835
		135 GR. PRACTICAL PISTOL™	.151	.149	44836
		150 GR. PRACTICAL PISTOL™	.168	.157	44839
10mm .400"		135 GR. HOLLOW POINT 250 QUANTITY BULK PACK	.121	.093	44838 44852
		150 GR. HOLLOW POINT	.134	.106	44849
		170 GR. HOLLOW POINT	.152	.137	44844
		180 GR. HOLLOW POINT	.161	.147	44837
45 .451"		185 GR. HOLLOW POINT 250 QUANTITY BULK PACK	.130	.142	42062 44847
		230 GR. FULL METAL JACKET	.162	.183	42064

RELOADING

NOSLER BULLETS

NOSLER PARTITION® BULLETS

The Nosler Partition® bullet earned its reputation among professional guides and serious hunters for one reason: it doesn't fail. The patented Partition® design offers a dual core that is unequallled in mushrooming, weight retention and hydrostatic shock.

Cal. Dia.	PARTITION®	BULLET WEIGHT AND STYLE	SECT. DENS.	BAL. COEF.	PART#
8mm .323"		200 GR. SPITZER	.274	.426	35277
338 .338"		210 GR. SPITZER	.263	.400	16337
		225 GR. SPITZER	.281	.454	16336
		250 GR. SPITZER	.313	.473	35644
35 .358"		225 GR. SPITZER	.251	.430	44800
		250 GR. SPITZER	.279	.446	44801
9.3mm .366"		286 GR. SPITZER (18.5 GRAM)	.307	.482	44750
375 .375"		260 GR. SPITZER	.264	.314	44850
		300 GR. SPITZER	.305	.398	44845

Cal. Dia.	PARTITION®	BULLET WEIGHT AND STYLE	SECT. DENS.	BAL. COEF.	PART#
6mm .243"		85 GR. SPITZER	.206	.315	16314
		95 GR. SPITZER	.230	.365	16315
		100 GR. SPITZER	.242	.384	35642
25 .257"		100 GR. SPITZER	.216	.377	16317
		115 GR. SPITZER	.249	.389	16318
		120 GR. SPITZER	.260	.391	35643
6.5mm .264"		100 GR. SPITZER	.205	.426	16319
		125 GR. SPITZER	.256	.449	16320
		140 GR. SPITZER	.287	.490	16321
270 .277"		130 GR. SPITZER	.242	.416	16322
		150 GR. SPITZER	.279	.465	16323
		160 GR. SEMI SPITZER	.298	.434	16324
7mm .284"		140 GR. SPITZER	.248	.434	16325
		150 GR. SPITZER	.266	.456	16326
		160 GR. SPITZER	.283	.475	16327
		175 GR. SPITZER	.310	.519	35645
30 .308"		150 GR. SPITZER	.226	.387	16329
		165 GR. SPITZER	.248	.410	16330
		170 GR. ROUND NOSE	.256	.252	16333
		180 GR. PROTECTED POINT	.271	.361	25396
		180 GR. SPITZER	.271	.474	16331
		200 GR. SPITZER	.301	.481	35626
		220 GR. SEMI SPITZER	.331	.351	16332

NOSLER BULLETS

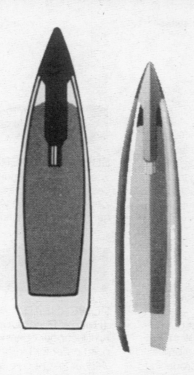

NOSLER BALLISTIC TIP® HUNTING BULLETS

Nosler has replaced the familiar lead point of the Spitzer with a tough polycarbonate tip. The purpose of this new Ballistic Tip® is to resist deforming in the magazine and feed ramp of many rifles. The Solid Base® design produces controlled expansion for excellent mushrooming and exceptional accuracy.

Cal. Dia.	SOLID BASE® BALLISTIC TIP® *Varmint*	BULLET WEIGHT AND STYLE	SECT. DENS.	BAL. COEF.	PART#
22 .224"		40 GR. SPITZER (ORANGE TIP)	.114	.221	39510
		250 CT. VARMINT PAK™			39555
		45 GR. HORNET (SOFT LEAD TIP)	.128	.144	35487
		50 GR. SPITZER (ORANGE TIP)	.142	.238	39522
		55 GR. SPITZER (ORANGE TIP)	.157	.267	39526
		250 CT. VARMINT PAK™			39560
6mm .243"		55 GR. SPITZER (PURPLE TIP)	.133	.276	24055
		70 GR. SPITZER (PURPLE TIP)	.169	.310	39532
25 .257"		85 GR. SPITZER (BLUE TIP)	.183	.331	43004

Cal. Dia.	SOLID BASE® BALLISTIC TIP® *Hunting*	BULLET WEIGHT AND STYLE	SECT. DENS.	BAL. COEF.	PART#
6mm .243"		95 GR. SPITZER (PURPLE TIP)	.230	.379	24095
25 .257"		100 GR. SPITZER (BLUE TIP)	.216	.393	25100
		115 GR. SPITZER (BLUE TIP)	.249	.453	25115
6.5mm .264"		100 GR. SPITZER (BROWN TIP)	.205	.350	26100
		120 GR. SPITZER (BROWN TIP)	.246	.458	26120
270 .277"		130 GR. SPITZER (YELLOW TIP)	.242	.433	27130
		140 GR. SPITZER (YELLOW TIP)	.261	.456	27140
		150 GR. SPITZER (YELLOW TIP)	.279	.496	27150
7mm .284"		120 GR. FLAT POINT (SOFT LEAD TIP)	.213	.195	28121
		120 GR. SPITZER (RED TIP)	.213	.417	28120
		140 GR. SPITZER (RED TIP)	.248	.485	28140
		150 GR. SPITZER (RED TIP)	.266	.493	28150
30 .308"		125 GR. SPITZER (GREEN TIP)	.188	.366	30125
		150 GR. SPITZER (GREEN TIP)	.226	.435	30150
		165 GR. SPITZER (GREEN TIP)	.248	.475	30165
		180 GR. SPITZER (GREEN TIP)	.271	.507	30180
338 .338"		180 GR. SPITZER (MAROON TIP)	.225	.372	33180
		200 GR. SPITZER (MAROON TIP)	.250	.414	33200
35 .358"		225 GR. WHELEN (BUCKSKIN TIP)	.251	.421	35225

SAKO BULLETS

PISTOL AND REVOLVER BULLETS

WC (Wad Cutter)
An accurate, highly popular bullet for target shooting that makes a hole that is easy to interpret. Low recoil.

SWC (Semi Wad Cutter)
Has greater speed and energy than the WC. Also intended for target shooting.

FMJ (Full Metal Jacket)
Good penetration and excellent feeding characteristics with semiautomatic weapons.

KPO
Contact-opening special bullet with jacket reliability when feeding from magazine. Electrolytic core will not separate.

RIFLE BULLETS

SPEEDHEAD FMJ
Intended chiefly for shooting game, the full-metal-jacket bullet is characterized by high accuracy.

SP (Soft Point)
Sako's semijacketed soft-point bullet is the most popular type of bullet for hunting. On hitting the prey the bullet spreads rapidly, immediately producing a fatal shock effect.

HP (Hollow Point)
The ballistic characteristics of the hollow-point bullet make it the ideal choice for target shooting. This bullet is also fast, making it well suited to varmint shooting.

HAMMERHEAD
The Sako Hammerhead is a heavy, lead tipped bullet especially designed for moose hunting and other big game.

SUPER HAMMERHEAD
The famous Hammerhead is designed in a light version for long-range hunting with better ballistic characteristics.

POWERHEAD (Hollow Point Copper)
An all-copper opening hollow-point bullet for big-game hunting without fear of core separation.

SP P = Soft Point Pointed
SP SP = Soft Point SemiPointed
SP RN = Soft Point Round Nose
SP FP = Soft Point Flat Point
HP = Hollow Point
HP BT = Hollow Point Boat Tail
HAMMERHEAD = Soft Point Bonded Core
SUPER HH = Hollow Point Bonded Core
POWERHEAD = Hollow Point Solid Copper

SIERRA BULLETS

RIFLE BULLETS

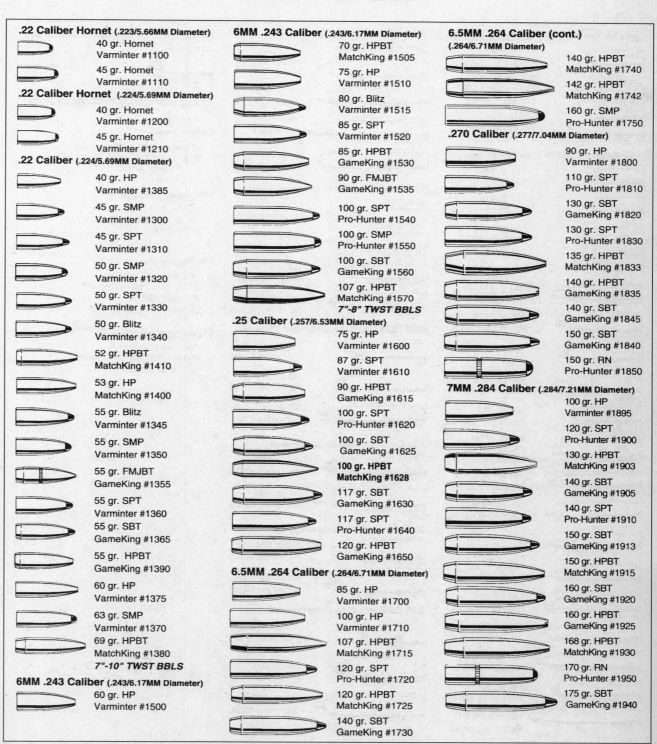

.22 Caliber Hornet (.223/5.66MM Diameter)
40 gr. Hornet
Varminter #1100

45 gr. Hornet
Varminter #1110

.22 Caliber Hornet (.224/5.69MM Diameter)
40 gr. Hornet
Varminter #1200

45 gr. Hornet
Varminter #1210

.22 Caliber (.224/5.69MM Diameter)
40 gr. HP
Varminter #1385

45 gr. SMP
Varminter #1300

45 gr. SPT
Varminter #1310

50 gr. SMP
Varminter #1320

50 gr. SPT
Varminter #1330

50 gr. Blitz
Varminter #1340

52 gr. HPBT
MatchKing #1410

53 gr. HP
MatchKing #1400

55 gr. Blitz
Varminter #1345

55 gr. SMP
Varminter #1350

55 gr. FMJBT
GameKing #1355

55 gr. SPT
Varminter #1360

55 gr. SBT
GameKing #1365

55 gr. HPBT
GameKing #1390

60 gr. HP
Varminter #1375

63 gr. SMP
Varminter #1370

69 gr. HPBT
MatchKing #1380

7"-10" TWST BBLS

6MM .243 Caliber (.243/6.17MM Diameter)
60 gr. HP
Varminter #1500

6MM .243 Caliber (.243/6.17MM Diameter)
70 gr. HPBT
MatchKing #1505

75 gr. HP
Varminter #1510

80 gr. Blitz
Varminter #1515

85 gr. SPT
Varminter #1520

85 gr. HPBT
GameKing #1530

90 gr. FMJBT
GameKing #1535

100 gr. SPT
Pro-Hunter #1540

100 gr. SMP
Pro-Hunter #1550

100 gr. SBT
GameKing #1560

107 gr. HPBT
MatchKing #1570

7"-8" TWST BBLS

.25 Caliber (.257/6.53MM Diameter)
75 gr. HP
Varminter #1600

87 gr. SPT
Varminter #1610

90 gr. HPBT
GameKing #1615

100 gr. SPT
Pro-Hunter #1620

100 gr. SBT
GameKing #1625

**100 gr. HPBT
MatchKing #1628**

117 gr. SBT
GameKing #1630

117 gr. SPT
Pro-Hunter #1640

120 gr. HPBT
GameKing #1650

6.5MM .264 Caliber (.264/6.71MM Diameter)
85 gr. HP
Varminter #1700

100 gr. HP
Varminter #1710

107 gr. HPBT
MatchKing #1715

120 gr. SPT
Pro-Hunter #1720

120 gr. HPBT
MatchKing #1725

140 gr. SBT
GameKing #1730

6.5MM .264 Caliber (cont.)
(.264/6.71MM Diameter)
140 gr. HPBT
MatchKing #1740

142 gr. HPBT
MatchKing #1742

160 gr. SMP
Pro-Hunter #1750

.270 Caliber (.277/7.04MM Diameter)
90 gr. HP
Varminter #1800

110 gr. SPT
Pro-Hunter #1810

130 gr. SBT
GameKing #1820

130 gr. SPT
Pro-Hunter #1830

135 gr. HPBT
MatchKing #1833

140 gr. HPBT
GameKing #1835

140 gr. SBT
GameKing #1845

150 gr. SBT
GameKing #1840

150 gr. RN
Pro-Hunter #1850

7MM .284 Caliber (.284/7.21MM Diameter)
100 gr. HP
Varminter #1895

120 gr. SPT
Pro-Hunter #1900

130 gr. HPBT
MatchKing #1903

140 gr. SBT
GameKing #1905

140 gr. SPT
Pro-Hunter #1910

150 gr. SBT
GameKing #1913

150 gr. HPBT
MatchKing #1915

160 gr. SBT
GameKing #1920

160 gr. HPBT
GameKing #1925

168 gr. HPBT
MatchKing #1930

170 gr. RN
Pro-Hunter #1950

175 gr. SBT
GameKing #1940

RELOADING

SIERRA BULLETS

RIFLE BULLETS

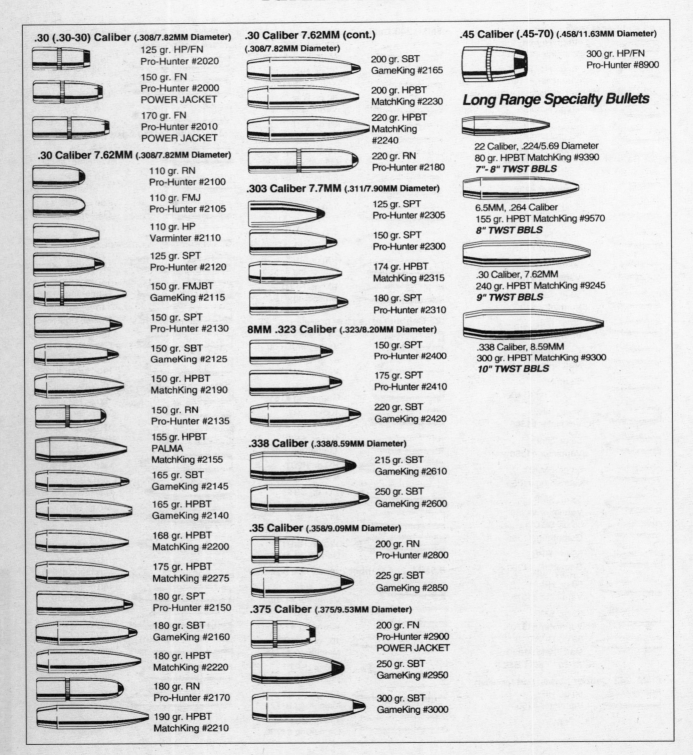

.30 (.30-30) Caliber (.308/7.82MM Diameter)

125 gr. HP/FN
Pro-Hunter #2020

150 gr. FN
Pro-Hunter #2000
POWER JACKET

170 gr. FN
Pro-Hunter #2010
POWER JACKET

.30 Caliber 7.62MM (.308/7.82MM Diameter)

110 gr. RN
Pro-Hunter #2100

110 gr. FMJ
Pro-Hunter #2105

110 gr. HP
Varminter #2110

125 gr. SPT
Pro-Hunter #2120

150 gr. FMJBT
GameKing #2115

150 gr. SPT
Pro-Hunter #2130

150 gr. SBT
GameKing #2125

150 gr. HPBT
MatchKing #2190

150 gr. RN
Pro-Hunter #2135

155 gr. HPBT
PALMA
MatchKing #2155

165 gr. SBT
GameKing #2145

165 gr. HPBT
GameKing #2140

168 gr. HPBT
MatchKing #2200

175 gr. HPBT
MatchKing #2275

180 gr. SPT
Pro-Hunter #2150

180 gr. SBT
GameKing #2160

180 gr. HPBT
MatchKing #2220

180 gr. RN
Pro-Hunter #2170

190 gr. HPBT
MatchKing #2210

.30 Caliber 7.62MM (cont.)
(.308/7.82MM Diameter)

200 gr. SBT
GameKing #2165

200 gr. HPBT
MatchKing #2230

220 gr. HPBT
MatchKing
#2240

220 gr. RN
Pro-Hunter #2180

.303 Caliber 7.7MM (.311/7.90MM Diameter)

125 gr. SPT
Pro-Hunter #2305

150 gr. SPT
Pro-Hunter #2300

174 gr. HPBT
MatchKing #2315

180 gr. SPT
Pro-Hunter #2310

8MM .323 Caliber (.323/8.20MM Diameter)

150 gr. SPT
Pro-Hunter #2400

175 gr. SPT
Pro-Hunter #2410

220 gr. SBT
GameKing #2420

.338 Caliber (.338/8.59MM Diameter)

215 gr. SBT
GameKing #2610

250 gr. SBT
GameKing #2600

.35 Caliber (.358/9.09MM Diameter)

200 gr. RN
Pro-Hunter #2800

225 gr. SBT
GameKing #2850

.375 Caliber (.375/9.53MM Diameter)

200 gr. FN
Pro-Hunter #2900
POWER JACKET

250 gr. SBT
GameKing #2950

300 gr. SBT
GameKing #3000

.45 Caliber (.45-70) (.458/11.63MM Diameter)

300 gr. HP/FN
Pro-Hunter #8900

Long Range Specialty Bullets

22 Caliber, .224/5.69 Diameter
80 gr. HPBT MatchKing #9390
7"- 8" TWST BBLS

6.5MM, .264 Caliber
155 gr. HPBT MatchKing #9570
8" TWST BBLS

.30 Caliber, 7.62MM
240 gr. HPBT MatchKing #9245
9" TWST BBLS

.338 Caliber, 8.59MM
300 gr. HPBT MatchKing #9300
10" TWST BBLS

SIERRA BULLETS

HANDGUN

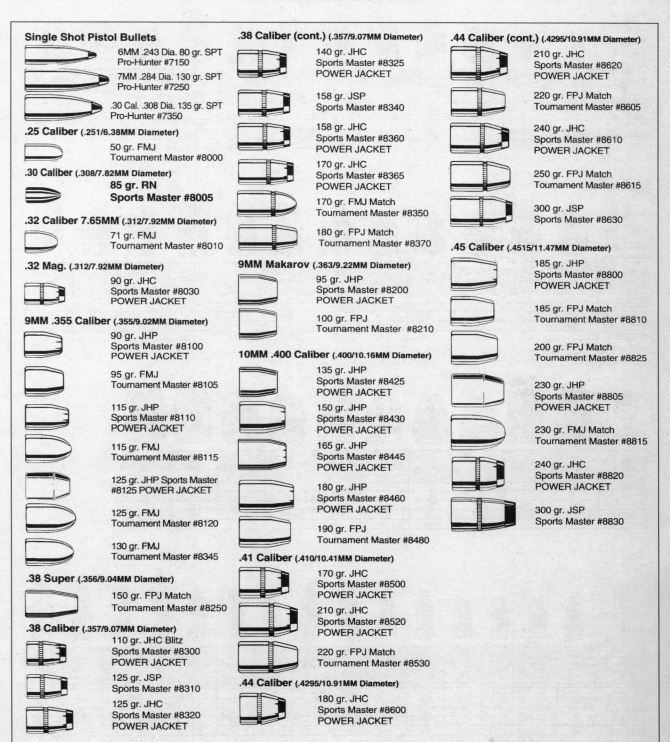

Single Shot Pistol Bullets

6MM .243 Dia. 80 gr. SPT
Pro-Hunter #7150

7MM .284 Dia. 130 gr. SPT
Pro-Hunter #7250

.30 Cal. .308 Dia. 135 gr. SPT
Pro-Hunter #7350

.25 Caliber (.251/6.38MM Diameter)

50 gr. FMJ
Tournament Master #8000

.30 Caliber (.308/7.82MM Diameter)

**85 gr. RN
Sports Master #8005**

.32 Caliber 7.65MM (.312/7.92MM Diameter)

71 gr. FMJ
Tournament Master #8010

.32 Mag. (.312/7.92MM Diameter)

90 gr. JHC
Sports Master #8030
POWER JACKET

9MM .355 Caliber (.355/9.02MM Diameter)

90 gr. JHP
Sports Master #8100
POWER JACKET

95 gr. FMJ
Tournament Master #8105

115 gr. JHP
Sports Master #8110
POWER JACKET

115 gr. FMJ
Tournament Master #8115

125 gr. JHP Sports Master
#8125 POWER JACKET

125 gr. FMJ
Tournament Master #8120

130 gr. FMJ
Tournament Master #8345

.38 Super (.356/9.04MM Diameter)

150 gr. FPJ Match
Tournament Master #8250

.38 Caliber (.357/9.07MM Diameter)

110 gr. JHC Blitz
Sports Master #8300
POWER JACKET

125 gr. JSP
Sports Master #8310

125 gr. JHC
Sports Master #8320
POWER JACKET

.38 Caliber (cont.) (.357/9.07MM Diameter)

140 gr. JHC
Sports Master #8325
POWER JACKET

158 gr. JSP
Sports Master #8340

158 gr. JHC
Sports Master #8360
POWER JACKET

170 gr. JHC
Sports Master #8365
POWER JACKET

170 gr. FMJ Match
Tournament Master #8350

180 gr. FPJ Match
Tournament Master #8370

9MM Makarov (.363/9.22MM Diameter)

95 gr. JHP
Sports Master #8200
POWER JACKET

100 gr. FPJ
Tournament Master #8210

10MM .400 Caliber (.400/10.16MM Diameter)

135 gr. JHP
Sports Master #8425
POWER JACKET

150 gr. JHP
Sports Master #8430
POWER JACKET

165 gr. JHP
Sports Master #8445
POWER JACKET

180 gr. JHP
Sports Master #8460
POWER JACKET

190 gr. FPJ
Tournament Master #8480

.41 Caliber (.410/10.41MM Diameter)

170 gr. JHC
Sports Master #8500
POWER JACKET

210 gr. JHC
Sports Master #8520
POWER JACKET

220 gr. FPJ Match
Tournament Master #8530

.44 Caliber (.4295/10.91MM Diameter)

180 gr. JHC
Sports Master #8600
POWER JACKET

.44 Caliber (cont.) (.4295/10.91MM Diameter)

210 gr. JHC
Sports Master #8620
POWER JACKET

220 gr. FPJ Match
Tournament Master #8605

240 gr. JHC
Sports Master #8610
POWER JACKET

250 gr. FPJ Match
Tournament Master #8615

300 gr. JSP
Sports Master #8630

.45 Caliber (.4515/11.47MM Diameter)

185 gr. JHP
Sports Master #8800
POWER JACKET

185 gr. FPJ Match
Tournament Master #8810

200 gr. FPJ Match
Tournament Master #8825

230 gr. JHP
Sports Master #8805
POWER JACKET

230 gr. FMJ Match
Tournament Master #8815

240 gr. JHC
Sports Master #8820
POWER JACKET

300 gr. JSP
Sports Master #8830

SPEER HANDGUN/RIFLE BULLETS

SPEER Handgun Bullets

Caliber & Type	25 Gold Dot Hollow Pt.	32 Gold Dot Hollow Pt.	9mm Gold Dot Hollow Pt.	9mm Gold Dot Hollow Pt.	9mm Gold Dot Hollow Pt.	9mm Gold Dot Hollow Pt.	357 Sig Gold Dot Hollow Pt.	38 Gold Dot Hollow Pt.	38 Gold Dot Hollow Pt.	9mm Makarov Gold Dot Hollow Pt.	40/10mm Gold Dot Hollow Pt.	40/10mm Gold Dot Hollow Pt.
Diameter	.251"	.311"	.355"	.355"	.355"	.355"	.355"	.357"	.357"	.364"	.400"	.400"
Weight (grs.)	35	60	90	115	124	147	125	125	158	90	155	165
Ballist. Coef.	0.091	0.118	0.101	0.125	0.134	0.164	0.141	0.140	0.168	0.107	0.123	0.138
Part Number	3985	3986	3992	3994	3998	4002	4360	4012	4215	3999	4400	4397
Box Count	100	100	100	100	100	100	100	100	100	100	100	100

SPEER Handgun Bullets

Caliber & Type	357 Sig TMJ	38 JHP	38 JSP	38 JHP	38 TMJ	38 JHP	38 JHP-SWC	38 TMJ	38 JHP	38 JSP	38 JSP-SWC	38 TMJ-Sil.
Diameter	.355"	.357"	.357"	.357"	.357"	.357"	.357"	.357"	.357"	.357"	.357"	.357"
Weight	125	110	125	125	125	140	146	158	158	158	160	180
Ballist. Coef.	0.147	0.122	0.140	0.135	0.146	0.152	0.159	0.173	0.158	0.158	0.170	0.230
Part Number	4362	4007	4011	4013	4015	4203	4205	4207	4211	4217	4223	4229
Box Count	100	100	100	100	100	100	100	100	100	100	100	100

SPEER Handgun Bullets

Caliber & Type	44 TMJ-Sil.	44 Mag. SP	45 TMJ-Match	45 TMJ-Match	45 JHP	45 Mag. JHP	45 TMJ	45 Mag. JHP	45 SP	50 AE HP
Diameter	.429"	.429"	.451"	.451"	.451"	.451"	.451"	.451"	.451"	.500"
Weight (grs.)	240	300	185	200	200	225	230	260	300	325
Ballist. Coef.	0.206	0.213	0.090	0.129	0.138	0.169	0.153	0.183	0.199	0.149
Part Number	4459	4463	4473	4475	4477	4479	4480	4481	4485	4495
Box Count	100	50	100	100	100	100	100	100	50	50

SPEER Rifle Bullets

Bullet Caliber & Type	22 Spitzer Soft Point	22 Spire Soft Point	22 Spitzer Soft Point	22 218 Bee Flat Soft Point w/Cann.	22 Spitzer Soft Point	22 "TNT" Hollow Point	22 Hollow Point	22 Hollow Point B.T. Match	22 FMJ B.T. w/Cann.	22 Spitzer Soft Point	22 Spitzer S.P. w/Cann.	22 FMJ B.T. w/Cann.	22 Semi-Spitzer Soft Point	6mm "TNT" Hollow Point	6mm Hollow Point
Diameter	.223"	.224"	.224"	.224"	.224"	.224"	.224"	.224"	.224"	.224"	.224"	.224"	.224"	.243"	.243"
Weight (grs.)	45	40	45	46	50	50	52	52	55	55	55	62	70	70	75
Ballist. Coef.	0.166	0.144	0.167	0.094	0.231	0.223	0.225	0.253	0.269	0.255	0.241	0.307	0.214	0.282	0.234
Part Number	1011	1017	1023	1024	1029	1030	1035	1036	1044	1047	1049	1050	1053	1206	1205
Box Count	100	100	100	100	100	100	100	100	100	100	100	100	100	100	100

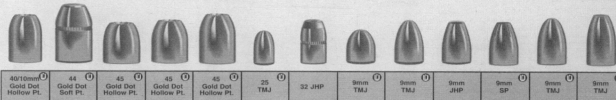

40/10mm (i) Gold Dot Hollow Pt.	44 (i) Gold Dot Soft Pt.	45 (i) Gold Dot Hollow Pt.	45 (i) Gold Dot Hollow Pt.	45 (i) Gold Dot Hollow Pt.	25 (i) TMJ	32 JHP	9mm (i) TMJ	9mm (i) TMJ	9mm JHP	9mm (i) SP	9mm (i) TMJ	9mm (i) TMJ
.400"	.429"	.451"	.451"	.451"	.251"	.312"	.355"	355"	355"	.355"	.355"	.355"
180	270	185	200	230	50	100	95	115	115	124	124	147
0.143	0.193	0.109	0.138	0.143	0.110	0.167	0.131	0.177	0.118	0.115	0.114	0.208
4406	4461	4470	4478	4483	3982	3981	4001	3995	3996	3997	4004	4006
100	50	100	100	100	100	100	100	100	100	100	100	100

38 TMJ-Sil.	9mm Mararov TMJ	40/10 mm TMJ	40/10mm (i) TMJ	40/10mm (i) TMJ	40/10mm (i) TMJ	41 JHP-SWC	41 JSP-SWC	44 Mag. JHP	44 JHP-SWC	44 JSP-SWC	44 Mag. JHP	44 Mag. JSP
.357"	.364"	.400"	.400"	.400"	.400"	.410"	.410"	.429"	.429"	.429"	.429"	.429"
200	95	155	165	180	200	200	220	200	225	240	240	240
0.236	0.127	0.125	0.135	0.143	0.208	0.113	0.137	0.122	0.146	0.157	0.165	0.164
4231	4375	4399	4410	4402	4403	4405	4417	4425	4435	4447	4453	4457
100	100	100	100	100	100	100	100	100	100	100	100	100

SPEER Handgun Bullets-Lead

Caliber & Type	32 HB-WC	9mm RN	38 BB-WC	38 DE-WC	38 HB-WC	38 SWC	38 HP-SWC	38 RN	44 SWC	45 SWC	45 RN	45 SWC
Diameter	.314"	.356"	.358"	.358"	.358"	.358"	.358"	.358"	.430"	.452"	.452"	.452"
Weight (grs.)	98	125	148	148	148	158	158	158	240	200	230	250
Part Number	--	4601	4605	--	4617	4623	4627	4647	4660	4677	4690	4683
Bulk Pkg.	4600	4602	4606	4611	4618	4624	4628	4648	4661	4678	4691	4684

6mm Spitzer Soft Point	6mm Spitzer Soft Point	6mm Spitzer Soft Point	6mm Spitzer Soft Point B.T.	6mm Spitzer Soft Point	25-20 Win. Flat Soft Point W/Cann.	25 Spitzer Soft Point	25 "TNT" Hollow Point	25 Spitzer Soft Point	25 Hollow Point	25 Spitzer Soft Point B.T.	25 Spitzer Soft Point B.T.	25 Spitzer Soft Point	6.5mm Spitzer Soft Point	6.5mm Spitzer Soft Point	270 "TNT" Hollow Point
.243"	.243"	.243"	.243"	.243"	.257"	.257"	.257"	.257"	.257"	.257"	.257"	.257"	.264"	.264"	.277"
80	85	90	100	105	75	87	87	100	100	100	120	120	120	140	90
-0.365	0.404	0.385	0.430	0.0443	0.133	0.300	0.310	0.369	0.255	0.393	0.435	0.41	0.433	0.496	0.275
1211	1213	1217	1220	1229	1237	1241	1246	1405	1407	1408	1410	1411	1435	1441	1446
100	100	100	100	100	100	100	100	100	100	100	100	100	100	100	100

SPEER RIFLE BULLETS

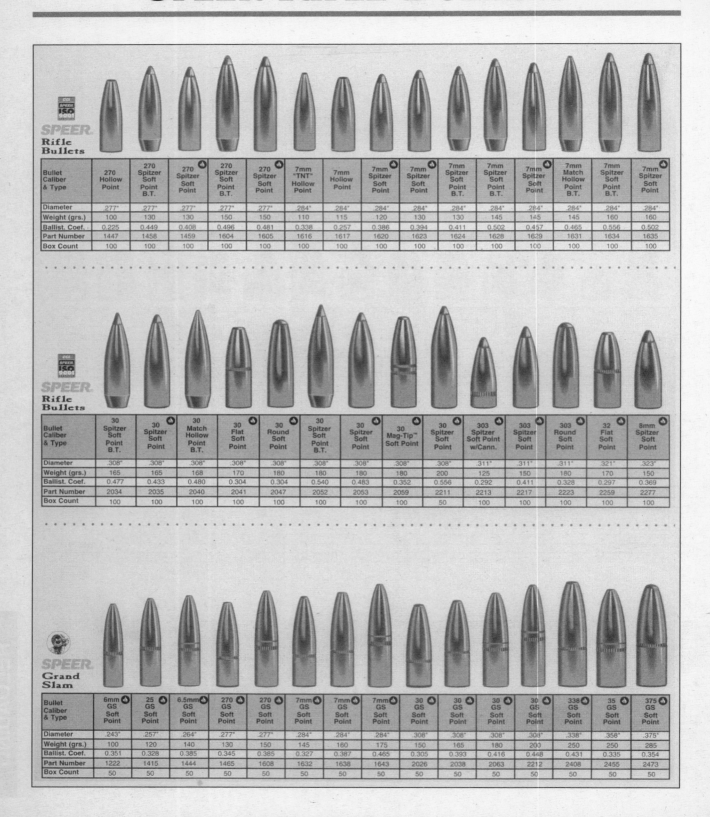

Rifle Bullets

Bullet Caliber & Type	270 Hollow Point	270 Spitzer Soft Point B.T.	270 Spitzer Soft Point	270 Spitzer Soft Point B.T.	270 Spitzer Soft Point	7mm "TNT" Hollow Point	7mm Hollow Point	7mm Spitzer Soft Point	7mm Spitzer Soft Point	7mm Spitzer Soft Point B.T.	7mm Spitzer Soft Point B.T.	7mm Spitzer Soft Point	7mm Match Hollow Point B.T.	7mm Spitzer Soft Point B.T.	7mm Spitzer Soft Point
Diameter	.277"	.277"	.277"	.277"	.277"	.284"	.284"	.284"	.284"	.284"	.284"	.284"	.284"	.284"	.284"
Weight (grs.)	100	130	130	150	150	110	115	120	130	130	145	145	145	160	160
Ballist. Coef.	0.225	0.449	0.408	0.496	0.481	0.338	0.257	0.386	0.394	0.411	0.502	0.457	0.465	0.556	0.502
Part Number	1447	1458	1459	1604	1605	1616	1617	1620	1623	1624	1628	1629	1631	1634	1635
Box Count	100	100	100	100	100	100	100	100	100	100	100	100	100	100	100

Rifle Bullets

Bullet Caliber & Type	30 Spitzer Soft Point B.T.	30 Spitzer Soft Point	30 Match Hollow Point B.T.	30 Flat Soft Point	30 Round Soft Point	30 Spitzer Soft Point B.T.	30 Spitzer Soft Point	30 Mag-Tip™ Soft Point	30 Spitzer Soft Point	303 Spitzer Soft Point w/Cann.	303 Spitzer Soft Point	303 Round Soft Point	32 Flat Soft Point	8mm Spitzer Soft Point
Diameter	.308"	.308"	.308"	.308"	.308"	.308"	.308"	.308"	.308"	.311"	.311"	.311"	321"	.323"
Weight (grs.)	165	165	168	170	180	180	180	180	200	125	150	180	170	150
Ballist. Coef.	0.477	0.433	0.480	0.304	0.304	0.540	0.483	0.352	0.556	0.292	0.411	0.328	0.297	0.369
Part Number	2034	2035	2040	2041	2047	2052	2053	2059	2211	2213	2217	2223	2259	2277
Box Count	100	100	100	100	100	100	100	100	50	100	100	100	100	100

Grand Slam

Bullet Caliber & Type	6mm GS Soft Point	25 GS Soft Point	6.5mm GS Soft Point	270 GS Soft Point	270 GS Soft Point	7mm GS Soft Point	7mm GS Soft Point	7mm GS Soft Point	30 GS Soft Point	30 GS Soft Point	30 GS Soft Point	30 GS Soft Point	338 GS Soft Point	35 GS Soft Point	375 GS Soft Point
Diameter	.243"	.257"	.264"	.277"	.277"	.284"	.284"	.284"	.308"	.308"	.308"	.308"	.338"	.358"	.375"
Weight (grs.)	100	120	140	130	150	145	160	175	150	165	180	200	250	250	285
Ballist. Coef.	0.351	0.328	0.385	0.345	0.385	0.327	0.387	0.465	0.305	0.393	0.416	0.448	0.431	0.335	0.354
Part Number	1222	1415	1444	1465	1608	1632	1638	1643	2026	2038	2063	2212	2408	2455	2473
Box Count	50	50	50	50	50	50	50	50	50	50	50	50	50	50	50

SPEER RIFLE BULLETS

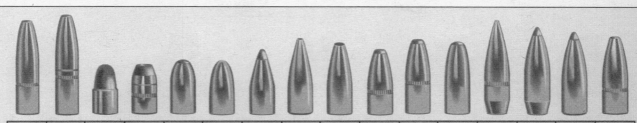

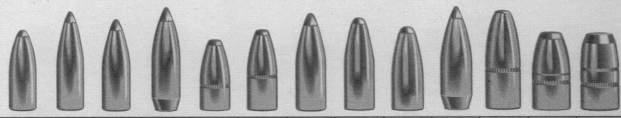

7mm Mag.Tip™ Soft Point	7mm Mag.Tip™ Soft Point	30 Round Soft Point Plinker™	30 Hollow Point	30 Round Soft Point	30 Carbine Round FMJ	30 Spire Soft Point	30 "TNT" Hollow Point	30 Hollow Point	30 Flat Soft Point	30 Flat Soft Point	30 Round Soft Point	30 FMJ B.T. w/Cann.	30 Spitzer Soft Point B.T.	30 Spitzer Soft Point	30 Mag-Tip™ Soft Point
.284"	.284"	.308"	.308"	.308"	.308"	.308"	.308"	.308"	.308"	.308"	.308"	.308"	.308"	.308"	.308"
160	175	100	110	110	110	110	125	130	130	150	150	150	150	150	150
0.354	0.385	0.124	0.136	0.144	0.179	0.273	0.326	0.263	0.248	0.268	0.266	0.425	0.423	0.389	0.301
1637	1641	1805	1835	1845	1846	1855	1986	2005	2007	2011	2017	2018	2022	2023	2025
100	100	100	100	100	100	100	100	100	100	100	100	100	100	100	100

8mm Semi-Spitzer Soft Point	8mm Spitzer Soft Point	338 Spitzer Soft Point	338 Spitzer Soft Point B.T.	35 Flat Soft Point	35 Flat Soft Point	35 Spitzer Soft Point	9.3mm Semi-Spitzer Soft Point	375 Semi-Spitzer Soft Point	375 Spitzer Soft Point B.T.	416 Mag Tip	45 Flat Soft Point	45 Flat Soft Point
.323"	.323"	.338"	.338"	.358"	.358"	.358"	.366"	.375"	.375"	.416"	.458"	.458"
170	200	200	225	180	220	250	270	235	270	350	350	400
0.354	0.411	0.448	0.484	0.245	0.316	0.446	0.361	0.317	0.429	0.332	0.232	0.214
2283	2285	2405	2406	2435	2439	2453	2459	2471	2472	2477	2478	2479
100	50	50	50	100	50	50	50	50	50	50	50	50

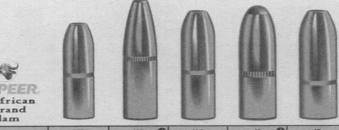

SPEER
African Grand Slam

Bullet Caliber & Type	375 AGS Tungsten Solid	416 AGS Soft Point	416 AGS Tungsten Solid	45 AGS Soft Point	45 AGS Tungsten Solid
Diameter	.375"	.416"	.416"	.458"	.458"
Weight (grs.)	300	400	400	500	500
Ballist. Coef.	0.258	0.318	0.262	0.285	0.277
Part Number	2474	2475	2476	2485	2486
Box Count	25	25	25	25	25

RELOADING

ALLIANT SMOKELESS POWDERS

HODGDON SMOKELESS POWDER

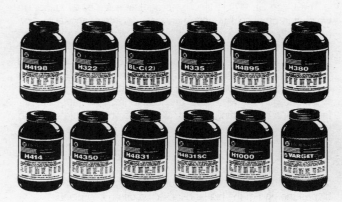

RIFLE POWDER

H4198
H4198 was developed especially for small and medium capacity cartridges.

H322
This powder fills the gap between H4198 and BL-C9(2). Performs best in small to medium capacity cases.

SPPHERICAL BL-C2
Best performance is in the 222, and in other cases smaller than 30/06.

SPHERICAL H335®
Similar to BL-C(2), H335 is popular for its performance in medium capacity cases, especially in 222 and 308 Winchester.

H4895®
4895 gives desirable performance in almost all cases from 222 Rem. to 458 Win. Reduced loads, to as low as 3/5 maximum, still give target accuracy.

SPHERICAL H380®
This number fills a gap between 4320 and 4350. It is excellent in 22/250, 220 Swift, the 6mm's, 257 and 30/06.

SPHERICAL H414®
In many popular medium to medium-large calibers, pressure velocity relationship is better.

H414®
A spherical powder developed epecially for 30-06, 220 Swift and 375 H&H.

H4350
This powder gives superb accuracy at optimum velocity for many large capacity metallic rifle cartridges.

H50 BMG
Designed for the 50 Browning Machine Gun cartridge. Highly insensitive to extreme temperature changes.

H4831®
Outstanding performance with medium and heavy bullets in the 6mm's, 25/06, 270 and Magnum calibers. Also available with shortened grains (H4831SC) for easy metering.

VARGET
Features small extruded grain powder for uniform metering, plus higher velocities/ normal pressures in such calibers as .223, 22-250, 306, 30-06, 375 H&H

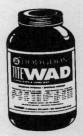

TITEGROUP
Excelllent for most straight-walled pistol cartridges, incl. 38 Spec., 44 Spec., 45 ACP. Low charge weights, clean burning; position insenstive and flawless ignition

TITEWAD
This new 12 ga. flattened spherical shotgun powder is ideal for 7/8, 1 and 1 1/8 oz. loads, with minimum recoil and mild muzzle report.

H1000 EXTRUDED POWDER
Fills the gap between H4831 and H870. Works especially well in overbore capacity cartridges (1,000-yard shooters take note).

HP38
A fast pistol powder for most pistol loading. Especially recommended for mid-range 38 specials.

CLAYS
Tailored for use in 12 ga., 7/8, 1-oz. and 1 1/8-oz. loads. Also performs well in many handgun applications, including .38 Special, .40 S&W and 45 ACP. Perfect for 1 1/8 and 1 oz. loads.

Universal Clays
Loads nearly all of the straight-wall pistol cartridges as well as 12 ga. 1.25 oz. thru 28 ga. 3/4 oz. target loads.

International Clays
Ideal for 12 and 20 ga. autoloaders who want reduced recoil.

HS-6 AND HS-7
HS-6 and HS-7 for Magnum field loads are unsurpassed, since they do not pack in the measure. They deliver uniform charges and are dense to allow sufficient wad column for best patterns.

H110
A spherical powder made especially for the 30 M1 carbine. H110 also does very well in 357, 44 spec., 44 Mag. or .410 ga. shotshell. Magnum primers are recommended for consistent ignition.

H4227
An extruded powder similar to H110, it is the fastest burning in Hodgdon's line. Recommended for the 22 Hornet and some specialized loading in the 45-70 caliber. Also excellent in magnum pistol and .410 shotgun.

DILLON PRECISION RELOADERS

Dillon Precision enters the shotgun shooting sports market with its new SL 900 progressive shotshell reloader. Based on Dillon's proven XL 650 O-frame design, it incorporates the same powerful compound linkage. The automatic case insert system, fed by an electric case collator, ranks high among the new features of this reloader. Adjustable shot and powder bars come as standard equipment. Both the powder and shot bars are case-activated, so no powder or shot can spill when no shell is at that station. Should the operator forget to insert a wad during the reloading process, the SL 900 will not dispense shot into the powder-charged hull. Both powder and shot systems are based on Dillon's adjustable powder bar design, which is accurate to within a few tenths of a grain. These systems also eliminate the need for fixed-volume bushings. Simply adjust the measures to dispense the exact charges required.

The Dillon SL 900 is the first progressive shotshell loader on which it is practical to change gauges. An interchangeable toolhead makes it quick and easy to change from one gauge to another. The SL 900 also has an extra large, remote shot hopper that holds an entire 25-pound bag of shot, making it easy to fill with a funnel. The unique shot reservoir/dispenser helps ensure that a consistent volume of shot is delivered to each shell.

For shotgunners who shoot and load for multiple gauges or different kinds of shooting, the SL 900's interchangeable toolhead feature makes quick work of changing from one gauge to another. It uses a collet-type sizing die that re-forms the base of the shotshell to factory specifications—a feature that ensure reliable feeding in all shotguns. The heat-treated steel crimp die forms and folds the hull before the final taper crimp die radiuses and blends the end of the hull and locks the crimp into place.

MODEL RL550B PROGRESSIVE LOADER

- Accomodates over 120 calibers
- Interchangeable toolhead assembly
- Auto/Powder priming systemsa
- Uses standard 7/8" by 14 dies
- Loading rate: 500-600 rounds per hour

Price: $298.95

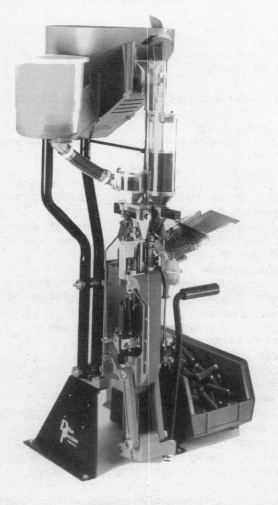

MODEL SL900
$799.95

DILLON PRECISION RELOADERS

MODEL SQUARE DEAL B
- Automatic Indexing
- Auto Powder/Priming Systems
- Available in 14 handgun calibers
- Loading rate: 400-500 rounds per hour
- Loading dies standard
- Factory adjusted, ready-to-use

Price: **$227.95**

MODEL RL 1050
- Automatic indexing
- Auto powder/priming systems
- Automatic casefeeder
- Commercial grade machine
- Swages military primer pockets
- Loading rate: 1000-1200 rounds per hour
- Weighs 54 lbs.
- Eight station

Price: **$1,079.95**

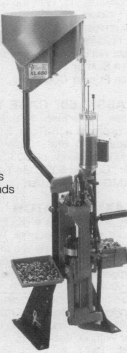

MODEL XL 650
- New primer system design (uses rotary indexing plate)
- Automatic indexing
- Uses standard 7/8" x 14 dies
- Loading rate: 800-1000 rounds per hour
- Five station interchangeable toolhead

Price: **$398.95**

MODEL AT-500
- Loads over 40 calibers
- Uses standard 7/8" by 14 dies
- Upgradeable to Model RL 550B
- Interchangeable toolhead
- Switch from one caliber to another in 30 seconds
- Universal shellplate

Price: **$179.95**

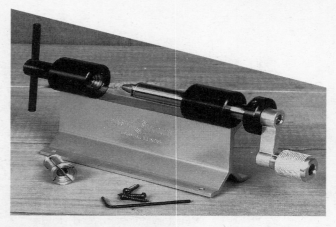

CO-AX® BENCH REST® RIFLE DIES

Bench Rest Rifle Dies are glass hard and polished mirror smooth with special attention given to headspace, tapers and diameters. Sizing die has an elevated expander button to ensure better alignment of case and neck.

BENCH REST® DIE SET $69.98
WEATHERBY BENCH REST DIE SET 69.98
ULTRA BENCH REST DIE SET 69.98
FULL LENGTH SIZER 32.98
BENCH REST SEATING DIE .39.98

HAND CASE TRIMMER

Shell holder is a Brown & Sharpe-type collet. Case and cartridge conditioning accessories include inside neck reamer, outside neck turner, deburring tool, hollow pointer and primer pocket cleaners. The case trimmer trims all cases, ranging from 17 to 458 Winchester caliber.
Price: $57.98

PRIMER SEATER
With "E-Z-Just" Shellholder

The Bonanza Primer Seater is designed so that primers are seated Co-Axially (primer in line with primer pocket). Mechanical leverage allows primers to be seated fully without crushing. With the addition of one extra set of Disc Shell Holders and one extra Primer Unit, all modern cases, rim or rimless, from 222 up to 458 Magnum, can be primed. Shell holders are easily adjusted to any case by rotating to contact rim or cannelure of the case.

PRIMER SEATER $69.00
PRIMER POCKET CLEANER 6.98

"CLASSIC 50" CASE TRIMMER (not shown)

Handles more than 100 different big bore calibers–500 Nitro Express, 416 Rigby, 50 Sharps, 475 H&H, etc. *Also available:* .50 BMG Case Trimmer, designed specifically for reloading needs of .50 Cal. BMG Shooters.

Price: "CLASSIC 50" CASE TRIMMER $95.50
.50 BMG CASE TRIMMER 99.50

CO-AX® INDICATOR

Bullets will not leave a rifle barrel at a uniform angle unless they are started uniformly. The Co-Ax Indicator provides a reading of how closely the axis of the bullet corresponds to the axis of the cartridge case. The Indicator features a springloaded plunger to hold cartridges against a recessed, adjustable rod while the cartridge is supported in a "V" block. To operate, simply rotate the cartridge with the fingers; the degree of misalignment is transferred to an indicator which measures in one-thousandths.

Price: Without dial $53.20
Indicator Dial 60.40

PRIMER SEATER

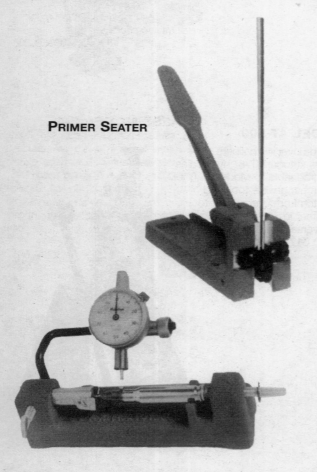

FORSTER RELOADING

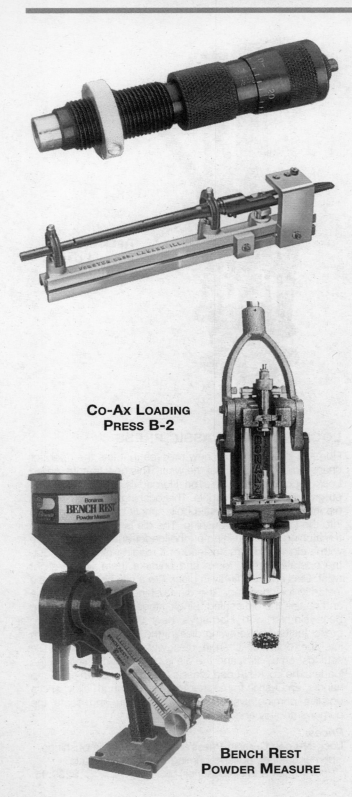

CO-AX LOADING PRESS B-2

BENCH REST POWDER MEASURE

ULTRA BULLET SEATER DIE

Forster's new Ultra Die is available in 56 calibers, more than any other brand of micrometer-style seater. Adjustment is identical to that of a precision micrometer—the head is graduated to .001" increments with .025" bullet movement per revolution. The cartridge case, bullet and seating stem are completely supported and perfectly aligned in a close-fitting chamber before and during the bullet seating operation.
Price: $62.98

UNIVERSAL SIGHT MOUNTING FIXTURE

This product fills the exacting requirements needed for drilling and tapping holes for the mounting of scopes, receiver sights, shotgun beads, etc. The fixture handles any single-barrel gun—bolt-action, lever-action or pump-action—as long as the barrel can be laid into the "V" blocks of the fixture. Tubular guns are drilled in the same manner by removing the magazine tube. The fixture's main body is made of aluminum casting. The two "V" blocks are adjustable for height and are made of hardened steel ground accurately on the "V" as well as the shaft.
Price: $368.00

CO-AX® LOADING PRESS MODEL B-2

Designed to make reloading easier and more accurate, this press offers the following features: Snap-in and snap-out die change • Positive spent primer catcher • Automatic self-acting shell holder • Floating guide rods • Working room for right- or left-hand operators • Top priming device seats primers to factory specifications • Uses any standard 7/8"X14 dies • No torque on the head • Perfect alignment of die and case • Three times the mechanical advantage of a "C" press
Price: $298.00

BENCH REST POWDER MEASURE

When operated uniformly, this measure will throw uniform charges from 2 1/2 grains Bullseye to 95 grains #4320. No extra drums are needed. Powder is metered from the charge arm, allowing a flow of powder without extremes in variation while minimizing powder shearing. Powder flows through its own built-in baffle so that powder enters the charge arm uniformly.
Price: $109.98

HORNADY

APEX 3.1 AUTO SHOTSHELL RELOADER

This versatile shotshell reloader features a new hold-fast shell plate. Other features include: extra-large shot hopper, short linkage arm, automatic dual-action crimp die, swing-out wad guide, and extra-long shot and powder feed tubes. The reloader is now available with Gas-Assist Indexing. With each downstroke of the handle the gas assist cylinder compresses, storing energy. Raise the handle and the gas cylinder transfers its energy to the shellplate, rotating it in one smooth motion, without jerking, and advancing the shells and primers with smooth control regardless of handle speed. The Apex 3.1 Auto Shotshell Loader with Gas Assist is available in four models: 12 ga., 20 ga., 28 ga., and 410 ga.

Prices:
APEX 3.1 SHOTSHELL LOADER (AUTOMATIC)
In 12 and 20 gauge $299.95
APEX SHOTSHELL LOADER WITH GAS ASSIST
In 12 and 20 gauge 349.95
In 28 and .410 gauge 369.95

APEX 3.1 SHOTSHELL LOADER w/GAS ASSIST

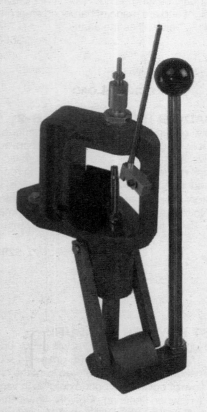

LOCK-N-LOAD CLASSIC RELOADING PRESS

LOCK-N-LOAD CLASSIC PRESS

Hornady introduces two new presses that lets the operator change dies with a flick of the wrist. This new feature, called Lock-N-Load, is available on Hornady's single stage and progressive reloader models. This bushing system locks the die into the press like a rifle bolt, simply by threading a die into the Lock-N-Load bushing. The die is then inserted into a matching press bushing on the loader and locked in place with a clockwise turn. Instead of threading dies in and out, the operator simply locks and unlocks them with a slight twist. Dies are held firmly in place like a rifle bolt, but release instantly for changing. The die bushing stays with the die and retains the die setting. Single stage reloading has never been simpler with Hornady's new Lock-N-Load Classic press. Instead of screwing dies in, the Lock-N-Load system lets the operator change dies with a simple twist. Die settings remain firm and the die is held perfectly solid in the loader. The Lock-N-Load Classic Press features an easy grip handle, an O-style frame made of high-strength alloy, and a positive priming system that feeds, align and seats the primer smoothly and automatically.

Prices:
LOCK-N-LOAD CLASSIC PRESS (includes three die bushings, primer catcher, positive priming system, Automatic Primer Feed and accessories) $239.95

HORNADY

LOCK-N-LOAD AUTO PROGRESSIVE PRESS

The Lock-N-Load Automatic Progressive reloading press, featuring the Lock-N-Load bushing system, delivers consistently accurate loaded rounds, changing forever the way handloaders switch from one caliber to another. This task can now be done with a flick of the wrist and allows the operator to stop loading, change dies and start loading another caliber in seconds. Five Lock-N-Load die stations offer the flexibility to add a roll or taper crimp die. Dies and powder measure are inserted into Lock-N-Load die bushings, which lock securely into the press. The bushings remain with the die and powder measure, retaining when a case is ready and removes in seconds. It also fits on other presses and mounts like dies using the Lock-N-Load bushing system. Other features include: Deluxe Powder Measure, Automatic Indexing, Off-Set Handle, Power-Pac Linkage, Case ejector.

LOCK-N-LOAD AUTO PROGRESSIVE PRESS (includes five die bushings, shellplate, primer catcher, Positive Priming System, powder drop, Deluxe Powder Measure, automatic primer feed) $349.95

MODEL 366 AUTO SHOTSHELL RELOADER

The 366 Auto features full-length resizing with each stroke, automatic primer feed, swing-out wad guide, three-state crimping featuring Taper-Loc for factory tapered crimp, automatic advance to the next station and automatic ejection. The turntable holds 8 shells for 8 operations with each stroke. The primer tube filler is fast. The automatic charge bar loads shot and powder. Right- or left-hand operation; interchangeable charge bushings, die sets and Magnum dies and crimp starters for 6 pint, 8 point and paper crimps.

MODEL 366 AUTO SHOTSHELL RELOADER:
12, 20, 28 gauge or .410 bore $340.00
PRIMER TUBE FILLER 12.25
POWDER AND SHOT BAFFLES (PER SET) 5.50
RISER LEGS (PER SET) 6.45
SHOT AND POWDER HOPPERS (EACH) 11.30

NEW DIMENSION CUSTOM GRADE RELOADING DIES

Features an Elliptical Expander that minimizes friction and reduces case neck stretch, plus the need for a tapered expander for "necking up" to the next larger caliber. Other recent design changes include a hardened steel decap pin that will not break, bend or crack even when depriming stubborn military cases. A bullet seater alignment sleeve guides the bullet and case neck into the die for in-line benchrest alignment. All New Dimension Reloading Dies include: collar and collar lock to center expander precisely; one-piece expander spindle with tapered bottom for easy cartridge insertion; wrench flats on die body, Sure-Loc™ lock rings and collar lock for easy tightening; and built-in crimper.

NEW DIMENSION CUSTOM GRADE RELOADING DIES:
SERIES I TWO-DIE RIFLE SET $26.95
SERIES I THREE-DIE RIFLE SET 28.59
SERIES II THREE-DIE PISTOL SET (w/Titanium Nitride) .37.75
SERIES III TWO-DIE RIFLE SET 32.25
SERIES IV SPECIALITY DIE SET 53.75
Also available:
50 CALIBER BMG DIES (TWO-DIE SET) $260.00

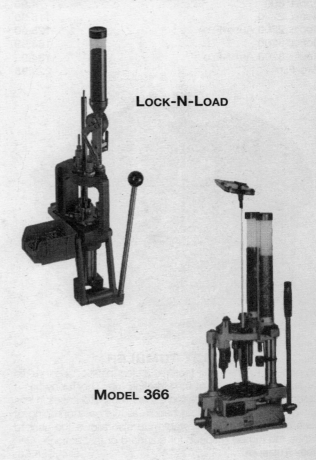

LOCK-N-LOAD

MODEL 366

LYMAN RELOADING TOOLS

MODEL 1200 CLASSIC TURBO TUMBLER

Features a redesigned base and drive system, plus a stronger suspension system and built-in exciters for better tumbling action and faster cleaning

MODEL 1200 CLASSIC	.$82.95
MODEL 1200 AUTO-FLO	.109.95
Also available:	
MODEL 600	.74.95
MODEL 2220	.116.95
MODEL 2200 AUTO-FLO	.125.00
MODEL 3200	.164.95
MODEL 3200 AUTO-FLO	.184.95
MAG-FLO	.229.95

"INSIDE/OUTSIDE" DEBURRING TOOL

This unique new tool features an adjustable cutting blade that adapts easily to any rifle or pistol case from 22 caliber to 45 caliber with a simple hex wrench adjustment. Inside deburring is completed by a conical internal section with slotted cutting edges, thus providing uniform inside and outside deburring in one simple operation. The deburring tool is mounted on an anodized aluminum handle that is machine-knurled for a sure grip.

DEBURRING TOOL $13.50

TUBBY TUMBLER

This popular tumbler now features a clear plastic "see thru" lid that fits on the outside of the vibrating tub. The Tubby has a polishing action that cleans more than 100 pistol cases in less than two hours. The built-in handle allows easy dumping of cases and media. An adjustable tab also allows the user to change the tumbling speed for standard or fast action.

TUBBY TUMBLER $58.50

MASTER CASTING KIT

Designed especially to meet the needs of blackpowder shooters, this new kit features Lyman's combination round ball and maxi ball mould blocks. It also contains a combination double cavity mould, mould handle, mini-mag furnace, lead dipper, bullet lube, a user's manual and a cast bullet guide. Kits are available in 45, 50 and 54 caliber.

MASTER CASTING KIT $154.00

LYMAN RELOADING TOOLS

FOR RIFLE OR PISTOL CARTRIDGES

POWER CASE TRIMMER

The new Lyman Power Trimmer is powered by a fan-cooled electric motor designed to withstand the severe demands of case trimming. The unit, which features the Universal™ Chuckhead, allows cases to be positioned for trimming or removed with fingertip ease. The Power Trimmer package includes Nine-Pilot Multi-Pack. In addition to two cutter heads, a pair of wire end brushes for cleaning primer pockets are included. Other features include safety guards, on-off rocker switch, heavy cast base with receptacles for nine pilots, and bolt holes for mounting on a work bench. Available for 110 V or 220 V systems.

Prices: 100 V Model $183.25
220 V Model 185.00

ACCULINE OUTSIDE NECK TURNER
(not shown)

To obtain perfectly concentric case necks, Lyman's Outside Neck Turner assures reloaders of uniform neck wall thickness and outside neck diameter. The unit fits Lyman's Universal Trimmer and AccuTrimmer. In use, each case is run over a mandrel, which centers the case for the turning operation. The cutter is carefully adjusted to remove a minimum amount of brass. Rate of feed is adjustable and a mechanical stop controls length of cut. Mandrels are available for calibers from .17 to .375; cutter blade can be adjusted for any diameter from .195" to .405".

OUTSIDE NECK TURNER w/extra blade, 6 mandrels . .$27.95
INDIVIDUAL MANDRELS 4.00

CRUSHER II PRO KIT

Includes press, loading block, case lube kit, primer tray, Model 500 Pro scale, powder funnel and *Lyman Reloading Handbook.*
STARTER KIT $149.95

LYMAN CRUSHER II RELOADING PRESS

The only press for rifle or pistol cartridges that offers the advantage of powerful compound leverage combined with a true Magnum press opening. A unique handle design transfers power easily where you want it to the center of the ram. A 4 1/2-inch press opening accommodates even the largest cartridges.

CRUSH II PRESS
With Priming Arm and Catcher $109.95

STARTER KIT

LYMAN RELOADING TOOLS

T-MAG II TURRET RELOADING PRESS

With the T-Mag II you can mount up to six different reloading dies on our turret. This means you can have all your dies set up, precisely mounted, locked in and ready to reload at all times. The T-Mag works with all 7/8 x 14 dies. The T-Mag II turret with its quick-disconnect release system is held in rock-solid alignment by a 3/4-inch steel stud.

Also featured is Lyman's Crusher II compound leverage system. It has a longer handle with a ball-type knob that mounts easily for right- or left-handed operation.

T-MAG II PRESS w/Priming Arm & Catcher $154.95
   Extra Turret Head 34.95
Also available:
EXPERT KIT that includes T-MAG II Press, Universal Case Trimmer and pilot Multi-Pak, Model 500 powder scale and Model 50 powder measure, plus accessories and Reloading Manual. Available in calibers 9mm Luger, 38/357, 44 Mag., 45 ACP and 30-06 ....$399.95

ELECTRONIC SCALE MODEL LE: 1000

Accurate to 1/10 grain, Lyman's new LE: 1000 measures up to 1000 grains of powder and easily converts to the gram mode for metric measurements. The push-button automatic calibration feature eliminates the need for calibrating with a screwdriver. The scale works off a single 9V battery or AC power adapter (included with each scale). Its compact design allows the LE: 1000 to be carried to the field easily. A sculpted carrying case is optional. 110 Volt or 220 Volt.

MODEL LE: 1000 ELECTRONIC SCALE $259.95
MODEL LE: 300 ELECTRONIC SCALE 166.50
MODEL LE: 500 ELECTRIC SCALE 183.25

MODEL LE-500 ELECTRONIC SCALE

PISTOL ACCUMEASURE

Lyman's Pistol AccuMeasure uses changeable brass rotors pre-drilled to drop precise charges of ball and flake pistol propellants (the tool is not intended for use with long grain IMR-type powders). Most of the rotors are drilled with two cavities for maximum accuracy and consistency. The brass operating handle, which can be shifted for left or right hand operation, can be removed. The Pistol AccuMeasure can be mounted on all turret and single station presses; it can also be hand held with no loss of accuracy.

PISTOL ACCUMEASURE w/3-rotor starter kit $35.00
Also available:
ROTOR SELECTION SET including 12 dual-cavity rotors and 4 single-cavity units. Enables reloaders to throw a variety of charges for all pistol calibers through 45 ....$46.00

ELECTRONIC DIGITAL MICROMETER $84.95

LYMAN RELOADING TOOLS

DRILL PRESS CASE TRIMMER

Intended for competitive shooters, varmint hunters, and other sportsmen who use large amounts of reloaded ammunition, this new drill press case trimmer consists of the Universal™ Chuckhead, a cutter shaft adapted for use in a drill press, and two quick-change cutter heads. Its two major advantages are speed and accuracy. An experienced operator can trim several hundred cases in an hour, and each will be trimmed to a precise length.

DRILL PRESS CASE TRIMMER $45.75

AUTO TRICKLER (NOT SHOWN)

This unique device allows reloaders to trickle the last few grains of powder automatically into their scale powder pans. The Auto-Trickler features vertical and horizontal height adjustments, enabling its use with both mechanical and the new electronic scales. It also offers a simple push-button operation. The powder reservoir is easily removed for cleaning. Handles all conventional ball, stick or flare powder types.

AUTO-TRICKLER $37.50

UNIVERSAL TRIMMER WITH NINE PILOT MULTI-PACK

This trimmer with patented chuckhead accepts all metallic rifle or pistol cases, regardless of rim thickness. To change calibers, simply change the case head pilot. Other features include coarse and fine cutter adjustments, an oil-impregnated bronze bearing, and a rugged cast base to assure precision alignment and years of service. Optional carbide cutter available. Trimmer Stop Ring includes 20 indicators as reference marks.

REPLACEMENT CARBIDE CUTTER $39.95
TRIMMER MULTI-PACK (incl. 9 pilots: 22, 24, 27,
     28/7mm, 30, 9mm, 35, 44 and 4A 64.95
NINE PILOT MULTI-PACK 10.50
POWER PACK TRIMMER 74.95
UNIVERSAL TRIMMER POWER ADAPTER 16.50

UNIVERSAL TRIMMER POWER ADAPTER

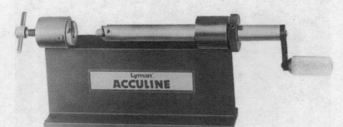

ACCU-TRIMMER

Lyman's Accu Trimmer can be used for all rifle and pistol cases from 22 to 458 Winchester Magnum. Standard shell-holders are used to position the case, and the trimmer incorporates standard Lyman cutter heads and pilots. Mounting options include bolting to a bench, C-clamp or vise.

ACCU TRIMMER w/9-pilot multi-pak $42.00

ELECTRONIC DIGITAL CALIPER
(not shown)

Lyman's 6" electronic caliper gives a direct digital readout for both inches and millimeters and can perform both inside and outside depth measurements. Its zeroing function allows the user to select zeroing dimensions and sort parts or cases by their plus or minus variation. The caliper works on a single, standard 1.5 volt silver oxide battery and comes with a fitted wooden storage case.

ELECTRONIC CALIPER $94.95

RELOADING

LYMAN RELOADING TOOLS

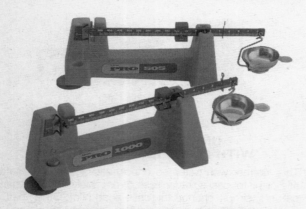

PRO 1000 & 505 RELOADING SCALES

Features include improved platform system; hi-tech base design of high-impact styrene; extra-large, smooth leveling wheel; dual agate bearings; larger damper for fast zeroing; built-in counter weight compartment; easy-to-read beam

PRO 1000 SCALE $56.95
PRO 500 SCALE 40.95

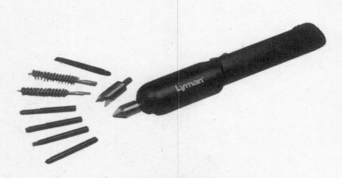

POWER DEBURRING KIT

Features a high torque, rechargeable power driver plus a complete set of accessories, including inside and outside deburr tools, large and small reamers and cleaners and case neck brushes. No threading or chucking required. Set also includes battery recharger and standard flat and phillips driver bits.

POWER DEBURRING KIT $54.95

AUTOSCALE

After setting this new autoscale to the desired powder charge, it dispenses the exact amount of powder with the push of a button, over and over again. Features solid-state electronics and is controlled by a photo transistor to ensure accurate powder charges.

AUTOSCALE $269.95

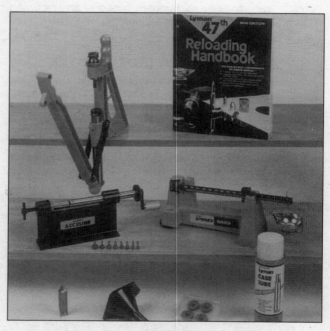

DELUXE RELOADERS' PRO KIT

Includes Accupress with compound leverage; Pro 505 Scale; Accutrimmer with 9 popular pilots; ram prime die; deburr tool; powder funnel; Quick Spray case lube; shellholders (4); Lyman's 47th *Reloading Handbook.*

DELUXE RELOADERS' PRO KIT $135.00

MEC Shotshell Reloaders

MODEL 600 JR. MARK V

This single-stage reloader features a cam-action crimp die to ensure that each shell returns to its original condition. MEC's 600 Jr. Mark 5 can load 6 to 8 boxes per hour and can be updated with the 285 CA primer feed. Press is adjustable for 3" shells. Die sets are available in 10, 12, 16, 20, 28 and .410 gauges at: $59.50
MODEL 600 . . . .$167.50

MODEL 600

MODEL 8567

MODEL 650

This reloader works on 6 shells at once. A reloaded shell is completed with every stroke. The MEC 650 does not resize except as a separate operation. Automatic Primer feed is standard. Simply fill it with a full box of primers and it will do the rest. Reloader has 3 crimping stations: the first one starts the crimp, the second closes the crimp, and the third places a taper on the shell. Available in 12, 16, 20 and 28 gauge and .410 bore. No die sets are available.
Price: $329.39

MODEL 650

MODEL 8567 GRABBER

This reloader features 12 different operations at all 6 stations, producing finished shells with each stroke of the handle. It includes a fully automatic primer feed and Auto-Cycle charging, plus MEC's exclusive 3-stage crimp. The "Power Ring" resizer ensures consistent, accurately sized shells without interrupting the reloading sequence. Simply put in the wads and shell casings, then remove the loaded shells with each pull of the handle. Optional kits to load 3" shells and steel shot make this reloader tops in its field. Resizes high and low base shells. Available in 12, 16, 20, 28 gauge and .410 bore. No die sets are available.
Price: $472.54

MODEL 8120 SIZEMASTER

Sizemaster's "Power Ring" collet resizer returns each base to factory specifications. This generation resizing station handles brass or steel heads, both high and low base. An 8-fingered collet squeezes the base back to original dimensions, then opens up to release the shell easily. The E-Z Prime auto primer feed is standard equipment (not offered in .410 bore). Press is adjustable for 3" shells and is available in 12, 16, 20, 28 gauge and .410 bore. Die sets are available at: $88.65 ($104.00 in 10 ga.)
MODEL 8120 . . . .$252.39

MODEL 8120

RELOADING

MEC Reloading

STEELMASTER SINGLE STATE

The only shotshell reloader equipped to load steel shotshells as well as lead ones. Every base is resized to factory specs by a precision "power ring" collet. Handles brass or steel heads in high or low base. The E-Z prime auto primer feed dispenses primers automatically and is standard equipment. Separate presses are available for 12 gauge 2 3/4", 3", 12 gauge 3 1/2" and 10 gauge.

STEELMASTER $262.65
In 12 ga. 3 1/2" only 289.08

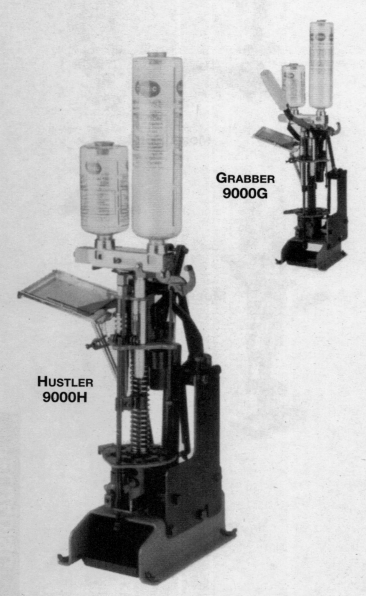

GRABBER 9000G

HUSTLER 9000H

E-Z PRIME "S" AND "V" AUTOMATIC PRIMER FEEDS

From carton to shell with security, these primer feeds provide safe, convenient primer positioning and increase rate of production. Reduce bench clutter, allowing more free area for wads and shells.

- Primers transfer directly from carton to reloader, tubes and tube fillers
- Positive mechanical feed (not dependent upon agitation of press)
- Visible supply
- Automatic. Eliminate hand motion
- Less susceptible to damage
- Adapt to all domestic and most foreign primers with adjustment of the cover
- May be purchased separately to replace tube-type primer feed or to update your present reloader

E-Z PRIME "S" (for Super 600, 650) or
E-Z PRIME "V" (for 600 Jr. Mark V & VersaMEC) . . .$39.70

MEC 9000 SERIES SHOTSHELL RELOADER

MEC's 9000 Series features automatic indexing and finished shell ejection for quicker and easier reloading. The factory set speed provides uniform movement through every reloading stage. Dropping the primer into the reprime station no longer requires operator "feel." The reloader requires only a minimal adjustment from low to high brass domestic shells, any one of which can be removed for inspection from any station. Can be set up for automatic or manual indexing. Available in 12, 16, 20 and 28 gauge and .410 bore. No die sets are available.

MEC 9000H $1,386.00
MEC 9000G SERIES 573.73

MTM Reloading

GUNSMITH'S MAINTENANCE CENTER

MTM's Gunsmiths Maintenance Center (RMC-5) is designed for mounting scopes and swivels, bedding actions or for cleaning rifles and shotguns. Multi-positional forks allow for eight holding combinations, making it possible to service firearm level, upright or upside down. The large middle section keeps tools and cleaning supplies in one area. Individual solvent compartments help to eliminate accidental spills. Cleaning rods stay where they are needed with the two built-in holders provided. Both forks (covered with a soft molded-on rubber pad) grip and protect the firearm. The RMC-5 is made of engineering- grade plastic for years of rugged use.

Dimensions: 29.5" X 9.5"
MODEL RMC-5 . . . .**$27.38**

PISTOL REST MODEL PR-30

MTM's new PR-30 Pistol Rest will accommodate any size handgun, from a Derringer to a 14" Contender. A locking front support leg adjusts up or down, allowing 20 different positions. Rubber padding molded to the tough polypropylene fork protects firearms from scratches. Fork clips into the base when not in use for compact storage.

Dimensions: 6" x 11" x 2.5
PISTOL REST MODEL PR-30 . . . .**$14.58**

CARD-GARD WITH WILD CAMO

The CASE-GARD SF-100 holds 100 shotshells in two removable trays. Designed primarily for hunters, this dust and moisture resistant carrier features a heavy-duty latch, fold-down handle, integral hinge and textured finish.

Price:
SF-100 12 or 20 ga.
   WILD CAMO SHOTSHELL BOX **$14.62**

RCBS RELOADING TOOLS

ROCK CHUCKER PRESS

With its easy operation, outstanding strength and versatility, a Rock Chucker press is ideal for beginner and pro alike. It can also be upgraded to a progressive press with an optional Piggyback II conversion unit.
- Heavy-duty cast iron for easy case-resizing
- 1" ram held in place by 12.5 sq. in. of rambearing surface
- Toggle blocks of ductile iron
- Compound leverage system
- Pins ground from hardened steel
- 1 1/4" - 12 thread for shotshell die kits and Piggyback II
- 7/8" - 14 thread for all standard reloading dies and accessories
- Milled slot and set screws accept optional RCBS automatic primer feed

Price: $130.95

ROCK CHUCKER MASTER RELOADING KIT

For reloaders who want the best equipment, the Rock Chucker Master Reloading Kit includes all the tools and accessories needed. Included are the following: • Rock Chucker Press • RCBS 505 Reloading Scale • Speer TrimPro Manual #12 • Uniflow Powder Measure • RCBS Rotary Case Trimmer-2 • deburring tool • case loading block • Primer Tray-2 • Automatic Primer Feed Combo • powder funnel • case lube pad • case neck brushes • fold-up hex ket set.

Price: $362.95

RELOADER SPECIAL-5

RELOADER SPECIAL-5

The Reloader Special press features a comfortable ball handle and a primer arm so that cases can be primed and resized at the same time.
- Compound leverage system
- Solid aluminum black "O" frame offset for unobstructed access
- Corrosion-resistant baked-powder finish
- Can be upgraded to progressive reloading with an optional Piggyback II conversion unit
- 1 1/4" - 12 thread for shotshell die kits and Piggyback II
- 7/8" - 14 thread for all standard reloading dies and accessories

Price: $101.95

AMMOMASTER RELOADING SYSTEM

The AmmoMaster offers the handloader the freedom to configure a press to his particular needs and preferences. It covers the complete spectrum of reloading, from single stage through fully automatic progressive reloading, from .32 Auto to .50 caliber. The AmmoMaster Auto has all the features of a five-station press.

SINGLE STAGE $177.95
AUTO 394.95

AMMOMASTER SINGLE STAGE

RCBS RELOADING TOOLS

APS BENCH-MOUNTED PRIMING TOOL

The APS Bench-Mounted Priming Tool was created for reloaders who prefer a separate, specialized tool dedicated to priming only. The handle of the bench-mounted tool is designed to provide hours of comfortable loading. Handle position can be adjusted for bench height.
Price: $85.95

APS PRIMER STRIP LOADER

For those who keep a supply of CCI primers in conventional packaging, the APS primer strip loader allows quick filling of empty strips. Each push of the handle seats 25 primers.
Price: $21.95

POW'R PULL BULLET PULLER (not shown)

The RCBS Pow'r Pull bullet puller features a three-jaw chuck that grips the case rim—just rap it on any solid surface like a hammer, and powder and bullet drop into the main chamber for re-use. A soft cushion protects bullets from damage. Works with most centerfire cartridges from .22 to .45 (not for use with rimfire cartridges).
Price: $24.95

APS BENCH-MOUNTED PRIMING TOOL

APS PRESS-MOUNTED PRIMING TOOL

This APS press-mounted priming tool provides the same features as the bench-mounted tool except it attaches to any single-stage press that accepts standard 7/8" x 14 dies.
Price: $54.95

RELOADING SCALE MODEL 5-0-5

This 511-grain capacity scale has a three-poise system with widely spaced, deep beam notches to keep them in place. Two smaller poises on right side adjust from 0.1 to 10 grains, larger one on left side adjusts in full 10-grain steps. The first scale to use magnetic dampening to eliminate beam oscillation, the 5-0-5 also has a sturdy die-cast base with large leveling legs for stability. Self-aligning agate bearings support the hardened steel beam pivots for a guaranteed sensitivity to 0.1 grains.
Price: $74.95

TRIM PRO™ CASE TRIMMER

Cartridge cases are trimmed quickly and easily with a few turns of the RCBS Trim Pro case trimmer. The lever-type handle is more accurate to use than draw collet systems. A flat plate shell holder keeps cases locked in place and aligned. A micrometer fine adjustment bushing offers trimming accuracy to within .001". Made of die-cast metal with hardened cutting blades. The power model is like having a personal lathe, delivering plenty of torque. Positive locking handle and in-line power switch make it simple and safe.
Price: Power $201.95
Manual $66.95
Also available:
TRIM PRO CASE TRIMMER STAND $13.95
CASE HOLDER ACCESSORY .31.95

RELOADING

RCBS RELOADING TOOLS

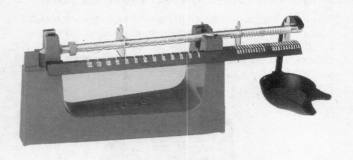

POWDER PRO™ DIGITAL SCALE

The RCBS Powder Pro Digital Scale has a 1500-grain capacity. Powder, bullets, even cases with accuracy up to 0.1 grain can be weighed. Includes infra-red data port for transferring information to the Powdermaster Electronic Powder Dispenser.
Price: $209.95

POWDERMASTER ELECTRONIC POWDER DISPENSER

Works in combination with the RCBS Powder Pro Digital Scale and with all types of smokeless powder. Can be used as a power trickler as well as a powder dispenser. Accurate to one-tenth of a grain.
Price: $220.95

RC-130 MECHANICAL SCALE

The new RC130 features a 130 grain capacity and maintenance-free movement, plus a magnetic dampening system for fast readings. A 3-poise design incorporates easy adjustments with a beam that is graduated in increments of 10 grains and one grain. A micrometer poise measures in 0.1 grain increments with acuracy to ±0.1 grain.
Price: $34.95

POWDER CHECKER (not shown)

Operates on a free-moving rod for simple, mechanical operation with nothing to break. Standard 7/8x14 die body can be used in any progressive loader that takes standard dies. Black oxide finish provides corrosion resistance with good color contrast for visibility.
Price: $22.59

RELOADING SCALE MODEL 10-10
Up to 1010 Grain Capacity

Normal capacity is 510 grains, which can be increased, without loss of sensitivity, by attaching the included extra weight.

Features include micrometer poise for quick, precise weighing, special approach-to-weight indicator, easy-to-read graduation, magnetic dampener, agate bearings, anti-tip pan, and dustproof lid snaps on to cover scale for storage. Sensitivity is guaranteed to 0.1 grains.
Price: $118.95

PARTNER ELECTRONIC POWDER SCALE

Accurate for +/- one-tenth of a grain up to 300 grains and +/- two-tenths up to 750 grains. Large LCD display is angled for easy reading over a wide range of positions. Powered by 9-volt battery.
Price: $150.95

REDDING RELOADING TOOLS

MODEL 721

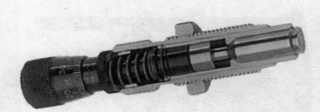

COMPETITION BUSHING NECK DIE

TYPE S BUSHING NECK DIE

MODEL 721 "THE BOSS" PRESS

This "O" type reloading press features a rigid cast iron frame whose 36° offset provides the best visibility and access of comparable presses. Its "Smart" primer arm moves in and out of position automatically with ram travel. The priming arm is positioned at the bottom of ram travel for lowest leverage and best feel. Model 721 accepts all standard 7/8-14 threaded dies and universal shell holders.

MODEL 721 "THE BOSS" $129.00
   With Shellholder and 10A Dies 165.00
Also available:
BOSS PRO-PAK DELUXE RELOADING KIT. Includes Boss Reloading Press, #2 Powder and Bullet Scale, Powder Trickler, Reloading Dies $336.00
   w/o dies and shellholder 289.50

ULTRAMAG MODEL 7000 (not shown)

Unlike other reloading presses that connect the linkage to the lower half of the press, the Ultramag's compound leverage system is connected at the top of the press frame. This allows the reloader to develop tons of pressure without the usual concern about press frame deflection. Huge frame opening will handle 50 x 3 1/4-inch Sharps with ease.

No. 700 PRESS, complete $289.50
No. 700K KIT, includes shell holder and
   one set of dies 324.00

BUSHING-STYLE NECK-SIZING DIES

Redding introduces two new Bushing Style Neck Sizing Dies—a simplified version (dubbed "Type S") and a Competition model—with interchangeable sizing bushings available in .001 increments. The Type S comes in 42 calibers and has an adjustable decapping rod to allow positioning of the bushing to resize only a portion of the neck length, if desired. The Competition Model features a cartridge case that is supported and aligned with the interchangeable sizing bushings before the sizing process begins.

COMPETITION BULLET SEATING DIE $96.00
TYPE S BUSHING NECK DIE 52.50
TYPE S FULL BUSHING DIE 52.50
COMPETITION BUSHING NECK DIE 96.00

METALLIC TURRET RELOADING PRESS
MODEL 25000 (not shown)

Extremely rugged, ideal for production reloading. No need to move shell, just rotate turret head to positive alignment. Ram accepts any standard snap-in shell holder. Includes primer arm for seating both small and large primers.

No. 25 PRESS, complete $289.50
No. 25K KIT, includes press, shell holder, and one
   set of dies 324.00

RELOADING

REDDING RELOADING TOOLS

MASTER POWDER MEASURE MODEL 3

Universal- or pistol-metering chambers interchange in seconds. Measures charges from 1/2 to 100 grains. Unit is fitted with lock ring for fast dump with large "clear" plastic reservoir. "See-thru" drop tube accepts all calibers from 22 to 600. Precision-fitted rotating drum is critically honed to prevent powder escape. Knife-edged powder chamber shears coarse-grained powders with ease, ensuring accurate charges.

No. 3 MASTER POWDER MEASURE (specify Universal-
  or Pistol-Metering chamber) $120.00
No. 3K KIT FORM, includes both Universal and
  Pistol Chambers 144.00
BENCH STAND 27.50

MODEL 3

MODEL 3BR

MASTER CASE TRIMMER MODEL 1400

This unit features a universal collet that accepts all rifle and pistol cases. The frame is solid cast iron with storage holes in the base for extra pilots. Both coarse and fine adjustments are provided for case length.

    The case-neck cleaning brush and primer pocket cleaners attached to the frame of this tool make it a very handy addition to the reloading bench. Trimmer comes complete with:
- New speed cutter shaft
- Six pilots (22, 6mm, 25, 270, 7mm and 30 cal.)
- Universal collet
- Two neck cleaning brushes (22 thru 30 cal.)
- Two primer pocket cleaners (large and small)

No. 1400 MASTER CASE TRIMMER complete $93.00
No. 1500 PILOTS 3.90

MASTER CASE TRIMMER MODEL 1400

COMPETITION MODEL BR-30 POWDER MEASURE (not shown)

This powder measure features a new drum and micrometer that limit the overall charging range from a low of 10 grains (depending on powder density) to a maximum of approx. 50 grains. For serious competitive shooters whose loading requirements are between 10 and 50 grains, this is the measure to choose. The diameter of Model 3BR's metering cavity has been reduced, and the metering plunger on the new model has a unique hemispherical or cup shape, creating a powder cavity that resembles the bottom of a test tube. The result: irregular powder setting is alleviated and charge-to-charge uniformity is enhance.

COMPETITION MODEL BR-30 POWDER MEASURE . .$180.00

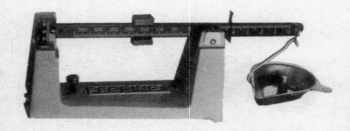

MATCH GRADE POWDER MEASURE MODEL 3BR

Designed for the most demanding reloaders—bench rest, silhouette and varmint shooters. The Model 3BR is unmatched for its precision and repeatability. Its special features include a powder baffle and zero backlash micrometer.

No. 3BR with Universal or
  Pistol Metering Chamber $150.00
No. 3BRK includes both metering chambers 189.00

STANDARD POWDER AND BULLET SCALE MODEL RS-1

For the beginner or veteran reloader. Only two counterpoises need to be moved to obtain the full capacity range of 1/10 grain to 380 grains. Clearly graduated with white numerals and lines on a black background. Total capacity of this scale is 380 grains. An over-and-under plate graduate in 10th grains allows checking of variations in powder charges or bullets without further adjustments.

MODEL NO. RS-1 . . . .$49.50
Also available: MASTER POWDER & BULLET SCALE. Same as standard model, but includes a magnetic dampened beam swing for extra fast readings. 505-grain capacity . .$75.00

Directory of Manufacturers & Suppliers   558

Caliberfinder   563

Gunfinder   572

Reference

DIRECTORY OF MANUFACTURERS AND SUPPLIERS

The following manufacturers, suppliers and distributors of firearms, reloading equipment, sights, scopes, ammo and accessories all appear with their products in the Specifications and/or "Manufacuters' Showcase" sections of this edition of SHOOTER'S BIBLE.

ACCURATE ARMS CO., INC.
5891 Hwy, 230W
McEwen, Tennessee 37101
Tel: 615-729-4207 Fax: 615-729-4211

AIMPOINT (sights, scopes, mounts)
420 West Main St.
Geneseo, Illinois 61254
Tel: 309-944-5631 Fax: 309-944-3676

ALLIANT TECH SYSTEMS (gunpowder)
Route 114, P.O. Box 6
Radford, Virginia 24141
Tel: 800-276-9337 Fax: 540-639-7189

AMERICAN ARMS (handguns; Franchi
  shotguns; Uberti handguns, rifles,
  blackpowder)
715 E. Armour Road
N. Kansas City, Missouri 64116
Tel: 816-474-3161 Fax: 816-474-1225

AMERICAN DERRINGER CORP. (handguns)
127 North Lacy Drive
Waco, Texas 76705
Tel: 817-799-9111 Fax: 817-799-7935

AMERICAN FRONTIER FIREARMS
  (black-powder arms)
P.O. Box 744
Aguanga, California 92536
Tel: 909-763-2209 Fax: 909-763-0014

ARCADIA MACHINE & TOOL INC.
  (AMT handguns, rifles)
6226 Santos Diaz Street
Irwindale, California 91702
Tel: 818-334-6629 Fax: 818-969-5247

ARMES DE CHASSE (AyA shotguns;
  Francotte rifles, shotguns)
P.O. Box 86
Hertford, North Carolina 27944
Tel: 919-426-2245 Fax: 919-426-1557

ARMSCOR (handguns, rifles, shotguns)
Available through K.B.I., Inc.

ARMSPORT, INC. (Bernardelli handguns,
  shotguns)
3590 NW 49th Street, P.O. Box 523066
Miami, Florida 33142
Tel: 305-635-7850 Fax: 305-633-2877

ARNOLD ARMS CO. INC. (rifles)
P.O. Box 1011
Arlington, Washington 98223
Tel: 360-435-1011 Fax: 360-435-7304

A-SQUARE COMPANY INC. (rifles)
One Industrial Park
Bedford, Kentucky 40006
Tel: 502-719-3006 Fax: 502-719-3030

ASTRA (handguns)
Available thru European American Amory

AUSTIN & HALLECK (blackpowder rifles)
1099 Welt
Weston, Missouri 64098
Tel: 816-386-2176 Fax: 816-386-2177

AUTO-ORDNANCE CORP. (handguns, rifles)
Williams Lane
West Hurley, New York 12491
Tel: 914-679-7225 Fax: 914-679-2698

AyA (shotguns)
Available through Armes de Chasse

BAUSCH & LOMB/BUSHNELL (scopes)
  Sports Optics Division
9200 Cody
Overland Park, Kansas 66214
Tel: 913-752-3433 Fax: 913-752-3489

BENELLI
Handguns available through European
  American Armory
Shotguns available through Heckler & Koch

BERETTA U.S.A. CORP. (handguns, rifles,
  shotguns)
17601 Beretta Drive
Accokeek, Maryland 20607
Tel: 301-283-2191 Fax: 301-283-0435

BERNARDELLI (handguns, shotguns)
Available through Armsport

BERSA (handguns)
Available through Eagle Imports Inc.

BLASER USA, INC. (rifles)
Available through Sigarms

BLUE BOOK PUBLICATIONS, INC. (books)
8009 34th Ave. South, Suite 175
Minneapolis, Minnesota 55425
Tel: 612-854-5229 Fax: 612-853-1486
(See P. 95 in Manufacturers' Showcase)

BLOUNT, INC. (RCBS reloading equipment;
  Speer bullets; Weaver scopes)
P.O. Box 856
Lewiston, Idaho 83501
Tel: 208-746-2351 Fax: 208-799-3904

BONANZA (reloading tools)
See Forster Products

BOND ARMS INC. (handguns)
P.O. Box 1296
Granbury, Texas 70048
Tel: 817-573-4445 Fax: 817-573-5636

BRNO (rifles)
Available through Euro-Imports

BROLIN ARMS (handguns, shotguns)
P.O. Box 698
Laverne, California 91750-0698
Tel: 909-392-2352 Fax. 909-392-2354

BROWN PRECISION, INC. (custom rifles)
7786 Molinos Avenue; P.O. Box 270 W.
Los Molinos, California 96055
Tel: 916-384-2506 Fax: 916-384-1638

BROWNING (handguns, rifles, shotguns,
  blackpowder guns)
One Browning Place
Morgan, Utah 84050
Tel: 801-876-2711 Fax: 801-876-3331

BURRIS COMPANY, INC. (scopes)
331 East Eighth Street, P.O. Box 1747
Greeley, Colorado 80631
Tel: 970-356-1670 Fax: 970-356-8702

CABELA'S INC. (blackpowder arms)
One Cabela Drive
Sidney, Nebraska 69160
Tel: 308-254-5505 Fax: 308-254-6669

CHRISTENSEN ARMS (rifles)
385 North 3050 East
St. George, Utah 84790
Tel: 801-674-9535 Fax: 801-674-9293

CLIFTON ARMS (custom rifles)
P.O. Box 1471
Medina, Texas 78055
Tel: 210-589-2666

COLT BLACKPOWDER ARMS CO.
  (blackpowder arms)
110 8th Street
Brooklyn, New York 11215
Tel: 718-499-4678 Fax: 718-768-8056

COLT'S MANUFACTURING CO., INC.
  (handguns, rifles)
P.O. Box 1868
Hartford, Connecticut 06144-1868
Tel: 800-962-COLT Fax: 860-244-1449

CONNECTICUT SHOTGUN MFG. CO.
  (A. H. Fox shotguns)
35 Woodland Street, P.O. Box 1692
New Britain, Connecticut 06051-1692
Tel: 860-225-6581 Fax: 860-832-8707

COONAN ARMS (handguns)
1745 Highway 36E
Maplewood, Minnesota 55109
Tel: 612-777-3156 Fax: 612-777-3683

COOPER FIREARMS (rifles)
P.O. Box 114
Stevensville, Montana 59870
Tel: 406-777-5534 Fax: 406-777-5228

COR-BON BULLET COMPANY (ammunition)
1311 Industry Road
Sturgis, South Dakota 57785
Tel: 605-347-4544 Fax: 605-347-5055
(See p.92 in Manufacturers' Showcase)

CUMBERLAND MOUNTAIN ARMS
  (blackpowder rifles)
1045 Dinah Shore Blvd., P.O. Box 710
Winchester, Tennessee 37398
Tel: 931-967-8414 Fax: 931-967-9199

CVA (blackpowder arms)
5988 Peachtree Corners East
Norcross, Georgia 30071
Tel: 800-251-9412 Fax: 770-242-8546

DAEWOO PRECISION (handguns)
Available through Kimber of America

DAKOTA (handguns)
Available through E.M.F. Co., Inc.

DAKOTA ARMS, INC. (rifles, shotguns)
HC 55, Box 326
Sturgis, South Dakota 57785
Tel: 605-347-4686 Fax: 605-347-4459

CHARLES DALY (shotguns)
Available through K.B.I., Inc.

DAVIS INDUSTRIES (handguns)
11186 Venture Drive
Mira Loma, California 91752
Tel: 909-360-5598 Fax: 909-360-1749

DESERT EAGLE (handguns)
Available through Magnum Research Inc.

DESERT MOUNTAIN MFG. (rifle rests)
P.O. Box 130184
Coram, Montana 59913
Tel: 800-477-6762 Fax: 406-387-5361
(see p. 94 in Manufacturers' Showcase)

J. DEWEY MFG. CO. (cleaning rods)
P.O. Box 2014
Southbury, Connecticut 06488
Tel: 203-264-3064 Fax: 203-262-6907

DILLON PRECISION PRODUCTS
  (reloading equipment)
8009 East Dillon's Way
Scottsdale, Arizona 85260
Tel: 800-223-4570 Fax: 602-998-2786

DIXIE GUN WORKS (blackpowder guns)
P.O. Box 130, Highway 51 S.
Union City, Tennessee 38261
Tel: 901-885-0561 Fax: 901-885-0440

DOCTER OPTIC TECHNOLOGIES
  (binoculars, scopes)
4685 Boulder Highway, Suite A
Las Vegas, Nevada 89121
Tel: 800-290-3634 Fax: 702-898-3737

DOWNSIZER CORPORATION (handguns)
P.O. Box 710316
Santee, California 92072-0316
Tel: 619-448-5510 Fax: 619-448-5780

DYNAMIT NOBEL/RWS (Rottweil shotguns)
81 Ruckman Road
Closter, New Jersey 07624
Tel: 201-767-1995 Fax: 201-767-1589

EAGLE IMPORTS, INC. (Bersa handguns)
1750 Brielle Avenue, Unit B1
Wanamassa, New Jersey 07712
Tel: 908-493-0333 Fax: 908-493-0301

E.M.F. COMPANY, INC. (Dakota handguns;
  Uberti handguns, blackpowder arms)
1900 East Warner Avenue 1-D
Santa Ana, California 92705
Tel: 714-261-6611 Fax: 714-756-0133

ENTRÉPRISE ARMS (handguns)
15861 Business Center Drive
Irwindale, California 91706
Tel: 626-962-8712 Fax: 626-962-4692

ERMA (handguns)
Available through Precision Sales Int'l.

EUROARMS OF AMERICA INC.
  (blackpowder guns)
208 E. Piccadilly St.,
P.O. Box 3277
Winchester, Virginia 22601
Tel: 540-662-1863

EURO-IMPORTS (Brno handguns)
614 Millar Avenue
El Cajon, California 92020
Tel: 619-442-7005 Fax: 619-442-7005

EUROPEAN AMERICAN ARMORY CORP.
  (Astra handguns; Benelli handguns;
   E.A.A. handguns, rifles)
P.O. Box 122
Sharpes, Florida 32959
Tel: 800-536-4442 Tel: 407-639-4842
Fax: 407-639-7006

FEDERAL CARTRIDGE CO. (ammunition)
900 Ehlen Drive
Anoka, Minnesota 55303-7503
Tel: 612-323-2300 Fax: 612-323-2506

FEG (handguns)
Available through Interarms and K.B.I., Inc.

FLINTLOCKS, ETC. (Pedersoli replica rifles)
160 Rossiter Road
Richmond, Massachusetts 01254
Tel: 413-698-3822 Fax: 413-698-3866

FORREST, INC. (ammo magazines)
P.O. Box 326
Lakeside, California 92040
Tel: 619-561-5800 Fax: 1-888-GUNCLIP
(see p. 95 in Manufacturers' Showcase)

FORSTER PRODUCTS (reloading)
82 East Lanark Avenue
Lanark, Illinois 61046
Tel: 815-493-6360 Fax: 815-493-2371

FORT WORTH FIREARMS (blackpower guns)
2006-B Martin Luther King Freeway
Fort Worth, Texas 76104
Tel: 817-536-0718 Fax: 817-535-0290

A. H. FOX (shotguns)
Available thru Connecticut Shotgun Mfg. Co.

FRANCHI (shotguns)
Available through American Arms

FRANCOTTE (rifles, shotguns)
Available through Armes de Chasse

FREEDOM ARMS (handguns)
One Freedom Lane, P.O. Box 1776
Freedom, Wyoming 83120
Tel: 307-883-2468 Fax: 307-883-2005

GARBI (shotguns)
Available through W. L. Moore & Co.

GLASER SAFETY SLUG, INC.
  (ammunition, gun accessories)
P.O. Box 8223
Foster City, California 94404
Tel: 800-221-3489 Fax: 415-345-8217
(See p. 91 in Manufacturers' Showcase)

GLOCK, INC. (handguns)
6000 Highlands Parkway
Smyrna, Georgia 30082
Tel: 770-432-1202 Fax: 770-433-8719

GONIC ARMS (blackpowder rifles)
134 Flagg Road
Gonic, New Hampshire 03839
603-332-8456 Fax: 603-332-8457

GRIZZLY INDUSTRIAL INC. (metal-working
  lathes, mills)
Bellingham, Washington/Williamsport,
Pennsylvania/Memphis, Tennessee
Tel: 800-523-4777 Fax: 800-438-5901
(see p. 89, 90, 91, 92 in Manufacturers' Showcase)

GSI (GUN SOUTH INC.) (Mauser rifles;
  Merkel shotguns; Steyr-Mannlicher rifles)
108 Morrow Ave., P.O. Box 129
Trussville, Alabama 35173
Tel: 205-655-8299 Fax: 205-655-7078

GUNLINE TOOLS (gun checkering tools)
2950-0 Saturn Street
Brea, California 92821
Tel: 714-993-5100 Fax: 714-572-4128
www.gunline.com
(See p. 93 in Manufacturers' Showcase)

GUTMANN CUTLERY, INC. (knives)
P.O. Box 2219
Bellingham, Washington 98227-2219
Tel: 800-288-5379 Fax: 360-715-2091
(See p. 90, 93 in Manufacturers' Showcase)

H&R 1871 INC. (see Harrington &
  Richardson or New England Firearms)

HÄMMERLI U.S.A. (handguns)
19296 Oak Grove Circle
Groveland, California 95321
Tel: 209-962-5311 Fax: 209-962-5931

HARRINGTON & RICHARDSON
(handguns, rifles, shotguns)
60 Industrial Rowe
Gardner, Massachusetts 01440
Tel: 978-632-9393 Fax: 978-632-2300
(see p. 89, 91, 93 in Manufacturers' Showcase)

HARRIS ENGINEERING INC. (bipods)
Barlow, Kentucky 42024
Tel: 502-334-3633 Fax: 502-334-3000
(see p. 94 in Manufacturers' Showcase)

HARRIS GUNWORKS (rifles)
3840 N. 28th Ave.
Phoenix, Arizona 85017-4733
Tel: 602-230-1414 Fax: 602-230-1422

HECKLER & KOCH (handguns, rifles; Benelli
and Fabarms shotguns)
21480 Pacific Boulevard
Sterling, Virginia 20166
Tel: 703-450-1900 Fax: 703-450-8160

HENRY REPEATING ARMS CO. (rifles)
110 8th Street
Brooklyn, New York 11215
Tel: 718-499-5600 Fax: 718-768-8056

HERITAGE MANUFACTURING (handguns)
4600 NW 135 St.
Opa Locka, Florida 33054
Tel: 305-685-5966 Fax: 305-687-6721

HI-POINT FIREARMS (handguns)
MKS Supply, Inc.
5990 Philadelphia Drive
Dayton, Ohio 45415
Tel/Fax: 513-275-4991

HIGH STANDARD MFG CO. (handguns)
4601 S. Pinemont, 2148B
Houston, Texas 77041
Tel: 713-462-4200 Fax: 713-462-6437

HODGDON POWDER CO., INC. (gunpowder)
6231 Robinson, P.O. Box 2932
Shawnee Mission, Kansas 66201
Tel: 913- 362-9455 Fax: 913-362-1307

HORNADY MANUFACTURING COMPANY
(ammunition, reloading)
P.O. Box 1848
Grand Island, Nebraska 68802-1848
Tel: 308-382-1390 Fax: 308-382-5761

HOWA (rifles)
Available through Interarms

ICC/KK AIR INTERNATIONAL (gun cases)
P.O. Box 9912
Spokane, Washington 99209
Tel: 800-261-3322 Fax: 509-326-5436
(See p. 94 in Manufacturers' Showcase)

IGA SHOTGUNS
Available through Stoeger Industries

IMR POWDER COMPANY (gunpowder)
1080 Military Turnpike
Plattsburgh, New York 12901
Tel: 518-563-2253

INTERARMS (FEG handguns; Howa rifles;
Rossi handguns, rifles; Star handguns;
Walther handguns)
10 Prince Street, Alexandria, Virginia 22314
Tel: 703-548-1400 Fax: 703-549-7826

ISRAEL ARMS INT'L. INC. (handguns)
5709 Hartsdale
Houston, Texas 77036
Tel: 713-789-0745 Fax: 713-789-7513

ITHACA GUN CO. (shotguns)
891 Route 34-B
Kings Ferry, New York 13081
Tel: 315-364-7171 Fax: 315-364-5134

JARRETT RIFLES INC. (custom rifles)
383 Brown Road
Jackson, South Carolina 29831
Tel: 803-471-3616

JENNINGS, INC. (handguns)
P.O. Box 20135
Carson City, Nevada 89721
Tel: 800-518-1666 Fax: 702-882-3129

KAHR ARMS (handguns)
P.O. Box 220
Blauvelt, New York 10913
Tel: 914-353-5996 Fax: 914-353-7833

K.B.I., INC. (Armscor rifles, handguns,
shotguns; Charles Daly shotguns; FEG
handguns)
P.O. Box 6346
Harrisburg, Pennsylvania 17112
Tel: 717-540-8518 Fax: 717-540-8567

KIMBER OF AMERICA, INC. (handguns,
rifles)
9039 Southeast Jannsen Road
Clackamas, Oregon 97015
Tel: 503-656-1704 Fax: 503-656-5357

KONGSBERG AMERICA (rifles)
Merwin's Associates
2 Merwin's Lane
Fairfield, Connecticut 06430
Tel: 203-259-0938 Fax: 203-259-2566

KOWA OPTIMED, INC. (scopes)
20001 South Vermont Avenue
Torrance, California 90502
Tel: 310-327-1913 Fax: 310-327-4177
(see p. 95 in Manufacturers' Showcase)

KRIEGHOFF INTERNATIONAL INC.
(rifles, shotguns)
337A Route 611, P.O. Box 549
Ottsville, Pennsylvania 18942
Tel: 610-847-5173 Fax: 610-847-8691

L.A.R. MANUFACTURING, INC. (Grizzly
handguns, rifles)
4133 West Farm Road
West Jordan, Utah 84084
Tel: 801-280-3505 Fax: 801-280-1972

LASERAIM TECHNOLOGIES INC.
(handguns, sights)
P.O. Box 3548
Little Rock, Arkansas 72203-3548
Tel: 501-375-2227 Fax: 501-372-1445

LAZZERONI ARMS CO. (rifles)
P.O. Box 26696
Tucson, Arizona 85726
Tel: 520-577-7500 Fax: 520-624-4250

LEUPOLD & STEVENS, INC.
(scopes, mounts)
1440 N.W. Greenbriar Parkway,
P.O. Box 688
Beaverton, Oregon 97075
Tel: 503-646-9171 Fax: 503-526-1455

LEICA CAMERA INC. (rifle scopes)
156 Ludlow Avenue
Northvale, New Jersey 07647
Tel: 800-222-0118 Fax: 201-767-8666

LLAMA (handguns)
Available through SGS Importers Int'l

LUGER, American Eagle (pistols)
Available through Stoeger Industries

LYMAN PRODUCTS CORP. (rifles,
blackpowder guns, reloading tools)
475 Smith Street
Middletown, Connecticut 06457
Tel: 860-632-2020 Fax: 860-632-1699

MAGNUM RESEARCH INC. (Desert Eagle
handguns; CZ handguns; Brno rifles)
7110 University Avenue N.E.
Minneapolis, Minnesota 55432
Tel: 612-574-1868 Fax: 612-574-0109

MAGTECH RECREATIONAL PRODUCTS
(shotguns)
5030 Paradise Rd., Ste A104
Las Vegas, Nevada 89119
Tel: 702-736-2043 Fax: 702-736-2140

MARKESBURY MUZZLELOADERS, INC.
(black-powder guns)
7785 Foundation Drive, Suite 6
Florence, Kentucky 41042
Tel: 606-342-5553- Fax: 606-342-2380

MARLIN FIREARMS COMPANY (rifles,
shotguns, blackpowder)
100 Kenna Drive
North Haven, Connecticut 06473
Tel: 203-239-5621 Fax: 203-234-7991

MAROCCHI (Conquista shotguns)
Available through Precision Sales Int'l.

MAUSER (rifles)
Available through GSI (Gun South Inc.)

MAVERICK OF MOSSBERG (shotguns)
Available through O. F. Mossberg

MEC INC. (reloading tools)
c/o Mayville Engineering Co.
715 South Street
Mayville, Wisconsin 53050
Tel: 414-387-4500 Fax: 414-387-2682

MERIT CORP. (sights)
P.O. Box 9044
Schenectady, New York 12309
Tel: 518-346-1420

MERKEL (shotguns)
Available through GSI (Gun South Inc.)

M.O.A. CORP. (handguns)
2451 Old Camden Pike
Eaton, Ohio 45302
Tel: 513-456-3669 Fax: 513-456-9331

MODERN MUZZLELOADING INC.
(Knight blackpowder guns)
P.O. Box 130, 234 Airport Rd.,
Centerville, Iowa 52544
Tel: 515-856-2626 Fax: 515-856-2628

WILLIAM L. MOORE & CO. (Garbi and
Piotti shotguns)
31360 Via Colinas, No. 109
Westlake Village, California 91361
Tel: 818-889-4160

O. F. MOSSBERG & SONS, INC. (shotguns)
7 Grasso Avenue; P.O. Box 497
North Haven, Connecticut 06473
Tel: 203-230-5300 Fax: 203-230-5420

MTM MOLDED PRODUCTS (reloading
tools)
P.O. Box 14117, Dayton, Ohio 45413
Tel: 513-890-7461 Fax: 513-890-1747
(See p. 92 in Manufacturers' Showcase)

MUZZLELOADING TECHNOLOGIES INC.
(black-powder guns)
25 E. Hwy. 40, Suite 330-12
Roosevelt, Utah 84066
Tel: 435-722-5996 Fax: 435-722-5909

NAVY ARMS COMPANY, INC. (handguns,
rifles, blackpowder guns)
689 Bergen Boulevard
Ridgefield, New Jersey 07657
Tel: 201-945-2500 Fax: 201-945-6859

NEW ENGLAND ARMS (Rizzini shotguns)
Lawrence Lane, P.O. Box 278
Kittery Point, Maine 03905
Tel: 207-439-0593 Fax: 207-439-6726

NEW ENGLAND FIREARMS CO., INC.
(handguns, rifles, shotguns)
60 Industrial Rowe
Gardner, Massachusetts 01440
Tel: 978-632-9393 Fax: 978-632-2300
(See p. 90 in Manufacturers' Showcase)

NIKON INC. (scopes)
1300 Walt Whitman Road
Melville, New York 11747
Tel: 516-547-4200 Fax: 516-547-0309

NORTH AMERICAN ARMS (handguns)
2150 South 950 East
Provo, Utah 84606
Tel: 801-374-9990 Fax: 801-374-9998

NOSLER BULLETS, INC. (bullets)
P.O. Box 671
Bend, Oregon 97709
Tel: 503-382-3921 Fax: 503-388-4667

NYGORD PRECISION PRODUCTS
(Unique handguns, rifles)
P.O. Box 12578
Prescott, Arizona 86304
Tel: 520-717-2315 Fax: 520-717-2198

OLIN/WINCHESTER (ammunition, primers,
cases)
427 No. Shamrock
East Alton, Illinois 62024
Tel: 618-258-2936 Fax: 618-258-3609

PARAGON COMPETITION (Rottweil shotguns)
1330 Glassel
Orange, California 92667
Tel: 714-538-3109

PARA-ORDNANCE (handguns)
980 Tapscott Road
Scarborough, Ontario, Canada M1X 1E7
Tel: 416-297-7855 Fax: 416-297-1289

PARKER REPRODUCTIONS (shotguns)
124 River Road
Middlesex, New Jersey 08846
Tel: 908-469-0100 Fax: 908-469-9692

PEDERSOLI, DAVIDE (replica rifles)
Available through Flintlocks Etc.

PENTAX (scopes)
35 Inverness Drive East
Englewood, Colorado 80112
Tel: 303-799-8000 Fax: 303-790-1131

PERAZZI U.S.A. (shotguns)
1207 S. Shamrock Ave.
Monrovia, California 91016
Tel: 818-303-0068 Fax: 818-303-2081

PIOTTI (shotguns)
Available through W. L. Moore & Co.

PRAIRIE GUN WORKS (rifles)
1-761 Marion St.
Winnipeg, Manitoba, Canada R2J 0K6
Tel: 204-231-2976

PRAIRIE RIVER ARMS LTD.
(blackpowder guns)
1220 North 6th St.
Princeton, Illinois 61356
Tel: 815-875-1616 Fax: 815-875-1402

PRECISION SALES INTERNATIONAL
(Erma handguns; Marocchi shotguns)
P.O. Box 1776
Westfield, Massachusetts 01086
Tel: 413-562-5055 Fax: 413-562-5056

PRECISION SMALL ARMS (handguns)
155 Carleton Rd.
Charlottesville, Virginia 22902
Tel: 804-293-6124 Fax: 804-295-0780

QUARTON USA (laser sights)
042 Alamo Downs Parkway, Suite 250
San Antonio, Texas 78238-4518
Tel: 800-520-8435 Fax: 210-520-8433
(see P. 90, 91, 92, 96 in Manufacturers' Showcase)

RCBS, INC. (reloading tools)
Available through Blount, Inc.

REDDING RELOADING EQUIPMENT
(reloading tools)
1089 Starr Road
Cortland, New York 13045
Tel: 607-753-3331 Fax: 607-756-8445

REDFIELD (scopes)
5800 East Jewell Avenue
Denver, Colorado 80227
Tel: 303-757-6411 Fax: 303-756-2338

REMINGTON ARMS COMPANY, INC.
(rifles, shotguns, blackpowder, ammunition)
870 Remington Drive, P.O. Box 700
Madison, North Carolina 27025-0700
Tel: 800-243-9700

RIDGELINE, INC. (hearing protectors)
P.O. Box 930
Dewey, Arizona 86327
Tel: 520-632-5800 Fax: 520-632-5900
(See p. 94 in Manufacturers' Showcase)

RIFLES, INC. (rifles)
873 West 5400 North
Cedar City, Utah 84720
Tel: 435-586-5995 Fax: 435-586-5996

RIZZINI (shotguns)
Available through New England Arms

ROSSI (handguns, rifles)
Available through Interarms

ROTTWEIL (shotguns)
Available through Paragon Competition

RUGER (handguns, rifles, shotguns,
blackpowder guns). See Sturm, Ruger
& Company, Inc.

SAFARI ARMS (handguns)
c/o Olympic Arms, Inc.
624 Old Pacific Highway Southeast
Olympia, Washington 98513
Tel: 360-459-7940 Fax: 360-491-3447

SAKO (rifles, actions, scope mounts, ammo)
Available through Stoeger Industries

SAUER (rifles)
c/o Paul Company, Inc.
27385 Pressonville Road
Wellsville, Kansas 66092
Tel: 913-883-4444 Fax: 913-883-2525

SAVAGE ARMS (rifles, shotguns)
100 Springdale Road
Westfield, Massachusetts 01085
Tel: 413-568-7001 Fax: 413-562-7764

SCHMIDT AND BENDER (scopes)
Schmidt & Bender U.S.A.
P.O. Box 134
Meriden, New Hampshire 03770
Tel: 800-468-3450 Fax: 603-469-3471

SGS IMPORTERS INTERNATIONAL INC.
(Llama handguns)
1750 Brielle Avenue
Wanamassa, New Jersey 07712
Tel: 908-493-0302 Fax: 908-493-0301

SHILOH RIFLE MFG. CO., INC. (Shiloh
Sharps blackpowder rifles)
P.O. Box 279, Industrial Park
Big Timber, Montana 59011
Tel: 406-932-4454 Fax: 406-932-5627

SIERRA BULLETS (bullets)
P.O. Box 818
1400 West Henry St.
Sedalia, Missouri 65301
Tel: 816-827-6300 Fax: 816-827-6300

SIGARMS INC. (Sig-Sauer shotguns and
    handguns, Blaser rifles)
Corporate Park
Exeter, New Hampshire 03833
Tel: 603-772-2302 Fax: 603-772-9082

SIMMONS OUTDOOR CORP. (scopes)
2120 Killarney Way
Tallahassee, Florida 32308-3402
Tel: 904-878-5100 Fax: 904-893-5472

SKB SHOTGUNS (shotguns)
4325 South 120th Street
P.O. Box 37669
Omaha, Nebraska 68137
Tel: 800-752-2767 Fax: 402-330-8029

SMITH & WESSON (handguns)
2100 Roosevelt Avenue
Springfield, Massachusetts 01102-2208
Tel: 800-331-0852 Tel: 413-781-8300
Fax: 413-731-8980

SPEER (bullets)
Available through Blount, Inc.

SPRINGFIELD INC. (handguns, rifles,
    Aimpoint scopes and sights)
420 West Main Street
Geneseo, Illinois 61254
Tel: 309-944-5631 Fax: 309-944-3676

STAR (handguns)
Available through Interarms

STEYR-MANNLICHER (rifles)
Available through GSI (Gun South Inc.)

STOEGER INDUSTRIES (American Eagle
    Luger; IGA shotguns; Sako ammo, bullets,
    actions, mounts, rifles; Tikka rifles, shotguns)
5 Mansard Court
Wayne, New Jersey 07470
Tel: 800-631-0722 Tel: 973-872-9500
Fax: 973-872-2230
(See pp. 89, 96 in Manufacturers' Showcase)

STURM, RUGER AND COMPANY, INC.
    (Ruger handguns, rifles, shotguns,
    blackpowder revolver)
Lacey Place
Southport, Connecticut 06490
Tel: 203-259-4537 Fax: 203-259-2167

SWAROVSKI OPTIK NORTH AMERICA
(scopes)
One Wholesale Way
Cranston, Rhode Island 02920
Tel: 800-426-3089 Fax: 401-946-2587

SWIFT BULLET CO. (bullets)
210 Main st., P.O. Box 27
Quinter, Kansas 67752
Tel: 913-754-3959 Fax: 913-754-2359

SWIFT INSTRUMENTS, INC.
    (scopes, mounts)
952 Dorchester Avenue
Boston, Massachusetts 02125
Tel: 800-446-1116 Fax: 617-436-3232

T&T ENTERPRISES (VersaMount handgun
    security boxes)
403 Hogle Street
Weatherford, Texas 76086
Tel: 817-599-9813 Fax: 817-596-5290
(see p. 93 in Manufacturers' Showcase)

TASCO (scopes, mounts)
7600 N.W. 26th Street
Miami, Florida 33122
Tel: 305-591-3670 Fax: 305-592-5895

TAURUS INT'L, INC. (handguns)
16175 N.W. 49th Avenue
Miami, Florida 33014-6314
Tel: 305-624-1115 Fax: 305-623-7506

THOMPSON/CENTER ARMS (handguns,
    rifles, reloading, blackpowder arms)
Farmington Road, P.O. Box 5002
Rochester, New Hampshire 03867
Tel: 603-332-2394 Fax: 603-332-5133

TIKKA (rifles, shotguns)
Available through Stoeger Industries

TRADITIONS, INC. (blackpowder arms)
1375 Boston Post Rd., P.O. Box 235
Deep River, Connecticut 06417
Tel: 203-526-9555 Fax: 203-526-4564

TRIPLE K MANUFACTURING CO. (shooting
    accessories)
2222 Commercial Street
San Diego, California 92113
Tel: 619-232-2066 or 800-521-5062
Fax: 619-232-7675
(See p. 95 in Manufacturers' Showcase)

TRISTAR SPORTING ARMS, LTD.
    (shotguns and rifles)
1814-16 Linn Street
North Kansas City, Missouri 64116
Tel: 816-421-1400 Fax: 816-421-4182

TRIUS PRODUCTS, INC. (traps, targets)
221 South Miami Avenue, P.O. Box 25
Cleves, Ohio 45002
Tel: 513-941-5682 Fax: 513-941-7970

UBERTI USA, INC. (handguns, rifles,
    blackpowder guns). See also American
    Arms, EMF, Navy Arms
362 Limerock Rd., P.O. Box 469
Lakeville, Connecticut 06039
Tel: 860-435-8068

ULTRA LIGHT ARMS COMPANY (rifles)
214 Price Street, P.O. Box 1270
Granville, West Virginia 26534
Tel: 304-599-5687 Fax: 304-599-5687

UNIQUE (handguns, rifles)
Available thru Nygord Precision Products

U.S.A. MAGAZINES, INC. (handgun and
    rifle magazines)
P.O. Box 39115
Downey, California 90239
Tel: 800-872-2577 Fax: 562-903-7857
(See p. 96 in Manufacturers' Showcase)

U.S. REPEATING ARMS CO. (Winchester
    rifles, shotguns)
275 Winchester Avenue
Morgan, Utah 84050
Tel: 801-876-3440 Fax: 801-876-3331

VOLQUARTSEN CUSTOM LTD.
    (custom conversions)
Route 1, P.O. Box 33A
Carroll, Iowa 51401
Tel: 712-792-4238 Fax: 712-792-2542
(See p. 96 in Manufacturers' Showcase)

WALTHER (handguns)
Available through Interarms

WEATHERBY, INC. (rifles, shotguns,
    handguns, ammunition)
3100 El Camino Real
Atascadero, California 93422
Tel: 805-466-1767 Fax: 805-466-2527

WEAVER (scopes, mount rings)
Available through Blount, Inc.

WICHITA ARMS (handguns)
P.O. Box 11371
Wichita, Kansas 67211
Tel: 316-265-0661

WILDEY INC. (handguns)
458 Danbury Road
New Milford, Connecticut 06776
Tel: 860-355-9000 Fax: 860-354-7759

WINCHESTER (ammunition, primers, cases)
Available through Olin/Winchester

WINCHESTER (rifles, shotguns)
Available through U.S. Repeating Arms Co.

ZEISS OPTICAL, INC. (scopes)
1015 Commerce Street
Petersburg, Virginia 23803
Tel: 804-863-1141 Fax: 804-733-4024

CALIBERFINDER

How to use this guide: To find a 22 LR handgun, look under that heading in the HANDGUNS section below. You'll find several models of that description, including the Beretta Model 21 Bobcat Pistol. Next, turn to the GUNFINDER section beginning on p.97, locate the heading for Pistols-Semiautomatic and find Beretta. The Model 21, you'll note, appears on p.105.

HANDGUNS

22 HORNET
Magnum Research Lone Eagle SS Action
MOA Maximum
Thompson/Center Contender Bull Barrel and Super "14"
Uberti 1871 Rolling Block Target

22 LONG RIFLE
American Derringer Models 1, 7, 11, 38 DA Derringer
Beretta Models 21 Bobcat and 89 Gold Standard Pistols, Model 87 Cheetah
Bernardelli Model PO10 Target Pistol
Bersa Model Thunder 22
Browning Buck Mark 22 and 5.5 Target Series (includes Bullseye, Silhouette, Varmint)
Colt .22 Semiauto DA and Target
Davis D-Series
European American Armory Small & Big Bore Bounty Hunter Models
FEG Mark II AP 22
Freedom Arms Model 252 Silhouette & Varmint Class
Hammerli Models 160 Free Pistol, 162 Electronic, 208S Standard Pistol, 280 Target Pistol
Harrington & Richardson Sportsman 999, Models 929 Sidekick, 949 Classic Western and 939 Premier Target
Heritage Rough Rider SA
High Standard Citation, Olympic, Trophy, Victor
Jennings T-22 Target
Magnum Research Mountain Eagle, Target & Compact
New England Firearms Standard Revolver, Ultra/Ultra Mag Revolver
North American Arms Mini-Revolvers and Mini-Master Series;
Rossi Model 515/518
Ruger Bisley SA Target, New Bearcat, Mark II Pistols, New Model Super Single-Six, Model SP101 Revolver
Smith & Wesson Models 17, 22A, 41, 63, 317 Airlite, 317 LadySmith, 617 (K-22 Masterpiece), 2206, 2206 Target, 2213/2214
Taurus Models 94, 96, PT-22
Thompson/Center Contender Bull Barrel, "Super 14" and "16"
Uberti 1871 Rolling Block Target Pistol
Unique Models DES 69U, Int'l Silhouette and Sport
Walther Model TPH DA
Wichita Arms International Pistol

22 RIMFIRE MAGNUM
American Derringer Models 7, 11
AMT 22 Automag II
Davis D-Series Derringer, Long-Bore D-Series, Big Bore
Freedom Arms Model 252
Heritage Rough Rider Revolver
North American Mini-Revolver and Mini-Master Series
Rossi Model 515/518 Revolver
Smith & Wesson Model 651 Kit Gun
Taurus Models 94 and 941 Revolver; Model 96
Uberti 1871 Rolling Block Target

Unique Model International Silhouette & Sport
Wichita Arms International Pistol

22 SHORT
Harrington & Richardson Model 929 Sidekick, Model 949 Classic Western, 939 Premier Target, Sportsman 999
High Standard Olympic Rapid Fire Pistol
New England Firearms Standard, Ultra/Ultra Mag.
North American Arms Mini-Revolvers
Unique Model DES 2000U Pistol

22 WIN. MAG.
American Derringer Model 1, 6
European American Armory Big and Small Bounty Hunter Models
Davis Long-Bore D-Series, D-Series Derringers, Big Bore D-Series
Heritage Rough Rider Revolver
MOA Maximum Single Shot Pistol
New England Firearms Ultra Revolver
North American Mini-Revolvers and Mini-Master Series
Thompson/Center Contender Bull Barrel
Uberti 1871 Rolling Block Target Pistol
Unique Int'l Silhouette and Sport Pistols

22-250
Magnum Research Lone Eagle Single Shot
Savage Arms "Striker" Models 510F, 516FSS, 516FSAK
Thompson/Center Encore
Weatherby Mark V CFP

223 REMINGTON
Magnum Research Lone Eagle SS Action
Thompson/Center Contender Bull Barrel, Encore, Hunter, "Super 14" and "16"

223 REM. COMM. AUTO
American Derringer Model 1

243
Magnum Research Lone Eagle SS Action
Savage Arms Models 510F, 516FSS, 516FSAK
Thompson/Center Encore

25 AUTO
Beretta Model 21 Bobcat, Model 950 Jetfire
Davis D-Series Derringers
Heritage Model H25S Semiauto
KBI Model PSP-25 Pistol
Precision Small Arms Model PSA-25 Pistol
Taurus Model PT-25
Walther Model TPH Pistol
Weatherby Mark V CFP

260 REM
Thompson/Center Encore

270 WIN.
Thompson/Center Encore

7mm BR
Magnum Research Lone Eagle SS Action
Thompson/Center Encore
Wichita Silhouette Pistol

7mm T.C.U.
Thompson/Center Contender Bull Barrel
Unique International Silhouette

7mm SUPER MAG.
Wichita Arms International Pistols

7mm-08
Magnum Research Model Lone Eagle Pistol & Lone Eagle SS Barreled Action
Thompson/Center Encore
Weatherby Mark V CFP

7x30 WATERS
Thompson/Center Super "14"
Wichita Arms International Pistol

30 CARBINE
American Derringer Model 1
AMT Automag III Pistol
Ruger New Model Blackhawk SA Revolver

30-06
Magnum Research Lone Eagle Pistol & Lone Eagle SS Barreled Action
Thompson/Center Encore

30-30 WIN.
American Derringer Model 1
Magnum Research Lone Eagle SS Action
Thompson/Center Contender Bull Barrel, Super "14"
Wichita Arms International Pistol

300 WHISPER
Thompson/Center Contender Super "14" and Bull Barrel

308 WINCHESTER
Magnum Research Lone Eagle Pistol & Lone Eagle SS Barreled Action
Savage "Striker" Models 510F, 516FSS, 516FSAK
Thompson/Center Encore
Weatherby Mark V CFP
Wichita Arms Silhouette Pistol

32 AUTO
Beretta Model 3032 Tomcat
Davis D-Series Derringers, Model P-32
Hammerli U.S.A. Model 280 Target
Sig-Sauer Model P232
Walther Model PPK & PPK/S

32 H&R MAGNUM
Davis Big-Bore D-Series Derringer, Long Bore D-Series
New England Firearms Lady Ultra
Wichita International Pistol

32 MAGNUM
American Derringer Models 1, 7, 11, Lady Derringer
Ruger Model SP101

32 S&W LONG
American Derringer Model 7
Hammerli Model 280 Target Pistol

32-20
American Derringer Model 1

35 REMINGTON
Magnum Research Lone Eagle SS Action

357 MAGNUM
American Arms Regulator Revolver, Mateba
American Derringer Models 1, 4, 6, 7, 11, 38 DA, Lady Derringer
Colt King Cobra, Python Elite Revolvers
Coonan Arms 357 Mag. Pistol & "Cadet" Compact
Downsizer Model WSP
EMF/Dakota Model 1873 Sixshooter, Single Action, 1890 Remington Police, Hartford Scroll Engraved Revolvers
European American Armory Big Bore Bounty Hunter, Windicator DA
Freedom Arms Model 353, Silhouette/Competition Models, Model 1997 Premier Grade
L.A.R. Mark I Grizzly Pistol
Magnum Research Desert Eagle Mark XIX Component System Pistol
Rossi Model 971 and 971 Compact, Model 877, Cyclops
Ruger New Model Blackhawk, Model GP-100, Model SP101, Bisley-Vaquero SA, Bisley SA Target Revolvers
Sig-Sauer Model P229 Pistol
Smith & Wesson Models 13 Military & Police, 19, LadySmith 36 and 60, Model 65 HB and LadySmith, 66, 586, 640 Centennial, 649 Bodyguard, 686, 686 Plus, 686 Powerport
Taurus Models 605, 606, 607, 608, 640 Centennial, 669, 689 Stainless
Thompson/Center Contender Bull Barrel Pistol
Uberti 1871 Rolling Block Target Pistol; 1873 Cattleman & 1875 Outlaw Revolvers
Unique Model Int'l Silhouette Pistol
Wichita Arms International Pistol

357 MAXIMUM
American Derringer Models 1, 4
Thompson/Center Contender Super "14"

357 SIG
AMT Backup Pistol
Laseraim Series III High Speed
Sig-Sauer Models P226, P239 Pistols

358 WINCHESTER
Magnum Research Lone Eagle SS Action
MOA Maximum Pistol

38 S&W
Smith and Wesson Models 10, 13, 14, 15, 36, 38 Bodyguard, 60, 64, 65, Model 442, Model 638, Model 649, LadySmith Models 36-LS and 60-LS Revolvers

38 SPECIAL
American Derringer 1, 7, 10, 11, Lady Derringer, DA 38, TexasDouble Derringer Comm.
Colt King Cobra DA, Python Elite DA, DS II Revolver
Davis Big-Bore D-Series, Long-Bore D-Series
European American Armory Windicator DA
Heritage Sentry DA Revolver
KBI Armscor Model M-2000DC
Rossi Models 68, M88, 851, Lady Rossi Revolvers
Smith & Wesson Models 10 & 13 Military & Police, Model 14 K-38 Masterpiece, Model 15 Combat Masterpiece, Model 19 & 66 Combat Magnum, Models 36 Chiefs Special, Models 36-LS & 60-LS LadySmith, Models 37 & 637 Chiefs Special Airweight, Model 38 and 638 Bodyguard Airweight, Models 49 & 649 Bodyguard, Model 64 Military & Police, Models 65 Heavy Barrel and LadySmith, Model 66 Combat, Model 67, Models 442 & 642 Centenial Airweight, Model 586

Distinguished Combat Magnum, Model 640 Centennial, Models 686, 686 Plus, 686 Powerport Revolvers
Taurus Models 82, 85, 606

38 SUPER
American Derringer Model 1
AMT Backup
Colt Combat Commander MKIV Series '80
Entreprise Tournament Shooters Models I, II, III
European American Armory Witness, Gold & Silver Teams
Ruger Model SP101
Sig-Sauer Model 220 "American" Pistol
Springfield Model 1911-A1 Standard Mil-Spec, Standard and Lightweight; PDP Series (Factory Comp, High-Capacity Factory Comp Pistols)

38-40
Colt Single Action Army Revolver
EMF/Dakota Model 1873, Hartford Model Revolvers

380 AUTO
American Arms Escort Pistol
American Derringer Models 1, 7 and 11
AMT Model Backup Pistol, 380 Backup II
Beretta Cheetah Models 84, 85 and 86 Pistols
Bernardelli PO18 Compact Target Pistol
Bersa Model Thunder 380, Series 95 Pistols
Browning Model BDA-380 Pistol
Colt Government Model, Mustang, Mustang Plus II, Mustang PocketLite 380 Pistols, Gov't 380 MK IV Pony Series 90
Davis P-380 Pistol
Downsizer Model WSP
European American Armory European SA Compact
FEG Models Mark II APK/AP
Hi-Point 380 Polymer Pistol
KBI FEG SMC Auto Pistol, FEG Model SMC-380
Llama Small Frame Automatic (Micro-Max)
Sig-Sauer Model 232 Pistol
Smith & Wesson Sigma Compact Series
Taurus Model PT-938 Compact
Walther Model PP DA, Model PPK and PPK/S

9mm PARABELLUM (LUGER)
American Derringer Model 1, Model DA 38 Double Derringer
Beretta Cougar Series (Compact Frame & Mini-Cougar), Models 92 FS, 92D, Centurion, Brigadier
Bernardelli Model PO18 Target and Compact Target Pistols
Bersa Thunder 9 DA Pistol
Browning 9mm Hi-Power, Model BDM DA
Davis Long-Bore D-Series, Big Bore D-Series
Downsizer Model WSP
European American Armory Witness, Witness Gold Team, Witness Silver Team, Witness Subcompact
Glock Model 26
Heckler and Koch Models P7M8, USP 9 & 40 Universal, Compact Universal, USP 45 Universal Self-Loading
Heritage Stealth Compact
Hi-Point Firearms Model 9mm Compact
Israel Arms & Firearms Models M-1500 & M-2500
Jennings Lazer Nine, Nine
Kahr Models K9, MK9 Micro-Compact, Lady K9
KBI Model PJK-9HP
Llama Maxi-1 (9 shot) Compact & Gov't
Ruger P-Series Pistols, SP101 Spurless DA
Sig-Sauer Models 210, 225, P229, P232, P239
Smith & Wesson Models 900 Series, 910, Model 940 Centennial, Model 3900 Compact Series, 5900 and 6900 Compact Series, Sigma Series Pistols, TSW Tactical Series
Springfield Model 1911-A1, Standard & Lightweight, High Capacity Ultra Compact, Trophy Match Bi-Tone
Stoeger American Eagle Luger
Taurus Models PT92, PT99, PT-911 Compact and PT-111
Walther Models P 5, P 88 Compact, P 99 Compact

10mm
American Derringer Model 1
Glock Model 29 Subcompact
L.A.R. Mark I Grizzly Pistol
Laseraim Technologies Laseraim Series
Smith & Wesson Model 610 Classic Hunter

40 AUTO
Beretta Cougar Series (Model 8040)
Ruger P-Series Pistols
Safari Arms Cohort, Enforcer, Matchmaster

400 COR-BON
AMT Backup DAO
Laseraim Series I, III Velocity High Speed

40 S&W
American Arms Aussie Semiauto
American Derringer Model 1, 38 DA Derringer
AMT Commando
Beretta Model 92/96 Series, Cougar Series (Compact Frame & Mini-Cougar)
Bernardelli Model P.018 Compact Target
Browning Hi Power SA
Downsizer Model WSP
Entreprise Tournament Shooters Models I, II, III
European American Armory Witness, Witness Fab, Gold & Silver Teams, Subcompact
Glock Models 22, 23, 27
Heckler and Koch HK USP 9 and 40 Universal, Compact Universal
Heritage Stealth Compact
Hi-Point Model 40
Israel Arms & Firearms Model 1500 & 2500
J.O. Arms Golan DA
Kahr Model K9, Lady K9
Laseraim Series I
Para-Ordnance Models P10, P14, P15 & P16
Sig-Sauer Model P226, 229, 239 Pistols
Smith & Wesson Model 410, Model 4000 Compact Series and Full Size, Sigma Series, TSW Tactical Series
Taurus Model PT-940

41 MAGNUM
American Derringer Model 1
Freedom Arms Silhouette/Competition, Model 555 Premier & Field Grades
Smith & Wesson Model 657 Stainless

.410
American Derringer Models 4 and 6

44 MAGNUM
American Derringer Models 1, 4
Colt Anaconda Revolver
European American Armory Big Boar Bounty Hunter
Freedom Arms 454 Casull and Model 555 Premier and Field Grades, Silhouette/Competition Models
Magnum Research Desert Eagle Mark XIX Component System, Lone Eagle SS Action
Ruger Redhawk, Super Redhawk, Super Redhawk Stainless, New Model Super Blackhawk SA, Bisley SA Target, Vaquero SA Revolvers
Smith & Wesson Model 29, Models 629, 629 Classic & Powerport; Series 4500 Compacts
Taurus Model 44 Revolver
Thompson/Center Contender Bull Barrel & Hunter, "Super 14", Encore
Unique Int'l Silhouette Pistol

440 COR BON/MARLIN
Magnum Research Lone Eagle Single Shot Action, One Pro Pistol
Thompson/Center Encore

44 SPECIAL
American Arms Regulator Deluxe
American Derringer Models 1, 7

Colt Anaconda
Rossi Model 720
Smith & Wesson Model 29, Models 629, 629 Classic and Powerport
Taurus Model 445 DA

44-40
American Arms Regulator SA and Deluxe
American Derringer Model 1, Texas Double Derringer Commemorative
EMF/Dakota Hartford Scroll Engraved SA, Models 1873, Sixshooter, Single Action 1873 Dakota SA, 1875 Outlaw, 1890 Remington Police
Navy Arms Replicas 1873 Colt-style SA, 1875 Schofield, Bisley Model SA
Ruger Vaquero SA Revolver
Uberti 1873 Cattleman, 1875 Outlaw/1890 Police Revolvers

444 MARLIN
Magnum Research Lone Eagle SS Action

45 ACP (AUTO)
American Derringer Models 1, 4, 6, 10
AMT Backup, Longslide, 1911 Government, 1911 Hardballer Models, Accelerator
Auto-Ordnance Model 1911A1 Thompson
Beretta Compact Frame Cougar (Model 8045)
Brolin Arms Legend, Gold and TAC-11 Models
Colt Anaconda, Combat Commander, Gold Cup Trophy, Match, Government Model, Model 1991A1 (Compact and Commander), Officer's ACP, Defender Lightweight Carry Series, Custom Tactical Models
Entreprise Elite P500, Tactical P500, Boxer P500, Tournament Shooters' Models I, II, III
European American Armory Big Boar Bounty Hunter, Witness, Gold and Silver Team, Subcompact
Downsizer Model WSP
Glock Model 21 Pistol, 30 Subcompact
Heckler and Koch Model HK USP Match, USP 45 Universal, Mark 23 Special Operations
Hi-Point Model 380 Polymer
Israel Arms & Firearms Model M-5000
Kimber Model Classic Series .45 (Custom, Custom Stainless, Custom Royal, Compact Stainless, Gold Match, Custom Target), Polymer Series
L.A.R. Mark I Grizzly Pistol
Laseraim Technologies Series I
Llama Maxi-I (7-shot) Compact & Gov't
Magnum Research One Pro 45 Pistol
Para-Ordnance Models P10, P12, P13, P14
Ruger P-Series Pistols
Safari Arms Cohort, Enforcer, Matchmaster
Sig-Sauer Model 220 American
Smith & Wesson Model 457, Model 625, Model 4500 Series Compact/Full Size, TSW Tactical Series
Springfield 11911-A1 Champion Series (Compact Mil-Spec, Lightweight Compact, Ultra Compact, Mil-Spec Champion), PDP Series High Capacity Factory Comp, Defender), Model 1911-A1 Standard, Mil-Spec, Lightweight Compact, Trophy Match, Ultra Compact Series, Super Tuned Series, 1911-A1 Bureau Model
Taurus Model PT-945
Uberti 1873 Cattleman, 1875 Outlaw/1890 Police

45 COLT
American Arms Regulator SA and Deluxe
American Derringer Lady Derringer, Models 1, 4, 6, 10, Texas Double Derringer Commemorative
Colt Single Action Army Revolver, Anaconda
EMF/Dakota Hartford Models (Artillery, Buntline Single Action, Sixshooter, Bisley, Cavalry Colt), 1893 Hartford Express Models 1873, 1873 Dakota SA, 1875 "Outlaw," Model 1890 Remington Police, Pinkerton Detective SA
European American Armory Big Bore Bounty Hunter

Navy Arms Replicas 1873 Colt-style SA, 1873 U.S. Cavalry, 1873 Pinched Frame SA, Flat Top Target Model SA, 1875 Schofield, Bisley Model SA, 1895 U.S. Artillery
Ruger Model Bisley SA Target, New Model Blackhawk, Vaquero, Stainless Redhawk, Vaquero SA and Bisley-Vaquero
Thompson/Center Contender Bull Barrel, Encore, Super "16"
Uberti 1873 Cattleman, 1875 Outlaw/1890 Police

45 WIN. MAG.
AMT Automag IV
American Derringer Model 1
L.A.R. Mark I Grizzly
Wildey Hunter and Survivor Pistols

45-70 GOV'T.
American Derringer Models 1 and 4
Thompson/Center Encore, Contender Super "16"

454 CASULL
American Arms Uberti SA
Freedom Arms 454 Casull, Model 555 Field and Premier Grades
Taurus "Raging Bull" DA

475 WILDEY MAG.
Wildey Hunter and Survivor Pistols

50 MAG. AE
Freedom Arms 454 Casull, Model 555 Premier & Field Grades
L.A.R. Grizzly 50 Mark 5
Magnum Research Desert Eagle Mark XIX Component System

RIFLES

CENTERFIRE BOLT ACTION STANDARD CALIBERS

17 BEE
Francotte Bolt Action

17 REMINGTON
Cooper Arms Model 21 Varmint Extreme, Custom & Western Classics
Sako Deluxe, Super Deluxe; Hunter Lightweight, Varmint
Ultra Light Model 20 Series

22LR
Unique Model T Dioptra Sporter, Model T UIT Standard, T/SM Silhouette

22 HORNET
KBI Model CDGA 4103 Field Grade
Ruger Model 77/22RH Hornet, K77/22VHZ Varmint
Ultra Light Model 20 Series

22 PPC
Cooper Arms Model 21 Benchrest, Varmint Extreme

22-250
AMT Standard Repeaters
A-Square Genghis Khan
Blaser Model R93
Browning A-Bolt II Series (except Gold Medallion)
Dakota 76 Classic Grades: Dakota 97 Varmint & Lightweight Hunter Series (add'l calibers available to 330 Dakota Mag.)
Harris Gunworks Classic Sporters, Stainless, Standard Sporters; Talon Sporter, Varminter
Howa Lightning
Marlin Model MR-7
Remington Models 700 BDL, Varmint LS & Synthetic
Ruger Models M-77VT MKII HB Target, M-77RP MKII All-Weather, K77RBZ
Sako Deluxe, Super Deluxe; Hunter, Varmint, Stainless Synthetic
Sauer Model 90

Savage Models Classic Hunter; Models 112 BVSS & 112FV Varmint, 112FVSS, 11F Hunter, 11G Classic American Hunter
Tikka Continental Varmint, Whitetail Hunter
Ultra Light Model 20 Series
Weatherby Mark V Sporter, Accumark, Stainless Synthetic
Winchester Models 70 Heavy Barrel Varmint, Sharpshooter II SS, Walnut Classic Featherweight

220 SWIFT
Harris Gunworks Varminter
Remington Model 700VS Varmint Synthetic
Ruger Model M-77VT MKII HB Target
Winchester Model 70 Heavy Barrel Varmint

221 FIREBALL
Cooper Arms Model 21 Varmint Extreme

222 REMINGTON
Cooper Arms Model 21 Varmint Extreme
Francotte Bolt Action
Magnum Research Mountain Eagle Varmint
Remington Models 700 ADL, BDL
Sako Deluxe, Super Deluxe; Hunter, Varmint
Ultra Light Model 20 Series

223 REMINGTON
AMT Standard Repeaters
Brown Precision High Country Youth and Tactical Elite
Browning A-Bolt II Series (except Gold Medallion)
Cooper Arms Models 21, Varmint Extreme, Custom & Western Classics Harris Gunworks Varminter
Howa Lightning
Magnum Research Mountain Eagle Varmint Edition
Remington Models Seven Carbine; 700 ADL, BDL; Varmint LS & Synthetic
Ruger Models Mark II M-77R, M-77RL Ultra Light, M-77RP All-Weather, M-77VT HB Target, K-77RBZ
Sako Deluxe, Super Deluxe, Hunter, Varmint
Savage Models 10FP, 110FP and 110FP Tactical, 110CY, 111G, 111F Classic Hunter; 11F Hunter, 112 BT Competition, 112FV/FVSS and 112BVSS Varmint; 116FSS "Weather Warrior", 10GY Ladies/Youth
Tikka Continental Varmint, Whitetail Hunter
Ultra Light Model 20 Series
Winchester Models 70 Ranger, Ranger Ladies/Youth, HB Varmint

243 WINCHESTER
AMT Standard, Repeater
Arnold Arms African Safari, African Synthetic, African Trophy, [note: these models also available in most calibers up to 458 Win. Mag.)
A-Square Genghis Khan
Blaser Model R93
Brown Precision High Country Youth
Browning A-Bolt II Series (except Eclipse, Varmint, Gold Medallion)
Francotte Bolt Action
Harris Gunworks Benchrest; Classic Sporter, Stainless, Standard Sporter; Talon Sporter, Varminter
Howa Lightning
Kongsberg Hunter 393 Series
Lazzeroni Model L2000ST/SA/SP
Marlin Model MR-7
Mauser Model 96, Model M94
Remington Models Seven Carbine, Stainless Synthetic, Youth; 700 BDL, BDL (DM), Mountain(DM), Varmint Synthetic, ADL Snythetic
Ruger Models Mark II M-77R, M-77RS, M-77VT HB & All-Weather
Sako Deluxe, Super Deluxe, Hunter, Stainless Synthetic
Sauer Models 90 & 202

Savage Models 110CY; 111G/111F Classic
  Hunter; 16FSS/116FSS "Weather Warrior",
  10FM Sierra Lightweight, 11G Classic Hunter,
  11F Hunter, 10GY Ladies/Youth
Steyr-Mannlicher SSG, SBS Mannlicher
  European Model
Tikka Whitetail Hunter
Ultra Light Model 20 Series
Unique Model TGC
Weatherby Mark V Sporter, Accumark/Ultra
  Lightweight, Carbine
Winchester Models 70 Classic Compact,
  Heavy Barrel Varmint; Ranger, Ranger Ladies/
  Youth; Classic Featherweight

6mm BR
Harris Gunworks Benchrest; Classic Sporter,
  Stainless, Standard Sporters

6mm PPC
AMT Standard Repeater
Harris Gunworks Benchrest

6mm REMINGTON
Brown Precision High Country Youth
Harris Gunworks Benchrest, Varminter, Classic
  & Stainless Sporter, Talon Sporter
Ruger Model M-77R MK II
Ultra Light Model 20 Series

25-06
AMT Standard Repeater
A-Square Hamilcar, Genghis Kahn
Browning A-Bolt II Composite & Stainless
  Stalker, Hunter, Medallion Harris Gunworks
  Classic Sporter, Stainless, Standard Sporters
Marlin Model MR-7
Mauser Model 96, Model M94
Remington Models 700, BDL, BDL (DM),
  Mountain (DM), Sendero
Ruger Models 77RS MKII, M-77VT MKII HB
  Target & All-Weather
Sako Deluxe, Super Deluxe; Hunter, TRG-S,
  Stainless Synthetic
Sauer Model 90, Model 202
Savage Models 110FP, 111G/111F Classic
  Hunter, 112 FVSS, 112BVSS Varmint
Steyr-Mannlicher SBS Mannlicher European Model
Tikka Whitetail Hunter, Continental Long-Range
  Hunting
Ultra Light Model 24 Series
Weatherby Mark V Sporter, Accumark, Ultra
  Lightweight
Winchester Model 70 Sporter, Ultimate Classic

257 ROBERTS
A-Square Hamilcar, Genghis Kahn
Dakota Arms Model 76 Classic
Harris Gunworks Classic Sporter, Talon
  Sporter, Varminter
Lazzeroni Models 2000 SP/ST
Ruger Model M-77R MKII, M-77RL MKII Ultra Light
Ultra Light Model 20 Series

260 REM.
Remington Mountain Rifle, BDL DM, ADL
  Synthetic, V-LS, Model Seven Carbine, Youth, SS

6.5x08
AMT Standard Repeater

6.5x55mm/SWEDISH
A-Square Hamilcar
Ruger Model M-77R MKII
Sako Model TRG-S Magnum
Winchester Classic Featherweight

6mm REM./BR
Harris Gunworks Classic Sporter

264 WINCHESTER
A-Square Hamilcar, Genghis Kahn
Lazzeroni Models L2000ST/SA/SP

270 WINCHESTER
AMT Standard, Repeater
A-Square Hamilcar
Beretta Mato
Blaser Model R93
Browning A-Bolt II Series (except Micro-
  Medallion, Varmint, Eclipse), Custom Trophy
Dakota Arms Model 76 Classic
Francotte Bolt Action
Harris Gunworks Alaskan; Classic Sporter,
  Stainless, Std. Sporters; Titanium Mtn.
Howa Lightning
Kongsberg Hunter 393 Series
Magnum Research Mountain Eagle
Marlin Model MR-7
Mauser Model 96, M94
Remington Models 700 ADL, BDL, BDL (DM),
  ADL, ADL Synthetic, Mountain (DM)
Ruger Models Mark II Series M-77RP/RSP All-
  Weather, M-77R MKII, M-77 RSM Express,
  M-77R/LR, M-77RL Ultra Light, M-77RS; M-
  77RSI Int'l. Mannlicher, K-77RBZ, K-77RSBZ
Sako Deluxe, Super Deluxe; Hunter, Stainless
  Synthetic, TRG-S
Sauer Models 90, 202, Model SHR 970 Synthetic
Savage Models 110CY; 111G, 111GC, 111F,
  111FAK Express, 111FC Classic Hunter;
  114CE "Classic European," 114CU "Classic
  Ultra"; 116FCS, 116FSK, 116FCS & 116FSS
  "Weather Warrior", 10FM Sierra Lightweight,
  116 Ultra Stainless
Steyr-Mannlicher SBS Mannlicher European,
  Pro Hunter, Forester
Tikka Continental Long-Range Hunting,
  Whitetail Hunter
Ultra Light Model 24 Series
Unique Model TGC
Weatherby Models Mark V Accumark,
  Eurosport, Sporter, Stainless, Synthetic
Winchester Models 70 Classic Series; Classic SM,
  Classic Laminated/Camo, Ultimate Classic, Classic
  Super Grade, Classic Sporter, Ranger, Featherweight,
  Stainless, Black Shadow

280 REMINGTON
A-Square Hamilcar
Beretta Mato
Browning A-Bolt II Composite/Stainless Stalker, Hunter,
  Medallion Dakota Arms Model 76 Classic
Harris Gunworks Classic Sporter, Stainless,
  Standard Sporters; Alaskan, Talon Sporter,
  Titanium Mountain
Magnum Research Mountain Eagle
Remington Models 700 BDL (DM), Mountain (DM)
Ruger Model M-77R MKII, M-77RP MKII All-Weather
Sako Deluxe, Super Deluxe, Hunter
Weatherby Mark V Sporter, Accumark & Accumark
  Ultra Lightweight, Stainless & Synthetic
Winchester Model 70 Classic Featherweight

284 WINCHESTER
Harris Gunworks Classic Sporter, Stainless,
  Standard Sporters; Talon Sporter
Ultra Light Model 20 Series

7mm BR
Harris Gunworks Classic Sporter, Stainless,
  Standard Sporters; Talon Sporter

7mm EXPRESS
Ultra Light Model 24 Series
7mm STW
A-Square Hamilcar
Harris Gunworks Classic Sporter
Winchester Models 70 Custom Classic
  Sporting Sharpshooter II, Classic Sporter,
  Ultimate Classic, Classic Laredo

7x57mm (ACKLEY/MAUSER)
Ruger Model M-77R MKII
Ultra Light Model 20 Series

7mm-08
Brown Precision High Country Youth
Browning A-Bolt II Series (except Gold
  Medallion, Varmint, Eclipse)
Harris Gunworks Classic Sporter, Stainless,
  Standard Sporters; National Match, Talon
  Sporter, Varminter
Remington Models Seven Carbine, Stainless
  Synthetic, Youth; 700 BDL (DM), BDL SS
  (DM), Mountain (DM)
Sako Deluxe, Super Deluxe; Hunter, Stainless
  Synthetic
Savage Models 111G/111F Classic Hunters
Steyr-Mannlicher SBS Mannlicher European
Ultra Light Model 20 Series
Unique Model TGC
Weatherby Mark V Sporter, Accumark &
  Accumark Ultra Lightweight, Carbine,
  Stainless Synthetic
Winchester Model 70 Walnut Classic
  Featherweight, Classic Compact

30-06
AMT Standard Repeater
A-Square Hamilcar
Beretta Mato
Blaser Model R 93
Browning A-Bolt II Series (except Micro
  Medallion, Varmint), Custom Trophy
Dakota Arms Model 76 Classic
Francotte Bolt Action
Harris Gunworks Alaskan; Classic Sporter,
  Stainless, Standard Sporters; Talon Sporter,
  Titanium Mountain
Howa Lightning
Kimber Mauser 98 Sporter
Kongsberg Hunter 393 Series
Magnum Research Mountain Eagle
Marlin Model MR-7B
Mauser Model 96, M94
Remington Models 700 ADL, ADL Synthetic,
  BDL, BDL (DM), BDL SS (DM), BDL Stainless
  Synthetic, Mountain (DM)
Ruger Models Mark II M-77RSM Express, M-
  77R/LR, M-77R MKII, M-77RL Ultra Light, M-
  77RP/RSP All-Weather, M-77RS; M-77RSI
  International Mannlicher, K-77RBZ, K-
  77RSBZ, K-77RSP
Sako Deluxe/Super Deluxe, Hunter, Model TRG-
  S, Stainless Synthetic
Sauer Models 90, 202, Model SHR 970 Synthetic
Savage Models 111F, 111FAK Express, 111FC,
  111G, 111GC Classic Hunters (112FVSS,
  112BVSS, 112FV Varmint); 114CE "Classic
  European," 110FP Tactical; 112FVSS,
  112BVSS Varmint; 116FCS, 116FCSAK,
  116FSK Kodiak, 116FSS, 10FM Sierra
  Lightweight, 116 Ultra Stainless
Steyr-Mannlicher SBS Mannlicher European
Tikka Whitetail Hunter
Ultra Light Model 24 Series
Unique Model TGC
Weatherby Mark V Accumark & Accumark Ultra
  Lightweight, Sporter, Stainless Synthetic
Winchester Models 70 Classic Featherweight
  Series; Sporter, Ultimate Classic,
  Sharpshooter II SS, Ranger, Super Grade,
  Classic Laminated/Camo, Black Shadow

300 SAVAGE
Ultra Light Model 20 Series

300 WINCHESTER
A-Square Hamilcar

308 WINCHESTER
AMT Standard Repeater
Blaser Model R 93
Browning A-Bolt II Short Action Series (except
  Gold Medallion)
Brown Precision High Country Youth, Tactical Elite

Francotte Bolt Action
Harris Gunworks Benchrest; Classic Sporter, Stainless, Standard Sporters; National Match, Talon Sporter, Varminter
Howa Lightning
Kongsberg Hunter 393 Series, Sporter 393 Thumbhole
Lazzeroni Models L2000 SP/SA
Marlin Model MR-7
Mauser Model 96, Model SR 86, M94
Remington Models 700 BDL (DM), BDL SS(DM), Varmint Synthetic and Stainless; Models Seven Carbine, Stainless Synthetic
Ruger Models M-77R, M-77RL Ultra Light, M-77RS, M-77VT HB Target; M-77RSI International Mannlicher
Sako Deluxe/Super Deluxe, Hunter, TRG-21, Stainless Synthetic
Sauer Models 90, 202
Savage Models 110CY; 110FP Tactical; Models 112FVSS & 112BVSS Varmint; 112BT Competition; 116 FSS "Weather Warrior", 10FP Tactical (short action), 15FSS Weather Warrior, 10FM Sierra Lightweight, 11F Hunter, 11G Classic Hunter, 10GY Ladies/Youth
Steyr-Mannlicher SSG Model, SBS Mannlicher European, Scout
Tikka Continental Varmint, Whitetail Hunter
Ultra Light Model 20
Unique Model TGC
Weatherby Mark V Sporter, Accumark & Ultra Lightweight, Carbine, Stainless & Synthetic
Winchester Models 70 Custom Classic Sharpshooter II SS; Heavy Barrel Varmint; Ranger Ladies/Youth; Classic Featherweight, Classic Compact

338-06
A-Square Hamilcar

35 WHELEN
Harris Gunworks Classic Sporter, Stainless Sporter, Alaskan
Winchester Model 70 Ultimate Classic

358 WINCHESTER
Ultra Light Model 20 Series

9.3x62mm
A-Square Hamilcar

CENTERFIRE BOLT ACTION MAGNUM CALIBERS

22 MAG.
Unique Model T Dioptera Sporter, T/SM Silhouette

222 REM. MAG.
Cooper Arms Model 21 Varmint Extreme
Ultra Light Model 20 Series

240 WBY. MAG.
Weatherby Mark V Sporter, Accumark & Ultra Lightweight, Stainless & Synthetic

243 Mag.
Arnold Arms Serengeti Synthetic (available also in other magnum calibers to 300 Mag.)

257 WBY. MAG
Arnold Arms Alaskan Synthetic, Alaskan Guide
Blaser Model R93
Harris Gunworks Classic Sporter, Stainless, Talon Sporter
Weatherby Models Mark V Accumark, Deluxe, Euromark, Eurosport, Lazermark, Stainless, Sporter, Synthetic

264 WIN. MAG.
Ultra Light Arms Model 28 Series
Winchester Models 70 Sporter, Ultimate Classic

270 WBY./WIN. MAG.
Sako Hunter, TRG-S Magnum, Deluxe, Super Deluxe
Winchester Models 70 Classic Sporter

7mm REM. MAG./7mm WBY. MAG.
AMT Standard Repeater
A-Square Caesar, Hamilcar
Beretta Mato
Blaser Model R93
Browning A-Bolt II Series (except Micro Medallion, Varmint), Custom Trophy
Dakota Arms Model 76 Classic Grade
Harris Gunworks Alaskan; Classic Sporter, Stainless, Standard Sporters; Long Range, Titanium Mountain
Howa Lightning
Kimber Mauser 98 Sporter
Kongsberg Hunter 393 Series
Magnum Research Mountain Eagle
Mauser Model 96, M94
Remington Models 700 ADL, ADL Synthetic, BDL, BDL (DMB),BDL SS (DM), BDL DM, BDL Synthetic; African Plains, Alaskan Wilderness, Sendero
Ruger Models Mark II M-77RSM Express, M-77R/LR, M-77RS, M-77RS/RSP All-Weather, K-77 RBZ, K-77 RSBZ, K-77RSP
Sako Deluxe/Super Deluxe, Hunter, Stainless Synthetic, TRG-S Magnum Sauer Models 90, 202
Savage Models 110 FP Tactical; 111GC, 111G, 111F, 111FC Classic Hunters; 112 FVSS, 112BVSS Varmint; 114CE "Classic European," 116FSK/FCSZK/116FSS "Weather Warrior", 116 Ultra Stainless
Tikka Continental Long-Range Hunting, Whitetail Hunter
Ultra Light Arms Model 28 Series
Unique Model TGC
Weatherby Mark V Accumark, Deluxe, SLS, Eurosport, Lazermark, Sporter, Stainless, Synthetic
Winchester Models 70 Ultimate Classic, Classic/Boss Stainless, Classic Sporter, Classic Laredo, Classic Featherweight/Boss All-Terrain, Classic Super Grade, Classic Laminated & Camo, Black Shadow

7mm STW
A-Square Caesar Model
Harris Gunworks Talon Sporter
Remington Sendero
Sako TRG-S Magnum, Hunter, Stainless Synthetic, Deluxe, Super Deluxe
Winchester Model 70 Classic Laredo

8mm REM. MAG.
A-Square Caesar and Hannibal
Remington Model 700 Safari, Safari KS, Classic

30-378
Sako Model TRG-S

300 H&H/DAKOTA MAGNUM
Dakota Arms Long Bow Tactical E.R.
Harris Gunworks Alaskan; Classic Sporter, Stainless, Standard Sporters; Talon Safari, Talon Sporter, Titanium Mountain
Winchester Model 70 Ultimate Classic

300 PEGASUS
A-Square Hannibal

300 PHOENIX
Harris Gunworks Long Range, Talon Safari, .300 Phoenix

300 WBY. MAG.
A-Square Caesar
Blaser Model 93
Harris Gunworks Classic Sporter, Stainless,

Standard Sporters; Alaskan, Talon Sporter, Titanium Mountain, Talon Safari
Magnum Research Mountain Eagle
Remington Models 700 BDL (DM), Sendero, African Plains, Alaskan Wilderness
Sako Deluxe/Super Deluxe, Hunter, Model TRG-S
Sauer Model 90, Model 202
Ultra Light Arms Model 40 Series
Weatherby Models Mark V Accumark, Deluxe, SLS, Euromark, Eurosport, Lazermark, Sporter, Stainless, Synthetic
Winchester Model 70 Classic Sporter, Ultimate Classic

300 WIN. MAG.
AMT Standard Repeater
Arnold Arms Alaskan Rifle, Alaskan Trophy, Grand Alaskan, Alaskan Synthetic, Serengeti, Synthetic
A-Square Caesar
Beretta Mato
Blaser Model R93
Brown Precision Tactical Elite
Browning A-Bolt II Series (except Micro Medallion, Varmint); Custom Trophy
Dakota Arms Model 76 Safari & Classic Grades
Francotte Bolt Action
Harris Gunworks Alaskan; Classic Sporter, Stainless Sporters; Talon Safari, Talon Sporter, Titanium Mountain, Long Range
Howa Lightning
Kimber Mauser 98 Sporter
Kongsberg Hunter 393 Series
Magnum Research Mountain Eagle
Mauser Model 96, M94
Remington Models 700 BDL, BDL (DM), BDL SS, BDL SS (DM) African Plains, Alaskan Wilderness, Classic, Sendero
Ruger Models Mark II M-77R, M-77R/LR, M-77RS, M-77RS/RSP All-Weather, M-77EXP Express, K-77RBZ, K-77RSP
Sako Deluxe/Super Deluxe, Hunter, Stainless Synthetic, TRG-S Magnum Sauer Models 90, 202
Savage Models 110 FP Tactical; 112 FVSS, 112BVSS Varmint; 114CE "Classic European," 116FCS, 116 FSS, 116FSK/FCSAK "Weather Warrior"; 116 Ultra Stainless
Tikka Continental Long-Range Hunting, Whitetail Hunter
Ultra Light Arms Model 28 Series
Unique Model TGC
Weatherby Models Mark V Accumark, SLS, Eurosport, Sporter, Stainless, Synthetic
Winchester Models 70 Classic/Boss Stainless, Classic Featherweight/Boss All-Terrain, Classic Laredo, Classic Sporter, Sporting Sharpshooter II, Super Grade, Ultimate Classic, Custom Fluted Take-Down, Laminated & Camo

308 WIN. MAG.
Remington BDL SS, BDL
Ruger Model K-77RSBZ, M77 All-Weather

308 NORMA
Remington Model 700 Classic

330 DAKOTA MAGNUM
Dakota Arms Long Bow Tachtical E.R.

338 A-SQUARE MAG.
A-Square Caesar, Hannibal

338 LAPUA MAG.
Dakota Arms Long Bow Tachtical E.R.
Harris Gunworks Long Range, Talon Safari
Sako Model TRG-S, TRG-21

338 WIN. MAG.
AMT Standard Repeater
Arnold Arms Alaskan Guide, Alaskan Synthetic, Grand African, Grand Alaskan
A-Square Caesar, Hannibal

Beretta Mato
Blaser Model R93
Browning A-Bolt II Series (except Micro Medallion, Gold Medallion, Varmint, Eclipse)
Dakota Arms Model 76 Safari & Classic Grades
Francotte Bolt Action
Harris Gunworks Classic Sporter, Stainless, Standard Sporters; Talon Safari, Talon Sporter, Titanium Mountain
Howa Lightning
Kimber Mauser 98 Sporter
Kongsberg Hunter 393 Series
Lazzeroni Models L2000 SP/SA
Magnum Research Mountain Eagle
Remington Models 700 African Plains, Alaskan Wilderness, BDL, BDL SS (DM), Classic
Ruger Models Mark II M-77R, M-77RSM Express, Mark II All-Weather, M-77RS, K-77RBZ, K-77RSBZ
Sako Deluxe/Super Deluxe, Hunter, Stainless Synthetic, TRG-S Magnum
Sauer Model 90
Savage Model 116FSK, 116FSS "Weather Warrior"; 116SE
Ultra Light Arms Model 28 Series
Weatherby Models Mark V SLS, Eurosport, Sporter, Stainless, Synthetic
Winchester Models 70 Classic/BOSS SM, Sporter, Super Grade, Ultimate Classic, Classic Laminated

340 WBY. MAG.
A-Square Caesar and Hannibal
Harris Gunworks Alaskan; Classic Sporter, Stainless, Standard Sporters; Talon Safari, Talon Sporter, Titanium Mountain
Magnum Research Mountain Eagle
Sako Hunter, TRG-S Magnum, Deluxe, Super Deluxe
Weatherby Models Mark V Deluxe, Lazermark, Euromark, Sporter, SLS, Accumark, Eurosport, Stainless, Synthetic

35 WHELEN
Harris Gunworks Talon Sporter, Titanium Mountain

350 REM. MAG.
Harris Gunworks Classic Sporter, Stainless, Standard Sporters; Talon Sporter, Varminter

357 MAG.
Magnum Research Mountain Eagle

358 WIN./NORMA
A-Square Hannibal
Harris Gunworks Alaskan, Classic Sporter, Titanium Mountain

358 STA
A-Square Caesar, Hannibal
Harris Gunworks Classic Sporter, Talon Sporter, Titanium Mountain

375 A-SQUARE MAG.
A-Square Caesar and Hannibal Models

375 H&H/DAKOTA MAGNUM
AMT Standard Repeater
A-Square Caesar, Hannibal
Beretta Mato
Blaser Model Safari
Browning Stainless Stalker
Dakota Arms Model 76 Safari, Classic Grades; Dakota 97 Varmint Hunter
Francotte Bolt Action
Harris Gunworks Alaskan; Classic Sporter, Stainless, Standard Sporters; Titanium Mountain, Talon Safari, Talon Sporter
Lazzeroni Models L2000 SP/ST
Magnum Research Mountain Eagle
Remington Models 700 African Plains, Alaskan Wilderness, Safari, Safari KS

Rifles, Inc. Lightweight Strata Stainless, Model 700 BDL SS
Ruger 77RSM MKII Magnum
Sako Deluxe/Super Deluxe, Hunter, Stainless Synthetic, TRG-S Magnum Sauer Models 90 and 202
Weatherby Models Mark V Euromark, Eurosport, Sporter, Stainless, Synthetic
Winchester Models 70 Custom Take-Down, Classic Super Express, Custom Classic Express

375 J.R.S.
A-Square Caesar, Hannibal

375 WEATHERBY
A-Square Caesar, Hannibal

375 WIN. MAG.
Sauer Model 202

378 WIN./WBY. MAG.
A-Square Hannibal
Harris Gunworks Talon Safari
Weatherby Models Mark V Deluxe, Euromark, Lazermark

404 JEFFERY
Dakota Arms 76 African Grade
Harris Gunworks Talon Safari

416 REM./WBY. MAG.
AMT Standard Repeater
Blaser Model R93
Harris Gunworks Alaskan; Classic Sporter, Stainless, Std. Sporters; Titanium Mountain, Talon Safari & Sporter
Lazzeroni Model L2000 SP/ST
Magnum Research Mountain Eagle
Remington Model 700 Safari, Safari KS
Sako Deluxe/Super Deluxe, Hunter, TRG-S Magnum
Weatherby Models Mark V Deluxe, Euromark, Lazermark
Winchester Models 70 Custom Classic Express, Custom Classic Super Express, Custom Take-Down

416 RIGBY/DAKOTA
AMT Standard Repeater
A-Square Hannibal
Dakota Arms 76 African Grade
Francotte Bolt Action
Harris Gunworks Talon Safari
Ruger 77RSM MKII Magnum
Ultra Light Arms Model 40 Series

416 TAYLOR and HOFFMAN
A-Square Caesar, Hannibal
Harris Gunworks Classic Sporter, Stainless Sporter, Alaskan, Talon Safari and Sporter, Titanium Mountain

425 EXPRESS
A-Square Caesar, Hannibal

44 MAG.
Ruger Model 77/44

450 ACKLEY/DAKOTA
A-Square Caesar, Hannibal
Dakota Arms 76 African Grade

458 WIN. MAG./LOTT
AMT Standard Repeater
Arnold Arms African Safari, Synthetic & Trophy; Alaskan Rifle, Synthetic, Trophy; Grand African & Alaskan
A-Square Caesar, Hannibal
Dakota Arms Model 76 Classic, Safari Grades
Francotte Bolt Action
Harris Gunworks Classic Sporter, Stainless; Talon Safari, Titanium Sporter, Titanium Mountain
Remington Models 700 Safari, Safari KS

Ruger Model M-77RS MKII
Sauer Safari
Savage Model 116SE Safari Express
Winchester Models 70 Custom Classic Express, Classic Super Express

460 SHORT
A-Square Caesar

460 WIN./WBY. MAG.
A-Square Hannibal
Francotte Bolt Action
Harris Gunworks Talon Safari
Weatherby Models Mark V Deluxe, Lazermark

470 CAPSTICK
A-Square Caesar, Hannibal

495 A-SQUARE MAG.
A-Square Caesar and Hanibal

505 GIBBS
Francotte Bolt Action

CENTERFIRE LEVER ACTION

22-250 REM.
Browning Model Lightning BLR

243 WINCHESTER
Browning Model Lightning BLR

270 WINCHESTER
Browning Model Lightning BLR
Winchester Model 1895 Grade 1

7mm-08 REM.
Browning Lightning BLR

300 Win. Mag.
Browning Lightning BLR

30-06 SPRGFLD.
Browning Lightning BLR
Winchester Model 1895 Grade 1, High Grade

30-30 WINCHESTER
Marlin Models 30AS, 336CS
Winchester Models 94 Checkered Walnut, Legacy, Ranger Compact, Ranger, Black Shadow, Trapper Carbine, Wrangler

307 WINCHESTER
Winchester Model 94 Big Bore Walnut

308 WINCHESTER
Browning Model Lightning BLR

35 REMINGTON
Marlin Model 336CS

356 WINCHESTER
Winchester Model 94 Big Bore Walnut

357 MAGNUM
EMF Model 1873 Sporting
Marlin Model 1894CS, 1894 Cowboy II, 1873 Winchester Sporting Rifle, 1892 Rifle, 1892 Short Rifle
Rossi Models M92 Stainless and SRC
Uberti 1873 Sporting, Carbine
Winchester Model 94 Trapper Carbine, Legacy, Trail's End, Ranger Compact, Model 1892 Grade 1

38 SPECIAL
EMF Model 1866 Yellow Boy Rifle/Carbine, Model 1873 Sporting
Marlin Model 1894CS, 1894 Cowboy II, 1866 Yellowboy Rifle/Carbine Rossi Model M92 SRC, SRS Old West Carbines
Uberti Models 1866 Sporting, Yellowboy Carbine

44 REM. MAG.
Marlin Model 1894S
Rossi Model 92 Old West Carbines (Large Loop & Stainless)
Winchester Model 94 Trapper Carbine, Wrangler, Black Shadow, Legacy, Trail's End

44 S&W SPECIAL
Marlin Model 1894S, 1894 Cowboy II
Winchester Model 94 Trapper Carbine, Wrangler, Black Shadow, Trail's End, Legacy

44-40
American Arms 1860 Henry, 1866 Winchester, 1873 Winchester
EMF Model 1860 Henry, 1866 Yellow Boy Rifle/Carbine, Model 1873 Sporting
Marlin Model 1894 Cowboy II, 1894S
Navy Arms 1866 Yellowboy Rifle/Carbine; Henry Military, Carbine, Iron Frame and Trapper Models, 1873 Winchester-Style and Winchester Sporting, 1892 Rifle, 1892 Brass Frame, 1892 Short
Uberti Model 1866 Sporting and Yellowboy Carbine, 1873 Sporting & Carbine; Henry Rifle Carbine
Winchester Model 94 Trail's End, Model 1892 Grade 1

444 MARLIN
Marlin Model 444SS
Winchester Model 94 Black Shadow, Big Bore

45 COLT
American Arms 1860 Henry, 1866 Winchester, 1873 Winchester & Deluxe
EMF Model 1860 Henry, 1866 Yellow Boy Rifle/Carbine
Marlin Model 1894S, 1894 Cowboy II
Navy Arms 1873 Winchester Sporting, Winchester-Style, Henry Military, 1866 Yellowboy Rifle/Carbine, Models 1892 Rifle/Brass Frame/Short
Rossi Model M92 (Large Loop & Stainless)
Uberti Model 1873 Sporting, Carbine; Henry Rifle
Winchester Model 94 Trapper Carbine, Legacy, Trail's End, Model 1892 Grade 1

45-70 GOV'T.
Marlin Model 1895SS
Winchester Model 1886 High Grade, Grade 1

CENTERFIRE SEMIAUTOMATIC

5.56mm
Springfield Model SAR-4800 Sporter

220 REMINGTON
Kimber Model 84C Classic & SuperAmerica

223 REMINGTON
Colt Competition H-Bar, Competition H-Bar II; Match Target, Match Target H-Bar, Match Target Lightweight, Accurized
Kimber Model 84C Classic, SuperAmerica & Varmint
Ruger K-Mini-14/5, Mini-14/5, Mini-14/5R Ranch

243 WINCHESTER
Browning BAR Mark II Safari
Remington Model 7400
Springfield M1A Standard

25-06
Browning BAR Mark II Safari

270 WIN.
Browning BAR Mark II Safari
Remington Model 7400

280 REM
Remington Model 7400

30-06
Browning BAR Mark II Safari
Remington Model 7400

300 WIN. MAG.
Browning BAR Mark II Safari

308 WINCHESTER
Browning BAR Mark II Safari
Remington Model 7400
Springfield Basic M1A, M1A National Match, M1A Standard, M1A-A1 Bush, Super Match

7.62x39
Colt Match Target Lightweight
Ruger Mini-30
Springfield Models SAR-8 and SAR-4800 Sporters

338 WIN. MAG.
Browning BAR Mark II Safari

40 AUTO
Ruger Model PC9 Carbine

45 ACP
Auto-Ordnance Thompson Models M1 Carbine, 1927A1, 1927A1C Lightweight
Marlin Model 45

7mm REM. MAG.
Browning BAR Mark II Safari

9mm
Colt Match Target Lightweight
Marlin Model 9 Camp Carbine

CENTERFIRE DOUBLE RIFLES

308
Krieghoff Model Classic S/S Standard
Tikka Model 512S

30-06
Krieghoff Models Classic S/S Standard
Tikka Model 512S

7x65R
Francotte Sidelock S/S, Boxlock S/S
Krieghoff Classic S/S Standard

8x57JRS
Francotte Sidelock S/S, Boxlock S/S
Krieghoff Classic S/S Standard
Pedersoli Kodiak Mark IV

8x57RS
Krieghoff Classic S/S Standard

9.3x74R
Francotte Sidelock S/S and Boxlock S/S
Krieghoff Classic S/S Standard
Pedersoli Kodiak Mark IV
Tikka Model 512S

375 FLANGED MAG. N.E.
Krieghoff Classic Side-by-Side

416 RIGBY/N.E.
Krieghoff Classic Side-by-Side

45-70
Navy Arms Deluxe/Kodiak Mark IV
Pedersoli Kodiak Mark IV

470 N.E., 500/416 N.E., 500 N.E.
Krieghoff Classic Side-by-Side

CENTERFIRE/RIMFIRE PUMP ACTION

22 S, L, LR
Remington Model 572 BDL Deluxe Fieldmaster
Rossi Models M62 SAC and SA

22 MAGNUM
Rossi Model 59

243 WIN./270 WIN. (CF)
Browning Model BPR
Dakota Arms Model 10 Single Shot (available in most calibers)
Remington Model 7600 (also calibers 280 Rem., 30-06, 308 Win., 35 Whelen)

308 WIN
Browning Model BPR

30-06
Browning Model BPR

7MM REM. MAG.
Browning Model BPR

300 WIN. MAG
Browning Model BPR

CENTERFIRE/RIMFIRE SINGLE SHOT

17 REMINGTON
Dakota Arms Model 10 (available in most calibers)
Kimber Model 84C Varmint

218 BEE
Ruger No. 1B Standard, No. 1S Medium Sporter

22 HORNET
AMT Single Shot Standard
Browning Model 1885 Low Wall
New England Handi-Rifle, Super Light Youth Handi-Rifle
Ruger No. 1B Standard
Thompson/Center Contender Series
Uberti Model 1871 Rolling Block Baby Carbine

22 MAG.
Marlin Model 25MN
Uberti Model 1871 Rolling Block Baby Carbine

22 PPC
AMT Single Shot Standard

22 S, L, LR
European American Armory HW 660 Weihrauch Rimfire Target
KBI Model M-12Y Youth
Kimber Model 82C SVT
Marlin 15YN "Little Buckaroo," Model 15N, Model 2000L
Remington Models 40-XR BR, 40-XR KS Target Rimfire Position
Savage Mark I-G
Thompson/Center Contender Series
Uberti Model 1871 Rolling Block Baby Carbine
Ultra Light Arms Model 20RF

22-250 REM.
AMT Single Shot Standard
Browning Model 1885 High Wall
Cooper Arms BR-50 Bench Rest, Model 22 Pro Varmint Extreme
Ruger No. 1B Standard, No. 1V Special Varminter
Savage Model 112FVSS, 112BVSS Varmint
Thompson/Center Encore

220 SWIFT
Cooper Arms BR-50 Bench Rest, Model 22 Pro Varmint Extreme
Ruger No. 1B Standard, No. 1V Special Varminter
Savage Models 112BVSS Varmint, 112FVSS

222 REMINGTON
AMT Single Shot Standard

223 REMINGTON
AMT Single Shot Standard
Browning Model 1885 Low Wall
Harrington & Richardson Ultra Varmint

Kimber Model 84C Varmint
New England Handi-Rifle
Ruger No. 1B Standard, No. 1V Special Varminter
Savage Model 112FVSS, 112BVSS Varmint
Thompson/Center Contender Series, Encore

243 WINCHESTER
AMT Single Shot Standard
Browning Model 1885 Low Wall
Cooper Arms BR-50 Bench Rest, Model 22 Pro Varmint Extreme
Harrington & Richardson Ultra Varmint
New England Handi-Rifle
Remington Model 7600
Ruger No. 1A Light Sporter, No. 1B Standard, No. 1 RSI International

25-06
Cooper Arms BR-50 Bench Rest, Model 22 Pro Varmint Extreme
Harrington & Richardson Ultra Single-Shot
Ruger No. 1B Standard, No. 1V Special Varminter

6mm PPC
AMT Single Shot Standard
Cooper Arms BR-50 Bench Rest, Model 22 Pro Varmint Extreme

6mm REMINGTON
Ruger No. 1B Standard, No. 1V Special Varminter

257 ROBERTS
Ruger No. 1B Standard

260 REM.
Thompson/Center Encore

270 WINCHESTER
Browning Model 1885 High Wall
Harrington & Richardson Ultra Comp
New England Handi-Rifle
Remington Model 7600
Ruger No. 1A Light Sporter, No. 1B Standard, No. 1 RSI International
Thompson/Center Encore

280 REMINGTON
New England Handi-Rifle
Remington Model 7600
Ruger No. 1B Standard
Thompson/Center Encore

30-06
Browning Model 1885 High Wall
Harrington & Richardson Ultra Comp
New England Handi-Rifle
Remington Model 7600
Ruger No. 1A Light Sporter, No. 1B Standard, No. 1 RSI International
Thompson/Center Encore

30-30 WIN.
Browning Model 1885 High Wall Traditional Hunter
Harrington & Richardson Whitetails Unlimited 1998 Commemorative Edition
New England Handi-Rifle
Thompson/Center Contender Series

300 WBY. MAG.
Ruger No. 1B Standard

300 WIN. MAG.
Ruger No. 1B Standard, No. 1S Medium Sporter
Savage Models 112FVSS, 112BVSS Varmint

308 WIN.
AMT Single Shot Standard
Cooper Arms BR-50 Bench Rest
Harrington & Richardson Ultra Single-Shot
Remington Model 7600

7mm REM. MAG.
Browning Model 1885 High Wall
Ruger No. 1S Medium Sporter, No. 1B Standard
Thompson/Center Encore

7x57mm
Ruger No. 1A Light Sporter

7mm-08
Thompson/Center Encore

7-30 WATERS
Thompson/Center Contender Series

338 WIN. MAG.
Ruger No. 1S Medium Sporter, No. 1B Standard

357 MAG.
Browning Low Wall Traditional Hunter
Pedersoli Calvary, Infantry, Long Range Creedmoor, Rolling Block Target
Uberti Model 1871 Rolling Block Baby Carbine

357 REM. MAX.
Harrington & Richardson Ultra Single Shot

375 H&H/WIN.
Ruger No. 1H Tropical

40-65
Browning Model 1885 BPCR

416 REM./RIGBY
Ruger No. 1H Tropical

44 REM. MAG.
Browning Low Wall Traditional Hunter
New England Handi-Rifle

45 COLT
Browning Low Wall Traditional Hunter

45-70 GOV'T.
Browning Model 1885 High Wall and BPCR
Navy Arms Remington Style Rolling Block Buffalo, Sharps Buffalo, Sharps Plains, 1873 Springfield Cavalry Carbine/Infantry, 1874 Sharps Cavalry Carbine, 1874 Sharps Sniper, No. 2 Creedmoor Target
New England Handi-Rifle
Pedersoli Calvary, Infantry, Long Range Creemoor, Rolling Block Target
Ruger No. 1S Medium Sporter

458 WIN. MAG.
Ruger No. 1H Tropical

45-90
Navy Arms Sharps Buffalo
10mm MAGNUM
Dakota 10 Magnum

50 BMG
L.A.R. Grizzly Big Boar Competitor

22 LR, 22 HORNET, 223 REM./12 or 20 Ga.
Savage Model 24F

22 LR/.410 Ga.
Springfield Model M-6 Scout

22 Hornet/.410 Ga.
Springfield Model M-6 Scout

45-70 GOVT./20 Ga.
Pedersoli Kodiak Mark IV

22 S, L, LR
Dakota Arms Model 22 LR Sporter
KBI M-12 Y Youth, Model CDGA 4103 Field Grade
Kimber Model 82C Series
Magtech Models MT 122.2.S/R/T
Marlin Models 25N, Model 81TS, 2000L
Remington Models 541-T and 581-S
Ruger Model 77/22 Series
Sako Finnfire
Savage Model 900TR Target Repeater
Ultra Light Arms Model 20, 20RF
Unique Model T Dioptra Sporter, T UIT Standard, T/SM Silhouette
Winchester Model 52B

22 MAGNUM RIMFIRE
Ruger Model 77/22 Series
Unique Model T Dioptera Sporter, Model T/SM Silhouette

22 WMR
Marlin Models 25MN
Remington Model 597 Magnum
Savage Models 93G, 93F, 93FVSS, 93 FSS Stainless, Model 900TR

22 S, L, LR
Browning Model BL-22 (Grades I and II)
Marlin Model Golden 39AS
Uberti Model 1866 Sporting, Yellowboy Carbine
Winchester Model 9422 Series, High Grade Series II, Wintuff, Legacy, Walnut, Trapper

22 MAG. (WMR)
Uberti Model 1866, Yellowboy Carbine
Winchester Models 9422 Walnut, Wintuff, Walnut, Trapper

22 S, L, LR
AMT Target Model
Brown Precision Custom Team Challenger
Browning Model 22 SemiAuto Grades I and VI
Cooper Arms Models 36 Classic, 36RF BR-50, 36RF/CF Featherweight, Custom Classic, Western Classic, Varmint Classic
KBI Models CDGA 6345 Enpire Grade, Standard M-20P
Marlin Models 39AS, 60/60SS, 60SB, 60SSK, 70PSS "Papoose," 795, 7000, 995SS
Remington Model 522 Viper, Model 552 BDL Deluxe Speedmaster, Model 597 Series
Ruger Model 10/22 Carbine Series
Savage Models Mark II-FV Heavy Barrel, Mark II-FSS, Mark II-LV, 64G, 64FV, 64F
Winchester Model 63 Grade 1 & High Grade

22 WMR
AMT Rimfire Magnum
Marlin Models 25MN, 882, 882L, 883, 883 SS, 922 Mag.

BLACKPOWDER HANDGUNS

30
Gonic Arms Model GA-90

31
Colt Blackpowder Colt 1849 Pocket
CVA New Model Pocket, Vest Pocket Derringer, 1849 Baby Dragoon

32

American Frontier Pocket Richards & Mason Navy Conversion, Richards 1861 Model Navy Conversion

36

American Arms 1851 Colt Navy
Armsport Models 5133, 5136
Colt Blackpowder Colt 1851 & 1861 Navy, Trapper Model 1862 Pocket Police, 1861 Custer
CVA Model 1851, Pocket Police
Dixie 1851 Navy Brass Frame Revolver, Spiller and Burr Revolver
EMF 1851 Sheriff's Model, Model 1862 Police, 1851 Navy
Navy Arms 1851 Navy "Yank" Revolver, Reb Sheriff's Model 1860, 1862 New Model Police Revolver, Reb Model 1860
Uberti 1851 and 1861 Navy, 1858 New Navy, Paterson

38

American Frontier 1871-2 Open-Top Frontier & Tiffany Models, Remington New Army Cavalry, Richards 1851 Navy Conversion, 1860 Army Model Conversion, Richards & Mason 1851 Navy Conversion
Dixie Mang Target Pistol

44

American Arms 1858 Remington Army and Army SS Target, 1860 Colt Army
American Frontier 1811-2 Open-Top Frontier & Tiffany Models, Remington New Army Cavalry Model, Richards 1851 Model Navy Conversion, Richards 1860 Army Model Conversion, Richards & Mason 1851 Navy Conversion
Colt Blackpowder Colt Third Model Dragoon, Colt 1860 Army, Colt Model 1860 Army Fluted Cylinder, Colt Cochise Dragoon, Cavalry Model 1860 Army, Colt 1847 Walker, Colt Walker 150th Anniversary Model, Colt 1860 Gold U.S. Cavalry
CVA 1851 and 1861 Navy Brass-Framed Revolvers, Remington Bison, 1858 Remington Army Revolvers, Walker
Dixie Pennsylvania Pistol, Remington 44 Army Revolver, Third Model Dragoon, Walker Revolver, Wyatt Earp Revolver
EMF Model 1860 Army, 1858 Remington Army, 1847 Walker, 1851 Navy, 1848 Dragoon, 1851 Sheriff's Model, Hartford 1863 Texas Dragoon, 1860 Army, 1851 Navy
Euroarms Rogers and Spencer Models 1005, 1006 and 1007, Remington 1858 New Model Army, Models 1020 & 1040, Model 1210 Colt 1860 Army Navy Arms Colt Walker 1847, 1851 Navy "Yank", 1858 Target Model, Reb Model 1860 Revolver, 1860 Army Revolver, Reb 60 Sheriff's Model, Rogers and Spencer Revolver, 1858 Target Remington and Deluxe New Model 1858 Revolvers, Le Mat Revolvers
Uberti 1st and 3rd Model Dragoon, Walker, 1858 Remington New Army, 1860 Army

44-40

Traditions 1875 Schofield

45

Dixie Charles Moore English Dueling Pistol, LePage Percussion Dueling Pistol
Navy Arms Kentucky Pistols
Ruger Old Army Cap & Ball
Traditions Pioneer, Schofield, Thunderer, 1894 Bisley, 1858 STARR DA, Model 1860 Army

50

CVA Kentucky Pistol, Hawken Pistol
Traditions Buckhunter Pro In-Line, Kentucky, William Parker & Trapper Pistols

54

Traditions Buckhunter In-Line Pistol

58

Navy Arms Harpers Ferry Pistol

RIFLES AND CARBINES

32

CVA Varmint
Navy Arms Pennsylvania Long
Thompson/Center Fire Hawk
Traditions Deerhunter

36

Markesbery Black Bear, Grizzly Bear, Brown Bear

40-65

Dixie 1874 Sharps Silhouette

45

Cabela Hawken
Dixie Hawken, Waadtlander, Pennsylvania
Markesbery Black Bear, Grizzly Bear, Brown Bear
Navy Arms Pennsylvania Long
Ruger Old Army Cap & Ball
Thompson/Center Hawken

45-70

Dixie 1874 Sharps Lightweight Target/Silhouette, 1873 Springfield Rifle/Carbine, Officer's Model
Shiloh Sharps Model 1874 Business, 1874 Sporting Rifle No.1 and No.3

45-90

Shiloh Sharps Model 1874 Business, 1874 Sporting Rifle No.1 and No.3

45-120

Shiloh Sharps Model 1874 Business, Sporting Rifle 21 and 23

50

Austin & Halleck Model 320/420, Mountain Rifle
Cabela Hawken, Rolling Black Rifle & Carbine
CVA Accubolt Pro, Firebolt Series, Eclipse Advantage Stag Horn, St. Louis Hawken
Dixie Tennessee Mountain, Hawken
Fort Worth Firearms Rio Grande, Rio Grande In-Line Percussion, Pecos In-Line Percussion; Brazos In-Line
Gonic Arms Model 93 Rifle Series; Mountain Classic, Magnum, Safari Classic, Deluxe
Lyman Trade Rifle, Deerstalker Rifle and Carbine, Great Plains, Cougar In-Line
Markesbery Black Bear, Grizzly Bear, Brown Bear
Marlin Model MLS-50
Modern Muzzleloading Knight MK-85 Series, BK-92 Black Knight, LK-93 Wolverine & Thumbhole Wolverine, Magnum Elite, Knight T-Bolt, American Knight, DISC Rifle
Navy Arms "Country Boy" In-Line, Smith Carbine
Prairie River Arms Bullpup & Classic
Ruger Model 77/50 SS All-Weather & RSO Rifle
Thompson/Center Fire Hawk Series, Hawken, New Englander, Pennsylvania Hunter (rifle and carbine), Thunder Hawk Shadow, Encore 209x50 Magnum, Black Diamond, System 1
Traditions Buckhunter & Buckhunter Pro In-Line Rifle Series, Buckskinner Carbine, Deerhunter, Kentucky, Tennessee, Lightning Bolt Action Series
Uberti Santa Fe Hawken

50-70

Shiloh Sharps 1874 Business, Sporting No.1 and No.3

50-90

Shiloh Sharps 1874 Business, Model 1874 Sporting No.1 and No.3

54

Cabela Hawken
CVA In-line Accubolt Pro, Firebolt Series, Stag Horn; St. Louis Hawken
Dixie Hawken, Sharps New Model 1859 Carbine and 1859 Military Rifle Euroarms U.S. 1803 Harpers Ferry Model 2305, U.S. 1841 Mississippi Model 2310, Eclipse Advantage Stag Horn, Stag Horn
Lyman Trade Rifle, Deerstalker In-Line Rifle, Great Plains, Cougar In-Line
Markesbery Black Bear, Grizzly Bear, Brown Bear
Marlin Model MLS-54
Modern Muzzleloading Knight MK-85 & 86 Series, LK-93 Wolverine & Thumbhole Wolverine
Navy Arms 1803 Harpers Ferry, 1841 Mississippi, 1859 Berdan Sharps, 1859 Sharps Cavalry Carbine
Prairie River Arms Bullpup & Classic
Thompson/Center Fire Hawk Series, Hawken, New Englander, System 1, Thunder Hawk, Shadow & Valve Pack
Traditions Buckhunter In-Line Rifle Series, Deerhunter, Lightning Bolt Action Series

58

Colt Blackpowder Colt Model 1861 Musket
Dixie 1858 Two-Band Enfield Rifle, U.S. Model 1861 Springfield, Mississippi, 1862 Three-Band Enfield Rifle Musket
Euroarms Model 2260 London Armory Co. Enfield 3-Band Rifle Musket, Models 2270 and 2280 London Armory Co. Enfield Rifled Muskets, Model 2300 Cook and Brother Confederate Carbine, J. P. Murray Carbine, 1861 Springfield, 1863 Remington Zouave, C. S. Richmond Model 2370 Musket, 1841 Mississippi Model 2310
Navy Arms Mississippi Model 1841, 1853 Enfield Rifle and Musket, 1861 Enfield Musketoon, 1861 Springfield, 1862 C. S. Richmond, Kodiak Double
Thompson/Center Big Boar Caplock, Firehawk

69

Dixie U.S. Model 1816 Flintlock Musket

75

Navy Arms Brown Bess Musket

DOUBLE RIFLES

45-70

Dixie Kodiak Mark IV Double Barrel

50

Cabela Kodiak Express

58

Cabela Kodiak Express

SHOTGUNS

10 GAUGE
Navy Arms Steel Shot Magnum

10GA./12 GA./20 GA.
Dixie Double-Barrel Magnum

12 GAUGE
CVA Trapper Single Barrel Shotgun, Classic Turkey Double Barrel Shotgun
Navy Arms Fowler, T&T Shotgun

GUNFINDER

To help you find the model of your choice, the following index includes every firearm found in this SHOOTER'S BIBLE 1999, listed by type of gun.

HANDGUNS

PISTOLS—COMPETITION TARGET

BERNARDELLI
Model P.010 Target 108
Model P.018 Compact Target 108
Model P.018 Target 108

BROWNING
Buck Mark 5.5 Target 113

COLT
Colt .22 Target 117
Custom Tactical Models 118

ENTREPRISE ARMS
Models I, II, III 125

GLOCK
Model 17L Competition 130
Model 24 Competition 130

HÄMMERLI
Model 160 Free, Model 162 Electronic 132
Model 208S Standard 132
Model 280 Target, Combo 132

GLOCK
Model 17L Competition 130
Model 24 Competition 130

HECKLER & KOCH
USP 45 Match 135

HIGH STANDARD
Olympic Rapid Fire 137
Citation, Supermatic Citation MS 138
Trophy 138
Supermatic Tournament 139

JENNINGS
Lazer Nine, T-22 Target 140

KIMBER
Classic 45 Gold Match 143
Custom Target 143
Polymer, Polymer Target 143

MAGNUM RESEARCH
Lone Eagle Single Shot 149

RUGER
Mark II Target Series 167, 168
P-512 22/45 Target 168

SMITH & WESSON
Model 41 Rimfire 177
Model 457 177
Model 22A Sport 177
Models 2213, 2214 Sportsman 177

THOMPSON/CENTER
Contender "Super 14" 197

UBERTI
1871 Rolling Block Target 198

UNIQUE
Model DES 32U 199
Model DES 69U 199
Model DES 2000U 199
Model I.S. Int'l Silhouette 199
Model I.S. International Sport 199

WICHITA ARMS
International, Silhouette 202

PISTOLS—DERRINGERS

AMERICAN DERRINGER
Models 1, 6, 7, 10, 11 99
Model 4, Model M-4 Alaskan Survival 100
Lady Derringer 100
Texas Double Derringer Commemorative 100

DAVIS
Long-Bore D-Series 120
D-25 Series Derringers 120

DOWNSIZER
Model WSP 121

PISTOLS SEMIAUTOMATIC
(See also PISTOLS COMPETITION/TARGET)

AMERICAN ARMS
Escort .380 98

AMT
Automag II, III, IV 102
Backup & 380 Backup II 101
1911 Government 101
1911 Government 45 ACP Longslide 101
1911 Hardballer 101

ARMSCOR. See KBI

AUTO-ORDNANCE
Model 1911A1 Deluxe, Pit Bull 103
WW II Parkerized 103
Model 1911A1 Thompson 103

BENELLI. See European American Armory

BERETTA
Model 21 Bobcat 105
Model 84 Cheetah 105
Models 85, 86, 87 Cheetah 106
Model 89 Gold Standard 106
Models 92D, 92F, 92F-EL, 92FS 107
Model 92 Centurion 107
Model 92 Compact L Type M 107
Models 96, 96 Centurion, 96D 107
Model 950 BS Jetfire 105
Model 3032 Tomcat 104
Models 8000/8040 Cougar & Mini-Cougar 104

BERSA
Series 95 109
Thunder 22 109
Thunder 380, 380 Deluxe 109

BROLIN ARMS
Legend Series Model L45, L45 Compact 110
Model TAC-11, Gold Model 110

BROWNING
Model BDA-380 112
Model BDM 9mm 111
Buck Mark Bullseye 113
Buck Mark 5.5 Field, Gold Target, Target 113
Buck Mark Silhouette, Varmint, Unltd. Silhouette 113
Hi-Power Capitan, HP-Practical 111
Hi-Power Mark III, Standard 111
Micro Buck Mark, Micro Plus, Standard 112

COLT
Combat Commander 114
MKIV Series 80 Pistols 114
Colt Defender Lightweight Carry Series 80 115
Combat Commander 114
Gold Cup Trophy 115
Government Model 380 Pony Series 115
M1991A1 Std. Series 80, Commander, Compact 114
Mustang 380, Pocketlite, Model LW380 116

COONAN ARMS
"Cadet" Compact 119
357 Magnum Pistol 119

DAVIS
Model P-32 120
Model P-380 120

ENTREPRISE
Elite P500 124
Tactical P500 124
Boxes P500 124

EUROPEAN AMERICAN ARMORY
European SA Compact 127
Witness DA 126
Witness Gold Team, Silver Team 126
Witness Subcompact 126

FEG/INTERARMS
Mark II APK, AP, AP22 128

FEG (See also KBI)

GLOCK
Model 17 130
Model 19 Compact 130
Models 20, 21 130
Models 22, 23 Compact 131
Models 26, 27 131
Model 30 Subcompact 131

HECKLER & KOCH
Mark 23 Special 135
Model HK USP 9 & 40 Universal 134
Model P7M8 Self-Loading 135
Model USP45 Universal Self-Loading 134

HERITAGE MFG.
Model H25S 136
Stealth Compact 136

HI-POINT FIREARMS
Models 9mm, 9mm Compact & 380 Polymer 137
Models 40, 45 137

HIGH Standard
Citation MS 138
Olympic 138
Supermatic Citation, MS 139
Trophy 138
Victor 22 LR 138

ISRAEL ARMS
Models M 1500, M-5000, M-2500 139

KAHR ARMS
Model K9 140

KBI
FEG Model PJK-9HP 141
FEG Model SMC Auto 141
FEG Model SMC-380 141

KIMBER
Model Custom .45 Series 142

L.A.R.
Grizzly Mark I & Mark V 144

LASERAIM TECHNOLOGIES
Dream Team 145
Series I, III 145

LLAMA
Government Model (table) 146
Maxi 7-Shot/9-Shot 147
Micro-Max 147

LUGER
American Eagle 148

MAGNUM RESEARCH
Lone Eagle Single Shot 149
Mark XIX Component System 149
One Pro 45 150

M.O.A.
Maximum 151

PARA-ORDNANCE
P Series Pistols 155, 156

RUGER
Mark II Series 167, 168
P-Series Pistols 166

SAFARI ARMS
Cohort, Enforcer, Matchmaster 169

SAVAGE ARMS
"Striker" Models 510F, 516FSS, 516GSAK 170

SIG-SAUER
Model P210 171
Model P220 "American" 171
Models P225, P226 171
Models P229, P232, P239 172

SMITH & WESSON
Model 410 175
Model 900 Series 175
Models 3900 Compact Series 173
Model 3913 LadySmith 173

Models 4006, 4043, 4046 Full-Size 174
Model 4506, 4566, 4586 Full-Size 174
Model 5904, 5906, 5946 Full-Size 175
Models 6904/6906 Compact 173
Sigma Series SW40F, SW380 176
TSW Tactical Series (3953TSW, 4013TSW, 4513TSW) 178

SPRINGFIELD
Champion Series 189
High-Capacity Series 188
Mil-Spec Champion 188
PDP Series (Defender, Factory Comp,
High-Capacity Factory Comp) 191
Lightweight Compact 188
Trophy Match 188
Ultra Compact Series 189, 190
Super Tuned Series 190

TAURUS
Models PT 22, PT 25 192
Models PT-92 193
Models PT-99 193
Model PT-911 Compact 192
Model PT-945 193
Model PT-938 Compact 192
Model PT 940 193

THOMPSON/CENTER
Contender Bull & Octagon Barrels 197
Contender Hunter 197
Contender "Super 14" & "Super 16" 197
Encore 197

UBERTI
1871 Rolling Block Target 198

WALTHER
Models P 5 DA 201
Model P 88 Compact 201
Model P 99 Compact 201
Models PP, PPK & PPK/S 200
Model TPH DA 200

WILDEY
Hunter & Survivor 202

Revolvers

AMERICAN ARMS
Mateba 98
Regulator SA, Deluxe 98
Uberti .454 SA 98

ARMSCOR. See KBI

COLT
Anaconda DA 118
DS II 117
King Cobra DA 117
The Peacemaker SA Army 117
Python Elite 118
Single Action Army 117

EMF/DAKOTA
Hartford Pinkerton 121
Cavalry Colt/Artillery 121
Hartford Single Action Models 122
1873 Hartford Buntline 122
1873 Hartford Sixshooter 122
1895 Hartford Bixley 122
1893 Hartford Express 122
Model 1873 Dakota SA 123
Model 1875 Outlaw 123
Model 1890 Remington Police 123

EUROPEAN AMERICAN ARMORY
Big Bore Bounty Hunter 127
Windicator DA 127

FREEDOM ARMS
Model 1997 Premier Grade 128
Model 252 Competition/Silhouette/Varmint 129
Model 353 Field/Premier 129
454 Casull Field/Premier 129
Model 555 Field/Premier 129

HARRINGTON & RICHARDSON
Model 929 Sidekick 91 133
Model 939 Premier Target 133
Model 949 Classic Western 133
Sportsman 999 133

HERITAGE MFG.
Rough Rider SA 136
Sentry DA 136

KBI
Armscor Model M-2000 DC/TC 141

NAVY ARMS
1873 "Pinched Frame" SA 151
"Flat Top" Target SA 151
1873 U.S. Cavalry 151
1873 Colt-Style SA 151

1875 Schofield 152
1895 U.S. Artillery 152
Bisley Model SA 152

NEW ENGLAND FIREARMS
Standard, Starter Revolver 153
Ultra, Ultra Mag & Lady Ultra 153

NORTH AMERICAN ARMS
Mini-Master Series 154
Mini Revolvers 154

ROSSI
Model 68 157
Model 88 157
Model 88 Lady Rossi 158
Models 515, 518 158
Model 720 157
Model 851 158
Model 877 158
Models 971, 971 VCR 159
Cyclops 159

RUGER
Bisley SA Target 165
GP-100 357 Mag. 164
Model SP101 Spurless 164
New Bearcat 165
New Model Blackhawk & Blackhawk Convertible (table) 162
New Model Single-Six 163
New Model Super Blackhawk 163
Fixed Sight New Model Super Single-Six 163
Redhawk Models (Stainless & Blued) 160
Super Redhawk Stainless DA 160
P-Series (P93, P94) 160
Bisley-Vaquero 161
Vaquero SA 161

SMITH & WESSON
Models 10 & 13 Military & Police 183
Model 14 K-38 Masterpiece 184
Model 15 Combat Masterpiece 184
Model 17 184
Model 19 Combat Magnum 185
Model 29 Magnum 186
Model 36 .38 Chiefs Special 179
Models 37 & 637 Chiefs Special Airweight 179
Model 38 Bodyguard Airweight 180
Model 60 .38 Chiefs Special Stainless 179
Model 60LS LadySmith 179
Model 317 Airlite, LadySmith 181
Model 63 Kit Gun 182
Model 64 M & P Stainless 183
Models 65 M & P, LadySmith 183
Model 66 Combat Magnum 185
Model 442 .38 Airweight 180
Model 586 Distinguished Combat Mag. 185
Model 617 K-22 Masterpiece 184
Model 610 Classic Hunter 187
Model 625 186
Model 629, 629 Classic/Classic DX 187
Model 629 Powerport 187
Model 640 Centennial 182
Model 642 Centennial Airweight, LadySmith 180
Model 649 Bodyguard 180
Model 651 Magnum Kit Gun 182
Model 657 Stainless 187
Model 686, 686 Plus, 686 Powerport 186
Model 696 180
Model 940 Centennial 181

TAURUS
Model 44 194
Model 82 194
Model 85 Series 194
Model 96 195
Model 454 Casull "Raging Bull" 194
Model 445 DA 195
Model 605 195
Model 606 Compact 196
Model 608 DA 196
Models 669 & 689 196
Model 941 195

UBERTI REPLICAS. See also American Arms
1873 Cattleman 198
1875 Outlaw/1890 Police 198

RIFLES

Centerfire Bolt Action

ARNOLD ARMS
African Safari, Synthetic, Trophy 206
Alaskan Series (Trophy, Grand Alaskan, Synthetic,
Alaskan Guide) 207
Grand African 206
Serengeti Synthetic 206

A-SQUARE
Caesar Model 208
Genghis Khan 208
Hamilcar & Hannibal 208

BERETTA
Mato Rifle 211

BLASER
Model R 93 211
Safari Model 211

BROWN PRECISION
High Country Youth 213
Pro-Hunter Elite, Pro-Varminter 212
Tactical Elite 213

BROWNING
A-Bolt II Eclipse, Stainless Stalker 217
A-Bolt II Hunter 216
A-Bolt II Gold Medallion 216, 217
Custom Trophy 217

CHRISTENSEN
CarbonCannon Series 219
CarbonTactical Series 219
CarbonOne Series 219
CarbonLite Series 219
CarbonFine Series 219
CarbonChallenge Series 219

COOPER ARMS
Varmint Extreme Series 222
Competition Series (Model 36) 223

DAKOTA ARMS
Dakota 76 224
Dakota 97 Varmint & Lightweight Hunter 225
Long Bow Tactical 225

FRANCOTTE
Bolt-Actions, Mountain Rifles 227

HARRIS GUNWORKS
Alaskan 229
Benchrest 231
Classic & Stainless Sporters 229
Long Range 231
National Match 231
Talon Safari 231
Talon Sporter 230
.300 Phoenix 230
Titanium Mountain 230
Varminter 230

HOWA
Lightning 233

JARRETT
Model No. 4 233

KIMBER
Mauser 98 Sporter 235

KONGSBERG
Model Hunter 393 237
Sporter 393 Thumbhole 237

LAZZERONI
Models L2000ST/SA/SP 239

MAGNUM RESEARCH
Mountain Eagle, Varmint Edition 240

MARLIN
Model MR-7B 245

MAUSER
Model 96 250

REMINGTON
Model Seven Series 265
Model 700 ADL 260, 262 (table)
Model 700 African Plains 263
Model 700 Alaskan Wilderness 263
Model 700 BDL Series 259, 260, 261 (table), 262 (table)
Model 700 Classic 263
Model 700 Mountain DM 262, 263 (tables)
Model 700 Safari, Safari KS 264
Model 700 Sendero 260, 261 (table), 262 (table)
Special, Sendero SF

RIFLES, INC.
Classic 269
Lightweight Strata SS 269
Safari 269

RUGER
Model Mark II Series 275
Mark II Series 277, 278
Model M-77 Mark II All-Weather 278
Model M-77RSI International Mannlicher 277
Model M-77VT MK II Heavy Barrel Target 278
Model 77/22RH Hornet 276
Ruger 77RSM MK II Magnum 278

SAKO
Model 75 Series (Hunter, Stainless Synthetic) 279, 284
Deluxe, Super Deluxe 282, 284

TRG-21, TRG-41, TRG-S	283, 284 (table)
Varmint	280, 284

SAUER

Model 90	286
Model SHR 970 Synthetic	286
Model 202 Supreme	286
Model .458 Safari	286

SAVAGE

Model 12BVSS/12FVSS/12FV Varmint	287
Model 110FP/10FP Tactical	288
Model 10FM Sierra Lightweight	288
Model 16FSS Weather Warrior	288
Model 11F Hunter	289
Model 10GY Ladies/Youth	289
Model 11G Classic American Style Hunter	289
Model 93 Series (Magnum, Stainless, FVSS)	294
Model 111 Classic Hunter Series	293
Models 112BT Competition, 112BVSS, 112FV, 112FVSS	290
Models 114CE, 114CU Classics	292
Model 116FCS, FSK Kodiak, FSAK, FSS Weather Warriors	291
Model 116SE Safari Express	292

STEYR-MANNLICHER

Steyr SSG-P1	300
Steyr Scout	300
Model SBS Mannlicher European	300

TIKKA

Continental Varmint & Long-Range Hunting	303
Whitetail Hunter & Synthetic	302

ULTRA LIGHT ARMS

Models 20, 24, 28 & 40 Series	306

UNIQUE Model TGC Centerfire | 307

WEATHERBY

Mark V Accumark & Lightweight	309, 310 (table)
Mark V Deluxe	308, 310 (table)
Mark V Euromark	310 (table), 312
Mark V Lazermark	310 (table), 311
Mark V Magnum Stainless	310 (table), 311
Mark V Sporter/Eurosport	310
Mark V Stainless & Synthetic	310 (table), 311
New Mark V Lightweight	310 (table), 313

WINCHESTER

Model 70 Classic Featherweight	316
Model 70 Classic Laredo	317 (table)
Model 70 Classic Compact	317 (table)
Model 70 Classic Camo Stainless	318
Model 70 Classic Sporter	319
Model 70 Classic Super Grade	316
Model 70 Custom Classics	314
Model 70 Heavy Barrel Varmint	318 (table)
Model 70 Black Shadow	317, 318
Ranger, Ranger Ladies'/Youth	318 (table), 319

CENTERFIRE LEVER ACTION

AMERICAN ARMS

180 Henry Replica	204
1866 Winchester Replica	204
1873 Winchester	204

BROWNING

Model Lightning BLR	218

EMF REPLICAS

1860 Henry	226
Model 1866 Yellow Boy	226
Model 1873 Sporting	226

MARLIN

Model 30AS	247
Model Golden 39AS	247
Models 336CS	247
Model 444SS	249
Model 1894 Cowboy	248
Models 1894CS & 1894S	248
Model 1895SS	249

NAVY ARMS

1892 Rifle	256
1892 Brass Frame	256
1892 Short Rifle	256

ROSSI

Models M92 Large Loop, Stainless	271

SAVAGE

Model 92SRC	271

WINCHESTER

Model 94 Big-Bore Walnut	321
Model 94 Standard Walnut	320
Model 94 Legacy	321
Model 94 Trail's End	321
Model 94 Ranger	321
Model 94 Walnut Trapper Carbine	320
Model 94 Win-Tuff	322

CENTERFIRE SEMIAUTOMATIC & SLIDE ACTION

AUTO-ORDNANCE

Thompson Model M1 Carbine	209
Thompson Model 1927 A1 Deluxe, Lightweight and Commando	209

BROWNING BAR Mark II Safari | 218

COLT

Accurized	221
Competition H-Bar, H-Bar II	221
Match Target, H-Bar & Lightweights	221

HECKLER & KOCH

Model HK PSG-1 High-Precision	232

MARLIN

Model 9 Camp Carbine	246
Model 45	246

REMINGTON Models 7400 & 7600 | 266

RUGER

Model PC9 Auto	271
Mini-14/5 Carbine, 14/5R Ranch Rifle	272
Model Mini-Thirty	272

SPRINGFIELD

M1A Standard, Nat'l Match, Super Match	299
M1A-A1 Bush	299
Model SAR-8 & SAR-4800 Sporters	298
STEYR-MANNLICHER	
Aug S.A.	291

CENTERFIRE SINGLE SHOT

AMT Single Shot Standard | 205

BROWNING

Model 1885 Low & High Wall	215
Model 1885	215
Model BPR Pump	218

HARRINGTON & RICHARDSON

Whitetails Unlimited 1998 Comm. Ed.	228
Ultra Single Shot Rifles	228

JARRETT

Models 1, 2, 3, 4	233

L.A.R.

Grizzly Big Boar Competitor	238

NAVY ARMS

Greener Harpoon Gun	255

NEW ENGLAND FIREARMS

Synthetic Handi-Rifle	257

RUGER

No. 1A Light & 1S Medium Sporters	274
No. 1B Standard/1V Special Varminter	274
No. 1H Tropical	274
No. 1RSI International	274

THOMPSON/CENTER

Contender Carbines	301
Encore	301

RIMFIRE BOLT ACTION & SINGLE SHOT

ARMSCOR. See KBI

DAKOTA ARMS

Dakota 10 Single Shot	224
22 LR Sporter	224

EUROPEAN AMERICAN ARMORY

HW660 Weihrauch Target	226

KBI/CHARLES DALY

Model CDGA 4103 Field Grade	234
Model M-12Y Youth	234
KIMBER	
Model 82C Series	235
Model 84C Single Shot Series	236

MAGTECH

Model MT 122.2 S, R, T	240

MARLIN

Model 81TS	245
Model MR-7	243
Model 15YN "Little Buckaroo"	244
Models 25MN & 25N	244
Models 882, 882L	245
Models 883 Magnum, 883SS	243
Model 922 Magnum	243
Model 2000L Target	250

NEW ENGLAND FIREARMS

Super Light Youth Handi-Rifle	257

REMINGTON

Models 40-XR KS Target Rimfire	264
Models 541-T	267
RUGER 77/22 Rimfire Series	276

SAKO Finnfire | 281, 284

SAVAGE

Mark I-G Single Shot	296
Model 93G Magnum	294
Model 900TR	297

THOMPSON/CENTER

Contender Carbines	294

ULTRA LIGHT

Model 20 RF	299

UNIQUE

Model T Dioptra Sporter	307
Model T/SM Silhouette	307
Model T UIT Standard	307

RIMFIRE LEVER ACTION

BROWNING

Model BL-22 (Grades I, II)	214

HENRY REPEATING ARMS

Henry Rifle	232
Lever Youth & Carbine	232
U.S. Survival	232

MARLIN

Golden 39AS	247

WINCHESTER

Model 9422 Series	322
Model 9422 Walnut	322

RIMFIRE SEMIAUTOMATIC & SLIDE ACTION

AMT

22 Rimfire Magnum & Target Model	205

BROWN PRECISION

Custom Team Challenger	213

BROWNING

22 Semiauto Grades I & VI	214

KBI/CHARLES DALY

Model CDGA6345 Empire Grade	234
Model CDGA M-20P	234

MARLIN

Models 60/60SS/60SB/SSK	241
Model 7000	242
Model 70PSS "Papoose"	242
Model 45	246
Model 9 Camp Carbine	246
Model 922 Magnum	243
Model 995SS	242

REMINGTON

Model 597 Series	268
Model 552 BDL Deluxe Speedmaster	267
Model 572 BDL Fieldmaster	267

ROSSI

Models M62 SA & SAC	271

RUGER

Model 10/22 Series	273

SAVAGE

Model 64 Series	295
Mark II-FV/FSS/LV	296
Model 900TR	297

DOUBLE RIFLES, ACTIONS & DRILLINGS

BERETTA

Express Rifles	210

BROWN PRECISION

Actions	212

FRANCOTTE

Boxlocks/Sidelocks	227

KRIEGHOFF

Classic Side-by-Side	238

NAVY ARMS

Kodiak MK IV, Deluxe	254

PEDERSOLI

Kodiak Mark IV	258

SAKO

Actions	285

REPLICA RIFLES

EMF
1860 Henry 226
1866 Yellowboy Carbine/Rifle 226
1873 Sporting Rifle & Carbine 226

NAVY ARMS
1866 "Yellowboy" Rifle & Carbine 252
1873 Springfield Cavalry Carbine 253
1873 Winchester Sporting 252
1874 Winchester-Style Rifle 252
1873 Winchester-Style Carbine & Rifle ... 252
1874 Sharps Cavalry Carbine & Infantry ... 253
1874 Sharps Sniper 253
Henry Carbine 251
Henry Iron Frame, Military, Trapper 251
Kodiak MK IV Double, Deluxe 254
No. 2 Creedmoor Target 255
Remington-Style Rolling Block Buffalo Rifle ... 255
Sharps Plains & Buffalo 254

PEDERSOLI
Kodiak Mark IV Double Rifle 258
Rolling Block Target 258
Sharps Carbine Model 766 258

UBERTI
Henry Carbine, Rifle 305
Model 1866 Sporting Rifle 304
Model 1866 Yellowboy Carbine 304
Model 1871 Rolling Block Baby Carbine ... 304
Model 1873 Carbine 305
Model 1873 Sporting Rifle 305

RIFLE/SHOTGUN COMBINATIONS
(See SHOTGUNS Shotgun/Rifle Combinations)

SHOTGUNS
AUTOLOADING

AMERICAN ARMS/FRANCHI
Model 610 Variopress System 325
Model 48/AL 327

BENELLI
Black Eagle Competition 330, 331
Super Black Eagle Slug Gun 328
Executive Series 331
Sport Model 330
Legacy 330
M1 Super 90 Series .... 331 (table), 332
M3 Super 90 Pump/Auto .... 331 (table), 332
Montefeltro Super 90VR .... 331 (table), 332
Specifications Table 331

BERETTA
Model A 390 Series (Silver Mallard, Camo) ... 337
Model 1201 FP Riot 336
Pintail, Pintail Rifled Slug 336
Model AL390 Silver Mallard (Synthetic, Camo, Standard) ... 337
Model AL390 Competition Sporting, Trap, Skeet, Youth ... 338

BROWNING
Auto-5 Series 341
Gold Hunter & Stalker 341

FRANCHI. See American Arms

HECKLER & KOCH
Fabarm Series (Red Lion, Gold Lion) 354

MOSSBERG
Model 9200 Series 369

REMINGTON
Model 11-87 Premier, Deer Gun 383
Model 11-87 Skeet/Trap 383
Model 11-87 Premier Sporting Clays 382
Model 11-87 SPS 384
Model 11-87 SPS/SPS Camo/SPST Turkey ... 384
Model 1100 Special Field Gun 385
Model 1100 LT-20 Special Field 385
Model 1100 LT-20 Youth 385
Model 1100 Synthetic 385
Model SP-10 Magnum, Camo 386
Model 11-96 Euro Lightweight 386

BOLT ACTION

BROWNING
A-Bolt Hunter, Stalker 345

MARLIN
Model 55 GDL Goose Gun 361
Model DL 512 Slugmaster 360, 361
Model 50DL 361

MOSSBERG
Model 695 370

SAVAGE
Model 210 "Master Shot" & Slug Gun 389

OVER-UNDER

AMERICAN ARMS
Silver I & II, Sporting 324
Specialty Models 326
Franchi Falconet 2000 327
Franchi Sporting 2000 327
Alcione 2000 SX 327

BERETTA
ASE Gold Skeet, Sporting Clays, Trap ... 336
Model 682 Gold Competition Skeet 333
Model 682 Gold Sporting 333
Model 686 Silver Essential 334
Model 686 Onyx 334
Model 686 Silver Essential 334
Silver Pigeon Field 334
Model ASE Gold Skeet 336
Model 687 Silver Pigeon Sporting 335
Model 687L Silver Pigeon Field 335
Model 687EL Gold Pigeon Field 335
Model 687EELL Diamond Pigeon 335
Model Ultralight 335

BROWNING
Citori Field Models 342
Citori Light Sporting, Special Sporting ... 343, 344
Citori Special Sporting Trap & Skeet ... 343, 344
Citori Sporting Clays Model 425 343
Citori Ultra Sporter 343
Light Sporting Model 802ES 343

CHARLES DALY
Field Hunter 347
Superior Sporting 347
Superior Skeet 347
Model Empire EDL 348
Diamond Grade 348

A.H. FOX
Custom Boxlock Models 350

HECKLER & KOCH
Fabarm Series (Model Silver Lion, Ultra Mag Lion, Super Light Lion, Max Lion) ... 354

KRIEGHOFF
Models K-80 Live Bird, Trap, Skeet 358
Sporting Clays 358
Model K-80 Specifications/Price Table ... 359

MAROCCHI
Conquista Series 362

MERKEL
Models 200E/201E Boxlocks 363
Models 202E/203E/303E Sidelocks 363

PERAZZI
Competition Series (Olympic, Double Trap, Pigeon, Skeet, Special/Sporting) ... 376
Game Models 375
Models SC3, SCO High Grades 376

PIOTTI
Sidelock 377

REMINGTON
Custom Model 396 Skeet & Sporting 378
Peerless 378

RIZZINI
Premier Sporting & Upland EL 387
Model S790 High Grade 387
Artemis EL High Grade 387

RUGER
Red Label 388
Sporting Clays 388
Woodside O/U 388

SIGARMS
Models SA3 & SA5 389

SKB
Model 505 390
Model 585 Series 391, 392
Model 785 Series 391, 392

STOEGER/IGA
Condor I & Supreme Single Trigger ... 394, 396 (table)
Waterfowl Model .... 394, 396 (table)
Deluxe Hunter Clay Model ... 395, 396 (table)
Trap Model .... 395, 396 (table)

TIKKA
Model 512S Premium Field 397
Sporting Clays Shotgun 397

WEATHERBY
Athena Grades IV & V .... 397, 398 (table)
Orion Grades I, II, III .... 397, 398 (table)

SIDE-BY-SIDE

AMERICAN ARMS
Brittany 325
Gentry 325
Specialty Model 326

AYA
Boxlock Models 329
Countryman 328
Sidelock Models 328

BERETTA
Model 470 Silver Hawk 338

BERNARDELLI
Hemingway Lightweight Boxlock 339
Holland & Holland-Type Sidelocks 3 339
Roma Series 339
S. Uberto 2 339

DAKOTA ARMS
American Legend 350

CHARLES DALY
Field Hunter S/S Series 349

FRANCOTTE
Boxlocks, Sidelocks 351

GARBI
Models 100, 101, 103A/103B, 200 351

HECKLER & KOCH
Fabarm Series (Classic Lion Grades I & II) ... 354

MERKEL
Models 47E/147E 364
Models 247S, 447SL 364

PIOTTI
Models King Extra & King No. 1 377
Model Lunik Sidelock 377
Model Piuma 377

SKB
Model 385 390

STOEGER/IGA
Coach Gun .... 393, 396 (table)
Uplander Series .... 393, 396 (table)
Turkey Model .... 394, 396 (table)
Deluxe Uplander .... 395, 396 (table)
Deluxe Coach Gun .... 395, 396 (table)

SINGLE BARREL

BERNARDELLI
Model 112 339

BROWNING
BT-100 Series 345

HARRINGTON & RICHARDSON
.410 Tamer Shotgun 352
Ultra Slug Hunter 352
Topper Series (Model 098, Youth, Junion Classic) ... 353
Topper Series Deluxe Model 098 353

KRIEGHOFF
Model KS-5 359

NEW ENGLAND FIREARMS
Pardner/Pardner Youth 372
Special Purpose Waterfowl SS 373
Survivor Series 372
Tracker Slug Gun 373
Tracker II Rifled Slug Gun 373
Turkey & Goose Gun 373

PARKER
A-1 Special 374

PERAZZI
American Trap Series 375

SLIDE ACTION

ARMSCOR. See KBI

BROLIN
Hawk Field Series 340
Hawk Lawman Series 340

BROWNING
BPS Magnum Series, Pump Series 346

HECKLER & KOCH
Fabarm Series Model FP6 355

ITHACA
Model 37 Deerslayer II 356
Model 37 Turkeyslayer 356
Classic 37, English Version 356

KBI
Armscor Field Models 357
Armscor Riot & Special Purpose Pumps 357

MAGTECH
Model 586.2 VR Series 360

MOSSBERG
Line Launcher 370
Model HS 410 Home Security 367
Model 500 American Field 365
Model 500 Crown Grade/Combos 365
Model 500 Mariner 367
Model 500 Sporting 365
Model 500 Wood& Camo 366
Model 500/590 Ghost Ring 367
Model 500/590 Special Purpose 367
Model 835 Ulti-Mag 368
Viking Series 371

MOSSBERG/MAVERICK
Model 31002 371

REMINGTON
Model 870 Express/Combo/Deer/Turkey 379, 380
Model 870 Express Syn. Home Defense 379
Model 870 Express Youth 379
Model 870 Express Super Magnum 380
Model 870 SP All Black Deer Gun 381
Model 870 SP Marine Magnum 381
Model 870 SPS-Camo, SPST Turkey 381
Model 870 Wingmaster Series 382

WINCHESTER
Model 1300 Deer, Field, Turkey 399
Model 1300 Defender Series 400
Model 1300 Ranger, Ranger Deer, Ladies'/Youth 399

BLACKPOWDER

MUSKETS, CARBINES & RIFLES

AUSTIN & HALLECK
Models 320, 420 Rifles 405
Mountain Rifle 405

CABELA'S
Hawken Rifle 406
Kodiak Express Double Rifle 406
Lightning Fire Rifle 406
Rolling Block Muzzleloader, Carbine 406

COLT BLACKPOWDER ARMS
Colt Model 1861 Musket 409

CVA
Accubolt Pro 412
Firebolt Series 412
St. Louis Hawken, Plainsman 411
Stag Horn In-Line 412
Eclipse Advantage Stag Horn Rifle 412

DIXIE
1858 Two-Band Enfield Rifle 412
1859 Sharps New Model Carbine/Military Rifle 415
1862 Three-Band Enfield Rifled Musket 418
1873 Springfield Rifle/Carbine & Officer's Model 417
1874 Sharps Lightweight Hunter 415
1874 Sharps Silhouette 415
Hawken 416
Kodiak Mark IV Double Barrel Rifle 417
Pennsylvania Rifle 416
Tennessee Mountain 416
U.S. Model 1816 Flintlock Musket 418
U.S. Model 1861 Springfield Rifle/Musket 418
Waadtlander Model 416

EUROARMS
Cook & Brother Confederate Carbine Model 2300 421
Cook & Brother Field Model 2301 421
C.S. Richmond Musket Model 2370 421
1803 Harpers Ferry Rifle Model 2305 423
1841 Mississippi Rifle Model 2310 423
1861 Springfield 423
1863 Remington Zouave Rifle 423
London Armory Co. Enfield Musketoon 423
London Armory Co. 2-Band Rifle Musket Model 2270 422
London Armory Co. 3-Band Enfield Musket Model 2260 422
London Armory Co. Musket Model 2261 422

FORT WORTH FIREARMS
Rio Grande In-Line 425
Pecos In-Line 425
Brazos In-Line 425
Sabine & Neches 425

GONIC
Model 93 Series (Mountain, Magnum, Safari) 426

LYMAN
Cougar In-Line 427
Deerstalker Rifle & Carbine 427
Great Plains Rifle 428
Trade Rifle 428

MARKESBERY
Black Bear, Brown Bear, Grizzly Bear Models 429

MARLIN
Models MLS-50 & MLS-54 430

MODERN MUZZLELOADING
American Knight 431
DISC Rifle 432
Model LK-93 Wolverine & Thumbhole Wolverine 432
Knight T-Bolt 431
Model MK-85 & MK-86 Series (Grand American, Hunter, Knight Hawk, Predator, Stalker) 430

NAVY ARMS
"Berdan" 1859 Sharps Rifle 439
Brown Bess Musket/Carbine 439
Country Boy In-Line Rifle 438
1803 Harpers Ferry 439
1853 Enfield Rifle Musket 437
1858 Enfield Rifle 437
1859 Sharps Cavalry, Carbine, Infantry Rifle 437
1861 Musketoon 437
1861 Springfield Rifles 438
1862 C.S. Richmond Rifle 440
Mississippi Rifle Model 1841 438
Pennsylvania Long Rifle 439
Smith Carbine 438

PRAIRIE RIVER ARMS
PRA Bullpup & Classic Rifles 441

REMINGTON
Model 700 ML & MLS 442
Model 700 ML Youth 442

RUGER
Model 77/50 All-Weather 443

SHILOH SHARPS
Model 1874 Business 444
Model 1874 Sporting Rifles No.1, No. 3 444

THOMPSON/CENTER
Black Diamond 446
Encore 209 X 50 Magnum 446
Fire Hawk Series 447
Hawken 448
New Englander Rifle 445
Pennsylvania Hunter/Carbine 445
System I Rifle 446
Thunder Hawk, Thunder Hawk Shadow 448

TRADITIONS
Buckhunter In-Line Rifle Series 456
Buckhunter Pro In-Line Rifles 456
Buckskinner Carbine/Deluxe 454
Deerhunter Rifle Series (Panther, Carbine) 452
Hawken Woodsman 453
Kentucky Rifle 454
Lightning Bolt-Action Rifles 455
Pennsylvania Rifle 453
Shenandoah Rifle 453

PISTOLS

CVA
Hawken, Kentucky 410

DIXIE
LePage Percussion Dueling 414
Mang Target 414
Charles Moore English Dueling 414
Queen Anne 414
Screw Barrel Pistol 414

NAVY ARMS
1806 Harpers Ferry 436
Kentucky Flint/Percussion 436

TRADITIONS
Buckhunter Pro In-Line 450
Kentucky 450
William Parker 449
Pioneer, Trapper 449

REVOLVERS

AMERICAN ARMS
1851 Colt Navy 402
1858 Army SS Target 402
1858 Remington Army 402
1860 Colt Army 402

AMERICAN FRONTIER FIREARMS
1871-2 Open-Top Frontier Model 403
1871-2 Open-Top Tiffany Model 403
Remington New Army Cavalry Model 403
Pocket Remington 403
Richards 1851 Model Navy Conversion 404
Richards 1860 Army Model Conversion 404
Richards & Mason 1851 Navy Conversion Model 404
Pocket Richards & Mason Navy Conversion Model 404
Richards 1861 Model Navy Conversion 404

COLT BLACKPOWDER ARMS
Colt 1849 Pocket 407
Colt 1851 Navy 407
Colt 1860 Army Model 408
Colt Model 1860 Army Fluted Cylinder 408
Colt 1861 Navy 408
Colt 1860 Gold U.S. Cavalry 409
Colt 1861 Custer 409
Colt Cochise Dragoon 409
Colt Third Model Dragoon 407
Colt 1847 Walker 407
Trapper Model 1862 Pocket Police 408

CVA
1851 Navy Brass Frame 410
1858 Army Steel Frame 410

DIXIE
1851 Navy Brass-Frame 413
1860 Army 413
Remington 44 Army 413
Walker 413
Spiller & Burr Brass-Frame 413
"Wyatt Earp" 413

EMF
Model 1851 Sheriff's 419
Model 1848 Dragoon 420
Model 1849 Baby Dragoon 420
Model 1850 Remington Army 420
Model 1851 Navy 420
Model 1860 Army 419
Model 1862 Police 419
Model 1863 Texas Dragoon 419
Model 1847 Walker 420

EUROARMS
Remington 1858 New Model Army Models 1010, 1020, 1040 424
Rogers & Spencer Models 1005, 1006 424
Rogers & Spencer London Gray Model 1007 424

NAVY ARMS
Colt 1847 Walker 433
1851 Navy "Yank" 434
First Model Dragoon 434
1858 New Model Army Remington Models 435
1860 Army 434
1862 New Model Police 433
Law & Order Set 433
Le Mat (Army, Navy, Cavalry, 18th Georgia, Beauregard) 433
REB Model 1860 434
REB 60 Sheriff's 435
Rogers & Spencer Models 433

RUGER
Old Army Cap & Ball 443

TRADITIONS
1875 Schofield 451
Thunderer 451
1894 Bisley 451
1873 Colt SA 451

UBERTI
1851 & 1861 Navy 458
1858 Remington New Navy 458
1860 Army 458
1st, 2nd, 3rd Model Dragoons 457
Paterson 457
Walker 457

SHOTGUNS

CVA
Classic Turkey Double 411
Trapper Single Barrel 411

DIXIE
Double Barrel Magnum 416

NAVY ARMS
Fowler 440
Model T & T 440
Steel Shot Magnum 440